MILLER'S

ANTIQUES

PRICE GUIDE 2008

MILLER'S ANTIQUES PRICE GUIDE 2008

Created and designed by
Miller's Publications
The Cellars, High Street
Tenterden, Kent, TN30 6BN
Tel: +44 (0) 1580 766411
Fax: +44 (0) 1580 766100

First published in Great Britain in 2007
by Miller's, a division of Mitchell Beazley,
imprints of Octopus Publishing Group Ltd,
2–4 Heron Quays, London E14 4JP
Miller's is a registered trademark of
Octopus Publishing Group Ltd,
an Hachette Livre UK Company

ISBN-978 1 84533 300 3

A CIP catalogue record for this book is
available from the British Library

Set in Frutiger

Colour origination by Colour Wheel Ltd, Whitstable, Kent
Additional colour origination by Ian Williamson, Pevensey Scanning
Printed and bound: Rotolito Lombarda, Italy

Consultant Editor: Jonty Hearnden
General Editor: Elizabeth Norfolk

Managing Editor: Valerie Lewis
Production Co-ordinator: Philip Hannath
Editorial Co-ordinator: Deborah Wanstall
Editorial Assistants: Melissa Hall, Joanna Hill
Production Assistants: Charlotte Smith, Mel Smith, Ethne Tragett
Advertising Executives: Michael Webb, Carol Woodcock
Advertising Co-ordinator & Administrator: Melinda Williams
Designer: Sam Ward
Indexers: Hilary Bird, Sally Roots
Production: Peter Hunt
Jacket Design: Tim Foster, Victoria Burley
Photographers: Elizabeth Field, Paul Harding,
Jeremy Martin, Dennis O'Reilly, Robin Saker

Front cover illustrations:
A painted beech marriage chest, c1760, 38½in (98cm) wide. **£11,500–12,500** **Robert Young Antiques** ⊞
A painted marriage chest, c1830, 42in (106.5) wide. **£3,000–3,500** **Robert Young Antiques** ⊞
A Yorkshire Toby jug, 1830–40, 10in (25.5cm) high. **£350–400** **Durham House Antiques** ⊞
A pair of Loetz glass candlesticks, Austria, c1895, 14in (35.5cm) high. **£3,500–4,000** **Afford Decorative Arts** ⊞
A set of four laminated walnut and vinyl side chairs, labelled and dated 1964. **£1,450–1,700** **Treadway** ⚒

Back cover illustrations:
A redware plate, America. **£4,500–5,000** **Raccoon Creek** ⊞
A bottle of Château Pétrus, Pomerol, Red Bordeaux, 1990. Vintage Rating: 10. **£2,500–3,000** **Berry Bros & Rudd** ⊞
A George III satinwood secretaire bookcase, c1770. **£30,000–35,000** **William Cooke** ⊞
A wall vase, China, Qianlong period, 1736–95, 8in (20.5cm) high. **£55,000–65,000** **Woolley & Wallis** ⚒

Photographs of Jonty Hearnden by Adrian Pope

Spine illustration:
A walnut marquetry longcase clock, c1690, 83in (211cm) high. **£6,000–7,200**
Half title illustration:
An Emile Gallé cameo glass vase, c1900. **£5,500–6,500** **Rago Arts** ⚒
Contents illustration:
A A painted We-Dan mask, Africa, Liberia, 1900–25. **£8,800–9,800** **Gordon Reece Gallery** ⊞

MILLER'S

ANTIQUES PRICE GUIDE 2008

ELIZABETH NORFOLK *GENERAL EDITOR*

JONTY HEARNDEN
CONSULTANT EDITOR

2008
VOLUME XXIX

HOW TO USE

To find a particular item, consult the contents list on page 7 to determine it can be found under the main heading – for example, Decorative Arts. You will find that larger sections have been sub-divided into more focused collecting areas. If you are looking for a particular factory, designer or craftsman, consult the index which starts on page 756.

FURNITURE 21

DINING & SIDE CHAIRS

DINING & SIDE CHAIRS

ESSENTIAL REFERENCE CHAIR BACK STYLES

Carolean (1665–85)

Solid vase-shape splat-back (1710–40)

Windsor (c1750–1850)

Hepplewhite shield back (1780–1800)

Gothic revival (1820–50)

Victorian button-back (c1860–90)

A pair of mahogany side chairs, with hoop backs, c1760.
£650–750
Woburn Abbey Antiques Centre ⊞

A set of six mahogany side chairs, with pierced and carved vase-shaped splats and drop-in seats, on leaf-carved cabriole front legs with webbed pad feet, Ireland, 18thC.
£18,000–22,000 **Mealy's**

A set of four Hepplewhite-style painted dining chairs, decorated with neo-classical motifs, the shield backs with plume crests, with stuff-over seats, on square tapered legs, c1780.
£2,000–2,500 **Sotheby's**

These chairs relate to ones illustrated in Hepplewhite's The Cabinet-Maker and Upholsterer's Guide *where reference is made to 'Japanned chairs' – 'a new and very elegant fashion...of finishing them with painted or japanned work, which gives a rich and splendid appearance...which allows a framework less massy than is requisite for Mahogany: and by assorting the prevailing colour to the furniture and light of the room affords...a pleasing and striking effect to the eye'.*

EXPERT'S EYE GEORGE III SIDE CHAIRS

Stile

The splat has been pierced, copying the line and designs of Thomas Chippendale.

During the 18th century drop in seats were generally larger than those of the 19th century.

Box stretcher. 18th-century chairs are also found with H-shaped stretchers. Make sure stretchers have not been replaced as this can effect value.

Although this toprail has been shaped, finer quality chairs of the period would be carved with much more attention to detail.

Shoe – 18th-century splats sit in a shoe, unlike later copies that tend to be an extension of the splat.

Square legs of this design were very fashionable and would sometimes be chamfered on the insides.

Early furniture was primitively constructed from solid wood, often reusing an old piece of timber. By the 18th century, construction was becoming increasingly sophisticated, with finely executed joints and a carcase that was well made. This is a set of five Chippendale-style side chairs from c1770.

£800–900 **Castlegate Antiques** ⊞

A set of six Chippendale-style side chairs, with pierced baluster splats, America, probably Delaware valley, late 18thC.
£3,250–3,750 **Freeman's**

Essential Reference
information on design styles, makers, designers, types of wares, decoration, marks etc.

Detail
this will either be a close-up of an interesting detail or an alternative view of the item.

Expert's Eye
a detailed focus on an item, pointing out component parts and/or specific areas of interest and craftsmanship.

Source code
refers to the Key to Illustrations on page 744 that lists the details of where the item was photographed. The icon indicates the item was sold at auction. The ⊞ icon indicates the item originated from a dealer.

Price guide
this is based on actual prices realized. Remember that Miller's is a price guide not a price list and prices are affected by many variables such as location, condition, desirability and so on. Don't forget that if you are selling it is quite likely you will be offered less than the price range. Price ranges for items sold at auction tend to include the buyer's premium and VAT if applicable.

BRITISH BRACKET, MANTEL & TABLE CLOCKS

An ebonized bracket clock, by William Hughes, London, the brass dial with silvered chapter ring, date and false pendulum apertures and strike/silent dial, the tic-tac escapement striking on a bell, the case with brass-bound door, brass pineapple finials and fishscale side frets, c1785, 15¾in (40cm) high.
£11,250–12,500
Derek Roberts Antiques

A mahogany bracket clock, by John Gilbertson, the silvered arched dial with sweep centre date and strike/silent dial, the triple-train six-pillar movement with verge escapement and striking the hours on a bell and the quarters on three further bells, the bell-top case with cast-brass finials and feet, c1785, 25in (63.5cm) high.
£4,750–5,250
Leigh Extence
John Gilbertson is recorded as working in Ripon, Yorkshire, from c1750 to his death in 1793. The quality and style of this clock would indicate that Gilbertson 'bought in' the movement, and quite probably the whole clock, from London, as it is almost identical to work by the top London makers of the period.

A George III mahogany bracket clock, by Richard Andrews, London, the brass dial with date aperture below strike/silent and regulator dials and signature, the twin-train fusee movement with verge escapement, the case with bell top, 18in (45.5cm) high.
£9,500–10,500
Country Lane Classics

A mahogany and brass-strung bracket clock, by James McCabe, London, the silvered dial with strike/silent dial, the twin-chain fusee movement striking on a bell, with trip repeat, the case with fret-cut brass panels to the sides, on brass bracket feet, late 18thC, 19¼in (49cm) high.
£6,000–7,500 Bearnes

A George III mahogany and brass-mounted bracket clock, by Thwaites & Read, London, No. 9843, the brass dial with silvered chapter ring and subsidiary fast/slow and date dials within pierced ormolu spandrels, the twin-train fusee movement striking on a bell, with engraved backplate and pendulum bob, on gilt-metal feet, 20in (51cm) high.
£4,250–5,000 Hy Duke

MILLER'S COMPARES

(L) A mahogany automaton bracket clock, by James Smith, London, the brass dial with silvered chapter ring, date aperture and automaton of people catching a pheasant, the eight-day fusee movement with verge escapement and striking the hours on a bell, the bell-top case with brass pineapple finials, c1790, 18½in (47cm) high.
£18,000–20,000
Derek Roberts Antiques

(R) A mahogany bracket clock, by John Pratt, Epsom, the brass dial with silvered chapter ring and cut-out for the signature plaque, strike/silent in the arch, the eight-day striking fusee movement with verge escapement, the bell-top case with pineapple finials, c1790, 18in (45.5cm) high.
£12,000–14,000
Derek Roberts Antiques

It is most unusual for a bracket clock to have anything other than strike/silent or rise/fall regulation dials in the arch, and the addition of a painted automaton scene dramatically adds to value. The clock shown on the left has an unusual automaton in that, rather than an arm or a bow for a musical instrument moving with the pendulum, it has a ratcheting device that causes a pheasant to emerge slowly from behind a bush and then rush back just as a gentleman wearing a hat tries to catch him. Further points to consider are the figuring and patina of the case, which are particularly good on the example on the left, and where the clock was made. A piece made in the provinces, such as the item on the right, will almost invariably sell for a lower price than one made in London. The best clockmakers tended to gravitate to the capital where they could command a higher price for their products from a more affluent clientele. James Smith of London was clockmaker to George III.

MARKET INFORMATION BRACKET CLOCKS

- Prices for standard bracket clocks have on the whole remained level, although they have dipped for lower-quality examples.
- Exceptional bracket clocks, by comparison, have continued to demand good prices.
- Collectors are looking for unusual features as well as good-quality clocks and eminent makers, all of which will boost value.

Miller's Compares
explains the difference in value between two similar-looking items.

Market Information
What's hot, what's not – up to date buying and selling information, revised each year, on all the major collecting fields.

Caption
provides a brief description of the item including the maker's name, medium, size, year it was made and in some cases condition.

Dates	British Monarch	British Period	French Period	German Period	U.S. Period	Style	Woods
1558–1603	Elizabeth I	Elizabethan	Renaissance			Gothic	Oak Period (to c1670)
1603–1625	James I	Jacobean		Renaissance			
1625–1649	Charles I	Carolean	Louis XIII (1610–1643)		Early Colonial	Baroque (c1620–1700)	
1649–1660	Common-wealth	Cromwellian	Louis XIV (1643–1715)	Renaissance/ Baroque (c1650–1700)			
1660–1685	Charles II	Restoration					Walnut period (c1670–1735)
1685–1689	James II	Restoration			William & Mary		
1689–1694	William & Mary	William & Mary			Dutch Colonial	Rococo (c1695–1760)	
1694–1702	William III	William III		Baroque (c1700–1730)	Queen Anne		
1702–1714	Anne	Queen Anne					
1714–1727	George I	Early Georgian	Régence (1715–1723)	Rococo (c1730–1760)	Chippendale (from 1750)		
1727–1760	George II	Early Georgian	Louis XV (1723–1774)	Neo–classicism (c1760–1800)	Early Federal (1790–1810)	Neo–classical (c1755–1805)	Early mahogany period (c1735–1770)
1760–1811	George III	Late Georgian	Louis XVI (1774–1793) Directoire (1793–1799) Empire (1799–1815)	Empire (c1800–1815)	American Directoire (1798–1804) American Empire (1804–1815)	Empire (c1799–1815)	Late mahogany period (c1770–1810)
1812–1820	George III	Regency	Restauration Charles X (1815–1830)	Biedermeier (c1815–1848)	Late Federal (1810–1830)	Regency (c1812–1830)	
1820–1830	George IV	Regency					
1830–1837	William IV	William IV	Louis Philippe (1830–1848)	Revivale (c1830–1880)		Eclectic (c1830–1880)	
1837–1901	Victoria	Victorian	2nd Empire Napoleon III (1848–1870) 3rd Republic (1871–1940)	Jugendstil (c1880–1920)	Victorian	Arts & Crafts (c1880–1900)	
1901–1910	Edward VII	Edwardian			Art Nouveau (c1900–1920)	Art Nouveau (c1900–1920)	

contents

MEET THE EXPERTS

The publishers would like to acknowledge the great assistance given by our consultants. We would also like to extend our thanks to all auction houses and their press offices, as well as dealers and collectors, who have assisted us in the production of this book.

EDITOR: **Elizabeth Norfolk** has been General Editor of *Miller's Antiques Price Guide* since 1995. She has a degree in French and trained as a numismatist at Stanley Gibbons, later working for Seaby's and Christie's. She has given radio interviews and talks about *Miller's Antiques Price Guide* and is still active in the field of numismatics.

US FURNITURE: **Anne Weston** has over 20 years' experience in decorative and fine arts. She has been an appraiser and consultant for auction houses, private galleries and collectors in the US and Europe. Until recently she worked for Northeast Auctions, New Hampshire but now has her own appraisal and consulting firm.

Anne Weston & Associates, LLC., 43 Pray Street, Portsmouth, New Hampshire 03801

BLACK FOREST FURNITURE: **Simon Daniels** has a gallery in Aspen, Colorado that is exclusively dedicated to Black Forest carvings. He is the author of *Swiss Carvings: The Art of the 'Black Forest' 1820–1940* and the world's leading expert in the field. Daniels is also a second-generation antique dealer and a Cambridge University graduate.

Simon Daniels Antiques, 431 East Hyman Ave, Aspen, Colorado, 81611

CLOCKS: **Robert Wren** is marketing manager at Derek Roberts Antiques, Tonbridge, consultant to Christie's South Kensington and assistant tutor on the Antique Clocks Conservation and Restoration programme at West Dean College, Chichester.

Robert Wren, Derek Roberts Antiques, 25 Shipbourne Road, Tonbridge, Kent TN10 3DN

AMERICAN CLOCKS: **Robert Schmitt** has been collecting clocks since 1969 and dealing in them for many years. He now holds consignment clock auctions from his base in New England. He is also active with the National Association of Watch & Clock Collectors, Columbia, PA.

Robert Schmitt, P O Box 162, Windham, NH 03087

BAROMETERS: **Derek and Tina Rayment** have 40 years' experience and are acknowledged in the trade as the leading specialists in English and Continental antique barometers, thermometers and barographs, including restoration undertaken for Europe and the US. They exhibit at major London antiques fairs.

Derek and Tina Rayment Antiques, Orchard House, Barton Road, Barton, Nr Farndon, Cheshire SY14 7HT

POTTERY: **Phil Howell** is Deputy Director of European Ceramics and Glass at Sotheby's, London, having previously been head of European and Oriental Ceramics at Sotheby's in Billingshurst, West Sussex. He has appeared on radio and television, is a member of the English Ceramics circle, the Derby Porcelain International Society and the Northern Ceramic Society.

Phil Howell, Sotheby's, Hammersmith Road, London W14 8UX

AMERICAN CERAMICS: **George R. Allen** runs Raccoon Creek Antiques with his partner, Gordon L. Wyckoff, focusing on American Folk Art with a specialized interest in ceramics. George is also a potter and lectures at colleges and civic organizations and has appeared on US national television.

George Allen, Raccoon Creek Antiques, 208 Spangsville Road, Oley, PA 19547

PORCELAIN: **John Axford** is head of the Ceramics, Glass and Oriental departments at Woolley and Wallis, Salisbury. He writes and lectures on ceramics and Oriental art and is a member of the BBC's *Antiques Roadshow* team. In 2005 John discovered the first Limehouse figure and discovered and identified The Alexander Vase.

John Axford, Woolley & Wallis, 50–51 Castle Street, Salisbury, Wilts SP1 3SU

ASIAN CERAMICS AND WORKS OF ART: **Peter Wain** is a leading specialist in Chinese and Japanese ceramics and works of art. He has written numerous books, catalogues and articles, broadcast on radio and television and lectured in the UK, USA and Australia.
Peter has been the Chairman of the Oriental Vetting Committees for many of the top international antiques fairs.

SILVER: **Hugh Gregory** joined Knight Frank & Rutley in 1962 and obtained the Gemmological Association's Diploma in 1966. In 1971 he joined Phillips, Bond Street, as an auctioneer in their silver department. He is presently with Thomson Roddick & Medcalf in Carlisle and Dumfries.

Hugh Gregory, Thomson Roddick & Medcalf, Coleridge House, Shaddongate, Carlisle, Cumbria, CA2 5TU

GLASS: **Simon Cottle** is a Director, auctioneer and Head of European Ceramics and Glass at Sotheby's London. He is Hon President of the Glass Circle and an Honorary Fellow of the Guild of Glass Engravers. Simon is also well respected for his knowledge of ceramics. He lectures widely, has appeared on television and radio and his books include *Sotheby's Concise Encyclopaedia of Glass*, now a standard reference work.

Simon Cottle, Sotheby's, Hammersmith Road, London W14 8UX

VINTAGE WINES: **Hugh Johnson** is the author of a dozen ground-breaking wine books, including *The World Atlas of Wine*, *The Story of Wine* and his memoirs, *Wine – A Life Uncorked*. His *Pocket Wine Book*, published annually since 1977 in a dozen languages, is the best-selling wine book of all time. His other passion is gardening.

VINTAGE WINES: **Bruce Cairnduff** is a second generation wine expert and a director and head of the wine department at Dreweatt Neate, the largest regional auctioneers of fine wine, holding three dedicated sales each year. They now offer an extensive and varied selection of fine wines for auction from private collections and cellars.

Bruce Cairnduff, Dreweatt Neate, Donnington Priory, Donnington, Newbury, Berks, RG14 2JE

VINTAGE WINES: **Berry Brothers**
We would like to thank Berry Brothers & Rudd Ltd for kindly allowing us to photograph the wine bottles and labels shown on pages 369–374.

JEWELLERY AND MICRO-MOSAICS: **John Benjamin** is an independent jewellery historian, valuer, lecturer and writer. Formerly International Director at Phillips, he is a member of BBC's *Antiques Roadshow* team of specialists. John is the author of *Starting to Collect Antique Jewellery* and co-author with Paul Atterbury of *Arts & Crafts to Art Deco: The Jewellery and Silver of H. G. Murphy.*

John Benjamin, P O Box 7, Aylesbury, Bucks HP22 5WB

FABERGE: **Geoffrey Munn** is the jewellery specialist on the BBC's *Antiques Roadshow* and the Managing Director of Wartski, the London-based firm of antiques dealers. He is also a Fellow of the Society of Antiquaries and a Liveryman of the Worshipful Companies of Goldsmiths and Painter-Stainers. Geoffrey Munn has published several books on jewellery.

Geoffrey Munn, Wartski Ltd, 14 Grafton Street, London W1S 4DE

ANTIQUITIES: **Peter Clayton FSA**, Egyptologist, archaeologist and numismatist, has been consultant to Seaby Antiquities since 1980. He has lectured for over 30 years and is often called upon to give live TV and radio interviews. Peter is also Expert Advisor to the Treasure Committee of the DCMS and many other institutions both national and local.

Peter A. Clayton, Seaby Antiquities, 14 Old Bond Street, London W1S 4PP

TRIBAL ART: **Gordon Reece** began his pioneering gallery in 1981 in Knaresborough, north Yorkshire. Since then he has presented over 200 exhibitions on non-European art and antiques and sells to major museums and collectors worldwide. He has also presented exhibitions in museums and galleries throughout Europe that have received both national and international acclaim.

Gordon Reece Galleries, Finkle Street, Knaresborough, Yorkshire, HG5 8AA

SCENT BOTTLES: **Heather Hemmings** has been an avid collector of glass and scent bottles for over 15 years and has dealt in scent bottles and Georgian glass for five years. Her collection of 18th-19th- and 20th-century scent bottles can be seen at Bourbon-Hanby Arcade.

Heather Hemmings, Bourbon-Hanby Antiques, 151 Sydney Street, London SW3 6NT

CARD CASES: **Graham Ellis** purchased his first card case over 40 years ago and still derives much pleasure from discovering cases he has not seen before. Graham has been a specialist dealer for the last ten years and shows at major national fairs.

Graham Ellis, Simply Antiques, Windsor House, High St, Moreton-in-Marsh, Glos GL56 0AD

WALKING CANES **Michael German** is a second generation antiques dealer specialising in walking canes and antique arms and armour, having set up his own business in 1972. In 1996 his son-in-law Dominic Strickland joined the business, thus ensuring its future. He is a member of the vetting Committees at the Grosvenor House Antiques Fair, the BADA Fair, and the Olympia Fairs.

Michael German Antiques, 38B Kensington Church St, London W8 4BX

AMERICAN FOLK ART: **Cynthia Tashjian** holds a masters in art history from Williams College and has worked for nearly 18 years for Skinner, Inc., auctioneers and appraisers of antiques and fine art, of Boston and Bolton, Massachusetts. Skinner holds four auctions each year featuring American Folk Art.

Skinner, Inc., 63 Park Plaza, Boston, MA 02116 / 357 Main Street, Bolton, MA 01740

RUGS & CARPETS: **Jonathan Wadsworth** is an internationally renowned specialist in European and Eastern carpets. He lectures on the academic and commercial aspects of carpets and the market both at home and abroad, as well as contributing to Miller's Publications and appearing on the BBC's *The Great Antiques Hunt*.

Jonathan Wadsworth, 2 St Nicholas, Houghton, Arundel, W. Sussex BN18 9LW

LAMPS & LIGHTING: **Jill Perry** and her husband Maurice run Norfolk Decorative Antiques, specialists in chandeliers and all forms of antique lighting and restoration. Jill buys and sells antique lighting from 1840 to 1990 and their clients include large organizations as well as private clients in the UK and Europe.

Jill Perry, Norfolk Decorative Antiques, Fakenham Industrial Estate, Fakenham, Norfolk NR21 8NW

SCIENTIFIC INSTRUMENTS & MARINE: **Charles Tomlinson** has been a dealer for 35 years, specializing in Scientific Instruments, early photographic material and cameras, with particular interest in microscopes, microscope slides, slide rules and mechanical calculating instruments. He is a member of The Oughtred Society, the international organization dedicated to the history and collection of sliderules and is also a member of the UK Slide Rule Circle.

charlestomlinson@tiscali.co.uk
Tel: 01244 318395

DECORATIVE ARTS: **Gordon Foster and Fiona MacSporran** established decorative arts@doune in 1999, specialising in Arts & Crafts silver, jewellery, furniture and unusual objects. They exhibit at several leading antique fairs including Olympia in London and regularly advise museums, institutions and private collectors. Fiona has published several monographs, contributed to magazines and collaborated on various exhibitions. Gordon has a passion for Scottish silver and has published articles and lectured widely on the subject.

Gordon Foster and Fiona Macsporran, decorative arts@doune, Scottish Antique & Arts Centre, Doune, Perthshire, FK16 6HD

TWENTIETH-CENTURY DESIGN: **Lisanne Dickson** is head of 1950s Modern Design for Treadway/Toomey Auctions, Chicago, which holds four 20th-Century Design sales a year. She has catalogued more than 6000 examples of furniture, pottery, glass, sculpture, lighting, jewellery and textiles dating from 1930 to 1980.

Lisanne Dickson, Treadway/Toomey Auctions, 2029 Madison Road, Cincinnati, Ohio 45208

PICASSO POTTERY: **Ralph Taylor** joined Sotheby's in 2005 after completing a Masters in 20th-Century European Art at the Courtauld Institute of Art. He also has a BA in English Literature and History of Art and spent 18 months with Christie's. In 2006 he became a specialist in the Contemporary Art and Impressionist & Modern Art departments at Sotheby's Olympia.

Ralph Taylor, Sotheby's, Hammersmith Road, London W14 8UX.

PRINTS: **Alexander Hayter** Alexander Hayter initially worked for Sotheby's as a print specialist and joined Bloomsbury Auctions in 2004 to set up their Modern & Contemporary Print Department. Since then his sales have become among the leading auctions of 20th-century prints in the UK, catering for collectors of British, European and American art.

Alexander Hayter, Bloomsbury Auctions, Bloomsbury House, 24 Maddox Street, London W1S 1PP.

INTRODUCTION

THE PAST YEAR in which I have worked with Miller's as Consultant Editor has been an exciting and stimulating one for me. A lot of thought has gone into the design and presentation of the 2008 edition and we very much hope that you will find the new approach a helpful one.

This 29th edition of the *Miller's Antiques Price Guide* includes advice and comment from over 400 contributors from auction rooms and dealers throughout the UK, Europe and the USA. Each major section has been verified by experts in their particular fields and the information they provide is well worth reading.

One of the major changes we have made this year is to segment furniture into categories, rather than by alphabetical listing. You will find complete sections on storage furniture, tables, writing furniture, seat furniture and others, including a special section on the distinctively ornate Black Forest furniture currently so popular in the United States. All items are presented as far as practical in date order. We have also amalgamated oak and country furniture into the appropriate sections, thus presenting a complete overview of each category. We believe that this approach makes it very much easier for readers to find their way around the Guide and to locate specific items.

In addition, we have included some fascinating new smaller sections dedicated to subjects that we feel are

A Black Forest lime-wood armchair, the back carved with entwined branches and resting bears, two cross-legged bears supporting the chair's arms, the front legs with climbing bears, Switzerland, c1900, 45in (114.5cm) high.

£10,000–11,000 Daniels Antiques

of particular interest. An exciting area is that of micro-mosaics, as used in the decoration of snuff boxes, jewellery and frames. These exquisite designs, where as many as 14,000 tiny pieces of glass can be set in a single square inch, are introduced by BBC's *Antiques Roadshow* jewellery expert John Benjamin. Fuelled by the current international demand for objects connected with the Grand Tour, the best examples stem from 18th- and 19th-century Rome and Florence. A top quality brooch by Castellani, for example, recently realized in excess of £22,000.

Card cases are the subject of another new section. These highly collectable items can range in price from

A micro-mosaic and gilt-bronze box, depicting views of Rome, flowers and doves, on claw feet, Italy, 19thC, 5¾in (14.5cm) wide.

£7,500–8,500 Freeman's

£50 to £3,000 depending on style, depth of carving and subject matter, with silver, tortoiseshell and ivory being the most sought after. However, it is still possible to find attractive cases in materials such as wood or Bakelite at very reasonable prices.

John Axford, a member of the *Antiques Roadshow* and expert writer and lecturer on ceramics, brings a new look to the porcelain section that highlights both British and European examples – one of the hotter areas for collectors. Much of the subject is now conveniently categorised under the factories in which it was made. Fellow *Antiques Roadshow* member Geoffrey Munn of Wartski's, who recently held a fabulous exhibition of Fabergé jewellery in their London gallery, has written an introduction to the art of Fabergé, and who better than Master of Wine, Hugh Johnson, to advise on investment in fine wines?

A special feature on Picasso ceramics is included in the 20th-Century Design section, and collectors may be surprised to know that limited editions approved by Picasso himself are still available in the £500 range rather than running into millions.

This year we have introduced a further new category looking at the increasing popularity and growth of interest in 20th-century prints, which have been particularly buoyant. Finally, the popular and eclectic pages on Decorative Arts have been given a makeover by Fiona MacSporran and Gordon Foster to focus on up-and-coming areas that are a must for collectors.

Readers should look out for two extremely useful new

features that appear throughout the Guide: the Expert's Eye, which examines an antique in close detail, illustrating and describing its specific characteristics, and Essential Reference, which includes additional information on the unique features of an antique that are vital in helping you in your identification and valuation.

The questions always asked by buyers and sellers alike are what's hot, what's not, what's going up and what's going down? Fashions change in antiques as in everything else in today's world and modern interior design in particular has had a powerful – and perhaps not always positive – effect on the antique furniture market. However, I see a strong future for a combination of ancient and modern, for antiques that happily thrive in a modern setting such as a bold abstract print hung above a Biedermeier chest of drawers, or a stark modern lamp placed on an antique mahogany sideboard. It just requires a little imagination.

There are certainly some exciting growth areas for collectors of antiques. Tribal Art of all kinds retains its appeal and an antique piece can look stunning in either a traditional or a modern setting. Quality Art Deco glass of good provenance is another area in which records are being smashed. Twentieth-Century design in general is increasingly popular and can be indulged in by buyers whatever the size of their pocket.

At the other end of the scale, the rapid expansion of the Chinese economy has led to China buying back its antiques, particularly ceramics, at prices that have caused shock waves around the world. For example, at the recent European Fine Art Fair, a 4th-century BC Chinese bronze wine pourer in the form of a tapir inlaid with gold and turquoise sold to a Chinese buyer for £6 million.

A teak sofa table, by Johannes Andersen for CFC Silkeborg, Denmark, 1950s–60s, 20½in (52cm) wide.
£700–850 Bukowskis

There is a strong emerging market in Russia for Russian paintings and works of art, especially for anything by Fabergé. The market in Asian antiquities and works of art has also been subject to rapid growth over the past three years, while contemporary Asian art – another hot tip – is said by some sources to have grown in excess of 350 per cent in just one year.

Major auction houses in general are celebrating a bumper year, with sales soaring over the past twelve months and reaching record heights as they focus on the upper end of the market. Sotheby's sold their most expensive painting ever – a Picasso – for a record price, while a further 12 works of art topped the $10 million mark. Likewise, Christie's achieved a large rise in sales, with a particularly buoyant market in post-war and modern art.

Moving on to a slightly less exalted level, a healthy proportion of respondents to a survey conducted by one of Britain's largest trade associations claimed to have increased their turnover during the past year. The survey also found that the United States continues to be Britain's biggest trading partner in the antiques business, involving more than 25 per cent of sales. It would appear that antique furniture prices have stabilized over recent months, suggesting that the market has levelled out. Early Victorian furniture remains a fashion victim but there are signs of a recovery in better quality 18th-century mahogany and walnut furniture.

On an upbeat note, I can assure you that opportunities for growth are always out there if you are prepared to go and look for them. There is still the chance to find something unusual and exciting in the antiques world. Remember that the everyday item, if in top condition, of genuine provenance and with rarity value, will always find a buyer. For example, an auction house in Boston Spa, North Yorkshire, recently sold a Bassett Lowke toy locomotive that had remained untouched since the 1960s. Nothing similar had been seen for more than ten years – it ticked all the right boxes and sold for the princely sum of £10,000.

One of the aims of *Miller's Antiques Price Guide* is to spot coming trends, check values and supply information on the ups and downs of the ever-changing antiques market. In this latest edition we provide you with superb pictures, descriptions, dates and valuations for a vast range of antiques covering every possible category. I hope it will stimulate your interest if you are a newcomer to the antiques trade, and that it will be your constant companion if you are an established dealer.

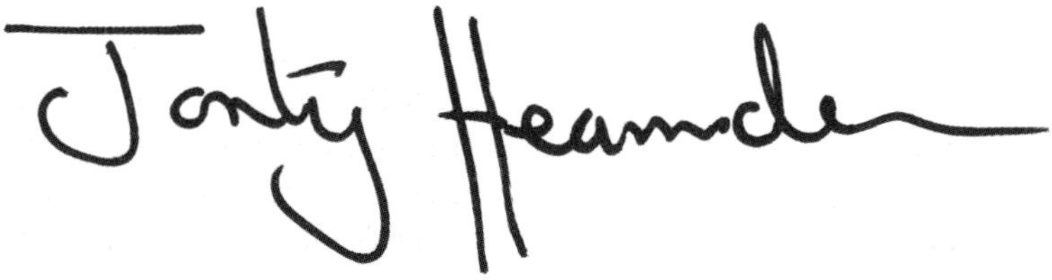

FURNITURE

STOOLS & BENCHES

An oak box stool, the hinged top above an arcaded frieze, 17thC, 19¼in (49cm) wide.

£1,250–1,500
Woolley & Wallis

An oak joined stool, the frieze carved with foliate scrolls, on reeded baluster-turned legs joined by a box stretcher, 17thC, 17¾in (45cm) wide.

£1,000–1,200 Skinner

An oak joined stool, with shaped apron, 1660–80, 21in (53.5cm) wide.

£1,250–1,400
Long Street Antiques

An oak and elm bench, with original paint, c1700, 46¼in (117.5cm) long.

£2,500–2,800 Robert Young Antiques

This unusual vernacular boarded seat incorporates massive hewn bases from two rare English Gothic period pew ends.

An oak box stool, in the form of a chest of drawers, c1700, 19in (48.5cm) wide.

£2,250–2,500
Period Oak

A walnut stool, the canted scrolled legs with pierced knees, with carved and pierced stretcher rails and turned H-shaped stretcher, one pierced stretcher rail replaced, early 18thC, 18in (45.5cm) wide.

£3,500–4,000 Sotheby's

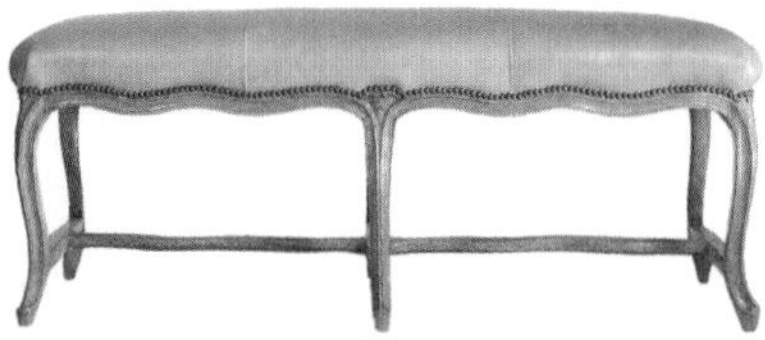

A beechwood banquette, with serpentine seat, on cabriole legs joined by stretchers, restored, France, mid-18thC, 53in (134.5cm) long.

£3,500–4,000 Sotheby's (NY)

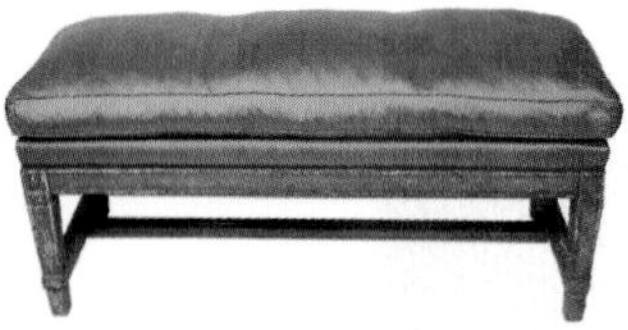

A painted wood stool, with stretcher, c1795, 49in (124.5cm) wide.

£3,500–4,000
Augustus Brandt

A mahogany piano stool, school of Duncan Phyfe, the seat on a brass swivel mount within a ring-turned pedestal, on acanthus-carved legs with hairy claw feet, America, New York, c1815, 30in (76cm) high.

£300–350
Northeast Auctions

A mahogany stool, with tapestry seat and turned legs, c1860.

£180–200
Hemswell Antique Centres

A walnut and parcel-gilt Gothic-style hall seat, the arcaded pierced ends with sphinx finials, on chamfered square legs and tapered feet, 19thC, 42½in (108cm) wide.

£1,000–1,200 Woolley & Wallis

EARLY CHAIRS

An oak wainscot chair, with carved decoration, c1610.
£5,700–6,500
Period Oak

An oak wainscot chair, with a carved back, Yorkshire, c1680.
£2,250–2,500
Castlegate Antiques

An oak panelled chair, with turned spindle arm supports, Scotland, 17thC.
£2,700–3,000
Oak & Country Furniture

A Charles II child's oak chair, the top rail branded with initials 'R. C.', with carved back and apron, on ring-tuned legs joined by stretchers.
£2,400–2,800
Sotheby's

An oak chair, the arcaded cresting rail with initials 'E. K.' and date, the back with carved and punchwork decoration, on square and ring-turned legs, restored, dated 1657.
£11,000–13,000 **Sotheby's**

An oak wainscot chair, with carved decoration, on turned legs joined by stretchers, Yorkshire, c1680, 46in (117cm) high.
£5,500–6,000
Period Oak

A walnut and beech armchair, with carved and crested rails and caned back and seat, c1690.
£2,200–2,400
Key Antiques

An oak elbow chair, with carved back panel, on square tapered legs, late 17thC.
£230–270
Gorringes (L)

An oak and ash back stool, with shaped back, the seat with moulded edge, on turned splay legs held by baluster stretchers, stamped inventory mark 'F' and a crown, late 17thC.
£3,000–3,300
Avon Antiques

An oak joined armchair, the back with carved decoration, the seat with 'dog tooth' carved edges, on turned front legs joined by stretchers, with later casters, 17thC and later.
£450–550
Penrith Farmers' & Kidd's

A walnut chair, in the style of Daniel Marot, late 17thC.
£1,600–1,750
Moxhams
Daniel Marot (1663–1752) was an influential Huguenot designer and architect to William II, Prince of Orange.

A beech open armchair, the back with pierced scrollwork crest and turned uprights, with moulded scrolled arms, on scroll-carved front legs joined by a pierced stretcher, c1695.
£1,250–1,500
Dreweatt Neate

COUNTRY CHAIRS

A fruitwood back stool, with rush seat, Wales, 1710.
£700–800
Oak & Country Furniture

An oak and walnut hooded armchair, 1710.
£7,000–8,000
Period Oak

An oak armchair, with drop-in seat, on front pad feet, early 18thC.
£1,600–1,800
Oak & Country Furniture

A set of six oak dining chairs, Wales, c1740.
£3,300–3,700
Mere Antiques

A turned cherrywood elbow chair, with rush seat, c1740.
£680–750
S & P Rumble

An elm and ash Windsor chair, with comb back and branded initials 'W. M.', c1750.
£2,800–3,200
Robert Young Antiques

An elm Windsor chair, with comb back, 18thC.
£520–580
Spurrier-Smith

A painted Windsor chair, the seat fitted for a commode, the baluster, spool and cylinder-turned splayed legs with tapered feet, America, Philadelphia, c1775.
£2,800–3,300
Northeast Auctions

A stained armchair, the back with a vase-shaped splat, with a rush seat, on square legs joined by a stretcher, America, probably southern Massachusetts, c1780.
£750–900
Northeast Auctions

A Shaker No. 6 rocking chair, with original finish, the arms on baluster-turned supports, the cylindrical legs joined by double box stretchers, the back slats impressed with the number '6', one rocker with transfer-printed label, taped seat later, America, Mount Lebanon, c1880.
£600–700 **Northeast Auctions**

Paul Hopwell Antiques

Early English Oak

Dressers, tables and chairs always in stock

A Queen Anne oak three drawer dresser base with geometric mouldings and cock-beaded shaped apron.
English c1705

A small Queen Anne oak chest of eight drawers supported on a bold baluster turned base. Excellent original colour, condition and patina.
English c1710

A George I oak single side table on bold baluster turned stretchers and legs. Excellent colour and patina.
English c1720

Furniture restoration service available

30 High Street, West Haddon, Northamptonshire NN6 7AP
Tel: 01788 510636 Fax: 01788 510044
Email: paulhopwell@antiqueoak.co.uk Website: www.antiqueoak.co.uk

WE WISH TO BUY 17TH & 18TH CENTURY OAK FURNITURE

A painted corner chair, with pierced splats, on square chamfered legs joined by a stretcher, America, probably Connecticut or Massachusetts, late 18thC.

£3,700–4,500
Northeast Auctions

A painted Windsor chair, on splayed turned legs joined by a turned stretcher, branded 'L. ALW' and 'I. Hamton', America, New York, late 18thC.

£4,000–5,000 **Northeast Auctions**

James and/or John Always worked in New York City with Joseph Hamton or Abraham Hamton during the 1790s.

An elm Windsor chair, c1800.

£800–900
Antiquesales.com

A set of eight elm dining chairs, with two carvers, c1800.

£4,500–5,000
Chair Set

An elm chair, with ratchet mechanism, East Anglia, c1800, 48in (122cm) high.

£2,250–2,500
S & P Rumble

A matched pair of yew and elm Windsor chairs, c1800.

£1,500–1,650
Mary Cruz Antiques

An ash and elm open armchair, c1800.

£225–250
Castlegate Antiques

An elm chair, with spindle back and rush seat, Lancashire, c1800.

£140–165
S & P Rumble

A fruitwood Mendlesham open armchair, with two turned rails and a rush seat, Suffolk, early 19thC.

£800–950 **Dreweatt Neate**

An ash and elm armchair, Evesham, Worcestershire, c1820.

£300–330
Long Street Antiques

A set of six painted chairs, the crest rails decorated with corncucopiae, grapes and vines, the splats shaped as stylized anthemion leaves centred by a roundel, the pierced bottom rails and front stretchers each with six gilt spheres, with rush seats, on turned legs with button feet, one later chair by Robert C. Whitely, decorated by David Guilment, America, probably Zanesville, Ohio, c1825.

£13,000–15,500 Northeast Auctions

An elm open armchair, the back with bobbin-turned uprights and shaped arms, on turned legs, early 19thC.

£300–350
Debden Antiques

An ash, elm and beech chair, with comb back and saddle seat, Wales, early 19thC.

£1,800–2,200
Peter Francis

A set of six ash and elm low-back Windsor chairs, by I. Godfrey, Worksop, stamped with maker's name, c1830.

£5,000–5,500 Swan Gallery

A matched set of eight yew-wood Windsor chairs, Thames Valley, 1830.

£8,100–8,900
Henry Baines

A yew-wood Windsor chair, 19thC.

£1,000–1,100
Castlegate Antiques

A child's pine play chair, with table and commode, with original paint, mid-19thC, 25in (63.5cm) high.

£700–800
Red Lion Antiques

A set of six cherrywood Roman pattern kitchen chairs, c1870.

£2,500–2,800
Peter Norden Antiques

A beech and elm carver chair, with turned spindles, late 19thC.

£140–175
Westville House Antiques

A Shaker No. 3 side chair, the slat back with acorn finials, upper slat with impressed number '3', with canvas tape seat, on tapered legs joined by double box stretchers, America, New Lebanon, New York, 1850–1900.

£600–750
Northeast Auctions

UPHOLSTERED CHAIRS

A walnut open armchair, with wavy stretchers, France, c1740.

£1,200–1,400
S & P Rumble

A pair of giltwood armchairs, in the manner of Cresson, the top and seat rails centred by a pomegranate flanked by foliage and rocaille, on cabriole legs, France, c1740.

£17,000–20,000 Sotheby's

The stylized pomegranates on the top and seat rails are similar to the work of Michel Cresson, the youngest son of the cabinet-maker Jean Cresson and brother of Louis. Michel worked in the rue de Cléry, Paris, and supplied seat furniture to the Prince de Condé at both the Palais Bourbon and Chantilly. However, it is possible that these chairs are the work of René Cresson (received Master 1738).

A pair of beechwood bergères, by Jean-Baptiste Tilliard, the moulded frames carved with C scrolls, foliage and rocaille, stamped maker's mark, France, mid-18thC.

£9,000–11,000 Sotheby's

Jean-Baptiste Tilliard was received Master in 1752.

A mahogany wing-backed armchair, c1780.

£1,800–2,000 Chair Set

An early George III mahogany armchair, with a serpentine front, the cabriole legs carved with shell and acanthus, with knurl toes, restored.

£2,500–3,000 Woolley & Wallis

A pair of giltwood bergères, by A. P. Dupain, the top rails with finials, the front rails carved with leaves, on fluted tapered legs, regilded, stamped maker's mark, France, late 18thC.

£7,000–8,500 Sotheby's

Adrien-Pierre Dupain was received Master in 1772. He was established in the rue Charonne, Paris, and under Louis XVI carried out commissions for various Royal residences.

A mahogany armchair, with moulded serpentine arms, on moulded legs, with a box stretcher, America, Massachusetts, c1790.

£2,800–3,200
Northeast Auctions

A mahogany armchair, with moulded serpentine arms, on square tapered moulded legs, with a box stretcher, America, Massachusetts, c1800.

£2,000–2,500 Northeast Auctions

A mahogany adjustable armchair, the shaped arms with turned supports, on square tapered legs, with reeded leg rest, damaged, America, possibly New England, c1800.

£3,500–4,000 Skinner

A mahogany wing-back armchair, on turned front legs, restored, c1795.

£1,200–1,400 **Dreweatt Neate**

A mahogany chair, with leather seat and back, on turned and reeded front legs, c1830.

£700–800
Woburn Abbey Antiques Centre

A painted *fauteuil*, on fluted tapered legs, France, 19thC.

£1,100–1,300
Mealy's

A pair of walnut open armchairs, with turned stretchers, c1850.

£5,500–6,000
Chair Set

A mahogany armchair, the lyre-shape back carved with acanthus leaves, the front legs carved with birds' wings, with lion-paw feet, America, 19thC.

£900–1,100 **Sotheby's (P)**

A carved walnut chair, with cabriole legs, c1870.

£900–1,000
S W Antiques

A pair of walnut armchairs, on turned front legs, c1880.

£3,500–4,250 **Sotheby's**

A late Victorian walnut button-back armchair, by Gillows, on turned front legs, stamped maker's mark.

£900–1,100 **Woolley & Wallis**

A painted beech open armchair, France, c1890.

£330–370
Period Furniture

A baroque-style armchair, in the manner of Andrea Brustolon, the armrests carved with reclining cherubs and supported by carved figures, on cabriole legs with mask feet and a shaped X-stretcher, Italy, late 19thC.

£4,000–4,500 **Sotheby's (NY)**

OPEN ARMCHAIRS

A carved walnut open armchair, c1680.

£1,200–1,400
Long Street Antiques

A George III mahogany corner chair, with pierced splats, turned uprights and drop-in seat, on chamfered legs.

£275–325 Sworders

A George III child's elbow chair, with a pierced splat, scroll armrests with detachable restraining bar and drop-in seat, on squared legs with adjustable foot rest.

£250–300 Greenslade Taylor Hunt

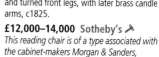

A mahogany open armchair, the shield back carved with wheat and drapes, the moulded arms carved with leaftips and rosette terminals, on reeded square tapered legs with with spade feet, America, New York, c1800.

£12,500–15,000
Northeast Auctions

George Hepplewhite's The Cabinet Maker and Uphosterers Guide *influenced furniture design for generations in Europe and America. The armchair shown here was originally part of a set of dining chairs and its desirability is based on a number of factors including condition, provenance and quality. American furniture collectors will pay high sums for pieces such as this that retain their original, or close to original, surface. This chair's overall proportions and quality of the carvings are very fine for American furniture. Its proven provenance is also well documented.*

A pair of marquetry-inlaid armchairs, on turned legs, Holland, 19thC.

£700–850 Mealy's

A mahogany reading chair, in the manner of Morgan & Sanders, with adjustable book rest and turned front legs, with later brass candle arms, c1825.

£12,000–14,000 Sotheby's

This reading chair is of a type associated with the cabinet-makers Morgan & Sanders, specialists in the manufacture of mechanical and metamorphic furniture.

A mahogany open armchair, with a leather seat, c1860.

£400–440
Period Furniture

A Georgian-style mahogany metamorphic chair, by J. Dent, with a caned seat, maker's stamp, c1880.

£3,500–4,000 Georgian Antiques

DINING & SIDE CHAIRS

A walnut side chair, c1710.

£2,700–3,000
Mary Cruz Antiques

A set of six mahogany dining chairs, with scroll-carved fiddle backs and drop-in seats, on shell and leaf-carved cabriole legs, 1725–50.

£22,000–25,000 Sotheby's

These chairs demonstrate the restraint of English chair design 20 years before the Chippendale period. Although carved, they rely more on form than surface adornment for their appeal. Their shell-carved knees, symbolizing the birth of Venus, are carried over onto the seat apron – a rare feature that is almost always the sign of a top maker. The splat and stiles are relatively plain and do not detract from the lower half of the chair.

A pair of mahogany side chairs, with hoop backs, c1760.

£650–750
Woburn Abbey Antiques Centre

A set of six mahogany side chairs, with pierced and carved vase-shaped splats and drop-in seats, on leaf-carved cabriole front legs with webbed pad feet, Ireland, 18thC.

£18,000–22,000 Mealy's

A set of seven George III mahogany dining chairs, with wavy splats above upholstered seats, on turned and fluted legs.

£2,250–2,750 Dreweatt Neate

A set of four Hepplewhite-style painted dining chairs, decorated with neo-classical motifs, the shield backs with plume crests, with stuff-over seats, on square tapered legs, c1780.

£2,000–2,500 Sotheby's

These chairs relate to ones illustrated in Hepplewhite's The Cabinet Maker and Upholsterer's Guide *where reference is made to 'Japanned chairs' – 'a new and very elegant fashion...of finishing them with painted or japanned work, which gives a rich and splendid appearance...which allows a framework less massy than is requisite for Mahogany: and by assorting the prevailing colour to the furniture and light of the room affords...a pleasing and striking effect to the eye'.*

EXPERT'S EYE GEORGE III SIDE CHAIRS

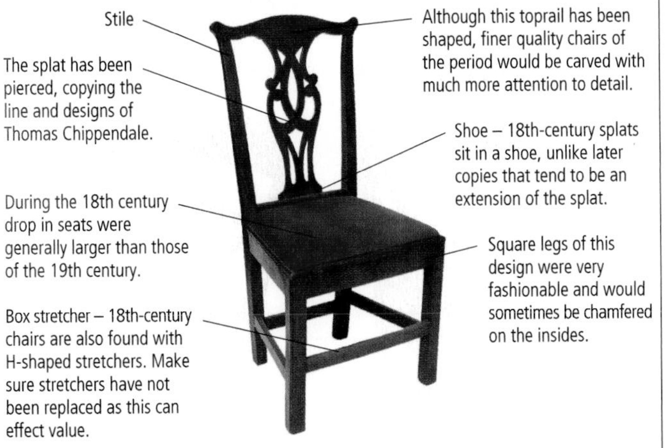
Stile
The splat has been pierced, copying the line and designs of Thomas Chippendale.
During the 18th century drop in seats were generally larger than those of the 19th century.
Box stretcher – 18th-century chairs are also found with H-shaped stretchers. Make sure stretchers have not been replaced as this can effect value.
Although this toprail has been shaped, finer quality chairs of the period would be carved with much more attention to detail.
Shoe – 18th-century splats sit in a shoe, unlike later copies that tend to be an extension of the splat.
Square legs of this design were very fashionable and would sometimes be chamfered on the insides.

Early furniture was primitively constructed from solid wood, often reusing an old piece of timber. By the 18th century, construction was becoming increasingly sophisticated, with finely executed joints and a carcase that was well made. This is a set of five Chippendale-style side chairs from c1770.

£800–900 Castlegate Antiques

A set of six Chippendale-style side chairs, with pierced baluster splats, America, probably Delaware Valley, late 18thC.

£3,250–3,750 Freeman's

A set of eight mahogany dining chairs, with bar backs and stuff-over seats, on square tapered legs with spade feet, c1790.

£5,500–6,500
Chair Set

A set of four Hepplewhite-style mahogany dining chairs, with drop-in seats, c1800.

£1,000–1,100
Swan at Tetsworth

A set of six mahogany side chairs, the scroll backs with reeded crests and acanthus and rosette-carved rails, on Grecian front legs, one chair later, America, Philadelphia, c1815.

£1,800–2,200 **Skinner**

A set of six ebonized side chairs, with rope-twist rails, the centre rail with a painted panel, with cane seats and sabre legs, c1810.

£4,500–5,000 **Chair Set**

A set four of ebonized and gilt-painted side chairs, with Trafalgar seats, on sabre legs, c1815.

£1,300–1,500
Chair Set

A set of eight Regency mahogany dining chairs, including two carvers.

£5,000–6,000
Tredantiques

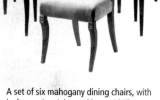

A set of six Regency mahogany dining chairs, with acanthus-carved top rails above pierced rails and caned seats, on gadrooned tapered legs.

£700–850 **Cheffins**

A set of four Regency rosewood dining chairs, with drop-in seats.

£750–850
Pantiles Spa Antiques

A set of six mahogany dining chairs, with leaf-carved uprights and legs, c1815.

£5,750–7,000
Sotheby's (O)

ESSENTIAL REFERENCE CHAIR BACK STYLES

Carolean (1665–85)

Solid vase-shape splat-back (1710–40)

Windsor (c1750–1850)

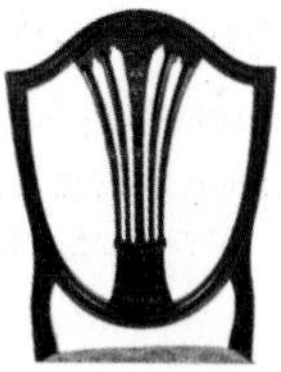

Hepplewhite shield back (1780–1800)

Gothic revival (1820–50)

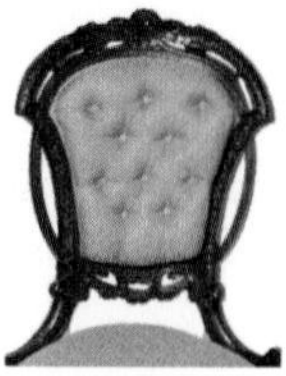

Victorian button-back (c1860–90)

A pair of mahogany chairs, each splat decorated in gilt-brass with a profile bust within a laurel wreath, on lion-paw feet, damaged, France, 1815–30.
£750–900
Sotheby's (P)

A set of six mahogany dining chairs, the rails with brass inlay, with drop-in seats and sabre legs, c1820.
£3,500–4,000 Chair Set

A set of eight mahogany dining chairs, including two carvers, with brass-inlaid top rails, rope-twist centre rails and drop-in seats, on sabre legs, c1820.
£8,000–9,000 Chair Set

A set of 14 mahogany dining chairs, including an armchair, with turned front legs, c1825.
£13,000–16,000
Sotheby's

A set of six George IV mahogany dining chairs, including two carvers, with drop-in seats, c1825.
£800–1,000 Woolley & Wallis

A set of eight painted dining chairs, including two carvers, with drop-in seats, northern Europe, 19thC.
£800–1,000
Sotheby's (Am)

A set of four mahogany chairs, with turned and reeded front legs, c1835.
£2,700–3,000
Woburn Antiques Centre

A set of six William IV mahogany dining chairs, the crest rails with carved acanthus leaf terminals, with drop-in seats and turned front legs.
£1,600–1,800 James Adam

A set of four mahogany dining chairs, with bar backs and drop-in seats, on turned and fluted front legs, c1835.
£1,300–1,500 Chair Set

A set of six mahogany dining chairs, with balloon backs and turned front legs, 19thC.

£4,000–4,500
Mary Cruz Antiques

An ebonized, partly painted and gilt chair, decorated with acanthus leaves and garlands of vines, fruits and palmettes, with a cane seat and paw feet, damaged, America, 1850–75.

£450–550 Sotheby's (P)

A set of six mahogany dining chairs, with balloon backs and turned front legs, c1860.

£1,800–2,000
Chair Set

A set of six painted Windsor side chairs, with simulated bamboo turning, America, New England, 19thC.

£800–1,000 Freeman's

A set of four walnut side chairs, inlaid with mother-of-pearl and bone, on cabriole legs, Syria, 19thC.

£5,000–6,000 Sotheby's (NY)

A pair of mahogany side chairs, with latticework backs, on tapered brass-capped legs, France, 1825–50.

£7,000–8,500 Sotheby's (NY)

A set of four rosewood dining chairs, the balloon backs with carved mid-rails above stuff-over serpentine seats, on tapered scroll legs, 19thC.

£400–500 Rosebery's

A set of 12 mahogany chairs, with balloon backs and turned front legs, c1850.

£1,700–1,900
Georgian Antiques

A Victorian papier-mâché chair, with mother-of-pearl inlay and a cane seat.

£300–350 Lorfords

HALL CHAIRS

A mahogany hall chair, with turned front legs, c1810.

£250–300 Swan at Tetsworth

A Regency mahogany hall chair, with a carved shell back.

£600–675 Georgian Antiques

A carved mahogany hall chair, c1820.

£1,100–1,250 Georgian Antiques

A pair of mahogany chairs, carved with stylized shells and leaves, on turned tapered legs, slight damage, c1820.

£450–550 Dreweatt Neate (N)

A pair of George IV mahogany hall chairs, the backs each with a carved and painted shield-shape crest.

£1,000–1,100 Woolley & Wallis

A pair of Geoge IV mahogany hall chairs, with panelled octagonal backs and baluster front legs.

£800–1,000 Sotheby's (O)

A set of four mahogany hall chairs, the moulded backs painted with a crest, on turned front legs, c1830.

£4,000–5,000 Sotheby's

A hall chair, with original paint, the back with the Winchester School crest, c1840.

£340–375 Woburn Antiques Centre

A pair of mahogany hall chairs, with shield-shaped backs, c1860.

£525–575 SW Antiques

SETTLES & SETTEES

An oak bench, the back with moulded panels, 16thC, 77¼in (196cm) wide.

£2,000–2,400
Sotheby's (P)

A Charles II oak settle, the panelled back with carving and inlay, the base with later bracing, 71in (180.5cm) wide.

£3,000–3,500 Sotheby's (O)

An oak settle/table, probably Wales, early 18thC, 44in (112cm) wide.

£1,200–1,400
Sotheby's (O)

An oak settle, the panelled back with carved cresting rail, with scrolled arms, on baluster legs with a carved front stretcher, restored, c1710, 71¼in (181cm) wide.

£3,300–4,000 Dreweatt Neate

An oak settle, with panelled back, on a stretcher base, early 18thC, 63in (160cm) wide.

£1,500–1,750 Gorringes (L)

A George III oak settee, with fielded panelled back, drop-in seat and scroll arms, on cabriole legs with pad feet joined by a turned and blocked stretcher, 71¼in (181cm) wide.

£1,700–2,000
James Adam

A George III oak settle, the fielded panelled back with mahogany crossbanding, with scroll arms and cabriole front legs, 75½in (192cm) wide.

£550–650
Penrith Farmers' & Kidd's

An elm and pine settle, with curved back, 18th–19thC, 59¾in (152cm) wide.

£1,800–2,200
Tennants

A Windsor settee, with simulated bamboo turning, slight damage, America, possibly Pennsylvania, c1810, 84in (313.5cm) wide.

£2,400–2,800 Skinner

A wooden settle, France, early 19thC.

£750–850
Henry Baines

CHAISE LONGUES & DAYBEDS

A plum and yew-wood drop-end day bed, with original drop-end support chains and tensioned rope seat, probably Wales, c1720, 54in (137cm) long.

£6,300–7,000 Robert Young Antiques

A Louis XVI-style painted *duchesse brisée*, on tapered reeded legs, slight damage, 19thC.

£4,000–5,000
Sotheby's (P)

A gilt-stencilled and part-ebonized daybed, with a scroll back and arm, above a plain frieze, on faceted legs, early 19thC, 50in (127cm) long.

£1,600–2,000 Skinner

A gadroon and leaf-carved coromandel daybed, with a scroll back, on paw feet, Ceylon, early 19thC, 76¼in (194cm) long.

£2,000–2,500
James Adam

An ebony, birch and rosewood daybed, Continental, early 19thC, 90in (228.5cm) long.

£7,500–9,000
Sotheby's (NY)

A William IV carved mahogany chaise longue, with a scrolled and reeded arm and footrest and a scrolled back, on turned legs, 64in (162.5cm) long.

£1,000–1,200 Northeast Auctions

A carved rosewood chaise longue, 19thC, 50in (127cm) long.

£2,700–3,000
Mary Cruz Antiques

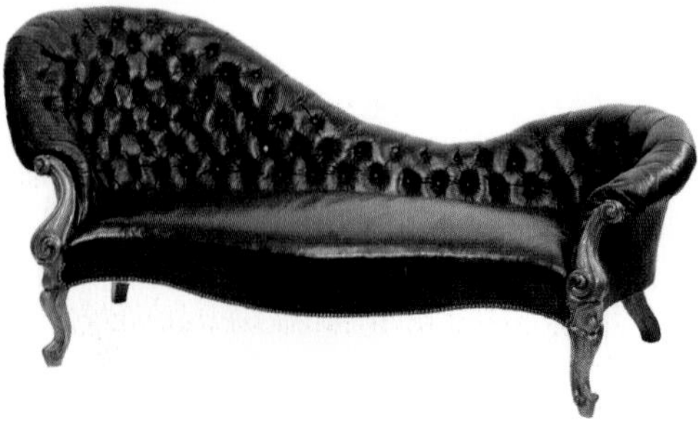

A Victorian walnut chaise longue, with leaf-carved arms, leather upholstery, on cabriole legs and scroll feet, 81in (205.5cm) long.

£750–900
Andrew Hartley

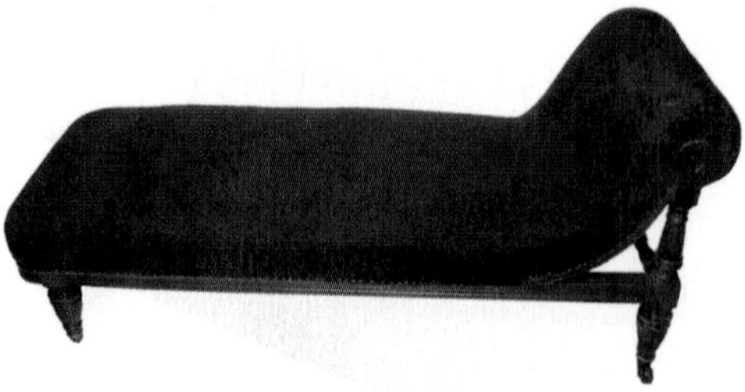

A rosewood daybed, by Collinson & Lock, attributed to Batley, c1880, 63in (160cm) long.

£7,000–8,000
Puritan Values

SETTEES & SOFAS

A George II mahogany double back settee, 54¼in (138cm) wide.

£9,000–11,000
Sotheby's (O)

A painted and parcel-gilt sofa, the curved and panelled backrest above two carved splats each with a laurel wreath and torch, the panelled seat rail and legs with paterae and pendant husks, Italy, c1800, 108in (274.5cm) wide.

£2,500–3,000 Skinner

A rococo painted sofa, with gilt detail, carved with rocailles and acanthus leaves, 1750–1800, Sweden, 67in (170cm) wide.

£6,500–7,000 Bukowskis

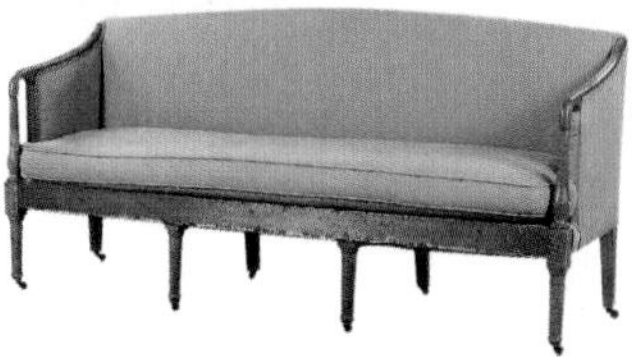

A tiger maple sofa, with downswept arms and vase-turned supports, on ring-turned front legs, America, New England, 1810–25, 77in (195.5cm) wide.

£1,400–1,800 Northeast Auctions

A George III mahogany sofa, with scroll arms, on square tapered front legs, c1800, 90¼in (229cm) wide.

£1,800–2,200
Dreweatt Neate

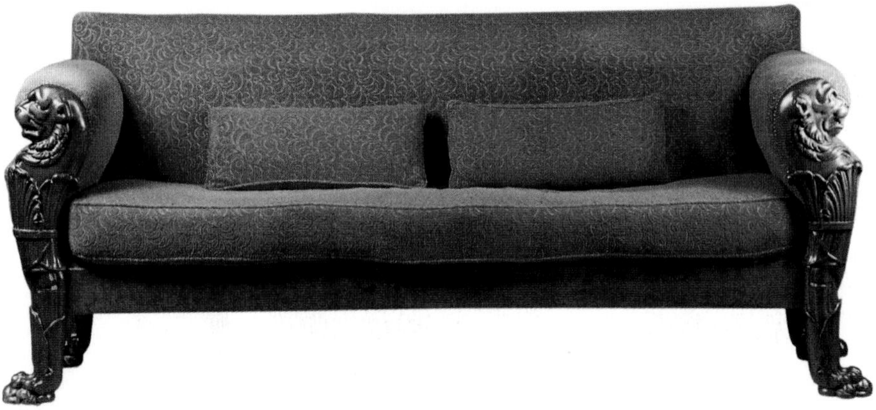

A mahogany sofa, in the manner of Thomas Hope, with scrolled arms, the arm facings carved with leopard monopodia, the carved feet with concealed brass and iron casters, c1815, 89¼in (226.5cm) wide.

£30,000–35,000 Sotheby's

The boldly carved monopodia supports of this sofa closely resemble the design for a tripod table in mahogany and gold illustrated in Hope's Household Furniture and Interior Decoration, *published in 1807. Thomas Hope was an influential Regency art collector whose published work reflected ideas and influences garnered from an eight-year Grand Tour. Hope also acknowledged being influenced by the leading French Empire designers Percier and Fontaine, whose publication* Recueil de Décorations Interieures *reflected the art of classical civilisation. Hope's direct influence can be seen in the designs of the architect and furniture designer George Smith (active 1804–28).*

A mahogany sofa, c1820, 74in (188cm) wide.

£4,500–5,000
Moxhams

A William IV mahogany sofa, with a rosette-carved scrolling padded back above scroll arms, on turned legs with gadrooned bun feet and inset brass casters, 85in (216cm) wide.

£1,000–1,200 Cheffins

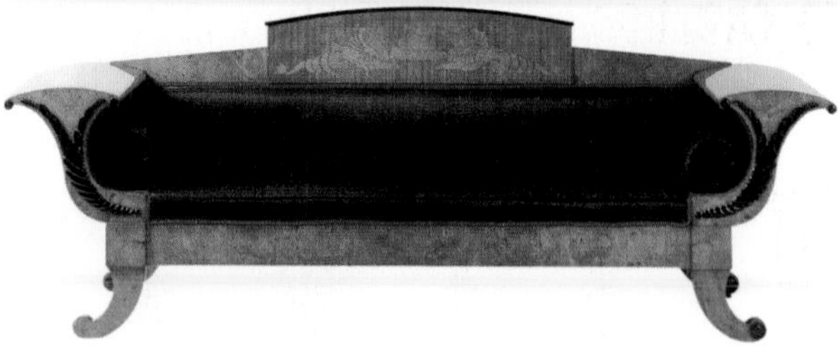

An ebonized, burr-elm, ash and mahogany settee, the arched backrest inlaid with a figure of Poseidon flanked by chimera, with cornucopia-shaped armrests, on splayed tapered legs, Continental, possibly Scandinavia, c1830, 99in (251.5cm) wide.

£7,500–9,000 **Sotheby's (NY)**

A carved walnut settee, France, 19thC, 55in (139.5cm) wide.

£1,350–1,500
Pennard House

A Biedermeier-style mahogany sofa, with scroll arms, Continental, 77in (195.5cm) wide.

£450–550
Woolley & Wallis

A mahogany sofa, carved with scrolling acanthus leaves and flowers, on lion-paw feet and casters, America, 19thC, 82in (208.5cm) wide.

£3,500–4,200 **Sotheby's (P)**

A pair of Louis XVI-style carved giltwood sofas, the frame carved with laurel leaves, acanthus and guilloche, regilded, Continental, 19thC, 75½in (192cm) wide.

£25,000–30,000 **Sotheby's**

A bronze-mounted mahogany settee, inlaid with fruitwood marquetry, France, 1850–1900, 52in (132cm) wide.

£3,750–4,500 **Sotheby's (Am)**

An early Victorian mahogany sofa, with arched top rail, scroll ends and turned feet, 87¾in (223cm) wide.

£600–700 **Sotheby's (O)**

A pair of walnut sofas, on turned legs, c1875, 52¾in (134cm) wide.

£5,000–6,000
Sotheby's (O)

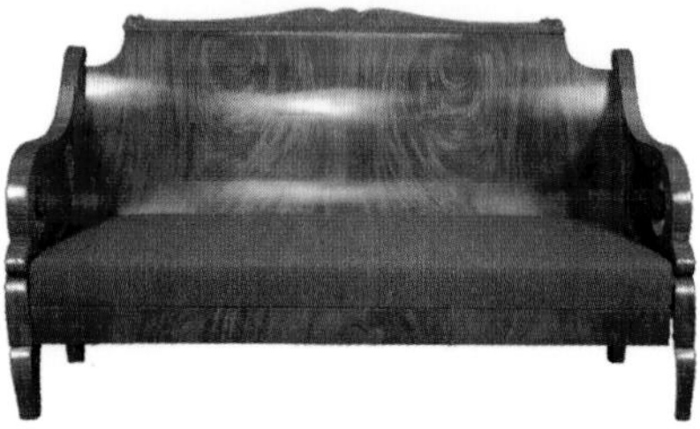

A Biedermeier-style mahogany settee, with scroll arms, on square section legs, c1860, 76in (193cm) wide.

£550–650 **Rosebery's**

A Victorian chesterfield, on petal-carved legs, 85in (216cm) wide.

£400–500
Woolley & Wallis

A Victorian settee, on turned walnut legs, with later button upholstery, 86in (218.5cm) wide.

£900–1,100 **Woolley & Wallis**

An ebonized and gilt settee, the frame with gilt-metal-mounted roundels surmounted by an arched pediment with winged seraphim mount, on turned and block legs, America, c1880, 76in (193cm) wide.

£2,800–3,400 **Hy Duke**

REFECTORY & FARMHOUSE TABLES

An oak and elm refectory table, the frieze with carved decoration, on six turned legs and square feet, early 17thC, 88¼in (224cm) long.

£15,000–18,000
Sotheby's

A Charles II oak refectory table, the boarded top above baluster legs and square feet, 100in (254cm) long.

£5,500–6,500
Sotheby's

A Charles II oak refectory table, the plank top on four chamfered legs, 108¼in (275cm) long.

£2,800–3,300
Sotheby's (O)

A Charles II oak refectory table, the board top above a carved frieze with punchwork, 59½in (151cm) long.

£2,000–2,500
Sotheby's (O)

An oak refectory table, with later alterations, late 17thC, 85in (216cm) long.

£6,200–6,800 Red Lion Antiques

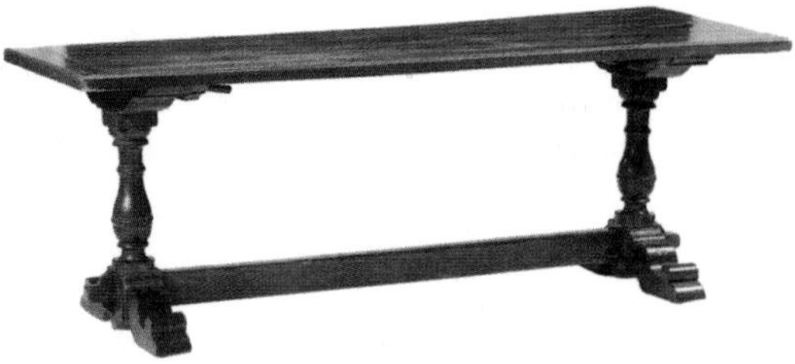

A walnut refectory table, the top on two turned columns and downswept legs, 17thC and later, 89½in (227.5cm) long.

£2,200–2,750 Freeman's

An ash farmhouse table, with a two-piece plank top and central stretcher, France, Normandy, 18thC, 89in (226cm) long.

£6,300–7,000 Oak & Country

A cherrywood farmhouse refectory table, with a drawer, mid-19thC, 80in (203cm) wide.

£3,500–4,000 Red Lion Antiques

GATELEG & DROP-LEAF TABLES

An oak gateleg table, with drawer, repaired, c1680, 65in (165cm) wide.
£6,300–7,000
Period Oak ⊞

An oak gateleg table, with bobbin-turned supports, late 17thC, 60in (152.5cm) wide.
£2,500–3,000 **Henry Baines** ⊞

A walnut and oak gateleg table, with square and turned legs on square Braganza feet, c1700, 51½in (131cm) extended.
£2,200–2,600 **Sotheby's (O)**

An oak double-action gateleg table, the frieze drawer above baluster-turned legs, restored, c1700, 67½in (171.5cm) extended.
£2,200–2,600 **Sotheby's (O)**

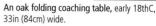

An oak folding coaching table, early 18thC, 33in (84cm) wide.
£800–900 **Oak & Country** ⊞

An oak gateleg table, c1720, 45½in (115.5cm) extended.
£1,300–1,500
Moxhams ⊞

An oak gateleg table, with turned legs and stretchers, c1720, 66in (167.5cm) wide.
£5,400–6,000 **Peter Norden Antiques** ⊞

An oak Westmorland-style gateleg table, with chamfered legs, mid-18thC, 45¾in (116cm) extended.
£2,000–2,200
Penrith Farmers' & Kidd's

An oak drop-leaf table, with drawer, 18thC, 42in (106.5cm) wide.
£420–480
Burford Antiques ⊞

A painted cherrywood and birch drop-leaf table, the tapered legs with pad feet, America, New England, late 18thC, 40in (101.5cm) extended.
£11,000–13,000
Northeast Auctions

. mahogany spider-leg drop-leaf table, estored, c1755, 26½in (67.5cm) wide.
2,000–2,500 Sotheby's

A mahogany drop-leaf table, with later frieze drawers, on cabriole legs and hoof feet, 18thC, 35in (89cm) wide.
£2,500–3,000 Mealy's

A mahogany drop-leaf table, with single leaf, cabriole legs and claw-and-ball feet, America, Massachusetts, c1760, 36in (91.5cm) extended.
£20,000–25,000
Northeast Auctions

Most drop-leaf tables made at this time have two leaves and those that only have one are generally regarded with suspicion by collectors as they are often faked. This table commanded a high price because of its rarity and its overall quality – the top has a moulded edge and the apron, which is original to the table, is scalloped. The C-scrolls at the top of the legs are a detail not often seen and the overall attenuation of the legs and crisp carving of the feet attest to the quality of the craftmanship.

. mahogany hunt table, with eight chamfered legs, Ireland, ite 18thC, 96in (244cm) wide.
12,000–14,000 Mealy's

. mahogany drop-leaf table, with tapered egs, France, c1800, 30¾in (78cm) wide.
700–850
otheby's (Am)

A mahogany and veneered drop-leaf table, with a rotating base, on claw feet, 1800–50, 38¾in (98.5cm) wide.
£2,300–2,750
Sotheby's (P)

A burr-walnut Sutherland table, with carved legs on casters, c1870, 34in (86.5cm) wide.
£1,100–1,250
Burford Antiques

DINING TABLES

n oak draw-leaf table, the plank top above a moulded ieze, on four bulbous turned legs, Holland, 17thC and iter, 83¾in (212.5cm) extended.
1,250–1,500 Andrew Hartley

A George III triple pedestal dining table, each pedestal with a tilt top, turned barrel supports and four downswept legs, slight damage, 104¾in (266cm) long.
£5,500–6,500 Woolley & Wallis

An inlaid mahogany triple dining table, with two hinged leaves, on swing legs with crossbanded cuffs, America, New York, c1800, 43in (109cm) extended.

£2,500–3,000 **Northeast Auctions**

A George III mahogany dining table, with drop-leaf centre section and extra leaf, 130in (332cm) extended.

£1,200–1,400
Thomson, Roddick & Medcalf (D)

A mahogany dining table, with two leaves, on turned supports and downswept legs with brass paw feet and casters, c1815, 90in (228.5cm) extended.

£3,000–3,500 **Freeman's**

A George IV mahogany dining table, with six leaves, the concertina frames on turned and ribbed legs, the later carved border decorated with foliage, putti and animals, 200in (508cm) extended.

£13,000–16,000 **Woolley & Wallis**

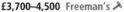

A George IV mahogany dining table, on turned and reeded legs, with central drop-leaf section, 111½in (283cm) long.

£1,400–1,800 **Drewett Neate**

A mahogany dining table, with two leaves, on tapered supports with downswept legs, America, Philadelphia, c1830, 94in (239cm) extende

£3,700–4,500 **Freeman's**

A George IV mahogany gate-leg dining table, in the manner of Gillow of Lancaster, on 12 reeded legs, 120in (305cm) long.

£15,000–18,000 **Sotheby's (O)**

A mahogany dining table, with two extra leaves, on a plinth base with claw feet, 1825–50, Holland, 92½in (235cm) diam.

£1,250–1,500 **Sotheby's (Am)**

A William IV mahogany dining table, on six turned legs with ebony rings, leaves missing, 48¾in (124cm) wide.

£1,500–1,800 **Sotheby's (O)**

A William IV mahogany dining table, with three extra leaves, on turned and reeded legs and brass casters, 45in (114.5cm) wide.

£1,800–2,200 **Drewett Neate**

A William IV mahogany dining table, with two extra leaves, on turne tapered legs and casters, 102½in (260.5cm) extended.

£2,400–2,800 **Greenslade Taylor Hunt**

A **mahogany dining table,** by Johnstone, Jupe & Co, after a design by Robert Jupe, ith eight small leaves and eight large leaves, the bead-moulded frieze above a aluster column and carved scroll feet, c1835, 84in (213.5cm) extended with rger leaves.

150,000–180,000 Sotheby's

A mahogany dining table, with six leaves, on turned legs and casters, c1830, 177in (450cm) extended, together with a mahogany stand containing the leaves.

£7,000–8,500
Sotheby's (Am)

Victorian walnut extending dining table, with three leaves, on carved cap and rned tapering legs, 116¼in (295cm) extended.

2,250–2,800
worders

A walnut dining table, with three leaves, the carved egg-and-dart top on a telescopic frame, on carved legs with claw-and-ball feet, late 19thC, 141in (358cm) extended.

£1,200–1,500 Woolley & Wallis

DRUM TABLES

satinwood drum table, with ebonized line nlay, c1790, 47¾in (121.5cm) diam.

6,000–7,000 Sotheby's (O)

A Regency mahogany drum table, the leather-inset top on a ring-turned column and four downswept legs, with brass caps and casters, 46½in (118cm) diam.

£1,800–2,200 Sworders

A Regency mahogany drum table, the top with four drawers and four dummy drawers, on a later base, 48¾in (124cm) diam.

£4,500–5,000
Sotheby's (O)

Regency rosewood drum table, with oxwood line inlay, 35¾in (91cm) diam.

3,800–4,500 Sotheby's (O)

A mahogany drum table, with four drawers and four dummy drawers, c1820, 48in (122cm) diam.

£5,000–6,000 Sotheby's (O)

A Gothic revival oak drum table, the top inset with a tooled leather writing surface above four short drawers, stamped 'Robert Strahan & Co', Ireland, 48in (122cm) wide.

£3,000–3,500 Hy Duke

LOWBOYS

An oak **lowboy,** 1710–20, 28in (71cm) wide.
£2,500–2,800
Long Street Antiques

An elm **lowboy,** with a cleated edge top, early 18thC, 23in (58.5cm) wide.
£550–650 Woolley & Wallis

An oak **lowboy,** with cabriole legs and figured apron, early 18thC, 34in (86.5cm) wide.
£1,250–1,400 Red Lion Antiques

A George II oak **lowboy,** the crossbanded top above three drawers, on cabriole legs and pad feet, 30¼in (77cm) wide.
£1,800–2,200 Tennants

A George III mahogany **lowboy,** the moulded top above one long and two short drawers, on cabriole legs, top possibly later, brass handles later, 36½in (92.5cm) wide.
£400–500 Woolley & Wallis

A burr-elm and walnut **lowboy,** the quarter-veneered and crossbanded top above three drawers, with a shaped apron, on cabriole legs, early 18thC, 30in (76cm) high.
£8,000–9,000 Chair Set

An oak Chippendale-style **lowboy,** with original handles, 1750–60, 36in (91.5cm) wide.
£2,200–2,500
Long Street Antiques

An oak **lowboy,** with crossbanded top, c1780, 28in (71cm) wide.
£1,100–1,250
Long Street Antiques

A George III oak **lowboy,** the board top above one long and two short drawers, lower drawers relined, 30¾in (78cm) wide.
£900–1,000 Woolley & Wallis

SIDE TABLES

joined oak folding side table, the folding
›p enclosing five compartments, above a
ırved frieze and three legs, mid-16thC,
5½in (90cm) wide.

70,000–85,000
reweatt Neate

his is one of the earliest surviving pieces of nglish secular furniture. It may have been sed as a writing, games, rent or tax table as ere is evidence of a former lock to keep aluable possessions safe from prying eyes. It ould have undoubtedly belonged to a erson of high status. It may have been tended to travel around with its owner as ere is evidence of three former hook-and-ye fastenings to the fold-over top.

An oak and **fruitwood side table,** the dentil frieze above a long drawer, on bobbin-turned legs, 1675–1700, 35in (89cm) wide.

£4,800–5,700 Sotheby's

A **walnut side table,** with a drawer, on columnar legs and bun feet, probably Italian, 17thC, 18½in (47cm) wide.

£1,300–1,500 Sotheby's (Am)

A rosewood **side table,** the crossbanded top with featherbanding and segmented oyster-veneered olivewood motifs, the frieze with a drawer, on spiral-twist legs and bun feet, late 17thC, 37in (94cm) wide.

£13,000–16,000 Sotheby's

An **oak side table,** with bobbin- and reel-turned legs, original ash drawer linings, c1690, 30in (76cm) wide.

£2,500–2,750 Swan Gallery

n **oak side table,** with chevron inlay, on spiral-turned legs, drawer ssociated, restored, late 17thC, 43¼in (110cm) wide.

2,800–3,500 Dreweatt Neate

An **oak side table,** on turned tapered and block legs with low stretcher, early 18thC, 38in (96.5cm) wide.

£1,600–2,000 Gorringes (L)

n **oak side table,** with drawer, on turned aluster legs, early 18thC, 30in (76cm) wide.

900–1,000
ong Street Antiques

An oak **side table,** the crossbanded top above a frieze drawer, on baluster-turned legs and cup feet, 18thC, 34in (86.5cm) wide.

£450–550 Cheffins

A **walnut marquetry side table,** the dished top above a long frieze drawer, Continental, 18thC, 32¾in (83cm) wide.

£900–1,100 Cheffins

A walnut side table, with a frieze drawer and shaped apron, on acanthus-carved cabriole legs and pad feet, Ireland, mid-18thC, 31in (78.5cm) wide.

£1,800–2,200 Freeman's

A mahogany side table, with carved Greek-key frieze, on square legs with carved spandrels and block feet, Ireland, mid-18thC, 82in (208.5cm) wide.

£11,000–13,000 James Adam

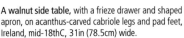

MARKET INFORMATION COUNTRY FURNITURE

- Early pieces, dating from the 16th and 17th centuries, are attracting higher prices than later examples.
- Refectory tables and beds continue to maintain good prices, reflecting the fact that rarity attracts value.
- Colour and condition are very important.
- Dressers with doors attract higher prices than those with just drawers.
- Prices for coffers have improved recently.
- Court cupboards and Windsor chairs are currently less popular.

A George III mahogany side table, the apron carved with scrolls, acanthus leaves and flowerheads, centred with a shell, on cabriole legs and paw feet, Ireland, 59¾in (152cm) wide.

£145,000–175,000 James Adam

Not only is this table of superb quality, it has an excellent provenance. Its ownership was traced back to Charles Brett of Belfast, a wine merchant during the 1780s.

A pair of harewood and marquetry side tables, with tulipwood, burr-walnut and purple-heart inlay, on square legs, height reduced, c1775, 44½in (113cm) wide.

£14,000–17,500 Sotheby's

A George III mahogany side table, the crossbanded top above a frieze drawer, on chamfered tapered legs, 29¾in (75.5cm) wide.

£450–550
Woolley & Wallis

A poplar side table, c1785, 34in (86.5cm) wide.

£1,000–1,100
Peter Norden Antiques

A mahogany kidney-shaped side table, c1800, 34in (86.5cm) wide.

£1,650–1,850 Chair Set

A mahogany side table, with a single flap, early 19thC, 30in (76cm) wide.

£600–700 Woolley & Wallis

A mahogany side table, with a frieze drawer, damaged, early 19thC, 36in (91.5cm) wide.

£500–600 Woolley & Wallis

An oak side table, with a carved frieze, on six turned legs, late 18thC, 24in (61cm) wide.

£1,800–2,000 Oak & Country

A mahogany and marquetry side table, with a drawer and two dummy drawers, on square tapered fluted legs, Holland, 28¾in (73cm) wide.

£450–550 Dreweatt Neate (N)

A mahogany bowfronted side table, with drawers, on tapered legs, altered, c1830, 42¼in (107.5cm) wide.

£500–600 Dreweatt Neate

A rosewood-veneered side table, the frieze with applied carved decoration, on tapered legs joined by a stretcher, c1835, 36¼in (92cm) wide.

£650–750 Dreweatt Neate

A mahogany breakfront side table, with three boxwood-strung frieze drawers, on ring-turned tapered legs, gallery missing, 19thC, 46in (117cm) wide.

£1,100–1,300 Dreweatt Neate

An oak side table, Holland, 19thC, 31in (78.5cm) high.

£2,200–2,500
Red Lion Antiques

A fruitwood side table, the oak-lined frieze drawer with a later handle, 19thC, 25in (63.5cm) wide.

£570–670 Woolley & Wallis

A mahogany silver table, the shaped frieze with carved shells, on leaf-carved cabriole legs and claw-and-ball feet, Ireland, 19thC, 27½in (70cm) wide.

£2,000–2,400 Mealy's

A Gothic-style oak side table, the moulded top above two frieze drawers, on sleigh feet joined by a carved stretcher, 19thC, 42¼in (107.5cm) wide.

£470–570
Cheffins

A Louis XV-style marquetry and gilt-bronze side table, France, Paris, c1880, 22in (56cm) wide.

£3,000–3,500
Sotheby's (O)

BREAKFAST TABLES

A mahogany breakfast table, on four downswept legs with brass caps and casters, c1800, 57in (145cm) diam.

£2,250–2,500 Hallidays

A Regency mahogany breakfast table, on four strung downswept legs with brass caps and casters, 43¾in (111cm) wide.

£280–350 Sworders

A William IV rosewood tilt-top breakfast table, on a baluster column, three lion-paw feet and casters, restored, 49¼in (125cm) diam.

£800–1,000 Dreweatt Neate (HAM)

A walnut breakfast table, with tilt-top, on a carved column and four carved legs, 19thC, 50in (127cm) diam.

£1,000–1,200 Ewbank Auctioneers

A Victorian burr-walnut breakfast table, the top with inlaid foliate decoration, on a turned pedestal with four conforming columns and acanthus-carved legs, 49¼in (125cm) diam.

£800–950 Rosebery's

A mahogany breakfast table, with later flap top, 19thC, 54in (137cm) wide.

£1,100–1,300 Sotheby's (Am)

A Victorian burr-walnut tilt-top breakfast table, on a carved column and scrolling legs, 58in (148cm) diam.

£3,000–3,500 Anderson & Garland

A mahogany tilt-top breakfast table, c1860, 44in (112cm) diam.

£800–900 Chair Set

CENTRE TABLES

A marquetry, ivory and bone-inlaid centre table, inlaid with scrolling flowers and a hunting scene, on spiral-turned legs, the X-stretcher centred by an urn, northern Italy, c1700, 59½in (151cm) wide.

£18,000–22,000 **Sotheby's (P)**

A birch table, with a scrubbed top, the base with original paint, America, New England, c1800, 39in (99cm) wide.

£2,300–3,000 **Northeast Auctions**

EXPERT'S EYE CENTRE TABLES

The crossbanded edge is a further detail that points to this table's quality.
The top, which demonstrates the quality of the craftmanship in this piece, is inlaid in satinwood with a band of trailing vines. Brass inlay was also used.
The centre has mirrored veneers, giving the top a sense of balance.
The feet have inset casters.
The carved C-scroll legs with their acanthus-leaf feet are more typical of early Victorian design.

This Regency rosewood centre table, which has a carved and inlaid base, has good proportions. It has faded to an even colour and has the added advantage of not having been restored. Rosewood is a tropical hardwood that smells sweet when cut; it was used extensively in the manufacture of quality furniture during the first half of the 19th century.

£15,000–16,500 **Ronald Chambers**

An oak pedestal centre table, by A. W. N. Pugin, on a carved and turned arcaded open base, c1830, 60½in (153.5cm) wide.

£5,000–6,000 Woolley & Wallis

Augustus Welby Northmore Pugin (1812–52) had his own business between 1829 and 1831 in Covent Garden, designing and making furniture and decorative details.

A mahogany centre table, on a turned and acanthus-carved support and paw feet, America, Philadelphia, c1830, 35in (99cm) diam.

£2,000–2,500 Freeman's

An ebony-inlaid tulipwood, flame mahogany and parquetry tilt-top centre table, decorated with a stylized flowerhead and Greek-key motif, Italy, Genoa, c1830, 48¼in (122.5cm) diam.

£15,000–18,000 Sotheby's

A rosewood and fruitwood marquetry centre table, the legs applied with gilt-bronze mounts, 19thC, 59in (150cm) wide.

£1,500–1,800 Sotheby's (Am)

A thuyawood, kingwood and parcel-gilt centre table, on three paw feet, Austria, c1840, 51in (129.5cm) diam.

£6,500–8,000 Sotheby's (NY)

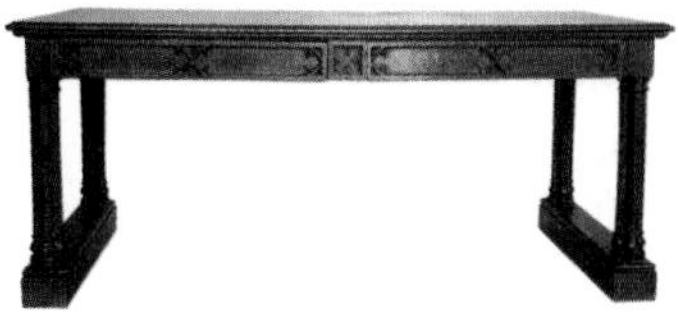

An oak and burr-oak centre table, the moulded top above a Gothic tracery frieze and two drawers, on column legs with end supports, c1850, 67in (170cm) wide.

£11,000–13,000 Bellmans

An early Victorian mahogany centre table, the crossbanded top over two frieze drawers and two dummy drawers, on turned supports and a platform base, 56in (142cm) wide.

£330–425 Sworders

A mahogany centre table, with a frieze drawer and paw feet, associated gilt-metal mounts, Russia, 19thC, 53in (134.5cm) diam.

£10,000–12,000 Sotheby's (NY)

A walnut and marquetry centre table, in the manner of Joseph Cremer, the top with a brass edge above a frieze drawer, on cabriole legs, France, mid-19thC, 54in (137cm) wide.

£3,200–3,800 Mealy's

A thuyawood and marquetry centre table, attributed to Holland & Sons, the quarter-veneered top inlaid with a ribbon-tied border of lilies, the four column supports centred by an urn, with gilt-brass mounts, c1860, 49in (124.5cm) wide.

£28,000–32,000 Sotheby's

Holland & Sons began life as Taprell, Stephen & Holland in 1803. Their style developed between 1851 and 1870, which was a period of great change in furniture-making in England. They exhibited at the Great Exhibition in Crystal Palace in 1851, in Paris in 1856 and again in London in 1862. This table typifies the quality of Holland & Sons' craftmanship – the French-influenced design was popular in Britain at this time.

A Victorian rosewood centre table, with crossbanding and stringing, the moulded top inlaid with a mother-of-pearl flowerhead, the turned and reeded stem flanked by three smaller columns carved with stiff-leaf banding, label for Johnson & Appleyards, Sheffield, 32¼in (82cm) diam.

£1,500–1,800 Andrew Hartley

A giltwood and gesso centre table, the marble top above a frieze with scrolling acanthus and paterae, the stretcher with an urn finial, France, 1900–25, 38½in (98cm) wide.

£400–500 Dreweatt Neate

PEMBROKE TABLES

A Georgian mahogany Pembroke table, with two end drawers, 35in (89cm) diam.

£1,350–1,500
Woburn Abbey Antiques

A Cuban mahogany Pembroke table, with a beaded drawer and opposing dummy drawer, c1770, 31in (78.5cm) wide.

£600–680 Swan at Tetsworth

A George III mahogany Pembroke table, with serpentine flaps, the bowed ends with a drawer and opposing dummy drawer, on square tapered legs, with Marlborough feet, 42in (106.5cm) wide.

£1,250–1,500 Northeast Auctions

A satinwood Pembroke table, with ebonized line inlay, c1790, 38¼in (97cm) wide.

£3,500–4,250
Sotheby's (O)

A Regency mahogany Pembroke table, with a drawer and opposing dummy drawer, on ring-turned tapered legs and brass casters, 25¾in (65.5cm) extended.

£1,500–1,650 J Collins

A mahogany Pembroke table, with a drawer and opposing dummy drawer, with holly and boxwood stinging and satinwood cross-banding, on tapered and reeded legs with brass casters, c1810, 34¼in (87cm) wide.

£2,250–2,500 J Collins

A mahogany Pembroke table, attributed to Michael Allison, with string inlay, a drawer and opposing dummy drawer, the tapered legs each inlaid with a patera depicting a Maltese Cross, a sword and a leaf, America, New York, c1810, 39in (99cm) extended.

£2,200–2,500 Northeast Auctions

A mahogany and satinwood-crossbanded Pembroke table, the shaped top over a frieze drawer and opposing dummy drawer, on square tapered sabre legs with brass caps and casters, c1820, 33¾in (85.5cm) wide.

£1,750–2,000 Freeman's

SOFA TABLES

ι **mahogany sofa table,** with satinwood and nahogany crossbanding, two frieze drawers o each side, c1800, 28¾in (73cm) extended.

1,600–2,000 Sotheby's (O)

A mahogany and satinwood-banded sofa table, with ebony and boxwood stringing,two frieze drawers, on sabre legs with brass caps and casters, c1810, 56¾in (144cm) wide.

£2,200–2,600 Sotheby's

A rosewood sofa table, with boxwood stringing, the frieze with two drawers, on sabre legs with brass caps and casters, c1810, 58¾in (149cm) wide.

£2,500–3,000 Sotheby's

\ **mahogany sofa table,** with two frieze drawers, on turned columns and sabre legs, brass caps and casters, early 19thC, 37in (94cm) wide.

£850–1,000 Sworders

An inlaid mahogany sofa table, with two frieze drawers and two dummy drawers, on trestle supports, downswept legs and brass casters, c1820, 35in (89cm) wide.

£2,200–2,800 Freeman's Fine Art

A mahogany sofa table, with two drawers and two dummy drawers, on downswept legs and brass casters, c1820, 37in (94cm) wide.

£1,100–1,300 Freeman's Fine Art

CONSOLE & PIER TABLES

A mahogany console table, with a marble top, Ireland, c1750, 37¾in (96cm) wide.

£3,800–4,250 Moxhams

A painted parcel-gilt console table, the top decorated with a grotesque scene, with a scalloped apron, on square tapered legs, restored, Italy, 18thC, 55in (139.5cm) wide.

£6,500–8,000 Sotheby's (NY)

A mahogany console table, the apron carved with foliage, with dolphin legs, marble top later, mid-18thC, 33½in (85cm) wide.

£7,000–8,500 Sotheby's

A wood console table, carved with acanthus leaves and garlands, on cabriole legs and paw feet, associated marble top, gilding worn, base missing, Germany, mid-18thC, 35½in (90cm) wide.

£3,200–3,800 Sotheby's (NY)

A pair of carved giltwood pier tables, in the manner of Seddon, Sons & Shackleton, each with a painted satinwood top above a fluted frieze, the legs with leaf-carved capitals and patera-centred stretchers, c1790, 28in (71cm) wide.

£28,000–35,000 Sotheby's

The design for these tables is derived from a pier table published by Thomas Sheraton in his The Cabinet-Maker & Upholsterer's Drawing Book: 1793. *Painted furniture of this type is often associated with the Seddon workshop, one of the leading cabinet-makers of the 18th century, whose clients included the Empress of Russia and the fifth Duke of Bedford.*

A bronzed and gilt console table, with a marble top, carved with rocailles, acanthus leaves, grapevines and pumpkins, slight damage, 1750–1800, 44in (112cm) wide.
£5,500–6,500 Bukowskis

A console table, the marble top above a guilloche-moulded frieze, on tapered legs, France, late 18thC, 38in (96.5cm) wide.
£1,350–1,600 Freeman's

A mahogany pier table, the marble top above exotic wood columns with brass caps, mirror back, on ebonized lion-paw feet, America, Philadelphia, c1825, 37in (94cm) high.
£6,500–7,500 Freeman's

A brass and mahogany console table, the marble top above a frieze drawer, on front supports with a female caryatid and inlaid with tulips, mirror back, possibly Holland, 1800–25, 37in (94cm) wide.
£5,000–6,000 Sotheby's

A mahogany pier table, with ring-turned supports and undershelf, on a plinth base, early 19thC, 42in (106.5cm) wide.
£600–700 Gorringes (L)

A giltwood console table, carved and pierced with scrolling acanthus, restored, marble top missing, Italy, probably Rome, 19thC, 44½in (113cm) wide.
£3,800–4,500 Sotheby's (Am)

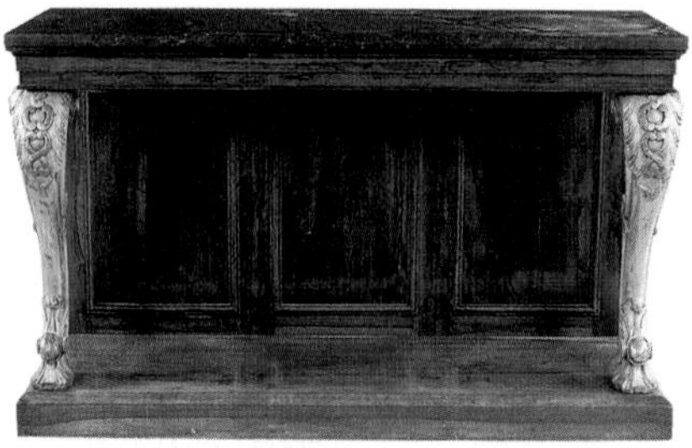

A William IV rosewood and parcel-gilt console table, the marble top on giltwood and gesso scroll supports, 61in (155cm) wide.
£2,250–2,750 Woolley & Wallis

A pair of painted and parcel-gilt pier tables, the marble tops, each support with a putto, restored, losses, 1825–50, 71in (180.5cm) wide.
£40,000–50,000 Sotheby's
Highly decorative tables such as these are currently very popular. The value of this particular pair is further enhanced because they were sold in a country house sale at Shrubland Hall, where they are documented in a receipt found in the house archives. It appears that they were supplied by Thomas Fairs of New Bond Street in London, and were possibly made by Messrs Morant, whose business was in the same street.

A painted and parcel-gilt demi-lune hall table, the frieze with foliate and gesso mask mounts, the tapered legs each with a female term, 19thC, 29¼in (74cm) wide.
£380–450 Rosebery's

A pair of carved giltwood console tables, with marble tops on carved leaf-moulded supports, 19thC, 28in (71cm) wide.
£3,250–4,000 Freeman's

An Empire-style painted beech console table, with gilded decoration and a marble top, France, c1900, 48in (122cm) wide.
£900–1,000 S W Antiques

SIDEBOARDS & SERVING TABLES

A **George II mahogany serving table,** the frieze centred with a carved shell, altered, 72¾in (185cm) wide.

£12,500–15,000 Sotheby's

This table belongs to a small group of tables distinguished by the use of exceptionally fine mahogany, crisply carved with fine detail. Each has the distinctive shell carving at the centre of the frieze, although they have cabriole legs. Another example, with square legs, was possibly made by William Bradshaw, a cabinet-maker working in London in the mid-18th century.

A **mahogany sideboard,** with three frieze drawers over two deep drawers, c1790, 56in (142cm) wide.

£1,750–2,000 Freeman's

A **mahogany sideboard,** with stringing, crossbanded borders and inlays, the central drawer flanked by a cellaret drawer and a deep drawer, on square tapered legs and spade feet, late 18thC, 84¾in (215.5cm) wide.

£5,000–6,000 Dreweatt Neate (N)

A **mahogany serving table,** with a brass gallery above a rope-moulded frieze, on rope-twist legs with brass lion-mask ring handles and paw feet with hairy hocks, Ireland, c1800, 82in (208.5cm) wide.

£18,000–22,000 James Adam

A **Sheraton-style mahogany sideboard,** with ebony and boxwood stringing, the drawer flanked by a cupboard and wine drawer, c1770, 67in (170cm) wide.

£9,000–10,000 Chair Set

A **George III mahogany bowfronted sideboard,** the top with crossbanding and boxwood stringing, with fitted frieze drawer and two bottle drawers, 56½in (143.5cm) wide.

£3,200–3,800 Anderson & Garland

A **Sheraton-style mahogany sideboard,** with flame birch panels, mahogany crossbanding and cockbeaded edges, the hinged front enclosing a fitted interior, America, New Hampshire, c1800, 57½in (146cm) wide.

£16,000–20,000 Northeast Auctions

Made in Portsmouth, New Hampshire, this piece not only has a Portsmouth family provenance but the use of flame birch – an indigenous wood – for the matched veneers provides contrast to the mahogany crossbanding and is typical of Portsmouth cabinet-makers. The design is unusual for the period and indicates an understanding of English fashion. Portsmouth furniture commands high prices for certain pieces and this example combines impeccable provenance, original surface, quality of cabinet-making and pleasing proportions.

A mahogany bowfronted sideboard, with three drawers above doors and bottle drawers, on ring-turned reeded tapering legs, restored, pulls later, slight damage, America, probably Boston, 1810–15, 71½in (181.5cm) wide.

£6,000–7,000 Skinner

A mahogany sideboard, with inlaid stringing and kingwood crossbanding, the bowfronted frieze drawer flanked by four cupboard doors with ivory escutcheons, on turned and reeded legs, possibly Channel Islands, 19thC, 91¼in (232cm) wide.

£1,600–2,000 Woolley & Wallis

A mahogany sideboard, the raised back carved with acanthus and central shell above an inverted breakfront top, over three frieze drawers with turned handles, on bun feet, Ireland, c1840, 73¼in (186cm) wide.

£600–700 Rosebery's

A mahogany breakfront sideboard, the mirror back flanked by foliate-mounted columns, above a frieze drawer and two cupboards, on platform supports, c1880, 72in (183cm) wide.

£650–800 Peter Francis

A Regency mahogany serving table, the moulded frieze flanked by lion masks, on tapered reeded legs, height reduced, 83½in (212cm) wide.

£1,400–1,700 Mealy's

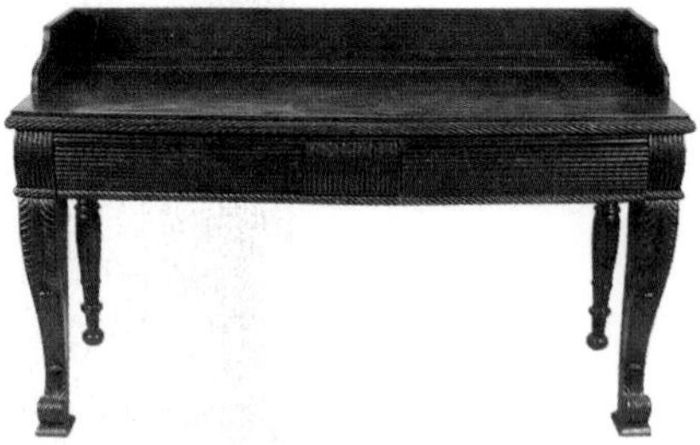

A George IV mahogany serving table, the top with rope moulding above two frieze drawers, on turned and scrolled legs, 70in (178cm) wide.

£4,500–5,500 James Adam

A cherrywood serving table, with two drawers and bread slide, France, c1860, 52in (132cm) wide.

£900–1,000 Gilbert & Dale

A mahogany sideboard, the raised back with a wreath, over cupboard doors flanked by pedestal cupboards, c1870, 78in (198cm) wide.

£1,300–1,400 Martin Taylor

A Louis XVI-style mahogany and gilt-bronze sideboard, with a marble top, France, Paris, c1900, 79¼in (201.5cm) wide.

£6,000–7,000 Sotheby's (O)

DRESSING TABLES

An amaranth and satinwood marquetry dressing table, mid-18thC, France, 37¾in (96cm) wide.

£3,200–3,800 Sotheby's (P)

A mahogany dressing table, the hinged top enclosing a mirror and a marble top, above a frieze drawer flanked by three drawers, France, c1790, 39¼in (100cm) wide.

£7,500–9,000 Sotheby's

A mahogany bowfronted dressing table, with a plate-glass top and three-quarter gallery, above two drawers, on turned legs, 19thC, 30in (76cm) wide.

£400–500 Greenslade Taylor Hunt

A cherrywood and mahogany dressing table, with two short and one long drawer, on turned tapering legs, slight damage, America, New England, 1800–25, 31in (78.5cm) wide.

£230–275 James D Julia

A painted wood dressing table, the drawer with gilded decoration, on square tapered legs, America, 1800–25, 36¼ (92cm) wide.

£5,500–6,500
Northeast Auctions

An oak dressing table, with one long and two short drawers, c1800, 28in (71cm) wide.

£630–700 Long Street Antiques

A painted pine dressing table, with a long drawer painted to resemble two drawers, over a further drawer, with pressed-brass handles, America, New England, 1825–30, 38¾in (98.5cm) wide.

£14,000–17,500 Northeast Auctions

WORK TABLES

A mahogany work table, with satinwood stringing, c1790, 30in (76cm) high.
£850–950 Long Street Antiques

A Regency rosewood work table, with satinwood banding and boxwood inlay, on square tapered legs, 17in (43cm) wide.
£2,250–2,500 Old Malthouse

A mahogany work table, with inlaid decoration, on sabre legs, Scotland, c1815, 19in (48.5cm) wide.
£650–725 C S Moreton Antiques

A Regency rosewood work table, 29½in (75cm) high.
£1,800–2,000
Georgian Antiques

A mahogany work table, with a drawer, on a tripod support, c1820, 20in (51cm) wide.
£1,300–1,500
Georgian Antiques

A rosewood drop-leaf work table, with inlaid stringing, with a frieze drawer and a bag, early 19thC, 15½in (39.5cm) wide.
£550–650 Woolley & Wallis

A rosewood work table, with two drawers, one with a fitted interior, on turned legs and brass casters, c1830, 29in (73.5cm) high.
£3,250–3,750 Mary Cruz Antiques

A William IV rosewood work box, with a fitted interior, on a turned and carved central column and carved paw feet, 18in (45.5cm) wide.
£800–900 Woburn Abbey Antiques

A William IV rosewood work table, with a turned stretcher, on lion-paw feet, 25in (63.5cm) wide.
£3,000–3,350 Georgian Antiques

A Victorian walnut games/work table, with stringing and foliate marquetry, folding swivel top inlaid with game boards, fitted frieze drawer over a sliding wooden basket, with leaf-carved trestle feet, 24in (61cm) wide.

£1,200–1,400
Andrew Hartley

A Victorian walnut work table, with inlaid decoration, 30in (76cm) high.

£1,500–1,650
Georgian Antiques

A Victorian mahogany drop-leaf work table, on turned legs, 27in (68.5cm) high.

£500–550
McBains

A Victorian papier-mâché and ebonized wood tripod work table, the hinged top decorated with butterflies and flowers, 16¼in (41.5cm) diam.

£1,000–1,200 **Bearnes**

GAMES TABLES

An oak games table, the two-leaf opening top supported by an extended opener, on turned legs joined by four stretchers, 18thC, 31in (78.5cm) wide.

£2,200–2,500 **Oak & Country**

An oak games table, 18thC, 28in (71cm) high.

£500–600
Skinner

A walnut games table, the baize-lined top with counter wells and inlaid backgammon board, with draughtboard slide and candle slides, on cabriole legs, mid-18thC, 31in (78.5cm) wide.

£6,000–7,000 **Woolley & Wallis**

A mahogany games table, the top with a leather inset, on square tapered reeded legs, with brass mounts, Russia, c1790, 53in (134.5cm) wide.

£10,000–12,000 **Sotheby's (NY)**

A Louis XV-style japanned games table, with a hinged top and baize-lined playing surface, with gilt-bronze mounts, 19thC, 32¾in (83cm) wide.

£6,000–7,000 **Freeman's**

A Victorian specimen wood games table, the inlaid chess board flanked by stars and lozenges, above inverted finials, on a pedestal of four ring-turned columns with acorn and leaf-carved cabriole legs and scrolled feet, 30¼in (77cm) wide.

£400–500 **Rosebery's**

A rosewood and satinwood games table, inlaid with chess and backgammon boards, c1850, 38in (96.5cm) wide.

£2,500–3,000 **Mary Cruz Antiques**

CARD TABLES

carved mahogany card table, attributed to
ohn Townsend, the hinged serpentine top
ith flute-carved edges, on moulded legs,
merica, Rhode Island, late 18thC,
2in (81.5cm) wide.
14,000–17,000 Northeast Auctions

A George II mahogany card table, the frieze with ribbon and flower moulding, on carved cabriole legs with claw-and-ball feet, probably Irish, 31in (78.5cm) wide.
£3,800–4,500 Mealy's

A mahogany card table, the shaped top with moulded edge above reeded and chamfered legs and six carved brackets, rebaized, c1760, 35in (89cm) wide.
£4,500–5,000
Langton Green Antiques

mahogany breakfront card table, with
andle and money well, on cabriole legs
ith claw-and-ball feet, c1770,
4in (86.5cm) wide.
2,700–3,000 Old Malthouse

A George III Sheraton-style satinwood **demi-lune card table,** with a ribbon- and floral-painted frieze on square tapered legs with spade feet, 36in (91.5cm) wide.
£1,750–2,000 Gorringes (L)

A George III **mahogany card table,** with a parquetry-inlaid fold-over top, on tapered legs with spade feet, 35¾in (91cm) wide.
£700–850 Cheffins

George III **satinwood card table,** the
ingwood-banded top above an inlaid frieze,
n four columns and cabriole legs and brass
asters, 34¼in (87cm) wide.
1,600–2,000 Cheffins

A **mahogany card table,** on tapered legs with carved feet, Ireland, c1780, 28in (71cm) wide.
£1,400–1,600
Woburn Abbey Antiques

A **mahogany demi-lune card table,** with a shaped frieze, c1790, 34in (86.5cm) wide.
£2,250–2,500
Woburn Abbey Antiques

A **satinwood card table,** with rosewood crossbanding and simulated bamboo turned tapered legs, c1790, 36in (91.5cm) wide.
£3,250–3,650 Mary Cruz Antiques

An **inlaid mahogany card table,** the hinged top above square tapered legs, with inlaid stringing, America, Massachusetts, c1800, 36in (91.5cm) wide.
£1,400–1,700 Northeast Auctions

A pair of rosewood card tables, with brass inlay, c1810, 36in (91.5cm) wide.

£13,000–15,000 Georgian Antiques

A rosewood card table, on a central column and four carved feet, c1825, 36in (91.5cm) wide.

£1,700–2,000 Swan at Tetsworth

A William IV satinwood card table, with ebony stringing and crossbanding, the top on a leaf-carved support, the quadripartite base with scroll and lion-paw feet, 33¾in (85.5cm) wide.

£2,000–2,200 Dee, Atkinson & Harrison

A rosewood card table, on an octagonal tapered central column and carved scroll feet, c1840, 36in (91.5cm) wide.

£1,300–1,500 Woburn Abbey Antiques

A Victorian carved walnut and burr-walnut-veneered loo table, the quarter-veneered tilt-top above a carved pedestal, on splayed scroll supports, 59in (150cm) diam.

£1,100–1,300 Bearnes

A rosewood card table, the top on an octagonal stem with reeded collar and lion-paw feet and brass casters, mid-19thC, 36in (91.5cm) wide.

£450–550 Bearnes

A Sheraton revival satinwood envelope card table, with counter wells and parquetry inlay, c1870, 31in (78.5cm) high.

£3,200–3,500 Mary Cruz Antiques

An inlaid mahogany card table, c1900, 22in (56cm) wide.

£650–750 Quayside Antiques

An Edwardian rosewood envelope card table, with foliate marquetry and stringing, swivel top and frieze drawer, on square tapered legs with spade feet and casters, 23½in (59.5cm) wide.

£850–1,000 Andrew Hartley

TEA TABLES

ɿ oak tea table, c1740, 32½in (82.5cm) wide.

3,000–3,250 Red Lion Antiques ⊞

A maplewood tea table, with tapered legs and pad feet, America, Rhode Island, c1760, 35in (89cm) wide.

£16,000–20,000
Northeast Auctions

A pine and maplewood tea table, with original paint and a drawer, the square moulded legs joined by an X-stretcher, America, New England, 1775–1800, 35in (89cm) wide.

£12,000–15,000 Northeast Auctions

George III mahogany tea table, 6in (91.5cm) wide.

500–575
urford Antiques ⊞

A George III mahogany and chequer-banded fold-over tea table, on reeded legs, 36in (91.5cm) wide.

£1,200–1,400 Long Street Antiques ⊞

A late Georgian mahogany fold-over tea table, on turned legs and brass casters, 36in (91.5cm) wide.

£750–850 Period Furniture ⊞

Regency mahogany tea table, on a turned olumn and four splayed legs with brass caps nd casters, 36in (91.5cm) wide.

800–900
emswell Antique Centres ⊞

A mahogany fold-over tea table, c1820, 34in (86.5cm) wide.

£900–1,000
Paul Weatherell ⊞

A mahogany fold-over tea table, with satinwood and rosewood crossbanding, on barley-twist legs, c1835, 36in (91.5cm) wide.

£1,800–2,000
Woburn Abbey Antiques ⊞

mahogany tea table, the quarter-veneered top above a haped frieze, on leaf-carved cabriole legs, France, 19thC, 35¾in (91cm) wide.

£650–750
ennants

A pair of mahogany tea tables, the foliate carved stems with scroll feet, mid-19thC, 36in (91.5cm) wide.

£4,000–5,000 Gorringes (L)

Pairs of tables are not as common as single examples and therefore much more desirable. It is probable that a single table of similar design would be valued at around £1,000–1,500.

OCCASIONAL TABLES

A mahogany tilt-top tripod table, 18thC, 29¾in (75.5cm) diam.

£1,200–1,400
Oak & Country Furniture ⊞

A mahogany tilt-top tripod table, on a leaf-carved stem, the legs in the form of eagles' legs, with claw feet, possibly Ireland, c1750, 37¾in (96cm) diam.

£15,000–18,000 Sotheby's ⚒

A chestnut tilt-top tripod table, on a turned baluster stem and splayed feet, c1760, 25in (63.5cm) diam.

£900–1,000 Swan Gallery ⊞

A George III mahogany and fruitwood tripod table, the moulded edge top on a triangular stem and flat scroll legs, 26in (66cm) diam.

£2,250–2,750
Woolley & Wallis ⚒

A mahogany revolving tripod table, with a birdcage mechanism, on cabriole legs, c1760, 26in (66cm) diam.

£1,650–1,850 J Collins ⊞

A mahogany tripod table, with an octagonal top, c1770, 26in (66cm) wide.

£1,500–1,650 J Collins ⊞

A painted pine tripod table, Sweden, c1770, 38in (96.5cm) wide.

£4,000–4,500
Robert Young Antiques ⊞

A George III oak and elm tilt-top tripod table, on a baluster-turned column and cabriole legs, 33in (84cm) diam.

£450–550 Cheffins ⚒

An ash, oak and walnut tripod candlestand, c1770, 18½in (47cm) diam.

£2,300–2,600
Robert Young Antiques ⊞

A painted wood tripod candlestand, on cabriole legs, America, New England, 1770–90, 16in (40.5cm) diam.

£8,500–10,000 **Northeast Auctions**

A mahogany tripod table, on a tapered column and cabriole legs, c1780, 28in (71cm) high.

£11,000–13,000 **Avon Antiques**

This table has a one-piece top, as opposed to the more usual plank construction and overall is of very delicate appearance. It also benefits from not having suffered any breaks or repairs.

An oak and elm child's table, with a drawer, on tapered square legs, c1790, 17in (43cm) wide.

£1,000–1,100 **Swan Gallery**

A sycamore, beech, oak and pine cricket table, 18thC, 25½in (65cm) diam.

£500–600 **Bellmans**

A mahogany tripod table, with a turned column, c1790, 24in (61cm) diam.

£900–1,000
Woburn Abbey Antiques

A mahogany tilt-top tripod table, with a dished top, c1795, 20in (51cm) diam.

£1,100–1,200
Graham Smith Antiques

A painted pine cricket table, early 19thC, 28in (71cm) high.

£630–700
Oak & Country Furniture

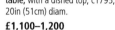

A nest of three painted tiger maple occasional tables, attributed to John and Thomas Seymour, the painting attributed to John Ritto Penniman, painted with floral sprays and fruit, on turned legs and trestle feet, America, c1805, largest 18½in (47cm) wide.

£40,000–50,000 **Northeast Auctions**

The design for this set of tables is based on one from Sheraton's Cabinet Directory *of 1803, where it was described as a quartetto table. They price this set achieved is due to rarity – only one other example is known to survive – and also because the cabinet-maker, John Seymour (1738–1818) and his son Thomas introduced the 'Federal' ie Adam, style to Boston, Massachusetts where they worked after emigrating from Devon, England in 1784. John Penniman rented a studio in Seymour's Boston Warehouse from 1808–10 and is known to have collaborated with Seymour. The delicate design, use of tiger maple and fine decorative painting are extremely rare features, all hightly sought after by American furniture collectors.*

A pair of mahogany and satinwood-banded wine tables, with line inlay, on vase-shaped pedestals, c1800, 33in (84cm) high.

£2,700–3,000
Chair Set

A mahogany occasional table, with two drawers, on a lyre-form pedestal and casters, America, 1800–50, 22in (56cm) wide.

£1,200–1,400
Sotheby's (P)

A mahogany tilt-top tripod table, c1820, 21in (53.5cm) wide.
£600–700
Graham Smith Antiques

A mahogany and rosewood-crossbanded tripod table, c1820, 19in (48.5cm) wide.
£850–950
Woburn Abbey Antiques

An occasional table, the top with trompe l'oeil painting and simulated brass inlay, on a turned and decorated pedestal, 1820–30, 23in (58.5cm) wide.
£8,000–9,000 **Avon Antiques**

A mahogany coaching table, with turned stretchers, c1825, 35in (89cm) wide.
£850–950
Peter Norden Antiques

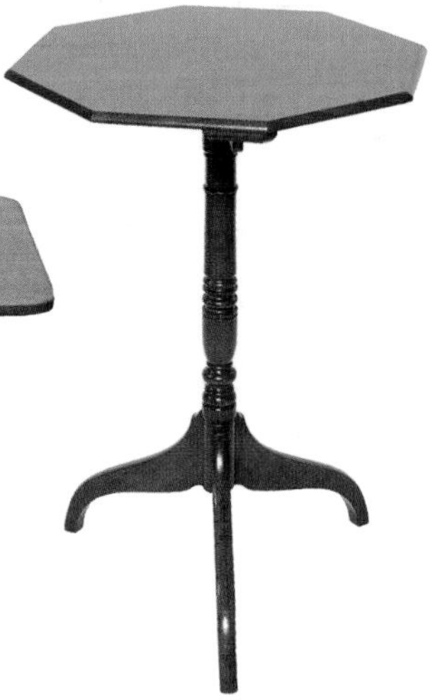

A mahogany tripod table, with an octagonal top, on a turned column, c1830, 20in (51cm) diam.
£325–375 **Swan at Tetsworth**

A walnut occasional table, the oyster-veneered top on a lappet-carved baluster stem, 1835, 19½in (50cm) diam.
£1,800–2,200 **Sotheby's**

A William IV rosewood occasional table, with hairy paw feet, 20in (51cm) diam.
£600–700 **Pantiles Spa Antiques**

A mahogany wine table, on a ring-turned column and four splayed legs, c1850, 17in (43cm) wide.
£270–300 **Swan at Tetsworth**

A mahogany wine table, on turned column, c1850, 12in (30.5cm) diam.
£600–700
Woburn Abbey Antiques

. rosewood pillar table, with a gallery, on a
·iform base and paw feet, c1860,
1in (78.5cm) high.

.1,200–1,350 Mere Antiques ⊞

A satinwood and purple heart parquetry occasional table, by Donald Ross, the inlaid top above a frieze drawer, on square tapered legs and a galleried undertier, with gilt-bronze mounts, c1860, 16½in (42cm) wide.

£2,500–3,000 Freeman's

A pair of mahogany tripod wine tables, each with barley-twist pedestal and three horseshoe feet, c1870, 18in (45.5cm) diam.

£300–350 Swan at Tetsworth ⊞

\ walnut occasional table, with a marquetry
op and gilt-metal mounts, c1870,
30in (76cm) wide.

£1,800–2,000 Martin Taylor ⊞

A rosewood two-tier occasional table, c1880, 34in (86.5cm) wide.

£450–500 Long Street Antiques ⊞

A mahogany two-tier occasional table, with crossbanded, painted and inlaid decoration, c1890, 31in (78.5cm) high.

£2,200–2,500 Georgian Antiques ⊞

A nest of four mahogany tables, with inlaid decoration, c1890, largest 22in (56cm) wide.

£1,400–1,600 Swan at Tetsworth ⊞

A carved wood occasional table, with an intaglio foliate top, Switzerland, c1900, 24in (61cm) diam.

£500–600 Jackson's

A burr-walnut and mother-of-pearl occasional table, the brass-bound top over an inlaid frieze, on square tapered legs, France, c1900, 19¾in (50cm) wide.

£1,100–1,300 Freeman's

LIBRARY TABLES

A Biedermeier burr-wood table, on curved supports joined by a stretcher, 1825–50, 73½in (192cm) wide.
£4,000–5,000 Sotheby's (NY)

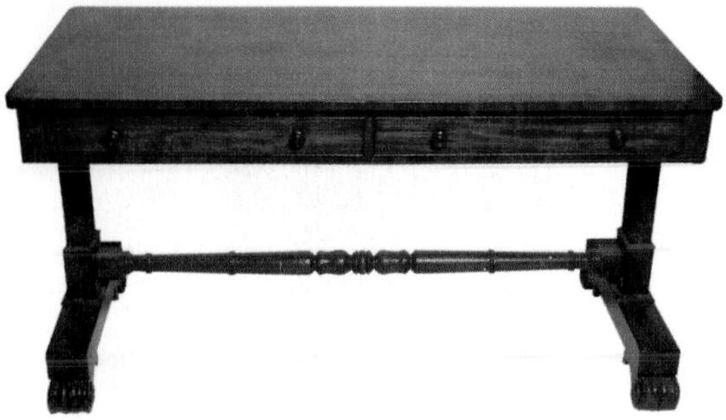

A mahogany library table, the crossbanded top above two drawers, c1820, 53in (134.5cm) wide.
£1,300–1,500 McBains of Exeter

A mahogany library table, with two frieze drawers, c1840, 47¾in (121.5cm) wide.
£2,750–3,250 Sotheby's (O)

A mahogany serpentine library table, c1860, 48in (122cm) wide.
£550–650 McBains of Exeter

A carved walnut library table, the leather-inset top above two drawers, c1870, 41in (104cm) wide.
£1,600–1,800 Newark Antiques

A pair of Victorian Gothic revival oak library tables, each top inset with leather, on four pillars and a cruciform base and casters, 51½in (131cm) diam.
£7,000–8,500 Tennants

A mahogany library table, 1880, 40in (101.5cm) wide.
£270–300
McBains of Exeter

A burr-walnut and rosewood library table, the stepped top above an ebonized acanthus-carved frieze, the stretcher with a seated putto and lobster, Continental, late 19thC, 51¼in (130cm) wide.
£800–950 Rosebery's

A cedarwood library table, with eight frieze drawers, on fluted baluster legs and porcelain casters, Australia, late 19thC, 96in (245cm) wide.
£1,400–1,800 Leonard Joel

:HESTS & COFFERS

ı oak coffer, the front decorated with arcaded chip carving, c1520, ;in (114.5cm) wide.

6,500–7,500 Period Oak

A walnut casket, Spain, c1550, 11in (28cm) wide.

£2,200–2,500 Period Oak

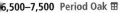

ı oak chest, with moulded top and kick-out et, c1610, 35½in (90cm) wide.

2,000–2,400 & P Rumble

An oak chest, the associated hinged top above a carved arcaded front frieze and geometric panel, early 17thC, 29in (74cm) wide.

£3,000–3,500 Sotheby's

An oak boarded chest, with cut-out end supports, slight damage, the top with later hinges, early 17thC, 28in (71cm) wide.

£280–350 Woolley & Wallis

ın oak coffer, with shaped ends, the top painted with a ıeart, c1650, 35in (89cm) wide.

:1,000–1,100 Moxhams

A Charles II oak coffer, the three-panelled front carved with lozenge and foliate decoration and converted to cupboard doors, 58in (147.5cm) wide.

£450–550 Hy Duke

An oak coffer, with a scroll-carved frame, the front with two panels, early 18thC, 32in (81.5cm) wide.

€500–600 Gorringes (L)

An oak mule chest, the hinged top above a frieze and panelled front with initials 'I. B.' and '1703', two frieze drawers, with double panelled sides, North Country, early 18thC, 47in (119.5cm) wide.

£400–500 Netherhampton Salerooms

A painted beech marriage chest, on shaped bracket feet, probably Channel Islands, c1760, 38½in (98cm) wide.

£11,000–12,500 Robert Young Antiques

A painted pine blanket chest, interior with open well, ti and secret compartment with original contents, on legs with half-moon cut-outs, America, New Hampshire, c1790, 42½in (108cm) wide.

£1,800–2,200 Northeast Auctions

An oak mule chest, with carved scroll panels and drawer to base, 18thC, 44in (119cm) wide.

£300–350 Holloway's

A George III oak dower chest, with a crossbanded fielded panel and two drawers, on ogee bracket feet, Wales, 50¼in (127.5cm) wide.

£650–750 Holloway's

An oak coffer, with applied ebonized mouldin drawer to the base, on bun feet, hinged top replaced, America, 18thC, 46in (117cm) wide

£1,300–1,600 Bearnes

A George III mahogany chest-on-stand, the upper section with a rising top and brass handles, the base with a drawer, on bracket feet with inset wooden casters, 48¾in (124cm) wide.

£1,000–1,200 Cheffins

A late George III mahogany mule chest, with a hinged top, the interior with a till and two drawers, the front with three dummy drawers over six drawers, Lancashire, 67½in (171.5cm) wide.

£1,100–1,300 Woolley & Wallis

A painted pine blanket chest, with two drawe painted to simulate tiger maple, America, New England, 1820–35, 38in (96.5cm) wide

£2,700–3,200 Northeast Auctions

A painted pine and poplar blanket chest, the borders painted and grained to simulate tiger maple, the front and side panels smoke-decorated, the interior with a till, America, New Jersey, 19thC, 43¼in (110cm) wide.

£2,200–2,500 Northeast Auctions

A painted marriage chest, decorated with naïve figure- and floral-painted panels within a jigsaw field, central Europe, c1830, 42in (106.5cm) wide.

£3,000–3,500 Robert Young Antiques

CUPBOARDS

A joined oak cupboard, with panels of carved tracery, the raised back with a shelf, over a cupboard door carved with a griffin, above an apron drawer, on square supports with an undertier, restored, France, 1475–1525 and later, 38¼in (97cm) wide.

£10,000–12,000
Dreweatt Neate

An oak court cupboard, with carved cup-and-cover columns, c1630, 56in (142cm) wide.

£8,900–9,900 Period Oak

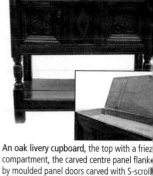

An oak livery cupboard, the top with a friez compartment, the carved centre panel flank by moulded panel doors carved with S-scrol and daisy wheels, the turned legs united by potboard, c1640, 49in (124.5cm) high 52½in (133.5cm) wide.

£8,000–9,000 Period Oak

A walnut corner cabinet, the panelled door enclosing shelves, c1725, 26in (66cm) wide.

£1,800–2,150 Sotheby's

A painted cupboard, the door panels with reserves depicting Bacchic figures, Italy, Le Marche, early 18thC, 69in (175.5cm) wide.

£7,000–8,500 Sotheby's (O)

A painted pine alcove cupboard, c1710, 43¼in (110cm) wide.

£2,000–2,200
S & P Rumble

An oak court cupboard, with three drawers, early 18thC, 54½in (138.5cm) high.

£5,800–6,500
Red Lion Antiques

An oak spice cupboard-on-stand, the coffered panelled door enclosing three drawers, early 18thC, 37in (94cm) high.

£400–500
Greenslade Taylor Hunt

A carved oak *buffet à deux corps*, with iror carrying handles, the cupboards with later shelves, restored, France, early 18thC, 59in (150cm) wide.

£3,500–4,200
Sotheby's (O)

›anelled and joined oak corner cupboard, thC, 32½in (82.5cm) high.

·20–400 eenslade Taylor Hunt

A fruitwood buffet, with four panelled doors and a shaped apron, France, 18thC, 49in (125cm) wide.

£600–700 Sworders

A George II walnut cupboard, with two fielded panel doors, interior with a drawer, on bracket feet, 53½in (136cm) wide.

£3,000–3,500 Tennants

walnut-veneered cupboard, the two doors th gilt-brass handles and escutcheons, closing shelves and two small drawers, er two short and two long drawers, maged, on later feet, Sweden, 1750–1800, ¾in (152cm) wide.

,500–4,250 Bukowskis

An oak hanging cupboard, Wales, 1760–1800, 70in (178cm) high.

£2,300–2,600 S & P Rumble

This cupboard would have been used for hanging meats such as ham.

A mahogany hanging corner cabinet, with dentil cornice, panelled door, fluted columns and serpentine shelves, c1780, 42in (106.5cm) high.

£1,700–1,850 Ronald Chambers

corner hanging cupboard, with painted noiserie decoration, c1780, 30in (76cm) high.

,300–1,500 Paul Weatherell Ants

An oak food cupboard, Shropshire, c1780, 39in (99cm) high.

£6,000–7,000 Oak & Country

A painted pine corner cupboard, France, 18thC, 42½in (108cm) wide.

£3,500–4,000 Antiquated

A chestnut and oak cupboard, the two panelled doors pierced with hearts, above a drawer, on square legs joined by a lower shelf with baluster-carved gallery, France, 18thC and later, 31½in (80cm) wide.

£600–700 Tennants

A Georgian painted pine corner cupboard, with glazed upper doors, 48in (122cm) wide.

£1,800–2,000
Pennard House

A painted corner cupboard, the moulded panelled doors enclosing shelves, slight damage, America, possibly Virginia, late 18thC, 46in (117cm) wide.

£3,500–4,200 Skinner

A cherrywood cupboard, with two doors and a central drawer, France, c1800, 86in (218.5cm) high.

£2,500–2,900
Gilbert & Dale

An oak corner cupboard, the cut corners carved with fluting, early 19thC, 42½in (108cm) wide.

£1,300–1,600
Sotheby's (Am)

An oak corner cupboard, the top with a glazed door, c1820, 36in (91.5cm) wide.

£2,200–2,500
Red Lion Antiques

A pine cupboard, the open to with scalloped sides and four shelves, the base with two drawers and a scalloped apron America, New England, mid-19thC, 46in (117cm) wide

£500–600 James D Julia

A painted and smoke-decorated corner cupboard, the upper section with a glazed door, above two fielded panelled doors and a shaped apron, upper section fitted for electricity, America, Pennsylvania, c1840, 45in (114.5cm) wide.

£30,000–36,000
Northeast Auctions

A painted pine and poplar cupboard, painted to resemble tiger maple and flame mahogany, with two doors enclosing shelves, America, New England, 19thC, 41in (104cm) wide.

£1,300–1,600 Northeast Auctions

An oak hanging corner cupboard, with a panelled doo enclosing shelves, 19thC, 26in (66cm) wide.

£300–360
Dee, Atkinson & Harrison

ıRMOIRES

oak armoire, the detachable cornice
ɔve two panelled doors, France, 18thC,
n (167.5cm) wide.

,000–1,200
ɔolley & Wallis

An oak marriage armoire, the frieze with relief-carved surmount, the two doors with floral-carved panels, enclosing three shelves, France, Normandy, 18thC, 58in (147.5cm) wide.

£1,700–2,000 Gorringes (L)

A carved oak armoire, with two panelled doors, France, late 18thC, 62¼in (158cm) wide.

£3,500–4,200 Sotheby's (O)

ash armoire, with two panelled doors and
Irawer, on block feet, France, 19thC,
¼in (158cm) wide.

,400–1,700 Dreweatt Neate

An oak armoire, with two panelled doors and decorative brasswork, France, c1800, 54in (137cm) wide.

£1,800–2,200 Burford Antiques

A walnut armoire, with a domed top and two moulded and panelled doors enclosing shelves, restored, France, 19thC, 59in (150cm) wide.

£2,800–3,500 Sotheby's (O)

:hestnut armoire, with two panelled doors
ɔve one short and two long drawers,
:h panelled sides, on stump feet, France,
thC, 69¼in (176cm) wide.

,500–1,800
'eenslade Taylor Hunt

A painted and parcel-gilt armoire, the domed top with a moulded frieze, the doors inset with prints of biblical subjects, with ribbed and scrolled canted corners and a shaped apron, on scroll feet, Italy, 19thC, 47¼in (120cm) wide.

£650–750 Dreweatt Neate

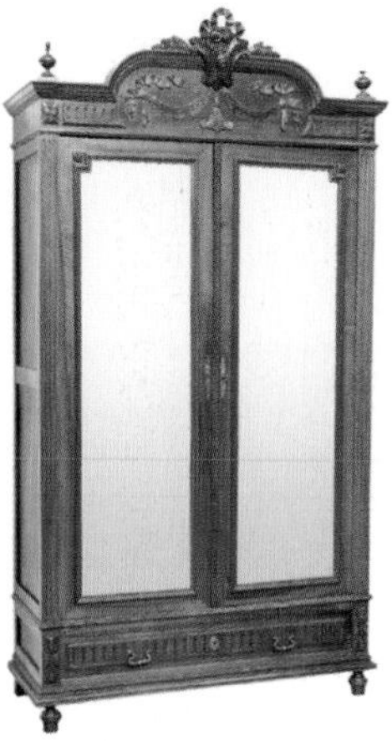

A walnut armoire, the arched moulded cornice with foliate surmount, with two mirrored doors flanked by fluted pilasters, above a drawer, on turned feet, 19thC, 53¾in (135.5cm) wide.

£550–650 Andrew Hartley

LINEN & CLOTHES PRESSES

EXPERT'S EYE GILLOWS LINEN PRESS

Fine detailing can be seen to the cornice which has dentil work above a frieze with pear drop and blind fret decoration. This intricate design is an indicator of the quality of craftsmanship. Similar designs can be seen on other pieces of Gillows furniture from the same period.

The flame mahogany-veneered panelled doors have been cleverly broken up by a raised shaped border with carved floral motifs to the corners.

Original brass drop handles are desirable as they are often replaced. (Check the insides of drawers as there may be evidence that handles have been removed.)

Ogee feet were fashionable between 1750 and 1780. This shaped ogee foot is an indicator of fine craftsmanship. Bracket feet were easier to construct and therefore more commonly found.

A mahogany linen press, attributed to Gillows, with two doors enclosing shelves, above two short and two long drawers, c1772, 50in (127cm) wide.

£10,000–12,000 Sotheby's

The overall richness and depth of colour adds to the attractiveness of the press which invariably increases value.

This piece is almost certainly made by Gillows of Lancaster – it has similar design elements to those shown in their sketch books and demonstrates the subtlety of Georgian craftmanship. The stylized elements of the cornice and panelled doors break up an otherwise square design.

An oak press cupboard, the top with two doors, the base with one short and two lon drawers, 18thC, 76½in (194.5cm) high.

£5,700–6,300 Red Lion Antiques

A George III oak clothes press, the upper section with two panelled doors flanked by fluted pilasters, the base with three dummy short drawers and two long drawers, on brac feet, with later handles, 53½in (136cm) wic

£1,100–1,300 Gilding's

A George III oak clothes press, the blind fret frieze above panelled doors flanked by quarter reeded columns enclosing hanging space, the base with two short and two long drawers, on bracket feet, 55in (140cm) wide.

£1,100–1,300
Penrith Farmers' & Kidd's

A mahogany linen press, with three drawers, the cupboard doors enclosing sides, c1790, 85in (216cm) high.

£2,700–3,000
Hemswell Antique Centres

A mahogany linen press, with ebonized lin and brass inlay, the swan-neck pediment abo two doors enclosing shelves, the base with four drawers, c1800, 50¾in (129cm) wide.

£11,000–13,000 Sotheby's (O)

ıahogany linen press, the two crossbanded
ɪ figured mahogany doors enclosing slides,
base with two short and two long drawers,
ıerica, probably Virginia, Norfolk, c1800,
¾in (129cm) wide.

,500–4,000 Northeast Auctions

A George III mahogany linen press, the two doors with applied panelling and enclosing slides, over two short and two long drawers, on bracket feet, 52in (132cm) wide.

£1,400–1,700 Andrew Hartley

A mahogany linen press, the top with two doors, over two short and one long drawers, on bracket feet, early 19thC, 76in (193cm) high.

£2,500–2,800 Andy Gibbs

ıahogany linen press, the top with two
ors, over two short and two long drawers,
bracket feet, c1820, 45in (114.5cm) wide.

,800–2,000
ırford Antiques

A mahogany linen press, the top with two doors, over three long drawers, on turned and reeded feet, c1825, 80in (203cm) high.

£1,600–1,800
Long Street Antiques

A mahogany linen press, the detachable cornice above two doors enclosing slides, over two short and two long drawers, with later brass handles, 19thC, 50¾in (129cm) wide.

£1,200–1,400 Woolley & Wallis

oak press cupboard, with two arched
nelled doors flanked by spiral-turned
lumns, the base with two short and two
ıg drawers, the turned knobs with mother-
-pearl insets, on pierced bracket feet,
ales, 19thC, 54in (137cm) wide.

,000–1,200 Peter Francis

A mahogany linen press, the two panelled doors with brass trim and enclosing slides, above two short and two long drawers with ebonized handles, mid-19thC, 51in (129.5cm) wide.

£1,100–1,300 Andrew Hartley

A satinwood linen press, with a fully fitted interior, c1860, 53in (134.5cm) wide.

£2,400–2,700
Burford Antiques

WARDROBES

A William IV mahogany breakfront wardrobe, by Mack, Williams & Gibton, the panels with rope edges, with two cupboard doors enclosing hanging space, over two short and two long drawers, flanked by conforming double-panel doors enclosing fitted interiors, on barley reeded legs, Ireland, 101in (256.5cm) wide.

£10,000–12,000 Mealy's

A pair of maple wardrobes, each with an ogee-moulde cornice above a mirrored door and a drawer, on ball fee America, Pennsylvania, c1830, 36¼in (92cm) wide.

£1,600–2,000 Freeman's

A mahogany wardrobe, the shaped pediment centred by a laurel wreath, above four doors with raised panels, on toupie feet, early 19thC, 96½in (245cm) wide.

£1,500–1,800 Sotheby's (Am)

A mahogany wardrobe, the C-scroll and leaf-moulded pediment over two panelled doors flanked by three-quarter turned pilasters, above a drawer with reeded turned handles, with a shaped apron, mid-19thC, 61½in (156cm) wide.

£1,100–1,300 Halls

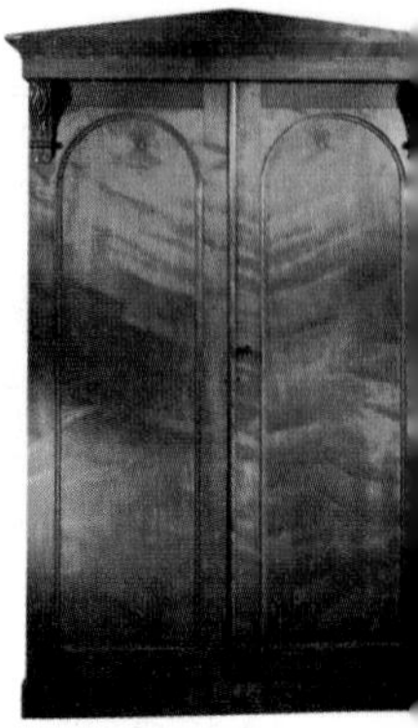

A mahogany wardrobe, the tv doors with arched panels and a drawer, 1850–75, 54in (137cm) wide.

£620–720 Sotheby's (O)

A Victorian pitch pine inverted breakfront combination wardrobe, with central panelled cupboard and three long and two short drawers, flanked by cupboards with turned pilasters, 82in (208.5cm) wide.

£480–580 Dee, Atkinson & Harrison

A mahogany wardrobe, the arched mirror-panel door enclosing a fitted interior, flanked by panelled burr-veneered doors, mid-19thC, 46½in (118cm) wide.

£375–450 Dreweatt Neate (N)

A burr-walnut breakfront wardrobe, the tv panelled doors over four graduated drawers flanked by two panelled doors enclosing hanging space, stamped 'Maple & Co', c1880, 76¾in (195cm) wide.

£1,500–1,800 Rosebery's

›RESSERS

oak low dresser, with three
›vers, on turned legs, 17thC,
ı (233.5cm) wide.
500–9,500
ɟ Lion Antiques

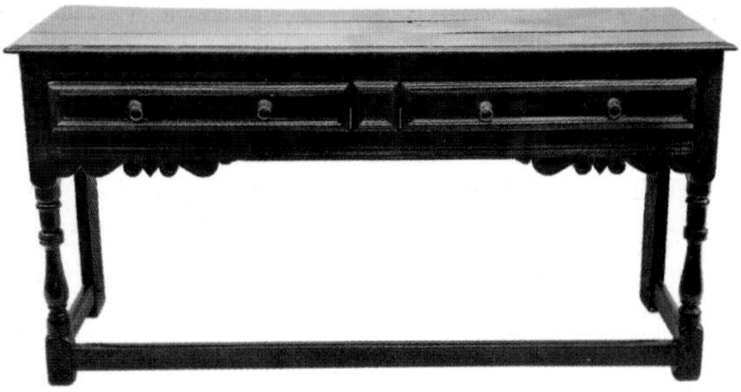

An oak low dresser, with two drawers, on turned legs joined by stretchers, c1650, 59in (150cm) wide.
£11,000–13,000 Period Oak

ueen Anne oak dresser, the associated
k above three drawers, on turned legs joined
noulded stretchers, 74in (188cm) wide.
,300–2,800 Hy Duke

A pine low dresser, with original paint and scrubbed top, c1750, 65¼in (165.5cm) wide.
£7,500–8,500
Robert Young Antiques

An oak dresser, the rack with a shaped frieze and three shelves, over three drawers, the arched panelled doors with H-shaped hinges, 18thC, 61in (155cm) wide.
£10,500–12,000 Swan Gallery

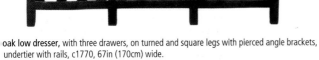

oak low dresser, with three drawers, on turned and square legs with pierced angle brackets,
undertier with rails, c1770, 67in (170cm) wide.
,000–9,500 Sotheby's

oak dresser, with three shelves over three
wers, on ring-turned front legs joined by a
:board and block feet, rack back later,
ıles, Montgomeryshire, c1760,
⁄in (198cm) wide.
,500–4,200 Halls

An oak dresser, the rack with a shaped frieze and sides, over three drawers, the arch fielded panelled doors flanking a further drawer and two panels, on stile feet, North Wales, 18thC, 58½in (148.5cm) wide.
£12,500–15,000 Woolley & Wallis

A George III oak dresser, the rack with open shelves, over three drawers and two spice drawers, with a fret-carved apron and a potboard, South Wales, 48in (122cm) wide.
£2,700–3,000
Greenslade Taylor Hunt

A George III oak and mahogany-crossbanded dresser, the rack with shaped sides, over seven drawers flanked by fluted quarter columns, on stile feet, cornice missing, 64½in (164cm) wide.

£2,000–2,500 Tennants

A George III oak dresser, the rack with reeded uprights, over three panelled drawers and two cupboard doors, on stile feet, rack associated, 69½in (176cm) wide.

£1,400–1,700
Penrith Farmers' & Kidd's

A George III oak dresser, the rack with a shaped frieze and three shelves flanked by cupboards, the base with three drawers, o cabriole legs with pad feet, rack later, 76in (193cm) wide.

£2,800–3,400 Tennants

An oak dresser, the rack with spice drawers, over six drawers and a pierced apron, with a potboard, late 18thC, 82in (208.5cm) high.

£6,500–7,200
Red Lion Antiques

A late George III oak and mahogany-banded dresser, with three drawers and three panelled doors, drawer handles later, plate rack missing, 78½in (199.5cm) wide.

£2,400–2,800 Woolley & Wallis

A joined oak dresser, the rack with a shaped frieze and sides, over three drawers and two fielded panel doors, on stile feet, 18thC and later, 55½in (141cm) wide.

£2,000–2,400 Tennants

An oak dresser, the rack with shaped sides, over six drawers a two panelled cupboard doors, n Wales, c1820, 61½in (156cm) w

£4,000–4,500
S & P Rumble

An oak dresser, the plate rack with two cupboards, over six drawers, on square legs, 19thC, 72½in (184cm) high.

£700–850 Sworders

A painted pine dresser, the base with three drawers over three doors, c1870, 63in (160cm) wide.

£1,300–1,500 Arcadia Antiques

An oak dresser, the base with two cupboar flanking a drawer, with a 'dog kennel' reces c1880, 70in (179cm) wide.

£700–850 Peter Francis

:ABINETS

valnut and featherbanded cabinet-on-
ɜst, with a cushion-moulded cornice
wer, over two doors enclosing 12 small
wers, with four drawers below, on later
ı feet, early 18thC, 43¼in (110cm) wide.
,000–11,000 Sotheby's

A mahogany estate cabinet, the upper section with two doors enclosing 24 pigeonholes, above a drop-flap and cupboard doors enclosing a fitted interior, the base with cupboard doors, on bracket feet, Ireland, c1770, 55in (139.5cm) wide.
£9,500–11,000 Mealy's

A mahogany, satinwood, tulipwood, amaranth and marquetry cabinet, with four doors, japanned with flowers, inlaid with fruitwood decoration, on stile feet, Holland, c1785, 63in (160cm) wide.
£30,000–35,000
Sotheby's (Am)

During the last phase of development of Dutch neo-classical furniture a distinct preference for light exotic veneers, such as satinwood, emerged. This new type of refined marquetry harmonized with the simplified geometric motifs that had become fashionable and relates to those produced in England at that time. It was probably inspired by the engraved furniture designs of Hepplewhite and Sheraton, which were published in 1788 and 1794 respectively. It is interesting that during this English-inspired phase of marquetry furniture, Dutch cabinet-makers often enriched their pieces with panels of Japanese or Chinese lacquer or with japanning.

walnut specimen cabinet,
th 20 drawers, c1880,
:in (132cm) high.
,800–2,000 McBaines

A Victorian mahogany specimen cabinet, the panelled doors enclosing 40 drawers with glazed covers, 38in (96.5cm) wide.
£1,500–1,800 Woolley & Wallis

:ABINETS-ON-STANDS

walnut cabinet-on-stand, with
vo drawers above two doors
ıclosing shelves, the stand with
frieze drawer, on five barley-
vist legs, restored, c1690,
3in (96.5cm) wide.
10,000–12,000
eriod Oak

A japanned cabinet-on-stand, the interior with 17 drawers above a frieze drawer, with parcel-gilt and mother-of-pearl chinoiserie decoration, restored, Holland, c1700, 24½in (62.5cm) wide.
£7,000–8,500
Sotheby's (Am)

An oak *vargueño*, the fall-front enclosing seven drawers and a cupboard of drawers, carved with figures, coats-of-arms and scrolling foliage, Spain, 18thC, 34in (86cm) wide.
£2,000–2,500
Greenslade Taylor Hunt

A mahogany cabinet-on-stand, in the manner of Gillows, the two panelled doors enclosing shelves, the fitted drawer with silver-mounted jewellery box, with ebony inlay, on reeded tapered supports joined by a stretcher, early 19thC, damaged, 26¾in (68cm) wide.
£2,000–2,500 Bearnes

DISPLAY CABINETS

A kingwood and tulipwood display cabinet, with gilt-bronze mounts, altered, France, mid-18thC, 35½in (90cm) wide.

£900–1,100 Sotheby's (Am)

A George III mahogany display cabinet, in the manner of Ince & Mayhew, with two glazed doors enclosing shelves, the stand with frieze drawer, on square moulded legs and stretchers, 40¼in (102cm) wide.

£5,500–6,500 Gilding's

A cherrywood and mahogany corner disp cabinet, the glazed door flanked by ebonize columns, above three drawers and two cupboard doors, on ebonized turned feet, Canada, Ontario, c1810, 44in (112cm) wid

£5,200–6,200 Northeast Auctions

A walnut marquetry display cabinet, with two glazed doors enclosing shelves, above panelled doors, on ball feet, Holland, 19thC, 64½in (164cm) wide.

£4,000–5,000 Cheffins

A calamander display cabinet, the two glazed doors enclosing a later mirrored interior, the base with a frieze drawer, with gilt-brass mounts, on cabriole legs with an undertier, early 19thC, 40¼in (102cm) wide.

£1,000–1,200 Bearnes

An Edwardian inlaid mahogany display cabinet, with two astragal-glazed doors flanked by recesses with turned columns, above two doors, on square tapered legs wi spade feet, 61¾in (157cm) wide.

£600–700 Rosebery's

An Edwardian mahogany display cabinet, the glazed doors surrounded by a frieze with neo-classical motifs, 83in (211cm) high.

£3,000–3,500 Mere Antiques

An Edwardian inlaid mahogany display cabinet, the glazed door enclosing a velvet-lined interior and a glass shelf, on bracket feet, 18in (48cm) wide.

£320–380 Greenslade Taylor Hunt

An Edwardian mahogany display cabinet, by Druce & Co, the base with two doors, losses, 42in (106.5cm) wide.

£550–650 Woolley & Wallis

Pugh's Antiques

Portley House
Old Ludlow Road
Leominster H36 0AA

opposite Leominster Reclamation Yard

There are six barns of furniture (6,000 sq. feet) Edwardian to Victorian. Furniture imported from France & Italy = Louis XV - country - French - armoires - dressers, etc. Speciality antique beds

OPEN MONDAY-SATURDAY

Tel: 01568 616546 Fax: 01568 616144

Email: sales@pughsantiques.com
Internet: www.pughsantiques.com

LAPADA MEMBER

LORRAINE SPOONER ANTIQUES

211 Watling Street West, Towcester
Northamptonshire NN12 6BX
Tel: 01327 358777
Email: lorraine@lsantiques.com
Website: www.lsantiques.com
Opening Hours: Tuesday~Saturday 9.30am~5.30pm
Or by Appointment

Period Furniture ~ Clocks ~ Silver ~ Porcelain
Glass ~ Paintings & Prints ~ Linens ~ Books

An Eye for Excellence ... at S W Antiques

A stunning collection of genuine 19th and early 20th century furniture for upstairs and downstairs, all beautifully displayed in our spacious showrooms just 6 miles from M5, J7. Plenty of easy on-site parking and a nationwide delivery service.

S W Antiques, Abbey Showrooms, Newlands (road), Pershore, Worcs

LAPADA MEMBER **Tel: 01386 555580 www.sw-antiques.co.uk**

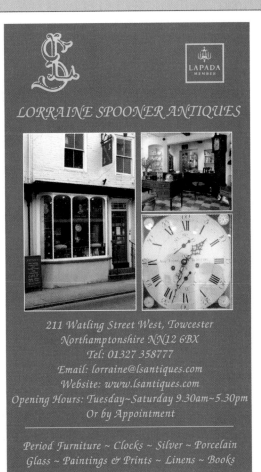

SIDE CABINETS

A George III mahogany bowfronted side cabinet, with two silk and wire-mesh doors, with boxwood stringing, on tapered legs, altered, 33½in (85cm) wide.

£3,200–3,800
Sotheby's

A marquetry side cabinet, the top crossbanded and quarter-veneered in rosewood and satinwood, with kingwood banding, decorated with portrait medallions of soldiers, Milan, Italy, c1800, 22½in (57cm) wide.

£5,000–6,000
James Adam

A rosewood side cabinet, with two imitation drawers, the two glazed doors enclosing shelves, on turned feet, c1830, 36in (91.5cm) wide.

£2,200–2,500
Woburn Abbey Antiques

A tulipwood and purple heart serpentine side cabinet, with a drawer above a tambour cupboard, with gilt-bronze mounts, on cabriole legs, Holland, late 18thC, 33½in (85cm) wide.

£2,000–2,500
Sotheby's (O)

A Regency rosewood and brass-inlaid side cabinet, the marble top above two doors with brass grilles, with giltwood stiles, superstructure missing, 36¼in (92cm) wide.

£10,000–12,000
Sotheby's (O)

In recent years heavily inlaid Regency furniture has fallen in price. However, this side cabinet, with its extraordinary attention to detail, demonstrates clearly that high prices can still be achieved for quality pieces.

A George IV gonçalo alves breakfront side cabinet, the top with rosewood banding, the two doors enclosing shelves, with gilt-metal mounts, interior with later paint, 35¼in (89.5cm) wide.

£550–650 Woolley & Wallis

Gonçalo alves is a tropical hardwood from central and south America. It is also known as tigerwood.

A harewood and satinwood buffet, the hin top above two slides, two drawers and two doors, Holland, late 18thC, 35in (89cm) wi

£8,000–10,000 Sotheby's (O)

A satinwood chiffonier, c1815, 36in (91.5cm) wide.

£7,000–8,000 Chair Set

A mahogany side cabinet, by Thomas King with two doors, c1824, 50in (127cm) wide.

£2,000–2,300 Swan at Tetsworth

Thomas King was an early 19th-century upholsterer and furniture designer. He produced in the region of 15 furniture patte books between 1829 and 1839.

A Victorian rosewood chiffonier, the mirrore back above a frieze drawer, over two panell doors flanked by pilasters, 48in (122cm) wide

£900–1,100 Anderson & Garland

igured walnut and marquetry credenza, the boxwood-strung frieze ›ve a door flanked by two glazed doors enclosing shelves, c1860, n (152.5cm) wide.

00–1,100 Halls

A Victorian ebonized breakfront side cabinet, with gilt-metal mounts, the satinwood-inlaid frieze above a panelled door flanked by two glazed doors, on a plinth base, 59½in (151cm) wide.

£350–420 Rosebery's

nahogany breakfront side cabinet, inlaid with marquetry, c1870, 72in (183cm) wide.

,500–2,900 Martin Taylor

A marquetry side cabinet, by Gillows, the mirrored back above two doors enclosing shelves, with gilt-brass mounts, inlaid with musical trophies, c1872, 82¼in (209cm) wide.

£17,000–20,000 Sotheby's

Victorian carved mahogany serpentine iffonier, with three cupboard doors closing shelves, 56½in (143.5cm) wide.

700–850 Woolley & Wallis

A Victorian walnut side cabinet, with gilt mounts and foliate inlay, the arched glazed door enclosing shelves, on a plinth base, 31½in (80cm) wide.

£580–680 Rosebery's

A walnut and tulipwood side cabinet, the cupboard door with a plaque depicting Louis XVI, with gilt-metal mounts, France, 19thC, 72½in (184cm) wide.

£5,000–6,000 Tennants

mahogany and marquetry-inlaid side cabinet, / Gillows, with satinwood crossbanding and ringing, the panelled door flanked by glazed oors, late 19thC, 48in (122cm) wide.

1,300–1,500 Andrew Hartley

A rosewood and marquetry-inlaid side cabinet, the glazed door enclosing shelves, with ebonized moulding, late 19thC, 31¼in (79.5cm) wide.

£350–420 Woolley & Wallis

An ebonized and tortoiseshell side cabinet, the marble top above a pair of panelled doors, with cut-brass mounts, France, late 19thC, 60½in (153cm) wide.

£900–1,100 Woolley & Wallis

EARLY CHESTS OF DRAWERS

An oak and snakewood-veneered chest of drawers, with fruitwood balusters, the cupboard doors enclosing drawers, c1660, 45in (114.5cm) wide.

£3,300–3,800 Moxhams

An oak chest of drawers, on bun feet, c1680, 42in (106.5cm) wide.

£2,500–2,800 Long Street Antiques

An oak chest of drawers, the boarded top above four long drawers, with later handles and feet, late 17thC, 44½in (113cm) wide.

£400–500 Woolley & Wallis

A walnut chest of drawers, with three long moulded drawers, with later brass-nailed initials, late 17thC, 43¾in (111cm) wide.

£14,000–16,500 Sotheby's

A William and Mary walnut and seaweed marquetry chest of drawers, with two short and three long drawers, bracket feet later, restored, 40in (101.5cm) wide.

£3,200–3,800 Sotheby's

An oak and cedarwood chest of drawers, wi two short and three long drawers, applied mouldings and cedar panels, on stile feet, restored, late 17thC, 40½in (103cm) wide.

£1,500–1,800 Dreweatt Neate

An oak chest of drawers, the four long drawers with applied split mouldings, on turned bun feet, later brass handles, late 17thC, 40in (101.5cm) wide.

£1,000–1,200 Woolley & Wallis

An oak chest of drawers, the four drawers with moulded panels, on later bun feet, some handles missing, late 17thC, 40¼in (102cm) wide.

£1,000–1,200 Sworders

A William and Mary oysterwood and elm ch of drawers, with two short and three long drawers, bracket feet later, 37in (94cm) wid

£3,500–4,200 John Nicholson

ESSENTIAL REFERENCE STYLES OF FURNITURE HANDLES

Late 17th-early 18thC

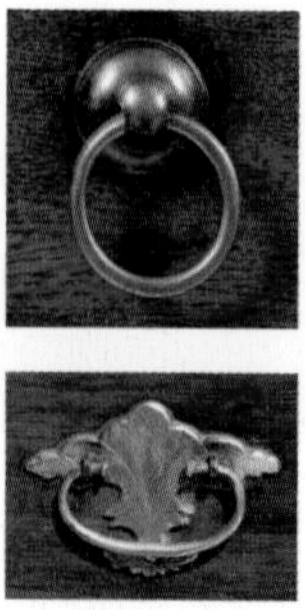

Early 18thC

Second quarter 18thC

Mid-18thC

Late 18thC-early 19thC

Late 19thC

18THC CHESTS OF DRAWERS

walnut and seaweed marquetry chest of awers, with two short and three long aduated drawers, on bracket feet, ·ly 18thC, 39in (99cm) wide.

2,000–38,000 Sotheby's

's marquetry chest is typical of work often sociated with the celebrated cabinet-maker rrit Jensen. Favoured by King William and een Mary, he also included many members the aristocracy among his patrons. He is own to have worked at Burghley House, atsworth, Arundel Castle, Boughton House d Petworth.

George I featherbanded walnut chelor's chest, the folding top above two le drawers, the front with a dummy drawer ove three long graduated drawers, bracket feet, 32in (81.5cm) wide.

13,000–15,000 Dreweatt Neate

George I lacquered chest of drawers, the o short and three long graduated drawers inted with gilt chinoiserie decoration, bracket feet, 39½in (100.5cm) wide.

2,000–2,500
reenslade Taylor Hunt

A burr-walnut and featherbanded chest of drawers, the quarter-veneered and crossbanded top above two short drawers and three long drawers, on turned bun feet, c1705, 39½in (100.5cm) wide.

£7,000–8,000 Richard Gardner

An oak chest of drawers, with two short over three long drawers, on turned bun feet, some handles missing, early 18thC, 38in (96.5cm) wide.

£850–1,000 Woolley & Wallis

A mahogany chest of drawers, the quarter-veneered and crossbanded top above two short and three long drawers, on bracket feet, c1740, 30¾in (78cm) wide.

£3,500–4,000 J Collins

A walnut chest of drawers, the quarter-veneered top above three short and three long graduated drawers, with crossbanding and herringbone stringing, on bracket feet, 18thC, 40¼in (102cm) wide.

£1,200–1,400
Dee, Atkinson & Harrison

A Queen Anne walnut chest of drawers, with two short over three long graduated drawers, bracket feet later, 38¼in (97cm) wide.

£4,000–5,000 Sotheby's

A walnut-veneered and oak chest of drawers, with four graduated drawers, with boxwood line inlay, on bracket feet, early 18thC, 33½in (85cm) wide.

£700–850 Skinner

A mahogany chest of drawers, by Joseph Rawson, with four long drawers, on ogee bracket feet, America, Rhode Island, 1750–80, 39in (99cm) wide.

£3,500–4,000
Northeast Auctions

A mahogany chest of drawers, with two short over three long drawers, on bracket feet, 18thC, 37in (94cm) wide.

£1,400–1,600 Spurrier-Smith

A George III oak chest of drawers, with four long drawers, on bracket feet, 39in (99cm) wide.

£380–450 Hy Duke

A mahogany chest of drawers, with a brushing slide above four long drawers, c1780, 34in (86.5cm) wide.

£3,500–4,000 Chair Set

A George III mahogany and satinwood chest of drawers, the crossbanded top above two short and three long graduated drawers, flanked by quarter pilasters and satinwood inlay, on ogee bracket feet, 40in (101.5cm) wide.

£2,000–2,500 Morphets

A George III brass-bound chest of drawers, the fold-over top enclosing a pop-up secretaire with brass candlesticks, above one dummy drawer and three long drawers, 31½in (80cm) wide

£10,000–11,000 Mealy's

A gonçalo alves quarter-veneered and crossbanded serpentine chest of drawers, with a brushing slide and four long drawers, on bracket feet, c1790, 41in (104cm) wide.

£15,000–18,000 Yoxall Antiques

A George III mahogany secretaire chest of drawers, the central baize-lined drawer fitted with two short drawers flanked by two further short drawers, above three long graduated drawers, on ogee bracket feet, 34in (86.5cm) wide.

£2,000–2,500 Cheffins

A mahogany bowfronted chest of drawers, th rosewood frieze with marquetry inlay above four graduated drawers, on splay feet, handles replaced, 18thC, 42in (106.5cm).

£1,700–2,000 Woburn Abbey Antiques

A pine mule chest, with a hinged top over two dummy drawers and two long drawers, on bracket feet, America, New England, c1790, 43in (109cm) wide.

£1,300–1,600 Northeast Auctions

A Louis XV-style oak chest of drawers, with shaped front and four drawers, Holland, 18thC, 35½in (90cm) wide.

£1,500–1,800 Sotheby's (Am)

A mahogany bowfronted chest of drawers, commemorating Admiral Lord Nelson, with four graduated drawers edged with ebony stringing, late 18thC, 36in (91.5cm) wide.

£2,500–2,800 Swan at Tetsworth

The reference to Nelson is taken from the backplate of the original handles. The design depicts a cannon, a trumpet, two laurel-leaf victory wreaths and the names of three of his campaigns – Nile, Copenhagen and Trafalgar.

19THC CHESTS OF DRAWERS

satinwood bowfronted chest of drawers, ith boxwood line inlay, marked 'GS' to nderside, c1800, 38¼in (97cm) wide.
3,500–4,200 **Sotheby's (O)**

A tiger maple chest of drawers, with four long graduated drawers, on French bracket feet, America, Pennsylvania, c1800, 38in (96.5cm) wide.
£2,500–3,000 **Freeman's**

An oak chest of drawers, with two short and three long drawers, c1800, 43in (109cm) wide.
£1,100–1,300
Spurrier-Smith

George III mahogany bowfronted chest of drawers, vith crossbanding and stringing, with three short drawers ver three long drawers flanked by quarter columns with nlaid fluting, on bracket feet, 48½in (123cm) wide.
:650–750 **Andrew Hartley**

A mahogany chest of drawers, with two short drawers over three long drawers, on bracket feet, c1800, 32in (81.5cm) wide.
£1,800–2,000
Woburn Abbey Antiques

A walnut *semainier*, with brass stringing and bronze and brass mounts, France, c1800, 26½in (67.5cm) wide.
£1,250–1,500
Sotheby's (P)

mahogany chest of drawers, with two short and three long drawers, early 19thC, 37½in (95.5cm) wide.
£700–850 **Dreweatt Neate**

A walnut and featherbanded chest of drawers, with two short and three long graduated drawers, on bun feet, early 19thC, 35½in (90cm) high.
£3,250–4,000 **Charterhouse**

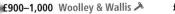

mahogany bowfronted chest of drawers, with two short and three long drawers, on splay feet, early 19thC, 40½in (103cm) wide.
£900–1,000 **Woolley & Wallis**

A Regency mahogany chest of drawers, with four long graduated drawers flanked by carved columns, on paw feet, 42½in (108cm) wide.
£2,200–2,500 **Hy Duke**

An oak chest of drawers, with clothes press and slide, early 19thC, 72in (183cm) high.
£2,000–2,300
Oak & Country

A pair of mahogany chests of drawers, each with two short and three long drawers, on splayed bracket feet, early 19thC, 37¾in (96cm) wide.

£5,000–6,000 **Sotheby's (O)**

A figured maple chest of drawers, with three short drawers and five long graduated drawers, with shaped apron and splayed legs, America, Pennsylvania, early 19thC, 41½in (105.5cm) wide.

£18,000–22,000 **Northeast Auctions**

The tall chest of drawers was especially popular in New England and Pennsylvania from c1750. The drawer configuration between New England and the Mid-Atlantic States differs primarily in that New England examples typically have a series of long graduated drawers and lack the smaller drawers at the top. This particular example is made in one piece in an indigenous wood, rather than a chest-on-chest from which the form is derived. The attention to detail such as the beaded edge to the drawers, the shaped apron, the high French feet and the unusual pressed-brass handles with beehive decoration are unusually fine for a provincial piece. The fact that it retains its original surface and has not been restored is reflected in the price. It was also part of a single-owner sale with a separate catalogue – a fact that often attracts higher prices, particularly when the owner is a well-known collector, as is the case here.

A mahogany bowfronted chest of drawers, the frieze inlaid with ebony stringing above two short and three long drawers, with shaped apron and splayed legs, c1820, 44½in (113cm) high.

£400–500 **Dreweatt Neate (N)**

A Regency oak chest of drawers, 41in (104cm) high.

£1,600–1,800 **Red Lion Antiques**

A cherrywood and maple chest of drawers, the raised back with stamped brass rosettes, above four long drawers, on turned tapered legs, America, Maine, 1800–50, 40in (101.5cm) wide.

£2,000–2,400 **Northeast Auctions**

An oak campaign chest of drawers, 19thC, 18in (45.5cm) wide.

£375–425 **Pennard House**

A walnut and brass-bound campaign chest of drawers, with a fitted secretaire compartment, 19thC, 38in (96.cm) wide.

£525–625 **Mealy's**

A mahogany bowfronted chest of drawers, with four drawers, c1830, 37in (94cm) wide.

£1,300–1,500 **Tredantiques**

A painted pine chest of drawers, with two short and three long drawers, on bracket feet, France, c1830, 41in (104cm) wide.

£700–800 **Top Banana**

A mahogany chest of drawers, with a marble top, frieze drawer and three long drawers, France, c1840, 51in (129.5cm) wide.

£1,300–1,500 **Gilbert & Dale**

A walnut chest of drawers, with a marble top, frieze drawer and three long drawers, France, c1850, 47in (119.5cm) wide.

£1,300–1,500 **Gilbert & Dale**

burr-walnut **Wellington chest,** with a hinged op and fall-front enclosing a secretaire ompartment, c1860, 49in (124.5cm) high.

6,000–6,500 Ronald Chambers ⊞

A Victorian walnut Wellington chest, the ebonized edged top above six drawers, with locking bar, on a plinth base, 25½in (65cm) high.

£900–1,000 Gorringes (L) 🔨

A painted pine chest of drawers, with two short and two long drawers, c1870, 29in (73.5cm) wide.

£520–580 Castlegate Antiques ⊞

A Victorian mahogany chest of drawers, with inverted breakfront top, the cushion frieze drawer over five long graduated drawers, flanked by turned columns, on a plinth base and bun feet, 52¾in (134cm) wide.

£550–650 Rosebery's 🔨

A Victorian mahogany bowfronted chest of drawers, with two short and three long graduated drawers, with later handles, on bracket feet, 42½in (108cm) wide.

£350–420
Greenslade Taylor Hunt 🔨

A Victorian mahogany bowfronted chest of drawers, with two short over three long drawers, on turned feet, 42in (106.5cm) wide.

£450–500 McBaines ⊞

A mahogany chest drawers, by Heal & Son, with two short and three long drawers, c1870, 41in (104cm) wide.

£1,000–1,100 Swan at Tetsworth ⊞

A Victorian mahogany bowfronted chest of drawers, with two short and three long drawers, on bun feet, 48in (122cm) wide.

£520–600 McBaines ⊞

A Victorian teak and brass-mounted secretaire campaign chest of drawers, the central fitted drawer flanked by two small drawers above three long drawers, with brass carrying handles, on turned feet, 40¼in (102cm) wide.

£1,600–1,800 Bearnes 🔨

A Victorian mahogany bowfronted chest of drawers, with two short and four long drawers, on bracket feet, 41in (104cm) wide.

£400–450 McBaines ⊞

A painted pine chest of drawers, by Heal & Son, with two short and three long drawers, on turned feet, c1880, 40in (101.5cm) wide.

£700–800 Piccadilly Antiques ⊞

CHESTS-ON-STANDS

A William and Mary oyster-veneered olivewood chest-on-stand, inlaid with stringing, with holly-wood banding, the stand with later elements, 41¾in (106cm) wide.

£15,000–18,000 Sotheby's

An oak chest-on-stand, the chest with five drawers, the stand with three drawers and cabriole legs, early 18thC, 31½in (80cm) wide.

£6,000–7,000 Sotheby's

An oak chest-on-stand, the chest with four short and one long drawers, the stand with two short drawers, on turned pillar legs, early 18thC, 39½in (100.5cm) wide.

£4,500–5,500 Tennants

A walnut chest-on-stand, the chest with a frieze drawer above two short and three long drawers, the stand on cabriole legs and pad feet, America, Massachusetts, 1730–50, 39¼in (99.5cm) wide.

£15,000–18,000 Skinner

A George II walnut chest-on-stand, the featherbanded and quartered top above two short and three long drawers, the later stand with three drawers and square cabriole legs, handles later, 41¾in (106cm) wide.

£1,700–2,000 Woolley & Wallis

A maplewood chest-on-chest, with seven drawers, on cabriole legs, America, Massachusetts, c1740, 36in (91.5cm) wide.

£7,500–9,000
Northeast Auctions

An oak chest-on-stand, with a shaped apron and cabriole legs, c1750, 53½in (136cm) high.

£2,500–2,800
Red Lion Antiques

An oak crossbanded chest-on-stand, the chest with two short and three long drawers, the stand with a long drawer, on pad feet, 18thC, 37in (94cm) wide.

£520–620 Greenslade Taylor Hunt

A painted tiger maple chest-on-stand, attributed to John Kimball, with eight drawers, on cabriole legs, restored, America, New Hampshire, c1765, 36½in (92.5cm) wide.

£40,000–50,000 Skinner

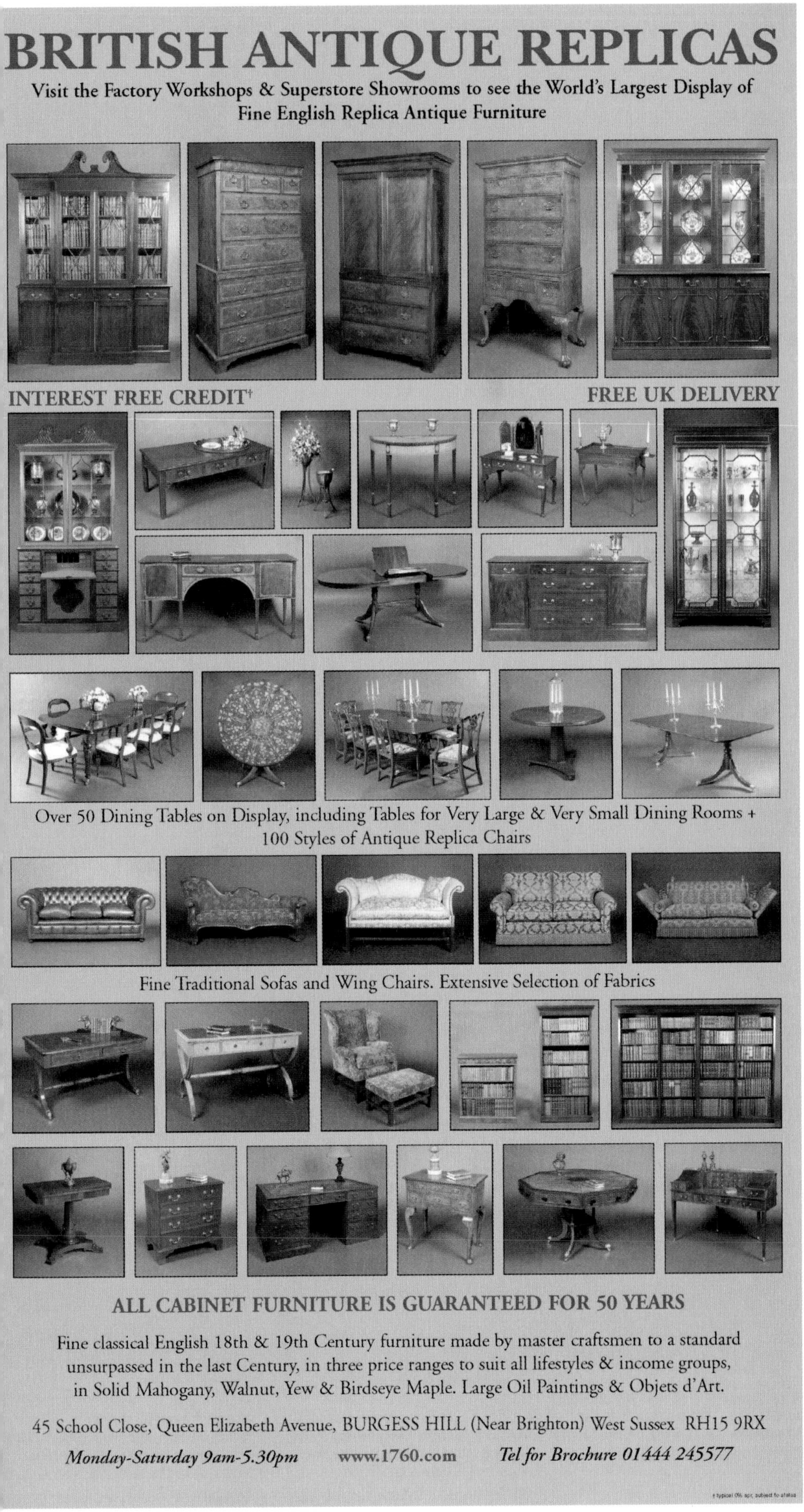
BRITISH ANTIQUE REPLICAS
Visit the Factory Workshops & Superstore Showrooms to see the World's Largest Display of Fine English Replica Antique Furniture
INTEREST FREE CREDIT†
FREE UK DELIVERY
Over 50 Dining Tables on Display, including Tables for Very Large & Very Small Dining Rooms + 100 Styles of Antique Replica Chairs
Fine Traditional Sofas and Wing Chairs. Extensive Selection of Fabrics
ALL CABINET FURNITURE IS GUARANTEED FOR 50 YEARS
Fine classical English 18th & 19th Century furniture made by master craftsmen to a standard unsurpassed in the last Century, in three price ranges to suit all lifestyles & income groups, in Solid Mahogany, Walnut, Yew & Birdseye Maple. Large Oil Paintings & Objets d'Art.
45 School Close, Queen Elizabeth Avenue, BURGESS HILL (Near Brighton) West Sussex RH15 9RX
Monday-Saturday 9am-5.30pm
www.1760.com
Tel for Brochure 01444 245577
† typical 0% apr, subject to status

COMMODES

A Louis XIV walnut serpentine commode, with two short drawers, two long drawers and a secret drawer, France, 49in (124.5cm) wide.

£9,000–10,000 Brandt Antiques

A walnut and marquetry commode, with locking mechanism, inlaid with strapwork, on bun feet, southern Germany, early 18thC, 54½in (138.5cm) wide.

£5,500–6,500 Sotheby's (NY)

A kingwood- and tulipwood-veneered commode, with a marble top and gilt-bronz mounts, reveneered, mid-18thC, 50¾in (129cm) wide.

£5,500–6,500 Sotheby's (P)

A Louis XVI oak commode, with two frieze drawers and three long moulded drawers, carved with garlands, on fluted tapered feet, France, 53in (134.5cm) wide.

£1,400–1,700 Gorringes (L)

A rosewood commode, with marquetry banding to the top and drawers, on cabriole legs, drawer pulls missing, northern Italy, mid-18thC, 54½in (138.5cm) wide.

£18,000–22,000 Sotheby's (NY)

A walnut, elm and painted hardwood commode, with limestone top and gilt-brass mounts, Sweden, 1750–1800, 43in (109cm) wide.

£5,500–6,500 Bukowskis

A George III mahogany commode, with three long drawers, on cabriole legs and scrolled feet, 42¼in (107.5cm) wide.

£6,000–7,000 Tennants

A walnut and parquetry commode, with three long drawers, on square tapered legs, Italy, Lombardy, late 18thC, 50½in (128.5cm) wide.

£5,000–5,700 Sotheby's (NY)

A mahogany and brass-mounted commode with three drawers, on tapered legs, Russia, late 18thC, 30¾in (78cm) wide.

£10,000–12,000 Sotheby's (NY)

A marquetry commode, with four graduated drawers flanked by cupboards, inlaid with classical urns, birds, flowers and insects, on claw-and-ball feet, Holland, 19thC, 32in (81cm) wide.

£1,600–2,000 Mealy's

A mahogany commode, with a marble top above four long drawers and a base drawer, France, c1830, 48¾in (124cm) wide.

£1,500–1,800 Sotheby's (Am)

A kingwood serpentine commode, with three drawers, bronze mounts and inlaid marquetry, c1900, 36in (91.5cm) wide.

£1,600–1,800 Tredantiques

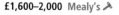

CHESTS-ON-CHESTS

figured walnut chest-on-
iest, c1715.

16,000–18,500
onald Chambers

A walnut chest-on-chest, with nine drawers, on bracket feet, mid-18thC, 40in (101.5cm) wide.

£2,000–2,500 Skinner

MILLER'S COMPARES

(L) A George II walnut chest-on-chest, with eight drawers and a slide, with featherbanded inlay, 42½in (108cm) wide.

£6,500–8,000
Sotheby's

(R) A George II burr-walnut and oak chest-on-chest, with nine drawers, bracket feet restored, 42¼in (107.5cm) wide.

£3,500–4,200
Sotheby's

The chest on the left has a very attractive patina and matched figured veneers, both of which give it a more striking appearance than the chest shown on the right. Moreover, the reeded canted corners to the upper section and the slide incorporated in the lower section demonstrate further that it is a superior piece. The example on the right is of lesser quality – the sides are made of oak, there is no slide and the bracket feet have been restored – all reasons why it sold for less than the item on the left.

mahogany chest-on-chest, with
entil-moulded cornice, on bracket
eet, c1760, 68½in (174cm) high.

4,000–4,500
antiles Spa Antiques

A George III mahogany chest-on-chest, with eight drawers, on bracket feet, 45¼in (115cm) wide.

£1,250–1,500
Dreweatt Neate (HAM)

George III mahogany chest-on-chest,
ith softwood sides and eight drawers,
n bracket feet, 43in (109cm) wide.

1,200–1,400
nderson & Garland

A mahogany chest-on-chest, with a blind-fret frieze, with nine drawers, on ogee bracket feet, late 18thC, 44in (112cm) wide.

£900–1,100
Dreweatt Neate

A painted maplewood chest-on-chest, attributed to Samuel Dunlap, the base with two dummy drawers, on cabriole legs, slight damage, America, New Hampshire, c1790, 38¾in (98.5cm) wide.

£55,000–65,000 Skinner

Pieces such as this which are attributable to a particular maker and have only minor imperfections will always command a premium.

18TH-CENTURY BOOKCASES

A walnut bureau bookcase, inlaid with box and ebony, the arched, moulded pediment above a glazed door and a candle slide, the base with a fall-front enclosing a fitted interior over a frieze drawer and two short and two long drawers, the lower drawer with inlaid concave sunburst, on bracket feet, altered and restored, early 18thC, 27in (68cm) wide.

£5,500–6,500 Toovey's

A breakfront library bookcase, in the manner of Thomas Chippendale, with four glazed doors, the base with four panelled doors, pediment missing, c1770, 59in (150cm) wide.

£15,000–18,000 Sotheby's

The design of this bookcase is similar to one by Thomas Chippendale for a library bookcase in The Gentleman and Cabinet-maker's Director *of 1754, which has similar glazing bars to the upper section. The S-shaped locks on this piece are also interesting. This unusual feature can be seen in other examples of furniture known to have been supplied by Chippendale.*

A Sheraton-style George III mahogany and satinwood-inlaid bookcase, the upper section with a pierced gallery over two astragal-glazed doors, the base with a drawer over two cupboard doors, on bracket feet, 47in (121cm) wide.

£8,000–9,500 James Adam

A George III mahogany secretaire bookcase, the detachable cornice above two astragal-glazed doors, the base with a fitted secretaire drawer over a long drawer and two cupboard doors enclosing drawers, 50in (127cm) wide.

£1,700–2,000 Woolley & Wallis

A Sheraton-style satinwood and ebony-inlaid bookcase, the top with three shelves on turned supports, above a cupboard, on square tapered legs, spade feet and casters, c1785, 21in (53.5cm) wide.

£11,000–12,500 Ronald Chambers

A Sheraton-style mahogany bureau bookcase, the tambour fall enclosing a fitted interior, c1790, 84in (213.5cm) high.

£11,000–13,000 Vanbrugh House

19TH-CENTURY BOOKCASES

. mahogany secretaire bookcase, ıe upper section with two stragal-glazed doors, above a tted secretaire drawer and two ɹpboard doors, with a shaped pron and splayed bracket feet, 1800, 43in (109cm) wide.

:9,000–11,000
ɪreweatt Neate (N)

An inlaid mahogany secretaire bookcase, the upper section with two glazed doors, over a hinged writing surface and three long drawers, on turned legs, America, Massachusetts, 40½in (103cm) wide.

£900–1,100
Northeast Auctions

A figured mahogany secretaire bookcase, with ebony and brass inlays, pilaster columns and sabre feet, c1815, 94½in (240cm) high.

£9,000–10,000
Moxhams

A mahogany bookcase, the three graduated shelves above two short drawers and two panelled doors, on splayed bracket feet, c1820, 22¾in (58cm) wide.

£1,200–1,500 Sotheby's

\ walnut 'Harvard' bookcase, the five ıraduated shelves above two panelled doors, ın turned feet, America, probably Massachusetts, ɐarly 19thC, 63½in (161.5cm) wide.

£9,000–11,000 Skinner

A mahogany secretaire bookcase, with two glazed doors above a fitted secretaire drawer, over two panelled doors, America, probably New York, c1820, 46¾in (119cm) wide.

£2,000–2,500 Skinner

A mahogany breakfront bookcase, with four glazed doors over four panelled doors, on lion-paw feet, America, Philadelphia, c1825, 84in (213.5cm) wide.

£15,000–18,000 Freeman's

\ George IV mahogany secretaire ɪookcase, inlaid with satinwood ınd ebony, with two glazed doors ıver a fitted secretaire drawer, ıbove three graduated drawers vith reeded handles, on square apered legs, 40in (101.5cm) wide.

£1,400–1,700 Morphets

A maple bookcase, with brass mounts, the upper section with two glazed doors, over two drawers and two cupboard doors, France, 1825–50, 53in (134.5cm) wide.

£4,000–5,000 Sotheby's (NY)

An oak inverted breakfront bookcase, with adjustable bookshelves flanked by cupboard doors with brass grilles, on a plinth base, c1830, 72¼in (183.5cm) wide.

£800–1,000
Sworders

A mahogany bookcase, with carved detail, the upper section doors with brass grilles, above two further doors, 1830, 87in (221cm) high.

£5,800–6,500 Georgian Antiques

A William IV mahogany secretaire bookcase, with two glazed doors, the base with a secretaire drawer above two cupboard doors flanked by fluted pilasters, on turned feet, 37in (94cm) wide.

£700–850 Greenslade Taylor Hunt

A cedar bookcase, with two glazed doors, the base with two panelled cupboard doors, Australia, 19thC, 55¼in (140.5cm) wide.

£3,500–4,200 Leonard Joel

An early Victorian mahogany bookcase, the upper section wi two glazed doors, above two drawers with turned rosewood handles and two panelled cupboard doors, on reeded bun feet, 45¼in (115cm) wide.

£3,500–4,200 Morphets

A mahogany bookcase, with two glazed doors over a drawer and two cupboard doors, c1850, 45in (114.5cm) wide.

£2,700–3,000 Old Cinema

A Victorian mahogany bookcase, the moulded cornice above two glazed doors, the base with a frieze drawer over two panelled doors flanked by turned pilasters, on a plinth base, 43½in (110.5cm) wide.

£550–650 Rosebery's

An oak inverted breakfront bookcase, c1860, 99¼in (252cm) wide.

£3,500–4,200 Sotheby's (O)

A Louis XVI-style kingwood and ormolu-mounted secretaire bookcase, the upper section mounted with hand-painted Sèvres-style porcelain plaques, above glazed panel doors, the base with glazed panel doors, France, mid- to late 19thC, 46in (117cm) wide.

£3,200–3,800 Jackson's

A flame mahogany bookcase, with two glazed doors over three drawers, c1890, 50in (127cm) wide.

£2,400–2,800 Hemswell Antique Centre

A Victorian mahogany breakfront open bookcase, with raised back and adjustable shelves, 114in (289.5cm) wide

£1,250–1,500 Woolley & Wallis

A pair of Victorian walnut inverted breakfront open bookcases, by Morant, Boyd & Morant, with chequer stringing, the backs cut for skirting boards, 66in (67.5cm) wi

£5,000–6,000 Woolley & Wallis

:SCRITOIRES & SECRETAIRES

'igured and burr-walnut escritoire, the cavetto ·nice revealing pigeon holes concealing secret ıwers, the fall-front enclosing a fitted interior d a fitted secret compartment, on later bun ·t, early 18thC, 47¾in (121.5cm) wide.

3,000–15,000 Sotheby's

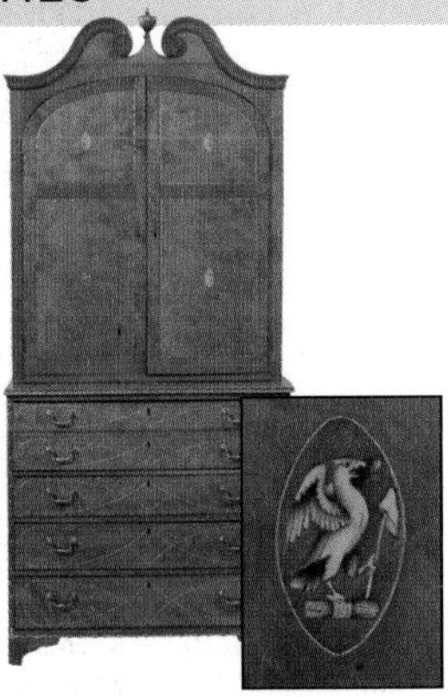

A cherrywood secretaire cabinet, the upper section with swan-neck pediment over two panelled doors inlaid with stringing enclosing shelves, each panel inlaid with a marquetry eagle clutching the Liberty Cap, the base with a fitted secretaire drawer and three graduated drawers with stringing, on bracket feet, drawer pulls replaced, America, probably Kentucky, c1800, 44½in (113cm) wide.

£70,000–85,000 Skinner

A rosewood and brass-inlaid writing cabinet, the crossbanded top over a fitted writing drawer, the scroll supports with ormolu mounts, c1820, 31in (78.5cm) wide.

£5,400–6,000 Ronald Chambers

:XPERT'S EYE SECRETAIRE BOOKCASE

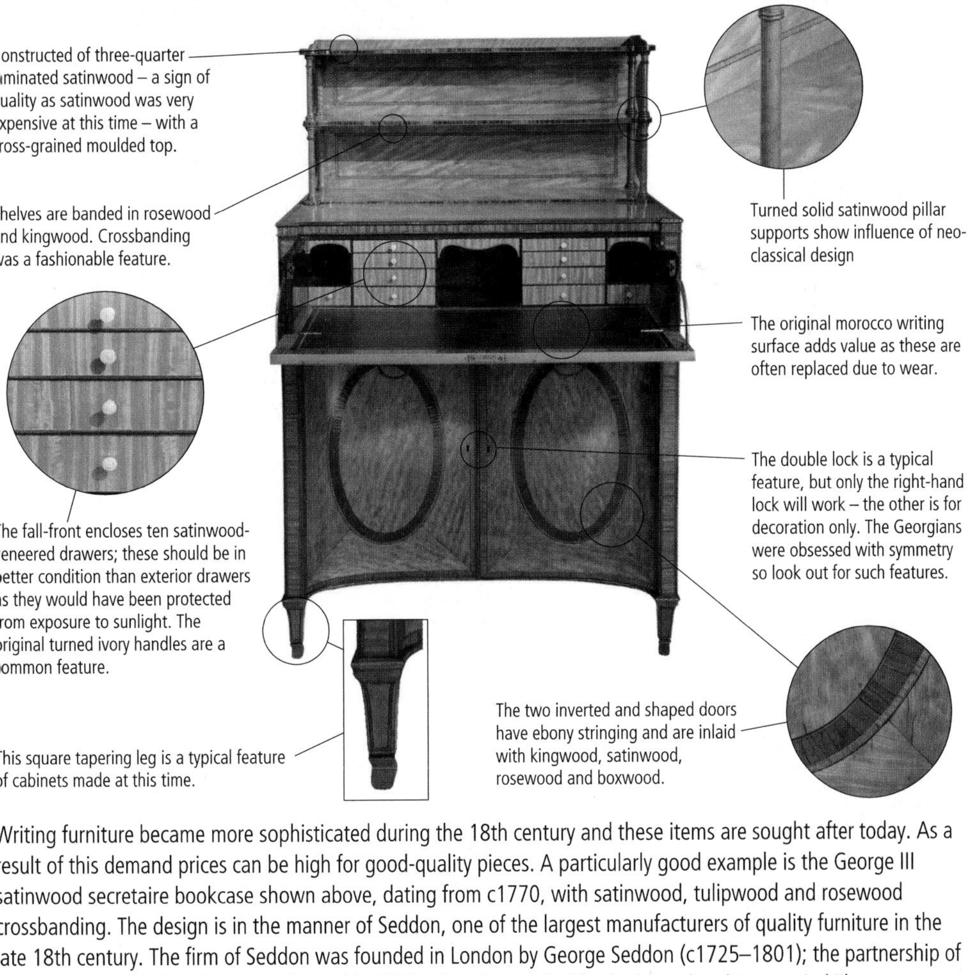

onstructed of three-quarter ıminated satinwood – a sign of uality as satinwood was very xpensive at this time – with a ross-grained moulded top.
helves are banded in rosewood nd kingwood. Crossbanding vas a fashionable feature.
'he fall-front encloses ten satinwood-eneered drawers; these should be in etter condition than exterior drawers ıs they would have been protected rom exposure to sunlight. The ›riginal turned ivory handles are a ommon feature.
'his square tapering leg is a typical feature ›f cabinets made at this time.
Turned solid satinwood pillar supports show influence of neo-classical design
The original morocco writing surface adds value as these are often replaced due to wear.
The double lock is a typical feature, but only the right-hand lock will work – the other is for decoration only. The Georgians were obsessed with symmetry so look out for such features.
The two inverted and shaped doors have ebony stringing and are inlaid with kingwood, satinwood, rosewood and boxwood.

Vriting furniture became more sophisticated during the 18th century and these items are sought after today. As a ·esult of this demand prices can be high for good-quality pieces. A particularly good example is the George III satinwood secretaire bookcase shown above, dating from c1770, with satinwood, tulipwood and rosewood :rossbanding. The design is in the manner of Seddon, one of the largest manufacturers of quality furniture in the ate 18th century. The firm of Seddon was founded in London by George Seddon (c1725–1801); the partnership of Seddon, Sons and Shackleton was formed in 1790 when George Seddon's eldest daughter married Thomas Shackleton, a cabinet-maker.

£30,000–35,000 William Cooke

BUREAU CABINETS

A George I walnut bureau cabinet, the bevelled mirror doors enclosing a fitted interior, the fall-front with a fitted interior above four drawers, altered, some later additions, probably Anglo-Dutch, 46in (117cm) wide.

£15,000–18,000 **Sotheby's**

A George I walnut and burr-walnut bureau cabinet, the upper section with two doors with bevelled mirror plates enclosing a fitted interior, the base with a fitted interior, mirror plates, engraved brass handles and escutcheons later, restored, 40¾in (103.5cm) wide.

£6,000–7,000 **Woolley & Wallis**

A mahogany bureau cabinet, the two doo with applied carving enclosing shelves, the fall-front enclosing a fitted interior, on gadroon-carved ogee bracket feet, c1760, 51¼in (130cm) wide.

£8,000–10,000 **Sotheby's**

A bureau bookcase, the broken-arch pediment with dentil-moulded cornice, c1760, 99in (251.5cm) high.

£10,500–11,500 **Ronald Chambers**

A carved cherrywood bureau cabinet, with two panelled doors over candle slides, the fall-front enclosing a fitted interior, above four drawers, on ogee bracket feet, America, Connecticut, c1780, 39in (99cm) wide.

£25,000–30,000
Northeast Auctions

This bureau cabinet is similar to others from the Hartford area. Connecticut furniture has long been considered 'quirky', a factor difficult to quantify but essentially relating to unusual methods of construction and carved detail. Furniture from this area has recently become sought after and this typically results in higher prices for a period of time. This bureau was particularly prized – it was sold as part of a single-owner sale and has a recent provenance from a well-established antique dealer. Moreover, the piece had not been restored and retained its original hardware, which also adds value in the American furniture market.

A mahogany bureau cabinet, the two door enclosing a fitted interior, above two candle slides, the fall-front enclosing a fitted interio with a secret compartment, over four graduate drawers, late 18thC, 45in (114.5cm) wide.

£4,000–5,000 **Mealy's**

An oak bureau cabinet, the upper section with two panelled doors, over a fall front and two short and two long drawers, c1780, 80in (203cm) high.

£2,000–2,300 **Pennard House**

A painted pine bureau cabinet, inscribed 'J. P. D.', Sweden, Jämtland Province, dated 1858, 46½in (118cm) wide.

£15,000–16,500
Robert Young Antiques

BUREAUX

A George I oak bureau, the fall-front enclosing a fitted interior and with an attached book rest above two short and two long graduated drawers, 38in (96.5cm) wide.

£800–1,000 Hy Duke

A George I walnut bureau, the fall-front enclosing a fitted interior, over two drawers, 27½in (70cm) wide.

£3,500–4,000 Sotheby's

A walnut-veneered bureau, with herringbone inlay, c1720, 33in (84cm) wide.

£8,000–9,000
Old Malthouse

A walnut bureau, attributed to William Parkman, the fall-front with 'mariner star' inlays and enclosing a fitted interior, over four graduated drawers inlaid with stringing, America, Massachusetts, c1740, 38in (96.5cm) wide.

£1,400–1,700 Northeast Auctions

A veneered palisander and rosewood bureau, the fall-front enclosing a fitted interior, slight damage, France, c1750, 37¼in (94.5cm) wide.

£2,700–3,200 Sotheby's (P)

An elm bureau, with brass swan-neck handles, on bracket feet, 1750–60, 36in (91.5cm) wide.

£2,800–3,200 Swan Gallery

A carved mahogany bureau, the fall-front enclosing a fitted shell-carved interior, over four long graduated drawers with brass fittings, America, New England, c1770, 36in (91.5cm) wide.

£10,000–12,000 Northeast Auctions

A George III mahogany bureau, the fall-front enclosing a fitted interior with secret compartments, above five drawers, on bracket feet, 38in (96.5cm) wide.

£550–650 Mealy's

A Georgian oak bureau-on-stand, the fall-front enclosing a fitted interior above two frieze drawers, on turned legs joined by plain stretchers, 38¼in (97cm) wide.

£320–400 Penrith Farmers' & Kidd's

A George III mahogany bureau, the fall-front over four drawers, 38in (96.5cm) wide.

£1,000–1,100 Tredantiques

A mahogany bureau, the fall-front enclosing a fitted interior, on bracket feet, late 18thC, 36in (91.5cm) wide.

£1,100–1,300
Castlegate Antiques

A mahogany bureau, the fall-front enclosing a fitted interior, above four long graduated drawers, handles and escutcheons later, c1780, 35¾in (91cm) wide.

£2,500–3,000 J Collins

A rosewood bureau, with gilt-brass mounts, the top with a pierced brass three-quarter galler above a fall-front enclosing a fitted interior, over three drawers and two cupboard doors, on sabre legs, France, 19thC, 39in (99cm) wid

£4,200–5,000 Mealy's

BONHEURS DU JOUR

A satinwood bonheur du jour, the detachable upper section with a handle, one long and two short drawers, the base with a drawer, on square tapered legs joined by a concave-fronted stretcher, c1800, 21¼in (54cm) wide.

£5,000–6,000
Sotheby's (O)

A walnut and tulipwood-banded bonheur du jour, with ormolu mounts, c1855, 36in (91.5cm) wide.

£3,500–3,800 Swan at Tetsworth

An inlaid satinwood bonheur du jour, the tambour front enclosing a fitted interior and a leather-lined folding writing surface, c1890, 29in (73.5cm) wide.

£5,800–6,500 Yoxall Antiques

A Louis XV-style kingwood bonheur du jou by Joseph-Emmanuel Zwiener, with gilt-bronze mounts, the *bombé* upper section with four drawers, the base with a shaped to over a drawer, impressed mark, France, c1900, 33½in (85cm) wide.

£25,000–30,000
Jackson's

German-born Joseph-Emmanuel Zwiener spent most of his working life in Paris. The individuality of his designs was an influence on François Linke, the leading cabinet-maker of the Belle Epoque period. Zwiener exhibite at the 1889 Exposition Universelle *in Paris, where he was awarded a gold medal.*

VRITING TABLES

ılipwood and marquetry ting table, with a pull-out ing surface, the side drawer n fitted interior, with ormolu ınts, on cabriole legs, France, '65, 22in (60cm) wide.

,500–10,000 theby's (NY)

A tulipwood writing table, the marble top above a drawer fitted with a writing slide and an inkwell, with ormolu mounts, on square tapered legs, France, c1785, 19½in (49.5cm) wide.

£5,000–6,000 Sotheby's (NY)

A mahogany writing table, with rosewood crossbanding and boxwood stringing, the leather-lined top above three frieze drawers, with handles to sides, on tapered legs and brass casters, c1790, 54in (137cm) wide.

£30,000–35,000 Sotheby's

The high value of this table is due to its fine proportions and to the fact that it is made of figured flame mahogany with rosewood crossbanding. The handles to both sides of the table are for the purpose of symmetry and the kneehole has been very delicately raised to add to the finesse of this table. The worn leather writing surface will not reduce the value but pieces with original leather in good condition will usually sell for a premium.

ruitwood and marquetry writing table, leather-inset top above two frieze wers, on tapered legs and brass casters, 18thC, 39in (99cm) wide.

8,000–22,000 Sotheby's

s writing table relates closely to the pieces duced by Christophe Wolff, received ster in 1755. He was of German origin and s a talented marquetry and cabinet maker. marquetry depicting rural landscapes is o reminiscent of the work of Gilbert and cret. All three are thought to have supplied ne marquetry panels to the furniture alers for them to integrate into furniture duced by other makers.

A rosewood writing table, with two drawers and two dummy drawers, with brass mounts and inlay, c1820, 50in (127cm) wide.

£25,000–30,000 Sotheby's

A mahogany writing desk, with four drawers, stamped 'William Priest London', c1830, 42in (106.5cm) wide.

£2,250–2,500 Swan at Tetsworth

William Priest was known in the 1830s as a furniture maker as well as an auctioneer, appraiser and upholsterer. A great many items of furniture bearing his trade label or stamp have survived, and as they range in date from the late 18th century to the mid-Victorian period, it is likely that he was also selling second-hand items that he labelled before selling.

A rosewood writing table, the leather-inset top above two drawers, with brass mounts, on cabriole legs, c1840, 56¼in (143cm) wide.

£3,250–4,000 Sotheby's (O)

walnut writing table, with original leather-et writing surface above two drawers, 870, 36in (91.5cm) wide.

,600–1,800 Swan at Tetsworth

A Louis XV-style kingwood *bureau plat*, the serpentine leather-inset top above two drawers, with gilt-metal mounts, on cabriole legs, France, late 19thC, 47¾in (121.5cm) wide.

£750–900 Rosebery's

An Edwardian mahogany writing table, the hinged top with inlaid cartouche with cypher AD and ducal crown, with leather fitted interior, on square supports united by a book rack, stamped 'English Patent No. 6425 AD 1902', 26½in (67cm) wide.

£650–725 Rosebery's

DESKS

An oak writing desk, the hinged top and fall front enclosing a fitted interior and two secret compartments, Holland, c1700, 33in (84cm) wide.

£1,700–2,000 Sotheby's (O)

An oak kneehole desk, with seven drawers and a kneehole cupboard, on bracket feet, 18thC, 32¼in (82cm) wide.

£1,500–1,800 Cheffins

A walnut and featherbanded kneehole d
c1720, 32in (81.5cm) wide.

£5,000–6,000 Sotheby's (O)

A figured walnut kneehole desk, with herringbone banding and bracket feet, 1720–40, 30in (76cm) wide.

£11,000–12,500 Moxhams

A maple, cherrywood and tiger maple desk, inlaid with bird's-eye maple, with two short drawers above three doors, over a fold-out writing surface and three drawers, slight damage, America, probably New Hampshire, 1810–15, 39¼in (99.5cm) wide.

£7,500–9,000 Skinner

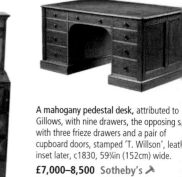

A mahogany pedestal desk, attributed to Gillows, with nine drawers, the opposing s with three frieze drawers and a pair of cupboard doors, stamped 'T. Willson', leat inset later, c1830, 59¾in (152cm) wide.

£7,000–8,500 Sotheby's

Thomas Willson established a cabinet retai firm in London in the early 19th century. It h been discovered that his stock was not onl second-hand furniture but also items made their own workshop. The fine quality of this added to the fact that Gillows was commissic to design a piece that is almost identical to suggests that it can almost certainly be attribu to Gillows and was most likely a piece retai rather than made by Thomas Willson.

A mahogany pedestal campaign writing desk, the leather-inset top with a folding gallery above nine drawers, on bun feet, 19thC, 39¾in (101cm) wide.

£850–1,000
Greenslade Taylor Hunt

A walnut pedestal writing desk, by Chindley & Sons, London, the leatherette-inset top above ten graduated drawers, stamped mark, retailer's label, 19thC, 58in (147.5cm) wide.

£5,000–6,000
Greenslade Taylor Hunt

A Victorian walnut and burr-walnut partners' desk, the leather-inset top above nine drawers, the opposing side with three frieze drawers and two cupboards, restored 54in (137cm) wide.

£1,500–1,800 Sotheby's (Am)

A mahogany kidney-shaped desk, by Gillows, the leather writing surface above nine drawers, the pedestals flanked by pilaster locking mechanisms, marked, 19thC, 51¼in (130cm) wide.

£21,000–25,000 Morphets

A Victorian burr-walnut pedestal desk, one drawer labelled 'T. H. Filmer & Sons', 49¼in (125cm) wide.

£850–1,000 Sotheby's (Am)

A mahogany partners' desk, with leather writing surface, c1850, 72½in (184cm) wide.
£5,250–6,000 Oak & Country

A satinwood pedestal desk, c1860, 48in (122cm) w
£1,400–1,600 Burford Antiques

A mahogany cylinder desk, c1860, 46in (117cm) wide.
£2,000–2,300 Burford Antiques

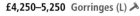

A Victorian mahogany desk, the leather-inset top above nine drawers, with fl carved canted corners, on ogee bracket feet, 60in (152.5cm) wide.
£4,250–5,250 Gorringes (L)

A late Victorian walnut pedestal desk, by Gillows, with nine drawers, leather inset later, marked, 54½in (138.5cm) wide.
£900–1,100 Woolley & Wallis

A late Victorian rosewood writing desk, with a gallery over a mirror and shelf flan by two cupboards, the tooled leather wri surface over two frieze drawers, on squa tapered legs, 38¼in (97cm) wide.
£550–650 Sworders

A mahogany cylinder desk, with crossbanded drawers, c1890, 32in (81.5cm) wide.
£1,100–1,300 Hemswell Antiques Centres

A Sheraton-revival painted satinwood writing desk, c1905, 22in (56cm) wide.
£2,000–2,400 Paul Weatherell

An Edwardian mahogany kidney-shaped with a leather-inset top, satinwood band and inlaid stringing, 48in (122cm) wide.
£1,700–2,000 Woolley & Wallis

·AVENPORTS

‧egency rosewood davenport, the sloping enclosing a fitted interior, with pen and drawer to the side, four short drawers and ‧my drawers, 20in (51cm) wide.

‧0–900 Hy Duke

A mahogany davenport, the hinged and sliding slope enclosing a fitted interior, above three drawers, on bun feet, c1825, 20in (51cm) wide.

£1,000–1,200 Dreweatt Neate

A rosewood davenport, by Gillows, the hinged and sliding slope with a fitted interior, above a slide and three graduated drawers, c1830, 21¾in (55.5cm) wide.

£6,000–7,000 Dreweatt Neate

ırr-walnut davenport, with a sliding top, ‧0, 22in (56cm) wide.

250–2,500
‧tlegate Antiques

A Victorian burr-walnut davenport, with a letter rack and piano front enclosing a fitted interior, above four drawers and four dummy drawers, 22in (56cm) wide.

£1,000–1,200 Dreweatt Neate

A burr-walnut davenport, the cylinder fall-front enclosing a fitted interior and adjustable writing slide, c1860, 30in (76cm) wide.

£5,200–6,000
Woburn Abbey Antiques

ictorian figured and inlaid walnut enport, the rising stationery compartment ‧ve a piano front enclosing a pull-out ‧ng slide and two drawers, ‧ve a cupboard enclosing four drawers, ‧in (62cm) wide.

000–6,000 Mealy's

A Victorian rosewood davenport, the raised hinged back with pierced three-quarter gallery enclosing a letter rack and pen trays over a sloping hinged top on leaf-carved scroll supports, four side drawers and opposing dummy drawers, on bun feet and casters, 37in (94cm) high.

£550–650 Dee, Atkinson & Harrison

A Victorian mahogany-banded satinwood and ebonized davenport, the raised stationery compartment with pierced gallery, a leather writing surface enclosing drawers on turned and fluted supports, with four side drawers, on bun feet and casters, 20¼in (51.5cm) wide.

£700–850 Andrew Hartley

BEDS

MILLER'S COMPARES

(L) **A James I carved oak tester bed,** the headboard carved with masks and dragons above floral panels flanked by herms and chevron banding, some parts later, 77¼in (196cm) high.

£20,000–25,000 Sotheby's (O)

(R) **A James I carved oak tester bed,** the headboard carved with serpents and arched panels, flanked by herms and caryatids, some parts later, 88¼in (224cm) high.

£12,500–15,000 Sotheby's (O)

The major factor contributing to the higher value of the bed on the left is that it has an outstanding provenance, having at one time been owned by the 6th Marquess of Bute and then been on display since the early 1980s in Warwick Castle, England. The bed on the left also has attractive inlay and a traditional deep color and patination, which is often more popular than the lighter color of the bed on the right. Additionally, the bed on the right is substantially taller, a major factor when not only considering the lower ceilings of modern houses, but also those of properties built early in American history.

An oak cradle, carved with griffins, 17thC, 36in (91.5cm) long.

£2,400–2,700 Chair Set

A mahogany four-poster bed, the canopy on fluted tapered posts, on ball-and-claw feet, North America, c1760, 62in (157.5cm) wide.

£2,500–3,000 Northeast Auctions

A brass four-poster bed, finia damaged, 19thC, 42½in (108cm) wide.

£1,300–1,600 Sotheby's (Am)

A burr-maple and walnut bed, carved with simulated drapery and beaded tassels, European, 19thC, 58in (147.5cm) wide.

£3,500–4,250 Sotheby's (NY)

A mahogany four-poster bed, later canopy, 19thC, 55½in (141cm) wide.

£500–600 Woolley & Wallis

A chestnut bed, with carved panels depict rural scenery, France, Brittany, c1890, 60i (152.5cm) wide.

£2,000–2,300 S W Antiques

EDSIDE CABINETS & COMMODES

ıahogany bedside cabinet, on cabriole
; and pad feet, repaired, 18thC,
n (48cm) wide.

50–425 Woolley & Wallis

A mahogany bedside cabinet, the tray top above two doors and a pot drawer, on square legs, c1760, 19¾in (50cm) wide.

£1,800–2,200 Sotheby's

A pair of mahogany bedside cabinets, with pot cupboards, the legs on leather casters, c1780, 21in (53.5cm) wide.

£8,000–9,000 Sotheby's (O)

nahogany bedside cabinet, with gallery
and tambour cupboard door, on cabriole
s, Holland, c1795, 21in (53.5cm) wide.

,400–2,700
oburn Abbey Antiques

A pair of mahogany bedside cabinets, c1810, 16in (40.5cm) wide.

£6,800–7,500 Moxhams

A mahogany bowfronted commode, the hinged top above a crossbanded and rosewood-strung panelled front and inner ceramic liner, above a dummy drawer, early 19thC, 28½in (72.5cm) wide.

£225–275 Woolley & Wallis

nahogany bedside cabinet/ bed steps,
:h leather insets, c1850, 24in (61cm) high.

,000–1,150
ɛorgian Antiques

A mahogany and mahogany-veneered drop-leaf bedside cabinet, the double-drawer front opening as a single drawer, America, 19thC, 16¾in (42.5cm) wide.

£1,100–1,300 Sotheby's (P)

A pair of mahogany bedside cabinets, c1860, 29½in (75cm) high.

£1,100–1,300 Georgian Antiques

RACKS & STANDS

A mahogany reading stand, with a telescopic tapered support and tripod base, c1760, 21¾in (55.5cm) wide.

£1,100–1,300 Sotheby's

A mahogany candlestand, with a fluted column, acanthus-carved knop and three leaf-carved cabriole legs, c1760, 33in (84cm) high.

£5,000–6,000 Richard Gardner

A pair of mahogany candlestands, the to edged with rosewood, each on a tapered co and three legs, c1770, 37in (94cm) high.

£2,250–2,500 Mere Antiques

A Regency mahogany book stand, attributed to Gillows, with a spindle gallery and a drawer, with beadwork moulding, 16¼in (41cm) wide.

£1,350–1,600 Sworders

A George IV mahogany folio stand, the hinged top for one or two folios, on a leaf-carved pillar and four legs, 30¾in (78cm) wide.

£4,500–5,500 Tennants

A mahogany folio stand, on a trestle base and bun feet, c1835, 34½in (87.5cm) wide

£1,200–1,500 Skinner

A turned and carved oak stick and umbrella stand, with tin liner, c1870, 34in (86.5cm) wide.

£800–900 Woburn Abbey Antiques

An oak and brass stick stand, with tin liner, c1890, 23in (58.5cm) wide.

£800–900 Woburn Abbey Antiques

A mahogany boot and whip stand, 19thC, 26in (66cm) wide.

£350–400 Long Street Antiques

An oak stick stand, in the manner of Jame Shoolbred, with brass mounts and zinc line 1875–1900, 23¼in (59cm) wide.

£1,500–1,800 Sotheby's (O)

ıahogany torchère, on a tripod
ıse, c1890, 48in (122cm) high.

,100–1,250
nald Chambers ⊞

An Edwardian oak and brass magazine rack, 34in (86.5cm) high.

£350–400 Top Banana ⊞

A mahogany three-tier cake stand, c1915, 35in (89cm) high.

£200–230 Castlegate Antques ⊞

:ANTERBURIES

ıahogany canterbury, on turned legs and
ıss casters, c1800, 18in (45.5cm) wide.

,700–2,000 Georgian Antiques ⊞

A mahogany canterbury, with a drawer, c1820, 19in (48.5cm) wide.

£2,000–2,200 Georgian Antiques ⊞

A walnut canterbury whatnot, with fretwork and barley-twist columns and feet, c1860, 38in (96.5cm) high.

£900–1,000 McBains ⊞

Victorian mahogany canterbury, the
ırced dividers above a drawer, on turned
ıs and brass casters, 20in (51cm) wide.

,350–1,500
'oburn Abbey Antiques ⊞

A walnut canterbury, c1880, 22in (56cm) wide.

£900–1,000
Period Furniture ⊞

A Victorian walnut canterbury, with pierced fretwork and a frieze drawer, on tapered legs and ceramic casters, 28½in (72.5cm) wide.

£700–850 Anderson & Garland

DUMB WAITERS

A Charles I oak three-tier court cupboard, with a drawer, 44in (112cm) wide.
£9,000–10,000 Sotheby's

A George III mahogany three-tier drop-leaf dumb waiter, on turned supports and a tripod base, 42¼in (107.5cm) high.
£2,000–2,500 Bearnes

A mahogany three-tier dumb waiter, on turned columns and three splayed legs, late 18thC, 45in (114.5cm) high.
£1,500–1,750 Long Street Antiques

A pair of mahogany three-tier dumb waiters, Ireland, c1790, 56in (142cm) high.
£11,000–13,000 Georgian Antiques

A mahogany three-tier dumb waiter, with ring-turned columns and brass rods, on bun feet and casters, c1830, 29¼in (74.5cm) wide.
£1,500–1,650 J Collins

A mahogany dumb waiter, c1860, 39in (99cm) wide.
£1,600–1,800 Quayside Antiques

A mahogany three-tier dumb w
on turned columns and brass casters, c1860, 41in (104cm) w
£800–900 Burford Antiques

An early Victorian mahogany three-tier telescopic dumb waiter, 21in (53.5cm) diam.
£2,200–2,500 Sotheby's (O)

A Victorian yew-wood three-tier dumb waiter, by Arthur Jones, carved with shamrocks and armorials, Ireland, Dublin, 29½in (100.5cm) wide.
£28,000–32,000 James Adam
This was probably made for the Dublin Industries Exhibition of 1853.

A walnut dumb waiter, on turned supports, c1900, 42in (106.5cm) wide.
£450–500 S W Antiques

WHATNOTS

George III mahogany five-tier whatnot, ith three drawers, on turned supports and eet, 65in (165cm) high.

1,200–1,500 Gorringes (L)

A mahogany whatnot, with a drawer and turned supports, on tapered legs and brass casters, America, c1800, 20in (51cm) wide.

£3,200–3,800 Northeast Auctions

A Regency mahogany whatnot, with rising top and fall front, 50in (127cm) high.

£3,000–3,500 Ronald Chambers

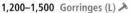

Regency mahogany four-tier whatnot, with urned columns and a drawer, 59in (150cm) high.

1,500–1,650 McBains

A mahogany whatnot, c1830, 36in (91.5cm) high.

£2,000–2,200 Spurrier-Smith

A mahogany whatnot, c1835, 31in (78.5cm) high.

£1,350–1,500 Woburn Abbey Antiques

mahogany three-tier whatnot, by Thomas ing, on scroll feet, c1840, 44in (112cm) high.

2,500–2,800 Andy Gibbs

A rosewood whatnot, with barley-twist supports, c1860, 23in (58.5cm) wide.

£650–750 Swan at Tetsworth

A walnut three-tier whatnot, c1870, 37in (94cm) high.

£700–800 Tredantiques

MUSIC STANDS

A gilt-metal and painted wood **music stand,** the support in the form of an arrow, with two copper candle branches, France, c1800, 49in (124.5cm) high.

£3,000–3,500 Sotheby's (NY)

A Regency *tôle peinte* music **stand,** decorated with oak leaves and acorns, with two candle branches and a cast-iron base, 19in (48.5cm) wide.

£1,100–1,300 Hy Duke

A walnut **duet stand,** with pierced adjustable slopes, on a turned column and tripod base, 19thC, 52in (132cm) high.

£700–850 Ewbank Auctioneers

A walnut **duet music stand,** c1870, 50in (127cm) high.

£1,700–2,000 Styles of Stow

WASHSTANDS

A George II mahogany **washstand,** the crossbanded fold-over top enclosing a fitted interior and adjustable mirror, above two dummy drawers and one long drawer, on square tapering legs, 24in (61cm) wide.

£500–600 Greenslade Taylor Hunt

A mahogany **washstand,** c1800, 13in (33cm) wide.

£450–500 Woburn Abbey Antiques

A Regency mahogany **washstand,** the roll-top enclosing a water tank and Staffordshire bowl transfer-printed with chinoiserie decoration, above a drawer and two cupboard doors, the side with a bidet, 24in (61cm) wide.

£3,200–3,800 Northeast Auctions

A burr-elm **washstand,** with a hinged top, France, c1820, 32in (81cm) wide.

£2,500–2,750 Red Lion Antiques

A pine **washstand,** c1900, 40in (101.5cm) wide.

£270–300 Harlequin Antiques

8TH-CENTURY MIRRORS

ouis XIV carved giltwood and gesso wall ror, France, 9¾in (50cm) wide.
,500–1,800 Sotheby's (O)

A japanned pier glass, the cushion frame decorated with chinoiserie scenes, with a cut-glass plate above the main plate, redecorated, c1705, 25½in (65cm) wide.
£1,800–2,200 Sotheby's (O)

A George II walnut and parcel-gilt wall mirror, with a swan-neck pediment centred by a cartouche, 26¾in (68cm) wide.
£1,350–1,600 Bellmans

carved and giltwood mirror, with pierced coration of rocailles, flowers, foliage and ticework, damaged and restored, 18thC, ½in (95.5cm) wide.
,000–7,500 Sotheby's (P)

A giltwood mirror, Sweden, 18thC, 40in (101.5cm) high.
£5,400–6,000 Augustus Brandt

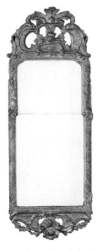

A gilt-bronze mirror, decorated with rocailles and flowers, slight damage, lower plate later, Sweden, Stockholm, 1750–1800, 20½in (52cm) wide.
£3,000–3,500 Bukowskis

mirror, the borders carved with leaves, ance, 1760–80, 29in (73.5cm) wide.
4,000–4,500 G D Blay

A giltwood mirror, France, late 18thC, 47in (119.5cm) high.
£6,000–7,000 Augustus Brandt

A pine mirror, with original painted decoration, Scandinavia, 1780–1800, 10¼in (26cm) wide.
£2,000–2,200 Robert Young Antiques

19TH-CENTURY MIRRORS

A mahogany mirror, outlined with brass-banded borders, the cresting and bottom rail inset with brass flutes, Russia, c1800, 26in (66cm) wide.

£4,500–5,500 Sotheby's (NY)

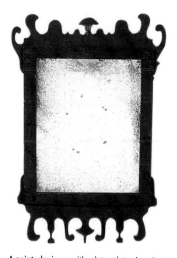

A painted mirror, with a later plate, America, c1800, 11½in (29cm) wide.

£8,000–9,500 Northeast Auctions

A mahogany and *verre églomisé* mirror, with a reeded frame and a tablet depicting sea battle, America, New England, early 19thC, 12½in (32cm) wide.

£500–600 Skinner

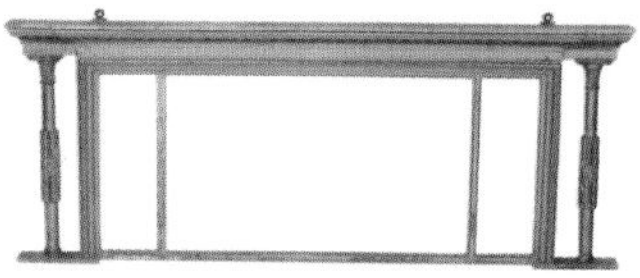

A Regency giltwood overmantel mirror, with a breakfront cornice above two ribbon-tied columns and three mirror plates, 60in (152.5cm) wide.

£350–425 Hy Duke

A giltwood convex wall mirror, surmounted by an eagle on an acanthus-decorated capital, the frame with ball decoration and acanthus leaves below, early 19thC, 41¼in (105cm) high.

£1,400–1,750 Bearnes

A Regency carved pine and giltwood overmantel mirror, with a reeded ebonized slip, the moulded frame with foliate cresting and lion-paw feet, 55in (140cm) wide.

£550–650 Sworders

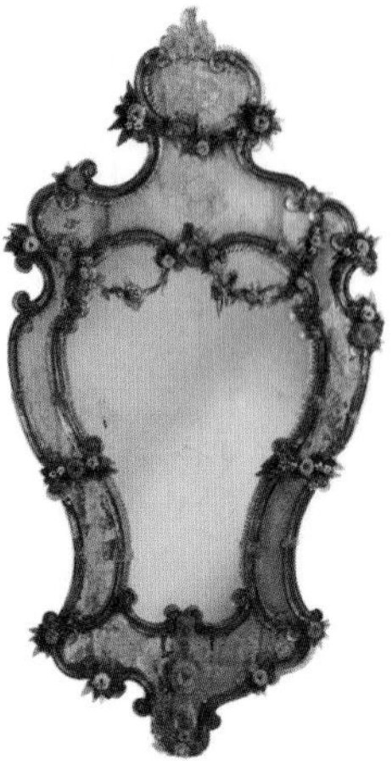

A Murano etched-glass mirror, decorated w coloured glass flower sprays and swags, slig damage, Italy, Venice, 19thC, 35in (89cm) wi

£5,000–6,000 Sotheby's (NY)

A rococo-style giltwood and gesso mirror, France, 19thC, 24½in (62cm) wide.

£1,500–1,800 Sotheby's (Am)

A giltwood girandole, by G. Nosotti, maker's plate to rear, c1825, 22in (56cm) wide.

£2,700–3,000 Chair Set

An Edwardian satinwood wall mirror, decorated with applied ormolu foliate and fruiting vines and reeded ormolu pilasters, with candle sconces, 50in (127cm) wide.

£1,750–2,000 Anderson & Garland

OILET MIRRORS

alnut toilet mirror, with herringbone
y, early 18thC, 29in (73.5cm) high.

500–1,650 ry Cruz Antiques

A George II walnut toilet mirror, with a moulded frame and brass fittings, 16½in (42cm) wide.

£280–320 Hy Duke

A George III mahogany toilet mirror, 25¼in (64cm) high.

£150–180 Sworders

HEVAL MIRRORS

eorge III mahogany cheval mirror,
square section frame with urn finials,
C-scroll supports, 26in (66cm) wide.

50–725 Rosebery's

A mahogany cheval mirror, with a ring-turned frame, on hipped splay feet with brass caps and casters, early 19thC, 26in (66cm) wide.

£550–650 Bearnes

A George IV mahogany cheval mirror, the spiral-turned frame with candlestands, on splay feet with brass paw caps and casters, 28in (71cm) wide.

£600–700 James Adam

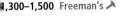

mahogany cheval mirror, with a moulded
diment, on acanthus-carved legs with
w feet, America, Philadelphia, c1825,
in (195.5cm) high.

,300–1,500 Freeman's

A mahogany cheval mirror, with adjustable brass candle sconces, on scrolled legs, 19thC, 26in (66cm) wide.

£475–575 Woolley & Wallis

A Victorian satin-birch cheval mirror, on scroll feet, 19thC, 33½in (85cm) wide.

£600–700 Holloway's

SCREENS

A mahogany pole screen, with a petit point panel, on a tripod base with cabriole legs and pad feet, c1740, 57in (145cm) high.

£400–500 Dreweatt Neate (N)

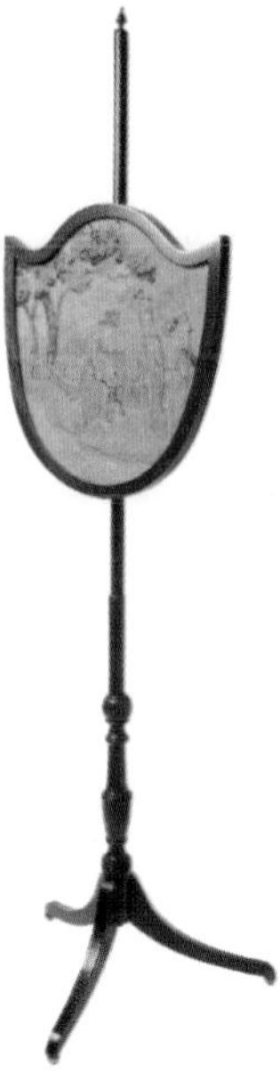

A Georgian mahogany polescreen, with a needlework panel, 56in (142cm) high.

£250–300 Pantiles Spa Antiques

A mahogany fire screen, with an adjustab tapestry panel, c1780, 32in (81.5cm) wide

£1,200–1,500 Sotheby's (O)

A rosewood fire screen, with original needlework, dated 1835, 45in (114.5cm) high.

£450–500 Long Street Antiques

A Louis XV-style carved giltwood fire screen, with a Gobelins tapestry panel signed by Jacques Neilson and dated 1820, frame 19thC, France, 29½in (75cm) wide.

£4,500–5,500 Sotheby's

A Victorian mahogany fire screen, carved with acanthus leaves, on scrolled splay feet 34in (86.5cm) wide.

£500–600 Anderson & Garland

An embossed leather four-fold screen, on an ebonized wood frame, 19thC, each panel 21in (53.5cm) wide.

£1,500–1,800 Sotheby's (Am)

A leather four-fold screen, painted and tooled with scrolling acanthus and floral sprays, 19thC, 119¾in (304cm) wide.

£380–450 Cheffins

A Louis XVI-style giltwood and gesso thre fold screen, each panel with asymmetrical C-scroll above a bevelled glass inset and lat fabric panel, 58¾in (149cm) wide.

£400–500 Dreweatt Neate (HAM)

BLACK FOREST WARES

IT IS OFTEN THOUGHT that Black Forest carvings originated in Germany but they were actually the creation of Swiss carvers. The wood carving industry of Switzerland began in the 1800s in the town of Brienz and by the end of the century it had become the industrial driving force of an entire community. The Swiss wood carvers achieved worldwide acclaim at international exhibitions including the Great Exhibition, London in 1851, the Centennial Exhibition, Philadelphia in 1876, the Chicago World's Fair in1893 and the *Exposition Universelle*, Paris in1900.

In Europe Black Forest wares became a symbol of luxury and wealth, with the finest pieces most often found in Royal collections or the homes of elite Victorian travellers. Popularity increased overseas as well – there was high demand for portrayals of animals native to America, such as bears, stags and eagles.

The genre has seen some tremendous changes over the past ten years. Specialist auctions and dealers have emerged in Europe and the United States and books have been written on the subject, adding to the previously sparse information available to collectors. For the first time pieces now surfacing at auctions that are being attributed to the master Swiss carvers. For instance, a pair of dogs attributed to Walter Mad recently turned up at Bonham's New York. Mader's ability to capture the dogs' expressions and moveme is unsurpassed.

As collectors and dealers become more knowledgeable they are far more discerning about th pieces they pursue. The quality of carving ranges fror indifferent to first rate, according to the ability of the carver. World-class examples rarely surface on the open market and, when they do, are readily snatchec up. Signed pieces and those by certain families such the Huggler family command a premium. The style, subject and detail of the piece also add value. Take t hall stands shown on page 114 for instance. The shaped tree hall stand with large cubs in the branche a cub strolling below and original colouring will bring the highest prices. Equally a hall stand with a dog ma bring double or triple the price of a bear hall stand d to the rarity and high skill required to produce it. As a greater understanding of the Black Forest genre com to light the importance of these works can only grow

Simon Danie

A Black Forest wood ashtray, carved with a bear, with a brass liner, Switzerland, c1900, 6in (15cm) wide.

£100–120 **Koh I Noor Antiques**

A Black Forest lime-wood bench, the supports carved as two standing bears, the back as four bears playing and working, Switzerland, c1870, 74in (188cm) wide.

£25,000–28,000 **Daniels Antiques**

A Black Forest wooden bench, carved as two bear cubs supporting the seat on their shoulders, with glass eyes, Switzerland, late 19thC, 38in (96.5cm) wide.

£6,000–7,000 **Jackson's**

A pair of Black Forest walnut candelabra, Switzerland, late 19thC, 34¼in (87cm) high.

£9,000–11,000 **Sotheby's (O)**

A Black Forest carved wood an marquetry musical chair, the back and seat inlaid with scenes of chamois, plays two airs when sat on, Switzerland, late 19thC.

£450–550 **Jackson's**

lack Forest lime-wood armchair, carved a seated bear with outstretched paws, itzerland, c1890, 47in (119.5cm) high.

0,000–22,000 Daniels Antiques

A Black Forest lime-wood armchair, the back carved with entwined branches and resting bears, two cross-legged bears supporting the chair's arms, the front legs with climbing bears, Switzerland, c1900, 45in (114.5cm) high.

£10,000–11,000 Daniels Antiques

A Black Forest wooden musical cigarette box and ashtray, carved with a bear, the ashtray with a brass liner, Germany, 1920s, 6in (15cm) high.

£100–110 Koh I Noor Antiques

A Black Forest hall rack, carved as a chamois trophy head, with coat hooks, c1870, 12in (30.5cm) high.

£350–400 Fenwick & Fenwick

Black Forest walnut frame, carved as a eath, with inset glazed panel, Switzerland, 900, 18in (45.5cm) diam.

00–500 Jackson's

A Black Forest walnut drinks stand, carved as a hiking bear with backpack, Switzerland, c1900, 18½in (47cm) high.

£2,400–2,750 Daniels Antiques

Victorian Black Forest walnut hall rack, rved with a stag's head, with a mirror, in (76cm) wide.

2,000–2,400 Northeast Auctions

A Black Forest hall rack, carved as a fox's head, with glass eyes, Switzerland, late 19thC, 12½in (32cm) high.

£650–750 Jackson's

A Black Forest lime-wood hall stand, carved as a mother bear shaking a tree with three cubs in the branches, Switzerland, c1870, 92in (233.5cm) high.

£17,000–20,000 Daniels Antiques

A Black Forest walnut hall **stand,** carved with a dog chasing a cat up a tree, Switzerland, c1870, 72in (183cm) high.

£20,000–25,000
Daniel's Antiques

A Black Forest lime-wood hall **stand,** probably by Louis Meichtry Brienz, carved as bear and a cub climbing a tree, with a mirror in a carved oak leaf frame, Switzerland, late 19thC, 89in (226cm) high.

£11,000–13,000
Jackson's

A Black Forest coloured lime-**wood hall stand,** carved with two cubs in a tree, a further bear at the base, Switzerland, c1890, 85in (216cm) high.

£17,000–20,000
Daniels Antiques

A Black Forest hall stand, damaged, Switzerland, c1900, 67¾in (172cm) high.

£2,000–2,400
Sotheby's (P)

A Black Forest inkwell, the hinged cover carved in the form of a goat's head, with glass eyes, Switzerland, 19thC, 8in (20.5cm) high.

£325–400 Andrew Hartley

A Black Forest tobacco jar, carved in the form of a dog smoking a pipe, Switzerland, c1890, 8in (20.5cm) high.

£10,000–12,000 Daniel's Antiques

A Black Forest jardinière, carved as a vine-covered basket, the stand carved as a branch Switzerland, late 19thC, 32in (81.5cm) high.

£650–750 Jackson's

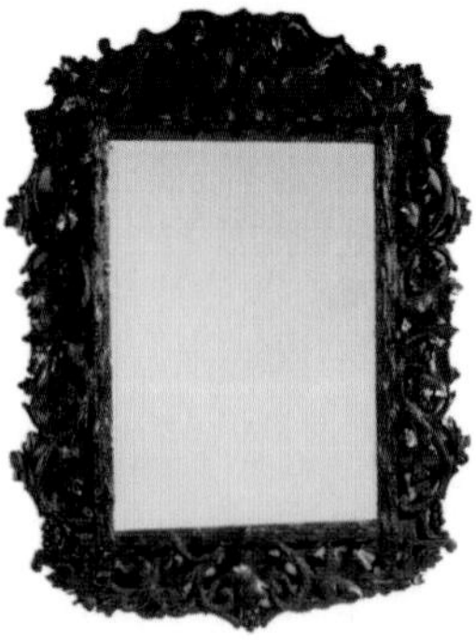

A Black Forest mirror, pierced and relief-carved with scrolling branches and grape clusters, with two birds in the crest, Switzerland, c1900, 41in (104cm) wide.

£2,000–2,400 Jackson's

A Black Forest carved model of a bear, with glass eyes, Switzerland, early 20thC, 12in (30.5cm) high.

£700–800 Gorringes (L)

A Black Forest carved model of a bear, with glass eyes, Switzerland, 19thC, 20in (51cm) long.

£1,800–2,200 Sworders

A Black Forest carved model of a bear with wood basket and axe, Switzerland, c1910, 5in (12.5cm) high.

£110–125 Long Street Antiques ⊞

A pair Black Forest carved walnut figures of soldiers, Switzerland, c1890, 11in (28cm) high.

£2,500–3,000 Daniel's Antiques ⊞

A Black Forest lime-wood walking stick stand, carved as a begging dog, with drip pan, Switzerland, c1890, 35in (89cm) high.

£11,000–13,000 Daniels Antiques ⊞

Black Forest lime-wood stick stand, arved with a chamois on a rocky outcrop, he base with copper drip pan, Switzerland, ate 19thC, 55in (139.5cm) high.

4,500–5,500 Jackson's

A Black Forest stick stand, carved as a bear cub, the base with copper drip pan, Switzerland, late 19thC, 34in (86.5cm) high.

£3,000–3,500 Jackson's

A Black Forest stick stand, carved as a bear holding a walking stick, the base with copper pan drip, Switzerland, late 19thC, 40in (101.5cm) high.

£1,300–1,600 Jackson's

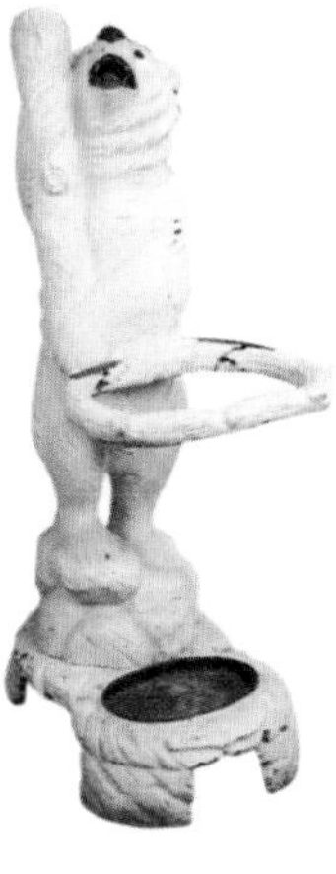

Black Forest softwood stick tand, carved as a bear holding tree stump, later painted, amaged, Switzerland, c1900, 5¾in (116cm) high.

1,000–1,200 Toovey's

A Black Forest walnut plant stand, carved in the form of a gnome, Switzerland, c1890, 36in (91.5cm) high.

£8,000–9,000
Daniel's Antiques ⊞

A Black Forest piano stool, carved as a kneeling bear cub supporting a revolving seat, Switzerland, c1870, 31in (78.5cm) high.

£7,000–8,000
Daniels Antiques ⊞

A Black Forest softwood smoker's companion table, the top carved with three bears, one a pipe rest, two standing on hinged compartments, supported by a tree trunk held by a bear, Switzerland, late 19thC, 34in (86.5cm) high.

£2,000–2,500 Toovey's

BOXES

A carved oak Bible/writing box, Westmorland, 17thC, 35in (89cm) wide.

£900–1,000 **Oak & Country** ⊞

A carved oak Bible box, repair to cover, c1680, 22½in (57cm) wide.

£675–750 **Period Oak** ⊞

A figured walnut tea caddy, with two compartments, c1730, 9in (23cm) high.

£350–400 **Fenwick & Fenwick** ⊞

A lacquered box, the domed top painted with men in an Oriental landscape, on scroll feet, Italy, Venice, mid-18thC, 9¾in (25cm) wide.

£12,000–15,000 **Sotheby's** ⚒

A tulipwood and stained sycamore casket, by David Roentgen, the brass-mounted cover enclosing a fitted interior with secret drawers, the sides with gilt-bronze handles, the apron with a concealed drawer, Germany, Neuwied, 1775–80, 9in (23cm) wide.

£25,000–30,000 **Sotheby's** ⚒

There are very few caskets recorded by David Roentgen. The majority are later than this one, veneered in plain mahogany with gilt-bronze mounts and very neo-classical in form. Caskets with rose marquetry such as this are extremely rare.

A papier-mâché tea caddy, attributed to Henry Clay, c1780, 5¼in (13.5cm) high.

£3,200–3,500
Richard Gardner ⊞

Henry Clay patented the papier-mâché manufacturing process in 1773.

A rosewood tea caddy, with three sections and spoon tray, with brass mounts and feet, c1780, 9in (23cm) wide.

£300–350 **Mostly Boxes** ⊞

A satinwood tea caddy, inlaid with stars and stringing, c1790, 4in (10cm) high.

£300–350 **Fenwick & Fenwick** ⊞

A mahogany and tulipwood-crossbanded tea caddy, by George Simson, the velvet-lined interior with two lidded boxes and central well with a plated handle, with trade labels, c1790, 12in (30.5cm) wide.

£400–500 **Sworders** ⚒

George Simson was an upholsterer, cabinet-maker and undertaker, trading from c1787 to 1840. He attracted commissions from a number of aristocratic clients and was named in a list of master cabinet-makers published by Sheraton in his Cabinet Directory *in 1803. The use of tulipwood crossbanding on this tea caddy is characteristic of his work.*

A mahogany tea caddy, with crossbanding and shell inlay, c1800, 9in (23cm) wide.

£350–400 **Mostly Boxes** ⊞

A figured mahogany wall-mounted knife box, c1790, 21in (53.5cm) high.

£350–400 **Fenwick & Fenwick** ⊞

ıorocco jewel box, c1800, 10in (25.5cm) wide.
80–200 Mostly Boxes ⊞

A mahogany and rosewood wall-mounted salt box, with drawer, c1810, 13in (33cm) high.
£350–400
Fenwick & Fenwick ⊞

A mahogany tea caddy, inlaid with stars, with two sections, c1815, 10in (25.5cm) wide.
£325–375 Mostly Boxes ⊞

ːegency japanned workbox, with ıoiserie decoration, 13½in (34.5cm) wide.
00–700 Sotheby's (O)

oak salt box, c1820, 16in (40.5cm) wide.
80–220
ːter Norden Antiques ⊞

An ormolu-mounted burr-amboyna document box, inlaid with mother-of-pearl, on winged paw feet, France, c1820, 23¼in (59cm) wide.
£4,000–5,000 Sotheby's (NY)

ɔapier-mâché box, by Stobwasser, inscribed ʼaria Stuart, Königin von Schottland', ırked, Germany, c1820, 4in (10cm) diam.
ː50–950 Hugh Mote ⊞

A rosewood writing slope, with brass inlay, original inkwells, candle sconces, secret drawers and false floor, c1820, 17in (43cm) long.
£1,100–1,200 Antique Boxes ⊞

A wooden box, printed with a view of Brighton Pavilion and the Brighton Patent Coach, with a drawer, early 19thC, 7½in (19cm) wide.
£800–950 Gorringes (L)

ɾosewood table box, inlaid with pewter and ɔther-of-pearl, c1830, 11in (28cm) wide.
150–175 Mostly Boxes ⊞

A William IV rosewood box, inlaid with mother-of-pearl, 8in (20.5cm) wide.
£250–300 Mostly Boxes

A rosewood writing box, with mahogany crossbanding and mother-of-pearl writing slope, c1835, 12in (30.5cm) wide.
£225–250 Mostly Boxes

A burr-walnut stationery box, the fitted interior with glass inkwells and pull-out folding writing slope, 19thC, 12½in (32cm) wide.
£1,000–1,200 Anderson & Garland

A carved walrus ivory sewing box, decorated with foliate scrolls, on bracket feet, Russia, Kholmogory, 19thC, 10¾in (27.5cm) wide.
£2,500–3,000 Sotheby's (NY)

A Sorrento ware tea caddy, decorated with marquetry figures and flowers, Italy, 19thC, 4in (10cm) wide.
£350–425 Dreweatt Neate

A tortoiseshell *bombé* tea caddy, with two sections, the cover with mother-of-pearl inlay, on carved ivory ball feet, c1840, 14in (35.5cm) wide.
£3,500–4,250 Freeman's

A walnut writing box, the cover with inlaid decoration, c1850, 12in (30.5cm) wide.
£150–175 Mostly Boxes

A Victorian rosewood workbox, inlaid with pewter and mother-of-pearl, with a fitted interior, 12in (30.5cm) wide.
£180–220 Dreweatt Neate

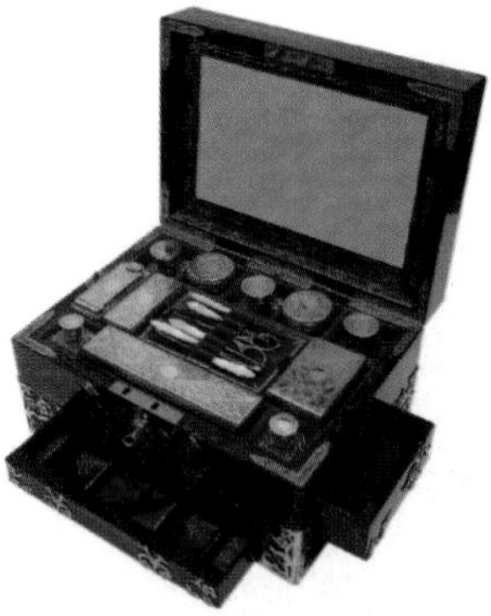

A brass-mounted coromandel lady's vanity box, the fitted interior with silver-mounted bottles and boxes, hallmarked, 1853, 13in (33cm) wide.
£2,700–3,000 Mostly Boxes

A Spa-ware wooden needle bo with hand-painted decoration, Belgium, c1860, 2½in (6.5cm) hig
£340–375
Eureka Antiques

A brass-mounted coromandel lady's vanity box, inlaid with brass stringing, engraved with scrolling foliage and 'Improved Patent Registered 3 April 1846', the trays and base drawer operated by a winding mechanism, fitted with nine silver-mounted bottles and an inkwell engraved with scrolling cartouches and a coat of arms, marked 'J. Vickery, London 1854', 19thC, 13in (33cm) wide.
£2,250–2,750 Sworders

A brass-banded walnut writing slope, with ebonized interior, c1870, 14in (35.5cm) wide.
£215–240 Mostly Boxes

rass-mounted walnut tea caddy, with two sections, c1870,
(20.5cm) wide.
50–175 Mostly Boxes

A lady's rosewood travelling box, the top and keyhole inlaid with mother-of-pearl, with original silver-mounted bottles, c1870, 12in (30.5cm) wide.
£375–425 Pantiles Spa Antiques

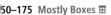

rass-banded rosewood jewel
d dressing box, the fitted
rior with silver-plated contents,
70, 12in (30.5cm) wide.
00–1,000
aham Smith Antiques

A walnut jewel box, c1880, 12in (30.5cm) wide.
£150–175 Mostly Boxes

A Victorian figured walnut writing slope, inlaid with mother-of-pearl and abalone in parquetry bands with pewter lines, the interior with replaced falls, inkwell and penrest, 11¾in (30cm) wide.
£240–280 Dreweatt Neate

rass-banded rosewood jewel box, c1880, 10in (25.5cm) wide.
15–240 Mostly Boxes

A walnut sewing box, inlaid with mother-of-pearl and herringbone stringing, with silk-lined fitted interior, c1890, 10in (25.5cm) wide.
£200–225 Pantiles Spa Antiques

igured walnut travelling writing
pe, with a black and white leather
erior and a brass handle, c1880,
n (30.5cm) wide.
70–300 Pantiles Spa Antiques

A rosewood and brass jewellery box, by Erard & Sohn, with a velvet lining, Austria, c1900, 6in (15cm) wide.
£350–385 Koh I Noor Antiques

An olive-wood Sorrento ware puzzle box, the cover with inlaid decoration, with a secret compartment, Italy, c1920, 9in (23cm) wide.
£200–225 Koh I Noor Antiques

CLOCKS

BRITISH BRACKET, MANTEL & TABLE CLOCKS

An ebonized bracket clock, by Isaac Papavoine, London, with brass dial, the silvered chapter ring with a date aperture, the eight-day pull quarter repeat fusee movement repeating the quarters on three bells and striking the hours on a further bell, the reinstated verge escapement with brass bob and shaped mask to the rear knife-edge suspension, backplate signed, c1690, 17in (43cm) high.

£20,000–22,000
Derek Roberts Antiques ⊞

An ebonized bracket clock, by John Clowes, London, the brass dial with silvered chapter ring, date and false pendulum apertures and strike/silent lever, the eight-day five-pillar fusee movement with verge escapement striking on a bell, pull quarter repeat work with barrel and gut line, the bell-top case with four finials, c1695, 14½in (37cm) high.

£20,000–22,000
Derek Roberts Antiques ⊞

An ebonized bracket clock, by Thomas Jackson, the brass dial with silvered chapter ring, false pendulum and date apertures and subsidiary dial for strike/silent, the twin fusee movement with verge escapement, striking the hours on a bell and quarter-hours with six hammers on six bells, the inverted bell-top case with later finials, c1730, 18¼in (46.5cm) high.

£5,250–6,250 Tennants

An ebonized bracket clock, by William Allam, London, the bra dial with date and false pendulu apertures and subsidiary dials strike/silent and rise/fall, the fi pillar striking fusee movement with verge escapement and tri repeat, in a brass-bound case, c1760, 15½in (39cm) high.

£22,000–25,000
Derek Roberts Antiques

William Allam is noted as havir produced a number of fine anc elegant bracket clocks and longcase clocks. They are alwa of the highest quality and with good proportions. This clock h the added advantage of being quite small.

An ebonized bracket clock, by Justin Vulliamy, London, with enamel dial and subsidiary dials for strike/silent and fast/slow, the five-pillar movement with verge escapement, in a bell-top case with brass block feet, c1765, 15¾in (40cm) high.

£45,000–50,000
Derek Roberts Antiques ⊞

A mahogany bracket clock, by William Wall, Richmond, the brass breakarch dial with silvered chapter ring, date aperture and strike/silent, the twin-train fusee movement with verge escapement striking the hours on a bell, c1770, 22in (56cm) high.

£11,500–12,500
Country Lane Classics ⊞

A George III mahogany bracket clock, by John Stone, Aylesbury, the silvered dial with subsidiary strike/silent and date dials, the eight-day twin-train fusee movement with verge escapement and trip repeat cord, the bell-top case with pineapple finials, side frets and bracket feet, 21in (53.5cm) high.

£3,750–4,500 Holloway's

A mahogany-veneered musica automaton clock, by William Rogers, London, the dial with subsidiary strike/silent and tun change dials, sweep calendar hand and automaton, six-pillar knife-edge triple-fusee moveme with verge escapement playing one of four tunes every hour or 12 bells and hammers, the case with brass finials and feet, c177 23½in (59.5cm) high.

£30,000–35,000
Clock-Work-Shop ⊞

MARKET INFORMATION BRACKET CLOCKS

- Prices for standard bracket clocks have on the whole remained level, although they have dipped for lower-quality examples.
- Exceptional bracket clocks, by comparison, have continued to demand good prices.
- Collectors are looking for unusual features as well as good-quality clocks and eminent makers, all of which will boost value.

ebonized bracket clock, by iam Hughes, London, the brass with silvered chapter ring, e and false pendulum rtures and strike/silent dial, tic-tac escapement striking a bell, the case with brass- nd door, brass pineapple als and fishscale side frets, 85, 15¾in (40cm) high.

1,250–12,500
rek Roberts Antiques

George III mahogany bracket ck, by Richard Andrews, don, the brass dial with date erture below strike/silent and ulator dials and signature, the n-train fusee movement with ge escapement, the case with l top, 18in (45.5cm) high.

,500–10,500
untry Lane Classics

Georges III mahogany and ass-mounted bracket clock, Thwaites & Read, London, No. 43, the brass dial with silvered apter ring and subsidiary st/slow and date dials within rced ormolu spandrels, the in-train fusee movement iking on a bell, with engraved ckplate and pendulum bob, on t-metal feet, 20in (51cm) high.

,250–5,000 Hy Duke

A mahogany bracket clock, by John Gilbertson, the silvered arched dial with sweep centre date and strike/silent dial, the triple-train six-pillar movement with verge escapement and striking the hours on a bell and the quarters on three further bells, the bell-top case with cast-brass finials and feet, c1785, 25in (63.5cm) high.

£4,750–5,250
Leigh Extence

John Gilbertson is recorded as working in Ripon, Yorkshire, from c1750 to his death in 1793. The quality and style of this clock would indicate that Gilbertson 'bought in' the movement, and quite probably the whole clock, from London, as it is almost identical to work by the top London makers of the period.

A mahogany and brass-strung bracket clock, by James McCabe, London, the silvered dial with strike/silent dial, the twin-chain fusee movement striking on a bell, with trip repeat, the case with fret-cut brass panels to the sides, on brass bracket feet, late 18thC, 19¼in (49cm) high.

£6,000–7,500 Bearnes

James McCabe was born into a watch and clockmaking family in Belfast. He came to London in the 1770s, settling at Royal Exchange in 1804. He gained his Freedom of the Clockmakers' Company in 1786 and became a Warden in 1811, the year he died. James McCabe was succeeded by his son, also James, and it is he who must be regarded as one of the most successful English clock and watchmakers of the 19th century, producing many fine examples.

MILLER'S COMPARES

(L) A mahogany automaton bracket clock, by James Smith, London, the brass dial with silvered chapter ring, date aperture and automaton of people catching a pheasant, the eight-day fusee movement with verge escapement and striking the hours on a bell, the bell-top case with brass pineapple finials, c1790, 18½in (47cm) high.

£18,000–20,000
Derek Roberts Antiques

(R) A mahogany bracket clock, by John Pratt, Epsom, the brass dial with silvered chapter ring and cut-out for the signature plaque, strike/silent in the arch, the eight-day striking fusee movement with verge escapement, the bell-top case with pineapple finials, c1790, 18in (45.5cm) high.

£12,000–14,000
Derek Roberts Antiques

It is most unusual for a bracket clock to have anything other than strike/silent or rise/fall regulation dials in the arch, and the addition of a painted automaton scene dramatically adds to value. The clock shown on the left has an unusual automaton in that, rather than an arm or a bow for a musical instrument moving with the pendulum, it has a ratcheting device that causes a pheasant to emerge slowly from behind a bush and then rush back just as a gentleman wearing a hat tries to catch him. Further points to consider are the figuring and patina of the case, which are particularly good on the example on the left, and where the clock was made. A piece made in the provinces, such as the item on the right, will almost invariably sell for a lower price than one made in London. The best clockmakers tended to gravitate to the capital where they could command a higher price for their products from a more affluent clientele. James Smith of London was clockmaker to George III.

A satinwood-veneered bracket clock, by Thomas Best, London, with enamel dial and brass hands, the double fusee striking movement with verge escapement, c1790, 17in (43cm) high.

£5,000–5,500 D S Pullen

A mahogany bracket clock, by Edward Green, with painted dial, the five-pillar eight-day movement with verge escapement and striking the hours on a bell with trip repeat, the pad-top case with brass fretwork and brass bracket feet, the rear of the dial signed 'Hewitt', c1810, 14½in (37cm) high.

£5,500–6,250 Leigh Extence

An ebonized bracket clock, by John Milward, London, the eight-day five-pillar movement with anchor escapement and striking and repeating the hours on a bell, the engraved pendulum with calibrated regulation, the case with brass mouldings, brass frets and brass ogee feet, c1810, 16in (40.5cm) high.

£6,000–6,750 P A Oxley

A mahogany bracket clock, by Richard Parsons, London, with painted dial, the five pillar, twin-fusee movement with anchor escapement and striking the hours on a bel the case with fishscale fretwork and engrav brass inlay, on brass bracket feet, c1810, 12½in (32cm) high.

£4,500–5,000 Leigh Extence

A Regency ebonized mantel timepiece, by M. Scott, Aylesbury, with enamel dial, the eight-day single fusee movement with arched plates and pendulum with a travelling clamp, the case with brass inlay, 10in (25.5cm) high.

£5,000–5,500
Derek Roberts Antiques

A mahogany musical clock, by William Redford, Leeds, with painted dial, the eight-day cylinder movement playing six airs on bells, c1815, 25in (63.5cm) high.

£12,000–14,000
Vanbrugh House Antiques

A mahogany bracket clock, by Smith & Sor Reading, with painted dial, the eight-day fu movement striking the hours on a bell mount on the backplate, anchor escapement, pendul and brass bob, the case with ogee top surmounted by a pineapple finial, inlaid wit brass, with ebony mouldings and fishscale fretwork with red silk, c1815, 20½in (52cm) h

£4,500–5,000
Derek Roberts Antiques

A Regency marble and bronze-mounted mantel timepiece, with an ormolu engine-turned dial, the eight-day single fusee movement signed 'Vulliamy, London', decorated with an eagle and two lions above a pierced bronze frieze, 18in (45.5cm) wide.

£17,500–20,000 Gardiner Houlgate

A rosewood bracket timepiece by William Strange, Kingston, with painted dial, the eight-day fusee movement with shaped plates, the chamfer-top case w a brass finial, brass fishscale sic frets, inlay and ball feet, c1820 19in (48.5cm) high.

£3,000–3,250
Leigh Extence

William Strange is recorded as working in Kingston, Surrey from befo 1828 until 1851 and was probably the son of Thomas Strange, who r recorded in Kingston from 1791 until 1824. William's son, Thomas, was working in Littlehampton, West Sussex, before moving to Kingst c1855, presumably to take over his father's business, as by 1862 the concern was known as Strange & Son.

egency-style mahogany bracket clock, Matthew Hick, York, with painted dial, eight-day fusee movement with anchor apement and striking the hours on a bell, chamfer-top case surmounted by a brass eapple finial and with brass stringing and scale frets, on brass feet, c1820, n (43cm) high.

,750–6,500
rek Roberts Antiques

tthew Hick was Free of the ırshipful Company of ckmakers in 1812, amberlain in 1832 and died on October, 1834. He is recorded working at Minstergate, York, tween 1823 and 1834.

A mahogany bracket clock, by Hendrick, Liverpool, the dial with subsidiary strike/silent dial, the twin-fusee movement with anchor escapement, trip repeat and striking on a bell, the case with pierced frets, on brass ball feet, dial hands later, c1820, 19in (48.5cm) high.

£1,250–1,500 Tennants

A gilt mantel clock, by Thomas Moss, London, gilt dial with engine-turned centre, the eight-day fusee movement signed on the backplate, the case on a marble plinth with a gilded floral swag, on engine-turned feet, c1820, 7¼in (18.5cm) high.

£3,750–4,250
Derek Roberts Antiques

Thomas Moss was a well-known maker who is noted as working between 1786 and 1827.

ebonized musical bracket nepiece, by George Wilkins, ndon, with enamel dial, the gle chain fusee movement th deadbeat escapement, the cape wheel mounted on the ckplate, the musical movement off by a weighted linkage aying three Scottish tunes with ght hammers, the case with a ass pineapple finial, brass inlay d fishscale frets, on brass ball et, c1820, 13½in (34.5cm) high.

1,500–13,000
erek Roberts Antiques

eorge Wilkins is noted as ɔrking in Frith Street, London tween 1810 and 1825. ne of his business rds/advertising leaflets is held the British Museum.

A late Regency mahogany bracket clock, by William Hislop, London, with an enamel dial and twin-train movement chiming the quarter-hours on eight bells, the Egyptian-style case in the manner of Thomas Hope, 20½in (52cm) high.

£7,000–7,800
Country Lane Classics

A rosewood bracket clock, by Joseph Moore, London, with painted dial and twin fusee trip repeat movement, the case with a gilt-bronze pineapple finial, brass-inlaid flower spandrels, fishscale frets and ball feet, early 19thC, 20½in (52cm) high.

£2,000–2,500 Sworders

A Regency mahogany bracket clock, by William Smith, Wingham, with painted dial, the eight-day five-pillar double fusee movement striking the hours on a bell, the case surmounted by a cast-brass pineapple finial, with brass inlay and ebonized mouldings, fishscale side frets, on brass ball feet, 21in (53.5cm) high.

£5,250–5,800
Leigh Extence

William Smith is recorded as working at Wingham, Kent from at least 1828 until 1838 when he moved to St Peters in Broadstairs, Kent working until at least 1874. The dial is signed Wingham but the ghost of the name St Peters is just visible, having been painted over it at a later stage. It is quite probable that Smith either had the clock in stock when he moved to Broadstairs and had the dial painter re-name it, or it came in for a repair and the place name was changed. It was always good publicity for the clockmaker if his correct address was known.

A mahogany bracket clock, by Joseph Moxon, London, with painted dial and twin-train striking fusee movement, the breakarch case with brass inlay, fishscale frets and feet, c1820, 16in (40.5cm) high.

£2,400–2,750 D S Pullen

A mahogany bracket clock, by John Smith, London, with painted dial and striking twin-train fusee movement, the pad-top case with fishscale frets and bracket feet, c1825, 13in (33cm) high.

£7,250–8,000 Styles of Stow

A William IV mahogany bracket clock, the painted dial signed 'Sibley, Portsmouth', the double fusee movement with trip repeat, the case with applied foliate and C-scroll carving, 19¼in (49cm) high.

£820–980 Gardiner Houlgate

An early Victorian bronze library mantel timepiece, by Alexander Purvis, London, with painted dial, the eight-day movement with chain fusee and anchor escapement, 7½in (19cm) high.

£2,250–2,500 Leigh Extence

A mahogany bracket clock, by Frodsham, London, with painted dial and twin-fusee repeat movement, backplate stamped, the scrolled case with carved decoration, losse mid-19thC, 18½in (47cm) high.

£450–525 Sworders

A burr-walnut mantel timepiece, by F. Villinger, with a silvered dial and single fusee movement with anchor escapement, c1850, 11½in (29cm) high.

£2,000–2,500 Tennants

A Victorian ebonized and gilt-metal-mounted bracket clock, the silvered dial with three subsidiary dials for slow/fast, chime/silent and Westminster, signed 'S. Smith & Son', the movement with Westminster chimes on eight bells, the case with brass panels and pineapple finials, 25in (63.5cm) high.

£1,250–1,500 Mealy's

A rosewood mantel clock, by Robert Molyneux, London, with engraved gilded di lever platform and Savage's two-pin platfor escapement, the case with spiral-twist columns, mid-19thC, 17in (43cm) high.

£2,250–2,750 Sworders

Savage's two-pin escapement is a form of lev escapement that was invented by George Sav

A rosewood timepiece, by Thomas Collingridge, London, with engraved silvered dial, the eight-day fusee movement with anchor escapement, the case with gadrooned top and wooden bun feet, c1845, 12½in (32cm) high.

£4,300–4,800 Clock-Work Shop

A Victorian Gothic-style burr-walnut musical bracket clock, by Alexander Guillaume, the silvered dial with strike/silent and regulator subsidiary dials, the eight-day fusee movement striking on eight bells and a gong, the case with pierced fretwork sides and bronze finials, on bun feet, 29¼in (74cm) high.

£3,500–4,250 Sworders

A mahogany five-glass timepiece, the silvered dial with gilt sightpiece and eight-d fusee movement with anchor escapement, c brass bun feet, c1890, 9in (23cm) high.

£3,700–4,200 Clock-Work Shop

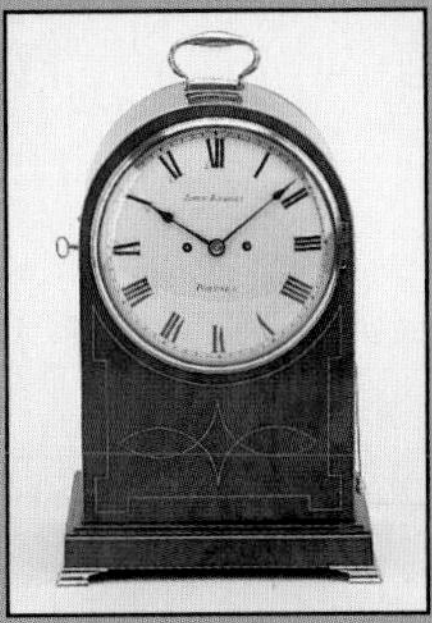

CONTINENTAL BRACKET, MANTEL & TABLE CLOCKS

A tortoiseshell and ormolu bracket clock, by Gilles Martinot, Paris, the ormolu dial with enamel numerals, the movement with outside countwheel striking on a bell, signed, France, early 18thC, 30½in (77.5cm) high.

£1,800–2,200 Lawrence Fine Art

A gilt-brass mounted and ebonized table clock, the gilt cast-brass dial with engraved and silvered chapter ring, alarm pointer and apertures for date and false pendulum, the trip-repeating triple-train movement striking on two bells, the case with a gilt foliate surmount, alarm removed, south Germany, c1730, 17¾in (45cm) high.

£1,500–1,750 Sotheby's (Am)

An ebonized mantel clock, by Laurentius Mi Freiburg, with silvered dial and chapter ring, aperture and subsidiary dial for strike/silen the triple-train verge movement converted eight-day fusee and chain, striking the qua hours on three bells, the case surmounted b carved figure of Chronos with pierced silver mounts, on claw-and-ball feet, signed, dat 1739, south Germany, 27¼in (69cm) high.

£2,800–3,200 Sotheby's (Am)

An ormolu mantel clock, with enamel dial, the movement with pull repeat and signed by Pierre Le Roy, Paris, the case surmounted by a classical figure slaying a dragon, France, c1740, 16½in (42cm) high.

£5,200–6,200 Sotheby's (NY)

An ormolu mantel clock, with enamel dial and countwheel bell-striking anchor movement, the case surmounted by an urn, the base with scrolls, trellis and a glass medallion, on a later ebonized plinth, dial replaced, France, c1775, 21¼in (54cm) high.

£1,200–1,400 Sotheby's (Am)

A Louis XV gilt-bronze elephant clock, by Hoguet, Paris, with a twin-train striking movement, the dial surmounted by a monk the elephant on a rocaille base, France, 16¼in (41.5cm) high.

£50,000–60,000 Sotheby's (P)

This clock is particularly desirable because t casting is of very good quality and elephant clocks are very popular.

A jacaranda-veneered rococo bracket clock, by Jacob Kock, with painted dial and twin-train striking movement, the case with gilt-bronze mounts, matching bracket, slight damage, Sweden, late 18thC, clock 34¾in (88.5cm) high.

£3,200–3,750 Bukowskis

A parcel-gilt mantel clock, the enamel dial with outer date marking, the anchor movement striking on a bell, the case surmounted by a figure of Ganimedes, the base supported by two putti on a moulded plinth, pendulum missing, Austria, 1775–1800, 25½in (65cm) high.

£1,000–1,200 Sotheby's (Am)

An ormolu-mounted marble portico mante clock, with enamel dial and trip repeating rack-striking verge movement, the case surmounted by an urn and supported by two fluted columns, Switzerland, c1780, 17¼in (44cm) high.

£1,000–1,200 Sotheby's (Am)

·ltwood mantel clock, by Johan Nyberg, painted wood dial surmounted by a swan resting on two sphinxes, with twin-train ‹ing movement, signed, Sweden, 18thC, 17¼in (44cm) high.

200–1,450 Bukowskis

ın Nyberg was received Master in ckholm in 1787.

A fruitwood inverted bell-top miniature bracket clock, the brass dial with enamelled chapter ring and alarm disc, the one-day movement striking on a bell, with repeat, alarm and strike/silent lever, Austria, c1790, 7in (18cm) high.

£3,800–4,200
Leigh Extence

A marble mantel clock, the enamel dial with month indicator, the eight-day movement striking the hours and half-hours on a bell, the case with original gilded castings, France, c1795, 21in (53.5cm) high.

£1,750–2,000
Kembery Antique Clocks

re-gilded and black patinated mantel ck, by Carl Adolph Talén, Stockholm, with ımel dial, the twin-train striking movement h a pendulum in the form of a dragonfly, case supported by a harlequin, the base unted with lion masks and palmettes, eden, early 19thC, 13in (33cm) high.

,250–6,250 Bukowskis

l Adolph Talén was working in Stockholm ween 1809 and 1815.

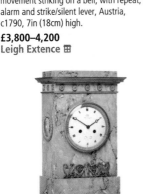

A Siena marble mantel clock, with enamel dial signed 'Ledure, Bronzier, Paris' and ''Hémen H.r.', the anchor movement striking on a bell, the case with ormolu mounts, France, c1820, 21½in (55cm) high.

£1,400–1,650 Sotheby's (Am)

An ormolu clock, the eight-day movement striking on a bell, France, c1820, 12in (30.5cm) wide.

£4,500–5,000
Country Lane Classics

ormolu figural mantel clock, by commun, Strasbourg, with twin-train vement striking on a bell, c1825, ınce, 19in (48.5cm) high.

,750–7,500
lings

An ebonized mantel clock, the ormolu dial with engine-turned and floral decoration, the anchor movement striking on a bell, on an ebonized base with pierced ormolu mounts, France, c1830, 21¼in (54cm) high.

£1,000–1,250 Sotheby's (Am)

An ormolu portico timepiece, by Raingo Frères, with a silvered engine-turned dial, the case with Corinthian columns and surmounted by a bull, France, c1845, 12½in (32cm) high.

£850–1,000
D S Pullen

An ebonized and painted cuckoo clock, with enamel dial, the domed top housing the cuckoo mechanism, Germany, 19thC, 17½in (44.5cm) high.

£1,000–1,200 Holloway's

An ormolu and polished steel mantel timepiece, the brass dial surrounded by simulated rocks with a figure of Jason holding the Golden Fleece, the plinth applied with a shield and weapons flanked by swords and wreaths, France, 19thC, 11½in (29cm) high.

£325–400 Toovey's

A gilt-cased mantel clock, the eight-day movement striking the hours and half-hou a gong, the dial and case with *champlevé* decoration, France, 19thC, 11¼in (28.5cm) h

£230–270 Dee, Atkinson & Harriso

A bronze and marble clock, the gilt dial with a gilt-bronze bezel, with twin-train striking movement, the case surmounted by a putto, numerals rubbed, France, 19thC, 20in (51cm) high.

£270–320 Jackson's

An ebony-veneered *haagse klok*, by P. Visbach Haghe, the velvet-covered dial with engraved silver chapter ring, the movement striking on a bell, the case with a moulded pediment, twisted half pilasters and a glazed door, signed, Holland, 19thC, 13in (33cm) high.

£2,800–3,200 Sotheby's (Am)

A boulle mantel clock, by Japy Frères, with ormolu dial, the eight-day movement striki the hours and half-hours on a gong, the tortoiseshell case inlaid with engraved bras and with cast-ormolu decoration, stamped m with stand, France, c1850, 16in (40.5cm) hig

£2,200–2,400 Leigh Extence

Japy Frères were well-known French maker both full clocks and movements supplied to c makers for finishing (roulant blancs). The busi was founded by Frédéric Japy of Beaucourt born 1749, who first made movements for clock industry at his factory in 1777, becon the largest and most commercially importa clockmaking concern in France. The busine was continued after his death by his sons.

A gilt-metal mantel clock, with a porcelain dial, the twin-drum movement striking on a bell, the case surmounted by an urn, with a porcelain panel, acanthus handles, ram's-head and scroll decoration, France, 19thC, 16in (40.5cm) high.

£540–640 Bearnes

A gilt-bronze figural mantel clock, the dial with enamel numerals, with twin-train striking movement, the case surmounted by a figure of Father Time, the sides pierced with lyres and masks, on leaf-and-ball feet, France, c1860, 27½in (70cm) high.

£2,800–3,200 Northeast Auctions

A Louis XVI-style ormolu clock, with enamel dial and twin-train striking movement, the case with shaped frets and original gilding, France, dated 1865, 13in (33cm) high.

£1,000–1,100 D S Pullen

A gilt-bronze mantel clock, by Marti, the enamel dial signed ' Ambercrombie & Co, Fournisse du Roi, Le Haye', the movemer with anchor escapement and r striking on a bell, France, c187 26½in (67cm) high.

£2,800–3,200 Sworders

ulle mantel clock, the cast
with enamel numerals, the
-day movement striking the
s and half-hours on a bell
signed 'Dufaud, Paris', the
with rococo mounts and
ulum aperture, the sides
with fretwork, France,
0, 18in (45.5cm) high.

00–1,750
bery Antique Clocks ⊞

A brass four-glass clock, with a two-piece enamel dial, the twin-train movement striking the hours and half-hours on a coiled gong, with a mercury pendulum, the case with fretwork decoration, France, c1880, 12in (30.5cm) high.

£1,200–1,400
Styles of Stow ⊞

A brass and *champlevé* enamel mantel clock, by E. Maurice, the silvered chapter ring with a brass repoussé centre, the eight-day movement with platform lever escapement striking the hours and half-hours on a gong, stamped mark, France, late 19thC, 10in (25.5cm) high.

£4,200–4,650
Leigh Extence ⊞

E. Maurice was one of the best of the late 19th-century French makers, known particularly for his decorative cases.

A patinated pedestal clock, by S. Marti & Co, the two-piece dial with an enamel cartouche, with a countwheel bell-striking movement, supported by a patinated classical figure on a moulded plinth, France, 1875–1900, 80¼in (204cm) high.

£4,300–5,100
Sotheby's (Am)

pper, gilt and patinated-bronze clock,
ial with enamel numerals, the case
ounted by a pair of entwined dragons,
decorated with birds, grasses and
sprays, the reverse with scalework,
inoiserie legs, slight damage,
inental, c1880, 16½in (42cm) high.

00–3,350 Northeast Auctions

A gilt-bronze and marble mantel clock, by Lemerle Charpentier, Paris, the enamel dial inscribed 'Paul Graselins/Auriel Charlot. 8', with twin-train striking movement, the case surmounted by berry finials, on a marble base inset with laurel leaves, on toupie feet, France, c1880, 18in (45.5cm) high.

£1,600–2,000 Northeast Auctions

An ormolu mantel clock, the dial marked with the signs of the zodiac, the eight-day movement striking on a bell, the case in the form of an eagle with outstretched wings, France, c1880, 14in (35.5cm) high.

£2,800–3,200
Country Lane Classics ⊞

labaster and ormolu four-
s clock, the dial with an
nel chapter ring and gilded
ne-turned centre, the eight-
movement striking the hours
half-hours on a coiled gong,
ce, c1880, 14in (35.5cm) high.

350–2,600
es of Stow ⊞

An ormolu mantel clock, with a marble dial, the eight-day movement striking on a bell, the case surmounted by a bronze bust of a maiden, the pedestal inset with hardstone panels, France, late 19thC, 18¼in (46.5cm) high.

£2,100–2,500 Toovey's

A gilt-bronze mantel clock, the dial with serpent hands, with a striking drum movement, the case modelled with cherubs, birds and a swan, on a lappet-cast stand with pieced panels, France, late 19thC, 16½in (42cm) high.

£1,200–1,500
Sworders

A gilt-bronze mantel clock, with enamel dial and striking drum movement, the case surmounted by a cherub and with porcelain panels, on a giltwood stand, France, late 19thC, 14½in (37cm) high.

£550–650 Sworders

A parquetry mantel clock, with enamel dial and eight-day striking movement by Japy Frères, France, c1900, 9in (23cm) high.

£1,200–1,300
Styles of Stow

A mahogany bracket clock, by Winterha & Hofmeier, with silvered dial and three-r quarter-striking movement, the case with inlay, the sides with pierced brass sound restored, slight damage, Germany, c1900 16in (40.5cm) high.

£335–400 R O Schmitt Fine Art

A marble mantel timepiece, by M. & Sohn, the gilt dial with enamel plaques, the case with bronze mounts, stamped with maker's name, Austria, c1900, 9¾in (25cm) high.

£380–450 Jackson's

A Louis XVI-style rosewood mantel clock, with enamel dial and twin-train striking movement, the marquetry case with ormolu mounts, France, c1900, 12in (30.5cm) high.

£1,150–1,250 D S Pullen

A marble and bronze mantel clock, the c with a gilded chapter ring, the eight-day movement striking the hours and half-hou on a gong, the case surmounted by a lion inset with classical scenes, stamped with trademark of Samuel Marti, the record of award of the Médaille d'Or at the Paris Exhibition of 1900, and the mark of Marc Corpet, Paris, France, c1910, 14½in (37cm)

£1,300–1,450 Leigh Extence

A mahogany bracket clock, with painted dial and eight-day French movement striking on a gong, the case with brass mounts and presentation plaque dated 1905, 19in (48.5cm) high.

£1,000–1,100
D S Pullen

A mahogany mantel clock, by H.A.C., with two-piece enamel dial and 14-day movement, the rear door with original paper label, slight damage, Germany, c1910, 10in (25.5cm) high.

£210–230 Collector's World

H.A.C. was formed in Germany in 1873 by Paul Landenberger and Phillip Lang. The company changed its name to Hamburg Amerikanische Uhrenfabrik and Hamburg American Clock Company (H.A.C.) in 1883. The crossed arrows that can be seen in the label reproduced above became their trademark in 1892, at which time the company started producing a variety of clocks, mainly for export to Great Britain and North America. In 1930 they merged with Junghans.

A Black Forest cuckoo shelf clock, the tw train spring-driven movement with cast-b lyre-shaped plates, the case carved with foliage, numerals missing from dial, hand replaced, top pediment missing from case Germany, c1915, 16in (40.5cm) high.

£280–350 R O Schmitt Fine Art

BRIAN LOOMES

Specialist dealer in antique British clocks.

ESTABLISHED 41 YEARS.

Internationally recognised authority and author of numerous text books on antique clocks.

Where else can you see 20 lantern clocks and a few good longcases?

Resident on premises. Prior phone call ESSENTIAL for directions & appointment.

Copies of all my current books always in stock.

CALF HAUGH FARM
PATELEY BRIDGE
NORTH YORKS
Tel: 01423 711163

(on B6265 Pateley-Grassington Road)

All stock on website

www.brianloomes.com

The Old Clock Shop

63 HIGH STREET
WEST MALLING
KENT
Tel: 01732 843246

Pretty Kent longcase clock, 10in square painted dial, birdcage movement, solid mahogany case, the maker Roberts, Ashford. Circa 1800.

Visit our five showrooms and see a fine selection of modestly priced clocks and barometers

Restoration service provided

Open 9am–5pm Mon–Sat

Proprietor: Ms S. L. LUCK
Website: www.theoldclockshop.co.uk

The Clock House

Antiquarian Horology

75 Pound Street, Carshalton, Surrey SM5 3PG

SPECIALISTS IN LONGCASE CLOCK RESTORATION

◆

DIALS RESTORED

◆

CASE RESTORATION UNDERTAKEN

◆

CASES BOUGHT, ANY CONDITION

◆

PART CLOCKS AND MOVEMENTS CONSIDERED

CLOCKS SOLD FULLY RESTORED

◆

CLOCKS SOLD NEEDING RESTORATION

◆

RESTORATION MATERIALS STOCKED (Bushes, Gut, Pendulums, Suspension, Springs, etc.

◆

TRADE AND ENTHUSIASTS WELCOME

OPENING HOURS: TUESDAY to FRIDAY .30am–4.30pm, SATURDAY 9.00am–6.00pm, or at other times by appointment

TELEPHONE: MARK COCKLIN
+44 (0)20 8773 4844 • Mobile 07850 363 317
Email: markcocklin@theclockhouse.co.uk
Website: www.theclockhouse.co.uk

ANTIQUE
clocks

Jonathan Beech

B.A.D.A. Dip

Specialising in 18th & 19th century clocks since 1982.
There is always a good range of clocks for sale in our workshop.
We only stock clocks which we consider original.
We also offer a complete restoration service.

www.jonathanbeechclocks.com

Workshop 3, Brewery Arts, Brewery Court,
Cirencester, Glos GL7 1JH

Tel: 07849609533

CARRIAGE CLOCKS

A gilt-bronze *pendule d'officier*, by Bonet, Aix, with signed enamel dial, the anchor movement with silk suspended pendulum, *petite sonnerie* striking on two bells, pull wind alarm on a bell, the case surmounted by two handles and four finials on claw feet, altered, France, 1800–25, 8¾in (22cm) high.

£2,000–2,500 Sotheby's (Am)

A brass *pendule d'officier*, with enamel dial, the countwheel movement with cylinder escapement, plain balance and striking on a bell, the case with four finials, a carrying handle and four turned feet, Switzerland, 1800–25, 5¼in (13.5cm) high.

£2,000–2,500 Sotheby's (Am)

A rosewood carriage clock, by James Gorh London, the silvered engraved dial with silve bezel, centre-sweep minute, hour and alarr hands, with twin-train chain fusee moveme and standing barrel for the alarm, lever platform escapement, c1835, 9in (23cm) h

£16,000–20,000
Derek Roberts Antiques

A gilt-brass *grande sonnerie* carriage clock, by A. Rechel, Vienna, the enamel dial with subsidiary seconds, date and alarm dials, the movement with platform cylinder escapement trip repeating and striking on a gong, with alarm on a bell, Austria, c1840, 6½in (16.5cm) high.

£2,300–2,750 Sotheby's (Am)

A carriage clock, by James McCabe, London, the engraved brass dial with subsidiary seconds dial and double fusee repeating movement, with a brass-bound mahogany travelling case, 19thC, 9¾in (25cm) high.

£17,000–20,000
Gildings

A gilt-brass miniature carriage timepiece, Drocourt, with enamel dial, the eight-day movement with platform lever escapement backplate stamped, with original numbere travelling box, France, 1850–1900, 3in (7.5cm) high.

£2,000–2,200 Leigh Extence

ESSENTIAL REFERENCE PAUL GARNIER

Paul Garnier (1801–69) is recognized as the founding father of the mass produced carriage clock industry in France. His clocks started with the early Series I, of which this is an example, with front wind and engine-turned dials, and progressed through to rear wind, usually with porcelain dials. Almost all of his clocks incorporated the chaffcutter escapement that he invented and patented in 1830.

This early small Series I clock (c1840) has its own carrying case.

£8,000–£10,000
Derek Roberts Antiques

All Garnier's early clocks and the majority of his later ones have his chaffcutter escapement. This could be easily mass produced and therefore lead to cost-effective methods of production.

Series I clocks had simple one-piece cases with thin carrying handles and no cutouts on the base. Series II clocks had cutouts on the base.

Garnier's carrying cases were almost always of this form with a brass carrying handle to the top, clasps to the side a a domed top to the case

All early Garnier clock had front wind and engine-turned and silvered dials.

t carriage clock, the enamel dial signed 'Lurasco
s, Amsterdam', with chaffcutter escapement and
twheel striking the hours and half-hours on a bell,
:e, c1850, 3½in (9cm) high.
00–2,200 Derek Roberts Antiques

ass drum-case timepiece carriage clock, with enamel
and eight-day chain fusee movement, France, c1880,
12.5cm) high.
0–1,000 D S Pullen
nusual to find a French clock with a fusee movement.

rriage clock, the enamel dial with
idiary date and alarm dials, the
ement with club-tooth lever escapement
silvered platform and striking the
ter-hours on bells, the case with
aved decoration, c1880, 6in (15cm) high.
000–4,500
ek Roberts Antiques

A brass *petite sonnerie* carriage clock, the eight-day twin-train movement with repeat and striking the hours and quarter-hours on two gongs, France, c1875, 6in (15cm) high.

£1,750–2,000
Styles of Stow

A gilt carriage clock, with enamel dial, the eight-day movement with lever platform escapement with five-minute repeat, rack-striking on a gong, minute hand replaced, France, c1880, 7½in (19cm) high.

£2,250–2,750
Penrith Farmers' & Kidd's

A gilt carriage clock, the silvered dial within a border of gilt scrolls and dragons, the movement with enamel alarm subsidiary mounted on the backplate, platform ratchet tooth lever escapement and rack-striking and alarm on a gong with repeat, France, c1880, 7½in (19cm) high, with a travelling case.

£1,700–2,000 Sotheby's (Am)

A gilt-brass carriage clock, by Aubert & Klaftenberger, Geneva, the enamel dial with engraved mask, the eight-day movement striking and repeating on a bell, with alarm, signed, Switzerland, c1880, 5in (12.5cm) high.

£3,750–4,250
Country Lane Classics

C. J. Klaftenberger (1795–1874), a skilled watchmaker and Vice-President of the British Horological Institute, operated in both London and Paris. During part of his career he was in partnership with Aubert and his name, either alone or in conjunction with Aubert, appears quite frequently on carriage clocks, nearly always of fine quality and usually supplied to him by one of the leading French makers. However, English carriage clocks bearing his name do occasionally appear .

A gilt-brass carriage clock, by Margaine, retailed by Payne & Co, Paris, with enamel dial, the eight-day movement with platform lever escapement and striking on a gong with push button repeat, backplate with maker's trademark and retailer's mark, France, 1850–1900, 5¾in (14.5cm) high.

£1,700–1,850
Leigh Extence

Margaine was one of the best carriage clock makers of the mid- to late 19th century, his pieces being of the highest quality. William Payne was a well known English maker and retailer and is recorded working at 163 New Bond Street, London from 1825 until the beginning of the 1900s when the company took over No. 165, now the premises of Asprey & Garrard.

A gilt *grande sonnerie* carriage **clock,** made in Paris for Maple & Co, with silvered dial, two striking settings, repeat button, France, c1885, 6in (15cm) high.

£2,700–3,000
Styles of Stow ⊞

A gilt carriage clock, by Joseph Soldano, the eight-day movement with lever escapement, the case with four porcelain panels decorated with birds, signed, France, c1880, 6¾in (17cm) high.

£6,000–7,000
Leigh Extence ⊞

A *grande sonnerie* striking carriage clock, by Achille Brocot, the enamel dial with alarm dial, movement stamped, France, Paris, c1890, 7in (18cm) high.

£4,500–5,000
Derek Roberts Antiques ⊞

A brass carriage timepiece, retailed by Dent, London, wi eight-day movement, France c1890, 5in (12.5cm) high.

£850–950
Jillings ⊞

A gilt carriage clock, the eight-day movement striking and repeating on a gong, France, c1890, 6in (15cm) high.

£2,250–2,500 **Jillings ⊞**

A *grande sonnerie champlevé* enamel carriage clock, the enamel dial with subsidiary alarm dial, the movement with lever platform escapement and striking the hours and quarter-hours on two bells, with selection lever for silent, quarters only and hours and quarters, numbered '1581', c1890, 7¾in (19.5cm) high, with original travelling case and key.

£5,500–6,250
Derek Roberts Antiques ⊞

A gilt carriage clock, retailed by Edward Sons, Paris, the enamel dial with subsidia alarm dial with a gilded and engraved ma the eight-day movement striking on a gor the movement numbered '123' and with trade mark 'A&B', the case in the shape c temple, France, c1890, 6½in (16.5cm) hig with original tooled leather travelling case

£2,500–2,750
Derek Roberts Antiques ⊞

A gilt carriage clock, retailed by W. Bruford & Son, Paris, the dial with a gilded mask, the eight-day movement striking the hours and half-hours on a gong with push button repeat, the backplate stamped with the serial number '1241', France, c1890, 6¼in (16cm) high.

£1,300–1,500 **Leigh Extence ⊞**

A brass miniature carriage clock, by H. Acier, the porcelain dial painted with a shepherd and shepherdess, the eight-day movement with lever escapement, France, late 19thC, 3¾in (9.5cm) high, with leather travelling case and key.

£1,300–1,500 **Woolley & Wallis**

A silver carriage timepiece, with enamel the eight-day movement with lever platfo escapement with cut bimetallic balance wheel, the spring barrel with stopwork, c marked London 1896, 7¾in (19.5cm) hig

£1,200–1,400
Jillings ⊞

ass carriage timepiece, with enamel dial an eight-day movement, the case with 'ex and concave mouldings and bun feet, ce, c1900, 4¼in (11cm) high.

0–400
nbery Antique Clocks ⊞

A brass carriage clock, with enamel dial and eight-day timepiece movement, the case with concave and convex mouldings, France, c1900, 4½in (11.5cm) high.

£280–320
Kembery Antique Clocks ⊞

A silver-gilt and enamel carriage clock, retailed by Hamilton & Co, Calcutta, with engine-turned silver dial, the eight-day movement with lever escapement and wheelwork with five crossings, on a lapis lazuli base, Switzerland, c1900, 3in (7.5cm) high.

£3,850–4,250
Leigh Extence ⊞

Hamilton & Co were well known retailers in Calcutta around the turn of the 19th century.

SSENTIAL REFERENCE REPLACEMENT ESCAPEMENTS

A carriage clock that has had its platform escapement (the part that ticks) changed will be worth considerably less an one that is all original. This 'repair' was often carried out when the original escapement became worn or oken as it was cheaper to replace it than restore it properly.

The two illustrations above show an original platform lever escapement and a modern replacement.

The original platform escapement (shown left) which is viewed from the top of the clock, is often silvered or gilded d occasionally plain brass. The cocks and bridges which taper have sharp corners. Typically they are hand graved 'SF' (Slow and Fast) and 'RA' (Retard and Avance) and sometimes with the maker's name. All the eelwork is polished and some of the smaller screws are blued – it is quite common to find them looking very dirty d tarnished, almost black, indicating that the clock is long overdue for a service.

You will notice that the replacement platform escapement (shown right) has frosted gilding, which is quite orange colour. The corners of the cocks and bridges are rounded and all the steelwork is very flat and matt in opearance. The 'SF' and 'RA' on the back cock is machine engraved.

It is worth checking that either type of escapement is actually working, as these delicate mechanisms are easily amaged and, as already mentioned, costly to repair.

CARTEL CLOCKS

A giltwood cartel timepiece, with engraved brass dial, the single-train movement with pendulum aperture, signed 'Paul Rimbault, London', 1750–75, 18in (45.5cm) high.

£2,250–2,750 Skinner

An ormolu cartel timepiece, with enamel dial, the movement with pull repeat, signed 'Moisy à Paris IV-536' and stamped 'St Germain', the case cast with rocaille and flowerheads above a musical trophy, France, c1755, 13in (33cm) high.

£5,500–6,500 Sotheby's (NY)

An ormolu cartel timepiece, with enamel c the movement with verge escapement and suspended pendulum, pull quarter repeatin on two bells, the case by Jean-Joseph de S Germain, France, c1755, 13in (33cm) high

£11,000–13,000 Sotheby's (Am)

Jean-Joseph de Saint-Germain (1719–91) became Master in 1748 and was one of th most celebrated bronzesmiths of his era. Many of his works are in museums worldw

An ormolu cartel clock, by Charles Le Roy, Paris, with enamel dial, the movement with anchor escapement and striking the hours on a bell, the case surmounted by an urn with ribbons, swags and a mask, stamped 'Osmond', France, c1770, 34in (86.5cm) high.

£12,000–14,000 Derek Roberts Antiques

A gilt-bronze cartel clock, by Pierre Gilles, Paris, with enamel dial, the twin-train striking movement with visible pendulum, the case surmounted by an urn and flanked by lions' heads, France, late 18thC, 26½in (67.5cm) high.

£4,000–5,000 Sotheby's (P)

A parcel-gilt and painted cartel clock, the engraved silvered dial with strike/silent lev the movement with anchor escapement, tr repeating *grande sonnerie* striking on two b the case surmounted by an eagle, pendulum missing, Austria, c1900, 32¾in (83cm) high

£1,000–1,200 Sotheby's (Am)

ELECTRIC CLOCKS

An electric mantel timepiece, by Eureka Clock Co, the enamel dial signed '1000 Day Electric Clock', on a mahogany base with battery compartment, with glass dome, slight damage, backplate dated c1906, 10¼in (26cm) high.

£400–500 Sworders

A brass and marble electric timepiece, the silvered dial with sweep seconds, France, c1910, 9¾in (25cm) high.

£1,500–1,800 Sotheby's (Am)

A brass electric Bulle patent mantel clock, with silvered chapter ring, on an ebonized plinth, with a cut-glass dome, France, 1920s, 14¼in (37.5cm) high.

£600–700 Toovey's

A brass four-glass electric timepiece, by Brillié, the enam dial with sweep seconds, the movement with brass plates a ball pendulum, on adjustable France, c1920, 21¾in (55.5cm)

£3,250–4,000 Sotheby's (Am)

ARNITURES

uis XVI-style marble and gilt-nze garniture, with porcelain the movement striking the rs and the half hours, France, hC, clock 27½in (70cm) high.

250–5,250
leria L C Morton

An ormolu garniture, the clock by Robbin, Paris, with a porcelain dial and twin-train striking movement, inset with Sèvres-style porcelain plaques, France, clock 14½in (37cm) high.

£1,100–1,300
Rosebery's

A slate and bronze garniture, the twin-barrel movement striking on a gong, backplate stamped 'Vincenti', the case surmounted by a figural group, c1880, clock 23¾in(60.5cm) high.

£640–760
Tennants

ANTERN CLOCKS

iron and brass lantern clock, painted dial with single hand, posted movement with verge apement, countwheel striking twice 1–6 on a bell, the case h brass finials, on turned t, with a stained oak wall cket, Italy, 1675–1700, n (22cm) high.

,750–4,500
theby's (Am)

A miniature lantern timepiece, by Thomas Bullock, Bath, the dial with single hand, the movement with alarm, the anchor escapement with rope drive, hoop and spikes, doors replaced, c1740, 8½in (21.5cm) high.

£5,000–6,000
Clock-Work-Shop

The replacement doors on this clock have been made from an old barometer dial.

A brass lantern wall timepiece, by Bachelot Achenneuiere, the posted movement with verge escapement and silk suspended pendulum, alarm on a bell, the front fret engraved with birds, France, 1725–50, 8¾in (22cm) high.

£4,000–5,000
Sotheby's (Am)

A brass lantern clock, by William Dunant, London, the brass dial with single hand and engraved alarm disc, the posted movement with verge escapement, countwheel striking and alarm on a bell, mid-18thC, 13¾in (35cm) high.

£1,400–1,650
Sotheby's (Am)

orass lantern clock, by John aper, Chelmsford, the brass dial h single hand and engraved rm disc, the posted movement h verge escapement, top unted bell for alarm, some parts er, c1770, 9in (23cm) high.

,200–1,400 **Tennants**

A brass hook and spike wall clock, the dial with single hand and central rotating alarm dial, 18thC, 7in (18cm) high.

£2,600–3,200
Holloway's

A brass lantern table clock, the engraved brass dial with silvered chapter ring, the spring-driven fusee and chain anchor movement, rack-striking the quarter-hours on two bells, on ball feet, 1825–50, 15¾in (40cm) high.

£2,000–2,500
Sotheby's (Am)

A patinated-brass lantern clock, the spring-driven movement striking the quarter-hours on two bells, c1880, 16in (40.5cm) high.

£1,200–1,350
D S Pullen

LONGCASE CLOCKS

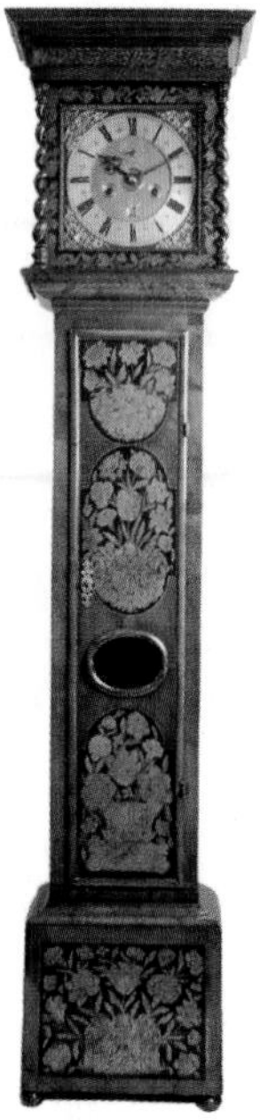

A marquetry and walnut longcase clock, by William Carter, Cambridge, the dial with inset seconds ring and calendar aperture, the five-pillar movement with internal countwheel and front-mounted bell stand, the case door with three floral panels and lenticle, convex inlaid moulding and barley twist columns, on bun feet, c1685, 82½in (209.5cm) high.

£25,000–28,000

Clock-Work-Shop ⊞

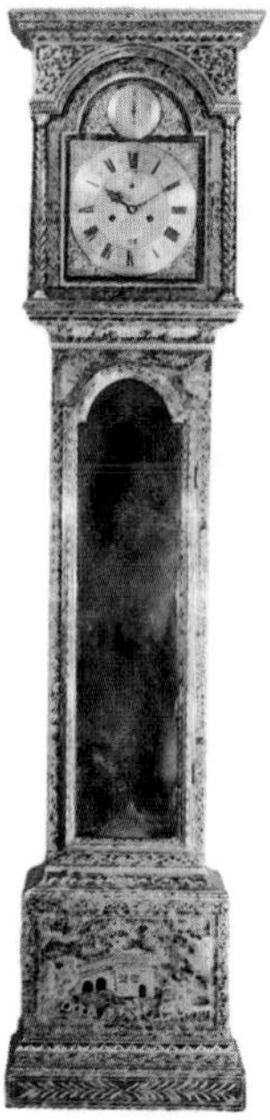

A *faux* tortoiseshell and chinoiserie lacquer longcase clock, by Francis Gregg, London, the dial with silvered chapter ring, subsidiary seconds, date aperture and fast/slow, with eight-day striking movement, the trunk door with a mirror, c1720, 89in (226cm) high.

£12,000–13,500

Allan Smith ⊞

An oak longcase clock, by John Hawkins, Southampton, the brass dial with silvered chapter ring, subsidiary seconds dial and date aperture, the five-pillar movement with anchor escapement and countwheel striking on a bell, the hood with arched pediment and turned columns, on later feet, c1730, 81¼in (206cm) high.

£1,000–1,250

Tennants

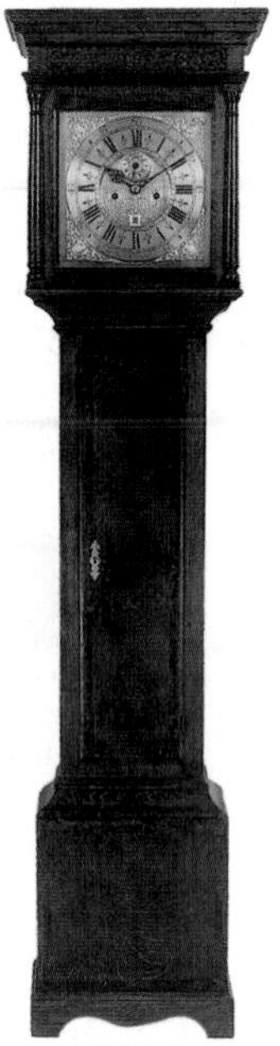

An oak longcase clock, by William Hough, the engraved b dial with silvered chapter ring subsidiary seconds dial and d aperture, the eight-day moven with four pillars and anchor escapement, striking the hour on a bell, the hood with turne angle pillars and blind sound c1735, 70in (178cm) high.

£7,000–7,750

P A Oxley ⊞

ESSENTIAL REFERENCE DATING FEATURES

- One way of dating late 17th/early 18th-century loncases is to examine the large moulding at the top of the trunk, just below the hood.
- The example on the right shows the convex moulding which was used on longcase clocks until c1700. This particular clock by Isaac Lownds, London, dates from c1690.
- The longcase clock on the far right shows the concave moulding which was introduced along with other developments c1700. The date of this particular example by James Hubert, London, is c1735.
- This fairly simple visual check enables you to quickly decide which side of the 1700 fence your clock falls.

A walnut-veneered and marquetry longcase clock, by Isaac Lownds, London, the brass dial with a silvered chapter ring and date aperture, the month duration movement partially latched, outside countwheel striking the hours on a bell, the hood with brass finials and barley-twist columns, c1690, 89in (226cm) high.

£38,000–42,000

Derek Roberts Antiques ⊞

A figured walnut longcase clock, by James Hubert, London, the brass dial with silvered chapter ring, date aperture, subsidiary seconds and strike/silent, dials wi a five-pillar month duration movemen the trunk door with crossbanding and wheatear stringing, base restored, c1735, 90in (229cm) high.

£18,000–20,000

Derek Roberts Antiques ⊞

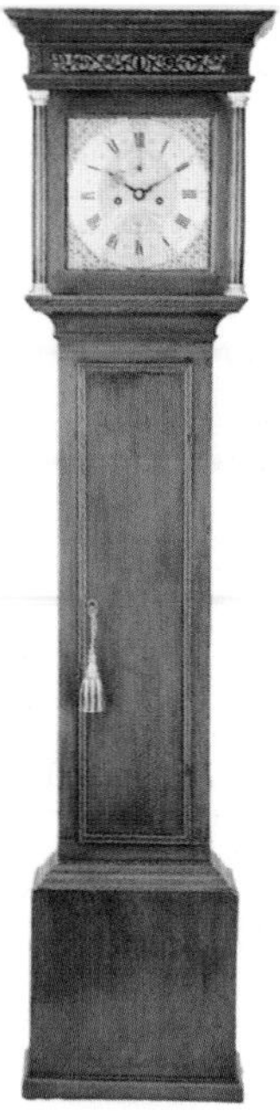

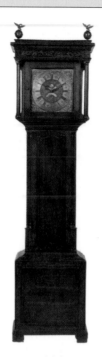

An oak longcase clock, by Wilsmhurst, Deal, the brass dial with silvered chapter ring, subsidiary seconds dial and date aperture, the eight-day movement with five pillars, c1735, 82¼in (209cm) high.

£7,000–7,750
Allan Smith ⊞

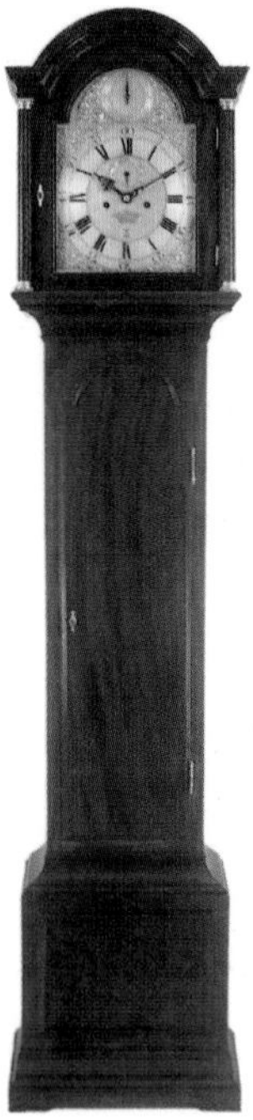

A mahogany longcase clock, by Henry Hurt, London, the brass dial with silvered chapter ring, subsidiary seconds dial, date aperture and strike/silent to arch, the eight-day five-pillar movement with anchor escapement and striking the hours on a bell, c1745, 89in (226cm) high.

£10,000–12,000
P A Oxley ⊞

A George II oak longcase clock, by John Stancliffe, the silvered chapter ring with central moonphase and date aperture, with 30-hour movement striking on a bell, the hood with gilt eagle, ball finials and turned columns, the trunk with quarter recessed columns, 88in (235cm) high.

£700–850 Hy Duke 🔨

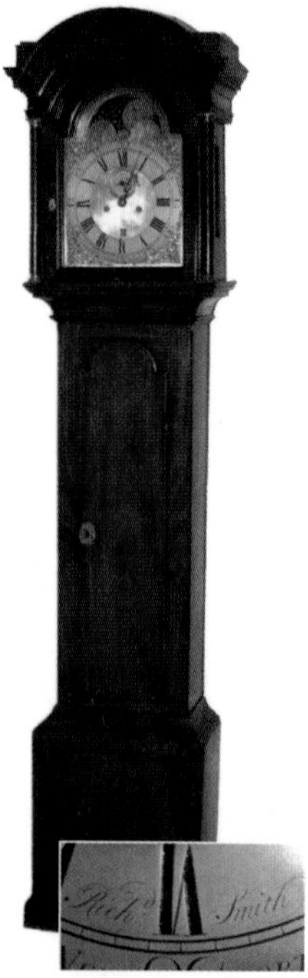

A mahogany longcase clock, by Richard Smith, Newport, the brass dial with subsidiary seconds, date aperture and moonphase, the eight-day movement striking the hours on a bell, the arched hood pediment with dentil cornice mouldings and brass-capped columns, Wales, c1745, 87¾in (223cm) high.

£5,250–5,750
Kembery Antique Clocks ⊞

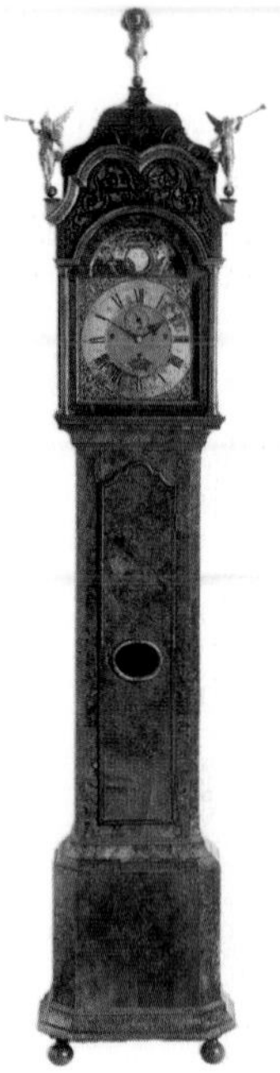

A burr-walnut musical longcase clock, by Pieter Paulus, Amsterdam, the brass dial with engraved silvered chapter ring, subsidiary seconds dial, date aperture, moonphase, strike/silent and play/not play, the triple-train six-pillar movement with anchor escapement, striking the half-hours on alternating bells, playing one of two tunes with 18 hammers on nine bells, the hood surmounted by a giltwood figure of Atlas and two angels, the canted trunk with lenticle to door, on ball feet, Holland, c1740, 110¼in (280cm) high.

£10,000–12,000
Sotheby's (Am) 🔨

An oak longcase clock, by Porthouse, Penrith, the brass dial with plaque inscribed 'Robt & Ester Dawson 1749', the four-pillar movement with anchor escapement and outside countwheel striking on a bell, 1749, 78¼in (199cm) high.

£1,400–1,650
Tennants 🔨

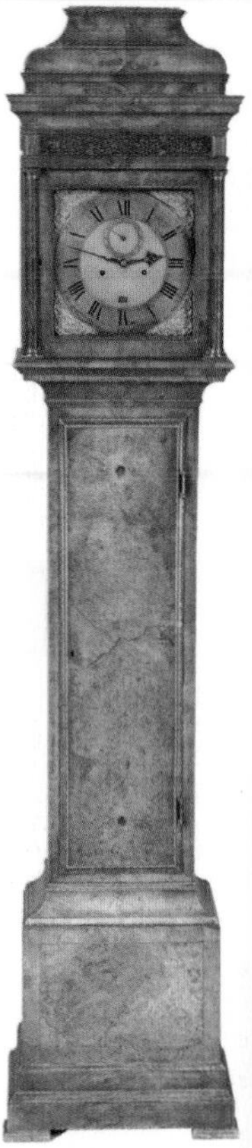

A burr-walnut longcase clock, by George Graham, London, th brass dial with subsidiary secon and calendar aperture, the five pillar latched movement with deadbeat escapement, bolt anc shutter maintaining power rack striking on a bell, movement ar winding key punch numbered 7 interior of trunk with inscriptio 'Set by ye church dial Jun ye 1s 1768', on later feet, c1740, 93¾in (238cm) high.

£160,000–200,000
Tennants 🔨

It is not often that such a fine a original clock by one of our mo eminent clockmakers comes or the open market. This longcase clock is of the finest quality anc has never suffered from overenthusiastic restoration. It even survived the 260 or so yea since its manufacture with its numbered winding key.

George Graham (1674–175 worked with and became a par of Thomas Tompion (the most famous British clockmaker) an married his niece. Graham succeeded to Tompion's busin and was also Fellow of the Ro Society and Master of the Worshipful Company of Clockm Throughout his career he was responsible for several importa horological inventions. On his death Graham was buried wit Tompion in Westminster Abbe a sign of how highly regarded both were in their lifetime.

The price realized is a substar amount for a longcase clock, a record for the auctioneers.

The Clock-Work-Shop
Winchester

6A Parchment St., Winchester SO23 8AT
Tel: 01962 842331 Open 9.00–5.00 Mon–Sat
or Mobile 07885 954302 anytime
Website: www.clock-work-shop.co.uk

8 Day mahogany longcase clock by William Hall of Nottingham

We offer for sale a wide range of lovingly restored quality antique clocks to suit most budgets.

Full repair/restoration service.

Delivery and set-up (or shipping) can be arranged.

Good prices paid for quality/interesting clocks.

All work carries a 3 year written guarantee

Coppelia Antiques
Valerie & Roy Clements

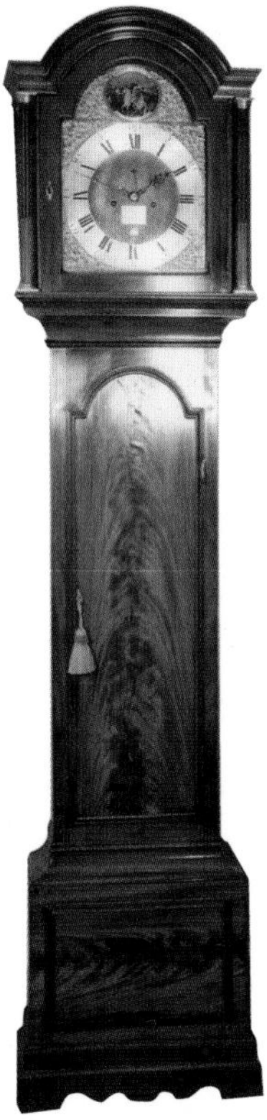

ANTIQUES
BOUGHT & SOLD

Holford Lodge
Plumley Moor Road
Nr Knutsford
Cheshire WA16 9RS

A superb c1795 8-day London mahogany arched brass dial longcase clock. The unusual feature of rocking horse automaton to arch with engraving H.R.H. The Duke of York above and Valciennes July 1793 below. The clock by John Davis Windsor showing all the typical good quality London case features. Outstanding flame-veneered mahogany. The 5-pillar movement striking hours on a single bell.

Similar good quality clocks and furniture always in stock.

TEL: 01565 722197
FAX: 01565 722744

Open 7 days by appointment

www.coppeliaantiques.co.uk

VISIT THE ANTIQUE CLOCK SPECIALIST
The Essence of Time

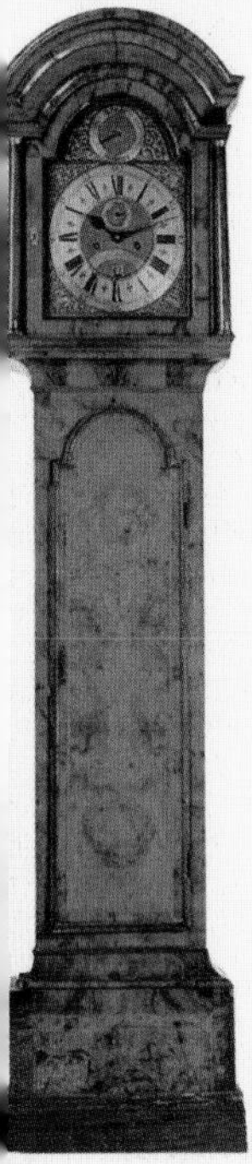

Established 1990

A FINE SELECTION OF LONGCASE GRAND FATHER, VIENNA AND OTHER DESIRABLE WALL, MANTEL AND NOVELTY CLOCKS - ALWAYS IN STOCK

ALWAYS CONSULT AN ESTABLISHED DEALER

Unit 2
Curborough Antiques & Craft Centre,
Curborough Hall Farm,
Watery Lane
Off Eastern Avenue By-Pass
LICHFIELD
Staffordshire WS13 8ES

SHOP OPEN
10.30am - 5.00pm
Every Wed/Thurs/Fri/Sat/Sun
Closed Mon/Tues Normally
But OPEN ALL BANK HOLIDAYS

Tel: Shop 01543 418239
Home (Evenings) 01902 764900
Mobile (Anytime) 07944 245064

Kembery Antique Clocks Ltd

We stock a range of longcase clocks including small cottage examples from 6ft 3in to taller 18th century clocks.

UK and overseas delivery arranged.

Overhauled and guaranteed.

Bracket, carriage and wall clocks also stocked.

Please telephone for an appointment or view our stock and photos on our website:

www.kdclocks.co.uk

Tel: 0117 956 5281

George Street Antique Centre
8 Edgar Buildings
George Street
Bath BA1 2EH

Email: kembery@kdclocks.co.uk

A japanned longcase clock, by Charles Clay, London, the brass dial with subsidiary seconds dial and date aperture, the arch with strike/silent, the four-pillar movement with anchor escapement and rack-striking on a bell, c1750, 86½in (220cm) high.

£1,600–2,000 **Tennants**

Charles Clay is listed as clockmaker to George II between 1730 and 1750.

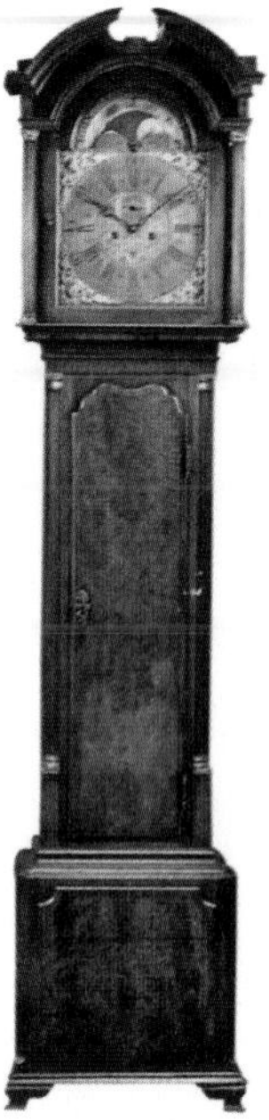

A figured mahogany longcase clock, by John Smith, Chester, the brass dial with subsidiary seconds dial, date aperture and moonphase, with eight-day striking movement, the hood with inset blue glass panels, the trunk with quarter reeded columns, on ogee bracket feet, 18thC, 91in (231cm) high.

£3,750–4,500 **Cheffins**

An inlaid mahogany longcase clock, by James Thristle, Stogursey, the silvered dial with moonphase and subsidiary dials for strike/silent, days of the week, months of the year and calendar and central sweep seconds, eight-day movement, 1753–1838, 89in (226cm) high.

£12,500–14,000
Styles of Stow

An oak longcase clock, by Willi Knight II, Petersfield, the engrav brass dial with subsidiary secor dial, the 30-hour rope-driven four-wheel train movement w countwheel striking, c1755, 78in (198cm) high.

£3,750–4,250
Clock-Work-Shop

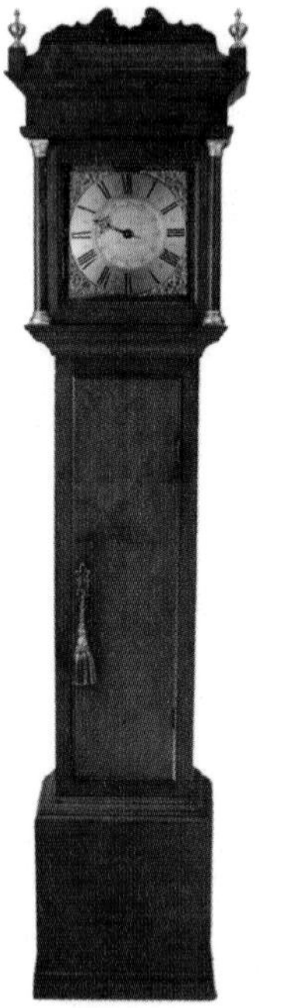

An oak longcase clock, by Edward Farmer, Monmouth, the engraved silvered-brass dial with single hand, the 30-hour posted frame movement with countwheel striking, Wales, c1760, 78in (198cm) high.

£4,000–4,500
Allan Smith

A walnut longcase clock, by Robert Hughes, Colchester, the brass dial with silvered chapter ring, seconds dial, calendar aperture and strike/silent, the five-pillar movement striking on a bell, the trunk with strung and crossbanded arched door, 18thC, 95in (241.5cm) high.

£3,000–3,500 **Sworders**

An oak longcase clock, by Thomas Stripling, Barwell, the brass dial with moonphase, with eight-day striking movement, 1760–70, 83in (211cm) high.

£6,000–7,000
Styles of Stow

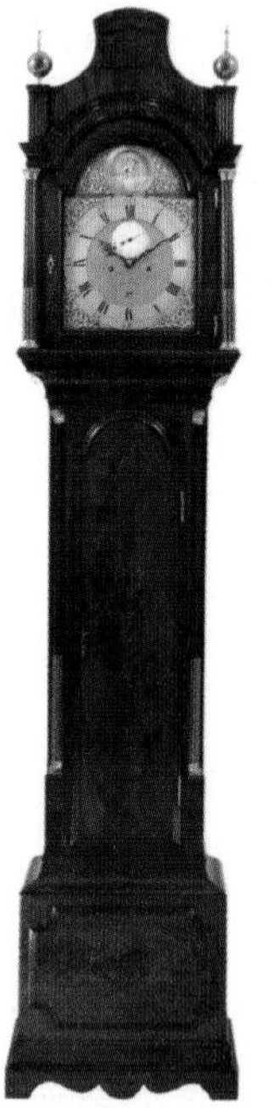

A mahogany-veneered longca clock, by Hugh Anderson, Lond the brass dial with date apertu and seconds dial, an automaton Chronos in the arch, with eigh day five-pillar movement striki the hours on a bell, the pagod top with brass finials, c1770, 93in (236cm) high.

£14,000–16,000
Derek Roberts Antiques

An oak and walnut-inlaid longcase clock, by David Collier, Gatley Green, the brass break-arch dial with silvered chapter ring, date disc and moonphase, the eight-day movement striking the hours on a bell, c1770, 87in (221cm) high.

£6,000–7,000
Essence of Time ⊞

An oak longcase clock, by John Woolley, Codnor, with brass dial, the four-pillar movement with anchor escapement and outside countwheel striking on a bell, later skirting to plinth, c1770, 83in (211cm) high.

£1,400–1,650
Tennants

An oak longcase clock, by J. Phillips, Oswestry, the brass dial with silvered chapter ring, calendar aperture and seconds dial, the eight-day movement with anchor escapement and striking on a bell, Wales, c1770, 78in (198cm) high.

£5,000–6,000
Clock-Work-Shop ⊞

A flame mahogany-veneered longcase clock, by Nathaniel Brown, Manchester, the break-a brass dial with silvered chapter ring, seconds dial, date apertu and moonphase, the eight-day four pillar movement rack-strik the hours on a bell, the hood w swan-neck pediment, c1775, 101in (256.5cm) high.

£14,700–16,300
Allan Smith ⊞

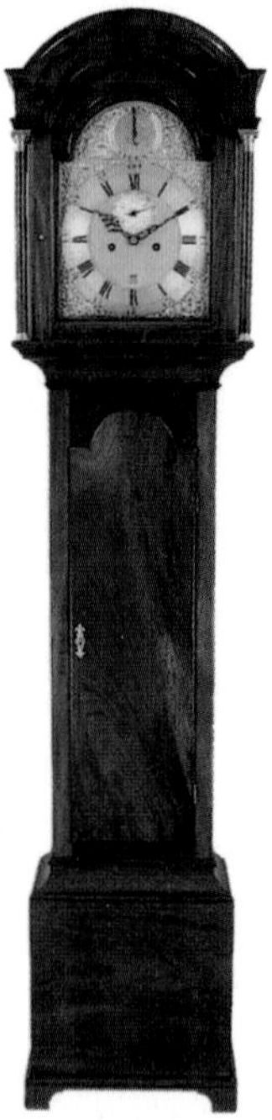

A mahogany longcase clock, by W. & J. Evill, Bath, the brass dial with silvered chapter ring, subsidiary seconds and date aperture, the eight-day movement striking the hours on a bell, the hood with break-arch top and brass-capped pillars, on bracket feet, c1775, 86in (218.5cm) high.

£8,000–9,500
P A Oxley ⊞

A figured mahogany longcase clock, by Thomas Ross, Hull, the brass dial with silvered chapter ring, subsidiary seconds dial, date aperture and strike/silent, the four-pillar movement with anchor escapement and rack-striking on a bell, dial and movement associated, c1780, 90½in (230cm) high.

£2,250–2,750 Tennants

A mahogany musical longcase clock, by Featherstone, Newcastle, the brass dial with silvered and engraved centre and moonphase, the triple-train movement striking the hours and playing a tune every three hours, the hood with swan-neck pediment and gilt rosettes, c1780, 87in (221cm) high.

£20,000–22,000
Styles of Stow ⊞

A flame mahogany-veneered longcase clock, by Peter Pohlma London, the dial with silvered chapter ring, subsidiary second and date ring, the triple-train movement with six knopped pi striking the quarter-hours on tw bells and the hours on a single bell, the pagoda hood with ree brass inlay and brass finials, th trunk with reeded brass-inlaid columns, c1780, 96in (244cm) h

£20,000–22,000
Derek Roberts Antiques

ɜrved oak longcase clock, by iam Vise, Wisbech, the brass with subsidiary seconds dial, e aperture and Father Time omaton to arch, with eight- movement striking on a bell, 80, 85in (216cm) high.

,000–4,500
les of Stow

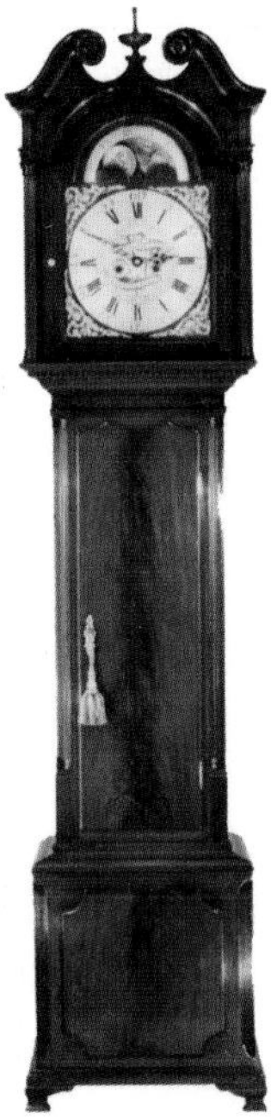

A mahogany longcase clock, by John Benson, Whitehaven, the engraved and silvered dial with moonphase and centre sweep date, the eight-day movement striking on a bell, c1780, 90in (229cm) high.

£11,000–13,000
Allan Smith Clocks

A George III mahogany longcase clock, by Thomas Gardner, London, the brass dial with subsidiary seconds dial and date aperture, the eight-day movement striking on a bell, 89in (226cm) high.

£2,000–2,500
Woolley & Wallis

An oak longcase clock, by Rouckliffte, Bridgwater, the painted dial with subsidiary seconds dial and date aperture, with eight-day four-pillar rack-striking movement, c1780, 77½in (197cm) high.

£4,500–5,000
Allan Smith

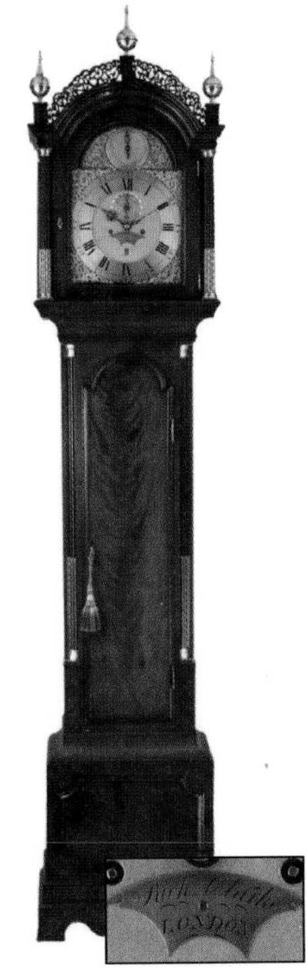

flame mahogany longcase ɔck, by Richard Clarke, London, e break-arch brass dial with vered chapter ring, strike/silent d date aperture, with eight- y five-pillar rack-striking ɔvement, c1780, 97in 46.5cm) high.

14,000–16,000
llan Smith

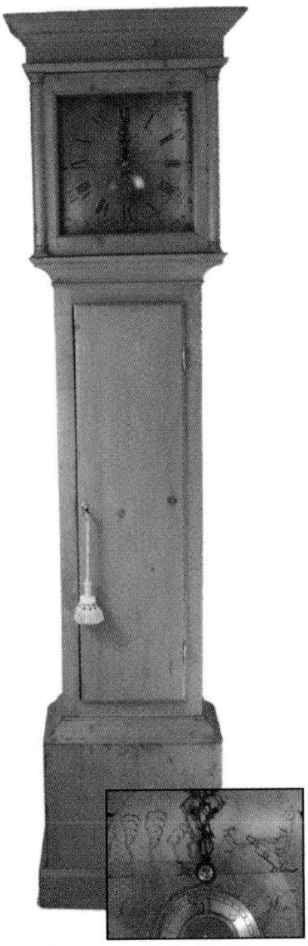

A pine longcase clock, by John Wood, Stroud, the silvered-brass dial with date aperture and engraved with a foundry and figures casting metal, with countwheel striking movement, c1780, 80in (203cm) high.

£3,000–3,500
Allan Smith

An oak longcase clock, by Richard Wright, Witham, the silvered and engraved brass dial with subsidiary seconds dial and date aperture, Father Time automaton to arch, the eight-day five-pillar movement striking the hours on a bell, c1780, 81in (206cm) high.

£6,000–7,000 P A Oxley

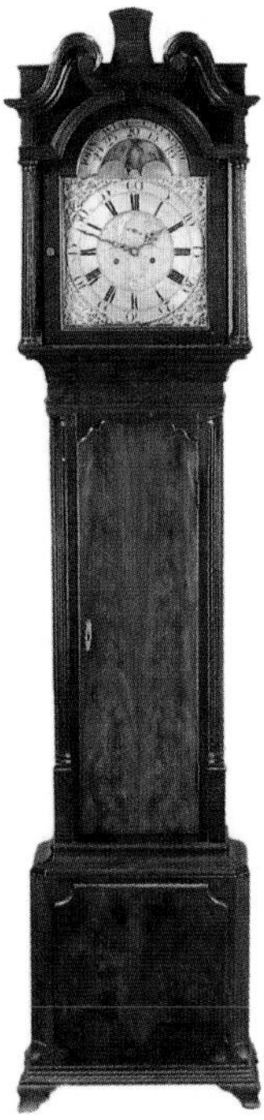

A mahogany longcase clock, by John Wyke, Liverpool, the brass dial with silvered chapter ring, subsidiary seconds dial, date aperture and moonphase to arch, the eight-day four-pillar movement with anchor escapement and striking on a bell, c1780, 96¾in (246cm) high.

£2,250–2,750 Tennants

A mahogany longcase clock, by John Warry, Bristol, the painted dial with rocking ship automaton to arch, with eight-day striking movement, the hood with swan-neck pediment and reeded columns, 1783–1821, 86in (218.5cm) high.

£8,000–9,000
Styles of Stow ⊞

A mahogany longcase clock, by William Coe, Cambridge, the brass dial with silvered chapter ring, sunken seconds, date aperture and rocking ship automaton, the eight-day, five-pillar movement striking the hours on a bell, the case with inlay, c1785, 89in (226cm) high.

£18,000–20,000
P A Oxley ⊞

A walnut longcase clock, by John Le Page, Guernsey, the painted dial with subsidiary seconds and date, eight-day movement striking the hours on a bell, c1785, 67½in (171.5cm) high.

£3,500–4,500
P A Oxley ⊞

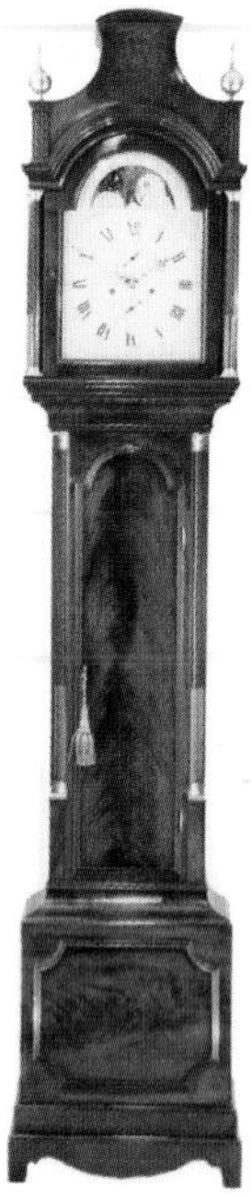

A flame mahogany longcase clock, by John Robinson, Lond the painted dial with subsidiar dials and moonphase, the hoo and trunk with brass-capped reeded columns and detachabl pagoda top, c1785, 94½in (240cm) high.

£15,000–16,500
Allan Smith ⊞

A mahogany longcase clock, by James Ivory, Dundee, with brass dial and silvered chapter ring with seconds and date, the eight-day movement striking the hours on a bell, the hood with swan-neck top and brass-capped angle pillars, on bracket feet, Scotland, c1785, 84in (213.5cm) high.

£8,500–10,000
P A Oxley ⊞

An oak longcase clock, by Thomas Lister (Jnr), Yorkshire, the brass dial with subsidiary seconds dial, date aperture and moonphase, with 30-hour striking movement, the hood with swan-neck pediment and brass-capped side pillars, the trunk with quadrant turned corner pilasters, date gear missing, late 18thC, 86in (218.5cm) high.

£1,300–1,600
Netherhampton Salerms

An oak longcase clock, by William Richardson, Edinburgh, the brass dial with silvered chapter ring and subsidiary seconds and date dials, with eight-day movement striking the hours on a bell, the hood with swan-neck pediment, brass finial, brass-capped pillars and satinwood sound frets, Scotland, c1785, 87in (221cm) high.

£8,000–9,000 **P A Oxley ⊞**

An oak and mahogany crossbanded longcase clock, by F. Careswell, Shrewsbury, the painted dial with subsidiary seconds dial, date aperture and rocking ship automaton to arch, the eight-day movement striking on a bell, hood and trunk with reeded columns, c1790, 90in (228.5cm) high.

£8,000–9,000
Clock-Work-Shop ⊞

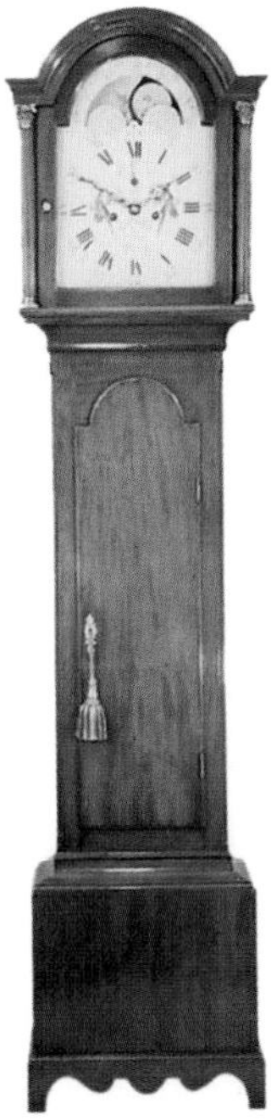

ahogany longcase clock, by iam Cox, Devizes, the Wilson with gesso decoration and onphase, the hood with ak-arch top, c1790, 81in 5.5cm) high.

500–8,500
an Smith Clocks ⊞

A mahogany longcase clock, by John Manley, Chatham, the brass dial with seconds dial and date aperture, the eight-day five-pillar movement with anchor escapement and rack striking on a bell, pediment and plinth reduced, c1790, 88in (224cm) high.

£2,300–2,750 Tennants

A mahogany longcase clock, by John Wyke, Liverpool, the engraved dial with moonphase and calendar, with eight-day movement, c1790, 89in (226cm) high.

£10,000–11,500
Essence of Time ⊞

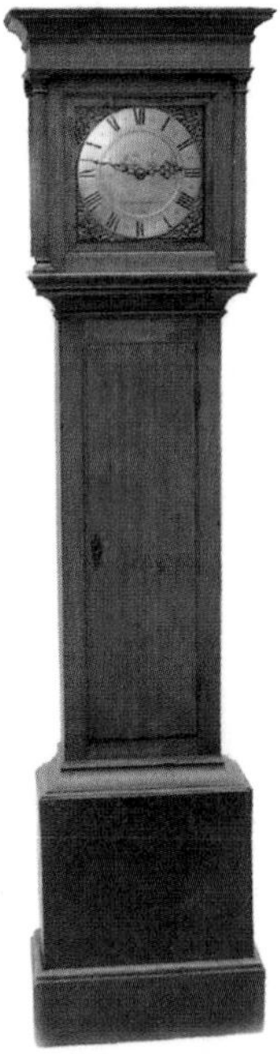

An oak longcase clock, by John Arnold, Child Okeford, the dial engraved with ships off Plymouth Hoe, the 30-hour movement with outside countwheel striking on a bell, late 18thC, 78in (198cm) high.

£800–1,000
Netherhampton Salerms

mahogany longcase clock, by chard Mason, St Albans, the inted arched dial with date d seconds indicators, the ght-day movement striking the urs on a bell, the hood with goda pediment, fluted hood lumns and Corinthian capitals, 790, 89¾in (228cm) high.

3,150–3,450
embery Antique Clocks ⊞

chard Mason is recorded in aillie's Clockmakers of the *orld as working 1777–95.*

An inlaid mahogany longcase clock, by J. Durward, Edinburgh, the dial with silvered chapter ring, subsidiary seconds and date dials, with eight-day striking movement, the case with swan-neck pediment with fretwork and shell inlay, Scotland, 1780, 86¼in (219cm) high.

£2,250–2,800
Penrith Farmers' & Kidd's

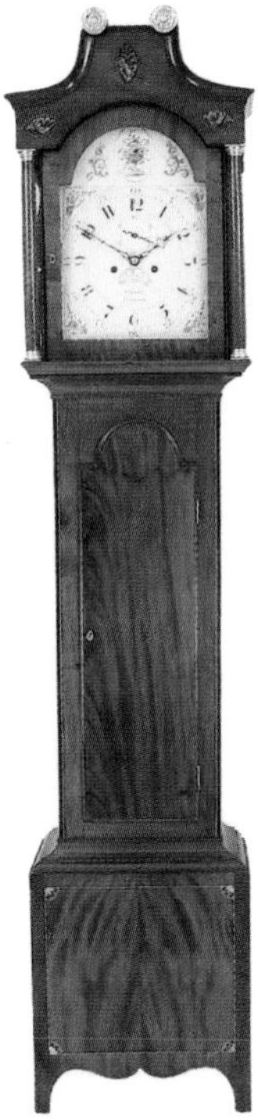

An inlaid mahogany longcase clock, by Crake, London, the painted dial with seconds dial and date aperture, the eight-day movement striking the hours on a bell, the hood with brass-capped pillars and brass paterae, c1795, 85in (216cm) high.

£5,000–6,000
P A Oxley ⊞

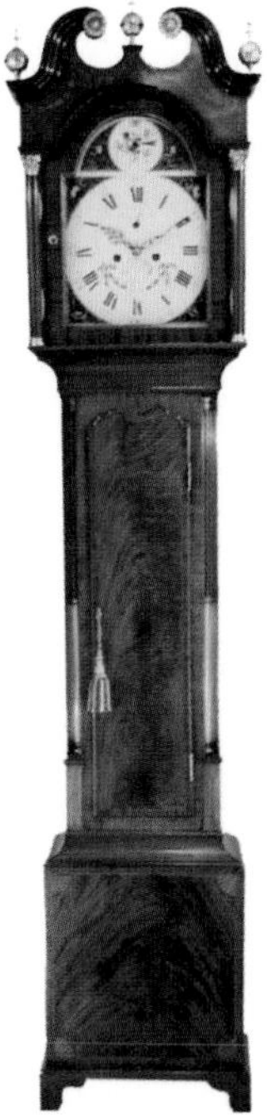

A mahogany longcase clock, by John Curle, Kelso, the Wilson dial painted with birds and flowers, with eight-day striking movement, the case with inlays and crossbanding, the hood with swan-neck pediment, Scotland, c1795, 90in (229cm) high.

£8,500–9,500
Allan Smith Clocks ⊞

An inlaid oak longcase clock, by William Plant, Walsall, with a painted arched dial, the eight-day movement striking on a bell, c1795, 86in (218.5cm) high.

£4,500–5,000
Essence of Time

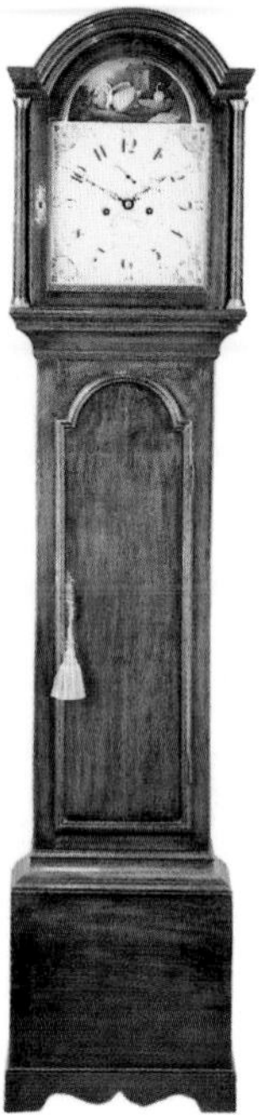

An oak longcase clock, by George Suggate, Halesworth, the painted dial with subsidiary seconds dial, date aperture and swan automaton, eight-day striking movement, c1795, 82½in (209.5cm) high.

£7,000–8,000
Allan Smith

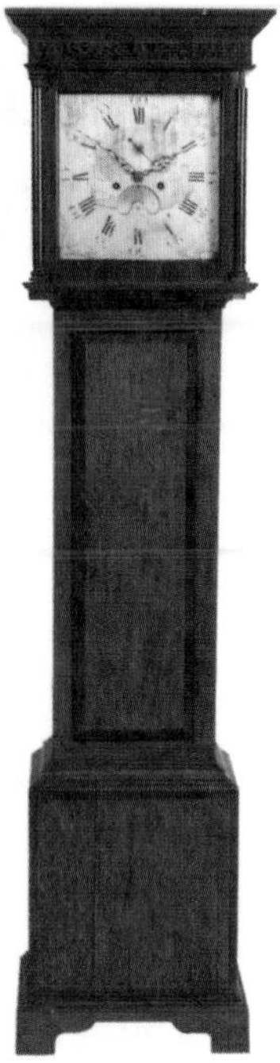

A George III oak longcase clock, by W. Curtis, Exeter the silvered dial with subsidiary seconds dial and date aperture, eight-day striking movement, the case with blind-fret decoration and turned columns, 78in (198cm) high.

£1,400–1,650 Hy Duke

A George III oak and mahog longcase clock, by W. Parkins Lancaster, the dial with silvere chapter ring and date aperture the 30-hour four-pillar movem striking on a bell, the case wit later carving, 82in (208.5cm) hi

£600–700 Halls

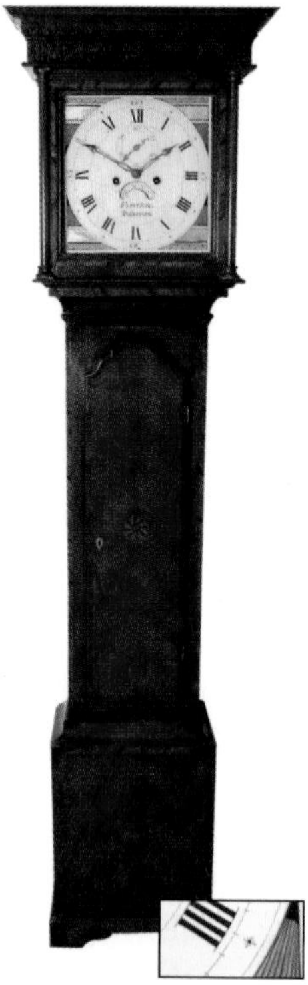

An oak longcase clock, by Fisher, Dulverton, with painted dial, the eight-day movement striking on a bell, the case with crossbanded and inlaid decoration, c1800, 79in (200.5cm) high.

£3,250–3,750
Styles of Stow

A stained cherrywood longcase clock, with painted dial, the iron-posted anchor movement with trip repeating rack-striking on two bells, the hood with a flowerbasket crest, Holland, c1800, 104in (264cm) high.

£1,000–1,200
Sotheby's (Am)

An oak longcase clock, by John Gartly, Aberdeen, the silvered-brass dial with subsidiary seconds, date and strike/silent dials, the eight-day five-pillar movement striking the hours on a bell, the hood with a carved acanthus leaf above brass-capped pillars, Scotland, c1800, 85in (215.9cm) high.

£5,000–6,000
P A Oxley

John Gartly was admitted to the incorporation of Hammermen in 1783. He is noted for making excellent pinions and arbors and perfected a hardening process.

A mahogany longcase clock, b James Gray, Edinburgh, the painted dial by Hipkiss & Harro with subsidiary seconds and da dials, the arch painted with scrolled gilt foliage and a classical building, the case with swan-neck pediment and brass paterae, Scotland, c1800, 91in (231cm) high.

£7,500–8,500
Derek Roberts Antiques

James Gray was admitted as a Freeman of the Incorporation o Hammermen in 1772. He became His Majesty's clock and watchmaker in Scotland.

Rare 8-day oval dial moonphase clock by Banister of Lichfield, 1783-95, in a fine mahogany and satinwood case

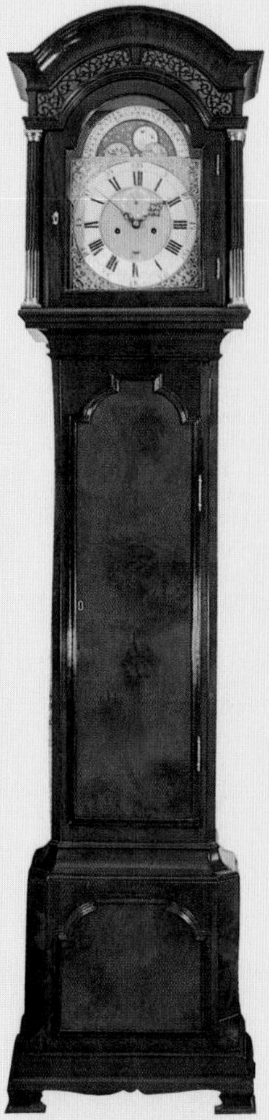

A fine 8-day arched brass dial high water at Bristol moonphase clock by John Plumley of Bristol, 1746-71, in an exceptional flame mahogany case

A mahogany longcase clock, by J. O'Donnel, Edinburgh, the painted dial with subsidiary seconds and date dials, the eight-day movement striking the hours on a bell, the case with figured veneers and boxwood stringing, Scotland, c1810, 80in (203cm) high.

£7,000–8,000 P A Oxley

A mahogany longcase clock, by Moses Abraham, Frome, the painted dial with moonphase, with eight-day striking movement, c1820, 82in (208.5cm) high.

£4,500–5,000
Styles of Stow

A mahogany longcase clock, the dial with subsidiary seconds and date dials, the twin-train movement striking on a bell, the hood surmounted with a brass finial, the panelled waisted door between quarter-turned pilasters, Scotland, early 19thC, 85½in (217cm) high.

£1,600–2,000 Bearnes

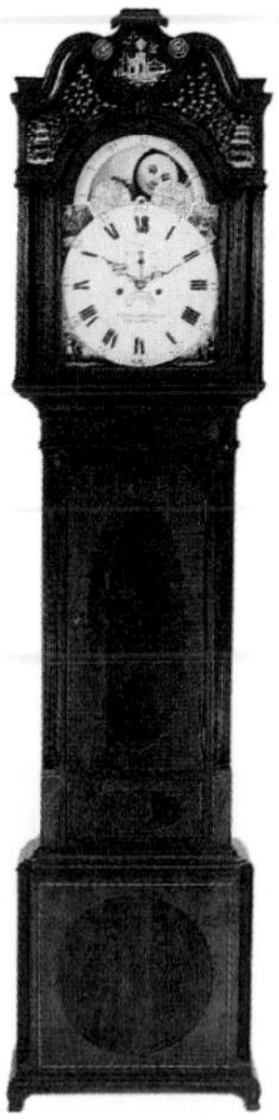

A mahogany longcase clock, by James Sharples, Liverpool, the painted dial with subsidiary seconds dial, date aperture and moonphase, the eight-day movement striking the hours on bell, the hood with blind glass sound frets painted with Orienta scenes and double reeded angle pillars, c1810, 94in (239cm) hig

£7,500–8,500 P A Oxley

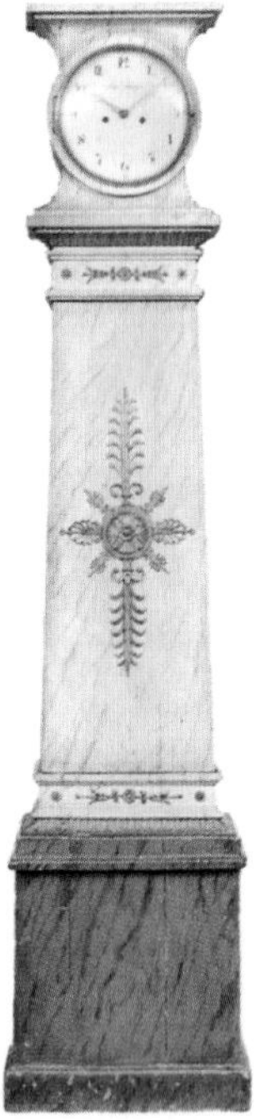

A painted longcase clock, by Petter Strand, with a lacquered dial and striking movement, the case with giltwood and bronzed lead mounts, Sweden, early 19thC, 88½in (225cm) high.

£2,750–3,250 Bukowskis

Petter Strand also made musical instruments and owned an organ-building workshop in Stockholm from 1791.

A painted pine longcase clock, the enamel face inscribed 'AAN Neiry', the lyre-form case with applied star and scrolls and a lenticle, Sweden, early 19thC, 91in (231cm) high.

£750–900
Northeast Auctions

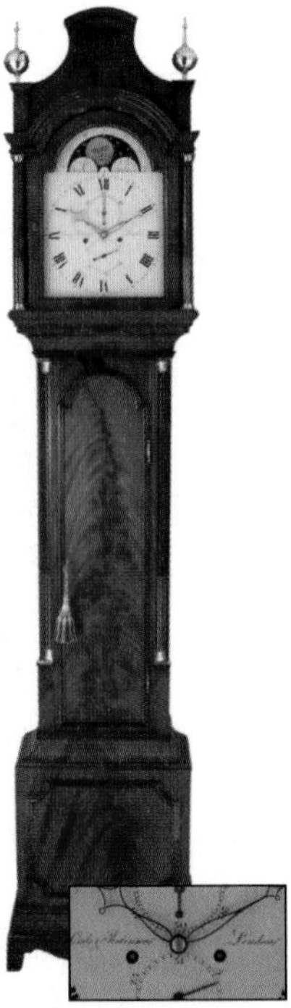

A flame mahogany longcase clock, by Cade & Robinson, London, the painted dial with subsidiary seconds and date dials and moonphase, the eight-day four-pillar rack movement striking the hours, the case with a pagoda top, early 19thC, 95¼in (242cm) high.

£15,000–16,500
Allan Smith

A mahogany longcase clock, by John McNab, Perth, the brass dial with silvered chapter ring and engraved silvered centre, with eight-day striking movement, the case with inlaid decoration and swan-neck pediment, Scotland, c1820, 86in (218.5cm) high.

£8,000–9,000
Essence of Time

EXPERT'S EYE LONGCASE CLOCK DIALS

The dial or face of a clock consists of a square, arched or round brass or iron plate. British longcase dials can be dated from their material, shape, size and additional features. Early dials tended to be small with narrow chapter rings and small spandrels. As time went by all of these features became larger. Breakarch dials appeared around 1820 and painted iron dials became fashionable c1770. This figured walnut longcase clock by James Hubert has a 12in (30.5cm) brass breakarch dial with silvered chapter rings; it was made c1730.

The back of the dial is just as important as the front in ascertaining its age and originality. The front is often bright and clean, possbily recently restored, but the rear is always left untouched and is very dull in comparison. You should check that it is without plugged or vacant holes, which may indicate a replacement dial. Punch marks may also suggest an engraved name has been removed or changed. Cast-iron false plates were often used to secure painted dials to the movement but were never used with brass dials.

£15,000–20,000 **Derek Roberts Antiques**

strike/silent dial
dial arch – arched tops appeared in the early 18th century. Various features can be found in this space, including signatures, coats-of-arms, strike/silent dials, moon dials, automatons, music selection and painted scenes.
subsidiary seconds dial
decorative half-hour marks
winding holes
minute track
date aperture
applied corner spandrels
Hands – the first hands were fairly simple with slender minute hands which were finely cut blued steel/iron with bevelled and facetted edges and turned centres. Over time the ornamentation spread to the entire minute hand and the hour hand was more open in its design. Matching hands, where the minute hand is an elongated version of the hour hand, were popular on both silvered and painted dials. Stamped brass hands are also found on painted dials – these were always gilded and often hac attractive hand punch mark decoration.

A mahogany longcase clock, by Webb & Son, Frome, the painted dial with subsidiary seconds and date dials and moonphase, the eight-day movement striking the hours on a bell, the case with crossbanding and ebony inlay, the hood with swan-neck pediment above capped and fluted Corinthian columns, c1820, 88in (223.5cm) high.

£4,500–5,000
Kembery Antique Clocks

Thomas and James Webb worked at Palmer Street and Market Place, Frome from 1810 to 1840. They are documented in A. J. Moore's Somerset Clockmakers.

A mahogany longcase clock, by Charles Merrilies, Edinburgh, the painted dial with subsidiary seconds and date dials, the eight-day movement striking the hours on a bell, the hood with brass-capped reeded pillars and a brass finial, Scotland, c1820, 90in (228.5cm) high.

£6,500–7,250 **P A Oxley**

An oak longcase clock, by Peatling, Boston, the painted dial with seconds dial, date aperture and moonphase, with eight-day striking movement, the case with swan-neck pediment, c1820, 80in (203cm) high.

£3,500–4,000
Styles of Stow

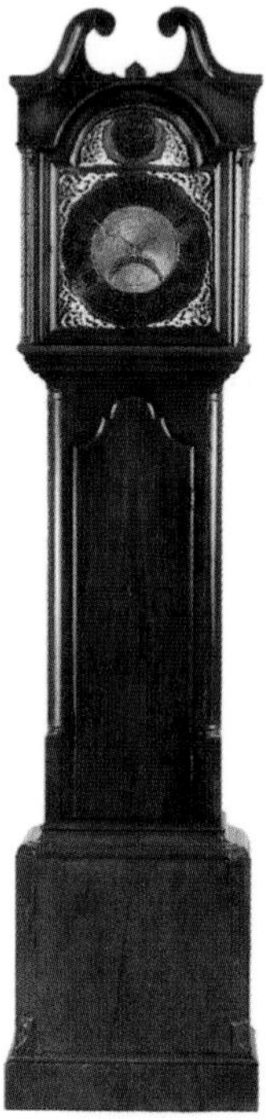

A mahogany longcase clock, b Thomas Pattinson, Winton, the brass dial with date aperture, with 30-hour movement, the hood with a swan-neck pedime and simulated bamboo pillars, the trunk with canted corners, c1829, 84in (213.5cm) high.

£1,200–1,500
Penrith Farmers' & Kidd's

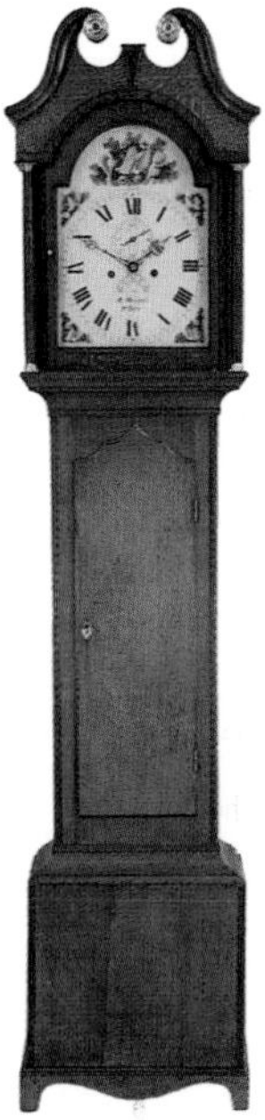

oak longcase clock, by John
nvile, St Ives, the painted dial
n subsidiary seconds dial and
e aperture, the eight-day
vement striking the hours on a
, the hood with swan-neck
iment and brass-capped pillars,
30, 83in (211cm) high.

,500–5,000
Oxley

A mahogany, kingwood-banded and marquetry-inlaid longcase clock, the brass dial with subsidiary seconds and silvered centre signed 'Edwd Bangor, Londini, 1760', the triple-train movement striking the quarter-hours on nine bells, 19thC, 94½in (239.5cm) high.

£3,500–4,250
Woolley & Wallis

A mahogany and boxwood-strung longcase clock, the painted dial signed 'Driffield', with subsidiary seconds dial and date aperture, the twin-train movement with anchor escapement striking on a bell, the hood with swan-neck pediment and turned columns, 19thC, 86½in (220cm) high.

£1,000–1,250 Bearnes

A mahogany longcase clock, the painted dial signed 'Jas. Sitchison, Cockburnsparth', with eight-day striking movement, the hood with swan-neck pediment, Scotland, 19thC, 86in (218.5cm) high.

£1,350–1,600
Anderson & Garland

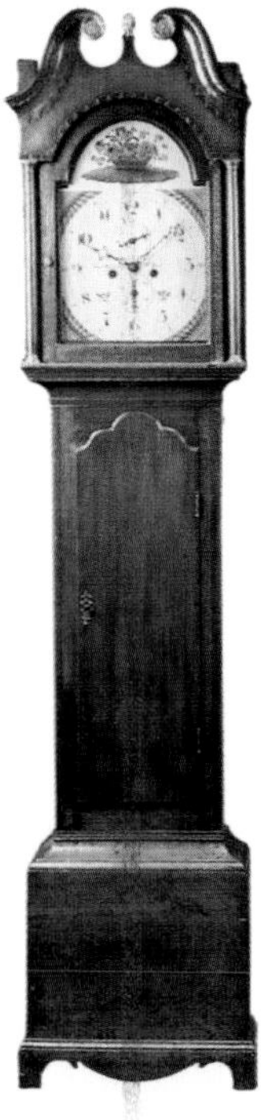

oak longcase clock, by Thomas
lson, St Ives, the painted dial
th subsidiary seconds and
endar dials, the eight-day
iking movement with Felton
seplate, the hood with swan-
ck pediment and dentil
ulding, case possibly associated,
thC, 82¾in (210cm) high.

,200–1,400 Cheffins

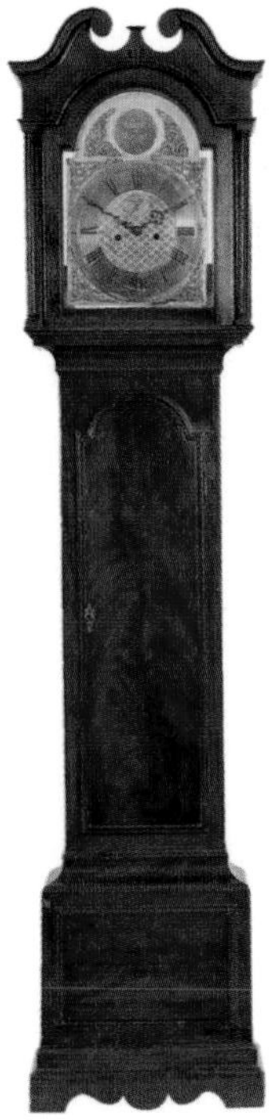

A mahogany longcase clock, the brass dial with subsidiary seconds dial, the twin-train movement with anchor escapement striking on a bell, the associated case with swan-neck pediment and fluted columns, 19thC, 91¼in (232cm) high.

£1,000–1,250
Bearnes

An inlaid mahogany longcase clock, by Mark Bartley, Bristol, the painted dial with subsidiary seconds dial, date aperture and rocking ship automaton, with eight-day four-pillar rack-striking movement, the case with swan-neck pediment, c1840, 82in (208.5cm) high.

£7,000–8,000 Allan Smith

An oak and mahogany-crossbanded clock, by Yeates & Sons, Penrith, the dial arch painted with a farmer harvesting, with eight-day striking movement, the case with swan-neck pediment, c1845, 85½in (217cm) high.

£600–700
Penrith Farmers' & Kidd's

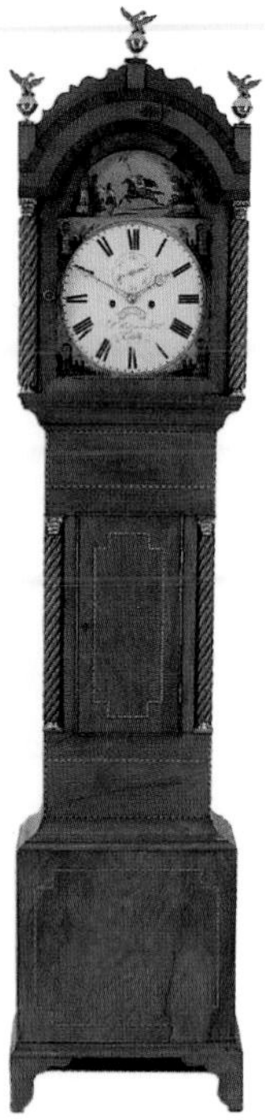

A mahogany longcase clock, by R. Heitzman & Co, Cardiff, the painted dial with subsidiary seconds dial and date aperture, the eight-day movement striking the hours on a bell, the case inlaid with chequered stringing, the top with three brass eagle finials, Wales, c1845, 90in (228.5cm) high.

£5,000–5,750 P A Oxley ⊞

A figured mahogany and rosewood crossbanded longcase clock, by Thomas Strange, Banbury, the painted dial with subsidiary seconds and date dials and moonphase, the twin-train movement striking on a bell, the case with swan-neck pediment with brass capitals and finial, c1850, 93in (236cm) high.

£5,750–6,500 Allan Smith ⊞

A mahogany longcase clock, by Charles Taylor, Bristol, the painted dial with subsic seconds dial, date aperture and moonphas with eight-day rack-striking movement, th case with rope-twist columns and a fret top mid-19thC, 90½in (230cm) high.

£6,600–7,300 Allan Smith ⊞

A burr-walnut longcase clock, the brass dial with silvered chapter ring, subsidiary seconds dial, date, day, month and moonphase apertures, signed 'Otto van Meurs, Amsterdam' the movement with anchor escapement rack quarter-striking on two bells, Holland, 1875–1900, 118¼in (300cm) high.

£7,500–9,000 Sotheby's (Am) ⚒

A boulle marquetry longcase clock, the cast-brass dial with enamel numeral cartouches, the eight-day movement striking the hours and half-hours on a bell, the case with cast-ormolu mounts, the trunk door with a lenticle, on splayed lion-paw feet, France, c1880, 83in (211cm) high.

£9,000–10,000 Kembery Antique Clocks ⊞

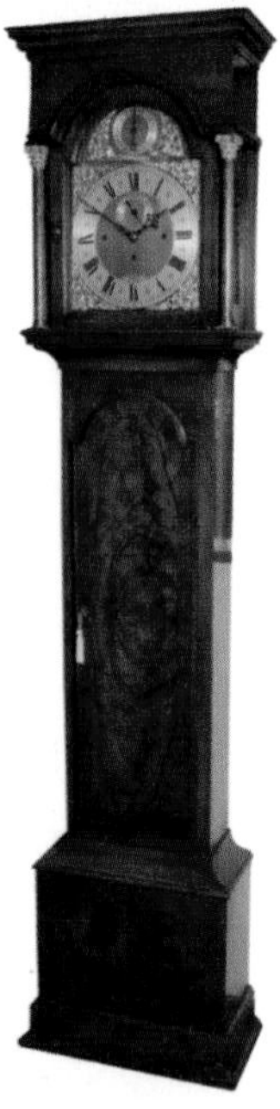

A burr-walnut musical longcase clock, by Goldsmiths and Silversmiths Co, London, the engraved brass dial with silvered chapter ring and subsidiary chime/silent and seconds dials, the triple-train eight-day brass movement chiming the quarter-hours, c1895, 89in (226cm) high.

£8,000–9,000 Essence of Time ⊞

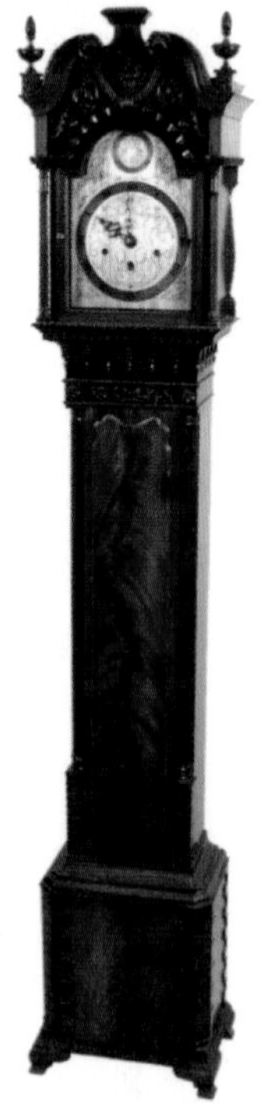

An Edwardian mahogany longcase clock, by Dimmer & Son, Chester, with arched silvered dial, the eight-day movement striking on gongs, 68in (172.5cm) high.

£5,750–7,000 Gorringes (L) ⚒

NOVELTY CLOCKS

ıetal figural timepiece, with ımel dial, the movement with hor escapement, in a painted e supported by a figure of a :k seller, on a mahogany base, ler a glass dome, Germany, I-19thC, 15in (38cm) high.

,500–3,000
theby's (Am)

A Louis XVI-style bisque 'cercles tournants' clock, the two chapter rings with enamel numerals, the rack bell-striking movement with club tooth lever platform escapement, the case in the form of an urn supported by a fluted column surrounded by the Three Graces, on a moulded bronze plinth, France, c1870, 29¼in (74cm) high.

£9,000–11,000
Sotheby's (Am)

A mystery timepiece, the movement with Brocot escapement, with gridiron-style pendulum, supported by a patinated-metal figure of a maiden, signed 'Auguste Moreau', France, late 19thC, 38¼in (97cm) high.

£2,750–3,250
Sotheby's (Am)

A figured marble gravity clock, by J. C. Vickery, London, supported by a mahogany frame with turned pillars, late 19thC, 15in (38cm) high.

£800–1,000 Holloway's

:old-painted bronze timepiece, in the form of a Moorish arch with a ıted maiden, the clock in the crest, movement by M. & Sohn, Karlstein, ck hands missing, late 19thC, Austria, Vienna, 16¾in (42.5cm) high.

,500–5,500 Skinner

An oak timepiece, in the form of a lighthouse, the four enamel dials each inscribed 'Hny Marc', the brass drum movement in the base, France, early 20thC, 15in (38cm) high.

£600–700 Sworders

SKELETON CLOCKS

skeleton clock, by A. B. Savory & Sons, ndon, with silvered chapter ring, the twin- in movement with chain fusees and ıeelwork with five crossings, the scroll frame four turned feet, on an ebonized base, with ȷlass dome, 19thC, 26in (66cm) high.

,000–4,500 Leigh Extence

A brass skeleton clock, by Parker & Pace, the gilded chapter ring with Breguet-style hands, the movement with bevelled-edge scroll asymmetric plates and individually cocked wheels and chain fusee, on a wooden base, dated 1840, 9¾in (25cm) high.

£1,800–2,000 D S Pullen

A skeleton clock, with silvered dial, the eight-day fusee movement with anchor escapement and wheelwork with five crossings including the hour wheel, with passing strike, on a mahogany base, with a glass dome, c1840, 14in (35.5cm) high.

£1,700–1,850 Leigh Extence

A brass skeleton clock, with silvered chapter ring, the movement with chain fusee, anchor escapement and passing strike on a bell at the hour, on a marble base, with a glass dome, mid-19thC, 18¼in (46cm) high.

£1,100–1,300 Sotheby's (Am)

A brass skeleton clock, with silvered brass dial, the movement with deadbeat escapement and striking the hours on a gong and half-hours on a bell, the marble and rosewood base with presentation plaque, c1850, 22½in (57cm) high.

£5,400–6,000
Derek Roberts Antiques

A Victorian skeleton timepiece, with silve dial, the eight-day movement with chain fus wheelwork with six crossings, adjustable 'beat' screw to pendulum and vase-style pillars, on a gilded-brass and ebonized bas with a glass dome, 13in (33cm) high.

£2,650–2,850 Leigh Extence

A brass skeleton timepiece, with enamel chapter ring and subsidiary dials for date and alarm, the movement with Brocot escapement, alarm striking on a bell, with a glass dome, dome damaged, France, c1850, 8¾in (22cm) high.

£1,250–1,500 Sotheby's (Am)

A skeleton clock, by Smiths, London, the twin-train fusee movement striking the hours and quarter-hours on two bells, on a later rosewood base, 1850–1900, 19in (48.5cm) high.

£7,000–7,500
Country Lane Classics

A brass skeleton clock, by J. Smith & Sons, London, in the form of Lichfield Cathedral, Staffordshire, the movement striking the ho on a coil gong and quarter-hours on a bell, on a marble plinth, with a glass dome, c186 17in (43cm) high.

£4,500–5,000 Country Lane Classics

A triple-frame skeleton clock, by Evans, Handsworth, the fretwork chapter ring with enamel plaques for the numerals, the movement with seven pillars and anchor escapement striking the hours on a bell, on a rosewood base with bun feet, with a glass dome, c1865, 21in (53.5cm) high.

£6,000–7,000
Derek Roberts Antiques

MARKET INFORMATION CLOCKS

- Early longcase and bracket clocks by well known makers such as the Knibb family, Thomas Tompion, Ahasuerus Fromanteel and Daniel Delander are extremely popular at the moment.
- Large sums are also being paid for rare and unusual clocks, for instance singing birdcage clocks and top of the range mystery and skeleton clocks.
- Eighteenth- and nineteenth-century clocks by prestigious makers such as Mudge & Dutton and the Vulliamy family are currently fetching high prices.
- Longcase and bracket clocks of small proportions are finding ready buyers, but bargains can be found in the more run-of-the-mill longcases.
- Provenance will invariably enhance the value of a clock. A Dent wall regulator once owned by Isambard Kingdom Brunel sold for a sum greatly in excess of the normal price for such a piece and a bracket clock by Vulliamy with a royal provenance that had later been bought back by the Vulliamy family sold in the US for over £100,000.

ENGLISH WALL CLOCKS

TO THE UNINITIATED, all English dial clocks are similar in appearance, whether they date from 1780 or 1890. However, the difference between the various types of these clocks is enormous and is reflected in their value. The one common feature of all of these clocks is that they used high quality English fusee movements which, certainly in the early striking examples, were almost identical to the movements that would have been used in English bracket clocks. They are fine timekeepers and, being relatively small, fit in well with modern houses and furnishing styles.

Not suprisingly, it is the earlier clocks that command the highest prices. These will almost always have either a silvered-brass dial or a painted wooden dial. They often have verge escapements, although some of the slightly later ones will have anchor escapements. If these clocks are by a well-known maker and also aesthetically attractive, their value is greatly enhanced. Two such clocks, both with silvered dials, are shown on these pages. One is a large English dial clock by Mudge & Dutton (see page 159) who made few dial clocks, making this example extremely rare. The second is an attractive chisel-bottomed drop-dial clock by Vulliamy (shown below).

The other feature that makes a great difference to the price of a clock is the size of the dial and, therefore, an 8in (20.5cm) early dial clock such as that shown by Robert Henderson (see page 159) would again command a considerable premium over a m standard 11in or 12in (28cm or 30.5cm) version.

Later dial clocks were made with painted metal d and in this category it is usually the aesthetics of th clock that determines price. Therefore those with convex dials and glass and only a small wooden surround to the cast bezel will fetch the highest pri A number of painted metal dial clocks can also be found with small trunks below the dial. These are usually known as drop-dial clocks and very often h attractive brass inlay and visible pendulums, featur which also add to value.

Mention should also be made of school and stati clocks. As with other clocks discussed here, they ha fine quality English fusee movements but have spu brass rather than cast-brass bezels. They usually ha a large expanse of wood around the bezel which detracts from the aesthetic quality of the clock and they almost always have flat painted metal dials, o with fairly thick and unattractive hands. Examples better hands and a thinner wood surround to the b will command the highest prices in this category.

It should also be noted that examples of English clocks that strike will sell for a higher price than no striking timepieces.

Robert W

EXPERT'S EYE DIAL CLOCKS

This dial clock is by the eminent maker Justin Vulliamy and displays many fine features which can also be found on clocks by less prominent makers that will consequently have a lower value.

£12,000–14,000

Derek Roberts Antiques

Dealers and collectors will often describe a dial clock as 8in (20.5cm), 10in (25.5cm) or 12in (30.5cm). This relates purely to the diameter of the dial and not the outside of the case. This particular 12in brass dial is silvered and has engraved and black wax-filled numerals. It has good overall colour and no losses to the black wax. Unlike a painted dial, a silvered dial can have its surface finish refreshed by a competent restorer without affecting its commercial value.

The opening glazed bezel is made of cast brass and has a silvered sight ring. This is solid and quite heavy unlike the later spun-brass examples.

The clock has an elegant narrow wooden surround. Later examples tended to have wider wooden surrounds.

Well known and respected make are always in demand by the tra and private collectors alike and i turn attract large premiums.

Only the better and more prol makers tended to number the clocks. This one is numbered 1612 on the dial, the moveme and even the pendulum bob, indicating that all pieces are original to the clock.

These wall clocks are often described as dial clocks or, as in this example, drop-dial clocks, which refers to the trunk below t dial. The trunk is veneered with c piece of beautifully figured mahogany which flows right through to the chisel-shaped bas including the lower door.

on wall clock, the pewter dial outer five-minute marking, t centre and engraved pierced , hands, the weight-driven ; movement with verge pement and countwheel ng on a bell, the case with rass cresting, front pendulum weights missing, south Germany,)–25, 9in (23cm) high.

'50–4,500
heby's (Am)

isian stained oak ***tstaart,*** the painted dial with m disc and ship automaton to arch, the brass posted anchor vement with countwheel king the quarter-hours on two 5, alarm on a single bell, the d surmounted by a figure of is and two angels, Holland, 80, 43¼in (110cm) high.

,800–3,400
theby's (Am)

A black lacquered tavern clock, by John Conell, London, with painted dial, the case door decorated with two deer in a landscape, mid-18thC, 44in (112cm) high.

£12,500–15,000
Sworders

A softwood wall clock, by Robert Burfield, Arundel, with a silvered dial, the plated frame movement with alarm, the case stained to simulate oak, c1780, 19½in (49.5cm) high.

£3,850–4,250
Clock-Work-Shop

A drop-dial wall clock, the movement with 'A' shape plates and anchor escapement, the silver dial ring with matching locking wooden bezel, the case with flame veneers, c1800, 23in (58.5cm) high.

£5,000–5,500
Clock-Work-Shop

A Frisian *stoelklok*, the painted dial with alarm disc and apertures for date and moonphase, the brass posted anchor movement with countwheel striking and alarm on a bell, Holland, c1760, 30¼in (77cm) high.

£2,800–3,200
Sworders

A mahogany wall clock, by Robert Henderson, London, the silvered dial with cut-out for false pendulum, the eight-day gut fusee movement with verge escapement and four pillars, c1790, dial 8in (20.5cm) diam.

£11,000–12,000
Derek Roberts Antiques

A mahogany wall clock, with wooden dial and brass hands, the Thwaites eight-day fusee movement with four pillars and striking the hours on a bell, movement stamped 'T. Thwaites 4243', 1808, 15½in (39.5cm) diam.

£7,000–8,000
Derek Roberts Antiques

A mahogany wall clock, by Mudge & Dutton, London, with silvered dial, the movement with five pillars and four-spoke wheelwork and gut fusee, the backplate with a counterweight for the minute hand, c1770, 31in (78.5cm) high.

£28,800–32,000
Derek Roberts Antiques

Thomas Mudge was born in 1715 and was apprenticed to and worked for George Graham. He started in business in Fleet Street after Graham's death in 1751. Mudge was one of the most eminent makers and invented the lever escapement in about 1757. He was particularly known for his high quality chronometers. He entered into partnership with William Dutton in 1755 which continued until 1790. Thomas Mudge moved to Plymouth in 1771, although it is thought that some of his clocks were still signed Mudge & Dutton, London after that date. Mudge & Dutton were particularly fine and sought-after makers and dial clocks by them are unusual. A clock of this size is particularly rare.

A black lacquer tavern clock, by James Calver, Diss, with a painted dials, the movement with stepped plates, the trunk door decorated in gilt and silver with birds, figures and trees, c1795, 55in (139.5cm) high.

£13,500–15,000
Derek Roberts Antiques

An unusual feature of this clock is that, to obtain the maximum fall of the weight, it is wound up through the seatboard towards the top of the case, where a pulley leads the line onto the barrel. James Calver was apprenticed to William Crisp of Wrentham in Suffolk in 1772 and died in 1809.

A Regency rosewood and brass-inlaid wall timepiece, with painted dial and eight-day fusee movement, 17in (43cm) wide.

£1,000–1,200
Hy Duke

A gilt-bronze striking wall clock, by Anders Lundberg, Stockholm, with enamel dial, surmounted by a helmet and crossed swords, flanked by dolphins, Sweden, 40¼in (102cm) high.

£1,750–2,200 Bukowskis

A Black Forest angelus wall clock, with painted dial, a ch in the arch with opening for a monk automaton, the anchor movement with countwheel striking on a gong, striking th angelus on two bells, Germar 1825–50, 17¼in (44cm) high

£2,300–2,750
Sotheby's (Am)

A Frisian stained oak *kantoortje*, the painted dial with alarm disc, the brass posted frame movement with anchor escapement, countwheel striking and alarm on a bell, with eight-day movement, the case surmounted by a giltwood figure of Atlas and two angels, Holland, 1825–50, 45in (114.5cm) high.

£800–1,000
Sotheby's (Am)

A satinwood-inlaid mahogany *Laterndluhr* wall clock, with enamel dial, the six-month movement with deadbeat escapement, Austria, c1830, 59in (150cm) high.

£26,000–30,000
Kembery Antique Clocks

A mahogany wall clock, by B. Russell, Norwich, with painted dial, the weight-driven movement with anchor escapement, striking the hours on a bell, c1830, 43in (109cm) high.

£2,700–3,000
Clock-Work-Shop

A mahogany timepiece, by Joseph Bramble, London, witl painted dial, the gut fusee movement with four pillars ar anchor escapement, with Thwaites & Reed label, proba for a repair, c1830, dial 12in (30.5cm) diam.

£3,850–4,250
Derek Roberts Antiques

A figured mahogany drop-dial wall clock, by W. H. Carter, Crawley, with painted dial, the eight-day day gut fusee movement with brass pendulum, c1840, 13in (33cm) high.

£2,800–3,200
Derek Roberts Antiques

A mahogany wall clock, by D. Blunt, Northampton, with painted dial, the eight-day fusee movement with four pillars and anchor escapement, c1840, dial 12in (30.5cm) diam.

£2,700–3,000 P A Oxley

A mahogany drop-dial wall timepiece, by J. Warry, Bristol, with painted dial, the eight-day fusee movement with anchor escapement, c1840, 19½in (49.5cm) high.

£2,000–2,250
Leigh Extence

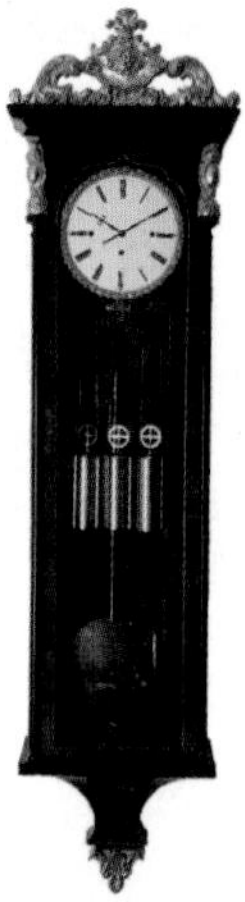

A Biedermeier rosewood *grar sonnerie* wall clock, with a ceramic dial, the movement wi strike/silent, deadbeat escapem and trip repeat striking the ho and quarter-hours on two gon the case with satinwood stringing and ebonized pillars with gilt capitals, surmounted by a gilt crest, Austria, c1840, 50in (127cm) high.

£11,000–12,500
Clock-Work-Shop

Gorringes
We don't just sell beautiful paintings for fabulous prices.
John William Godward oil painting sold for £500,000.
tary general service medal
- 1814, sold for £3,100.
A black Steiff teddy bear
sold for £23,000.
If you need to sell an individual piece worth from £50 to £500,000, a collection or an entire house contents, we have the experience and expertise to guide you through the auction process.
We hold select fine art and antique auctions every six weeks which are now linked worldwide to eBay live, and the largest weekly antique / general auctions in Southern England.
For an auction appraisal, probate or insurance valuations in Sussex, Kent, Surrey or London, telephone :
01273 472503
01903 238999
www.gorringes.co.uk email: clientservices@gorringes.co.uk
que crickets vase
or £4,600.
A signed
Francoise Linke
kingwood vitrine
sold for £12,000.
nton floor vase
for £7,000.
A 19th century hour
repeating bracket clock
sold for £10,000.
of Edwardian
nd bracelets
or £14,000.
Alice's Adventures in Wonderland,
first published edition, sold for £14,000.
An 18th century Danish gold
and enamel box sold for £16,000.
A Fifty Pounds Lloyds patriotic fund sword
and a Welsh presentation sword
sold for £44,000 and £23,000 respectively.

A mahogany wall clock, by S. Fehrenbach & Son, London, with painted dial, the eight-day fusee movement with anchor escapement, c1845, dial 12in (30.5cm) diam.

£2,400–2,750
P A Oxley

A mahogany wall timepiece, by C. C. Webb, London, with painted dial, the eight-day movement with chain fusee, c1850, 16¾in (42.5cm) diam.

£1,650–1,850
Leigh Extence
Charles Clark Webb is recorded as working in London from 1839 until 1881, having become free of the Clockmakers Company by redemption in 1847.

A mahogany night watchm clock, the silvered dial with ring inscribed 'Knights patent Register', the case with a d c1850, 17¾in (45cm) high.

£3,750–4,500
Sworders
This clock is a very rare exar of Patent No. 5494, 'Appar for ascertaining the attenda to duty of any watchman or other person...' taken out b Henry Knight in 1827. There other example recorded.

A carved mahogany wall timepiece, by B. L. Vulliamy, London, with silvered dial, the eight-day chain fusee movement with anchor escapement and Vulliamy-style steel rod pendulum, backplate signed 'Vulliamy, London No. 1904', dated 1851, dial 12in (30.5cm) diam.

£7,000–8,000
Derek Roberts Antiques
Vulliamy was clockmaker to Queen Victoria, and this piece is an exceptional example of his work.

A mahogany wall clock, by William Dutton, London, the silvered dial engraved with a crown and initial, the Thwaites & Reed movement with anchor escapement, dated 1854, dial 13¼in (33.5cm) diam.

£6,250–7,000
P A Oxley

A Black Forest carved musical wall clock, the brass movement with anchor escapement and countwheel striking on a gong, playing on eight wooden pipes connected to the hornblower automaton, Germany, 1850–75, 39in (99cm) high.

£3,250–3,750
Sotheby's (Am)

An ebonized Vienna regula with enamel two-piece dial, eight-day movement with dea escapement, maintaining pow adjustable beat regulation a striking the hours and half-h on a gong, the backplate ar movement stamped with ma trademark and '74832', the pediment with carved decor the case with turned finials canted corners, Germany, c1 50in (127cm) high.

£1,650–1,800
Leigh Extence

A Victorian mahogany drop-dial wall clock, by J. W. Benson, London, with a painted dial, the eight-day chain fusee movement with anchor escapement, backplate signed 'London 11351', 13in (33cm) high.

£2,600–2,850 **Leigh Extence**
J. W. Benson was a well-known clock and watchmaker who is recorded as working in the mid- to late Victorian period. The company made many high-class clocks and watches for retail, the railway companies and city workers. The script signature on the dial, which was Benson's trade-mark at the time, is unusual on a wall clock.

A mahogany drop-dial wall timepiece, by J. W. Benson, London, with painted dial, the eight-day chain fusee movement with anchor escapement, c1880, 19½in (49.5cm) high.

£1,500–1,650
Leigh Extence

ll timepiece, with a two-
enamel dial, the eight-day
ment with spring-driven
or escapement and mock
on pendulum, the case stained
semble walnut, Germany,
0, 17in (43cm) high.

,50–1,850 k-Work-Shop

A burr-walnut and ebonized wall clock, the enamel dial with subsidiary seconds dial, the twin-weight-driven movement with deadbeat escapement, Germany, c1890, 52½in (133.5cm) high.

£1,250–1,500 Tennants

A walnut wall clock, by Werner Uhrenfabrik, with a two-piece enamel dial, the eight-day twin-train movement striking on a melodious gong rod, Germany, c1890, 47in (119.5cm) high.

£250–300 R O Schmitt

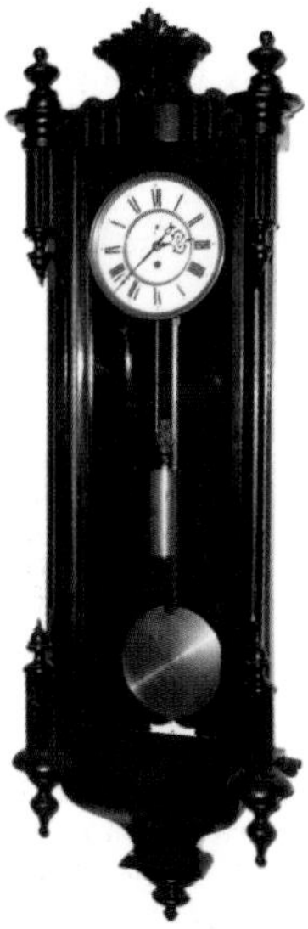

An ebonized walnut timepiece, by Gebr. Resch, the movement marked with retailer's name 'F. Kroeber, N. Y.' and No. 88222, four finials and top trim replaced, Austria, c1895, 45in (114.5cm) high.

£450–500 R O Schmitt

SSENTIAL REFERENCE VIENNESE WALL CLOCK STYLES

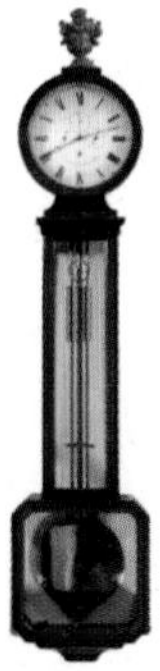

rly *Laterndluhr* (1790–1820)

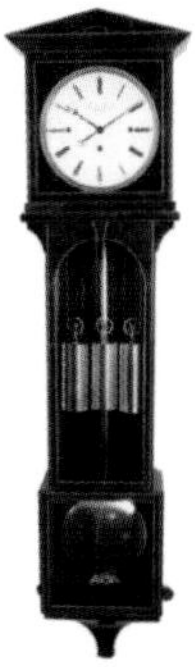

Fully-formed *Laterndluhr* (1820–50)

Dachluhr (1820–50)

Early Biedermeier (1840–60)

Late Biedermeier (1850–70)

German mass-production (1860–1900)

Viennese wall clocks were first produced from c1790. The early cases often had round tops and octagonal
toms. The case styles were very individual, although they eventually took on a more uniform appearance.
fully-formed *Laterndluhr* dates from c1820 onwards.

Laterndluhrs and *Dachluhrs* produced from 1820 to 1850 had edge stringing, usually in boxwood.

Laterndluhrs and some of the early *Dachluhrs* had lift-out rather than opening doors. The quality of cabinetwork
s superb. *Laterndluhrs* almost always have all inside edges veneered.

In addition to the more normal roof-top shapes, curved tops were occasionally fitted. They were all exceedingly
in and stylish.

In the early Biedermeier period, c1840–60, case embellishments, sometimes in gesso, and carved tops begin to
seen. Cases were still very elegant.

Dachluhrs and early Biedermeiers normally had six-light cases, ie six pieces of glass, two at the front and two at
her side.

Late Biedermeier cases had much more exuberant decoration and occasionally turned pillars. The quality of
ework was now not so good.

Very late Biedermeier and German mass-produced clocks had turned pillars and finials, two-piece dials and were
ally made from poorer quality woods.

AMERICAN CLOCKS

A pine tallcase clock, the painted dial with sweep seconds and calendar dials, with twin-train striking movement, the case stained to resemble mahogany, the hood with brass finials, New England, 1750–80, 85in (216cm) high.

£300–350
Northeast Auctions

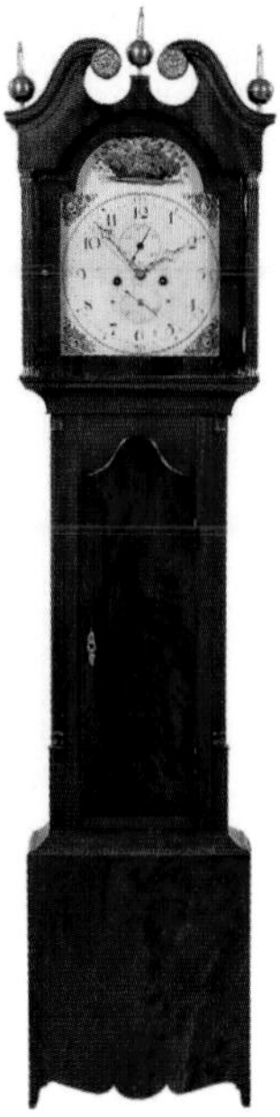

A mahogany tallcase clock, with a painted dial and eight-day striking movement, the hood with swan-neck pediment and brass finials, c1780, 79in (200.5cm) high.

£3,500–4,250
Northeast Auctions

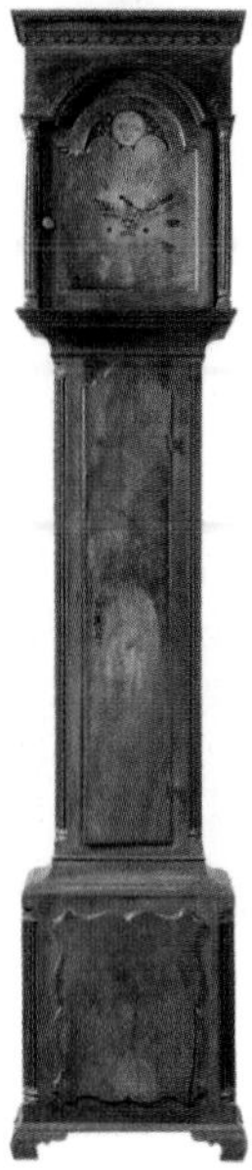

A walnut tallcase clock, by Richard Miller, the brass dial with moonphase, the hood with brass-capped fluted columns, 18thC, 95in (241.5cm) high.

£15,000–18,000
Northeast Auctions
Richard Miller (active 1710–20), worked in New York and Williamsburg, Virginia.

An inlaid mahogany tallcas clock, the painted dial with subsidiary seconds dial, caler dial and moonphase, with ei day twin-train striking mover the swan-neck pediment with star terminals, the hood with b capped columns, the case wit inlaid quarter columns, New Y or New Jersey, c1790, 88in (223.5cm) high.

£1,800–2,200
Northeast Auctions

A mahogany and *verre églomisé* shelf clock, by Aaron Willard, Boston, the case with reeded pediment, brass ball and eagle finial flanked by fretwork, the base with ebony stringing and brass ball feet, Massachusetts, c1800, 38in (96.5cm) high.

£22,000–27,000
Northeast Auctions

A pine tallcase clock, by Aaron Smith, Ipswich, the brass dial with silvered chapter ring and filigree ormolu spandrels, Massachusetts, 1797, 76in (193cm) high.

£5,500–6,500
Northeast Auctions
A card on the inside of the door states 'This clock was made by Aaron Smith, Ipswich, in 1797.'

A mahogany and crossbanded shelf clock, by Elnathan Taber, Roxbury, the enamel dial with gilt-painted cornucopiae, Massachusetts, c1805, 38in (96.5cm) high.

£3,750–4,500
Northeast Auctions
Elnathan Taber (1767–1854) was formerly an apprentice of Simon Willard, from whom he bought his business, tools and goodwill.

A cherry tallcase clock, by Jc Osgood, Haverhill, the dial w subsidiary seconds dial and calendar aperture, with eight weight-driven striking mover the hood with scrolled fretwc and brass ball finials, Massach 1810–15, 92in (233.5cm) hi

£6,300–7,500 **Skinner**

inted and *faux* rosewood
ned pine tallcase clock, by Riley
ing, Winchester, the dial with
ep minute hand and painted
Masonic symbols, with striking
ement, the case door with
ged decoration, Connecticut,
0, 84in (213.5cm) high.

500–5,500
theast Auctions

A mahogany and *verre églomisé* **banjo timepiece,** by Elnathan Taber, Roxbury, with painted iron dial and brass eight-day weight-driven movement, with a brass eagle finial, Massachusetts, c1820, 38in (96.5cm) high.

£2,800–3,200
Skinner

An inlaid mahogany **tallcase clock,** by S. Curtis, Boston, the painted dial with subsidiary seconds dial and date aperture, the hood with pierced fretwork and brass finials, the Roxbury case with stringing, inlaid crossbanded border and fluted quarter columns, early 19thC, 96in (244cm) high.

£17,000–20,000
Northeast Auctions

A giltwood and *verre églomisé* **banjo clock,** by Aaron Willard, Boston, with painted dial, the case with a grapevine above the figure of 'blind justice', the base depicting a sea battle, early 19thC, 33in (84cm) high.

£2,000–2,400
Northeast Auctions

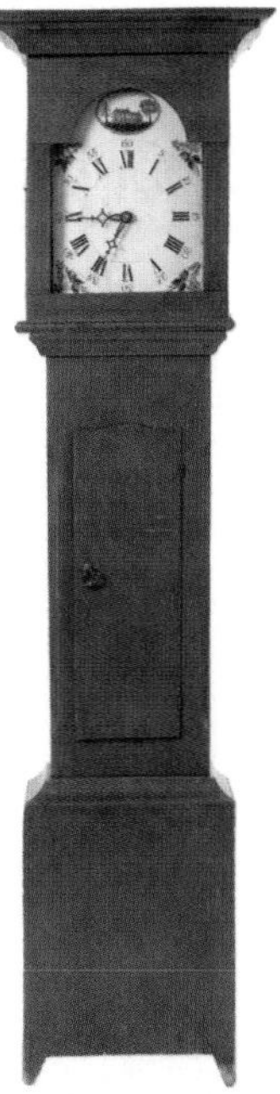

ainted pine tallcase clock,
a painted wood dial, early
hC, 80in (203cm) high.

300–4,000
rtheast Auctions

A grained and painted **tallcase clock,** by Riley Whiting, Winchester, with painted dial and wooden movement, the hood with swan-neck pediment, the trunk door stencilled with a floral bouquet, Connecticut, early 19thC, 71½in (181.5cm) high.

£3,750–4,500
Northeast Auctions

A carved mahogany and veneered **shelf clock,** with a gilt and painted wood dial and 30-hour wooden movement, with label 'Manufactured by Moses Barrett, Amherst, N.S.', on acanthus-carved hairy paw feet, c1825, 33½in (85cm) high.

£1,700–2,000
Skinner

A mahogany-veneered **shelf clock,** by Atkins & Porter, Bristol, with a painted metal dial and 30-hour weight-driven striking movement, with a glass Fenn tablet depicting curtains and flowers, Connecticut, c1845, 25in (63.5cm) high.

£100–120 R O Schmitt

The most notable creator of stencil designs for clock tablets was William B. Fenn of Plymouth, Connecticut (1813–90). Fenn worked for Seth Thomas between 1830 and 1840, then started his own business supplying these tablets to Connecticut clock manufacturers. Between 1840 and 1864 Fenn was a major supplier to makers such as Seth Thomas, Silas Hoadley, Brewster & Ingraham and Birge & Fuller.

MARKET INFORMATION THE AMERICAN MARKET

- American weight-driven wall clocks have proved to be a good investment, particularly those by E. Howard & Co Boston. No other category of clock has seen such appreciation in value.
- Regulators are another area where values are increasing. At a recent auction in New Hampshire, a Seth Thoma Connecticut, model No. 16 weight regulator sold for a record price of £21,000. In Mebane, North Carolina, a set five Figure Eight wall regulators by E. Howard & Co, Boston, sold for a combined price of approximately £550,00 setting a new world record around 50 per cent above previous highs.
- Weight-driven clocks from England and the Continent seem to have experienced a similar up-turn in price, bot in the US and Europe.
- Investment predictions for the future are: floor or wall clocks made for precision scientific use, such as for an observatory or laboratory and those made for main train stations, where, before the days of electronics, accurate time was essential to prevent collisions.

A rotary pendulum clock, by John C. Briggs, with painted dial and brass mechanism, on an ebonized base with iron claw feet, with a glass dome, mid-19thC, 6¼in (16cm) high.

£200–240 Sworders

A rosewood and mahogany-veneered shelf clock, by Brewster Manufacturing Co, with painted dial and eight-day striking movement, losses and slight damage, c1852, 19¾in (50cm) high.

£350–420 R O Schmitt

A grain-painted cottage timepiece, by H Sperry & Co, New York, with painted dial and 30-hour movement, c1855, 12in (30.5cm) high.

£450–550 R O Schmitt

A veneered shelf calendar clock, by Ithaca Calendar Clock Co, No. 5, with painted dials and eight-day striking movement, one dial papered over, slight damage, repaired, c1875, 22½in (57cm) high.

£270–320 R O Schmitt

A walnut 'Triumph' clock, by Ansonia Clock Co, with eight-day striking movement, movement restored, damaged, statues replaced, c1880, 24in (61cm) high.

£180–220
R O Schmitt

A rosewood and rosewood-veneered 'Gerster VP' mantel clock, by Welch, Spri & Co, with eight-day striking movement, hands replaced, case restored, pendulum replaced, c1880, 16½in (42cm) high.

£400–500 R O Schmitt

sewood-veneered 'Cabinet T' cottage piece, by Seth Thomas Clock Co, with a ted dial and eight-day movement, c1881, (23cm) high.

0–240 R O Schmitt

An enamelled iron 'Imogene' mantel clock, by Ansonia Clock Co, the porcelain dial with open escapement, with eight-day striking movement, gilding restored, pendulum replaced, c1885, 10½in (26.5cm) high.

£160–200 R O Schmitt

A brass-cased four-glass mantel timepiece, by Vermont Clock Co, Fairhaven, with porcelain dial, the eight-day movement with jewelled lever escapement, gilding worn, c1900, 9½in (24cm) high.

£230–270 R O Schmitt

SSENTIAL REFERENCE WEIGHT-DRIVEN WALL CLOCKS

eight-driven wall clocks are popular with collectors because they e both attractive and fascinating. Hung in a choice position they hance the room – whether a simple design in oak or a fancy rved model in walnut or cherry, the original artisan's work is splayed at eye level where it can be easily appreciated by the server. Furthermore, although all wall clocks have grown in pularity, weight-driven models seem to captivate the echanical instinct in many collectors. Nothing seems to bring ore joy than the act of placing the crank over the winding hole d turning it the 14 turns that are usually required to raise the eight from the bottom of the clock to its top position, ready to ave gravity alone power the clock for the coming week.

mahogany wall clock, by Ansonia Clock Co, with eight-day gong-striking ovement and two weights, the case with bronze mounts, losses, America, ew York, c1900, 46½in (118cm) high.

3,500–4,500 R O Schmitt

orcelain clock, by Waterbury ck Co, with enamel dial, ts missing, c1900, ⁄in (31cm) high.

00–270
leria L C Morton

A walnut 'Regulator A' school clock, by Ansonia Clock Co, with eight-day striking movement, c1906, 32in (81.5cm) high.

£220–260
R O Schmitt

An oak 'Clinton' drop-dial timepiece, by Sessions Clock Co, with eight-day movement, dial papered over, repaired, c1910, 27½in (70cm) high.

£155–185 R O Schmitt

A 'Progress No. 56' wall clock, by William L. Gilbert, No. 56, the case decorated with owls, damage and repair, c1910, 24½in (62cm) high.

£280–330 R O Schmitt

BRITISH REGULATORS

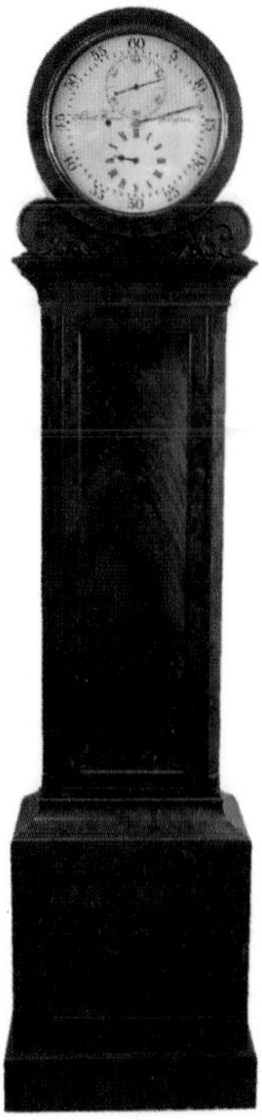

A figured mahogany longcase regulator, by Albert Winser, Brighton, with painted observatory dial, the eight-day five-pillar movement with deadbeat escapement and maintaining power, the trunk door glazed, c1820, 79½in (202cm) high.

£4,000–5,000
Sworders

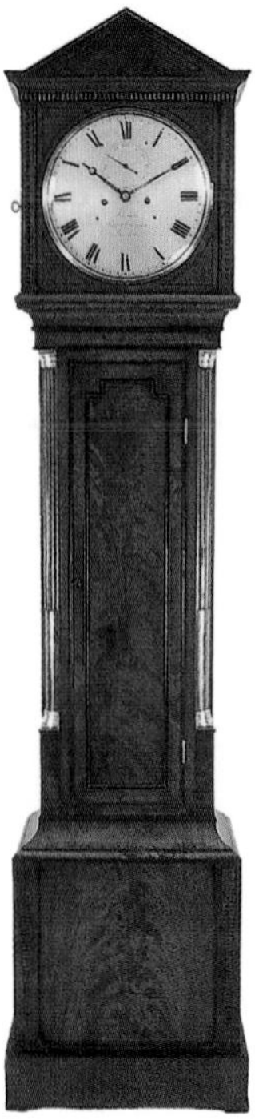

A mahogany-veneered longcase regulator, by Santiago James Moore French, London, the silvered dial with subsidiary seconds dial and strike/silent, the eight-day five-pillar movement with deadbeat escapement and wood rod pendulum with calibrated rating, striking the hours on a bell, c1820, 84in (213.5cm) high.

£15,000–18,000 P A Oxley

A figured mahogany longcase regulator, by Archibald Haswell, London, with silvered dial, the movement with Graham's deadbeat escapement and maintaining power, the wheelwork with six crossings, c1845, 74in (188cm) high.

£15,000–16,500
Derek Roberts Antiques

A mahogany longcase **regulator,** by G. Blackie, Lon
with painted 24-hour dial, th
eight-day four-pillar moveme
with Graham's deadbeat
escapement and maintaining
power, the wheelwork with fc
crossings, the trunk with a gl
door, c1845, 72in (183cm) hi

£16,000–18,500
Derek Roberts Antiques

George Blackie was born in 1
and died in 1885. He was an
escapement maker and made
chronometer escapements for
William Birch. He became
treasurer of the BHI in 1863 a
worked mostly from Amwell
Street in Clerkenwell, London

CONTINENTAL REGULATORS

An ormolu table regulator, by Jean-Joseph Lepaute, Paris, the enamel dial with lunar aperture, concentric calendar and centre seconds, the movement with pinwheel escapement, outside countwheel and striking on two bells, gridiron pendulum, knife edge and beat adjustment replaced, the case with egg-and-dart moulded cornice, fluted corners and bun feet, France, late 18thC, 15in (38cm) high.

£55,000–65,000 Sotheby's

Jean-Joseph Lepaute, the nephew of Pierre Basile Lepaute, was born in 1768 and worked with his uncle in Paris between 1798 and 1811. He then set up on his own at the Place de Palais Royale, calling himself Lepaute neveu à Paris.

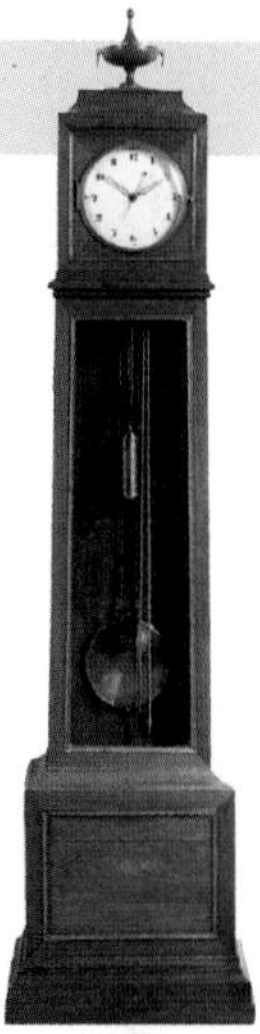

A mahogany longcase regulator timepiece, with enamel dial, the weight-driven movement with deadbeat escapement and gridiron pendulum, the case with brass line inlay and surmounted by an urn finial, France, c1790, 83in (211cm) high.

£4,000–5,000
Sotheby's (Am)

A gilded four-glass table regul
by Basile Charles Le Roy, Paris
with two-piece enamel dial, th
14-day movement with visible
coupe perdue escapement an
gridiron compensating pendul
striking the hours and half-ho
on a bell, backplate signed wi
maker's name, No. 7012 and
'Honoré Pons', France, c1840,
18in (45.5cm) high.

£6,000–6,500
Leigh Extence

3AROMETERS

TICK BAROMETERS

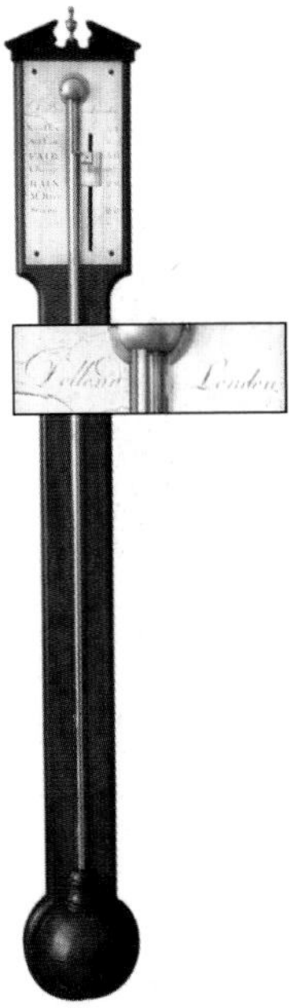

ıahogany stick barometer, Dollond, London, c1780, ı (94cm) high.

,000–3,500
an Walker ⊞

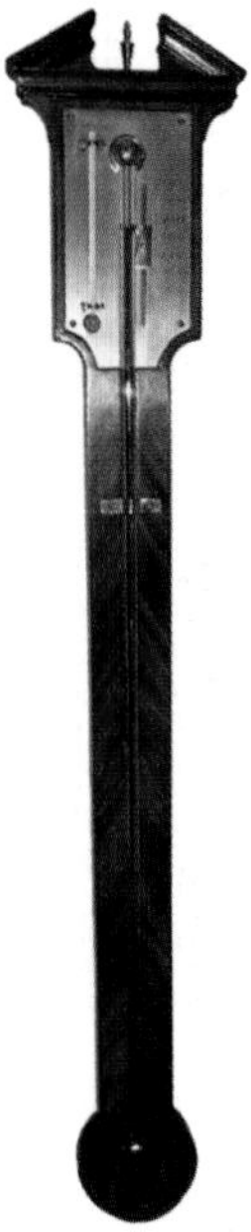

A mahogany stick barometer, by Simms, London, with silvered scale and manual vernier, c1785, 38in (96.5cm) high.

£1,500–1,750
Barometer Fair ⊞

The overhanging top pediment, extended lower part of the scale and maker are indicators of an early date.

A George III mahogany stick barometer, dial signed 'Dk. Gatty, Lewis', with silvered scale and thermometer, with ivory-mounted reservoir cover, 39in (99cm) high.

£800–950 Hy Duke

A mahogany stick barometer, by Manticha & Co, London, with chevron bands and breakarch pediment, signed, c1790, 37in (94cm) high.

£3,200–3,600 Alan Walker ⊞

mahogany stick barometer, by ward Nairne, London, c1790, in (99cm) high.

,250–4,750
& T Rayment ⊞

A mahogany stick barometer, by D. Torre, Glasgow, with triple stringing, the base with lily patera, signed, Scotland, c1800, 38in (96.5cm) high.

£2,800–3,200
Alan Walker ⊞

A mahogany stick barometer, by P. Caminada, c1810, 37in (94cm) high.

£3,000–3,300 Alan Walker ⊞

P. Caminada is recorded working in Taunton between 1810 and 1842.

A mahogany stick barometer, by Negretti & Co, Gloucester, c1820, 38in (96.5cm) high.

£2,250–2,500
D & T Rayment ⊞

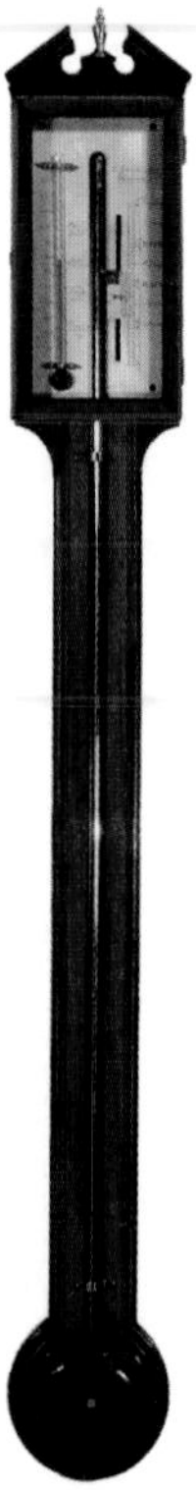

A mahogany stick barometer, by Charles Jacopi, Shrewsbury, the case inlaid with kingwood, ebony and boxwood stringing, repaired, 1820–30, 38¼in (97cm) high.

£2,000–2,400
Charles Edwin

An inlaid stick barometer, the silvered scale inscribed 'Chas. Aiano', early 19thC, 39in (99cm) high.

£600–700
Anderson & Garland

Charles Aiano is recorded working in Canterbury betwwen 1826 and 1841.

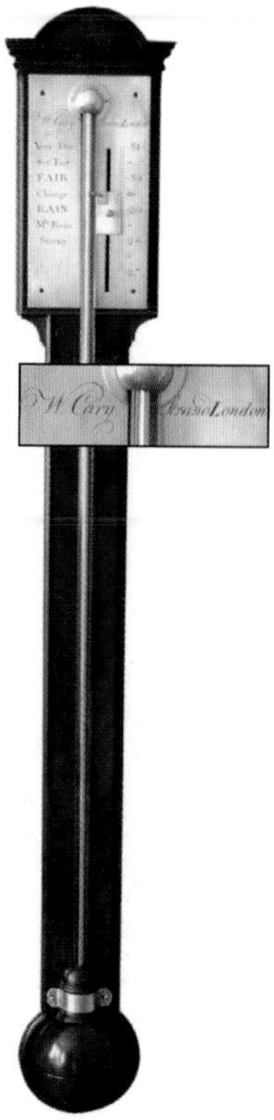

A mahogany stick barometer, by William Cary, London, with arched pediment, c1830, 37in (94cm) high.

£3,000–3,300
Alan Walker

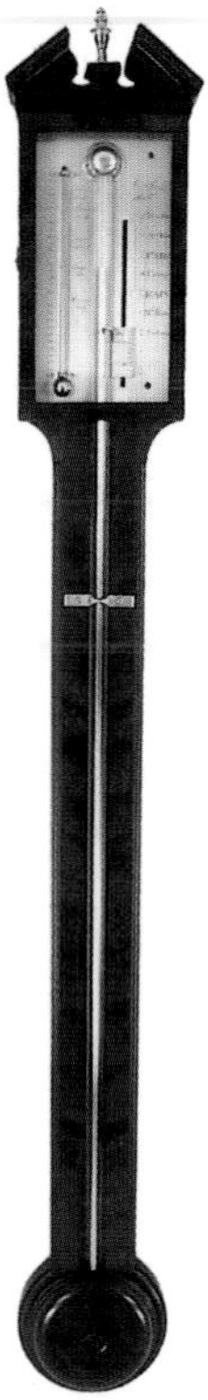

A mahogany stick barometer Northern, Hull, the silvered-br scale engraved with weather indicators, the case with herringbone veneers, c1830.

£2,700–3,000 **P A Oxley**

A mahogany sympiesometer, by Adie & Son, Edinburgh, dial signed, No. 1616, Scotland, c1850, 23in (58.5cm) high.

£3,800–4,200
Alan Walker

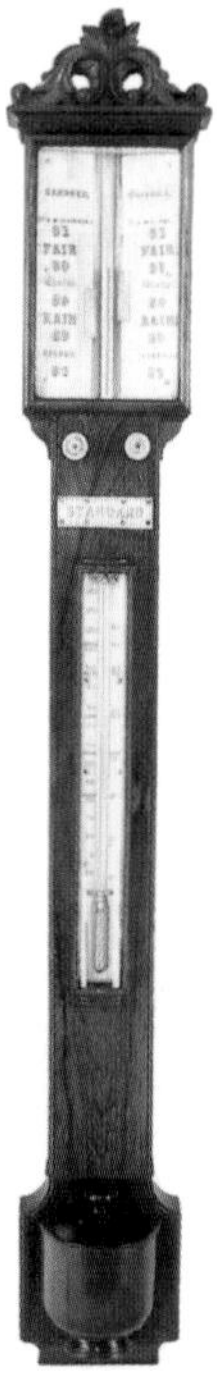

A rosewood stick barometer, by Gardner, Greenock, the double vernier with ivory setting keys, with a bone scale thermometer, Scotland, c1850, 38in (96.5cm) high.

£2,400–2,700 **P A Oxley**

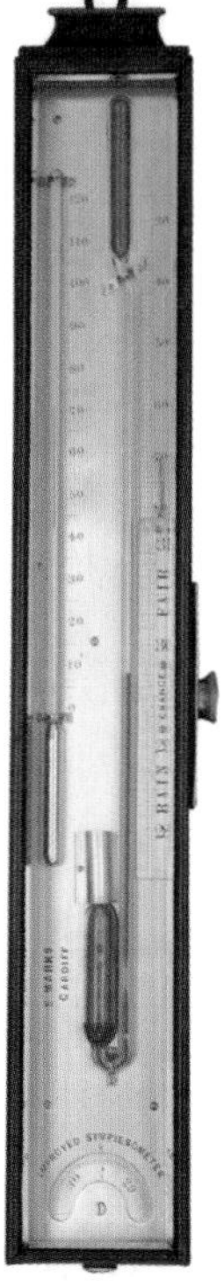

A mahogany sympiesometer, by Solomon Marks, Cardiff, Wales, c1850, 22in (56cm) high.

£2,200–2,600
Alan Walker

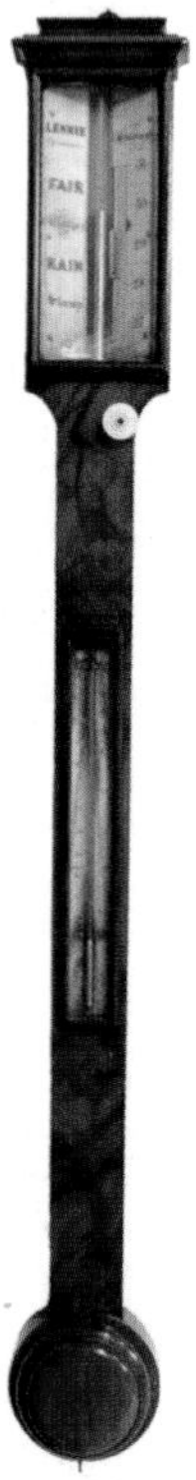

A Victorian walnut stick barome with thermometer, the ivory regis signed 'Lennie Optician, Edinbur with ivory handle, Scotland, c18 37¼in (94.5cm) high.

£850–1,000 **Andrew Hart**

ictorian mahogany ricultural' stick barometer, ı ivory dial, 34¼in (87cm) high.

00–600
olley & Wallis

A mahogany and brass Kew pattern barometer, by Negretti & Zambra, London, c1870, 44in (112cm) high.

£1,200–1,400
D & T Rayment

An oak stick barometer, by Baird, Glasgow, with cushion top, ivory register plates and twin verniers, mercury thermometer, Scotland, c1880, 37in (94cm) high.

£800–900
Barometer Fair

A walnut stick barometer, by E. Bevan, Birkenhead, with arched top, ivory register plates and twin verniers, mercury thermometer, c1870, 37in (94cm) high.

£1,200–1,300
Barometer Fair

DMIRAL FITZROY BAROMETERS

oak Admiral Fitzroy Royal ytechnic barometer, by ɘph Davis, London, c1880, n (109cm) high.

600–1,800 **Alan Walker**

An oak Admiral Fitzroy barometer, by Negretti & Zambra, London, c1880, 41in (104cm) high.

£2,200–2,600
Alan Walker

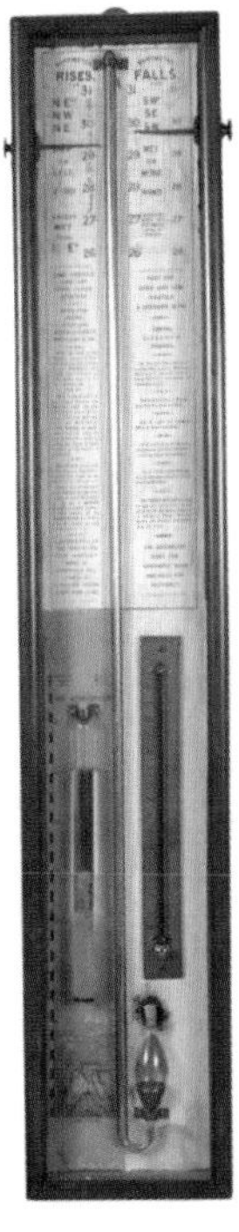

A mahogany Admiral Fitzroy barometer, c1880, 33in (84cm) high.

£650–750
D & T Rayment

An oak Admiral Fitzroy barometer, with original paper charts, c1880, 45in (114.5cm) high.

£1,600–1,750
D & T Rayment

WHEEL BAROMETERS

A mahogany wheel barometer, by Charles Somalvico, London, with engraved silver dial, hygrometer and thermometer, c1750, 39in (99cm) high.

£3,400–3,750 D & T Rayment

MILLER'S COMPARES

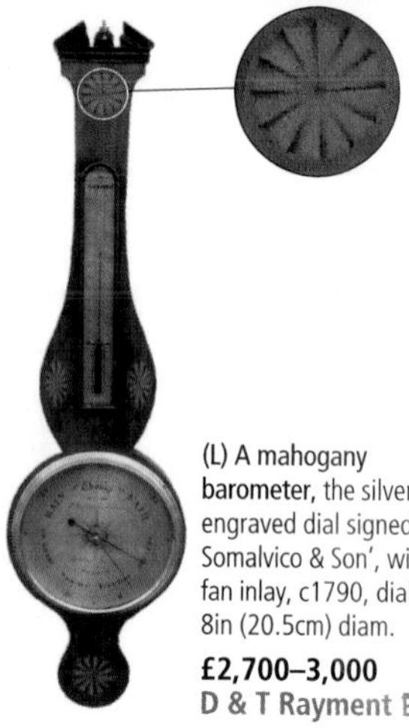

(L) A mahogany **barometer,** the silvered engraved dial signed 'J. Somalvico & Son', with fan inlay, c1790, dial 8in (20.5cm) diam.

£2,700–3,000
D & T Rayment

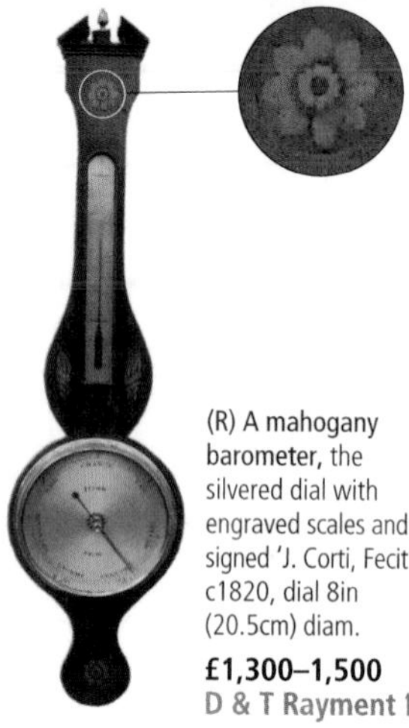

(R) A mahogany **barometer,** the silvered dial with engraved scales and signed 'J. Corti, Fecit' c1820, dial 8in (20.5cm) diam.

£1,300–1,500
D & T Rayment

Although similar in appearance to the item on the right, the barometer on the left is worth approximately twice as much. This is because in the 30 years between the dates of their manufacture, barometers became almost entirely mass produced and craftsmanship inevitably declined. This can be seen clearly when considering the quality of the inlay in the two pieces: th round inlays at the top and bottom of earlier examples tend to be larger ir diameter and are often fan inlays rather than flower or shell; additionally the oval inlays on the lower part of the thermometer box are usually sligh bigger and made up of larger sections. Another feature of the item on the lef is that the veneers are hand cut and laid horizontally rather than around the case, and it has a narrow shoulder at the top and a wider portion above th dial, which is more elegant. Finally, the engraving on the dial is far superic to that of the barometer on the right, and the brass bezel is fitted closer to th edge of the case, which further adds to its aesthetic appeal and higher value

An inlaid mahogany wheel **barometer,** by J. M. Ronketti, London, with engraved dial and thermometer, c1790, 37in (94cm) high.

£2,700–3,000
Alan Walker

A mahogany-veneered wheel **barometer,** by Joseph Teste, London, with engraved dial and thermometer, the case inlaid with chequer stringing, fan and shell paterae, signed, c1800, 36in (91.5cm) high.

£1,750–1,900
Barometer Fair

A mahogany and inlaid barometer, by P. Martinelli, Ronchetti & Co, Birmingham, with engraved and silvered dial and thermometer, c1810, 40in (101.5cm) high.

£2,700–3,000
D & T Rayment

A mahogany barometer, by W A. Barttelot, with engraved and silvered dial, signed and dated, 1815, 38in (96.5cm) high.

£1,700–1,850
D & T Rayment

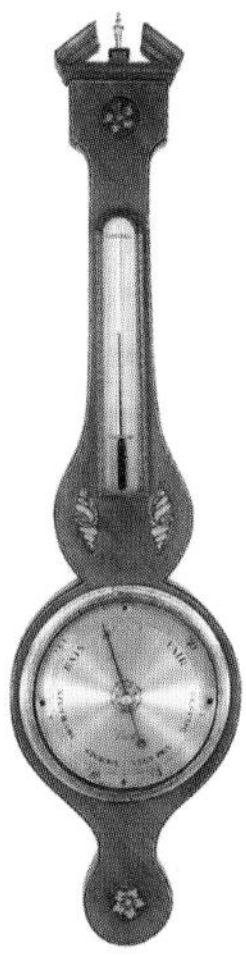

ahogany wheel barometer, erga, Bath, with silvered brass , the case with boxwood and y stringing and inlaid with s and flowers, c1815, 8in (20.5cm) diam.

400–1,600 P A Oxley

A mahogany wheel barometer, signed 'A. Salla, London', the case with chequered stringing and inlaid with shells and flowers, c1820, 38½in (98cm) high.

£650–750 Tennants

A mahogany barometer, by J. Urio, Bristol, with silvered dial and thermometer, the case with shell inlay, c1820, 38in (96.5cm) high.

£1,100–1,200
D & T Rayment

A mahogany barometer, by Mathew Woller, Birmingham, with silvered dial and thermometer, c1825, 47in (119.5cm) high.

£1,500–1,700
Essence of Time

SSENTIAL REFERENCE PEDIMENT STYLES

e most common pediment styles encountered on mercury barometers include:

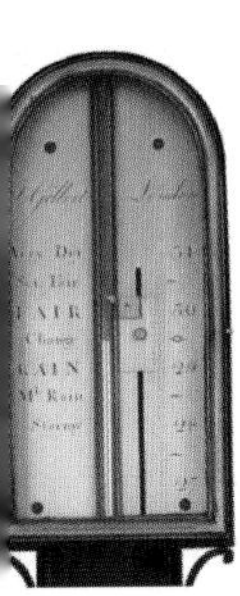

Round or Arched

Swan-neck

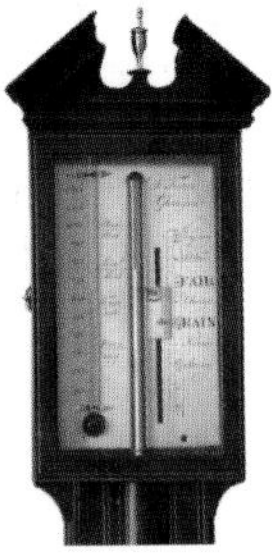

Break-arch or Architectural

Onion

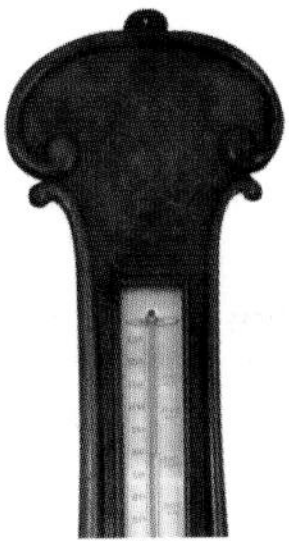

Scroll

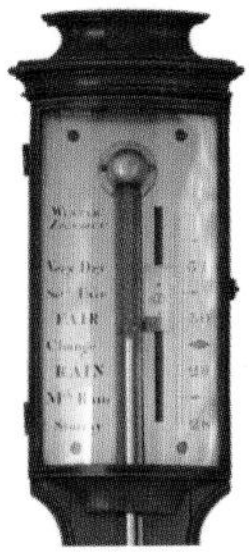

Caddy

nahogany wheel barometer, Agnew & Zanetti, Manchester, h silvered brass dial, hygrometer d thermometer, the case with nging and crossbanding, ivory al, c1830, 48in (122cm) high.

,000–3,500
rometer Fair

A mahogany wheel barometer, by Thomas Bolton, London, with silvered brass dial, hygrometer, mercury thermometer and spirit level, c1835, 39in (99cm) high.

£1,100–1,200
Barometer Fair

A mahogany-veneered wheel barometer, by L. Caminada, the top with a silvered humidor above a thermometer, the base with a spirit level, c1840, dial 8in (20.5cm) diam.

£350–420
Netherhampton Salerms

A mahogany barometer, with silvered dial, c1850, 39in (99cm) high.

£650–750
D & T Rayment

CONTINENTAL BAROMETERS

A pair of giltwood barometers, calibrated according to the Casati and Huyghens system, carved with rocailles and foliage and surmounted by a crown, France, dated 1750, 48½in (123cm) high.

£14,000–17,000
Sotheby's (P)

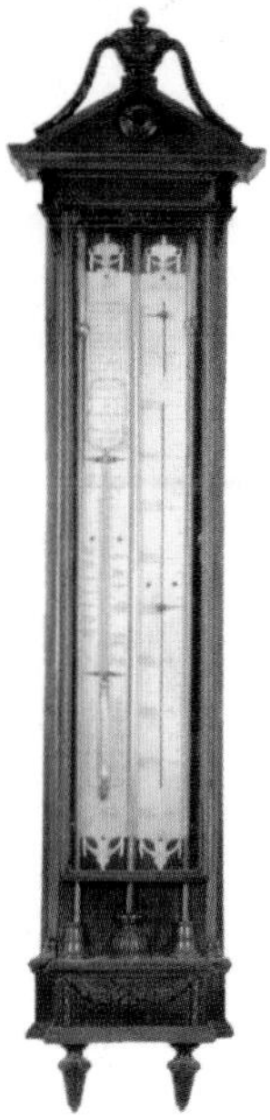

A mahogany barometer, the engraved silvered plates signed 'P. Wast en Zoonen Amsterdam', the pediment surmounted by an urn and carved garlands, above a glazed door flanked by quarter columns, Holland, 1775–1800, 49¾in (126.5cm) high.

£4,500–5,500
Sotheby's (Am)

A gilt wheel barometer, with painted dial, France, c1783, 43in (109cm) high.

£1,600–1,750
Barometer Fair

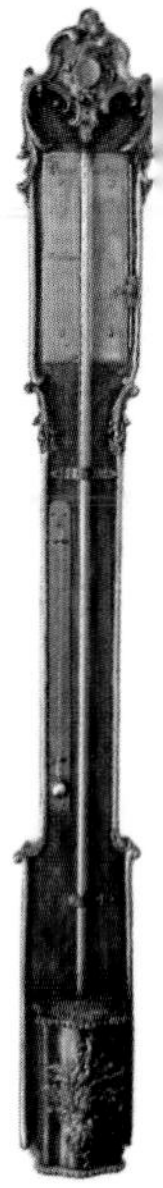

A parcel-gilt sti barometer, silve register and thermometer, register plate ma with initials 'R. D Austria, 1775–1 38½in (98cm) hi

£3,500–4,00
Charles Edwi

A carved giltwood barometer, by Godot, Paris, decorated with lovebirds and dolphins, signed, France, c1790, 39in (99cm) high.

£8,500–9,500
D & T Rayment

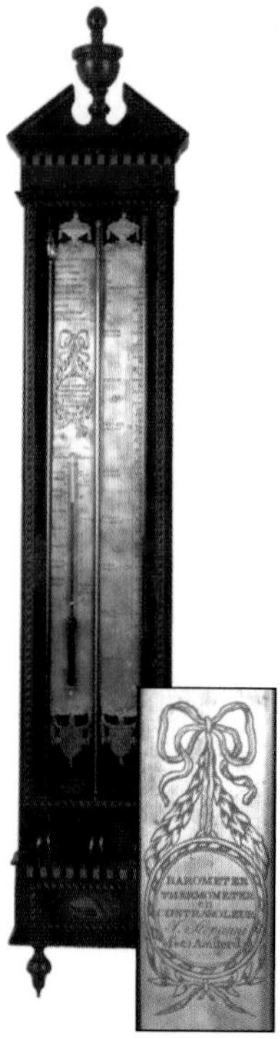

A mahogany barometer, by F. Stopanni, Amsterdam, with engraved pewter scales, signed, Holland, c1820, 49in (124.5cm) high.

£6,500–7,500
D & T Rayment

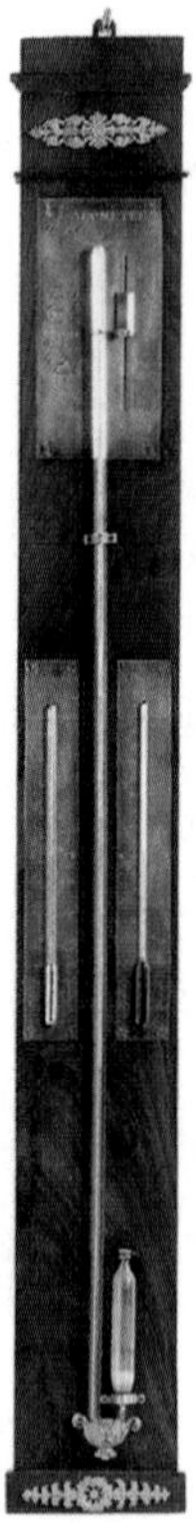

A mahogany stick barometer, the silvered plate with vernier, with ormolu mounts, signed 'Soleil Opticien du Roi', France, c1830, 43in (109cm) high.

£1,300–1,500
Sotheby's (Am)

A painted stick barometer, by A. Goubeaux, Paris, signed, France, c1 37in (94cm) high.

£1,100–1,200
D & T Raymen

ANEROID BAROMETERS

A pocket aneroid barometer/ altimeter, by J. Hicks, London, with thermometer on dial, c1880, dial 2in (5cm) diam.

£300–350 D & T Rayment

A gilt-brass travelling aneroid barometer, the two hinged doors fitted with mercury thermometer and compass set, inscribed 'A. & N. C. S. Ltd, Westminster', late 19thC, 3½in (9cm) high.

£300–350 Toovey's

An ivory double-sided pocket barometer, by Dollond, No. 5636, with opposing thermometer and compass on calibrated ground, in fitted leather case, early 20thC, dial 2in (5cm) diam.

£350–420 Gorringes (L)

A carved oak chrono-aneroid barometer, by H. Hughes & Son, Liverpool, the silvered dial with clock and two thermometers, c1910, 9in (23cm) diam.

£1,800–2,000 Richard Twort

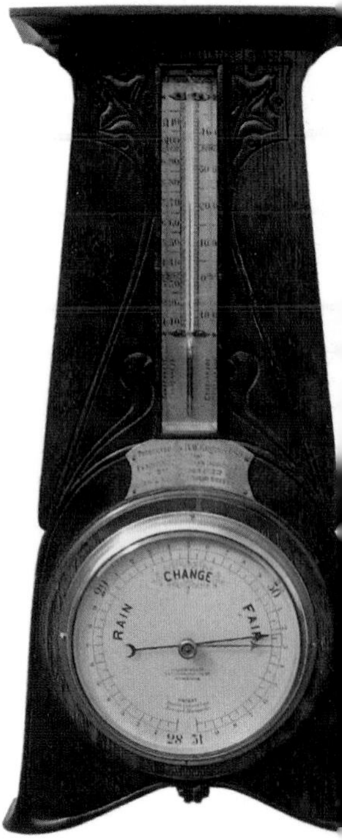

An oak aneroid barometer, c1920, 24in (61cm) high.

£600–650
D & T Rayment

BAROGRAPHS

A mahogany barograph, by Richard Frères, Paris, France, late 19thC, 11in (28cm) high.

£350–400 Richard Twort

A mahogany wall barograph, by J. Hicks, London, c1880, 10in (25.5cm) high.

£1,200–1,400 Richard Twort

A carved mahogany barograph, by Short & Mason, London, c1910, 16in (40.5cm) wid

£1,800–2,200 Alan Walker

A mahogany barograph, by Short & Mason, London, with chart drawer, early 20thC, 14½in (37cm) wide.

£500–600 Andrew Hartley

A mahogany barograph, by Kelvin, White & Hutton, London, with ancillary dial, c1915, 15in (38cm) wide.

£1,500–1,700 Alan Walker

An oak barograph, by Sharman D. Neil, Belfast, with supplementary dial, c1925, 14½in (37cm) wide.

£1,800–2,000 Richard Twort

WATCHES

OCKET WATCHES

ilver pair-cased verge pocket tch, by D. Threlkeld, Newcastle, '00, 2¼in (5.5cm) diam.

,000–1,100
vorders

A gilt-metal verge 'Oignon' pocket watch, by Piquet, Rennes, with gilt fusee movement and verge escapement, slight damage and losses, France, c1700, 2¼in (5.5cm) diam.

£1,100–1,300 Tennants

A horn verge pocket watch, by Jean Deonna, Geneva, with sun and moon silver *champlevé* dial and fusee movement, case associated, Switzerland, c1715, 2¼in (5.5cm) diam.

£1,500–1,800 Sworders

A gold pair-cased pocket watch, by Claud Viet, London, with enamel dial, fusee movement signed, the case decorated with a scene depicting Diana and an attendant, 1727, 2in (5cm) diam.

£2,500–3,000 Sotheby's

ilver pair-cased verge pocket tch, by Thomas Moore, Ipswich, h enamel dial, fusee and chain vement with worm and wheel rrel, signed, case with maker's ırk 'HT', marked London 1756, ı (5cm) diam.

50–950
eces of Time

A silver pair-cased verge pocket watch, by John Rayment, Huntingdon, with enamel dial, marked London 1762.

£300–350
Lawrence Fine Art

An 18ct gold pair-cased pocket watch, by Justin Vulliamy, with enamel dial and full-plate movement, cylinder escapement, case with maker's mark and London 1764, 2in (5cm) diam, with Vulliamy perpetual calendar watch paper.

£1,800–2,200
Sotheby's

A 22ct gold pair-cased pocket watch, by Nicholas Daventry, the dial with engine-turned decoration, fusee lever movement with Harrison's maintaining power and Bosley regulator, marked London 1766, 2in (5cm) diam.

£1,200–1,350
Pieces of Time

jilt-metal and leather pair-cased rge pocket watch, by George ɔr, London, the enamel dial with kish numerals, fusee and chain ɔvement with worm and wheel rrel, signed, restored, leather ver later, c1780, 2¼in (5.5cm) diam.

,000–2,250
eces of Time

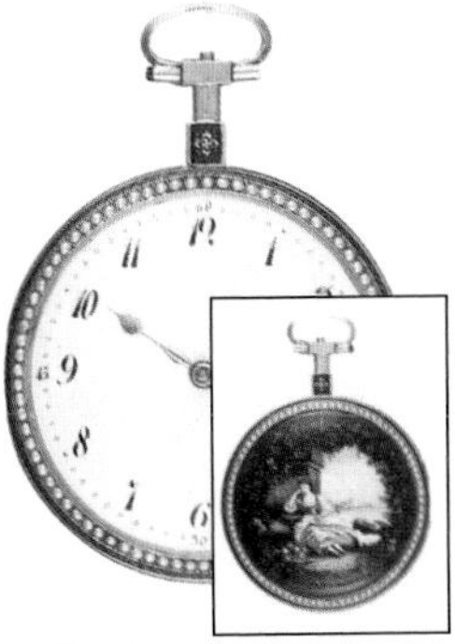

A gold and enamel verge pocket watch, with enamel dial and gilt-fusee movement, the case set with pearls, the enamel back decorated with a shepherdess, restored, Switzerland, c1790, 2in (5cm) diam.

£4,000–4,500
Pieces of Time

A tortoiseshell pair-cased verge pocket watch, by Thomas Hebard, London, with enamel dial and fusee movement, c1800, 2in (5cm) diam.

£630–700
Pieces of Time

A gilt verge automaton pocket watch, the enamel ring dial surrounded by chased and engraved classical figures with moving arms, the fusee movement quarter-repeating on two gongs, Switzerland, c1810, 2¼in (5.5cm) diam.

£3,000–3,500
Pieces of Time

An 18ct gold pair-cased pocket watch, by Lamb & Webb, London, the enamel dial with subsidiary dial, movement No. 41132, the cock engraved with Masonic motifs, dated 1820.

£1,100–1,300 Sworders

A silver niello hunter pocket watch, with enamel dial and lever movement, with gold Russian inscription, 19thC, 2in (5cm) diam.

£350–400
Worcester Antiques

An 18ct gold pocket watch, by Rentzsch, London, the gold dial with subsidiary seconds, with fusee movement, the case engraved with a coat-of-arms and inscription, marked 1819, 2¼in (5.5cm) diam.

£3,500–4,250 Sotheby's

An 18ct gold cylinder pocket w by Bautte & Moynier, Geneva, engine-turned gold dial, keywi movement quarter repeating c two gongs, Switzerland, c182 1¾in (4.5cm) diam.

£700–800 Pieces of Time

An 18ct gold fusee cylinder pocket watch, by John Taylor, London, with guilloche dial, fire-gilt full-plate movement, London 1825, 1¾in (4.5cm) diam.

£1,000–1,200
Fossack & Furkle

An 18ct gold cylinder pocket watch, by Robert Whatley, London, the two-tone gold dial with brass detachable dustcover, marked London 1828, 1¾in (4.5cm) diam.

£1,250–1,350
Fossack & Furkle

An 18ct gold pocket watch, by Patek Philippe, the enamel dial with subsidiary seconds, keyless movement with bi-metallic compensation balance, signed, Switzerland, c1855, 1¾in (4.5cm) diam.

£1,500–1,800 Sotheby's

An 18ct gold pocket watch, with enamel dial and keyless movement, London 1885, 1½in (4cm) diam.

£250–300
Pieces of Time

An 18ct gold pocket chronometer, by L. W. Zimmerman, three-quarter plate fire-gilt movement with Earnshaws spring detent escapement, London 1897, 2in (5cm) diam.

£4,500–5,000 Fossack & Furkle

A 9ct gold hunter pocket watch, by Waltha Watch Co, the enamel dial with subsidiary seconds and keyless movement, America, marked Chester 1922, 2in (5cm) diam.

£750–850 Pieces of Time

VRISTWATCHES

artier diamond
stwatch, signed,
30s, with inscribed
d case.

,500–3,000
theby's

A Hanhart chromed-brass button chronograph **wristwatch,** the dial with luminous numerals and hands, subsidiary dials for seconds and 30 minutes, signed, Germany, c1940.

£1,200–1,500 Sotheby's

The Hanhart factory, founded in 1882, produced high-quality pilots' watches during WWII. Production ceased after the war but in 1997 they began to make limited edition models of their original pilots' chronograph.

An International Watch Co steel **automatic wristwatch,** Switzerland, c1950.

£800–900 Tempus

An International Watch Co stainless steel Mark XI military **wristwatch,** signed, Switzerland, c1952.

£2,200–2,500
Pieces of Time

International Watch Co 9ct gold wristwatch,
itzerland, c1950.

00–1,000 Tempus

A Longines stainless steel Lindbergh aviator's **wristwatch,** with silvered dial, bezel calibrated for 150 degrees, signed, Switzerland, c1947, with original leather strap with silver buckle.

£3,000–3,500 Sotheby's (Am)

A Longines 9ct gold **wristwatch,** with seconds dial, Switzerland, c1930.

£1,100–1,200 Tempus

Longines **wristwatch,** with
conds dial and five-piece
rmetic clip-on case back,
vitzerland, c1943.

1,800–2,000
empus

A Movado stainless steel **wristwatch,** with lever movement, signed, Switzerland, c1945.

£550–600 Tennants

A Nivada Grenchen Antarctic V steel **wristwatch,** Switzerland, c1940s.

£450–500 Harpers

An Omega stainless steel calendar **wristwatch,** the silvered dial with apertures for day, month and moonphase, subsidiary seconds, signed, Switzerland, c1945.

£1,800–2,200 Sotheby's

An Omega steel wristwatch, with subsidiary seconds, case and movement signed, Switzerland, c1945.

£500–550
Anthony Green Antiques

A Rolex silver Prince chronometer wristwatch, the signed movement with protective cap, signed Rolex hairspring, the case with Swiss control mark, British import marks, signed 'RWC Ltd', c1930.

£2,800–3,200
Anthony Green Antiques

A Rolex 9ct gold cushion-shaped Oyster wristwatch, dial, movement, winder and c signed, case with international patents and British import marks, c1933.

£2,200–2,500
Anthony Green Antiques

A Rolex Prince 18ct gold duo-dial wristwatch, two-tone silvered dial with subsidiary seconds, signed, Switzerland, c1950.

£4,750–5,500 **Sotheby's**

A Vacheron & Constantin 18ct gold bracelet watch, with two-tone copper dial, signed, Switzerland, c1935.

£2,400–2,800
Sotheby's

A Vacheron & Constantin 18ct gold wristwatch, the di with gold hands and subsidiary seconds, signed, Switzerland, 1950s.

£1,100–1,300
Greenslade Taylor Hunt

A Vertex diamond wristwatch, with silvered dial, case stamped with maker's name and numbered 520/7032, with a fitted case by Collingwood & Son Ltd, Darlington, c1930.

£1,000–1,200 **Tennants**

An 18ct gold and enamel wristwatch, with gilt dial and lever movement, with import marks for London 1911, on a three-colour gold mesh link bracelet, with case.

£380–420 **Toovey's**

A diamond cocktail watch, 1920s, 7in (18cm) long.

£4,500–5,000
Sotheby's

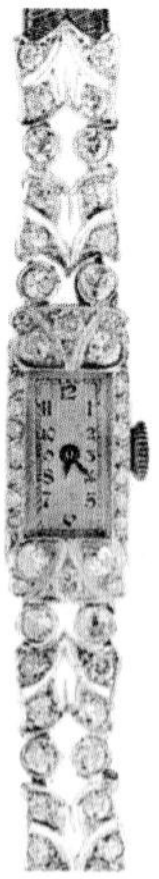

A platinum and 18ct gold wristwatch, set with diamonds, 1930s.

£500–550
Bukowskis

A platinum cockta wristwatch, set wi diamonds, c1935.

£650–720
Anthony Green Antiques

?OTTERY

?NGLISH DELFTWARE

D ELFTWARE IS A TYPE of tin-glazed earthenware, known as maiolica in Italy and faïence in France. It was first developed in the 9th century in Iraq ı spread to Spain and Italy in the Middle Ages. In the h century Italian potters introduced the technique to ıce and also to Antwerp in Belgium. From there it de its way to Holland, England and north Germany. ngland it was known as galleyware, a term used il well into the 18th century, when it became wn as delftware, reflecting the fact that by then Dutch town of Delft had become the most ortant centre of production in Europe.

lanufacture of tin-glazed earthenware in England jan with the arrival in 1567 of two Flemish potters, o set up potteries in Norwich and London. Another ortant factory was set up in Southwark c1618 by a tchman but it was not until after the Restoration in 50 that the number of potteries increased. London ters moved to Brislington in Avon and then to stol and in the 18th century delftware potteries ead to Liverpool, Glasgow, Dublin and Belfast – all ts with access to raw materials.

he influence of Chinese porcelain can be plainly n in 18th-century English delftware. Other forms of decoration include European landscapes, biblical subjects, inscribed and commemorative pieces. Although nearly all surviving delftware is decorated, most utilitarian wares were plain white. Among sought-after items are blue-dash chargers, produced at London and Bristol from c1650 to1740. Decorated with distinctive blue dashes around the rim, these large dishes depicted contemporary heroes, particularly Royalty, and biblical subjects. A feature peculiar to English delft was the introduction of *bianco-sopra-bianco*, which consisted of a border pattern of flowers, pine cones and scrollwork being painted in white enamel on a slightly bluish-tinged glaze. Another distinctive type of decoration is the so-called Fazackerley palette; primarily associated with Liverpool from c1750 the colours include sage-green, manganese, pale blue, yellow and red.

The fashion for delftware in the British Isles lasted until the 1770s when it was superseded by creamware which was cheap to make, far more durable and could be stamped, moulded and pierced, lending itself to mass-production. By the end of the 18th century the manufacture of delftware in Britain had virtually ceased.

Phil Howell

ondon delft blue-dash charger, c1680, n (30.5cm) diam.
,500–5,000 Erna Hiscock

A Bristol delft blue-dash charger, decorated with Adam and Eve, c1700, 13½in (34.5cm) diam.
£2,250–2,750 Skinner

A Vauxhall delft pottery plate, painted with flowers, c1720, 6in (15cm) diam.
£300–350 Moxhams

lelft charger, Bristol or London, with decoration underside, c1730, 14in (35.5cm) diam.
00–1,000 Moxhams

A Bristol delft dish, c1730, 13in (33cm) diam.
£850–950 Moxhams

A Bristol delft pottery dish, decorated with sparring cockerels, c1730, 13in (33cm) diam.
£850–950 Moxhams

A delft plate, probably Bristol, painted with a cockerel among sponged trees, c1730, 8¾in (22cm) diam.

£3,200–3,800 Sotheby's (O)

A Bristol delft plate, decorated with mimosa, c1740, 9in (23cm) diam.

£225–250 Offa's Dyke

A delft plate, painted with ducks and a peony, with initials 'B. I. I.' slight damage, dated 1745, 8½in (21.5cm) diam.

£950–1,150 Sworders

Documentary pieces, ie with dates and ini invariably sell for a premium.

A Lambeth delft charger, decorated with a Chinese man within a floral and foliate border, mid-18thC, 13¼in (33.5cm) diam.

£500–600 Skinner

A delft plate, painted with flowers, 18thC, 10½in (26.5cm) diam.

£180–200 Guest & Gray

A delft plate, decorated with peonies issu from urns, c1750, 8½in (21.5cm) diam.

£100–120 Guest & Gray

ESSENTIAL REFERENCE ENGLISH DELFTWARES

The function of some delftwares is not immediately apparent from the shape, as shown by the following examples

Apothecary jar: two principal shapes contained wet (shown on left) or dry drugs.

Flower brick: a small brick-like holder with holes in the top for cut flowers.

Posset pot: a two-handled pot used for alcoholic gruel or porridge from the mid-17th century to the mid-18th century. The liquid was drunk from the spout.

Plate: some of the most sought-after delft subjects include the 'farmyard' series of plates decorated with birds and animals. The polychrome versions are more valuable than the blue and white.

- Delft is tin-glazed earthenware; it originated in Iraq in the 9th century.
- Tin-glazed earthenware was also made in England using similar techniques to those employed by the Dutch and is referred to as English delft or delftware.
- London was the most important early centre of production for English delft but after c1660 centres were established in Bristol, Brislington, Liverpool, Glasgow and Dublin.
- The glaze on English delft is smoother than that of Dutch Delft and chips more easily. However, despite damage, early pieces still command high prices as they are so rare.
- After about 1720 English delft became more distinctive. A wide variety of wares was produced and can be decorated with British landscapes, figures, flowers or birds. Chinoiserie themes also featured.
- The end of 18th century saw a rise in popularity of creamware, and production of English delft virtually ceased as a result.

Puzzle jug: the challenge is to drink from the jug without spilling the liquid through the numerous holes. This is possible by means of a hidden tube which runs from the spout, round the rim and down the handle into the base of the vessel.

Pill slab: used (despite the name) as pharmacy window displays. Usually decorated in blue with a coat-of-arms belonging to the Worshipful Society of Apothecaries.

ndon delft plate, decorated with two
ese men, c1750, 9in (23cm) diam.
00–1,100 Roger de Ville

A London delft plate, painted with panels of flower sprays and bamboo on a manganese ground, slight damage, mid-18thC, 8¾in (22cm) diam.
£400–500 Dreweatt Neate (N)

A Liverpool delft dish, decorated with a seated man, c1760, 12in (30.5cm) diam.
£270–300 Moxhams

r of London delft plates, decorated with birds and flowering
s, c1760, 9in (23cm) diam.
5–600 Moxhams

A delft pottery plate, decorated with a bird and flowers, c1760, 9in (23cm) diam.
£150–180 Dee, Atkinson & Harrison

lft soup plate, decorated with two Oriental ladies in a garden with
er and a bird, the rim with fences and flowers, slight damage,
0, 8¼in (21cm) diam.
0–180 Guest & Gray

A delft bowl, probably London, c1770, 9in (23cm) diam.
£270–300 M V S Antiques

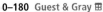

lft pottery plate, decorated with a floral pattern,
70, 9in (23cm) diam.
0–350 Moxhams

A pair of London delft plates, decorated with hot air balloons above buildings, within a border of flower swags, slight damage, c1785, 9in (23cm) diam.
£1,500–1,800 Sotheby's (O)
These plates probably commemorate an ascent by Vincent Lunardi in the London area in September 1784.

A pair of Liverpool delft flower bricks, painted with flower sprays in the Fazackerley palette, 18thC, 6in (15cm) wide.

£3,750–4,500 Hy Duke

The Fazackerley palette is associated with Liverpool delftware from the 1750s. The colours used were predominantly manganese, sage-green, blue, yellow and red. The name derives from a pair of Liverpool delftware mugs dedicated to a Thomas and Catherine Fazackerley and painted in this distinctive bright palette. Similar colours are less often seen on Bristol delftware, often in combination with bianco-sopra-bianco *borders.*

A delft posset pot and cover, probably Bristol, painted with Oriental figures at various pursuits, the handles applied with serpents, slight damage, c1700–15, 8¾in (33cm) high

£35,000–40,000 Sotheby's (NY)

This piece is rare because of its early date, polychrome decoration and very unusual handles. Moreover, it is painted with figures rather than the more usual birds or flowers.

A Liverpool delft puzzle jug, inscribed w a verse flanked by floral sprays, the neck pierced with hearts and ovals, c1765, 6¾in (17cm) high.

£1,500–1,800 Northeast Auction

A pair of delft shoes, London or Bristol, painted with flowers and initials 'W. I. M', dated 1729, 5½in (14cm) long.

£6,000–7,000 Gorringes (L)

A delft tile, depicting a shepherdess, c17 5in (12.5cm) wide.

£130–150 Moxhams

A Liverpool delft tile, decorated with Chinese figures, c1750, 5in (12.5cm) wide.

£380–425 Moxhams

A delft pottery tile, decorated with a man fishing, c1750, 5in (12.5cm) wide.

£125–140 Moxhams

A delft pottery tile, probably London, decorated with a boat and a castle, c1750, 5in (12.5cm) wide.

£125–140 Moxhams

A delft pottery tile, decorated with a light-house on a rock, c1750, 5in (12.5cm) wide.

£100–120 Moxhams

A Liverpool delft pottery tile, painted in t Fazackerley palette with a vase of flowers, c1760, 5in (12.5cm) wide.

£300–350 Moxhams

LIPWARE

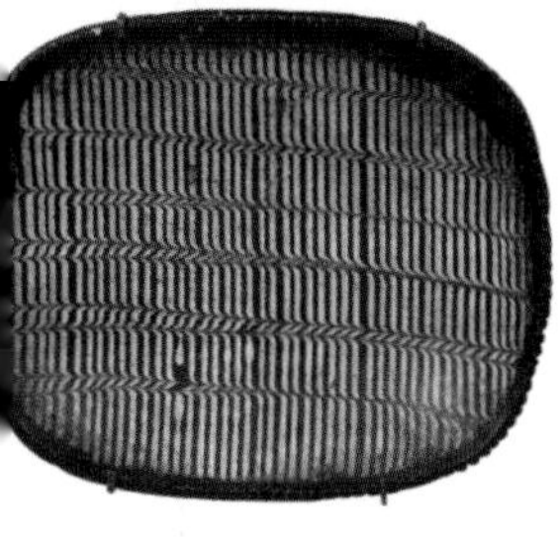

\bbott slipware dish, with combed
ration and a piecrust rim, impressed
ott Potter', 1781–83, 15in (38cm) wide.

000–2,500 Sworders

rew Abbott of Lane End, Staffordshire is d as using the mark impressed on this dish veen 1781 and 1783.

A slipware dish, northeast England, c1900, 15in (38cm) wide.

£130–150 Offa's Dyke

laypits Pottery slipware dish, Wales,
nny, c1930, 10in (25.5cm) diam.

30–150 Offa's Dyke

e has been a thriving ceramics business ınd the village of Ewenny near Bridgend in th Wales since medieval times, due to the ndance of red clay in the area. The Claypits ery was established in the 18th century.

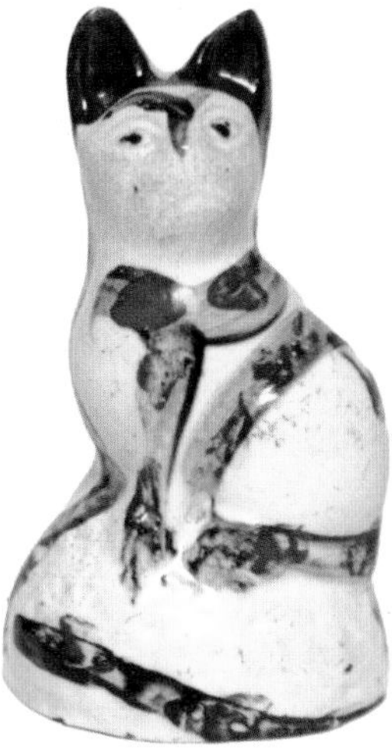

A slipware model of a cat, c1770, 5in (12.5cm) high.

£425–475 Roger de Ville

A slipware three-tier hens-and-chickens money box, Yorkshire, c1900, 13in (33cm) high.

£320–350 Offa's Dyke

ALT-GLAZED STONEWARE

rampton salt-glazed stoneware coffee pot,
byshire, moulded with roses and foliage, with an
nthus-moulded handle, the cover with a flower finial,
ıC, 13½in (34.5cm) high.

50–420 Dreweatt Neate (N)

A salt-glazed stoneware commode pot, with roulette decoration, c1840, 11in (28cm) diam.

£130–140 Offa's Dyke

A salt-glazed stoneware jardinière, north Midlands, c1890, 8in (20.5cm) high.

£90–100 Offa's Dyke

A salt-glazed stoneware flask, commemorating the Duke of York, impressed 'Samuel Garrett, Duke of York Wine & Spirit Vaults, Shadwell', c1830, 8in (20.5cm) high.

£800–900 Roger de Ville

EXPERT'S EYE SALT-GLAZED STONEWARE

Salt-glazed stoneware has a distinctive pitted surface which was formed by throwing salt into the kiln during the high-temperature firing process. The sodium in the salt fused with silicates in the clay to form a glassy surface. This Staffordshire teapot from c1760 would have had its body thrown on a wheel, with the handle and spout created from a mould and added separately.

£1,700–2,000 Roger de Ville

The process uses a single firing for both hardening and glazing.

Salt-glazed stoneware can also be found in brown or light buff colour.

The pitted surface of the glaze is also known as 'orange peel'.

These vibrant enamel colours are typical on white salt-glazed stoneware.

A Mortlake Pottery salt-glazed stoneware **hunting jug,** by Joseph Kishere, applied with drinkers under a tree and a hunting scene, the cover with a silver mount, c1800, 9¾in (25cm) high.

£300–350 Bearnes

A Herculaneum salt-glazed stoneware jug, applied with three groups of putti above a leaftip border, the neck with engine-turned decoration, impressed maker's mark, c1805, 8¾in (22cm) high.

£800–950 Northeast Auctions

A salt-glazed stoneware elephant money box, c1820, 5in (12.5cm) high.

£850–950 John Howard

A salt-glazed stoneware tankard, with a silver-mounted rim, early 18thC, 7½in (19cm) high.

£2,500–3,000 Hy Duke

A Brampton salt-glazed stoneware tankard, Derbyshire, c1835, 5in (12.5cm) high.

£160–180 Offa's Dyke

A salt-glazed stoneware treacle pot/wet drug jar, Yorkshire, c1840, 8in (20.5cm) h

£140–160 Offa's Dyke

RED STONEWARE

A red stoneware money bank, applied with 19 birds, inscribed 'Jane Sorey...1834', 7½in (19cm) high.

£400–500 Northeast Auctions

A red stoneware coffee pot, with engine-turned decoration, seal mark, cover missing, c1770, 7in (18cm) high.

£400–450 Offa's Dyke

A red stoneware teapot, with sprigged decoration, repaired, c1760, 5in (12.5cm) diam.

£250–280 Offa's Dyke

REAMWARE

erced creamware basket, c1780, 5in (12.5cm) wide.
0–400 John Howard ⊞

A creamware bowl, transfer-printed with Masonic symbols and a ship, damaged, c1790, 9in (23cm) diam.
£135–150 Offa's Dyke ⊞
This bowl would be worth approximately £400 if undamaged.

eamware bowl and cover, decorated flowers, late 18thC, 6in (15cm) diam.
0–400 Moxhams ⊞

A creamware bowl, c1790, 9in (23cm) wide.
£400–450 John Howard ⊞

A pair of Heath creamware candlesticks, c1790, 9in (23cm) high.
£1,100–1,200 John Howard ⊞

eeds creamware coffee pot, with metal ınts, decorated with flowers, restored, ıt damage, c1760, 11¼in (28.5cm) high.
00–700 Guest & Gray ⊞

A creamware coffee pot, probably Leeds, painted with flowers, with entwined strap handle, restored, c1770, 11½in (29cm) high.
£160–200 Sworders

A creamware coffee pot, Dutch-decorated with a view of Samuel anointing Saul's head within a scroll cartouche, with entwined strap handle, the cover with a floral knop, c1780, 11¾in (30cm) high.
£180–220 Northeast Auctions

reamware coffee pot, with bat-printed oration and strap handle, c1790, 10in high.
25–475 Typically English ⊞

A Whieldon-style creamware coffee pot, moulded in relief with a cartouche enclosing a pineapple in a basket, with a scroll spout, the cover with a floral knop, 18thC, 9½in (24cm) high.
£650–800 Hy Duke

A Yorkshire creamware cup and saucer, decorated with flowers, c1775.
£200–220 Offa's Dyke ⊞

A pair of creamware figures of Antony and Cleopatra, she with an asp, restored, c1780, 12½in (31.5cm) long.
£300–350 Sworders

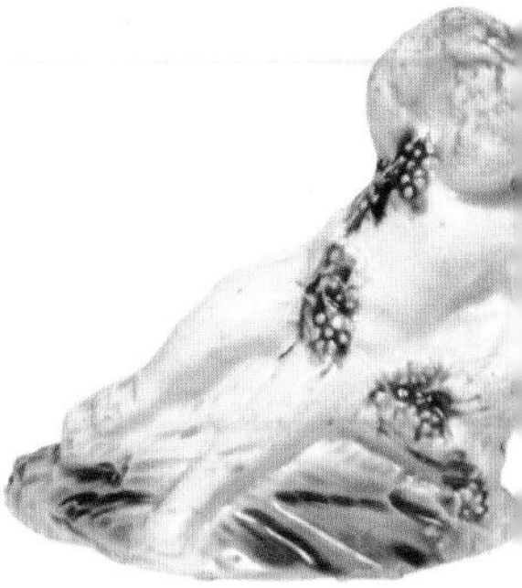

A creamware figure of a boy with grape c1790, 2½in (6.5cm) high.
£375–420 Moxhams

A Whitehead creamware jug, decorated with a hunting scene, reverse inscribed 'John Harvey 1778', 10¼in (26cm) high.
£1,800–2,000 Erna Hiscock

A Derbyshire creamware jug, c1785, 9in (23cm) high.
£1,350–1,500 Erna Hiscock

A creamware jug, commemorating Admir Lord Nelson and the Battle of the Nile, c1 9in (23cm) high.
£1,350–1,500 Roger de Ville

A creamware jug, transfer-printed with a fishing boat and a sailing ship, c1810, 7in (18cm) high.
£520–600 Roger de Ville

A creamware jug, transfer-printed and enamel-decorated with Masonic symbols and a ship, inscribed 'R. J. J.', c1811, 10¾in (27.5cm) high.
£2,000–2,400 Northeast Auctions

A creamware jug, commemorating Georg Washington, c1880, 5in (12.5cm) high.
£450–500 John Howard

A creamware model of a ram, c1780, 3½in (9cm) long.
£225–250 M V S Antiques

A creamware model of a sheep, c1790, 3in (7.5cm) long.
£325–375 Moxhams

eamware model of a sheep, c1800,
(10cm) long.
30–325 Moxhams

A creamware model of a goat, decorated in Pratt colours, Scotland, c1820, 9in (23cm) high.
£2,700–3,000 John Howard

A creamware mug, probably Liverpool, transfer-printed with a scene of a girl and a man, inscribed 'Friendship Love and Unity, Accept this Pledge of Affection', early 19thC, 6in (15cm) high.
£375–425 Cheffins

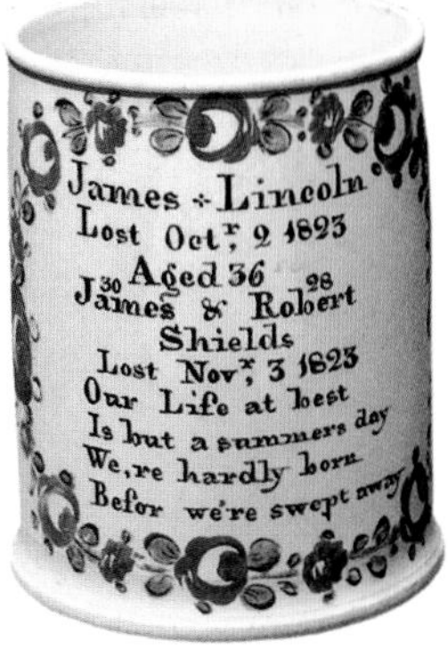

reamware mug, enamel-decorated with
nscription within a floral wreath,
ed 1823, 5¾in (14.5cm) high.
50–300 Northeast Auctions

A Staffordshire plate, decorated with Whieldon-type glazes, mid-18thC, 8¾in (22.5cm) diam.
£160–200 Sworders

A creamware plate, with pierced decoration, c1780, 8¾in (22cm) diam.
£125–140 Erna Hiscock

reamware plate, probably Swansea,
sibly painted by William Weston Young
h a named view of the River Lee, near
fford, the rim painted and gilded with vines,
ht damage, early 19thC, 7½in (19cm) high.
,000–1,200 Bearnes

A Swansea Pottery child's creamware plate, with transfer-printed and enamel decoration, Wales, c1815, 6½in (16.5cm) diam.
£120–140 Offa's Dyke

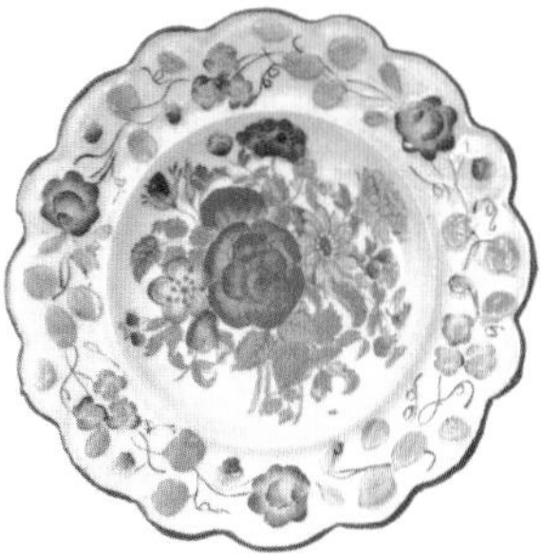

A Swansea Pottery creamware plate, with transfer-printed and enamel decoration, Wales, c1815, 7in (18cm) diam.
£120–140 Offa's Dyke

Swansea Pottery creamware plate,
h pierced rim, Wales, c1820,
(20.5cm) diam.
0–100 Offa's Dyke

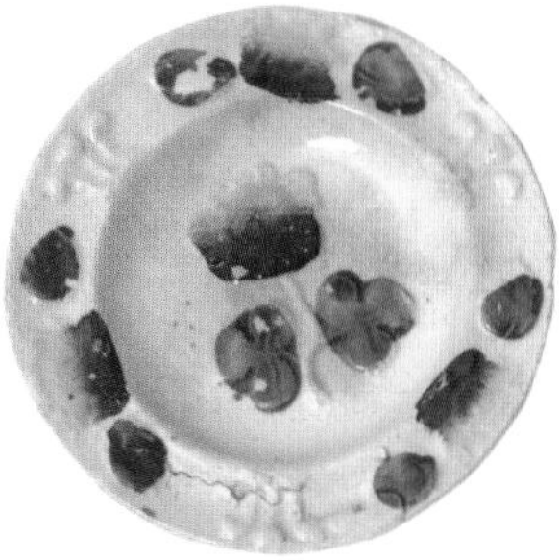

A creamware miniature plate, c1820, 3½in (9cm) diam.
£120–140 Offa's Dyke

A Staffordshire creamware punch pot, decorated with Whieldon-type lead glazes, with crabstock spout and foliate moulded handle, 18thC, 7in (18cm) high.
£600–700 Skinner

A creamware miniature tea bowl and saucer, c1780, bowl 2in (5cm) diam.

£250–280 Offa's Dyke

A creamware tea canister, decorated in iron-red with a pastoral scene, c1760, 4½in (11.5cm) high.

£380–420 Guest & Gray

A Staffordshire creamware teapot, decorated with Whieldon-type glazes, the handle and spout modelled as twigs, the cover with a bi finial, restored, c1760, 6in (15cm) high.

£450–500 Dreweatt Neate (N)

A Leeds creamware teapot, decorated with a farming scene and harvesting tools, inscribed 'J. Allan, Milk Now, 1775', the cover with a flower knop, cover glued to body, spout restored, c1775, 5¼in (13.5cm) high.

£2,000–2,200 Penrith Farmers' & Kidd's

A Leeds creamware teapot, probably painted by David Rhodes, decorated with Masonic symbols, c1775, 5in (12.5cm) diam.

£2,700–3,000 Roger de Ville

Robinson & Rhodes ran a decorating studio in Leeds and David Rhoc painted a great deal of Wedgwood and Leeds creamware. Rhodes' palette was mostly confined to red and black, with touches of green, rosy purple and yellow.

PEARLWARE

A Bristol pearlware spirit barrel, by W. Fifield, with enamel decoration, Bristol, c1820, 9in (23cm) long.

£360–400 Offa's Dyke

A pearlware barrel, decorated in Pratt colours and with initials 'J. N. 1821', 4½in (11.5cm) high.

£480–550 Moxhams

A pearlware basket and stand, c1820, 11in (28cm) wide.

£270–300 Hugh Mote

A pearlware bowl, the interior painted in Pratt colours with a fish and inscription 'Keep Me Swimming', the rim with swags, slight damage, c1790, 9¾in (24.5cm) diam.

£1,300–1,600 Sworders

A pearlware bowl, decorated with profiles of George III and Queen Charlotte within a foliate cartouche, inscribed 'A King Revered a Queen Beloved' and 'Long May They Live', c1810, 10¼in (26cm) diam.

£700–850 Special Auction Services

A pearlware box, decorated in Pratt colours with screw-on cover, c1820, 3in (7.5cm) hi

£550–600 John Howard

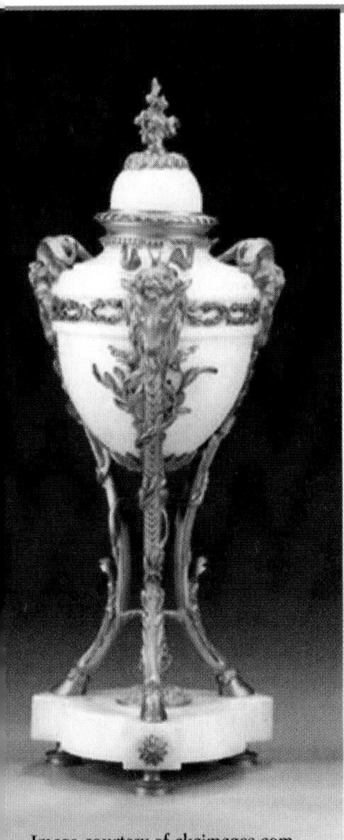

A pearlware comport, probably Swansea, painted by Thomas Pardoe with landscape panels within foliate borders, restored, Wales, early 19thC, 14½in (37cm) wide.

£240–275 Bearnes

A Wood family pearlware jug, relief-moulded with a parson, clerk and sexton flanked by trees, within leaf-tip borders, impressed 'Wood', c1790, 8¾in (22cm) high.

£250–300 Northeast Auctions

A pearlware mug, decorated in Pratt colours, moulded with profiles of George III and Queen Charlotte within foliate borders, the rim decorated with foliage entwined with ribbon, the handle moulded with acanthus leaf mounts, restored, c1793, 5¾in (145cm) high.

£2,750–3,250
Special Auction Services

A Baker, Bevans & Irwin pearlware plate, Wales, Swansea, 1813–38, 7in (18cm) diam.

£120–135 Old Corner House

A pearlware 'Pope and Devil' drinking cup, decorated in Pratt colours, repaired, c1800, 5½in (14cm) high.

£350–400 Moxhams

A pearlware jug, decorated in Pratt colours, commemorating the Duke of York, c1798, 6in (15cm) high.

£650–725 Roger de Ville

A pearlware tea canister, decorated in Pratt colours, moulded with profiles of George III, the shoulders banded in pink lustre, slight crack, c1793, 6in (15cm) high.

£1,800–2,200
Special Auction Services

A Staffordshire pearlware jug, modelled Bacchus seated on a barrel, the spout in t form of a dolphin, the handle a monkey, late 18thC, 12½in (32cm) high.

£950–1,150 Skinner

A pearlware jug, transfer-printed with hu scenes and inscription 'Commercial Coffee House, Boston', c1805, 9¼in (23.5cm) high

£2,500–3,000 Northeast Auctions

This piece was made in England for the American market.

A pearlware cornucopia wall vase, decorated in Pratt colours, relief-moulded with a child with a brazier and a quiver of arrows, c1808, 12½in (32cm) high.

£300–350 Northeast Auctions

OCHA WARE

cha ware jug, decorated in slip marbled pattern, c1780, 19.5cm) high.

)0–1,800 Northeast Auctions

A Mocha ware water jug, decorated in slip with cats' eyes and trails, c1820, 7¾in (19.5cm) high.

£850–1,000 Northeast Auctions

A Mocha ware water jug, decorated in slip with tulip stems and dots, c1830, 7in (19cm) high.

£600–720 Northeast Auctions

A Mocha ware mustard pot, decorated with a geometric pattern, c1820, 5in (12.5cm) high.

£270–300 Erna Hiscock

cha ware tankard, decorated with ed, c1820, 4¾in (12cm) high.

–800 Erna Hiscock

A Mocha ware tea canister, decorated with a marbled and combed pattern, c1790, 4¾in (12cm) high.

£850–950 Erna Hiscock

A Mocha ware teapot, encrusted with pieces of clay, with engine-turned and berry-and-leaf borders, finial replaced, c1795, 4½in (11.5cm) high.

£280–350 Northeast Auctions

SENTIAL REFERENCE MOCHA WARE

:ha ware derives its name from the tree-like marks found type of agate that was shipped across the world from port of Mocha in Yemen. The technique, which was)duced on English creamware c1770, consisted of ping a special 'tea' of acidic liquid including tobacco juice) a surface dipped in coloured alkaline slip. The reaction veen the acid and alkali caused a tree-like pattern to ad across the surface. The term Mocha ware is often nded to other abstract designs and is most commonly on mugs and jugs. Some of the more collectable erns are given names such as 'earthworm' and 'cat's-eye'. .ha ware is avidly collected in the US and it is here most early pieces are seen. With its primitive charm :s happily with American folk art. Prices have risen endously in recent times, no doubt helped by *Mocha and ted Dipped Wares 1770–1939* by Jonathan Rickard, ntly published by the University Press of New England.

A Mocha ware tankard, decorated with earthworms and cats' eyes, c1810, 5in (12.5cm) high.

£700–800 Erna Hiscock

COW CREAMERS

A St Anthony's Pottery cow creamer, with a milkmaid, early 19thC, 6in (15cm) high.
£1,150–1,300 Roger de Ville

A pearlware cow creamer, possibly Yorkshire, with a milkmaid, slight damage, restored, early 19thC, 5¾in (14.5cm) high.
£330–400 Dreweatt Neate

A pair of Staffordshire cow creamers, w milkmaids, the hats forming the lids, c18 6in (15cm) high.
£850–950 John Howard

TOBY & CHARACTER JUGS

A Staffordshire pearlware Bacchus character jug, cover restored, slight damage, c1790, 11¼in (28.5cm) high.
£9,000–11,000 Sotheby's (NY)
This is a very rare model.

A Toby jug, c1790, 10in (25.5cm) high.
£1,800–2,000 Judi Bland

A pearlware Toby jug, c1800, 9½in (24cm)
£600–700 Skinner

A pearlware Toby jug, c1800, 9½in (24cm) high.
£1,500–1,800 M V S Antiques

A Toby jug, decorated in Pratt colours, c1810, 10in (25.5cm) high.
£1,400–1,600 M V S Antiques

A Toby jug, attributed to Swillington Bri Pottery, decorated in Pratt colours, impre mark, early 19thC, 10in (25.5cm) high.
£1,300–1,500 Skinner

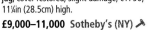

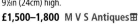

WEDGWOOD

A Wedgwood creamware basket and stand, c1785, 8in (20.5cm) wide.

£500–550
John Howard

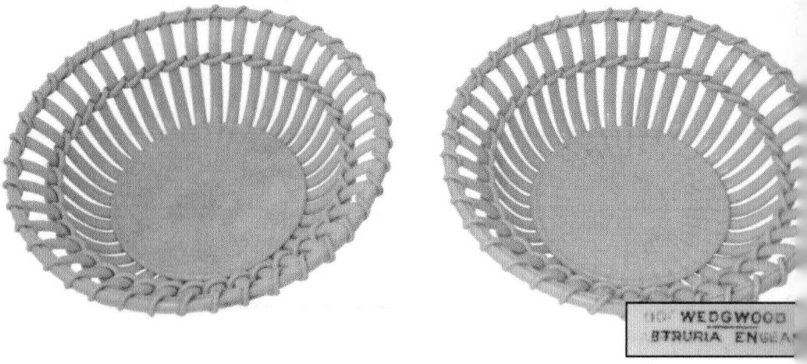

A pair of Wedgwood creamware baskets, dated 1916, 9in (23cm) diam.

£120–140 Offa's Dyke

A Wedgwood jasper ware bough pot, decorated with cherubs and arched palm trees, impressed mark, restored, c1800, 6½in (16.5cm) high.

£900–1,100
Woolley & Wallis

A Wedgwood & Bentley black basalt bust of Socrates, inscribed title, impressed mark, c1775, 19¾in (50cm) high.

£2,250–2,750 Skinner

A pair of Wedgwood creamware butter boats, c1780, 3in (7.5cm) wide.

£350–400
Offa's Dyke

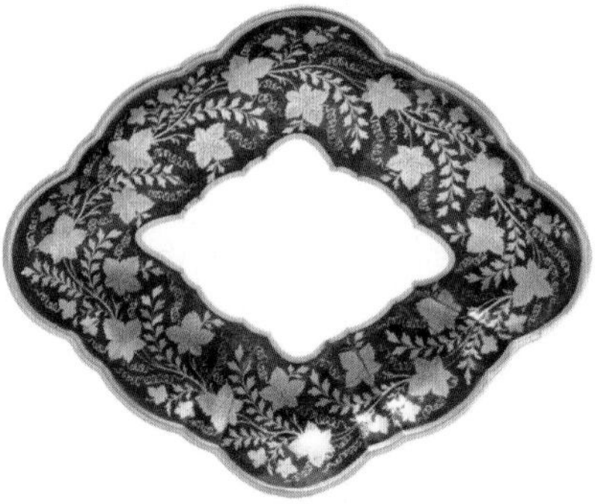

A Wedgwood dish, with elaborate gilt decoration, c1810, 11½in (29cm) wide.

£220–250 Stockspring Antiques

A Wedgwood black basalt fi of Triton, candle sconce dama 19thC, 11in (28cm) high.

£225–275
Woolley & Wallis

A pair of Wedgwood & Bentley creamware cassolettes and covers, each with a gilt medallion depicting classical figures, on black basalt bases, marked, c1775, 10¼in (26cm) high.

£6,000–7,000 Sotheby's

These are used to emit perfume by placing a pastille inside.

A pair of Wedgwood black basalt models of griffins, after Sir William Chambers, the heads surmounted by candle sconces, late 18thC, 13½in (34.5cm) high.

£10,000–12,000 Sotheby's

A Wedgwood jasper ware jardinière, impressed mark, late 19thC, 8in (20.5cm) hig

£160–200 Waddingto

'r of Wedgwood black basalt plaques,), 9in (23cm) high.
0–600
M Antiques

A Wedgwood Queen's ware platter, decorated with Corinthian ruins, impressed mark, late 18thC, 19¾in (50cm) wide.
£800–950 Skinner

A Wedgwood dessert service, comprising 15 pieces, painted with flowers within basket moulded borders, impressed mark, early 19thC.
£175–200 Sworders

dgwood majolica dessert service, comprising ›ieces, decorated with strawberries, ged, impressed marks, c1880.
–180
dington's

A Wedgwood rosso antico teapot, metal repair, c1810, 7in (18cm) wide.
£100–120 Offa's Dyke

A Wedgwood black basalt teapot and jug, c1840, teapot 8in (20.5cm) wide.
£250–280 Hugh Mote

edgwood caneware miniature tea and coffee ce, comprising 19 pieces, losses and damage, essed mark, c1790, tray 16¾in (42.5cm) wide.
00–3,500 Sotheby's (O)

edgwood creamware sauce tureen, cover and d, in the form of a shell, painted with leaves, essed mark, 19thC, 5½in (14cm) high.
0–200 Sworder's

ir of Wedgwood jasper ware vases and covers, ormolu mounts, c1860, 10½in (26.5cm) high.
00–3,500 Hugh Mote

MILLER'S COMPARES

(L) A Wedgwood jasper ware vase, the handles with coiled snakes, impressed mark, late 18thC, 14in (35.5cm) high.
£2,800–3,500 Skinner

(R) A Wedgwood pearlware vase, the handles with coiled snakes, depicting a mother and child, the reverse with a nymph, impressed mark, c1870, 14¾in (37.5cm) high.
£700–850 Skinner

The snake-handled vase shown on the left was Wedgwood's most popular vase in the late 18th century. It is made of jasper ware, a type of unglazed semi-porcelain introduced by Wedgwood in 1774. The continuing popularity of the shape can be seen with the vase on the right, made almost 100 years later. The body is pearlware which was a development from creamware – the glaze contains cobalt blue which gives it its distinctive bluish tinge. The vase is painted after a portrait by Sir Joshua Reynolds. The higher value of the jasper ware vase on the left is attributable to it being a much earlier piece and to the applied neo-classical ornament, which appears more suitable to the shape of the vase.

TRANSFER-PRINTED WARE

A pair of Copeland & Garrett earthenware garden seats, transfer-printed with a titled view, 'Thun', from the Byron Views series, slight damage, printed and impressed marks, c1840, 19in (48.5cm) high.

£6,500–7,250 Sotheby's (O)

Thun is the name of both a town and a lake in Switzerland. The views of various European countries are based on engravings in Finden's Landscape and Portrait Illustrations to the Life and Works of Lord Byron.

A Minton jug, transfer-printed with portraits of William IV and Queen Adelaide, slight damage, c1830, 6¼in (16cm) high.

£230–270 Bearnes

An earthenware jug, transfer-printed with portrait of Queen Victoria flanked by flags, the reverse with Britannia and the British Lion, c1837, 7¾in (19.5cm) high.

£300–350
Special Auction Services

ESSENTIAL REFERENCE BLUE & WHITE POTTERY BORDERS

- When blue and white transfer pottery was first made it was classed as simple utlilitarian domestic ware.
- The decoration was produced using underglaze blue transfer prints taken from engraved copper plates and fired once
- The earliest pieces were inspired by Chinese ceramics.
- The peak of manufacture was from the late 18th century to the mid-19th century.
- Many items were made in a series, with each piece having a different central picture while all share the same borde some of which are illustrated below:

Crown, Acorn & Leaf border series, c1825: produced by Tom Meir this pattern takes its name from the border of oak leaves and acorns and the crown on the backstamp above the name of the place illustrated. The series mostly featured views of country houses.

Bluebell border series, c1815–20: produced by William Adams and J. & R. Clews, this series included 23 views by one maker and 18 views by another. The only known shared view is of St Mary's Abbey in York and it was produced in two shades of blue – the darker shade for export to the US, the light one for the home market.

Foliage border series, c1820: produced b William Adams. J. & R. Clews and an unknown maker whose pieces were most likely made for the North American marke The exported pieces were a very dark blue making the scenes indistinct.

Tulip border series, c1820–25: produced by an unknown maker, this border extends inwards much further than is usual with other borders.

Pineapple border series, c1820: produced by an unknown maker, this border mainly surrounds views of ruined castles and abbeys.

Grapevine border series, c1820: produce by Enoch Wood, this series contains over 65 patterns.

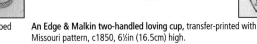

ving cup, commemorating the centenary of Methodism, inscribed
e Feast', depicting John Wesley, c1839, 5in (12.5cm) high.
'5–750 Roger de Ville

An Edge & Malkin two-handled loving cup, transfer-printed with Missouri pattern, c1850, 6½in (16.5cm) high.
£250–300 Greystoke Antiques

ate, transfer-printed with The Drover from
Durham Ox series, c1820,
(21.5cm) diam.
0–280 Old Corner House

A Don Pottery plate, transfer-printed with Obelisk at Catania pattern, c1820, 10in (25.5cm) diam.
£135–150 Greystoke Antiques

A Staffordshire plate, from the Commemorative series, depicting George III and a child, inscribed 'I hope the time will come when every poor child in my dominions will be able to read the Bible', c1820, 10½in (26.5cm) diam.
£450–550 Bamfords

alph Hall plate, transfer-printed with
tered Peasants pattern, 1822–36,
(25.5cm) diam.
0–120 Greystoke Antiques

A Minton plate, from the Monk Rock series, transfer-printed with a watermill scene, c1825, 9½in (24cm) diam.
£135–150 Greystoke Antiques

A William Mason platter, transfer-printed with a view of Furness Abbey, c1810, 20in (51cm) wide.
£600–680 Winson Antiques

atter, transfer-printed with Fisherman with Nets
ern, c1820, 14in (35.5cm) wide.
:0–140 Sworders

A pearlware platter, transfer-printed with fishermen within a border of Turkish figures, c1820, 19in (48.5cm) wide.
£150–180 Thomson, Roddick & Medcalf (C)

A John & Richard Riley platter, transfer-printed with Europa pattern, 1810–28, 19in (48.5cm) wide.

£525–600 Greystoke Antiques ⊞

A Ridgway platter, from the Oxford and Cambridge series, decoratec with a view of All Souls and St Mary's Oxford, c1820, 20½in (52cm) wid

£1,350–1,500 Peter Scott ⊞

A Davenport platter, transfer-printed with Montreal pattern, c1835, 18in (45.5cm) wide.

£275–325 Waddington's

A Lake platter, transfer-printed with a view of Hallowell, 19thC, 19in (48.5cm) wide.

£160–200 Waddington's

Lake is a little-known maker, who produced a series of views of America. Hallowell is in Maine, USA.

A platter, probably by Thomas Mayer, transfer-printed with Bullfight pattern withi a vine leaf border, slight damage, c1835, 15in (38cm) wide.

£110–125 Church Hill Antiques ⊞

A platter, transfer-printed with Ladies Cabin pattern, from the Boston Mails series, c1840, 15in (38cm) wide.

£450–500 Dwyer Antiques ⊞

A Davenport part dinner service, comprising 20 pieces, transfer-printed with scrolling foliage borders and landscape scenes, printed and impressed marks, with a platter and dish by Daws damaged, 19thC.

£900–1,100 Rosebery's

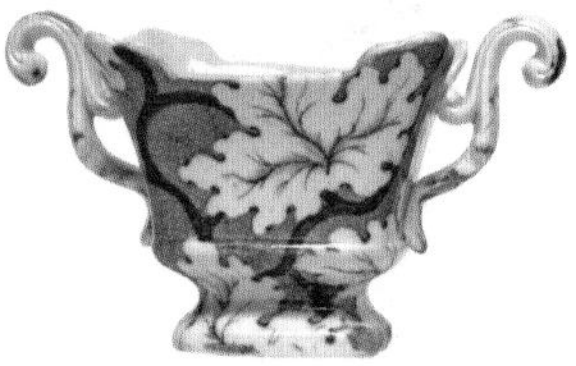

A pair of Henshall salts, transfer-printed with Flowers and Leaves pattern, c1820, 2in (5cm) high.

£300–350 Gillian Neale ⊞

A Spode pearlware soup tureen, cover and stand, transfer-printed with Italian pattern, slight damage, impressed marks, c1820, 17in (43cm) wide.

£140–175 Woolley & Wallis

An Enoch Wood tureen, cover and stand, transfer-printed with views of Sherborne Castle and Cokelthorpe Park, from the Grapevine Border series, c1820, 7in (18cm) wide.

£350–400 Gillian Neale ⊞

A John Meir & Son tureen, cover and sta transfer-printed with Italian Scenery patte c1840, 8in (20.5cm) high.

£75–85
Old Corner House ⊞

IRONSTONE

A pair of ironstone conservatory seats, decorated with Imari pattern, slight damage, mid-19thC, 20½in (52cm) high.
£2,000–2,500
Dreweatt Neate (HAM)

A Mason's Ironstone foot bath, decorated with Pheasant pattern, 1815–25, 16in (40.5cm) wide.
£1,800–2,000
Winson Antiques

A Mason's Ironstone pot pc jar, decorated with Japan Fe pattern, 1820–30, 6in (15cm)
£600–700
Winson Antiques

A Mason's Ironstone jardinière and stand, c1840, 4in (10cm) high.
£600–700 Roger de Ville

A Mason's Ironstone Fenton jug, decorated with Old School House pattern, c1820, 9in (23cm) high.
£1,100–1,300 Winson Antiques

An ironstone jug, decorated in the Imari palette, with a snake handle, slight damag c1820, 9¾in (25cm) high.
£200–250 Woolley & Wallis

A Spode part dinner service, comprising 50 pieces, printed and painted with chinoiserie pattern No. 2879, slight damage, early 19thC.
£400–500 Bearnes

A Victorian Mason's Ironstone part dinner service, comprising 54 pieces, painted and enamelled with chinoiserie pattern No. 9799.
£1,000–1,200 Andrew Hartley

An Ashworths ironstone dinner service, comprising 67 pieces, decorated with Japan pattern, slight damage, late 19thC.
£850–1,000 Bearnes

A Spode sugar box and cover, decorated with pattern No. 2117, c1820, 7in (18cm) wide.
£115–130 Stockspring Antiques

̶TAFFORDSHIRE FIGURES & MODELS

›del of a pug dog, c1800,
7.5cm) high.
0–500 Moxhams ⊞

A Staffordshire pearlware figural spill vase, decorated in Pratt colours, c1800, 8in (20.5cm) high.
£2,250–2,500 John Howard ⊞

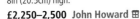

A Staffordshire bull-baiting group, slight damage, c1810, 5½in (14cm) high.
£600–700 Dreweatt Neate

affordshire pearlware group of
rtainers, c1820, 10in (25.5cm) high.
500–2,800 John Howard ⊞

A Staffordshire pearlware figure, inscribed 'Walton', c1820, 7in (18cm) high.
£700–800 Roger de Ville ⊞

A Staffordshire pearlware figural group of a gentleman dressing a lady's hair, c1820, 10in (25.5cm) high.
£1,250–1,400 Roger de Ville ⊞

SSENTIAL REFERENCE NAPOLEONIC BEAR JUGS

ar-baiting was popular in England until the 19th century.
ars would be chained to a post in a fenced arena or pit and
en set upon by dogs. This form of jug derives from the white
d brown salt-glazed stoneware bear-baiting jugs made in
affordshire and Nottingham in the mid-18th century. Usually
e bear was modelled grasping a small
g in its paws but in this example, the
g has been replaced by a small
ure of Napoleon portrayed as a
onkey. Napoleon's military
ccesses brought him to the
tention of English satirists. The
ely inspiration for the group is a
uikshank print entitled 'John Bull shewing
e Corsican monkey', which depicts Napoleon as a monkey
rched on a bear.

Staffordshire Napoleonic bear jug, with hand-painted decoration,
820, 10in (25.5cm) high.
,800–2,000 Hugh Mote ⊞

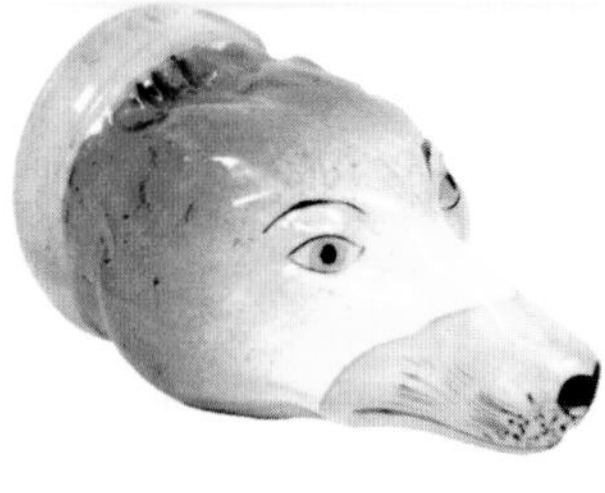

A Staffordshire stirrup cup, in the form of a fox mask, early 19thC, 4in (10cm) wide.

£670–750 Mary Cruz Antiques ⊞

A Staffordshire figure, entitled 'Widow', early 19thC, 8½in (21.5cm) high.

£225–250 Islwyn Watkins ⊞

A Staffordshire pearlware figural vase, c1830, 6¾in (17cm) high.

£400–450 Serendipity ⊞

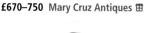

A Staffordshire Tithe Pig group, c1830, 9in (23cm) high.

£1,100–1,250 John Howard ⊞

The Tithe Pig was a popular ceramic subject. Examples in Derby porcelain, Staffordshire pottery and as printed scenes are found in the late 18th and early 19th centuries. The scene depicts a parson standing with a pig in his hand and a farmer and his wife. The farmer's wife is refusing to part with a tenth (or tithe) pig unless the parson takes her tenth child also.

A Staffordshire model of sheep, before bocage, c1830, 4¾in (12cm) high.

£250–280 Serendipity ⊞

A pair of Staffordshire figures, c1835, 9in (23cm) high.

£1,350–1,500 John Howard ⊞

This pair of figures is previously unrecorde

A pair of Staffordshire models of wolves, c1840, 8¼in (21cm) high.

£2,500–2,750 Richard Gardner ⊞

A pair of Staffordshire models of spaniels, c1840, 4in (10cm) high.

£250–275 Serendipity ⊞

A Staffordshire figure of a sleeping boy leaning on his dog, 19thC, 7in (18cm) wi

£675–750 Mary Cruz Antiques ⊞

A pair of Staffordshire models of poodles, c1845, 4in (10cm) high.

£680–750 Mary Cruz Antiques ⊞

A pair of Victorian Staffordshire spill vases, each modelled with a horse and a foal, 6½in (16.5cm) high.

£650–725 Woolley & Wallis

ʳr of Staffordshire Disraeli dogs, holding baskets of ʳrs in their mouths, c1850, 8in (20.5cm) high.
00–1,850 John Howard

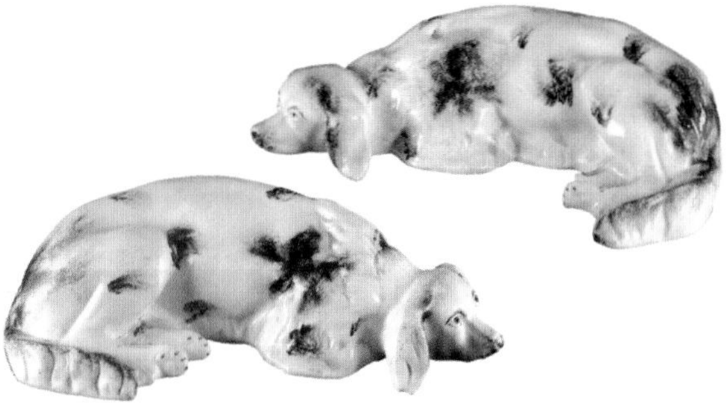

A pair of Staffordshire models of dogs, slight damage, 1850–1900, 8¾in (22cm) wide.
£600–700 Woolley & Wallis

affordshire figural group of children bird ing, c1850, 8in (20cm) high.
0–350 Serendipity

A Staffordshire figure of Sir Robert Peel on horseback, the base with flowers and an inscription, c1850, 11in (28cm) high.
£1,350–1,500 John Howard

A Staffordshire spill vase, in the form of an elephant, c1855, 6in (15cm) high.
£675–750 John Howard

air of Victorian Staffordshire models of s, with lambs, 10¼in (26cm) high.
000–3,500 Woolley & Wallis

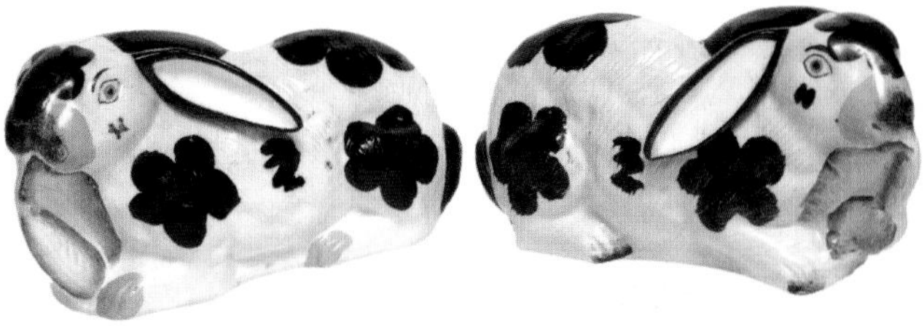

A pair of Staffordshire models of rabbits, c1855, 10in (25.5cm) wide.
£5,500–6,000 John Howard

air of Staffordshire models of spaniels, seated on cushions, 50, 5in (12.5cm) high.
800–2,200 Richard Gardner

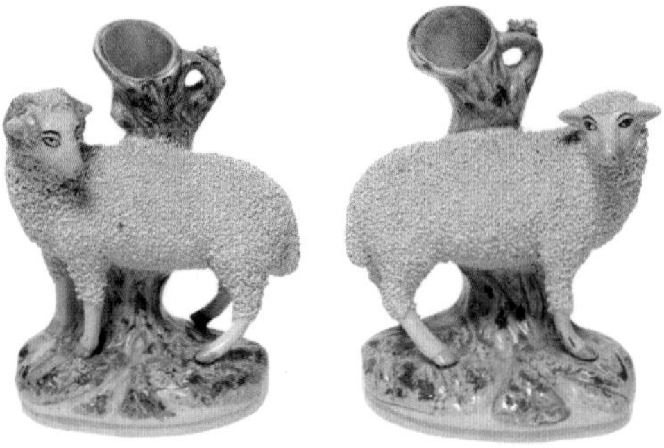

A pair of Staffordshire spill vases, with sheep, 1860, 8in (20.5cm) high.
£450–500 Offa's Dyke

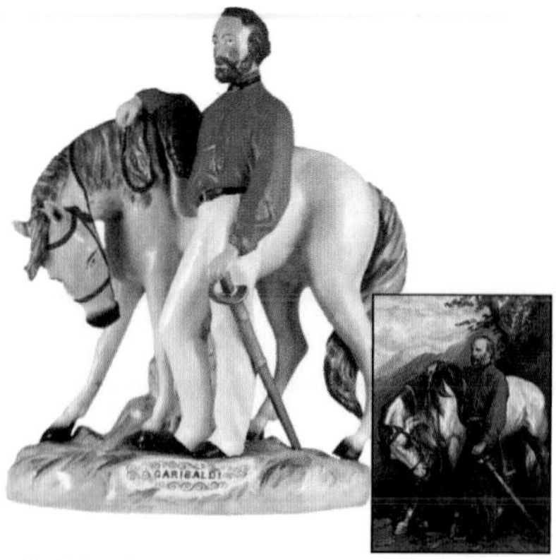

A Staffordshire figure of Garibaldi standing beside his horse, 19thC, 14½in (37cm) high.

£475–575 Woolley & Wallis

A pair of Staffordshire models of zebras, c1860, 6in (15cm) high.

£450–500 John Howard

A pair of Staffordshire models of dogs with children, c1860, 12in (30.5cm) high.

£2,000–2,200 John Howard

A Staffordshire tureen, in the form of a h on a nest, c1875, 8in (20.5cm) wide.

£400–450 John Howard

A pair of Victorian Staffordshire Disraeli **models of greyhounds,** 10¾in (27.5cm) high.

£475–575 Woolley & Wallis

So-called Disraeli models were named after Queen Victoria's prime minister, Benjamin Disraeli who had distinctive curly hair.

A Staffordshire figure of a boy with rabbits, c1875, 7in (18cm) high.

£225–250 John Howard

A pair of Staffordshire models of lions, e standing on a figure of Napoleon Bonapar c1875, 9in (23cm) high.

£900–1,000 John Howard

A Staffordshire model of Jumbo the **Elephant,** late 19thC, titled, 11¼in (28.5cm) high.

£1,750–2,000 Woolley & Wallis

Jumbo became the highlight of Phileas Barnum's circus in 1882, touring the US and Canada. On 15 September 1885 he was hit by a train and killed. Barnum had a taxidermist immortalize the six-ton elephant and later told the world that Jumbo had charged the train in an attempt to save Alice, a smaller elephant, which he billed as Jumbo's widow.

A Staffordshire spill vase, with a lion and cubs beneath a tree entwined with a snake, late 19thC, 12in (30.5cm) high.

£350–425 Andrew Hartley

A Staffordshire tobacco jar, surmounted b clown and a cherub, damaged, c1880, 12½in (32cm) high.

£375–425 Serendipity

ИAJOLICA

eorge Jones majolica cheese bell, c1860, (28cm) diam.

500–4,000 Britannia

A Joseph Holdcroft majolica cheese dish, moulded with fish and weed, c1870, 10in (25.5cm) high.

£750–900 Dreweatt Neate (Ham)

A majolica cheese dish and cover, moulded with bamboo and wickerwork, painted mark, c1880, 12½in (32cm) wide.

£900–1,100 Woolley & Wallis

air of Minton majolica figural comports, in the form of a merman mermaid supporting seashells, impressed mark, c1870, 15in :m) high.

800–4,500 Skinner

An Etruscan majolica salad comport, moulded with daisies, America, 19thC, 9in (23cm) diam.

£200–250 Jackson's

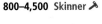

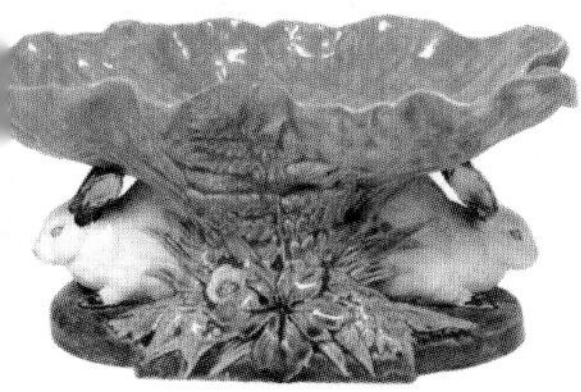

Iinton majolica leaf dish, the base delled with rabbits and foliage, c1860, ı (25.5cm) wide.

500–4,000 Britannia

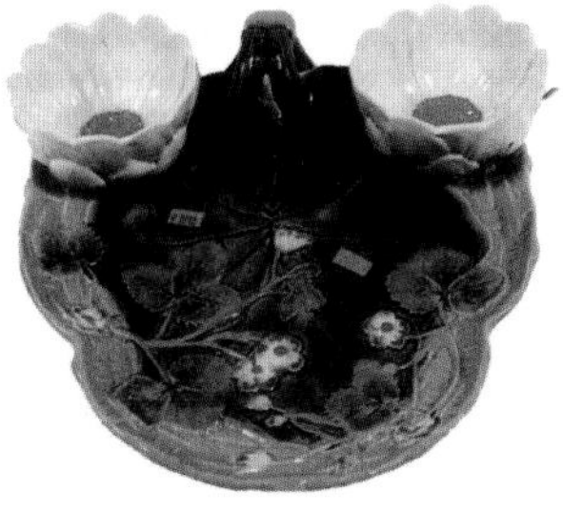

A Minton majolica strawberry dish, by George Jones, with two fixed bowls in the form of water lilies, 19thC, 10in (25.5cm) wide.

£400–500 Mealy's

Iinton majolica figure of man and a pe basket, 19thC, 10in (25.5cm) high.

00–600 Mealy's

A Minton majolica jardinière, moulded with cherubs and lion masks, c1870, 13in (33cm) high.

£650–725 Mealy's

A Victorian majolica jardinière, moulded with female masks and shells, on square tapering scrolling supports headed by grotesque masks, on a triform base, 19in (48.5cm) high.

£250–300
Dee, Atkinson & Harrison

A George Jones majolica jardinière, the body moulded with flowering water lilies, slight damage, impressed crescent mark with monogram, c1873, 16in (40.5cm) high.

£850–1,000 Sworders

A Minton majolica jardinière, with applied snake handles, slight damage, impressed date code for 1878, 19¾in (50cm) wide.

£1,500–1,800 Toovey's

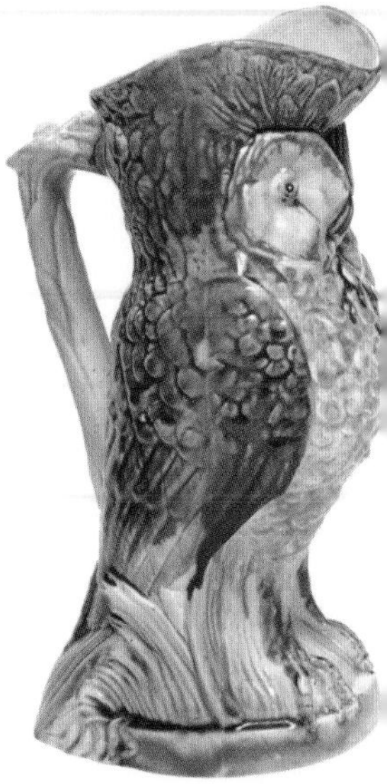

A majolica jug, in the form of an owl, c18
11in (28cm) high.

£280–320 Long Street Antiques

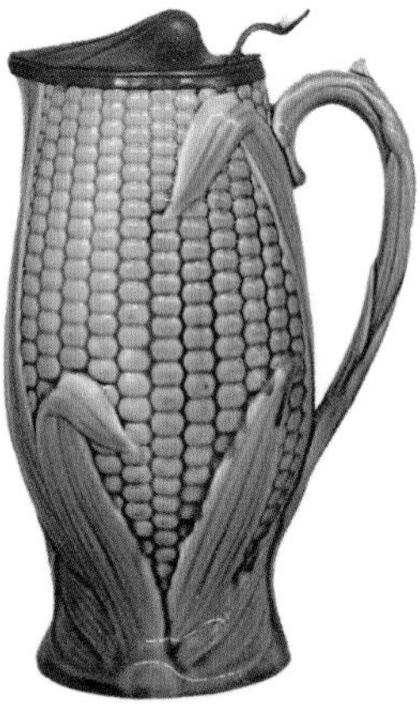

A majolica jug, in the form of a corn on the cob, with a hinged pewter cover, seal mark, 19thC, 9¼in (23.5cm) high.

£180–220 Peter Francis

A majolica jug, in the form of an Oriental man, c1880, 8in (20.5cm) high.

£120–140 Long Street Antiques

A majolica jug, moulded with a ram's hea
c1880, 9in (23cm) high.

£135–150 Long Street Antiques

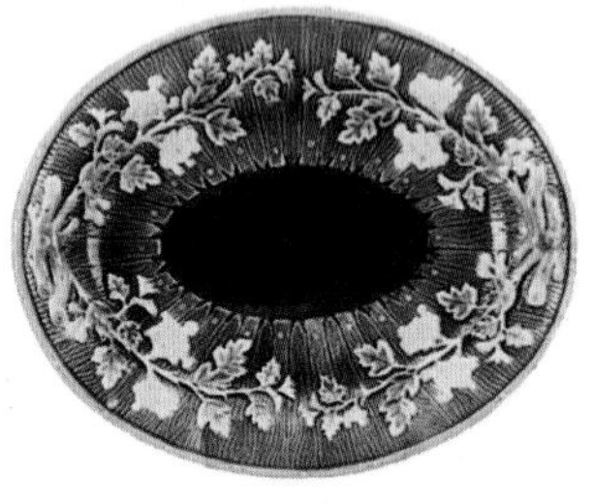

A majolica platter, c1880, 13¾in (35cm) wide.

£140–175 Waddington's

A majolica part dinner service, comprising eight pieces, each in the form of a lily pad, c1880, plates 9in (23cm) diam.

£240–280 Sworders

A majolica teapot, c1880, 6in (15cm) high

£125–140 Church Hill Antiques

A George Jones majolica tureen and cover, moulded with rabbits, the cover surmounted by a quail and chicks, slight damage, repaired, painted mark, registration mark for 1873, 14½in (37cm) wide.

£15,000–18,000 Sotheby's

A pair of Minton majolica vases, each moulded with two portrait busts, represent
Africa, America, Europe and Asia, slight damage, impressed mark, c1870, 13½in (34.5cm) high.

£1,400–1,700 Toovey's

VEMYSS

'emyss basin, painted with apples, land, c1900, 15in (38cm) diam.
)0–800 Fair Finds

A Wemyss basket, painted with wild roses, impressed mark, retailer's mark for T. Goode & Co, Scotland, c1900, 12in (30.5cm) wide.
£900–1,000 Rogers de Rin

A Wemyss bulb bowl, painted with carnations, impressed mark, Scotland, 1890–1900, 14in (35.5cm) diam.
£1,800–2,000 Rogers de Rin

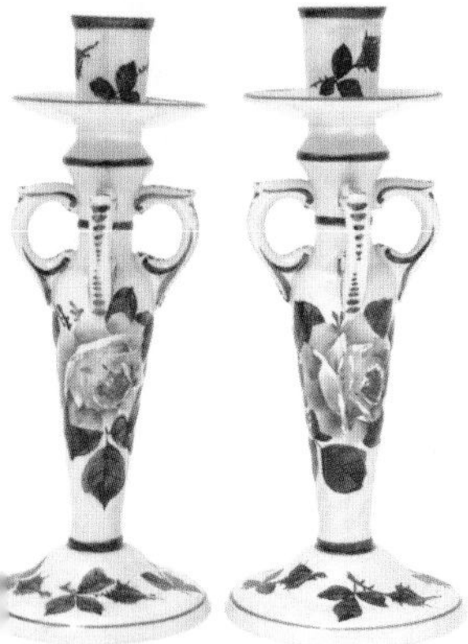

air of Wemyss Kintore candlesticks, nted with roses, impressed mark, retailer's k for T. Goode & Co, Scotland, c1900, (23cm) high.
50–400 Rogers de Rin

A Bovey Pottery Wemyss model of a cat, painted by Joseph Nekola with shamrocks, with glass eyes, script mark, c1930, 12in (31cm) high.
£6,000–7,000 Sotheby's
This cat has a distinctive script mark that can be attributed to Joseph Nekola at Bovey Tracey. The last 'S' is punctuated by a serif and a full stop follows the mark.

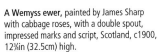

A Wemyss chamber pot, painted with cherries, Scotland, c1900, 9in (23cm) diam.
£300–350 Ruskin Decorative Arts

Vemyss honey box, cover and stand, nted with bees and hives, Scotland, c1900, (18cm) square.
75–750 Humbleyard Fine Art

A Wemyss ewer, painted by James Sharp with cabbage roses, with a double spout, impressed marks and script, Scotland, c1900, 12¾in (32.5cm) high.
£3,500–4,000 Sotheby's

Vemyss jam pot and cover, painted h blackcurrants, Scotland, early 20thC, (10cm) high.
50–180 Holloways

A Wemyss jug, painted with nesting rooks, inscribed 'Earlshall Faire' and 'As the many wintered crow; that leads the clanging rookery home', impressed mark, Scotland, dated 1914, 7½in (19cm) high.
£800–950 Sotheby's

A Wemyss jug, decorated with lemons, 1940s, 7in (18cm) high.
£500–550 Sandra Deas

A **Wemyss mug,** painted with lilac, impressed mark, Scotland, c1900, 5½in (14cm) high.

£500–550 Rogers de Rin

A **Wemyss model of a pig,** painted with shamrocks, impressed mark, Scotland, c1900, 6¾in (17cm) wide.

£650–800 Sotheby's

A **Bovey Pottery Wemyss model of a pig,** painted by Joseph Nekola with clover and leaves, restored, marked, 1930s, 17¼in (44cm) wide.

£1,200–1,400 Sotheby's

The Bovey Pottery company in Bovey Trace Devon, bought the rights to the Fife Potter in 1930.

A **Wemyss tea cup and saucer,** painted with a cockerel, inscribed 'Bon Jour', impressed mark, retailer's mark for T. Goode & Co, Scotland, c1920.

£500–550 Rogers de Rin

A **Wemyss two-handled tray,** painted with pheasants, restored, impressed marks, Scotland, c1900, 17in (43cm) wide.

£2,500–3,000 Sotheby's

A **Wemyss tyg,** impressed mark, Scotland, c1900, 9in (23cm) diam.

£1,000–1,200 Rogers de Rin

A **Wemyss vase,** possibly painted by Karel Nekola with cabbage roses, impressed mar and script, Scotland, c1900, 16½in (42cm) wi

£1,500–1,800 Sotheby's

ESSENTIAL REFERENCE KAREL NEKOLA

Karel Nekola is the most well-known of the Wemyss artists. He came to Britain from Bohemia in 1883 to work for Robert Heron at the Fife Pottery and it was at this time that the distinctive Wemyss wares were introduced. The company became famous for its brightly-painted designs and models of pigs and cats. Shown here is one of a rare set of birds of prey plates depicting eagles, hawks, falcons and owls. The likely inspiration for the bird images was J. C. Werner's *Atlas des Oiseaux d'Europe* published in Paris between 1826 and 1842. The overall crazing to the glaze is a typical feature of this creamy earthenware.

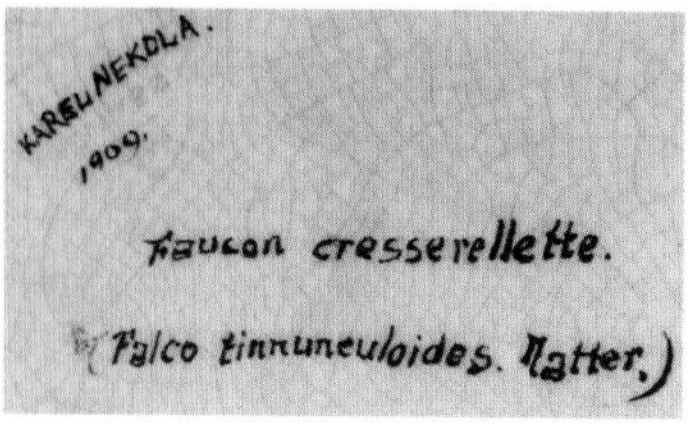

A **Wemyss plate,** painted by Karel Nekola with a kestrel, signed, impressed mark, Scotland, dated 1909, 8¼in (21cm) diam.

£3,000–3,500 Sotheby's

USTREWARE

underland lustre jug, attributed to
lison, Falconer & Co, printed with a
sonic pattern depicting Charity, Justice and
pe, with figures and symbols, inscribed
tish Slavery' and 'Sailor's Farewell',
rked 'Newcastle Pottery', early 19thC,
(23cm) high.

00–600 **Northeast Auctions**

*political cartoon 'British Slavery', taken
n a James Gillray engraving of 1792,
npares the poor conditions of the newly
rated French populace to the more
pitious state of the unliberated British.*

A Sunderland lustre puzzle jug, printed with verses and a mariner's compass, early 19thC, 7¾in (19.5cm) high.

£475–575 **Northeast Auctions**

A Sunderland lustre jug, transfer-printed with a view of Northumberland Life Boat and a verse, early 19thC, 8½in (21.5cm) high.

£550–650 **Northeast Auctions**

A Sunderland lustre jug, inscribed 'Women make men love, love makes them sad; sadness makes them drink, and drinking sets them mad', the reverse with another verse, early 19thC, 5¾in (14.5cm) high.

£300–350 **Northeast Auctions**

underland lustre mug, printed on one
e with 'The Agamemnon in a Storm' the
er with 'Manchester Unity Independent
der of Odd Fellows', the interior with
ulded frog, early 19thC, 4¾in (12cm) high.

20–270 **Northeast Auctions**

A creamware lustre mug, painted with a crown flanked by flowers of the Union, c1821, 4¾in (12cm) high.

£550–650 **Special Auction Services**

A Sunderland lustre plaque, attributed to Dixon & Co at the Garrison Pottery, decorated and inscribed with 'A west view of the cast iron bridge over the River Wear', c1850, 9in (23cm) wide.

£250–275 **Church Hill Antiques**

Newcastle lustre mug, commemorating
T. Liddell's election at Alnwick, dated 1826,
n (10cm) high.

00–700 **Roger de Ville**

*is election is one of the most commemorated
all local elections due to the huge sums spent
supporters on both sides to ensure their
ndidates' election. There were two Tory
ndidates, Bell and Liddell, and two Whig
ndidates, Beaumont and Lord Howick, the
ries being finally elected. Each arranged for the
oduction of mugs, jugs and bowls to celebrate
eir success and to present to their supporters.*

A Sunderland lustre chamber pot, damaged, c1850, 9in (23cm) diam.

£250–280 **Offa's Dyke**

POT LIDS

'The Queen God Bless Her', in a copper-plated mount, c1840, 4in (10cm) diam.

£100–120 Offa's Dyke

'Belle Vue Tavern', c1850, 4¾in (12cm) diam.

£900–1,100 Special Auction Services

'Queen Victoria and Prince Albert', by F. & R. Pratt, with base, c1850, 5in (12.5cm) diam.

£180–220 Bamfords

'The Great Exhibition of 1851, Opening Ceremony', c1851, 5in (12.5cm) diam.

£1,600–2,000
Special Auction Services

'Piesse & Lubin Parfumeurs London', c185
2½in (6.5cm) diam.

£230–275
Special Auction Services

A pot lid, decorated with flowers, with gilt-lined base, c1855, 2½in (6.5cm) diam.

£250–300 Special Auction Services

'Shakespeare's Birthplace', c1855, 4in (10cm) diam.

£250–300 Special Auction Services

'Mrs Filce's Ointment', restored, c1880, 2¾in (7cm) diam.

£650–800 BBR

'J. J. Matthias Unrivalled Cherry Toothpaste', with a portrait of the Prince of Wales, slight damage, c1880, 3in (7.5cm) diam.

£425–525 BBR

'Dr Ziemer's Alexandra Tooth Paste', depicting Princess Alexandra, c1905, 3¾in (9.5cm) diam.

£200–250 BBR

A Mason's Ironstone china footbath decorated in the Japan Fence pattern. C1820-1830

MISCELLANEOUS

A Glamorgan Pottery child's plate, Wales, 1814–38, 7in (18cm) diam.

£180–200 Swan at Tetsworth ⊞

A Staffordshire child's cup and saucer, sponge-decorated with a peafowl, early 19thC.

£100–120 Humbleyard Fine Art ⊞

A Victorian pottery jug, possibly Poutney & Allies or Poutney & Goldney, transfer-printed and painted with flowers and vignettes, 16in (40.5cm) high.

£2,500–3,000 Hy Duke

A child's mug, inscribed 'William', c1830, 3in (7.5cm) diam.

£280–320 Roger de Ville ⊞

A stoneware cheese dish and stand, probably Dudson, applied with a hunting scene, impressed mark, 1800–50, 12½in (32cm) diam.

£350–425 Woolley & Wallis

An iron-glazed jar, early 19thC, 8in (20.5cm) high.

£100–120 Islwyn Watkins ⊞

A Bargeware teapot, inscribed 'J & E Whittaker', dated 1878, 12in (30.5cm) high.

£130–150 Bradley Gent ⊞

MERICAN REDWARE

ɗware charger, attributed to Norwalk ·ry, with slip-trail inscription 'Chicken e', America, Connecticut, 1860–80, n (31cm) diam.

›00–9,000 Raccoon Creek ⊞

t plates were made by skilled potters in 9th century and examples can be found slogans, mottoes and names. This piece :ts the popularity of chicken pot pie in ⁄ households.

A redware flask, in the form of a pig, attributed to Wallace and Cornwall Kirkpatrick, Anna Pottery, incised 'Railroad & River Guide with a little Good Old Rye in' and the names of local landmarks, slight damage, America, Illinois, c1880, 7½in (19cm) wide.

£4,000–5,000 Skinner

A redware model of a dog, with scratch decoration, ochre and manganese underglaze, America, Pennsylvania or Virginia, 1860s, 4½in (11.5cm) wide.

£4,500–5,200 Raccoon Creek ⊞

Pieces such as this were produced by potters for their children, and are therefore not often found in good condition.

ɗware pitcher, by John Brownscombe, ɑged, Canada, Ontario, Kinloss ıship, 19thC, 10½in (26.5cm) high.

300–2,200 Waddington's

A redware plate, decorated with a stylized tulip, America, Pennsylvania, Berks County, 1840–60, 8½in (21.5cm) diam.

£4,500–5,000 Raccoon Creek ⊞

Occasionally decorators of slipware plates would produce a piece with a more realistic design than usual. It is believed that they were made for display or a special occasion and are therefore not commonly found.

A redware two-handled urn, with manganese brush decoration and a clear lead glaze, America, Pennsylvania, 1825–50, 9½in (24cm) high.

£2,000–2,200 Raccoon Creek ⊞

This urn is a good example of how an attractive glaze can distinguish a fairly common early form.

SSENTIAL REFERENCE REDWARE DECORATION

-unctional redware, made from alluvial clay, was first made in America m c1625, and manufacture continued well into the 19th century.

Red earthenware, made largely in Connecticut and decorated with trailed ›, is often referred to as Pennsylvania slipware.

Pieces are often found in the form of deep plates, pans and pie dishes but items were used frequently they are often found in worn condition.

To differentiate between modern earthenware and early pieces, pick up : item, look at it closely and feel it. Older pieces have usually developed a tina and surface quality that is hard to copy.

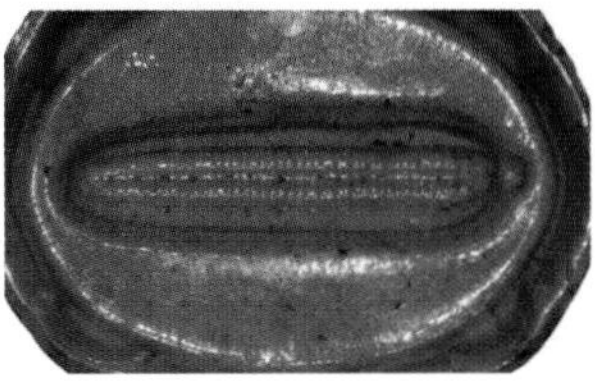

Impressed

Spotted

Incised

Sponged

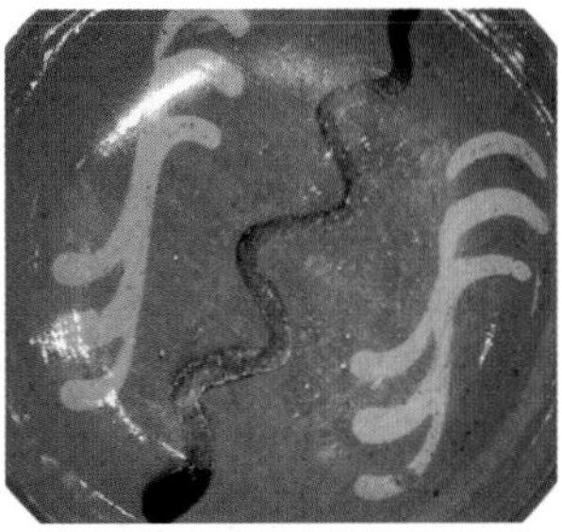

Slip-trailed

AMERICAN STONEWARE

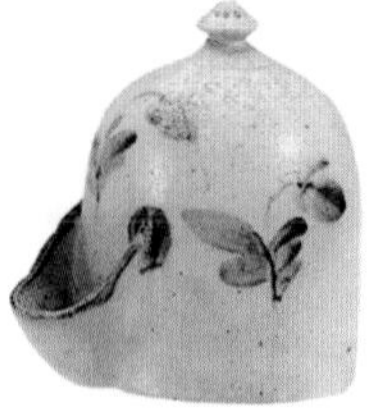

A stoneware bird feeder, decorated with flowers, America, Pennsylvania, 19thC, 6in (15cm) high.

£1,800–2,200 Freeman's

A stoneware cake pot, decorated with grapes, America, Philadelphia, 1860–80, 8½in (21.5cm) diam.

£700–800 Raccoon Creek

These forms were used to store cake in the 19th century. This example is particularly well decorated with a cobalt brushed design encircling the whole pot.

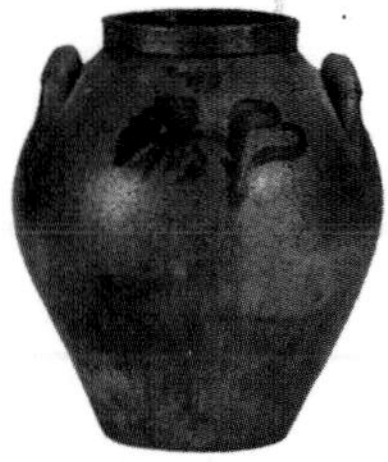

A stoneware pot, by D. Fisk, decorated w a flower, America, Ohio, Akron, early 19th 13in (33cm) high.

£80–100 Waddington's

A stoneware crock, with stencilled inscription 'Hamilton Jones, Greensboro, PA', America, 10in (25.5cm) high.

£75–90 Jackson's

An N. A. White & Son stoneware crock, decorated with a flower, America, Utica, late 19thC, 8½in (21.5cm) high.

£65–80 Waddington's

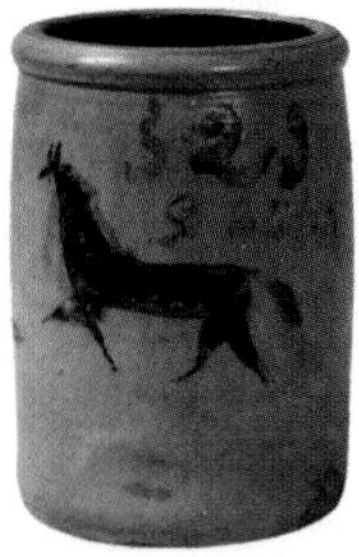

A salt-glazed stoneware jar, incised with horse, America, early 19thC, 11in (28cm) h

£2,000–2,400 Skinner

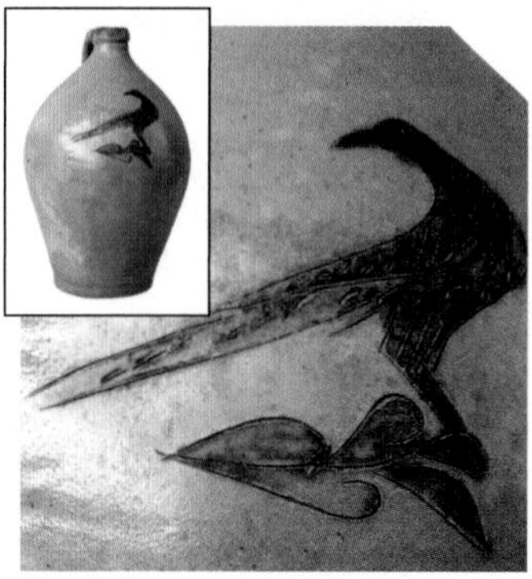

A stoneware jug, incised with a bird, America, New York/Connecticut Valley, 1810–30, 12½in (32cm) high.

£2,300–2,600 Raccoon Creek

Pieces such as this were decorated when wet. The bird would have been etched into the wet clay and further enhanced by a cobalt brushed glaze, then salted.

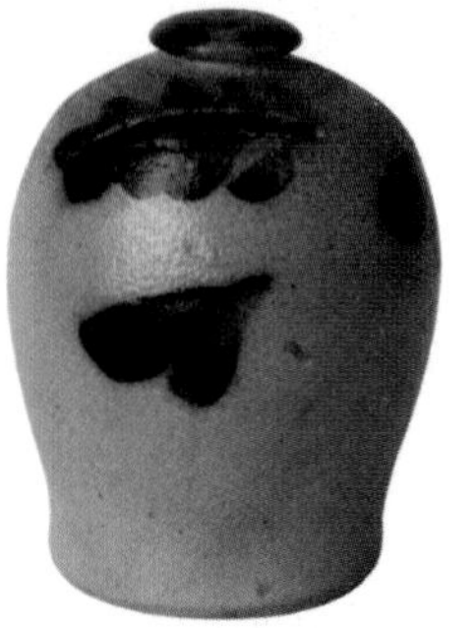

A Remmey Pottery stoneware money bank, with a button finial, America, Philadelphia, c1880, 4½in (11.5cm) high.

£4,700–5,200 Raccoon Creek

Money banks such as this were made for sale to the public and often custom-made for special people and events. The Richard Clinton Remmey Factory produced three classic styles during the 19th century.

A stoneware pitcher, decorated with birds and floral baskets, the handle as a snake, America, Delaware Valley, damaged, 1830–50, 8½in (21.5cm) high.

£22,000–26,000 Raccoon Creek

Unusual pieces such as this were made for presentation and are rarely seen. This pitch was probably made as an anniversary toke and, although cracked, is sought after by collectors of decorated stoneware.

MARKET INFORMATION REDWARE & STONEWARE

- The complex and diverse objects made by American potters of the 18th and 19th centuries continue to interest American collectors at all levels. Redware and stoneware in particular are fetching very high prices.
- Stoneware incised with human figures and/or animals continues to set records, regardless of condition. A flask with incised double bird and heart decoration, brushed with cobalt and ochre recently fetched approximately £20,000 at a New York auction despite being severely cracked.
- A redware slip-decorated plate with polychrome floral decoration achieved over £16,500 in a recent Pennsylvan auction, again illustrating that better and rarer pieces achieve high prices.
- Although still popular with collectors, everyday redware and stoneware items are selling slowly, with the more common items currently remaining on the shelf.

ONTINENTAL MAIOLICA

aiolica charger, decorated with an
l kissing a nymph, Italy, 19thC,
(63.5cm) diam.
000–1,200 Freeman's

A Cantagalli maiolica charger, painted with the head of an angel and an inscription, Italy, late 19thC, 18¾in (47.5cm) diam.
£2,500–3,000 Cheffins

A maiolica drug jar, decorated with fruits and scrolling foliage clusters, the handles with mask terminals, Italy, 17thC, 14in (35.5cm) high.
£4,500–5,000 Sotheby's

ir of maiolica drug jars, marked 'Ung.
olice' and 'Ung. d'Ossisep di Merc', Italy,
0, 7¼in (18.5cm) high.
5–750 Hugh Mote

A Ligurian maiolica wet drug jar, painted with a border of rabbits and fruit, Italy, 18thC, 7¾in (19.5cm) high.
£700–850 Gorringes (L)

A Castelli maiolica plate, painted in the manner of Carlo Antonio Grue with a bear hunt, Italy, c1720, 6¾in (17cm) diam.
£1,300–1,600 Sotheby's (Am)

eruta maiolica tazza, painted by Del
gimento with a biblical scene of Virgin
with a saint kissing the Christ child,
aged and restored, Italy, c1710,
in (32cm) diam.
700–3,000 Guest & Gray

air of maiolica two-handled vases,
ted with battle scenes, the snake handles
mask terminals, restored, Italy,
19thC, 27½in (70cm) high.
0–1,100 Sworders

ESSENTIAL REFERENCE CANTAGALLI

This maiolica vase is signed with the cockerel mark of the Cantagalli factory which was founded by Ulysse Cantagalli and his brother Giuseppe at Doccia, near Florence. From 1878, it produced copies of early Italian maiolica, Middle Eastern and Hispano-Moresque pottery. This vase is derived from a 16th-century example made at Urbino. From about 1899 earthenware vases decorated with stylized animal and plant forms were made in the Art Nouveau manner and in 1901 the factory produced vases and dishes from designs by the English potter, William de Morgan.

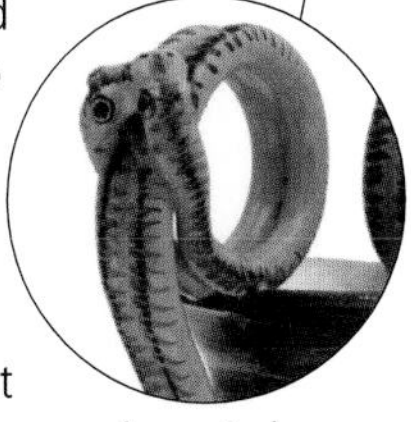

A Cantagalli maiolica two-handled vase, hand-painted with an Italianate scene, with serpent handles, marked, Italy, c1885, 15in (38cm) high.
£1,600–1,800 Griffin

DUTCH DELFT

A Dutch Delft barber's bowl, decorated with floral sprigs, restored, slight damage, 18thC, 10¾in (27cm) diam.

£900–1,100 Guest & Gray

A Dutch Delft charger, possibly by Gÿsbrecht Gruyck, Holland, 1663–71, 13in (33cm) diam.

£500–550 Moxhams

A Dutch Delft charger, decorated with a deer, slight damage, Holland, c1750, 13½in (34.5cm) diam.

£800–900 Guest & Gray

A Dutch Delft flask, painted with people drinking coffee, the reverse with a bird, Chinese emblems and vases, the sides with pierced rocks and flowering plants, Holland, mid-18thC, 7½in (19cm) high.

£2,500–3,000 Sotheby's (Am)

A Dutch Delft shoe brush back, slight damage, Holland, early 18thC, 5½in (14cm) high.

£2,000–2,500 Sotheby's (NY)

A Dutch Delft charger, decorated with a man in lion form, Holland, c1780, 13¾in (35cm) diam.

£450–500 Hugh Mote

A pair of Dutch Delft wall plaques, each painted with rustic scenes of figures, farm animals and buildings, one plaque restored, Holland, 19thC, 22in (56cm) high.

£350–425 Sworders

A Dutch Delft candlestick, painted with a monogram beneath a crown flanked by laurels, Holland, 1660–70, 8¾in (22cm) hi

£2,000–2,500 Sotheby's (O)

A Dutch Delft Factory De Porceleyne Clae charger, maker's marks, Holland, 18thC, 12¼in (31cm) diam.

£320–360 Guest & Gray

A pair of Dutch Delft chargers, Holland, c1790, 12in (30.5cm) diam.

£700–800 Hugh Mote

A Dutch Delft wall plaque, painted with a townscape above a mask within a mouldec border, Holland, 19thC, 22½in (57cm) higr

£800–1,000 Sworders

ıtch Delft plate, painted with a half-length crowned portrait of am III flanked by the initials 'K' and 'W', within a scroll border, the ɘrside with number 20, slight damage, c1689, 8½in (21.5cm) diam.

000–2,500 Special Auction Services

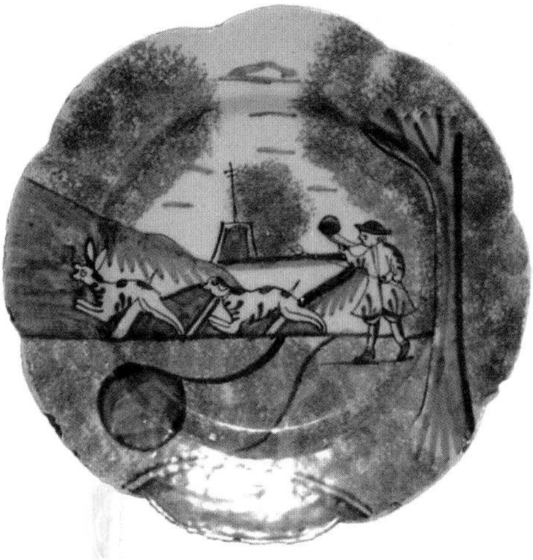

A Dutch Delft plate, decorated with a hunter and dog chasing a hare, Holland, c1750, 9in (23cm) diam.

£500–550 Guest & Gray

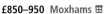

air of Dutch Delft plates, Holland, c1750, (23cm) diam.

50–950 Moxhams

A Dutch Delft plate, decorated with a leopard, Holland, c1750, 14in (35.5cm) diam.

£850–950 Moxhams

A Dutch Delft plate, painted with flowers, Holland, c1750, 9in (23cm) diam.

£250–275 Moxhams

ıtch Delft plate, painted in manganese ı a rose, Holland, c1760, 9in (23cm) diam.

20–140 Moxhams

A Dutch Delft plate, decorated with flowers, Holland, c1790, 9in (23cm) diam.

£90–100 Peter Norden

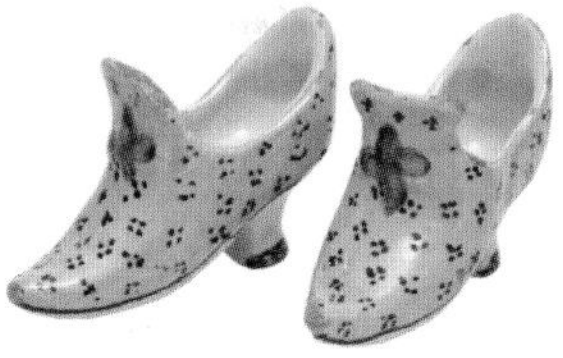

A pair of Dutch Delft shoes, Holland, c1780, 3¼in (8.5cm) long.

£450–500 Hugh Mote

ɘe Dutch Delft tiles, painted in the manner of Dürer with animals, Holland, y 19thC, each tile 6in (15cm) wide.

25–475 Moxhams

A Dutch Delft vase, decorated with chinoiserie figures in a garden, damaged, Holland, late 17thC, 6in (15cm) high.

£600–700 Guest & Gray

A Dutch Delft De Drye Clocken factory garniture of vases, painted with a river scene, factory mark, restored, early 18thC, largest 11¾in (30cm) high.

£3,250–4,000 Sotheby's (NY)

A pair of Dutch Delft Factory De Porceley Bijl vases, moulded and painted with a cartouche panel of figures in boats, with windmills in river landscapes, mark in blue, Holland, 18thC, 8¾in (22.5cm) high.

£750–850 Guest & Gray

A Dutch Delft vase, decorated with flowers and birds, Holland, 18thC, 11in (28cm) high.

£400–500 Holloway's

A pair of Dutch Delft covered vases, the knops modelled as dogs of *Fo*, Holland, c1780, 11in (28cm) high.

£1,800–2,000 Hugh Mote

A Dutch Delft wig stand, decorated with figures, on a baluster stem, Holland, c170 8½in (21.5cm) high.

£2,500–3,000 Sotheby's

FRENCH FAIENCE

A faïence bowl, decorated with three birds, France, c1800, 13in (33cm) diam.

£475–525 Moxhams

A Moustiers faïence dish, decorated with the arms of the Lambesti family, France, c1760, 17in (43cm) wide.

£430–480 Guest & Gray

A Strasbourg faïence plate, marked H/23 for Paul Honnogg, France, c1780, 9½in (24cm) diam.

£220–250 Stockspring Antiques

A Malicorne faïence plate, France, 19thC, 10in (25.5cm) diam.

£140–160
Scottish Antique & Arts

A faïence tulip vase, formed in two sections, the upper part pierced with rows of holes, the base with a moulded satyr mask at each side, damaged and restored, France, mid-18thC, 12¼in (31cm) high.

£1,200–1,400 Guest & Gray

A faïence tureen and cover, in the form of a recumbent cow, on a stand, interior with painted number 4, damaged, France, 19thC 9¾in (25cm) wide.

£120–150 Dreweatt Neate (HAM)

;ERMAN FAIENCE

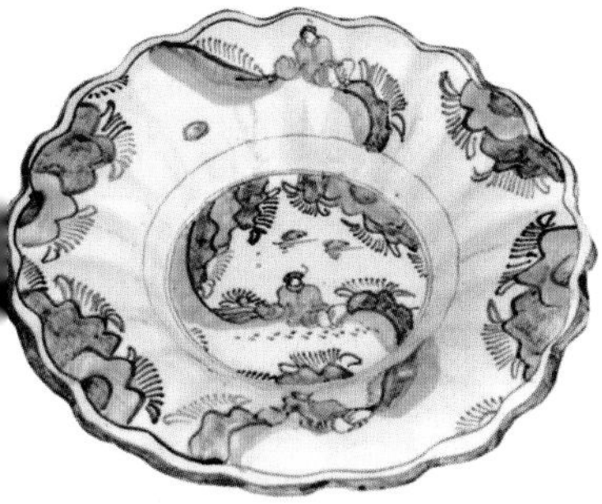

aïence bowl, with a fluted rim, painted with chinoiserie oration, Germany, 18thC, 8¼in (21cm) diam.

00–250 Holloway's

lanau faïence pewter-mounted armorial jug, the er struck with an angel and initial 'H', Germany, cover bably Frankfurt, 1720–30, 12in (30.5cm) high.

,250–4,000 Sotheby's (O)

A Magdeburg faïence plate, with a pierced rim, painted with a flower spray, Germany, c1775, 9in (23cm) diam.

£700–850 Sotheby's (O)

A pair of Niederviller faïence figures of musicians, playing bagpipes and a mandolin, each standing on a grassy base and with a tree stump support, damaged and repaired, Germany, 1760–80, 5¼in (13.5cm) high.

£1,500–1,800
Sotheby's (O)

lurenberg faïence pewter-mounted kard, painted with a pastoral scene ked by cornucopiae and flowers, the cover et with a medallion of St John Nepomuk, many, c1740, 9in (23cm) high.

,300–1,600 Sotheby's (O)

A faïence pewter-mounted tankard, painted with towers among trees, the cover with a medallion possibly showing the Annunciation, Germany, c1760, 9½in (24cm) high.

£1,100–1,250 Guest & Gray

A faïence vase, painted with figures and a pine tree, restored, painted mark, Germany, 18thC, 7½in (19cm) high.

£250–300
Woolley & Wallis

GERMAN STONEWARE

A stoneware pewter-mounted bellarmine, decorated with a face mask, foliate scrollwork, acanthus leaves and six medallions with an image of a religious figure, slight damage, Germany, probably Cologne, c1550, 8in (20.5cm) high.

£900–1,100 BBR

A stoneware bellarmine, decorated with three relief-moulded medallions enclosing a coat-of-arms and date 1607, slight damage, pewter cover missing, Germany, possibly Cologne, early 17thC, 14¼in (36cm) high.

£6,000–7,000 Sotheby's (Am)

A stoneware bellarmine, decorated with a beared mask over a floret, damaged, Germany, c1680, 5½in (14cm) high.

£750–900 Sworders

A salt-glazed stoneware wine bottle, Germany, 18thC, 12in (30.5cm) high.

£160–180 Offa's Dyke

A Creussen stoneware hexagonal pewter mounted flask, each side moulded with a titled saint within beaded arcaded panels, slight damage, Germany, late 17thC, 9½in (24cm) high.

£2,500–3,000 Sotheby's (O)

EXPERT'S EYE BELLARMINES

Bellarmines are brown-glazed stoneware jugs from Cologne or Frechen. They are allegedly named after the notorious and much-hated Cardinal Bellarmine. Most of the vessels are applied with small medallions or an armorial device, which is sometimes the arms of Elizabeth I of England.

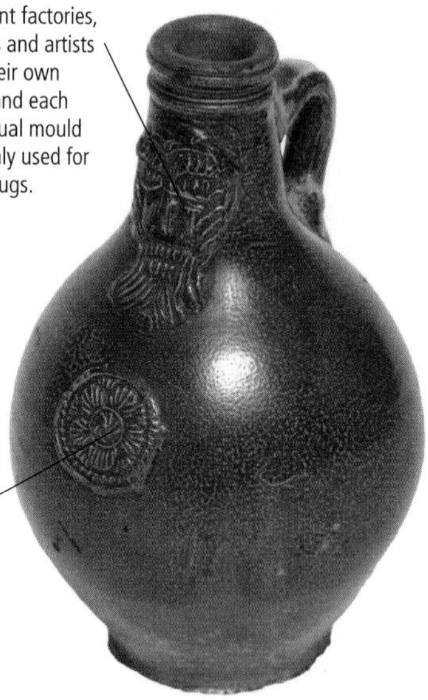

Different factories, potters and artists had their own ideas and each individual mould was only used for a few jugs.

Jugs can be found with up to three medallions.

The beard is too tightly curled and mechanical.

The applied medallions have a thick edge.

A fake bellarmine should be easy to spot as they have a more regular appearance. The genuine bellarmine above is from the late 17th century.

£500–600

ISCELLANEOUS CONTINENTAL POTTERY

ence punchbowl, with floral decoration and monogram, slight
ıge, Continental, c1800, 12¾in (32.5cm) diam.

0–850 Sotheby's (NY)

An earthenware centrepiece, by Louis Carrier-Belleuse, in the form of a terrace, each end with a pierced basket and three putti, restored, incised maker's name, France, late 19thC, 36in (91.5cm) wide.

£2,500–3,000 Sotheby's (O)

Louis (1848–1912) was the son of Albert Carrier-Belleuse. He became Art Director at the Choisy-le-Roi factory and is known for producing terracotta busts and took a keen interest in mythological subjects.

spano-Moresque-style charger, painted
a monogram 'Y' below a coronet, the
vith stylized motifs and shields, Spain,
0, 17¼in (44cm) diam.

0–150 Halls

A maiolica dish, decorated with a castle with two towers in a landscape, slight damage, Spain, Aragon, 18thC, 12½in (32cm) diam.

£850–950 Guest & Gray

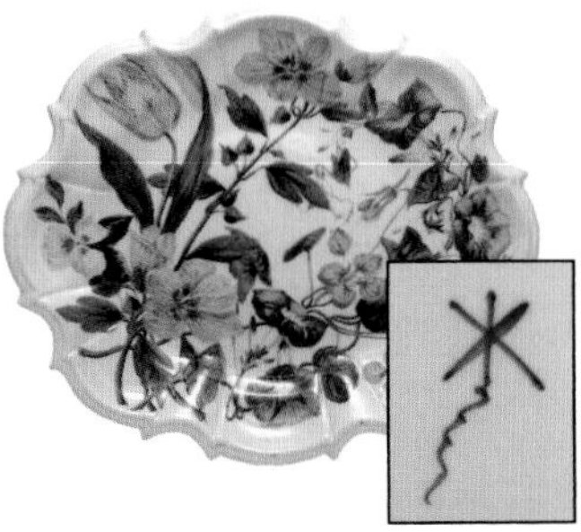

A Nove dish, with floral decoration, mark to base, Italy, c1860, 15¾in (40cm) wide.

£350–400 Hugh Mote

t of three Creil plates, decorated
military scenes, France, c1810,
(20.5cm) diam.

0–500 Moxhams

A Sèvres-style urn, painted after François Gerard with a scene of Napoleon Bonaparte at the Battle of Austerlitz, with gilt-metal handles and base, pseudo-Sèvres marks and 'Austerlitz', France, late 19thC, 38½in (98cm) high.

£4,500–5,500 Dreweatt Neate

The original work was designed for the chamber of the Conseil d'Etats *and shows General Rapp presenting Bonaparte with captured colours taken from the combined Russo-Austrian army at Austerlitz on 2 December 1805, often considered one of his greatest battles. The painting was exhibited at the Salon of 1810 and is at Versailles.*

ïence tureen, cover and stand, in the
of a red cabbage, the cover with a snail
l, slight damage, restored, probably
ssels, late 18thC, 10¼in (26cm) wide.

200–3,800 Sotheby's (NY)

A pair of Gabel redware vases, relief-decorated with lizards, satyrs and flowers, damaged, Bohemia, early 18thC, 11¾in (30cm) high.

£2,200–2,750 Bukowskis

PORCELAIN

CHELSEA

A Chelsea basket, the interior painted in the Kakiemon style with flowers and phoenix roundels, rim ground, c1755, 8in (20.5cm) diam.

£900–1,100 Woolley & Wallis

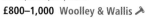

A Chelsea beaker, painted with flowers, c1775, 2¾in (7cm) diam.

£800–1,000 Woolley & Wallis

A Chelsea beaker and saucer, moulded bands of acanthus leaves and painted wi flowers, slight damage, red anchor mark, c

£1,500–1,800 Woolley & Wallis

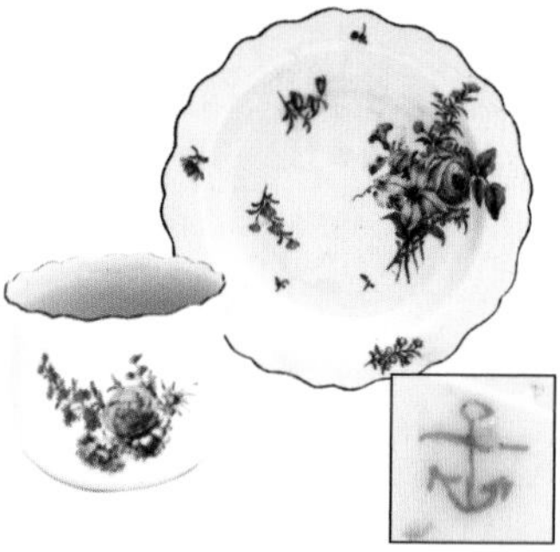

A Chelsea finger bowl and stand, painted with flowers, red anchor mark, c1755, stand 6in (15cm) diam.

£1,000–1,200 David March

A Chelsea cup, painted in the Kakiemon style with flowers, handle replaced, c1750.

£400–500 Woolley & Wallis

A Chelsea coffee cup, teabowl and sauc painted with flowers and gilt panels, gold anchor marks, 1760–65.

£3,800–4,500 Sotheby's (NY)

A Chelsea dish, painted in the Kakiemon style with a tiger and a flowering shrub, slight damage, restored, 1750–55, 15½in (39.5cm) wide.

£900–1,100 Woolley & Wallis

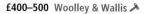

A Chelsea dish, painted with flowers, painted mark, 1752–56, 8½in (21.5cm) wide.

£600–700 Gorringes (L)

A Chelsea dish, painted with fruit and insects, painted mark, 1752–56, 10¼in (26cm) wide.

£400–500 Gorringes (L)

A Chelsea dish, painted with exotic birds in a landscape, 1752–58, 10in (25.5cm) wide.

£1,200–1,400 Louisa Francis & Walker

A Chelsea dish, painted with fruit and vegetables, brown anchor mark, c1760, 8¼in (21cm) wide.

£1,200–1,400 Woolley & Wallis

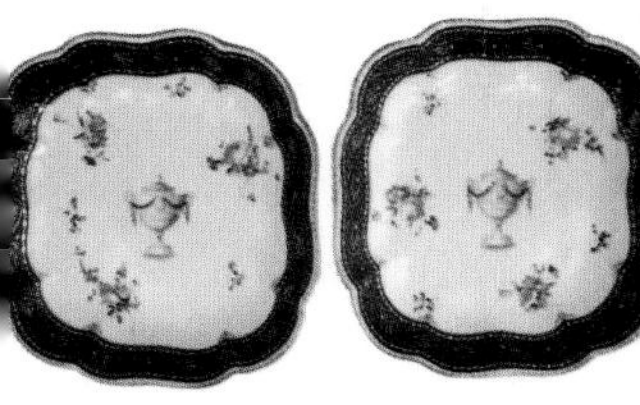

r of Chelsea Derby dessert dishes, each painted loral bouquets surrounding a central urn, with led' and gilt-beaded borders, gilt painted mark, , 7¾in (19.5cm) wide.

–600 Dreweatt Neate (HAM)

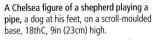

A Chelsea figure of a shepherd playing a pipe, a dog at his feet, on a scroll-moulded base, 18thC, 9in (23cm) high.

£525–625 Andrew Hartley

A Chelsea allegorical figure of Summer, c1775, 5in (12.5cm) high.

£4,500–5,500 Woolley & Wallis

elsea goat and bee jug, painted and moulded with rs and insects, restored, incised triangle mark, –49, 4½in (11.5cm) high.

00–8,500 Sotheby's (NY)

A Chelsea cream jug, painted with Lady in a Pavilion pattern, damaged, repaired, raised anchor mark, c1750, 4¼in (10.5cm) high.

£375–450 Woolley & Wallis

XPERT'S EYE CHELSEA FIGURES

elsea, along with many other British tories, made close copies of Meissen ures, as well as taking their inspiration m prints. Figures produced during the d anchor period (1756–69) are netimes elaborate and can command h prices. This pair of sweetmeat ures c1765 have all the 18th-century ments a buyer should look for.

,000–2,250 David March

Pastel colours were favoured.

Costumes were usually heavily decorated.

ures usually stood on bases which were ly applied with floral bocage. When the age was used as a backdrop, the groups e designed to be displayed on a shelf, some are marked on the back instead he base.

The thin glaze is very glassy and tends to pool and craze, particularly around the bases.

A Chelsea plate, painted with flower sprays, painted mark, 1752–56, 8¾in (22cm) wide.

£400–500 Gorringes (L)

A Chelsea plate, painted with fruit, c1758, 8½in (21.5cm) diam.

£350–380 Stockspring Antiques

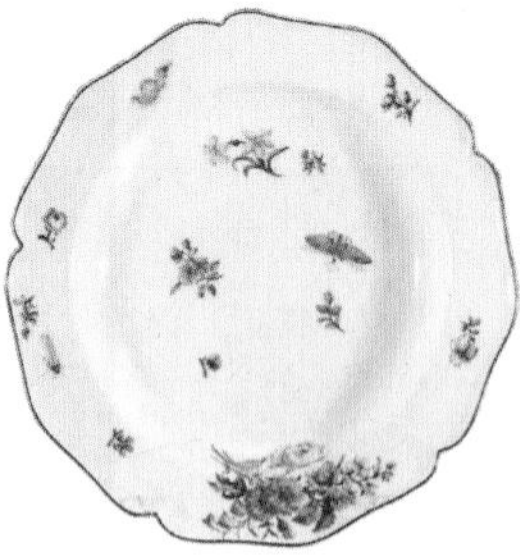

A Chelsea soup plate, painted with flowers and insects, slight wear, red anchor mark, c1755, 9in (23cm) diam.

£900–1,100 Sotheby's (O)

A Chelsea teabowl and saucer, decorated in the manner of Jeffryes Hamett O'Neale with scenes from Aesop's *Fables* after Francis Barlow, the teabowl with 'The Tiger and the Fox', the saucer with 'The Young Kite and His Mother', damaged, c1752.

£9,000–11,000 Woolley & Wallis

A Chelsea teabowl and saucer, painted with a view of a church within a gilt border, painted mark, 1756–69.

£2,250–2,750 Gorringes (L)

A Chelsea plate, painted with birds among branches and rocks within a feather-moulded rim, red anchor mark, c1755, 8¾in (22cm) diam.

£280–320 Dreweatt Neate (N)

A pair of Chelsea potpourri vases and covers, painted with birds and insects, damaged, gold anchor marks, c1765, 7½in (19cm) high.

£5,000–6,000 Sotheby's (NY)

A Chelsea Derby tankard, painted with flowers, gold anchor and 'D' mark, c1775, 5in (12.5cm) high.

£280–320 Dreweatt Neate (N)

A Chelsea Derby teabowl and saucer, painted with flowers, swags and a lattice border within a gilt rim, blue crown over 'D' mark, c1770.

£180–220 Dreweatt Neate (N)

A Chelsea plate, painted with bamboo flowers, rim chip, red anchor mark, c17 9¾in (24.5cm) diam.

£550–650 Woolley & Wallis

A Chelsea saucer, decorated with spray of flowers, red anchor mark, c1753, 4½in (11.5cm) diam.

£700–800 Stockspring Antique

A Chelsea Derby neo-classical vase, the moulded with florets, with two faun-mas handles, the base with paw feet, incised No. 8, patch marks, c1770, 9in (23cm) h

£350–425 Dreweatt Neate (N)

Derby pieces were supported in the kiln three or four balls of clay, about the size marbles, which left marks on the base w removed. They are known as patch mark are a diagnostic feature of 18th-century and Chelsea Derby.

BOW & LONGTON HALL

Bow basket, painted with Quail pattern, 770, 6in (15cm) diam.

,100–1,300 Gorringes (L)

A Bow bowl, decorated with a dragon and pearl pattern, 1762–65, 6in (15cm) diam.

£450–500 Stockspring Antiques

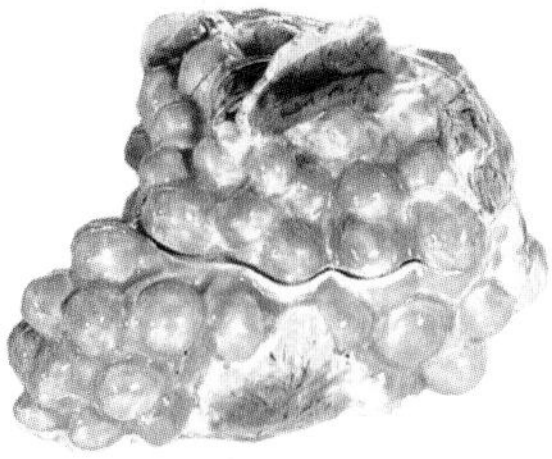

A Longton Hall box and cover, in the form of a bunch of grapes, restored, c1755, 5in (12.5cm) wide.

£2,000–2,500 Sotheby's (NY)

air of Bow candlesticks, each painted h flowers, moulded with scrollwork and ll motifs, slight damage, restored, c1760, n (11.5cm) high.

,200–1,400 Sotheby's (NY)

A Bow coffee can, painted in the *famille rose* style with chrysanthemums and rockwork, c1750, 2½in (6.5cm) high.

£200–250 Dreweatt Neate (N)

A Bow coffee can, painted with Cross-legged Chinaman pattern, the reverse with a fisherman in a boat, slight damage, c1750, 2¼in (5.5cm) high.

£450–550 Woolley & Wallis

SSENTIAL REFERENCE CUP HANDLES

andles on porcelain cups and mugs can help identify a maker and the period of manufacture.

e loop handle form can be und over a long period from e 18th to the 20th century d was used by factories such Vincennes, Sèvres, Chelsea, rby and many others.

This scroll handle with thumb rest and spur is capped with acanthus leaves, which are popular motifs accross a wide range of the applied arts.

The wishbone or clip handle derives from Meissen shapes of the 1740s.

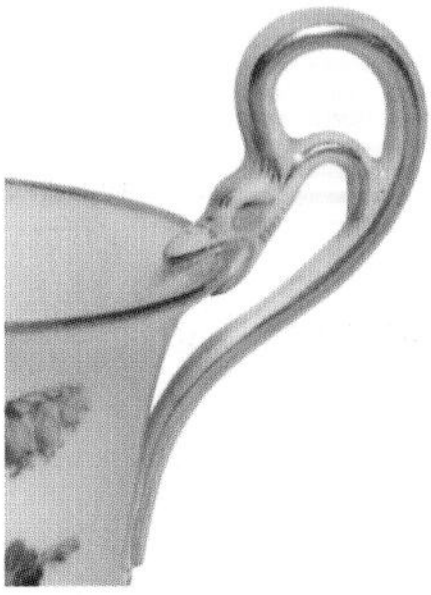

The swan handle first appeared at the beginning of the 19th century. It is associated with Regency and Empire forms.

7' handle is typically a)-classical design.

The ring handle was popular in the second half of the 19th century and early 20th century.

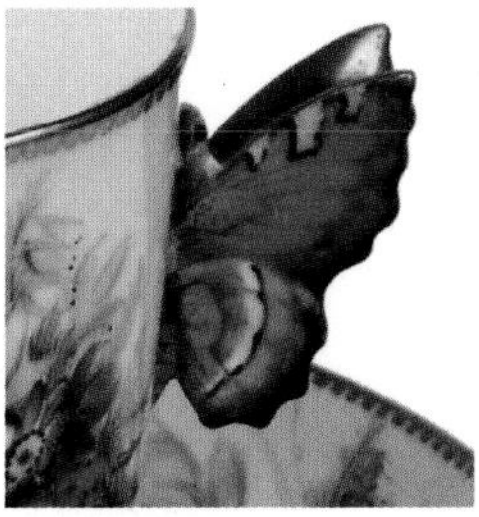

Butterfly handles are fairly uncommon. They appeared from around the 1830s and were used by a number of different English factories.

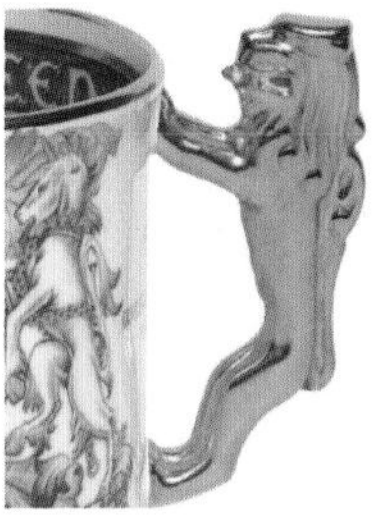

The lion handle form is only found on commemorative mugs.

A Bow coffee can, painted with a willow tree and rockwork, No. 19 to base, 1755–58, 2½in (6.5cm) high.

£300–350 Dreweatt Neate

A Bow leaf dish, painted in the Kakiemon style with Quail pattern, later incised triangle mark, slight damage, 1750–55, 7in (17.5cm) wide.

£450–550 Woolley & Wallis

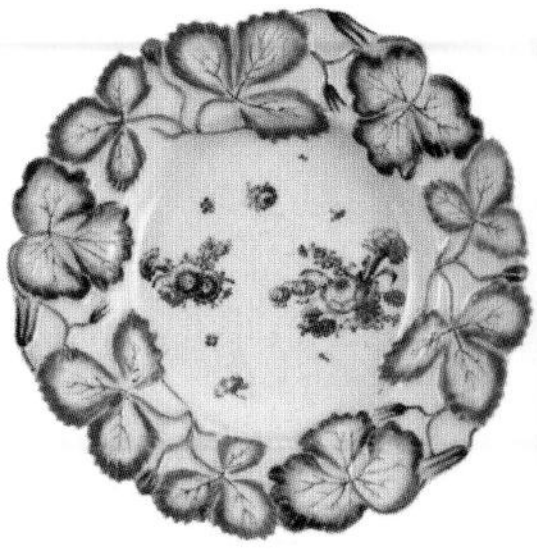

A Longton Hall strawberry dish, painted wi flowers within a moulded border, restored, c1755, 8¾in (22cm) diam.

£450–550 Woolley & Wallis

A Longton Hall figure of Hercules and the Nemean lion, the plinth painted with a landscape panel, slight damage, restored, c1755, 7½in (19cm) high.

£3,800–4,500 Sotheby's (NY)

A Bow figure of Columbine, after Meissen, c1755–58, 5in (12.5cm) high.

£1,000–1,100 David March

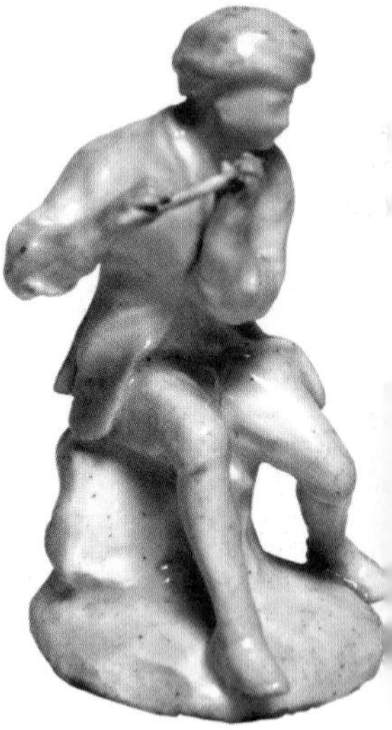

A Bow figure of a flautist, c1756, 4in (10cm) high.

£1,100–1,250 David March

A pair of Bow figures of a monk and a nun, c1758, 4¾in (12cm) high.

£450–550 Dreweatt Neate (N)

A Bow figure of Autumn, from the Rustic Seasons series, c1758, 6in (15cm) high.

£1,350–1,500 David March

A Longton Hall figure of Winter, c1758, 5in (12.5cm) high.

£475–525 David March

A Bow figure of a nun, restored, c1760, 5½in (14cm) high.

£450–500 Hugh Mote

›w figure of Piping Harlequin, c1760, 12.5cm) high.

‹00–2,000 David March

›w plate, painted with a boat in a pagoda ›scape, 1750–55, 8¾in (22cm) diam.

›0–850 Woolley & Wallis

›ngton Hall teabowl and saucer, painted geese, damaged, 1755–60.

›0–1,100 Woolley & Wallis

›ngton Hall teapot and cover, in the form melon, on three leaf legs, slight damage, 55, 4¼in (11cm) high.

›,000–25,000 Sotheby's (NY)

›gton Hall produced a number of ›aordinarily idiosyncratic shapes unlike ›hing by any other 18th-century factory.

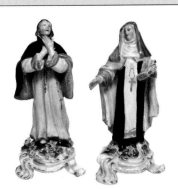

A pair of Bow figures of a Prior and Prioress, c1765, 6in (15cm) high.

£2,200–2,500 David March

A Bow plate, painted with Golfer and Caddy pattern, c1758, 9½in (24cm) diam.

£400–500 Dreweatt Neate (N)

A Bow mug, painted in the *famille rose* style with flowers, leaves and rocks, slight damage, c1755, 4¾in (12cm) high.

£350–425 Woolley & Wallis

A Bow saucer, painted with a Golfer and Caddy pattern, c1760, 4in (10cm) diam.

£300–350 Helen Girton

A miniature Bow tea service, painted with Fruiting Vine pattern, c1758, teapot 2½in (6.5cm) high.

£4,000–4,500 Louisa Francis & Walker

A Bow bottle vase, decorated with flowers, c1758, 6in (15cm) high.

£1,300–1,500 Helen Girton

A Bow vase and cover, pierced and applied with flowers, painted with butterflies, dragonflies, ladybirds and foliage, with female mask handles, the cover with a bird finial, c1765, 11¾in (30cm) high.

£750–900 Dreweatt Neate (N)

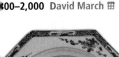

EARLY WORCESTER

DR WALL'S FACTORY AT WORCESTER was among the earliest in England and today is one of the most collected. The factory was founded following the two year venture by Benjamin Lund at Bristol, whereby his Bristol factory was purchased and moved further up the river Severn in 1751. Worcester porcelain had one great advantage over most of its English competitors in that the soft-paste porcelain recipe contained soapstone. This soapstone made the porcelain paste stable in the firing, so that there were fewer kiln losses, a problem that dogged their competitors; it also made the finished porcelain wares resistant to thermal shock, so that the teapots didn't crack the moment boiling water was poured in – this, incidentally, is where the term 'flying teapots' originates from.

In the 18th century, Worcester concentrated on the middle market, making tea and coffee services and a great number of blue and white wares designed to compete with the imports from the Orient. Quite a number of the patterns are direct copies from either Chinese or Japanese porcelains and even use pseudo Chinese marks. Stylistically, the shapes and patterns follow the predominant styles of the century, moving from rococo and chinoiseries in the 1750s and '60s towards neo-classicism by the 1780s and '90s, and again through to the richly gilded wares of the Regency period in the early 19th century. While al periods of Worcester are collected, among the mo highly prized are the small and understated pieces from the first few years. This was nicely demonstra recently when a small jug wrongly described on eb sold for £220, and then properly identified as Worc of c1751 fetched £46,800 at a UK auction house.

The last five years have seen a number of high pr auctions and exhibitions of early Worcester, notab among which is the Zorensky collection of over 14 pieces. The sale, divided into three parts, clearly demonstrates the continued interest among collec The first sale was held at Bonhams in 2004, and w a few lots did fetch five-figure sums, including an elegant rococo sauceboat of c1755 at £13,000 an pair of large baluster vases and covers c1765 at £29,000, the majority of pieces sold for under £1,(The final auction in 2006 again proved a sell-out.

Worcester was such a prolific factory in the 18th century that, 250 years later, collectors really do ha a terrific opportunity to hunt down and purchase pieces at all price levels from a great variety both o form and decoration.

John Axt

A Worcester basket, decorated with Pine Cone pattern, the pierced rim moulded with flowerheads, crescent mark, 18thC, 7¾in (19.5cm) high.

£600–700 **Gorringes (L)**

A Worcester Flight & Barr coffee can, scratched 'B' mark, 1792–1807.

£240–280 **Mere Antiques**

A Chamberlain's Worcester coffee can a saucer, decorated in the Imari style, c182

£220–250 **Guest & Gray**

A Worcester low Chelsea ewer, decorated with a Chinese garden scene, on a moulded acanthus base, c1770, 4¼in (11cm) high.

£225–275 **Sworders**

A Worcester cup and saucer, decorated with an Imari floral pattern, with seal mark, c1770.

£450–500 **Stockspring Antiques**

A Worcester 'Blind Earl' dish, decorated Gilt Queen's pattern, c1765, 6in (15cm) w

£350–425 **Dreweatt Neate (N)**

This pattern is named after the Earl of Cove who lost his sight in a hunting accident. It said that he owned a Worcester set of this pattern and could feel the embossed leav

orcester high Chelsea ewer, painted Chinese figures in a garden, 1765–70, (9cm) high.

0–380 Woolley & Wallis

sea ewers appear in two forms, high and Characteristically the body is lobed, fluted has acanthus moulding rising from the The shape is copied from a rare Chelsea on of the red anchor period, c1755, after h they are named. They were copied at cester, Caughley, Chamberlain's, Newhall other English factories.

A Worcester jug, with gilt and enamelled panels of birds and insects, fretted square mark, c1770, 8in (20cm) high.

£2,200–2,750 Bearnes

A Worcester Flight & Barr jug, decorated with Hop pattern and a view of Buildwas Abbey, c1800, 8in (20.5cm) high.

£2,250–2,500 Mere Antiques

Buildwas Abbey is on the banks of the River Severn. The Abbey was closed in 1536 by the orders of Henry VIII.

'orcester mug, painted with Zigzag Fence ern, scratch line mark and workman's mark, it damage, c1754, 3¾in (9.5cm) high.

400–1,800 Woolley & Wallis

A Worcester plate, decorated in the Chinese style with Hundred Antiques pattern, with pseudo Oriental mark, c1770, 7½in (19cm) diam.

£320–350 Stockspring Antiques

A Chamberlain's Worcester plate, from the Sir James Yeo service, c1815, 9in (23cm) diam.

£625–700 John Newton

This service , made for Sir James Yeo, was ordered in 1815. The border is pattern No. 298 and the centre was decorated with Sir James's crest. He commanded all the Naval Forces on the lakes of Canada during the war of 1812.

/orcester sauce boat, painted with Oriental figures and emblems, aired, c1753, 7½in (19cm) wide.

50–850 Guest & Gray

A Chamberlain's Worcester dinner service, decorated with stylized flowers within gadroon-moulded borders, 1786–1840.

£2,200–2,750 James Adam

SSENTIAL REFERENCE TYPES OF PORCELAIN

Porcelain bodies can be divided into two categories, ard paste and soft paste. This difference can be an d when identifying unmarked pieces.

Hard-paste porcelain was discovered by the cient Chinese and developed using a combination kaolin, *petuntse* and quartz. It was first made in rope by Meissen and has a smooth texture that sembles icing sugar.

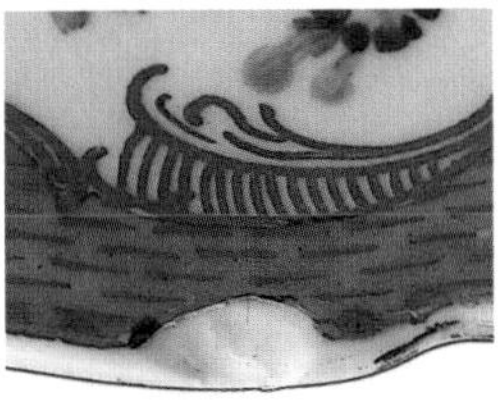

A hard-paste porcelain chip is shiny and resembles a broken flint.

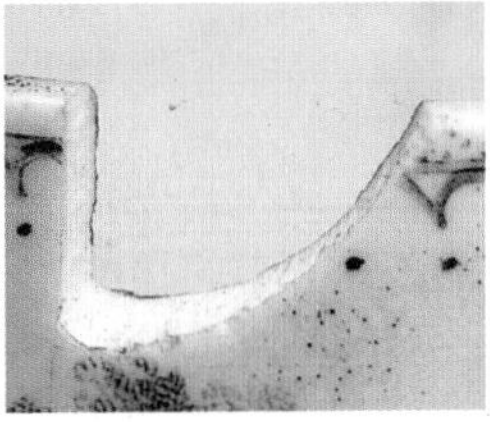

A soft-paste porcelain chip appears granular.

Soft-paste porcelain differs mainly in that it does ot contain kaolin. It was developed in Europe before the secret of making true porcelain was discovered. ie colour can vary from white to grey according to the minerals used and this can help with identification. ie texture is slightly more granular and any chips may have a rougher appearance.

A Worcester Flight Barr & Barr dinner service, comprising approximately 78 pieces, printed with an armorial vignette of a Bishop's mitre and a dove, printed and impressed marks, 1813–40.

£5,500–6,500 Hy Duke

A Worcester mug, printed with a half-length profile of a gentleman pinned with the Garter Star, a Man o'War to the reverse, c1760, 6¼in (16cm) high.

£1,500–1,800 Special Auction Services

A Worcester teapot, painted with Quail pattern, c1770, 7½in (19cm) wide.

£400–500 Dreweatt Neate (N)

This is an unusual version of Quail pattern.

A Worcester Flight & Barr teapot, cover and stand, decorated with Tea Plant pattern, with incised 'B' mark, c1800, 7½in (19cm) high.

£250–280 Stockspring Antiques

A pair of Chamberlain's Worcester sauce tureens, decorated with exotic birds and flowers, c1820, 9in (23cm) high.

£900–1,000 John Newton

A pair of Worcester Flight Barr & Barr vas decorated by Henry Stinton with flowers a insects, c1825, 9in (23cm) high.

£5,000–5,500 Mere Antiques

ROYAL WORCESTER

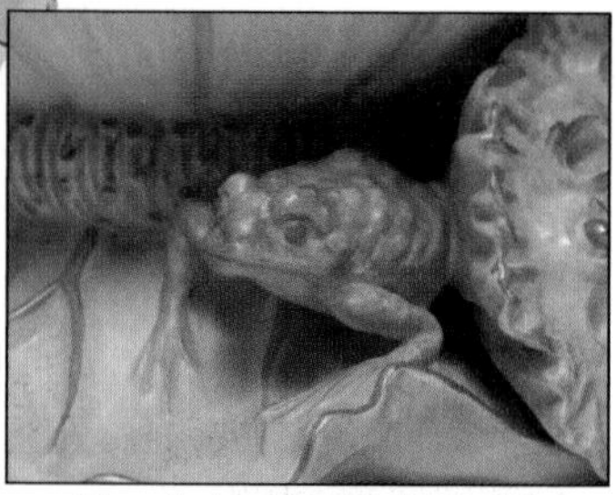

A Royal Worcester bowl, in the form of a lily, the foot with a frog and flower buds, c1880, 12in (30.5cm) diam.

£750–850 Tony Horsley

A Royal Worcester bust of Qu Victoria, modelled by James Hadley, on an integral square column relief-moulded with a bust of Edward, Prince of Wal printed mark and registration, moulded Hadley signature, c1887, 23½in (60cm) high.

£700–850 Sworders

This item would have been produced to celebrate Queen Victoria's Golden Jubilee. In th model, Victoria usually wears a crown, but here it is missing a appears never to have been exta

A Royal Worcester bowl, with reticulated and 'jewelled' decoration, c1890, 4½in (11.5cm) high.

£1,350–1,500 David Brower

A Royal Worcester dish, decorated with flowers and insects, within a gilt and fretwork border, signed 'E. Raby', c1890, 9in (23cm) diam.

£350–400 Tony Horsley

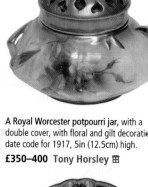

A Royal Worcester figure, after Sir Thomas Brock, entitled 'The Bather Surprised', impressed mark, dated 1893, 26in (66cm) high.

£1,400–1,750 Andrew Hartley

A pair of Royal Worcester figures, each in the form of a classical maiden, gilt printed marks and date code for 1903, 10in (25.5cm) high.

£900–1,000 Sworders

A Royal Worcester potpourri jar, with a double cover, with floral and gilt decorati date code for 1917, 5in (12.5cm) high.

£350–400 Tony Horsley

A Royal Worcester plate, decorated in gil and hand-painted with fruit, signed 'R. Sebright', 1917, 9in (23cm) diam.

£525–600 Tony Horsley

A Royal Worcester tea service, comprising five pieces, applied with lilies, printed marks, c1893, teapot 6in (15cm) high.

£200–240 Freeman's Fine Art

A pair of Royal Worcester tazzas, c1910, 4in (10cm) diam.

£100–110 K & M Antiques

A Royal Worcester tea service, comprising 23 pieces, painted by E. Townsend, Mosely, H. Price and H. Ayrton with fruit, marked, c1934.

£5,000–6,000 Anderson & Garland

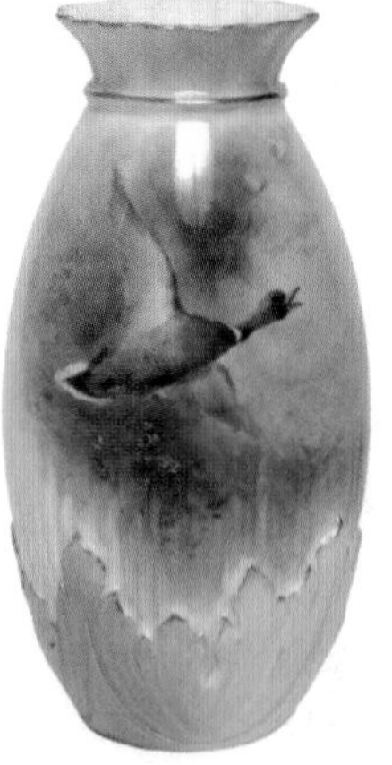

A Royal Worcester vase, signed 'Jas Stinton', date code for 1907, 5¾in (14.5cm) high.

£1,000–1,100 Tony Horsley

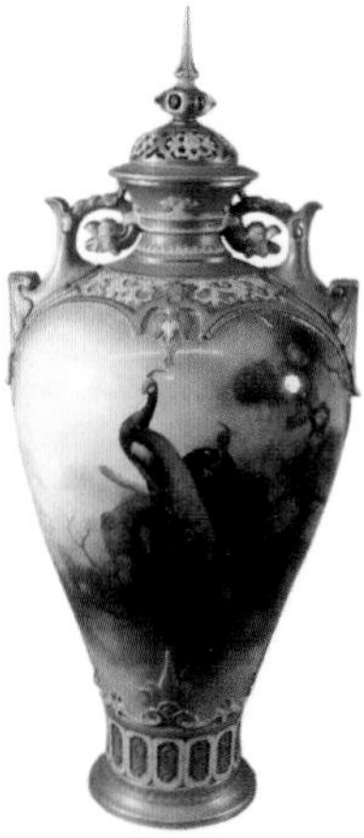

A Royal Worcester vase and cover, by N. White, decorated with a peacock, date code for 1909, 15¾in (40cm) high.

£2,500–3,000 Penrith Farmers' & Kidd's

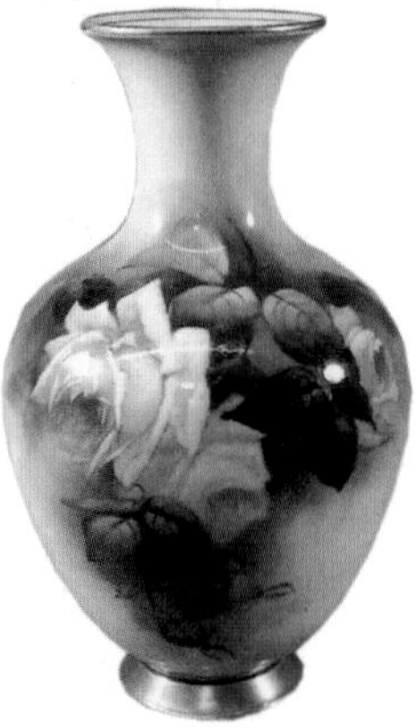

A Royal Worcester vase, by R. Austin, hand-painted with roses, date code for 1911, 8in (20.5cm) high.

£250–300 Penrith Farmers' & Kidd's

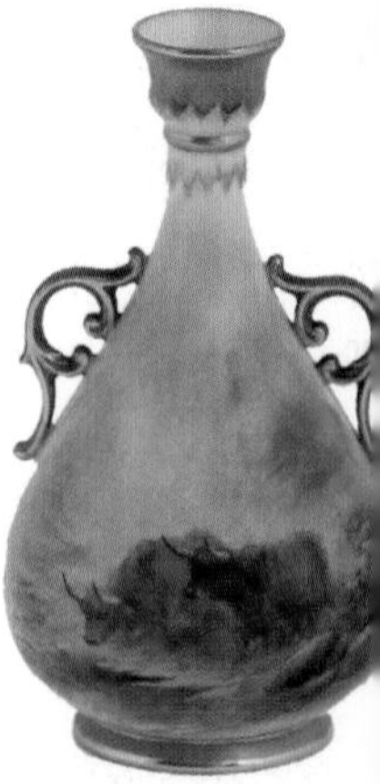

A Royal Worcester vase, pain by Harry Stinton with Highland cattle, shape No. G995, printe marks, date code for 1912, 6in (15cm) high.

£1,100–1,250 Bearnes

OWESTOFT, CAUGHLEY & LIVERPOOL

chard Chaffers Liverpool bowl, painted with a Chinese lady fishing
eath a willow tree, slight damage, c1760, 5¾in (14.5cm) diam.
0–600 **Woolley & Wallis**

A Richard Chaffers Liverpool bowl, painted with peony and willow issuing from rockwork, 1760–70, 6in (15cm) diam.
£300–350 **Woolley & Wallis**

verpool bowl, printed with figures and
ep, slight damage, 1770–80,
1 (21cm) high.
60–200 **Woolley & Wallis**

A Caughley fluted bowl and cover, c1785, 4¼in (11cm) diam.
£280–320 **Stockspring Antiques**

'aughley caddy spoon, transfer-printed
1 a pagoda, 1780–85, 4¼in (11cm) wide.
50–800 **Woolley & Wallis**

A Samuel Gilbody Liverpool coffee cup, painted with flowers and bamboo issuing from rocks, 1755–60.
£1,000–1,200 **Woolley & Wallis**

A Richard Chaffers Liverpool coffee can, painted with a figure, slight damage, c1760, 2½in (6.5cm) high.
£400–500 **Woolley & Wallis**

Richard Chaffers Liverpool coffee
), c1760, 2¼in (5.5cm) high.
00–220 **Guest & Gray**

A Lowestoft coffee cup and saucer, painted with Mansfield pattern, painted marks, repaired, 1760–70.
£250–300 **Woolley & Wallis**

A Lowestoft butter dish and cover, decorated with Fisherman pattern, 1760–65, 5½in (14cm) wide.
£5,000–6,000
Penrith Farmers' & Kidd's

iverpool coffee can, c1765,
n (6.5cm) high.
50–300 **M V S Antiques**

A Lowestoft cream boat, in the Chelsea ewer shape, painted with flowers and leaves, c1775, 3¾in (9.5cm) wide.
£350–425 **Tennants**

A Caughley pickle dish, c1780, 4¾in (12cm) wide.

£250–300 M V S Antiques

A Caughley egg drainer, printed with Fisherman pattern, 1785–99, 3in (7.5cm) diam.

£400–450 Louisa Francis & Walker

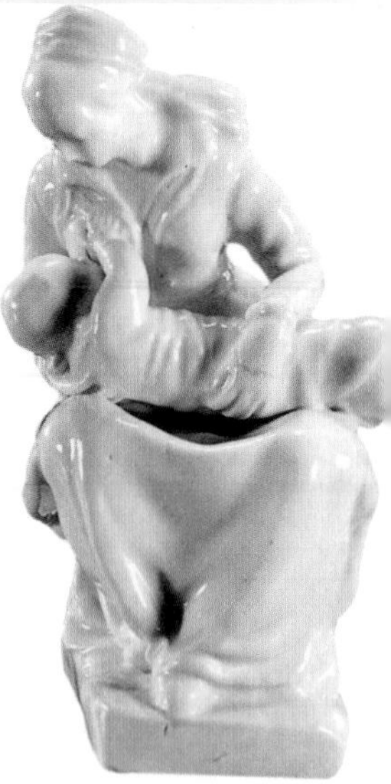

A Richard Chaffers Liverpool figure of La Nourrice, slight damage, 1758–60, 5¾in (14.5cm) high.

£4,000–5,000 Sotheby's

A Lowestoft sparrow beak milk jug, painted with Oriental-style flowering branches and rockwork, c1780, 3½in (9cm) high.

£650–750 Louisa Francis & Walker

The handle terminal is characteristic of Lowestoft pieces.

A Caughley jug, with cabbage leaf moulding and mask spout, printed with versions of the Fisherman and Cormorant pattern, c1785, 7½in (19cm) high.

£180–220 Bearnes

A Liverpool cream jug, c1770, 3½in (9cm) high.

£550–600 M V S Antiques

A Lowestoft teabowl, c1765, 3in (7.5cm) high.

£300–350 M V S Antiques

A Liverpool teabowl and saucer, c1775.

£140–160 Stockspring Antiques

A Caughley miniature teabowl and sauce
printed with Fisherman pattern, with 'S' ma
c1785, 1¾in (4.5cm) diam.

£275–300 Stockspring Antiques

A Caughley tea canister, c1780, 5in (12.5cm) high.

£225–250 M V S Antiques

A Richard Chaffers Liverpool teapot and cover, painted with figures, restored, slight damage, c1760, 8¼in (21cm) high.

£375–450 Woolley & Wallis

A Lowestoft saucer, painted with a figure, c1760, 4¾in (12cm) diam.

£400–500 Dreweatt Neate (N)

ARLY DERBY

erby bough pot, slight damage, restored,
ted marks, c1800, 9¾in (25cm) wide.
0–280 **Waddington's**

erby coffee can, probably by Thomas
tin Randall, decorated with a view of the
Forest, Hampshire, pattern No. 743,
ked, 1796–1800, 2½in (6.5cm) high.
0–350 **Dreweatte Neate (N)**

**air of Derby figures of Ranelagh
ncers,** 1765–70, 10in (25.5cm) high.
500–4,000 **Moxhams**
elagh Gardens were an 18th-century lic pleasure ground in the Chelsea/Fulham , which at the time was on the outskirts ondon, and is now the site of the annual lsea Flower Show. It was a very popular ue, particularly for romantic assignations, included a rococo rotunda where Mozart formed in 1765 at the age of nine, a nese pavilion, an ornamental lake and a nber of walks.

**air of Derby figures of Crying Boy and
ghing Girl,** c1770, 8in (20.5cm) high.
00–1,000 **David March**

A pair of Derby candlesticks, applied with rabbits and flowering shrubs, c1775, 9in (23cm) high.
£2,000–2,200 **David March**

A Derby figure of Autumn, slight damage, c1760, 4¾in (12cm) high.
£2,000–2,500 **Sotheby's**

A pair of Derby figures, entitled 'The Mansion House Dwarves', c1770, 8in (20.5cm) high.
£1,350–1,500 **David March**
This type of figure was first made at Derby in 1784 and named after the dwarf figures that stood outside the Mansion House, London, bearing annoucements of plays and sales.

A pair of Derby figures of dancers, c1775, 8in (20.5cm) high.
£2,250–2,500 **David March**

A Derby coffee can, with a wishbone handle, c1790, 2½in (6.5cm) high.
£90–100 **Stockspring Antiques**

A Derby figural group of Venus and Cupid, slight damage, c1760, 7¾in (19.5cm) high.
£800–1,000 **Sotheby's**

A Derby figure of John Wilkes, c1780, 12in (30.5cm) high.
£1,100–1,200 **David March**
Politician and journalist John Wilkes was a celebrated champion of Liberty.

A Derby figure of Winter, c1780, 9in (23cm) high.

£850–950 David March

A Derby model of a cow, c1810, 3½in (9cm) high.

£425–475 David March

A pair of Derby dressing table pots and covers, painted with figures, landscapes and horses, with flower finials, restored, patch marks, c1770, 2¾in (7cm) high.

£1,100–1,300 Sotheby's (O)

A Derby trio, by John Brewer, painted with views of Derbyshire, with gilt borders, c1815.

£450–550 Dreweatt Neate (N)

A Bloor Derby figural group of a shoe mender and a lady, c1830, 7in (18cm) high.

£700–800 David March

Robert Bloor acquired the Derby factory in 1811. However he became ill and the business declined until the factory closed in 1848.

A Derby plate, decorated with sprays of flowers, with puce mark, '127' pattern mark with impressed letter, c1785, 8½in (21.5cm) diam.

£270–300 Stockspring Antiques

A Derby sauce boat, painted and encrusted with flowers, c1765, 6¾in (17cm) wide.

£280–320 Dreweatt Neate (N)

A pair of Bloor Derby vases, probably painted by Daniel Lucas Senior with views of Chatsworth and Geneva, slight damage, painted mark, c1825, 14¾in (37.5cm) high.

£10,000–12,000 Sotheby's

A Derby ice pail, decorated with flowers a butterflies, c1800, 10in (25.5cm) high.

£800–900 Stockspring Antiques

This ice pail is decorated with designs afte those found on Vienna wares of the 1780

A Derby plate, painted after Richard Aske with putti riding a ram, with gilt decoratio marked, c1820, 9in (23cm) diam.

£225–275 Dreweatt Neate (N)

A Derby part tea service, decorated with exotic birds, with gilt rims, painted marks, late 18thC.

£1,800–2,200 Ewbank Auctioneers

A Bloor Derby vase, applied with flowers, slight damage, printed mark, c1825, 6¾in (17cm) high.

£200–250 Dreweatt Neate (Bri)

ATER DERBY

ɔyal Crown Derby miniature basket, date
for 1912, 3in (7.5cm) wide.
50–400 K & M Antiques

A Royal Crown Derby miniature coffee pot, date code for 1913, 3in (7.5cm) high.
£475–525 K & M Antiques

A Royal Crown Derby cup and saucer, date code for 1929.
£110–125 K & M Antiques

erby cabinet plate, decorated with a
dscape titled 'High Tor Matlock', within a
ef-moulded gilt border, signed 'E. Trowell',
'8–90, 8¾in (22cm) diam.
00–700 Greenslade Taylor Hunt

A pair of Derby Crown Porcelain vases, decorated with stylized flowers, printed marks, date code for 1880, 7in (18cm) high.
£325–400 Bamfords
Derby Crown Porcelain became Royal Crown Derby in 1890 when granted a Royal Warrant by Queen Victoria.

A pair of Royal Crown Derby vases and covers, signed 'A. Gregory', date code for 1905, 6in (15cm) high.
£2,000–2,300 Tony Horsley

air of Derby Crown Porcelain vases,
lied with gilt flowers and insects, printed
rk, date code for 1889, 7in (18cm) high.
00–600 Bamfords

A Royal Crown Derby vase and cover, decorated with gilt and hand-painted with a bird, signed 'C. Harris', date code for 1897, 7in (18cm) wide.
£1,000–1,100 Tony Horsley

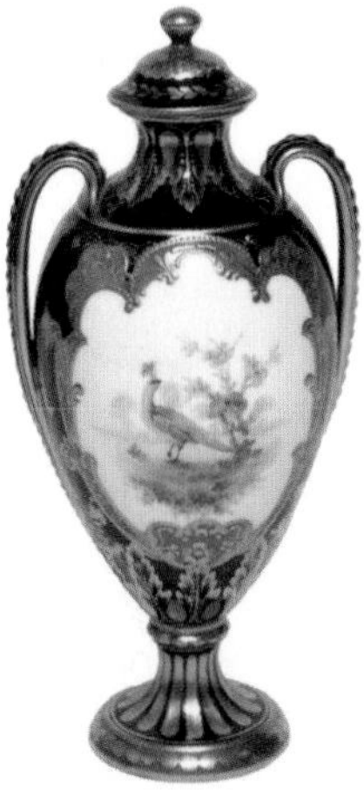

loyal Crown Derby vase and cover, hand-
nted with a peacock, with gilt decoration,
e code for 1897, 6½in (16.5cm) high.
,000–1,100 Tony Horsley

A Royal Crown Derby vase and cover, signed 'W. E. J. Dean', date code for 1918, 7in (18cm) high.
£800–900 Mere Antiques

A Royal Crown Derby vase and cover, painted by A. Gregory with flowers, signed, date code for 1921, 7in (18cm) high.
£900–1,000 Mere Antiques

PLYMOUTH, BRISTOL & NEW HALL

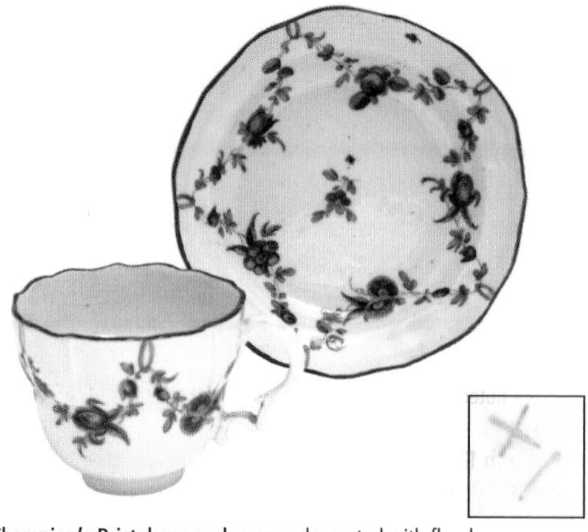

A Champion's Bristol cup and saucer, decorated with floral swags, marked X1, c1773.

£450–500 David March

A Champion's Bristol trio, decorated with apples within a gilt bord 1773–75.

£650–750 David March

A Champion's Bristol cup and saucer, with floral swag decoration, 1773–75.

£850–950 David March

A Champion's Bristol cup and saucer, painted with swags in the French style, marked, 1773–76 .

£550–600 David March

A Champion's Bristol hard-paste porcelain chocolate cup, with basket-weave moulding, 1773–76.

£750–850 David March

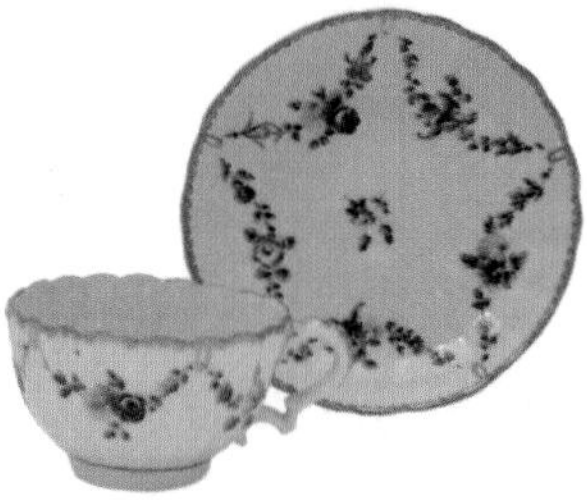

A Champion's Bristol cup and saucer, decorated with flowers issuing from gold hoops, c1775, 3in (7.5cm) diam.

£1,000–1,100 Helen Girton

A Plymouth figure of a toper, 1768–70, 6in (15cm) high.

£1,600–1,800 David March

A New Hall teabowl and saucer, pattern No. 191, c1800, saucer 5¼in (13.5cm) diam.

£115–130 Stockspring Antiques

A Bristol pickle dish, in the shape of a maple leaf, with vein decoration to underside, 1770s, 3in (7.5cm) wide.

£900–1,000 David March

Although this shape is the most commonly found of Bristol wares, they are rarely seen with a printed design.

ɪstol figure of a hurdy gurdy player,
'5, 7in (18cm) high.
200–2,500 David March

A Plymouth sauce boat, with a fluted body and floral decoration, maker's mark, 1768–70, 8in (20.5cm) long.
£1,000–1,100 David March
This piece is marked with Plymouth's 24 factory mark which is the chemical symbol for tin. Tin mining was one of the main industries in the area at that time.

ɔokworthy Plymouth sauce boat, moulded with scrolls and hand-
ted with flowers, 1768–70, 5½in (14cm) wide.
500–2,800 Helen Girton

A Plymouth sauceboat, moulded with scrolls and hand-painted with Oriental flowers, slight damage, marked, c1770, 5½in (14cm) wide.
£1,600–2,000 Sotheby's (O)

ɪristol part tea service, comprising 26 pieces, painted with garlands of flowers,
ıaged, c1775.
,600–2,000 Sotheby's

A Bristol teapot and cover, painted with flowers, damaged, marked, c1765, 7in (18cm) wide.
£240–280 Dreweatt Neate (N)

ɪristol teapot, with hand-painted
.oration and acorn finial, underglaze
ssed swords mark with overglazed X10,
'0s, 5¼in (13.5cm) high.
25–600 David March

A New Hall teapot, cover and stand, painted with flowers and leaves, pattern No. 856, restored, early 19thC.
£320–380 Woolley & Wallis

STAFFORDSHIRE FACTORIES

A set of three Spode cachepots and stands, painted with landscapes, pattern No. 1926, c1820, 6in (15cm) diam.

£3,000–3,500 Mere Antiques

A Spode cream jug, decorated with pattern No. 868, c1810, 6in (15cm) wide.

£200–220 John Newton

An H. & R. Daniel cup and saucer, decorated with pattern No. 4412, the cup on flower feet, c1825.

£250–300 Clive & Lynn Jackson

A Spode dish, with Imari-style decoration, No. 715, c1810, 11in (28cm) diam.

£270–300 Stockspring Antiques

This is known as the Dollar pattern and appears in different colour combinations.

A Minton nodding figure of a coachman, c1835, 7in (18cm) high.

£500–550 Tony Horsley

A Minton *pâte-sur-pâte* jar and cover, by Alboin Birks, c1900, 5½in (14cm) high.

£2,000–2,400 Tony Horsley

A Samuel Alcock jug, designed by Eyre, entitled 'The Royal Patriotic', printed with a Crimean war scene and a grieving family, registration lozenge, dated 1855, 8in (20cm) high.

£250–300 Sworder's

A pair of Minton plates, by Antoine Boullemier, presented to Thomas Minton on his marriage in 1872, 10in (25.5cm) diam.

£1,600–1,850 each Mario's Antiques

A pair of Ridgway plates, painted with vases of flowers, pattern No. 6/4554, damaged, c1830, 9¼in (23.5cm) diam.

£120–150 Woolley & Wallis

A pair of Ridgway plates, each painted with flowers, with gilt borders, 1830–40, 9in (23cm) diam.

£175–220 Woolley & Wallis

A set of 24 Minton dinner plates, decorated with a floral motif, within a Greek-key and acid-etched fruiting vine border, printed marks, date mark for 1881, 10¼in (26cm) diam.

£2,750–3,200 Freeman's

A Minton cabinet plate, decorated with a young girl eating an apple, gilt borders, impressed mark, c1881, 9½in (24cm) diam.

£180–200 K & M Antiques

linton *pâte-sur-pâte* plate, depicting a 'ub, with gilt decoration, date code for 4, 9½in (24cm) diam.

300–1,500 David Brower

A Minton Parian dessert plate, with a *pâte-sur-pâte* cameo by Louis Solon, within a pierced and moulded border, signed, c1890, 9in (23cm) diam.

£2,250–2,750 Dreweatt Neate (N)

A Minton porcelain plate, with gilt decoration, c1912, 9in (23cm) diam.

£1,600–1,850 Mario's Antiques

idgway part dessert service, comprising pieces, painted with flowers, damaged, 20, comport 15½in (39.5cm) wide.

.100–1,300 eweatt Neate (HAM)

An H. & R. Daniel part dessert service, comprising nine pieces, painted with landscapes within gilt borders, pattern No. 3970, slight damage, 1820–30, tazza 12¾in (32.5cm) diam.

£500–600 Woolley & Wallis

A Spode part dessert service, comprising seven pieces, painted with summer flowers, pattern No. 3139, marked, c1825.

£900–1,100 Tennants

pode tea service, comprising 38 pieces, painted mark, c1830, teapot 6in (15cm) high.

,200–1,500 Freeman's

A Staffordshire model of a tulip, c1840, 4in (10cm) high.

£350–400 Hugh Mote

Spode spill vase, decorated in the Imari 'ette, pattern No. 967, c1815, in (11.5cm) high.

'40–280 Stockspring Antiques

A Spode *sucrier*, decorated with pattern No.1020, c1805, 7in (18cm) wide.

£240–270 John Newton

A pair of Minton vases and covers, with pierced rims and shoulders, painted with chrysanthemums, with gilt borders, c1895, 7in (18cm) high.

£850–950 Mere Antiques

A pair of Minton *pâte-sur-pâte* vases, decorated by Alboin Birks, depicting Minerva, Cupid and Venus, signed, printed marks, c1910, 7¾in (19.5cm) high.

£4,500–5,500 Sotheby's

OTHER BRITISH FACTORIES

A beaker, depicting Baltimore, Maryland, early 19thC, 3½in (9cm) high.

£3,000–3,500 Northeast Auctions

A Vauxhall bowl, painted with a stylized pine tree and a rocky island, c1755, 5½in (14cm) diam.

£800–1,000 Woolley & Wallis

A Vauxhall coffee can, painted in coloured enamels with a garden scene, rockwork and flowers, damaged, c1762, 2½in (6.5cm) high.

£400–450 Guest & Gray

A Coalport breakfast cup and saucer, c1815.

£160–180 Stockspring Antiques

A Coalport dish, painted by Stephen Lawrance, c1840, 13in (33cm) diam.

£580–650 Mere Antiques

A Charles Gouyn St James's *bonbonnière*, in the form of an egg, painted with flowers, the gold hinged mount with inscription, 1749–55, 1¾in (4.5cm) high.

£3,200–3,800 Sotheby's

A punchbowl, decorated in gilt with Egyptian-style flowerheads and leaves, c1820, 13¾in (35cm) diam, with fitted case.

£550–650 Tennants

A Miles Mason coffee cup and saucer, decorated with Boy in the Door pattern, 1805–10.

£140–160 Winson Antiques

A Hicks & Meigh ewer, decorated with pattern No. 206, c1830, 8in (20.5cm) high.

£580–650 John Rogers

A pair of Pinxton bough pots, decorated with landscapes, with metal liners, c1790, 7in (18cm) wide.

£5,000–5,500 Hugh Mote

A pair of cachepots and stands, painted w floral panels on gilt vermiculation, with moulded ring handles, worn, c1810, 4¼in (11cm) high.

£350–425 Sworders

A Miles Mason tea cup and saucer, with g decoration, c1810.

£220–250 Stockspring Antiques

A pair of Dudson figures, entitled 'Bird Hunters', c1835, 6½in (16.5cm) high.

£425–480 David March

A jug, moulded with a crowned portrait flanked by initials 'G.R.' and flowers of the Union, c1821, 4¼in (10.5cm) high.

£500–600 Special Auction Services

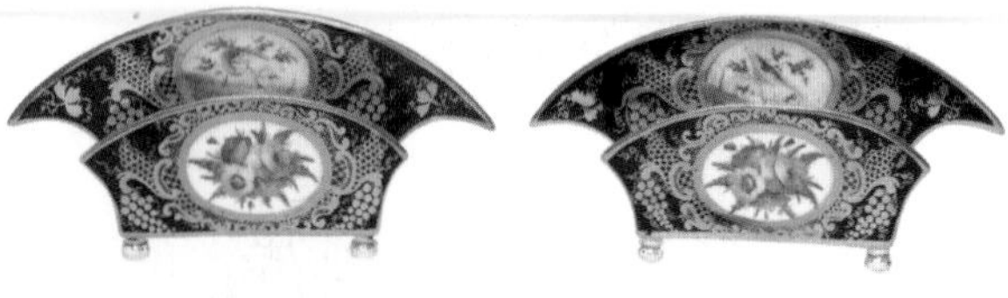

A pair of letter racks, with gilt decoration, c1820, 6in (15cm) wide.

£1,100–1,200 Mere Antiques

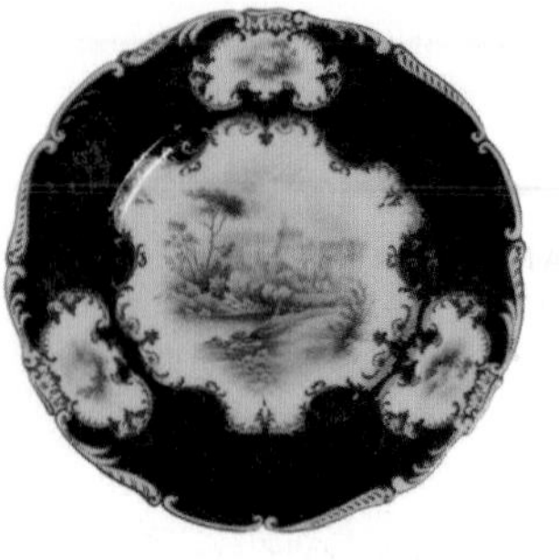

A set of 12 Coalport plates, depicting Windsor Castle, 1900–10, 10in (25.5cm) diam.

£3,500–4,000 Scottow Antiques

A Turner plate, decorated with an Imari-inspired pattern, c1805, 8in (20.5cm) diam

£230–260 Stockspring Antiques

A Coalport plate, by Frederick Chivers, c1900, 9in (23cm) diam.

£580–650 Scottow Antiques

A part dessert service, comprising 10 pieces, decorated with a Greek key border, scrolling foliage and a lion rampant crest, c1810, bowl 11in (28cm) diam.

£1,100–1,300 Sworders

A part tea and coffee service, comprising 28 pieces, decorated in the Japanese style with ribbons and flowers, 19thC.

£650–800 Gilding's

A Coalport pot pourri jar and cover, by Arthur Perry, c1900, 8in (20.5cm) high.

£1,100–1,250 David Brower

A Coalport trio, London shape, c1815.

£250–280 Stockspring Antiques

A Coalport neo-classical-style vase, c1800, 11in (28cm) high.

£1,400–1,600 Moxhams

A George Jones porcelain vase, c1900, 11in (28cm) high.

£270–300 Candice Horley

A pair of George Jones *pâte-sur-pâte* vases, depicting maidens in gardens, impressed mark, c1880, 9¼in (23.5cm) high.

£900–1,100 Skinner

/WANSEA & NANTGARW

ntgarw bowl, enamelled with bouquets
wers and urns, Wales, early 19thC,
18cm) diam.

0–280 **Bearnes**

A Nantgarw coffee cup and saucer, painted with flowers, worn, Wales, c1820.

£500–600 **Woolley & Wallis**

A Swansea teacup and saucer, decorated with an Imari pattern, marked, Wales, c1820.

£320–380 **Woolley & Wallis**

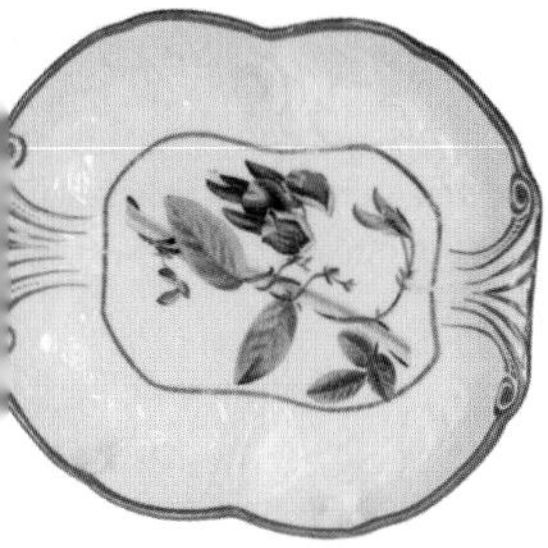

ir of Swansea dessert dishes, decorated
floral sprays, early 19thC, Wales,
(24cm) wide.

0–300 **Bearnes**

A Nantgarw dish, decorated with an eagle crest and motto, the border with gilt anthemia, damaged, impressed mark, Wales, c1820, 19¾in (50cm) wide.

£800–1,000 **Woolley & Wallis**

A Swansea dish, decorated with the Marquis of Anglesey pattern, impressed marks, Wales, c1820, 8¾in (22cm) diam.

£850–1,000 **Woolley & Wallis**

ir of Swansea plates, decorated with
ers within a gilt border, slight damage,
/ 19thC, Wales, 8in (20.5cm) diam.

i0–300 **Bearnes**

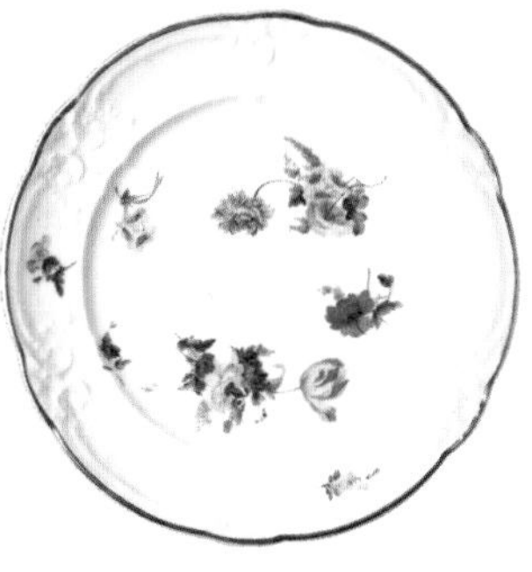

A Nantgarw plate, with flower decoration attributed to Moses Webster, Wales, c1819, 8½in (21.5cm) diam.

£3,500–4,000 **David Phillips**

A Nantgarw plate, London-decorated with flowers, fruit and insects, probably by Robins and Randall, impressed marks, Wales, c1820, 10in (25.5cm) diam.

£5,500–6,500 **Woolley & Wallis**

This plate was made in Wales at the Nantgarw factory but sent to London as a blank to be painted and gilded. This short-lived factory produced some of the finest Regency porcelain and developed a beautiful translucent white porcelain body in an attempt to rival Sèvres. Today, both Nantgarw and Swansea pieces are highly prized, with the best examples, such as this plate, fetching high prices.

vansea teapot, cover and stand, painted with panels of flowers, printed marks, Wales, c1817.

250–2,750 **Woolley & Wallis**

A Swansea teapot, cover and stand, printed with panels of flowers on an Imari-style ground, restored, painted marks, Wales, c1820.

£850–1,000 **Woolley & Wallis**

PARIAN

A Copeland Parian bust of Queen Victoria, inscribed 'J. Sherwood, Westmacott', impressed mark, dated 1853, 10¾in (27.5cm) high.

£500–600 Woolley & Wallis

A Copeland Parian bust of Poetry, 1874, 14in (35.5cm) high.

£500–575 Clive & Lynn Jackson

A Copeland Parian group, by Joseph Dur entitled 'Go to Sleep', with Art Union of London inscription, slight damage, dated 1862, 17½in (44.5cm) high.

£1,000–1,150 Langton Green Antiques

A Minton Parian group, by J. B. Klagman after the marble original by W. Greef, entitled 'Lion in Love', impressed marks, slight damage, c1872, 15in (38cm) high.

£800–950 Sworders

A Robinson & Leadbeater Parian bust of Handel, c1860, 19in (48.5cm) high.

£700–800 John Newton

A Worcester Parian figural group of Hen and Hafed, c1860, 13in (33cm) high.

£700–800 John Newton

A Parian figural group of Jesus Christ, John the Baptist and an angel, after the model by John Hancock, slight damage, c1855, 23¼in (59cm) high.

£450–550 Sworders

A Parian figure of Queen Elizabeth I, c1878, 13in (33cm) high.

£200–220 Serendipity

A Parian figure of a woman seated on a rock, 19thC, 15¾in (40cm) high.

£270–300 Rosebery's

ELLEEK

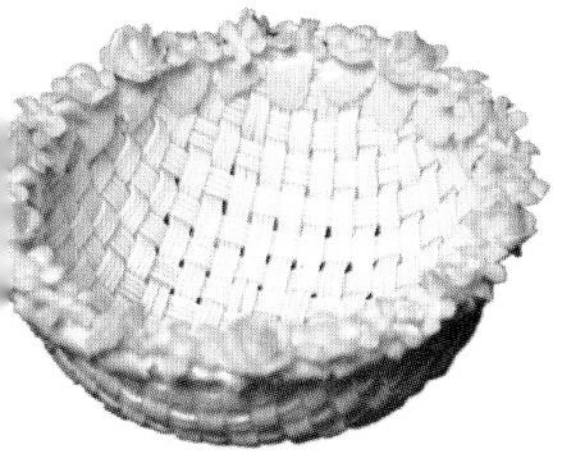

lleek Bird's Nest basket, Ireland, Second
d, 1891–1926, 4in (10cm) diam.

5–240 Bac to Basic ⊞

A Belleek basket and cover, Ireland, c1940,
13in (33cm) wide.

£1,250–1,400 Delphi Antiques ⊞

A Belleek Institute cup and saucer, black
mark, Ireland, Second Period, 1891–1926.

£160–185 Bac to Basic ⊞

lleek flask, Ireland, First Period,
3–90, 6in (15cm) high.

0–450 Era Antiques ⊞

A Belleek Echinus cream jug, Ireland, First
Period, 1863–90, 3in (7.5cm) high.

£160–180 Bac to Basic ⊞

A Belleek Acorn milk jug, black mark, Ireland,
Second Period, 1891–1926, 6in (15cm) high.

£200–225 Bac to Basic ⊞

A Belleek Shamrock cream jug and sugar bowl, Ireland, Second Period, 1891–1926,
jug 4in (10cm) high.

£110–125 Scottish Antique & Arts ⊞

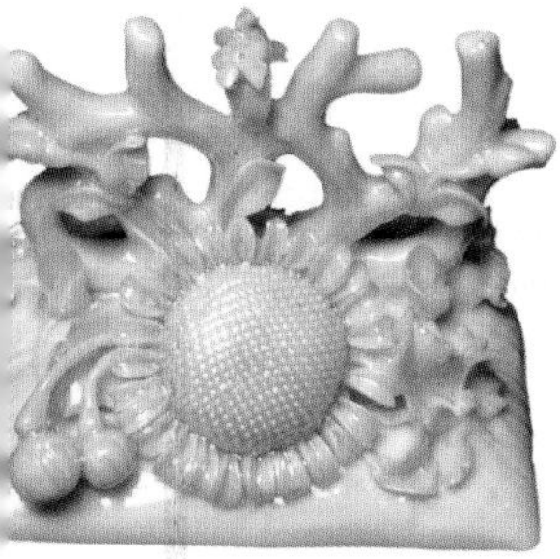

elleek menu holder, Ireland, Second
od, 1891–1926, 2½in (6.5cm) wide.

0–550 Marion Langham ⊞

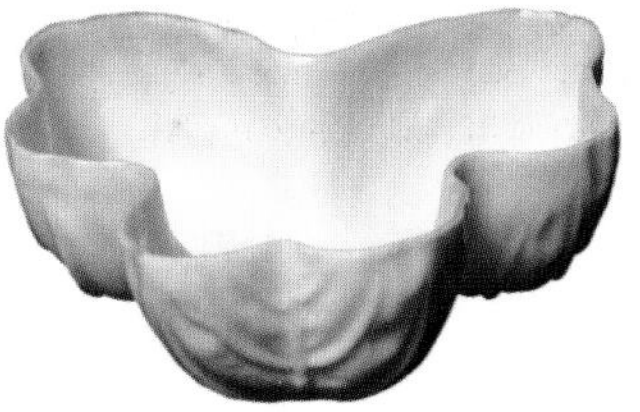

A Belleek Shamrock salt dish, Ireland, Second
Period, 1891–1926, 3in (7.5cm) diam.

£50–60 Bac to Basic ⊞

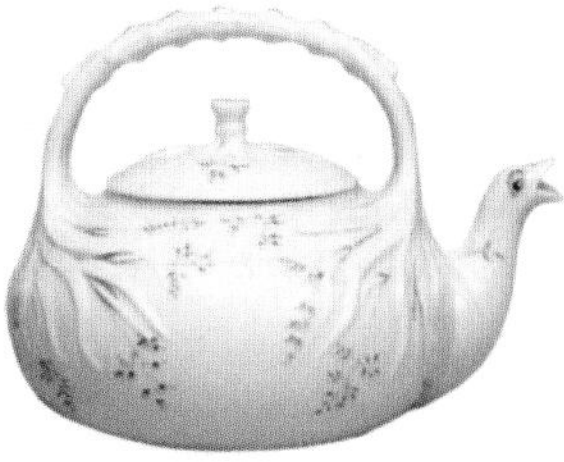

A Belleek Grass teapot and cover, Ireland,
First Period, 1863–90, 8in (20.5cm) wide.

£1,400–1,800 Paul Beighton

elleek Shamrock teapot, Ireland, Second
od, 1891–1926, 8in (20.5cm) wide.

0–280 Woburn Abbey Antiques ⊞

A Belleek Tridacna teapot, black mark,
Ireland, Second Period, 1891–1926,
5in (12.5cm) diam.

£140–160 Ruskin Decorative Arts ⊞

A Belleek Shell vase, black mark, Ireland,
Second Period, 1891–1926, 7in (18cm) high.

£750–900 Anderson & Garland

VINCENNES & SEVRES

A Vincennes cup and saucer, painted with birds and gilt trelliswork, marked, painter's mark possibly for Pierre François Yvernel, slight damage, France, c1753.

£2,750–3,250 Sotheby's (NY)

A Sèvres cup and saucer, painted with figures at work within gilt borders, marked, painter's mark for Vieillard *père*, c1765.

£1,000–1,200 Sotheby's (NY)

A Sèvres coffee can and saucer, painted panels of flowers and gilt with scrolls, da code for 1778, France.

£1,750–2,000 Woolley & Wallis

A Sèvres coffee can, decorated with a named study of *Rhododendron Ponticum*, marked, painter's code 119, date code for 1783, France.

£800–1,000 Sworders

A pair of Sèvres coffee cans and saucers, decorated with bands of gilt and blue, marked, France, late 18thC.

£600–700 Woolley & Wallis

A Sèvres coffee can and saucer, painted with flowers, marked, date code for 1783, France.

£600–700 Woolley & Wallis

A Sèvres cup and saucer, decorated with flowers and gilt rims, marked, date code for 1780, France.

£340–380 Hugh Mote

A Sèvres cup and saucer, sight damage, marked, France, late 18thC.

£160–200 Waddington's

ESSENTIAL REFERENCE SEVRES MARKS

- The Sèvres factory mark was a Royal symbol – the interlaced or mirrored letter 'L' was the cypher of Louis XV.
- Sèvres added a code system using letters or symbols that uniquely identified the painters and gilders who had worked on each item, as well as the year of production.
- A single letter was placed in the centre of the cypher to represent the year, beginning with A in 1753, B in 1754 and so on.

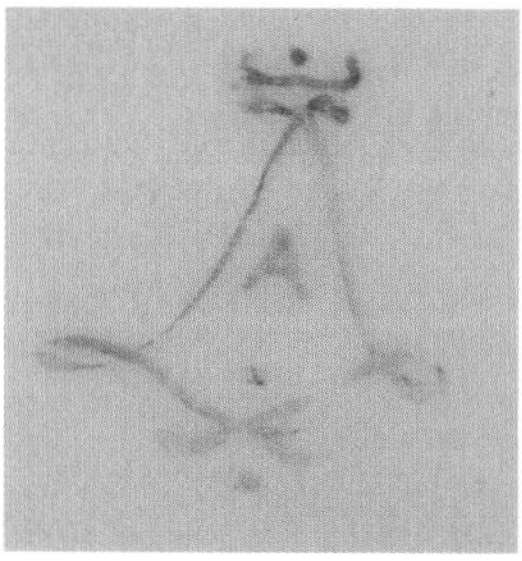

Year code A for 1753, the first year this system was used. The painter's mark at the top is for the landscape painter André-Vincent Vieillard.

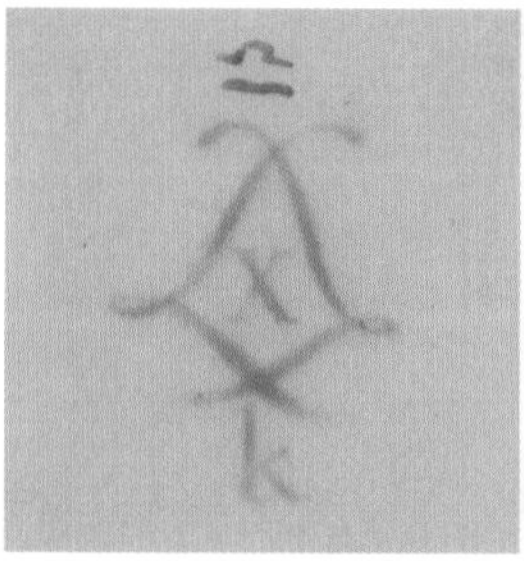

Year code X for 1775 and painter's mark at the bottom is for figure-painter Charles-Nicolas Dodin. The gilder's mark at the top is for Guillaume Noel.

vres cabinet cup, with a bull's
' base, decorated with gilding,
.ed, incised 'JB', France,
;–24, 6½in (16.5cm) high.
)00–6,000 Sotheby's

A Sèvres dish, moulded with lotus and painted with flowers, painter's mark for François Binet, date code for 1764, France, 9in (23cm) diam.
£340–380 Stockspring Antiques

A Sèvres *écuelle*, cover and stand, painted with panels of putti within gilt borders, marked, France, 1770–75, stand 8½in (21.5cm) wide.
£5,000–6,000 Sotheby's (NY)

vres *écuelle*, cover and stand, later-
ted with shepherds and shepherdesses,
ıt damage, marked, painter's mark 'B',
ce, 18thC, stand 9in (23cm) wide.
500–3,000 Sotheby's

A Sèvres biscuit group of L'Autel de l'Amitié, modelled with Venus and Cupid burning Cupid's arrows at the altar, losses and repairs, incised 'B' and No. 7, France, c1770, 12½in (32cm) high.
£3,500–4,250 Sotheby's (NY)

A Sèvres biscuit figural group of Pygmalion, after Etienne Maurice Falconet, the base with gilt decoration, marked, France, c1770, 14in (35.5cm) high.
£11,000–13,000 Sotheby's (NY)

èvres biscuit group of La Fête du Chateau,
lelled by E. M. Falconet, damaged, incised
rance, c1770, 8in (20.5cm) high.
,000–2,400 Sotheby's (O)

èvres ice pail, painted and gilt with
vers on a *bleu céleste* ground, some
oration probably later, marked, painter's
'k'V', date code for 1754, France,
ı (16.5cm) high.
600–2,000 Sotheby's

A Vincennes potpourri jar and cover, by Jean-Claude Duplessis, painted with flowers, with later ormolu mounts, restored, marked, c1752, 9¾in (25cm) high.
£7,500–9,000 Sotheby's (NY)

A Vincennes potpourri jar and cover, by Jean-Claude Duplessis, painted and applied with flowers, ground and gilding probably later, marked, painter's mark, restored, France, 1752–56, 7¾in (19.5cm) high.
£3,200–3,800 Sotheby's (NY)

A **Sèvres plate,** painted and gilded with flowers within bead and leaf garland borders, France, c1775, 9in (23cm) diam.

£300–350 Hy Duke

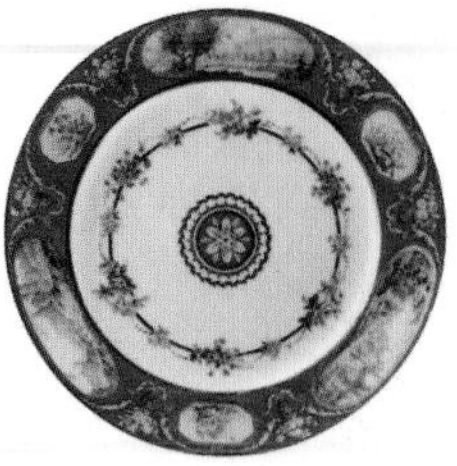

A **Sèvres plate,** painted by Bouillat *père* and gilded by Henry-François Vincent with flowers, marked, painter's and gilder's marks, date code for 1790, France, 9½in (24cm) diam.

£2,800–3,200 Sotheby's (O)

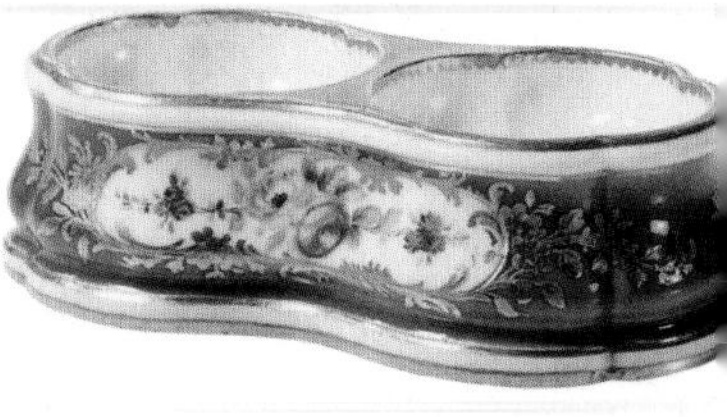

A **Sèvres double salt,** painted by François le Vavasseu with flowers, with gilt flowers and scrollwork, slight damage, marked, painter's mark, date code for 1760, France, 5in (12.5cm) high.

£2,500–3,000 Sotheby's (NY)

A **Sèvres part tea service,** comprising 17 pieces, painted *en grisaille* with a putto and trophies of love and war, France, 1770–75, teapot 5¾in (14.5cm) high.

£9,000–11,000 Sotheby's (NY)

A **Sèvres cabaret service,** comprising nine pieces, late decorated in the style of Morin with quayside scenes o *vermiculé* ground, slight damage, marked, France, 18t teapot 4in (10cm) high, in a silk-lined leather-covered

£4,500–5,500 Sotheby's (NY)

A **Sèvres tête-a-tête,** painted by Michaud, slight damage, marked, painter's mark, date code for 1775, France, teapot 4in (10cm) high.

£4,000–5,000 Sotheby's (P)

A **Sèvres teapot,** painted by André Vincent Vieillard wi a landscape and seascape and a laurel wreath band, marked, painter's mark, date code for 1778, France, 4¾in (12cm) high.

£2,200–2,750 Sotheby's (O)

A **Sèvres footed vase and cover,** painted with a scene of lovers in a landscape and a flower spray, the rims with laurel borders, France, restored, 1775–85, 8½in (21.5cm) high.

£2,000–2,500 Sotheby's (O)

A **Vincennes wine cooler,** painted with a landscape, slight damage, central divider missing, marked, painter's mark possibly for Matel, date code for 1755–56, France, 12½in (32cm) wic

£1,600–2,000 Sotheby's (NY)

:VRES-STYLE

A Sèvres-style coffee can and saucer, with 'jewelled' and painted decoration, France, c1880.

£1,500–1,650 Mario's Antiques

A Sèvres-style coffee cup and saucer, signed, France, 1901.

£300–350 Mario's Antiques

res-style bowl, painted with trailing rs and gilt with scrollwork, with gilt- handles and stand, painted marks, e, mid-19thC, 8¾in (22cm) high.

5–625 Sworders

A Sèvres-style miniature tea set, comprising three pieces, painted with roundels depicting courting couples and flowers within gilded cartouches, the covers with bud finials, France, 19thC, teapot 4in (10cm) high.

£350–425 Andrew Hartley

r of Sèvres-style gilt-metal nted scent bottles, France, c1860, (30.5cm) high.

250–2,500 Mario's Antiques

A pair of Sèvres-style ormolu-mounted covered vases, France, c1880, 15in (38cm) high.

£7,500–8,250 David Brower

A pair of Sèvres-style covered vases, decorated with painted panels on a gilt and *rose Pompadour* ground, France, c1880, 17in (43cm) high.

£4,250–5,000 Mario's Antiques

Rose Pompadour is a rare colour.

SSENTIAL REFERENCE SEVRES-STYLE

me Sèvres-style porcelain was made in the th century using old Sèvres blanks, in tories in Paris, Limoges and sometimes even England, to copy the famous old porcelain t was proudly displayed in museums. res-style pieces usually bear fake 18th- tury marks and the date letters are often early for the style of decoration. Vast antities were made and sold, even then, as vres'. This term became generic and it is w usual to find copies referred to in auction alogues as 'Sèvres' today. Sèvres-style is a ferable description as this implies the piece a copy and not made at the Sèvres factory.

èvres-style covered vase, painted and gilded with a ne depicting Napoleon on horseback and other unted officers, the cover with a berry finial, on a socle se, France, 19thC, 37½in (95.3cm) high.

,000–11,000 Freeman's

A pair of Sèvres-style gilt-metal-mounted covered vases, painted with scenes of lovers and riverside landscapes, on socle bases, signed 'M. Gravey', France, early 20thC, 30½in (76cm) high.

£1,750–2,000 Freeman's

PARIS

An ormolu-mounted Paris basket, painted with summer fruits and the Rothschild family arms, *faux* Sèvres marks, France, c1850, 10in (25.5cm) diam.

£1,500–1,800 John Newton

A Paris box, painted with a scene of two cavaliers, marked, France, c1900, 3in (7.5cm) wide.

£270–300 John Newton

A pair of Paris coffee cans, painted with gentleman and a lady in panels on a gilt ground, crowned RF marks, France, c1800

£375–450 Sworder's

A pair of Paris sweetmeat dishes and covers, painted in enamel and gilt with trailing leaves and berries, France, c1800, 10¾in (27.5cm) wide.

£280–340 Sworder's

A Paris coffee can and saucer, the can applied with a bust in the antique style, the field decorated with attributes of war on a marble ground, France, c1800.

£2,000–2,400 Sotheby's (P)

A Paris figure group, modelled as a mother and child seated on a mule, with three attendants, marked, repaired, France, c1880, 14½in (37cm) high.

£375–450 Sworder's

A Paris allegorical figural group, depictir three people and a bird cage, France, c19 6in (15cm) high.

£550–625 John Newton

A pair of Paris ice pails, with covers and liners, painted and gilt with flowers, France, c1790, 10¾in (27cm) high.

£6,000–7,000 Sotheby's (P)

A Paris inkstand, decorated with flowers, France, c1810, 5½in (14cm) wide.

£350–400 Moxhams

A pair of Paris oil lamp stands, the spiral columns with Corinthian capitals, the bases with bust portraits after the antique Daphne, Amphitrite, Bacchus, Saturn, Nep Apollo, Rhee and Ariane, one restored, Fr c1800, 17½in (44.5cm) high.

£6,500–8,000 Sotheby's

A Paris tea and coffee service, comprising 32 pieces, decorated in gilt with scrolling foliage, with an associated creamer, France, 19thC, coffee pot 10in (25.5cm) high.

£2,000–2,400 Freeman's

THER FRENCH FACTORIES

oisy le Roi dinner service, comprising 62 ıs, decorated with birds, impressed mark, ce, late 19thC.

,00–13,000 Sotheby's (Am)

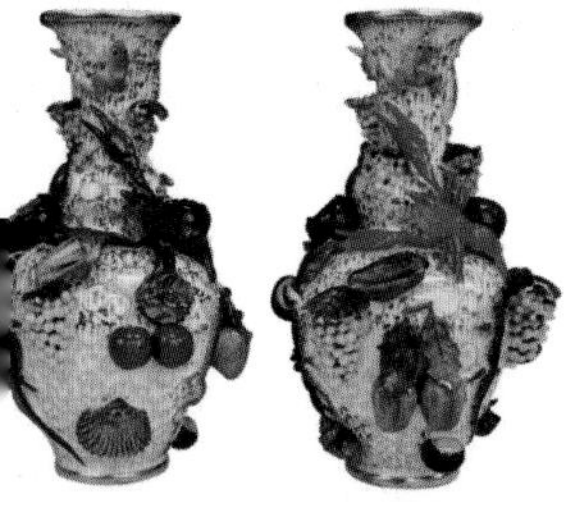

ir of Jacob Petit vases, relief-decorated reptiles, shells and fruit on a gilt scroll nd, damaged, France, mid-19thC, n (32cm) high.

0–550 Toovey's

ir of Samson dishes, decorated in the of Chinese export wares, France, c1900, in (26.5cm) wide.

0–265 John Newton

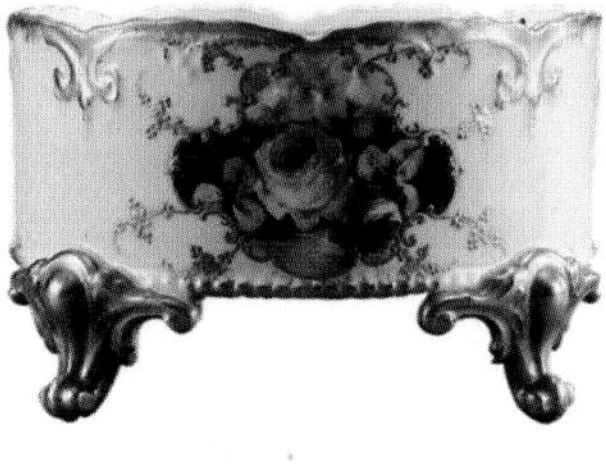

A Limoges jardinière, with a bisque insert, marked 'AK', France, c1900, 7½in (19cm) diam.

£160–200 Jackson's

A Samson box, painted with exotic birds, the cover with a parlour scene, crossed swords mark, France, c1890, 3½in (9cm) high.

£440–485 John Newton

A Tournai plate, decorated in the Chinese style, the border with flowers in iron-red highlighted with gilt, crossed swords and gilt crosses marks, France, c1770, 9¼in (23.5cm) diam.

£5,000–6,000 Sotheby's (P)

A Mennecy figure of a Chinese man, with later ormolu mounts, restored, France, c1750, 5¾in (14.5cm) high.

£2,250–2,750 Sotheby's (NY)

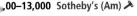

A Samson dish, with Chinese-style decoration, France, c1880, 16in (40.5cm) diam.

£850–950 David Brower

A Tournai *sucrier* and cover, marked, France, 18thC, 4¼in (11cm) diam.

£2,800–3,200 Sotheby's (P)

urnai dinner service, comprising 193 pieces, painted with flowering branches and rated with La Ronda pattern, slight damage, marked, France, 19thC.

,000–18,000 Sotheby's (Am)

A Tournai teapot, decorated with battle scenes, France, c1765, 4¾in (12cm) high.

£12,000–15,000 Sotheby's (P)

MEISSEN

A Meissen bowl, enamelled in the manner of Höroldt with Summer and Winter landscape panels and Kakiemon sprays, the interior with a further landscape panel, marked, slight damage, Germany, c1735, 6¼in (16cm) diam.

£850–1,000 Bearnes

A Meissen Louis XV-style mantel clock, the gilt dial with numeral cartouches, with countwheel bell-striking movement, the case surmounted by an urn with flowers and putti, movement signed 'Lenzkirch', Germany, c1870, 21in (53.5cm) high.

£3,800–4,500 Sotheby's (Am)

A Meissen box and cover, Germany, c1870, 3½in (9cm) diam.

£270–300 Mario's Antiques

A pair of Meissen figural candelabra, Germany, c1860, 8in (20.5cm) high.

£2,800–3,250 David Brower

A Meissen coffee pot and cover, with hand-painted decoration, Germany, Academic period, c1765, 9½in (24cm) high.

£850–950 Hugh Mote

A Meissen centrepiece, Germany, c1860, 8in (20.5cm) high.

£1,650–1,850 Mario's Antiques

A Meissen two-handled cup and saucer, hand-painted with a harbour scene, Germany, c1750.

£1,350–1,500 K & M Antiques

ESSENTIAL REFERENCE MEISSEN MARKS

- The shape and form of the Meissen crossed swords are an invaluable guide to dating.
- The swords were usually painted in the centre of the base, but some mid-18th-century figures with rough bases and no glaze were given a mark at the back of the model, near the base.
- The Academic and Marcolini marks are the most commonly faked Meissen marks.
- Post-Marcolini marks were more loosely painted but became more precise from 1840 to c1920.

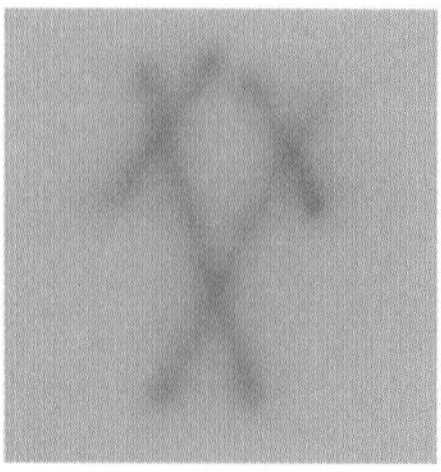

Straight swords, c1750.

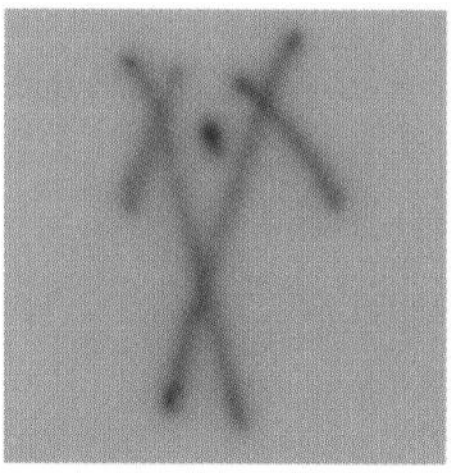

Dot between the hilts, Academic period, 1763–74.

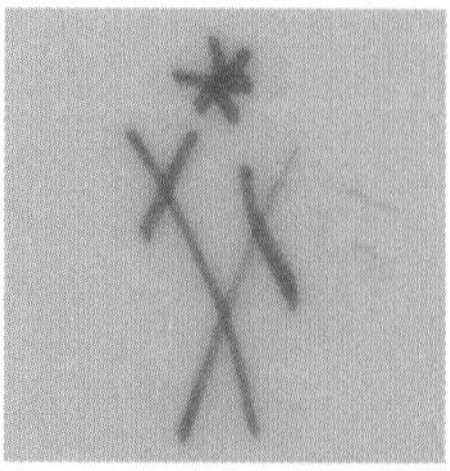

Star above the swords, Marcolini period, 1774–1814.

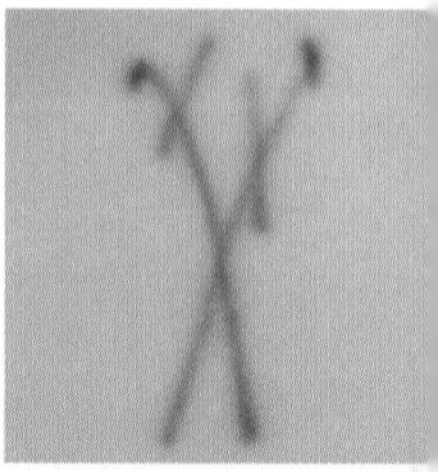

Curved swords with pommels, 1850–1900.

XPERT'S EYE MEISSEN CUPS & SAUCERS

s Meissen cup and saucer made '60 was probably part of a series tems all decorated in the same tern. Cups and saucers on their n are popular with collectors as y are easy to display.
0–250

reverse side would be ked in the usual way with crossed swords and possibly an impressed number.

nochrome decoration was ionable in the mid-18th ury; puce was a particularly ular in the German rococo od (c1730–60).

The idyllic landscape subject and the absence of a frame around the painting are also typical rococo features.

The limited gilding is a characteristic of much early German porcelain.

The moulding on this cup is of prunus flowers and leaves. It is copied from Chinese *blanc-de-Chine* porcelain dating from the early 18th century.

issen cup and saucer, painted with rs, Germany, c1880.
0–120 K & M Antiques

A Meissen demi-tasse cup and saucer, painted with flowers and butterflies, with a swan handle, Germany, c1900.
£270–300 John Newton

A Meissen dish, decorated with flower sprays and garlands, Germany, c1760, 10in (25.5cm) diam.
£280–320 Stockspring Antiques
This was a popular early neo-classical design – Champion's Bristol used a similar pattern, as did Chelsea-Derby.

issen figure of a vintner, by J. J. Kändler, the Peasant Farmer series, Germany, 0, 8in (20.5cm) high.
00–4,000 Yvonne Adams

A Meissen miniature figure of a Dutch peasant, modelled by P. Reinicke, Germany, c1748, 3½in (9cm) high.
£2,200–2,500 Yvonne Adams

A Meissen figure of a child vintner, by J. J. Kändler, from the Gardening Children series, Germany, c1750, 4in (10cm) high.
£1,800–2,000 Yvonne Adams

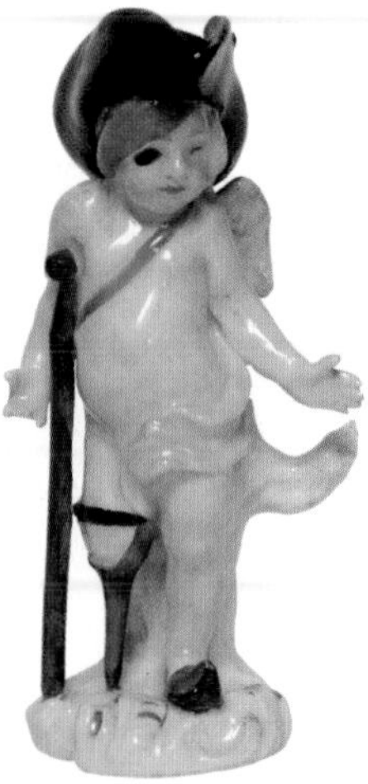

A Meissen figure of Cupid disguised as a beggar, by J. J. Kändler, Germany, c1760, 4in (10cm) high.

£1,500–1,800
Yvonne Adams

A Meissen figure of a shepherd, by M. V. Acier, Germany, c1775, 12in (30.5cm) high.

£1,500–1,800
Yvonne Adams

A Meissen figure of a fisherman, Marcolini period, Germany, 1774–1814, 5in (12.5cm) high.

£2,500–2,800
Mario's Antiques

A Meissen figure of a Turk, Germany, c1850, 7in (18cm) high.

£2,250–2,500
Mario's Antiques

A Meissen figural group, from the Harvest Children series, Germany, c1860, 8in (20.5cm) high.

£2,500–2,800
Mario's Antiques

A Meissen model of a monkey playing a violin, from a series of 21 Monkey Band models, Germany, 1860–80, 5in (12.5cm) high.

£1,200–1,400
David Brower

A Meissen figure of Cupid, entitled '*Je découvre tout*', Germany, c1870, 5in (12.5cm) high.

£750–850
Mario's Antiques

A Meissen figure of a child with a toy, Germany, c1870 7in (18cm) high.

£1,300–1,500
Mario's Antiques

A Meissen figure of Ortolona, slight damage, restored, painted and inscribed marks, Germany, c1870, 5½in (14cm) high.

£450–550 **Sworders**

A Meissen figural group of Venus and Cupid, Germany, c1880, 8in (20.5cm) high.

£900–1,000
John Newton

A Meissen group of children feeding swans, Germany, c1880, 9in (23cm) high.

£3,000–3,500
Mario's Antiques

A Meissen group of Cupid hunting with hounds, after model by Joseph Ringler, Ge c1895, 6in (15cm) high.

£1,500–1,800
John Newton

ɪr of Meissen figures of a man and a ɑn, standing beside tree trunks, on r-encrusted bases, Germany, c1900, ı (49.5cm) high

0–800
rith Farmers' & Kidd's

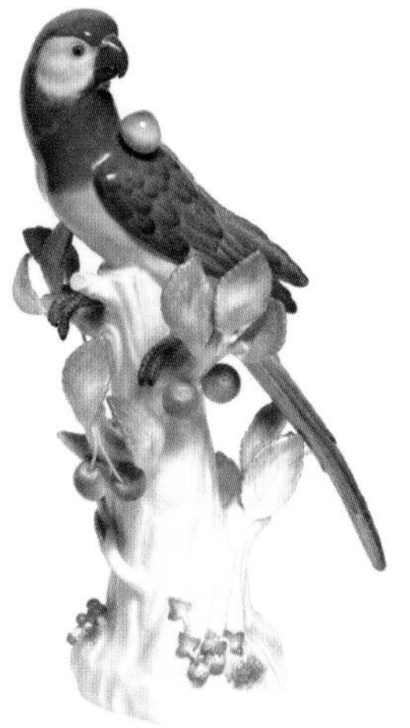

A Meissen model of a parrot on a tree, Germany, late 19thC, 13in (33cm) high.

£450–500 Humbleyard Fine Art

A Meissen part table service, painted with flowers within gilt borders, the tureen covers modelled with figures of Roman soldiers and muses, slight damage, marked, Germany, c1761.

£200,000–240,000 Sotheby's

This service is one of a number of important Meissen royal services. It was ordered by the Prussian King Frederick the Great in 1761 and comprises over 150 pieces. The service displays rococo forms, shells, scrolls, recumbent Roman soldiers and scantily-clad maidens.

ɪissen soup plate, decorated with birds nsects, marked, Germany, Marcolini d, c1790, 9in (23cm) diam.

0–280 Hugh Mote

A pair of Meissen sauce boats, painted with flower sprigs, the handles with moulded flower terminals, damaged, one with crossed swords mark, Germany, c1750, 9in (23cm) wide.

£800–950 Sotheby's

ɪissen dessert service, comprising six pieces, decorated with n pattern, 19thC, largest dish 11¼in (28.5cm) diam.

0–500 Dorotheum

A Meissen dessert service, comprising 17 pieces, each with a pierced border and painted with flowers, large bowl damaged, Germany, c1880, plates 9½in (24cm) diam.

£3,250–4,000 Sworder's

ver-mounted Meissen tankard, bly painted by Christian rich Herold with a scene of a ary camp, the cover mounted a figure of a Roman soldier narked for Dresden, Germany, 0, 7½in (19cm) high.

,000–18,000
otheum

A Meissen bottle vase, encrusted with flowers and fruit, painted with butterflies and insects, damaged, Germany, 19thC, 13¼in (33.5cm) high.

£375–450 Rosebery's

A Meissen *Schneeballen* vase, encrusted with flowers and birds, Germany, c1870, 23in (58.5cm) high.

£30,000–35,000
David Brower

A Meissen vase, with double serpent handles, Germany, c1900, 15½in (39.5cm) high.

£1,100–1,300
Sotheby's (Am)

BERLIN

A KPM Berlin cabinet cup and saucer, hand-painted with flowers, Germany, c1890.

£115–130 K & M Antiques

A pair of Berlin allegorical figures, modelled as children harvesting, inscribed 'Julius' and 'Augustus', sceptre marks, Germany, 19thC, 4in (10cm) high.

£400–450 Guest & Gray

A Berlin model of a dog sitting on a cushi repaired, Germany, c1830, 2¾in (7cm) hi

£320–380 Dorotheum

A KPM Berlin plaque, entitled 'La Chocolatière', Germany, c1880, 9½ x 6in (24 x 15cm).

£3,400–3,750 David Brower

A KPM Berlin plaque, painted with a portrait of a girl, impressed KPM and sceptre mark, Germany, late 19thC, 7in (18cm) high, framed.

£1,000–1,200 Freeman's

A Berlin plaque, depicting 'Psyche in Moonlight', Germany, late 19thC, 5¾ x 3¾in (14.5 x 9.5cm), framed.

£1,400–1,750 Freeman's

A Berlin plaque, painted after Richter with Queen Louise, Germany, late 19thC, 9½ x 6in (24 x 15cm), framed.

£2,000–2,500 Freeman's

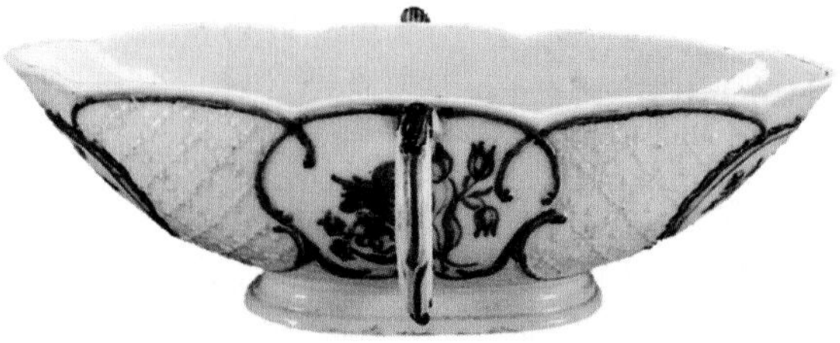

A Wegely Berlin sauce boat, with two handles, with underglaze blue and relief decoration, Germany, 18thC, 9¼in (23.5cm) wide.

£1,500–1,800 Bukowskis

A Berlin plate, painted with lilies of the valley, the gilt rim with scrolling foliage, slight restoration, marked, Germany, 1817–23, 9½in (24cm) diam.

£1,500–1,800 Sotheby's (Am)

A Berlin solitaire, each piece painted wit named view, with moulded gilt scroll bor handles and finials, slight damage, Germa 1849–70, tray 16¾in (42.5cm) wide.

£8,500–10,000 Sotheby's

THER GERMAN FACTORIES

r of candlesticks, probably Wallendorf, ed with flowers sprigs and birds, ed, Germany, Thuringia, c1775, (25.5cm) high.

00–1,800 **Sotheby's**

A Dresden centrepiece, the base with applied figures, Germany, c1890, 12in (30.5cm) high.

£500–550
Millroyale Antiques

A Nymphenburg cabinet cup and saucer, decorated with a view of Halle and a crest, crest to base of cup, marked, Germany, c1820.

£2,500–2,800 **Hugh Mote**

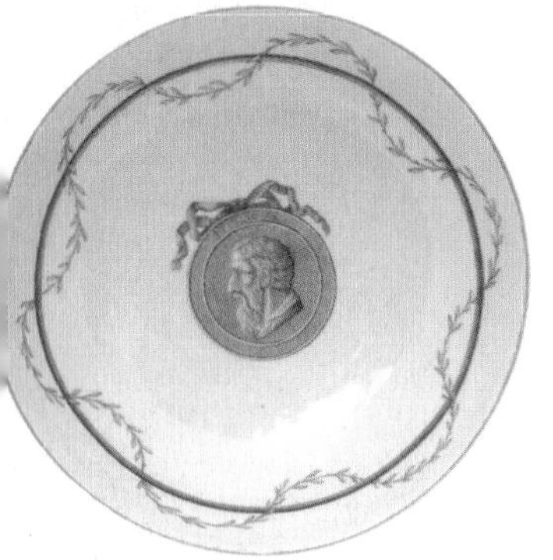

stenberg saucer dish, the centre with a cameo, ed, Germany, 1780–85, 8in (20.5cm) diam.

)–260
kspring Antiques

A Höchst figural group of a sleeping boy and a girl, by Johann Peter Melchior, restored, wheel mark, Germany, c1770, 7in (18cm) high.

£2,000–2,500 **Sotheby's (NY)**

A Frankenthal allegorical figure of December, modelled by Konrad Link, from a series of the months, marked, Germany, c1765, 7¼in (18.5cm) high.

£2,500–3,000
Sotheby's (O)

mphemburg Commedia dell'Arte e, Lucinda, after the model by Franz n Bustelli, slight damage, marked, any, c1900, 7½in (19cm) high.

00–1,300 **Sotheby's (O)**

A pair of Ludwigsburg flower pots and covers, painted with portraits flanked by moulded ribbon-tied swags, the covers each with a leaf finial, marked, Germany, 1775–1800, 4¼in (11cm) high.

£1,500–1,800 **Sotheby's (O)**

A pair of Ludwigsburg potpourri jars and covers, painted with figures in landscapes, applied with mask handles, Germany, 1765–75, 14in (35.5cm) high.

£9,500–11,500 **Sotheby's (NY)**

A Dresden vase, painted and gilded with panels of flowers and lovers, cover missing, Germany, c1890, 13½in (34cm) high.

£140–175
Sworders

VIENNA

A pair of Du Paquier Vienna teabowls, decorated with *indianische Blumen*, Austria, c1725, 2in (5cm) high.

£4,700–5,500 Dorotheum

A Vienna charger, decorated with a scene depicting Diana, Austria, c1817, 17in (43cm) wide.

£5,000–5,500 Mario's Antiques

A Vienna coffee can and saucer, ename with stylized flowers between bands of vermiculation, blue shield and impressed marks, Austria, c1795.

£280–350 Sworders

A Vienna cup and saucer, decorated with floral sprays, with a gilt border, shield mark and impressed number, Austria, c1780.

£180–220 Stockspring Antiques

A Vienna cup, saucer and cover, decorated by Anton Kothgasser with a scene of Venus and Cupid, with gilded motifs *en grisaille*, slight damage, impressed date mark and painter's marks, Austria, c1802.

£2,500–3,000 Sotheby's (O)

A Vienna coffee can and saucer, decora with cornflowers, with gilt borders, Austr date code for 1807.

£400–500 Dorotheum

A Vienna cup and saucer, decorated with gilt between coloured bands, the cup inscribed 'Glück', Austria, date code for 1828.

£250–300 Dorotheum

A Vienna-style cup, cover and saucer, entitled 'Achelous und Hercules', painted classical scenes, marked, Austria, c1880.

£775–875 John Newton

In ancient mythology, Achelous and Herc fought for the hand of the beautiful Deja During the fight Achelous turned first int snake, then a bull, but was defeated by Hercules, who ripped a horn from his hea It was taken by the goddess of Plenty wh called it cornucopia, the horn of Plenty.

A Vienna figure of a flower girl, with gilt-bronze mounts, slight damage, Austria, c1765, 9in (23cm) high.

£750–900 Dorotheum

A Vienna figure of a pretzel seller, Austria, c1762, 8in (20.5cm) high.

£700–850 Dorotheum

A Vienna bull-baiting group, shield mar Austria, late 19thC, 8in (20.5cm) wide.

£350–425 Dreweatt Neate

ır of Vienna plates, with hand-painted decoration, d 'Gurner', Austria, c1880, 9½in (24cm) diam.

'50–2,500 Mario's Antiques

A set of 12 Vienna plates, each painted with a maiden in a landscape, marked, titled to reverse, Austria, late 19thC, 9in (23cm) diam.

£7,500–9,000 Freeman's

ɜnna plate, entitled 'The Bathers', with -painted decoration, signed 'Wagner', 0, 9in (23cm) diam.

ɔ00–1,200 Mario's Antiques

A Vienna plate, depicting Ruth, with hand-painted decoration, Austria, c1880, 9½in (24cm) diam.

£1,100–1,250 Mario's Antiques

A Vienna plate, with hand-painted and gilt decoration, Austria, c1880, 8½in (21.5cm) diam.

£1,650–1,850 Mario's Antiques

ɛnna plate, depicting Lorelei, hand-ted and gilded, Austria, c1880, (24cm) diam.

500–1,650 Mario's Antiques

ɜrman folklore, Lorelei was a siren who sat rock near St Goarshausen on the Rhine. rs were so captivated by her beauty that were lured onto the rocks and shipwrecked.

A Vienna plate, entitled 'Amors Revanche', decorated with a mythological scene, Austria, c1880, 9½in (24cm) diam.

£800–900 David Brower

A Vienna plate, entitled 'Hoffnung', gilded and painted with a portrait, Austria, c1890, 9½in (24cm) diam.

£1,000–1,100 David Brower

ɛnna-style cabinet plate, entitled 'The ıction of Amymone', painted with a ological scene, Austria, c1890, 20.5cm) diam.

0–900 John Newton

ɾeek mythology, Amymone was rescued by idon from a satyr who was about to rape her.

A Vienna two-handled vase, decorated with gilt scrolls and a painted panel of two ladies in a garden, on a plinth, signed 'Legles', marked, cover missing, Austria, 19thC, 14½in (37cm) high.

£600–700 Rosebery's

A Vienna two-handled vase, painted with Napoleonic scenes, with gilded decoration, Austria, late 19thC, 29in (73.5cm) high.

£8,000–9,500 Freeman's

RUSSIAN FACTORIES

A cup and saucer, possibly by Gardner, Russia, late 18thC.

£1,500–1,800 Bukowskis

A Gardner figure of a berry gatherer, restored, marked, Russia, c1830, 4¾in (12cm) high.

£1,200–1,500 Sotheby's (O)

An Imperial Porcelain Manufactory dinner plate, decorated with an interior scene, the border with gilt palmettes, Russia, St Petersburg, 1825–55, 10in (25.5cm) diam.

£12,000–15,000 Bukowskis

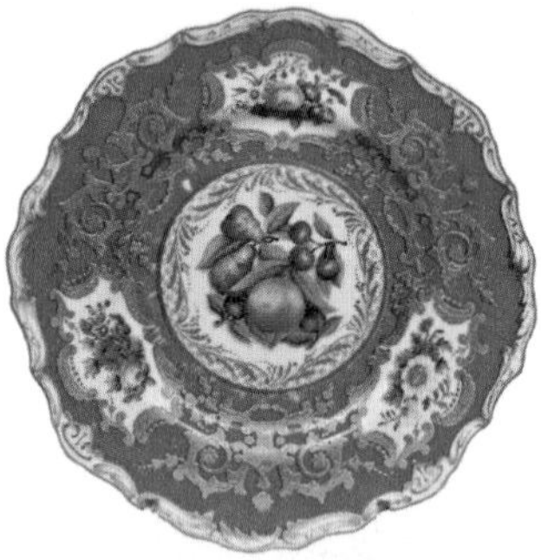

An Imperial Porcelain Manufactory cabinet plate, decorated with fruit and flowers, slight damage, Russia, 1825–55, 9¼in (23.5cm) diam.

£1,500–1,800 Dorotheum

An Alexander Popov cabinet plate, decorated with a waterside view, marked, Russia, Moscow, c1830, 9½in (24cm) diam.

£1,300–1,600 Dorotheum

An Imperial Porcelain Manufactory dinr plate, with painted and gilded decoratior Russia, St Petersburg, 1855–81, 9½in (24cm) diam.

£1,000–1,200 Bukowskis

A pair of Imperial Porcelain Manufactory plates, from the Raphael service, marked and dated, Russia, 1886 and 1894, 8½in (21.5cm) diam.

£20,000–25,000 Waddington's

The Raphael service was commissioned in 1883 for the Catherine Palace in Tsarskoye Selo by Emperor Alexander III (1845–94). Its classical motifs originate from the Italian frescoes in the Imperial Hermitage that had been designed for Catherine II by Giacomo Quarenghi who was influenced by the Vatican's Raphael Loggia. Leonard Leonardovich Schaufelberger, head of the Imperial Porcelain Manufactory, supervised the creation of the service for 50 people. It was completed in 1903 for the personal use of the Empress Maria Feodorovna.

A Gardner tea service, comprising 43 pieces, marked, Russia, late 19thC, teapot 4¾in (12cm) high.

£1,200–1,400 Sotheby's (O)

An Imperial Porcelain Manufactory ture cover and fixed stand, in the form of a mel printed mark, Russia, late 19thC, 10in (25.5cm) high.

£450–550 Sworders

A Kornilov part dinner service, comprising 30 pieces, decorated with troika, hunting and farming scenes, marked 'Made in Russian by Kornilow Bros for Tiffany & Co, New York', Rus St Petersburg, dinner plate 11in (28cm) diam.

£18,000–22,000 Northeast Auctions

THER CONTINENTAL FACTORIES

ef-moulded casket, the cover surmounted by a fox and hunting trophies, des with dogs and dead game, on paw feet, probably Italy, early 19thC, (33cm) wide.

0–1,100 Mealy's

A Cozzi coffee can, painted with sprays of flowers, red anchor mark, Italy, c1765, 2in (5cm) high.

£270–300 Helen Girton

The red anchor mark, although a different shape, can be confused with the Chelsea red anchor.

ccia coffee pot and cover, painted with flower ys, with a bird spout, painted No. '16', Italy, c1775, (23.5cm) high.

0–1,000 Sotheby's (NY)

A Riessner, Stellmacher & Kessel figure of a boy, unglazed, Bohemia, c1900, 14in (35.5cm) high.

£375–425 Oakwood Antiques

A pair of Fischer & Reichenbach vases, decorated with views of Carlsbad to the East and West, Bohemia, Pirkenhammer, 1810–46, 6¼in (16cm) high.

£9,500–11,500 Dorotheum

erend tea service, comprising 15 pieces, damaged and repaired, marked, Hungary, c1900.

500–6,500 Dorotheum

double-walled reticulated design derives from 18th-century Chinese porcelain.

A pair of Naples vases, gilded and painted with classical figures and with two gilt rams' masks, with associated covers, slight damage, marked, Italy, c1790, 10in (25cm) high.

£8,500–10,000 Sotheby's

A SELECTION OF CHINESE DYNASTIES & MARKS

EARLY DYNASTIES

Neolithic	10th – early 1st millennium BC
Shang Dynasty	16th century–c1050 BC
Zhou Dynasty	c1050–221 BC
Warring States 480–221 BC	
Qin Dynasty	221–206 BC
Han Dynasty	206 BC – AD 220
Six Dynasties	AD 222–589
Wei Dynasty AD 386–557	
Sui Dynasty	AD 581–618
Tang Dynasty	AD 618–
Five Dynasties	AD 907–
Liao Dynasty	AD 907–1
Song Dynasty	AD 960–1
Northern Song AD 960–1127	
Southern Song AD 1127–1279	
Xixia Dynasty	AD 1038–1
Jin Dynasty	AD 1115–1
Yuan Dynasty	AD 1279–1

MING DYNASTY MARKS

Hongwu
1368–1398

Yongle
1403–1424

Xuande
1426–1435

Chenghua
1465–1487

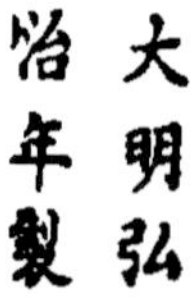
Hongzhi
1488–1505

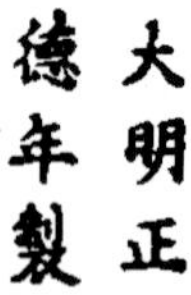
Zhengde
1506–1521

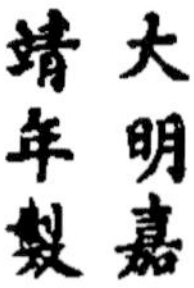
Jiajing
1522–1566

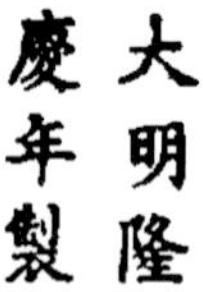
Longqing
1567–1572

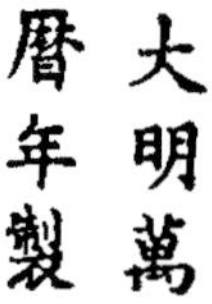
Wanli
1573–1619

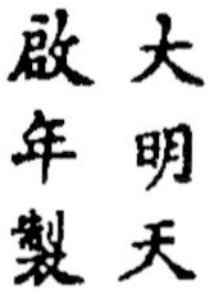
Tianqi
1621–1627

Chongzhe
1628–164

QING DYNASTY MARKS

Shunzhi
1644–1661

Kangxi
1662–1722

Yongzheng
1723–1735

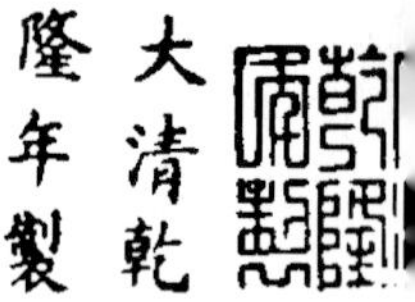
Qianlong
1736–1795

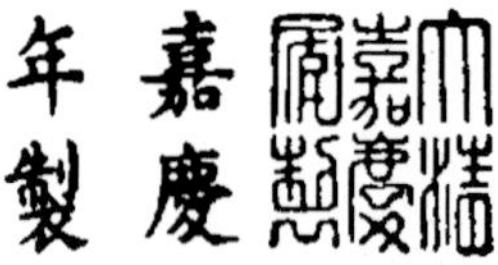
Jiaqing
1796–1820

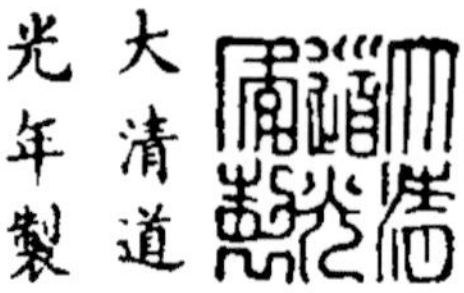
Daoguang
1821–1850

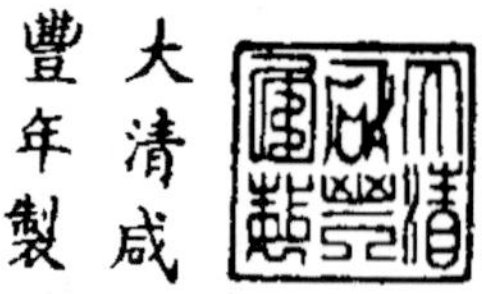
Xianfeng
1851–1861

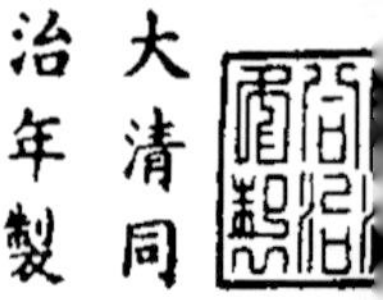
Tongzhi
1862–1874

Guangxu
1875–1908

Xuantong
1909–1911

Hongxian
1916

CHINESE CERAMICS

EARLY CERAMICS

black pottery amphora, Warring States riod, 480–221 BC, 12in (30.5cm) high.
350–950 Glade Antiques

A pair of Honan ware bowls, Song Dynasty, AD 960–1279, 5½in (14cm) diam.
£1,250–1,500 Skinner

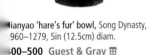

ianyao 'hare's fur' bowl, Song Dynasty, 960–1279, 5in (12.5cm) diam.
00–500 Guest & Gray

A black-glazed bowl, Song Dynasty, AD 960–1279, 8in (20.5cm) diam.
£700–800 Glade Antiques

A Yingqing bowl and cover, Song Dynasty, c1100, 3½in (9cm) high.
£600–650 Guest & Gray

izhou bowl, decorated with paper-cut nels and mottos, Southern Song Dynasty, 27–1279, 4½in (11.5cm) diam.
,500–5,500 Sotheby's (NY)

A celadon bowl, with sgraffito decoration, Song Dynasty, AD 960–1279, 5in (12.5cm) diam.
£800–1,000 Skinner

pod censer, on lion-paw feet, Tang asty, AD 618–907, 4¾in (12cm) diam.
000–8,500 Sotheby's

A Honan ware censer, Song Dynasty, AD 960–1279, 5½in (14cm) diam.
£1,100–1,300 Skinner

A Yaozhou celadon censer, carved with acanthus leaves and lotus flowers, Northern Song Dynasty, AD 960–1127, 5¼in (13.5cm) diam.
£1,800–2,200 Skinner

A pottery cup, moulded with floral bands, Tang Dynasty, AD 618–907, 3¾in (9.5cm) diam.

£2,000–2,500 Sotheby's

A Xing ewer, Tang Dynasty, AD 618–907, 8¼in (21cm) high.

£6,500–8,000 Sotheby's (NY)

A *sancai*-glazed figure of Tianwang, standing above a recumbent bull, Tang Dynasty, AD 618–907, 41in (104cm) high.

£8,000–9,500 Sotheby's

Tianwang is a Lokapala, one of the Guardian Kings of the Four Quarters.

A Yaozhou celadon dish, interior applied with biscuit fish, Northern Song Dynasty, AD 960–1127, 3in (7.5cm) diam.

£2,000–2,500 Glade Antiques

A Yue ware celadon ewer, cover missing, 11thC, 5in (12.5cm) diam.

£1,200–1,400 Skinner

A *sancai*-glazed pilgrim flask, moulded with floral scrolls, Tang Dynasty, AD 618–907, 6in (15cm) high.

£4,000–4,500 Sotheby's

A pottery jar, with carved decoration, Han Dynasty, 206 BC–AD 220, 14in (35.5cm) high.

£600–700 Skinner

A Yaozhou dish, Song Dynasty, AD 960–1279, 6in (15cm) diam.

£6,500–8,000 Sotheby's (NY)

Yaozhou is the name of a kiln site in Norther China during the Song Dynasty.
It is famous for its high-quality celadons.

A pair of glazed pottery figures of ladies of the court, Sui Dynasty, AD 581–618, 8in (20.5cm) high.

£215–240 Pastimes

A pottery jar, Neolithic period, 3,000–2,000 12in (30.5cm) high.

£1,500–1,800 Skinner

A jar, Tang Dynasty, AD 618–907, 6¾in (17cm) high.

£6,000–7,000 Sotheby's

During the Tang Dynasty blue glaze was created by using expensive imported cobal from Persia. Wares decorated with blue splashes were therefore held in high esteer

ncai-glazed jar, Tang Dynasty, 18–907, 7¾in (19.5cm) high.

500–9,000 Sotheby's (NY)

ttery model of a horse, Han Dynasty, BC–AD 220, 24in (61cm) long.

0–700 Skinner

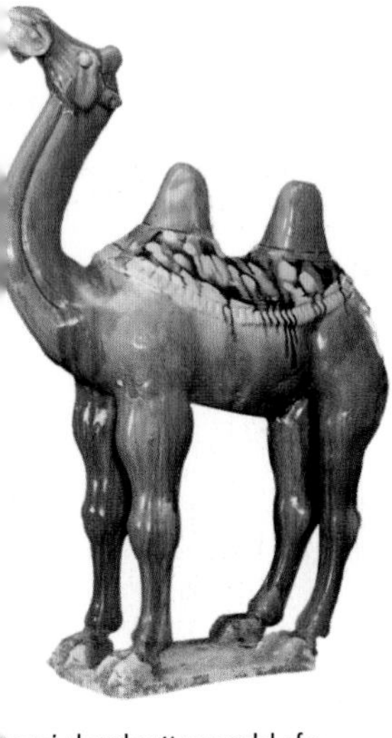

ancai-glazed pottery model of a trian camel, Tang Dynasty, AD 618–907, in (59cm) high.

000–6,000 Sotheby's

eladon model of a lion, Northern Song asty, AD 960–1127, 2in (5cm) high.

50–625 R & G McPherson

A *sancai*-glazed jar, Tang Dynasty, AD 618–907, 7in (18cm) high.

£10,000–12,000 Sotheby's

The decoration on these types of Tang Dynasty jars usually reflects contemporary textile designs.

A pottery model of a wild boar, Wei Dynasty, AD 386–557, 6in (15cm) long.

£100–120 Pastimes

A pottery model of a buffalo, slight damage, possibly Liao Dynasty, 10th/11thC, 4in (10cm) wide.

£500–575 R & G McPherson

A Jian hare's fur teabowl, inscribed 'San', Song Dynasty, AD 960–1279, 5½in (14cm) diam.

£14,000–18,000 Sotheby's

The inscription on the base of this bowl reads 'San' which means 'three'. It is suggested that numerals may refer to a particular kiln or to the precise location within a kiln where the bowls would be fired.

A pottery model of a duck, Han Dynasty, 206 BC–AD 220, 7in (18cm) high.

£850–1,000 Woolley & Wallis

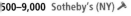

A pottery model of a cockerel, slight damage, Tang Dynasty, AD 618–907, 4¼in (11cm) high.

£340–380 Guest & Gray

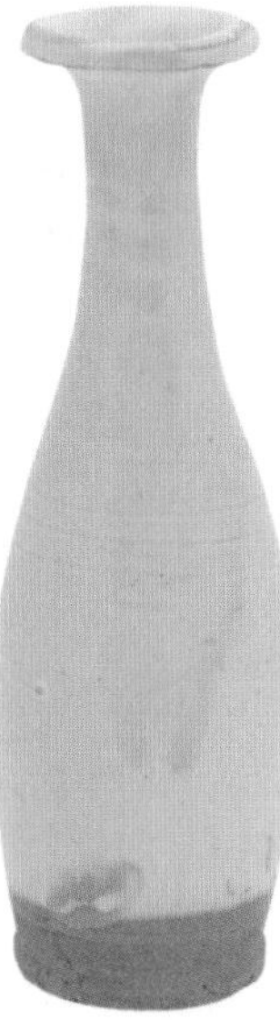

A Cizhou ware vase, Song/Yuan Dynasty, 12/14thC, 7in (18cm) high.

£575–650
R & G McPherson

Cizhou ware changed little over the years. However, the form and potting point to this vase being either Song or Yuan Dynasty. It has a thick layer of creamy white slip which has then been applied with a layer of clear glaze. The potter's finger marks can clearly be seen in the the slip towards the bottom of the vase.

BLUE & WHITE

A Chinese export bough pot, painted with flowering lotus, Qianlong period, 1736–95, 8in (20.5cm) diam.

£650–800 Lawrence Fine Art

A bowl, the interior decorated with a central roundel with two pomegranates, the outside decorated with pine, bamboo, plantain and cherry blossom, restored, Wanli period, 1573–1619, 10in (25.5cm) diam.

£1,100–1,200 Guest & Gray

A bowl and cover, applied with metal handles and finial, Kangxi period, 1662–1722, 9in (23cm) diam.

£1,100–1,300 Woolley & Wallis

A bowl, from the Nanking cargo, decorated with peonies and rocks, c1750, 6in (15cm) diam.

£250–280 Roger Bradbury

Nanking (now Nanjing) is a port on the east coast of China from where most of its Chinese porcelain of the 18th century was exported to the west. The name Nanking has now become a generic term for a type of underglaze blue porcelain. There were many hundreds of cargos of Nanking wares sent to the west, the most famous being that aboard the Geldermalsen *which sank off Java in 1751. Although there was little in the cargo to excite the purist collector of Asian ceramics, the story of the salvage attracted intense public interest, which was reflected in the prices achieved when the pieces were sold at auction in 1986. Items from this cargo still command a premium over comparable pieces of Chinese export porcelain.*

A bowl and saucer, from the *Diana* cargo, decorated with Diving Birds pattern, 1817, saucer 4¼in (11cm) diam.

£315–350 Roger Bradbury

The Diana *sank off the coast of Malacca in 1817 and the cargo was recovered in 1985.*

A bowl, from the *Tek Sing* cargo, with flowered rim, painted with a young boy holding blossom, c1822, 6in (15cm) diam.

£225–250 Roger Bradbury

The Tek Sing *sank in the Gaspar Straits, east of Java, in 1822.*

A porcelain brushpot, decorated with text, marked, Kangxi period, 1662–1722, 6¼in (16cm) high.

£35,000–42,000 Toovey's

The inscription on this brushpot was obviously of great significance to Chinese collectors, resulting in a realized price that far exceeded the saleroom estimate.

A brushpot, painted with warriors and a landscape in underglaze blue, incised with leaf-scroll borders, Kangxi period, 1662–1722, 8in (20.5cm) high.

£2,250–2,750 Gorringes (L)

A porcelain brushpot, painted with shrubs, insects and a bird, slight damage, Kangxi period, 1662–1722, 4¾in (12cm) high.

£500–600 Tennants

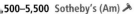

harger, painted with a *qilin*, 17thC,
ı (35.5cm) diam.
,500–5,500 Sotheby's (Am)

A stem cup, decorated with cherry blossom, Kangxi period, 1662–1722, 4½in (11.5cm) high.
£1,500–1,800 Bukowskis

A stem cup, painted with alternating panels of plants, Kangxi period, 1662–1722, 4¾in (12cm) high.
£1,000–1,200 Guest & Gray

›air of *ko-sometsuke* porcelain dishes, for the Japanese market, each decorated with a
ɛery landscape and a figure, slight damage, c1625, 6in (15cm) square.
,350–1,500 R & G McPherson
sometsuke wares were produced during the Tianqi period (1621–27) for the Japanese market.

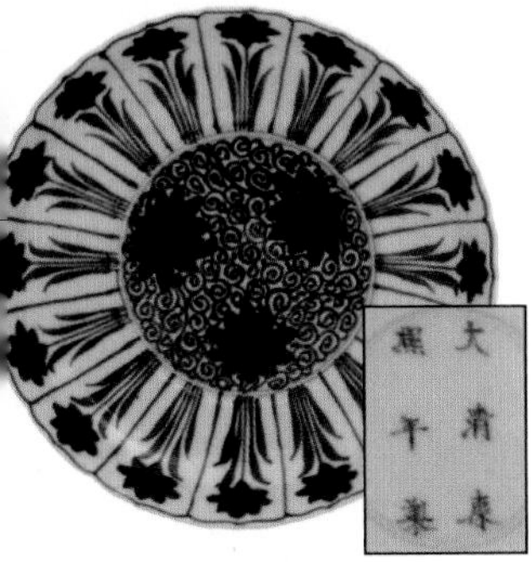

›air of dishes, decorated with Aster
ɛtern, six character Kangxi mark and of the
ɾiod, 1662–1722, 6in (15cm) diam.
',200–2,500 R & G McPherson

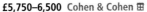

A set of six dishes, painted with birds, insects and flowering plants, Kangxi period, c1700, 9in (23cm) diam.
£5,750–6,500 Cohen & Cohen

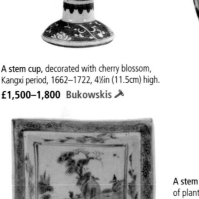

A silver-mounted ewer, painted with an official and his attendant, slight damage, cover associated, silver 19thC, c1650, 8¼in (21cm) high.
£1,000–1,200 Sotheby's (Am)

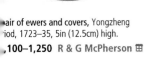

›air of ewers and covers, Yongzheng
ɾiod, 1723–35, 5in (12.5cm) high.
,100–1,250 R & G McPherson

A moon flask, decorated with peaches and bats, neck reduced, slight damage, marked, Qianlong period, 1736–95, 8½in (21.5cm) high.
£2,500–3,000 David Lay

A garden seat, decorated with peacocks, rockwork, bamboo and *lingzhi*, with lion-mask handles, Jiajing period, 1522–66, 15½in (39.5cm) high.
£13,000–16,000 Sotheby's (HK)

A garden seat, 19thC, 19¼in (49cm) high.

£240–300 Penrith Farmers' & Kidd's

A jar, painted with figures in a landscape, slight damage, marked, c1650, 8in (20.5cm) high.

£1,000–1,200 Sotheby's (Am)

A jar and cover, painted with prunus blossoms, Kangxi period, 1662–1722, 9¼in (23.5cm) high.

£4,000–5,000 Sotheby's (NY)

A storage jar, 19thC, 9½in (24cm) high.

£200–240 Waddington's

A jardinière, painted with panels of officials and their attendant, silver handles later, sligh damage, Kangxi period, 1662–1722, 7¾in (19.5cm) high.

£1,600–2,000 Sotheby's (Am)

A *kendi*, in the form of an elephant, with a double spout, Wanli period, 1573–1619, 8in (20.5cm) high.

£9,000–11,000 Sotheby's

A porcelain *kendi*, painted with precious objects, late Ming Dynasty, early 17thC, 8in (20.5cm) high.

£900–1,100 Holloway's

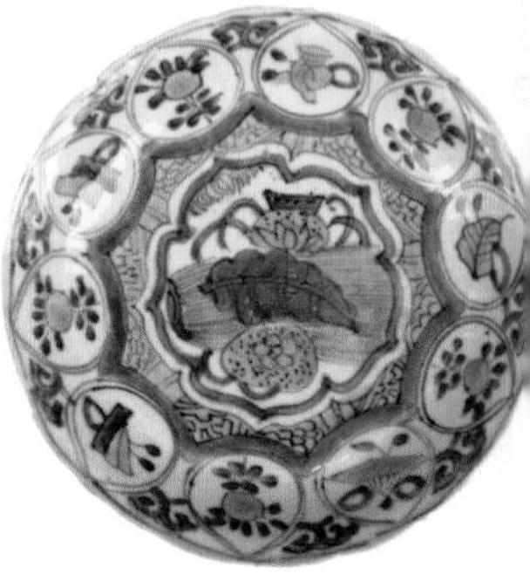

A *kraak* dish, decorated with leaves and objects, slight damage, Wanli period, 1573–1619, 8¼in (21cm) diam.

£400–450 Guest & Gray

A plate, with *kraak* decoration, Wanli period, 1573–1619, 11in (28cm) diam.

£580–650 Guest & Gray

Production of porcelain for export increased greatly during the reign of the Emperor Wanli. Pieces were predominantly blue and white, much of it kraak *porcelain, so-called because a cargo of such pieces was captured by the Dutch from a Portuguese carrack (*kraak *in Dutch) in 1603 and subsequently auctioned in Amsterdam amid great excitement. The decoration on this type of porcelain is enclosed in panels and the most common themes found are floral, precious objects or symbols tied with ribbons, crickets, beetles and butterflies.*

A set of eight Master of the Rocks-style plates, painted with a fisherman and figures, slight damage, one plate repaired, marked, Kangxi period, 1662–1722, 8¾in (22cm) diam.

£3,750–4,500 Sotheby's (Am)

The Master of the Rocks style is characterized by repeating close-knit lines defining the landscape elements. Very often these rock masses with twisting rhythms running through the design are very similar to the style of painting of Dong Qichang, a painter of the later Ming period, whose influence was enormous.

hinese-export Dutch Delft-style porcelain plate, decorated with s, slight damage, Yongzheng period, 1723–35, 8½in (21.5cm) diam.
75–650 R & G McPherson

A plate, decorated with trellis and vines, c1750, 9in (23cm) diam.
£115–130 Moxhams

hinese export platter, with European-e decoration, slight damage, Qianlong iod, 1736–95, 18¼in (46.5cm) wide.
50–425 Bukowskis

A platter, painted with peonies and bamboo in a garden, slight damage, c1750, 14¼in (36cm) wide.
£300–350 Sworders

A Nanking platter, painted with a pagoda and river landscape, Qianlong period, c1780, 16in (40.5cm) wide.
£475–525 Moxhams

Nanking platter, depicting a fisherman and boy, c1780, in (28cm) wide.
80–200 Moxhams

A Nanking sauce boat, c1770, 9in (23cm) wide.
£180–200 Peter Norden

part dinner service, comprising 11 pieces, each painted with a figure and a river ene, Qianlong period, 1736–95, platter 17¼in (44cm) diam.
,500–1,800 Sotheby's

A dinner service, comprising 88 pieces, decorated with plants, with an osier border, damaged, Qianlong period, 1736–95.
£4,000–5,000 Bukowskis

A part dinner service, comprising 57 pieces, Jiaqing period, 1796–1820, plate 10in (25.5cm) diam.

£10,000–12,000 Bukowskis

A tazza, decorated with a dragon, Qianlong mark and of the period, 1736–95, 9in (23cm) diam.

£5,000–6,000 Sotheby's (NY)

A teapot, decorated with figures and a monster' head, silver cover later, Chenghua mark, Chongzhen period, 1628–43, 4½in (11.5cm) hig

£750–850 Guest & Gray

A Chinese export teapot and cover, slight damage, Yongzheng period, 1723–35, 4½in (11.5cm) high.

£400–450 R & G McPherson

A tureen and cover, Kangxi period, 1662–1722, 6in (15cm) diam.

£1,750–2,000 R & G McPherson

A Chinese export porcelain tureen stand, painted with deer beneath a pine tree, Qianlor period, 1736–95, 15½in (39.5cm) wide.

£325–400 Toovey's

A pair of tureens, covers and stands, Qianlong period, 1736–95, 5in (12.5cm) wide.

£1,800–2,000 Cohen & Cohen

A tureen, cover and stand, painted with flower motifs and stylized scrolls, slight damage, Qianlong period, 1736–95, tureen 12¾in (32.5cm) wide.

£1,600–2,000 Sotheby's (Am)

A *meiping*, decorated with scholars and flowers, Chenghua period, 1465–87, 9in (23cm) high.

£9,000–11,000 Sotheby's

A double-gourd vase, decorated with officials and soldiers, wooden stopper later, Jiajing period, 1522–66, 13½in (34.5cm) high.

£20,000–25,000 Sotheby's (HK)

The double-gourd shape of this vase is always popular and, when combined with good painting, colour and condition, such pieces can be expected to reach a high price.

A vase, painted with figures and immortals a landscape, repaired, Transitional period, c1650, 17in (43cm) high.

£3,750–4,500 Sotheby's (Am)

air of vases and covers, each painted with figures in garden
lions, Kangxi period, 1662–1722, 13in (33cm) high.

000–6,000 Sotheby's (NY)

A vase, decorated with mountains, landscapes and inscriptions, Xuande mark, Kangxi period, 1662–1722, 20½in (52cm) high.

£1,500–1,800 Hy Duke

A *yen yen* vase, painted with dragons chasing a pearl, Kangxi period, 1662–1722, 18in (45.5cm) high.

£1,800–2,200 Tennants

orcelain vase, slight damage,
ngxi period, c1700,
(23cm) high.

,100–1,250
& G McPherson

A porcelain crocus vase, with six apertures, decorated with prunus blossoms and vignettes of vases, 19thC, 10¼in (26cm) high.

£300–350 James Adam

A porcelain double-gourd vase, decorated with Lotus pattern, 19thC.

£1,250–1,500
Waddington's

A pair of baluster vases, painted with peony scrolls, 19thC, 17¾in (45cm) high.

£450–550 Waddington's

A pair of vases, each decorated with two dragons chasing a flaming pearl among powdered clouds, c1900, 17¼in (43.5cm) high.

£500–600 Sworders

pair of vases, each painted with a *qilin* and phoenix among clouds,
900, 22¾in (57.5cm) high.

50–420 Sworders

A pair of wall vases, in the form of carp, slight damage, Jiaqing period, 1796–1820, 9¼in (23.5cm) long.

£1,250–1,500 Sotheby's (Am)

FAMILLE ROSE

A pair of *famille rose* **bowls,** painted with floral sprays, *Minyao* marks, Yongzheng period, 1723–35, 7¼in (18.5cm) diam.

£6,000–7,000 Sotheby's (NY)

Minyao *literally translates as 'popular ware'.*

A *famille rose* **bowl,** decorated with bats and a fruiting vine, seal mark, Qianlong period, 1736–95, 6¾in (17cm) diam.

£6,500–8,000 Sotheby's (HK)

A *famille rose* **bowl,** painted with a hunting scene, the interior with a panel of a mother feeding her child, damaged and repaired, Qianlong period, 1736–95, 11½in (29cm) diam.

£600–700 Toovey's

A Chinese export *famille rose* **punchbowl,** decorated with a fence garden, Qianlong period, 1736–95, 15¾in (40cm) diam.

£650–800 Hy Duke

A Chinese export *famille rose* **bowl,** enamelled with peonies and flowers, Qianlong period, 1736–95, 15in (38cm) diam.

£240–280 Hy Duke

A *famille rose* **punchbowl,** decorated with a pagoda by a lake and mountains, Qianlong period, c1760, 15½in (39.5cm) diam.

£4,500–5,000 Cohen & Cohen

A Chinese export *famille rose* **punchbow** decorated with Masonic emblems, early 19thC, 12½in (32cm) diam.

£4,000–5,000 Northeast Auctions

EXPERT'S EYE MEDALLION BOWLS

Chinese medallion bowls are so-named because they have four round *famille rose* medallions reserved on a coloured ground and a single underglaze blue medallion on the inside. Bowls of this type can be found with blue, ruby/pink and yellow grounds. First made during the Qianlong period, their popularity reached a peak during the Daoguang period (1821–50), although they continued to be made until the end of the 19th century. This is one of a pair of Chinese Imperial bowls dating from the Daoguang period.

£25,000–30,000 Hy Duke

The interior is painted in underglaze blue only with a central medallion of flowers and ribbons above waves crashing on rocks.

Yellow ground bowls are most desirable as yellow was the Emperor's own personal colour. The medallions are often painted with symbolic designs which can be the 'four seasons' flowers, the sacred and profane 'one hundred antiquities' or symbols of longevity and prosperity. This medallion bowl is painted with peaches, which have a vast range of symbolic meanings including those of spring, immortality and marriage.

The well-painted Imperial mark says 'Great Qing Dao Guang Period Made'.

mille rose **bowl,** painted with exotic flowers, the interior with a
allion of a rabbit, seal mark, Daoguang period, 1821–50,
15cm) diam.

000–8,500 Sotheby's (HK)

A *famille rose* **bowl,** decorated with stylized lotus blooms, fruit and bats, seal mark, Daoguang period, 1821–50, 6¾in (17cm) diam.

£7,500–9,000 Sotheby's (HK)

ir of *famille rose* **medallion bowls,** decorated with panels of blossom trees and flower sprigs,
interiors with a medallion of a rabbit, seal mark, Daoguang period, 1821–50, 6in (16cm) diam.

,000–22,000 Sotheby's (HK)

A *famille rose* **bowl,** painted with flowering shrubs, on a hardwood stand, 19thC, 10in (25.5cm) diam.

£1,800–2,200 Gorringes (L)

anton *famille rose* **bowl,** painted with
els of figures within panels of key fret and
cious objects, c1870, 10¼in (26cm) diam.

50–550 Sworders

A Chinese export *famille rose* **bowl,** decorated with figures, c1870, 9½in (24cm) diam.

£150–180 Waddington's

These colourful chunky pieces of famille rose *were produced in large quantities at the end of the 19th century for sale to Chinese people living in Singapore, Malaya, etc.*

A Chinese export *famille rose* **dish,** decorated with chrysanthemums and gilt birds, Qianlong period, c1750, 14½in (37cm) diam.

£900–1,100
Dreweatt Neate (HAM)

hinese export *famille rose* **figure of a**
man holding a vase, restored, Qianlong
iod, 1736–95, 7½in (19cm) high.

45–160 R & G McPherson

A pair of *famille rose* **figural candlesticks,** in the form of court ladies, Qianlong Period, c1770, 11in (28cm) high.

£16,000–18,000 Cohen & Cohen

A *famille rose* **figure of a woman holding fruit,** losses, Qianlong period, 1736–95, 7½in (19cm) high.

£1,600–1,800 Guest & Gray

A *famille rose* figure of Guandi, slight damage and losses, Jiaqing period, 1796–1820, 8in (20.5cm) high.

£500–600 Guest & Gray

A *famille rose* fish bowl, painted with nine five-clawed dragons chasing the flaming pearl between *ruyi* and a wavy border, the interior with five goldfish among seaweed, 19thC, 21in (53.5cm) diam.

£4,500–5,500 Sotheby's (Am)

A pair of Canton *famille rose* moon flasks, decorated with figures, plants and dragons, one converted to a la Qing Dynasty, 19thC, 15¾in (40cm) high.

£4,500–5,500 Bukowskis

A *famille rose* garden seat, 19thC, 18in (45.5cm) high.

£1,100–1,200 R & G McPherson

A pair of *famille rose* gilt-bronze-mounted jardinières/wine coolers, each decorated with an armorial and flowers, with rams'-mask handles, the bases cast with guilloches, the porcelain 18thC, 10in (25.5cm) high.

£11,000–13,000 Sotheby's

A *famille rose* jardinière, painted with Shoulao and attendants, 19thC, 16in (40.5cm) diam.

£425–525 Waddington's

ESSENTIAL REFERENCE COLOUR CLASSIFICATION

Coloured enamelling on Chinese porcelain became popular in the early 18th century and was named after the predominant background colour.

- The predominant colour of *famille verte* porcelain is green, with the additional use of yellow, manganese, purple and violet enamels. The red colour is a flat iron-red, introduced during the Kangxi period (1662–1722). This was the standard form of decoration until the introduction of *famille rose* c1720.
- *Famille rose* enamelling was introduced around 1720, with the best examples dating from the reign of Yongzheng (1723–35). It was one of the few ceramic innovations to be introduced to China by Europe, and by the mid-18th century the demand for this type of decoration for export wares almost equalled that for blue and white. The opaque pink colour, derived from colloidal gold, was initially used sparingly. The smallest amount of rose enamel is sufficient to classify a piece as *famille rose*.
- *Famille noire* has a black ground washed over with a transparent green enamel and decoration in the *famille verte* palette. The process involved applying a copper-green lead-based enamel over an unfired coating of the dry black cobalt that was used in the outlines. Most pieces of *famille noire* and *jaune* were manufactured in the 19th century. Some later pieces involve black enamel added as an extra layer on early Kangxi pieces.

Famille verte

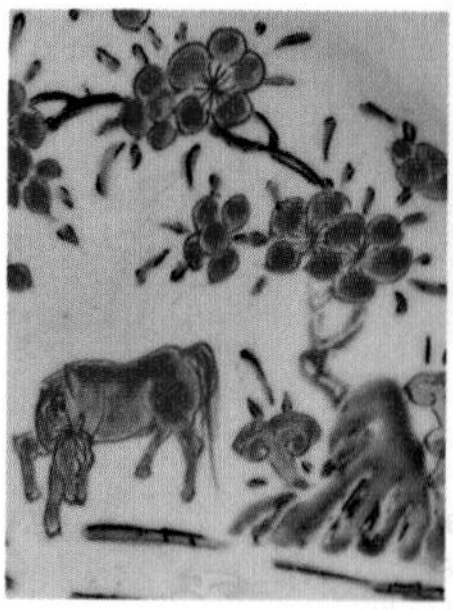

Famille rose

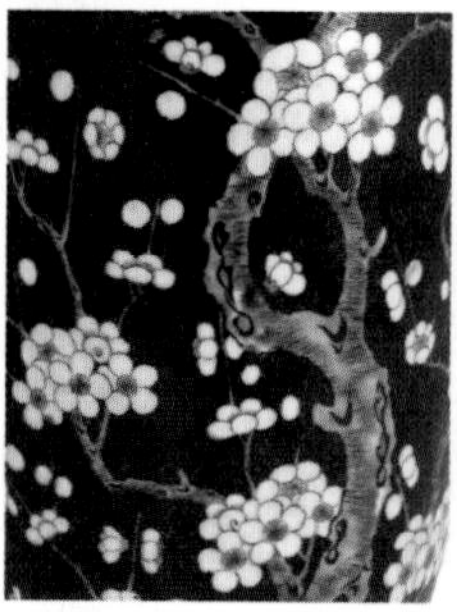

Famille noir

Famille jaune

- *Famille jaune*, another variant of the *famille verte* palette, has a predominantly yellow ground. As with *famille noire* it was often added at a later stage to Kangxi pieces.

ɪir of *famille rose* **jardinières,** each decorated with the Eight Daoist Immortals Shoulao, some sailing on a log boat, 19thC, 18¼in (46.5cm) diam.

500–5,500 Woolley & Wallis

A pair of Chinese export *famille rose* **jardinières,** each painted with panels of animals and flowers, c1900, 13¾in (35cm) high.

£2,000–2,500 Sotheby's (NY)

ɪir of *famille rose* **models of pheasants,** ʝ Dynasty, 18thC, 8½in (21.5cm) high.

,000–16,000 Sotheby's (NY)

A pair of gilt-bronze-mounted *famille rose* **models of birds,** Jiaqing period, 1796–1820, 9¼in (23.5cm) high.

£15,000–18,000 Bukowskis

A *famille rose* **mug,** painted in enamels with figures and birds, c1750, 5in (12.5cm) high.

£160–200 Sworders

ɪmille rose **mug,** decorated with Chinese ɜs and children, Qianlong period, c1765, (12.5cm) high.

ʼ5–425 Moxhams

A pair of Canton *famille rose* **mugs,** decorated with panels of figures and flowers, 19thC, 5¾in (14.5cm) high.

£350–425 Woolley & Wallis

A pair of *famille rose* **plates,** each decorated with chrysanthemums, peony branches and a butterfly, Yongzheng period, 1723–35, 8in (20.5cm) diam.

£4,500–5,500 Sotheby's (Am)

ɪir of Chinese export *famille rose* **soup** ꞓes, each decorated with a mythological ɪe of Cybele by a reclining lion, Qianlong ɔd, c1755, 9in (23cm) diam.

200–3,500 Cohen & Cohen

A Chinese *famille rose* **platter,** decorated with flowers, slight damage, Qianlong period, 1736–95, 11½in (29cm) wide.

£675–750 Guest & Gray

A *famille rose* **platter,** decorated with crickets, insects and flowers, slight damage, Xianfeng mark and of the period, 1851–61, 16½in (42cm) wide.

£500–600 Bukowskis

A *famille rose* **sauce boat,** painted with a panel of figures by a house with oxen, slight damage, Qianlong period, 1736–95, 7¾in (19.5cm) wide.

£350–400 Guest & Gray

A *famille rose* **tea service,** painted with birds and flowers within a Y-diaper border, Yongzheng period, c1730, teapot 5in (12.5cm) high.

£7,000–8,000 Cohen & Cohen

A *famille rose* **part service,** comprising 16 pieces, each painted with a peony, damaged and repaired, Qianlong period, 1736–95, largest 14¼in (36cm) diam.

£3,500–4,000 Sotheby's

A Chinese export *famille rose* **part dinner service,** comprising 48 pieces, decorated with floral motifs, c1760.

£1,250–1,500 Northeast Auctions

A *famille rose* **spittoon,** decorated with flowers and insects, Qianlong period, c1740 5in (12.5cm) high.

£1,350–1,500 Cohen & Cohen

A Chinese export *famille rose* **tureen stand,** decorated with an ox-head, restored, Qianlong period, 1736–95, 15½in (39.5cm) wide.

£25,00–30,000 Bukowskis

This is a very rare item.

A Chinese export *famille rose* **tankard,** decorated with panels of flowers on a chicken-skin ground, the handle with *ruyi* terminals, slight damage, Qianlong period, 1736–95, 4¾in (12cm) high.

£120–150 Dreweatt Neate (HAM)

Chicken skin is a term for a thick, opaque white glaze used for the background of ceramic items.

A Chinese export *famille rose* **teapot and cover,** decorated in the Mandarin palette with figures and a pavilion, late 18thC, 6½in (16.5cm) high.

£250–300 Hy Duke

A *famille rose* **teapot,** decorated with flowers, Qianlong period, c1760, 5in (12.5cm) high.

£800–900 Cohen & Cohen

A pair of *famille rose* **tureens and covers,** Qianlong period, 1736–95, 8in (20.5cm) wide.

£12,000–15,000 Bukowskis

A *famille rose* **tureen and cover,** decorate with peacocks in a garden, Qianlong period 1736–95, 14in (35.5cm) wide.

£3,250–4,000 Bukowskis

mille rose **tureen, cover and stand,**
painted and gilt decoration, c1825,
d 18½in (47cm) wide.
400–1,750 Leonard Joel

A pair of *famille rose* **vases,** each decorated with eight boy musicians and a figure riding a *qilin*, c1730, 7½in (19cm) high.
£650–800 Woolley & Wallis

mille rose **garniture of vases,** comprising five pieces, each with
f decoration, the cover finials in the form of a seated animal,
ored, Qianlong period, 1736–95, 13in (33cm) high.
000–3,500 Sotheby's (Am)

A pair of Chinese export *famille rose* **vases,** each decorated with panels of vases and flowers, late 18thC, 11½in (29cm) high.
£900–1,100 Hy Duke

A Canton *famille rose* **vase,** painted with panels of warriors and applied with *chilong*, with Buddhist lion handles, mid-19thC, 35in (89cm) high.
£3,200–3,800 Sworders

air of *famille rose* **vases and covers,** decorated with raised panels
owers, scrolls and butterflies on a chicken-skin ground, with red
gilt serpent handles, Qianlong period, c1780, 19in (48.5cm) high.
,000–18,000 Cohen & Cohen

anton *famille rose* **vase,**
orated with butterflies,
scrolled handles, c1875,
n (14cm) high.
50–800 Sworders

A Canton *famille rose* **vase,** decorated with figures, with gilt dragon and lion dog handles, late 19thC, 17½in (44.5cm) high.
£375–450 Greenslade Taylor Hunt
Thousands of this type of vase were imported by Liberty & Co.

A Canton *famille rose* **vase,** decorated with moulded panels of figures, slight damage, base drilled, 19thC, 23¼in (59cm) high.
£2,200–2,600 Sotheby's (Am)
Although the predominant colour of this vase is green, the slight use of rose enamel classified it as a famille rose *piece.*

A *famille rose* **bottle vase,** decorated with a landscape, the neck with inscription, seal marks, early 20thC, 8in (20.5cm) high.
£3,000–4,000 Sotheby's (HK)

FAMILLE VERTE

EXPERT'S EYE LION CENSERS

Chinese models of mythical beasts are usually found in pairs with their heads turned to face each other. They were used as guardian beasts in Buddhist temples, usually placed on each side of a statue. These censers from the Kangxi period are modelled as dogs of *Fo* but unusually are standing four-square rather than in the normal squat position. It is rare for Kangxi period *famille verte* to appeal to both Western and Chinese tastes, but these censers do and the potential market is therefore enormous, as reflected by their high price.

£35,000–40,000 **Sotheby's**

It is more usual for the incense to be poured into the body of the beast, then ignited. These censers have incense stick holders protruding from their mouths, thus enabling them to be refilled quickly and easily.

This pair is of exceptional quality *famille verte* enamel ware, the bold use of iron-red swirls contrasting with the green.

A ***famille verte* charger,** decorated with a garden scene, slight damage, Kangxi period, 1662–1722, 13¾in (35cm) diam.

£13,000–16,000 **Bukowskis**

A ***famille verte* dish,** decorated with birds on a flowering branch, the border with phoenix, Kangxi period, 1662–1722, 9½in (24cm) diam.

£8,200–9,750 **Bukowskis**

A pair of *famille verte* saucer dishes, eac painted with two butterflies above peonies both with slight damage, conch mark to bases, Kangxi period, 1662–1722, 13¼in (33.5cm) diam.

£3,500–4,250 **Sotheby's**

A ***famille verte* moulded dish,** painted with a dragon and phoenix fighting within panels depicting Buddhist lions and birds, slight damage, Kangxi period, 1662–1722, 9¾in (25cm) diam.

£3,200–3,800 **Sotheby's (Am)**

A Chinese export *famille verte* figure of a man, restored, early 18thC, 3in (7.5cm) wide.

£175–200 **R & G McPherson**

A ***famille verte* figure group of a man wi his horse,** restored and damaged, Kangxi period, 1662–1722, 6½in (16.5cm) high.

£22,000–28,000 **Sotheby's (Am)**

This model is extremely rare.

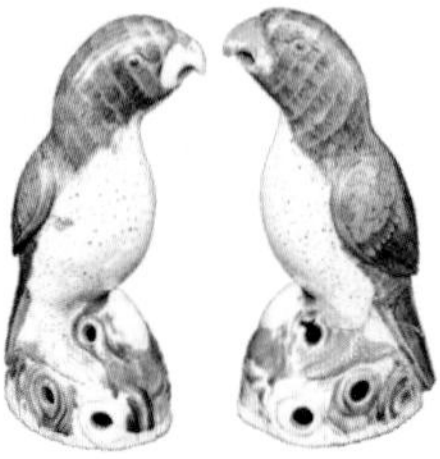

A pair of *famille verte* models of parrots, one damaged, Kangxi period, 1662–1722, 5in (12.5cm) high.

£1,300–1,500 **Guest & Gray**

A ***famille verte* figure of a boy,** restored, Kangxi period, 1662–1722, 6½in (16.5cm) high.

£11,000–12,000 **Guest & Gray**

A ***famille verte* model of a elephant,** the howdah decorated with flowerheads on a dia ground, restored, 19thC, 8¼in (21cm) high.

£1,100–1,300 **Sotheby's (Am)**

ɜir of Chinese export *famille verte* ɫels of cockerels, slight damage, one ɔred, 19thC, 16½in (42cm) high.

800–2,200 Sotheby's (NY)

A *famille verte* plate, decorated with floral scrolls, with a pierced border, slight damage, Kangxi period, 1662–1722, 8¼in (21cm) diam.

£750–850 Guest & Gray

A *famille verte* plate, after a design by Cornelis Pronk, the reverse with a stylized ornamental border, 18thC, 7in (18cm) diam.

£2,000–2,500 Sotheby's (Am)

ɑir of *famille verte* vases, decorated ɦ precious objects and flanked by two gilt ' head handles, painted with panels of ɫs, mythical creatures, landscape scenes ɫ flowers, mounted as lamps, slight ɲage, Kangxi period, 1662–1722, ¼in (60.5cm) high.

5,000–18,000 Sotheby's

s type of vase is currently particularly ɔular with interior designers.

A pair of *famille verte* vases, with enamelled decoration, each decorated with a *ruyi* collar and floral bouquets, Kangxi period, 1662–1722, 15in (38cm) high.

£16,000–20,000 Sotheby's

A *famille verte* vase, the body enamelled with a maiden and two boys, the base with a *faux* Chenghua mark, Kangxi period, 1662–1722, 9¾in (25cm) high.

£2,500–3,000 Sotheby's (NY)

A pair of *famille verte* vases, decorated with alternating panels of flowers and precious objects, the shoulders with scrolling flowers, one restored, Kangxi period, 1662–1722, 18in (45.5cm) high.

£2,000–2,200 Guest & Gray

'amille verte baluster vase, painted with ɖs in a magnolia tree, restored, Kangxi 'iod, c1700, 4¾in (12cm) high.

00–600 Sworders

A pair of *famille verte* vases, enamelled with figures of courtesans in a garden landscape, 19thC, 9½in (24cm) high.

£300–350 James Adams

A *famille verte* vase and cover, decorated with flowers and stylized foliage, with a lambrequin border, late 19thC, 25¼in (64cm) high.

£1,550–1,850 Sotheby's (P)

IMARI

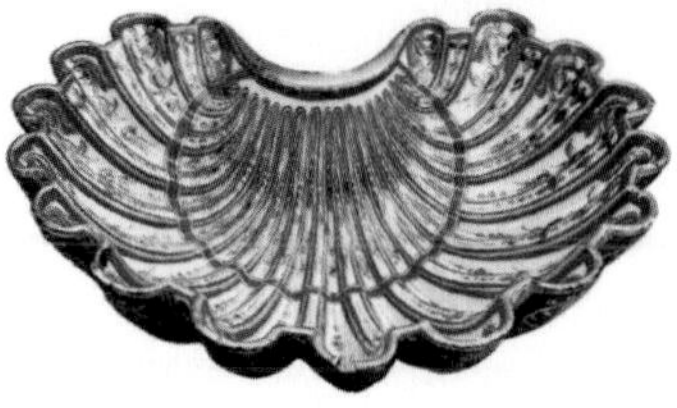

An Imari basin, in the form of a shell, Kangxi period, 1662–1722, 14¾in (37.5cm) wide.
£2,400–2,750 Bukowskis

An Imari barber's bowl, decorated with peonies and flowers, Kangxi period, early 18thC, 12½in (32cm) diam.
£1,000–1,100 Guest & Gray

A pair of Imari dishes, each painted with a basket of flowers, Qing Dynasty, Kangxi period, 1662–1722, 13¾in (35cm) diam.
£2,500–3,000 Sotheby's

An Imari cup and saucer, 18thC, 4½in (11.5cm) diam.
£300–350 Guest & Gray

An Imari dish, decorated with peony, rock and bamboo, slight damage, Qianlong period, 1736–95, 10¼in (26cm) diam.
£450–500 Guest & Gray

An Imari mug, painted with flowers and foliage, Qianlong period, 1736–95, 6¼in (16cm) high.
£500–550 Guest & Gray

A Chinese Imari tea canister, Kangxi peric early 18thC, 4in (10cm) high.
£135–150 Offa's Dyke

An Imari teapot, decorated with bunches of grapes on vines, late Kangxi period, 1710–35, 4in (10cm) high.
£750–850 R & G McPherson

An Imari teapot, c1715, 5in (12.5cm) high.
£525–585 R & G McPherson

An Imari teapot and cover, decorated with peonies and chrysanthemums, restored, Qianlong period, 1736–95, 5½in (14cm) hi
£340–380 Guest & Gray

A pair of Imari tureens, Kangxi period, c1710, 8in (20.5cm) high.
£3,000–3,500 R & G McPherson

An Imari garniture of vases, comprising five pieces, with lion finials, some damage and restoration, 18thC, largest 12½in (32cm) high.
£1,800–2,200 Sotheby's (Am)

DDITIONAL COLOURS

inese export 'Spanish coin' box and
', enamelled with a portrait of King
es IV of Spain, with a Latin inscription,
ase with Spanish Royal coat-of-arms,
ıg period, c1808, 2½in (6.5cm) diam.
00–10,000 **Sotheby's**

A box and cover, decorated *en grisaille* with the Empress Dowager pattern, the base with an inscription, seal mark, Guangxu period, late 19thC, 12½in (32cm) diam.
£7,000–8,500 **Woolley & Wallis**

A coffee pot and cover, decorated with a crest, slight damage, 18thC, 9in (23cm) high.
£180–200
Woolley & Wallis

SSENTIAL REFERENCE SYMBOLISM

n Chinese art and design, the meaning of a particular symbol is important in both cultural and religious terms.
ny of the symbols have been used since prehistoric times, particularly as decoration on bronzes.

'he meaning is often duplicated, as in the deer and the crane, which both represent immortality.

ach of the four seasons is represented by a flower: prunus for winter and symbolic of beauty; peony for spring
d wealth; lotus for summer and purity; and the chrysanthemum for autumn and steadfast friendship.

Jo one single symbol is more important than another, and each has its own place and historic meaning.
ey are used on all objects irrespective of medium and function.

Aany of these symbols became popular motifs on export works of art made for the Western market but to the
sterner the traditional meaning would be lost.

onies represent love, beauty, happiness
d honour.

Dragons represent authority, strength, wisdom and the Emperor.

Deer symbolize longevity as they are believed to live to a long age. They are also thought to be the only animals capable of finding the sacred fungus of longevity, *lingzhi*.

e pine, prunus and bamboo together are
o known as the 'Three Friends of Winter'
d denote spiritual harmony.

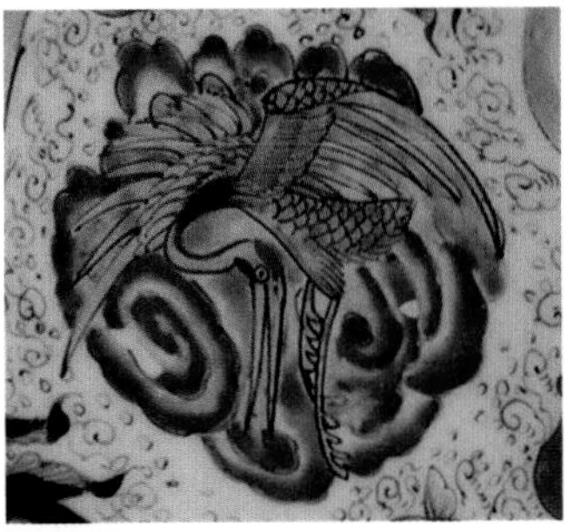

Cranes represent longevity and transport for the Immortals.

Fish symbolize fertility, wealth and abundance. Paired fish are a symbol of marital bliss and harmony.

A dish, decorated with birds and flowers, Tianqi period, 1621–27, 5¼in (13.5cm) square.

£600–650 Guest & Gray

This dish was produced for the Japanese market.

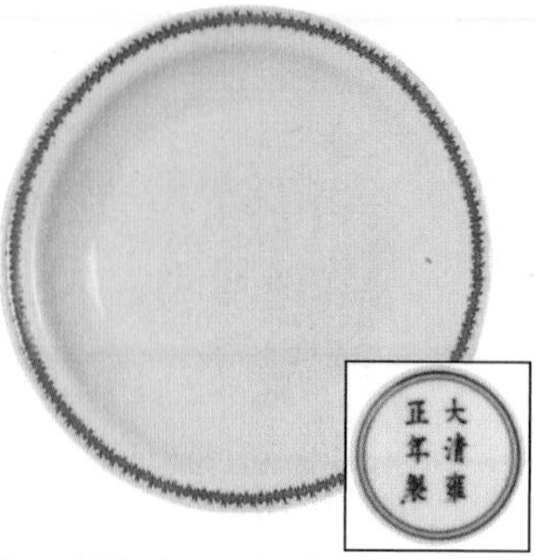

A footed dish, decorated with an *anhua shou* character and dragons within a border of bats, marked, Yongzheng period, 1723–35, 6¾in (17cm) diam.

£14,000–17,500 Sotheby's (HK)

A footed dish, decorated with dragons chasing a flaming pearl, Qianlong period, 1736–95, 10in (25.5cm) diam.

£5,000–6,000 Sotheby's (NY)

A dish, decorated with a dog of *Fo* chasing a ball, marked, Qianlong period, 1736–95, 5¼in (13.5cm) diam.

£900–1,100 Woolley & Wallis

A Chinese export porcelain dish, decorated with Tobacco Leaf pattern, late 18thC, 12in (30.5cm) long.

£5,000–6,000 Northeast Auctions

A pottery ridge tile, surmount a bearded figure riding a myt beast, damaged, restored, M Dynasty, 14½in (37cm) high.

£500–600 Guest & Gra

A figural group of the Gods of Mirth (Hehe Erxian), slight damage, Qianlong period, 1736–95, 6½in (16.5cm) high.

£1,100–1,300 Guest & Gray

A pair of porcelain figures of Shoulao, wearing robes decorated with the *shou* character, slight damage, Qianlong period, 1736–95, 8in (20.5cm) high.

£625–685 R & G McPherson

Shoulau was the Deity of Long Life and Old Age.

A pair of Canton clay figures of a lady ar gentleman, with nodding heads, wearing court robes, c1800, 12½in (32cm) high.

£11,000–13,000 Sotheby's

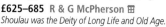

MARKET INFORMATION ASIAN CERAMICS

- As with other areas of antiques, the market for Asian ceramics is volatile. Much sought-after rarities are in demand whereas less desirable pieces are proving difficult to sell.
- Demand for Chinese Imperial porcelain continues unabated, especially in the home market. Other good quality rare pieces are as eagerly sought after. In contrast, less important pieces are failing to sell. A recent international sale saw fifty per cent of items remaining unsold.
- When an item unexpectedly achieves a high price, such as two or three times the estimate, one of the knock-on effects can be that similar items are put up sale. When this happens, supply can often outstrip demand, as seen in 2006 when a Chinese export 'Spanish Coin' box (see page 285) sold for a record price of £8,400. As a result, two more such boxes were put put up for sale but both failed to reach their reserves of £3,000–4,000.

·*cai* **jar,** decorated with mythical beasts
ːaves, damaged, mid-17thC,
ı (32cm) high.
.00–1,800 Toovey's

A *doucai* jar, decorated with a dragon, the shoulder with a ring of Eight Buddhist Emblems, seal mark, Daoguang period, 1821–50, 5¼in (13.5cm) high.
£8,000–10,000 Sotheby's (NY)

A jardinière, painted with a panel of figures in a garden, late 19thC, 9in (23cm) high.
£375–450 Gorringes (L)

ır of East India Company models of hounds,
·red, Qianlong period, 1736–95, 7in (18cm) high.
300–2,200 Sotheby's (Am)

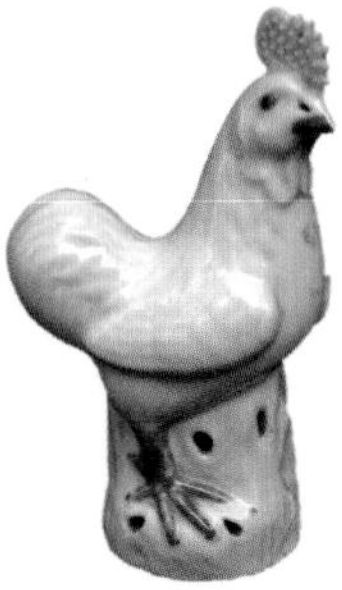

A model of a cockerel, some wear, 18th/19thC, 6¾in (17cm) high.
£580–650 Guest & Gray

A pair of *sancai* stoneware models of Buddhist lions, one with a cub, one with a ball, 19thC, 8in (20.5cm) high.
£300–350 Waddington's

ırcelain mug, decorated in the Mandarin
·te, Qianlong period, c1780,
12.5cm) high.
5–600 R & G McPherson

A Chinese export mug, moulded with the head of Bacchus, c1785, 4in (10cm) high.
£2,000–2,500 Sotheby's (Am)

A Chinese export dinner plate, painted *en grisaille* and gilt with the resurrection of Christ, Qianlong period, c1745, 9in (23cm) diam.
£2,250–2,500 Cohen & Cohen

ıinese export plate, decorated in gilt and
ːnel with a coat-of-arms, worn, Qianlong
ɔd, c1755, 14in (35.5cm) diam.
300–1,600 Skinner

A pair of Chinese export plates, Qianlong period, c1775, 9in (23cm) diam.
£800–900 Moxhams
These plates were made for the French market.

A pair of Canton saucers, painted with figures, flowers and fruits, Qianlong period, 1736–95, 5in (12.5cm) diam.

£1,250–1,500 Sotheby's (Am)

A Chinese export platter, decorated with the arms of Bushay, Sheriff of Dumfries, c1790, 13in (33cm) wide

£850–950 Moxhams

A teabowl and saucer, Kangxi period, 1662–1722, saucer 4¼in (11cm) diam.

£225–250 Guest & Gray

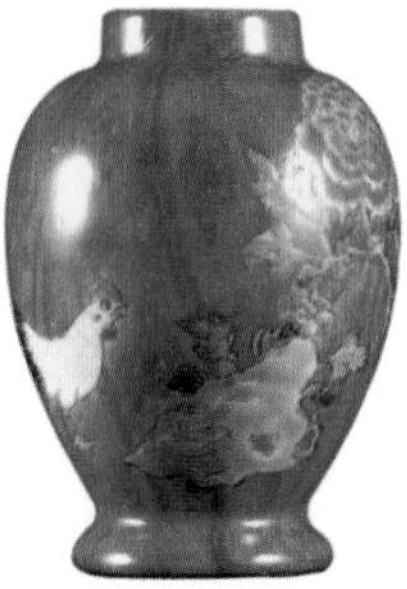

A tea canister, decorated to resemble wood with a peony, rockwork and a cockerel, restored, 18thC, 4in (10cm) high.

£300–350 Woolley & Wallis

A porcelain teapot, painted with a pheas among flowers, 18thC, 4in (12cm) high.

£100–120 Holloway's

A Yixing teapot, the cover with a dog of *Fo* finial, 19thC, 4½in (11.5cm) high.

£130–150 Guest & Gray

A tureen, stand and cover, cover repaired, Jiaqing period, 1796–1822, tureen 12¼in (31cm) wide.

£2,000–2,500 Bukowskis

A pair of gilt-bronze-mounted tureens, in the form of quails, repaired, Qianlong peri 1736–95, 8¼in (21cm) wide.

£45,000–55,000 Bukowskis

Quails always appear in pairs. They are symb of affinity and a long-lasting relationship. Chinese export quail tureens are quite rare and always fetch good prices. These turee have been mounted in superb 18th-centu gilded bronze specifically designed and ma for them. Ormolu mounts are very popular the Continent and it is the quality of the mounts that has raised the value of this pa

A *wucai* vase, decorated with figures and a horse, slight damage, Shunzhi period, 1644–61, 14½in (37cm) high.

£3,000–3,500 Sotheby's (Am)

An ormolu-mounted *wucai* vase, decorated with the Eight Daoist Immortals, mounted as a lamp, c1650, (40cm) high.

£3,000–3,500 Sotheby's (NY)

A pair of bottle vases, each painted with three lions, Kangxi period, 1662–1722, 5¾in (14.5cm) high.

£2,250–2,750 Sotheby's (NY)

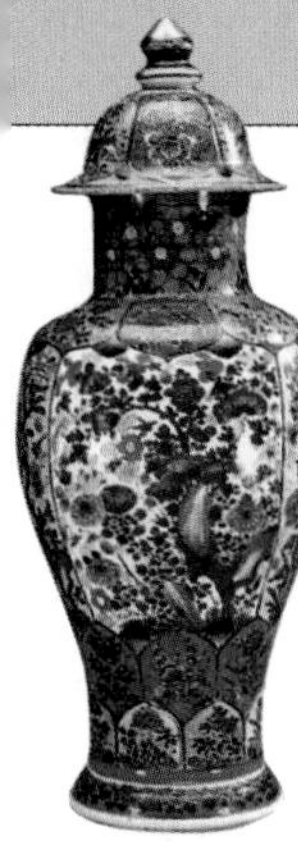

se, decorated with panels of
en motifs, slight damage,
gxi period, 1662–1722,
(53.5cm) high.
)00–3,500 Bukowskis

A Chinese export garniture of vases, comprising five pieces, iron-red and gilt highlights added in Holland, early 18thC, largest 15¾in (40cm) high.
£7,500–9,000 Northeast Auctions

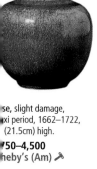

se, slight damage,
xi period, 1662–1722,
(21.5cm) high.
750–4,500
heby's (Am)

A wall vase, painted with millefleurs, with gilt animal-head mask handles, seal mark, Qianlong period, 1736–95, 8in (20.5cm) high.
£55,000–65,000
Woolley & Wallis
The decoration commonly known as millefleurs juxtaposes hundreds of chrysanthemums, peonies, lilies, convolvulus, roses, magnolias, irises, asters, begonias, camellias and many other flowers so that the porcelain surface is entirely covered, giving a tapestry-style effect that becomes almost abstract.

A vase and cover, moulded with swags, painted with landscapes, Qianlong period, late 18thC, 16¾in (42.5cm) high.
£3,000–3,500
Woolley & Wallis
This shape has been traced back to late 16th-century designs by Stefano della Bella when he was working for Ferdinand de Medici. These designs were first published in England by Israel Sylvester and a later edition by Sayer was faithfully reproduced by Wedgwood. The Wedgwood version was the model the Chinese copied, although the design was also copied by the Marieburg factory in Sweden.

A vase, mounted as a lamp, 18thC, 21in (53.5cm) high.
£800–1,000 Sotheby's (P)

A bottle vase, decorated with gilt dogs of *Fo*, 19thC, 15½in (39.5cm) high.
£800–1,000 James Adam

se, painted with herons,
rs and foliage, applied with
s and lions, 19thC,
(93.5cm) high.
0–650 Rosebery's

A vase, decorated with vignettes of figures, birds, dragons and vases of flowers, 19thC, 8¼in (46.5cm) high.
£500–600 James Adam

A vase, painted and gilded in iron-red with Immortals and sea monsters, six-character Qianlong seal mark, c1880, 10¾in (27cm) high.
£1,500–1,800 Sworders

A pair of vases, decorated with exotic birds, butterflies and flowers below pleated rims, damaged, c1900, 14¼in (36cm) high.
£225–275 Sworders

BLANC DE CHINE

A *blanc-de-Chine* **censer,** moulded with a geometric band, on three feet, 17thC, 5in (12.5cm) high.

£350–425 Woolley & Wallis

A *blanc-de-Chine* **censer,** slight damage, 17thC, 7in (18cm) diam.

£600–700
Guest & Gray

A *blanc-de-Chine* **figure grou**
slight damage, c1680,
3in (7.5cm) high.

£450–500 Guest & Gray

ESSENTIAL REFERENCE BLANC-DE-CHINE

Dehua, in Fujian Province, is the home of *blanc-de-Chine* porcelain. These wares were very popular in the West in the late 17th and 18th centuries and imported in large numbers. Figures of the Buddhist and Taoist deities have always been the most popular wares .

A pair of *blanc-de-Chine* **figures of Guan Yu/Guandi,** restored, c1700, 8½in (21.5cm) high.

£2,250–2,750 Woolley & Wallis

Guan Yu was a great general in the 2nd century AD, who later became worshipped as Guandi, the Chinese god of War.

A *blanc-de-Chine* **figure of Lu Dongbin,** restored, Qianlong period, 1736–95, 9in (23cm) high.

£470–520 Guest & Gray

Lu Dongbin was the patron of scholars.

A *blanc-de-Chine* **figure of Guanyin,** on a lotus wave scr
base, seal mark, 18thC,
22in (56cm) high.

£4,500–5,500
Sotheby's (HK)

Three *blanc-de-Chine* **figures,** from the Nanking cargo, c1750, 4in (10cm) high.

£350–400
Roger Bradbury

A pair of *blanc-de-Chine* **models of dogs of Fo,** on hardwood stands, c1900, 5in (13cm) high.

£200–250 Sworders

A *blanc-de-Chine* **snuff bottle,** carved w
monks, 19thC, 2½in (6.5cm) high.

£130–160
Waddington's

ELADON

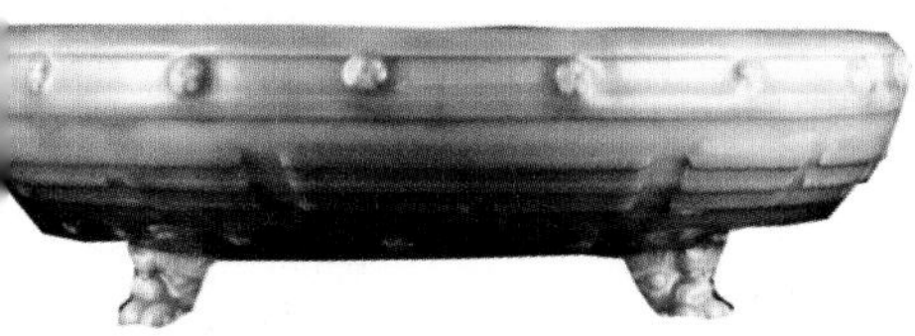

ladon censer, moulded with the Eight Trigrams, on three mask damaged, 15thC, 12¼in (31cm) diam, on a wooden stand.

0–300 Woolley & Wallis

Two celadon garden seats, decorated with Buddhistic lions, banana plants, peonies and cash symbols, slight damage, Longqing period, 1567–72, 16½in (42cm) high.

£16,000–20,000 Bukowskis

SSENTIAL REFERENCE THE EIGHT TRIGRAMS

e Eight Trigrams are groups of lines arranged in ranks. They formed the basis of the *gua*, which is an ancient system of philosophy and divination. The symbols were sequently used as a decorative motif on many Chinese items.

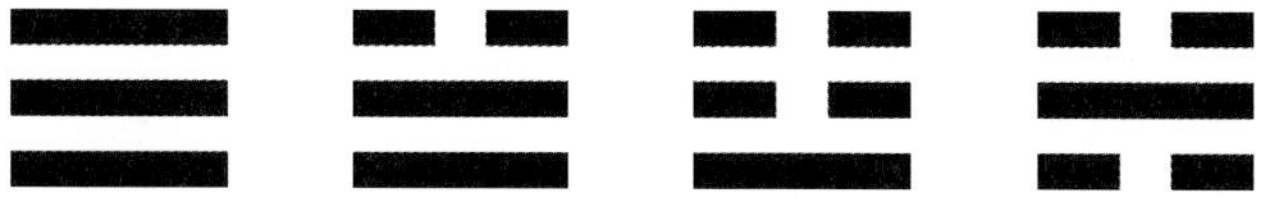

Qian
Sky; expansive energy

Dui
Marsh; joy, satisfaction, stagnation

Zhen
Thunder; excitation, revolution, division

Kan
Water; danger, rapid rivers, the abyss, the moon

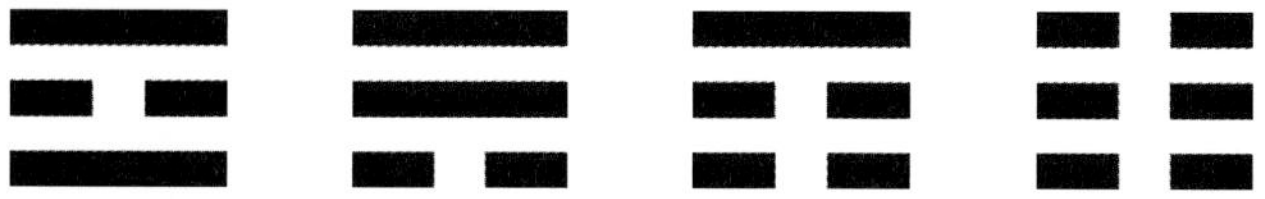

Li
Fire; rapid movement, radiance, the sun

Xun
Wind; gentle penetration, flexibility

Gen
Mountain; stillness, immovability

Kun
Earth; receptive energy, that which yields

A celadon and biscuit figure of Guanyin, flanked by two birds Ming Dynasty, 1368–1644, 10¾in (27.5cm) high.

£8,000–10,000 Sotheby's

ir of celadon vases, elled in relief with birds in ches, the necks applied with ant heads, damaged, 9thC, 23¼in (59cm) high.

5–450 Bearnes

EXPERT'S EYE STEM CUPS

The beautifully painted mark, contained within a double circle, reads 'Da Qing Yong Zheng Nian Zhi' which means 'Made during the Yongzheng period of the great Qing Dynasty'.

The rim of the cup is always the most vulnerable part of the piece. The rim of this cup has been carefully re-inforced with an extra layer of glaze to give it a lip. This subtle but practical technique has added to the overall appeal of its shape.

Stem cups of this shape and glaze are rare. The perfectly balanced shape is a fine example of a master thrower's art. In Chinese ceramics the potter (or thrower) is considered an artisan and does not receive the recognition he perhaps should. The celebrated kiln supervisor Tang Ying was appointed in 1728 during the reign of the emperor Yongzheng and one of his major successes was the development of fine monochrome celadon glazes which enhance sophisticated and exquisite forms. This stem cup is one such example. **£6,500–8,000 Sotheby's**

MISCELLANEOUS MONOCHROMES

An eggshell porcelain teabowl, Yongzheng mark and of the period, 1723–35, 3½in (9cm) diam.

£1,100–1,300 Bukowskis

A stem bowl, Zhi ben Tang mark, Jiaqing period, 1796–1820, 3¼in (8.5cm) dian

£3,000–4,000 Sotheby's (HK)

The Zhi ben Tang was a private kiln operating during the Jiaqing reign.

A saucer dish, incised with Buddhist symbols, Yongzheng mark and of the period, 1723–35, 4¾in (12cm) diam.

£2,750–3,250 Bukowskis

A 'claire-de-lune' jardinière and stand, applied with a moulded band, on four *ruyi* feet, Qianlong period, 1736–95, 4½in (11.5cm) high.

£2,500–3,000 Sotheby's

A stand, in the form of a low table, the legs with masks, Kangxi period, 1662–1722, 9½in (24cm) wide.

£3,000–3,500 Sotheby's

A pair of vases, 18thC, 10¼in (26cm) high.

£3,250–4,000
Bukowskis

A bottle vase, mounted as a lamp, damaged, c1800, 27½in (70cm) high.

£6,500–8,000 Sotheby

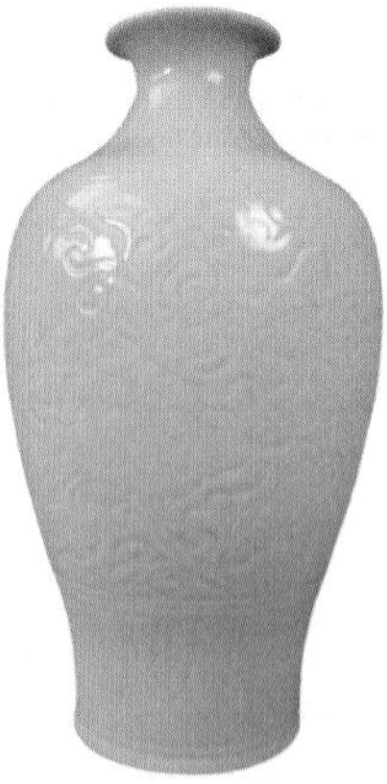

A vase, incised with stylized foliage and a band of scrolling flowers and foliage, 19thC, 35in (89cm) high.

£350–425 Rosebery's

A pair of vases, each with a crackled glaze, 19thC, 16in (40.5cm) high.

£2,500–3,000
Sotheby's

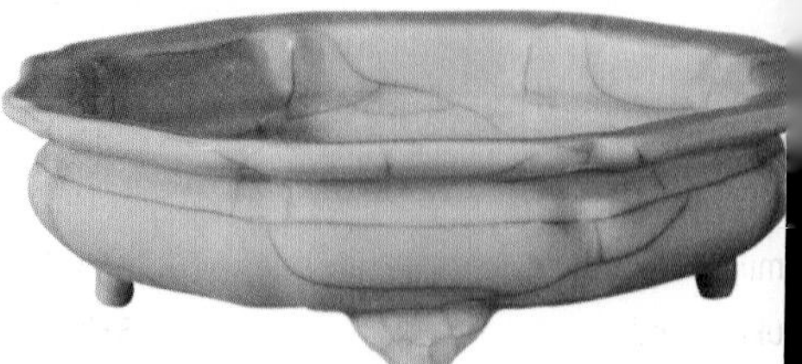

A brush washer, with crackle glaze, on *ruyi* feet, Qing Dynasty, 18
7¼in (18.5cm) diam.

£10,000–12,000 Sotheby's (HK)

APANESE CERAMICS

ISHES & PLATES

rita dish, decorated with the VOC
gram, *ho-o* birds, flowers and
granates, the rim with panels of bamboo
owers, c1800, 12¼in (31cm) diam.

00–8,000 Sotheby's (Am)

's the motif for the Dutch East India
any (Vereengde Oostindische
agnie), which imported large quantities
anese Arita porcelain in the late 17th
ry. Many of these pieces were marked
the VOC motif.

An Arita plate, decorated with flowers issuing from rockwork, early 18thC, 12½in (32cm) diam.

£2,000–2,200 Guest & Gray

An Arita saucer dish, painted with banded hedges, prunus and chrysanthemum *mons*, cracked, early 18thC, 7¼in (18.5cm) diam.

£300–350 Guest & Gray

An Arita plate, with gilded decoration, c1700, 10in (25.5cm) diam.

£350–385 Moxhams

An Imari dish, painted with a basket of flowers within panels of *shishi*, *ruyi* lappets and garden scenes, early 20thC, 24in (61cm) diam.

£600–700 Cheffins

tsuma plate by Kinkozan, painted and
d with a tree, figures and buildings,
ed, gilt and impressed signatures,
period, 1868–1911, 7½in (19cm) diam.

0–220 Toovey's

A pair of Imari dishes, painted with lions in a garden, the borders with *mon* and stylized flowers, 1850–75, 13½in (34.5cm) diam.

£200–250 Dreweatt Neate (N)

A Satsuma octagonal dish, decorated with four geishas and other figures, six-character mark, late 19thC, 6in (15cm) diam.

£160–200 Mealy's

SSENTIAL REFERENCE JAPANESE CHRONOLOGY CHART

non (Neolithic) period	c10,000–100 BC	Muromachi (Ashikaga) period	1333–1568
yoi period	c200 BC–AD 200	Momoyama period	1568–1600
nulus (Kofun) period	200–552	Edo (Tokugawa) period	1600–1868
ka period	552–710	*Genroku period*	*1688–1703*
ra period	710–794	Meiji period	1868–1911
an period	794–1185	Taisho period	1912–1926
nakura period	1185–1333	Showa period	1926–1989

FIGURES

A pair of Imari figures of *bijin*, their hands clasped, one repaired, c1700, 10in (25.5cm) high.

£2,000–2,200 **Guest & Gray**

An Imari figure of a reclining *bijin* holding a sconce, Edo period, c1710, 10in (25.5cm) high.

£11,000–12,000 **Cohen & Cohen**

This figure is very rare.

A pair of Imari porcelain figures of actors Japan, 18thC, 18in (45.5cm) high.

£12,000–15,000 **Sotheby's (NY)**

A figure of a *bijin*, by Kinkozan, decorated in gilt enamels, signed and impressed seal mark, Meiji period, 1868–1911, 11½in (29cm) high.

£3,500–4,250 **Sotheby's**

A Satsuma figure of one of the Seven Lucky Gods, signed, Meiji period, 1868–1911, 3in (7.5cm) high.

£700–800 **David Brower**

A pair of figures of geisha girls, both holc bowls, with gilt decoration, Meiji period, 1868–1911, 12¾in (32.5cm) high.

£380–450 **Bamfords**

KOROS

A Satsuma *koro*, painted with warriors and ladies in a garden, the pierced cover with a moulded leaf finial, signed, on a hardwood stand, 19thC, 9½in (24cm) wide.

£500–600 **Andrew Hartley**

A Yasuda *koro* and cover, by Ryozan, painted with a continuous scene of revellers, signed, Yasuda company trade mark, Meiji period, 1868–1911, 5in (12.5cm) high.

£3,200–3,800 **Sotheby's**

A Satsuma *koro* and cover, decorated in gilt and enamels with peonies, chrysanthemun and prunus blossom, repaired eleven-character mark, Meiji p 1868–1911, 5in (12.5cm) hi

£200–250 **Dreweatt Neate (HAM)**

ASES

ıari vase, Edo period, –1868, 19¾in (50cm) high.

50–2,500 st & Gray

A pair of Arita vases, painted with mountain landscapes, 1650–1700, 10in (25.5cm) high.

£2,000–2,400 Sotheby's

A vase and cover, painted and gilt with *ho-o* birds among *kiku* blooms, drapery, *shishi* and peonies, the cover with a *shishi* finial, c1690, 24in (61cm) high.

£5,400–6,000 Guest & Gray

· of Imari jars and covers, the covers ıted with models of dogs of *Fo*, one ged, c1700, 17¾in (45cm) high.

00–1,800 Bukowskis

A pair of Imari vases and covers, painted with panels of flowers, c1800, 23¼in (59cm) high.

£8,500–10,000 Sotheby's

ıari garniture of four vases, comprising two baluster vases and covers and two trumpet vases, ated with flower sprays and medallions, each cover surmounted by a Buddhist lion, damaged, 18thC, ;t 19in (48.5cm) high.

00–3,000 Sotheby's (Am)

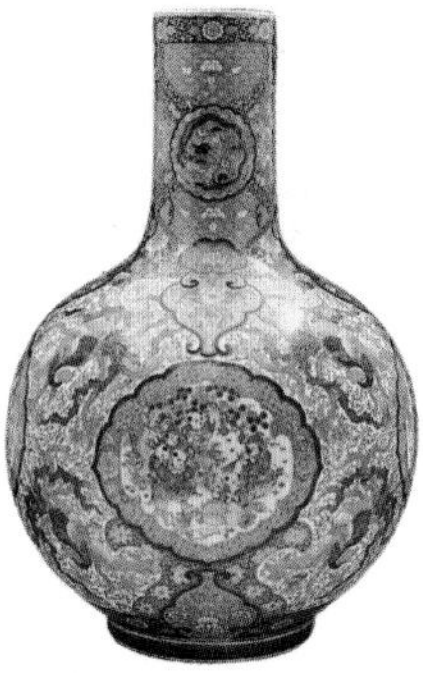

An Imari bottle vase, decorated with leafy scrolls above four cartouches, two with musicians, two with vases of flowers, eight-character mark, 19thC, 23in (58.5cm) high.

£2,250–2,750 Gilding's

ɾ of Imari bottle vases, decorated with prunus and ı trees, *ho-o* birds, flowers and *mon*, Meiji period, –1911, 24½in (62cm) high.

00–2,500 Dreweatt Neate (HAM)

A pair of Satsuma vases, each side decorated with flowers in a pot, a vase or growing from rockwork, marked, 19thC, 9½in (24cm) high.

£1,400–1,800 Sotheby's (Am)

A Satsuma hexagonal vase, painted with landscape panels, chrysanthemum and wisteria, Meiji period, 1868–1911, 9¾in (25cm) high.

£2,250–2,750 Woolley & Wallis

A Satsuma vase, by Taizan, decorated in enamel and gilt with peonies and butterflies, signed, Meiji period, 1868–1911, 12¼in (31cm) high.

£2,250–2,750 Sotheby's

The Taizan family operated from a workshop in Awata, Kyoto. Their highly decorated opulent vases were exported to Europe in large quantities.

A pair of Kyoto earthenware vases and covers, decorated in coloured and gold enamels with *ho-o* birds on a lattice grou the neck pierced, 19thC, 21in (53.5cm) h

£2,500–3,000 Sotheby's

A pair of earthenware vases, each decorated with a cockerel, hen and flocks of small birds, with gilt detail, five-character mark of Kinkozan, Meiji period, 1868–1911, 9¾in (25cm) high.

£1,300–1,600 Tennants

A Fukagawa vase, decorated with banana leaves, signed, c1900, 15½in (39.5cm) high.

£2,000–2,400 Sotheby's

A porcelain vase, by Makuzu Kozan, pai with irises, the carved wood cover with *k* finial, on three feet, signed, early 20thC, 6¼in (16cm) high.

£2,800–3,500 Sotheby's

MISCELLANEOUS

An Imari barber's bowl, c1700, 10in (25.5cm) diam.

£850–950 Guest & Gray

An Imari panelled jar and cover, decorated with garden, lake and stylized floral scenes, the cover with a *shishi* finial, mid-19thC, 18½in (47cm) high.

£400–500 Dreweatt Neate (N)

An Arita jug, painted with p of peonies growing from rock on a *karakusa* scrolling grou c1690, 11in (28cm) high.

£1,300–1,600 Sotheby's (Am)

Karakusa or Chinese grasses a common decoration on Japanese ceramics.

ASIAN WORKS OF ART

LOISONNE & ENAMEL

isonné basin, decorated with stylized flowerheads
wan-diaper ground, China, Qing Dynasty, 18thC,
n (42.5cm) diam.

00–6,000 Sotheby's

A *plique-à-jour* **bowl,** worked with maple leaves and cherry blossom in silver and coloured glass, slight damage, Japan, c1900, 5in (12.5cm) diam.

£500–550 Guest & Gray

que-à-jour **bowl,** worked with peacock
ers in silver wire and enamels, with
ed silver rims, Japan, Meiji period,
–1911, 3in (7.5cm) diam.

00–5,500 Sotheby's

A cloisonné box and cover, decorated with a phoenix on a rock, the sides with bats and *bajixiang* on a ground of cloud scrolls, interior with later metal lining, China, Qianlong period, 1736–95, 8½in (21.5cm) diam.

£2,000–2,500 Sotheby's

Bajixiang *is box-form decoration.*

A *famille rose* **censer,** painted with *bajixiang* and lotus on scrolling stems, the S-shaped handles and rim with keyfret bands, on three feet, six-character seal mark, China, Qianlong period, 1736–95, 13¾in (35cm) wide.

£18,000–22,000 Sotheby's

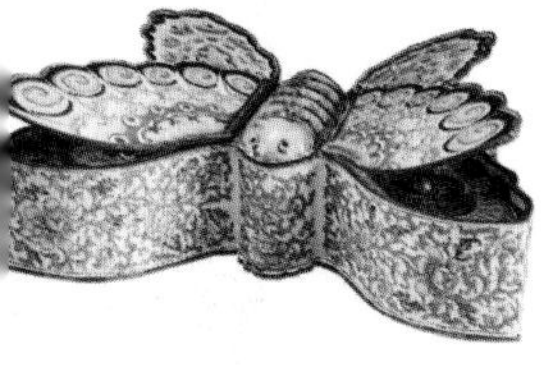

nton scholar's enamel desk set, in the
of a butterfly with hinged wings, each
partment enclosing two boxes, one with a
glass beaker, one with a pierced metal
, China, Qianlong period, 1736–95,
23cm) wide.

00–11,000 Sotheby's

A cloisonné dish, decorated with scrolls and a band of lotus, China, 17thC, 9in (23cm) diam.

£1,000–1,200 Guest & Gray

isonné dish, decorated with stylized lotus,
a, 18thC, 4in (10cm) diam.

0–350 Woolley & Wallis

A cloisonné fish bowl, decorated with mountains and deer, the sky with cranes among cloud scrolls, China, Qianlong period, 1736–95, 28in (71cm) diam.

£12,000–14,000 Sotheby's

A Canton enamel lantern, decorated with bats, flowers, fruit and auspicious objects, damaged, China, 18th/19thC, 11¾in (30cm) high.

£500–600 Woolley & Wallis

A Canton enamel quatrefoil teapot, decorated with four figural vignettes on a cell pattern ground, Qianlong character mark, China, Qianlong period, 1736–95, 7½in (19cm) high.

£1,250–1,500 Northeast Auctions

An enamel double gourd vase, decorated with butterflies among flowering and fruiting gourd vines, with applied gilt-metal birds and insects, China, 18thC, 6½in (16.5cm) high.

£5,500–6,500 Sotheby's

This vase is a rare example of the fine quality of painted enamel wares produced by artisans working in Guangzhou during the 18th century. The design is rich in symbolism – the gourd and butterflies for numerous descendants and the bats and butterflies for happiness and prosperity. The doubly auspicious design of a gourd-shaped vessel decorated with gourds was especially favoured by potters at the Imperial kilns at Jingdezhen.

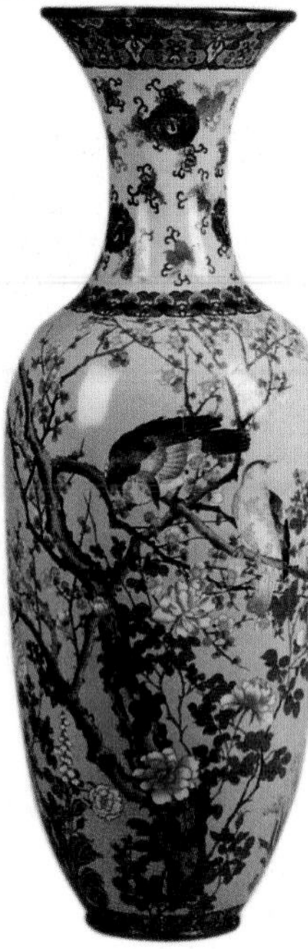

A cloisonné vase, decorated with birds and flowers, repaired, Japan, Meiji period, 1868–1911, 42in (106.5cm) high.

£1,300–1,500 Skinner

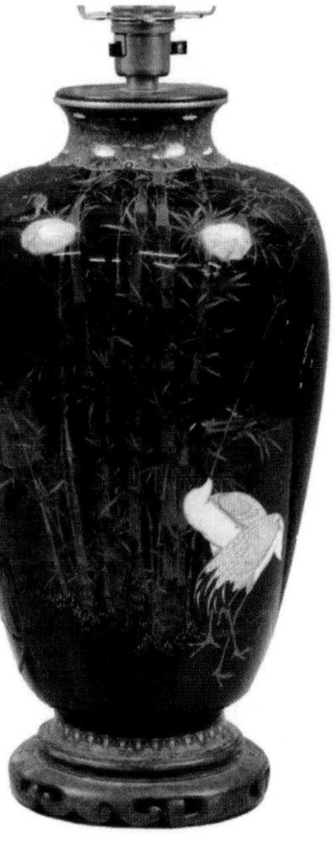

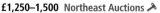

A cloisonné vase, decorated with storks among bamboo, mounted as a lamp, Japan, Meiji period, 1868–1911, 12in (30.5cm) high.

£1,100–1,300 Gorringes (L)

A cloisonné vase, in the style of Hayashi Kodenji, worked with butterflies, Japan, Meiji period, 1868–1911, 4in (10cm) high.

£3,800–4,500 Sotheby's

A ***moriage*** **cloisonné vase,** attributed to Kamei Fukutaro, decorated with birds flying over waves on a hammered silver ground, stamped mark, Japan, late 19thC, 18¾in (47.5cm) high, with box.

£950–1,150 Sworders

Moriage is a raised enamel technique.

A pair of cloisonné vases, studio mark, Japan, Meiji period, 1868–1911, 6in (15cm) high.

£1,400–1,600 David Brower

A pair of cloisonné vases, decorated with birds among branches of wisteria, slight damage, Japan, late 19thC, 7in (18cm) high.

£1,800–2,000 Guest & Gray

LASS

y-flashed glass beaker, carved with
-mask handles and dragon strapwork,
a, Qianlong period, 1736–95,
0cm) high.
00–3,500 Sotheby's

A celadon glass footed bowl and cover, China, c1800, 4in (10cm) diam.
£1,200–1,400 Sotheby's

A Peking glass bowl, carved with flowers and birds, China, probably 19thC, 7¼in (18.5cm) diam.
£140–175 Hy Duke

A Peking cameo glass brushpot, in triple overlay, carved with dragons, clouds and pearls, above waves, China, c1880, 6½in (16.5cm) high.
£200–240 Sworders

verse painting on glass, depicting a
herdess in a landscape, China, c1760,
gilt frame, 16¼ x 18¼in (41.5 x 46.5cm).
250–4,000 Woolley & Wallis

A pair of paintings on glass, one depicting a European couple by a tree, the other an Oriental woman and a boy by a river, China, c1785, in hardwood frames, 6¼ x 3¾in (16 x 9.5cm).
£4,750–5,750 Sotheby's

A reverse painting on glass, depicting female figures in an interior, a lake beyond, China, 19thC, 19 x 13½in (48.5 x 34.5cm).
£120–150 Holloway's

king overlaid glass bottle
, carved with a scene of
es and mythical beasts
ng pavilions, rocks and pine
, incised seal mark, China,
long period, 1736–95,
n (26.5cm) high.
200–3,800 Sotheby's

A glass bottle vase, four-character Qianlong mark and of the period, China, 1736–95, 11¼in (28.5cm) high.
£3,000–3,500 Woolley & Wallis

A Peking overlaid glass vase, carved with scenes of warriors before a city, with *lingzhi* handles, China, Qianlong period, 1736–95, 6¾in (17cm) high.
£4,500–5,500 Skinner

An overlaid glass vase, carved with flowering lilies and a butterfly, China, early 20thC, 9in (23cm) high.
£1,000–1,200 Sotheby's

JADE

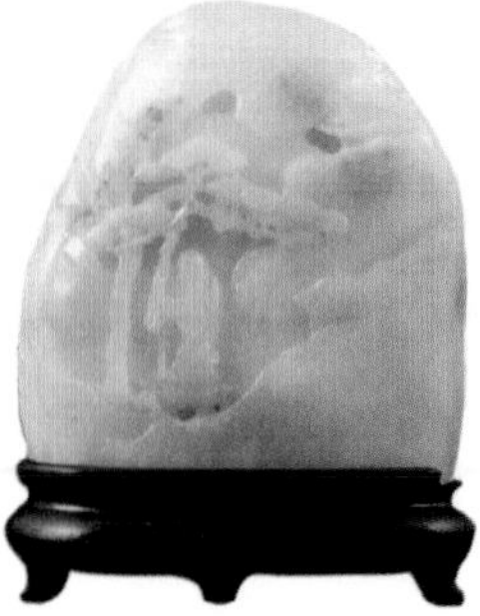

A **white jade boulder carving,** depicting Shoulao beneath a pine tree in a cave, the reverse with a deer among rocks, China, 18th/19thC, on a wood stand, 3¼in (8.5cm) high.

£3,200–3,800 Woolley & Wallis

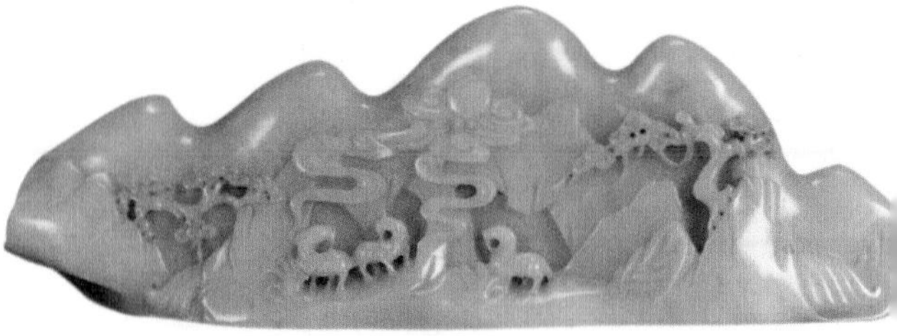

A **celadon jade brush rest,** in the form of a mountain with clouds, pine trees and rams, the reverse with seals, China, 19thC, 9in (23cm) wide.

£4,000–5,000 Skinner

A **white jade bowl,** China, 18thC, 4½in (11.5cm) diam.

£7,500–9,000 Skinner

A **jade censer and cover,** carved with tw *taotie* masks, with carved animal mask handles, China, Qianlong period, 1736–9 6½in (16.5cm) wide.

£4,000–5,000 Sotheby's

A **celadon jade censer,** carved with *taotie* masks, on four legs with mythical beast masks, China, Qianlong period, 1736–95, 6½in (16.5cm) high.

£3,800–4,500 Sotheby's

A **jade censer,** with animal-form handles, the cover surmounted by a pair of dogs of *Fo*, Chir 18th/19thC, 5in (12.5cm) high.

£9,500–11,500 Skinner

A **jadeite censer and cover,** carved with *taotie* masks, with horned dragon-head handles, on three feet, 19thC, 5¾in (14.5cm) wide.

£14,000–18,000 Sotheby's (HK)

A **white jade censer and cover,** with lion-head handles, the cover with a finial in the form of a lion cub, on ball feet, China, early 20thC, 4in (10cm) wide.

£8,000–9,500 Sotheby's (HK)

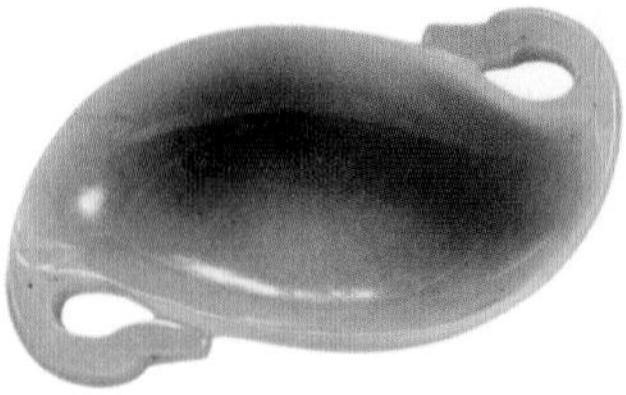

A **Mughal-style jade cup,** carved as a pair of ducks, their heads and necks forming the handles, China, Qianlong period, 1736–95, 4in (10cm) wide.

£1,400–1,750 Sotheby's

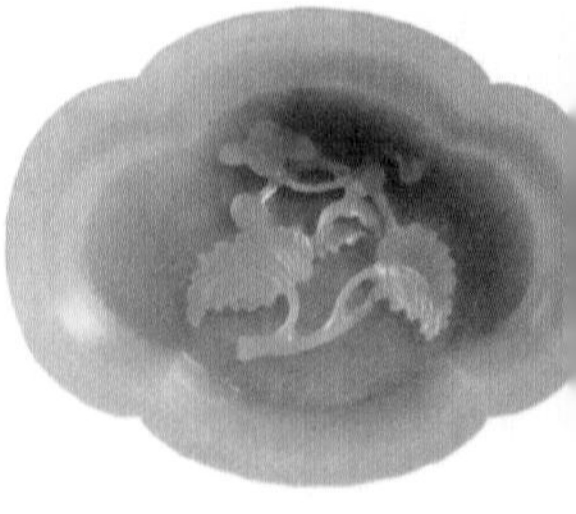

A **nephrite dish,** carved with a flowering sprig, on bracket feet, China, Qing Dynast probably late 18thC, 3¼in (8.5cm) wide.

£2,750–3,250 Tennants

ɪir of jade and gilt-copper lanterns, engraved with river landscapes, China, ı/19thC, 5¼in (13.5cm) high.
,000–13,000 Skinner

A carved jade model of a mandarin duck, on a lotus leaf, China, Ming Dynasty, 1368–1644, 2½in (6.5cm) wide.
£4,500–5,500 Sotheby's

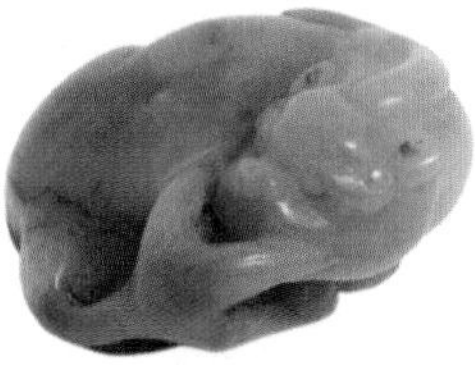

ıde model of an animal, China, Ming asty, 1368–1644, 2in (5cm) wide.
000–1,200 David Bowden

A jade model of a lion, China, Ming Dynasty, 1368–1644, 2½in (6.5cm) wide.
£1,450–1,600 David Bowden

A jade model of a *shishi*, on a wood stand, China, Ming Dynasty, 1368–1644, 3in (7.5cm) wide.
£1,250–1,400 David Bowden

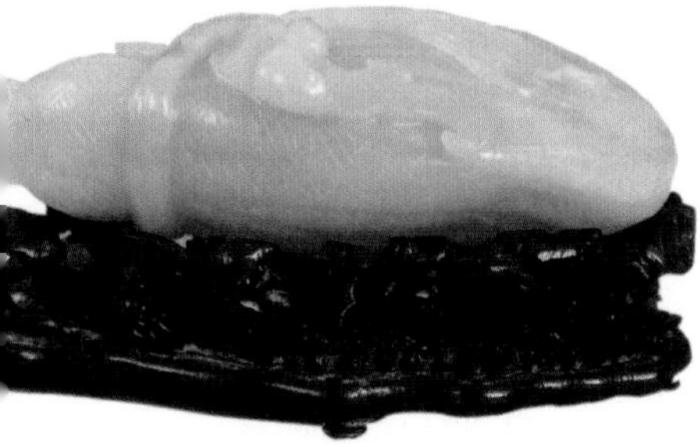

ephrite carving of a money bag and bat, on a hardwood stand ɾed as a bat flying among waves, China, late 18thC, 3½in (9cm) long.
000–7,000 Tennants

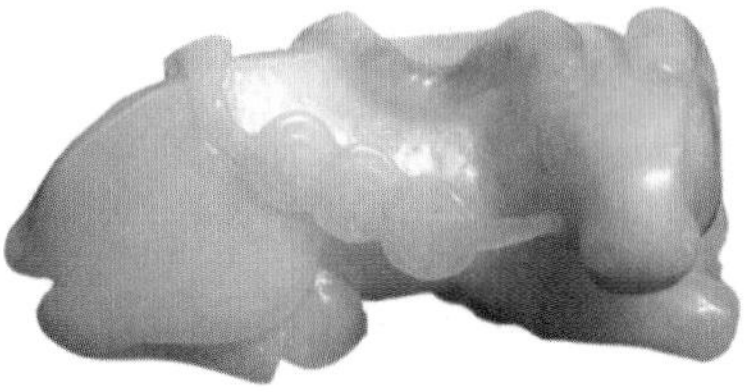

A jade model of a goat, China, Qianlong period, 1736–95, 2½in (6.5cm) wide.
£1,450–1,600 David Bowden

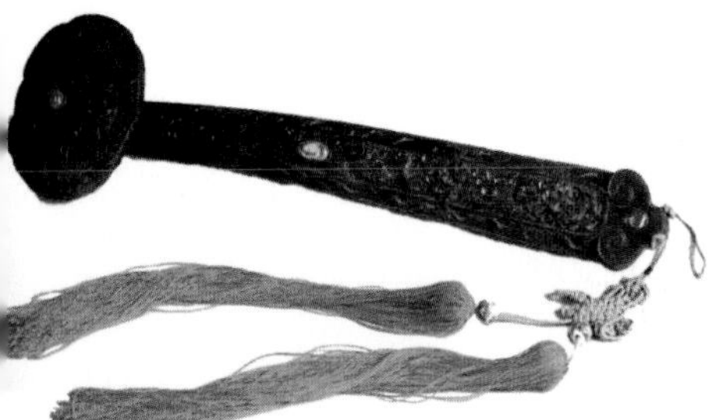

ıde *ruyi* sceptre, carved with dragons, bats and clouds, inlaid with ɛe rubies, China, early 20thC, 15½in (39.5cm) long.
,800–3,500 Skinner
ıyi is a presentation sceptre.

A jade vase, cover and stand, carved with a cat and butterfly, the reverse with a water buffalo, marked, China, Qianlong period, 1736–95, 8½in (21.5cm) high.
£6,000–7,000 Skinner

A jade *gu*-shape vase, on a carved wood base, China, c1800, vase 5in (12.5cm) high.
£320–380 Rosebery's

LACQUER

A lacquer box and cover, carved with peonies, China, Yongle/Xuande period, early 15thC, 5¼in (13.5cm) diam.

£24,000–28,000 Sotheby's

This box is over 500 years old and is in excellent condition for its age. It is one of only four known to exist – rare and good-quality work is currently in great demand by the Chinese.

A lacquer box and cover, carved with a dragon in pursuit of a flaming pearl among cloud scrolls above rocks and waves, on a floral diaper ground, China, 17th/18thC, 3in (7.5cm) diam.

£2,400–2,800 Sotheby's

A lacquer dish, carved in the form of a flower, the interior carved with a diaper medallion, peonies and morning glory, China, early 17thC, 7in (18cm) diam.

£6,500–8,000 Sotheby's (HK)

A lacquer moon flask, carved with immortals in a sea with crashing waves, the neck, shoulders and foot with lotus, meander and keyfret, China, 19thC, 9½in (24cm) high.

£2,500–3,000 Sotheby's

Moon flasks are always popular with collectors and lacquer examples are quite rare.

A lacquer pedestal stand, the floret diaper-carved top on four *ruyi*-shaped legs carved with fruiting melon vines, on a stretcher with four bracket feet, China, Qianlong period, 1736–95, 8¾in (22cm) high.

£7,000–8,500 Sotheby's

A *lacque burgauté* tray, China, Kangxi period, 1668–1722, 20in (51cm) square.

£135–150 Guest & Gray

A lacquer vase, carved with panels of flow on a floral and diaper ground, restored, China, 19thC, 15½in (39.5cm) high.

£2,200–2,600 Sotheby's (Am)

ESSENTIAL REFERENCE LACQUER

Chinese lacquer comes from the sap of the tree *Rhus verniciflua*, which is native to China and grows wild in the central and southern areas of the country. The sap is coloured by adding pigments, and up to 200 layers of lacquer can be applied to an item.

A carved lacquer tripod vessel and cover, carved with archaistic bird and *taotie* scrolls on a key-fret ground, China, Qianlong period, 1736–95, 81/4in (21cm) high.

£4,500–5,500 Sotheby's

A lacquer and *shibayama* tray, inlaid with mother-of-pearl, coral, ivory and silver mounts, with cloisonné detail, Japan, Meiji period, 1868–1911, 9in (23cm) wide

£13,500–15,000 David Brower

This tray illustrates the different lacquer techniques that were used during the Meiji period.

ıETALWARE

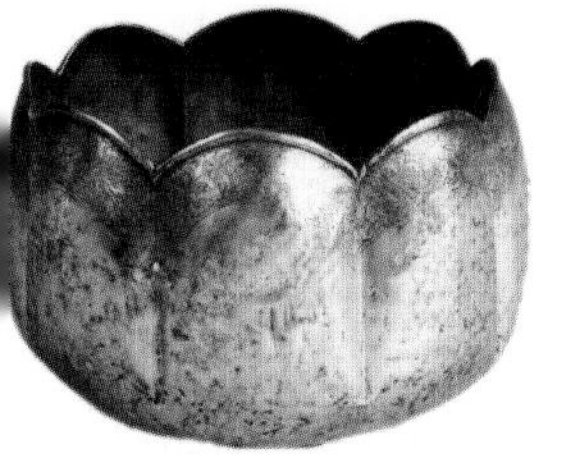

ıver wine-warming bowl, with a band
ɔral decoration on a punched ground,
ɪa, Song Dynasty, 960–1279,
(18cm) diam.

300–1,500 Skinner

**air of Chinese export paktong
dlesticks,** with candle rings, China,
18thC, 9¼in (23.5cm) high.

**500–5,500
rtheast Auctions**

ronze double gourd censer and cover,
h side cast with a Buddhist lion and a
bboned ball, the handle formed as
fronting lions chasing a flaming pearl, the
ced cover with a flowering bud finial,
na, 17th/18thC, 6¾in (17cm) high.

200–3,800 Sotheby's (NY)

A silver bowl, embossed with a hunting scene, with a vacant armorial shield flanked by ibex supporters, on an embossed foot, India, c1880, 16in (40.5cm) diam, 115oz.

£1,800–2,200 Sotheby's (O)

A silver-inlaid parcel-gilt bronze censer, cast with flowering plants between inlaid silver wire keyfret bands, on butterfly feet, with a carved and pierced hardwood cover with a stained carved bone knop, incised mark for Hu Wenming zhi, China, Wanli period, 1573–1619, 3¼in (8.5cm) high.

£8,000–9,500 Sotheby's (HK)

Hu Wenming was a celebrated 17th-century metalworker.

A bronze censer and cover, cast with mythical beasts and sea creatures, the cover pierced with a dragon and phoenix among clouds, China, 17th/18thC, 5¾in (14.5cm) high.

£7,500–9,000 Sotheby's (NY)

A parcel-gilt silver cup, in the form of a flower, the base repoussé-decorated and chased with a lotus motif, the petals decorated with flower and bird roundels, China, 7thC AD, 3¼in (8.5cm) diam.

£2,400–2,800 Skinner

A silver- and gold-inlaid iron miniature cabinet and cover, by Komai, with two sabre handles, the front and back inset with named landmarks, the doors enclosing an arrangement of seven drawers with grapevine handles, the cover and shoulder decorated with *mon* and leaves below a pierced *kiku* knop, signed, Japan, Meiji period, 1868–1911, 7in (18cm) high.

£9,000–11,000 Sotheby's

A pair of bronze chariot bells, with geometric decoration, China, Warring States period, 6thC BC, 6½in (16.5cm) high.

£550–650 Skinner

A pair of bronze chariot fittings, decorated with lions devouring human figures, China, 5thC BC, 2½in (6.5cm) high.

£650–750 Skinner

A Chinese export silver egg cup stand, possibly by Cut Shing, with six cups and six spoons, pseudo hallmarks and letters 'P' and 'CU', China, c1835, stand 8in (20.5cm) high.

£2,500–3,000 Northeast Auctions

A bronze wine ewer, with a dragon spout, lion handle and bear feet, China, 2ndC AD, 5½in (14cm) high.

£600–700 Skinner

A pair of bronze fittings, decorated with *taotie* masks, China, Warring States period, 6thC BC, 2in (5cm) long.

£350–425 Skinner

A gilt-bronze fitting, the pierced palmette around a central boss, China, Tang Dynast 618–907, 3½in (9cm) diam.

£200–250 Skinner

A gilt-bronze fitting, decorated with scrolls and human-headed birds, China, Tang Dynasty, 618–907, 3½in (9cm) wide.

£550–650 Skinner

A pair of gilt-bronze harness fittings, with floral relief decoration, China, 11thC, 3in (7.5cm) wide.

£200–250 Skinner

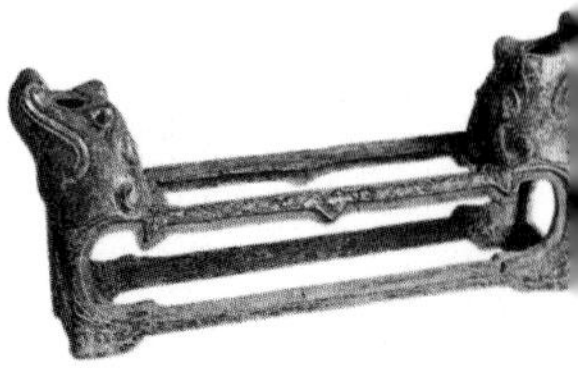

A gilt-bronze headrest, the finials in the fo of stags' heads, China, 2ndC BC, 19in (48.5cm) long.

£3,750–4,500 Skinner

A parcel-gilt bronze jar with a *zitan* cover and stand, relief-decorated with 128 gilt *shou* characters, with zoomorphic-mask ring handles, the cover pierced and carved with two bats and two *shou* characters against cloud scrolls, with a carved *lingzhi* fungus knop, the stand with five cabriole feet, China, early 17thC, 7in (18cm) high.

£12,000–15,000 Sotheby's (HK)

A bronze lamp stand, the base in the form of a man above a roundel of animals, China, Han Dynasty, 206 BC – AD 220, 11½in (29cm) high.

£1,400–1,750 Skinner

A bronze lamp stand, the base decorated with scrolling animals, China, Han Dynasty, 206 BC – AD 220, 6in (15cm) high.

£700–850 Skinner

A bronze mirror, China, Han Dynasty, 206 BC – AD 220, 4¾in (12cm) diam.

£400–450 Guest & Gray

A Chinese export silver hand mirror, by Hung Chong, slight damage, c1890, 9¾in (25cm) long.

£580–650 Daniel Bexfield

A bronze spittoon, decorated with hunting scenes, geometric patterns and elephants, China, 4thC BC, 9in (23cm) high.

£2,400–2,800 Skinner

-bronze spittoon, carved with a stag being
:d by a dog, with stylized scrolling, China,
ynasty, 206 BC – AD 220, 4in (10cm) high.
:00–3,800 Skinner

›nze ritual tripod, with basketweave
ration, China, 9thC BC, 5in (12.5cm) diam.
;00–2,000 Skinner

ixed metal vase, decorated with budding
ers, with wheel handles, Japan, Meiji
›d, 1868–1911, 9in (23cm) high.
250–2,750 Skinner

ronze ikebana vase, the top decorated
turtles, the stem with sea birds,
›orted on four dragons, signed, Japan,
i period, 1868–1911, 11½in (29cm) high.
;0–425 Bukowskis

Chinese export silver three-piece tea service, the covers with dog of *Fo* finials, China, c1870, teapot 8in (20.5cm) high.
£3,150–3,500 Daniel Bexfield

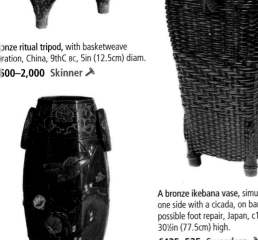

A bronze ikebana vase, simulating wicker, one side with a cicada, on bamboo feet, possible foot repair, Japan, c1860, 30½in (77.5cm) high.
£425–525 Sworders

An inlaid bronze vase, by the Inoue Co, Kyoto, decorated in copper, silver, *shakudo* and gold *takazogan* with butterflies and moths over a peony, signed, maker's mark, Japan, Meiji period, 1868–1911, 14in (35.5cm) high.
£3,800–4,500 Sotheby's

A bronze *ding*, decorated with a band of dragons and *taotie* masks, with loop handles, on three legs, China, Shang Dynasty, 16thC–c1050 BC, 8in (20.5cm) high.
£12,000–15,000 Sotheby's

A bronze ritual vessel, decorated with a duck and spiral scrolling, China, 4thC BC, 10½in (26.5cm) high.
£3,750–4,500 Skinner

A bronze ritual vessel, decorated with scrolling, with *taotie*-mask ring handles, China, 4thC BC, 8in (20.5cm) high.

£3,500–4,250 Skinner

A bronze vessel, China, Warring States period, 480–221 BC, 3½in (9cm) high.

£700–800 Guest & Gray

A gilt-bronze water vessel, in the form o hollowed peach on a gnarled leafy stem v seven smaller peaches, decorated with gil splashes, China, 17thC, 2½in (6.5cm) hig

£3,800–4,500 Sotheby's

WOOD

A bamboo brushpot, carved with a scene of scholars in a pine grove, slight damage, China, 18thC, 6in (15cm) high.

£900–1,100 Skinner

A bamboo brushpot, carved with the twin beauties in a fenced garden pavilion, on bracket feet, China, 18th/19thC, 5¾in (14.5cm) high.

£6,500–8,000 Sotheby's (NY)

A bamboo brushpot, carved with a landsc and a poem, China, 19thC, 5in (12.5cm) high.

£380–450 Skinner

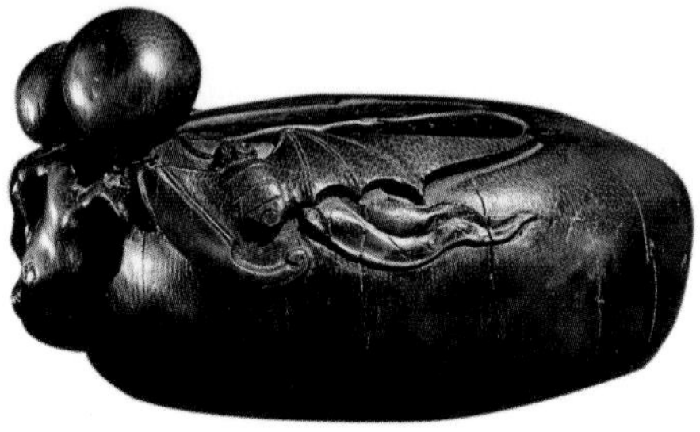

A bamboo brush washer, in the form of a peach, carved with a bat, two small peaches and a branch, China, 19thC, 5¾in (14.5cm) diam.

£2,200–2,600 Sotheby's (Am)

A carved and lacquered wood dish, decorated with re and black scrolling patterns with geometric borders, with two lugs, one engraved with two characters, Chin 2ndC BC, 5½in (14cm) wide.

£225–275 Skinner

A lacquered wood ewer, decorated with animals and swirling scrolls, five-character inscription to base, damaged, China, 2ndC BC, 11in (28cm) long.

£1,100–1,300 Skinner

A wooden panel from a ceremonial chariot, India, Kerala c1750, 24in (61cm) high.

£3,000–3,500 Jeremy Knowles

A carved and inlaid *zitan* table stand, in t form of a miniature daybed, inlaid with a ja panel centred by a *lingzhi* sprig, flanked by jade panels, the armrests inlaid with a jade medallion, on four bow legs and stretchers inlaid with silver wire, China, 18thC, 12½in (32cm) wide.

£10,000–12,000 Sotheby's (HK)

RMS & ARMOUR

ather, iron and lacquer suit of armour, ed 'Yoshihisa', Japan, helmet bowl omachi period, c1550, armour Edo d, c1700, 53¾in (136.5cm) high.

500–8,000 Sotheby's

e were two makers named Yoshihisa king between 1532 and 1554.

A lacquered iron helmet (*kabuto to-kamuri*), with applied lacquered decoration, slight damage, Japan, c1820, 12in (30.5cm) high.

£2,000–2,350 Michael Long

A chain mail head covering (*khula zirah*), India, c1790, 12in (30.5cm) high.

£1,800–2,000 Arbour Antiques

A steel helmet (*khula khud*), with gold and silver damascening, India, 19thC, 8in (20.5cm) high.

£1,800–2,000 Arbour Antiques

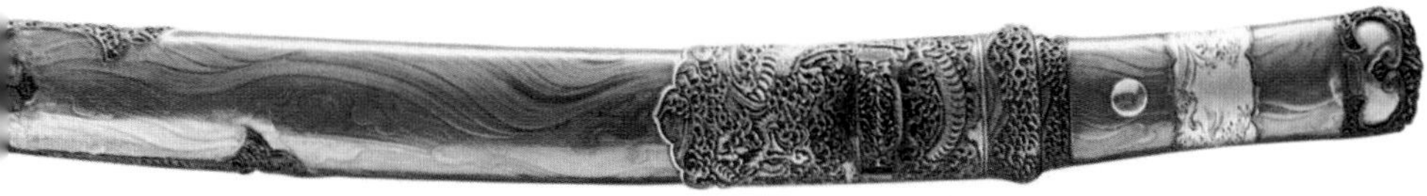

agger (*aikuchi*), the scabbard with silver mounts decorated with dragons, blade signed 'Kanefusa', Japan, 18thC, 11in (28cm) long.

000–8,500 Sotheby's

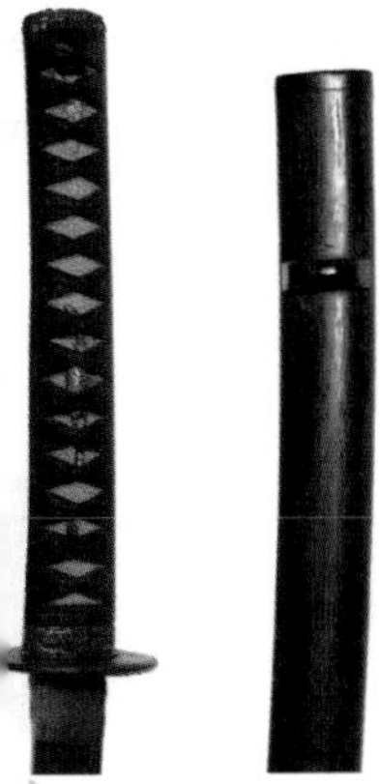

izen blade, with gilt mounts, an, c1500, mounts later, n (101.5cm) long.

,800–3,250
e Lanes Armoury

en is a Japanese province which s once one of the main centres swordsmithing.

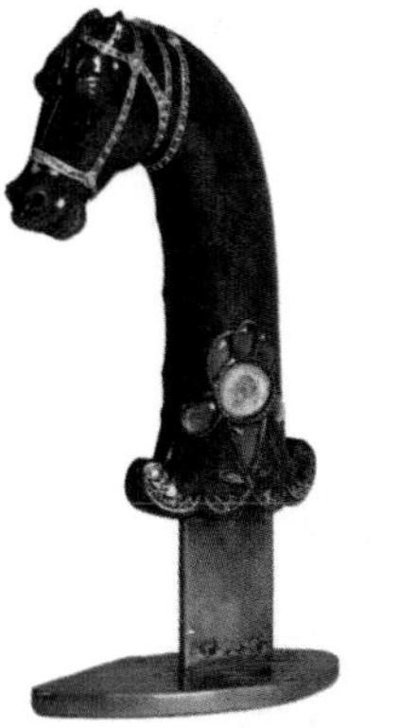

A jade dagger hilt, in the form of a horse's head, inset with crystals and turquoise set in gold and silver, India, 17thC, 5½in (14cm) high.

£10,000–12,000 Skinner

A gilt-bronze dagger, with a gilt ring pommel, China, Warring states period, 480–221 BC, 8in (20.5cm) long.

£475–575 Skinner

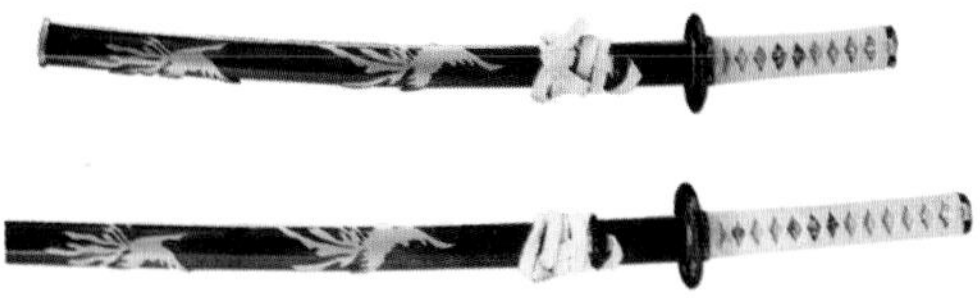

A pair of swords (*daisho*), comprising a *katana* and *wakazashi*, Japan, Meiji period, 19thC, *katana* blade 27¾in (70.5cm) long, *wakazashi* blade 18¼in (46.5cm) long.

£9,000–11,000 Sotheby's

A Bizen sword (*katana*), with inscription, signed 'Toshiteru', Japan, 16th/17thC, mounts 19thC, 24¼in (61.5cm) long, with lacquered scabbard.

£5,750–7,000 Sotheby's

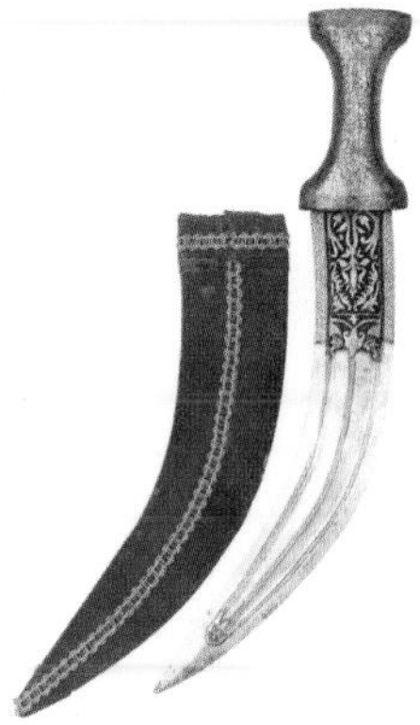

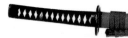

A dagger (*jambiya*), with a gold floral panel and an iron hilt, Indo-Persian, early 19thC, blade 11½in (29cm) long, with velvet-covered sheath.

£500–600 Wallis & Wallis

A sword (*katana*), signed 'Tsuda Echizen no Kami Sukehiro', blade repolished, Japan, dated 1674, blade 24½in (62cm) long, with lacquered scabbard.

£4,500–5,500 Wallis & Wallis

A bronze dagger axe (*ko*), decorated with snakes, China, 4thC BC, 8in (20.5cm) long.

£1,500–1,800 Skinner

A sword (*katana*), *handachi* mounts, Japan, 18thC, blade 39½in (100.5cm) long.

£3,250–3,750 The Lanes Armoury

A silvered-bronze mace or sceptre, the handle with a chain, China, 2ndC AD, 22½in (57cm) long.

£1,300–1,500 Skinner

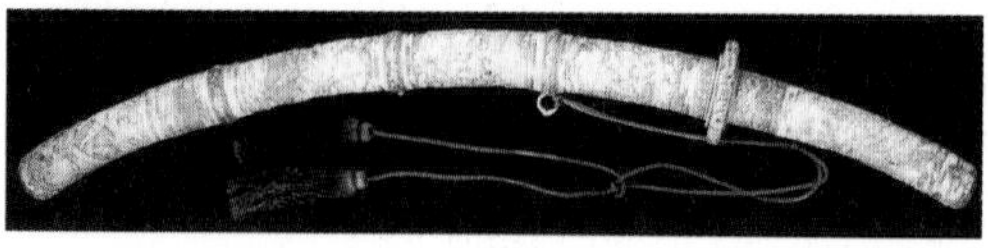

An ivory-mounted sword, the hilt carved with children watching a street performer, the scabbard carved in relief with figures and animals, the *tsuba* carved with *ho-o* birds, Japan, Meiji period, 1868–1911, 24¼in (87cm) long.

£4,250–5,250 Sotheby's

A Koto-style *tachi* (long sword), the wood-grained scabbard with bird *mon* in gold *takamakie*, silvered hilt, Japan, blade possibly 15thC, mounts 19thC, 27½in (70cm) long.

£4,750–5,750 Sotheby's

A court long sword (*tachi*), mounted with dragons, blade c1600, mounts 19thC, 44in (112cm) long.

£6,300–7,000 The Lanes Armoury

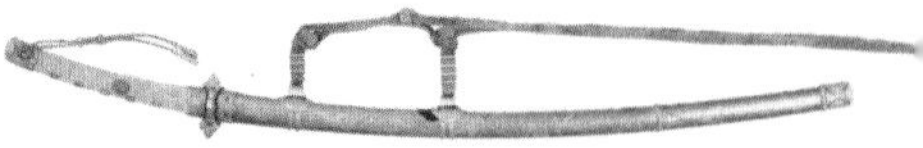

A long sword (*tachi*), with gilded brass mounts, the lacquer scabba decorated with leaves and *ho-o* birds, slight damage, Japan, 18thC, 27½in (70cm) long.

£1,300–1,500 Wallis & Wallis

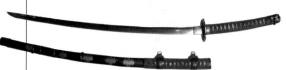

A Samurai long sword (*tachi*), with Bizen blade, signature, Japan, c1930, 40in (101.5cm) long.

£5,400–6,000 The Lanes Armoury

A dagger (*tanto*), the hardwood scabbard carved with dragons and clouds, hilt collar missing, Japan, c1600, 10in (25.5cm) long.

£750–900 Wallis & Wallis

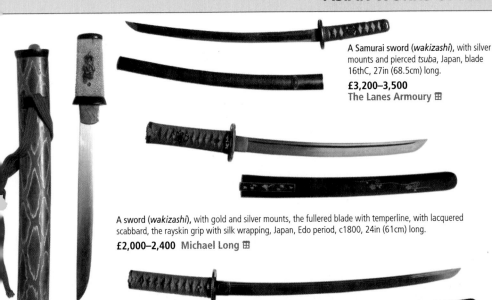

A Samurai sword (*wakizashi*), with silver mounts and pierced *tsuba*, Japan, blade 16thC, 27in (68.5cm) long.

£3,200–3,500 **The Lanes Armoury**

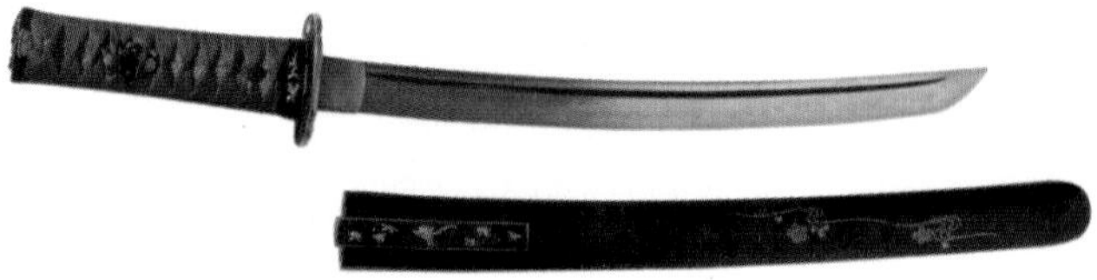

A sword (*wakizashi*), with gold and silver mounts, the fullered blade with temperline, with lacquered scabbard, the rayskin grip with silk wrapping, Japan, Edo period, c1800, 24in (61cm) long.

£2,000–2,400 **Michael Long**

agger (*tanto*), signed
oshige, Japan, Meiji period,
ed 1878, 14in (35.5cm) long.

100–1,250
rth Vincent

A sword (*wakizashi*), the rayskin grip with silk wrapping, the copper *tsuba* with brass rim, black lacquered scabbard with signed knife, Japan, Edo period, c1810, 24in (61cm) long.

£1,800–2,000 **Michael Long**

SUBA

Choshu School iron *tsuba*, carved with a
scape, mountains and temples, the reverse
h a figure, signed, Japan, 18thC,
n (8.5cm) diam.

,000–1,200 **Sotheby's**

An iron *tsuba*, carved with a guardian figure holding a bird, the reverse with calligraphy, with inscription and gilt monogram, Japan, 19thC, 3¼in (8.5cm) diam.

£2,500–3,000 **Sotheby's**

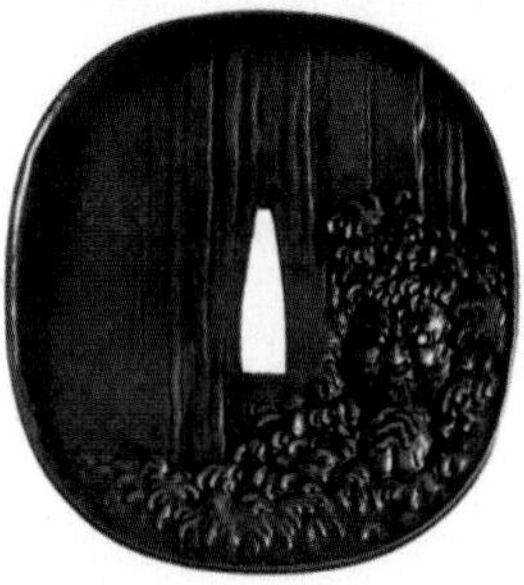

A Yokoya school copper *tsuba*, carved with Mongaku Shonin doing penance, the eyes inlaid with *shibuichi*, signed 'Kiryusai Somin' marked, Japan, 19thC, 3¾in (9.5cm) wide.

£3,500–4,250 **Sotheby's**

Endo Morito fell in love with the wife of a Samurai. Plotting to assassinate her husband, he killed her by mistake. Overcome with grief, Endo Morito became a monk under the new name of Mongaku and went to repent beneath the waterfall of Machi.

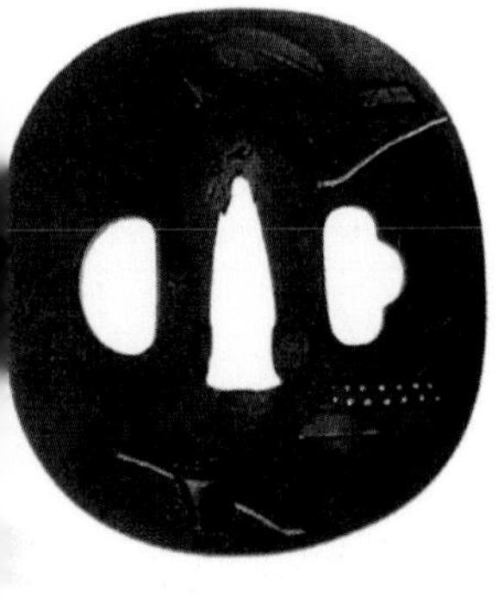

bronze *tsuba*, carved with a tea ceremony,
aid with silver studs and gilt eyes, signed,
pan, c1820, 2¾in (7cm) high.

00–120 **Bloomsbury**

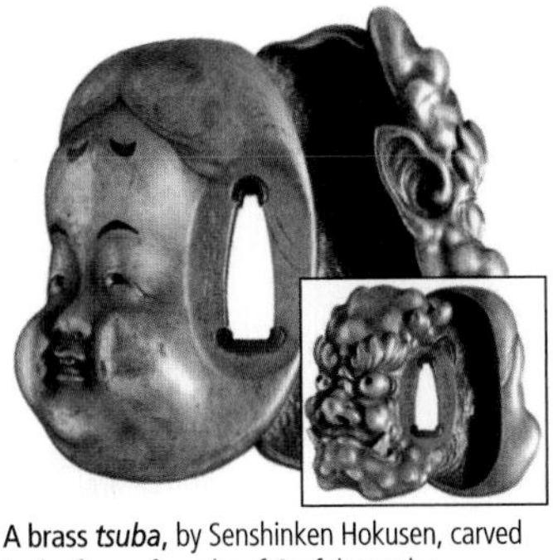

A brass *tsuba*, by Senshinken Hokusen, carved in the form of masks of Otafuku and a demon, with inscription, signed, Japan, dated 1848, 3¾in (9.5cm) wide.

£3,250–4,000 **Sotheby's**

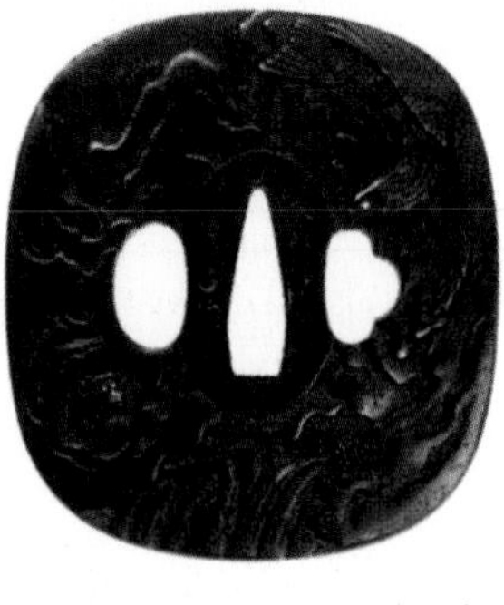

An iron *tsuba*, carved with an eagle and a monkey in a landscape, inlaid with gilt eyes, signed, Japan, c1860, 3¼in (8.5cm) wide.

£225–275 **Bloomsbury**

BOXES

A lacquered wooden box, decorated with birds and mythical creatures, with bronze *taotie* mask mounts, the base with inscription, China, c200 BC, 7in (18cm) high.

£900–1,100 Skinner

A lacquered wooden box, decorated with Oriental scenes, Chinese, early 17thC, 16in (40.5cm) wide.

£1,100–1,250 Guest & Gray

A bronze box, pierced and chased with flo scrolls, the cover with a lotus finial, India, Mughal period, probably 17thC, 5in (12.5cm) diam.

£550–650 Skinner

A *huanghuali* box and cover, inlaid with mother-of-pearl, bone, soapstone and jade flowers and antiques, the cover decorated with a *qilin*, China, 18thC, 14½in (37cm) wide.

£7,000–8,500 Sotheby's

A silver-gilt filigree box, the hinged cover inset with a glass panel depicting a lady, China, 18thC, 4¼in (11cm) wide.

£3,500–4,250 Woolley & Wallis

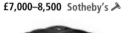

A pair of *huanghuali* Weiqi boxes and covers, China, 18thC, 4¼in (11cm) diam.

£3,000–3,500 Sotheby's (NY)

Weiqi is Chinese chess; it is usually known by the Japanese term 'Go'.

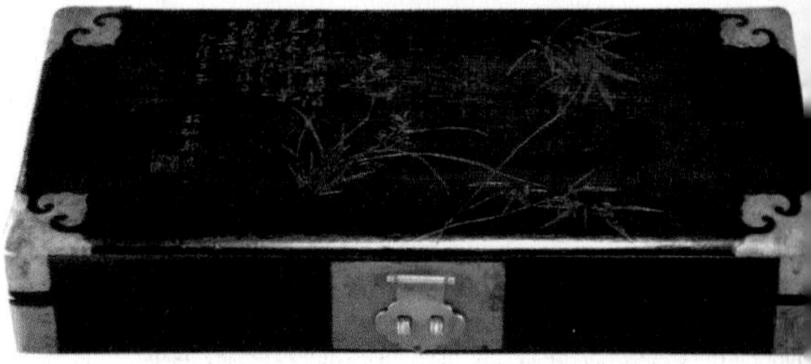

A hardwood and metal-bound writing box, carved with irises and bamboo, with date, verse and inscription, China, dated 1762, 13¾in (35cm) wide.

£2,250–2,750 Sotheby's

Dated items are popular with collectors.

A Chinese export lacquer tea caddy, decorated with pavilions, pagodas, figures and foliage, the centre with an armorial and motto, the interior with three pewter containers, early 19thC, 16in (40.5cm) wide.

£1,000–1,200 Hy Duke

A Chinese export lacquer games box, the interior with boxes and ca trays, on carved wood and gilt feet, c1830, 15in (38cm) wide.

£750–850 Moxhams

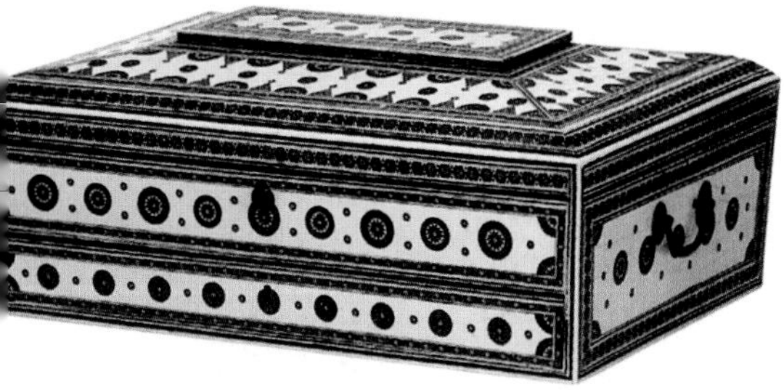

ivory writing casket, with a fitted interior, the front with a drawer inset with a ng surface, slight damage, India, Vizagapatam, 19thC, 19¼in (49cm) wide.

00–2,400 Sotheby's (Am)

An ivory casket, carved, pierced and undercut with figures, flowers and pagodas, the hinged cover enclosing a velvet-lined tray, China, mid-19thC, 6¼in (16cm) wide.

£1,200–1,400 Guest & Gray

nton ivory casket, the interior with ovable tray, damaged, China, mid-19thC, (17cm) wide.

0–850 Sworder's

An ivory work box, attributed to Shedashboodoo, decorated with bands of flowers and foliage, the hinged lid enclosing compartments, on gadrooned bun feet, India, Vizagapatam, c1855, 10in (25.5cm) wide.

£3,000–3,500 Gorringes (L)

A papier-mâché box, painted with panels of figures and gods, India, Kashmir, mid-19thC, 10in (25.5cm) high.

£450–550 Sworder's

vory and sandalwood work box, decorated with scrolling foliage flowers, the hinged cover enclosing compartments, on horn bun , India, Vizagapatam, c1855, 10½in (26.5cm) wide.

0–850 Gorringes (L)

A lacquer tea caddy, painted with figures in a landscape, the interior with a pewter box, China, 19thC, 13½in (34.5cm) wide.

£1,200–1,400 Sotheby's (Am)

ivory *fukura suzume* (box), by Tomonobu, in the form of a stylized rrow, Japan, 19thC, 1½in (4cm) wide.

,800–2,000 David Bowden

A brass jewellery box, China, 19thC, 7in (18cm) wide.

£100–120 Mostly Boxes

FIGURES & MODELS

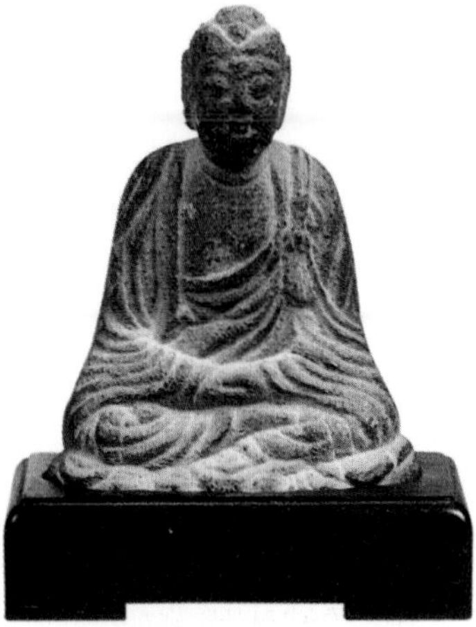

A bronze figure of Amida Buddha, China, Tang Dynasty, 618–907, 4in (10cm) high.

£550–650 Skinner

A bronze figure of the Hindu goddess Gauri, India, 8thC, 8½in (21.5cm) high.

£6,750–7,500 Jeremy Knowles

A marble figure of Vishnuchakramurti, Ir c800 AD, 16½in (42cm) high.

£15,000–17,000 Jeremy Knowles

A gilt-bronze figure in court costume, China, Ming Dynasty, 1368–1644, 3¾in (9.5cm) high.

£600–700 Skinner

A brass figure of Narasimha and consort, India, Himachal Pradesh, 15thC, 7¾in (19.5cm) high.

£6,750–7,500
Jeremy Knowles

Narasimha was the fourth incarnation of the Hindu god Vishnu.

A carved wood figure of Avalokiteshvara Guan Yin, with painted and lacquered decoration, Vietnam, 17th/18thC, 41in (104cm) high.

£3,200–3,800 Skinner

A pair of carved wood figures, China, 18thC, 9in (23cm) high.

£2,500–2,800
Mary Cruz Antiques

An iron figure of Guandi, with a dedicatory inscription on the reverse, China, Jiajing period, 1522–66, 25¼in (64cm) high.

£4,500–5,000
Guest & Gray

Guandi is the Chinese God of War. Guan Yu was a general during the Three Kingdoms period (220–80 AD) when he helped defeat Cao Cao of the northern kingdom of Wei. He became a folk hero to many groups in Chinese society and was identified as the god of loyalty, wealth, literature and protector of temples. In 1614, the Ming Dynasty government awarded Guan Yu imperial rank, designating him as Guandi, the God of War. He is still one of the most revered of Chinese gods and his image is often used in the arts.

A bamboo figure of Dongfan Shuo, sitting on a recumbent deer, China, 17th/18thC, 6½in (16.5cm) high.

£5,500–6,500 Sotheby's

Dongfang Shuo was a very witt who lived during the Han Dyn

A carved ivory figure of Shoula wooden cap later, China, 18th 13in (33cm) high.

£1,500–1,800 Skinner

t-bronze figure of Manjusri, holding
t a sword, blade missing, Tibet, 18thC,
(17cm) high.

800–3,500 **Woolley & Wallis**

jusri was a Tibetan Buddhist Bodhisattva.

A bronze figural group, with temple dedication inscription and guardian naming, slight damage, Japan, dated to Kansei period, (1789–1801), 14in (35.5cm) high.

£1,100–1,250
Guest & Gray

A carved rootwood figure of the God of Literature, standing on a dragon, with glass eyes, China, 18th/19thC, 35in (89cm) high.

£1,100–1,300
Skinner

A carved ivory figure of Lan Caihe, China, 19thC, 10in (25.5cm) high.

£900–1,100 **Skinner**

Lan Caihe is one of the Eight Immortals – a group of legendary transcendents in Chinese mythology.

oxwood figure of Guan Yin, 19thC,
1 (35.5cm) high.

,500–6,500 **Freeman's**

*an Yin was the Buddhist Goddess of
rcy. She is the embodiment of wisdom,
passion and love and is often depicted
ng or standing on a lotus flower, a symbol
urity. It is commonly believed that anyone
o prays to Guan Yin will be cured of illness.*

A set of seven carved wood deities, with gilt highlights, China, 19thC, 15in (38cm) high.

£900–1,100 **Skinner**

**ivory figure of a lady writing
a book,** Japan, 19thC,
(15cm) high.

,000–2,400
vid Bowden

An ivory *okimono* of two figures catching a giant carp, signed, Japan, 19thC, 4in (10cm) high.

£1,350–1,500
K & M Antiques

An ivory figure of a lady, Japan, 19thC, 6in (15cm) high.

£1,100–1,250
David Bowden

A Tokyo school ivory figural group of a man and a child, Japan, 19thC, 5in (12.5cm) high.

£1,400–1,600
K & M Antiques

A bronze model of a lion, signed, on a carved hardwood stand, Japan, 19thC, 12in (30.5cm) wide.

£375–450 Gilding's

A bronze model of a tiger attacking a water buffalo, signed, Japan, 19thC, 8in (20.5cm) w

£380–425 K & M Antiques

A wood *okimono* of a family of rats, by Itsumin, Japan, 19thC, 1¾in (4.5cm) high.

£1,500–1,650
K & M Antiques

A carved ivory figure of a basket maker, signed 'Eiitsu', Japan, Meiji period, 1868–1911, 2½in (6.5cm) high.

£2,000–2,400 Laura Bordignon

An ivory *okimono* of two rats, signed, Japan, Meiji period, 1868–1911, 1¾in (4.5cm) wide.

£400–500 Hy Duke

A carved ivory figural group of a farmer and child, signed, Japan, Meiji period, 1868–1911, 8in (20.5cm) high.

£2,000–2,200
David Brower

An ivory figural group of two travellers, signed in a red seal 'Seiko', Japan, Meiji period, 1868–1911, 6in (15cm) high.

£5,000–5,500
Laura Bordignon

An ivory figure of a scholar, signed 'Hidemasa', Japan, Meiji period, 1868–1911, 4in (10cm) high.

£3,000–3,500
Laura Bordignon

A carved ivory *okimono* of a geisha, a child and a cat, Japan, Meiji period, 1868–19
3½in (9cm) high.

£280–350
Holloway's

A pair of carved wood figures of dancers, attributed to Takamura Toun, damaged, signed, Japan, Meiji period, 1868–1911, 13¾in (35cm) high.

£1,600–2,000 Sotheby's

A carved ivory *okimono* of a *bijin* and child being drawn on a rickshaw, Japan, Meiji period, 1868–1911, 3in (7.5cm) high.

£900–1,000
David Brower

A bronze group of a water buffalo and ric signed, Japan, Meiji period, 1868–1911, 18in (45.5cm) wide.

£2,800–3,500
Gorringes (L)

…arved ivory *okimono* of …nnon riding a carp, signed …isai', Japan, Meiji period, …8–1911, 4½in (11.5cm) high.

…50–300 **Holloway's**

…nnon was the principal …hisattva of Mahayana Buddhism.

A carved ivory figure of a puppeteer, signed, Japan, Meiji period, 1868–1911, 13½in (34.5cm) high.

£1,450–1,650
Woolley & Wallis

An ivory figural group of men fighting, signed 'Ryukosai Shugyoku' in a seal, Japan, Meiji period, 1868–1911, 4in (10in) high.

£4,500–5,000 **Laura Bordignon**

… ivory figural group of a … painter with assistant, …ned, Japan, late 19thC, … (23cm) high.

…,000–4,500
…& M Antiques

A bronze figure of Genji, holding a temple bell, signed 'Miyao' in a seal , Japan, Meiji period, c1900, 20in (51cm) high.

£12,000–14,000
Laura Bordignon

A bronze model of a Pekinese dog, Japan, Meiji period, 1868–1911, 13in (33cm) long.

£2,700–3,000
David Brower

A carved ivory Luohan group, on a wooden stand, China, c1900, 10¼in (26cm) high.

£7,000–8,500 **Sotheby's**

An ivory figure of a man and a snake, Japan, Meiji period, c1900, 3½in (9cm) high.

£1,600–1,800
Laura Bordignon

…wood and ivory figural group of two entertainers, with gold lacquer, …ned 'Seiti' in a red seal, Japan, Meiji period, c1900, 12in (30.5cm) wide.

…0,000–11,000 **Laura Bordignon**

A silver articulated model of a dragon, signed, China, early 20thC, 16½in (42cm) high.

£3,200–3,800 **Gorringes (L)**

FURNITURE

A lacquer *bonheur du jour*, the two doors enclosing a fitted interior, the base with a detachable work box with a double hinged top and two drawers, on cabriole legs with hairy paw feet, slight wear, China, c1850, 61¾in (157cm) high.

£800–1,000
Dreweatt Neate

EXPERT'S EYE VIZAGAPATAM

This is an important Anglo-Indian hardwood cabinet-on-stand that belongs to a group of exotic ivory-veneered furniture made under the direction of the Dutch and English companies at Vizagapatam on the Coromandel Coast during the second half of the 18th century. The cabinet is profusely inlaid all over with etched ivory in typical Vizagapatam style.

It is normal for Anglo-Indian furniture of this period to have cabriole legs and claw-and-ball feet in the classical English style.

The cabinet was acquired in India by Major General Sir Eyrie Coote, who helped to suppress Bonnie Prince Charlie's uprising in Scotland before going to India where his prompt action ensured the victory at Plassey in June 1757. This provenance is an important factor in the high price attained.

An ivory-inlaid padouk and hardwood cabinet-on-stand, the later glazed doors enclosi three long and four short drawers, the conforming stan with a frieze drawer, on cabrio legs with claw-and-ball feet, Anglo-Indian, Vizagapatam, 18thC, 36½in (92.5cm) wide.

£160,000–180,000
Mealy's

A japanned lacquer table cabinet, with scenic decoration, the two doors enclosing drawers, China, early 19thC, 11in (28cm) high.

£2,500–3,000 Avon Antiques

An iron-bound padouk table cabinet, China, 19thC, 28in (71cm) wide.

£1,100–1,300
Sotheby's (O)

A pair of cinnabar lacquered chairs, carve with dragons, phoenixes and clouds, restor China, 18th/19thC.

£7,000–8,000 Skinner

An ivory-inlaid teak writing desk, the hinged top enclosing a parquetry-inlaid sandalwood interior with three pigeonholes, India, Vizagapatam, c1870, 24½in (62cm) wide.

£7,000–8,500 Sotheby's

A painted toilet mirror, with floral decoration, the bevelled plate supported on spiral-twist columns, on a base with two drawers, Kashmir, late 19thC, 20¾in (52.5cm) high.

£320–380 Sworders

A lacquer five-fold screen, decorated with figures in a landscape, the reverse with birc amid foliage, China, c1910, each panel 15 (38.5cm) wide.

£1,100–1,300 Woolley & Wallis

..rved rosewood stand, with a ..ble top, China, c1850, .. (91.5cm) high.
..0–380 S W Antiques

A carved rosewood stand, with an inset marble top, China, c1900, 31in (78.5cm) high.
£300–350 Sworders

A walnut stool, with a drop-in needlework seat, on shell- and foliate-carved cabriole legs with claw-and-ball feet, Anglo-Indian, early 20thC, 39¾in (101cm) wide.
£550–650 Woolley & Wallis

A lacquer low table, inlaid with mother-of-pearl peony scrolls, China, 17thC, 25in (63.5cm) wide.
£1,600–2,000
Skinner

..**osewood occasional table,** with ivory inlay and white-metal mounts, .. top inlaid with a geometric design, above three drawers, the ..estal on a platform base with carved paw feet, damaged, Anglo- ..an, c1850, 24in (61cm) wide.
..000–1,200 Gorringes (L)

A lacquered wood occasional table, Kashmir, 1850–80, 28½in (72.5cm) wide.
£4,500–5,000 Jeremy Knowles

..**est of four carved and ..ulded hardwood tables,** ..na, early 20thC, largest ..n (71cm) high.
..50–650
..oolley & Wallis

A mother-of-pearl-inlaid trunk, decorated with panels of birds and foliage, the front panel with hinged doors, China, 19thC, 31in (78.5cm) wide.
£450–550
Gorringes (L)

A pair of carved and pierced rosewood and ivory table screens, decorated with scenes of Immortals, China, 19thC, 10¼in (26cm) high.
£5,000–6,000 Skinner

INRO

A gold lacquer four-case *inro*, each side decorated with *Shibayama* inlay, the front with an entertainer blowing bubbles, the reverse with a hanging basket in the form of a boat filled with flowers, with a *nashiji* interior, Japan, 19thC, 2¾in (7cm) high.

£3,000–3,500 Sotheby's

A gold lacquer four-case *inro* and an ivory *netsuke* of a puppy with an abalone shell, the *inro* with *Shibayama* inlay of the rabbit in the moon, signed, with a carnelian *ojime*, slight damage to *netsuke*, Japan, 19thC.

£1,700–2,000 Skinner

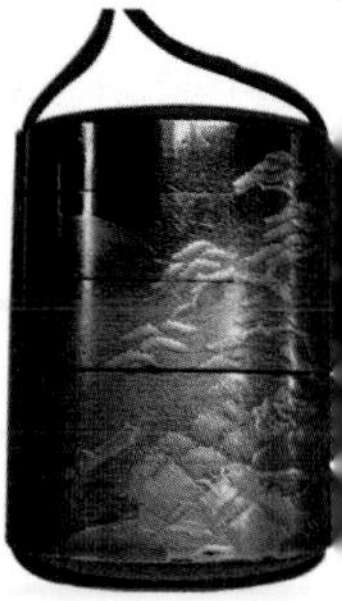

A lacquer five-case *inro*, decc with figures on the banks of lake, Japan, Meiji period, 1868–1911, 3in (7.5cm) hig

£350–425 Hy Duke

A four-case *inro* and a wooden *netsuke* of a puppy, the *inro* decorated with an exotic bird a prunus branch, with a shell *ojime*, Japan, c1900, 3¼in (8.5cm) high.

£650–800 Woolley & Wallis

JEWELLERY

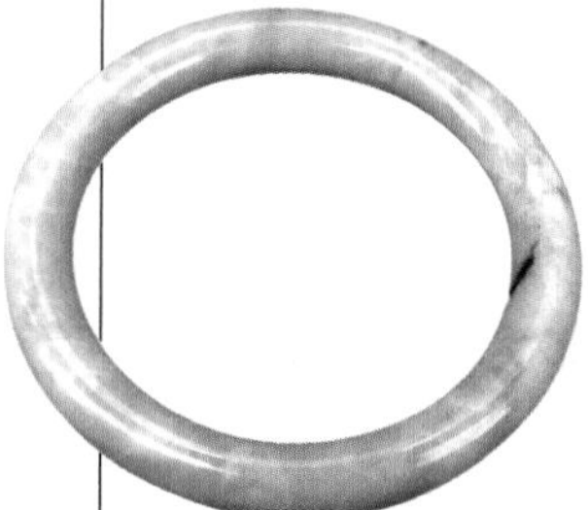

A jade bangle, China, 19thC.

£900–1,000 Guest & Gray

A pair of silver-gilt bracelets, decorated with designs of cash coins, with animal-head finials, China, 11th–12thC.

£300–350 Skinner

An amber, coral and glass court necklace, suspending glass medallion in a gilt-metal frame with kingfisher in China, 18thC.

£1,600–2,000 Sotheby's (NY)

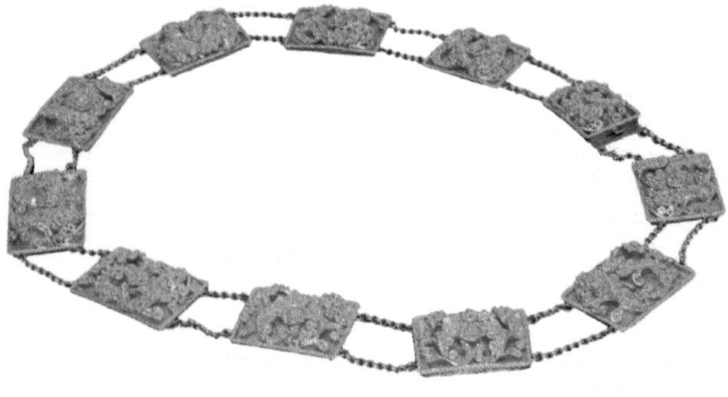

A gold filigree necklace, with 11 graduated plaques on a chain, with a concealed clasp, India, c1850.

£380–450 Gorringes (L)

A gold pendant necklace, set with gems a seed pearls, India, late 19thC.

£350–425 Rosebery's

:TSUKE

›e *netsuke* of a *shishi* **on a rock,** slight
Japan, 18thC, 1¾in (4.5cm) high.
–350 **Sworders**

An ivory *netsuke* **of a parrot on a perch,** Japan, 19thC, 2in (5cm) high.
£700–850 **Skinner**

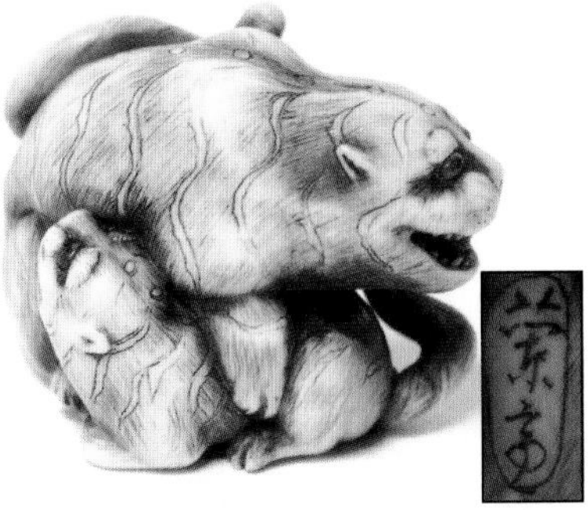

A ivory *netsuke* **of a tigress and cub,** by Rantei, signed, Japan, 19thC, 1¼in (3cm) high.
£3,400–3,750 **K & M Antiques**

›oden *netsuke* **of a mask,** with mother-
arl eyes and lacquered detail,
ture on a silver plaque, Japan, 19thC,
(4.5cm) high.
)–750 **Skinner**

An ivory *netsuke* **of a pair of quail with millet plants,** by Okatomo, signed, Japan, 19thC, 1½in (4cm) high.
£1,100–1,300 **Skinner**

A boxwood *netsuke* **of three terrapins,** by Chuichi, Japan, 19thC, 2in (5cm) wide.
£2,250–2,500 **David Bowden**

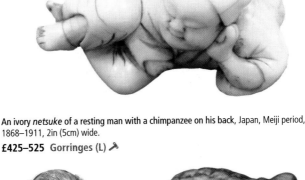

›ved ivory *netsuke* **of a monkey**
hing an insect on a gourd, by
ıtomo, signed, losses, Japan, Meiji
›d, 1868–1911, 1½in (4cm) high.
0–700 **Holloway's**

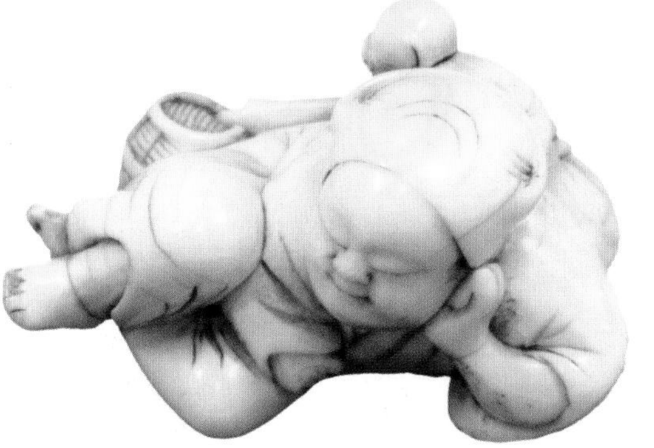

An ivory *netsuke* **of a resting man with a chimpanzee on his back,** Japan, Meiji period, 1868–1911, 2in (5cm) wide.
£425–525 **Gorringes (L)**

›ory *netsuke* **of a skeleton beside a**
: fruit, signed, Japan, Meiji period,
3–1911, 2in (5cm) wide.
›0–300
Duke

A carved ivory *netsuke* **of a monkey dressing her baby,** by Masamoto, signed, Japan, Meiji period, 1868–1911, 1½in (4cm) high.
£650–800 **Holloway's**

An ivory *netsuke* **of a toad on a rope sandal,** by Tamakazu, signed, Japan, late 19thC, 1½in (4cm) wide.
£200–250 **Sworders**

ROBES & COSTUME

A pair of boots for bound feet, China, c1920.
£230–260 Elizabeth Gibbons

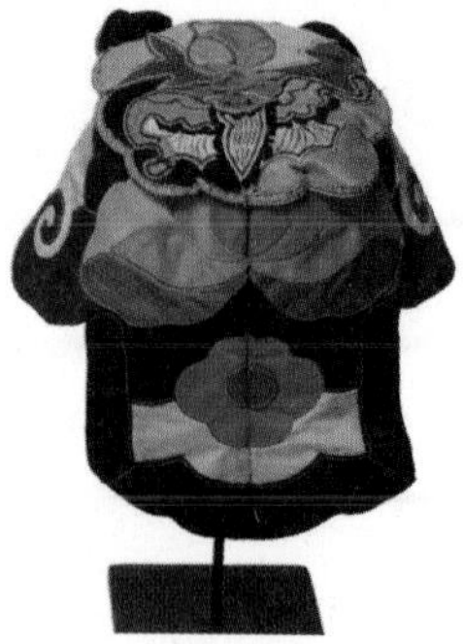

A child's embroidered silk festival hat, China, c1900.
£135–150
Elizabeth Gibbons

A Manchu woman's horsehair and kingfisher feath headdress, decorated with tourmaline, jade, pearls, coral and rubies, some losses, China, 19thC.
£13,000–15,000 Skinner

A silk gauze dragon robe, worked with eight five-clawed dragons in pursuit of flaming pearls, China, early 19thC.
£4,500–5,500 Sotheby's (NY)

A silk robe, embroidered with eight dragon roundels a a sea wave border, China, late 19thC.
£6,000–7,000 Woolley & Wallis

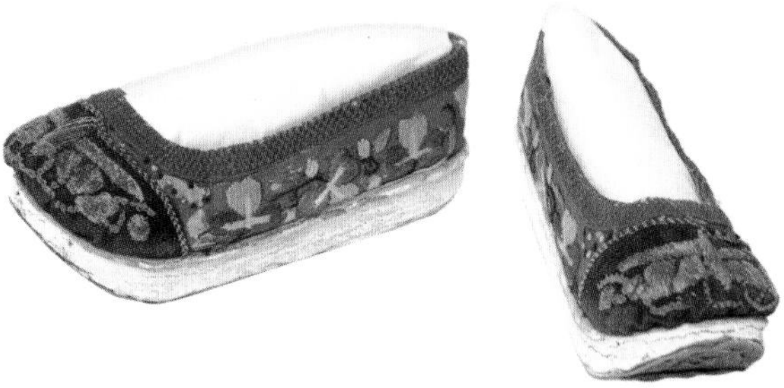

A pair of child's shoes, with embroidered decoration, China, Manchuria, 1890s.
£150–175 Elizabeth Gibbons

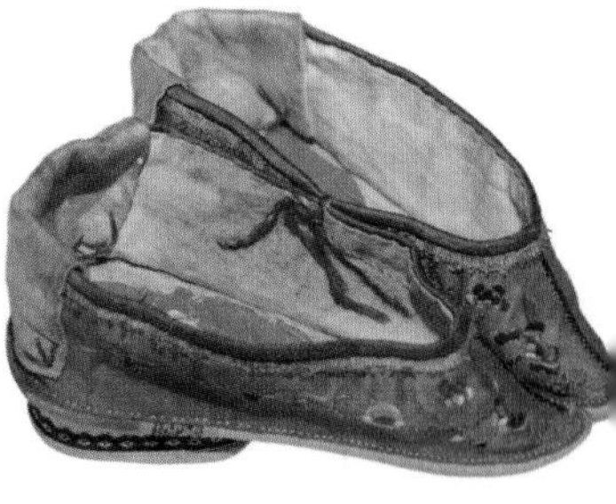

A pair of silk shoes, with embroidered decoration, Ch early 20thC.
£75–85 Joanna Proops

A pair of silk shoes, with leather soles, China, Manchuria, 1920s, 6in (15cm) long.
£80–90 Le Boudoir
These shoes come from the Manchu region where bound feet were banned.

A pair of silk shoes, embroidered with lotus flowers, China, c1920 6in (15cm) long.
£90–100 Le Boudoir

ꞁUFF BOTTLES

ite jade snuff bottle and tray, the bottle lightly engraved a scholar, the reverse with a landscape, with lion mask ꞁes and a tourmaline stopper, the tray engraved with a China, 18thC, bottle 2¾in (7cm) high.

'50–2,750 Skinner

A cinnabar snuff bottle, carved with phoenixes and clouds, China, 18thC, 3in (7.5cm) high.

£800–1,000 Skinner

A glass snuff bottle, with red overlay, China, 18thC, 2½in (6.5cm) high.

£900–1,000 David Bowden

ɟate snuff bottle, China, 18thC, '.5cm) high.

ᴉ00–2,000 David Bowden

A glass snuff bottle, with red overlay, China, 18thC, 3in (7.5cm) high.

£1,600–1,800 David Bowden

A jadeite snuff bottle, with a pink quartz stopper, China, 19thC, 2¼in (5.5cm) high.

£1,650–1,800 Guest & Gray

odstone snuff bottle, China, 18thC, '(6.5cm) high.

)–700 Skinner

An amber snuff bottle, carved with *ruyi* sceptres tied with ribbons, China, c1900, 2½in (6.5cm) high.

£2,000–2,500 Skinner

A Suzhou School agate snuff bottle, carved with a man seated on a terrace with a crane flying overhead, China, 19thC, 2¾in (7cm) high.

£3,500–4,250 Sotheby's (Am)

A glass snuff bottle, overlaid with three monkeys and a tree, slight damage, China, 19thC, 2¾in (7cm) high.
£200–220 Guest & Gray

A coral snuff bottle, by Tao Feng, carved with women in a garden scene, on a carved ivory stand, slight damage, signed, China, 19thC.
£1,600–2,000 Skinner

An agate snuff bottle, with carved handle and a glass stopper, China, 19thC, 2¼in (6cm) high.
£160–180 Guest & Gray

A shadow agate snuff bottle, carved with a figure of Li Po, China, 19thC, 2½in (6.5cm) high.
£2,500–3,000 Skinner
Li Bai (Li Po) was a famous poet of the Tang Dynasty.

A glass snuff bottle, by Ma Shaoxian, China, late 19thC, 3in (7.5cm) high.
£3,500–4,000 David Bowden

A rock crystal snuff bottle, by Ma Hsiao Hsuan, interior-painted with butterflies ar album leaves, signed, China, early 20thC, 2½in (6.5cm) high.
£475–575 Skinner

TEXTILES

A woven cotton baby carrier, China, Dai nation, early 20thC, 28 x 26in (71 x 66cm).
£230–260 Peter Wain

A Chinese export satin coverlet, embroidered with a central lotus medallion, floral scrolls, birds and foliate swags, relined, late 18thC, 82 x 92in (208.5 x 233.5cm).
£5,000–6,000 Sotheby's

A silk brocade hanging, with three depic of Buddha, above the Eighteen Luohans a the Guardians of the Four Directions, Chi Qianlong period, 1736–95, 57in (145cm) long.
£15,000–18,000 Sotheby's (HK)

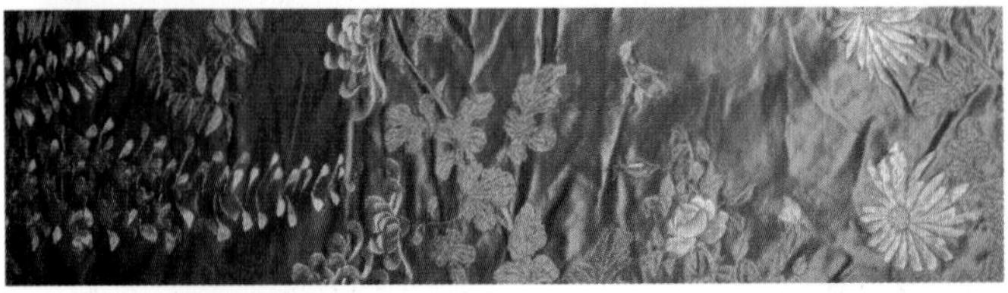

A silk quilt, with hand-embroidered decoration, probably Japanese, c1880, 80 x 74in (203 x 188cm).
£450–500 Joanna Proops

ILVER

ASKETS

er sugar basket, possibly by John
, pierced and chased with scrolling
s, glass liner later, London 1770,
0cm) high, 1¾oz.

–800 Bearnes

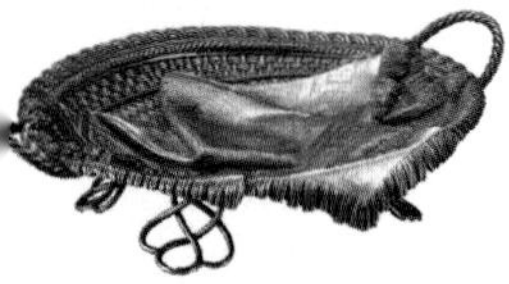

er basket, by Gustav Klingert, Russia,
w 1892, 14½in (37cm) wide.

0–4,250 Heritage

A George III silver fruit basket, with pierced decoration, fluted handle and bright-cut engraving, later coat-of-arms and monogram, London 1804, 13in (33cm) wide.

£1,500–1,800 Jeffrey Neal

A silver basket, pierced and applied with grapes and vines, Chester 1901, 6in (15cm) wide.

£350–400 Andrew Campbell

A Victorian silver two-handled basket, with foliate and scroll cast decoration, on a lobed foot, London 1840, 11¾in (30cm) high.

£380–450 Rosebery's

A sterling silver basket, by Gorham Manufacturing Co, with removable silver-plated liner, America, early 20thC, 14½in (37cm) high, 43½oz.

£900–1,100 Jackson's

OWLS

er monteith, with detachable rim, chased
-scrolls, foliage and masks, anchor mark,
, Galway, c1700, 8¾in (22cm) diam, 288oz.

00–13,000 Bearnes

er two-handled bowl, by F. Elkington,
sed with a band of classical figures,
lt interior, Birmingham 1875,
(31cm) diam, 78oz.

0–2,800
son, Roddick & Medcalf (E)

A silver porringer, by William Jones, engraved 'Z-GD', marked 'WI', America, Massachusetts, early 18thC, 5in (12.5cm) diam, 7oz.

£2,500–3,000 Northeast Auctions

A silver bowl, by Josiah Austin, engraved 'LS', America, Massachusetts, late 18thC, 7¼in (18.5cm) diam, 15oz.

£2,200–2,600 Northeast Auctions

A silver two-handled bowl, by Tiffany & Co, America, New York, late 19thC, 12in (30.5cm) wide, 27oz.

£1,800–2,200 Waddington's

A pair of silver bowls and covers, decorated with putti and scrolls, crest to side, the covers with acorn finials, 1880, 9in (23cm) diam.

£700–800 Jeffrey Neal

A silver bowl, by W. Gibson & J. Langman, embossed and chased masks, fruit, foliage and fluting, on four stylized dragon scroll supp London 1890, 8¼in (21cm) diam, 21½oz.

£225–275 Sworders

A silver bowl, engraved with equestrian and figural panels, Russia, c1900, 19in (48.5cm) wide, 93oz.

£750–900 Freeman's

A sterling silver bowl, by Kirk & Sons, repoussé-decorated with garden scenes and flowers, stamped marks, America, c1900, 9¼in (23.5cm) diam, 25¾oz.

£1,200–1,500 Jackson's

BOXES

A silver, gilt and niello box and cover, the cover inset with a medallion depicting Catherine II as Minerva, the base with entwined initials 'AK', Russia, 18thC, 3¼in (8cm) wide.

£2,500–3,000 Rosebery's

A silver and tortoiseshell trinket box, in the form of a tortoise, London 1882, 4½in (11.5cm) wide.

£225–275 Andrew Hartley

A silver cigar box, by Thornhill, London 1888, 7¾in (19.5cm) wide.

£1,600–1,800 Shapiro

For Snuff Boxes please see our speci feature on pages 345–47.

A silver biscuit box and cover, by Huttons, with engine-turned decoration, on claw-and-ball feet, London 1899, 8¼in (21cm) wide, 36oz.

£800–1,000 Anderson & Garland

A silver playing card box, Birmingham 1904, 5in (12.5cm) high.

£2,200–2,500 Andrew Campbell

A dressing table box and cover, probab Whiting Manufactory Co, decorated in lov with ribbon-like scrolls, marked and initi 'MAG', America, c1900, 3½in (9cm) high

£320–380 Woolley & Wallis

ADDY SPOONS

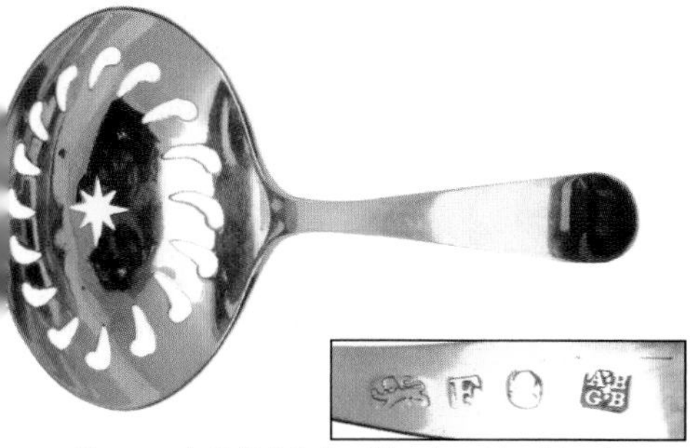

ver caddy spoon, by D. B. & G. B., with a pierced bowl, London
, 3in (7.5cm) long.
5–150 Jennifer Lloyd

A silver caddy spoon, by Cocks & Bettridge, with a leaf-shaped bowl and engraved decoration, initialled 'FW', Birmingham 1806, 3½in (9cm) long.
£170–200 Woolley & Wallis

ver filigree caddy spoon, 1818, 3in (7.5cm) long.
0–300 Jennifer Lloyd

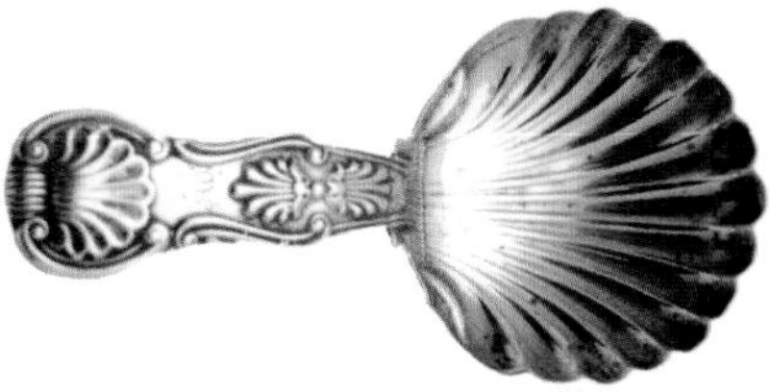

A silver caddy spoon, by John Watson, with embossed decoration, Newcastle 1837, 3in (7.5cm) long.
£60–65 Greystoke Antiques

ANDLESTICKS & CHAMBERSTICKS

ver taperstick, by
ezer Coker, London 1759,
(13.5cm) high, 5½oz.
500–1,850
iel Bexfield

A pair of silver candlesticks, by Matthew Boulton, with detachable nozzles and loaded bases, Birmingham 1808, 12in (30.5cm) high.
£1,800–2,200 Sotheby's (O)

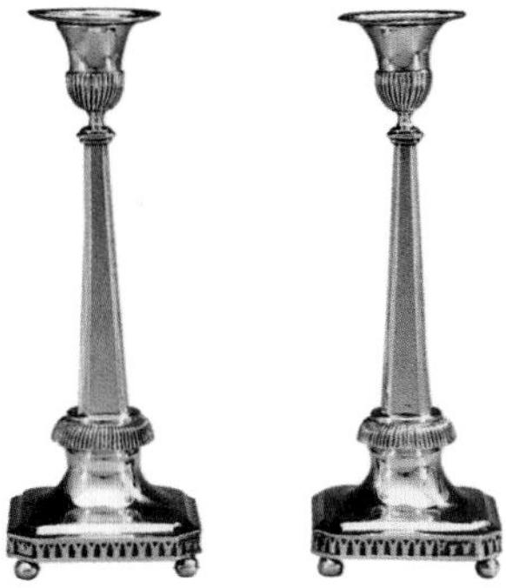

A pair of silver candlesticks, by Olof Bergström, Sweden, Uppsala 1816, 9¾in (25cm) high.
£2,500–3,000 Bukowskis

r of silver chambersticks, by Robert Garrard,
detachable nozzles and snuffers, London 1843,
5cm) diam, 30¾oz.
00–1,750 Sotheby's (O)

A silver and gilt candelabra centrepiece, London 1846, 30in (76cm) high.
£23,000–26,000
Bourbon-Hanby

A pair of silver candlesticks, Birmingham 1889, 6in (15cm) high.
£350–400 Pantiles Spa Antiques

A pair of silver candlesticks, Sheffield 1893, 12in (30.5cm) high.
£2,000–2,200 Bourbon-Hanby

A pair of silver candlesticks, London 1896, 3½in (9cm) high.
£280–320 Pantiles Spa Antiques

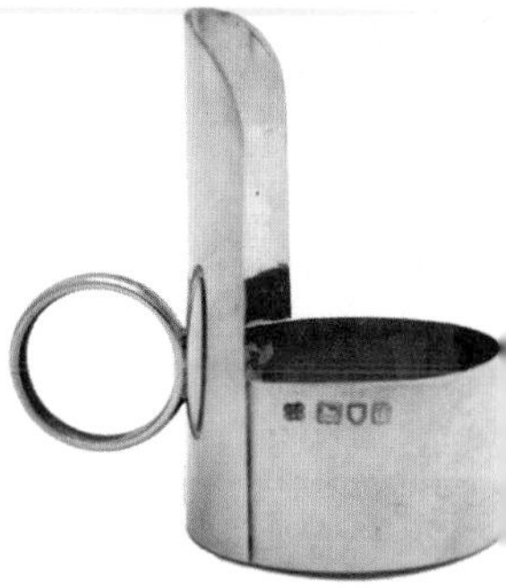

A silver candle holder, 1896, 3in (7.5cm) h
£225–250 Jeffrey Neal

A set of six silver candlesticks and two candelabra, by Herbert Charles Lambert, London 1910, 12½in (32cm) high.
£14,000–16,000 Daniel Bexfield

A pair of silver candlesticks, by William Hutton, London 1910, 11in (28cm) high.
£1,350–1,500 Lucy Harris

A pair of silver candlesticks, by Francis Coombe, Sheffield 1924, 7in (18cm) high
£450–500 Andrew Campbell

EXPERT'S EYE CANDLESTICKS

Candlesticks were made in a diverse range of sizes and styles but the basic form of a base, vertical stem, nozzle and, on most examples, a drip pan of some description is essentially the same. Early 18th-century candlesticks tend to be plain with minimal decoration and often consist of a square or octagonal base with a baluster square column. By the 1730s candlesticks, such as this example, had become taller with richer ornamentation consisting of pleated or lobed forms. This 1769 cast candlestick is one of pair by John Scofield. He was renowned for his elegant fluted candlesticks and his designs are highly sought after today.
£5,400–6,000 pair Daniel Bexfield

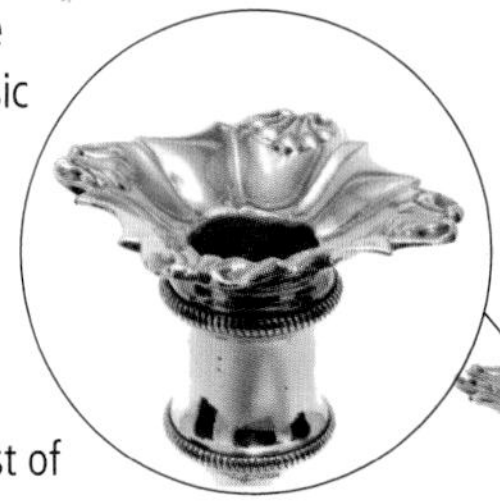

The detachable nozzle fits into the socket to hold the candle and stop the wax dripping down the inside of the stem. Detachable nozzles, which co be cleaned, were typical from the 1740s. The sha of the nozzle usually mirrors that of the base. The nozzles are usually marked but this is not essenti the design should match that of the stem and foo

The socket, also known as the sconce or capital, is the cylindric holder attached to the top of the column that the candle fits into. is a separate piece that is soldere to the column and should bear maker's marks or an assay mark

Some candlesticks feature a ledge above the nozzle that catches dripping wax and is known as a drip pan; others feature a tray between the stem and the base to catch the drips.

The candlestick stem is also known as the column.

A protruding ornament on the stem is called a knop.

The lowest part of the candlestick is known as the base or foot and should be fully marked, either underneath or along the edge.

Soldered join.

ASTERS

er caster, by Charles Adam, knopped finial, London , 6in (15cm) high, 4¼oz.

–1,100 **Bearnes**

A silver caster, by John Potwine, marked, America, Boston, c1730, 3¼in (8.5cm) high, 2oz.

£3,250–3,750
Sotheby's (NY)

A silver caster, by Thomas Daniell, with rope decoration, 1774, 5¼in (13.5cm) high.

£400–450 **Schredds**

A silver caster, by Henry Chawner and John Emes, London 1796, 3½in (9cm) high.

£130–150
Greystoke Antiques

er caster, by Thomas s, with reeded decoration, , 3½in (9cm) high.

)–425 **Schredds**

A silver caster, London 1810, 3½in (9cm) high.

£200–220
Greystoke Antiques

A silver caster, by Nathan & Hayes, chased with flowers and scrolls, Chester 1899, 7½in (19cm) high.

£225–275
Greenslade Taylor Hunt

A silver caster, by Robert Patrick Fry, London 1910, 4½in (11.5cm) high.

£700–800
Daniel Bexfield

XPERT'S EYE CASTERS

sters are so-called because they 'cast' their ntents over food. They were used for sugar, pper and mustard and first appeared in the ond half of the 17th century. Single casters desirable, but complete sets even more so. se casters by Samuel Wastell are dated don 1714 and have a crest that incorporates eaf of wheat. **£2,500–3,000 pair** **Tennants**

Pierced caps can be prone to damage and wear so check for splits and repairs.
Cap should fit snugly.
Mouldings can be worn through on corners; look for soldered filling.
Foot can be pushed into base and splits can occur inside.
Examine for splits and wear to mouldings.

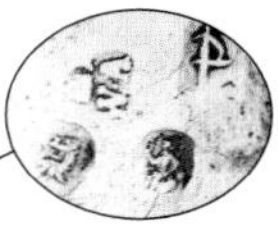

The cap should bear part marks which correspond to those on the base.

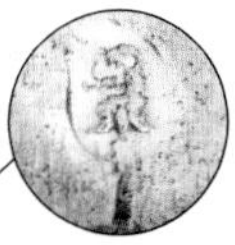

The marks should be complete and easy to read. Look inside the base to see that the punch impressions are visible and correspond. If there are no impressions the mark may have been transposed from another item, either as an outright forgery or to avoid duty.

Any crest or inscription should be nearly contemporary with the piece.

CHOCOLATE, COFFEE & TEAPOTS

A silver chocolate pot, by Henry Daniell, with a leaf-capped swan-neck spout, wooden finial later, Ireland, Dublin, 1715–20, 9¾in (25cm) high, 29oz.

£18,000–22,000 Tennants

A silver coffee pot, by J. Swift, monogrammed, London 1733, 11in (28cm) high.

£900–1,100 Sworders

A silver teapot, by Conrad Gadd, with wooden handle, wooden covering missin from finial, feet probably later, Sweden, Kristiansstad 1734, 6¾in (17cm) high.

£2,250–2,750 Bukowskis

A silver teapot, by Richard Gurney and Thomas Cook, engraved with an armorial, London 1736, 5¼in (13.5cm) high, 13½oz.

£1,500–1,800 Bearnes

A silver coffee pot, possibly by William Kidney, later-decorated with crests and rococo chasing and embossing, with artichoke finial, ebonized handle, London 1739, 9in (23cm) high, 28oz.

£1,500–1,800 Anderson & Garland

A silver coffee pot, by John Langlands, Newcastle 1798, 12in (30.5cm) high.

£2,600–3,000 Andrew Campbel

A silver teapot, by John Walton, Newcastle 1823, 7in (18cm) wide.

£525–575 Andrew Campbell

A silver teapot, by Charles Fox, London 1828, 7in (18cm) diam.

£575–650 Bourbon-Hanby

A bachelor's teapot, by W. B., with chase decoration, London 1834, 7in (18cm) wide.

£270–300 Jennifer Lloyd

A silver teapot, by Ivan Semenovich Gubkin, with palmette and shell border, ivory scroll handle and finial, Russia, Moscow 1837, 16¾oz.

£600–700 Heritage

A silver teapot, by Frederick Elkington, with bright-cut garland an ribbon-tied engraved decoration, ivory handle and finial, London 1 9¾in (24.5cm) wide, 17¼oz.

£280–350 Bearnes

ƆFFEE & TEA SERVICES

'er tea service, by William Patrick
ingham, with bright-cut engraved
ation, London 1788, 10in (25.5cm) high.
00–2,750 Andrew Campbell

A silver tea service, by John and Joseph Angel, comprising three pieces, with engraved crests, London 1835–36, 45oz.
£550–650 Gilding's

ver coffee service, by Ball, Tompkins &
, comprising three pieces, America,
York, c1850 and later, teapot 9in
ı) high, 81½oz.
0–900 Waddington's

A silver coffee service, by Ball, Tompkins & Black, comprising four pieces, embossed and chased with fruiting vines, America, New York, 1851–76, teapot 10in (25.5cm) high, 97oz.
£900–1,100 Freemans

in silver tea service, by Gorham Manufacturing Co, comprising
pieces, decorated with Medallion pattern, with applied beaded
the handles cast with ribbon-tied portrait medallions, America,
9, teapot 6in (15cm) high, 45oz.
00–1,200 Northeast Auctions

A silver tea service, by Michelsen, comprising three pieces, stamped marks, Denmark, Copenhagen, c1862, teapot 5¼in (13.5cm) high.
£320–380 Tennants

ver-gilt miniature tea service,
ce, c1870, with fitted case.
200–1,400 Bourbon-Hanby

A silver tea and coffee service, by Tiffany & Co, comprising six pieces, each monogrammed 'ERA 1893' and marked with a globe for the 1893 World's Columbian Exposition in Chicago, maker's marks, America, 1890–93, kettle and burner 11in (28cm) high.
£10,000–12,000 Northeast Auctions

CONDIMENT POTS & CRUETS

A silver Warwick cruet, the stand with a vacant lion mask and rococo cartouche, with three casters and two silver-mounted cut-glass bottles, London 1759, 8¼in (21cm) high, 31oz.

£2,750–3,250 Bearnes

A silver mustard pot, by John Langlands, Newcastle, c1774, 2½in (6.5cm) diam.

£600–700 Andrew Campbell

A George III silver mustard pot, by Peter Ann Bateman, with a reeded rim, anthem thumbpiece and blue glass liner, London 4in (10cm) high.

£300–350 Manor House Antique

A pair of silver salts, by Anders Hildén, with gilt interiors, Finland, Brahestad 1786, 3in (7.5cm) diam.

£5,000–6,000 Bukowskis

A pair of silver salts, by Craddock & Reid, the legs decorated with female masks, on scrolled feet, London 1823, 4in (10cm) diam.

£600–700 Lucy Harris

A silver mustard, by John, Henry and Charles Lias, London 1832, 3in (7.5cm) wide.

£350–400 Greystoke Antiques

A set of three silver table salts and matching spoons, by William Bateman, in the form of convolvulus flowers, with gilt bowls, two dated 1834, one 1832, 3½in (9cm) diam, 13oz.

£850–1,000 Holloway's

A silver cruet, by Henry Wilkinson, with glass pots, London/Birmingham, 1873, salt spoon Chester 1926, mustard spoon Sheffield 1922, 4½in (11.5cm) wide.

£400–450 Daniel Bexfield

A silver mustard pot, by Nathan & Hayes, with blue glass liner, Chester 1899, 2½in (6.5cm) diam.

£160–180 Greystoke Antiques

A set of four silver trencher salts, Chester 1906, 3in (7.5cm) diam, with box.

£450–500 Andrew Campbell

CUPS & GOBLETS

A silver two-handled cup, by John Hamilton, Ireland, Dublin 1736, 8½in (21.5cm) high, 41oz.

£4,750–5,750 Waddingtons

A silver-gilt two-handled cup and cover, by Gabriel Sleath, with embossed and engraved decoration, London 1740, on an ebonized stand, 10¾in (27.5cm) high.

£4,750–5,750 Sotheby's

Born in 1674, Gabriel Sleath was apprenticed to Thomas Cooper and freed in 1701 after a seven-year apprenticeship. Sleath had an extensive business in the production of hollow wares until his death in 1756, his major works being the wine cisterns in the Hermitage, St Petersburg and the Grocers' Company, London.

A silver loving cup, by John Langlands, on a pedestal foot, later embossed, Newcastle 1772, 7in (18cm) high.

£580–650 Andrew Campbell

A silver cup and spiral-fluted cover, by Louisa Courtauld and George Cowles, decorated with swags, rosettes and acanthus leaves, with reeded handles, London 1776, 16½in (42cm) high, 63oz.

£1,700–2,000 Sotheby's (O)

A silver two-handled loving cup, by Langlands & Robertson, Newcastle 1790, 12in (30.5cm) high.

£800–900 Andrew Campbell

A silver cup and cover, by Henry Chawne later-engraved with a crest and presentati inscription, with reeded handles, London 1792, 16½in (42cm) high, 52oz.

£1,000–1,200 Hy Duke

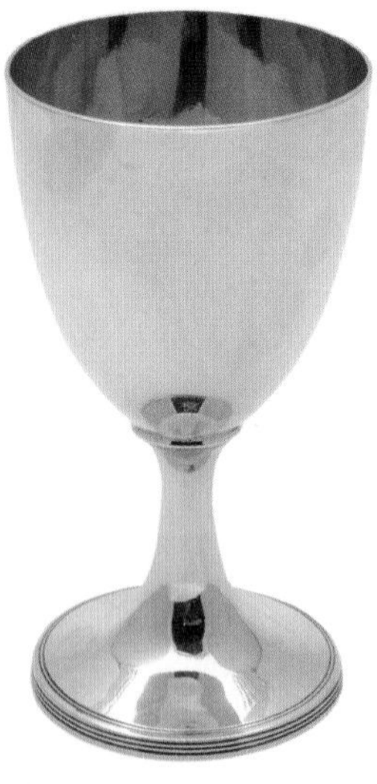

A silver goblet, by Peter, Ann and William Bateman, with gilt interior, London 1802, 6¾in (17cm) high.

£450–500 Manor House Antiques

A silver-mounted coconut cup, by Phipps & Robinson, with carved decoration, c1810, 7in (18cm) high.

£540–600 Jennifer Lloyd

A silver cup, by Harry Atkin, inscribed 'Bes Fat Beast In The Yard', Sheffield 1897, 10in (25.5cm) high, 13oz.

£400–450 Daniel Bexfield

UTLERY

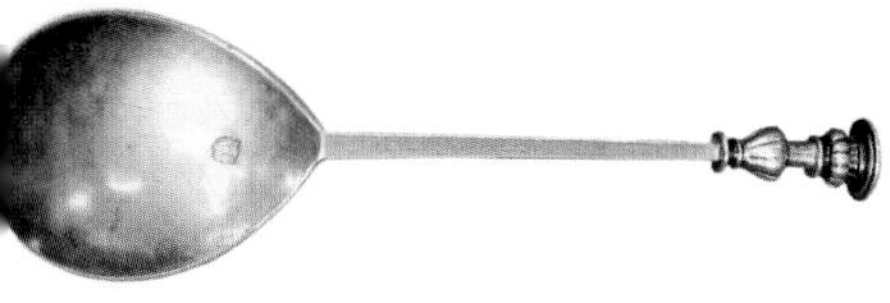

ver seal-top spoon, the gilt terminal with pricked initials 'P/TA', owl with traces of gilding, London 1586, 7in (18cm) long.
250–2,750 Hy Duke

A silver seal-top spoon, by William Dobson I, with a parcel-gilt terminal, inside of bowl and back of shaft with a fleurs-de-lys, maker's mark WD, Lewes, c1630, 6½in (16.5cm) long.
£1,300–1,600 Gorringes (L)

arles II child's silver Puritan spoon, with scratched initials 'SC' to everse and 'V' on the rattail, maker's mark IC above a chanticleer, ably London, 5½in (14cm) long, ½oz.
0–700 Woolley & Wallis

A silver basting spoon, by Michael Keating, with a hook top, Ireland, Dublin, c1770, 3½oz.
£500–600 Mealy's

ver teaspoon, by Paul Revere Jr, the handle with bright-cut wrigglework lers, the terminal with monogram 'EAT', the bowl with a leafy moulded drop, rica, Boston, 18thC, 5½in (14cm) long, 1oz.
800–3,500 Northeast Auctions

A set of six silver knives, by Julius Marianus Bergs, Sweden, Stockholm 1784, 24¾oz.
£600–700 Bukowskis

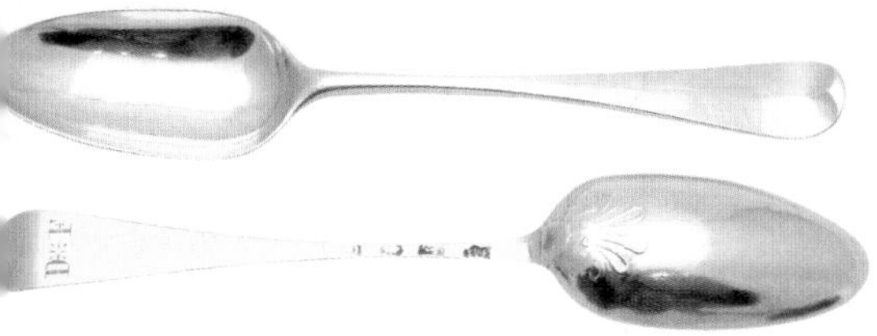

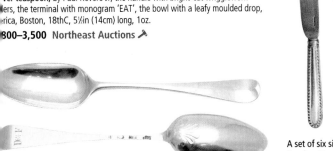

air of George III silver shell-back tablespoons, homas and William Chawner, 8in (20.5cm) long.
70–200 Greystoke Antiques

A silver basting or stuffing spoon, by William Fearn, London 1794, 12in (30.5cm) long.
£200–220 Greystoke Antiques

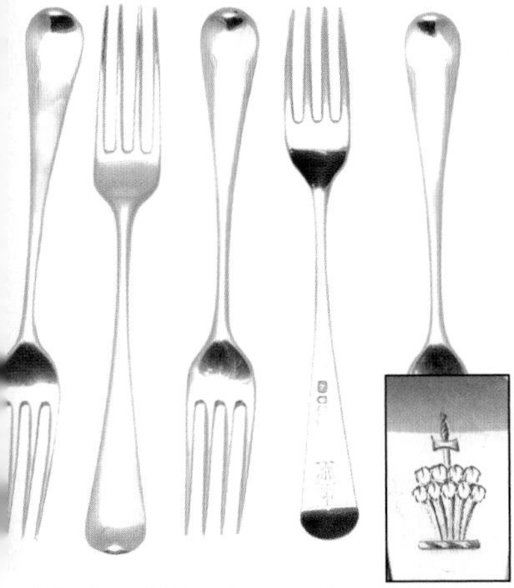

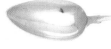

et of six silver Old English pattern dinner forks, Richard Crossley, each with a crest to the reverse, don 1787, 8in (20.5cm) long.
00–240 Manor House Antiques

A silver Fiddle pattern gravy spoon, by John Walton, Newcastle 1806, 12in (30.5cm) long.
£220–250 Andrew Campbell

A pair of silver Fiddle pattern stuffing spoons, by W. Woodman, Exeter 1826, 12in (30.5cm) long.
£300–340 Schredds

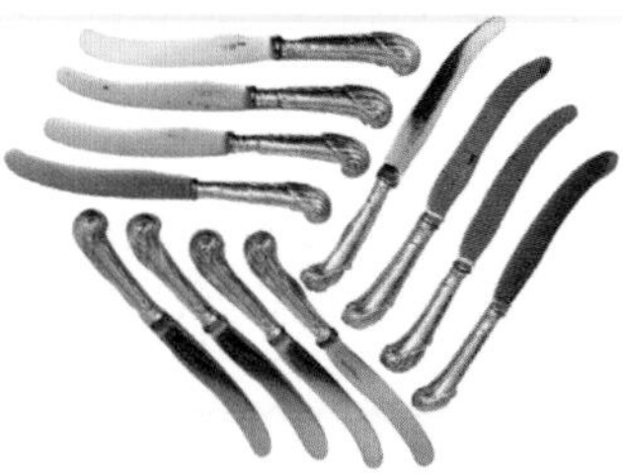

A set of 12 silver knives, by Francis Higgins, the pistol handles with spray terminals and moulded scrolls and engraved with a crest, with steel blades, London 1844.

£550–650
Netherhampton Salerooms

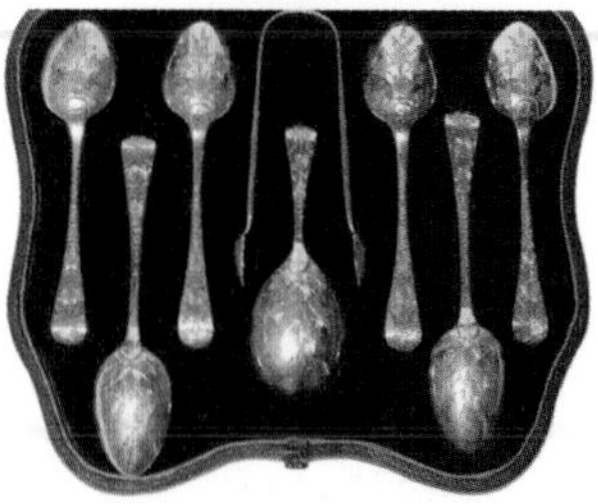

A set of silver-gilt teaspoons with sugar tongs and a sugar spoon, London 1878, 5in (12.5cm) long, with case.

£500–550 Judy & Brian Harden

A set of four silver-gilt fruit spoons, by R London 1892, with case, 11in (28cm) wic

£1,200–1,400
Paul Cranny

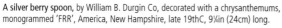

A silver berry spoon, by William B. Durgin Co, decorated with a chrysanthemums, monogrammed 'FRR', America, New Hampshire, late 19thC, 9¼in (24cm) long.

£300–350 Heritage

A silver Dresden pattern flatware servic by Whiting Manufacturing Co, America, N York, late 19thC, 3¼in (8.5cm) high, 58½

£650–800 Heritage

ESSENTIAL REFERENCE HALLMARKS

In 1300 Edward I introduced the use of a hallmark to define standards of manufacture and try to prevent fraud. Maker's marks later became mandatory and Assay offices were established across the country, although only five are in operation today: London, Birmingham, Dublin, Edinburgh and Sheffield.

- British sterling silver usually bears at least four marks – the maker's mark, standard mark, town mark and date letter. These are accompanied by a duty mark.
- Some items also bear a mark commemorating a public event or anniversary, but these are optional and not strictly hallmarks. In Britain, marks have been used to commemorate the Silver Jubilee of George V and Queen Mary in 1934–35, the coronation of Elizabeth II in 1953 and her Silver Jubilee in 1977.
- Assay marks have always been applied to both the main body and any detachable parts. These detachable parts should bear an incomplete part mark which usually included the maker's and standard mark.
- Marks on flatware are struck vertically, ie reading top to bottom rather than horizontally or left to right, to prevent them being lifted and soldered to another item. For instance, a cream jug with a flatware-type mark around its foot should be treated with suspicion.

Maker's mark
Used on silver from 1363, the early marks were signs or symbols as few people could read. In the late 17th century symbols and initials were combined, the symbols falling from use during the next 100 years. Maker's marks on sterling silver (925 parts per 1,000) show the initials of the first name and surname; those on Britannia standard (958 parts per 1,000) are the first two letters of the surname.

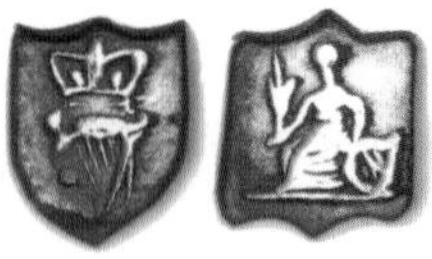

Town mark
This varied according to the assay office of the individual town. Sometimes the London mark was used on provincial silver in addition to the town mark.

Date letter
This appears in London from 1478 and later in other parts of the country. It is unique from year to year and assay office to assay office, but usually follows an alphabetical sequence. The letter is always enclosed by a shield.

Duty mark
In the form of a sovereign's head, this mark was used between 1784 and 1890 (and in Dublin from 1807) to indicate that duty has been paid on the item.

Standard mark
This indicates that the silver was of the legally required standard. From 1300 the mark for sterling silver wa a leopard's head, replaced in 1544 b a lion passant. Britannia standard is a higher standard of silver and the sterling marks were replaced by Britannia and a lion's head in profil

)ISHES

ilver sweatmeat dish, punched with ized flowers and buds and with 'SA' nogram, with shell handles, marked on rim l handles, London 1659, 9¾in (25cm) wide.

,800–3,500 Sotheby's (O)

A silver sweetmeat dish, with pricked initials 'IAH', 'IG' and scratched 'DB', on a domed foot, Denmark, Copenhagen 1727, 5¼in (13.5cm) wide.

£450–550 Woolley & Wallis

A pair of meat dishes, by Robert Breading, engraved with an armorial, crest and motto, with gadroon borders, Ireland, Dublin 1795, 14¼in (36cm) wide, 69½oz.

£3,650–4,350 Bearnes

:ilver entrée dish and cover, by Walter Brind, engraved with an norial and a motto, with leaf-wrapped handles, the base with a drooned border, London 1772, 14½in (37cm) wide, 33½oz.

:,000–2,500 Bearnes

A silver pap boat, by Hester Bateman, with a beaded border, London, 1778, 5in (12.5cm) long.

£380–425 Manor House Antiques

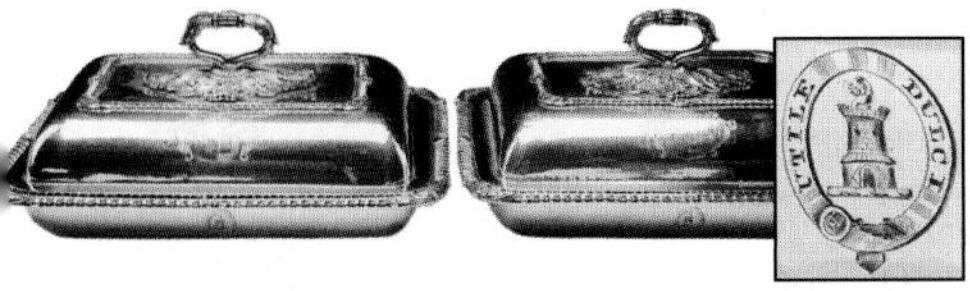

)air of silver entrée dishes and covers, possibly by John Harris, the vers with a cartouche with a coat-of-arms and a motto, the bases :h gadrooned borders and shell corners, slight repair, London 1812, ¼in (30cm) wide, 131oz.

,000–2,500 James D Julia

A set of six silver serving dishes, by Barnard & Son, London 1850, largest 20½in (52cm) wide, 290oz.

£6,000–7,000 Sotheby's (O)

silver bonbon dish, embossed with cherubs d chased with a classical scene, import ırks for London 1887, 5in (12.5cm) wide.

'20–250 Swan at Tetsworth

An embossed silver dish, by Fenton Brothers, Sheffield 1895, 9½in (24cm) wide, 31oz.

£400–500 Daniel Bexfield

A silver muffin dish, by William Hutton & Sons, London 1896, 7in (18cm) wide.

£350–400 Swan at Tetsworth

Edwardian silver butter dish and cover, Martin Hall & Co , modelled as a shell sting on coral feet, monogrammed, 10oz, effield, 5in (13cm) wide.

!50–300 Sworders

A pierced silver dish, by Whiting Manufacturing Co, modelled as a ladle, decorated with scrolling foliage, marked, America, c1910, 9¾in (25cm) long, 8½oz.

£250–300 Sworders

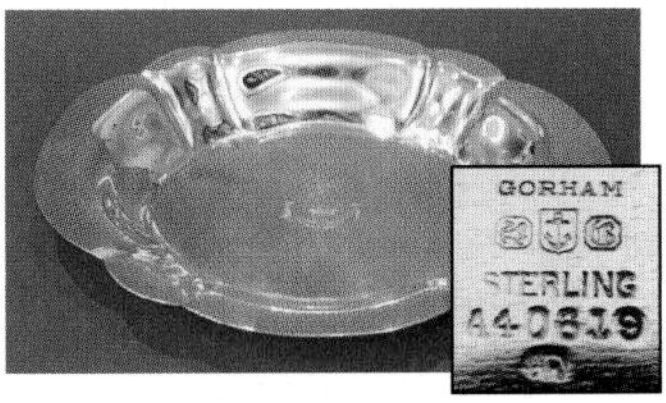

A silver dish, by Gorham Manufacturing Co, manufacturer's mark, America, c1930, 7½in (19cm) wide.

£300–350 Daniel Bexfield

FRAMES

A silver photograph frame, by William Comyns, with embossed decoration, London 1893, 8 x 6¾in (20 x 17cm).

£350–400 Riccardo Sansoni

A silver photograph frame, embossed with floral scrolls and a cartouche, Birmingham 1900, 6in (15cm) high.

£170–200 Gorringes (L)

A silver photograph frame, by H. M. H. Matthews, with embossed decoration, Birmingham, c1903, 9¼in (23.5 cm) high.

£300–350 Riccardo Sansoni

A silver photograph frame, by C. S. Green & Co, relief-decorated with a native American Indian outside a teepee, inscribed 'Feed the Fire of Friendship and the Winds will Fan the Flame', slight damage, Birmingham 1904, 11in (28cm) high.

£500–600 Woolley & Wallis

The inscription is from H. W. Longfellow's poem 'Hiawatha'.

A silver photograph frame, by M. & C. Lister Ltd, with embossed decoration of a girl on a bench by a pond, Birmingham 1906, 8½in (21cm) high.

£600–700 Woolley & Wallis

A pair of silver photograph frames, by Messrs Aitken, Aitken & Ashford, relief-decorated with fairies, imps and pixies, Birmingham 1909, 9in (23cm) high.

£1,400–1,800 Woolley & Wallis

INKWELLS & STANDS

A silver inkstand, possibly by Henry Hyde, with two ink bottles and a taperstick, the tray rim with lattice and flowerhead decoration, on scroll and shell feet, maker's mark 'HH', 1829, 9in (23cm) wide, 19oz.

£500–600 Lawrence Fine Art

A silver, gold and glass travelling inkwell, by Thomas Dicks, London 1838, 2¼in (5.5cm) diam.

£540–600 Daniel Bexfield

ver inkstand, by Gorham Manufacturing Co, the pierced gallery a cartouche, above a compartment with three sections, the cover a gadrooned top, inscribed 'Multa Paucis', America, Rhode Island 2, 7¾in (19.5cm) wide.

0–300 Heritage

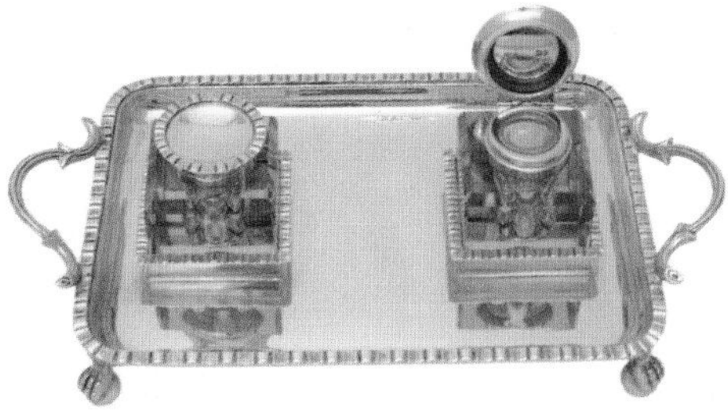

A silver inkstand, with two glass bottles, London 1898, 13in (33cm) wide.

£800–900 Grey-Harris

ver inkwell, London 1905, 5in (12.5cm) diam.

0–350 Bourbon-Hanby

A silver treasury inkstand, by Sebastian Garrard, with thumbnail decoration, on bun feet, London 1908, 9in (23cm) wide.

£2,000–2,250 Percy's

A silver inkstand, by Charles Stuart Harris & Sons, with two glass bottles, London 1909, 7¼in (18.5cm) wide, 8oz.

£250–300 Woolley & Wallis

JGS

ilver cream jug, with chinoiserie oration, maker's mark worn, 1756, n (8.5cm) high, 2oz. (65g).

00–700 Daniel Bexfield

A silver cream jug, by Benjamin Burt, inscribed 'Maria B. Motley', the base engraved 'HG' and marked 'B. Burt' , America, Boston, c1760, 3¾in (9.5cm) high, 3oz.

£2,500–3,000 Northeast Auctions

This piece is accompanied by a copy of a hand-written record of ownership passed down through the family.

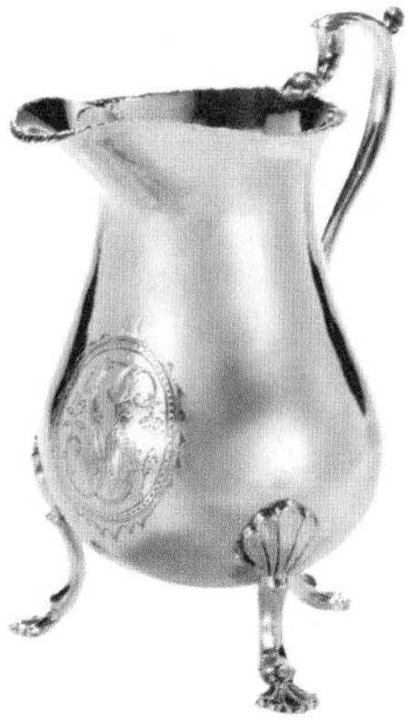

A silver cream jug, probably by Anthony Dubois, with a monogram flanked by bright-cut leafy sprays, America, Philadelphia 1780–90, 4¾in (12cm) high.

£1,500–1,800 Sotheby's (NY)

silver cream jug, by Solomon Hougham, h a gilt interior, London 1802, (10cm) high.

20–360 Greystoke Antiques

A silver hot milk jug, the cover with a button finial, maker's mark 'IIM', Portugal, Lisbon, c1820, 6¾in (17cm) high.

£450–550 Sotheby's

A silver creamer, with an embossed band of eagles, hunting trophies and portrait medallions, with a gilt interior and a burwood scroll handle, Russia, Moscow 1829, 3¼in (8.5cm) high, 9¾oz.

£475–575 Heritage

A silver hot water jug, by B. Smith, engraved with an armorial, with a leaf-capped reeded scroll handle, the cover with a flower finial, London 1830, 9¼in (23.5cm) high, 29oz.

£700–850 Sworders

A silver cream jug, by Edward and John Barnard, London 1856, 5in (12.5cm) high, 7¼oz.

£580–650 Daniel Bexfield

A silver cream jug, 1886, 4¼in (11cm) hig

£340–380 Shapiro

A silver cream jug, by Thomas Prime, Birmingham 1891, 3½in (9cm) high.

£150–175 Greystoke Antiques

A silver and cut-glass jug, by John Heath and John Middleton, Birmingham 1895, 8in (20.5cm) high.

£280–325 Andrew Campbell

A silver jug, by Howard & Co, with a C-scr foliate handle, the spout decorated with acanthus, slight wear, America, New York, c1902, 12¼in (31.5cm) high.

£800–950 Heritage

MIRRORS

A silver mirror, with a crested medallion, the corners with acanthus leaves, maker's mark 'WE', c1690, 24½in (62cm) high.

£3,750–4,250 Sotheby's (O)

A silver hand mirror, France, c1880, 10¼in (26cm) long.

£575–650 Daniel Bexfield

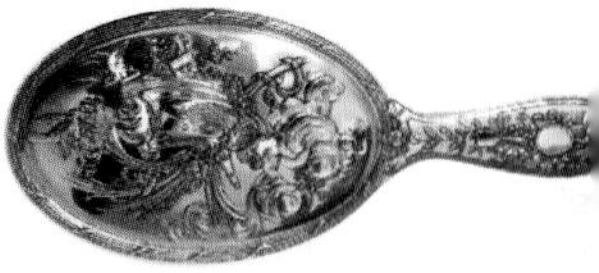

A silver hand mirror, by Boulanger, France, c1890, 12in (30.5cm) long.

£400–450 Daniel Bexfield

A silver dressing table mirror, by William Comyns, pierced and embossed with birds and grotesque masks, London 1896, 11in (28cm) high, in a case.

£600–700 Sworders

IUGS & TANKARDS

lver tankard, by Arvid Falk, chased with , figures and horses, on ball feet, Sweden, kholm, c1675, 5¾in (14.5cm) high.

000–5,000 Bukowskis

A Britannia standard silver mug, by Thomas Parr, with scroll handle, inscribed 'WB', London 1713, 5½in (14cm) high, 20oz.

£1,500–1,800 Sotheby's (O)

A silver mug, by John Kincaid, with crest, London 1746, 4in (10cm) high, 7¾oz.

£280–350 Waddington's

lver mug, by Thomas Grant, with scroll dle, inscribed 'JGL', marked, America, ssachusetts, c1770, 6in (15cm) high, 11oz.

500–4,250 Northeast Auctions

A silver mug, by Joshua Jackson, London 1781, 3¼in (8.5cm) high.

£600–700 Daniel Bexfield

A pair of silver mugs, by Peter, Ann and William Bateman, each ring-turned and engraved with a stork, London 1801, 5¾in (14.5cm) high, 42oz.

£3,000–3,500 James D Julia

ilver mug, by John Emes, with gilt interior, idon 1801, 3in (7.5cm) high, 10oz.

50–1,000 Hy Duke

A pair of silver tankards, by John Clarke, each engraved with a crest between reeded bands, London 1807, 5¾in (14.5cm) high, 31oz.

£2,250–2,750 Sotheby's (O)

silver christening mug, chased with wers, maker's mark WK, London 1831, 1 (10cm) high.

:30–260 Jennifer Lloyd

A silver mug, by Edward Charles Brown, decorated with foliage, London 1894, 4in (10cm) high.

£425–475 Shapiro

A silver mug, by Harry Atkins, with embossed decoration, Sheffield 1897, 3½in (9cm) high.

£130–150 Greystoke Antiques

PINCUSHIONS

A silver pincushion, in the form of a recumbent cow, Sheffield 1837, 2½in (6.5cm) high.

£250–300 Andrew Hartley

A silver pincushion, in the form of a shoe, cast with putti, probably Holland, re-assay mark for London 188 5in (12.5cm) long, 4½oz.

£230–380 Holloway's

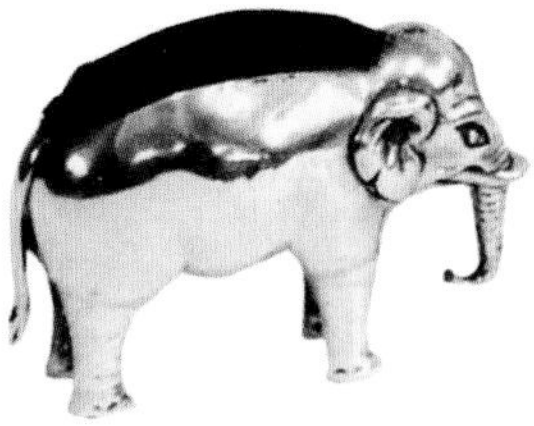

A silver pincushion, in the form of an elephant, Birmingham 1905, 2in (5cm) long.

£200–250 Andrew Hartley

A silver pincushion, by Adie & Lovekin, in the form of a pig, Birmingham 1905, 2in (5cm) long.

£100–120 Woolley & Wallis

A silver pincushion, in the form of a rabbi Birmingham 1906, 2in (5cm) high.

£350–425 Andrew Hartley

A silver pincushion, in the form of a watering can, Sheffield 1906, 3in (7.5cm) high.

£675–750 Shapiro

A silver pincushion, possibly by H. V. P & Co, in the form of a camel, maker's mark rubbed, Birmingham 1906, 2¾in (7cm) high.

£350–425 Bearnes

A silver pincushion, by Boots Pure Drug Co in the form of a fledgling bird, Birmingham 1908, 2in (5cm) high.

£675–750 Daniel Bexfield

SALVERS, TRAYS & WAITERS

A silver salver, by William Lukin, engraved with a crest within a moulded border, London 1706, 8in (20.5cm) diam, 9oz.

£1,000–1,200 Bearnes

A silver salver, by W. Aytoun, with a bath border, Scotland, 1737, 7¾in (19.5cm) dia

£1,100–1,250 Schredds

A bath border consists of moulded applied pairs of shallow curves meeting at a point intersected by short straight sections. It is used for waiters and salvers.

A silver waiter, with flat chasing and ngraved coat-of-arms, maker's mark listorted, London 1745, 7in (18cm) diam.

:225–275 Woolley & Wallis

A silver waiter, by John Robinson, decorated with a coat-of-arms, husk and scroll border and flat chasing, London 1750, 6¾in (17cm) diam, 8oz.

£280–320 Woolley & Wallis

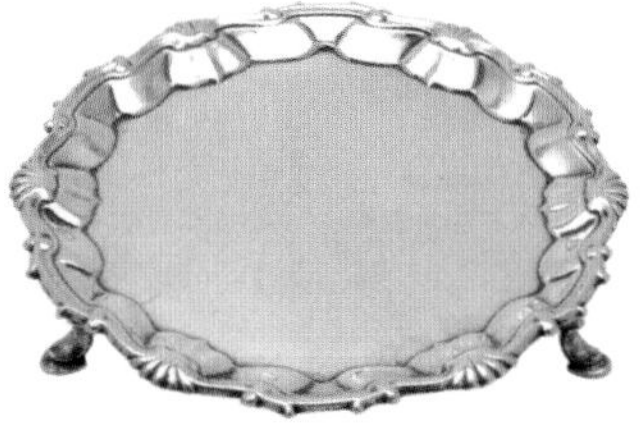

A silver waiter, by W. I., London 1753, 7in (18cm) diam.

£230–260 Jennifer Lloyd

silver salver, by Isaac Cookson, with a nell and scroll border, with presentation scription, armorial later, on hoof feet, ewcastle 1753, 12in (30.5cm) diam, 29oz.

450–550 Hy Duke

A silver waiter, by Richard Rugg, on three claw-and-ball feet, London 1774, 6in (15cm) diam.

£540–600 Andrew Campbell

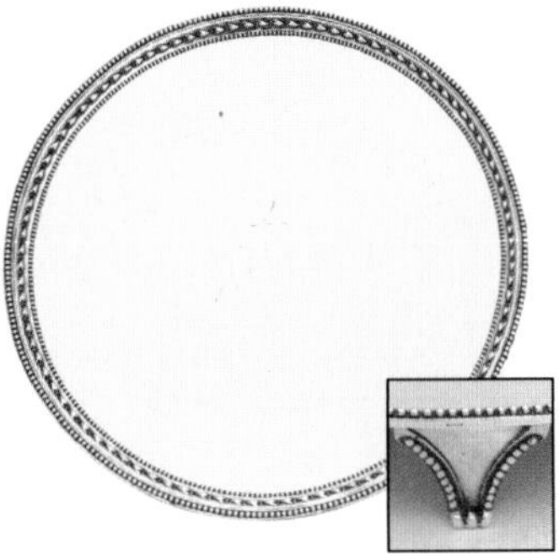

A silver salver, by Hannam & Crouch, with beaded edging, London 1786, 12¼in (31cm) diam.

£1,800–2,000 Schredds

silver tray, by Solomon Hougham, with engraved borders and a vacant rtouche, London 1802, 21½in (54.5cm) wide, 58oz.

1,600–2,000 Sotheby's (O)

A silver salver, by Hunt & Roskell, on four feet, London 1866, 12in (30.5cm) diam.

£650–750 Greystoke Antiques

silver tea tray, by Howard & Co, with a gadroon and engraved initials, America, New York, c1884, in (66cm) wide, 157oz.

,400–1,750 Sotheby's (O)

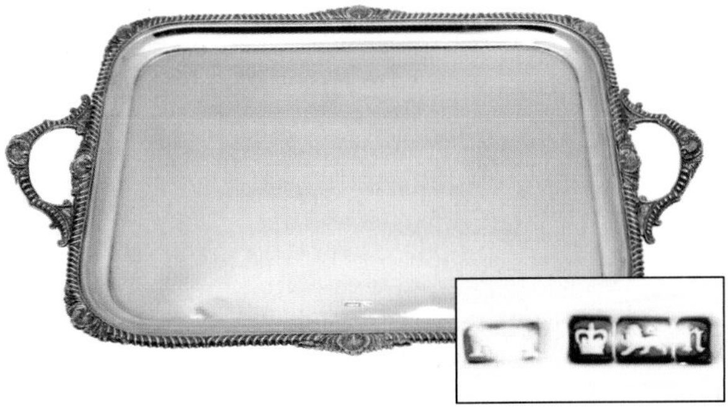

A silver tray, by Harry Atkins, with gadroon and shell decoration, Sheffield 1905, 25in (63.5cm) wide.

£1,800–2,000 Greystoke Antiques

SAUCE & CREAM BOATS

A silver sauce boat, by Paul Crespin, with crest, London 1744, 9in (23cm) wide, 19½oz.

£3,000–3,500 Waddington's

A silver sauce boat, on cabriole legs and hoof feet, crested and initialled, maker's mark possibly 'J.W.', Dublin, mid-18thC, 6¼in (16cm) wide, 5oz.

£750–900 Bearnes

A pair of silver sauce boats, by Daniel Smith and Robert Sharp, London 1761, 9in (23cm) wide, 25¼oz.

£3,250–3,650 Daniel Bexfield

A pair of sauce boats, possibly by Richard Tudor, each chased with rural scenes and animals and on three feet, one damaged, Ireland, Dublin 1765, 8½in (21.5cm) wide, 30oz.

£4,750–5,750 Mealy's

A silver sauce boat, by John Langlands, with scroll handle and pad feet, Newcastle 1769, 6in (15cm) wide.

£350–400 Manor House Antiques

A silver cream boat, by Pehr Zethelius, chased with a flowering sprig, with gilt interior, Sweden, Stockholm 1774, 8in (20.5cm) wide.

£3,000–3,500 Bukowskis

A silver sauce boat, by William Bond, Ireland, Dublin 1787, 7in (18cm) wide.

£700–800 Andrew Campbell

A silver sauce boat, by Tiffany & Co, with repoussé decoration and acanthus handle terminating in a ram's head, America, New York, 1875–76, 7¾in (19.5cm) wide.

£1,750–2,000 Heritage

A silver sauce boat, by Tiffany & Co, the rim cast with scrolls, with monogram and inscription, America, 1890–94, 3¾in (9.5cm) high, 8oz.

£350–425 Northeast Auctions

A pair of silver sauce boats, Continental, c1900, 9in (23cm) wide, 32

£1,650–1,850 Daniel Bexfield

ERVING IMPLEMENTS

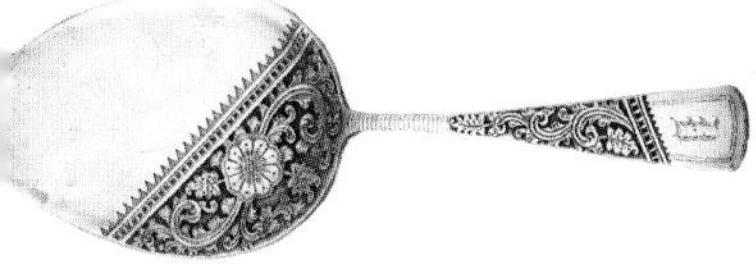

lver cake server, by Gorham Manufacturing Co, orated with a Persian-style pattern, America, Rhode nd, c1885, 9½in (24.5cm) long.

)0–850 Heritage

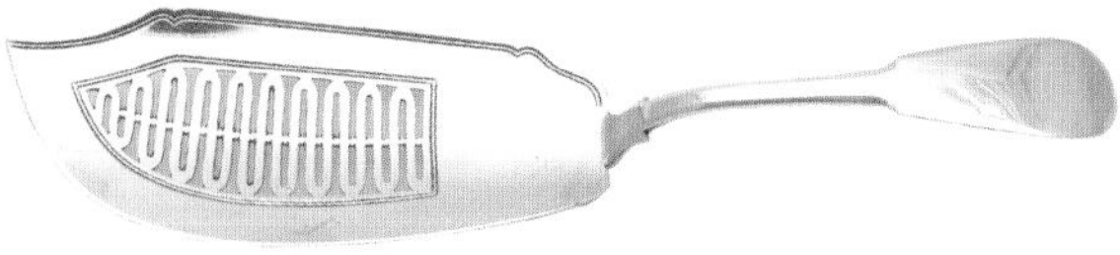

A silver Fiddle pattern fish slice, by Richard Turner, London 1806, 11½in (29cm) long.

£90–100 Manor House Antiques

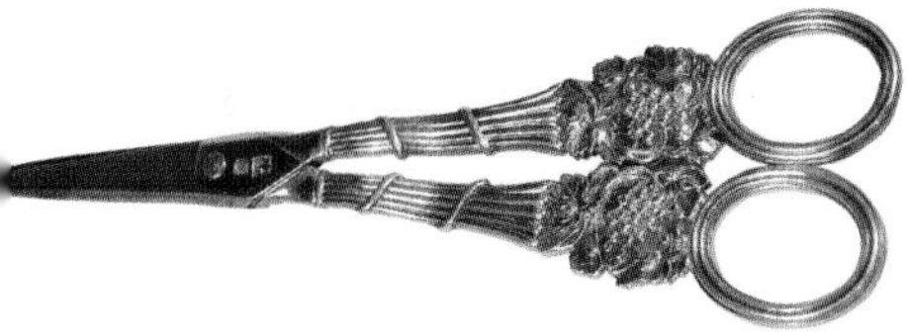

air of silver-gilt grape scissors, by B. & J. Smith, decorated with s, London 1808, 7in (17.5cm) long.

)0–700 Sworders

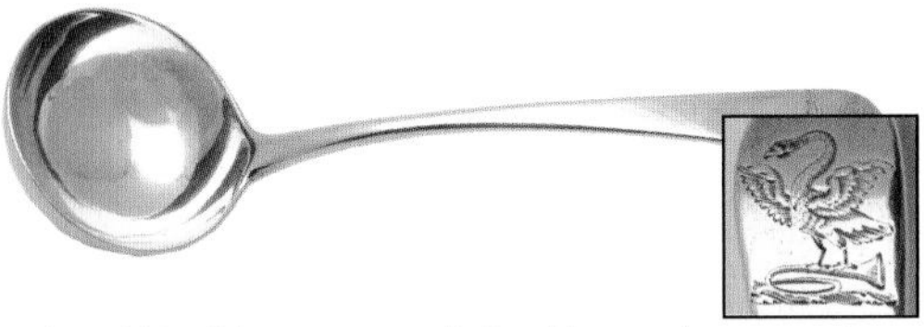

A silver Old English pattern sauce ladle, with a swan/trumpet crest, London 1768, 7in (18cm) long.

£115–130 Manor House Antiques

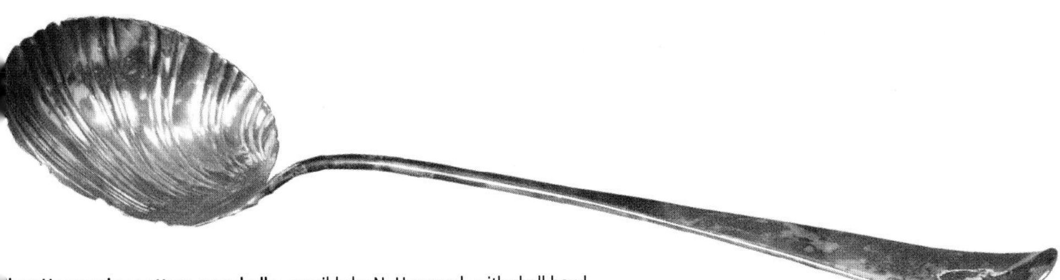

lver Hanoverian pattern soup ladle, possibly by N. Horwood, with shell bowl, nogrammed and crested, London 1760, 14¾in (37.5cm) long.

25–400 Sworders

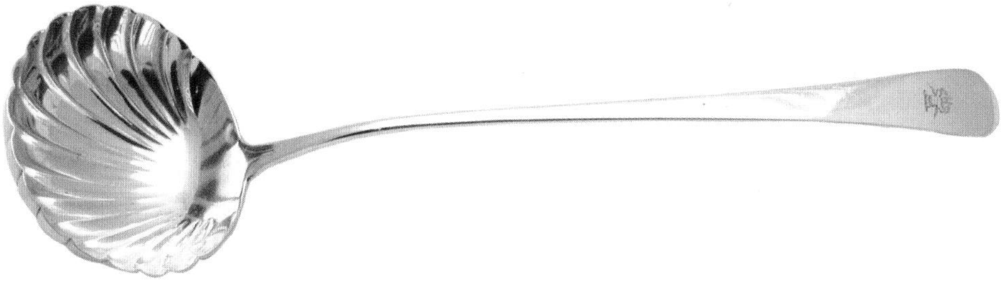

ilver Old English pattern soup ladle, by William Sumner, with a scallop bowl, London 1787, 13in (33cm) long.

70–300 Manor House Antiques

ilver Fiddle pattern marrow scoop, by Barber, Cattle & North, sed with a crest, York 1830, 9in (23cm) long.

00–500 Andrew Hartley

et of 11 parcel-gilt oyster forks, Gorham Manufacturing Co, ased and engraved with sprays of flowers, America, New York,)00, 5in (12.5cm) long, 6oz, in a fitted case.

50–800 Tennants

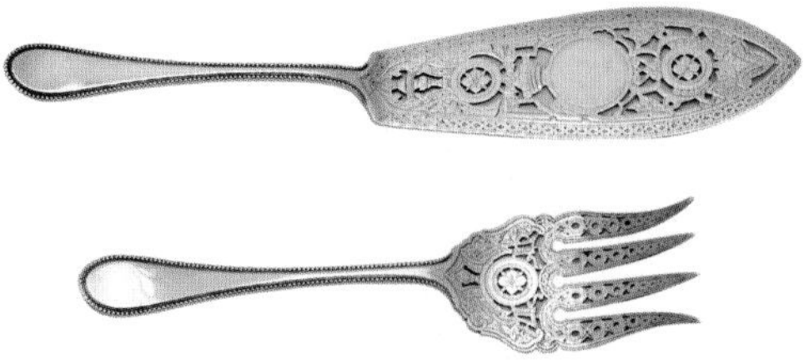

A pair of silver fish servers, by Martin Hall & Co, Sheffield 1862, 13in (33cm) long.

£220–250 Greystoke Antiques

A pair of silver servers, by Reed & Barton, America, Massachusetts, c1900, 10in (25.5cm) long, 11oz.

£150–180 Waddington's

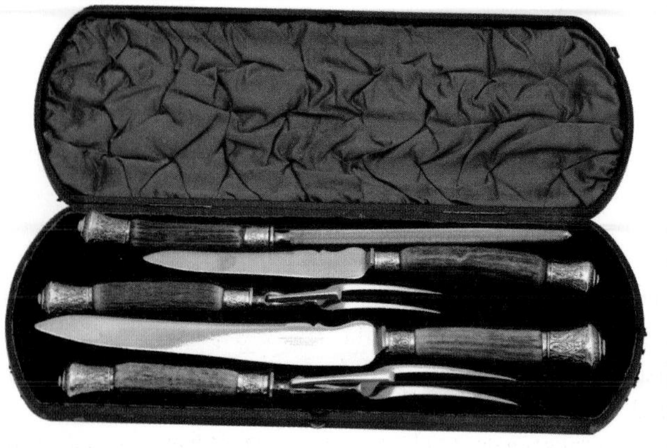

A silver-mounted steel carving set, by Joseph Braham, comprising five pieces, with stag-horn handles, in original leather case, Sheffield 1880, 17in (43cm) wide.

£350–385 Greystoke Antiques

A pair of silver servers, America, c1900, 9½in (24cm) long, 8¾oz.

£200–250 Waddington's

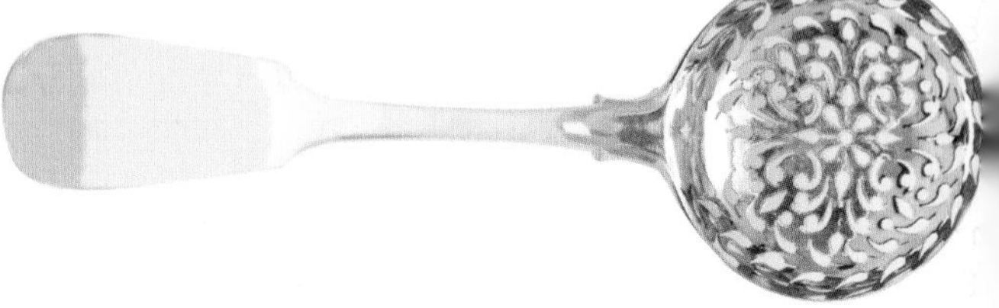

A silver sifter spoon, by William Eaton, London 1833, 7in (18cm) long.

£100–120 Greystoke Antiques

A silver presentation set, by Christian John Reid II, comprising butter knife, caddy spoon, sugar spoon and sugar tongs, Newcastle 1869, 9in (23cm) wide, in a fitted case.

£425–475 Andrew Campbell

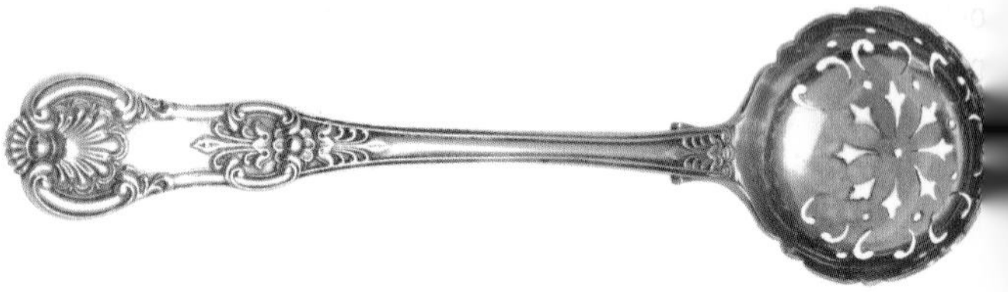

A silver Queen's pattern sifter spoon, by J. A., Scotland, Glasgow 1834, 7in (18cm) long.

£100–110 Manor House Antiques

A silver Fiddle pattern straining spoon, by John Pittar, Ireland, Dublin 1809, 13in (33cm) long, 5oz.

£400–500 Andrew Hartley

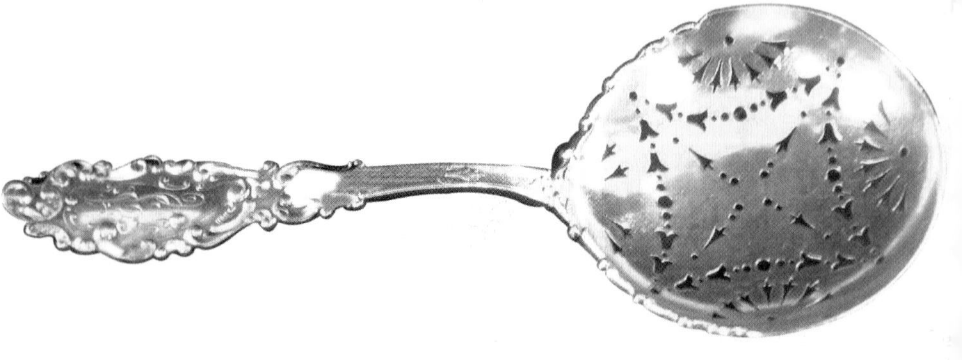

A silver-gilt pea serving spoon, by Gorham Manufacturing Co, America, 1880, 8¼in (21cm) long.

£300–350 Alter Silver Gallery

NUFF BOXES

HE INTRODUCTION OF TOBACCO in the 16th century created a demand for tightly-closed pocket-sized containers in which to carry ground acco, or snuff. The huge variety of materials used snuff boxes gives endless scope for collectors, the most popular material was silver, the interior ıg gilded to resist corrosion. These boxes were n engraved with inscriptions and testimonials, ch can add to the historical interest of the piece. ger boxes were designed for table use and, as they e less likely to be become worn with use or oped, can often be found in good condition. though snuff boxes of the 17th and early 18th turies are occasionally found, it is those of the mid- h to 19th centuries that are more common. By the 18th century snuff box manufacture was centred irmingham and, although mass-produced, the lity and variety of design was good. A prolific ker was Nathaniel Mills, active from about 1825 to i0, whose standard of work was always high, even modest pieces. His speciality was the manufacture castle-top' boxes (see page 347), so-called because y are decorated with scenes of castles, notable ıses, churches and historic buildings. A box with of the more common views, such as Newstead oey or Windsor Castle, could fetch £350–500 and es for these have remained steady for a few years. Boxes with rare views such as Bar Gate, Southampton, have increased in value, particularly if the condition is good, and one should expect to pay £1,200–1,500 for such a piece.

Snuff boxes were intended for everyday use, often in social situations, so they were prone to wear. It is important to check for damaged joints, worn engraving and inscriptions, holes, splits and rubbed corners. Any piece that appears to have been restored should be avoided. Small boxes, often with rounded corners, sometimes curved to fit the waistcoat pocket, are frequently seen. These come in a huge variety of shapes with engraved, engine-turned or ribbed decoration and make an interesting collecting field. A box of this type can be found for about £150–350, but value depends on attractiveness of design and condition is vital.

The variety of snuff boxes made on the Continent is equally large. The superb gold, enamelled and bejewelled boxes produced in France and Switzerland can fetch four-figure sums but many high-quality examples that were produced in Russia, where niello enamel is a speciality, are available at more modest prices. Continental snuff boxes can often be found for comparatively small sums and offer great potential for an interesting and varied collection, as can be seen in the following pages.

Hugh Gregory

lver snuff box, the cover inset with a fabric medallion, ground engraved with birds and leafy scrolls, the base n putti, maker's mark, 1680–90, 2¾in (7cm) wide.
,000–1,200 **Sotheby's (NY)**

A silver snuff box, in the form of a heart engraved with an eagle, with initials IC, America, 18thC, 1¾in (4.5cm) long, 5oz.
£4,000–5,000 **Northeast Auctions**

A silver snuff box, with chased reserves of shells and scrolls, gilt interior, maker's mark I&R, possibly altered from Lothian & Robertson, Scotland, 1750–60, 2in (5cm) high.
£2,800–3,500
Woolley & Wallis

ilver-mounted stone snuff box, c1780, (7.5cm) wide.
10–125 **Mostly Boxes**

A silver snuff box, by James Kennedy, Ireland, Dublin, c1785, 3in (7.5cm) wide.
£2,250–2,500 **J. W. Weldon**

A coin silver snuff box, by Joseph Anthony, America, Philadelphia, late 18thC, 3¼in (8.5cm) long.
£170–200 **Heritage**

SNUFF BOXES

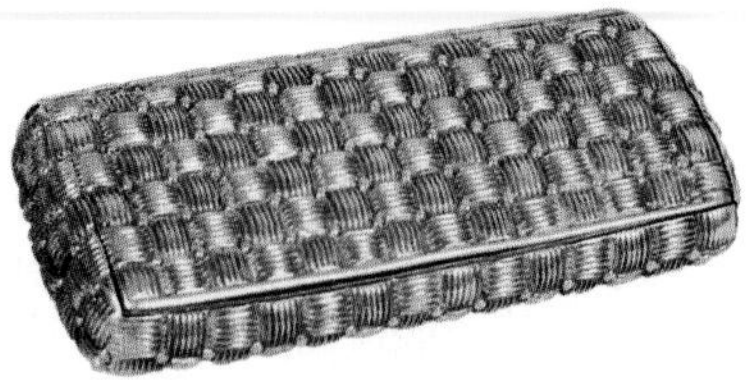

A silver snuff box, with basket-weave pattern and gilt interior, London 1803, 3in (7.5cm) wide.

£325–400 Greenslade Taylor Hunt

A silver snuff box, by Joseph Ash I, decorated with a hunting scene London 1809, 3¼in (8.5cm) wide.

£1,200–1,400 Daniel Bexfield

A silver-mounted mother-of-pearl snuff box, early 19thC, 3in (7.5cm) wide.

£120–140 Long Street Antiques

A silver table snuff box, by John Shaw, Birmingham 1817, 3½in (9cm) wide.

£1,300–1,500 Daniel Bexfield

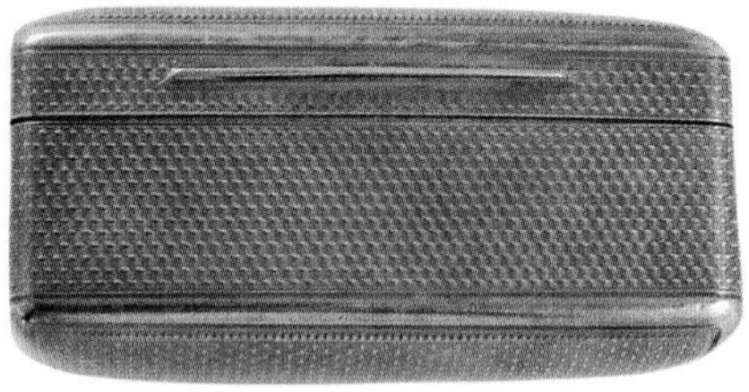

A silver-gilt snuff box, by A. J. Strachan, with engine-turned decoration, London 1818, 3¼in (8.5cm) long, .

£350–425 Woolley & Wallis

A silver snuff box, by John Linnit, the cover embossed with a pedlar, with gilt interior, London 1825, 4¾in (10cm) wide, 6½oz.

£2,000–2,500 Sotheby's (NY)

A silver snuff box, by Thomas Shaw, Birmingham 1826, 3in (7.5cm) wide, 2¾oz.

£300–350 Waddington's

A parcel-gilt and niello snuff box, possibly by I. Kaltykov, assay master Nikolay Dubrov the cover depicting Peter the Great on horseback, with Russian inscription 'To Pete Catherine II', the sides with architectural scenes, the base with military trophies, Russia, Moscow 1829, 1¼in (3.5cm) wide.

£1,100–1,300 Sworders

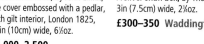

A silver table snuff box, by Nathaniel Mills, Birmingham 1834, 3½in (9cm) wide.

£2,400–2,700 Daniel Bexfield

A silver snuff box, by Joseph Wilmore, in the form of a fox mask, with engine-turne cover, chased foliate border and gilt interior, Birmingham 1835, 3½in (9cm) wide.

£4,000–5,000 Woolley & Wallis

ver castle-top snuff box, by Joseph Wilmore, the cover with
ew of Dryburgh Abbey, the base with initials, Birmingham 1835,
(7cm) wide.

0–1,000 Woolley & Wallis

A silver-gilt snuff box, by J. W., with engine-turned decoration and a cartouche with a monogram, interior with an inscription, Scotland, Glasgow 1836, 3¼in (8.5cm) wide.

£280–350 Hy Duke

lver snuff box, by Joseph Wilmore, with presentation inscription
in a border of Masonic emblems, with gilt interior, Birmingham
7, 3¾in (9.5cm) wide.

000–1,200 Woolley & Wallis

A silver snuff box, by Nathaniel Mills, with engine-turned decoration and cartouche with a monogram, Birmingham 1847, 3½in (9cm) wide, 4oz.

£450–550 Andrew Hartley

lver-mounted cowrie shell snuff box,
nogrammed 'PH', America, 19thC,
n (4cm) wide.

50–800 Heritage

A silver snuff box, embossed with chinoiserie scenes, with silver-gilt interior, Continental, 19thC, 2in (5.5cm) wide.

£160–200 Heritage

A silver and niello snuff box, the cover etched with a village, silver-gilt interior worn, Russia, Moscow 1856, 2½in (6.5cm) wide.

£150–180 Heritage

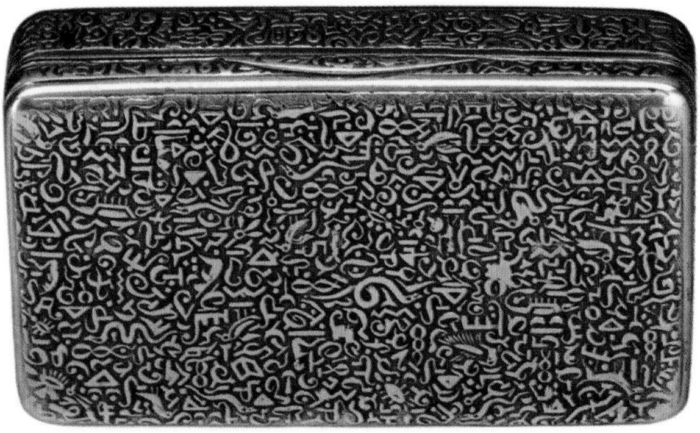

ilver snuff box, by Karl Verlin, decorated with hieroglyphics, with silver-gilt interior, Russia,
Petersburg, c1880, 3in (7.5cm) wide.

50–800 Heritage

A silver snuff box, by Fischmeister, the cover set with a porcelain plaque depicting two young girls, Austro-Hungarian, late 19th century, 2½in (6.5cm) wide.

£300–350 Woolley & Wallis

TEA CADDIES

A silver tea caddy, by Peter Archambo, London 1723, 4¼in (11cm) high.

£3,500–4,250 Sotheby's (O)

A silver tea caddy, Holland, Amsterdam 1767, 4¾in (12cm) high.

£2,000–2,250 Daniel Bexfield

A pair of silver tea caddies, applied with Oriental figures, shells and scrolls, one with marks for John Welding or James Wiburd, London 1778, 5¼in (14cm) high, 39½oz.

£2,500–3,000 Sotheby's (O)

A silver tea caddy, by George M. Jackson and David Fullerton, London 1897, 4in (10cm) high.

£200–230 Greystoke Antiques

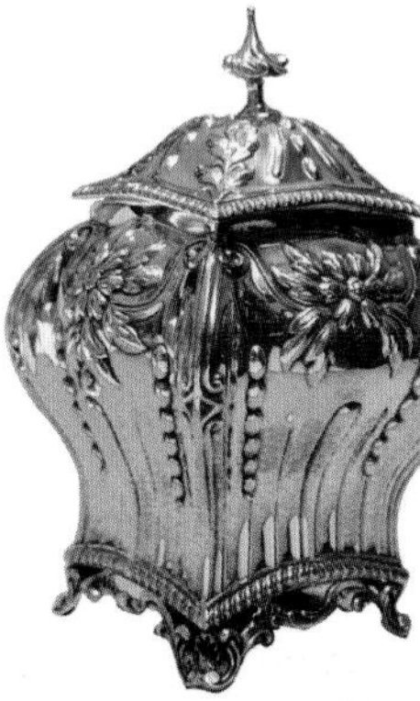

A silver tea caddy, by W. Fordham and A. Faulkner, Sheffield 1908, 6in (15cm) high, 9½oz.

£1,100–1,250 Daniel Bexfield

A silver tea caddy, by Roberts & Belk, Sheffield 1912, 4½in (11.5cm) high, 5¾oz.

£540–600 Daniel Bexfield

TOAST RACKS

A silver toast rack, by John Emes, London 1802, 6¼in (16cm) high, 5¾oz.

£225–275 Waddington's

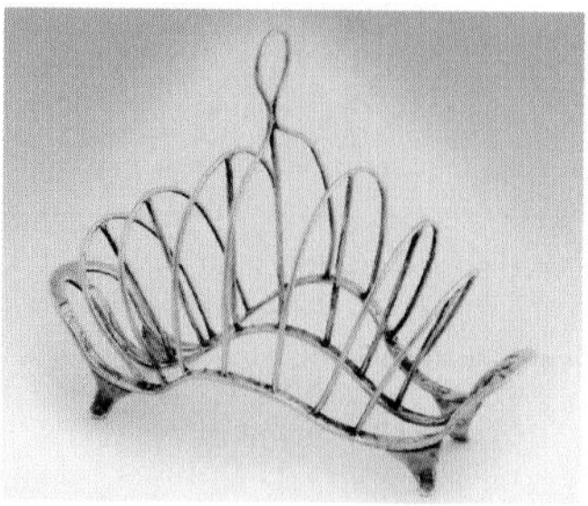

A silver toast rack, by William Welch, Exeter 1802, 8in (20.5cm) long, 7½oz.

£350–425 Bearnes

A silver toast rack, by Richard Sawyer Jr, Ireland, Dublin 1831, 6in (15cm) wide, 11½

£450–550 Netherhampton Salerooms

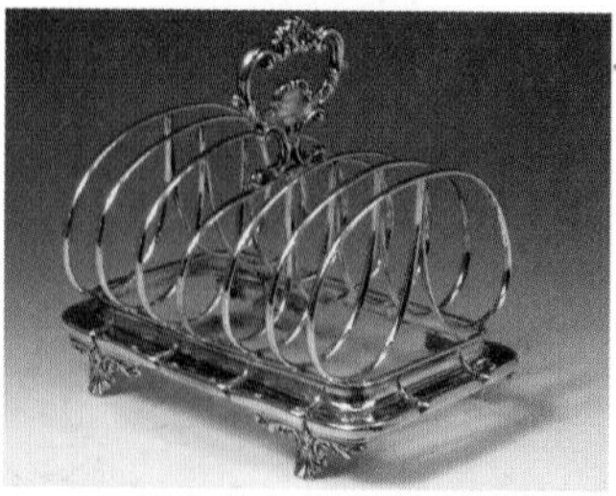

A silver toast rack, by William Bateman, on shell feet, London 1837, 6¾in (17cm) wide.

£350–425 Sworders

A silver toast rack, cast with fruit and masks, maker's mark indistinct, London 1868, 7½in (19cm) wide.

£250–300 Woolley & Wallis

A silver toast rack, by J. Bradbury & J. Henderson, London 1878, 6¼in (16cm) high

£600–700 Daniel Bexfield

UREENS

ilver soup tureen and cover, by Thomas in, the cover with a lion finial, on lion-sk and paw feet, 1741, 17in (43cm) wide.
,000–8,500 Gorringes (L)

A pair of silver sauce tureens, London 1790, 8in (20.5cm) wide.
£2,500–2,750 Andrew Campbell

A pair of silver soup tureens, by John Houle, the covers with spiral fluting, the bases engraved with an armorial, on lion-paw feet, London 1818, 17in (43cm) wide, 342oz.
£25,000–30,000 Tennant's

'ESTA CASES

ilver vesta/snuff case, the hinged cover losing two compartments, one with ker, Birmingham 1867, 2in (5cm) wide.
00–250 Andrew Hartley

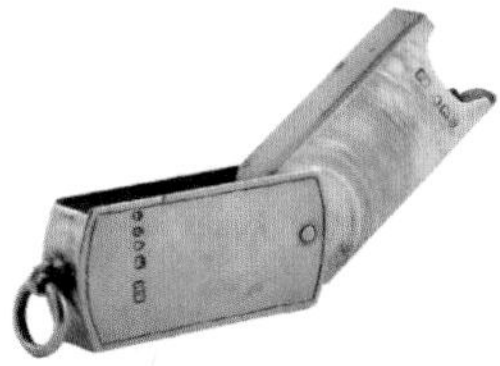

A silver vesta case, by Sampson Mordan, with sliding compartment and ring attachment, London 1880.
£175–200 Woolley & Wallis

A silver vesta case, by W. F. Wright, enamelled with the head of a terrier, applied gold monogram, London 1896.
£225–275 Woolley & Wallis

silver vesta case, by David & Lionel Spiers, the form of a mussel, Birmingham 1897, (5cm) long.
,100–1,250 Daniel Bexfield

A silver and enamel vesta case, Birmingham 1903, 2in (5cm) high.
£1,100–1,250 Shapiro

A silver vesta case, by E. Smith & W. Bartlam, Birmingham 1908, 1¾in (4.5cm) long.
£200–230 Daniel Bexfield

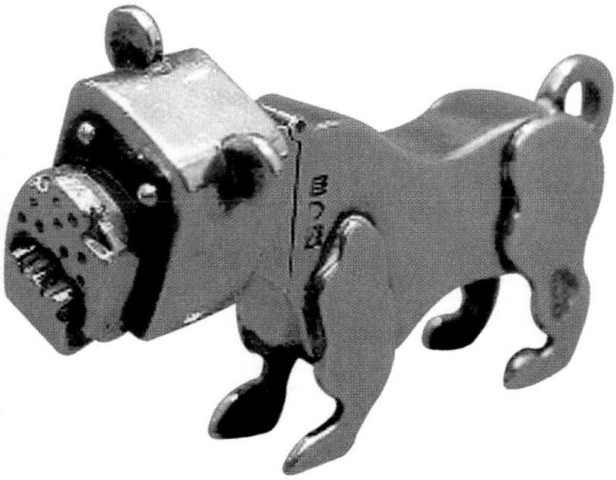

silver vesta case, by Goldsmiths & Silversmiths Co, in the form of a dog, London 07, 2in (5cm) long.
,750–4,250 Daniel Bexfield

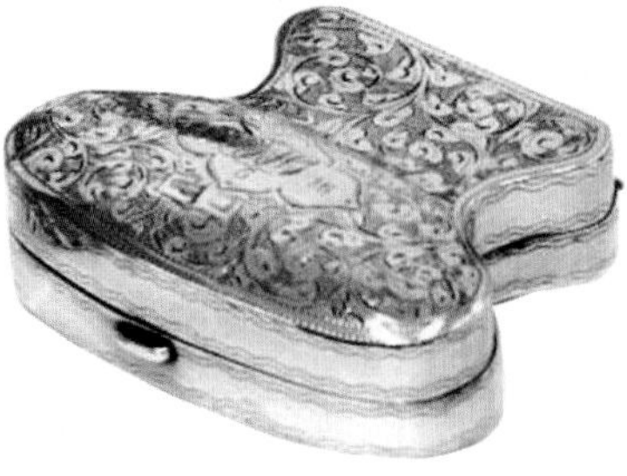

An Edwardian silver vesta case, chased with foliate scrolls, the hinged cover enclosing compartments for matches and pipe top, 2¾in (7cm) wide.
£280–350 Andrew Hartley

VINAIGRETTES

A silver-gilt vinaigrette, by John Reily, with engine-turned decoration, London 1815, 1½in (3.5cm) wide.

£200–250 Woolley & Wallis

A silver vinaigrette, by Samuel Pemberton, with engraved decoration, initialled 'GR', the grille pierced with flowers, Birmingham 1817, 1¼in (3cm) wide.

£180–220 Woolley & Wallis

A parcel-gilt vinaigrette, by Joseph Wilmor in the form of the Royal crown, the grille pierced with flowers and scrolls, Birminghar 1820, 1¼in (3cm) wide, with a morocco cas

£2,200–2,800 Woolley & Wallis

This vinaigrette was probably made to commemorate the Coronation of King George

A silver vinaigrette, by Thomas Shaw, the cover with an engine-turned panel, monogram and floral border, Birmingham 1827, 4in (10cm) wide.

£475–525 Anthony Green

A silver locket vinaigrette, by Lawrence & Co, Birmingham 1829, 1in (2.5cm) diam.

£540–600 Daniel Bexfield

A silver vinaigrette, by Nathaniel Mills, depict Windsor Castle in relief within raised floral borders, Birmingham 1840, 1½in (4cm) wide

£1,000–1,200 Woolley & Wallis

A silver vinaigrette, by Yapp & Woodward, with engraved decoration, Birmingham 1844, 1¼in (3cm) wide.

£150–180 Woolley & Wallis

A silver vinaigrette, in the form of an articulated fish, with garnet eyes, Germany, mid-19thC, 3¼in (8.5cm) long.

£300–350 Heritage

A silver vinaigrette, by George Unite, with engine-turned decoration and crest, with gilt interior, Birmingham 1853, 1¾in (4.5cm) long.

£170–200 Woolley & Wallis

A silver vinaigrette, by Edward Smith, the engine-turned cover with monogram, Birmingham 1864, 1½in (4cm) wide, ½oz.

£150–180 Penrith Farmers' & Kidd's

A silver vinaigrette, in the form of a curling stone, the silver-gilt interior with pierced scroll grille, suspension chain with loop, America, late 19thC, 1in (3cm) diam.

£200–240 Heritage

GLASS

LE, SPIRIT & WINE GLASSES

ner, the stem applied with erry prunts below an iled band, on an everted with spun trailing, Germany, C, 8in (20.5cm) high.

00–6,000
eby's (Am)

A wine glass, the funnel bowl with a teared solid base and collar over a teared triple-knopped stem and folded conical foot, c1720, 5¼in (13.5cm) high.

£1,500–1,800
Woolley & Wallis

A heavy baluster goblet, with a trumpet bowl, on a tiered inverted baluster stem and folded foot, c1700, 5in (12.5cm) high.

£2,700–3,000
Jeanette Hayhurst

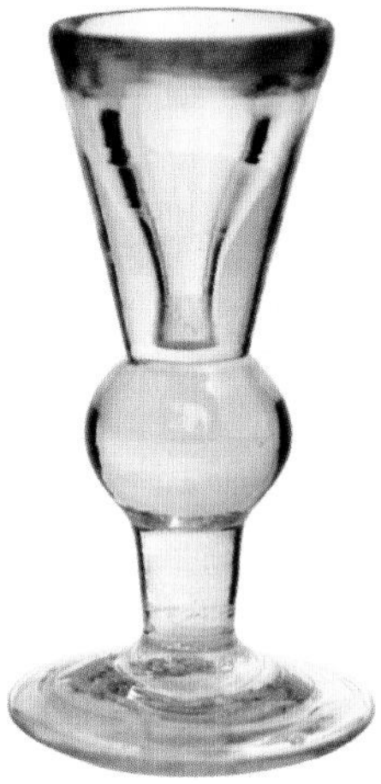

A toastmaster's glass, the funnel bowl on an inverted baluster stem and folded conical foot, c1710, 4in (10cm) high.

£950–1,100
Rapparee

SSENTIAL REFERENCE BOWL SHAPES

Tulip Bowl

Lipped Bowl

Pan-topped Bowl

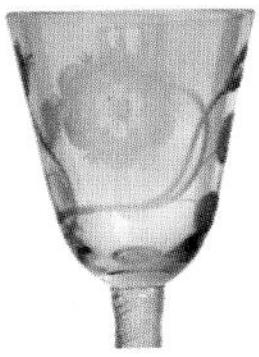

Funnel Bowl

Cup Bowl

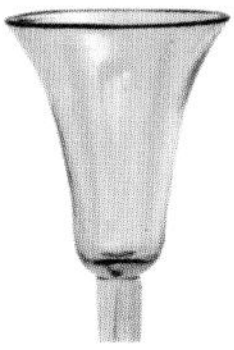

Bell Bowl

Bucket Bowl

Ogee Bowl

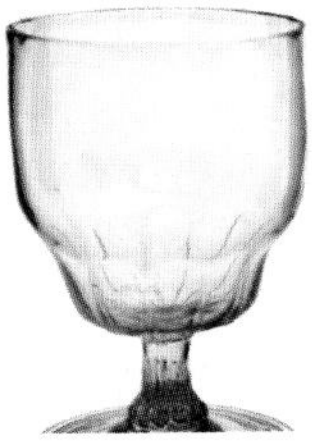

Double ogee Bowl

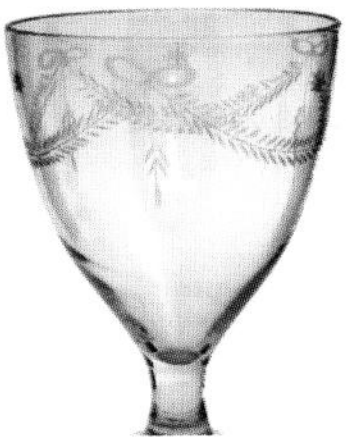

Ovoid Bowl

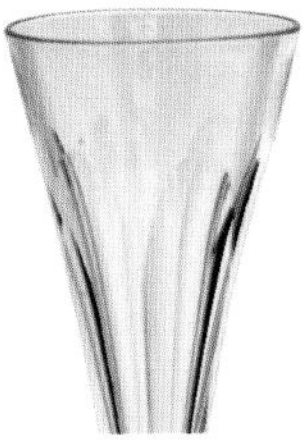

Trumpet Bowl

There are many different combinations of bowl shape and stem form in 18th-century drinking glasses. The earliest asses, known as heavy balusters, had mainly pointed, round, funnel and conical bowls, while some were made th bell and thistle-shaped bowls.

The drawn trumpet bowl is particularly associated with the air-twist stem, while the ovoid bowl was found on any facet-stemmed glasses. Opaque-twist stems often had round funnel, bell or ogee bowls.

The bowls of 18th-century drinking glasses may seem small when compared to those made today. This is ecause, rather than being filled with wine to accompany meals, these glasses were used as toasting vessels and ould be recharged several times.

A goblet, the thistle-shaped bowl on a solid base with a collar, with a four-sided pedestal-moulded stem with a tear, on a conical foot, c1710, 6½in (16.5cm) high.

£2,500–3,000 **Sotheby's**

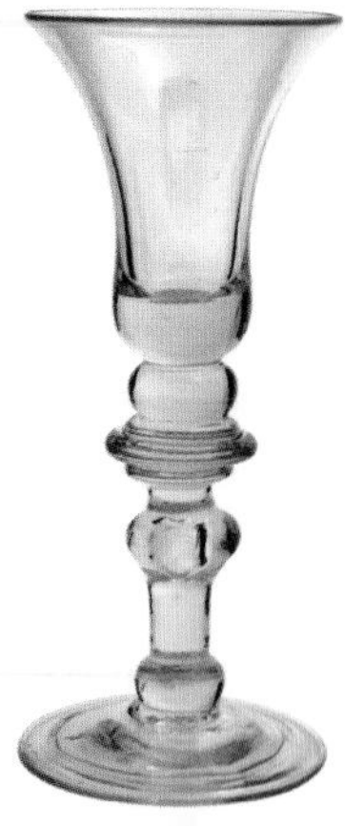

A wine glass, the bell-shaped bowl with a solid base, on a flattened ball knop and triple annulated knop, over a basal knop and a folded conical foot, c1715, 6in (15cm) high.

£1,400–1,600 **Rapparee**

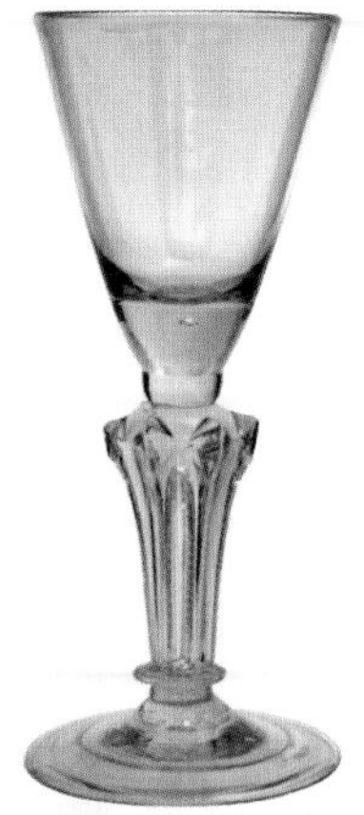

A wine glass, the funnel bowl on a six-sided pedestal-moulded stem with diamond-cut shoulders and a basal collar, on a folded foot, c1720, 6in (15cm) high.

£1,200–1,300 **Rapparee**

A baluster goblet, the bell- bowl with a solid base, on a ringed annulated knop over flattened knop and baluster on a folded conical foot, c1 8¼in (21cm) high.

£4,750–5,750 **Sotheby**

This is a rare knop formatio

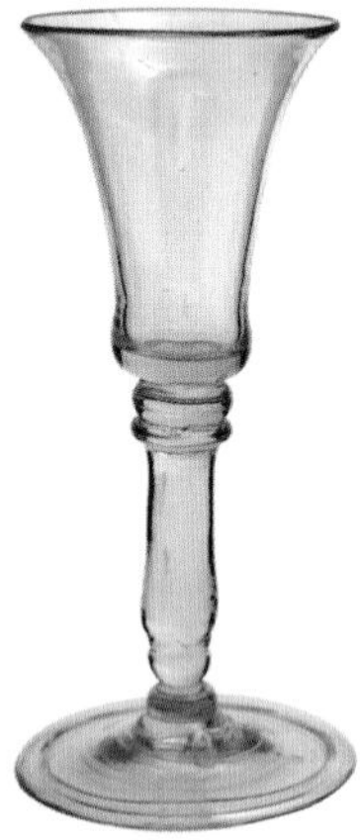

A baluster wine glass, the bell-shaped bowl on a flattened knop above a collar with cylinder and basal knops, on a conical folded foot, c1725, 6in (15cm) high.

£500–600 **Rapparee**

A wine glass, with a bell-shaped bowl and beaded solid base, on an annulated knop and inverted baluster with a plain conical foot, c1725, 6½in (16.5cm) high.

£450–550 **Hy Duke**

A wine glass, the engraved funnel bowl with an everted rim, on a triple annulated knop and stem with a basal knop, on a domed and folded foot, possibly Holland or Germany, c1730, 7in (18cm) high.

£450–550 **Dreweatt Neate (HAM)**

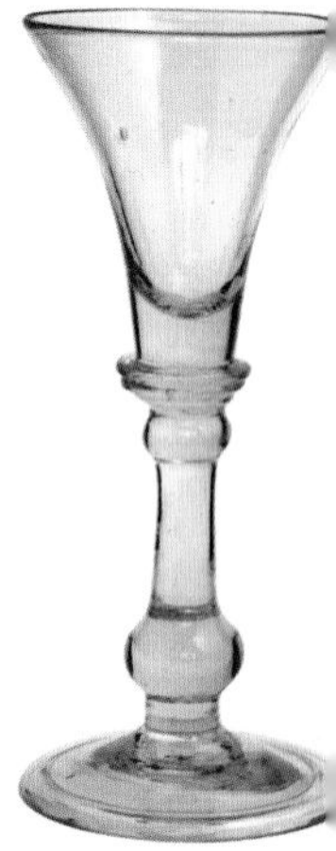

A baluster wine glass, the f bowl with a solid base, on a annulated collar above a flat ball knop and baluster, on a conical foot, c1730, 6in (15cm

£1,500–1,800 **Rappare**

A wine glass, the flared conical bowl engraved with a cockerel and hen in a landscape, on a double-knopped stem and conical foot, c1730, 6¾in (17cm) high.

£1,800–2,200 **Hy Duke**

A toastmaster's glass, the bell-shaped bowl on a plain stem and folded conical foot, c1740, 7in (18cm) high.

£1,200–1,500 **Sotheby's (O)**

A Jacobite wine glass, the funnel bowl engraved with a rose and rose buds, on a multi-spiral air-twist stem and conical foot, c1745, 4½in (11.5cm) high.

£1,000–1,200 **Jeanette Hayhurst**

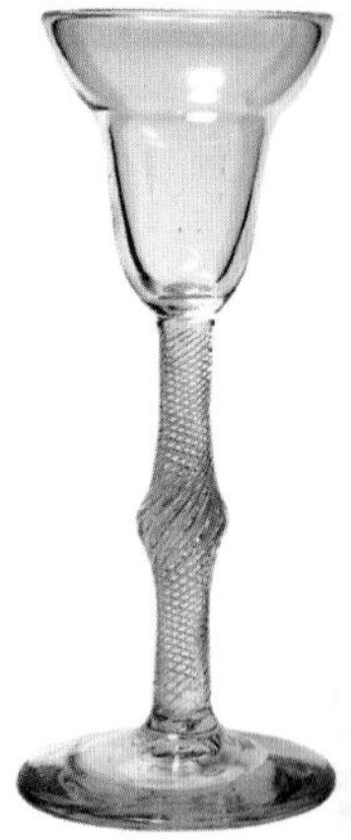

A wine glass, the pan-top bo on a multi-spiral air-twist ster and conical foot, c1750, 6in (15cm) high.

£550–625 **Frank Dux**

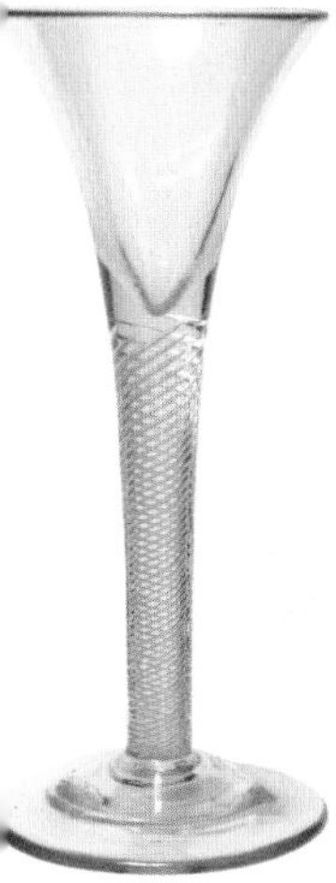

ıe glass, the drawn trumpet on a multi-spiral air-twist and conical foot, c1750, 8cm) high.

0–950 Frank Dux

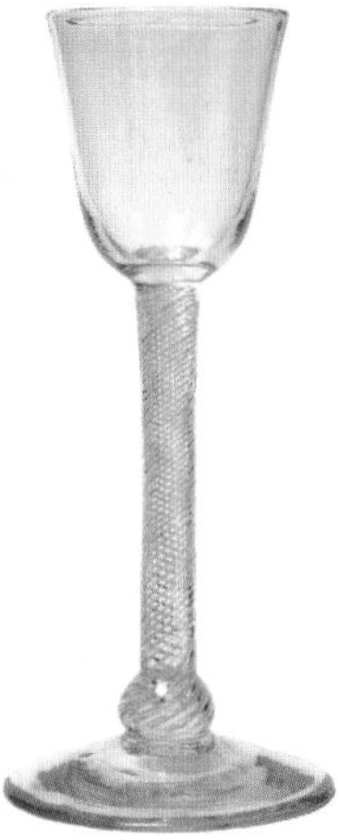

A cordial glass, the funnel bowl on a multi-spiral air-twist stem with a basal knop and conical foot, c1750, 6in (15cm) high.

£750–850 Frank Dux

A wine glass, the round funnel bowl on a multi-spiral air-twist stem and conical foot, c1750, 7in (17.5cm) high.

£500–550 Brian Watson

A baluster wine glass, the flared bucket bowl on a knopped stem with a tear and folded conical foot, c1750, 6in (15cm) high.

£700–800 Rapparee

XPERT'S EYE THE COMPOSITE STEM

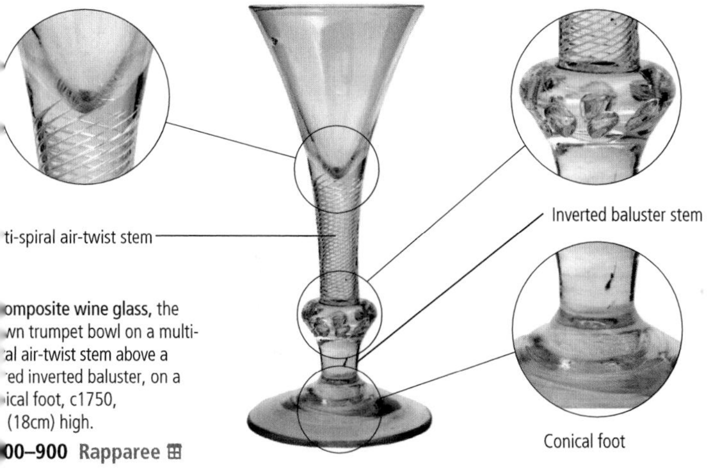

omposite wine glass, the wn trumpet bowl on a multi-al air-twist stem above a ed inverted baluster, on a ical foot, c1750, (18cm) high.

00–900 Rapparee

ıe glasses and goblets featuring an interesting combination of plain stems with twists or opaque-twists and occasionally all three were particularly popular in gland, Holland and Scandinavia in the mid-18th century.

ey were particularly well-made glasses because extra care and craftsmanship was uired due to the complexity of their construction. Also featuring drawn trumpet, and tulip-shaped bowls, some of those with round funnels were especially chosen engraving by Dutch masters such as Jacob Sang. The traditional examples and s the most common are those with a squat or low baluster knop incorporating air ads into which a plain, multi-spiral air-twist or opaque-twist stem is positioned. ese often had a domed foot, some of which have a folded rim.

glass is made up of several sections – the bowl, stem and foot, each individually med from gathers of molten glass. However, most opaque-twist stems were made ependently of the bowl and foot and were connected by the gradual melting on h connecting end.

e should be aware that a composite may be a marriage of two or more damaged sses. The tell-tale concentric line, perhaps microscopically chipped at the edges, at connections of the knops, stems and bowls is a good indicator.

fashions for air-twist and opaque-twist stems overlap in the period after 1750 may run concurrently, though the latter survived for longer, possibly until c1780.

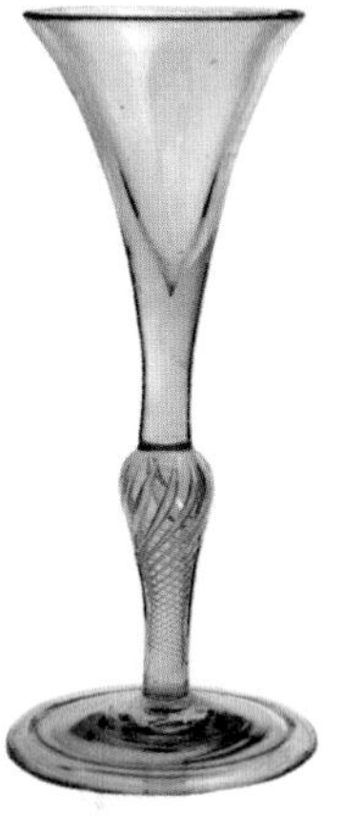

A composite wine glass, the drawn trumpet bowl on a multi-spiral air-twist inverted baluster stem, on a folded conical foot, c1750, 6½in (16.5cm) high.

£600–700 Rapparee

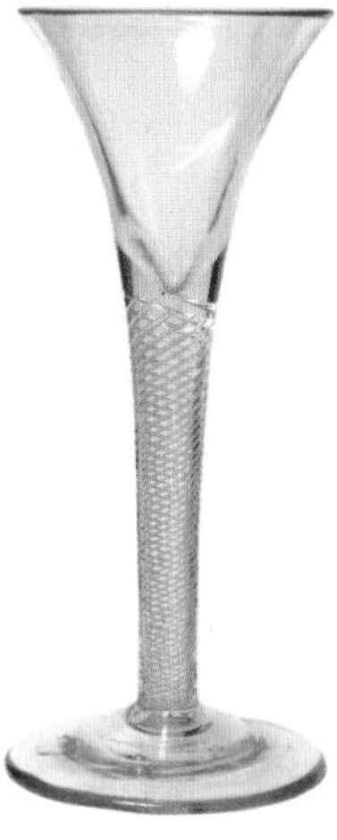

A wine glass, the trumpet bowl on a multi-spiral air-twist stem and conical foot, c1750, 7in (18cm) high.

£250–280 Frank Dux

A wine glass, with a honeycomb-moulded funnel-shaped bowl, on a knopped air-twist stem and conical foot, c1750, 6¾in (17cm) high.

£300–350 Hy Duke

EXPERT'S EYE OPAQUE-TWIST STEMS

- The opaque-twist was developed slightly later than the air-twist stem, about 1755.
- It is manufactured from preformed cylindrical 'canes' of opaque white glass, equidistantly placed either in a mould, laid in grooves, or laid side by side in a ceramic or metallic plate and heated until soft.
- The positioning of thicker and thinner canes is crucial to their finished appearance, either as a fine cotton-thread-like gauze core, pairs of thick entwined tapes, multi-spiral cotton threads, or a combination of these.
- The canes are then picked up on the outside of a heated gather of glass and rolled together.
- Both ends of the gather are then drawn out and twisted so that it becomes narrower and elongated. As the completed rod cools the glassmaker cuts it into three- or four-inch long sections to which a bowl and foot are added separately. This then creates a series of glasses each bearing an identical stem form.

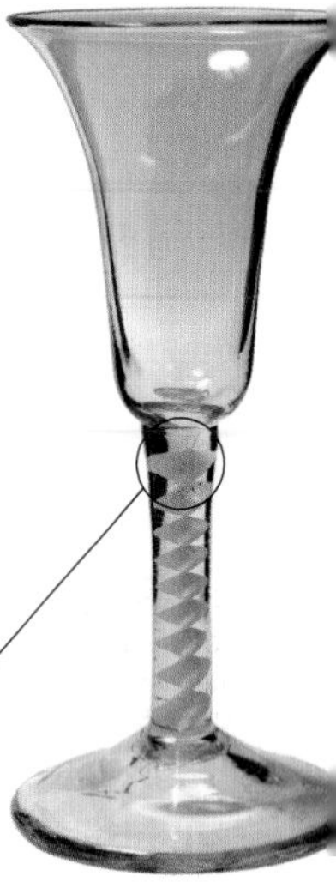

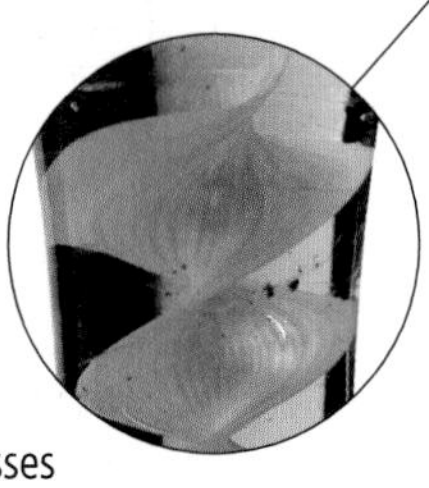

A wine glass, with a bell bo on a single-series opaque-tw stem and conical foot, c176 7in (18cm) high.

£520–580 Brian Watson

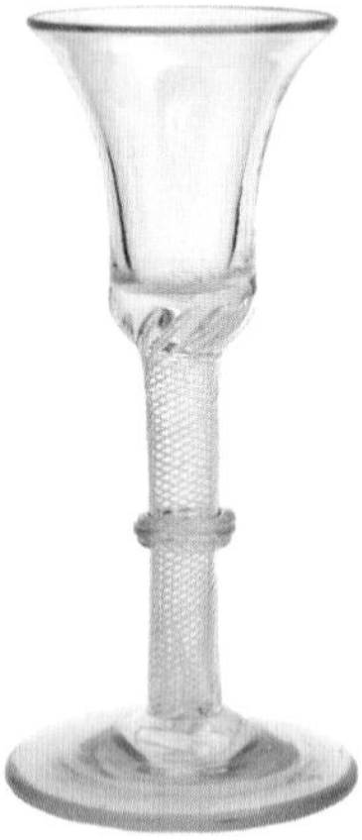

A wine glass, the drawn bell bowl with a solid base, on a multi-spiral air-twist stem, the spiral extending into the bowl with a triple-plaited collar, on a conical foot, c1760, 6in (15cm) high.

£650–700 Rapparee

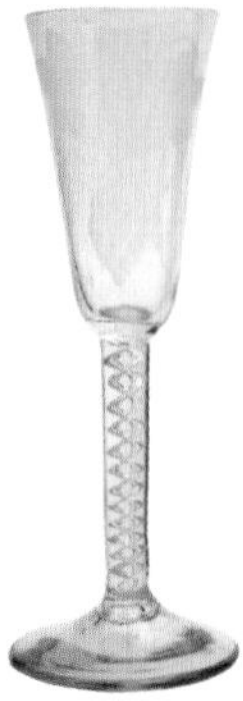

An ale glass, the funnel bowl engraved with hops and barley, on a single-series mercury air-twist stem and conical foot, c1760, 7in (18cm) high.

£580–650 Rapparee

A cordial glass, the bucket bowl engraved with a floral spray and a bird, on a double-series air-twist stem and conical foot, c1760, 7in (18cm) high.

£1,300–1,500 Rapparee

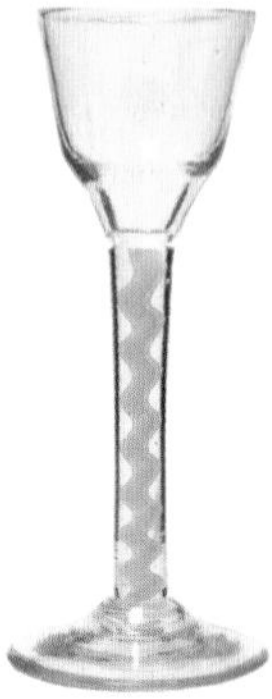

A cordial glass, the ogee bo on a single-series opaque-tw stem with a corkscrew spiral gauze and conical foot, c176 6in (15cm) high.

£500–550 Frank Dux

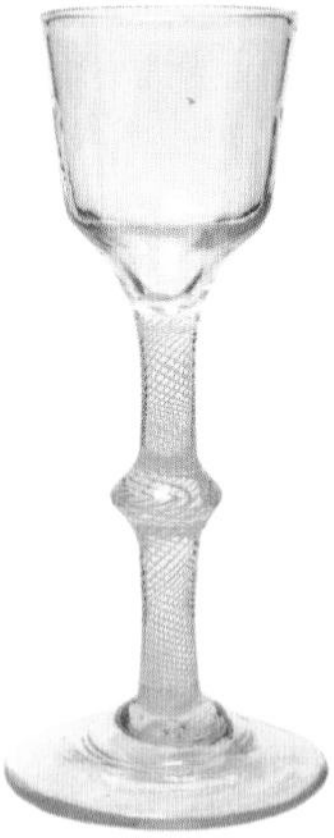

A wine glass, the hammer-moulded ogee bowl on a multi-spiral air-twist stem with a central swelling, on a conical foot, c1760, 6in (15cm) high.

£380–440 Frank Dux

A dram glass, the ogee bowl on a single-series opaque-twist stem and domed foot, c1760, 5in (12.5cm) high.

£680–750 Rapparee

A dwarf ale glass, with a wrythen bowl and knopped stem, c1760, 5in (12.5cm) high.

£100–120 Guest & Gray

A goblet, the ogee bowl on a double-series opaque-twist s and conical foot, c1760, 7¾in (19.5cm) high.

£750–850 Brian Watsc

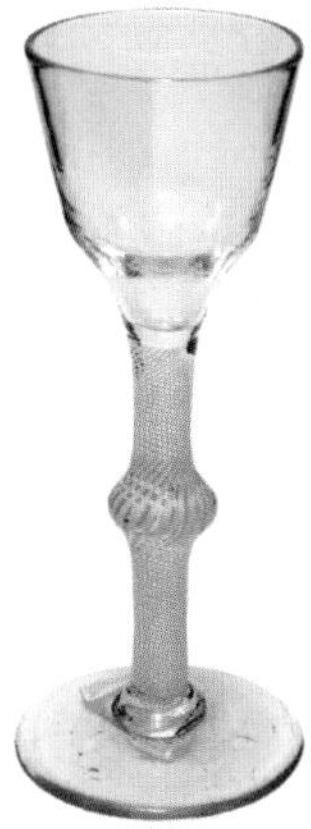

ıe glass, the ogee bowl on ti-spiral opaque-twist with a central swelling onical foot, c1765, 5cm) high.

)–460 **ette Hayhurst ⊞**

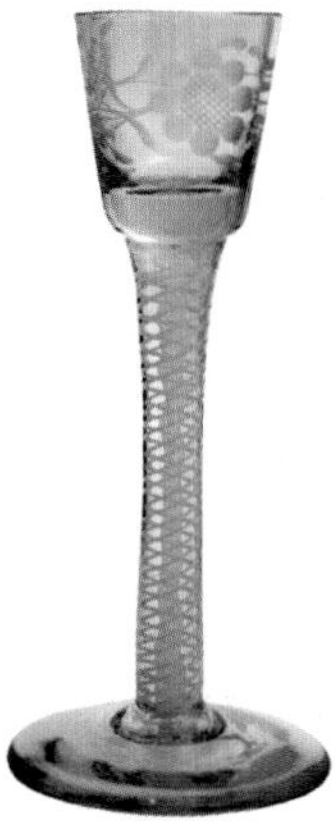

A cordial glass, the bucket bowl engraved with a stylized flowerhead and foliage, on an opaque-twist stem with four spiral threads around a vertical gauze, on a conical foot, c1765, 6½in (16.5cm) high.

£700–800 **Rapparee ⊞**

An ale glass, the bowl with a fluted base, on a double-series opaque-twist stem and conical foot, c1765, 7½in (19cm) high.

£400–450
Jeanette Hayhurst ⊞

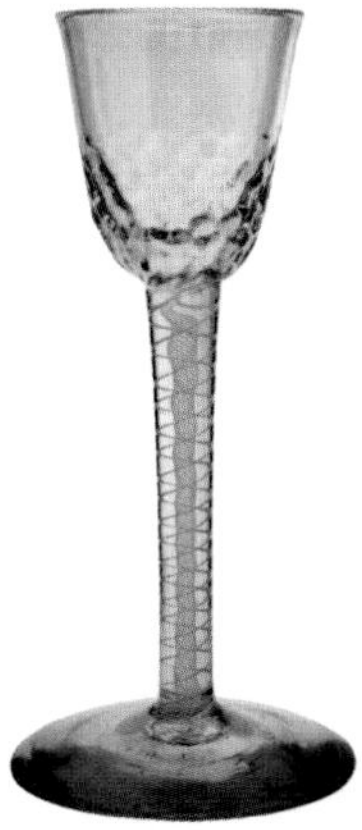

A wine glass, with a hammered funnel bowl, the opaque-twist stem with a pair of spiral threads outside a vertical gauze, on a conical foot, c1765, 6in (15cm) high.

£525–600 **Rapparee ⊞**

nmer, the bowl engraved with a neo-cal leafy band, on a lemon squeezer 1770–80, 5½in (14cm) high.

)–125 **Glass etc ⊞**

MARKET INFORMATION GLASS

- As with most collecting areas, there has been a polarization in market prices between rare glass and general run-of-the-mill examples. The traditional collecting field of English 18th-century drinking glasses offers extremes at both ends of the spectrum and is a worthwhile investment for the established collector.
- Early English heavy balusters (1700–20), Beilby enamelled glass and delicate colour-twists of the second half of the 18th century continue to improve in value.
- Today, the new collector can find rarities among the opaque-twist and air-twist stemmed glasses at more moderate prices. However, as supply diminishes prices for even the most humble examples are set to rise.
- English 19th-century engraved glass in the neo-classical manner and imitation rock crystal in the Aesthetic style – generally from Stourbridge – have shown a rise in value.
- English cameo glass of the same period has seen steady price levels with the exception of rarities or pieces of the highest quality – prices for these have soared. Signed and attributed examples by named glass craftsmen – George Woodall, Lionel Pearce and William Fritsche in particular – are rising significantly in value.

ıg glass, the ogee bowl with a polished band, on a diamond facet stem and foot, c1790, 5in (12.5cm) high.

)–150 **Frank Dux ⊞**

A rummer, the bowl engraved with neo-classical ribbons and bows, Ireland, Cork, 1790–1820, 4½in (11.5cm) high.

£110–125 **Glass etc ⊞**

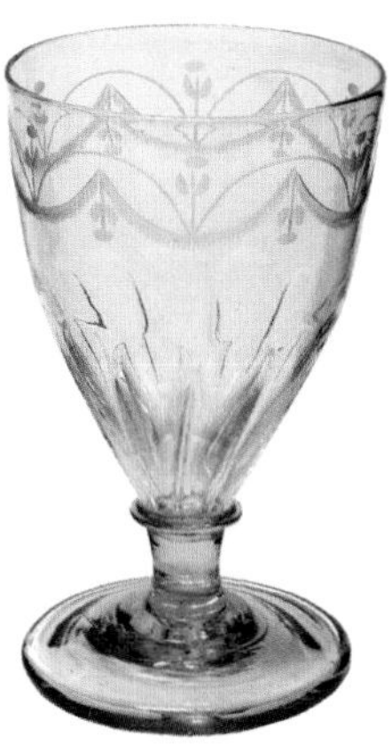

A pair of rummers, the ovoid bowls engraved with swags and tassels, c1800, 6in (15cm) high.

£320–350 **Bourbon-Hanby ⊞**

A rummer, the bowl engraved with initials 'AAW' within a cartouche framed by vine leaves above a leafy festoon, the reverse engraved with intertwined roses and thistles, on a lemon squeezer foot, c1807, 4½in (11.5cm) high.

£130–150 Glass etc

This rummer was probably made in commemoration of the centenary of the Act of Union between England and Scotland in 1707.

A rummer, the ovoid bowl engraved with a branch of leaves and tied ribbons, on a plain stem and foot, c1810, 6in (15cm) high.

£100–110 Rapparee

A goblet, the bucket bowl with a guilloch cut band over slice-cut panelling, the hol knop enclosing a George II silver coin, on a star cut foot, early 19thC, 10¾in (27.5cm) high.

£400–500 Tennants

A goblet, the cup-shaped bowl with a stop-cut base, the stem with a faceted knop on a star-cut foot, Ireland, c1830, 5½in (14cm) high.

£60–70 Offa's Dyke

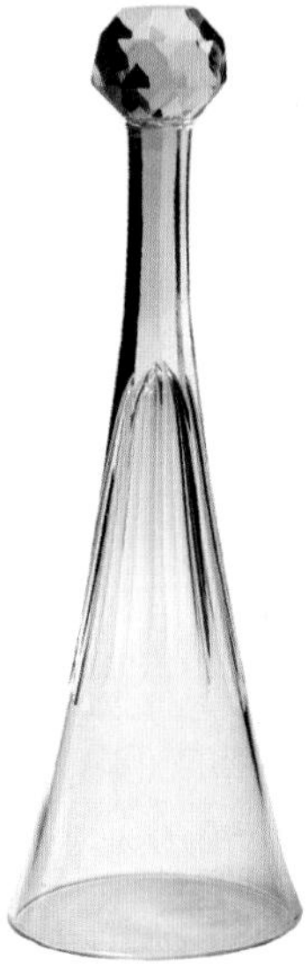

A stirrup glass, the panel-cut drawn trumpet bowl with a slice-cut stem and faceted ball knop, c1830, 6¾in (17cm) high.

£120–135 Brian Watson

A set of four Gothic-style goblets, the bo cut with hollow diamonds, 1845–50, 6¼in (15.5cm) high.

£180–200 Glass etc

A goblet, the ogee bowl cut with arched panels and basal facets, on a hollow stem with three knops and plain foot, c1870, 7in (18cm) high.

£90–100 Rapparee

A set of six Louis Philippe-style wine goblets, with cut bowls on pedestal stems, France, 1880–1900, 5¾in (14.5cm) high.

£130–150 Glass etc

A Venetian glass marriage cup, with enamelled and decoration, Italy, c1900, 6in (15.5cm) high.

£800–900 Brian Watson

This is an imitation of the 15th-century Barovier marriage cup.

:AKERS & TUMBLERS

:emian **Koula School beaker,** with
:ed and matt engraving of two putti
:rting a basket of flowers and a heart
:ed 'IHS' within a heart-shaped reserve,
verse with a German inscription,
:se with flowers and berries,
7thC, 4¾in (12cm) high,
: fitted case.
:–425 Rosebery's

A Bohemian beaker, with Baroque engraved decoration within geometric cartouches, c1740, 6½in (16.5cm) high.
£110–125 Glass etc

A tumbler, engraved with the Sunderland Bridge and a two-masted ship, c1820, 4in (10cm) high.
£340–380 Frank Dux

ESSENTIAL REFERENCE ANTON KOTHGASSER

Anton Kothgasser (1769–1851) was a painter at the Royal porcelain factory in Vienna. He was also a prolific decorator of glass tumblers and beakers using thin transparent enamels. Early examples were simple straight-sided types but from 1814 the *ranftbecher*, which had a waisted or tapered body and a thick cogwheel-cut base, became popular. Kothgasser's enamelled decorations resembled romantic watercolours and his designs included landscapes, floral sprays, city views (particularly of Vienna), portraits and allegorical and neo-classical subjects, generally within elaborate gilt frames.

A ***ranftbecher,*** by Anton Kothgasser, transparent-enamelled and gilt-decorated, Austria, Vienna, c1825, 4¾in (12cm) high.
£11,000–13,000 Dorotheum

:emian *ranftbecher,* by
:ch Egermann, transparent-
:elled with gilt bands
:ing insects, slight damage,
, c1850, 5½in (14cm) high.
:00–1,800 Dorotheum

:emian beaker, in the style of Karl Pfohl,
:ated with a medallion enclosing a
:ing horse, the reverse cut with a lens
: monogram, c1850, 5¼in (13.5cm) high.
:–900 Dorotheum

A Bohemian faceted beaker, by Josef Riedel, decorated with a coat-of-arms, the reverse with a German motto, c1860, 4¾in (12cm) high.
£400–500 Dorotheum

A Lobmeyr Persian-style beaker, designed by Schmoranz and Machtyka, with an everted rim, painted and gilt with two panels of geometric scrolls within panels and bands of stylized flowers and circles, monogrammed 'JLL', restored, Austria, Vienna, c1878, 5½in (14cm) high.
£3,500–4,250 Sotheby's

BOTTLES, CARAFES & DECANTERS

A wine bottle, of shaft-and-globe form, with an applied string rim and kick-in base, slight damage, c1650, 8¼in (21cm) high.
£5,000–6,000 Sotheby's

A bladder wine bottle, the neck applied with a string rim, the seal inscribed 'Io: Collard 1725', slight damage, 8in (20.5cm) high.
£5,000–6,000 BBR

A glass decanter, the neck with a triple rim over a cruciform section body, c1740, 9¼in (23.5cm) high.
£300–350 David Lay

A wine bottle, the seal inscr 'H Hopper Esq 1786', 12in (30.5cm) high.
£700–850 Gorringes (L)

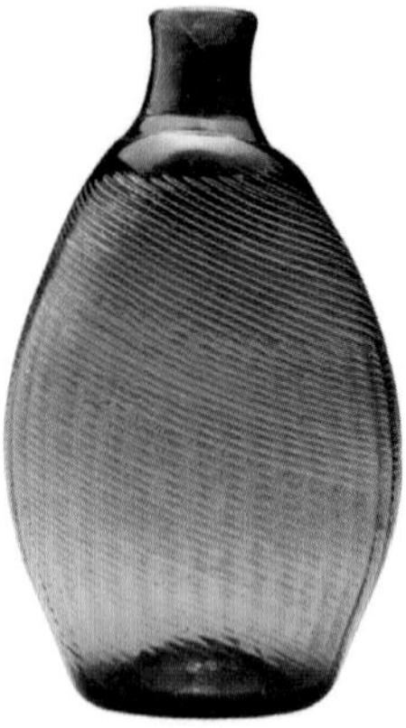

A blown moulded glass pitkin, with broken swirl ribs, America, 1790–1830, 6¾in (17cm) high.
£550–650 Northeast Auctions

A Prussian-shaped glass decanter, with three applied neck rings and matching stopper, possibly Irish, 1810–25, 8½in (21.5cm) high.
£180–200 Glass etc

A Prussian-shaped glass decanter, cut with diamonds, flutes and sunbursts, 1815–20, 8½in (21.5cm) high.
£130–150 Glass etc

A cylinder bottle, with a too lip and string rim, the seal w ducal coronet above initial 'F within a lined border, c1820, 10in (25.5cm) high.
£200–250 BBR

ESSENTIAL REFERENCE DECANTER SHAPES

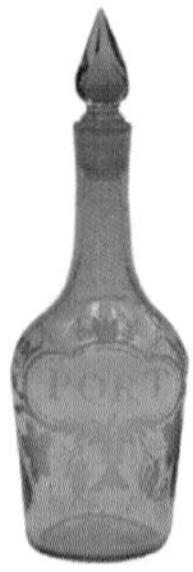

Shouldered – c1765

Tapered – c1780

Prussian – c1790–1820

Ship's – c1800–30

Cruciform – c1800–3C

- Late 17th- early 18th-century decanters were made from heavy, mould-blown glass with high kicks in the base. As with sealed bottles they were used for serving, and stoppers, where found, were loose corks or plugs secured with stri
- True decanter shapes began to appear in the mid-18th century. They were usually left undecorated to show the colour of the liquid. Glass stoppers began to be used and were less heavy than their predecessors, perhaps due to the tax levied on glass at the time.

ilsea-style cranberry-tinted glass gimmel flask, c1830, 10in (25.5cm) long.
0–300 Just Glass ⊞

A mallet-shaped glass decanter, with a mushroom stopper, slice-cut shoulders and triple neck rings, the body engraved with a laurel-edged panel enclosing a ship in full sail and inscribed 'Success to Sarah & Mary' and 'R & J Edmond' to the reverse, 1850–1900, 9¾in (25cm) high.
£325–400 Bearnes

t-glass decanter, with a -cut neck, the body engraved roses, thistles and shamrocks, 0, 12in (30.5cm) high.
0–250
ette Hayhurst ⊞

A pair of cut-glass decanters, with blown stoppers, scale-cut necks, lens flute and diamond-cut bodies, 1870–80, 13in (33cm) high.
£200–220
Jeanette Hayhurst ⊞

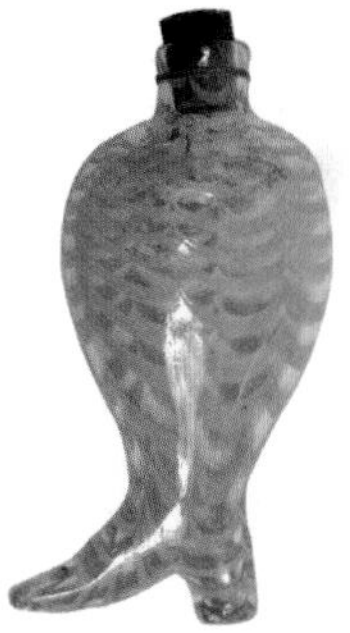

A Nailsea-style glass spirit flask, in the form of a boot, c1875, 7in (18cm) wide.
£150–170 Just Glass ⊞

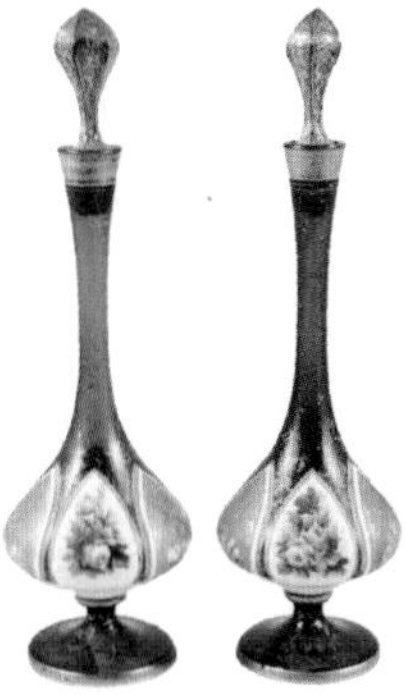

A pair of Bohemian cased glass bottles and stoppers, carved with panels painted with floral bouquets and gilt motifs, c1870, 10¾in (27.5cm) high.
£750–900
Dreweatt Neate (HAM)

ir of ruby glass carafes, c1880, 18cm) high.
0–175 Just Glass ⊞

A cranberry glass water carafe and beaker, with enamelled and gilded decoration, c1880, 7in (18cm) high.
£180–200 Just Glass ⊞

uare – c1810 | Fancy (Royal) – c1830 | Claret jug – Victorian | Bell – c1845–60 | Shaft & Globe – 1730–50 and c1850 | Wine decanter – c1880

eck rings evolved towards the end of the 18th century, both for decoration and to ensure safer handling.

ctorian decanters were influenced by late Georgian and Regency styles but were more elaborate, often with ed styles of cutting and bands of engraving. The commonest form is the shaft-and-globe, which has a fat round / and a long neck. These are relatively easy to find and therefore need to be in mint condition to have any value.

alue is affected by size, rarity of shape and decoration. Heavy cutting and labels are features to look for.

BOWLS

A glass bowl, cut with facets, with a knopped stem and lemon-squeezer foot, slight damage, Ireland, c1790, 8½in (21.5cm) high.

£1,100–1,300 Sotheby's (O)

A cut-glass bowl, Ireland, c1800, 10in (25.5cm) wide.

£900–1,000 Offa's Dyke

A glass punch bowl, cover and ladle, engr with leaves, heightened with gilding, prob Russia, 1850–1900, 12¼in (31.5cm) diar

£500–600 Bukowskis

A Thomas Webb rock-crystal-style glass bowl, by George Woodall, engraved with leaves, signed, c1890, 9½in (24cm) diam.

£9,000–11,000 Sotheby's

Although primarily regarded as one of the foremost English cameo glass engravers, George Woodall is also known to have produced some imitation rock crystal glass in the late 19th century. Such pieces are quite rare but reveal Woodall's extreme versatility. It is likely that he was inspired by the work of the Bohemian engravers working in the Stourbridge glass industry such as William Fritsche.

A George Davidson & Co pressed jet glass sugar bowl and jug, c1890, bowl 6in (15cm) d

£80–90 Just Glass

A cut-glass centre bowl, America, early 20thC, 10½in (26.5cm) wide.

£160–200 Jackson's

A cut-glass bowl, with fan-cut rim, on a pedestal foot, c1920, 8¾in (22.5cm) high

£230–275 Sworders

CENTREPIECES

A lead-glass tazza, probably by George Ravenscroft, Savoy Glasshouse, with folded rim and gadrooning, on a trumpet foot, 1675–80, 3½in (9cm) high.

£8,000–10,000 Sotheby's

A moulded glass tazza, on a domed and folded foot, c1750, 6¼in (16cm) high.

£450–500 Brian Watson

A Falcon Glassworks cut-glass sulphide tazza, probably by Apsley Pellatt, cut with strawberry diamonds, the stem inset with classical maiden, c1820, 6¼in (16cm) hig

£900–1,100 Sotheby's (O)

hemian cased glass and silver centrepiece, enamel-
ed with flowers, c1835, 8¾in (22cm) high.

)–500 Dorotheum

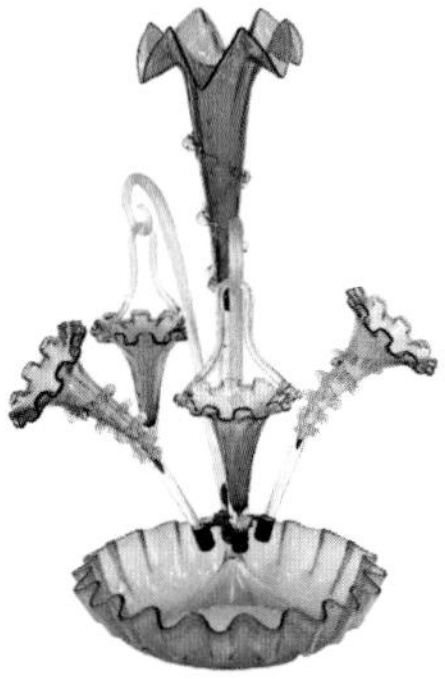

A Victorian cranberry glass **épergne,** with trailed decoration, 19½in (49.5cm) high.

£325–400
Andrew Hartley

A cut-glass and gilt-bronze épergne, probably by Osler, Birmingham, c1880, 12in (30.5cm) diam.

£2,000–2,250 Ronald Chambers

A tinted glass épergne, c1900, 16in (40.5cm) high.

£400–450 Just Glass

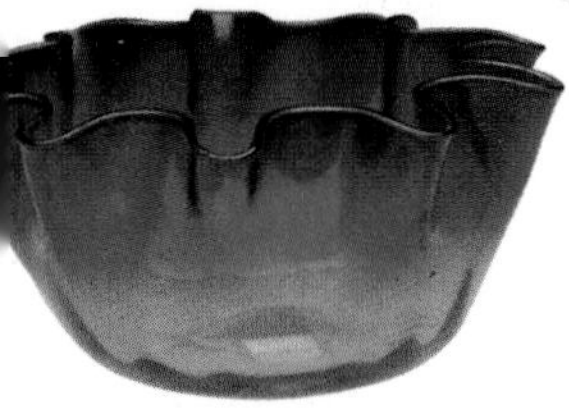

**)unt Washington Glass Works glass
'epiece bowl,** America, c1885,
(14cm) wide.

)–260 James D Julia

A George Davidson & Co vaseline pressed glass comport, c1895, 9in (23cm) diam.

£180–200 Just Glass

ELLY & SWEETMEAT GLASSES

ly glass, with blade and
knops above a domed foot,
;0, 4¼in (11cm) high.

)0–220
nette Hayhurst

A sweetmeat glass, with a double ogee bowl, on a domed and folded foot, mid-18thC, 7in (18cm) high.

£300–350
Jeanette Hayhurst

A slice-cut sweetmeat glass, on a pedestal stem, c1750, 6¼in (15.5cm) high.

£150–175 Glass etc

A jelly glass, with folded inverted lip, late 18thC, 4in (10cm) high.

£40–45 Frank Dux

rythen jelly glass, with
rted lip on a cushion knop,
18thC, 4in (10cm) high.

)–55 Frank Dux

A sweetmeat glass, with a double ogee bowl, on a multi-spiral opaque twist stem with a shoulder knop, c1770, 3½in (9cm) high.

£475–525 Rapparee

A pair of jelly glasses, with lipped funnel bowls, the stems with collar knops, on lemon-squeezer feet, c1800, 4in (10cm) high.

£100–110 Frank Dux

JUGS

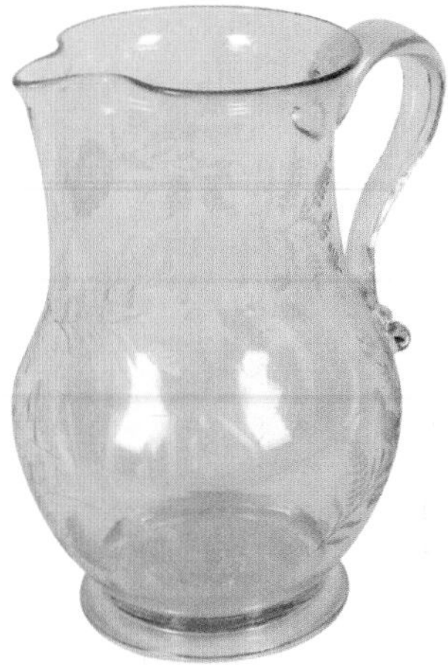

A glass jug, with engraved decoration, inscribed 'B. P. Meanley', 18thC, 9in (23cm) high.

£550–650 **James Adam**

A step-cut-glass water jug, with slice-cut handle and star-cut base, slight damage, c1820, 6¼in (16cm) high.

£1,100–1,300 **Sotheby's (O)**

A glass cream jug, with applied decoration and foot, America, early 19thC, 5in (12.5cm) high.

£1,500–1,800 **Notheast Auction**

MARKET INFORMATION CONDITION

- Although there may be fewer opportunities to buy rare, good and standard examples of glass from the 16th century to the end of the 19th, today's lower prices provide an affordable field for the new collector.
- Condition is critical and may significantly affect value. However, an honest chip or minor crack should be perceived as the wear and tear that might be expected on an old object and not deter the would-be collector. The removal of chips can cause damage and change the proportions of a item considerably. New methods of repair with resin – a reversible technique – may provide a useful disguise without being invasive. Glass is there to be seen and admired.

A glass jug, c1850, 7in (18cm) high.

£140–160 **Just Glass**

A cut-glass jug, America, c1900, 6½in (16.5cm) high.

£120–150 **Jackson's**

A Bohemian glass jug, with gilt-metal decoration and mounts, c1860, 12¼in (31cm) high.

£450–550 **Dorotheum**

A Bohemian quatrefoil glass jug, by Moser Glassworks, enamelled with oak leaves and insects, c1885, 12in (30.5cm) high.

£3,500–4,000 **Bourbon-Hanby**

A Georgian-style cut-glass water jug, c1890, 7in (18cm) high.

£270–300 **Brian Watson**

PAPERWEIGHTS

Baccarat paperweight, with double lematis, star-cut base, France, mid-19thC, ½in (6.5cm) diam.

1,200–1,500 Gorringes (L)

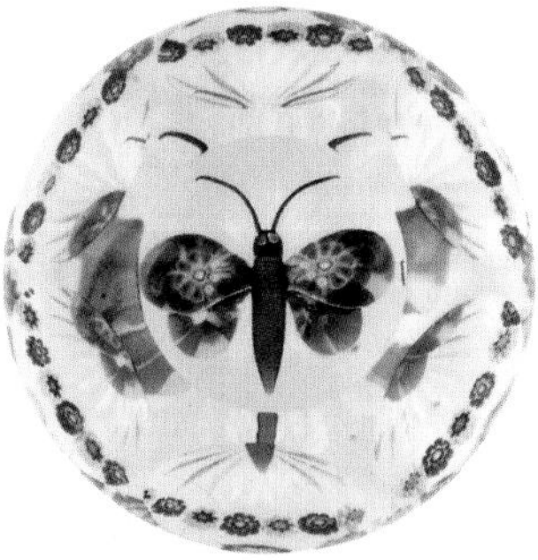

A Baccarat paperweight, with a butterfly within a garland of canes, star-cut base, France, c1850, 2¾in (7cm) diam.

£2,500–3,000 Sotheby's (O)

A Baccarat paperweight, with double clematis on an upset muslin ground, France, c1850, 3¼in (8.5cm) diam.

£2,500–2,750 Dunlop Collection

Baccarat closepack millefiori paperweight, ith silhouettes of a goat, cockerel, flower and itterfly, France, c1850, 3¼in (8.5cm) diam.

850–1,000 Rosebery's

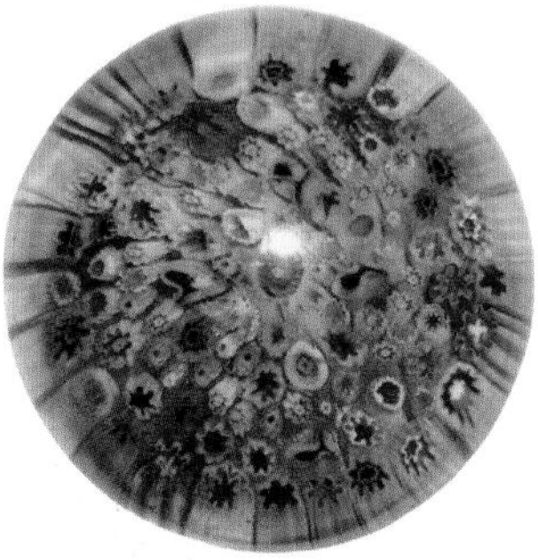

A Bacchus & Co scrambled paperweight, with four silhouette head canes, c1850, 3in (7.5cm) diam.

£700–800 Sweetbriar Gallery

A Bacchus & Co paperweight, with Queen Victoria silhouette cane, c1850, 2½in (6.5cm) diam.

£630–700 Sweetbriar Gallery

MARKET INFORMATION PAPERWEIGHTS

- Paperweights have not risen greatly in value, possibly because fewer collections have come on to the market, especially in America where, since he 1970s, the major buyers have been located.
- Classic French paperweights of Baccarat, St Louis and Clichy are still sought after at a higher price level.
- There appears to be growing interest in the modern weights of Scotland and America.

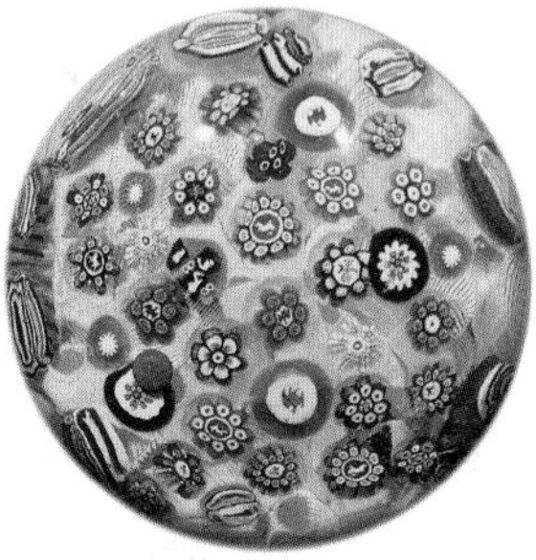

A Bohemian glass spaced millefiori paperweight, with upset muslin ground, dated 1848, 2¾in (7cm) diam.

£1,200–1,350 Dunlop Collection

Clichy closepack millefiori paperweight, nce, c1850, 3¼in (8.5cm) diam.

,000–4,400 Dunlop Collection

A Clichy concentric millefiori paperweight, France, c1850, 3¼in (8.5cm) diam.

£3,250–3,750 Dunlop Collection

A Clichy moss-ground millefiori paperweight, France, c1850, 3in (7.5cm) diam.

£13,000–15,000 Gorringes (L)

This is a rare paperweight. The mossy ground is formed from shredded glass canes.

A Clichy **paperweight**, with a viola, France, c1850, 3in (7.5cm) diam.

£4,000–4,500 Sweetbriar Gallery

A Clichy **paperweight**, with a swirl, France, c1850, 3in (7.5cm) diam.

£1,000–1,200 Sweetbriar Gallery

A Clichy closepack millefiori **paperweight**, France, c1850, 2¾in (7cm) diam.

£1,800–2,000 Sweetbriar Gallery

A New England Glass Co scrambled **paperweight**, America, c1850, 2¼in (5.5cm) diam.

£270–300 Sweetbriar Gallery

A New England Glass Co magnum **paperweight**, with a floral bouquet on a *latticinio* ground, c1860, 4in (10cm) diam.

£4,500–5,500 Freeman's

Paperweights that are 4in (10cm) in diameter or larger are called magnums.

A St Louis **paperweight**, with a dog cane, France, 1845–60, 2½in (6.5cm) diam.

£900–1,000 Sweetbriar Gallery

A St Louis closepack millefiori cruciform **paperweight**, France, c1850, 2½in (6.5cm) diam.

£6,750–7,500 Dunlop Collection

A St Louis concentric **paperweight**, with a date cane, France, 1848, 3in (7.5cm) diam.

£3,000–3,500 Sweetbriar Gallery

A St Louis **paperweight**, with a pompom on a *latticinio* ground, France, 1845–60, 2½in (6.5cm) diam.

£700–800 Sweetbriar Gallery

A St Louis mushroom millefiori **paperweight**, with canes and thread, on a *latticinio* ground, six printies, France, c1850, 3¼in (8.5cm) diam.

£1,200–1,500 Sotheby's (O)

A St Louis nosegay **paperweight**, on a *latticinio* ground, France, c1850, 3in (7.5cm) diam.

£1,300–1,500 Sweetbriar Gallery

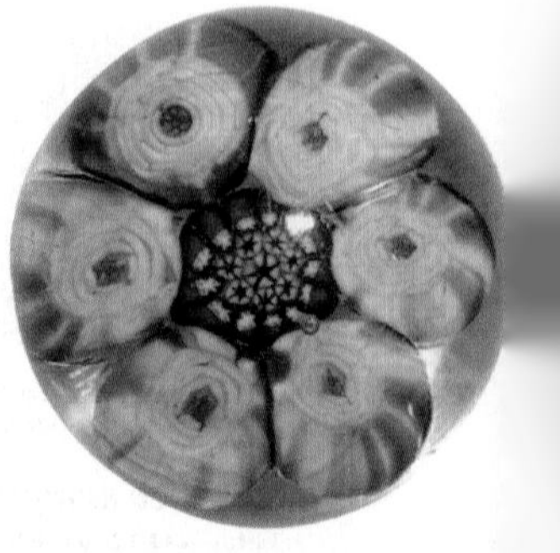

A miniature **paperweight**, with six roses, 1845–60, 1¾in (4.5cm) diam.

£540–600 Sweetbriar Gallery

VASES & URNS

A glass vase, cut with fans and 'lunate' eye-shapes, on a ball-knop stem and star-cut foot, 1785–95, 8in (20cm) high.

£110–125 **Glass etc**

A pair of opaline glass vases, probably by Baccarat, possibly painted by Jean-François Robert with sprays of flowers, with gilt banding, France, 1845–50, 17¾in (45cm) high.

£10,000–12,000
Sotheby's

A glass vase and cover, decalcomania-decorated with chinoiserie scenes of dragons, figures, rocks and temples, Italian, 1800–50, 23¾in (60.5cm) high.

£3,200–3,800 **Sotheby's**

Decalcomania is a process in which a design is transferred from prepared paper onto another surface such as porcelain, glass or paper.

A Bohemian opaque glass vase, decorated in gilt and enamels with scrolls and flower sprays, mid-19thC, 12¼in (31cm) high.

£650–800 **Sworders**

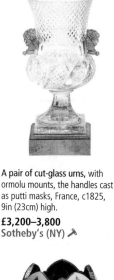

A pair of cut-glass urns, with ormolu mounts, the handles cast as putti masks, France, c1825, 9in (23cm) high.

£3,200–3,800
Sotheby's (NY)

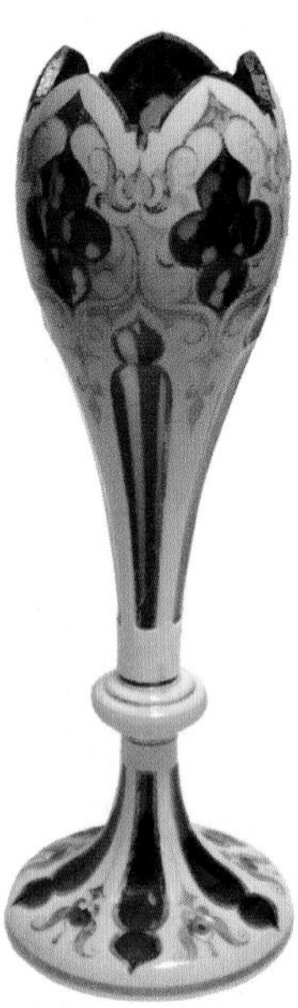

A Bohemian cased-glass vase, with enamel and gilt decoration, c1860, 16in (40.5cm) high.

£225–250 **Just Glass**

An opaline glass vase, by La Hautin & Co, decorated with animals, birds and stylized flo after Ferdinand Audry, Franc 1845, 27½in (70cm) high.

£7,500–9,000
Dorotheum

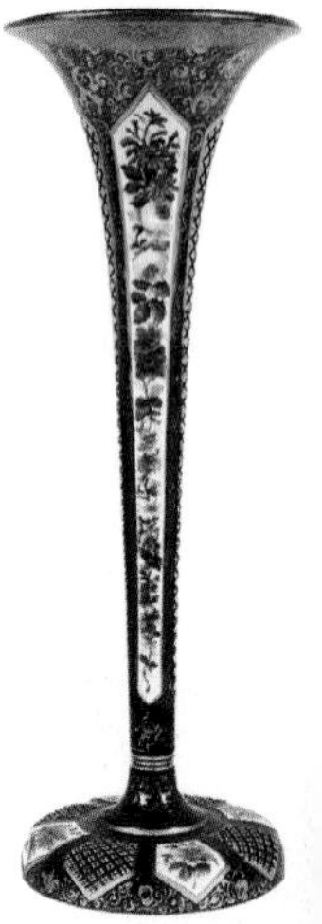

A Bohemian glass vase, decorated in enamel with pa of flowers within gilt scrollwo c1870, 16½in (42cm) high.

£550–650 **James Adam**

A pair of Bohemian gilded glass vases, with spiral collars, c1870, 11in (28cm) high.

£150–180 **James Adam**

A pair of copper-mounted glass vases and a jardinière, painted with birds, bamboo and reeds, the neck and feet mounted with dragons, slight damage, France, c1880, vases 18¼in (46.5cm) high.

£4,500–5,500 **Dorotheum**

alachite pressed glass
e, by Edward Moore, c1880,
(18cm) high.
35–150 Just Glass

A pair of Bohemian Mary Gregory-style cranberry glass vases, with enamelled decoration, c1890, 13in (33cm) high.
£540–600 Just Glass

A Bohemian glass trumpet vase, with enamel panels painted with flowers, restored, late 19thC, 17in (43cm) high.
£280–350 Sworders

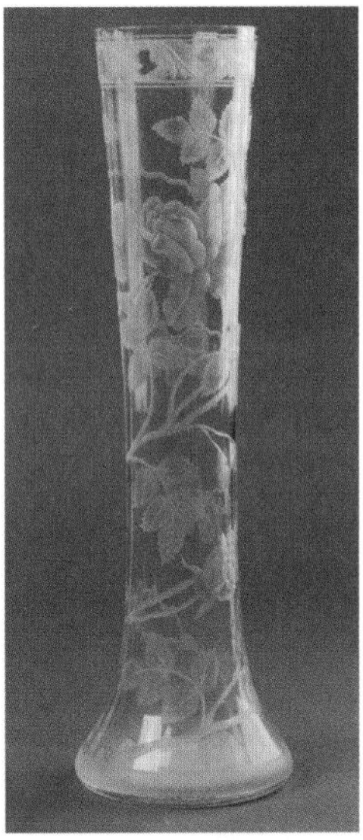

A Victorian glass vase, engraved with roses, 18in (45.5cm) high.
£175–220 Hy Duke

ohemian cut-glass vase, by Moser
ssworks, c1900, 9in (23cm) high.
00–800 Mike Weedon

A pair of Bohemian glass vases, each painted with fruit and flowers, the reverse cut with a lens, c1900, 6in (15cm) high.
£280–350 Dreweatte Neate (HAM)

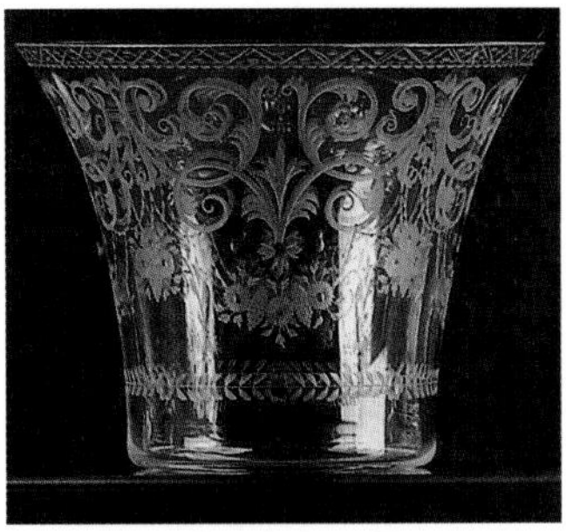

A Lobmeyr glass vase, designed by Stefan Rath, engraved with borders and bands of flowers, marked, Austria, Vienna, c1905, 6in (15cm) high.
£450–550 Dorotheum

. G. Hawkes Glass Co cut-glass vase,
orated with Queens pattern, signed, America,
w York, early 20thC, 11in (28cm) high.
50–550 Jackson's

MARKET INFORMATION CONTINENTAL

- Continental glass has been dogged by the continuing poor economic conditions in Germany – traditionally the most popular centre for collectors of European glass – but there are signs of improvement.
- Dutch glass such as the finely engraved light balusters of the 1740s–60s are impressive works or art and should be focused on.
- Current market trends are very positive for rare Venetian glass of the 16th and 17th centuries, good late 19th-century French glass by Baccarat and others and decorative Bohemian glass from the 1840s and '50s.
- Collectors from the Far and Middle East are once more collecting decorative pieces from the late 19th century, while average academic examples from the 17th and 18th centuries are finding it more difficult to attract buyers. Consequently, the spotlight has slightly dimmed for the more impressive pieces. The reduction in value of such glass at all levels offers a perfect opportunity for new collectors to enter the market and snap up some high quality examples at affordable prices.
- One of the most significant areas of improvement has been for European enamelled glass in the Islamic style. For example, the works of J. & L. Lobmeyr of Vienna and Philippe-Joseph Brocard of Paris have trebled in value over the last five years. Strong interest from America and the Middle East has fuelled this resurgence.

MISCELLANEOUS

A cut-glass box, with ormolu mounts, on paw feet, France, 19thC, 10½in (26.5cm) wide.
£4,750–5,750 Sotheby's (NY)

A blown and notch-cut glass cruet set, comprising three pieces, c1770, 7¼in (18.5cm) high.
£200–225 Glass etc

A cut-glass preserve pot and cover, c1810, 6¼in (16cm) high.
£50–55 Glass etc

A glass tankard, moulded with flutes, enclosing a sixpence, slight damage, late 18thC, 8in (20cm) high.
£280–350 Sworders

A pair of cut-glass candlesticks, c1830, 8in (20.5cm) high.
£540–600 Rapparee

A pinwheel- and fan-cut-glass inkwell, America, c1900, 3in (7.5cm) high.
£475–575 Jackson's

A cut-glass preserve jar and cover, c1810, 11½in (29cm) high.
£225–275 Hy Duke

A cut-glass tea canister, cut with vertical and horizontal prisms and strawberry diamonds, with stopper, c1815, 5½in (14cm) high.
£80–90 Glass etc

A hob- and lace-cut-glass charger, with laurel wreath decoration, America, c1900, 13½in (34.5cm) diam.
£200–250 Jackson's

A Sowerby Queens ware pressed glass plate on a tripod stand, 1879, 10in (25.5cm) diam.
£135–150 Just Glass

A Bohemian cased glass sugar box, cut and decorated in enamels with flowers, the cover painted with cattle in a landscape, with gilt-metal mounts, c1860, 5½in (14cm) wide.
£800–1,000 Dorotheum

A pair of toddy lifters, with panel-cut shoulde and neck rings, c1800, 4½in (11.5cm) high.
£220–250 Frank Dux

A toddy lifter was used to transfer punch from bowl to glass using a syphon principle. The bulbous end of the decanter-shaped bottle is lowered into the punch and a finge placed over a neck hole. When the thumb is removed, the punch pours out into the glas

/INTAGE WINES

) N THE FACE OF IT investing in wine is a racing cert. The best ones go inexorably up; the rest paddle along behind. Art is not so different – pt that the fashionable view of what's best is, , fashionable. It's not that wine is immune from ion – just that very few wines cut the mustard, larly, famously, and internationally. And there's ther reason: wine takes time, and time is on the stor's side.

e routine is this: you contact a mainstream wine chant or, better, several. You wait until the release good new vintage. En primeur signifies it is still in el, at its opening price, with a year or more to go it is bottled, shipped and taxes become due. read all the glowing reports, wine by wine ysis, and pick your horse. Past form is readily lable – go to winesearcher.com for the current es of almost any wine.

ordeaux is the classic: the Derby, the Grand National Cheltenham rolled into one. Why? Because there big enough quantity, and a wide enough range, to e a real market. Even more important, because the t keep and improve – in a good vintage for up to 30 or 40 years – time for multiple dealings.

Entry into a blue chip market is never cheap or indeed easy. The racing-cert labels tend to be on allocation to people who have got there already. If Château Pétrus always goes up, your chance of buying any is conditional on backing other Châteaux from the same stable, not necessarily so quick on their feet.

Burgundy, red and white, is a more ticklish purchase, calling for study so close it can become obsessive. It varies from vineyard to vineyard, producer to producer and vintage to vintage too widely for general rules to apply. Do your homework, though, and rewards will come – for instance among certain Rhône valley producers, and in such outside bets as super Tuscans, super Spaniards and even vintage Madeira, Tokay and Germany's rare Trockenbeerenauslesen. Port has long been considered mainstream; it just calls for patience.

In musical chairs the music stops; in wine-investing, too. Wine is a perishable commodity whose sell-by date remains a secret. The canny only wait until they have doubled their money, then sell half and drink half for free.

Hugh Johnson

Prices shown on these pages are for single bottles, except for those marked (12) which are for cases of 12 x 75cl bottles.

eau Cheval Blanc St Emilion Grand Cru
Bordeaux

2 Vintage Rating: 10
0–550 Chicago Wine Co

5 Vintage Rating: 8
0–350 Fine & Rare Wines

9 Vintage Rating: 9
0–220 Farr Vintners

0 Vintage Rating: 10
0–950 Fine & Rare Wines

5 Vintage Rating: 9
000–2,400 (12) Justerini & Brooks

6 Vintage Rating: 9
400–1,800 (12) Farr Vintners

0 Vintage Rating: 9
0–800 Berry Bros & Rudd

Château Figeac St Emilion Grand Cru
Red Bordeaux

1982 Vintage Rating: 10
£750–850 Corney & Barrow

1985 Vintage Rating: 8
£575–675 (12) Sotheby's

1989 Vintage Rating: 9
£575–675 (12) Sotheby's

1990 Vintage Rating: 10
£100–130 Fine & Rare Wines

1995 Vintage Rating: 9
£70–85 Dreweatt Neate

1996 Vintage Rating: 9
£45–55 Dreweatt Neate

2000 Vintage Rating: 9
£550–650 (12) Fine & Rare Wines

Château Haut Brion 1st growth
Red Bordeaux

1982 Vintage Rating: 10
£200–250 Dreweatt Neate

1985 Vintage Rating: 8
£120–150 Chicago Wine Co

1989 Vintage Rating: 9
£5,750–6,750 (12) Sotheby's

1990 Vintage Rating 10
£4,000–5,000 (12) Sotheby's (NY)

1995 Vintage Rating: 9
£2,000–2,500 (12) Farr Vintners

1996 Vintage Rating: 9
£220–250 Berry Bros & Rudd

2000 Vintage Rating: 9
£380–420 Berry Bros & Rudd

Château Lafite Rothschild 1st growth
Red Bordeaux

1982 Vintage Rating: 10
£550–650 Dreweatt Neate

1985 Vintage Rating: 8
£160–200 Fine & Rare Wines

1989 Vintage Rating: 9
£100–200 Dreweatt Neate

1990 Vintage Rating: 10
£400–450 Berry Bros & Rudd

1995 Vintage Rating: 9
£2,500–3,000 (12) Corney & Barrow

1996 Vintage Rating: 9
£80–120 Dreweatt Neate

2000 Vintage Rating: 9
£320–380 Chicago Wine Co

Château Latour 1st growth
Red Bordeaux

1982 Vintage Rating: 10
£10,000–12,000 (12) Sotheby's

1985 Vintage Rating: 8
£2,400–2,800 (12) Corney & Barrow

1989 Vintage Rating: 9
£150–180 Chicago Wine Co

1990 Vintage Rating: 10
£200–250 Dreweatt Neate

1995 Vintage Rating: 9
£2,750–3,250 (12) Justerini & Brooks

1996 Vintage Rating: 9
£180–220 Chicago Wine Co

2000 Vintage Rating: 9
£700–770 Berry Bros & Rudd

Château Margaux 1st growth
Red Bordeaux

1982 Vintage Rating: 10
£350–420 Chicago Wine Co

1985 Vintage Rating: 8
£350–380 Berry Bros & Rudd

1989 Vintage Rating: 9
£300–340 Berry Bros & Rudd

1990 Vintage Rating: 10
£300–340 Chicago Wine Co

1995 Vintage Rating: 9
£2,000–2,500 (12) Sotheby's

1996 Vintage Rating: 9
£470–520 Berry Bros & Rudd

2000 Vintage Rating: 9
£7,750–8,750 (12) Sotheby's (NY

GROWTH CLASSIFICATION

The classification system was introduced to help maintain quality. In 1855 several of the main wine-producing regions of Bordeaux ranked their top red wines in a classification system from First to Fifth growths, or crus. There has been only one change to the First growth classification – in 197 when Mouton Rothschild was promoted to First growth status. Other regions, such as Saint Emilion and Pessac-Léognan have subsequently introduced additional classifications and modifications. The Pomerol regio home to Pétrus and Le Pin, has no official classification system. In some cases the classification system is outdated – there are many unclassed wines which are produced to a very high quality, and several of the highly classified wines could possibly achieve a lower classification if Bordeaux wines were reclassified today.

Château Mouton Rothschild 1st growth
Red Bordeaux

1982 Vintage Rating: 10
£900–1,000 Berry Bros & Rudd

1985 Vintage Rating: 8
£1,700–2,000 (12) Corney & Barrow

1989 Vintage Rating: 9
£1,500–1,800 (12) Sotheby's

1990 Vintage Rating: 10
£1,800–2,200 (12) Sotheby's (NY)

1995 Vintage Rating: 9
£220–250 Berry Bros & Rudd

1996 Vintage Rating: 9
£1,800–2,200 (12) Justerini & Brooks

2000 Vintage Rating: 9
£2,800–3,500 (12) Sotheby's

Château Cos d'Estournel 2nd growth
Red Bordeaux

1982 Vintage Rating: 10
£180–220 Farr Vintners

1985 Vintage Rating: 8
£140–175 Berry Bros & Rudd

1989 Vintage Rating: 9
£850–1,000 (12) Corney & Barrow

1990 Vintage Rating: 10
£160–200 Berry Bros & Rudd

1995 Vintage Rating: 9
£65–80 Fine and Rare Wines

1996 Vintage Rating: 9
£1,100–1,400 (12) Sotheby's (NY)

2000 Vintage Rating: 9
£525–625 (12) Sotheby's

teau Ducru Beaucaillou 2nd growth
Bordeaux

2 Vintage Rating: 10
30–160 Fine and Rare Wines

5 Vintage Rating: 8
30–220 Dreweatt Neate

9 Vintage Rating: 9
25–750 (12) Justerini & Brooks

0 Vintage Rating: 10
)–70 Fine and Rare Wines

5 Vintage Rating: 9
100–1,300 (12) Sotheby's (NY)

6 Vintage Rating: 9
300–1,600 (12) Sotheby's (NY)

0 Vintage Rating: 9
0–100 Berry Bros & Rudd

Château Léoville Barton 2nd growth
Red Bordeaux

1982 Vintage Rating: 10
£1,200–1,500 (12)
Fine and Rare Wines

1985 Vintage Rating: 8
£55–65 Dreweatt Neate

1989 Vintage Rating: 9
£100–120 Dreweatt Neate

1990 Vintage Rating: 10
£70–85 Dreweatt Neate

1995 Vintage Rating: 9
£90–110 Chicago Wine Co

1996 Vintage Rating: 9
£500–600 (12) Justerini & Brooks

2000 Vintage Rating: 9
£100–120 Berry Bros & Rudd

Château Léoville Lascases 2nd growth
Red Bordeaux

1982 Vintage Rating: 10
£3,500–4,200 (12)
Justerini & Brooks

1985 Vintage Rating: 8
£120–150 Berry Bros & Rudd

1989 Vintage Rating: 9
£1,350–1,600 (12) Sotheby's (NY)

1990 Vintage Rating: 10
£220–250 Berry Bros & Rudd

1995 Vintage Rating: 9
£1,500–1,800 (12) Sotheby's (NY)

1996 Vintage Rating: 9
£175–200 Berry Bros & Rudd

2000 Vintage Rating: 9
£160–200 Fine and Rare Wines

âteau Montrose 2nd growth
d Bordeaux

32 Vintage Rating: 10
,200–1,500 (12) Corney & Barrow

35 Vintage Rating: 8
00–720 (12) Corney & Barrow

39 Vintage Rating: 9
,800–2,200 (12) Farr Vintners

90 Vintage Rating: 10
00–370 Berry Bros & Rudd

95 Vintage Rating: 9
50–650 Farr Vintners

96 Vintage Rating: 9
5–70 Berry Bros & Rudd

00 Vintage Reading: 9
00–120 Berry Bros & Rudd

Château Pichon Lalande 2nd growth
Red Bordeaux

1982 Vintage Rating: 10
£400–500 Dreweatt Neate

1985 Vintage Rating: 8
£140–165 Berry Bros & Rudd

1989 Vintage Rating: 9
£120–150 Berry Bros & Rudd

1990 Vintage Rating: 10
£900–1,100 (12) Farr Vintners

1995 Vintage Rating: 9
£80–100 Fine and Rare Wines

1996 Vintage Rating: 9
£120–150 Berry Bros & Rudd

2000 Vintage Rating: 9
£1,000–1,200 (12) Sotheby's

Château Palmer 3rd growth
Red Bordeaux

1982 Vintage Rating: 10
£100–130 Fine and Rare Wines

1985 Vintage Rating: 8
£75–90 Farr Vintners

1989 Vintage Rating: 9
£1,600–2,000 (12) Farr Vintners

1990 Vintage Rating: 10
£100–130 Fine and Rare Wines

1995 Vintage Rating: 9
£80–100 Dreweatt Neate

1996 Vintage Rating: 9
£80–100 Berry Bros & Rudd

2000 Vintage Rating: 9
£950–1,150 (12) Sotheby's

Château Talbot 4th growth
Red Bordeaux

1982 Vintage Rating: 10
£1,300–1,600 (12) Sotheby's (NY)

1985 Vintage Rating: 8
£45–55 Fine and Rare Wines

1989 Vintage Rating: 9
£45–55 Fine and Rare Wines

1990 Vintage Rating: 9
£45–55 Fine and Rare Wines

1995 Vintage Rating: 9
£350–450 (12) Farr Vintners

1996 Vintage Rating: 9
£30–40 Fine and Rare Wines

2000 Vintage Rating: 9
£50–60 Berry Bros & Rudd

Château Pétrus, Pomerol
Red Bordeaux

1982 Vintage Rating: 10
£1,100–1,300 Dreweatt Neate

1985 Vintage Rating: 8
£3,400–4,200 (12) Sotheby's (NY)

1989 Vintage Rating: 9
£2,000–2,300 Berry Bros & Rudd

1990 Vintage Rating: 10
£2,500–3,000 Berry Bros & Rudd

1995 Vintage Rating: 9
£3,400–4,200 (12) Sotheby's (NY)

1996 Vintage Rating: 9
£1,800–2,200 (12) Sotheby's (NY)

2000 Vintage Rating: 9
£2,250–2,650 Fine and Rare Wines

VINTAGE RATING

The vintage rating system is based on the quality of the vintage relative to other vintages of wines from the same region – ten being the highest score and one the lowest. In general, vintages with a higher score can be kept for longer than vintages with a low score. As with all subjective methods of scoring, generalizations are unavoidable and, within each wine-growing area, some wines will be of relatively better quality than the score implies and some will be of poorer quality.

Château Le Pin, Pomerol
Red Bordeaux

1982 Vintage Rating: 10
£30,000–35,000 (12)
Corney & Barrow

1985 Vintage Rating: 8
£12,000–15,000 (12)
Corney & Barrow

1989 Vintage Rating: 9
£1,100–1,400 Fine and Rare Wines

1990 Vintage Rating: 10
£3,500–3,800 Berry Bros & Rudd

1995 Vintage Rating: 9
£6,000–7,000 (12) Sotheby's (NY)

1996 Vintage Rating: 9
£3,500–4,200 (12) Sotheby's

2000 Vintage Rating: 9
£16,000–20,000 (12)
Corney & Barrow

Château Lynch Bages 5th growth
Red Bordeaux

1982 Vintage Rating: 10
£140–180 Farr Vintners

1985 Vintage Rating: 8
£1,300–1,600 Corney & Barrow

1989 Vintage Rating: 9
£1,200–1,500 (12) Sotheby's (NY)

1990 Vintage Rating: 10
£100–120 Dreweatt Neate

1995 Vintage Rating: 9
£65–80 Berry Bros & Rudd

1996 Vintage Rating: 9
£80–100 Berry Bros & Rudd

2000 Vintage Rating: 9
£65–85 Chicago Wine Co

Richebourg Grand Cru, Domaine de la Romanée Conti
Red Burgundy

1986 Vintage Rating: 7
£300–370 Fine and Rare Wines

1989 Vintage Rating: 9
£550–650 Fine and Rare Wines

1990 Vintage Rating: 10
£1,200–1,400 Berry Bros & Rudd

1995 Vintage Rating: 8
£550–650 Fine and Rare Wines

1996 Vintage Rating: 9
£550–650 Fine and Rare Wines

2000 Vintage Rating: 7
£270–300 Berry Bros & Rudd

2002 Vintage Rating: 8
£700–800 Fine and Rare Wines

·trachet Grand Cru, Domaine de la
·anée Conti
·e Burgundy

·5 Vintage Rating: 7
·,000–22,000 (12) Sotheby's (NY)

·9 Vintage Rating: 9
·300–2,750 Fine and Rare Wines

·0 Vintage Rating: 10
·,000–25,000 (12) Sotheby's (NY)

·5 Vintage Rating: 8
·000–1,200 Fine and Rare Wines

·6 Vintage Rating: 9
·000–2,200 Berry Bros & Rudd

·0 Vintage Rating: 7
·300–1,600 Berry Bros & Rudd

·2 Vintage Rating: 8
·250–1,500 Justerini & Brooks

Château Climens
White Bordeaux

1983 Vintage Rating: 9
£900–1,100 (12) Justerini & Brooks

1986 Vintage Rating: 8
£70–85 Fine and Rare Wines

1988 Vintage Rating: 10
£50–60 Chicago Wine Co

1989 Vintage Rating: 9
£45–55 Dreweatt Neate

1990 Vintage Rating: 10
£90–110 Dreweatt Neate

1995 Vintage Rating: 9
£28–35 Fine and Rare Wines

2001 Vintage Rating: 10
£200–240 Berry Bros & Rudd

Château Rieussec
White Bordeaux

1983 Vintage Rating: 9
£100–120 Berry Bros & Rudd

1986 Vintage Rating: 8
£40–50 Fine and Rare Wines

1988 Vintage Rating: 10
£400–500 (12) Dreweatt Neate

1989 Vintage Rating: 9
£50–60 Berry Bros & Rudd

1990 Vintage Rating: 10
£400–500 (12) Sotheby's

1995 Vintage Rating: 9
£35–40 Berry Bros & Rudd

2001 Vintage Rating: 10
£100–120 Berry Bros & Rudd

·âteau Suduiraut
·ite Bordeaux

·33 Vintage Rating: 9
·20–380 (12) Sotheby's

·36 Vintage Rating: 8
·00–350 (12) Sotheby's

·38 Vintage Rating: 10
·8–32 Dreweatt Neate

·39 Vintage Rating: 9
·5–45 Fine and Rare Wines

·90 Vintage Rating: 10
·8–45 Dreweatt Neate

·95 Vintage Rating: 9
·75–220 (12) Dreweatt Neate

·01 Vintage Rating: 10
·5–80 Berry Bros & Rudd

Château d'Yquem
White Bordeaux

1983 Vintage Rating: 9
£2,750–3,250 (12) Sotheby's

1986 Vintage Rating: 8
£240–270 Berry Bros & Rudd

1988 Vintage Rating: 10
£160–200 Chicago Wine Co

1989 Vintage Rating: 9
£320–350 Berry Bros & Rudd

1990 Vintage Rating: 10
£300–350 Berry Bros & Rudd

1995 Vintage Rating: 9
£130–160 Fine and Rare Wines

2001 Vintage Rating: 10
£3,500–4,500 (12) Farr Vintners

Dom Pérignon
Champagne

1982 Vintage Rating: 9
£80–100 Chicago Wine Co

1985 Vintage Rating: 9
£100–120 Chicago Wine Co

1988 Vintage Rating: 8
£150–180 Farr Vintners

1990 Vintage Rating: 10
£120–140 Corney & Barrow

1996 Vintage Rating: 9
£65–80 Dreweatt Neate

1998 Vintage Rating: 9
£80–100 Berry Bros & Rudd

1999 Vintage Rating: 8
£700–850 (12) Fine and Rare Wines

Penfold's Grange
Australia

1990 Vintage Rating: 10
£250–300 Fine and Rare Wines

1991 Vintage Rating: 10
£150–175 Justerini & Brooks

1994 Vintage Rating: 9
£130–150 Fine and Rare Wines

1996 Vintage Rating: 10
£125–150 Fine and Rare Wines

1998 Vintage Rating: 10
£200–250 Berry Bros & Rudd

2000 Vintage Rating: 8
£150–200 Berry Bros & Rudd

2001 Vintage Rating: 9
£1,500–1,750 (12) Farr Vintners

Dow
Port

1963 Vintage Rating: 10
£90–100 Fine and Rare Wines

1970 Vintage Rating: 9
£120–140 Berry Bros & Rudd

1977 Vintage Rating: 8
£70–90 Berry Bros & Rudd

1983 Vintage Rating: 8
£300–350 (12) Fine and Rare Wines

1985 Vintage Rating: 8
£55–60 Berry Bros & Rudd

1994 Vintage Rating: 10
£40–50 Dreweatt Neate

1997 Vintage Rating: 8
£300–350 (12) Sotheby's

Fonseca
Port

1963 Vintage Rating: 10
£230–250 Berry Bros & Rudd

1970 Vintage Rating: 9
£80–100 Dreweatt Neate

1977 Vintage Rating: 8
£80–100 Corney & Barrow

1983 Vintage Rating: 8
£35–45 Dreweatt Neate

1985 Vintage Rating: 8
£55–70 Berry Bros & Rudd

1994 Vintage Rating: 10
£100–120 Berry Bros & Rudd

1997 Vintage Rating: 8
£420–520 (12) Justerini & Brooks

We would like to thank Berry Brothers & Rudd Ltd for kindly allowing us to photograph the wine bottles and labels shown on these pages.

Graham
Port

1963 Vintage Rating: 10
£90–100 Dreweatt Neate

1970 Vintage Rating: 9
£100–125 Berry Bros & Rudd

1977 Vintage Rating: 8
£30–40 Chicago Wine Co

1983 Vintage Rating: 8
£350–420 (12) Sotheby's

1985 Vintage Rating: 8
£60–70 Berry Bros & Rudd

1994 Vintage Rating: 10
£28–35 Dreweatt Neate

1997 Vintage Rating: 8
£280–350 (12) Justerini & Brooks

Taylor
Port

1963 Vintage Rating: 10
£100–120 Dreweatt Neate

1970 Vintage Rating: 9
£60–75 Farr Vintners

1977 Vintage Rating: 8
£100–120 Berry Bros & Rudd

1983 Vintage Rating: 8
£35–42 Dreweatt Neate

1985 Vintage Rating: 8
£375–450 (12) Sotheby's

1994 Vintage Rating: 10
£70–80 Corney & Barrow

1997 Vintage Rating: 8
£45–55 Berry Bros & Rudd

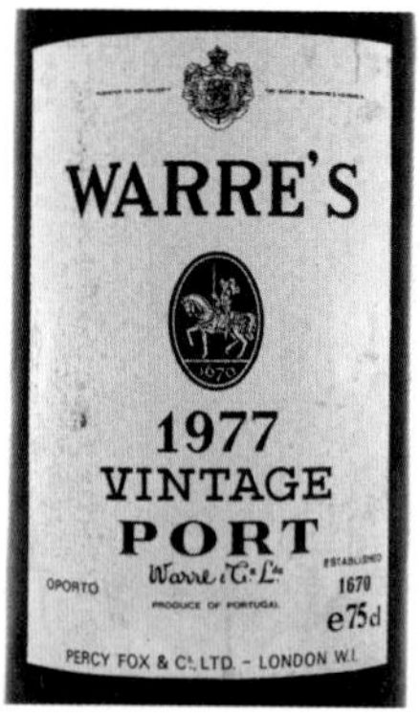

Warre
Port

1963 Vintage Rating: 10
£950–1,150 (12) Justerini & Brooks

1970 Vintage Rating: 9
£100–120 Berry Bros & Rudd

1977 Vintage Rating: 8
£55–65 Berry Bros & Rudd

1983 Vintage Rating: 8
£45–50 Berry Bros & Rudd

1985 Vintage Rating: 8
£35–40 Fine and Rare Wines

1994 Vintage Rating: 10
£350–400 (12) Dreweatt Neate

1997 Vintage Rating: 8
£20–25 Farr Vintners

WINE ANTIQUES

ɘramic port barrel, cover
ꞩing, c1900, 13in (33cm) high.
0–120 Junktion

A pair of silver bottle holders, by Robert Smith, chased and pierced with scrolling vines, with Vernon crest, Dublin 1844, Ireland, 5¾in (14.5cm) high, 59oz.
£22,000–25,000 Mealy's
The provenance of these bottle holders is exceptional, having originally been owned by the Vernon family of Clontarf Castle and more recently by the Guinness heir, the Hon Garech Browne.

A silver-mounted glass claret jug, by John Grinsell & Son, engraved with a figure of a milkmaid, the silver mount in the form of a milk churn, Birmingham 1876, 12in (30.5cm) high.
£3,250–3,750 Percy's

ilver-mounted rock-crystal ss claret jug, by William & ɔrge Sissons, engraved with nes, birds and insects beside a d in the manner of Stevens & liams of Stourbridge, Sheffield 78, 10¾in (27cm) high.
,750–3,250 Bearnes

A pair of silver-mounted cut-glass claret jugs, by Finley & Taylor, monogrammed 'IRSR', London 1891, 12¼in (31cm) high, with fitted case.
£4,500–5,500 Sotheby's (O)

A silver-mounted cut-glass claret jug, with engraved decoration, maker's mark 'CEN', Sheffield 1894, 12in (31cm) high.
£600–700 Penrith Farmers' & Kidd's

A silver-mounted cut-glass claret jug, by Atkin Bros, with pierced and embossed decoration, Sheffield 1896, 8¾in (22cm) high.
£325–400 Cheffins

air of silver coasters, by Richard Makepeace, pierced with scrolling foliage and engraved h Middleton crest, on turned wooden bases, London 1772, 4¾in (12cm) diam.
,750–5,750 Sotheby's

A set of four silver coasters, by Henry Wilkinson & Co, Sheffield 1835, 8in (20.5cm) diam.
£6,250–7,000 Andrew Campbell

ɔair of silver coasters, London 1840, 7in (18cm) diam.
,250–3,750 Bourbon-Hanby

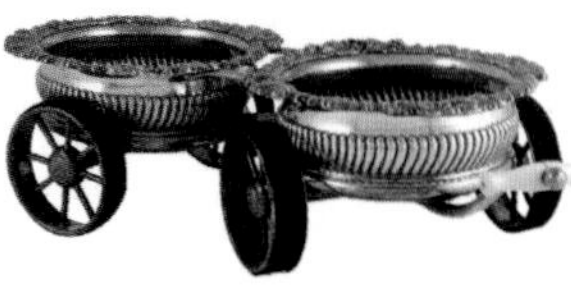

An Old Sheffield-plated double coaster trolley, with spoked wheels and an ivory handle, c1840, 16½in (41.7cm) long.
£900–1,100 Woolley & Wallis

A set of four papier-mâché coasters, decorated with gilt butterflies and foliage, mid-19thC, 5¼in (13.5cm) diam.

£450–550 Woolley & Wallis

A steel Kings's Screw corkscrew, with turned ivory handles, marked 'Machin, Leadenhall', c1820, 11in (28cm) extended.

£850–1,000 Sworders

A silver-plated Napier cocktail shaker, with 15 cocktail recipes, America, patented 1932, 11in (28cm) high.

£225–250 Greystoke Antiques

The 'Tells-You-How-Mixer' was Napier's first cocktail shaker. The outer sleeve rotates to reveal engraved recipes for 15 different classic cocktails, some with as many as six different ingredients. The shaker was originally available only through Saks Fifth Avenue. Napier products have very thin silver plating that is often in poor condition.

A Thomason patent corkscrew, with turne wooden handle and cast-bronze barrel, wi 'Gothic window' decoration, early 19thC, 7½in (19cm) long.

£550–650 Gorringes (L)

A mahogany decanter box, containing six glass bottles, 19thC, 9in (23cm) wide.

£1,300–1,450 Ronald Chambers

A mahogany decanter box, c1800, 12in (30.5cm) wide.

£450–500 Mostly Boxes

A brass-bound decanter box, with four decanters and six glasses, c1820, 8¼in (21cm) wide.

£650–725 Antiquesales.com.au

An ebonized decanter box, containing four etched-glass decanters and 16 glasses in a fitted interior, France, c1880, 13in (33cm) wide.

£900–1,000 Woburn Abbey

A pair of silver and parcel-gilt wine ewers, by George Fox, each in the form of a griffin, with glass eyes, London 1868 and 1872, 8¼in (21cm) high, 52¼oz.

£6,000–7,000 Dreweatt Neate (N)

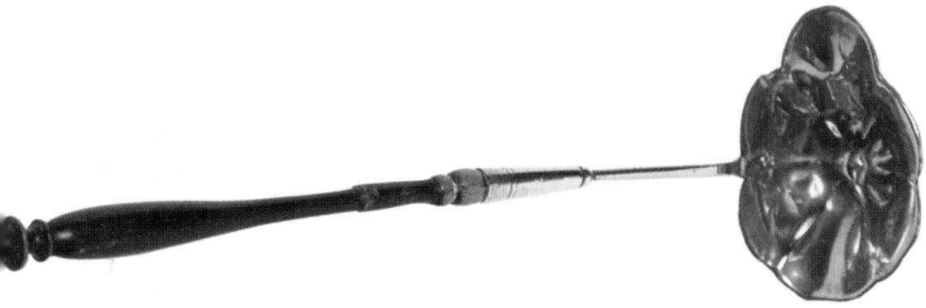

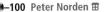

›pper and brass toddy ladle, with a turned wood handle, France, c1810, 11in (28cm) long.

›–100 Peter Norden ⊞

A silver nutmeg grater, by Joseph Taylor, with a domed screw cover above bright-engraving and a screw base, crested, Birmingham 1799, 1¼in (3cm) high.

£400–500
Woolley & Wallis

Nutmeg was used to spice toddies and mulled wine.

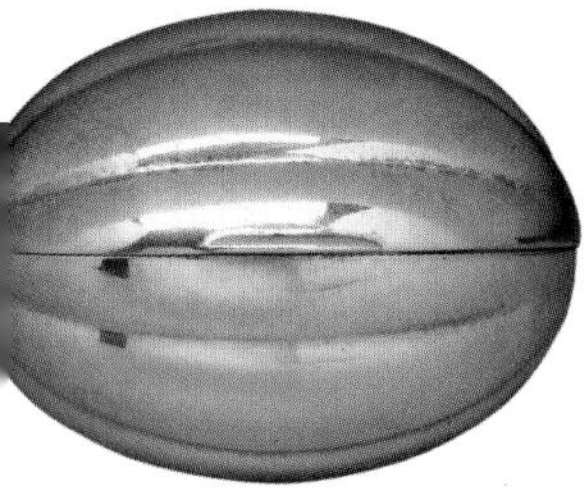

›lver nutmeg grater, by Gorham ›ufacturing Co, in the form of a melon, › a hinged steel grater, America, Rhode ›d 1869, 2in (5cm) long.

30–350 Heritage

A set of four glass whisky tots, with silver covers, Birmingham 1912, 4in (10cm) high, in a fitted case.

£1,000–1,200 Bourbon-Hanby ⊞

A silver wine funnel, marked 'I.P.', London 1791, 6in (15cm) high.

£900–1,000
Shapiro & Co ⊞

›ictorian silver-plated wine ›ler, with embossed cartouches › vines on an engraved ground, ›n (24cm) high.

00–500
›wrence Fine Art

A silver wine funnel, by Hester Bateman, London 1782, 5¼in (13.5cm) long, 2oz.

£550–650 Waddington's

A silver wine label, by Sandilands Drinkwater, London, chased with a border of fruiting vines, incised 'CAPE', marked, c1745.

£700–850 Woolley & Wallis

A silver wine label, by Hester Bateman, London, bright-cut with a border of flowers and scrolls, incised 'FRONTINIAC', marked, c1775.

£700–850 Woolley & Wallis

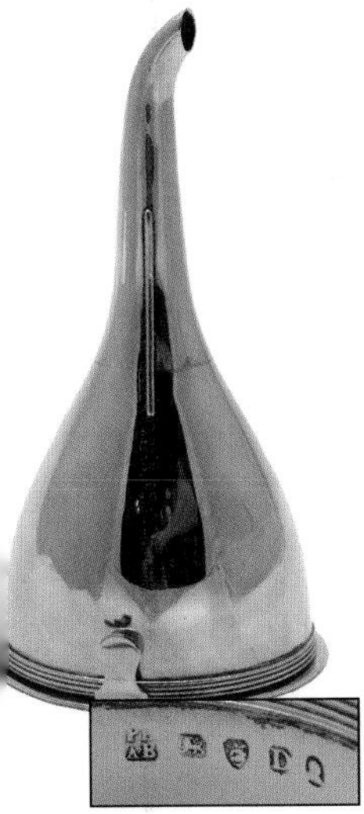

›ilver wine funnel, by Peter & ›n Bateman, London 1799, ›in (12cm) high.

›75–750
›nnifer Lloyd ⊞

A silver wine label, by Elizabeth Morely, pierced and bright-cut engraved 'MADEIRA', London 1799, 2in (5cm) wide.

£400–500 Gorringes (L)

A George III mother-of-pearl wine label, with border engraving, incised and filled with 'CALCAVELLA'.

£200–250 Woolley & Wallis

JEWELLERY

BANGLES & BRACELETS

A gold serpent bangle, with engraved decoration, set with enamel, rubies and diamonds, c1845, with case.
£1,400–1,600 Gorringes (L)

An early Victorian pinchbeck bracelet, set with five amethysts.
£375–450 Webb's

A Victorian 15ct gold bracelet, with integral flattened lozenge section strapwork.
£3,200–3,500 Wimpole Antiques

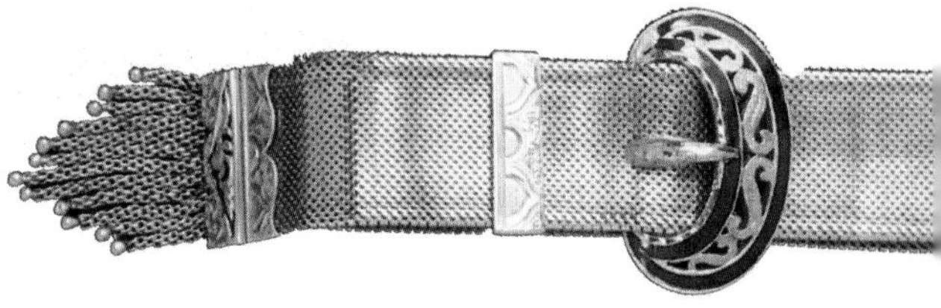

A pair of Victorian 14ct gold and enamel Milanese pattern *jarretière* bracelets, with scrol buckles and foxtail fringes, slight damage.
£700–850 Skinner

A pair of Victorian 14ct gold bracelets, decorated with tracery enamel birds and foliate motifs.
£300–350 Skinner

ESSENTIAL REFERENCE ROBERT PHILLIPS

Robert Phillips (1810–81), known as 'Robert Phillips of Cockspur Street', was an important English goldsmith and one of the leading exponents of the 'archaeological' style of jewellery popular in the 1860s and 1870s. At the Paris Exposition of 1867 he exhibited a range of gold pieces inspired by Assyrian, Babylonian and Egyptian themes. He was also noted for his use of coral and polychrome enamels. After his death the business was continued by his son, Alfred. Robert Phillips signed his jewellery with a stylized Prince of Wales feather motif in a lozenge.

An archaeological-style gold bangle, by Robert Phillips & Sons, with applied beade wirework and two lapis lazuli hinged pane with internal inscription '19th September 1878', with maker's mark.
£4,500–5,500 Bearnes

A Victorian 15ct gold bangle, set with half pearls, 2½in (6.5cm) diam.
£1,100–1,300 Wimpole Antiques

A gold bangle, decorated with enamel and set with onyx and rubies Russia, c1885, 3in (7.5cm) diam.
£1,400–1,750 Lyon & Turnbull

ROOCHES

edgwood jasper ware Slave allion, depicting a chained . and moulded with the iption 'Am I not a Man and other', impressed mark, gold mount, late 18thC, (3cm) high.

500–3,000
heby's (NY)

Slave Medallion was modelled /illiam Hackwood at Josiah gwood's request as a design he seal of the Society for the ition of Slavery, c1787. gwood was an ardent itionist and cameos and seals ing this subject were both and given away.

ESSENTIAL REFERENCE MOURNING JEWELLERY

The evolution of mourning jewellery offers collectors a fascinating insight into changing social tastes and fashions over a two hundred-year period. In the late 17th century memento mori slides and rings contained gruesome enamelled skulls and coffins. After the death of Prince Albert in 1861 Queen Victoria went into prolonged mourning and the fashion for mourning jewellery really took off, largely due to the huge popularity of Whitby jet.

The brooch illustrated is a prime example of late 18th-century neo-classical mourning jewellery – a finely enamelled funerary urn painted with a miniature of an inconsolable maiden clutching a tomb bearing an appropriately tragic inscription. Pearls signified tears and such jewels invariably exhibited a weeping willow tree picked out in human hair. This was sentimentality at its most heart-rending.

A gold and enamel mourning brooch, mounted with seed pearls, with a miniature of a maiden embracing a tomb inscribed 'E.W. Not Lost but Gone Before' and incorporating hair, the reverse inscribed 'AD 1787', late 18thC, together with a hand-written note.

£1,400–1,750 Bearnes

ietra dura **brooch,** set with hardstones in orm of a butterfly, in a gold frame with scroll ng, Italy, Florence, early 19thC, with case.

0–500 Gorringes (L)

A carved coral brooch, in the form of a putto, suspending three amphora-shaped drops, one drop damaged, c1840.

£650–750 Bearnes

A gold brooch, set with graduated emeralds, with a tassel drop and suspending chain loop, c1850.

£750–850 Bearnes

old brooch, set with foil-backed ethysts, rock crystals and freshwater rls, Scotland, c1850, 2in (5cm) diam.

,000–1,200 Wimpole Antiques

ilver knot brooch, set with agate, tland, c1860, 3in (7.5cm) wide.

50–400 Wimpole Antiques

A silver brooch, in the form of a flower, set with agate panels, Scotland, c1860, 2in (5cm) diam.

£250–300 Aurum

A gold brooch, by Castellani, set with spinels and seed pearls, signed, Italy, c1860.

£3,800–4,500 Sotheby's (NY)

A Victorian 18ct gold brooch, set with turquoise and pearls, the rear with a glazed panel, 2in (5cm) high.

£500–550 Anthony Green Antiques

A Victorian silver pebble brooch, set with agate, sard and malachite panels, 2in (5cm) diam.

£135–150 Vetta Decorative Arts

A Victorian bicolour gold brooch, with applied bead a ropetwist decoration, pin replaced, 2½in (6.5cm) long.

£180–220 Skinner

A Victorian gold locket brooch, in the form of a heart, set with a ruby within a pearl border, reverse engraved 'Evelyn from Stanley 11th June 1888', 1in (2.5cm) high.

£900–1,000 Wimpole Antiques

A Victorian neo-classical-style 18ct gold brooch, with a jasper ware panel enclosed by pearl and guilloche enamel borders, 1¾in (4.5cm) high.

£1,500–1,650 Wimpole Antiques

A Victorian 14ct gold and enamel brooc the carved rock crystal depicting an ancier Egyptian, set with diamonds and seed pea 2in (5cm) long.

£700–850 Skinner

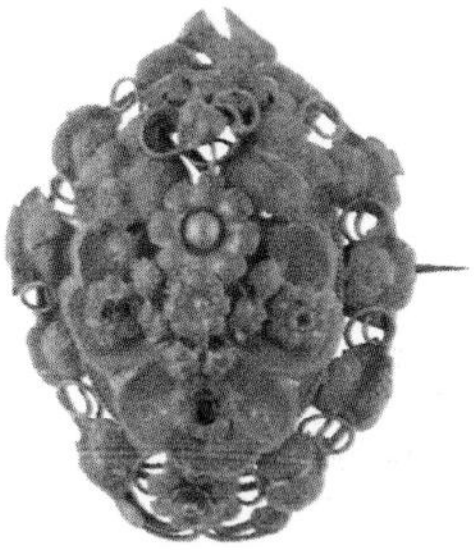

A 15ct gold locket brooch, moulded with vine leaves, tendrils and flowers, with engraved decoration and set with four paste stones, the hinged panel enclosing a glazed locket, Australia, c1870.

£175–200 Leonard Joel

A Victorian 15ct gold brooch, set with a faceted citrine within an enamel border, 2in (5cm) wide.

£1,150–1,300 Wimpole Antiques

A gold and enamel brooch, in the form of a knot with suspended tassel, Australia, c1870.

£400–500 Leonard Joel

A silver and gold brooch, mounted *en tremb* and set with diamonds, c1880, 2¾in (7cm) h

£2,000–2,400 Bukowskis

ver and gold brooch, c1880,
(4cm) wide.
0–150 Aurum

A silver and gold brooch, in the form of a fly, set with rubies and diamonds, with a later detachable brooch fitting, c1890, 1½in (4cm) wide.
£3,500–4,250 Cheffins

A Victorian diamond brooch, in the form of a star, the points interspaced with single diamonds on knife-bars.
£800–1,000 Hy Duke

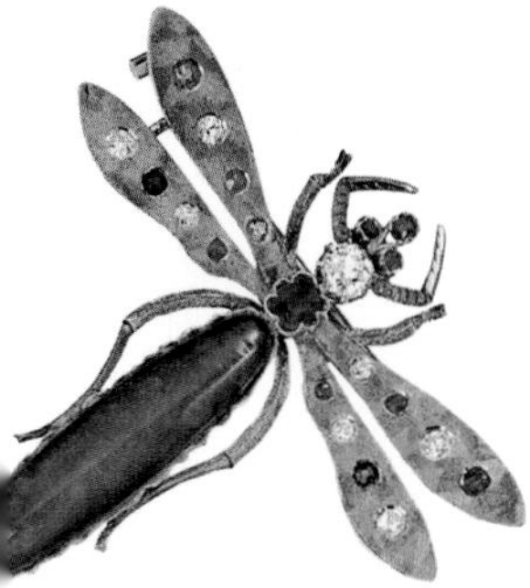

4ct gold brooch, by A. J. Hedges & Co,
e form of a dragonfly, set with rubies,
ralds, sapphires and an opal cabochon,
ked, America, c1890.
500–6,500 Sotheby's (NY)
*rew J. Hedges was born in Florham Park,
Jersey in 1828. After working for several
l jewellery firms, he established A. J.
ges & Co in 1877 with the aid of his
her Wallace. The company's output
ided a line of 14ct gold jewellery set with
nonds and other stones, and novelty
els featuring insects and reptiles.*

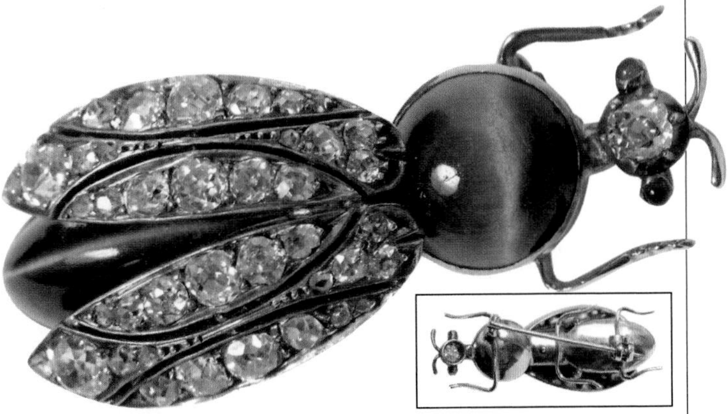

A Victorian 15ct gold and silver brooch, in the form of a beetle, set with tiger's eye cabochon, diamonds and garnets, 1¾in (4.5cm) long.
£3,400–3,750 Wimpole Antiques

An 18ct gold and enamel brooch, by Plisson & Hartz, France, c1900, 1in (2.5cm) diam.
£2,200–2,500 Wimpole Antiques
Maison Plisson & Hartz, Paris, was notable for pioneering dragon brooches known as broches-chimères.

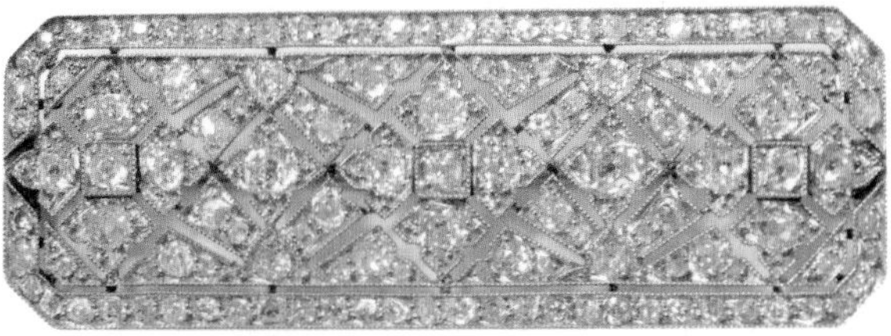

A platinum brooch, set with diamonds, with a gold pin, c1900, 2½in (6.5cm) wide.
£4,250–4,750 Wimpole Antiques

4ct gold brooch, set with onyx, enamel and
d pearls, depicting a putto driving a chariot,
nce, late 19thC, 1½in (4cm) high.
00–700 Skinner
*s miniature is a prime example of 'Limoges
ival' enamel in monochrome colours known as
grisaille. Neo-classical subjects such as putti
play were particularly popular in this medium.*

A platinum-mounted silver brooch, by Tiffany & Co, in the form of a bow, set with diamonds and pearls, America, early 20thC, 2in (5cm) wide.
£1,800–2,200 Skinner

An Edwardian platinum brooch, set with diamonds, with a gold pin, 2in (5cm) high.
£2,000–2,200 Wimpole Antiques

CAMEOS

A cameo bracelet, carved with a classical maiden, set in an 18ct gold mount, mid-19thC, 2in (5cm) wide.

£1,100–1,200 Anthony Green Antiques

A shell cameo bracelet, comprising five cameos carved with Cupid at various pursuits, within gold frames, set in gold, Italy, c1870, 6¾in (17cm) long.

£3,500–4,250 Sothebys (NY)

The design of this bracelet is strongly redolent of Castellani, who specialized in Classical Revival archaeological jewellery with applied gold shotwork and twisted wire decoration.

MILLER'S COMPARES

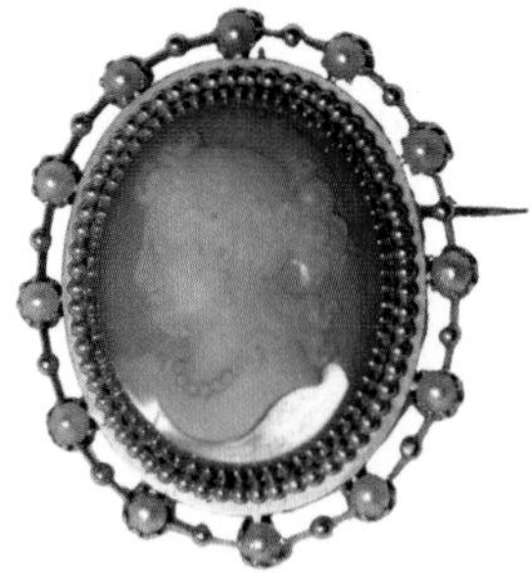

(L) A sardonyx cameo brooch, in a gold wirework and half pearl frame, c1850, 1½in (4cm) high.

£1,300–1,500 Grey-Harris

(R) A shell cameo brooch, in a gold mount, c1865, 2in (5cm) high.

£350–400 Grey-Harris

Although these two Victorian cameo brooches are broadly similar, having attractive cameos and gold frames, the key factor that determines the value of the cameo on the left is that it is carved from brown and white sardonyx, while the item on the right is fashioned from shell. The detail in the carving of the item on the left is intricate and finely observed – sardonyx is very hard and takes a far better polish, whereas the shell cameo on the right is worn in several places – an enduring problem with natural shell which is soft, brittle and frequently sustains wear and damage. Damage or repair to the frame will reduce value even further.

A lava cameo brooch, in a 15ct gold mount, c1860, 2in (5cm) wide.

£180–200 Grey-Harris

A shell cameo brooch, carved with two classical female warriors, in a gold wirework frame, late 19thC, with case.

£700–850 Bearnes

A cameo brooch, carved with the head of Classical Greek scholar, set in a gold leaf scroll mount, c1850, 2in (5cm) high.

£275–300 Amelie Caswell

A hardstone cameo brooch, carved with and a woman in a chariot, within a gold and beadwork frame, signed 'E. Guyetant', c

£3,250–4,000 Sotheby's (NY)

A cameo brooch, carved with a profile of a man, signed 'Barbarti Sculpt', Italy, c1860, 2in (5cm) high, with fitted box.

£380–450 Webb's

It was the fashion for gentlemen undertaki the Grand Tour to have their portraits carve in a shell cameo by specialist craftsmen suc as Saulini and Barbarti.

A Victorian coral cameo pendant/brooch, carved with a portrait of Diana, in a 14ct g frame, 2in (5cm) high.

£180–200 Skinner

JFFLINKS

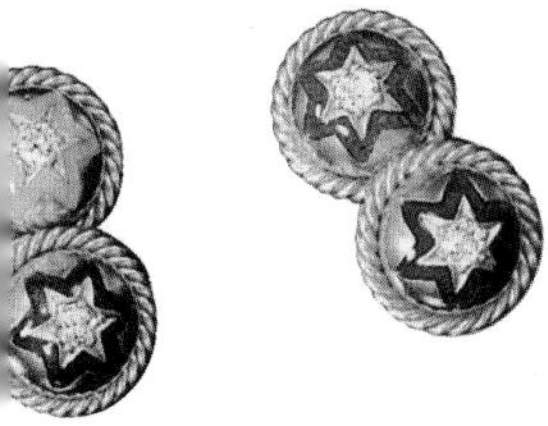

: of enamel cufflinks, decorated with el star motifs set with diamonds, late 19thC.
00–1,500 Sotheby's

A pair of 15ct gold cufflinks, decorated with scroll engraving, Birmingham 1900.
£350–400 Grey-Harris

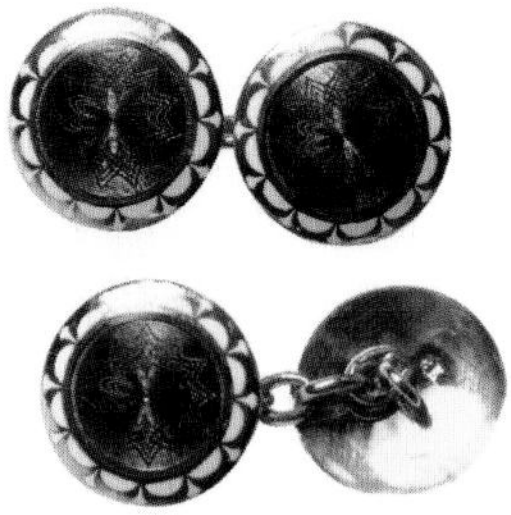

A pair of 18ct gold and enamel cufflinks, with engraved centres, c1930.
£475–525 Grey-Harris

SSENTIAL REFERENCE RUBIES

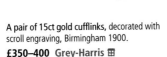

y should one ruby be worth £50,000 and another £500? In the nplex world of gemstones there are four key factors which ect value: size, colour, clarity and – crucial for all precious gems ountry of origin. The best rubies in the world come from Burma l the best Burmese rubies were mined and polished before the 20s – so-called 'old mine' goods. Today, fine rubies are mitted for laboratory testing, not only to establish origin but o to confirm they have not been treated to improve colour. A antique Burmese ruby can fetch over £70,000 per carat at ction proving that, size for size, they are among the rarest and st expensive gems in the world.

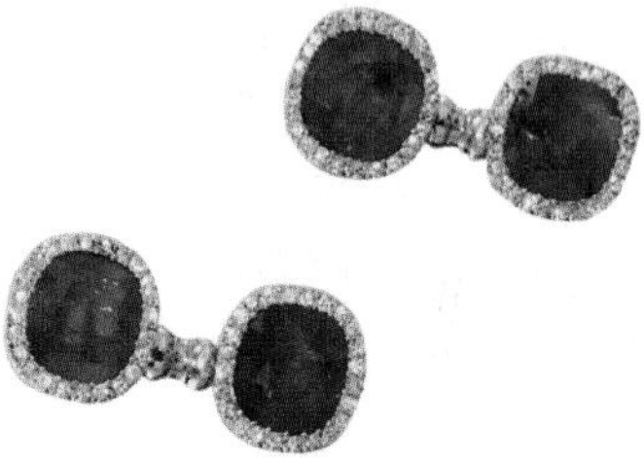

A pair of platinum and gold cufflinks, set with Burmese rubies and diamonds, French assay marks, c1900.
£25,000–30,000 Sotheby's (G)

ARRINGS

ir of 18ct gold earrings, set with faceted thysts, with later pearl drops, c1850, (4cm) long.
0–650 Grey-Harris

A pair of Victorian gold and enamel earrings, each set with a pearl.
£240–280 Webb's

A pair of Egyptian revival 15ct gold and enamel earrings, each set with a portrait, c1875, 2in (5cm) long.
£1,650–1,850 Wimpole Antiques

air of silver and gold earrings, set with nonds, c1890.
200–1,400 Wimpole Antiques

A pair of diamond earrings, each set with a sapphire, c1900, 1½in (4cm) high.
£1,200–1,500 Wimpole Antiques

A pair of silver and gold earrings, set with diamonds, c1900.
£1,600–1,800 Gorringes (L)

NECKLACES

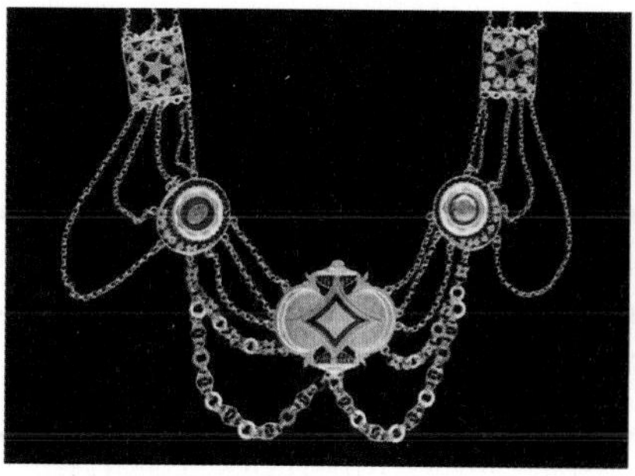

A gold and enamel necklace, by O. Jeansson, slight damage, Sweden, early 19thC.

£2,000–2,500 **Bukowskis**

A gold necklace, set with amethysts, repaired, c1830, 15½in (39.5cm) long.

£1,800–2,200 **Bukowskis**

A gold and *pietra dura* necklace, with five panels depicting butterflies, Italy, 19thC.

£2,000–2,500
Dreweatt Neate (HAM)

A gold snake necklace, set with garnets and diamonds, the reverse with glazed compartment, c1845, 16½in (42cm) long.

£4,500–5,500 **Sotheby's (NY)**

A gold and enamel necklace, set with fo backed stones and garnets, the links in the of boys riding dolphins, the three pendan with seed pearls, c1870, 16in (40.5cm) l

£3,800–4,200 **Sotheby's (NY)**

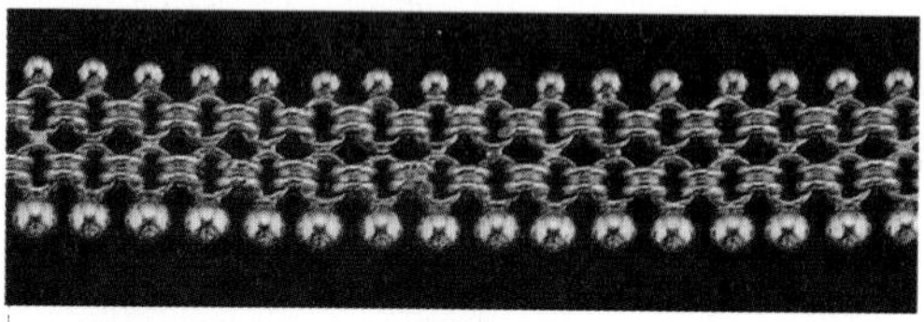

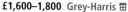

A Victorian 18ct gold collar, with bolt-ring clasp.

£850–1,000 **Woolley & Wallis**

A gold necklace, set with graduated opals, c1890, 16in (40.5cm) long, with a fitted case.

£1,600–1,800 **Grey-Harris**

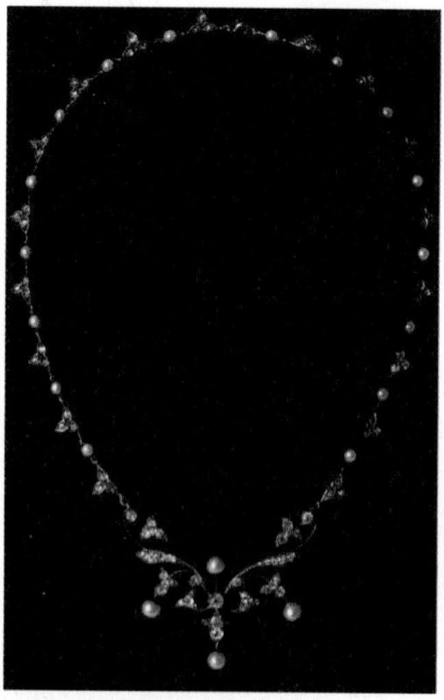

A diamond and pearl necklace, with trefoil clusters, Austria, c1895, 20in (51cm) long.

£8,500–9,500 **Grey-Harris**

An amethyst necklace, late 19thC, 18½in (47cm) long.

£2,200–2,600 **Sotheby's**

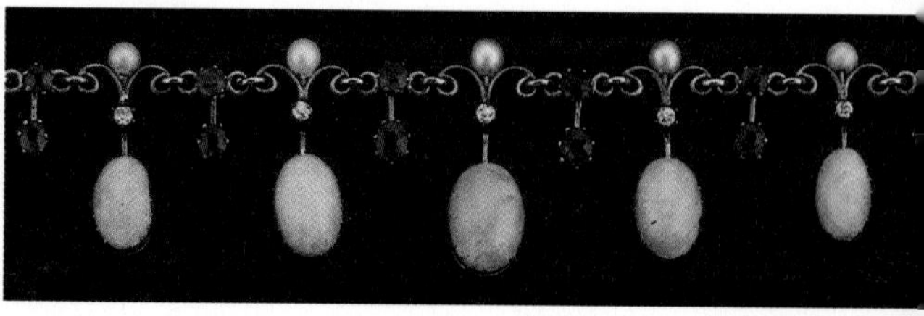

An Edwardian gold necklace, set with opal cabochons, rubies, diamonds and pearls, with a fitted case.

£1,700–2,000 **Woolley & Wallis**

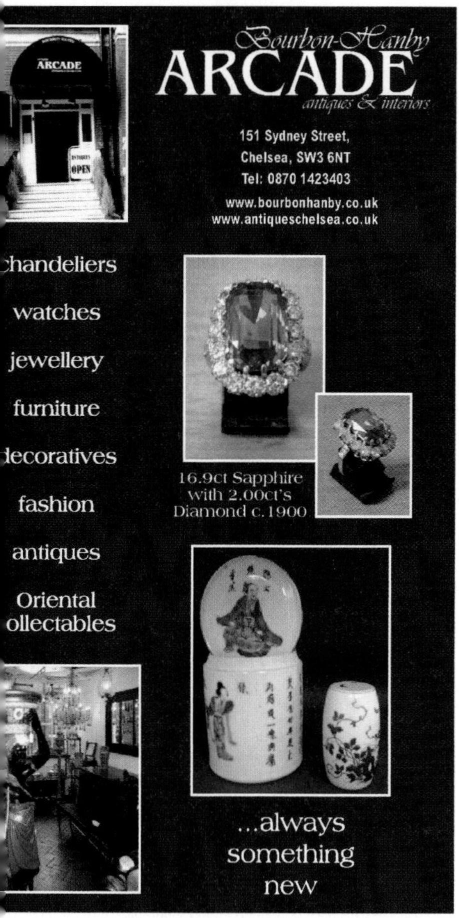
Bourbon-Hanby
ARCADE
antiques & interiors
151 Sydney Street,
Chelsea, SW3 6NT
Tel: 0870 1423403
www.bourbonhanby.co.uk
www.antiqueschelsea.co.uk
handeliers
watches
jewellery
furniture
ecoratives
fashion
antiques
Oriental
ollectables
16.9ct Sapphire
with 2.00ct's
Diamond c.1900
...always
something
new

SHAPIRO & CO
Jewels • Silver • Objects d'Art
From our collection of Fabergé for the perfect gift
STAND 380, GRAY'S ANTIQUE MARKET,
58 DAVIES ST., LONDON W1Y 5LP
TELEPHONE: 020 7491 2710

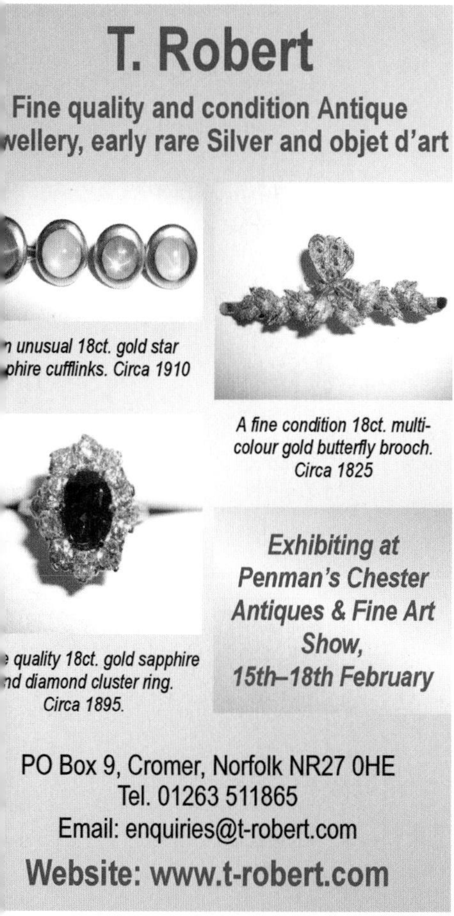
T. Robert
Fine quality and condition Antique
wellery, early rare Silver and objet d'art
n unusual 18ct. gold star
phire cufflinks. Circa 1910
A fine condition 18ct. multi-
colour gold butterfly brooch.
Circa 1825
quality 18ct. gold sapphire
nd diamond cluster ring.
Circa 1895.
Exhibiting at
Penman's Chester
Antiques & Fine Art
Show,
15th–18th February
PO Box 9, Cromer, Norfolk NR27 0HE
Tel. 01263 511865
Email: enquiries@t-robert.com
Website: www.t-robert.com

Gorringes
We don't just sell beautiful paintings for fabulous prices.
A military general service medal
1793 – 1814, sold for £3,100.
John William Godward oil painting sold for £500,000.
A black Steiff teddy bear
sold for £23,000.
If you need to sell an individual piece worth
from £50 to £500,000, a collection or an entire
house contents, we have the experience and
expertise to guide you through the auction
process.
A Lalique crickets vase
sold for £4,600.
We hold select fine art and antique auctions
every six weeks which are now linked
worldwide to eBay live, and the largest weekly
antique / general auctions in Southern England.
A signed
Francoise Linke
kingwood vitrine
sold for £12,000.
For an auction appraisal, probate or
insurance valuations in Sussex,
Kent, Surrey or London, telephone :
01273 472503
01903 238999
A Minton floor vase
sold for £7,000.
www.gorringes.co.uk email: clientservices@gorringes.co.uk
A 19th century hour
repeating bracket clock
sold for £10,000.
A pair of Edwardian
diamond bracelets
sold for £14,000.
Alice's Adventures in Wonderland,
first published edition, sold for £14,000.
An 18th century Danish gold
and enamel box sold for £16,000.
A Fifty Pounds Lloyds patriotic fund sword
and a Welsh presentation sword
sold for £44,000 and £23,000 respectively.

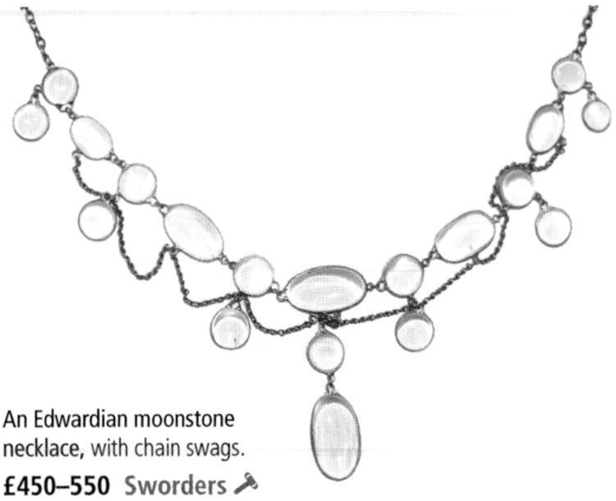

An Edwardian moonstone necklace, with chain swags.
£450–550 Sworders

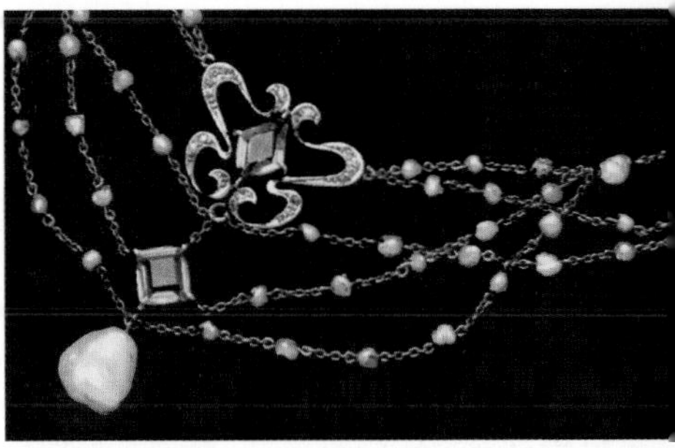

An Edwardian 14ct gold necklace, set with peridots, diamonds and freshwater pearls, 16in (40.5cm) long.
£1,100–1,300 Skinner

An Edwardian opal and diamond necklace.
£3,200–3,800 Dreweatt Neate (HAM)

An opal, ruby and diamond necklace, early 20thC, 20½in (52cm) long, with a fitted case.
£2,400–2,800 Sotheby's

SETS & PARURES

A Victorian 15ct gold demi-parure, comprising a pair of earrings and a brooch with glazed locket to reverse, dated 1846–47, in a fitted leather case.
£1,000–1,200 Leonard Joel

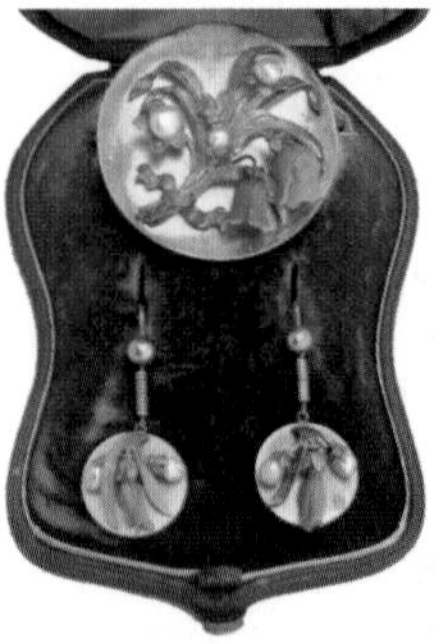

A gold brooch and earring set, by MacKay Cunningham & Co, set with pearls and coral flowers, Scotland, Edinburgh, c1850, 1½in (4cm) diam, with fitted case.
£800–900
Anthony Green Antiques

A gold demi-parure, comprising a bracelet, drop earrings and brooch, set with diamonds within enamel mounts, c1855, in a fitted leather case.
£2,500–3,000
Bearnes

A garnet and diamond pendant and earring set, France, c1870, pendant 1in (2.5cm) high.
£1,800–2,000
Wimpole Antiques

A gold and enamel mourning brooch and earrings set, set with pearls, the brooch with locket compartment to reverse, c1870, brooch 2in (5cm) wide.
£450–550 Lawrence Fine Art

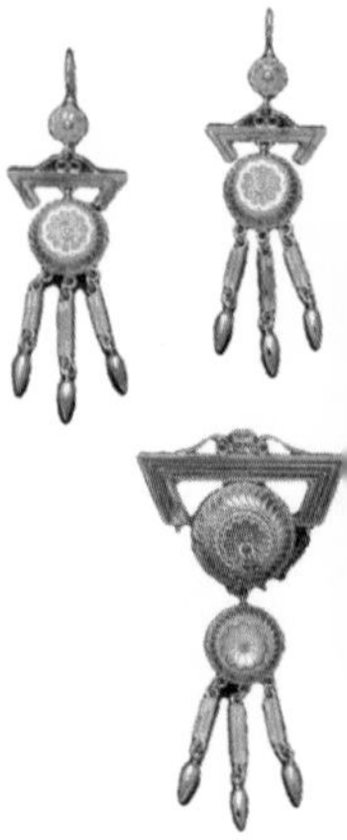

A 14ct gold demi-parure, comprising brooch and earri[ngs,] clasp replaced, c1875.
£400–500 Skinner

ENDANTS

ld pendant, set with rubies and paste
es, the reverse with enamel, suspension
later, probably Hungary, c1700,
(4cm) high.
00–2,200 Sotheby's (NY)

A gold mourning pendant, with a sepia miniature depicting a woman by a memorial inscribed 'Jane' beneath a weeping willow of hair, the reverse with flowers and initials 'J. M. V. D. M.', c1785, 5in (12.5cm) high.
£550–650 Bearnes

A gold pendant, set with emeralds and diamonds, the reverse with a compartment containing hair, c1870.
£1,400–1,750 Bearnes

ct gold and guilloché enamel pendant,
ed with a diamond-set star, the reverse
a locket, France, c1875, 1½in (4cm) high.
00–3,000 Wimpole Antiques

A 9ct gold locket, in the form of a heart, set with a diamond, c1880, 1in (2.5cm) high.
£100–120 Sylvie Spectrum

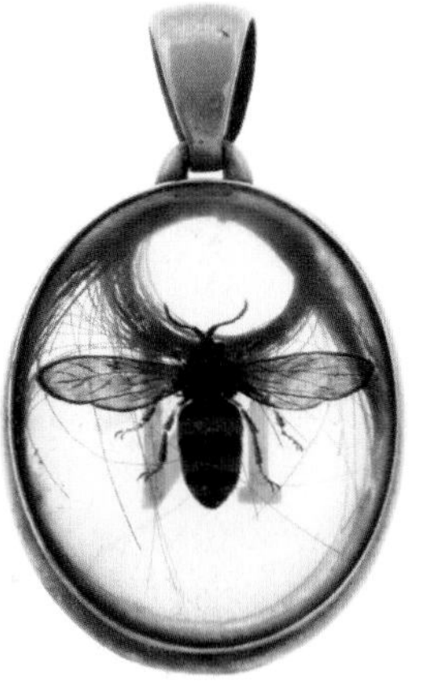

A reverse-painted crystal intaglio mounted pendant, depicting a bee, in a gold frame, the reverse hair compartment with the initial 'N', late 19thC.
£350–450 Bearnes

nperial gold and Siberian jasper egg
ant, by E. Dimitriev, Russia, St
sburg, 1896–1907, ¾in (2cm) high.
00–2,750 Shapiro & Co

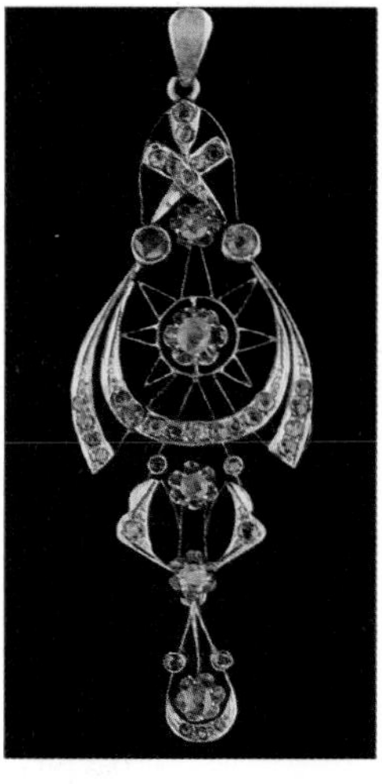

A 14ct gold pendant, set with demantoid garnets, chain later, Russia, St Petersburg, c1900, 2¾in (7cm) high.
£1,300–1,600 Bukowskis

A platinum, gold and pearl suffragette pendant, set with amethysts, demantoid garnets and white enamel, c1900, 1¾in (4.5cm) long.
£4,250–4,750 Wimpole Antiques

Pieces of jewellery incorporating these stones were often worn by members of the suffragette movement. The initial letters of the colours of the jewels – green, white and violet signify 'Give Women Votes' but in Victorian jewellery language the colours also represent Hope, Purity and Loyalty respectively.

RINGS

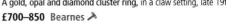

A platinum, gold and diamond ring, set with a marquise diamond in a pierced openwork frame, c1890.
£2,800–3,250 Wimpole Antiques ⊞

A gold, opal and diamond cluster ring, in a claw setting, late 19thC.
£700–850 Bearnes

An 18ct gold ring, set with pearls and diamonds, c1890.
£1,100–1,250 Grey-Harris ⊞

A Victorian 9ct gold ring, set with coral and a diamon
£115–125 Vetta Decorative Arts ⊞

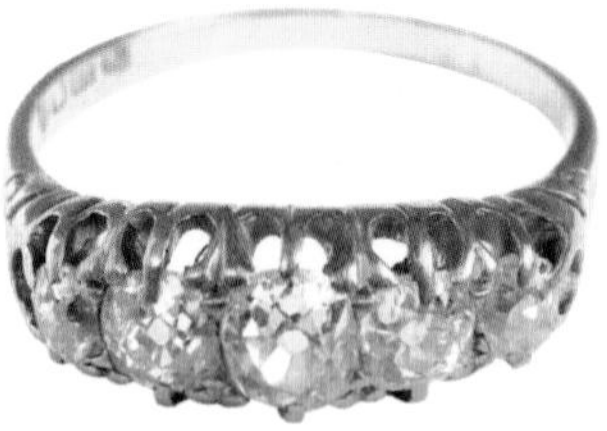

An 18ct gold ring, set with five graduated diamonds, c1900.
£225–275 Rosebery's

A gold and platinum ring, set with a diamond in a *pavé* diamond tablet field, c1910.
£1,000–1,100 Sylvie Spectrum ⊞

A diamond ring, set in a crossover format on a waved band, c1915.
£8,500–9,500 Lyon & Turnbull

STICKPINS

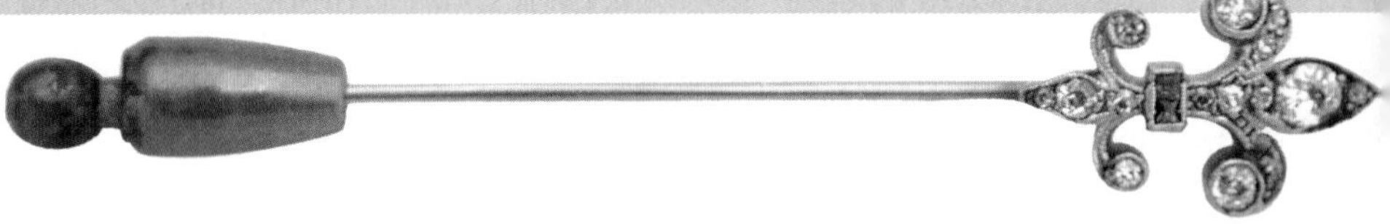

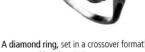

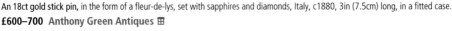

An 18ct gold stick pin, in the form of a fleur-de-lys, set with sapphires and diamonds, Italy, c1880, 3in (7.5cm) long, in a fitted case.
£600–700 Anthony Green Antiques ⊞

An enamelled stick pin, depicting a dog, signed 'WB Ford', 1872.
£380–450
Woolley & Wallis
William Bishop Ford (1832–1922) was a prolific enameller who produced a large range of high quality gold tie pins depicting many breeds of dogs.

An 18ct gold and oxidized silver stick pin, modelled with a dog, c1900.
£115–135
Leonard Joel

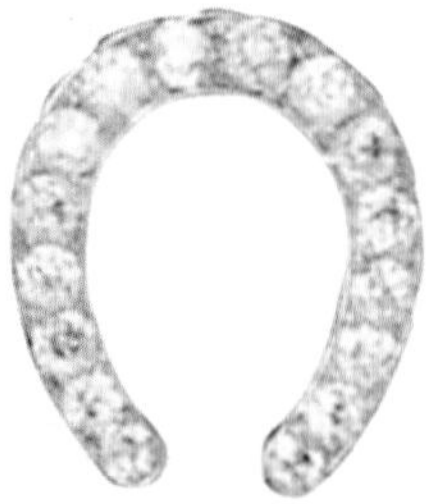

An Edwardian platinum and diamond stick pin, in the form of a horseshoe.
£200–240
Skinner

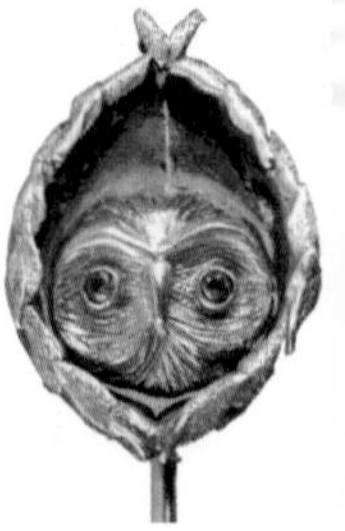

A gold and *plique-a-jour* enamel stick pin, modelled w an owl's head within a wrea chased border, early 20thC.
£650–800
Dreweatt Neate (HAM)

MICRO-MOSAICS

MICRO-MOSAICS require high levels of skills to produce and are found in a wide range of objects including snuff boxes, jewellery and ɿes. In recent times value has risen steeply, fuelled nternational demand for artefacts of the Grand r and a better understanding of the craft.

e art of setting minute pieces of coloured glass or e known as tesserae to form a recognizable design icture has its roots in the Renaissance, although e early craftsmen had taken their inspiration from mosaic floors and frescoes of ancient Italy. By the -18th century there were two principal areas of duction, Rome and Florence. The Roman artisans cialized in using tiny fragments of glass cut from ı, thin rods called *smalti filati* which were invariably que, although the addition of gold or silver leaf duced a shiny, metallic finish. In Florence the aicists set larger and more expensive sections of ured hardstone and semi-precious gems into a of black marble – a technique known as *pietra* a. The particles were set into cement and grouted ı coloured wax, which in turn was smoothed and shed. The quality of the mosaic is key to identifying age and associated value. The best 18th- and early 19th-century examples are composed of tiny cubes of tesserae – as many as 1400 per square inch – set so deftly that the surface texture is extremely smooth. Cheaper 19th-century examples have far fewer particles and are uneven to the touch.

Subject matter includes architectural sites, such as the Colosseum, found on Grand Tour souvenirs, and landscapes, putti and animals, typical of the early 19th-century Romantic movement. One classical subject, Pliny's Doves (see pp 390 and 391), was a popular motif for snuff boxes and *objets d'art*. Quality declined in the mid- to late 19th century with the growth of the tourist industry and rising costs of production. By the 1860s rather unimaginative flower studies and coarse 'classical' designs such as architectural ruins and animals replaced the earlier, finely executed examples. Even so, these later mosaics can achieve astonishing results. Recently a top quality mid-19th century gold brooch mounted with a micro-mosaic of a spaniel by the celebrated goldsmith Castellani fetched £22,000 against an estimate of £4,000–6,000 – an excellent result for top craftsmanship and technical virtuosity combined. **John Benjamin**

cro-mosaic and burrwood powder box, depicting a swan n a silvered-metal mount, Italy, c1800, 3¼in (8.5cm) diam.
000–5,000 Sotheby's (NY)

A micro-mosaic and gold snuff box, depicting figures by a river landscape, set with rubies within chased foliage, France, c1815, 2½in (6.5cm) wide.
£11,000–13,000 Sotheby's (NY)

cro-mosaic and 18ct gold box, by G. Petochi for Carimati, depicting the sseum within an onyx frame, signed, Italy, mosiac c1830, 4¾in (12cm) wide.
750–3,250 Sotheby's (NY)

A micro-mosaic and gilt-bronze box, depicting views of Rome, flowers and doves, on claw feet, Italy, 19thC, 5¾in (14.5cm) wide.
£7,500–8,500 Freeman's

A micro-mosaic and gold brooch, depicting the Capitoline Doves of Pliny the Elder, Italy, mid-19thC, 1¾in (4.5cm) wide.

£3,500–4,250 Sotheby's (NY)

Pliny's doves was a popular subject for micro-mosaic craftsmen, allowing plenty of scope for fine detailing and interesting blends of coloured tesserae. Please also see the central roundel of the table top shown on page 391.

A micro-mosaic and gold brooch and earrings set, depicting doves and flowers, with bead fringes, Italy, c1870.

£1,800–2,200 Sotheby's (NY)

A micro-mosaic and 15ct gold brooch/pendant, with locket back, Italy, c1870, 3in (7.5cm) high.

£3,000–3,250 Wimpole Antiques

A pair of micro-mosaic and 18ct gold earrings, depicting flowers and a dove, Italy, c1870.

£3,200–3,600 Beverley R

A micro-mosaic and glass wall mirror, Ita late 19thC, 39½in (100.5cm) high.

£2,000–2,500 Sotheby's (O)

A micro-mosaic and moulded glass wall mirror, Italy, c1880, 47in (120cm) wide.

£18,000–22,000 Sotheby's (O)

A micro-mosaic and 18ct gold parure, comprising pendant/brooch, bracelet and earrings, depicting doves, Italy, c1870.

£10,000–11,000 Beverley R

A micro-mosaic plaque, depicting an Italian landscape after Claude Lorrain, set in a gilt frame and applied to a later nephrite box, Italy, early 19thC, 3¾in (9.5cm) wid

£8,000–9,500 Sotheby's

A micro-mosaic Grand Tour souvenir plaque, depictin the Colosseum, in an ebonized frame, Italy, early 19th 5¾in (14.5cm) wide.

£3,500–4,200 Greenslade Taylor Hunt

cro-mosaic plaque, depicting a bull-baiting scene, in a metal frame, early 19thC, Italy, 7.5cm) wide.

500–5,500 Sotheby's (NY)

A micro-mosaic plaque, depicting a tiger, in an ebonized circular frame, Italy, early 19thC, 4½in (11.5cm) diam.

£4,500–5,500 Gorringes (L)

icro-mosaic plaque, depicting a King les spaniel, in a metal frame, Italy,)–40, 1½in (4cm) wide.

000–3,500 Sotheby's (NY)

A micro-mosaic plaque, in the manner of Biagio Barzotti, depicting a view of Rome, Italy, 19thC, 46½in (118cm) wide, in a giltwood frame.

£55,000–65,000 Leonard Joel

icro-mosaic plaque, depicting St Peter's are, Rome, Italy, 19thC, 11in (28cm) wide.

500–11,500 Freeman's

A micro-mosaic and gold snuff box, with three panels depicting flowers and a ruined temple, each within an aventurine glass frame, engraved 'Meüsel et Fils à Genève', c1835, 3in (7.5cm) wide.

£3,250–3,750
Sotheby's

A micro-mosaic plaque, by Federico Campanili, depicting a vase of flowers, fruit and exotic birds, printed label, Italy, 1858–64, 32¾in (83cm) wide, in a giltwood and painted frame.

£65,000–75,000
Sotheby's

Pieces by known makers are always particularly sought after.

icro-mosiac roundel, depicting figures and a sical ruin, set within a marble surround into sewood occasional table inlaid with quetry trophies, 19thC, 23in (58.5cm) wide.

000–2,500 Andrew Hartley

A micro-mosaic table top, depicting the Capitoline Doves of Pliny the Elder within views of Rome, within a malachite border, Italy, 19thC, 22in (56cm) diam.

£22,000–26,000 Freeman's

A micro-mosaic roundel, depicting the Forum Romanum within a floral border, set into a giltwood table, Italy, c1850, 20in (51cm) diam.

£20,000–25,000
Sotheby's (Am)

FABERGE

CARL FABERGÉ was born in St Petersburg in 1846 of Huguenot stock, the family having fled persecution in their native France in the late 17th century, ending up in Russia by the mid-19th century. His father was a goldsmith and jeweller who retired to Dresden in 1860 and, from the age of 16, Carl's education and apprenticeship took place in Germany with visits to England, Italy and Paris. French art and culture and the work of the Florentine enamellers and goldsmiths remained lifelong influences and these early experiences furnished him with the skills and confidence to take over control of the family business when he returned to St Petersburg in 1870.

By the 1880s, Carl's brother Agathon had joined the company which by now was producing small decorative objects. These pieces were first put on show in the Pan-Russian Exhibition held in Moscow in 1882 and the company was awarded a gold medal. It was around this time that the brothers began discussing the production of an Easter egg containing a surprise for the Tsarina. The first one was presented in 1884 and was such a success that the Tsar commissioned the firm to produce one every year.

Objects by Fabergé became the 'must-haves' of th time. At the 1900 Exposition Internationale Univers in Paris the company displayed for the first time all Easter eggs they had made with a selection of their other wares. Fabergé was declared Maître and awarded the Légion d'Honneur. Other royal commissions followed – gifts for Edward VII to pres to Queen Alexandra and carvings in various coloure stones of the domestic animals at Sandringham. Th company's star began to fade at the outbreak of W when the workshops were increasingly given over t the manufacture of small arms and medical supplie. It was finally extinguished in 1917 by the Russian Revolution when the Communists took over private businesses and Carl Fabergé, like his Huguenot ancestors, was forced to flee. He died in exile in Lausanne in 1920.

The fascination with Fabergé remains to this day. A recent exhibition in London had people queuing in t street and, even in these difficult times for the antiqu trade, these exquisite works of art continue to comma large sums whenever they appear on the market.

Geoffrey M

A Fabergé gold mesh evening bag, the clasp decorated with enamel and set with rubies and diamonds, Russia, c1910, 7in (18cm) wide.

£22,500–25,000
Wartski

A Fabergé parcel-gilt basket, one side engraved with initials, the other 'Zvenigorod', with a strap handle, Imperial Warrant and Fabergé marks, Russia, Moscow, c1894, 4¾in (12cm) wide.

£3,250–4,000 Sotheby's (O)

A Fabergé silver basket, by Alexander Wäkevä, with gilt interior, marked, Russia Moscow, 1908–17, 9½in (24cm) wide, 22

£9,000–11,000
Bukowskis

A Fabergé enamelled gold bell push, set with a moonstone and diamonds, on gold gadrooned feet, Russia, c1900, 1¾in (4.5cm) square.

£22,500–25,000
Wartski

A Fabergé silver-mounted agate bowl, by Karl Gustav Armfelt, with a silver parrot on the rim, Russia, St Petersburg, 1899–1908, 7in (18cm) diam.

£135,000–160,000
Bukowskis

A Fabergé gold-mounted nephrite box, decorated with a diamond-set trellis and cabochon ruby, Russia, c1900, 1½in (4cm) diam.

£30,000–35,000
Wartski

abergé enamelled gold and gem-set box, sia, c1910, 1¼in (3cm) diam.

5,000–20,000 Wartski

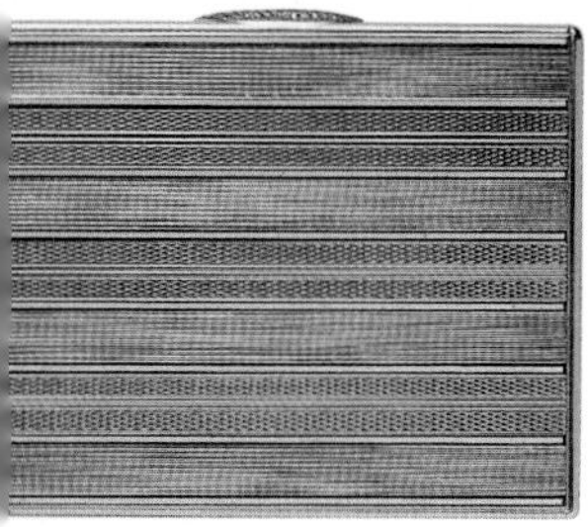

abergé gold cigarette case, decorated h bands of coloured gold and enamel, thumbpiece set with diamonds, Russia, 00, 3¼in (8.5cm) wide.

,300–7,000 Wartski

e Fabergé Nobel Jubilee clock, in the m of the fire worshippers' temple, silver-unted granite set with rhodonite 'flames' d a plaque showing a map of Azerbaijan, rear with a further plaque depicting a female ure holding an oil lamp, an altar with a rning flame, a view of the Nobel oil rigs and temple of Zoroaster, silver mounts by Karl stav Armfelt, Russia, St Petersburg, 1908–17, ¾in (68cm) high, in original oak case.

,500,000 + Bukowskis

is clock was commissioned by Emmanuel bel of the Nobel Brothers' Petroleum Co d nephew of Alfred Nobel, founder of the bel Prize. The fire worshipper's temple tside Baku, Azerbaijan, was the symbol of Nobel Oil Company. The Zoroaster temple s the company's symbol because roastrianism was once the dominant igion in the district. Fire was central to the igion and also gave Azerbaijan its name, hich translates as 'Land of Fire'. The map on front of clock includes an image of the rld's first oil tanker, the Zoroaster, nceived by Ludvig Nobel and built in eden. It arrived at Baku in 1878.

A Fabergé gold brooch, set with an amethyst and diamonds, marked 'KF', Russia, St Petersburg, c1890, 2in (5cm) long.

£7,500–9,000 Sotheby's (O)

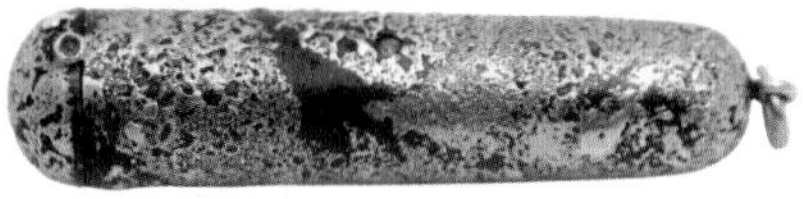

A Fabergé woven gold and gunmetal cigar/cigarette box, in the Samorodok style, set with gemstones, Russia, c1900, 2½in (6.5cm) long.

£2,500–2,750 Shapiro & Co

A Fabergé silver candlestick, the socle decorated with roses, marked 'KF', Russia, Moscow, c1890, 5¾in (14.5cm) high.

£4,500–5,500 Sotheby's (O)

A Fabergé enamel cigarette case, workmaster Henrik Wigström, with engine-turned decoration and a diamond-set thumbpiece, marked, Russia, St Petersburg, c1910, 3¼in (8.5cm) wide.

£17,000–20,000 Freeman's

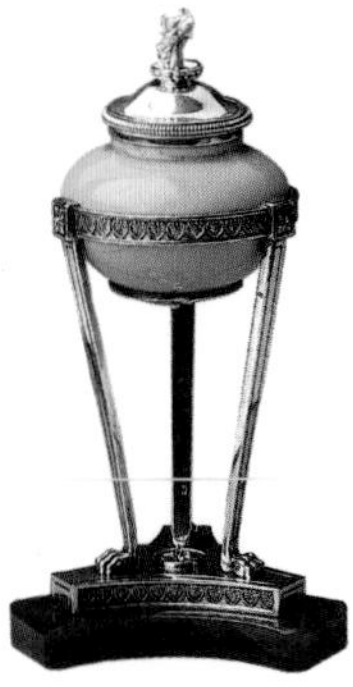

A Fabergé enamelled silver and hardstone cigar lighter, Russia, c1900, 4¾in (12cm) high.

£7,200–8,000 Wartski

A Fabergé enamelled silver cloak clasp, each piece set with an aquamarine, Russia, c1890, 4¾in (12cm) wide.

£10,250–11,500 Wartski

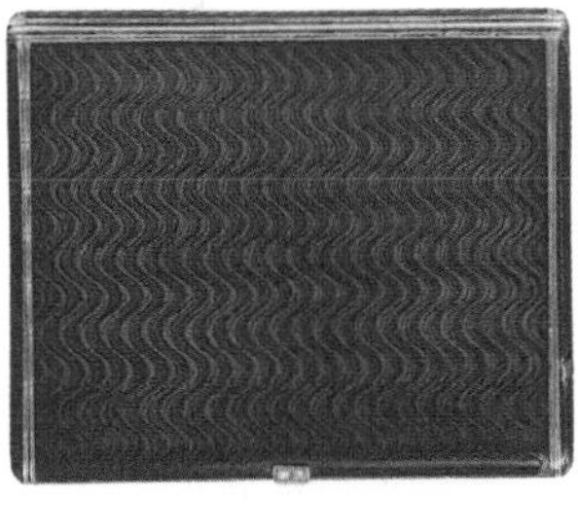

A Fabergé silver-gilt and enamel compact, workmaster Andrei Astreyden, with engine-turned decoration and diamond-set thumbpiece, damaged, marked, Russia, St Petersburg, 1908–17, 3¼in (8.5cm) wide.

£2,000–2,500 Sotheby's (O)

A Fabergé wood, silver and enamel desk pad holder, with mecca-stone finials, Russia, c1900, 5½in (14cm) wide.

£13,500–15,000 Wartski

A **Fabergé silver** *kovsch*, workmaster Alexander Wäkevä, set with semi-precious stones, with presentation inscription, Imperial Warrant and Fabergé marks, Russia, St Petersburg, c1907, 13½in (34.5cm) long, 37¾oz.

£55,000–65,000 Heritage

A **Fabergé silver-gilt cream jug,** Imperial Warrant and later Soviet control marks, Russia, Moscow, 1908–17, 5¼in (13.5cm) high, 7oz.

£1,300–1,600 Bukowskis

A **Fabergé carved obsidian model of an elephant,** with rose-cut diamond eyes, slig damage, Russia, c1910, 1¾in (4.5cm) high

£3,500–4,000
Dreweatt Neate (HAM)

Using hardstones that were native to Russi Fabergé began producing and selling hardstone animals in the 1890s. They were prized throughout Europe for their detail, realism and endearing features. A number famous collections of these animals have been built up by clients including the Britis Royal family.

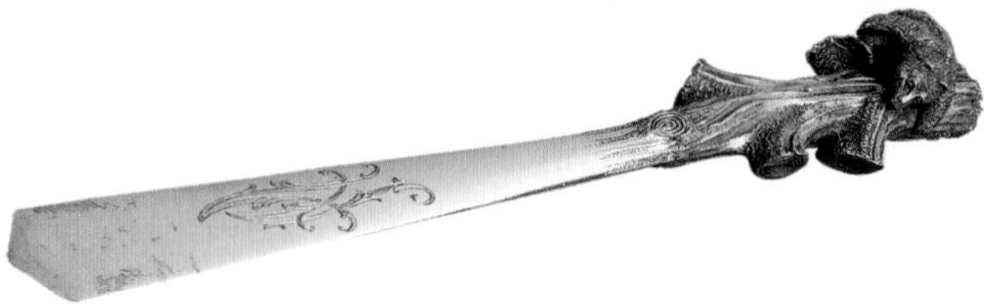

A **Fabergé silver paper knife,** in the form of a bear climbing over a log, Russia, c1900, 7½in (19cm) long.

£6,300–7,000 Wartski

A **Fabergé nephrite pendant,** in the form o an elephant, with diamond-set eyes, Russia c1900, ¾in (2cm) wide.

£13,500–15,000 Wartski

A **Fabergé silver fish platter,** Russia, Moscow, 1908–17, 27½in (69cm) wide, 70¾oz.

£8,500–10,000 Bukowskis

A **Fabergé silver teapot,** moulded with a band of anthemia and papyrus leaves, the cover with a bud finial, ivory handle, Imperi Warrant, Fabergé mark and workmaster's initials 'JW', Russia, Moscow, 1899–1908, 6¼in (16cm) high.

£3,800–4,500 Sotheby's (O)

A **Fabergé silver quill holder,** chased with Pan-Slavic motifs, gilt interior, Imperial Warrant and Fabergé marks, Russia, Moscow, 1899–1908, 4½in (11.5cm) high.

£3,000–3,500 Sotheby's (O)

A **Fabergé silver-mounted wooden spoon,** workmaster Anders Nevalainen, marked, Russia, St Petersburg, 1899–1908, 8¾in (22cm) long.

£4,000–5,000 Sotheby's (O)

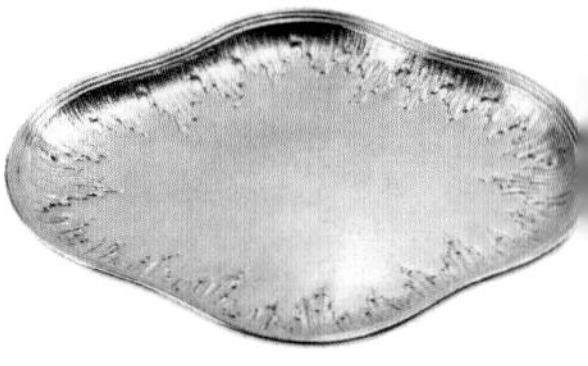

A **Fabergé silver tray,** workmaster Julius Rappaport, with cast and chased decoratior Russia, Moscow 1896, 10in (25.5cm) wide.

£4,000–5,000
Sotheby's (O)

ʾORTRAIT MINIATURES

ɔrtrait miniature of a gentleman, by id des Granges, on vellum, c1675, in a ·metal frame, 2¾in (7cm) high.

,000–8,500 **Sotheby's**

A portrait miniature of the Countess Amalia Lewenhaupt, Swedish School, gouache, early 18thC, 2½in (6.5cm) high.

£350–425 **Bukowskis**

A portrait miniature of a gentleman, 18thC, 2in (5cm) high.

£1,600–2,000 **Sotheby's (Am)**

ɔortrait miniature of a lady, American ool, oil on ivory, 18thC, gilt locket losure, 1¾in (4.5cm) high.

,000–1,200 **Freeman's**

A portrait miniature of a gentleman, American School, oil on ivory, 18thC, gilt locket enclosure, 1¾in (4.5cm) high.

£9,000–11,000 **Freeman's**

A portrait miniature of a gentleman, by Gervase Spencer, signed, dated 1758, 1¼in (3cm) high.

£750–850 **Ellison Fine Art**

ɔortrait miniature of a gentleman, tercolour on ivory, the glass reverse with plait hair and initials, c1775, 2½in (6.5cm) high.

.00–500 **Northeast Auctions**

A portrait miniature of a gentleman, by John Smart, signed, dated 1779, later gold frame with brooch attachment, 1½in (4cm) high.

£5,750–6,750 **Sotheby's (NY)**

A portrait of a lady, by Philip Jean, in a gold frame, late 18thC, 2¼in (5.5cm) high.

£7,000–8,500 **Sotheby's**

A portrait miniature of Lady Elford, attributed to George Engleheart, with initials and inscription, late 18thC, in a gilt-metal pendant frame, 3¼in (8.5cm) high.

£4,000–5,000 Cheffins

A Georgian portrait miniature of a gentleman, by Horace Hone, watercolour on ivory, 2¼in (5.5cm) high.

£350–425 Gorringes (L)

A portrait miniature of a gentleman, by Samuel Shelley, c1790, in a gold frame, 1¾in (4.5cm) high.

£550–650 Sotheby's (NY)

A portrait miniature of Captain James Marsden, by Frederick Buck, with lock of hair and initials 'JM' to reverse, Ireland, c1790, in a gold frame, 2½in (6.5cm) high.

£2,000–2,300 Silver Shop

A portrait miniature of an officer, by George Engleheart, c1795, 2¾in (7cm) high.

£14,000–16,000 Ellison Fine Art

A portrait miniature of a man, circle of Abraham Daniel, c1800, 2¼in (6cm) long.

£500–600 Bearnes

A portrait of Robert Milligan, by Henry Bone, signed, early 19thC, 5¼ x 4in (13.5 x 10cm), in a gilt-metal easel frame.

£1,300–1,600 Woolley & Wallis

Robert Milligan was a wealthy merchant and ship owner whose family had extensive sugar plantations in Jamaica. This miniature was painted by Henry Bone who was enamel painter to George III and HRH The Prince Regent.

A portrait miniature of Anne Jones, by William Wood, c1800, 3in (7.5cm) high.

£7,000–8,000 Ellison Fine Art

A pair of portrait miniatures of Aaron and Theodosia Burr, by John Wesley Jarvis, watercolour and ink on paper, signed and dated 1802, 5½ x 4in (14 x 10cm), framed.

£1,000–1,200 Freeman's

John Wesley Jarvis was an English-born American who became a popular portrait painter in New York.

›rtrait miniature of a gentleman, ›rcolour on ivory, c1810, in a gold locket ›e, the glazed reverse with lock of hair split pearls, 2½in (6.5cm) high.

'5–450 Bloomsbury

A portrait miniature of an officer, by Eric Reuterborg, the gold frame with glazed reverse enclosing lock of hair, signed and dated 1815, 2¼ x 1¾in (5.5 x 4.5cm), in an ebonized wood frame.

£500–600 Sotheby's

A portrait miniature of a gentleman, English School, on ivory, the reverse with a portrait of a child, early 19thC, in a copper frame, 2½in (6.5cm) high.

£500–600 Andrew Hartley

›rtrait miniature of a lady, English ›ol, early 19thC, in a gilt-metal frame, › (6.5cm) high.

200–1,500 Sotheby's (NY)

A portrait miniature of Count Sixten David Sparre, by Carl Viertel, gouache, Denmark, c1800, 2¾in (7cm) high.

£700–850 Bukowskis

A portrait miniature of a woman, 19thC, in a metal frame mounted with pearls, 1½in (4cm) high.

£230–280 Ewbank Auctioneers

ortrait miniature of a young officer, eved to be Thomas Francis Wade, nadier Guards, watercolour, 19thC, n (6.5cm) high, in an ebonized frame.

50–425 Holloway's

A portrait miniature of an officer, by William Armfield Hobday, watercolour, the reverse with artist's visiting card, c1800, 2½in (6.5cm) high, in an ebonized frame.

£8,000–10,000 Holloway's

A portrait miniature of a lady, by Frederick Buck, Ireland, c1810, 4½in (11.5cm) high.

£1,450–1,600 Silver Shop

A portrait miniature of an officer in the 33rd Regiment of Foot, believed to be Francis Ralph West, 19thC, 1½in (3.5cm) high, framed.

£800–1,000 **Charterhouse**

Major West is believed to have served with Wellington throughout his campaigns in India as Second in Command of his regiment.

A portrait miniature of a lady, American School, watercolour on ivory, c1825, 2¾in (7cm) high, framed.

£300–350 **Northeast Auctions**

A portrait miniature of a lady, by Wm. S. Sn watercolour, pen and ink on card, signed a dated 1828, 5¾ x 4¾in (14.5 x 12cm).

£375–450 **Northeast Auctions**

A double portrait miniature of a boy and a girl facing a memorial, watercolour, pencil and ink, America, 1830–40, framed, 4 x 7in (10 x18cm).

£4,750–5,750 **Northeast Auctions**

A portrait miniature of a gentleman, American School, oil on glass, 19thC, 2¾in (7cm) high.

£1,200–1,500
Galeria Louis C Morton

A portrait miniature of a girl, by S. Richard Schwager, on ivory, signed, Austria, 19thC, 1½in (4cm) high, in a gilt brooch mount.

£800–950 **Lawrence Fine Art**

A portrait miniature of John Mathew Car by Reginald Easton, c1861, 3½in (9cm) hig

£3,000–3,500 **Ellison Fine Art**

A portrait miniature of General John Adams Dix, by M. Perine, watercolour on ivory, signed, 19thC, 3¼ x 2¼in (8.5 x 5.5cm), in a gilt-metal and rosewood frame.

£1,100–1,300 **Skinner**

John Dix served as a junior officer in the War of 1812. He was appointed as Secretary of State of New York from 1833 to 1839, and later became Governor of New York. Fort Dix in New Jersey is named after him.

A portrait miniature of a shepherd, a lady and a flock of sheep, watercolour, c1900, in a brass easel-back frame, 2¼in (5.5cm) wide, in original leather case stamped J. C. Vickery, Regent Street.

£380–420 **Anthony Green Antiques**

A portrait miniature of a dachshund, watercolour on iv c1910, 5 x 4in (12.5 x 10cm).

£520–580
Long Street Antiques

SCULPTURE

ırved oak group of The Deposition, depicting saints
e, John, Mary and Mary Magdelen, slight damage,
ɔably Brussels, c1500, 12in (30.5cm) high.

800–4,500 Dreweatt Neate

Deposition group formed part of an rpiece below the figure of Christ being ered from the cross. In northern Europe altarpiece was an important type of ɔden sculpture.

A marble figure of Hercules, on a marble base, slight damage, Italy, late 16thC, 29½in (75cm) high.

£8,000–10,000 Sotheby's (NY)

A carved limewood group of the Virgin and Child, with gold leaf and silver-gilt decoration, Continental, c1680, 23½in (60cm) high.

£6,000–7,000 S & P Rumble

ast-bronze model of a Maribou stork,
Christophe Fratin, France, c1840,
n (22cm) high.

700–3,000 David Hickmet

istophe Fratin (1800–64) was born in tz, France. The son of a taxidermist, he uired a sound knowledge of anatomy n his father. Fratin began exhibiting at the s Salon in 1831 and worked exclusively as animalier producing numerous small dels of dogs, horses, domestic animals and r prey. Among his best known works is group of two eagles guarding their prey in v York's Central Park.

A bronze figure of an Ethiopian gazelle, by Antoine Louis Barye, on a marble plinth, signed, France, dated 1837, 3½in (9cm) high.

£950–1,150 Jackson's

A terracotta bust of Madeleine Guimard, by Gaetano Merchi, signed, Italy, dated 1779, 28¾in (73cm) high.

£4,250–5,250 Cheffins

Madeleine Guimard was a celebrated dancer with the Comédie Française *in Paris.*

A bronze group, by Alexei Petrovitch Gratchev, entitled 'The Farewell Kiss', signed, foundry mark, Russia, 19thC, 9in (23cm) high.

£3,500–4,250 Weschler's

A bronze group, by Jan Jozef Jaquet, entitled 'The Lion Slayer', signed, Belgium, 19thC, 32¼in (82cm) high.

£3,000–3,600 Bukowskis

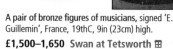

A bronze figure of Ambroise Paré, by Pierre Jean David, signed, F. Barbedienne foundry mark, France, dated 1840, 18½in (47cm) high.

£700–850 Jackson's

A pair of bronze figures of musicians, signed 'E. Guillemin', France, 19thC, 9in (23cm) high.

£1,500–1,650 Swan at Tetsworth

A marble group of Ariadne and the Pantl after J. H. Von Dannecker, 19thC, 30in (76cm) high.

£1,800–2,200 Jackson's

A bronze figure of Diane de Gabies, inscribed 'F. Barbedienne Fondeur', France, 19thC, 21in (53.5cm) high.

£2,300–2,600
Swan at Tetsworth

A bronze model of a pheasant, by Jules Moigniez, signed, on a marble base, France, 19thC, 21in (53.5cm) high.

£4,000–5,000 John Nicholson

An alabaster bust of a young woman, by Fiaschi, signed, Italy, 19thC, 18in (45.5cm) hi

£600–700 James D Julia

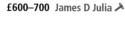

A bronze model of a racehorse, by Pierre Lenordez, entitled 'Baron Brod', with inscription, France, 19thC, 14¼in (36cm) wide.

£1,800–2,200 Sotheby's (Am)

A bronze model of a donkey, by Auguste Cain, entitled 'Âne d'Afrique', France, c1850, 5½in (14cm) high.

£3,800–4,200 Richard Gardner

An ivory bust of a general, Russia, dated 1855, 6in (15.5cm) high.

£2,700–3,200 Heritage

A bronze sculpture, representing Art, Industry and Science, the globe inscribed 'Exp'tion Universelle 1851 signed 'Ateliers Desir et Arquiche', France, c1850, 21¼in (54cm) wide.

£1,600–2,000 Sotheby's (O)

ɪair of bronze figures, by Emile Victor Blavier, ɪtled 'Jeunes Voyageurs', France, dated 1854, ɪin (54.5cm) high.

ɪ000–9,000 Garret & Hurst

A bronze model of a Roman bull, by Jean-Baptiste Clésinger, signed, France, 1857, 9¾in (25cm) wide.

£500–600 Jackson's

ɪronze figural group of two putti, by Charles Roux, ɪtled 'The Lovers', on a giltwood plinth, signed, France, ɪ60, 18in (45.5cm) wide.

ɪ,650–1,850 Ronald Chambers

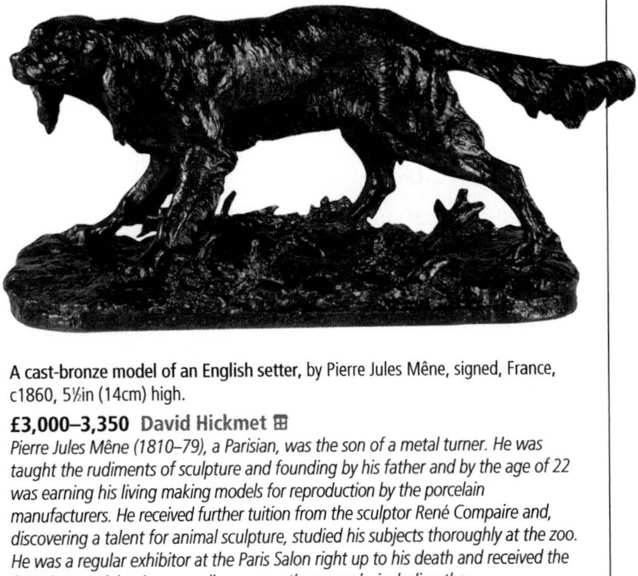

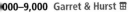

A cast-bronze model of an English setter, by Pierre Jules Mêne, signed, France, c1860, 5½in (14cm) high.

£3,000–3,350 David Hickmet

Pierre Jules Mêne (1810–79), a Parisian, was the son of a metal turner. He was taught the rudiments of sculpture and founding by his father and by the age of 22 was earning his living making models for reproduction by the porcelain manufacturers. He received further tuition from the sculptor René Compaire and, discovering a talent for animal sculpture, studied his subjects thoroughly at the zoo. He was a regular exhibitor at the Paris Salon right up to his death and received the first class medal twice, as well as many other awards, including the Légion d'Honneur *in 1861.*

ɪronze figure, entitled 'The Dying Gaul', France, c1860, ɪin (43cm) wide.

ɪ,000–2,250 Ronald Chambers

A bronze figural group of two slaves, by Louis-Auguste-Edouard Levêque, signed, France, 19thC, 19in (48.5cm) high.

£4,500–5,500 Sotheby's (P)

A marble bust of a young man, by Sir John Steell, signed, Scotland, dated 1865, 28in (71cm) high.

£2,250–2,750 Freeman's

Sir John Steell studied in Edinburgh and Rome and became a member of the Royal Scottish Academy in 1829. He is perhaps most well known for his statue of Sir Walter Scott in the Scott memorial in Edinburgh. He was knighted by Queen Victoria in 1876.

ɪronze model of a ewe, by Pierre Jules Mêne, entitled ɪanding Ewe', signed, France, dated 1864, 9in (23cm) wide.

ɪ,000–3,300 Richard Gardner

A plaster figural group, by John Rogers, entitled 'The Council of War', slight damage, America, dated 1868, 24in (61cm) high.

£1,400–1,750 James D Julia

A bronze model of the Derby winner 'Kinscem', by Isidore Bonheur, signed, Peyrol foundry stamp, France, c1870, 8¼in (21cm) high.

£4,500–5,000 David Hickmet

Isidore Bonheur (1827–1901) was born in Bordeaux, the third child of Raymond Bonheur anc brother of Rosa Bonheur. In 1849 he enrolled at the Ecole des Beaux Arts, though he had ma his debut at the Paris Salon the previous year. He exhibited regularly at the Royal Academy in London and won a medal in 1889.

A bronze model of a stag, by Antoine Louis Barye, signed, F. Barbedienne foundry mark, France, c1870, 8¼in (21cm) high.

£3,300–3,650 David Hickmet

A bronze model of an elephant, by Antoine Louis Barye, entitled 'Eléphant d'Asie', signed, France, c1870, 5in (12.5cm) high.

£6,750–7,500 Richard Gardner

Antoine Louis Barye (1796–1875) was born in Paris and took up sculpture in 1817, working in the studios of Bosio & Gros. In 1819 he took part in the competition of the École des Beaux Arts where he was runner up. Barye exhibited at the Paris Salon from 1827 onwards. In a career spanning half a century his output was prodigious; his bronzes are imbued with realism and there is meticulous attention to anatomical detail.

A bronze group of a soldier on horseback, by Evgeni Alexandrovich Lanceray, signed, Russia, dated 1873, 11½in (29cm) wide.

£11,000–13,000 Sotheby's (O)

A bronze model of a doe, by Alfred Dubucand, c1875, 5in (12.5cm) wide.

£2,000–2,350 Garret & Hurst

A bronze model of a running elephant, by Antoine Louis Barye, entitled 'Eléphant du Sénégal', France, c1875, 5¼in (13.5cm) high.

£18,000–20,000 Richard Gardner

This cast was awarded the prestigious gold 'FB' mark from the F. Barbedienne foundry.

A bronze figure, by Adrien Etienne Gaudez, entitled 'L'Armurier', Voyave St Ame Bruxelles foundry mark, Belgium, c1875, 23½in (59.5cm) high.

£3,800–4,250 Garret & Hurst

Stay in the know
all year round
with the online
Miller's Club
Why not sign up today?
MILLER'S
REGISTER FREE TODAY AT
www.millersbooks.com
Miller's Collectables Price Guide 2008
OUT THIS OCTOBER

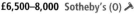

A bronze group, by Evgeni Alexandrovich Lanceray, entitled 'Cossack Lovers saying Goodbye', signed 'F. Chopin', Russia, dated 1878, 13¾in (35cm) wide.

£6,500–8,000 **Sotheby's (O)**

A bronze group, by Evgeny Naps, entitled 'The Return of the Bear Hunters', Woerffel Foundry mark, signed, Russia, dated 1879, 10½in (26.5cm) wide.

£8,000–10,000 **Sotheby's (O)**

A bronze group of two hunt dogs, by Prosper Lecourtier, entitled 'Chien au Relais', Fra c1880, 15in (38cm) high.

£6,000–7,000
Richard Gardner

A gilt-bronze figure, by Albert Carrier-Belleuse, entitled 'Liseuse', France, c1880, 8in (20.5cm) high.

£2,250–2,500 **Clarion Antiques**

A bronze figure of a youth with a lyre, by R. Marino, c1880, 19in (48.5cm) high.

£3,200–3,500
Ronald Chambers

A bronze figure, by Adrien Etienne Gaude entitled 'Défense du Foyer', c1880, 13½in (34.5cm) high.

£2,000–2,400 **Garret & Hurst**

A bronze model of a horse and rider, by Arthur Marie (Comte du Passage) Gabriel, entitled 'Le Contrebandier', France, 19thC, 21¾in (55cm) high.

£4,500–5,500
Bearnes

A bronze figure of a muse, by Henri Michel Antoine Chapu, with Thiebaut Frères foundry mark, on a wooden shelf, signed, France, 19thC, 14in (35.5.cm) high.

£380–450 **Jackson's**

A bronze figure of Jason and Fleece, by Alfred Désiré Lanso signed, France, 19thC, 19½in (49.5cm) high.

£2,800–3,200 **Sotheby's**

A bronze figure, by Jean Alexandre Joseph Falguière, entitled 'Le Vainqueur au Combat de Coqs', signed, 19thC, 13¾in (35cm) high.

£750–900 Jackson's

A bronze group of George and the Dragon, by Emmanuel Fremiet, No. 195, France, c1882, 20½in (52cm) high.

£9,500–11,000 Garret & Hurst

A bronze model of two hunting dogs, by Auguste-Nicholas Cain, signed, France, 1850–1900, 16½in (42cm) wide.

£2,500–3,000 Sotheby's (Am)

bronze model of a horse, by Pierre Jules Mêne, inscribed 'Rallye 1884 Prix des Dames', late 19thC, 26¾in (68cm) wide.

20,000–24,000 Garret & Hurst

A bronze figure of a soldier, by Alexei Petrovitch Gratchev, signed, Russia, dated 1889, 9¼in (23.5cm) high.

£2,500–3,000
Northeast Auctions

A bronze figure of a fisher boy, by Eugène Emile Thomas, signed, foundry mark, France, c1890, 15in (38cm) high.

£2,700–3,000 David Hickmet

Eugène Emile Thomas (1817–82) was born in Paris and studied under the Swiss sculptor Jean-Jacques Pradier. He exhibited at the Paris Salon from 1843 onwards.

ronze model of a lady, by George van der aeten, Belgium, late 19thC, n (43cm) high.

00–1,000 Gorringes (L)

A bronze figure, by Eutrope Bouret, entitled 'La Fiancée du Marin', France, c1890, 23¼in (59cm) high.

£3,500–4,000 Garret & Hurst

A marble figure of The Madonna, by Professor Giuseppe Bessi, signed, c1890, 20in (51cm) high.

£1,700–2,000 Mary Cruz Antiques

A marble figure of a woman, by Cesare Lapini, signed, Italy, c1890, 34¾in (87cm) high.

£7,000–8,500
Bukowskis

A bronze figure, by Henry Weisse, entitled 'Charmeur de Serpent', Germany, c1890, 8½in (21.5cm) high.

£1,200–1,400
Garret & Hurst

A bronze figure of a woman, by Mathurin Moreau, entitled 'At the Spring', signed, France, 19thC, 24in (61cm) high.

£1,800–2,200
Freeman's

A bronze figure of a young maiden playing pipes, by Édouar Drouot, entitled 'Muse des Bois', with gilt highlights, on a marble plinth, signed, c1890, 29½in (75cm) high.

£3,500–4,000
David Hickmet

A marble bust of a woman, Continental, late 19thC, 20¾in (52.5cm) high.

£800–1,000
Dreweatt Neate

A bronze group of a Native American on horseback, by Prince Paulo Troubetzkoy, signed and dated 1893, 16¾in (43cm) wide.

£18,000–22,000
Sotheby's (O)

A bronze model of a hunting dog, by Eglantine Lemaitre signed and stamped, France, c1900, 10¼in (26cm) high.

£3,000–3,350 David Hickmet

Eglantine Lemaitre (1852–1920) mainly produced works depicting dogs. She also used her maiden name Eglantin Robert-Houdin.

A bronze figural inkwell, by Roland Hinton Perry, entitled 'The Siren', signed, America, dated 1902, 16½in (42cm) wide.

£2,200–2,600 Jackson's

A bronze figure of a man sitting on a rock, by Julien Monier, on a marble base, France, dated 1904, 22½in (57cm) high.

£1,600–2,000 Sotheby's (P)

A gold-plated nickel figure of Ernest Meissonier, by Vincenz Gemito, signed, Italy, 1909, 2C (52cm) high, on a marble base

£2,000–2,500 Jackson's

onze model of a tethered dog, by les Valton, entitled 'Passez au Large', ce, c1910, 10¼in (26cm) high.

00–7,000 Richard Gardner ⊞

ld-painted bronze figural group of a ve American and child, by Franz Bergman, marble base, Austria, early 20thC, 20.5cm) high.

100–1,300 Freeman's

onze figure of a girl with a ball, ed 'Barillot Paris', France, c1920, (43cm) high.

600–1,800
an at Tetsworth ⊞

A bronze figure, by Georges Colin, entitled 'The Oarsman', on a marble plinth, France, c1910, 33in (84cm) high.

£6,000–6,500
Richard Gardner ⊞
Georges Colin exhibited at the Paris Salon from 1899 to 1914.

A bronze figure of Icarus, by Türpe, signed, Germany, early 20thC, 31¼in (79.5cm) high.

£2,000–2,500
Sotheby's (O)

A bronze figure of a man, by Schmidt Felling, entitled 'Captive', Germany, 1920s, 15½in (39.5cm) high.

£1,800–2,000 Clarion Antiques ⊞

A bronze model of woman, by Albin Polasek, signed, marked 'Roman Bronze Works, NY', America, dated 1914, 16in (40.5cm) high.

£2,500–3,000 Freeman's

A bronze group of three children playing by a duck pond, by Antoine Bofill, entitled 'Les Trois Enfants', with cold-painted silver and gold decoration, signed and stamped to base, Spain, c1920, 16½in (42cm) wide.

£2,250–2,500 Richard Gardner ⊞
Antoine Bofill was a student of the Academy of Beaux Arts in Barcelona. He specialized in small figures and groups and exhibited at the Paris Salon of the Société des Artistes Français in the early 20th century.

A bronze group of a sow and her piglets, by Hansen Aksel, signed, dated 1928, Denmark, 7¼in (18.5cm) high.

£3,500–4,000 Richard Gardner ⊞

A bronze figure of Otto Schmidt riding 'Marmor', by A. V. Gunter, c1930, 14in (35.5cm) high.

£2,250–2,500 Swan at Tetsworth ⊞

ANTIQUITIES

A limestone vessel, with two pierced lug handles, rim damaged, Egypt, Old Kingdom, 3rd Millennium BC, 4in (10cm) high.

£400–450 Helios Gallery

An alabaster bowl, restored, slight damage, Egypt, 3100–2700 BC, 3½in (9cm) diam.

£450–500 Ancient & Gothic

A limestone stele, carved with figures ar hieroglyphs, Egypt, 13th Dynasty, 1759–1640 BC, 11¼in (28.5cm) high.

£7,000–8,500 Sotheby's (NY)

ESSENTIAL REFERENCE USHABTIS

After scarabs, ushabtis are the most frequently found Egyptian antiquity. They can be made of stone, wood and, more generally, faïence and were provided in the burial to stand in place of the deceased in the next world – some dead were buried with several hundred ushabtis. Higher class ushabtis are inscribed with the Sixth Chapter of the Book of the Dead (the ushabti chapter). Values depend on condition and desirability. Ushabtis from royal tombs can achieve three- or even four-figure sums. A good average piece, with inscription, can be bought for around £200, while poor, small, late examples are obtainable for as little as a few pounds.

A wooden ushabti of Bakenkhonsu, with painted decoration and inscription from the Sixth Chapter of the Book of the Dead, Egypt, 18th/19th Dynasty, 1540–1190 BC, 8½in (21.5cm) high.

£3,500–4,250 Sotheby's (NY)

A composition ushabti figure, incised with hieroglyphs, Egypt, 380–300 BC, 5in (12.5cm) high.

£450–500 Millennia

A carved limestone head of a woman, with painted decoration, Egypt, 19th Dynasty, 1292–1190 BC, 3in (7.5cm) high.

£2,500–3,000 Sotheby's (NY)

A granite figure of Osiris, Egypt, 25th/early 26th Dynasty, 700–600 BC, 15¼in (38.5cm) high.

£7,750–9,250 Sotheby's (NY)

A basalt bust of a man, restored, Egypt, 26th Dynasty, 589–525 BC, 8¾in (22cm) high.

£3,500–4,250 Sotheby's (NY)

A cast-bronze figure of Isis nursing the infant Horus, with traces of original gilding, slight damage, Egypt, Late Dynastic Period, 730–332 BC, 4in (10cm) high.

£580–650 Helios Gallery

During Egypt's history, Isis was the country's greatest goddess whose love encompassed every living creature. She was worshiped beyond Egypt and there was even a temple built for her in Roman London.

A pair of painte wood panels, probably from th sides of an ornat coffin, painted w zoomorphic deiti slight damage, Egypt, late Ptole or Roman Period 1st Century BC/AI 27¼in (69cm) hig

£2,250–2,500 Helios Galler

A stone object, Bactria, late 3rd/early 2nd Millennium BC, 12¾in (32.5cm) high.

£1,500–1,800 Sotheby's (NY)

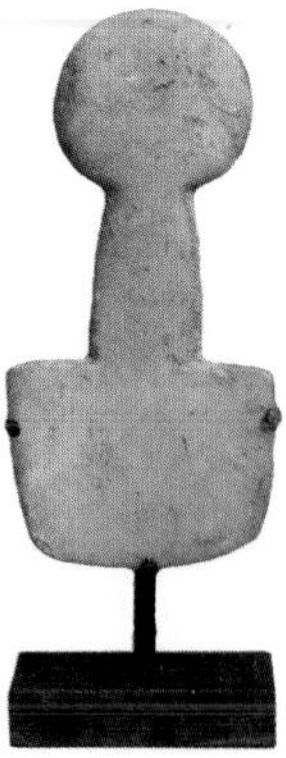

A marble idol, Ancient Near East, Early Bronze Age II, 2700–2400 BC, 3¼in (8.5cm) high.

£1,600–2,000 Sotheby's (NY)

A cornelian and gold necklace, string and clasp later, Syria/Holy or Mesopotamia, early to mid-2nd millennium BC, 18½in (47cm) lo

£580–650 Helios Gallery

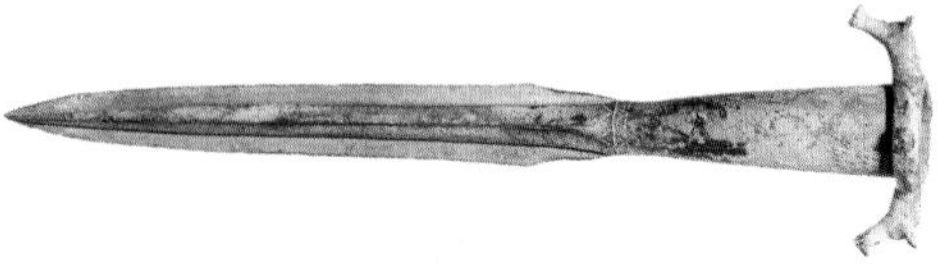

A bronze lance point, with geometric engraving and stylized animal heads, Hittite, c1500 BC, 15in (38cm) long.

£700–850 Hermann Historica

A calcite dish, on a pedestal foot, The Levant, 14th/13thC BC, 4¾in (12cm) diam.

£3,500–4,250 Sotheby's (NY)

A silver beaker, decorated with winged bulls and lions, foot decorated with a sunburst, Persia, Achaemenid Period, 4thC BC, 5in (12.5cm) high.

£20,000–25,000 Skinner

A pottery amphora, painted with Greek-influenced geometric decoration, the two strap handles decorated with a trellis pattern, restored, Magna Graecia, 750–725 BC, 15in (38cm) high.

£1,000–1,200 Helios Gallery

An Italo-Corinthian pottery olpe, painted w friezes of sphinxes, bulls, lions, geese, boa and deer, 575–550 BC, 17¼in (43.5cm) hi

£2,500–3,000 Sotheby's (NY)

> The items in this section have been arranged in sequence of civilizations, namely Egyptian, Near Eastern, Greek, Cypriot, Etruscan, Roman, Byzantine, western European, British, Anglo-Saxon and Medieval.

A pottery dish, with wishbone handles, Cyprus, 1050–650 BC, 12in (30.5cm) diam.

£200–220 Helios Gallery

A pottery amphora, painted with bands and columns of concentric circles, Cyprus, 750–475 BC, 19½in (49.5cm) high.

£6,500–8,000 Sotheby's (NY)

A pottery askos, attributed to the Randaz group, in the form of a mouse, Sicily, 450–410 BC, 4¼in (11cm) wide.

£6,500–8,000 Sotheby's (NY)

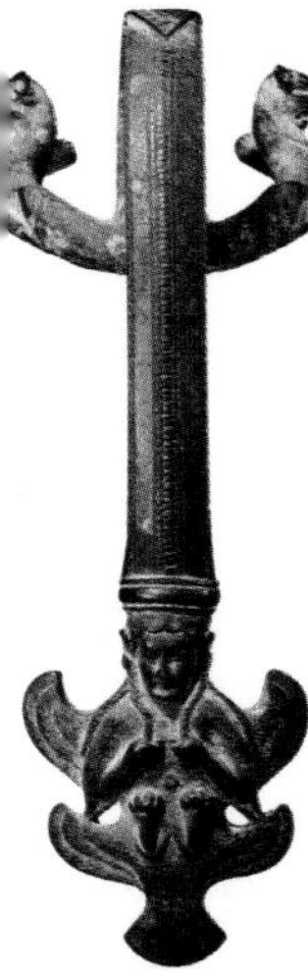

:truscan bronze oinochoe
dle, the lower section in the
of a siren, Ancient Greece,
5thC BC, 10¼in (26cm) high.
750–5,750
heby's (NY)

An Etruscan terracotta head of a boy, 2ndC BC, 11in (28cm) high.
£10,000–12,000 Sotheby's (NY)

A Roman terracotta fragment, modelled in relief with a kneeling satyr, 1stC BC/AD, 8½in (21.5cm) wide.
£6,000–7,000 Sotheby's (NY)

MARKET INFORMATION ANTIQUITIES

- The antiquities market is now very much governed by provenance, and objects with good provenance or from noted collections always command higher prices.
- Items from named collections invariably have special catalogues prepared, consequently prices achieved are usually higher than for similar items from other sources.
- The market is particularly strong for top-end items such as good Egyptian sculptures (especially if inscribed), decorated wooden coffins and funerary masks; large Greek and Roman bronzes; good-quality Greek black- and red-figure pottery, especially if signed by the potter and/or painter, or examples of identified classes and schools; Imperial Roman emperor portraits; decorated stone sarcophagi.
- Many antiquities dealers have noted that there is a dearth of fresh material and middle-range pieces.
- It has become more noticeable in recent years that there are fewer small shops dealing solely in antiquities; dealers increasingly have to rely on issuing printed lists or advertising their goods on the internet.

oman marble herm head of a
nan, nose restored, 1stC AD,
1 (25cm) high.
800–4,500
theby's (NY)

oman marble head of a goddess, crown
sing, 2ndC AD, 11¾in (30cm) high.
3,000–16,000 Sotheby's (NY)

A Roman marble cinerarium, decorated with birds, eagles and hares, with inscription, 2ndC AD, 14¼in (36cm) wide.
£13,000–16,000 Sotheby's (NY)

A Roman bronze model of a bull, 1stC AD, 3½in (9cm) wide.
£5,750–7,000 Sotheby's (NY)

A Roman iron dagger, slight damage, 1stC AD, 10½in (26.5cm) long.
£2,500–3,000 Hermann Historica

A Roman cast-bronze appliqué, in the form of a bust of Bacchus, 1st/2ndC AD, 2½in (6.5cm) high.

£1,200–1,350 Helios Gallery

This was probably part of a banqueting couch, forming the main decorated finial on top of the front of the back-rest. Bacchus was the god of wine and merriment, the Roman equivalent of Dionysus.

A Roman bronze chest/box fitting, cast and chased with a lion's head, 2ndC AD, 6in (15cm) diam.

£300–350 Skinner

A Roman pottery oil lamp, decorated with a pair of dramatic masks, maker's mark, repair 1st or early 2ndC AD, 4¼in (11cm) wide.

£135–150 Helios Gallery

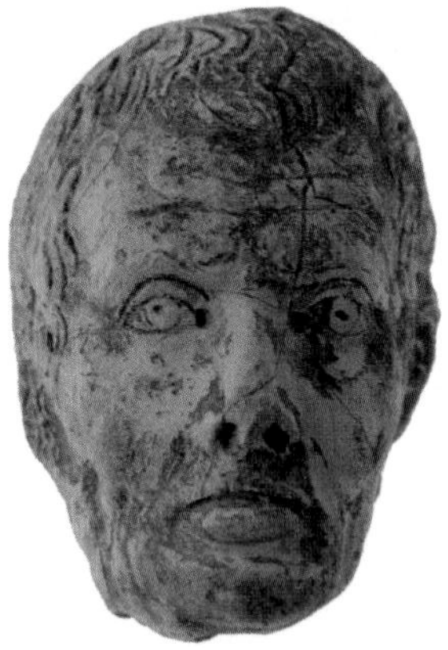

A Roman terracotta model of a male head, hollow, slight damage, c250 AD, 3½in (8.5cm) high.

£200–250 Bloomsbury

A Roman glass bottle, with strap handle, 1st/2ndC AD, 5in (13cm) high.

£500–550 Guest & Grey

A Roman glass flask, decorated with ribbin c3rd/4thC AD, 6¾in (17cm) high.

£3,500–4,250 Sotheby's (NY)

A Roman glass flask, with threaded neck, 4th/5thC AD, 8in (20.5cm) high.

£2,000–2,400 Hurst Gallery

A Roman glass unguentarium, with double loop handles, 5thC AD, 11½in (29cm) high.

£3,200–3,500 Hurst Gallery

A Byzantine bronze reliquary cross, c700–1000 AD, 2in (5cm) high.

£125–150 Jackson's

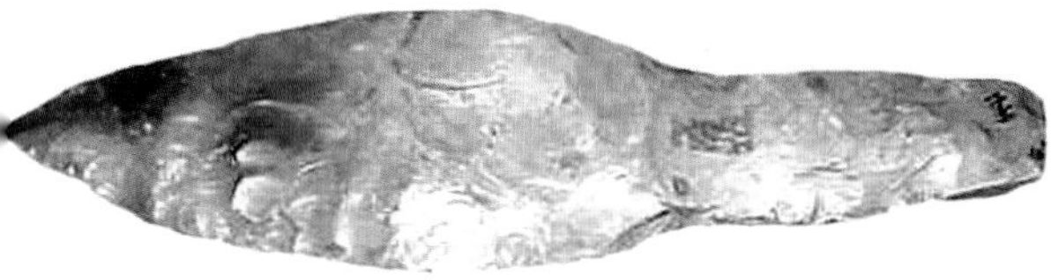

t dagger, Denmark, Neolithic Period, c2000 BC, 6in (15cm) long.

0–650 Helios Gallery

nze sword, with engraved decoration, central Europe, Bronze Age, c1000 BC, (61cm) long.

00–3,500 Hermann Historica

onze axe, restored, central Europe, Bronze Age, c1000 BC, 7in (18cm) long.

0–850 Hermann Historica

ast-bronze profile of a horse's head, with elled decoration, central Europe,)–1000 AD, 2in (5cm) long.

45–160 Helios Gallery

A bronze axe head, Britain, Bronze Age, c600 BC, 3½in (9cm) long.

£250–300 Bloomsbury

SSENTIAL REFERENCE CAUTION

'hen considering buying antiquities it is important to be aware of e following:

Objects from certain countries, especially Mali, Iraq and Iran, are not ceptable unless they have indisputable paperwork supporting their iginal appearance on the market before the dates of any relevant laws acted in the countries concerned.

Export licenses are required for any objects found in Britain and also rtain items identified in auction sale catalogues, subject to advice from e expert advisors to the Department for Culture, Media and Sport.

The problem of antiquities illicitly appearing on the market, whether from useums, private collections or the product of illegal excavation and export om their country of origin, continues to bedevil the trade – to the point here it could stamp out the the collecting of antiquities altogether.

A gold hair ring, central Europe, c1500 BC, 1¼in (3cm) diam.

£1,200–1,400 Hermann Historica

A bronze comb helmet, minor restoration, central Europe, Iron Age, 9th/8thC BC, 12¾in (32.5cm) high.

£15,000–18,000 Hermann Historica

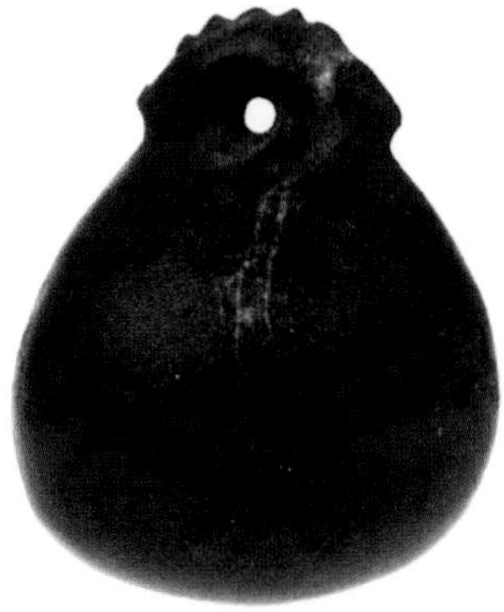

A stone steelyard weight, with quartz crystal streak, Britain, c1300, 2½in (6.5cm) high.

£280–350 Bloomsbury

A silver-gilt brooch, slight damage, Britain, 14thC AD, ¾in (1.5cm) diam.

£200–220 Helios Gallery

These brooches were usually worn in pairs and pinned to the upper part of a dress.

TRIBAL ART

A Native American Mescalero Apache beaded buffalo hide bow case and quiver, with bow and ten arrow shafts, slight damage, Southern Plains, 1870s, 42in (106½in) long.

£4,500–5,500 Skinner

A Native American Apache basket ***olla,*** 10¾in (27.5cm) high.

£280–350 Jackson's

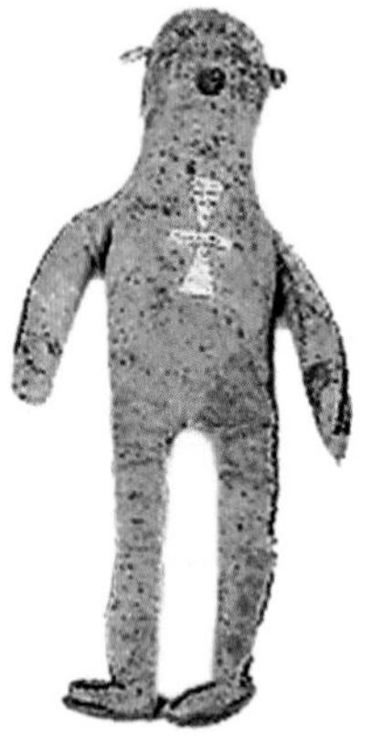

A Native American Apache hide doll, with beaded decoration, slight damage, 1875–1900, 12½in (32cm) high.

£1,400–1,750 Skinner

MARKET INFORMATION TRIBAL ART

- The market for tribal artefacts (as opposed to ethnographic items) has seen a marked increase in interest and an upsurge in business.
- Many auction records have gone through the ceiling, and for the first time a mas has sold for over £3.5 million.
- A new type of serious art buyer has emerged who wants to acquire fine tribal masks and figures to put alongside contemporary artworks.
- The market has been further stimulated by the break-up and sale of numerous major tribal collections that were formed between the 1920s and 1950s.
- Quick to latch on to this movement and seeking to emulate its effects are interior decorators who are now keen to place tribal pieces in their minimalist interiors.
- This is having a strong effect on supply and demand but the downside is that trib pieces will be manufactured to meet demand, and all too often these items confuse the novice collector.
- It is difficult to tell the difference between reproductions, modern copies and downright forgeries from the real thing, so do buy from established, reputable source
- Provenance is a critical factor in estimating the value of tribal artefacts. For example, two figures made as a pair by the same maker at the same time become separated after a time. One arrives in Europe and is purchased by a well-known artist. On his death, it is sold through a major auction house to a collector in the US who lends it to several exhibitions. It is again auctioned and has by reputation been accepted as desirable by several authorities. If now compared with its partner the price differential will be substantial – perhaps £3,500 for the 'unknown' item and £35,000 for the one with provenance.

A Native American Hopi cottonwood ***katchina*** **dance board,** with painted decoration, c1900, 15½in (39.5cm) wide.

£8,000–10,000 Skinner

This object, known as a moisture tablet, is part of a costume for a number of katsinam *characters. Important figures such as the Red Tail Hawk and Eagle* katsinam *wear such devices on their backs. The six discs at the corners and middle section represent four directions. The green paint is copper carbonate and would have originally been blue before it oxidized.*

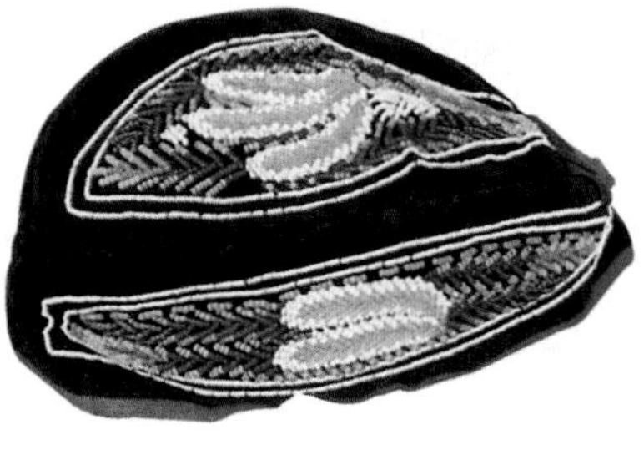

A Native American Iroquois cloth cap, with beaded decoration, late 19thC.

£200–250 Skinner

A Native American Lakota muslin dance sh with a wooden frame, painted with a hawk Central Plains, late 19thC, 17in (43cm) dia

£4,000–5,000 Skinner

ative American Lakota hide bag, decorated with glass metallic seed beads, Central s, slight damage, late C, 31in (78.5cm) long.

200–2,600 Skinner

A Native American Navajo saddle blanket, late 19thC, 30½in (77.5cm) wide.

£1,000–1,200 Skinner

A Native American Navajo leather bow guard, set with nine turquoise stones, 1900–25, 5in (12.5cm) long.

£1,750–2,000 Skinner

A Native American Ute hide amulet, decorated with sun, moon and human faces, with brass-bead fringe, Southern Plains, 3¾in (9.5cm) diam.

£2,500–3,000 Skinner

A Native American child's cloth dress, decorated with carved bone simulated elk teeth, with glass beads, Northern Plains, 1900–25, 35in (89cm) long.

£2,400–2,800 Skinner

This amulet was collected in 1895.

A Native American horse-tooth necklace, with painted decoration and brass spacers, Plains, 1850–1900, 21in (53.5cm) long.

£700–850 Skinner

ative American hide fleche, with painted oration, Northern Plains, 19thC, 27in (68.5cm) long.

00–1,100 Skinner

A Native American Pomo coiled basketwork bowl, decorated with feathers and clam shells, California, 7¼in (18.5cm) diam.

£1,600–2,000 Skinner

A Native American cloth flat bag, depicting a mounted warrior and flower motifs, slight damage, Plateau, 1900–25, 12½ x 11in (32 x 28cm).

£1,250–1,500 Skinner

ative American Salish carved wood roof post finial, in the form of an animal head, n painted decoration, 1850–1900, 13in (33cm) long.

50–1,000 Waddington's

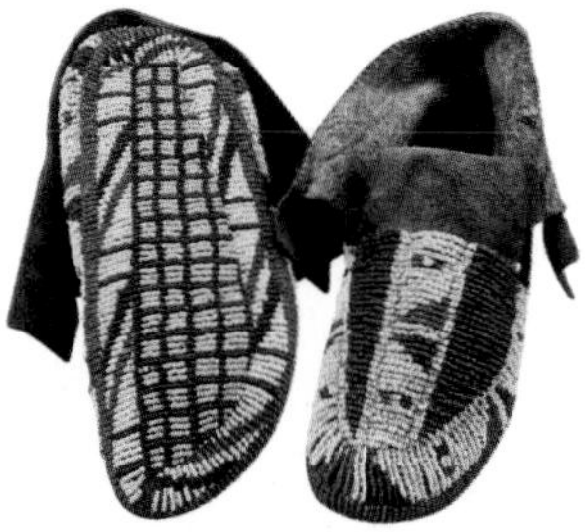

A pair of Native American Sioux moccasins, with beaded decoration, c1900, 7¾in (19.5cm) long.

£750–900 Jackson's

A Native American Tsimshian maplewood, hide and canvas frontlet, decorated with seal-lion whiskers and abalone, 1850–1900, 9in (23cm) wide.

£25,000–28,000 Waddington's

The Tsimshian lived on the coast of British Columbia and Alaska. Their society encompassed nobles, commoners and slaves and was based on a matrilineal line of descent. The four lineages were Raven, Wolf, Eagle and Killer Whale. These lineages held the rights to family crests, myths, dances, songs and a combination of economic resources. The frontlet was part of the formal attire worn by high-ranking Tsimshian society members. They were carved to represent the lineage of the owner.

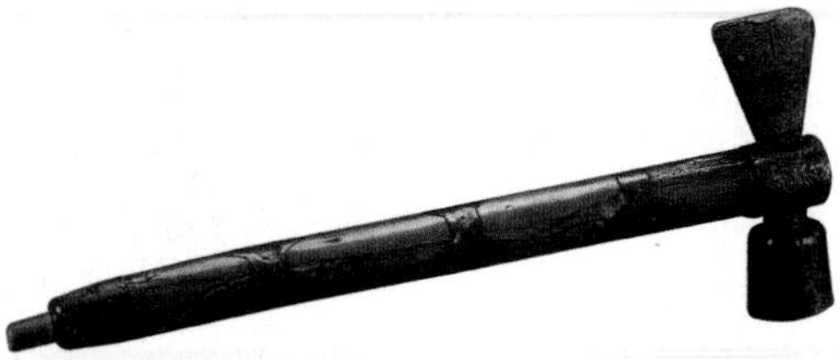

A Native American pewter and wood pipe, in the form of an axe, c1890, 8¾in (22cm) long.

£400–500 Jackson's

An Algonquin birch bark storage box and cover, slight damage, Canada, 1875–1900, 13½in (34.5cm) diam.

£400–500 Skinner

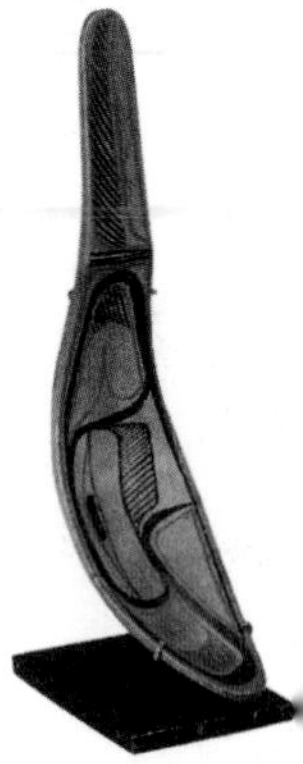

A Kwakwaka'wakw wooden s with painted decoration, Can late 19thC, 9½in (24cm) long.

£350–425 Waddington'

A Tlingit cloth wall pocket, beaded with an eagle, frog and bear with flowers, Canada, late 19thC, 27½in (70cm) long.

£3,000–3,500 Skinner

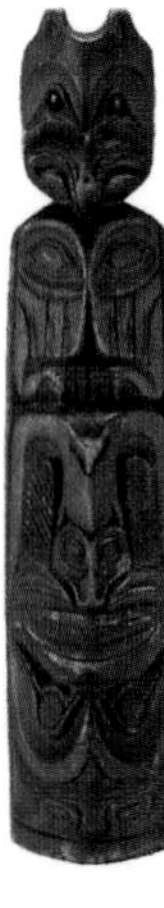

A Tlingit carved wood totem pole, with metal eyes, Canada, c1896, 14½in (37cm) high.

£2,200–2,600 Waddington's

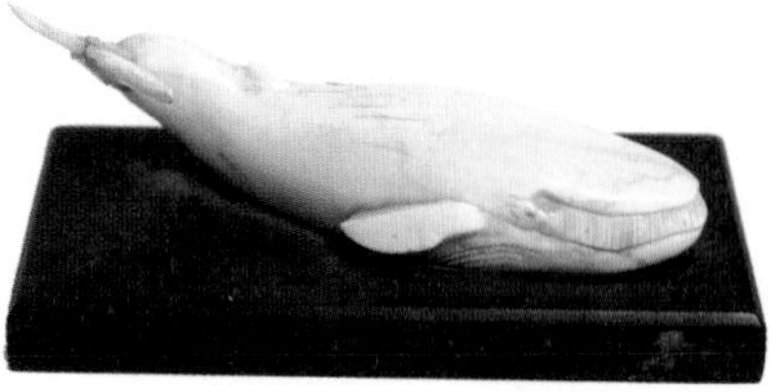

An Inuit carved ivory model of a whale, early 20thC, 5in (12.5cm)

£160–175 Humbleyard Fine Art

A pair of Inuit carved whalebone models of hunters and seals, c1950, 10in (25.5cm) high.

£1,400–1,750 Waddington's

An Inuit carved soapstone model of a seal eating a fish, signed, c1950, 12in (30.5cm) high.

£175–220 Skinner

An Inuit carved wood mask, early 20thC, 8½in (21.5cm) high.

£1,000–1,200 Skinner

An Inuit carved soapstone figure of a hunter, with ivory eyes, c1955, 16in (40.5cm) hi

£15,000–18,000 Waddington's

arved wood chair, Africa, Ethiopia,
.0–30, 34in (86.5cm) high.
00–600 Tribal Gathering ⊞
style and construction of this chair shows uropean influence.

A Baule ivory comb, incised with a face below a rooster, Africa, Ivory Coast, 3½in (9cm) high.
£2,250–2,750
Sotheby's (NY)

MILLER'S COMPARES

(L) **A Baule figure of a woman,** Africa, Ivory Coast, 19thC, 15in (38cm) high.
£5,800–6,500
Gordon Reece Gallery ⊞

(R) **A Baule figure of a man,** Africa, Ivory Coast, mid-20thC, 15¾in (40cm) high.
£1,750–2,000
Gordon Reece Gallery ⊞

Both these Baule figures have a fine libation-induced patination that is correct for the piece and the date, and the quality of carving is comparable. There are two factors that contribute to the price difference between them. The style of the female shown on the left is refined and belongs to the 19th-century aesthetic, whereas the more robust form of the male figure shown on the right is typical of the mid-20th century. Furthermore, the female figure was bought from a private collection, which almost invariably increases value.

amana carved wood door latch, in the
n of a woman, with incised decoration,
ca, Mali, 18in (45.5cm) high.
20–260 **Skinner**

A painted We-Dan mask, Africa, Liberia, 1900–25, 8¼in (21cm) high.
£8,800–9,800 **Gordon Reece Gallery** ⊞

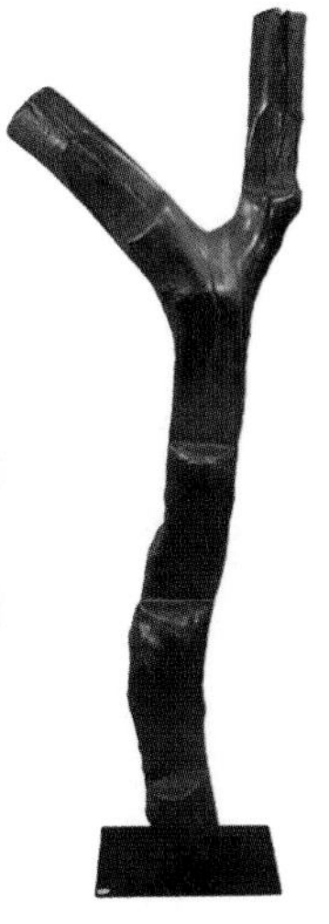

ogon ceremonial ladder,
ca, Mali, Somba, 1900–25,
in (130cm) high.
,650–1,800 **Gordon**
ece Gallery ⊞

A Tutsi wooden bracelet, with copper decoration, Africa, Rwanda, 8¾in (22.5cm) diam.
£2,250–2,750 **Sotheby's (NY)**

A wooden headrest, in the form of a cart, slight damage, southeast Africa, 6¼in (16cm) long.
£3,500–4,000 **Sotheby's (P)**
This item was acquired by the vendor from the Pitt Rivers collection, assembled by the archaeologist and anthropologist Augustus Pitt Rivers in the late 19th century.

A Wongo wooden divination bowl, Africa, Democratic Republic of Congo, 1900–25, 16½in (42cm) wide.
£7,000–7,800 **Gordon Reece Gallery** ⊞

A Sumba carved fertility figure, Indonesia, 1900–25, 27½in (70cm) high.

£4,000–4,400 Gordon Reece Gallery

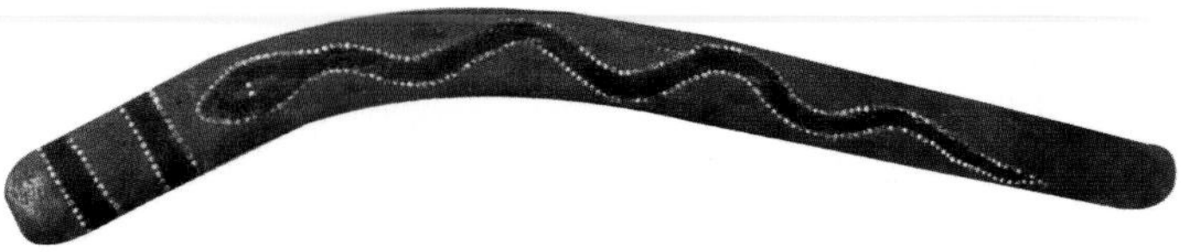

An Aboriginal boomerang, painted with a snake, Australia, 1900–2 19in (48.5cm) long.

£275–325 Skinner

A Maori *hei tiki* greenstone pendant, New Zealand, 3¾in (9.5cm) long.

£6,000–7,000 Sotheby's (NY)

A Kerewa *gope* board, decorated with a figure, Papuan Gulf, 75¼in (191cm) high.

£9,500–11,500 Sotheby's (NY)

In the Papuan Gulf, boards like this were made to house an imunu (spirit) and were placed among other boards of like-minded spirits in a shrine devoted to the earthly well-being of a particular family.

An Aboriginal wooden spear-thrower, engraved and painted with vegetable dyes, Australia, 28in (71cm) long.

£1,800–2,200 Sotheby's (P)

A ceremonial axe, with a ston blade, the wooden handle bou with vegetable fibre and wool, decorated on each side with a stylized face, New Caledonia, 19½in (49.5cm) long.

£3,250–4,000 Sotheby's (P)

A Polynesian carved wood *u'u* club, with carved decoration, Marquesas Islands, 1875–1900, 36½in (92.5cm) long.

£2,400–2,800 Skinner

U'u clubs were highly stylized weapons with anthropomorphic decoration that were made for individual members of the warrior caste and mercenaries who would hire out their services.

A sperm whale tooth *tabua*, with coconut fibre chain, Fiji, 7½in (19cm) long.

£1,100–1,300 Sotheby's (P)

These necklaces – tabua – were precious items, handed down through the generations. They were used as currency, to ratify documents or promises and also betrothals.

A Polynesian carved wood *kava* bowl, in the form of a stylized animal, Fiji ,19thC, 20½in (52cm) diam.

£1,800–2,200 Skinner

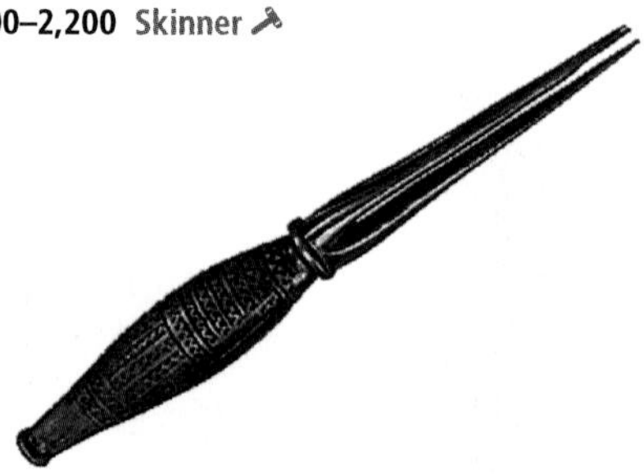

A wooden *bulutoko*, with four prongs, Fiji, 10¼in (26cm) long.

£6,000–7,000 Sotheby's (P)

Bulutoko – *cannibal forks – were used exclusively by priests and chieftains, whose lips should never touch food.*

TREEN

ʳved burrwood tobacco box, ·dinavia, c1870, 6in (15cm) wide.
5–150 Mostly Boxes ⊞

A turned rosewood cruet set, c1840, 11in (28cm) high.
£3,000–3,300 Avon Antiques ⊞

A wooden pilgrim's flask, with food hole and turned and chip-carved decoration, 18thC, 15in (38cm) high.
£500–550 Mostly Boxes ⊞

urnum goblet, 1680–90, 15cm) high.
0–580
k Seabrook ⊞

A tobacco jar, carved in the form of a dog, Germany, 1920, 7in (18cm) high.
£200–225 Koh I Noor Antiques ⊞

A birchwood ceremonial *kasa*, carved with a serpent's head and tail, painted with roses, with inscription, Norway, dated 1858, 14in (35.5cm) wide.
£15,000–16,500 Avon Antiques ⊞

itwood knitting sheath, c1750, 9in (23cm) long.
0–500 Mark Seabrook ⊞

A fruitwood knitting sheath, in the form of a fish, c1840, 5in (12.5cm) long.
£450–500 Sue Killinger ⊞

rved wood lighter, in the of Scottie dog, with glass , c1930, 5in (12.5cm) high.
–80 Mostly Boxes ⊞

A carved oak mangle board, dated 1782, 27½in (70cm) long.
£540–600 Period Oak ⊞

A sycamore muffineer, 1780–90, 5in (12.5cm) high.
£520–575
Mark Seabrook ⊞

A turned boxwood pestle, c1670, 10in (25.5cm) long.
£160–175 Mark Seabrook

A lignum vitae pestle and mortar, 18thC, mortar 7in (18cm) high.
£450–500 Period Oak

A walnut and w iron rush light, 15in (38cm) hig
£400–450 Period Oak

A walnut snuff box, decorated with Masonic symbols, the interior with tortoiseshell lining, France, early 19thC, 3¼in (8.5cm) diam.
£300–350 Woolley & Wallis

An applewood bonnet or wig stand, the turned pedestal carved with a pineapple, the base carved with a heraldic swan, stag and birds, Scotland, c1850, 27in (68.5cm) high.
£3,000–3,500 Avon Antiques

A lignum vitae string barrel, c1825, 7in (18cm) high.
£130–150 Fenwick & Fenwick

A turned lignum vitae string box, blade missing, 10¾in (27.5cm) high.
£400–500 Woolley & Wallis
The large and unusual form of this box would suggest it was made for a shop.

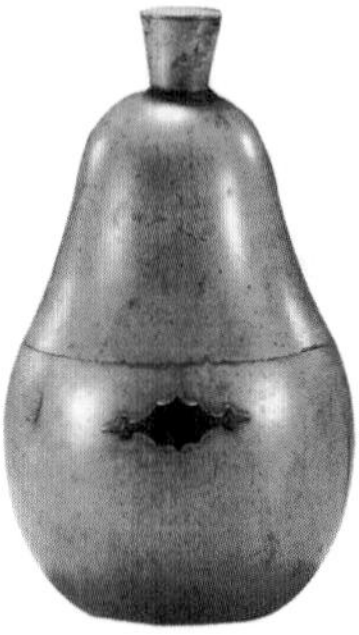

A fruitwood tea caddy, with a silvered-metal finial, c1800, 7in (18cm) high.
£1,500–1,800 Sotheby's (O)

A turned lignum vitae wassail bowl and cover, late 17thC, 9¾in (25cm) diam.
£9,000–11,000 Sotheby's (O)
Wassailing is a term used to describe community drinking, usually associated w festive occasions. Recipes vary according t local customs. Good ale or, in some cases, wine were the bases to which sugar, clove and cardamoms were added together wit small roasted apple for each drinker. Egg white was added to produce froth giving to the name 'lamb's wool'. The goblet on top of this bowl may well have had a cove and been used as a spice box.

A Regency wooden tea caddy, in the form of a pagoda, with ebonized moulding and one drawer, 9½in (24cm) high.
£2,700–3,200 Hy Duke

A turned oak wassail bowl and cover, repaired, 18thC, 10½in (26.5cm) high.
£475–575 Woolley & Wallis

TUNBRIDGE WARE

A Tunbridge ware rosewood box, with a velvet-lined interior, c1860, 3½in (9cm) wide.

£70–80 Mostly Boxes

A Tunbridge ware rosewood box, inlaid with a view of abbey ruins, slight damage, 19thC, 9in (23cm) wide.

£200–240 Woolley & Wallis

Tunbridge ware walnut box, c1900, 0in (25.5cm) wide.

120–135 Swan at Tetsworth

A pair of Tunbridge ware oak candlesticks, with geometric mosaic, c1900, 10in (25.5cm) high.

£540–600 Amherst Antiques

A Tunbridge ware chamberstick, with cube decoration, stickware candle sconce and handle, c1880, 3½in (9cm) diam.

£180–200 Amherst Antiques

Tunbridge ware clamp, with painted decoration, thimble holder and eedlecases, c1820, 9in (23cm) high.

580–650 Rogers de Rin

A Tunbridge Ware dressing table compendium, with four bottles, a ring tree, watch stand and pincushion, c1860, 11in (28cm) wide.

£1,600–1,800 Amherst Antiques

Tunbridge ware inkstand, with glass inkwell and mosaic cover, c1850, in (9cm) wide.

70–300 Amherst Antiques

A Tunbridge ware hat or stick pin, c1890, 3in (7.5cm) long.

£200–220
Amherst Antiques

A Tunbridge ware coromandel letter box, by Edmund Nye, decorated with roses, with label, 19thC, 5¼in (13.5cm) wide.

£675–800 Woolley & Wallis

A set of brass postal scales, on a Tunbridge ware coromandel base by Thomas Barton, scales by John Co & Son, c1870, 7½in (19cm) wide.

£1,000–1,200 Amherst Antiques

A Tunbridge ware snuff box, with geometric mosaic, c1860, 3in (7.5cm) diam.

£270–300 Amherst Antiques

A Tunbridge ware spice box, with painted decoration, c1810, 8in (20.5cm) diam.

£180–200 Fenwick & Fenwick

A Tunbridge ware knitting tool, with painted decoration, c1820, 5in (12.5cm) long.

£400–450 Rogers de Rin

A Tunbridge ware rosewood string box, by Thomas Barton, c1890, 3¼in (8.5cm) high.

£180–200 Amherst Antiques

A Tunbridge ware tea caddy, the interior with two lidded canisters and glass blending bowl, on bun feet, 19thC, 12¼in (31cm) wide.

£725–875 Bearnes

A Tunbridge ware coromande veneered thermometer stand by Henry Hollamby, inlaid with pointer, c1870, 7in (18cm) hig

£500–550
Amherst Antiques

A Tunbridge ware thread winder, c1870, 2in (5cm) diam.

£160–180 Amherst Antiques

A Tunbridge ware rosewood workbox, decorated with a stag and doe, with Berlinwork border, the interior with removable tray, 19thC, 10¾in (27.5cm) wide.

£500–600 Bearnes

A Tunbridge ware rosewood writing slope the cover decorated with ruins within a flor border, 19thC, 12¼in (31cm) wide.

£400–500 Toovey's

)BJETS DE VERTU

:ARD CASES

ARD CASES WERE FIRST USED in England around 1800 and were made of silver and leather with fine gilt tooling. The earliest French es, c1760, were made of gold, silver and enamel, netimes with ivory panels or beadwork. Eventually ry material imaginable was used and cases were duced until c1935.

ith the advent of popular tourism in the 19th tury, card cases were made to depict places of rest and examples include silver castle-top cases, ttish Mauchline ware and Tartan ware and, from and, Killarney ware. Among silver cases castle-tops the most valuable, with the popular versions of ndsor, Warwick, Kenilworth and Abbotsford selling around £700–2,000; rarer examples fetch much her prices. Cases with engraved patterns by thaniel Mills, Yapp & Woodward and Taylor & Perry t from £200 to £500. However, engraved scenes or dings by these makers start at £700. Georgian toiseshell cases inlaid with mother-of-pearl flowers :h around £400–800 and mother-of-pearl cases m £150 to £700. As with all antiques, values depend on condition, quality and rarity.

Simple cases can be found from £50 upwards in materials such as wood, Bakelite and various other media. Ivory card cases depend very much on the quality, clarity and subject matter and the depth of carving, whether Indian or Chinese. Values start at £50, rising to £3,000. Japanese *Shibayama* cases can vary from £800 to £9,000 depending on subject and decoration, which can be coral, horn, nephrite, silver, gold and various semi-precious stones. Metalwork from Japan in bronze, *komai* and *shakudo* can often be very interesting.

Many cases were made for exhibition purposes only especially in fragile materials such as glass or porcelain. Over a period of 50 years card case values have performed very well, but still sell for less than the cost of making them today, especially the exotic examples, while of course, ivory, tortoiseshell and mother-of-pearl are no longer legally obtainable for manufacture.

Graham Ellis

acquer card case, gilded and painted in chinoiserie style, c1825, 4in (10cm) high.

20–360 Simply Antiques

A silver castle-top card case, by Taylor & Perry, decorated with a view of Newstead Abbey, Birmingham 1835, 3¾in (9.5cm) high, 3¼oz.

£1,300–1,450
Daniel Bexfield

This piece has a 'seam' at the top on both sides which looks like a repair, but is not. It was originally made this way by the silversmiths, who have used a die from a top-opening card case. This is a good quality example of the view of Newstead Abbey, which was Lord Byron's house. Note also the detail in the trees, the ducks and the ripples on the lakes.

A silver castle-top card case, decorated with a view of Abbotsford, dated 1835, 4in (10cm) high.

£1,100–1,250 Shapiro

ilver card case, embossed on both sides ı a fountain, with grapevine and scroll oration, America, 1840, 3¼in (8.5cm) high.

75–325 Heritage

A silver castle-top card case, by David Pettifer, embossed with a view of Crystal Palace, Birmingham 1850, 4in (10cm) high.

£2,500–2,800 Nicholas Shaw

EXPERT'S EYE CASTLE-TOP CARD CASES

Various silversmiths are associated with castle-top cases, including Joseph Willmore and Taylor & Perry. From the mid-1820s cases had a flat appearance with a building on both sides surrounded by embossed scrolls or acanthus leaves and sometimes a stippled background giving a frosted effect. Other examples have pierced surfaces.

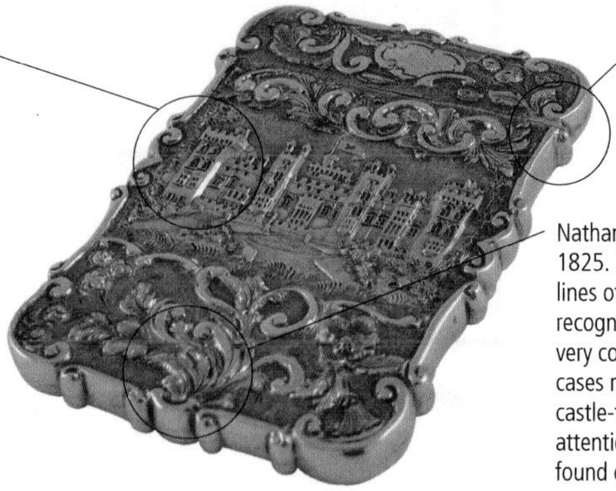

Note the protruding hinge. The hinges on earlier cases were flush with the sides of the case

Nathaniel Mills registered his assay mark in 1825. His attention to detail and flowing lines of decoration are immediately recognizable and examples such as this are very collectable. The rising prices of card cases made by top silversmiths, particularly castle-top examples, have attracted the attention of fraudsters, and fakes can be found on the open market.

Silver castle-top card cases were so-called because they were embossed with castles, country houses and cathedrals. This silver case by the sought-after maker Nathaniel Mills, depicts views of Warwick Castle and Windso Castle and is hallmarked Birminghan 1843. While not outstanding, it is of good quality decorated with a popular design. Prices for castle-top cases depend on clarity and detail. **£1,000–1,200** **Woolley & Wallis**

A silver card case, by Leonard & Wilson, engraved with a view of a bridge on an engine-turned ground, the reverse monogrammed 'BMV', America, Philadelphia, Pennsylvania, 1847–50, 3½in (9cm) high.

£180–220 **Heritage**

A tortoiseshell card case, set with abalone inlaid with flowers, c1850, 4in (10cm) high.

£425–475 **Simply Antiques**

A silver card case, engraved with a country landscape on an engine-turned ground, the reverse with a scroll cartouche inscribed 'Ellen, Christmas, 1856', America, c1855, 3½in (9cm) high.

£200–250 **Heritage**

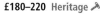

A silver card case, by Hilliard & Thomason, engraved with a basket of flowers, Birmingham 1857, 4in (10cm) high.

£230–275 **Gorringes (L)**

The presence of a Celtic belt cartouche may indicate that the first owner was Scottish.

A Dieppe ivory card case, carved with a panel of flowers, France, Dieppe, c1860, 4in (10cm) high.

£525–575 **Simply Antiques**

An ivory card case, damaged, 19thC, 5in (12.5cm) high.

£160–175 **Long Street Antiques**

This is a quality case but the damage has affected the price considerably.

nother-of-pearl card case, c1860, (10cm) wide.

50–275 Eureka Antiques

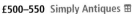

A nautilus shell card case, decorated with flowers within an abalone border, c1860, 4in (10cm) high.

£500–550 Simply Antiques

A tortoiseshell card case, impressed with a classical scene, c1860, 5in (12.5cm) high.

£350–400 Long Street Antiques

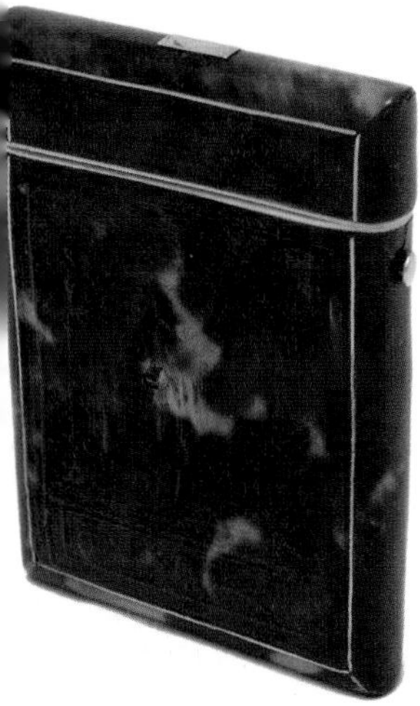

tortoiseshell and silver card case, impressed ith a classical scene, c1870, 4in (10cm) high.

350–400 Eureka Antiques

An ivory card case, carved with figures and buildings, China, c1880, 4½in (11.5cm) high.

£1,000–1,200 Simply Antiques

An ivory card case, engraved with scenes of monkeys and an insect, signed, Japan, c1880, 4in (10cm) high.

£1,400–1,600 Simply Antiques

mother-of-pearl card case, engraved with owers within an abalone border, c1880, n (10cm) high.

130–145 Long Street Antiques

An ivory and *Shibayama* card case, Japan, c1890, 4in (10cm) high.

£6,000–6,800 Simply Antiques

A silver castle-top card case, decorated with a view of Windsor Castle, Birmingham 1905, 4in (10cm) high.

£850–950 Shapiro

SCENT BOTTLES

SCENT BOTTLES HAVE BEEN in existence since around 1000 BC and offer an intriguing glimpse into the fine art and culture of the time. It is perhaps not widely known that colour is often significant, for example red bottles indicate life and energy, green long life and health. Famous producers such as the Staffordshire factories, Lalique, Baccarat and Sampson Mordan & Co have produced some fine examples. In 1907 René Lalique teamed up with perfumier François Coty; this was one of the best partnerships in scent bottle history – the bottles created for Coty by Lalique were works of art and gave a visual theme to the fragrance within. The first bottle, which is decorated with a dragonfly, called 'Libellule', is now very rare. Lalique also produced bottles for other perfumiers, such as Houbigant's 'La Belle Saison' (1924), a very beautiful bottle with a portrait of a woman's face surrounded by radiating flowers which is now worth about £1,500.

More unusual is Vigny's 'Jack', 'Jill' and 'Junior' from the 1920s, a set consisting of three black glass scent bottles, decorated as gollies, in a pink presentation box. When originally produced the bottles were advertised as 'golliwoggs', a term that is unacceptable these days, but these bottles retain their appeal and the set is worth in the region of £1,800.

Demand for scent bottles continues to increase, rangi from the hobby collectors to the more serious aficionad who are looking for top quality bottles as an investmen coupled with the pleasure of owning a piece of history.

Always check the condition of any bottle you find, especially whether it has its original stopper, whether there are dents or holes in the case of silver bottles, anc whether there has been any restoration or repair. A goc dealer will bring such faults to your attention and they will be reflected in the price. I don't recommend buying on the internet, you need to see and hold the item in order to examine it properly. High quality bottles are in limited supply, so get to know your dealer as he will be able to advise you and help you make an informed decision. The American market is the strongest and higl prices are being achieved as a result of online bidding. At a recent auction at Rago Arts in New Jersey most sce bottles exceeded their esitmates. A Lalique presentation bottle of 'Trésor de la Mer' for Saks Fifth Avenue c1936, estimated at £13,500–19,000 sold for £117,000. Numbered 72 of a limited edition of 100, it was in mint condition, complete with its original red velvet box and original price tag.

Heather Hemmin

A gold scent bottle, chased with flowers, dragonflies and a squirrel, 1740–50, 2¾in (7cm) high.

£4,500–5,500
Sotheby's (NY)

Scent bottles sold in New York will achieve higher prices due to an avid collectors' market. They are also very popular in Australia.

A gold scent bottle, chased with Telemachus and Calypso, with a glass liner, c1750, 3¼in (8.5cm) high.

£2,000–2,400
Sotheby's (NY)

A Chelsea porcelain scent bottle and stopper, in the form of entwined fish and an eel, restored, mounts missing, stopper replaced, c1755, 4in (10cm) high.

£1,300–1,600
Sotheby's (NY)

This bottle was produced during the Red Anchor period.

A 20ct gold and enamel scent bottle, by Frantz Bergs, decorated with trailing flowers, Sweden, Stockholm 1760, 3¾in (9.5cm) high.

£22,000–26,000
Bukowskis

This scent bottle was made by one of Sweden's most celebrate 18th-century goldsmiths. Only a exceptionally talented craftsman could achieve such quality enamel decoration. At this time gold items such as scent bottles and boxes were frequently giver as payments and were therefore often melted down for their gol content, which makes surviving pieces very rare.

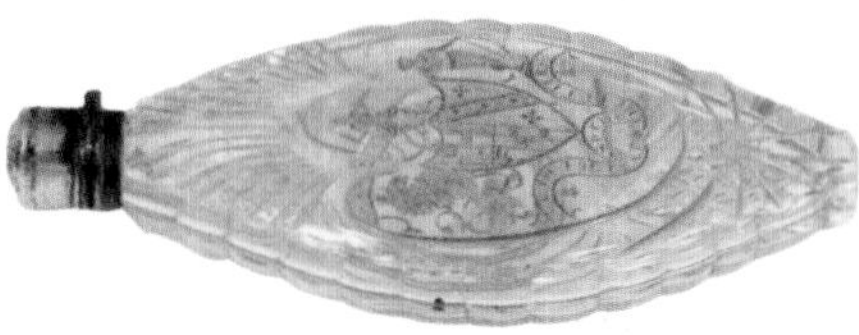

A George III cut-glass scent bottle, with silver-plated top, engraved with a coat-of-arms and motto, the reverse with initials, 6¼in (16cm) long.

£400–500 **Bearnes**

ɔair of glass scent bottles, possibly painted ɟilt by James Giles with flowers, birds, ldings and a maiden, slight damage, c1765, ın (4.5cm) high, in a gilt-metal case.

50–900 Sotheby's (NY)

A porcelain Palais Royale group, in the form of a woman seated on a donkey, her feet in a pannier, the reverse with two cut-glass scent bottles, France, Paris, mid 19thC, 8¼in (21cm) high.

£525–625 Sworders

A double overlay glass scent bottle, with silver-gilt mounts, France, c1850, 4½in (11.5cm) long.

£550–650 Vivienne King

:SSENTIAL REFERENCE BOULLEWORK

oulle is a type of decorative inlay using ɔrtoiseshell and other materials such as brass, ewter, ebony and mother-of-pearl. It was amed after the master cabinet-maker to Louis ⁊IV, André-Charles Boulle (1642–1732) who ›erfected the technique, although there were ılso other workshops in Paris undertaking this ype of work at the time. Boulle used only the ınest quality materials to make tables, cabinets ınd small items such as the casket shown here. ⁊ntique boulle commands very high prices, eflecting the excellent craftmanship, and nulticolour inlay is particularly popular. Beware ›f buying damaged pieces as they can be very ›xpensive to repair.

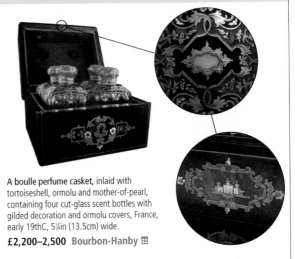

A boulle perfume casket, inlaid with tortoiseshell, ormolu and mother-of-pearl, containing four cut-glass scent bottles with gilded decoration and ormolu covers, France, early 19thC, 5¼in (13.5cm) wide.

£2,200–2,500 Bourbon-Hanby

pair of Baccarat ruby-flash cut-lass scent bottles, France, 1870, 8in (20.5cm) high.

750–850
ɜourbon-Hanby

A milk-glass scent bottle, c1880, 6in (15cm) high.

£60–65
Durham House Antiques

An opaline glass scent bottle, by Mellish, London, the silver-metal top set with coral, c1880, 3½in (9cm) long.

£400–450
Bourbon-Hanby

A Coalport porcelain double scent bottle, with 'jewelled' and gilded decoration, marked, c1880, 4in (10cm) high.

£340–380
Bourbon-Hanby

A Victorian ruby-flash glass scent bottle, with silver mounts, with etched decoration, 4½in (11cm) long.

£220–260 Woolley & Wallis

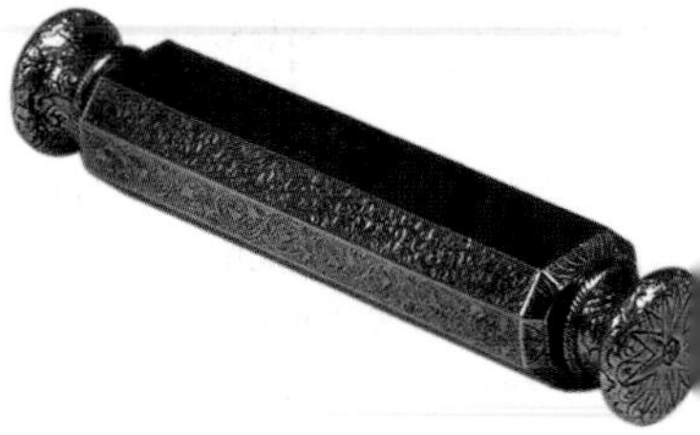

A parcel-gilt double-ended scent bottle, possibly India 19thC, 4¾in (12cm) long.

£160–200 Sworders

A glass scent bottle, with connected tops joined by a link chain, c1880, 3in (7.5cm) long.

£120–140 Bourbon-Hanby

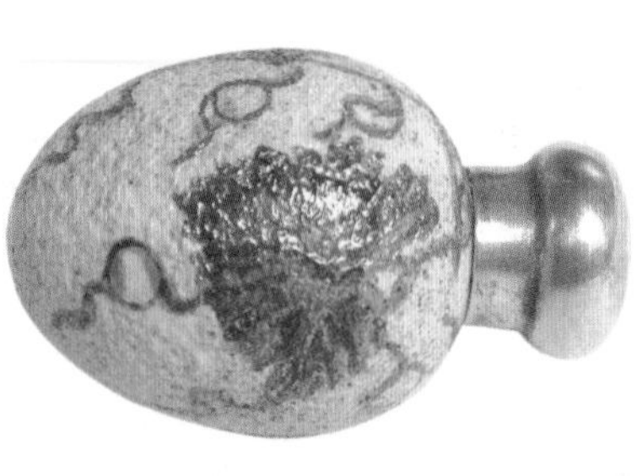

A porcelain scent bottle, with silver mounts, in the form of an egg, 1880, 2in (5cm) long.

£120–150 Lynda Brine

This type of scent bottle can also be found made from an ostrich egg.

A porcelain scent bottle, probably by Sampson Mordan & Co, with silver mounts, decorated with an Imari pattern, marked, London 1885, 2¼in (5.5cm) high.

£200–240 Sworders

A silver scent bottle, by Horton & Allday, enamelled with a daffodil, Birmingham 1885, cased.

£1,000–1,200 Hy Duke

This bottle is particularly desirable as it is still in its original presentation box.

A Bohemian opaline glass scent bottle, with gilt and enamel decoration, c1900, 6in (15cm) high.

£200–230 Vivienne King

A silver scent bottle, by Hilliard & Thomason, Birmingham 1893, 2in (5cm) high, with original presentation box.

£300–350 Durham House Antiques

A ruby glass scent bottle, with silver mounts, Birmingham 189 3in (7.5cm) high.

£250–280 Bourbon-Hanby

A glass scent bottle, with silver overlay, c1900, 6in (15cm) high.

£220–250 Durham House Antiques

A glass scent bottle, with silver mounts, with inner glass stopper, Birmingham 1906, 2½in (6.5cm) high.

£240–270 Bourbon-Hanby

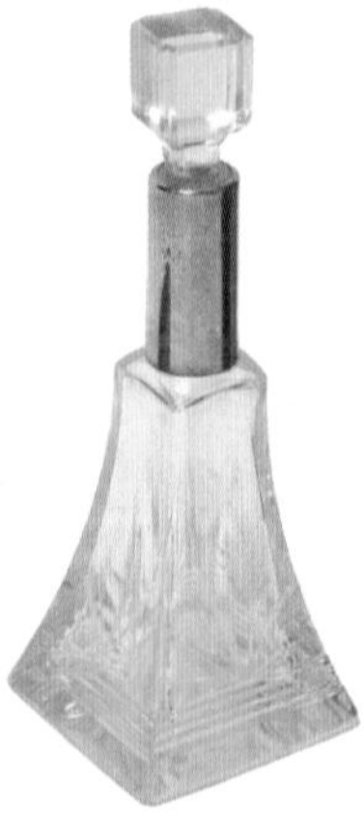

A cut-glass scent bottle, with silver mounts, London 1913, 5in (12.5cm) high.

£180–200 Bourbon-Hanby

VALKING CANES

THE WALKING CANE was once a necessity for the majority of the population and was part of everyday dress. During the 17th and 18th ıturies walking canes were mainly carried by people of ık. In the late 17th century men of substance would ry an ivory-handled silver *piqué*-inlaid cane, often ted and highly prized at that time. King Charles I, ıen on the scaffold in Whitehall, London, gave, ıong other items, two of his *piqué* canes to friends d one of these handles can still be viewed today in Carisbrooke Castle Museum on the Isle of Wight. he fashion for walking canes was most popular in period from the 1830s to WWI, when wealth in rope was at its height. In 1900, there were over 60 ops selling canes in London alone. The dress code was follows: a malacca or bamboo cane for daytime, a ely mounted hardwood cane for the evening and, visiting the country, a plainer folk art one would be choice. The more exotic and costly the cane the ore important the owner or occasion and canes used society events were inlaid with gold, ivory, enamels d precious stones. It is highly probable that the erage Victorian household would have had in the gion of 20 canes and parasols in the hall stand, often bought for special occasions such as birthdays, Christmas or given as retirement gifts.

For the collector of today the possibilities are endless, but do bear in mind that each cane is an individual work of art and it is extremely rare to find an exact match from the multitude produced. One reference book, *Cane Curiosa* by Catherine Dike, published by Editions de l'Amateur, 1983, lists over 1,600 canes with a dual purpose including: sword canes, gun canes and cosh canes for self defence; canes containing cigarettes, cigars, snuff, pipe cleaners etc for smokers and canes with watches, telescopes and musical instruments. These canes were usually very plain in appearance in order to avoid attracting attention to their valuable contents or to disguise their deadly intent. Few were signed but the name Brigg of London is often encountered – they were mainly known to be the largest retailer of canes but they also patented and manufactured some. Other names are Asprey, Henry Howell and Ben Cox in the UK, Tiffany and Gorham in America, Antoine in France and Fabergé in Russia, all of whom supplied superb canes. Fortunately for the collector of today, good examples can regularly be found.

Michael German

malacca walking cane, the ld handle with chased coration and an engraved est, c1800, 35in (89cm) long.

1,000–1,200
ichael German ⊞

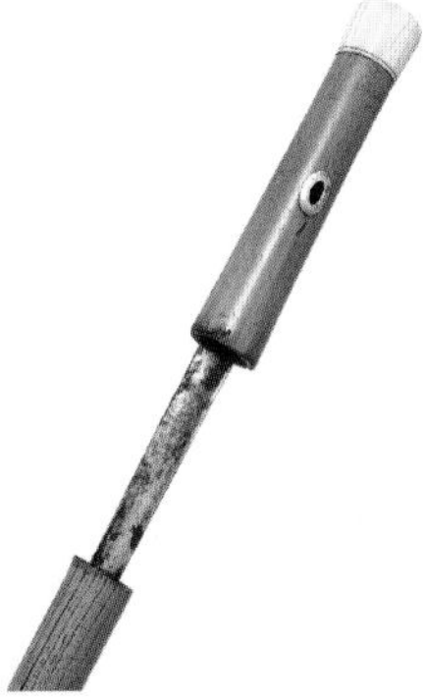

A malacca sword cane, with an ivory top and an etched triangular blade, early 19thC, 35in (89cm) long.

£340–375
Chiltern Antiques ⊞

An ebonized hardwood walking cane, the porcelain handle in the form of two children's faces back-to-back, with a gilt collar, c1850, 35in (89cm) long.

£1,000–1,100
Michael German ⊞

An ebony walking cane, the handle carved in the form of a jester, with a gold collar, c1860, 35in (89cm) long.

£600–700 Michael German ⊞

Victorian walking cane, the ivory handle carved in the rm of a duck, with glass eyes and an articulated beak, sses to hinge mechanism, 34in (86.5cm) long.

350–420 Gorringes (L)

A Victorian whalebone walking cane, with a whale-tooth handle, 75¼in (191cm) long.

£650–800 Sworders

EXPERT'S EYE PIQUE CANES

Produced for a limited period from approximately 1650 to1720, *piqué* canes were carried by professionals such as doctors and lawyers, and men of rank. The handles were always made from elephant ivory inlaid with patterns of silver *piqué* work, often with a central cord hole. Examples can be found with either the owner's initials or a two-number date, or both for example 'NF98'.

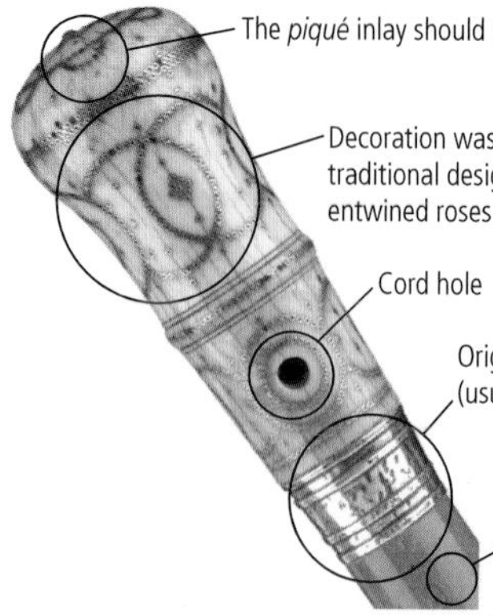
The *piqué* inlay should be intact
Decoration was usually a traditional design such as entwined roses or tulips
Cord hole
Original collar (usually silver)
The shaft was always made from malacca

A silver piqué walking cane, dated 1700, 35in (89cm) long.

£2,500–3,000 Michael German ⊞

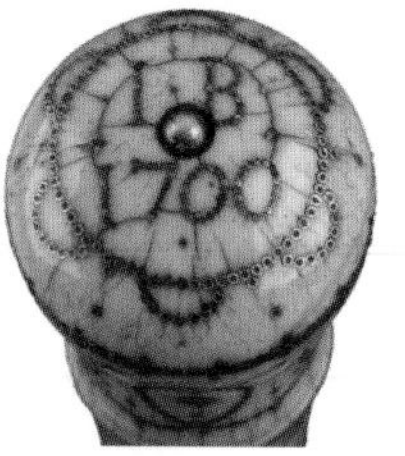

The top sometimes has the owner's initials and date (usually the last two numbers only)

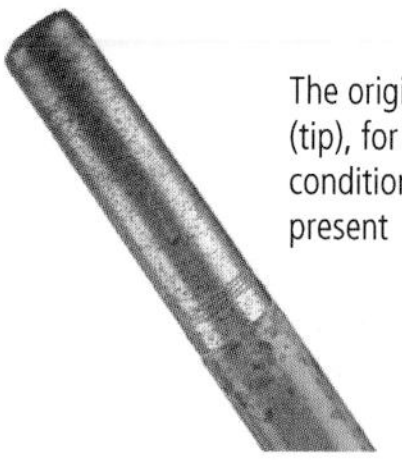

The original long ferrule (tip), for use in muddy conditions, should be present

A wooden walking cane, by Richard R. Haines, the handle carved in the form of a bird of prey with a rabbit, signed, America, New York, 19thC, 34½in (87.5cm) long.

£1,100–1,300 Freeman's

A snakewood walking cane, the ivory handle carved with a bust of Franz Liszt, c1870, 35in (89cm) long.

£800–900
Michael German ⊞
Walking sticks with snakewood shafts are rarely found.

A malacca walking cane, the hardwood handle carved with a monkey's head, with a silver collar, c1880, 35in (89cm) long.

£180–220
Geoffrey Breeze ⊞

A walking cane, the woven wooden strips with metal pins, the crook with a metal cap, France, c1880, 35in (89cm) long.

£340–380
Michael German ⊞

A bamboo sword cane, the whale-tooth handle with a silver collar, the shaft with a hollow-ground blade, c1880, 35in (89cm) long.

£300–350
Chiltern Antiques ⊞

An ebonized walking cane, the ivory handle carved in the form of a snarling dog's head, with a silver collar, c1880, 36in (91.5cm) long.

£270–300
Geoffrey Breeze ⊞

A hardwood walking cane, the stained ivory handle carved in the form of a rosebud, with a gilt-metal collar, c1890, 35in (89cm) long.

£620–680
Michael German ⊞

A Palais Royale bamboo walking cane, by Antoine, the brass handle in the form of a coiled serpent among vines and grapes, stamped maker's mark, France, Paris, c1890, 35in (89cm) long.

£380–450
Michael German ⊞
Antoine was the leading Paris maker in the 19th century and is still in business today.

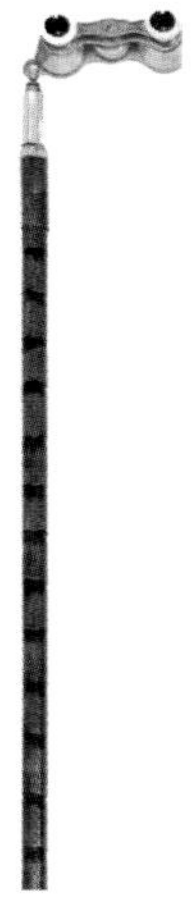

A simulated bamboo walking cane, mounted with a pair of hinged mother-of-pearl, gilt and enamel opera glasses, France, late 19thC, 36½in (92.5cm) long.

£350–425 Freeman's

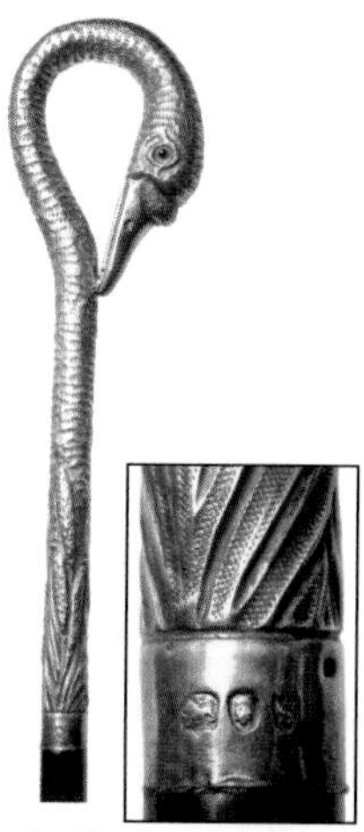

An ebonized hardwood walking cane, the silver handle in the form of a swan's head with glass eyes, London 1893, 35in (89cm) long.

£400–450
Michael German

A malacca sword cane, retailed by Brigg, London, the silver-mounted handle inset with hardstone, the blade inscribed 'Cordoba 1891', Spain, 1894, 37¼in (95cm) long.

£500–600 Sworders

An ebonized walking cane, the carved horn handle in the form of a stylized greyhound's head, with a silver collar, 1898, 35in (89cm) long.

£180–220
Geoffrey Breeze

A malacca walking cane, the handle carved in the form of a greyhound's head, with a silver collar, London 1900, 36in (91.5cm) long.

£280–320
Geoffrey Breeze

A malacca walking cane, the Black Forest handle carved as a cat's head with articulated ears and glass eyes, with a silver collar, London 1900, mounted onto an umbrella.

£400–500 Toovey's

A briar wood walking cane, the antler handle carved with a dachshund's head, with a silver collar, Alpine, c1900, 36in (91.5cm) long.

£600–660
Geoffrey Breeze

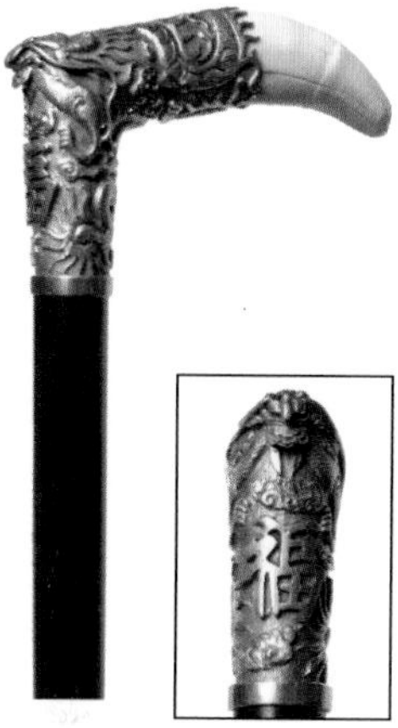

A hardwood walking cane, the silver handle with chased decoration, mounted with a tiger's tooth terminal, China, c1890, 35in (89cm) long.

£700–800
Michael German

A hardwood walking cane, the horn handle carved in the form of a gargoyle's head with glass eyes, c1890, 35in (89cm) long.

£520–600
Michael German

A malacca walking cane, the silver handle embossed with Indian figures and engraved with the owner's name and address, Anglo-Indian, c1890, 33in (84cm) long.

£130–150 Geoffrey Breeze

A hardwood walking cane, with a cloisonné handle, Japan, c1890, 35in (89cm) long.

£300–350
Michael German

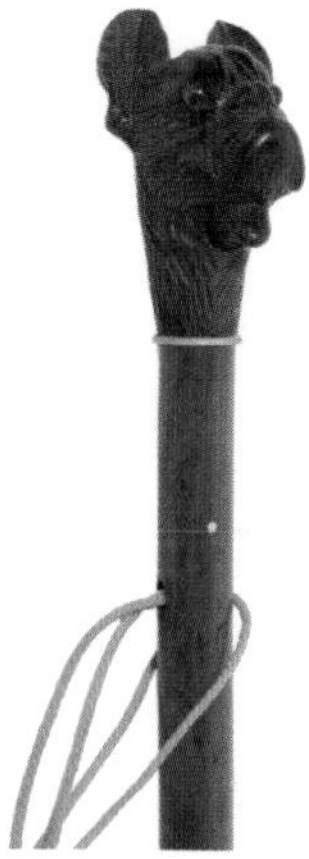

A mahogany cane, the wooden handle carved in the form of a bulldog's head with an articulated glove-holder jaw, France, c1890, 35in (89cm) long.

£180–200 Geoffrey Breeze

KITCHENWARE

A carved walnut bread box, France, 19thC, 39in (99cm) high.

£425–475 Castlegate Antiques

A cedarwood butter churn, 19thC, 18in (45.5cm) high.

£90–100 Clarenbridge Antiques

A wooden butter churn, with crank handle, marked 'Standard Churn Co', America, c1890, 30in (76cm) high.

£125–150 Jackson's

A ceramic butter dish and cover, c1910, 8in (20.5cm) wide.

£130–150 Skip & Janie Smithson

A wooden butter mould, carved with a cow, Wales, c1880, 9in (23cm) wide.

£180–200 Long Street Antiques

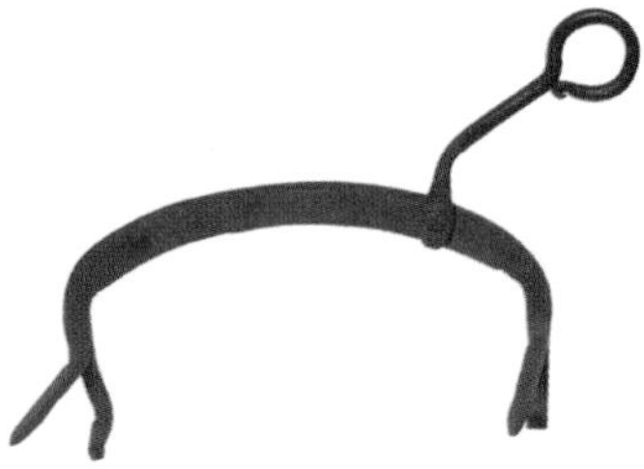

A cast-iron cauldron tilt, 18thC, 12in (30.5cm) long.

£130–150 Long Street Antiques

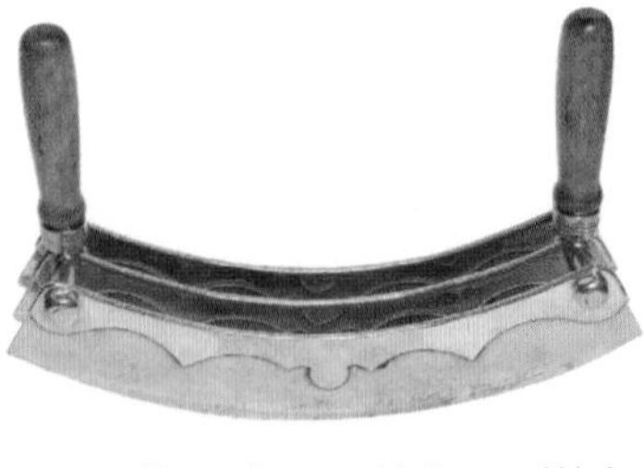

A copper and brass chopper, with three steel blades and two wooden handles, 19thC, 13in (33cm) wide.

£240–265 Long Street Antiques

A Kenrick & Co cast-iron and brass coffee grinder, No 00, c1880, 4in (10cm) high.

£100–120 Skip & Janie Smithson

A ceramic and metal Diadem egg beater, the whisk with a wooden handle, c1880, 11in (28cm) high.

£130–150 Skip & Janie Smithson

ɔle peinte **egg coddler,** transfer-printed attendants in a landscape, the hinged enclosing a two-tier stand, with gilt swan dles and paw feet, some repainting, ,ce, early 19thC, 11in (28cm) high.
ɔ0–900 Olivers

A **cast-iron charcoal iron,** with dragon's head chimney and wooden handle, Germany, c1880, 6in (15cm) wide.
£270–300 Long Street Antiques

A **Wedgwood ceramic milk jug,** 8 quart capacity, c1910, 13in (33cm) high.
£300–350 Skip & Janie Smithson

iron kettle tilter, 19thC, 13in (33cm) high.
30–200 Long Street Antiques
item allowed water to be poured from the kettle without removing ɔm the hearth. It would have been hung from a pot hook on the ɪe of the chimney bar, the kettle resting on the upturned hooks.

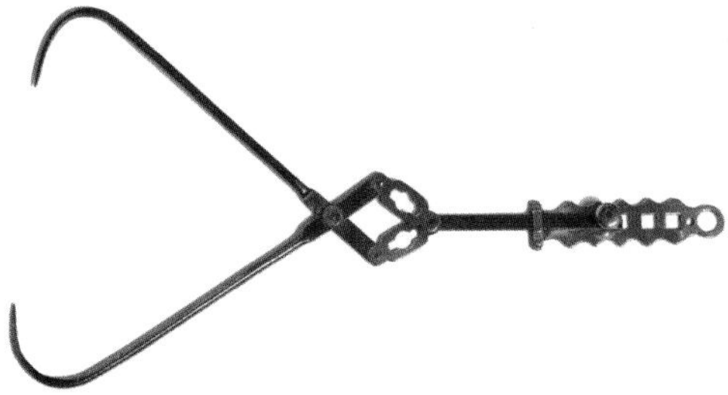

An **iron and brass adjustable meat hook,** 18th/19thC, 21¼in (54cm) long.
£180–200 Long Street Antiques

arved wood gingerbread mould, decorated on both sides, Holland, c1770, 17in (43cm) wide.
25–250 Peter Norden Antiques

A **brass muffineer,** c1785, 6in (15cm) high.
£70–75 Mark Seabrook

ilver pepper caster, London 1728, n (9cm) high, 2½oz.
00–850 Bearnes

A **turned ivory pepper grinder,** with silver mounts, 3½in (9cm) high, 2½oz.
£200–250 Holloway's

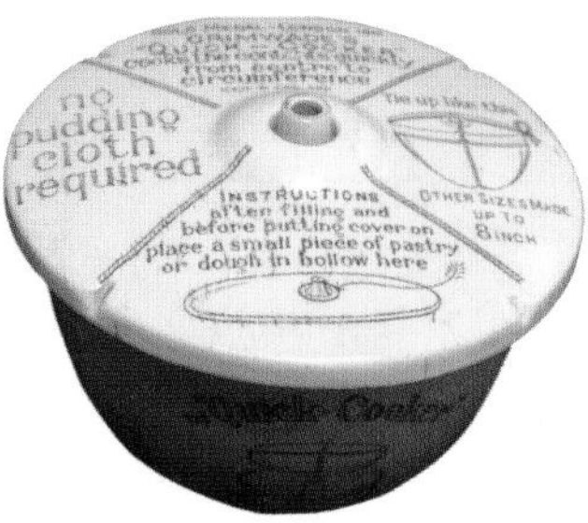

A **Grimwade's ceramic quick cooker,** c1910, 5in (12.5cm) diam.
£135–150 Skip & Janie Smithson

A pair of brass servers, with ebonized handles, c1840, 14in (35.5cm) long.

£220–250 Peter Norden Antiques

A turned wood spice box, with three compartments for 'Cinnamon', 'Ginger' and 'Nutmeg', 5½in (14cm) high.

£320–360 Hy Duke

A stoneware storage jar, Scotland, c1880
9in (23cm) high.

£90–100 Skip & Janie Smithson

Four Grimwade's storage jars, with transfer-printed decoration, c1910, 6in (15cm) high.

£135–150 each Skip & Janie Smithson

A brass strainer, c1760, 10in (25.5cm) dia

£430–480 Mark Seabrook

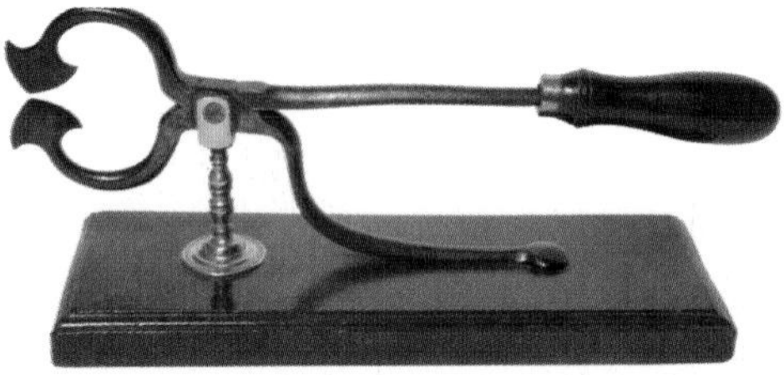

A cast-iron table sugar cutter, on a fruitwood base, c1800, 14in (35.5cm) wide.

£250–285 Fenwick & Fenwick

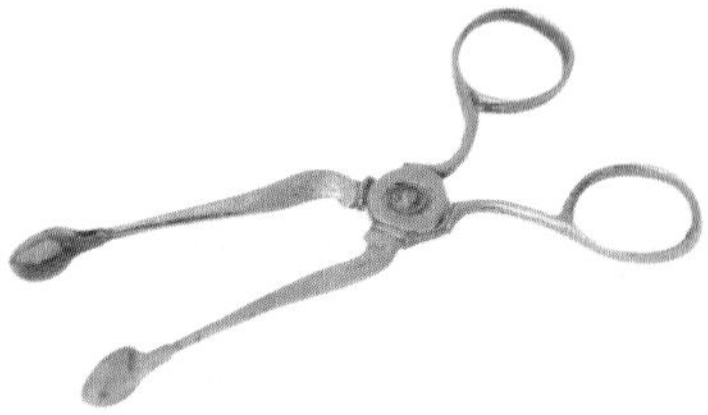

A pair of brass sugar tongs, c1750, 4in (10cm) long.

£250–280 Mark Seabrook

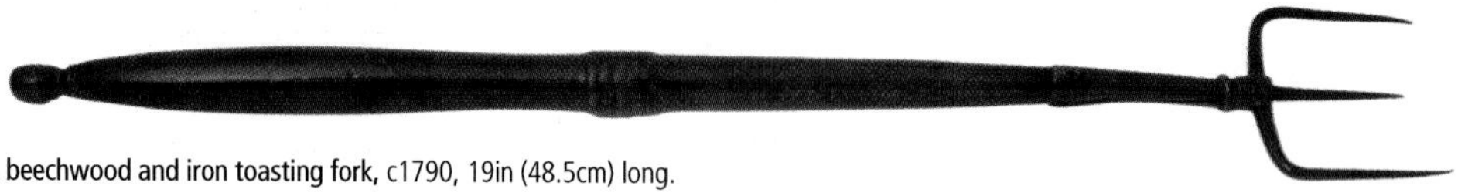

A beechwood and iron toasting fork, c1790, 19in (48.5cm) long.

£180–200 Mark Seabrook

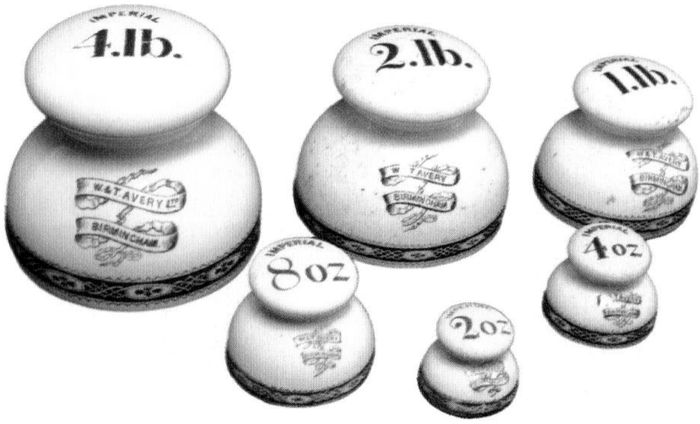

A set of six Avery ceramic weights, c1910, largest 4in (10cm) high.

£1,300–1,500 Skip & Janie Smithson

A Shenstons ceramic weight, early 20thC,
3in (7.5cm) high.

£135–150 Skip & Janie Smithson

AMERICAN FOLK ART

AMERICAN FOLK ART is one of the most intriguing areas of antiques and collectables. It is not limited to a period, school or region and ıdes paintings, sculptures, textiles and ceramics ɔng its forms. Themes range from patriotic, ɔrical and religious to purely decorative. By strict nition, folk art is the creation of an untrained ;an – its strength and appeal lies in its ightforward individual quality. Mundane objects materials become vibrant statements inspired by maker's social, cultural and historical experiences. e, for example, the whimsical whirligig of the man tting a bumblebee, or the three rooster weather es shown on page 440, each of which is a distinct rpretation of the same subject. Consider, too, the ed eagle by John Haley Bellamy on page 437. amy was an accomplished carver, but the folk art ector is attracted to the eagle for its colour and iotic theme, as well as its form. Objects also can creations in an unusual medium, such as the sand ure in a bottle on page 439.

lk art was first perceived as collectable relatively y in the 20th century. Early collections of American folk art generally focused on 18th- and 19th-century objects of Anglo-Saxon, Dutch and German heritage as unique expressions of historical and cultural commentary. It was several decades before the appeal of African-American, Hispanic and other cultural and ethnic creations were considered. Some collections concentrated on one aspect such as weather vanes, flags or a particular painter, others were characterized by region or period.

Constantly evolving, the market for folk art is very strong today. New York auctions recently saw an Edward Hicks painting realize £3,335,000 and a work by Ammi Phillips sell for £670,000. Strong as the market is, however, new collectors can gain a foothold and share in the enjoyment of this wonderful aspect of American art. There are items available to suit all purses in every category imaginable. Considerations include form, visual appeal and condition; if provenance can be established, it can add significantly to the value of a piece. Whether acquired as an investment or for the sheer enjoyment of it, folk art undeniably continues to be one of the most vibrant and exciting areas of collectable Americana.

Cynthia Tashjian

atercolour and ink birth record, ibuted to Moses Connor Jr, painted with s and inscription, New Hampshire, 1804, × 6¼in (21.5 x 16cm), in a wooden frame.

500–3,000 Skinner

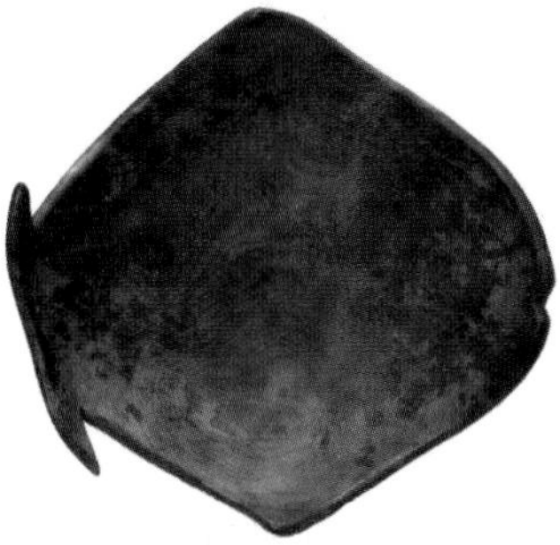

A burrwood bowl, in the shape of a fish, restored, Maine, New England, early 19thC, 14¼in (36cm) wide.

£6,000–6,750
Raccoon Creek

A carved wood wall box, pierced with a heart above three compartments, restored, probably Pennsylvania, late 18thC, 13in (33cm) wide.

£3,000–3,500 Sotheby's (NY)

Folk Art is a very broad term, encompassing many collecting areas. For other examples refer to the sections on Kitchenware, Marine, Metalware, Treen, Boxes, Textiles and Toys.

oplar box, with painted decoration, slight damage, New York, early 19thC, ¼in (65.5cm) wide.

,000–6,000 Skinner

A pasteboard bandbox, by S. M. Hurlbert, decorated with hand-block printed paper depicting men's hats, gloves and umbrellas, Boston, c1835, 9in (23cm) high.

£14,000–18,000 Northeast Auctions

A bandbox, decorated with floral wallpaper, lined with newsprint, Pennsylvania, c1840, 12½in (32cm) high.

£600–700 Northeast Auctions

A tin document box, painted with stylized flowers, Pennsylvania, c1840, 9¼in (23.5cm) wide.

£16,000–20,000 Northeast Auctions

A tramp art wooden storage box, with coin slots and lamps, c1900, 19in (48.5cm) high.

£4,000–5,000 Skinner

A wooden candle box, carved with fans, late 18thC, 12in (30.5cm) wide.

£5,000–6,000 Skinner

A tin coffee pot, possibly by Filley Tinshop, painted with flowers, Philadelphia, c1840, 11in (28cm) high.

£24,000–28,000 Northeast Auctions

A Shaker wooden container, stencilled 'H. F. Lonbaid', c1800, 13in (33cm) diam.

£250–300 James D Julia

This container is believed to have been an insert in a wooden firkin or pail thus creating two compartments for storage.

A carved, gilded and painted pine coat-o arms, carved with a pony, steer's head, do and foliage, slight damage, late 19thC, 33in (84cm) high.

£2,500–3,000 Sotheby's (NY)

A carved and painted model of a drake, attributed to Ira Hudson, Virginia, Chincoteague, 1920s, 21¼in (54cm) long.

£20,000–25,000 Northeast Auctions

A carved pine model of an eagle, holding a document, possibly the Constitution, painted wi the colours of the American flag over original gilding, slight damage, Bucksport, Maine, c180 54½in (138.5cm) wide.

£11,000–13,000 Skinner

ʼved and painted pine model of an
ɛ, with incised decoration and original
ıg, standing on a shield, Maine, Saco,
19thC, 38in (96.5cm) high.

ı00–9,000 **Sotheby's (NY)**

nvas family register, by Polly Giles, worked
silk threads on linen with a family register
e Giles family, signed, Massachusetts,
19thC, 21½ x 17in (54.5 x 43cm), in later
s-eye maple frame.

ı00–3,000 **Skinner**

*vas worked by one of the daughters of John
: and his second wife Mary. She probably
ɛd stitching it while attending the Groton
ale Seminary in Groton, Massachusetts.*

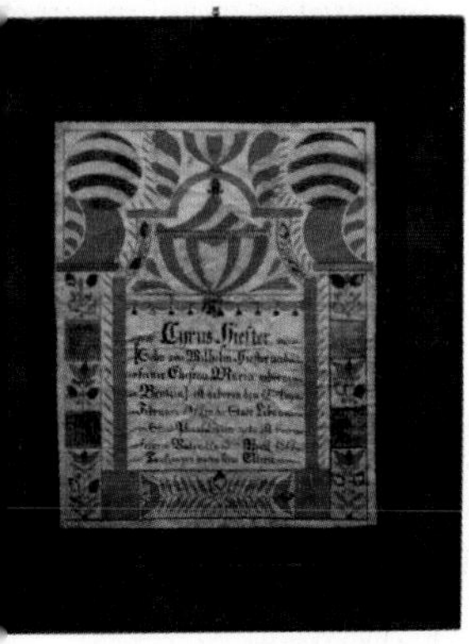

ıtercolour fraktur, Philadelphia, Lancaster
nty, 1817, 11¾ x 8¾in (30 x 22cm), framed.

750–5,250 **Raccoon Creek**

*turs are watercolour and ink paintings
ɛted by the Pennsylvanian Dutch during
18th and 19th centuries and usually took
form of marriage blessings, birth and
ism certificates etc. They were often
ırated with calligraphy and motifs such as
;, tulips, mermaids and unicorns.*

A carved eagle plaque, by John Haley Bellamy, with banner inscribed 'E Pluribus Unum', 1870–90, 26in (66cm) wide.

£18,000–22,000 **Northeast Auctions**

John Haley Bellamy (1836–1914) worked in Boston for the ship carver Laban Smith Beecher and later attended the New Hampton Literary Institute. After 1857, Bellamy began his career as a carver, working first at a shop in Boston and later in Maine. In addition to his well-known eagles, Bellamy's output included clock cases, signs, frames, animal figures and furniture.

A leather ceremonial fire bucket, painted with an eagle above flames and inscription 'Ancient Fire Society, Jos. F. Tufts', Massachusetts, Charlestown, dated 1815, 13in (33cm) high.

£9,000–11,000 **Sotheby's (NY)**

A watercolour fraktur, by David Auger, slight damage, New England, Vermont, 1840, 16 x 12in (40.5 x 30.5cm), framed.

£4,750–5,250 **Raccoon Creek**

A printed silk American flag, c1837, 31½ x 35in (80 x 89cm), framed.

£3,200–3,800 **Freeman's**

A watercolour fraktur, Delaware Valley, 1780, 10¾ x 8¼in (27.5 x 21cm), framed.

£2,300–2,600 **Raccoon Creek**

A watercolour fraktur, for 'Ruth P. Wallin', Pennsylvania, 1830–50, 7½ x 9½in (19 x 24cm), framed.

£1,350–1,600 **Raccoon Creek**

A tree-root frame, c1900, aperture 13½ x 17in (34.5 x 43cm).
£2,500–3,000 Skinner

A copper-plate printed handkerchief, commemorating George Washington, inscr 'The Effect of Principle Behold the Man', 19thC, framed, 12in (30.5cm) square.
£380–450 Freeman's

A painted wood ceremonial parade fire hat, painted with emblems, Fairmont, Philadelphia, 1830–40, 13½in (34.5cm) diam.
£11,000–13,000 Northeast Auctions

A carved wood jigger, in the form of a man, with a felt tie and coat tails, c1900, 16½in (42cm) high.
£200–240 Jackson's

A chalkware and plaster model of a bird slight damage, probably Pennsylvania, 1840–80, 6in (15cm) high.
£1,800–2,000 Raccoon Creek

A watercolour and ink painting, 19thC, framed, 13½ x 15in (34.5 x 38cm).
£200–240 Freeman's

A Pennsylvania/German School egg tempera and ink painting, depicting a bird on a perch, 19thC, 4¾ x 4in (12 x 10cm), framed.
£1,650–1,950 Skinner

A oil painting, on chestnut panel, depictir man and his dog, 1840–60, 14 x 10in (35.5 x 25.5cm), framed.
£7,000–8,000 Raccoon Creek

A carved and painted wood plaque, of the Buffalo Insurance Company, depicting symbols of 19thC industry, occupation and abundance, New York State, 19thC, 29¼in (74.5cm) diam.
£4,750–5,750 Skinner

An oil painting, on canvas, depicting an eagle and flags, 19thC, 41¼in (105cm) diam.
£5,000–6,000 Freeman's

n rug, depicting urns of flowers, 1830–40, 24 x 65in (61 x 165cm).
00–9,000 Northeast Auctions

ol and cotton hooked rug, depicting an urn of flowers, wooden stretcher, 19thC, 20 x 34in (51 x 86.5cm).
'50–3,250 Skinner

A Shaker-style silk, felt and wool hooked and braided rug, New England, c1890, 25¾ x 41½in (65.5 x 105.5cm).
£1,800–2,000 Raccoon Creek

on and silk hooked rug, uted to Grenfell Labrador tries, depicting ducks, mounted wooden stretcher, early 20thC, x 39¾in (134 x 101cm).
00–3,500 Skinner

A hooked rug, by Edna Bullard, worked with 117 squares depicting flowers and objects, Wisconsin, 1946, 144 x 108in (365.5 x 274cm).
£3,250–4,000 Freeman's

A sand picture in a bottle, by Andrew Clemens, depicting the ship *Wm H. Cook*, the reverse with eagle and US flag, Iowa, McGregor, dated 1888, 6¾in (17cm) high.
£6,000–7,000 Skinner
Andrew Clemens was born in Dubuque, Iowa, in 1857. Using sand from river bluffs near his home, he earned his livelihood by arranging it into pictures in glass bottles.

rved and painted pine shop depicting a Native American ess, on a stand, 1875–1900, n (166.5cm) high.
,000–14,000 theast Auctions

A carved and painted pine Oddfellows staff, 19thC, 62½in (160cm) long.
£600–700 Freeman's

A cast-iron coin-operated strength tester, in the form of Uncle Sam, early 20thC, 30in (76cm) high.
£6,500–8,000 Freeman's

A cast-iron tobacco store figure, in the form of a Native American princess holding tobacco leaves, 19thC, 25in (63.5cm) high.

£2,400–2,800 Freeman's

A wooden Victrola cabinet, by Adelard Roy, inlaid with pictures of Army generals, pictures of the ship *The Tuscania*, the American flag and other portraits, slight damage, Maine, 1922, 27in (68.5cm) diam.

£34,000–40,000 James D Julia

Seventeen different types of wood were used to make this cabinet.

An iron weathervane, in the form of a rooster, Pennsylvania, 1860–80, 21in (53.5cm) wide.

£7,000–8,000 Raccoon Creek

A copper weathervane, attributed to J. W. Fiske, in the form of horse and driver 'St Julien with Sulky', sl damage, New York, 1875–1900, 40in (102cm) wide.

£13,000–16,000 Skinner

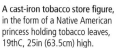

A copper weathervane, in the form of a running horse, with zinc ears, probably New England, 19thC, 35in (89cm) wide.

£4,750–5,750
Sotheby's (NY)

A cast-iron and copper weathervane, in the form of a running horse, damaged, late 19thC, 28in (71cm) wide.

£900–1,100 Skinner

A copper weathervane, attributed to William Hennis, in the form of a rooster, Philadelphia, early 20thC, 15in (38cm) wide.

£2,800–3,400
Northeast Auctions

A carved and painted metal and wood whirligig, in the form of a man swatting a bumblebee, late 19thC, 20in (51cm) high.

£2,000–2,500 Northeast Auctions

A carved and painted pine whirligig, in t form of a soldier with rotating arms, on a wooden base, America, late 19thC, 32¼in (82cm) high.

£1,900–2,200 Skinner

EXTILES

OVERS & QUILTS

ɔollen patchwork coverlet, the centre a double-headed eagle with a chequered rial shield, the patches and motifs edged rd, 18thC, 69¼ x 55¼in (176 x 140.5cm).

0–800 Kerry Taylor

A wool and linsey-woolsey zigzag quilt, with a crenellated pattern, slight damage, America, c1820, 94 x 72in (239 x 183cm).

£2,500–3,000 Skinner

A coverlet, the border with a graduated diamond design, with a Cumbrian weave and wool wadding backing, 1820–40, 86½ x 78¾in (220 x 200cm).

£180–220 Penrith Farmers' & Kidd's

tton-faced patchwork chintz Durham quilt, backed wool, c1850, 90 x 80in (228.5 x 203cm).

0–650 Joanna Proops

An appliqué quilt, the ground of rose blocks hand-quilted in feather and leaf wreaths, the oak leaves with a lattice pattern ground, America, 19thC, 84 x 82½in (213.5 x 209.5cm).

£220–260 Whitaker

An appliqué pieced friendship quilt, with floral wreath, heart, star and bird motifs, quilted with tulips, leaves, scrolls and geometric designs, one corner monogrammed 'S. E. G ', America, New Jersey, c1850, 102 x 86in (259 x 218.5cm).

£9,000–11,000 Northeast Auctions

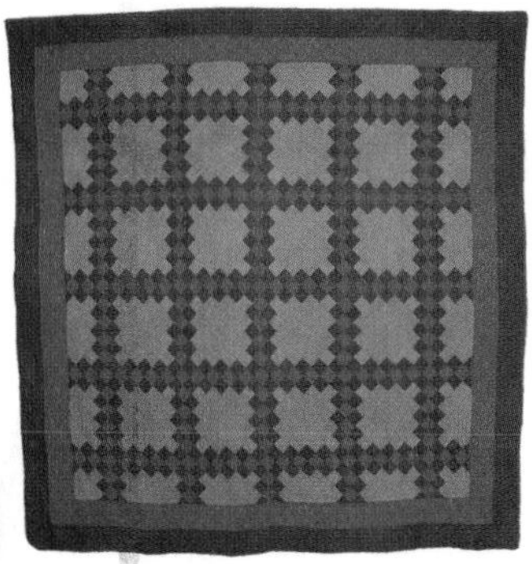

eeplechase quilt, America, Pennsylvania, c1850, 84in (221 x 213.5cm).

600–1,800 Rocky Mountain

name Steeplechase probably came from the fences on eplechase course. Steeplechase and Irish Chain quilts basically the same pattern, except for the orientation. eeplechase pattern is set horizontally/vertically on a and an Irish Chain is set diagonally. This piece is very ual due to the use of taupe calico (an extremely rare c) for the joining blocks.

A Prince's Feather quilt, double line-quilted and decorated with hand-appliquéd Confederate maple leaves in the corners and field, America, Pennsylvania, c1850, 84 x 82in (213.5 x 208.5cm).

£1,600–1,800
Rocky Mountain

A Patriotic Basket quilt, America, Pennsylvania, c1880, 78 x 68in (198 x 172.5 cm).

£900–1,000 Rocky Mountain

This is termed a Patriotic quilt because it is red, white and blue.

An Odd Fellows candlewick **bridal cover,** embroidered with the initials 'A.B.' and the date, surrounded by a leafy flowering vine and various devices, with an outer border of swags, flowerheads, butterflies and leaves, America, Pennsylvania, Lancaster County, dated 1884, 80 x 60in (203 x 152.5cm).
£900–1,100 **Freeman's**

A **quilt,** comprising 30 panels depicting fans, America, late 19thC, 69¾ x 60¾in (177 x 154.5cm).
£1,000–1,200 **Sotheby's (Am)**

A **child's silk Durham quilt,** with crochet edging, c1890, 60 x 50in (152.5 x 127cm
£230–260 **Joanna Proops**

An **Oak Leaf and Reel quilt,** America, New York, c1880, 77 x 76in (195.5 x 193cm).
£1,000–1,200 **Rocky Mountain**

An **embellished wool Crazy quilt,** America, Maine, c1890, 89 x 76in (226 x 193cm).
£1,100–1,250 **Rocky Mountain**

A **calico Star of Bethlehem quilt,** with pie and appliquéd vases of flowers and eight-point stars, America, Pennsylvania, c1890 80in (203cm) square.
£600–750 **Skinner**

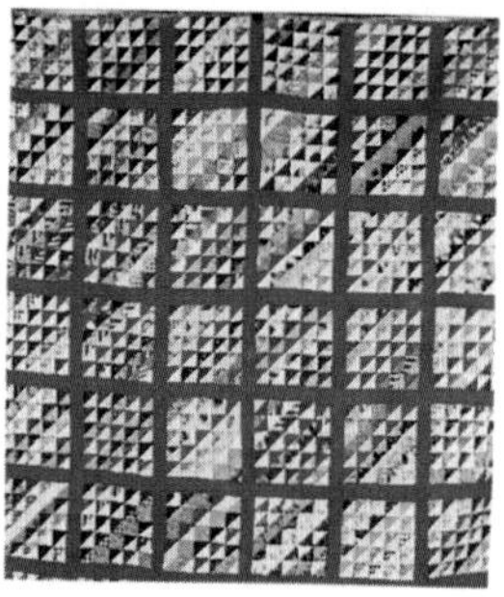

A **calico patchwork quilt,** late 19thC, 79½ x 66in (202x 167.5cm).
£110–130 **Waddington's**

An **Amish Joseph's Coat/Bars Variation quilt,** America, Pennsylvania, 70 x 67in (187 x 170cm).
£1,000–1,250 **Rocky Mountain**

A **silk quilt,** with machine stitching, c192C 80 x 68in (203 x 172.5cm).
£250–300 **Joanna Proops**

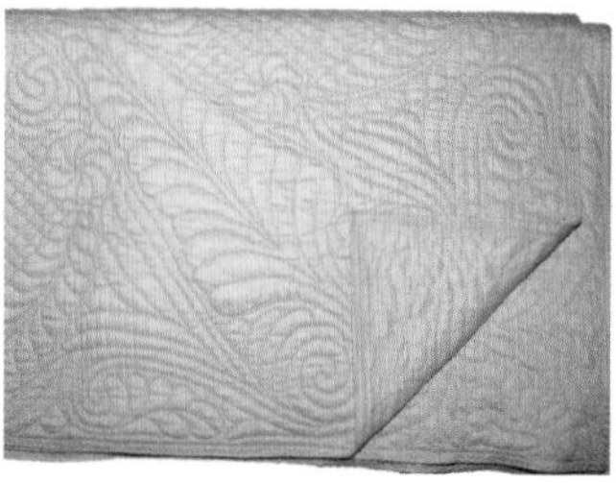

A **Durham wedding quilt,** 1920s, 132 x 84in (335.5 x 213.5cm).
£530–600 **Joanna Proops**

A **Durham quilt,** with chintz backing, c1920, 100 x 80in (254 x 203cm).
£530–600 **Joanna Proops**

A **pieced quilt,** hand-stictche 1930s, 70 x 80in (178 x 203c
£100–120 **Jackson's**

ИBROIDERY & NEEDLEWORK

‹ **embroidery,** decorated with silver
ıd, European, c1650, 6 x 9in (15 x 23cm).
0–520 **Joanna Proops** ⊞

An embroidered picture, with a central tent-stitched vignette, c1675, framed, 15¼ x 19¼in (39 x 49cm).
£3,500–4,250 **Sotheby's (O)**

A silver wire and embroidered raised work panel, depicting kings and queens, a shepherd and a man riding a goat, c1675, in an ebonized frame, 11¾ x 15¼in (30 x 39cm).
£2,750–3,250 **Bearnes**

edlework picture, by Hester Ford,
'ed 'The Offering of Isaac', signed,
18thC, 14 x 16½in (35.5 x 42cm).
500–4,250 **Woolley & Wallis**

A gros and petit point needlework panel, depicting Jesus Christ with three disciples blessing a kneeling woman, 18thC, framed, 19 x 25in (48.5 x 63.5cm).
£1,000–1,200 **Gorringes (L)**

A Quaker friendship token needlework, signed to reverse, America, Burlington County, New Jersey, 1810–30, 4 x 5¼in (10 x13.5cm), framed.
£400–450 **Raccoon Creek** ⊞

ıir of needlework pictures, possibly
vell School, Philadelphia, one inscribed 'In
ɪory of an Affectionate Father', the other
Virtue be your Guide', America, early
ıC, 7¼ x 8in (18.5 x 20.5cm), each in
'nal giltwood frame.
000–6,000 **Skinner**

A needlework mourning picture, for George Washington, by Charlotte Poe, worked in silk, chenille, watercolour and ink on a silk ground, America, 1816, 14½ x 16½in (37 x 42cm).
£4,500–5,500 **Freeman's**

A needlework family record, by Polly Holman, depicting a tree stitched with the names of six of her seven children, inscription to reverse, slight damage, America, early 19thC, 12 x 13½in (30.5 x 34.5cm).
£900–1,100 **Skinner**

ıir of embroidered and painted pictures,
ıt damage, Sweden, c1825, 8¼ x 9¾in
‹ 25cm), framed.
300–1,500 **Bukowskis**

A needlework picture, c1830, 22 x 16in (56 x 40.5cm), framed.
£450–500
Fair Finds ⊞

A beadwork picture of a parrot, 19thC, 14in (35.5cm) high, in a wooden frame.
£630–700
Durham House Antiques ⊞

A needlework picture, the border with carnations and strawberries, America, Pennsylvania, 1845–80, 24½ x 25in (62 x 63.5cm), in original frame.

£2,800–3,200 Raccoon Creek ⊞

A velvet and embroidery almanac book cover, c1845, 5in (12.5cm) wide.

£140–160 Joanna Proops ⊞

A crewelwork-covered casket, c1850, 13in (33cm) wide.

£300–350 Period Oak ⊞

A cotton velvet bolster, embroidered with metallic-wrapped thread, c1850, 30in (76cm) wide.

£630–700 Brandt Antiques ⊞

A cotton velvet cushion, embroidered with metallic-wrapped thread, c1850, 30in (76cm) wide.

£630–700 Brandt Antiques ⊞

An embroidered silk pelmet, c1860, 74in (188cm) long.

£180–200 Durham House Antiques ⊞

A beadwork panel, c1870, 34in (86.5cm) long.

£200–220 Durham House ⊞

A beadwork and tapestry cushion, c1880, 16in (40.5cm) wide.

£200–220 Durham House Antiques

A beadwork and tapestry fragment, c1880, 19in (48.5cm) long.

£200–230
Durham House Antiques ⊞

A beadwork and tapestry panel, c1880, 40in (101.5cm) long.

£170–185 Durham House Antiques ⊞

ir of crewelwork curtains, worked in wool on linen, late 19thC, 30in (203 x 76cm).
300–2,000 Joanna Proops

A beaded and needlepoint cushion piece, c1880, 18in (45.5cm) square.
£140–160 Durham House Antiques

aded bag, with floral embroidery and aded frame, the clasp with enamelled ers, France, c1900, 7in (18cm) wide.
0–350 Lynda Brine

A length of crewelwork, worked in wool on linen, early 20thC, 50 x 33in (127 x 84cm).
£350–400 Joanna Proops

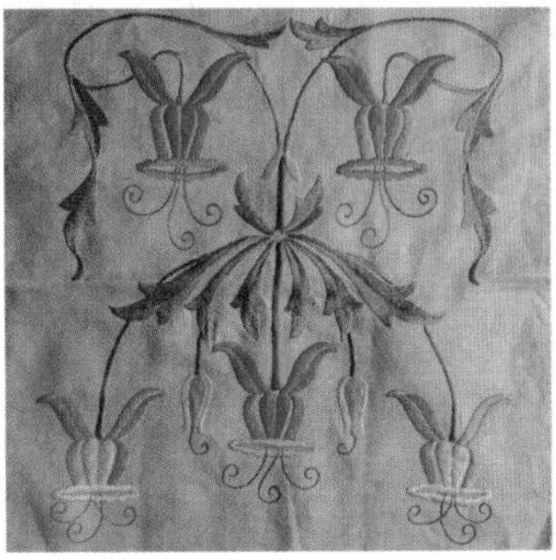

An embroidered panel, on linen, c1890, 23in (58.5cm) square.
£100–110 Hillhaven

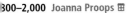

ACE

oint de France lace collar, slight age, c1700, 27in (68.5cm) wide.
70–200 Whitaker

A Brussels lace flounce, worked with floral sprays and swags, slight damage, Belgium, early 19thC, 290in (736.5cm) long.
£200–240 Whitaker

A Chantilly lace flounce, worked with floral bouquets and garlands above scalloped swags, France, 1860s, 78in (198cm) long.
£425–525 Whitaker

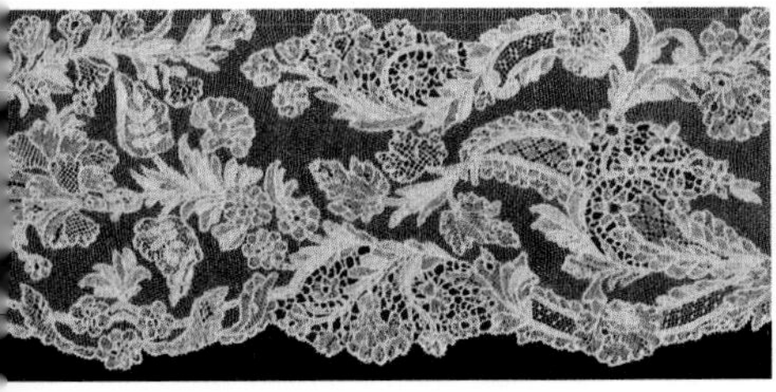

760s-style Brussels needlepoint dress flounce, worked with nation sprays and leaf forms, Belgium, 19thC, in (2700cm) long, and a fragment.
00–500 Kerry Taylor

A Brussels needlepoint dress flounce, with leafy and floret border and worked with blooms and spots, Belgium, c1860, 382in (970cm) long.
£800–1,000 Kerry Taylor

SAMPLERS

A sampler, embroidered with text and vignettes, 1749, 13¾ x 10¼in (35 x 26cm), framed.

£3,500–4,250 Dreweatt Neate (N)

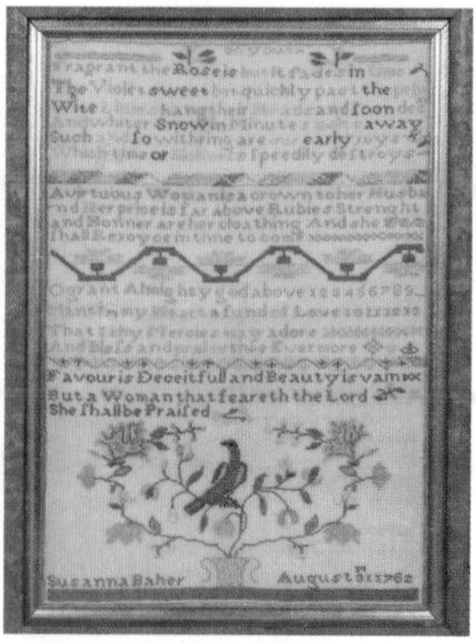

A sampler, by Suzanna Baker, 1762, 12¼in (31cm) high, framed.

£520–600 Hiscock & Shepherd

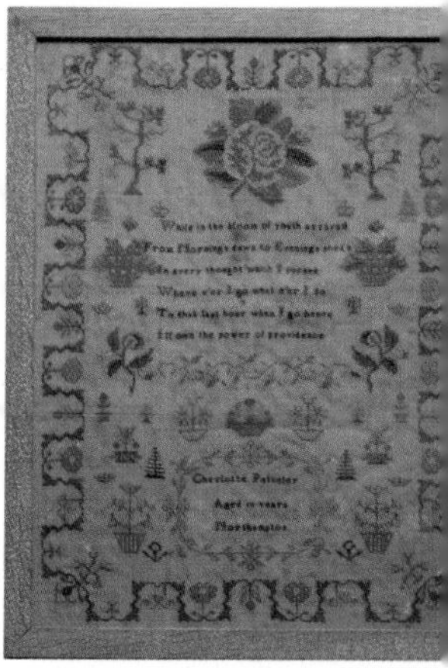

A sampler, by Charlotte Pettefer, c1790, 15in (38cm) high, framed.

£450–500 Durham House Antique

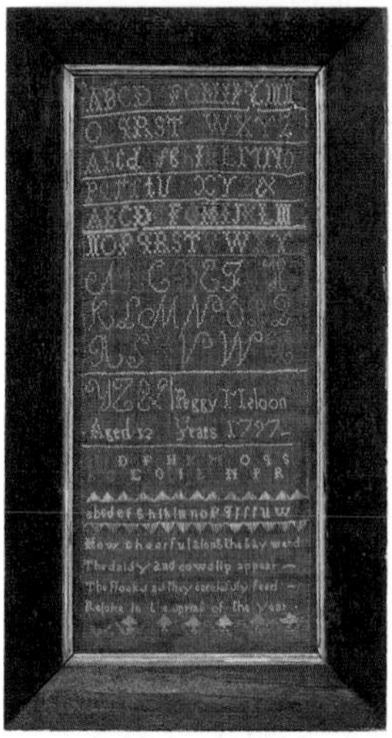

A sampler, by Peggy Meloon, worked with an alphabet and verse, slight damage, America, possibly New Hampshire, 1797, 17 x 7in (43 x 18cm), in a painted pine frame.

£1,000–1,200 Skinner

A sampler, by Eliza Quinby, worked in silk with an alphabet and numerals, signed, slight damage, America, Massachusetts, 1797, 11½ x 7in (29 x 18cm), framed.

£13,000–15,000 Raccoon Creek

A sampler, worked in silk, c1800, 16 x 12in (40.5 x 30.5cm), framed.

£800–900 Swan at Tetsworth

A sampler, by Jane Barnes, on linen, in original frame, c1800, 14in (35.5cm) wide.

£450–500 Durham House Antiques

A sampler, Scotland, c1800, 16½in (42cm) high, frame

£2,250–2,500 Hiscock & Shepherd

The flat-topped 'A' is indicative of Scottish samplers.

A sampler, by Sarah Porter, worked in silk on linen, 1800, 11 x 13in (28x 33cm), framed.

£500–600 Swan at Tetsworth ⊞

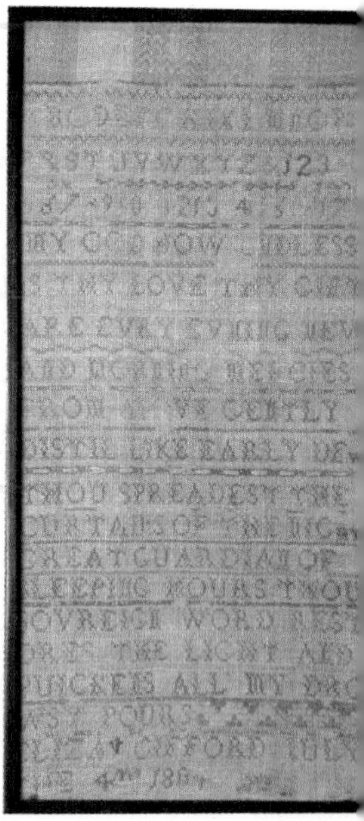

A sampler, by Mrs Eliza Clifford, worked in wool on linen, 1804, 21 x 10in (53.5 x 25.5cm), framed.

£140–160 Joanna Proops ⊞

A sampler, by Jannet Lidsy, worked with the alphabet, monograms and a house within a geometric floral border, slight fading, America, Pennsylvania, 1807, 17 x 13in (43 x 33cm).

£3,800–4,500 Skinner

A sampler, worked on linen with peacocks and flowers, Scotland, 1812, 16 x 7in (40.5 x 18cm), framed.

£430–480 Swan at Tetsworth ⊞

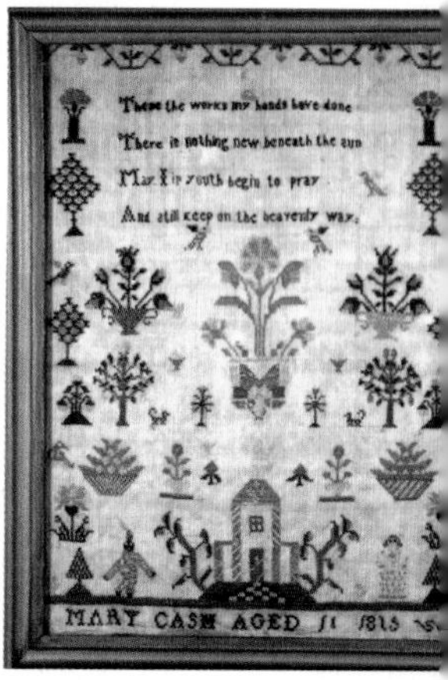

A sampler, by Mary Cash, worked in woo a verse over a folly flanked by figures, fol animals and birds, 1815, in a gilt frame.

£250–300 Andrew Hartley

A sampler, by Mary Brown, 1816, framed.

£350–400
Hiscock & Shepherd ⊞

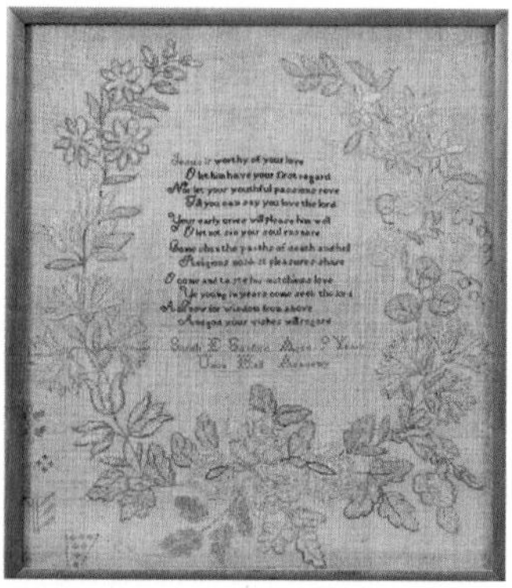

A sampler, by Sarah E. Sanford, worked in silk with a verse within a wreath, America, New York, 1818, 20 x 18in (51 x 45.5cm), framed.

£550–650 Freeman's

A note on the reverse of this sampler reads 'Sampler made in 1818 by Sarah Sanford married to James MacNight'.

A sampler, by Lucy Adams, worked with family register flanked by a flowering vine America, Massachusetts, 1819, 16¼ x 16½in (41.5 x 42cm).

£1,500–1,800 Skinner

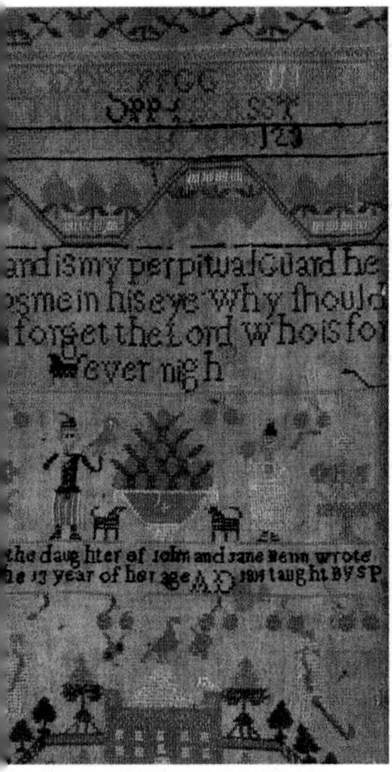

mpler, by Hannah Benn, worked with lphabet, numbers, strawberries, a figure animals, a house and birds, 1819, 12in (51 x 30.5cm).

'5–200
rith Farmers' & Kidd's

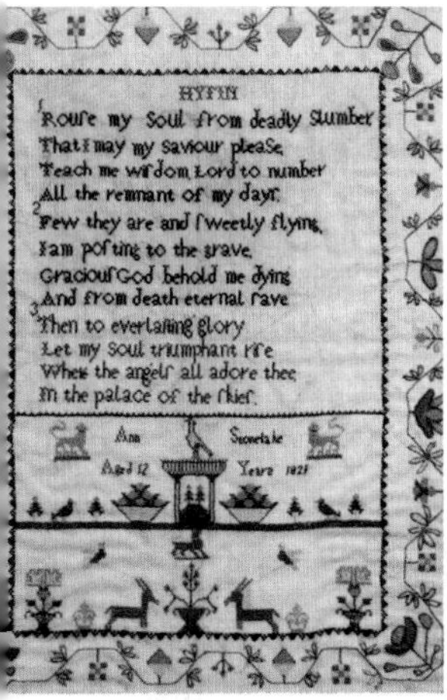

mpler, by Ann Stonelake, worked with rse, animals and birds within a floral ler, slight damage, 1821, 16¾ x 13in 5 x 33cm), in an ebonized frame.

0–350 Canterbury Auctions

mpler, by Jane Richings, framed, land, 1824, 12¼in (31cm) high, framed.

0–900 Hiscock & Shepherd

ssical house with a lawn in front is ative of Scottish samplers.

A sampler, by Ann McKenzie, worked in silk on linen, Scotland, c1820, 17 x 10in (43 x 25.5cm), framed.

£450–500 Swan at Tetsworth

A sampler, by Lucia Carpenter, worked in silk on linen with alphabets, numbers and two houses in a garden, slight damage, America, probably New Hampshire, 1822, 17½ x 12¾in (44.5 x 32.5cm), framed.

£2,000–2,500 Skinner

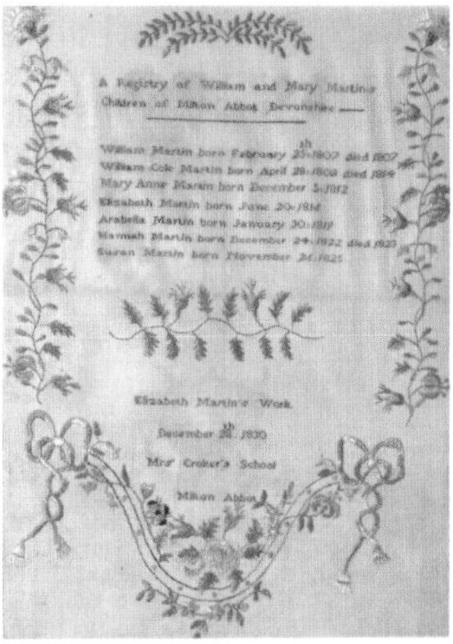

A school sampler, by Elizabeth Martin, worked in silk with a family record, 1830, 17 x 13in (43 x 33cm), framed.

£630–700 Joanna Proops

A sampler, by M. B. Huddleson, worked with Quaker-style spot motifs, slight damage, America, Pennsylvania, 1820, 24¼ x 22½in (61.5 x 57cm), framed.

£7,000–8,000 Raccoon Creek

A sampler, worked in silk with an urn of flowers, initialled 'H. S', America, Pennsylvania, Chester County, 1820–30, 12¼in (31cm) square, framed

£1,800–2,000 Raccoon Creek

A sampler, worked with Adam and Eve and a serpent motif, 19thC, 15in (38cm) square.

£300–330 Elizabeth Gibbons

An embroidered sampler, worked with a tiger and a house among flowers, 1830, 11¾in (30cm) high, framed.

£900–1,000 Hiscock & Shepherd

A sampler, by Hannah Alsbury, depicting Adam and Eve and the Tree of Life, 1831, 16 x 12in (40.5 x 30.5cm), framed.

£450–520 Swan at Tetsworth

A sampler, by Margaret Brown, worked with verses, trees and flowers within a zigzag floral border, 1833, 16¾ x 15¼in (42.5 x 38.5cm), framed.

£500–600 Andrew Hartley

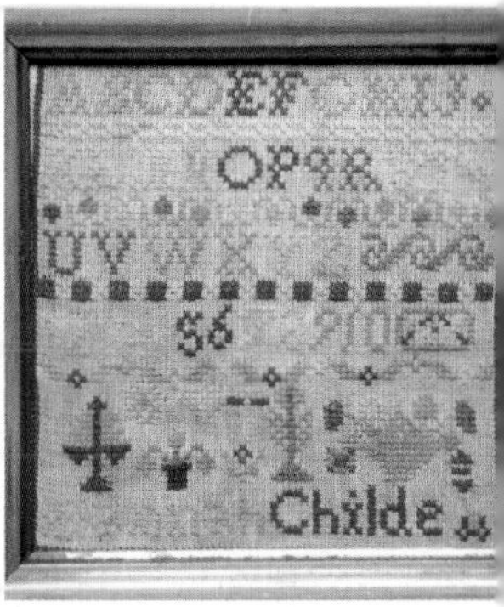

A sampler, by Hannah Childe, in linen, c1840, 6in (15cm) square, framed.

£150–165 Joanna Proops

A sampler, by Emmeline Harding, worked with an alphabet, numbers and the Tree of Life flanked by Adam and Eve, with a floral meander border, 19thC, 13¼ x 9in (33.5 x 23cm).

£550–650 Bearnes

A sampler, by Eliza Seibert, worked in wool on linen with floral sprigs, wreaths, vases of flowers and an inscription within a flowering vine, trimmed with ribbon, slight damage, America, Pennsylvania, 1840, 26½ x 26in (67.5 x 66cm), in a mahogany-veneered frame.

£320–380 Freeman's

A school sampler, by Jane Smith, Isle of Wight, 1844, 7in (18cm) high, framed.

£450–500 Hiscock & Shepherd

A sampler, by Mary Ann Dear, worked with a verse within a stylized border, 1846, 18in (45.5cm) square, framed.

£375–450 Sworders

A sampler, worked with a verse, a deer, initials and the date 1847, 11in (28cm) high, framed.

£900–1,000 Hiscock & Shepherd

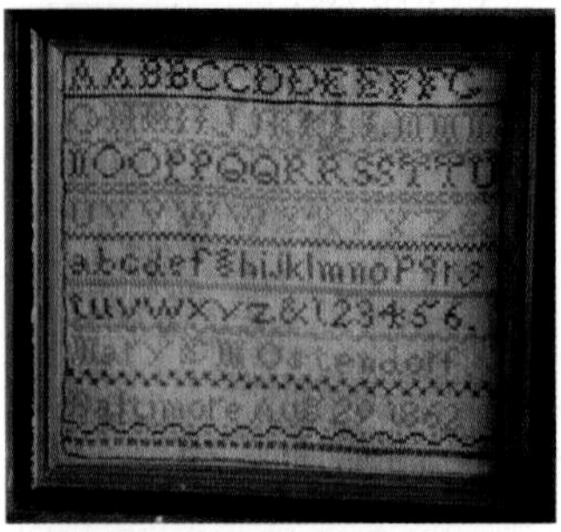

A sampler, by Mary E. M. Ostendorf, worked with the alphabet and numerals, America, Baltimore, 1862, 8½ x 7½in (21.5 x 19cm), framed.

£400–500 Weschler's

An Edwardian sampler, worked with a map of England and Wales, 20½ x 19¼in (52 x 49cm), framed.

£160–200 Halls

A sampler, worked in wool on linen, dated 1881, 12 x 8in (30.5x 20.5cm), framed.

£400–450 Joanna Proops

APESTRIES

pestry fragment, woven in l and silk with a mythological e, slight damage and losses, ored, Flanders, late 16thC, x 62¼in (245 x 158cm).

000–5,000 heby's (P)

A tapestry, woven in wool and silk with a mythological landscape with Paris, Hera, Athena and Aphrodite, within a floral border, slight damage, parts of border later, Flanders, 17thC, 119 x 205in (302 x 521cm).

£6,250–7,500 Bukowskis

A tapestry, depicting Esther pleading to Ahasuerus, Flanders, 17thC, 66¼ x 56in (168.5 x 142cm).

£2,800–3,200 Tennants

russels tapestry, after Pieter Van Lint, en by the Van Leefdael-Van der Strecken kshop, depicting the Emperor and his er, with a Latin cartouche, Belgium, 60, 126 x 61½in (320 x 156cm).

500–5,500 Sotheby's (NY)

A tapestry, depicting a woodland clearing with a heron and an eel on a riverbank, a woodman, birds and trees, within a floral and ribbon border, France/Belgium, late 17thC, 109 x 67in (277 x 170cm).

£3,800–4,500 Sotheby's

An Aubusson tapestry, depicting a shepherd and shepherdess within a flowering vine border, France, 1750–1800, 109½ x 65½in (278 x 166.5cm).

£3,800–4,500 Sotheby's (NY)

pestry, depicting a bird in a landscape, Flanders, 18thC, x 57in (88 x 145cm).

000–8,000 Orientalist Rugs

An Aubusson tapestry, depicting a rural scene with two figures with two goats and a kid, France, 19thC, 115 x 185in (292 x 470cm).

£7,000–8,000 Orientalist Rugs

COSTUME

A silk floral brocade gown, with a quilted silk petticoat, America, c1740.

£380–450 Freeman's

A silk brocade bodice, with self-covered buttons and linen and silk linings, worn, late 18thC.

£280–320 Whitaker

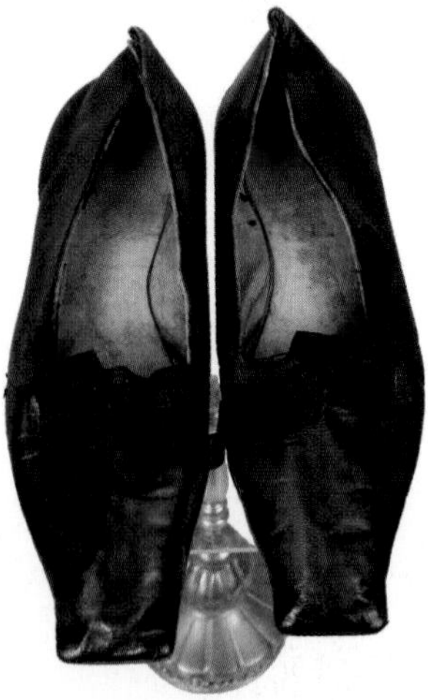

A pair of gentleman's leather evening shoes, with ribbon-tie latchets and leather lining , slight wear, America, c1835.

£750–900 Whitaker

A satin damask and silk brocade open gown, slight repair, c1770.

£1,400–1,700 Whitaker

A silk and net ball gown, with 'peacock eye' trimming and satin piping, wear and repair, c1815.

£250–300 Whitaker

A gentleman's embroidered satin waistc decorated wth flower sprigs, tulips and sequins, c1775.

£400–500 Kerry Taylor

A child's linen frock coat, with frogging, toggles and loops, the cuffs with metal hooks and eyes, the back seams decorate with chain stitch, the pockets lined with pink linen, c1780.

£3,250–4,000 Kerry Taylor

A pair of Victorian child's leather boots.

£120–140 Elizabeth Gibbons

ɔrgandie wedding gown, with a boned lined bodice, trimmed with silk ribbons bobbin lace, slight wear, 1850s.

30–280 Whitaker

A wool and silk Lyons shawl, woven with a quatrefoil flanked by stylized acanthus with shaped lobes, France, mid-19thC, 72in (183cm) square.

£420–465 Joanna Proops

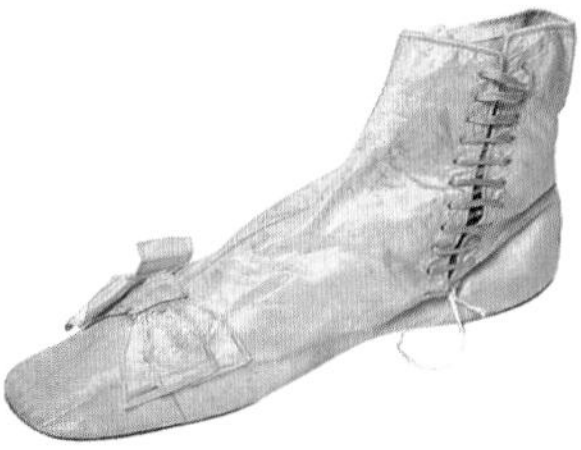

A pair of silk boots, the vamps decorated with a bow, mid-19thC.

£180–200 Elizabeth Gibbons

A pair of leather 'prize' shoes, the uppers embroidered with crowns and foliage, with satin insoles, c1860.

£1,750–2,000 Kerry Taylor

During the first half of the 19th century competitions were organized with money prizes to encourage excellent shoe workmanship. Many examples were made from materials not normally used for shoes, with narrow soles, fancy heels and delicate embroidery. They were hand-sewn with often between 30 and 40 stitches to the inch. Later, shoes were made specially for display at trade exhibitions such as the Great Exhibition of 1851. These particular slippers were never intended to be worn, but were for display and may have been used in a shop window to demonstrate the expertise of the shoemaker.

traw wedding bonnet, trimmed with cloth ıs and lace, with original hand-decorated , slight wear, 1869.

50–400 Whitaker

voven silk shawl, France, c1870, x 136in (162.5 x 345.5cm).

30–480 Durham House Antiques

A silk taffeta two-piece dress, trimmed with a silk fringe, pleated red tulle and later velvet ribbon, altered, c1871.

£350–400 Whitaker

A cotton two-piece outfit, c1880.
£340–375 Decades

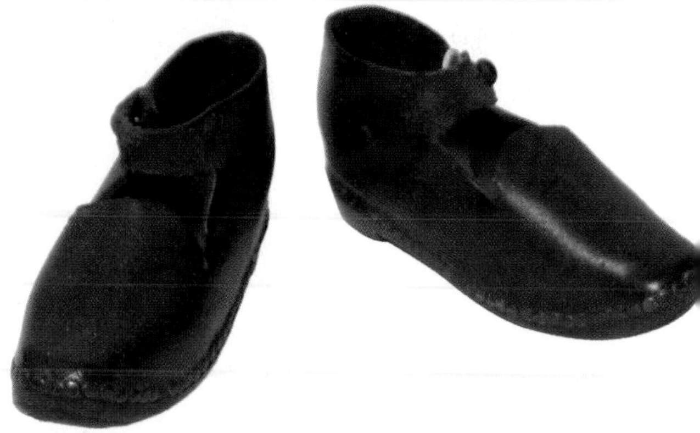

A Victorian child's pair of leather clogs.
£120–140 Elizabeth Gibbons

A wool and silk Paisley shawl, Scotland, c1880, 64in (162.5cm) long.
£340–380 Durham House Antiques

A child's pair of leather boots , c1880.
£140–155 Le Boudoir

A wedding hat, with silver-work embroidered ribbon, Bohemia, late 19thC.
£160–175 Elizabeth Gibbons

A lacework cape, c1900.
£150–170 Clobber

A crepe silk two-piece tea gown, the bodice with gold button-decorated velvet ribbons, the silk sash with velvet ribbon bands, with a silk lining, slight wear, c1905.
£230–275 Whitaker

An Edwardian lace dress.
£165–185 Echoes

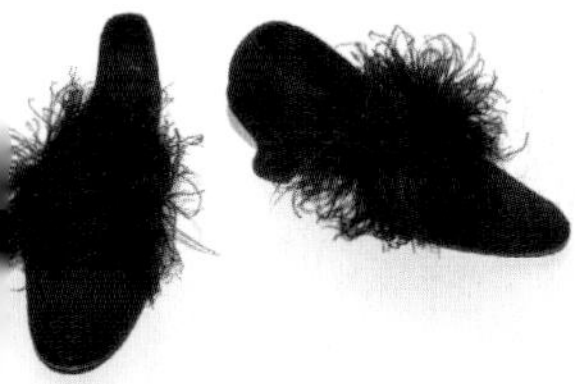

air of Edwardian cloqué and ostrich-
her slippers.

30–145 Tin Tin

air of leather boots, with wooden
s, c1914.

30–145 Peter Campbell

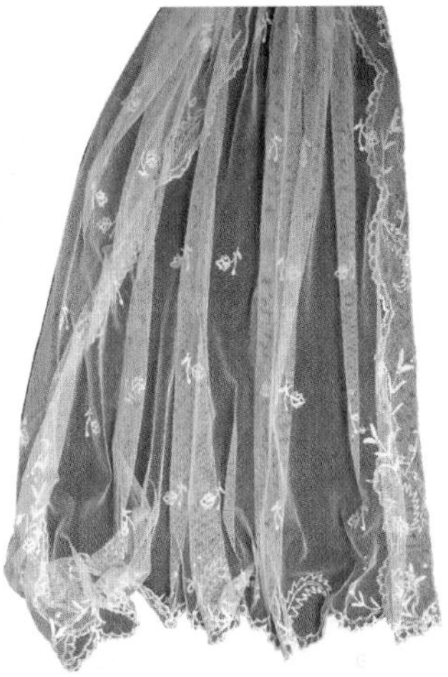

An Edwardian net wedding veil, 72in (183cm) long.

£235–260 Margaret Williamson

A child's pair of leather boots, c1920.

£100–110 Bradley Gent

A woollen opera coat, decorated with tambour stitch embroidery, with pleated silk collar and cuffs and a Chinoisere printed silk faille lining worked with cranes and lanterns, slight damage, America, c1910.

£400–500 Whitaker

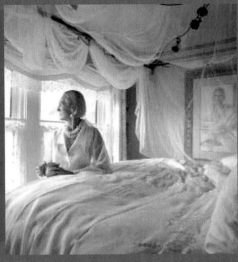

RUGS & CARPETS

An Aubusson carpet, France, c1860, 158 x 148in (401.5 x 376cm).

£3,000–3,500 Northeast Auctions

An Aubusson carpet, restored, France, c1850, 128 x 109in (325 x 277cm).

£4,000–4,500 Sotheby's (NY)

An Aubusson rug, France, c1850, 144 x 132in (366 x 335cm).

£7,000–8,000 Karel Weijand

A needlepoint carpet, possibly reduced, borders pieced together and later applied, c1850, 102 x 101in (259 x 256.5cm).

£6,500–8,000 Sotheby's (NY)

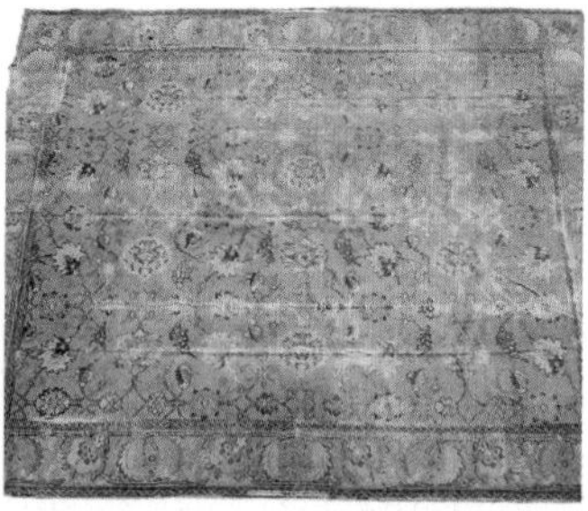

A carpet, damaged, possibly English, early 19thC, 170 x 150in (432 x 381cm).

£16,000–20,000

Netherhampton Salerooms

English carpets with an Oriental (Persian) pattern are very rare. This is an extremely good example of an all-over Oriental design in soft colours and is probably of English origin. Rare and decorative carpets such as this achieve high prices, regardless of condition.

An Aubusson carpet, slight damage, Franc early 20thC, 130 x 95in (330 x 241.5cm).

£4,000–4,500 Sotheby's (NY)

MARKET INFORMATION RUGS & CARPETS

- Large, decorative carpets of, say, 192 x 144in (488 x 365cm) with a large open design, overall repeat pattern and muted colours are highly sought after and command high prices. Carpets that fall into this category include those made in the late 19th and early 20th centuries from northwest Persia, known as Ziegler or Sultanabad, and Ushak in West Turkey.
- Carpets with more traditional deep colours and intricate patterns remain unfashionable, even if finely knotted, and can be found at bargain prices. The exceptions are detailed patterned Tabriz carpets in soft, pale colours – often described as Hadji Jalili type, after a maker from the early 20th century.
- Caucasian rugs made in the 19th century are highly sought after and can command high prices if condition is perfect and the dyes are vegetable based. Categories included Kazak, Shirvan and Kuba rugs.
- Persian and Turkish rugs and carpets of traditional size and colour and medium to low quality are currently less popular.
- Condition is critical; damage and wear generally have a negative impact on value.
- Proven provenance will usually enhance value, regardless of condition.

Kirshehir wool prayer rug, Anatolia, 870, 65 x 47¼in (165 x 120cm).
,200–3,500 Karel Weijand

An Obruk prayer rug, Turkey, c1880, 66¼ x 48in (168 x 122cm).
£3,400–3,800 Karel Weijand

A Kuba rug, northeast Caucasus, c1850, 93 x 45in (236 x 114.5cm).
£2,750–3,250 D & A North

Kuba rug, northeast Caucasus, c1880, 3 x 53in (211 x 134.5cm).
5,200–6,000 M & N Oriental

A Melas wool rug, worked with a star design, Anatolia, c1890, 55 x 39¼in (140 x 100cm).
£4,000–4,500 Karel Weijand

Yürük wool rug, Turkey, c1920, 72 x 45¼in (183 x 115cm).
1,800–2,000 Karel Weijand

A Chelaberd Karabagh rug, southwest Caucasus, early 20thC, 91 x 61in (231 x 155cm).
£2,000–2,500 Netherhampton

An Afshar Kerman rug, some repair, southwest Persia, late 19thC, 83 x 55in (211 x 139.5cm).

£675–800
Netherhampton Salerooms

An Afshar wool rug, southwest Persia, c1900, 74¾ x 50½in (190 x 128cm).

£2,700–3,000 Karel Weijand

A Heriz rug, northwest Persia, c1900, 81 x 57in (206 x 145cm).

£2,800–3,200 Karel Weijand

ESSENTIAL REFERENCE RUG MOTIFS & DECORATIONS

- Motifs play an important part in identifying the origin of a rug or carpet, although it must be remembered that the same motifs were used in many carpet-making areas.
- Motifs can be divided into three groups: field motifs, border motifs and decorative motifs.
- Field motifs are repeat designs used to decorate the whole field of the carpet, such as *boteh* and *herati* motifs.
- Border motifs, as the name indicates, decorate the lateral bands of carpets; these include designs such as *kufic* and serrated leaf borders and palmette, vine and flowerhead continuous linked borders.
- Decorative motifs serve to complete the field decoration. The best known are the eight-pointed star, the palmette and the Fylfot (swastika).

Herati
This is a central diamond flanked by four serrated leaves. Found on many weavings from Persia, particularly from Feraghan.

Dragon
Dragons are found in the mythology of many countries. In the Caucasus dragon motifs were highly stylized, but in Tibet and China they retain a more natural form.

Boteh
This motif is thought to represent a leaf form and can be curvilinear or stylized. It was favoured by village, tribal and city weavers in many of the world's major rug-weaving regions.

Harshang
These motifs, which resemble crabs, are widely found on rugs made in the Caucasus, as well as on pieces from Azerbaijan and the western areas of Persia.

Animals
Stylized animals are found on many Persian tribal and Caucasian village rugs.

Gül
A repeat pattern of hexagonal or sometimes octagonal form used to decorate the fields of carpets. Traditionally, each tribe had its own *gül* design. This one was used by the Tekke tribe, but was widely copied from 1900.

A Karadja rug, northwest Persia, c1900, 73 x 59in (185.5 x 150cm).
£400–500 Wadsworth's

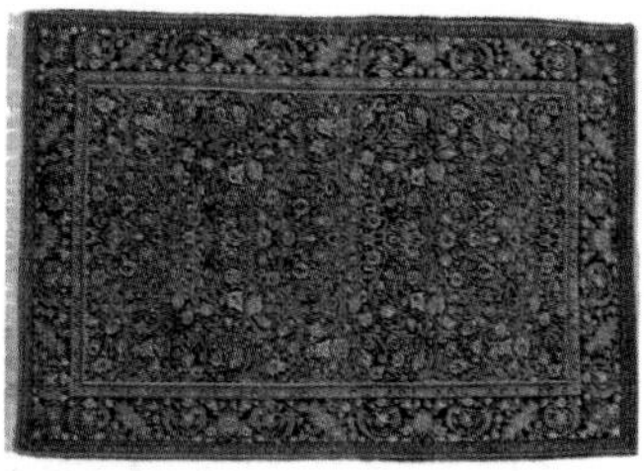

A Motashem Kashan rug, Persia, c1880, 78 x 54in (198 x 137cm.
£6,250–7,000 Karel Weijand
The term Motashem is used to describe a superior quality product of fine, soft, lustrous wool, finely woven, the side cords overwrapped in magenta silk or cotton. The designs are intricate, and visually very attractive. Motashem is the name of a known designer, although very few pieces are actually signed 'Motashem'. This example is not overwrapped in magenta silk, but the quality is consistent with the appearance of fine pieces usually attributed to the Motashem workshops.

A Kashan carpet, central Persia, c1900, 78 x 52in (198 x 132cm).
£4,500–5,000 Karel Weijand

A Kashan rug, central Persia, c1910, 76 x 53in (193 x 134.5cm).
£5,200–6,000 M & N Oriental

A Kashgai rug, southwest Persia, c1880, 92 x 58in (233.5 x 147.5cm).
£5,500–6,000 M & N Oriental

A Kashgai kilim, southwest Persia, c1900, 31 x 62in (78.5 x 157.5cm).
£675–750 Knights Antiques

A Kashgai flatweave kilim, southwest Persia, 1850–1900, 107 x 56in (272 x 142cm).
£280–350 Woolley & Wallis

A Kashgai rug, southwest Persia, c1900, 94½ x 55in (240 x 140cm).
£1,500–1,650 Samarkand Rugs

ESSENTIAL REFERENCE LAYOUT OF A CARPET

- Most Oriental and European rugs and carpets have a central field surrounded by a main border, which is edged on either side by narrow secondary borders (inner and outer guardstripes).
- Within the field, three basic designs are used, directional, medallion and non-directional.
- The directional design, with spandrels at one end, is often found on prayer rugs; these incorporate a mihrab triangle-shaped niche that is pointed in the direction of Mecca. The non-directional design is an all-over pattern that allows the carpet to be placed in any position in a room.
- The most commonly found design is the medallion, placed either centrally on its own or in repeating columns within the field. Spandrels are not always present, but the borders and guardstripes appear on nearly all weavings. The source of this design has been traced to early Islamic manuscript illuminations.

A Kurdish rug, northwest Persia, c1890, 84 x 36in (213.5 x 91.5cm).

£1,100–1,250 Wadsworth's

A Kurdish rug, northwest Persia, c1910, 87 x 53in (221 x 134.5cm).

£700–850 Wadsworth's

A Malayer *khelleh*, slight damage, repair and losses, west Persia, dated AH 1319, 183 x 74in (468 x 188cm).

£1,700–2,000 Bukowskis

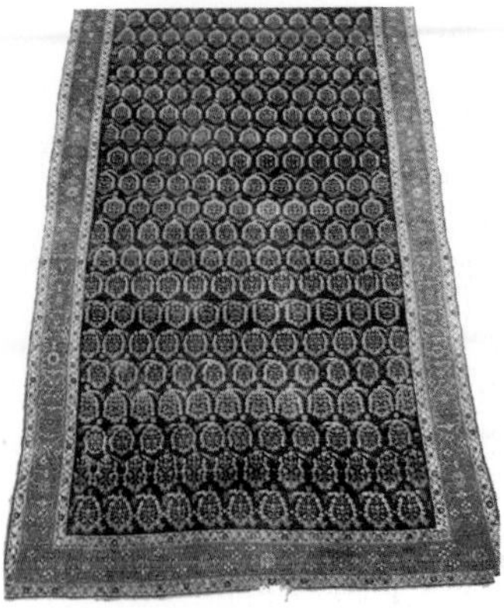

A Kurdish *kelleh*, northwest Persia, late 19thC, 165 x 83in (418.5 x 211cm).

£1,000–1,200 Netherhampton Salerooms

A Ziegler Mahal carpet, restored, central Persia, c1900, 166 x 122in (421.5 x 310cm).

£3,000–3,600 Sotheby's (O)

Messrs Ziegler & Co, a British/Swiss firm, opened offices in the Sultanabad area of Persia in the late 19th century to cater for the increased demand for room-sized carpets from the rapidly expanding upper and middle classes of Europe and north America. By the late 1880s, in response to specific requests from European clients, they became actively involved in the production of carpets, employing local carpet designers to create new designs. Traditional patterns were adapted, and more carpets of the large format that was so much in demand in the west, were woven. Ziegler carpets are distinguished by their all-over, large scale, lattice vine patterns often based on classical Persian designs of the 17th century. Medallions are rarely seen.

A Sarouk rug, west Persia, c1900, 63½ x 42¼in (161 x 107cm).

£1,500–1,650 Samarkand Rugs

A Kurdish runner, repairs, northwest Persia, c1900, 159 x 41¾in (404 x 106cm).

£280–350 Woolley & Wallis

A Sarouk rug, west Persia, c1900, 59¾ x 41in (152 x 104cm).

£2,500–2,800 Karel Weijand

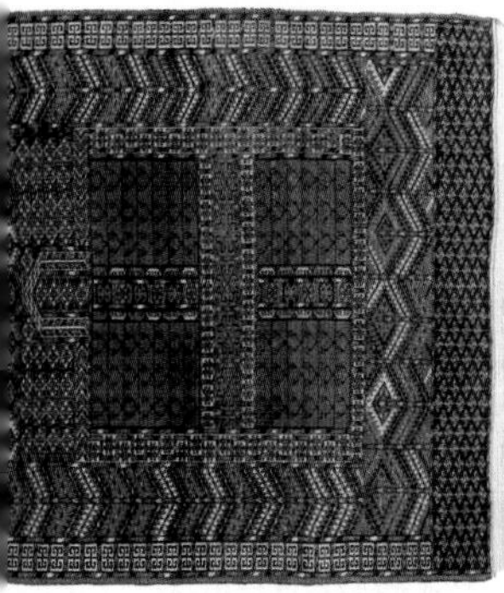

ekke *ensi*, west Turkestan, late 19thC, x 55¼in (134.5 x 150.5cm).

,200–2,600 Dorotheum

Ersari rug, Afghanistan, c1900, x 44in (127 x 112cm).

,250–1,400 Karel Weijand

pair of Agra rugs, India, c1880, 3¼ x 32¼in (186 x 82cm).

8,000–9,000 Karel Weijand

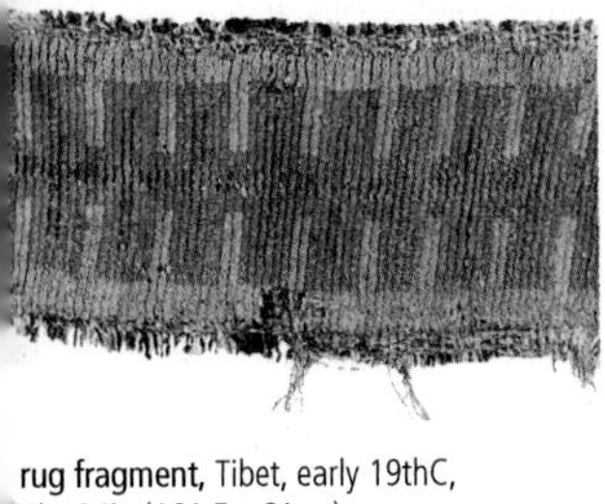

rug fragment, Tibet, early 19thC, 3½ x 24in (161.5 x 61cm).

1,100–1,300 Sotheby's (O)

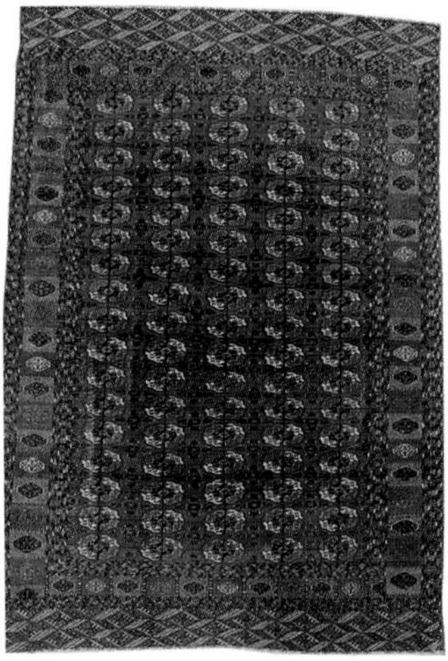

A Tekke carpet, west Turkestan, c1900, 151½ x 104¼in (385 x 265cm).

£1,300–1,450 Sotheby's (Am)

Tekke carpets made c1900 are invariably crowded with motifs and rows of repeat gül motifs. Earlier examples are more sparingly decorated with fewer rows of güls and are more 'open' in design.

A Yomut carpet, with *kepse güls*, slight damage and repair, northwest Turkestan, c1850, 118 x 65½in (299.5 x 166.5cm).

£3,200–3,800 Woolley & Wallis

The term kepse *refers to the shape and style of the repeat güls in the offset rows of the field.*

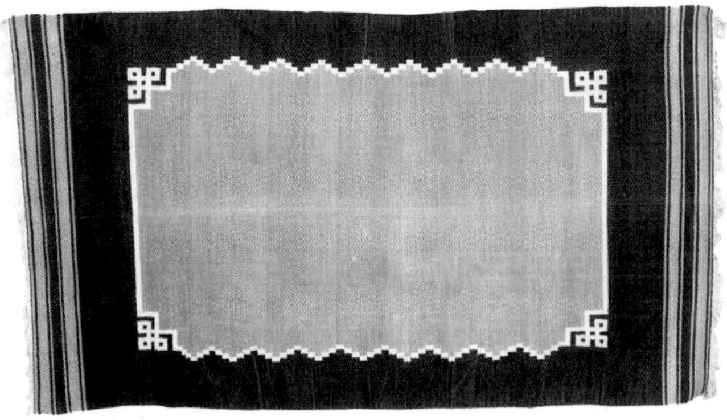

A *dhurrie*, India, c1900, 91¼ x 50¾in (232 x 129cm).

£1,200–1,500 Sotheby's (O)

A Ninghsia gallery carpet, slight damage, repair, China, early 19thC, 167 x 77in (424 x 195.5cm).

£30,000–35,000 Sotheby's (NY)

A Pao-Tao rug, China, c1910, 116¼ x 95in (295 x 241cm).

£6,250–7,000 Karel Weijand

A Pao-Tao is a type of Chinese carpet which was made in the early years of the 20th century, typically using ivory as the main field colour, and two shades of blue, as can be seen in this example.

LAMPS & LIGHTING

ANTIQUE LIGHTING has become a highly successful part of the general antiques trade, surviving the downturns and thriving through the minimalist decorating phase. It appeals to younger buyers, as well as interior designers and down-shifters – everyone needs good lighting. The glossy magazines and TV makeover programmes have particularly encouraged the market for chandeliers, although traditional Art Nouveau and Edwardian lighting remains popular. Naturally, good antique chandeliers are preferable to reproductions – the metalwork is finer and the glass is better cut.

Early candle chandeliers have solid glass or metal arms and must be wired over the arm when converted to electricity. Chandeliers made for gas have hollow arms and are therefore easier to convert, as are wall-mounted lights, sconces and appliqués, although many of these have 1920s' conversions that need updating.

There is confusion about the correct terminology for antique lighting, so it might be helpful to clarify it here: chandeliers and gasoliers, being made for candles or gas, have light sources that point upwards; electroliers were manufactured in period style in the late 19th century after the advent of domestic electricity and they therefore often have light sources pointing downwards.

Plain Georgian period lanterns (especially Irish examples) made for candles or oil are rare and attract very high prices at auction, as do flat-backe two- or three-armed wall lights in giltwood, limewood or brass and ormolu, particularly if they d not project too far from the wall. There has been a decline in the sale of converted oil lamps both as wall light fittings and table lamps, perhaps becaus they don't fit in with modern interiors.

It is fortunate that many fine examples of early lighting exist, due mainly to the fact that they were hung high up out of harm's way. Please note that a antique lighting should be converted by an expert and have a relevant electrical safety certificate.

Jill Pe

CHANDELIERS

A brass 12-branch chandelier, surmounted by a double eagle finial, the arms cast with masks, Germany, 18thC, 28¼in (72cm) high.

£7,500–9,000 Sotheby's (Am)

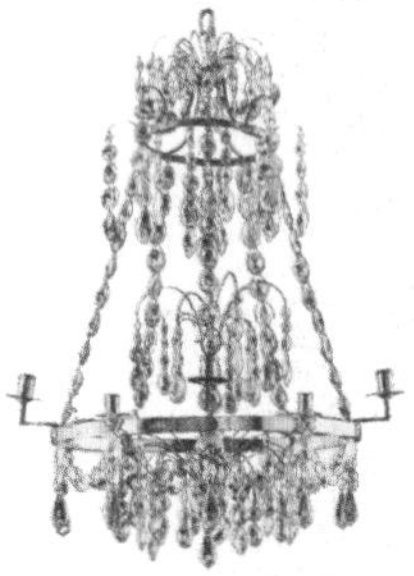

A gilt-brass and glass five-branch chandelier, Sweden, c1775, 37½in (95.5cm) high.

£7,000–8,500 Bukowskis

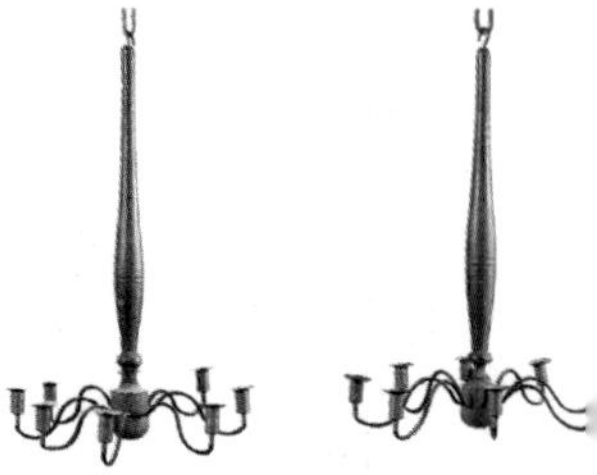

A pair of painted eight-branch chandeliers each with tinware candle cups, some cups later, America, c1800, 26in (66cm) high.

£20,000–25,000 Northeast Auctions

A Meissen porcelain eight-branch chandelier, decorated with women playing instruments, rocailles, flowers, and birds, slight damage, Germany, 1800–50, 45¼in (115cm) high.

£6,500–8,000 Dorotheum

A brass and cut-glass seven-branch chandelier, Sweden, c1800, 41¼in (105cm) high.

£2,500–3,000 Bukowskis (F)

A Regency brass and cut-glass eight-branch chandelier, restored, c1815, 43in (109cm) hig

£4,000–5,000 Sotheby's (NY)

gilt-brass and bronze colza chandelier, with a leaf-cast
it terminal, decorated with bacchic masks, anthemea and
ves, adapted for electricity, c1820, 28½in (72.5cm) high.

,750–5,750 Mealy's

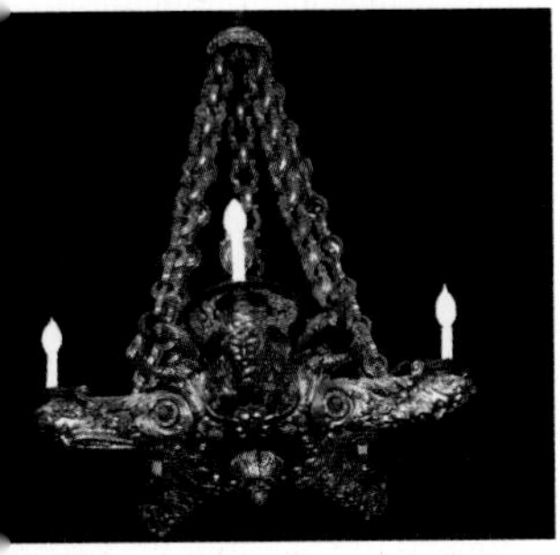

lacquered-metal five-branch chandelier,
ecorated with gilt-bronze acanthus mounts,
asks, garlands and a crested vase, fitted for
ectricity, France, 19thC, 39¾in (101cm) high.

7,500–9,000
aleria Louis C Morton

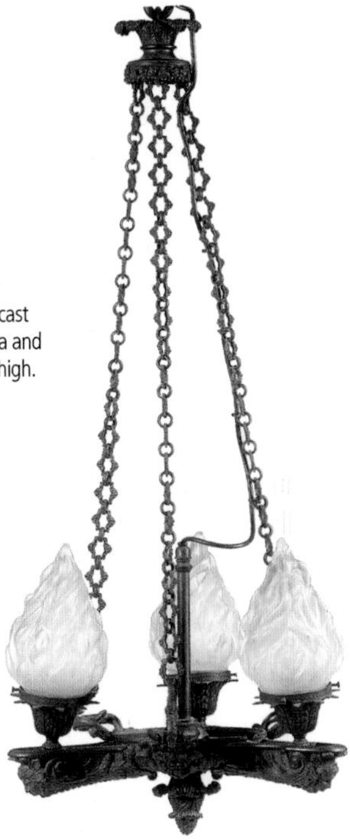

A bronze colza three-branch chandelier, fitted for electricity, c1825, shades c1900.

£1,400–1,750 Sotheby's

A gilt-bronze colza chandelier, by Hancock & Rixon, the central urn cast with masks, c1826, 18in (45.5cm) high.

£14,000–17,500 Sotheby's

Hancock & Rixon was an important firm of glass manufacturers from the late 18th century to the mid-19th century. They supplied chandeliers to wealthy patrons from the near East and India, including the palace in Constantinople.

EXPERT'S EYE CUT-GLASS CHANDELIER

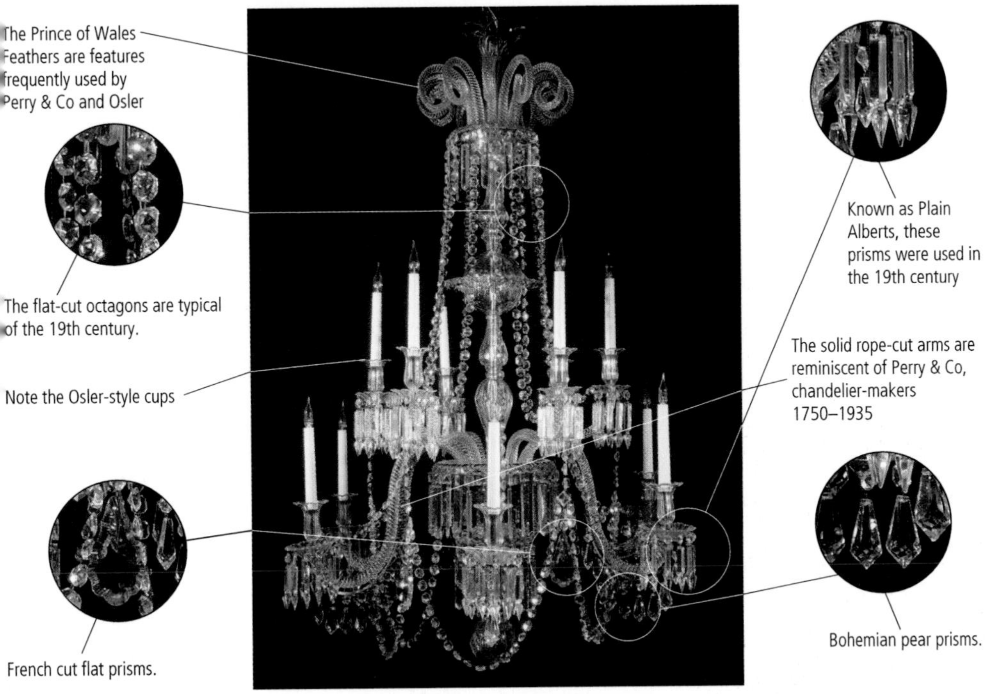
The Prince of Wales Feathers are features frequently used by Perry & Co and Osler
The flat-cut octagons are typical of the 19th century.
Note the Osler-style cups
French cut flat prisms.
Known as Plain Alberts, these prisms were used in the 19th century
The solid rope-cut arms are reminiscent of Perry & Co, chandelier-makers 1750–1935
Bohemian pear prisms.

After the repeal of the Glass Excise Act in 1832 chandeliers became heavier and more ornate. This typical example from the mid-Victorian period (c1870) is of great quality and formerly hung in the Chrysler Building in New York. It employs all the fashionable features of the great chandelier makers such as Perry & Co and Osler and was probably made in both London and Birmingham using some glass imported from Bohemia; the metal parts are silver plated.

£13,000–15,000 Norfolk Decorative

A tole three-branch hanging lamp, with original painted decoration, fitted for electricity, France, c1880, 20in (51cm) high.
£1,350–1,500 Mary Cruz Antiques ⊞

A brass and gilt chandelier, fitted for electricity, France, late 19thC, 46in (117cm) high.
£10,500–12,000 Norfolk Decorative ⊞

A chandelier, the glass engraved with famil and ecclesiastical crests, fitted for electricity, France, Burgundy, c1900, 47¼in (120cm) hi
£3,000–3,300 Norfolk Decorative

A Federal-style silver-plated eight-branch chandelier, America, c1900, 40in (101.5cm) high.
£20,000–22,000 Chameleon ⊞

A bronze and iron armorial chandelier, America, c1920, 28½in (72.5cm) high.
£5,000–5,500 Chameleon ⊞

A pair of white metal cut-glass table chandeliers, fitted for electricity, France, 1920s, 28in (71cm) high.
£1,600–1,800 Norfolk Decorative

A wrought-iron four-branch chandelier, fitted for electricity, France, c1930, 22in (56cm) high.
£630–700 Norfolk Decorative ⊞

A cast-brass and cut-glass chandelier, Italy, c1930, 29in (73.5cm) high.
£2,000–2,350 Norfolk Decorative ⊞

A Murano glass eight-branch chandelier, w gold colouring, Italy, 1930s, 37¾in (96cm) hig
£2,700–3,000 Norfolk Decorative

ANTERNS & HANGING LIGHTS

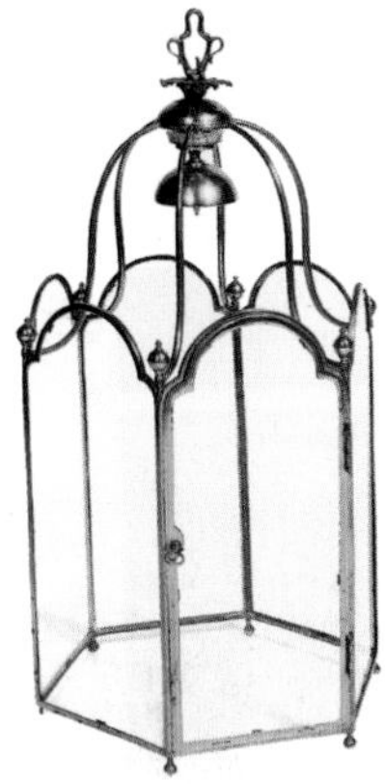

ate Georgian brass and glass hall lantern, Hanbury, with six urn finials, stamped rks, Ireland, Dublin, 28in (71cm) high.

2,000–26,000 Mealy's

A brass two-branch gas light, with two counterweights and replacement shades, fitted for electricity, c1870, 40in (101.5cm) wide.

£500–550 Exeter Antique Lighting

A cast-glass *plaffonier*, America, c1900, 17in (43cm) diam.

£1,800–2,000 Chameleon

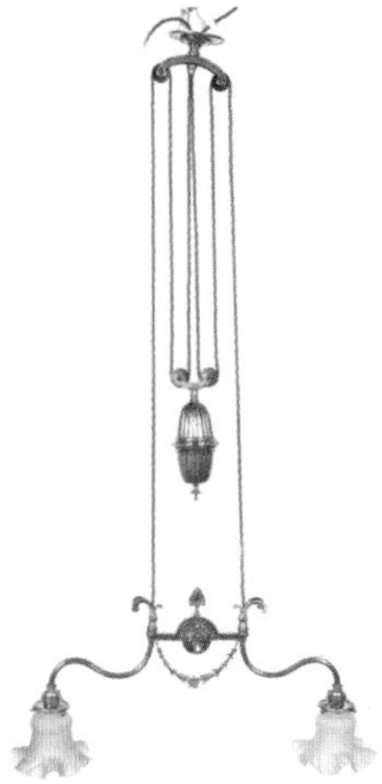

brass rise-and-fall light, with ram's head d swag detail, etched glass shades later, 900, 20in (51cm) wide.

540–600 Norfolk Decorative

A brass and glass hall lantern, with later four-light fitting, 19thC, 34½in (87.5cm) high.

£2,000–2,500 Woolley & Wallis

A brass three-branch ceiling lamp, with cut-glass pineapple shades, c1910, 25in (63.5cm) diam.

£400–450 Exeter Antique Lighting

wrought-iron electrolier, with frosted nd cut-glass shades, France, c1910, 7in (94cm) high.

800–900 Exeter Antique Lighting

A silhouette hanging light, Italy, c1915, 30in (76cm) high.

£900–1,000 Norfolk Decorative

This hanging light was made to reflect light from candles. It was hung with tiny pear drops on two concentric circles with no external or internal light source.

A Gothic-style embossed brass and stained-glass lantern, c1920, 19in (48.5cm) high.

£300–350 Sworders

WALL BRACKETS & APPLIQUES

A pair of gilt-metal and ormolu wall lights, each decorated with lion, ram and eagle heads and foliate mounts, 19thC, 24½in (62cm) high.

£12,000–14,000
Anderson & Garland

A pair of Louis XV-style gilt-bronze three-branch wall lights, fitted for electricity, 19thC, 29in (73.5cm) high.

£6,000–7,000 Sotheby's

A pair of Renaissance-style carved pine two-branch wall lights, 19thC, 31½in (80cm) high.

£4,000–4,400 LASSCO (sm)

A bronze wall sconce, by E. F. Caldwell, America, New York, c1900, 9in (23cm) high.

£1,200–1,400 Chameleon

A pair of Federal-style bronze two-branch wall sconces, by E. F. Caldwell, America, New York, c1910, 12in (30.5cm) high.

£2,000–2,200 Chameleon

A pair of silvered-brass two-branch wall sconces, by General Electric Co, decorated with swags and acanthus leaves, c1910, 14in (35.5cm) high.

£720–800 Norfolk Decorative

A pair of painted wrought-iron wall sconces, with coloured glass drops, France, c1930, 12in (30.5cm) high.

£450–500 Norfolk Decorative

A chinoiserie-style bronze, enamel and jade two-branch sconce, by E. F. Caldwell, with crystal drops, America, New York, c1910, 9in (23cm) high.

£3,750–4,250 Chameleon

TANDARD, TABLE & OIL LAMPS

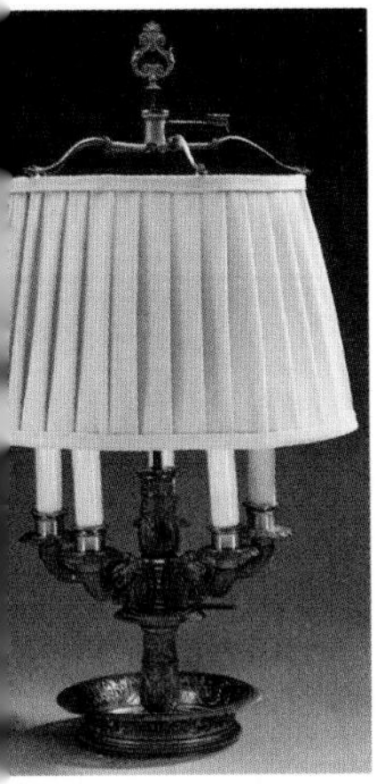

ilt-bronze five-branch table ıp, with a silk shade, fitted for :tricity, France, early 19thC, ı (66cm) high.

,600–2,000 Bukowskis

A pair of patinated and gilt-bronze two-branch Argand oil lamps, with frosted glass shades, retailer's plate embossed 'B. Gardiner, New York', America, c1830, 20in (51cm) high.

£2,500–3,000 Northeast Auctions

A pair of amethyst pressed glass oil lamps, by the Boston & Sandwich Glass Co, each with a pewter collar, America, Massachusetts, c1850, 9½in (24cm) high.

£1,400–1,600 Northeast Auctions

nid-Victorian gilt-bronze and gilt oil np, by Palmer & Co, with an etched glass ade and a snuffer, 32¾in (83cm) high.

i00–700 Sworders

A patinated-brass figural oil lamp, attributed to Henry N. Hooper & Co, with a frosted-glass shade, America, Boston, c1850, 26¾in (68cm) high.

£2,500–3,000 Northeast Auctions

A neo-classical-style brass lamp, by Cornelius & Baker, with an acanthus-moulded standard, the base with floral garlands and classical masks, repaired, America, Philadelphia, c1860, 25in (63.5cm) high.

£575–700 Weschler's

gilt-brass newel post lamp, fitted for ectricity, c1880, 19in (48.5cm) high.

450–500 Exeter Antique Lighting

A hand-painted opal glass and ormolu oil table lamp, fitted for electricity, America, c1875, 25in (63.5cm) high.

£300–350 Jackson's

A ruby glass oil table lamp, with ormolu mounts, America, Connecticut, late 19thC, 21in (53.5cm) high.

£125–150 Jackson's

A bronze student oil lamp, with a vaseline glass shade and adjustable arm, America, late 19thC, 21in (53.5cm) high.

£220–260 **Jackson's**

Student lamps were designed so that they did not cast a shadow.

A gilt-brass and cut-glass three-branch table lamp, fitted for electricity, 19thC, 18in (45.5cm) high.

£180–220 **Woolley & Wallis**

A brass electric table lamp, with scallop glass shade, on a tripod base, c1900, 21in (53.5cm) high.

£450–500 **Exeter Antique Lighting**

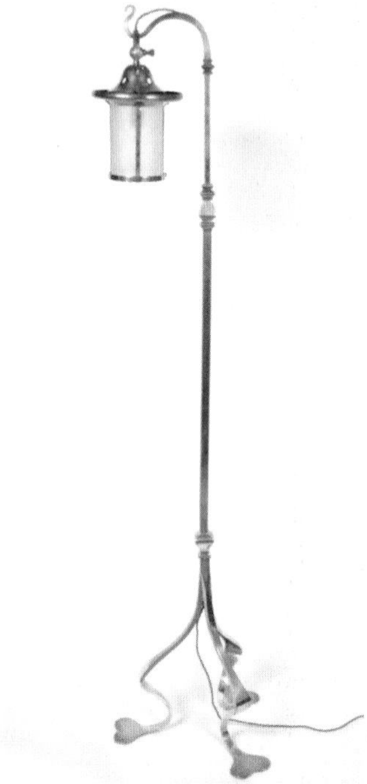

A silvered-brass telescopic floor lamp, by the Faraday Co, stamped 'No. 29', original glass to shade, fitted for electricity, c1900, 69in (175.5cm) high.

£1,000–1,200 **Norfolk Decorative**

A marble and gilt-bronze standard lamp, with glass beading and crystals, France, Paris, c1900, 75½in (192cm) high.

£7,500–9,000 **Sotheby's (O)**

A silver-gilt and enamel lamp, with a *pliq à-jour* shade, probably America, c1910, 6¼in (16cm) high.

£2,500–3,000 **Sotheby's (O)**

A nickel-plated brass Queen's oil reading lamp, c1915, 23in (58.5cm) high.

£250–275 **Exeter Antique Lighting**

The Queen's lamp, which does not cast a shadow, was also known as a student lamp .

A pair of brass and cut-glass table lamps, Continental, 20thC, 22¾in (58cm) high.

£1,200–1,500 **Sotheby's (O)**

An alabaster figural lamp, Italy, c1920, 61in (155cm) high.

£5,500–6,500 **Sotheby's (O)**

ARCHITECTURAL ANTIQUES

RONZE

onze lantern, early 20thC, (114cm) high.
200–1,500 **Sotheby's (S)**

A bronze and copper wall lantern, with bracket, early 20thC, 35in (89cm) high.
£1,800–2,200 Sotheby's (S)

A pair of cast-bronze wall plaques, with portraits of Native Americans, America, 1850–1900, 21½in (54.5cm) wide.
£45,000–52,000
Newell Art Galleries
The value of these plaques lies in their size, popular subject matter and, of course, the quality and patina of the casting.

ERAMIC

air of stoneware chimney pots, probably lashfield, c1870, 50in (127cm) high.
800–2,200 Sotheby's (S)

A pair of stoneware niches, late 19thC, 31in (78cm) diam.
£2,500–3,000 Sotheby's (S)

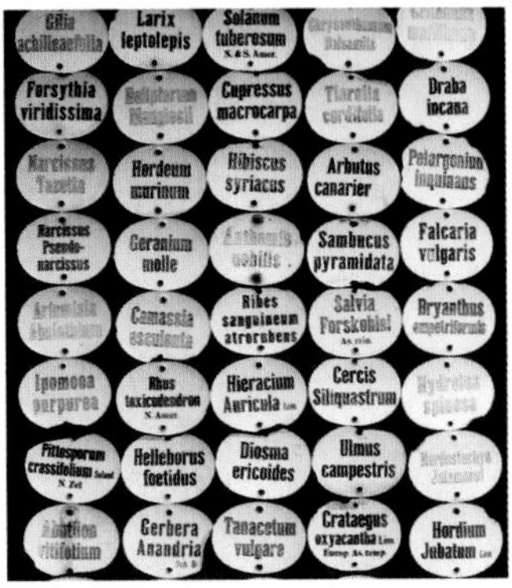

A collection of 53 porcelain plant labels, 1850–1900, 4in (10cm) wide.
£1,500–1,800 Sotheby's (S)

linton Hollins tile, c1910, (20.5cm) square.
5–65 Olliff's Architectural

A set of six Minton tiles, depicting Warwickshire houses, c1880, 6in (15cm) square.
£500–550 Olliff's Architectural

A set of four Minton tiles, decorated with birds, c1890, 6in (15cm) square.
£225–250 Olliffs Architectural

IRON

A pair of cast-iron park bench ends, c1900, 32in (81.5cm) high.

£350–400 **Antique Garden**

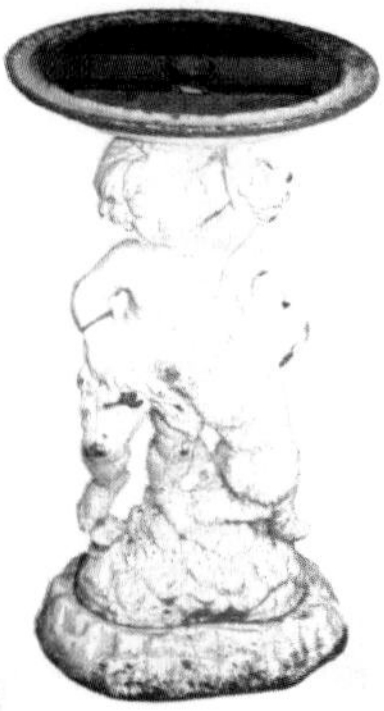

A cast-iron bird bath, c1890, 12in (30.5cm) high.

£300–350 **Antique Garden**

A pair of Coalbrookdale cast-iron and gl overmantel cabinets, c1882, late 19thC, 23¼in (59cm) wide.

£2,800–3,500 **Lyon & Turnbull**

A pair of painted cast-iron Corinthian capitals, America, late 19thC, 28½in (72.5cm) wide.

£350–420 **Skinner**

A cast-iron fire mark, for the Fireman's Insurance Co of Washington and Georgetown, with painted decoration, America, mid-19thC, 14in (35.5cm) high.

£350–400 **Weschler's**

A cast-iron radiator, the three columns decorated with a rococo pattern, 1900–25 32in (81.5cm) high.

£380–420 **LASSCO (bh)**

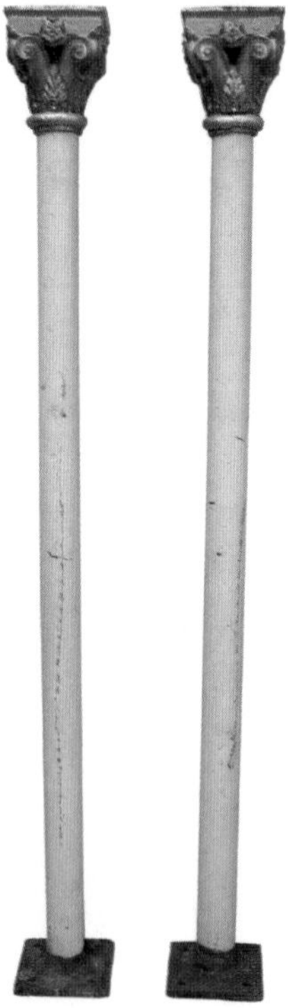

A pair of cast-iron columns, with moulded capitals, c1860, 82¼in (209cm) high.

£900–1,100 **Robert Mills**

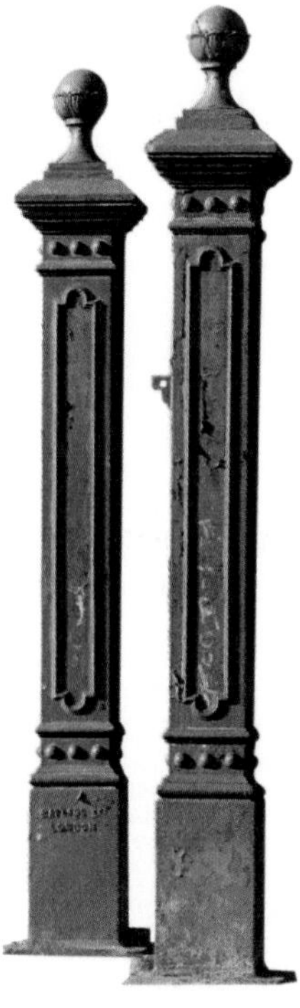

A pair of cast-iron gate piers, stamped 'Baylis, London', late 19thC.

£1,600–2,000 **Sotheby's (S)**

A set of three Victorian Fletcher, Russell & Co cast-iron heaters, with parcel-gilt floral decoration, 36¼in (92cm) high.

£600–700 **Cheffins**

st-iron stick stand, c1880,
(71cm) high.
0–170 Spurrier-Smith ⊞

A cast-iron umbrella/whip stand, c1890,
32in (81.5cm) high.
£300–350 Piccadilly Antiques ⊞

An Abram Cox Stove Co cast-iron stove plate, decorated with three witches and a verse, heightened in gilt, marked, America, Philadelphia and Chicago, late 19thC, 30 x 24in (76 x 61cm).
£2,000–2,500 Freeman's ⚒
The witches and verse are from Shakespeare's play Macbeth.

EAD

ad cistern, with strapwork, armorials and
als, dated 1723, 83in (216cm) wide.
,000–20,000 Sotheby's ⚒

A lead cistern, dated 1727,
26in (66cm) wide.
£2,000–2,500 Sotheby's (S) ⚒

A lead corner cistern, decorated with florets and crowns, initialled 'WB' and dated 1783, 16in (40.5cm) wide.
£1,000–1,200 Woolley & Wallis ⚒

ARBLE

air of Cipolin marble columns, 19thC,
(182cm) high.
500–3,000 Sotheby's (S) ⚒

A pair of carved marble drum pedestals, late 18thC, 17in (43cm) high.
£2,200–2,600 Sotheby's (S) ⚒

A Victorian marble plant stand, top missing, 38in (96.5cm) high.
£200–220 Robert Mills ⊞

STONE

A near pair of carved sandstone finials, c1870, 29½in (75cm) high.
£1,400–1,750 Sotheby's (S)

A pair of composition stone finials, late 19thC, 38in (96.5cm) high.
£1,400–1,750 Sotheby's (S)

A set of four carved sandstone flower va each supported by three putti, 19thC, 39½in (100.5cm) high.
£15,000–18,000 Sotheby's (Am)

A pair of carved Bath stone niches, c1800, 106½in (270cm) high.
£13,000–16,000 Sotheby's (S)

A carved Istrian stone wellhead, c1900, 12½in (32cm) high.
£14,000–17,500 Sotheby's (S)

TERRACOTTA & CLAY

A clay chimney pot, in the form of a creature with facial features and limbs, 18thC, 12in (30.5cm) high.
£320–380 Gorringes (L)

A pair of terracotta pots, decorated with scrolls, early 20thC, 14in (36cm) high.
£1,900–2,200 Sotheby's (S)

A terracotta house tile, c1880, 9in (23cm) wide.
£75–90 LASSCO (bh)

'OOD

. E. Wilson & Co mahogany bell board, 0, 21in (53.5cm) wide.
0–200 Walcot Reclamations

A pair of carved oak brackets, c1900, 16in (40.5cm) high.
£800–900 Robert Mills

t of four oak panels, carved with portraits, numbered, mid-16thC, est 14½ x 10¼in (37 x 26cm).
000–8,500 Dreweatt Neate

An oak newel post, carved with a lion, Belgium, c1820, 54in (137cm) high.
£1,200–1,400
Peter Norden Antiques

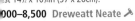

ve oak linenfold panels, 1500–50, est 16½ x 10½in (42 x 26.5cm).
)0–700 Dreweatt Neate

A pair of stripped pine fluted columns, c1890, 114in (289.5cm) high.
£2,400–2,800 Robert Mills

oak panel, carved with frogs playing musical instruments, 19thC, 10 x 33½in (25.5 x 85cm).
80–450 Jackson's

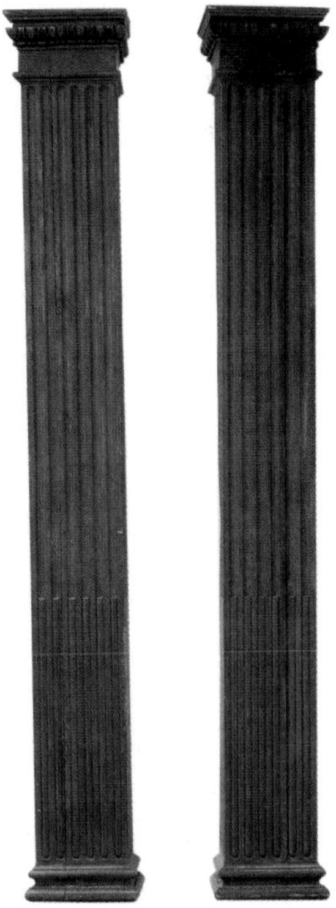

A pair of oak corner pilasters, each capital with an egg-and-dart border, France, c1770, 166in (421.5cm) high.
£4,000–5,000 Sotheby's (NY)

BATHROOM FITTINGS

A Shanks & Co cast-iron and enamel bath, with soap tray, plunger and taps, c1900, 80in (203cm) long.

£3,850–4,250 Drummonds ⊞

A C. Berlie & Co fire-glazed earthenware bath, France, c1900, 65½in (166.5cm) long.

£10,000–11,000 LASSCO (bh) ⊞

An iron slipper bath, c1900, 61in (155cm) long.

£900–1,000 Catchpole & Rye ⊞

A tin bateau bath, with hand-painted decoration of a flaming torch flanked by swans, c1918, 61½in (156cm) long.

£3,500–4,000 LASSCO (bh) ⊞

A Doulton cistern, c1900, 24in (61cm) long.

£800–1,000 Catchpole & Rye ⊞

A T. A. Harris burnished cast-iron Black F
cistern, c1905, 15in (38cm) wide.

£600–700 LASSCO (bh) ⊞

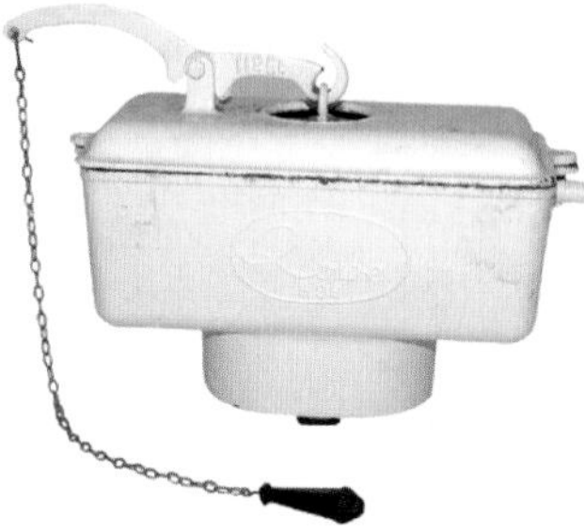

A cast-iron Rowe cistern, c1910, 19in (48.5cm) wide.

£160–180 Walcot Reclamations ⊞

A Doulton Simplicitas lavatory pan, c1880, 17in (43cm) high.

£600–700 Walcot Reclamations ⊞

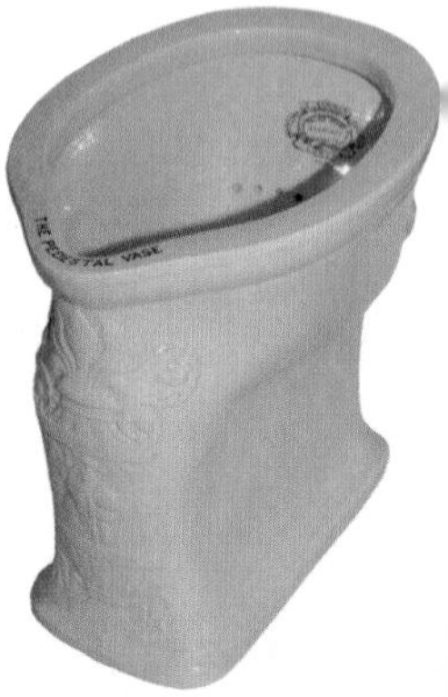

A George Jennings & Co porcelain Pedes
Vase lavatory pan, c1880, 26in (66cm) hi

£675–750 Walcot Reclamations

A salt-glazed stoneware Excelsior lavatory pan, c1898, 16in (40.5cm) high.

£600–650 Walcot Reclamations ⊞

A ceramic Waterfall lavatory pan, decorated with flowers, c1900, 17in (43cm) high.

£1,300–1,500 Drummonds ⊞

A P. E. F. .J. painted lavatory pan, c1900, 15in (38cm) high.

£800–900 Olliff's Architectural ⊞

air of chrome bath taps, with porcelain inserts and
ed spouts, 1930s, 7in (18cm) high.
25–475 LASSCO (bh) ⊞

A pair of brass basin taps, restored, early 20thC, 6in (15cm) high.
£130–150 LASSCO (bh) ⊞

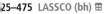

Taylor & Sons ceramic corner wash basin, c1890,
n (63.5cm) wide.
00–800 Walcot Reclamations ⊞

A ceramic wash basin, hand-painted and transfer-printed with flowers, c1880, 27½in (70cm) wide.
£2,400–2,700 LASSCO (bh) ⊞

hanks & Co wash basin, with brass bracket,
910, 27in (68.5cm) wide.
50–950 Olliff's Architectural ⊞

A Porcher porcelain double basin and pedestal, France, Paris, 1930s, 55in (139.5cm) wide.
£3,000–3,300 LASSCO (bh) ⊞

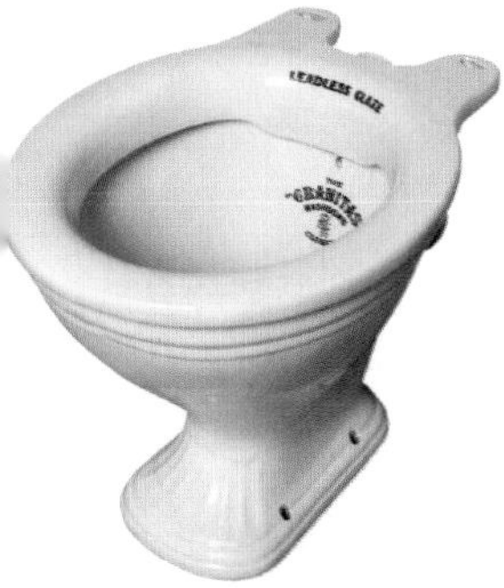

eramic Granitas lavatory pan, 1900–25,
n (48.5cm) diam.
,400–1,600 LASSCO (bh) ⊞

A ceramic pedestal wash basin, transfer-printed with The Pheasant pattern, c1910, 37½in (95cm) wide.
£4,750–5,250 LASSCO (bh) ⊞

A Jacob Delafon fire-glazed earthenware double wash basin, France, Paris, 1925–50, 39in (99cm) wide.
£4,750–5,250 LASSCO (bh) ⊞

DOORS & DOOR FURNITURE

A pine door frame, carved with tulips and berries, slight damage, America, Connecticut, 18thC, 38½in (98cm) wide, with two carved door panels.

£7,500–9,000 Northeast Auctions

A pine door, with raised and fielded glazed panels, c1830, 35in (89cm) wide.

£250–300 Walcot Reclamations

A stripped pitch pine door, with glazed panels, c1880, 42in (107cm) wide.

£200–240 Robert Mills

A pair of pine doors, with glazed panels, c1840, 49in (124.5cm) wide.

£520–600 Walcot Reclamations

A Gothic-style pitch pine door, c1910, 31¼in (79.5cm) wide.

£600–700 Robert Mills

A painted wood door, with coloured glass panels, c1900, 32in (81.5cm) wide.

£350–400 Walcot Reclamations

A cast-iron door knocker, c1800, 8in (20.5cm) high.

£220–250 Olliff's Architectural

A pair of cast-iron door handles, with integrated door plates, c1880, 16in (40.5cm) high.

£130–150 Olliff's Architectural

A cast-iron door knocker, c1835, 10in (25.5cm) high.

£270–300 Olliff's Architectural

'ictorian cast-iron door knocker, 1 (28cm) high.
00–230 LASSCO (sm)

A brass door knocker, c1860, 9in (23cm) high.
£130–150 Fenwick & Fenwick

A Victorian brass mortice set, with a pair of matching escutcheons, door handles 2in (5cm) diam.
£120–150 LASSCO (sm)

'uitwood door pediment, carved with a female mask flanked by floral scrolls I fruiting vines, France, late 18thC, 40in (101.5cm) wide.
50–425 Gorringes (L)

A set of four pine door pediments, with oak-effect finish and armorial plaques, c1870, 66½in (169cm) wide.
£1,700–2,000 Robert Mills

GATES & RAILINGS

pair of wrought-iron gates, with later bases and lock plates, France, c1750, ½in (90cm) wide overall.
:,300–2,750 Sotheby's (S)

A pair of wrought-iron gates, 1850–1900, 92in (233.5cm) wide overall.
£2,200–2,600 Sotheby's (S)

painted cast-iron gate, by D. Wilder, nerica, c1870, 27in (68.5cm) wide.
,600–2,000 Sotheby's (NY)

A section of Victorian wrought-iron railings, 87½in (222.5cm) wide.
£150–175 Robert Mills

FIREPLACES

A neo-classical marble fire surround, Belgium, 1775–1800, 68½in (174cm) wide.

£3,000–3,600 Sotheby's (Am)

A marble fire surround, after Thomas Hope, c1830, 76in (193cm) wide.

£1,100–1,200 Olliff's Architectural

A white marble fire surround, with carved baskets of fruit and flowers above caryatids, early 19thC, 46in (117cm) high.

£23,000–27,000 Sworders

A pine and composition fire surround, attributed to Robert Wellford, with original paint, America, Philadelphia, c1815, 79in (200.5cm) wide.

£8,500–10,000 Northeast Auctions

Robert Wellford arrived in Philadelphia from London in 1797 and by 1807 had founded the American Manufactory of Composition Ornament. This material was durable and easier to carve than plaster, and was less expensive than wood.

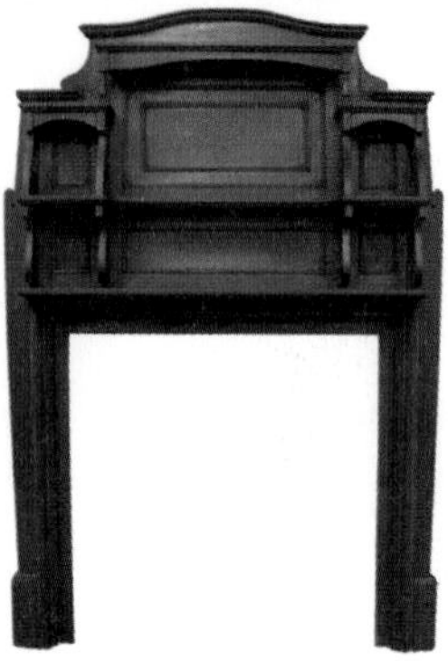

An Edwardian oak fire surround, 51¼in (130cm) wide.

£475–525 Robert Mills

A George III cast-iron hob grate, 24in (61cm) high.

£800–900 LASSCO (sm)

A cast-iron hob grate, c1820, 33in (84cm) wide.

£900–1,000 Walcot Reclamations

A cast-iron fireplace, c1835, 36in (91.5cm) wide.

£1,100–1,200 Olliff's Architectural

A Victorian cast-iron fireplace, 29¾in (75.5cm) wide.

£225–250 Robert Mills

A cast-iron hob register grate, c1850, 24in (61cm) wide.

£500–575 Walcot Reclamations

An Edwardian polished cast-iron fireplace, 36in (91.5cm) high.

£550–650 LASSCO (sm)

A cast-iron portable range, by The Metal Agencies 'Go Ahead' Co Ltd, Bristol, early 20thC, 36in (91.5cm) wide.

£700–800 Walcot Reclamations

IREPLACE ACCESSORIES

ir of Clark's patent mechanical bellows, c1835, (48.5cm) long.

5–185 Red Lion Antiques

A Victorian japanned coal scuttle and cover, with gilt decoration and cast-iron handles, on scrolled feet, 21in (53.5cm) high.

£425–500 Sworders

A brass-mounted steel fender, with sheet iron baseplate, 1850–75, 62¼in (158cm) wide.

£2,000–2,400 Dreweatt Neate

rought-iron fire basket, fleur-de-lys finials, c1900, in (59.5cm) wide.

50–280 Robert Mills

A George III brass-mounted cast-iron fire grate, the back cast with a two-handled urn draped with husks, restored, 18½in (47cm) wide.

£2,300–2,750 Tennants

A brass mounted cast-iron fire grate, decorated with stylized wolves' heads, 19thC, 31¼in (79.5cm) wide.

£400–500 Dreweatt Neate (HAM)

vrought- and cast-iron firegrate, with a rced apron, 19thC, 28in (71cm) wide.

,000–2,400 Dreweatt Neate

A set of three early Victorian steel and gilt bronze fire tools, the pierced handles with flowerheads, some repair.

£450–550 Woolley & Wallis

A cast-iron fireback, decorated with a religious scene, Flanders, c1740, 33in (84cm) wide.

£700–800 Peter Norden Antiques

pair of brass andirons, c1900, n (78.5cm) high.

,450–1,600 Robert Mills

A brass and copper-bound log bin, with lion-mask handles, late 19thC, 12½in (32cm) diam.

£230–275 Woolley & Wallis

A wrought-iron trivet, with a plate shelf, c1780, 12in (30.5cm) wide.

£165–185 Peter Norden Antiques

FOUNTAINS

A terracotta pedestal fountain, the column decorated with three cranes, on a triangular base, 19thC, 73in (185.5cm) high.

£38,000–42,000 LASSCO (sm)

A marble fountain, Italy, c1870, 39½in (100.5cm) high.

£7,500–9,000 Sotheby's (S)

A lead fountain figure of a girl, with a posy of flowers, early 20thC, 31½in (80cm) high.

£1,200–1,400 Sotheby's (S)

A bronze figural fountain, by Edward Berge, entitled 'Duck Mother', signed, America, c19 41in (104cm) high.

£20,000–25,000 Northeast Auctions

SEATING

A carved marble seat, 19thC, 45¼in (115cm) wide.

£12,000–15,000 Sotheby's (S)

A wrought-iron seat, Scotland, c1850, 36in (91.5cm) wide.

£1,200–1,500 Sotheby's (S)

A Victorian Coalbrookdale painted Gothic pattern cast-iron seat, 61¾in (157cm) wide.

£1,400–1,800 Woolley & Wallis

A carved stone seat, 19thC, 101in (256.5cm) wide.

£6,500–8,000 Sotheby's (S)

A carved marble seat, Italy, 1850–1900, 59in (150cm) wide.

£12,000–15,000 Sotheby's (S)

A Val d'Osne cast-iron seat, France, c1870, 39in (99cm) wide.

£1,200–1,500 Sotheby's (S)

A Coalbrookdale cast-iron seat, stamped, No. 104848, registration No. 27, 19thC, 52in (132cm) wide.

£2,500–3,000 Sotheby's (S)

...oalbrookdale cast iron seat, decorated with oak and ...leaves, c1880, 42½in (108cm) wide.

...000–4,500 Olliff's Architectural

A Victorian painted iron garden elbow seat and a single seat, each with an openwork swirl seat and backrest.

£160–200 Greenslade Taylor Hunt

A pair of iron and wood garden elbow chairs, France, c1880.

£400–450 Millers

...pair of wirework chairs, in the form of daisies, 1900–50.

...,800–4,500 Sotheby's (S)

A pair of composition stone seats, France, c1940, 33in (84cm) high.

£680–750 Olliff's Architectural

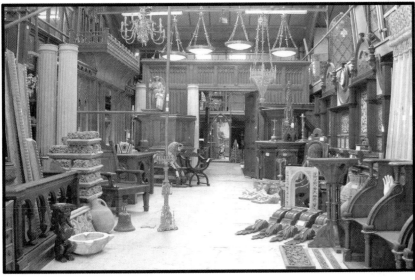

STATUARY

A marble figure of a putto, by Nicolas Blasset, inscribed 'N Blasset Arch et Sculp du Roy', dated 1656, 21in (53.3cm) high.

£22,000–26,000 Sotheby's (S)

Nicolas Blasset (1600–59) was the son of the sculptor Philippe Blasset. He became a master sculptor in 1625 and in 1637 became the Architecte et Sculpteur Ordinaire du Roi. *Many of his works can be seen in Amiens Cathedral.*

A carved and painted gritstone putto, by Jan Pieter van Bauerscheit the Elder, holding a dog and a seal, damaged, signed, Holland, early 18thC, 35½in (90cm) high.

£14,000–17,500 Sotheby's (Am)

Jan Pieter van Bauerscheit the Elder (1668–1728) worked mainly in marble and gritstone, producing a number of pairs of urns decorated with allegorical and mythological subjects. He was also responsible for several groups of putti which are similar in style to this.

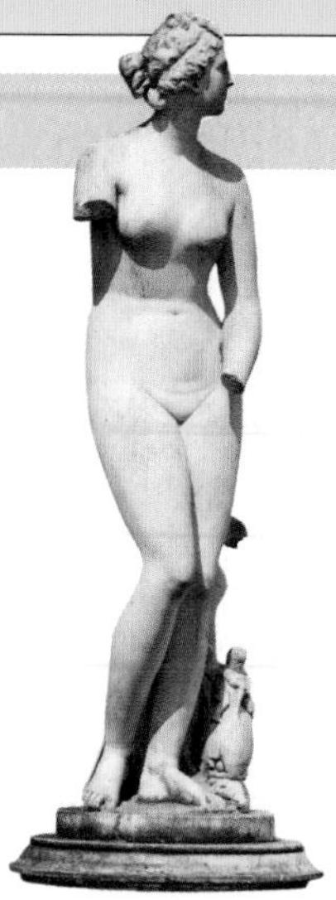

A marble figure of the Medici Venus, 1800–50, 78in (198cm) high.

£8,000–10,000 Sotheby's (S)

The Venus de Medici was first definitely recorded in 1638 at the Villa Medici in Rom By 1688 the statue was moved to the Uffizi Florence and in 1800 it moved again to Sici for protection from the French. In 1802 it w ceded to the French but was returned in 18 and resumed its position in the Uffizi where still stands to this day. Although its origins a unknown it is believed to be a 1st-century co of an Athenian bronze.

A composition stone model of a phoenix rising from a bed of fire, early 19thC, 78in (198cm) high.

£5,400–6,000 LASSCO (sm)

A pair of Austin & Seeley composition stone gate pier eagles, c1850, 37in (94cm) high.

£9,500–11,000
Sotheby's (S)

A marble garden statue of Ceres, after the antique, c1880 54in (137cm) high.

£8,500–9,500
Olliffs' Architectural

A pair of cast-iron Newfoundland dogs, attributed to J. W. Fiske, America, late 19thC, 46in (117cm) long.

£6,000–7,000 Northeast Auctions

A pair of Crowther & Son lead statues of peacocks, 1900–20, 24in (61cm) high.

£1,800–2,000
Olliff's Architectural

A cast-iron cherub, c1920, 21in (53.5cm) high.

£300–330
Olliff's Architectural

UNDIALS

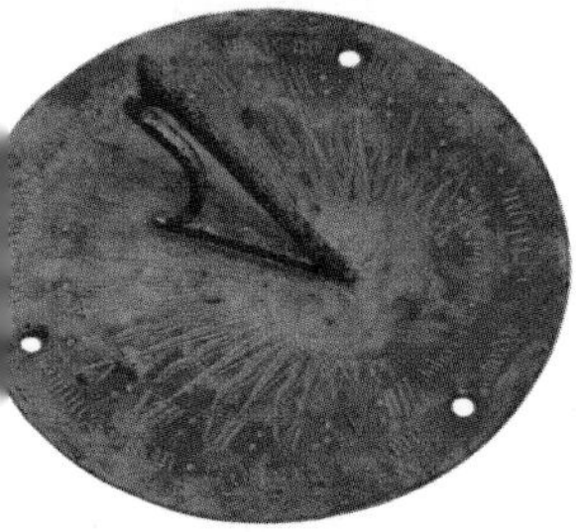

rass sundial, by John Seth, Bristol, dated
57, 9in (23cm) diam.
00–800 Grimes Militaria

A cast-iron sundial, marked 'Anno 1735', Sweden, 12½in (32cm) square.
£1,400–1,750 Bukowskis

A bronze sundial, by Cole of London, dated 1769, 8¾in (22cm) diam.
£700–800 Walpoles

arved stone polar sundial, c1800,
in (137cm) high.
,000–3,600 Sotheby's (S)
oss dials are an ingenious way of combining
ar dials with direct east and west dials.

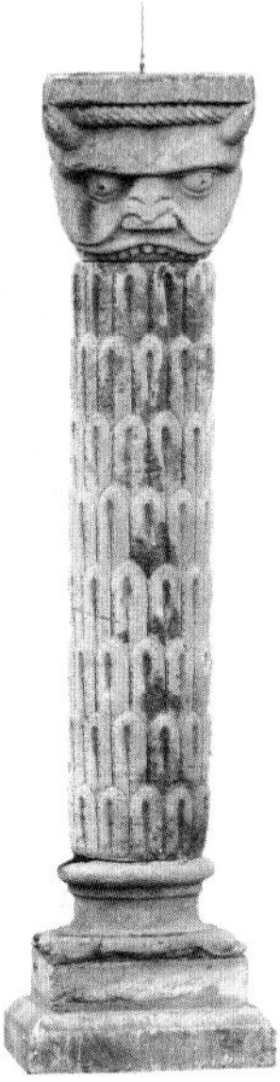

A carved stone sundial, with a brass plate, north European, 19thC, 53in (134.5cm) high.
£3,800–4,500 Sotheby's (S)

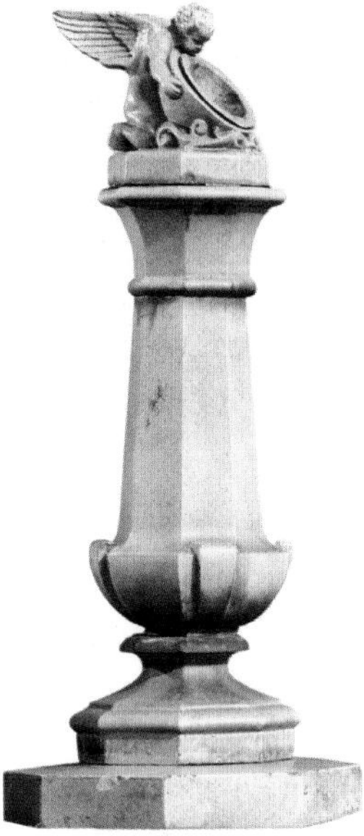

A glazed earthenware sundial, probably by Doulton, the dish with a hemispherical bronze dial, early 20thC, 44in (112cm) high.
£1,800–2,200 Sotheby's (S)

JRNS

pair of marble urns, on carved gritstone
destals, c1800, 38½in (98cm) high.
,000–7,000 Sotheby's (Am)

A terracotta urn and cover, the fluted lid with an acorn finial, the body modelled with rams-head handles and swags, on a socle foot, 19thC, 29½in (75cm) high.
£1,500–1,800 LASSCO (sm)

A terracotta urn, the body decorated with fairies, on a stone base, France, c1840, 35in (89cm) high.
£1,100–1,300 Robert Mills

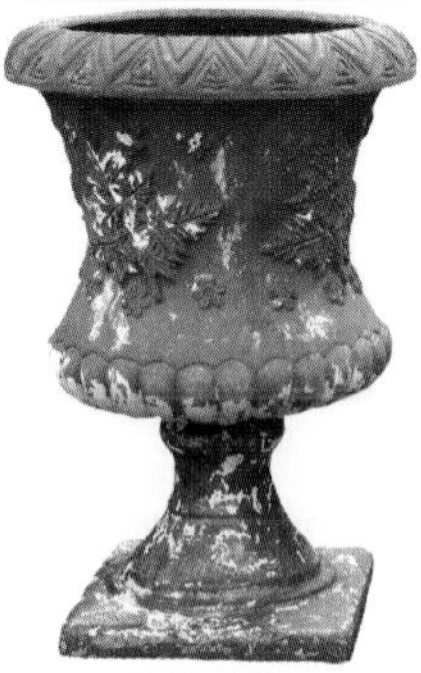

A pair of Victorian terracotta **urns,** with original paint, 20¼in (51.5cm) high.

£700–800 Robert Mills

A pair of Victorian painted cast-iron urns, decorated with figures and leaves, 26½in (67.5cm) high.

£1,200–1,400 Penrith Farmers' & Kidd's

A pair of Victorian painted cast-iron gard urns, 9½in (24cm) high.

£160–200 Dee, Atkinson & Harriso

A Handyside cast-iron garden urn, c1890, 36in (91.5cm) diam.

£2,250–2,500 Olliff's Architectural

Andrew Handyside (1806-87) purchased th Britannia Iron Works in Derby in 1848. In 18 at the Great Exhibition, Handyside was awarc a medal for his exhibits, which included reduc copies of the Medici urn and portrait busts various notables. The quality of casting was exceptional and the foundry went from strength to strength from that moment on. In 1873 the business became a limited company and in the following year it publish catalogue of its ornamental wares.

A pair of Victorian cast-iron garden urns, each with a moulded rim and lobed body, on a fluted foot with foliate banding and a plinth, 10in (25.5cm) high.

£200–250 Andrew Hartley

A pair of fireclay urns, after the antique, Scotland, c1870, 36in (91.5cm) high.

£3,500–4,250 Sotheby's (S)

WINDOWS

A pair of stained glass fanlights, 1900, 34in (86.5cm) wide.

£2,000–2,400
Robert Mills

A Victorian stained glass panel, incorporating a coat-of-arms with a cockerel, 17in (43cm) wide.

£280–350 Charterhouse

A pair of stained glass windows, decorated with flower patterns, c1860, 23¾in (60.5cm) wide.

£580–650 Robert Mills

A pair of rosewood pelmets, fretted and carved with ribbon cresting and leaf scroll swags, Portuguese East Indies, 19thC, 72in (183cm) wide.

£300–350 Canterbury Auctions

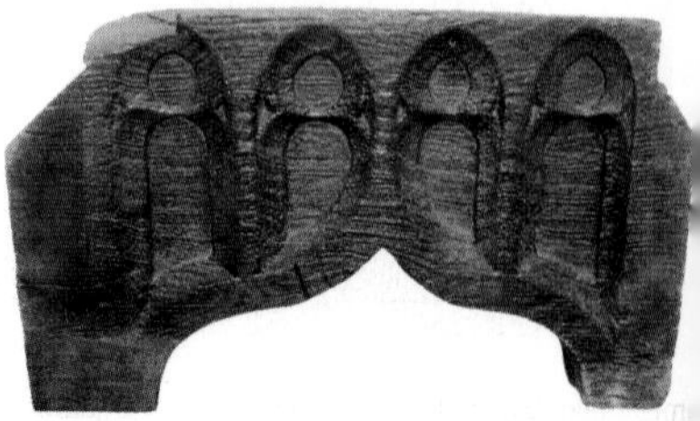

An oak window head, carved with recessed lancets, carpenter's mark, 15thC, 21¾in (55.5cm) wide.

£375–450 Dreweatt Neate

3OOKS & BOOK LLUSTRATIONS

niniature almanack, published for Company Stationers, London, first edition, 1783, x 1¾in (6 x 4cm), engraved frontispiece d calendar, morocco with calf onlays d gilt decoration.

25–525 Bloomsbury

J. M. Barrie, *Peter and Wendy*, published by Hodder & Stoughton, London, first edition, 1911, 8°, title and 12 plates by Francis Bedford, gilt cloth, gift inscription to endpaper.

£200–250 Rosebery's

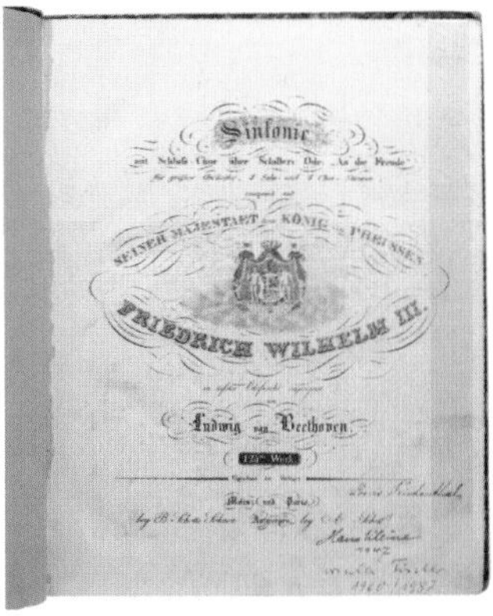

Ludwig van Beethoven, full score of his Ninth Symphony, published by B. Schotts Söhnen, Mainz and Paris, first edition, 1826, 2°, three-quarter calf with marbled boards, with a clamshell box.

£22,500–25,000 Bauman Rare Books

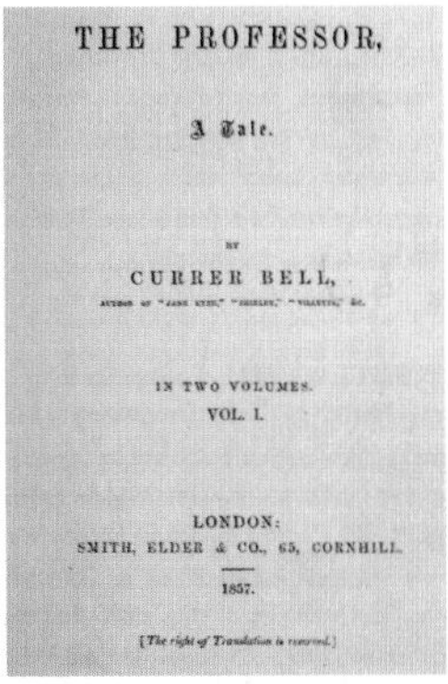

THE PROFESSOR,

A Tale.

BY

CURRER BELL,

AUTHOR OF "JANE EYRE," "SHIRLEY," "VILLETTE," &c.

IN TWO VOLUMES.

VOL. I.

LONDON:

SMITH, ELDER & CO., 65, CORNHILL.

1857.

[The right of Translation is reserved.]

ırrer Bell (Charlotte Brontë), *The Professor, Tale*, published by Smith, Elder & Co, ndon, 1857, 8°, 2 vols, cloth.

00–500 Lawrence Fine Art

The Holy Bible, printed by John Hayes, Cambridge, 4°, 1675, calf decorated with gilt scrolls and flowerheads.

£1,600–2,000 Anderson & Garland

The Holy Bible, published by John G. Murdoch, London, 1878, 14in (35.5cm) high, illustrated, leather with brass fittings.

£180–200 Durham House Antiques

mes Boyd, *Drums*, illustrated by N. C. yeth, published by Charles Scribner's Sons, ew York, 1928, 4°, edition of 525, signed by yd and Wyeth, cloth.

220–260 Waddington's

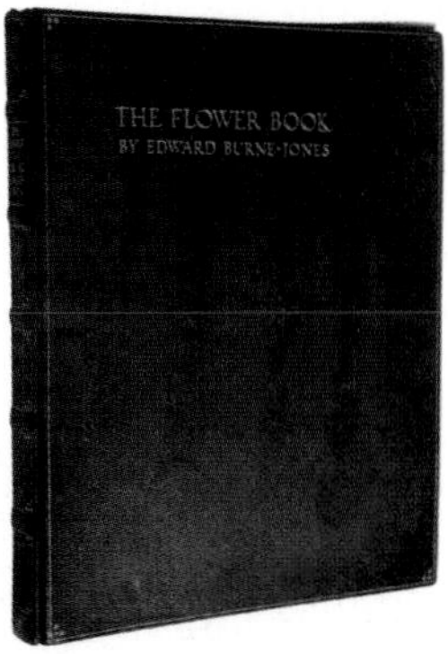

Edward Burne-Jones, *The Flower Book*, 1927, 13 x 10in (33 x 25.5cm), edition of 300, leather bound.

£1,800–2,000 Addyman Books

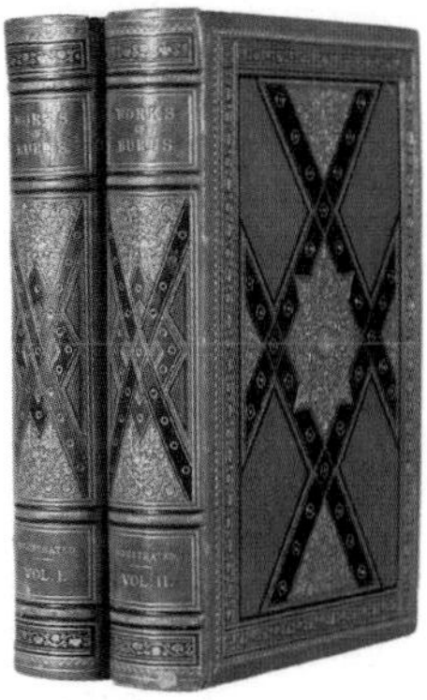

Robert Burns, *The Works*, 1878, 8°, 2 vols, engraved titles and plates, morocco with morocco onlays and gilt stamping.

£700–850 Bloomsbury

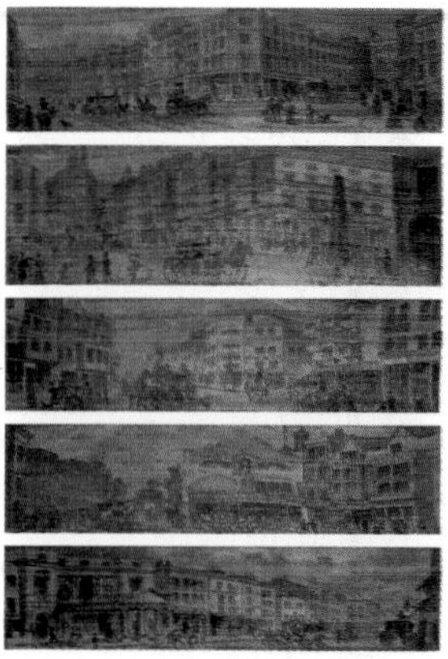

Lord George Gordon Noel Byron, *The Works*, London, 1814–24, 8°, 5 vols, engraved plates, each volume with watercolour fore-edge painting of a different street scene in central London, gilt-tooled morocco.

£2,250–2,750 Toovey's

George Catlin, *North American Indians*, published by John Grant, Edinburgh, 1926, large 8°, 2 vols, 180 colour plates, 3 maps, gilt cloth, gilt edges.

£1,600–1,800 Peter Harrington

A young lawyer turned portraitist, George Catlin set out in 1830 from his home in Pennsylvania to record on canvas the indigenous tribes of North America and their way of life. His eight years among the major tribes of the Great Plains and the Rocky Mountains resulted in his 'Indian Gallery', an enormous collection of artefacts as well as more than 400 paintings, including portraits and scenes of tribal life.

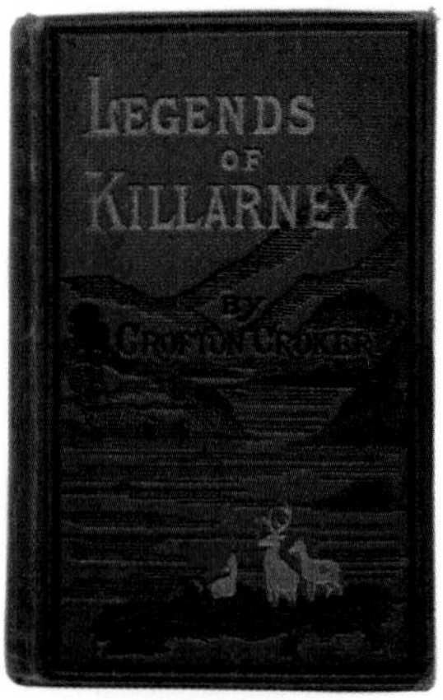

Crofton Croker, *Legends of Killarney*, published by William Tegg & Co, London, c1870, 6½in (16.5cm) high.

£100–120 Vanessa Parker

Lewis Carroll (Reverend Charles Lutwidge Dodgson), *The Nursery Alice*, published by Macmillan, London, first published edition, 1889, small 4°, 20 colour illustrations, cloth, with morocco-backed collector's box.

£7,500–8,500 Peter Harrington

The first printing of this condensed version of Alice was discarded by Carroll in much the same way as its 1865 predecessor; 500 copies were sent for issue in the USA but even they were destroyed.

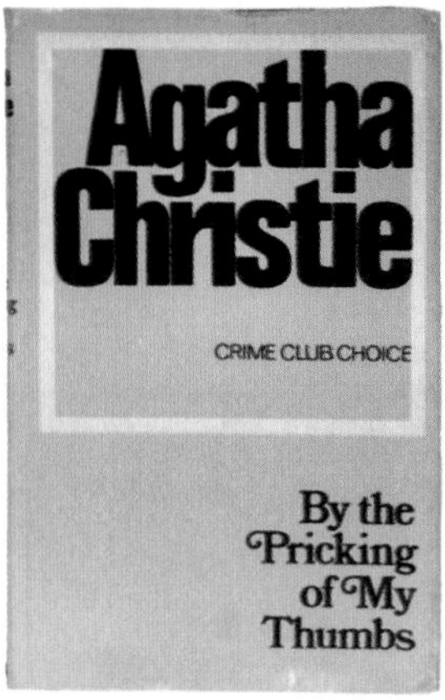

Agatha Christie, *By the Pricking of My Thumbs*, published by Collins Crime Club, first edition, 1968, 8°, inscribed by the author to her daughter Rosalind, cloth, dust jacket.

£2,000–2,400 Bearnes

Thomas Davidson, *Rowan Tree & Red Thread*, published by Oliver & Boyd, Edinburgh, first edition, 1949, 8¾ x 5½in (22 x 14cm), dust jacket.

£130–150 Barter Books

Lewis Caroll (Reverend Charles Lutwidge Dodgson), *Alice in Wonderland*, illustrated Mabel Lucie Attwell, published by Raphael Tu & Sons, London, 1910, 10in (25.5cm) high.

£150–170 Vanessa Parker

Winston S. Churchill, *The Second World W The Gathering Storm, Their Finest Hour, The Grand Alliance, The Hinge of Fate, Closing the Ring, Triumph and Tragedy*, published by Cassell, London, 1948–54, 8°, 6 vols, first vol inscribed by author to Nellie Soames, cloth, dust jackets.

£6,750–7,500 Bauman Rare Books

Joseph Crawhall, *Olde Tayles Newlye Relayt* published by Field Tuer, Leadenhall Press, London, 1883, 11¼ x 8in (28.5 x 22.5cm), c200 wood engravings, cloth.

£130–150 Barter Books

Charles Dickens, *Great Expectations*, publishec by Chapman & Hall, first edition, fifth issue, 1861, 8°, 3 vols, cloth, spines lettered in gilt

£5,000–6,000 Sotheby's

This first edition, fifth issue, was published o 30 October 1861. The first issue had appearec on 6 July; the second, third and fourth issues also termed 'editions' on the title pages, wer published on 5 August, 17 August and 17 September respectively. All these issues were published in identical bindings of violet wavy grained cloth.

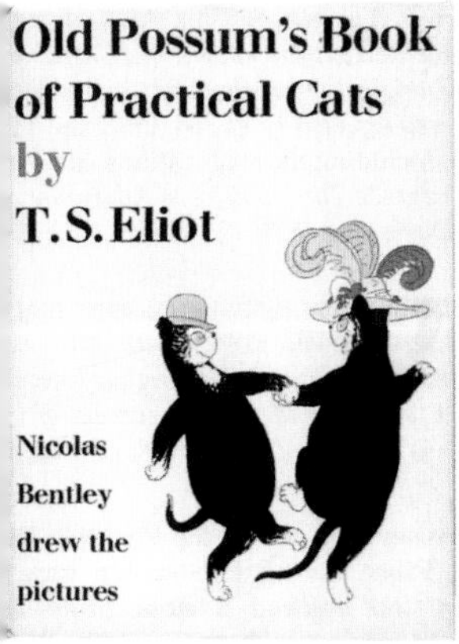

Old Possum's Book of Practical Cats
by
T.S. Eliot
Nicolas Bentley drew the pictures

S. Eliot, *Old Possum's Book of Practical* *ts*, illustrated by Nicolas Bentley, published Faber & Faber, first illustrated edition, 40, 8°, pictorial cloth, dust jacket.

700–850 Bloomsbury

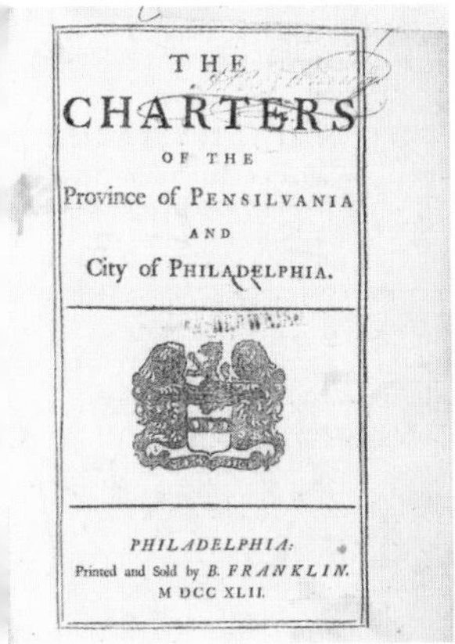

Printed and Sold by B. FRANKLIN.
M DCC XLII.

he Charters of the Province of Pensilvania ***nd City of Philadelphia***, printed by Benjamin anklin, Philadelphia, 1742, 2°, disbound.

500–600 Freeman's

liver Goldsmith, *The Vicar of Wakefield*, lustrated by William Mulready, published by ohn van Voorst, London, 1843, large 8°, osway binding by Rivière & Son, crushed orocco, spine and boards with gilt ecoration, front board with miniature ortrait of Goldsmith by Miss Currie mounted ehind glass, watered silk endpapers, gilt dges, marbled paper leather-entry slipcase.

4,250–4,750 Peter Harrington

his is a good example of a genuine Cosway inding, so-called after the famous Regency iniaturist Richard Cosway. This style of binding vas executed by Rivière & Son in the early 0th century for Henry Sotheran booksellers, vith miniatures by Miss C. B. Currie mounted nder glass on the front cover.

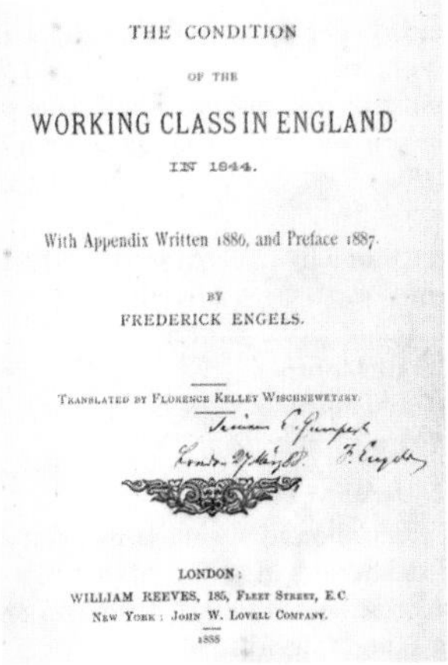

THE CONDITION
OF THE
WORKING CLASS IN ENGLAND
IN 1844.
With Appendix Written 1886, and Preface 1887.
BY
FREDERICK ENGELS.
LONDON:
WILLIAM REEVES, 185, FLEET STREET, E.C.
NEW YORK: JOHN W. LOVELL COMPANY.
1888

Frederick Engels, *The Condition of the Working Class in England in 1844*, translated by Florence Keley Wischnewetzky, published by William Reeves, London and New York, first English edition, 1888, 8°, presentation copy signed by the author, cloth.

£4,000–5,000 Bloomsbury

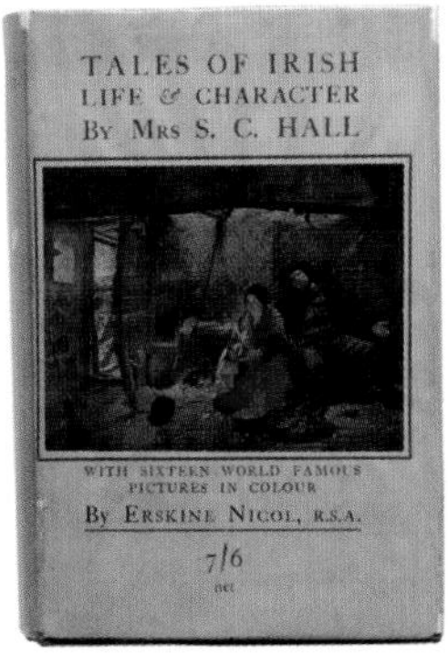

TALES OF IRISH
LIFE & CHARACTER
BY MRS S. C. HALL
WITH SIXTEEN WORLD FAMOUS PICTURES IN COLOUR
BY ERSKINE NICOL, R.S.A.
7/6

Mrs S. C. Hall, *Tales of Irish Life & Character*, illustrated by Erskine Nicol, published by T. N. Foulis, Edinburgh and London, 1910, 8in (20.5cm) high, dust jacket.

£90–100 Vanessa Parker

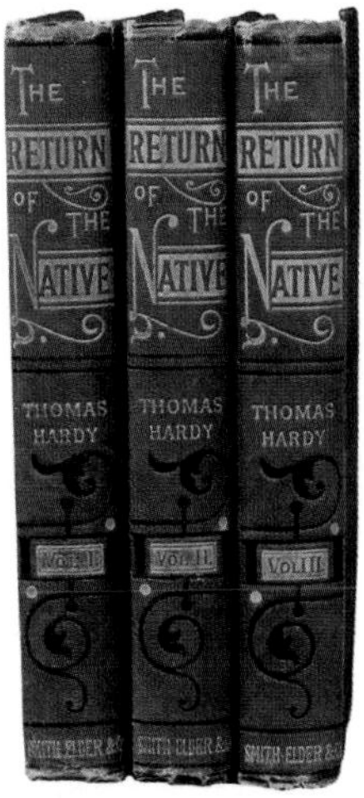

Thomas Hardy, *The Return of the Native*, published by Smith, Elder & Co, London, first edition, 1878, 8°, 3 vols, vol 1 with sketch map fontispiece and receipt signed by Hardy for an episode of the novel *Belgravia* loosely inserted, cloth with gilt-lettered spines, folding cloth cases and quarter morocco slipcases.

£3,500–4,250 Sotheby's

F. Scott Fitzgerald, *All The Sad Young Men*, published by Charles Scribner's Sons, New York, first edition, 1926, 8°, cloth, spines lettered in gilt, dust jacket.

£2,000–2,250 Peter Harrington

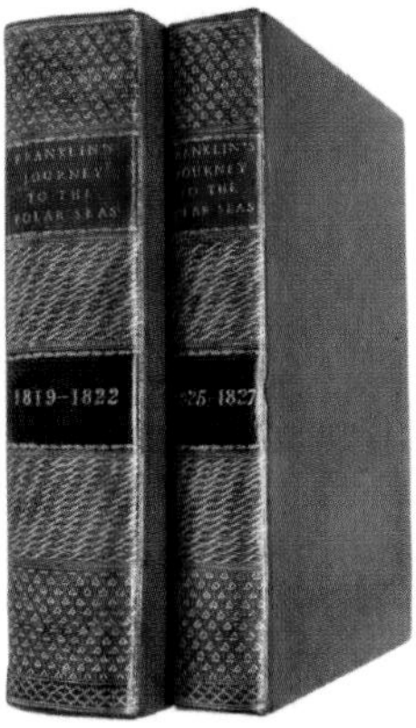

Captain John Franklin, *Franklin's Journey to the Polar Seas*, published by John Murray, London, first editions, 1823 and 1828, 4°, 2 vols, coloured plates, folding maps, speckled calf with gilt spines.

£5,400–6,000 Adrian Harrington

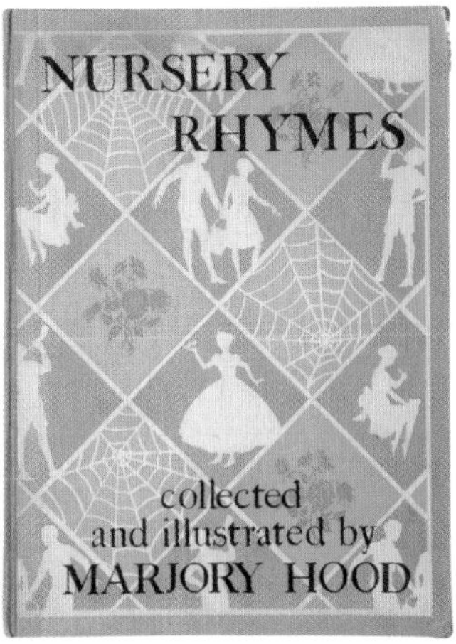

Margory Hood (compiler and illustrator), *Nursery Rhymes*, published by Eyre & Spottiswoode, 1930, 13in (33cm) high.

£130–150 Vanessa Parker

Bob Hope, *They Got Me Covered*, published by the author, Hollywood, first edition, 1941, 8°, presentation copy inscribed by author to Bing Crosby, introduction by Bing Crosby, illustrated, morocco-backed pictorial laminate boards, gilt titles to spine, cloth slipcase, damaged.

£2,000–2,250 **Peter Harrington**

Samuel Johnson, *A Dictionary of the English Language*, 1822, 4°, 2 vols, engraved portrait frontispiece, gilt calf.

£600–700 **Anderson & Garland**

Rudyard Kipling, *The Jungle Book*, illustrated by Kipling, W. H. Drake and P. Frenzeny, published by Macmillan, London, 1897, 7½in (19cm) high, cloth.

£220–250 **George Bayntun**

F. Edward Hulme, *Familiar Wild Flowers*, published by Cassell & Co, London, 1902, 8 x 6in (20.5 x 15cm), 7 vols, coloured plates, cloth, gilt titles, 1902.

£100–120 **George Bayntun**

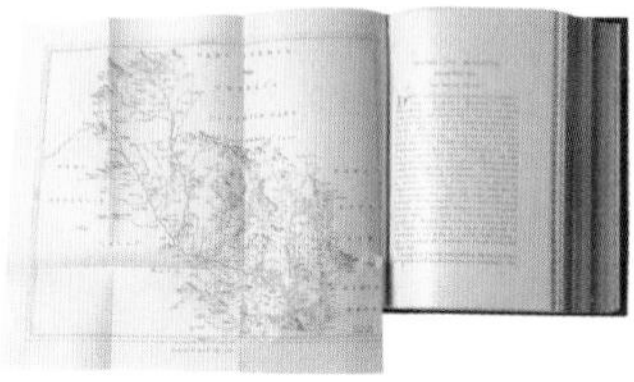

John and Robert Hyslop, *Langholm As It Was*, published by Hills & Co, Sunderland, first edition, 1912, 9in (23cm) high.

£300–360 **Barter Books**

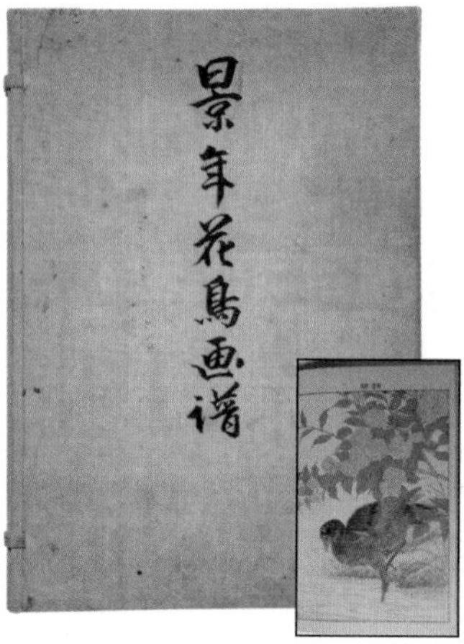

Imao Keinen, *Bird and Flower Albums*, published by Sozaemon Nishimura, Kyoto, first edition, 1891–92, 2°, 4 vols, hand-coloured woodblock prints, card wraps, cloth slipcase.

£3,500–3,800 **Adrian Harrington**

These volumes are bound in the traditional fukurotoji *style, sewn with purple thread through five holes. It is rare to find a complete set (Spring, Summer, Autumn, Winter) as they are usually broken for prints. Imao Keinen (1845–1923) was born in Kyoto and studied* ukiyo-e *(pictures of the floating world), painting with Umegata Tokyo and Suzuki Hyakunen. In 1880 he began to teach as a professor at the Kyoto Prefecture School of painting. In 1904 he became a member of the Art committee of the Imperial Household and in 1919 a member of the Imperial Art Academy. An important Japanese style painter, Keinen specialized in Kacho-ga (flower and bird prints) with very realistic detail.* Keinen Kacho Gafu, *his best-known work, was carved by Tanaka Hirokichi and printed by Miki Jinzaburo.*

Fergus W. Hume, *The Mystery of a Hansom Cab*, published by The Hansom Cab Publishing Co London, 1890s, 8°, advertisemen pictorial wrappers.

£200–240 **Bloomsbury**

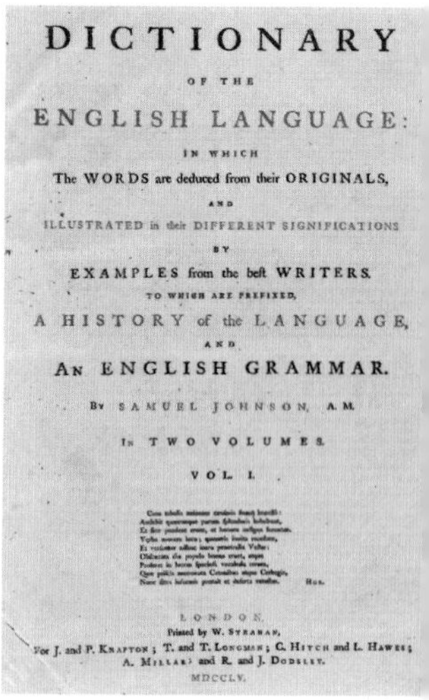

DICTIONARY
OF THE
ENGLISH LANGUAGE:
IN WHICH
The WORDS are deduced from their ORIGINALS,
AND
ILLUSTRATED in their DIFFERENT SIGNIFICATIONS
BY
EXAMPLES from the best WRITERS.
TO WHICH ARE PREFIXED,
A HISTORY of the LANGUAGE,
AND
AN ENGLISH GRAMMAR.
By SAMUEL JOHNSON, A.M.
IN TWO VOLUMES.
VOL. I.

LONDON,
Printed by W. STRAHAN,
For J. and P. KNAPTON; T. and T. LONGMAN; C. HITCH and L. HAWES;
A. MILLAR; and R. and J. DODSLEY.
MDCCLV.

Samuel Johnson, *A Dictionary of the English Language*, printed by W. Strahan, first editio 1755, 2°, 2 vols, marbled endpapers, woodcut tailpieces, later half morocco, morocco-cloth covers.

£6,000–7,000 **Sotheby's**

This is a first edition of the first standard Englis dictionary. Two thousand copies were printed

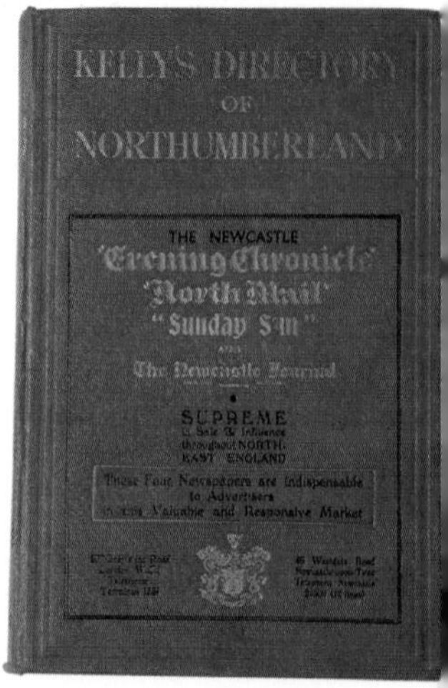

Kelly's Directory of Northumberland, London, 1938, 10½in (26.5cm) high.

£115–130 **Barter Books**

Andrew Lang (editor), *The Green Fairy Book*, illustrated by H. J. Ford, published by Longmans, Green & Co, first edition, 1892, 7½in (19cm) high.

£160–175 George Bayntun

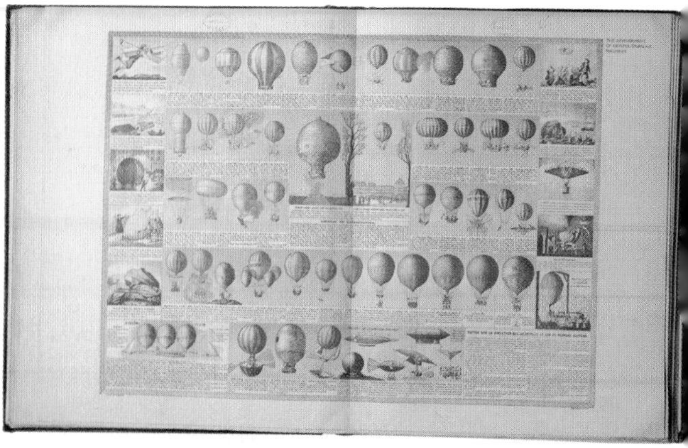

W. Lockwood Marsh, *Aeronautical Prints & Drawings*, published by Halton & Truscott Smith, London, first edition, 1924, 12½ x 9¾in (31.5 x 25cm), foreword by Sir Frederick H. Sykes, 7 colour plates, 87 plates, gilt cloth.

£120–140 Barter Books

Harriet Martineau, *The English Lakes*, published by John Garnett, Windermere, 1858, 11½ x 9in (29 x 23cm), woodcuts by J. W. Linton, 6 steel engravings, 3 mountain outline pages, 40 vignettes, gilt cloth.

£100–120 Barter Books

Arthur Miller, *Death of a Salesman*, published by Viking Press, New York, first edition, 1949, 8°, illustrated boards, dust jacket.

£600–700 Dreweatt Neate (N)

A. A. Milne, *A Gallery of Children*, illustrated by Henriette Willebeek Le Mair, published by Stanley Paul, 1925, 10in (25.5cm) high, gilt cloth.

£340–380 Vanessa Parker

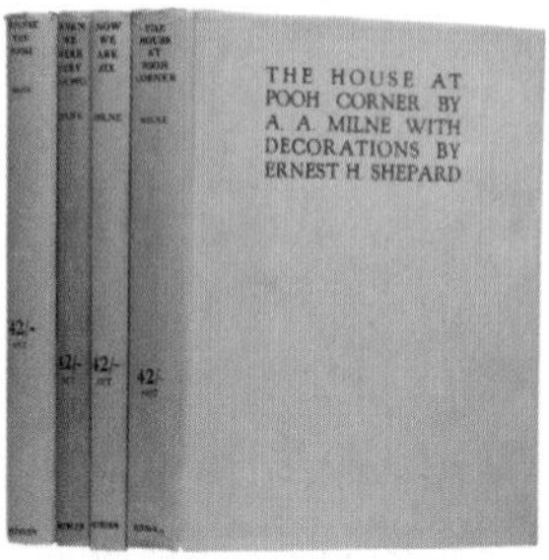

A. A. Milne, *When We Were Very Young, Winnie The Pooh, Now We Are Six, The House At Pooh Corner*, illustrated by Ernest H. Shepard, published by Methuen, first editions, 1924–28, signed by Milne and Shepard, large square 8°, 4 vols, half cloth, dust jackets, chemise and half morocco slipcase.

£30,000–35,000 Bauman Rare Books

John Milton, *The Poetical Works*, 1835, 8°, 6 vols, engraved frontispieces and titles after Turner, later half morocco, gilt spines.

£160–200 Bloomsbury

Charles Morren, *La Belgique Horticole*, 1851–69, 8°, 9in (23cm) high, 19 vols, hand-coloured plates, wood engravings and lithographs, quarter morocco, cloth boards.

£4,000–4,500 Adrian Harrington

Beverley R. Morris, *British Game Birds and Wildfowl*, published by Groombridge & Sons, (1899), 4°, 60 hand-coloured plates, gilt cloth.

£600–700 Lawrence Fine Art

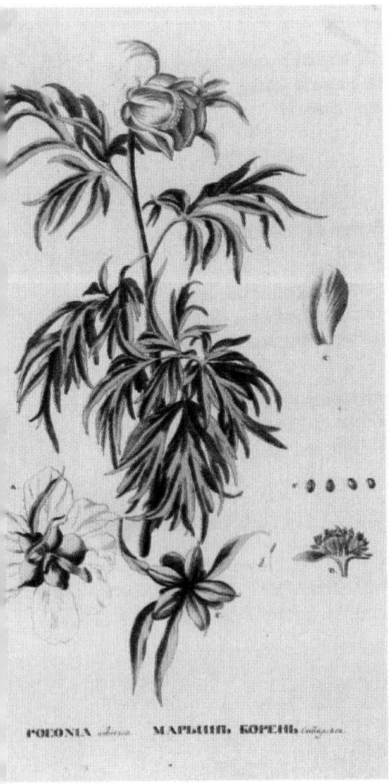

›eter Simon Pallas, *Flora Rossica*, published J. J. Weitbrecht, St Petersburg, first edition, 784–88, 2°, 101 hand-coloured engraved ›ates, captions in Latin and Russian, half calf.

11,000–13,000 Sotheby's

›is beatifully illustrated pioneering work on ıssian botany by the eminent German ›turalist Peter Simon Pallas is based on his ›servations made during the Academic ›peditions of 1768–74, in the course of which › collected many plant specimens. Pallas had ›en invited in 1767 by Catherine the Great to ›ork in the St Petersburg Academy of Sciences ›d for more than 40 years he was associated ›clusively with the development of Russian ›ience. Pallas's aim was to create a complete ›talogue of the plants and animals of Russia ›d although this project remained ›finished, his achievements in zoology and ›tany were of great importance.

›nna Sewell, *Black Beauty*, published by Jarrold › Sons, London, first edition, (1877), 8°, ›rontispiece, 8pp publisher's advertisements, ›ilt-decorated cloth.

£8,500–9,500 Peter Harrington

Willy Pogany (illustrator), *The Rime of the Ancient Mariner*, by Samuel Taylor Coleridge, signed by Pogany, published by Thomas Y. Crowell & Co, New York, (1910), 4°, edition of 525, pictorial endpapers, colour plates, colour and monochrome illustrations, top edge gilt, tooled calf, gilt titles to spine.

£1,800–2,000 Peter Harrington

Arthur Rackham (illustrator), *Grimm's Fairy Tales*, translated by Mrs Edgar Lucas, published by Constable, London, signed by the author, 1909, 4°, 40 colour illustrations, top edge gilt, vellum with pictorial decoration to spine and front board.

£3,000–3,500 Peter Harrington

This is a deluxe issue of 750.

Arthur Rackham (illustrator), *The Legend of Sleepy Hollow*, by Irving Washington, published by George G. Harrap & Co, London, 1928, 4°, signed by Rackham, edition of 250, pictorial endpapers, 8 colour plates, top edge gilt, vellum, gilt titles and decoration.

£2,500–2,750 Peter Harrington

W. Heath Robinson, *Hunlikely!*, published by Duckworth, London, first edition, 1916, 9¾ x 8in (25.5x 20.5cm), 24 full-page illustrations and cartoons, cloth spine, pictorial boards.

£100–120 Barter Books

Sacheverel Sitwell and William Blunt, *Great Flower Books 1700–1900*, published by Collins, 1956, 20 x 14in (51 x 35.6cm).

£300–350 George Bayntun

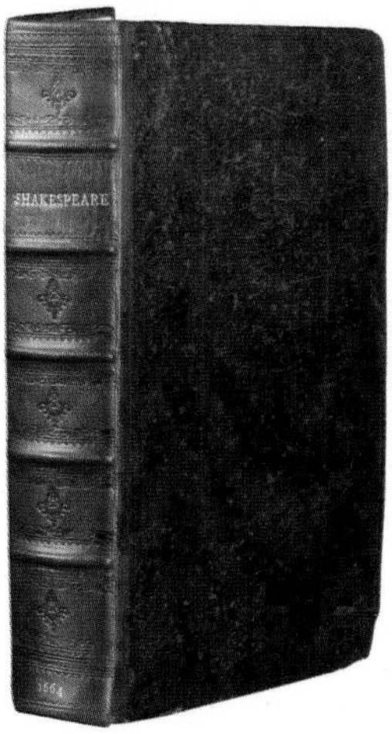

William Shakespeare, *Comedies, Histories and Tragedies*, published for Philip Chetwind, 1664, 2°, 3 parts in 1 vol, second issue, woodcut head-pieces and initials, mottled calf, upper and lower covers with blind fillets and decorative borders, rebacked, new endpapers.

£28,000–34,000 Sotheby's

This is the third folio of Shakespeare's plays, generally regarded to be the rarest of the 17th-century folio editions. An unknown number of copies are thought to have been destroyed in the Great Fire of London of 1666. The third folio is a page-for-page reprint of the second edition (1632) as far as the text is concerned. This second issue adds seven plays at the end, the last six of which are spurious, although the first, Pericles, appears here for the first time in any of the folio editions.

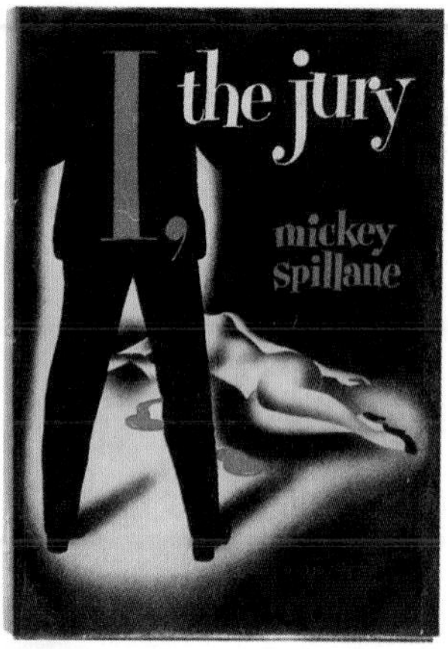

Mickey Spillane, *I, the Jury*, published by E. P. Dutton & Co, first edition, 1947, New York, 8°, bookplate signed by author, dust jacket, minor restoration.

£800–1,000 Bloomsbury

Gertrude Stein, *Chicago Inscriptions*, privately printed for Bobsy Goodspeed, Chicago, first edition, 1934, 8°, wire-stitched.

£1,100–1,300
Peter Harrington
This is a very rare book, apparently one of less than 50 copies distributed as a Christmas card by the wife of the noted bookseller Charles Goodspeed.

George Tate, *The History of the Borough, Castle and Barony of Alnwick*, 1866–69, 8¾ x 5½in (22 x 14cm), 2 vols, 21 plates and plans, half-leather with cloth board

£450–500 Barter Books

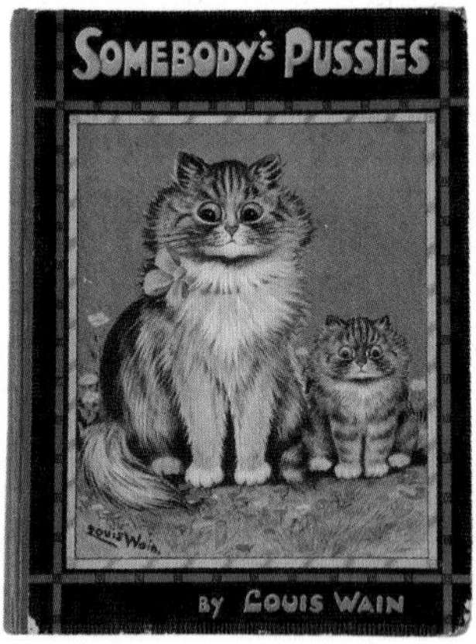

Louis Wain, *Somebody's Pussies*, published by Raphael Tuck & Sons, London, 1925, 10 x 8in (25.5 x 20.5cm).

£700–800 Biblion

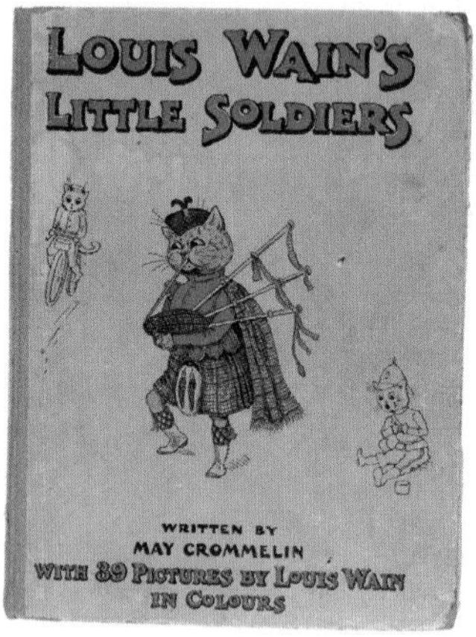

Louis Wain (illustrator), *Little Soldiers*, by May Crommelin, published by Hutchinson, London, c1930, 10 x 8in (25.5 x 20.5cm).

£400–450 Biblion

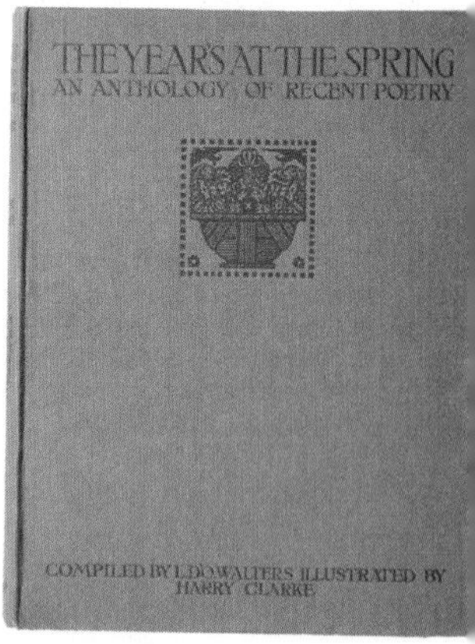

L. D'Oyly Walters (compiler), *The Year's at the Spring – an Anthology of Recent Poetry*, illustrated by Harry Clarke, published by George G. Harrap & Co, London, 1920, 10½in (26.5cm) high.

£280–320 Vanessa Parker

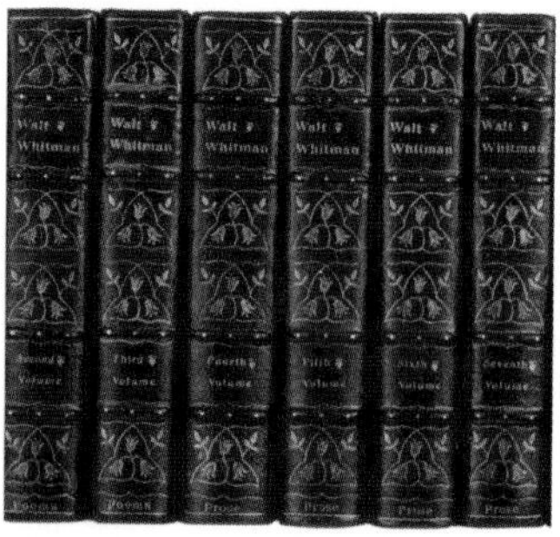

Walt Whitman, *The Complete Writings*, published by G. P. Putnam's Sons for the Knickerbocker Press, New York and London, 1902, large 8°, 10 vols, edition of 32 sets, signed by the publisher, marbled endpapers, frontispieces, tissue guards, top edges gilt, morocco, gilt titles and decoration.

£16,000–18,000 Peter Harrington
These volumes were published just ten years after Whitman's death and issued under the editorial supervision of his literary executors, with additional bibliographical and critical material prepared by Oscar Lovell Triggs. This edition contains a page of Whitman's manuscript and a notarized statement dated 19 May 1902 authenticating the manuscript.

Oscar Wilde, *The Happy Prince and Other Tales*, illustrated by Walter Crane and Jacomb Good, published by David Nutt, London, 1888, 4°, edition of 75, signed by Wilde and Nutt, handmade paper, publisher's paper binding over card, cloth sleeve and slipcase with calf spine and gilt titles.

£8,500–9,500 Adrian Harrington

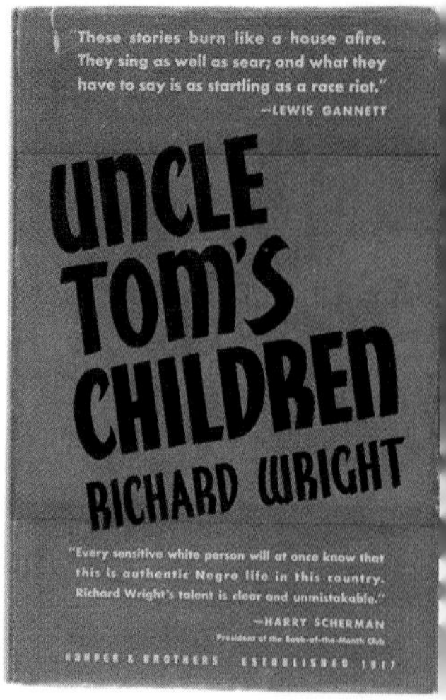

Richard Wright, *Uncle Tom's Children*, published by Harper & Bros, New York and London, first edition, 1938, 8°, cloth, dust jacket.

£600–700 Bloomsbury
This book is extremely scarce with its dust jacket.

MAPS & ATLASES

WORLD

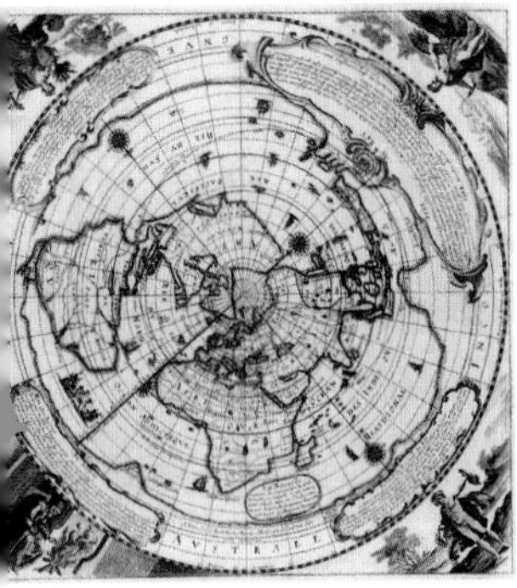

uis de Mayerne-Turquet, an engraved and nd-coloured map of the world, North Pole ojection, France, Paris, 1648, ½in (44.5cm) square.

2,250–2,750 **Sotheby's**

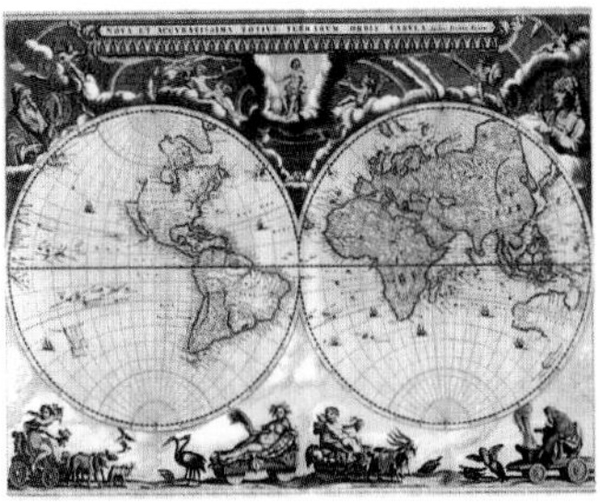

Jan Blaeu, *Nova et Accuratissima totius Terrarum Orbis Tabula*, an engraved and hand-coloured map, heightened in gold, repaired, Holland, Amsterdam, 1662 or later, 16¾ x 21¾in (42.5 x 55.5cm).

£7,500–9,000
Greenslade Taylor Hunt

John Seller, an engraved map of the world, published by Mount & Page, with later hand colouring, c1675, 18 x 21in (45.5 x 53.5cm).

£4,500–5,000 **John Travers**

rank De Wit and Louis Renard, a coloured opperplate Planisphere, Holland, msterdam, 1680–1715, 7 x 11in (43 x 28cm).

1,000–1,200 **Jonathan Potter**

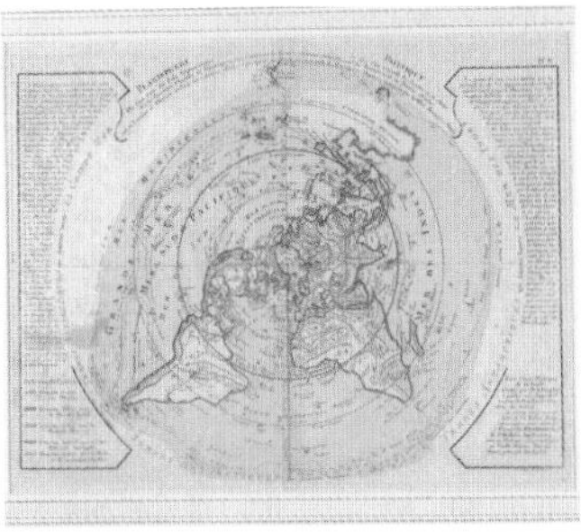

Philippe Buache and J. Dezauche, a coloured copperplate map of the world, France, c1780, 13 x 17in (33 x 43cm).

£580–650 **Jonathan Potter**

This map was orginally published by Guillaume De L'Isle in c1700 but was reissued in the late 18th century by Buache and Dezauche.

Carington Bowles, *Bowles's Universal Atlas*, published by Bowles & Carver, 1794–98, 2°, with engraved and hand-coloured maps of the world with surrounding vignettes, calf-backed boards, damaged.

£7,500–9,000 **Bloomsbury**

AFRICA & ARABIA

laudius Ptolemy, *Arabia*, a hand-coloured ouble-page woodcut map of the Arabian eninsula, slight damage, Austria, Vienna, 541, 10¾ x 18¼in (27.5 x 46.5cm).

700–850 **Sotheby's**

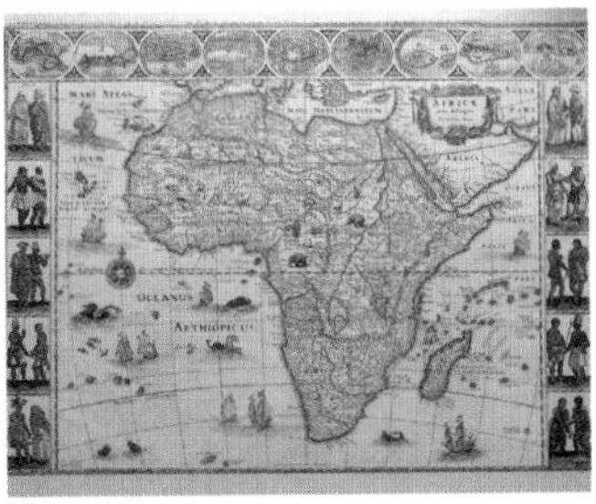

Willem Blaeu, a hand-coloured copper engraving of Africa, Holland, Amsterdam, 1645, 16 x 22in (40.5 x 56cm).

£5,800–6,500 **Antique Print Shop**

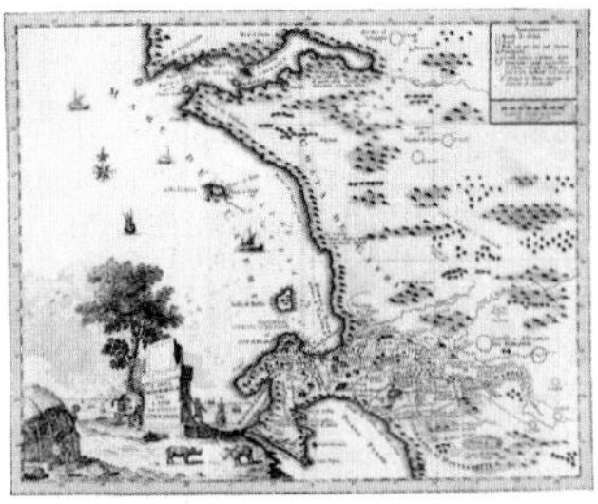

Guillaume de L'Isle, *Carta Geografica del di Buona Speranza*, an engraved and hand-coloured map of the west coast of South Africa, with title vignettes, Venice, c1750, 13 x 17in (33 x 43cm).

£280–320 **Bloomsbury**

AMERICAS

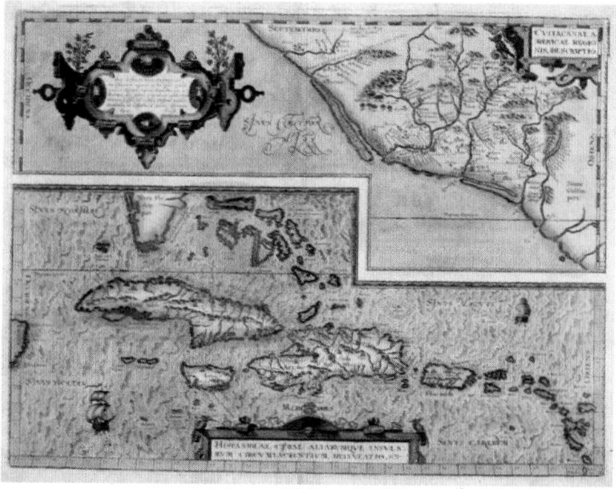

Abraham Ortelius, *Culiacanae Americae Regionis Descripio; Hispaniolae, Cubae, Aliarumuque Insularum Circumiacientium Delineato*, engraved and hand-coloured maps of western Mexico, Cuba, Haiti and Jamaica, slight damage, Belgium, Antwerp, c1579, 14¼ x 19¾in (36 x 50cm).

£850–1,000 Bloomsbury

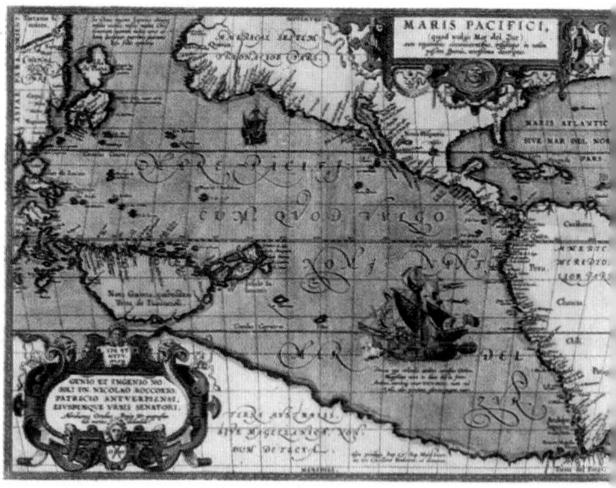

Abraham Ortelius, *Maris Pacifici*, double-page engraved and hand-coloured map of the Pacific, showing North and South America, New Guinea and Australia, Belgium, Antwerp, 1592, 13½ x 19½in (34.5 x 49.5cm).

£3,500–4,250 Sotheby's

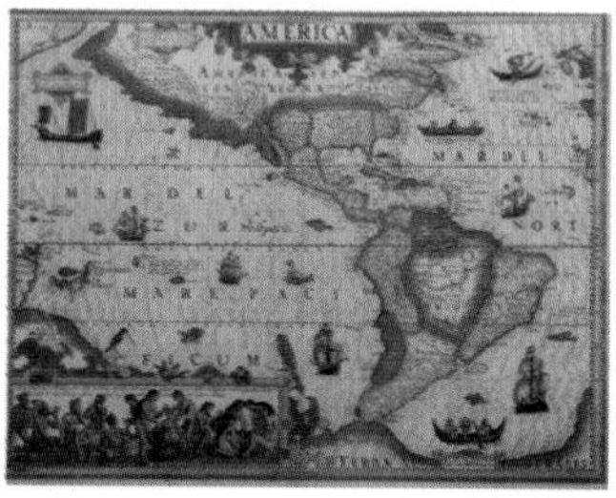

Jodocus Hondius, a hand-coloured map of the Americas, 1606–12, 15 x 20in (38 x 51cm).

£3,500–4,000 John Travers

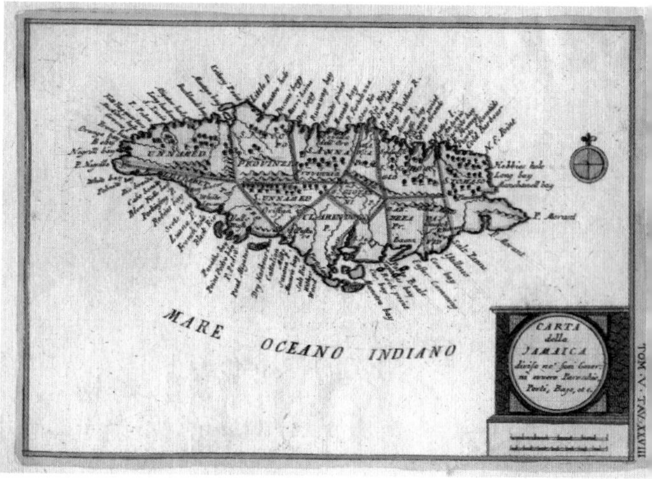

A coloured copperplate map of Jamaica, showing 13 provinces, c1740, 6¾ x 9¾in (17 x 25cm).

£320–360 Jonathan Potter

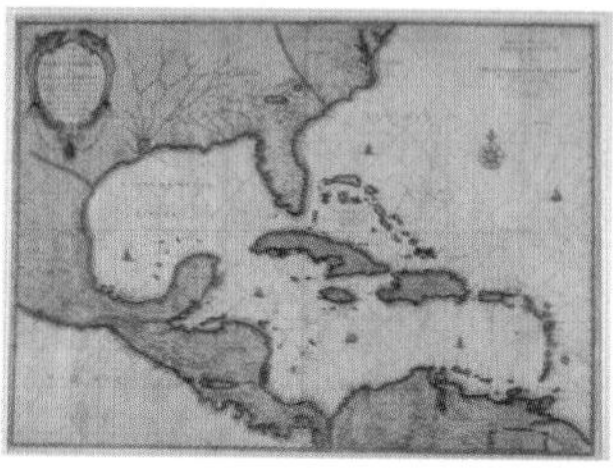

Johannes Vingboons, a coloured copperplate chart of the West Indies, published by Valck & Schenk, Holland, Amsterdam, 1655–1720, 20 x 28in (51 x 71cm).

£5,000–5,500 Jonathan Potter

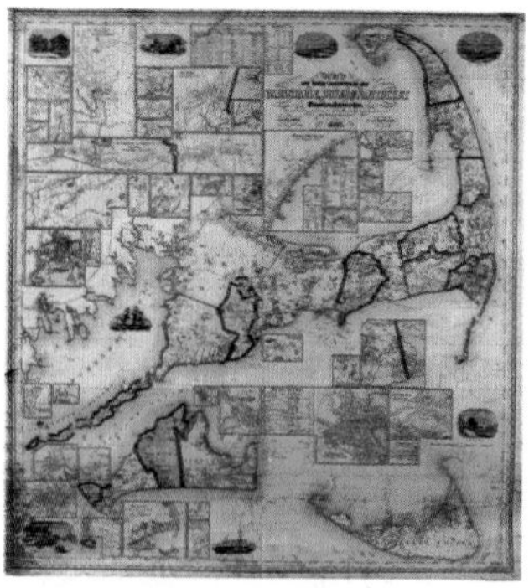

Henry F. Walling, an engraved map of Massachusetts, published by D. R. Smith & Co, America, Boston, 1858, 59 x 62in (150 x 157.5cm).

£4,000–5,000 Northeast Auctions

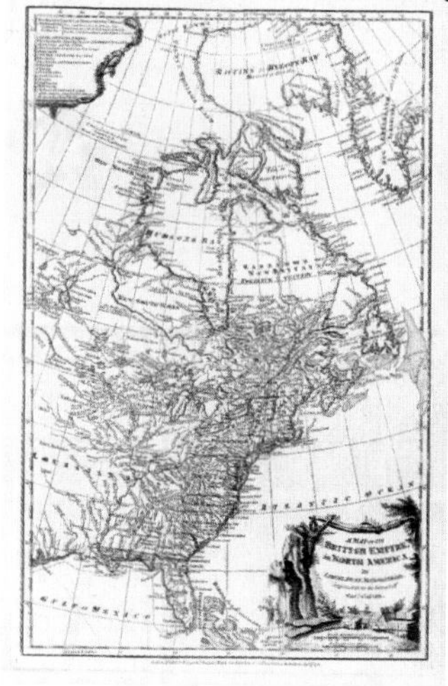

Thomas Jeffreys, *The American Atlas*, published by Sayer & Bennett, London, 1778, 2°, 30 hand-coloured copperplate maps of America, later calf.

£55,000–65,000 Freeman's

Illustrated Historical Atlas of the Counties of Lincoln & Welland, published by H. R. Page, Canada, Toronto, 1876, 2°, cloth.

£230–275 Waddington's

\SIA & AUSTRALASIA

illem Blaeu, *Asia Noviter Delineata*, an
graved and hand-coloured map of Asia,
ıstrated with figures, city views and plans,
ght damage, Holland, Amsterdam, c1650,
¼ x 22in (41.5 x 56cm).

1,800–2,200 Bloomsbury

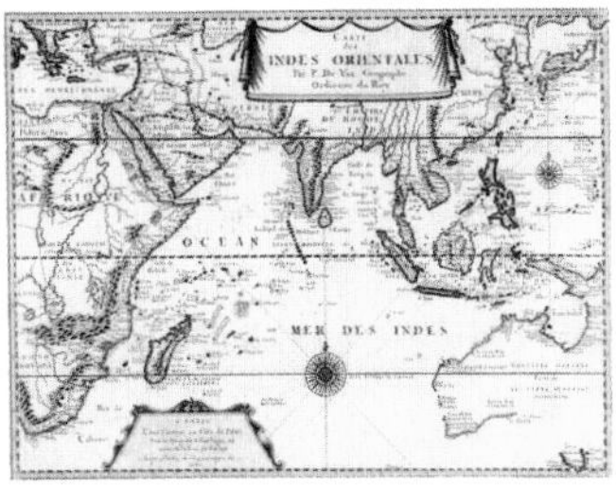

Pierre du Val, *Carte des Indes Orientales*, an engaved and hand-coloured double-page map of the Indian Ocean from the Cape of Good Hope to Australia, France, Paris, 1661, 15½ x 21in (39.5 x 53.5cm).

£750–900 Sotheby's

Du Val's map is one of the earliest maps in a terrestrial atlas to show Australia defined by Abel Tasman's two voyages c1643. Abel Tasman was the first recorded European to reach New Zealand and Tasmania.

Giovanni Maria Cassini, *La Nuova Zelanda Delineata Sulle Osservazioni del Capitan Cook*, an engraved and hand-coloured map of New Zealand, with vignette of a ship, officers and natives, Italy, Rome, 1798, 19 x 13¾in (48.5 x 35cm).

£3,000–3,500 Bloomsbury

EUROPE

map of Malta, engraved, Italy,
ome, 1565?, 10 x 7½in
25.5 x 19cm).

5,000–6,000 Sotheby's

his is an extremely rare map of
he island relating to the Great
iege of Malta in 1565 and is one
f only two copies known.

Abraham Ortelius, *Regni Hispaniae Postomnium Editiones Locvpletissima Descriptio*, an engraved and hand-coloured map of Spain and Portugal, illustrated with ships and sea monsters, damaged, Belgium, Antwerp, 1598 or later, 19½ x 15in (38 x 49.5cm).

£300–350 Bloomsbury

Abraham Ortelius, *Europae*, an engraved and hand-coloured map, Belgium, Antwerp, c1603, 13½ x 18½in (34.5 x 47cm).

£650–800 Greenslade Taylor Hunt

Henricus Hondius, *Novissima Russiae tabula*,
an engraved and hand-coloured map of
Russia, after Isaac Massa, some damage and
epair, Holland, Amsterdam, c1633, 18½ x
21¾in (47 x 55.5cm).

£400–500 Sotheby's

Joan and Willem Blaeu, *Cyprus Insula*, an engraved and hand-coloured map of Cyprus, with a female figure in a shell chariot harnessed to two swans, Holland, Amsterdam, 1655, 15¼ x 19¾in (38.5 x 50cm).

£1,000–1,200 Bloomsbury

Claes Janszoon Visscher, a hand-coloured map of Germany, Holland, Amsterdam, c1660, 19 x 23in (48.5 x 58.5cm).

£450–500 Swan at Tetsworth

Willem Blaeu, *Tabula Russiae*, a double-page engraved and hand-coloured map of Russia, after Hessel Gerritsz, inset with a plan of Moscow, Holland, Amsterdam, 1664, 16¾ x 21½in (42.5 x 54.5cm).

£1,600–2,000 Sotheby's

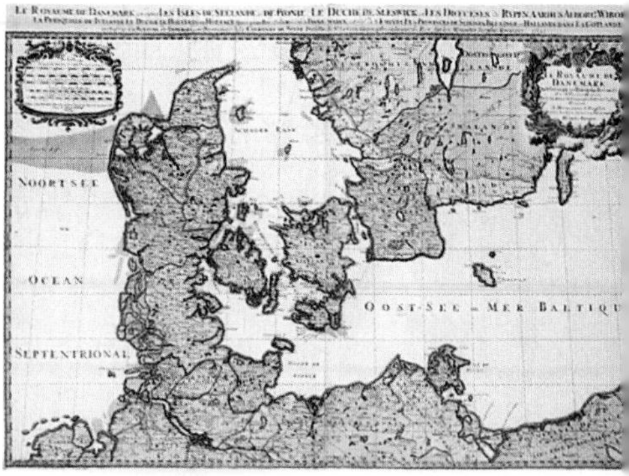

Nicolas Sanson, *Le Royaume de Danemark, Subdivisé en ses Principales Provinces*, an engraved and hand-coloured map of Denmark, with northern Germany and southern Sweden, slight damage, France, Paris, 1692, 23 x 34¾in (58.5 x 88.5cm).

£200–250 Bloomsbury

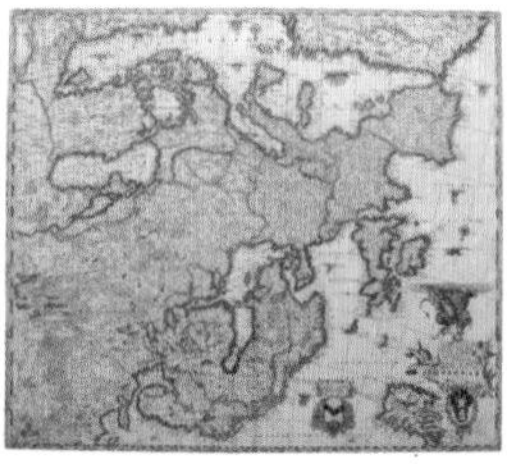

Philip Lea, a map of Europe, London, 1690, 19 x 22in (48.5 x 56cm).

£750–850 John Travers

Frederic de Wit, a map of Italy, Holland, Amsterdam, c1707, 19 x 22in (48.5 x 56cm).

£350–400 John Travers

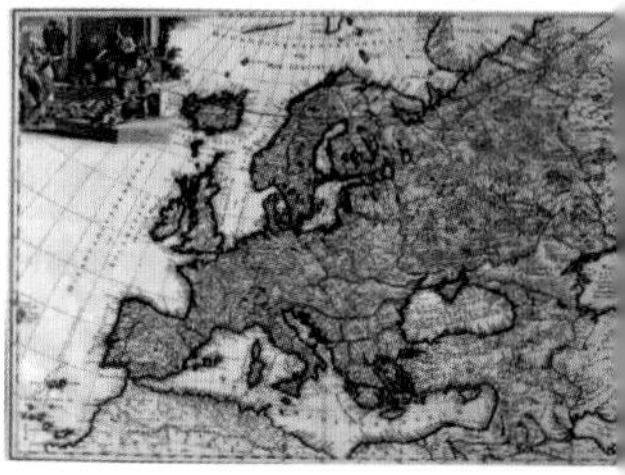

Pieter Van Der Aa, *Europa In Praecipius Ipsiu Partes*, a coloured copperplate map of Europ with allegorical cartouche by Jan Goeree, Holland, Leiden, 1713, 19½ x 25¾in (49.5 x 65.5cm).

£1,200–1,400 Jonathon Potter

Hermann Moll, an engraved and hand-coloured map of Russia, inscribed 'To his most Serene and August Majesty Peter Alexovitz absolute lord of Russia', London, 1728, 23¾ x 38½in (60.5 x 98cm).

£6,500–8,000 Sotheby's

Nolin and Tillemont, a coloured map of Denmark and Norway, France, 1749, 19¾ x 22½in (50 x 57cm).

£550–650 Bukowskis (F)

Isaak Tirion, *Carta Geografica del Regno di Corsica*, an engraved and hand-coloured map of Corsica with vignette of a coastal scene, Holland, Amsterdam, mid-18thC, 13½ x 17¼in (34.5 x 44cm).

£230–275 Bloomsbury

Isaak Tirion, *Carta Geografica del Governo della Provenza*, an engraved and hand-coloured map of Provence, with vignette of a coastal scene, Italy, Venice, mid-18thC, 13½ x 17½in (34.5 x 44.5cm).

£150–180 Bloomsbury

;REAT BRITAIN & IRELAND

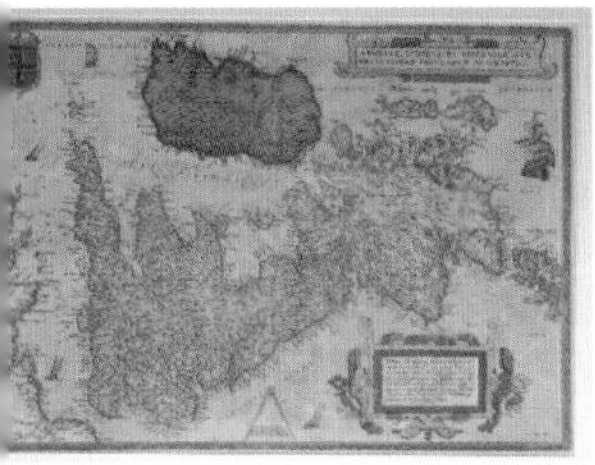

;aham Ortelius, a map of the British Isles, ;gium, Antwerp, c1584, x 20in (35.5 x 51cm).

50–850 John Travers

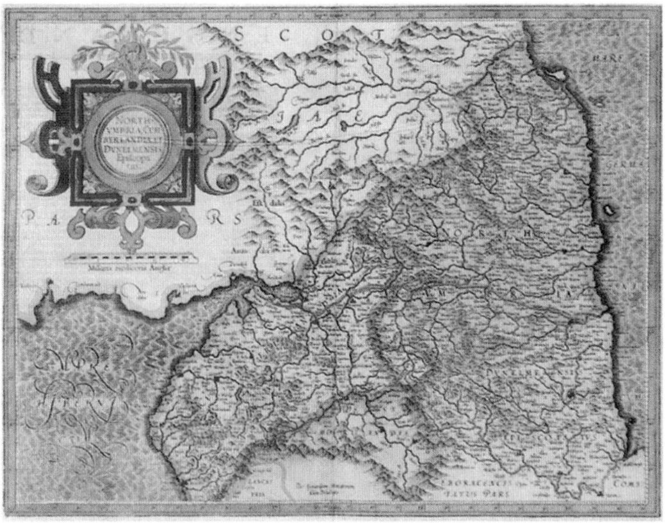

Gerard Mercator, *Northumbria, Cumberlandia, et Dunelmensis Episcopatus*, Holland, Amsterdam, 1595 or later, 14¼ x 18¼in (36 x 46.5cm).

£250–300 Bloomsbury

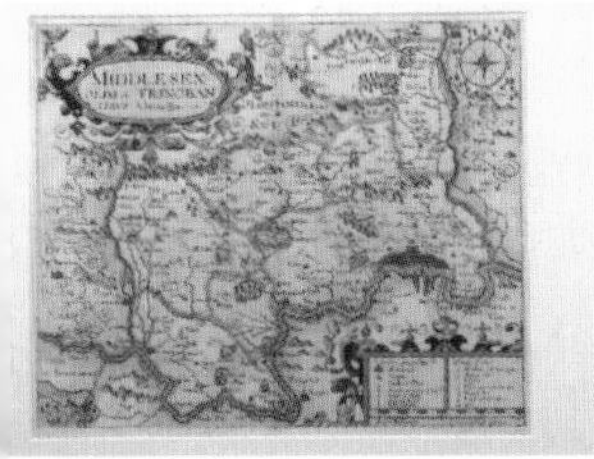

'iam Hole, a map of Middlesex, c1610, x 14in (28 x 35.5cm).

00–330 John Travers

lliam Kip and John Norden, a hand-coloured and engraved map of 'tfordshire, with grapes watermark, c1610, 11 x 13½in (28 x 34.5cm).

40–170 Sworders

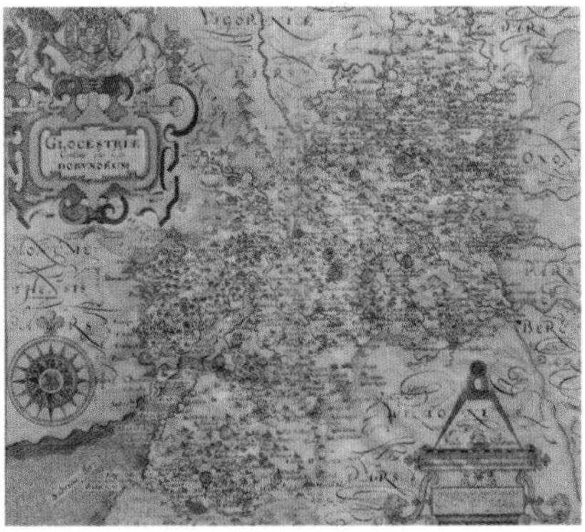

Christopher Saxton and John Norden, *Glocestriae*, an original county map of Gloucestershire taken from the 1607 Latin edition of Camden's *Britannia*, engraved by William Hole and William Kip, 1607, 12 x 13in (30.5 x 33cm).

£300–325 Swan at Tetsworth

The maps in the 1607 edition of Camden's Britannia *were reprinted in 1610 and again in 1637. Editions can be dated by looking at the reverse. The 1607 edition has Latin writing on the back but the 1610 edition does not, and 1637 has a map number on the lower corner.*

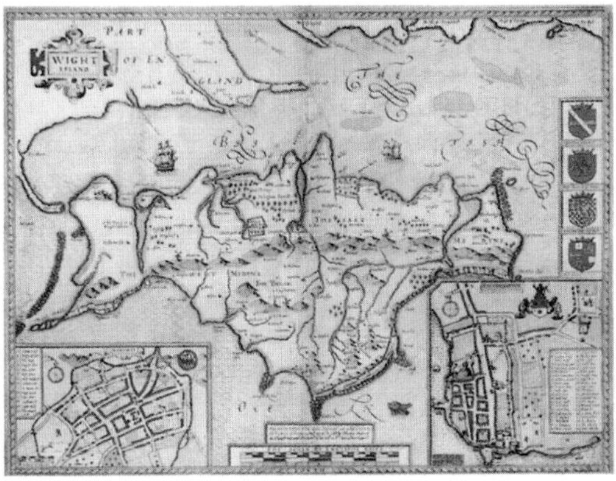

.n Speed, *Wight Island*, an engraved and hand-coloured map of the Isle of ;ght, with inset plans of Newport and Southampton, published by William White, tored, slight damage, c1614, 15½ x 20½in (39.5 x 52cm).

30–275 Greenslade Taylor Hunt

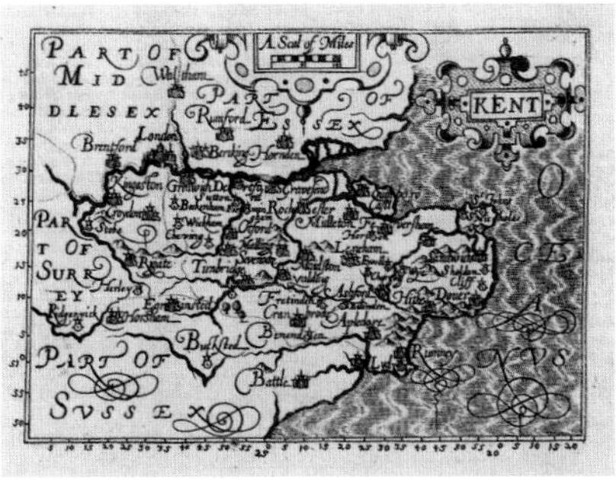

William Camden and John Bill, *The Abridgment of Camden's Britannia with the maps of severall shires of England and Wales*, London, 1626, small oblong 4°, engraved pictorial title, general map and 51 county maps, disbound.

£10,000–12,000 Sotheby's

This copy includes the general map A Tipe of England *which is not present in some copies. The maps are the earliest known county maps to bear longitudinal markings.*

Joan and Willem Blaeu, *Scotiae Provintiae, inter Taum Fluvium et Septentrionales oras Angliae*, an engraved and hand-coloured map of southern Scotland, Holland, Amsterdam, c1630 or later, 17½ x 21in (44.5 x 53.5cm).

£175–200 Bloomsbury

Christopher Saxton & John Norden, a county map of Kent, from the 1637 English edition of Camden's *Britannia*, engraved by William Hole and William Kip, 1637, 12 x 15in (30.5 x 38cm).

£300–330 Swan at Tetsworth

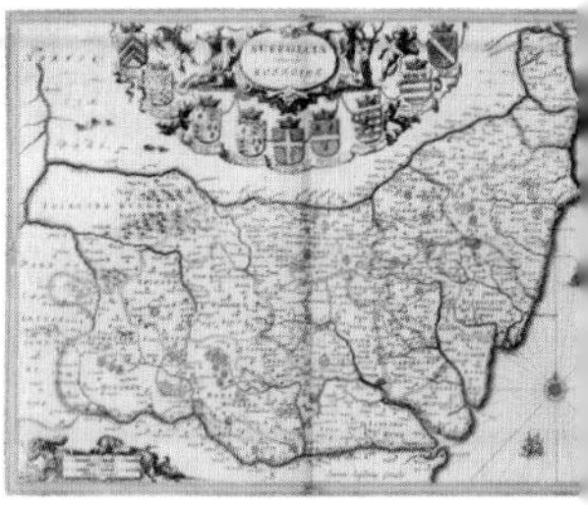

Jan Jansson, *Suffolcia, Vernacula Suffolke*, engraved and hand-coloured map of Suffolk, putti, deer and coats-of-arms, Holland, Amste 1644 or later, 15¼ x 19¾in (38.5 x 50cm).

£240–280 Bloomsbury

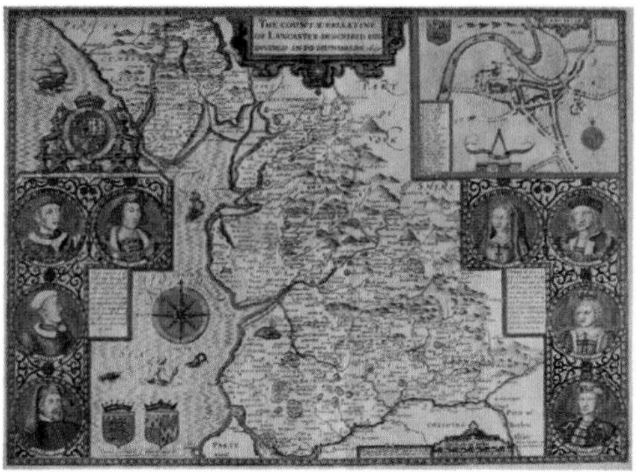

John Speed, *The Countie Pallatine of Lancaster, Described and Divided into Hundreds*, Jodocus Hondius' map of Lancashire, engraved and hand-coloured, with inset plan of Lancaster, portrait medallions of Houses Lancaser and York and a compass, 1646, 15¼ x 20¼in (38.5 x 51.5cm).

£450–550 Bloomsbury

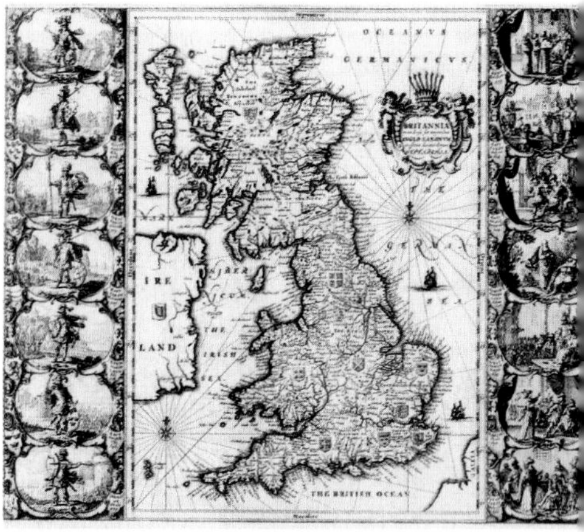

Jan Jansson, *Britannia prout divisa fuit temporibus Anglo-Saxonum, praesertim durante illorum Heptarchia*, a double-page map of the British Isles, based on Blaeu with 14 vignettes of Anglo-Saxon histor Holland, Amsterdam, 1649, 16¾ x 20¾in (42.5 x 52.5cm).

£1,000–1,200 Sotheby's

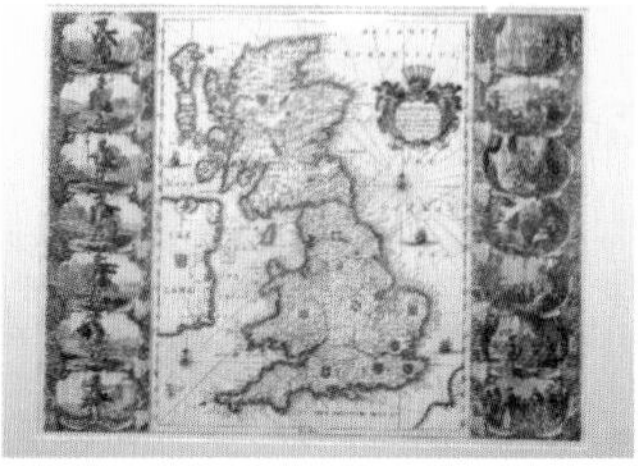

Jan Jansson, *Heptarchy (Saxon division of the British Isles)*, Holland, Amsterdam, c1652, 17 x 21in (43 x 53.5cm).

£2,000–2,400 John Travers

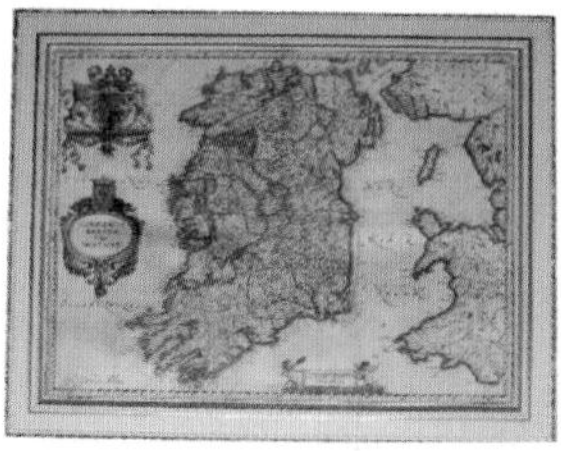

Joan Blaeu, a hand-coloured map of Ireland, Holland, Amsterdam, 1654, 16 x 20in (40.5 x 51cm).

£1,100–1,250 Neptune Gallery

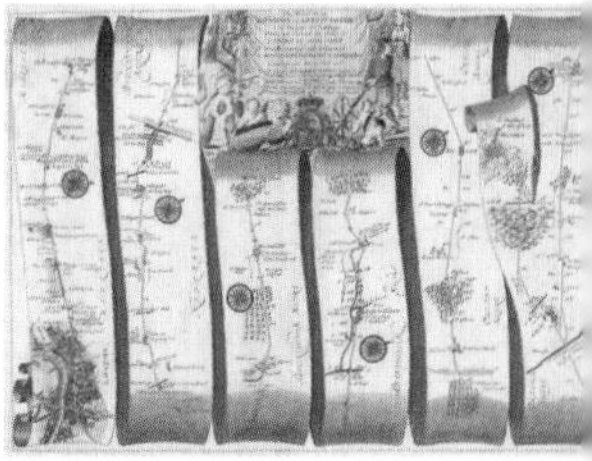

John Ogilby, *The Road From London to Aberistwith*, sheet 1, the section from Lond to Oxford, an engraved and hand-coloured map, c1675, 12¾ x 17¼in (32.5 x 44cm).

£140–175 Bloomsbury

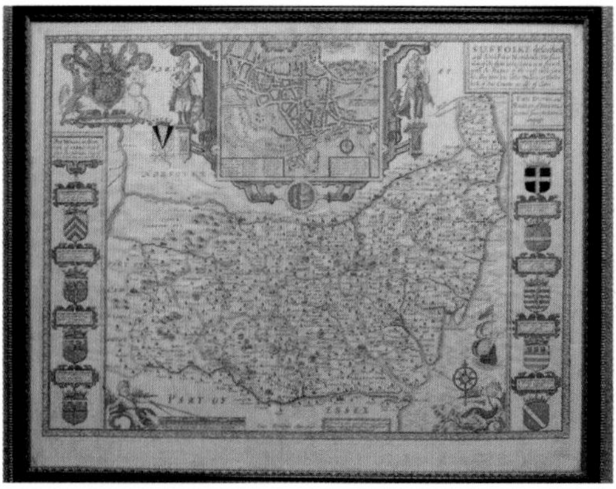

John Speed, *Suffolke*, a hand-coloured county map from *Theatre of the Great Britaine*, with inset plan of Ipswich and arms of the noble families of the island, c1676, 15 x 20in (38 x 51cm).

£550–620 Swan at Tetsworth

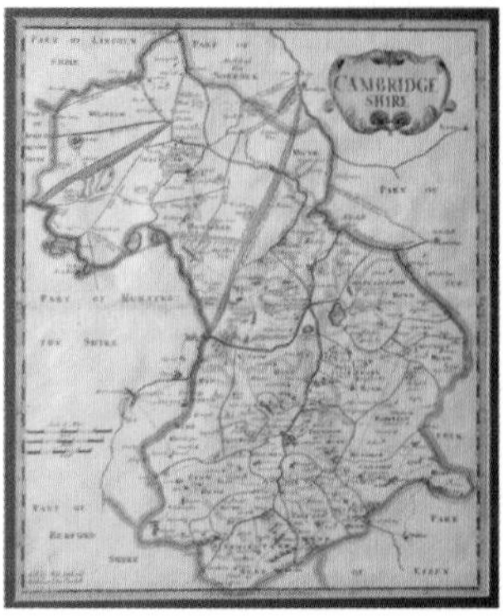

Robert Morden, *Cambridgeshire*, hand-coloured county map of Cambridgeshire from Gibson's revised edition of Camden's *Britannia*, c1695, 16 x 14in (40.5 x 35.5cm).

£100–120 Swan at Tetsworth

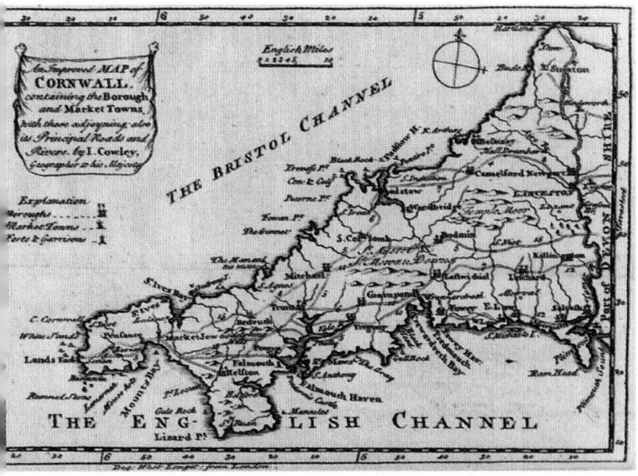

ɔert Dodsley and John Cowley, *The Geography of England*, first edition, 1744, 3 engraved general maps and 52 county maps, all folding, gilt calf, slight damage.
,800–2,200 Sotheby's

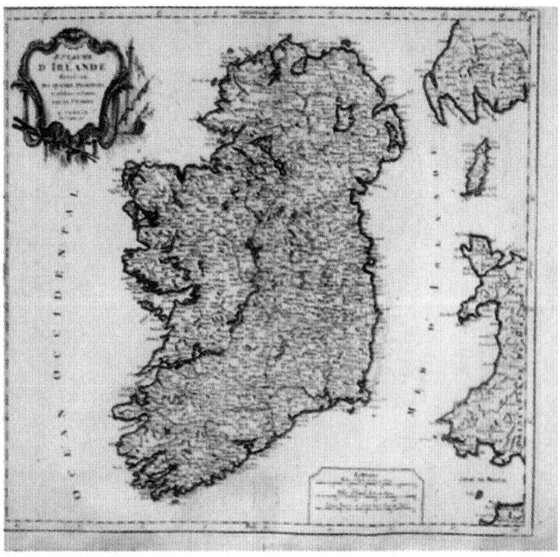

François Santini, *Royaume d'Irlande*, Italy, Venice, 1778, 20 x 22½in (51 x 57cm).
£600–700 Mealy's

'OWN & CITY PLANS

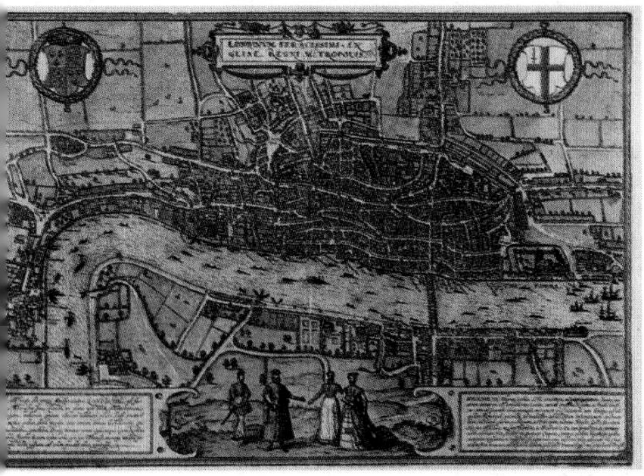

org Braun and Franz Hogenberg, *Londinum Feracissimi Angliae ɲni Metropolis*, an engraved and hand-coloured double-page spective plan, Germany, Cologne, c1590, 11¾ x 19in (30 x 48.5cm).
,750–5,750 Sotheby's

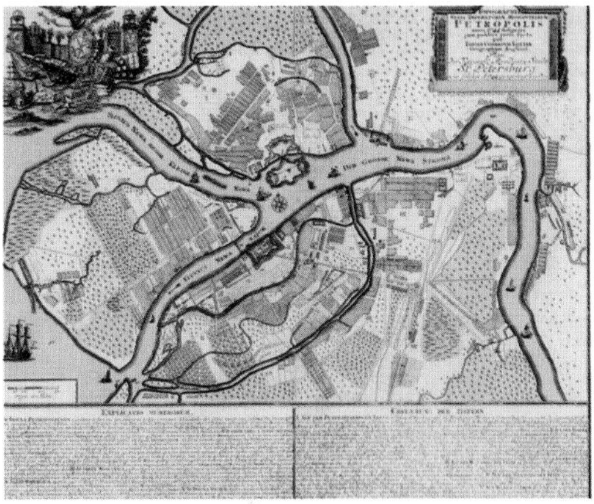

Tobias Conrad Lotter, *Petropolis*, a coloured map of St Petersburg, Germany, 1744, 20¼ x 22¾in (51.5 x 58cm).
£700–850 Bukowskis (F)

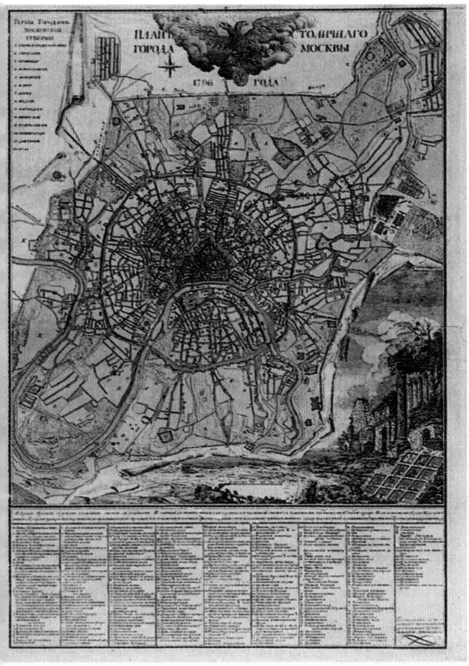

ɿofei Polezhaiv, *Plan Stolichnago Goroda Moskvy*, a double-page ɪraved broadsheet plan of Moscow, with detailed key, Russia, ɔscow, 1796, 30 x 19¼in (76 x 49cm).
,500–4,250 Sotheby's

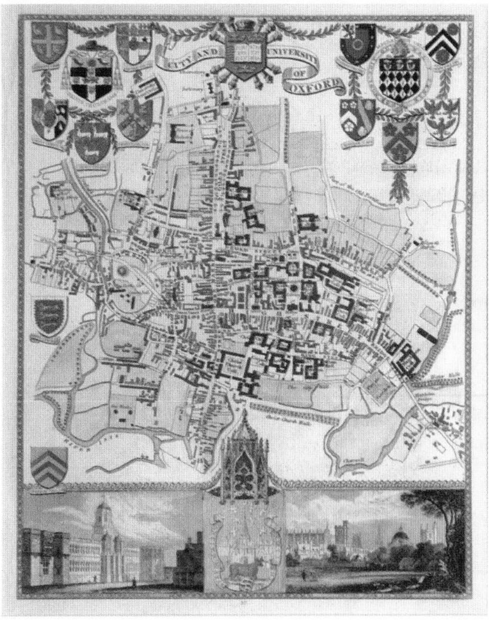

Thomas Moule, an engraved and hand-coloured map of Oxford, c1845, 10 x 8in (25.5 x 20.5cm).
£80–90 John Travers

MUSIC

CYLINDER MUSICAL BOXES

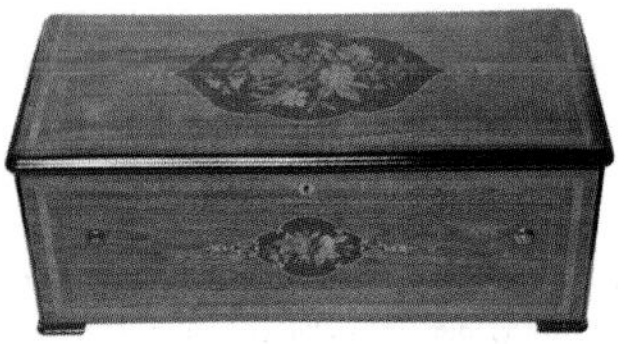

A cylinder musical box, by Weil & Harburg, playing ten airs, with drum bells and castanet, retailer's label for Van Grusen, Switzerland, Geneva, c1870, 26in (66cm) wide.

£5,800–6,500 Vanbrugh House

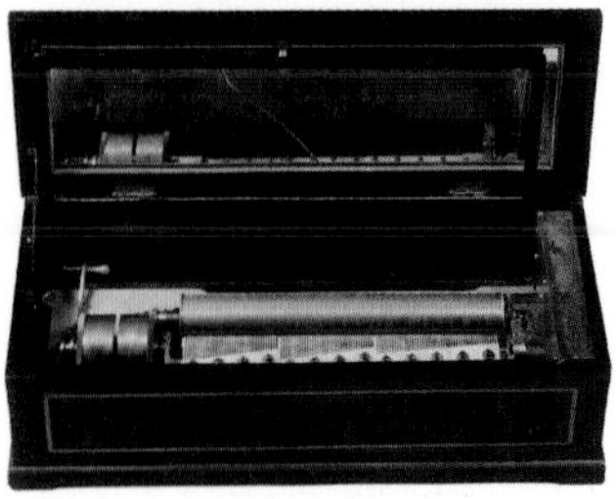

A Sublime Harmony cylinder musical box, playing eight airs on four combs, with a lever-wound double motor, the rosewood case with ebonized mouldings, brass stringing and later brass handles, Switzerland, c1875, 31in (78.5cm) wide.

£1,200–1,500 Sotheby's

A Tunbridge ware musical box, playing thr airs, c1880, 5in (12.5cm) wide.

£340–380 Worcester Antiques

A musical box and butterflies automaton, playing eight airs, with three bells, in an inlaid rosewood case, Switzerland, c1895, 18in (45.5cm) wide.

£1,500–1,650 Worcester Antiques

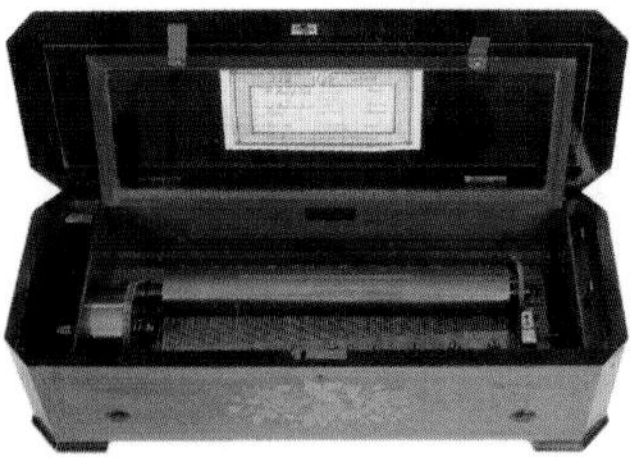

A cylinder musical box, playing six airs, with a lever-wound movement, in a rosewood and marquetry case, Switzerland, late 19thC, cylinder 12¾in (32.5cm) wide.

£1,400–1,750 Bearnes

A musical box, by G. B. & Co, playing eight airs, with three bells, in a rosewood veneere case, c1890, 13in (33cm) wide.

£1,300–1,500 Kembery Clocks

DISC MUSICAL BOXES

A Symphonion disc musical box, with 14 discs, in a mahogany case, late 19thC, 10½in (26.5cm) wide.

£380–450 Dee, Atkinson & Harrison

A Regina disc musical box, with a double comb movement and 36 discs, in a mahogany case and cabinet, America, late 19thC, 47in (119.5cm) high.

£2,300–2,800 Jackson's

A Regina disc musical box, No. 18016, wit 25 original discs and a comb, in an oak case with rope-twist mouldings, back comb missing, c1900, 21in (53.5cm) wide.

£1,250–1,500 Skinner

/IECHANICAL MUSIC

ıte George III mahogany table-top barrel an, with a rising top and removable side front panels, 11½in (29cm) wide.

50–650 Lawrence Fine Art

A singing nightingale in a cage automaton, by Bontems, France, Paris, c1880, 19in (48.5cm) high.

£4,500–5,000 Vanbrugh House

A tinplate singing bird in a cage automaton, Germany, late 19thC, 9in (23cm) high.

£180–200
Humbleyard Fine Art

ıcquered and gilt-metal singing bird omaton musical box, the sides inlaid with ıraved gilt panels, with a silvered key in form of a bird, Switzerland, c1880, (10cm) wide.

,000–2,300 Pieces of Time

A silver, enamel and carved ivory singing bird automaton musical box, Germany, 19thC, 4¼in (11cm) wide.

£2,500–3,000 Freeman's

A singing bird musical box, the tortoiseshell case with a hinged and engraved silver lid and a pierced grille, slight damage, Continental, late 19thC, 4in (10cm) wide.

£700–850 Gorringes (L)

ırass revolving cylinder sical Christmas tree stand, J. C. Eckardt, playing two ols, Germany, Stuttgart, 395, 13in (33cm) diam.

50–500
nbrugh House

A singing bird musical box, Germany, c1890, 4in (10cm) wide.

£1,800–2,000
AutomatomaniA

/urlitzer Style 125 Military Band Organ, with 116 boxed re-cut s, in an oak case, America, New York, c1956, 41in (104cm) wide.

,000–11,000 Skinner

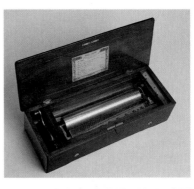

MUSICAL INSTRUMENTS

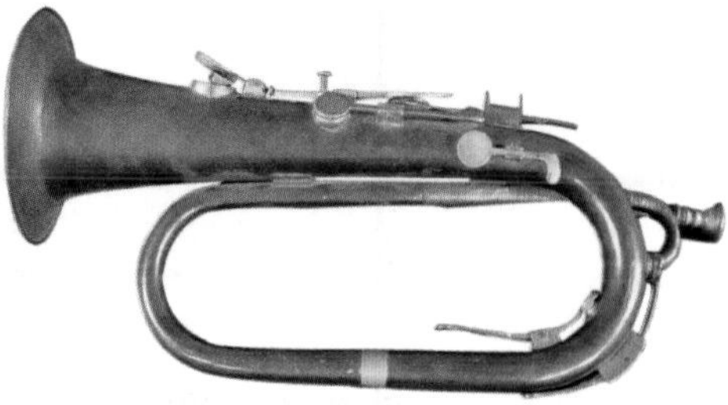

A brass bugle, with six keys and a nickel mouthpiece, c1850.
£600–700 Ewbank Auctioneers

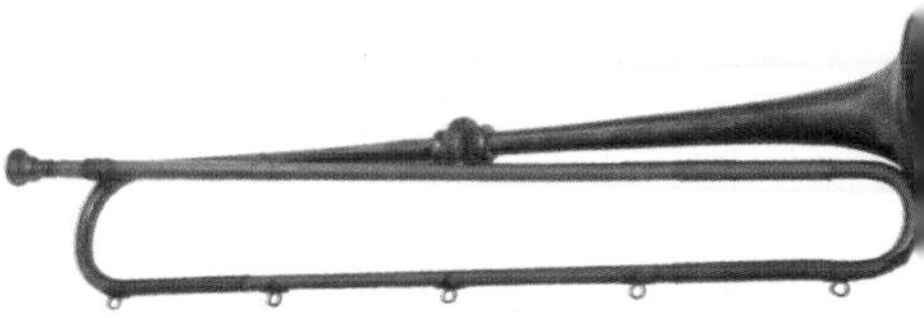

A brass herald's bugle, Ireland, c1880, 27in (68.5cm) long.
£115–130 Grimes Militaria

A cello, by William Forster II, with label, dated 1795, length of back 30in (76cm).
£13,000–15,000 Ewbank Auctioneers

A cello, probably by Joseph Kloz, Germany, late 18thC, length of back 30in (76cm).
£14,000–17,500 Sotheby's

A Neuner School cello, Germany, c1820, length of back 29½in (75cm).
£3,500–4,250 Gardiner Houlgate

A cello, by Alexis Villaume, labelled and branded, France, Troyes, c1830, length of back 30in (76cm).
£6,500–8,000 Sotheby's

A cello, by Jul. Heinr. Zimmerman, No. 1797, with maker's label, Germany, Leipzig, 19thC, length of back 30in (76cm).
£700–850 Rosebery's

A leather-bound wood cornettino, with a later mouthpiece by Christopher Monk, possibly Italy, 17thC, 16½in (42cm) long.
£5,500–6,500 Sotheby's

ɔsewood single flageolet, by William Bainbridge, London, with ivory mounts, silver pins and ılver key cover, stamped maker's marks, c1825, 8½in (21.5cm) long.

ɔ0–1,000 Sotheby's

ɔsewood flute, by Rudall & Rose, with silver mounts and keywork, c1840, ¼in (58cm) long, in original case.

,800–2,200 Sotheby's

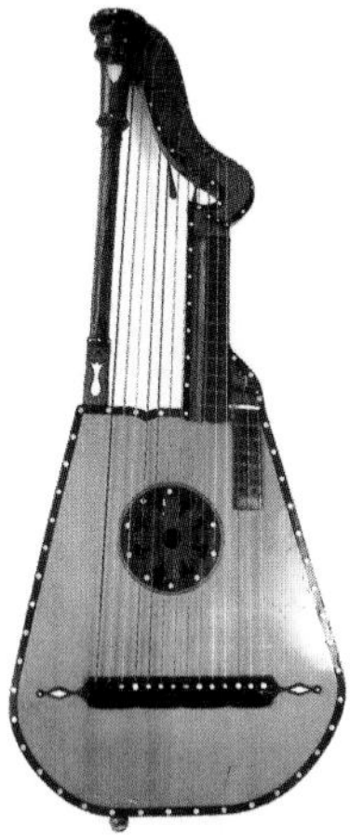

mulated rosewood, stained fruitwood and r-wood harp lute, on brass ball feet, early ıhC, 33¾in (85.5cm) long, in original case.

ɔ0–700 Rosebery's

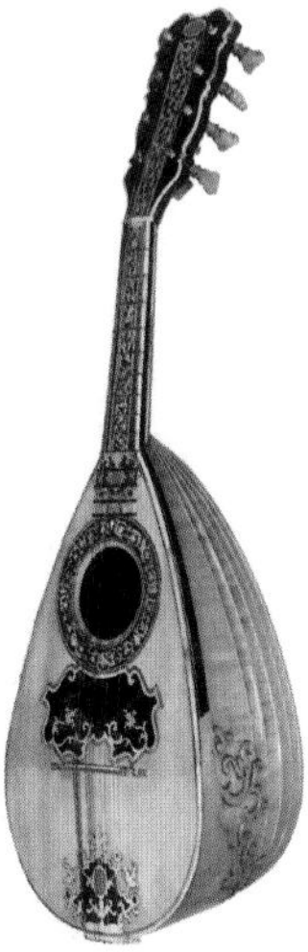

A mandolin, by Donato Filano, decorated with mother-of-pearl and tortoiseshell inlay and coral plaques, Italy, Naples, dated 1781, 22½in (57cm) long, in original case.

£7,500–9,000 Sotheby's

An ebonized, parcel-gilt, silvered and lacquered harp, with carved and painted decoration, signed 'Hermès à Paris', France, late 18thC, 65in (165cm) high.

£30,000–35,000 Sotheby's (NY)

Harps had become enormously popular in France towards the end of the 18th century. It is possible that this was due to the fact that Queen Marie Antoinette herself was an accomplished harpist and appears in a number of portraits entertaining her friends at court.

ıahogany square piano, by Clemanti & London, with chequer stringing, late ıhC, 66¼in (168.5cm) wide.

ı0–700 Dreweatt Neate (HAM)

ebonized model B grand piano, by ıway & Sons, c1896, 40in (101.5cm) ɔ, with an ebonized bench seat.

ɔ000–7,000 Jackson's

A model B grand piano, by C. Bechstein, No. 78080, retailed by Waring & Gillow, Germany, c1905, 80in (203cm) wide.

£1,150–1,350 Sworders

An ebonized baby grand piano, by Steinway & Sons, No. 272096, America, 1931, 58in (147.5cm) wide, with an ebonized bench with a needlepoint seat.

£7,000–8,000 James D Julia

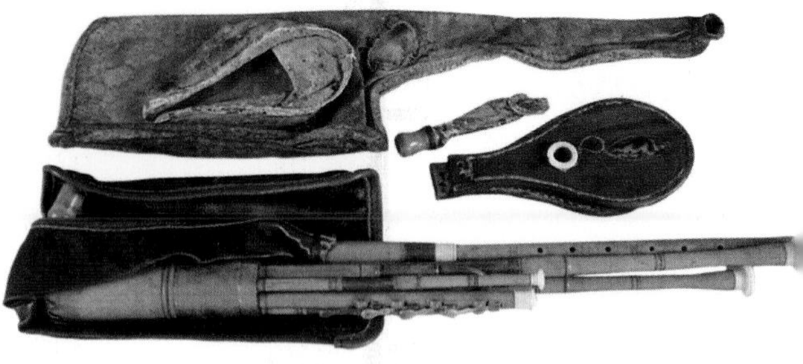

A set of boxwood, ivory, brass and leather Union pipes, by Timothy Kenna, some losses, Ireland, Dublin, c1800, 13½in (34.5cm) long.

£7,500–9,000 Ewbank Auctioneers

A leather-bound wooden serpent, by Huggett, London, with 14 brass keys and mounts, c1840, 93in (236cm) total length.

£2,000–2,500 Sotheby's

A mahogany bentside spinet, by John Harrison, London, decorated with holly and ebony stringing and mahogany crossbanding, the ebony and ivory keys inscribed 'J. Burr', dated 175 78in (198cm) wide.

£18,000–22,000 Sotheby's

A bentside is a type of spinet possibly developed c1630 by Italian harpsichord maker Girolamo Zenti.

A viola, attributed to Carlo Antonio Testore, with label, Italy, Milan, dated 1730, length of back 15½in (39.5cm).

£14,000–17,500 Sotheby's

A viola, attributed to Pietro Paolo Desideri, with label, Italy, c1900, length of back 16¼in (41.5cm), and a silver-mounted bow by Mathias Thoma, cased.

£6,000–7,000 Sotheby's

A violin, attributed to Carlo Ferdinando Landolfi, with label, Italy, 18thC, length of back 14in (35.5cm), cased.

£8,000–10,000 Sotheby's

A violin, attributed to Lorenzo Carcassi, with label, Italy, Florence, c1750, length of ba 14in (35.5cm).

£6,500–8,000 Sotheby's

olin, attributed to Vincenzo
ormo, France/Italy, late
ıC, length of back
ı (35.5cm), cased.
,000–20,000
rdiner Houlgate

A violin, by Astor, London, with label, early 19thC, length of back 14in (35.5cm), cased.
£1,400–1,750
Gardiner Houlgate

A violin, by W. A. Cross, Sheffield, with label and stamp, 19thC, length of back 14¼in (36cm), and a nickel-mounted bow, cased.
£450–550 Rosebery's

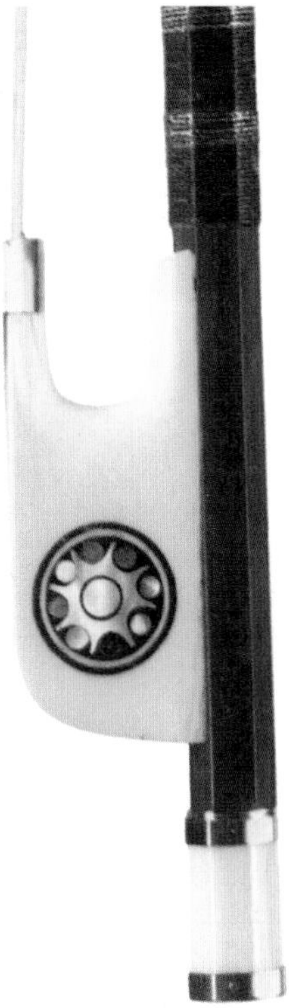

A Tourte School gold and ivory-mounted violin bow, the ivory frog inlaid with a mother-of-pearl star and dots within an ebony circle, France, early 19thC, 54.5 grams.
£4,000–5,000 Sotheby's

lver-mounted violin bow,
ames Tubbs, the ebony frog
ı pearl eyes and a silver
ılaid adjuster, stamped
er's mark, c1890, 62.5 grams.
800–4,500 Sotheby's

A silver-mounted ebony violin bow, by Joseph Alfred Lamy, the ebony frog with pearl eyes, the adjuster with two silver bands, stamped mark, France, c1900, 60 grams.
£3,800–4,500 Sotheby's

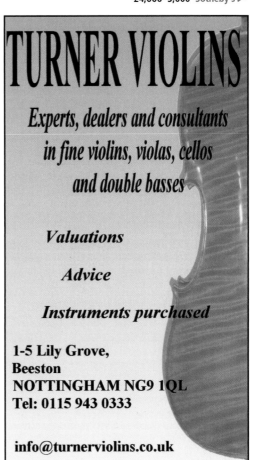

DOLLS

SELECTED MAKERS

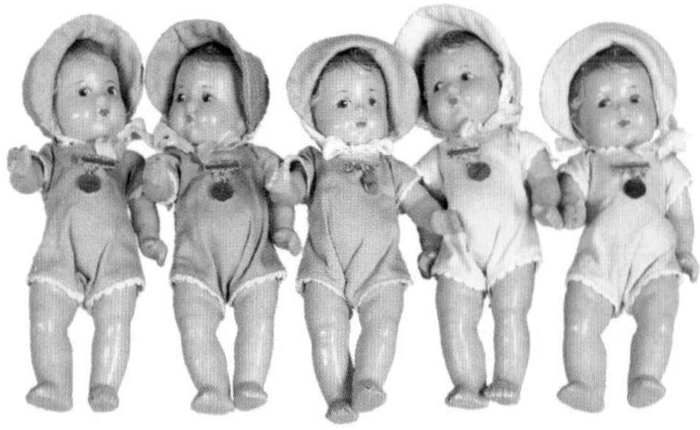

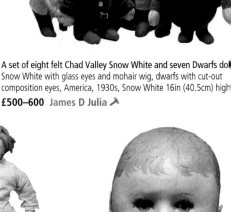

A set of Alexander Doll Co composition Quintuplet toddler dolls, with painted eyes and hair, heads and bodies marked 'Alexander', golden bar and pendant name pins later, America, 1930s, 7¼in (18.5cm) high.

£320–400 Skinner

Beatrice Behrman, whose trade name was Madame Alexander, first made cloth and then composition dolls for the Alexander Doll Co during and after WWI.

A set of eight felt Chad Valley Snow White and seven Dwarfs do Snow White with glass eyes and mohair wig, dwarfs with cut-out composition eyes, America, 1930s, Snow White 16in (40.5cm) high

£500–600 James D Julia

A Bru papier-mâché, composition and wood *bébé* doll, with weighted glass eyes, porcelain teeth, mohair wig, wearing original muslin dress with traces of *Bébé* Bru label, undergarments and leather shoes, marked, France, c1890, 19in (48.5cm) high, with original box labelled '*Bébé* Bru No. 9'.

£2,200–2,500 Theriault's

A Bru fashion doll, with Mona Lisa smile, weighted glass eyes, pierced ears, original mohair wig, kid body, wearing antique costume, original leather boots, incised mark, France, 1880–90, 18in (45.5cm) high.

£2,200–2,600 James D Julia

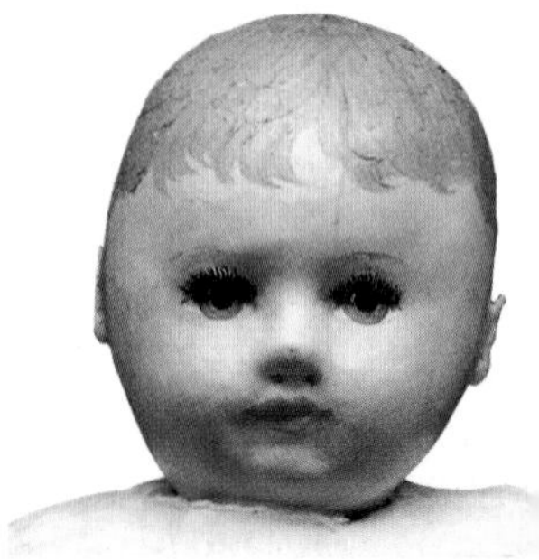

A Martha Chase cloth doll, stamped 'repaired by the Chase Stockinet Doll Co', America, 1920–30, 19½in (49.5cm) high.

£180–220 James D Julia

A François Gaultier bisque-headed bride doll, with kid leather body, France, c1870, 12in (30.5cm) high.

£1,350–1,500 Amelia Dolls

A François Gaultier bisque shoulder-head, with fixed eyes and pierced ears, original cork pate and lace bonnet, France, c1880, 3in (7.5cm) high.

£135–150 Babara Ann Newman

A François Gaultier bisque doll, with ope closed mouth, the jointed body with fused w scroll mark, France, c1890, 16in (40.5cm) h

£2,500–2,850 Amelia Dolls

rnst Heubach bisque-
ded doll, with fixed eyes and
position body, Germany,
10, 7in (18cm) high.
0–200 Amelia Dolls

A Jumeau bisque-headed doll, No. 8, with weighted glass eyes, jointed composition body, mohair wig, France, 1880s–90s, 20in (51cm) high.
£3,800–4,500 James D Julia

A Jumeau bisque-headed doll, with eight-ball-jointed wood and composition body, incised 'Déposé', France, 1886–89, 17in (43cm) high.
£3,400–3,800 Amelia Dolls

A Tête Jumeau doll, No. 7, with fully-jointed wood and composition body, France, c1890, 17in (43cm) high.
£270–300 Amelia Dolls

meau bisque-headed *bébé* doll, No. 12, with
ghted glass eyes, pierced ears, mohair wig, fully-
ted wooden body, wearing antique costume, marked,
ce, c1888, 26in (66cm) high.
800–4,500 Theriault's

A Jumeau bisque-headed *bébé* doll, with weighted glass eyes, porcelain teeth, pierced ears, mohair wig, wood and composition jointed body, wearing original costume, marked '12', France, c1895, 27in (68.5cm) high.
£2,500–3,000 Theriault's

A Jumeau doll, with sleeping glass eyes and open mouth, France, c1900, 23½in (60cm) high.
£575–700 Bertoia

ämmer & Reinhardt bisque-
ded boy doll, with sleeping
s eyes and jointed body,
many, c1900,
n (38cm) high.
50–500 Amelia Dolls

A Kämmer & Reinhardt bisque-headed doll, with sleeping glass eyes, original wig and five-piece composition body, Germany, c1910, 7in (18cm) high.
£220–250 Amelia Dolls

A Kämmer & Reinhardt bisque-headed boy doll, No. 115/A, with sleeping eyes, closed mouth, mohair wig, fully jointed composition body, wearing original costume, impressed mark, Germany, 1911–27, 16in (40.5cm) high.
£2,000–2,400 Skinner

A Kestner bisque-headed doll, No. 12, with glass eyes, composition body with fixed wrists, impressed mark, Germany, c1895, 23in (58.5cm) high.
£1,800–2,000 Doll Antiques

A Kestner bisque-headed doll, with sleeping glass eyes, original mohair wig, fully-jointed composition Handwerck body, wearing antique costume, Germany, 1890–1900, 14in (35.5cm) high.

£800–1,000 James D Julia

A Kestner bisque-headed doll, No. 171, with sleeping glass eyes and jointed composition body, Germany, c1900, 12in (30.5cm) high.

£540–600 Amelia Dolls

A Kestner bisque-headed doll, No. 171, with sleeping eyes, Germany, c1900, 13in (33cm) high.

£450–500 Pantiles Spa Antiques

A Kley & Hahn bisque-headed character doll, No. 536, with sleeping glass eyes, pierced ears, mohair wig, composition body with jointed wrists, wearing original costume, Germany, c1915, 13in (33cm) high, with original box labelled 'Mein Goldherz Baby' and additional costume pieces.

£1,500–1,800 Theriault's

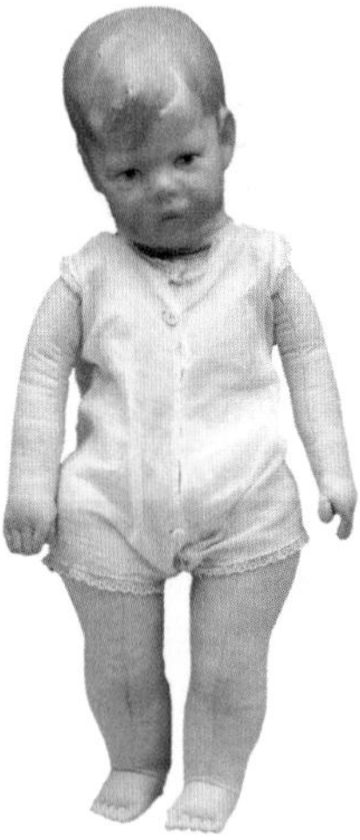

A Käthe Kruse Type 1 cloth doll, wearing original costume, slight damage, stamped mark, Germany, 1920s, 16½in (42cm) high.

£1,800–2,200
James D Julia

An Armand Marseille bisque-headed doll, Germany, 1890s, 17in (43cm) high.

£300–330
Barbara Ann Newman

An Armand Marseille bisque-headed character doll, No. 345, with painted eyes, mohair wig, Sonneberg composition and wooden fully-jointed body, wearing original costume, marked, Germany, c1912, 10in (25.5cm) high.

£700–850 Theriault's

An Armand Marseille bisque-headed baby doll, No. 351, with sleeping glass eyes and five-piece composition body, Germany, c1920, 15in (38cm) high.

£270–300 Amelia Dolls

A Rabery & Delphieu bisque-headed *bébé* doll, with jointed composition body, costume and wig later, France, 1880–90, 22in (56cm) high.

£1,300–1,600
James D Julia

chmitt et Fils bisque-headed *bébé* doll, ı glass eyes, pierced ears and hand-tied ıan hair wig, composition and wooden ted body, marked, France, c1880, ı (45.5cm) high.

000–7,000 **Theriault's**

A Schmitt et Fils *bébé* doll, with paperweight eyes, wearing antique costume, incised marks, France, 1880s, 15in (38cm) high.

£9,5000–11,500 **James D Julia**

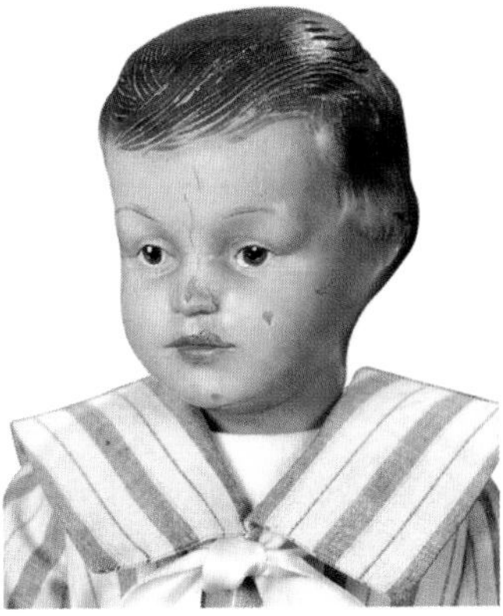

A Schoenhut wooden character doll, No. 205, with carved hair, intaglio eyes, spring-jointed body, wearing Schoenhut-style suit and original Schoenhut shoes, marked, America, c1912, 16in (40.5cm) high.

£1,100–1,300 **Theriault's**

imon & Halbig bisque-headed character l, No. 719, with weighted glass eyes, ıt-ball-jointed composition body, wearing ique clothing, wig replaced, Germany, 30–90, 19in (48.5cm) high.

,800–2,200 **James D Julia**

A Simon & Halbig bisque-headed child doll, No. 939, with glass eyes, porcelain teeth, pierced ears, antique hand-tied human hair wig, composition and wooden ball-jointed body, marked, Germany, c1890, 40in (101.5cm) high.

£4,000–5,000 **Theriault's**

A Simon & Halbig bisque-headed doll, with composition body, Germany, c1890, 4in (10cm) high.

£140–160 **Amelia Dolls**

imon & Halbig bisque-headed Oriental l, with sleeping eyes, open mouth, pierced s, original mohair wig, fully articulated nposition body, wearing embroidered silk nese costume, impressed marks, Germany, ly 20thC, 28in (71cm) high.

,000–2,500 **Skinner**

A Jules Steiner bisque-headed doll, with sleeping eyes, pierced ears, composition body, wearing original undergarments, marked, France, c1887, 16in (40.5cm) high.

£2,500–3,000
Netherhampton Salerooms

An Izannah F. Walker doll, with painted features, wearing original undergarments, jacket later, America, 1880s, 17in (43cm) high.

£4,500–5,500 **James D Julia**

UNKNOWN MAKERS

A carved chestnut doll, 17thC, 10¼in (26cm) high.

£800–1,000 Dreweatt Neate

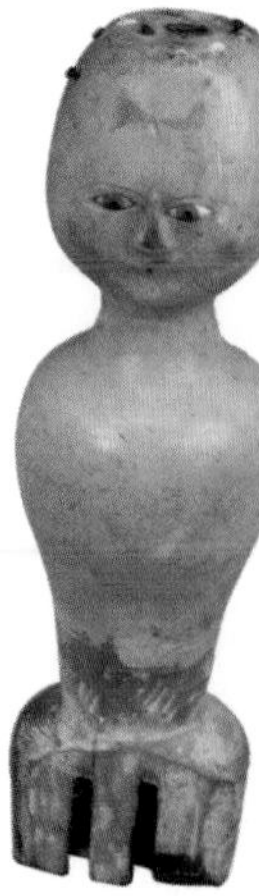

A wooden doll, with gesso face and inset enamel eyes, 18thC, 12in (30.5cm) high.

£280–350 Gorringes (L)

A George III wood and gesso doll, with glass eyes and painted features, open mouth with four teeth, jointed kid leather body, 33in (84cm) high.

£600–700 Gorringes (L)

A late Georgian painted woo doll, wearing full-length dress 12½in (32cm) high.

£450–550 Gorringes (L)

A papier-mâché doll, with brown glass eyes, painted hair, open mouth with bamboo teeth, kid body, individually wired fingers, wearing antique silk dress with embroidered trim, hat missing, France, 1850s, 14½in (37cm) high.

£950–1,100 Dolls and Lace

This doll was displayed for over 40 years in the Mary Merritt Doll Museum Collection.

A wax fairy doll, c1870, 14in (35.5cm) high.

£125–135 Amelia Dolls

A wax doll, with glass eyes, mohair wig, cloth body with bellows in torso, wax over composition limbs, wearing American dres bellows damaged, 1870s, 16in (40.5cm) h

£600–700 Skinner

A wax over composition doll, with glass eyes, cloth body and wooden limbs, late 19thC, 11in (28cm) high.

£200–240 Gorringes (L)

A bisque girl doll, with articulated head, kid-lined socket, mohair wig and peg-strung limbs, wearing original costume, France, c1880, 5in (12.5cm) high.

£1,100–1,300 Skinner

A wax and cloth doll, some parts missing, 19thC, 22in (56cm) high.

£230–275 Gorringes (L)

sque-headed boy doll, Germany, c1880,
10cm) high.
–100 **Amelia Dolls**

A bisque-headed Paris *bébé* doll, with weighted glass eyes and composition body, France, Paris, 1880–90, 28in (71cm) high.
£3,400–4,000
James D Julia

A bisque mignonette doll, with glass eyes, mohair wig, peg-jointed bisque arms with ball-joints at elbows, wearing original costume, France, c1880, 5½in (14cm) high.
£3,500–4,200 **Theriault's**

sque-headed doll, with glass
erweight eyes, wood and composition
/, Germany, c1890, 11½in (29cm) high.
50–650 **Bertoia**

sque baby doll, in layette basket, c1900,
10cm) high.
20–135 **Amelia Dolls**

A bisque doll, wearing original Chinese costume, c1915, 9in (23cm) high.
£65–75 **Pollyanna**

A composition doll, c1920,
7in (18cm) high.
£70–80 **Amelia Dolls**

TEDDY BEARS

An Ideal teddy bear, with shoe-button eyes, America, 1906–10, 13in (33cm) high.

£550–600 Teddy Bears of Witney

A Steiff mohair teddy bear, with shoe-button eyes and squeaker, Germany, c1908, 12½in (32cm) high.

£2,000–2,200 Teddy Bears of Witney

A Steiff teddy bear, with shoe-button eyes, Germany, ear button missing, c1908, 9½in (24cm) high.

£300–350 Teddy Bears of Witney

A Steiff teddy bear, with shoe-button eyes, felt pads later, ear button missing, c1910, 16in (40.5cm) high, with certificate of authenticity.

£2,000–2,400 James D Julia

A Steiff plush teddy bear, with shoe-button eyes, stitched nose, mouth and claws, excelsior stuffed, with ear button, some wear, Germany, c1915, 11½in (29cm) high.

£500–600 Dolls and Lace

A Steiff mohair teddy bear, with ear button and growler, Germany, c1920, 13in (33cm) high.

£900–1,000 Bourton Bears

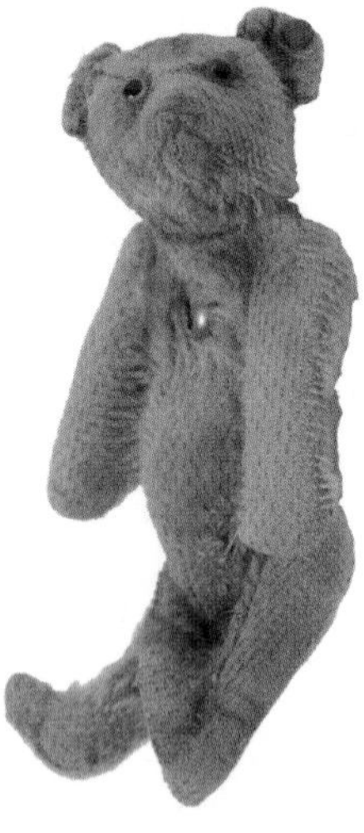

A Steiff rattle teddy bear, with glass eyes, with original bell and hooks, with ear button, Germany, c1920, 5½in (14cm) high.

£500–550 Teddy Bears of Witney

The hooks on this bear enabled it to be hung on the edge of a crib.

A mohair teddy bear, possibly France, early 20thC, 12½in (32cm) high.

£115–130 Teddy Bears of Whitney

A plush panda bear, with glass eyes, stitched nose and velvet pads, 1900–50, 24in (61cm) high.

£180–220 James D Julia

TOYS

AEROPLANES & AIRSHIPS

An Eagle tinplate 'Victory' biplane, with pilot and disc wheels, America, c1919, 5in (12.5cm) wide.

£350–420 Bertoia

A Hubley cast-iron 'America' aeroplane, propellers spin when pushed along, with two pilots, America, 1930s, 17in (43cm) wide.

£1,100–1,300 James D Julia

A Hubley 'Lindy' aeroplane, gear-assisted drive activates propeller, America, 1920s–30s, 10in (25.5cm) wide.

£1,100–1,300 James D Julia

A Kenton air mail aeroplane, America, 1920s–30s, 8in (20.5cm) wide.

£1,000–1,200 James D Julia

A Kilgore 'Sea Gull' aeroplane, America, 1930s, 8½in (21.5cm) wide.

£1,000–1,200 James D Julia

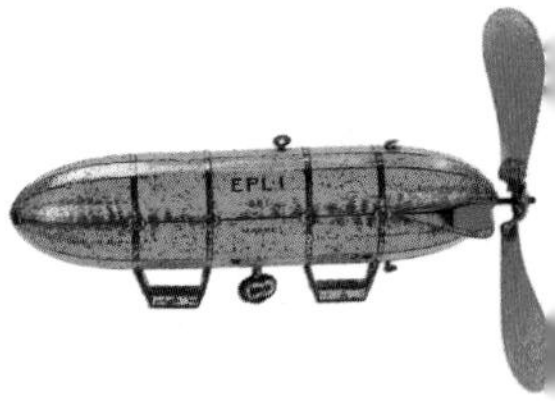

A Lehmann lithographed tin mechanical 'Los Angeles' airship, EPL model 767, Germany, c1925, 9in (23cm) long.

£450–550 Theriault's

BOATS

A J. Bekker & Zoon lithographed tin 'Holland' ocean liner, the hinged cabin opens to reveal storage space, on four wheels, Holland, c1920, 24in (61cm) long.

£2,700–3,300 Theriault's

A Bing clockwork three-funnelled liner, with GBN label, masts, rudder and guard missing, slight damage, Germany, c1920, 8¼in (21cm) long.

£175–220 Sworders

A Bowman Models aluminium and wood live steam 'Sea Jay' Super Cruiser, main mast missing, 1930s, 31in (78.5cm) long, with original box.

£1,100–1,300 Vectis

A painted metal electric-powered steamboat, c1930, 40in (101.5cm) long.

£220–240 Piccadilly Antiques

A Weeden tinplate steam-powered 'Water Witch' stear losses, America, 19thC, 12in (30.5cm) long, with original b

£3,300–4,000 James D Julia

ΛECHANICAL TOYS

Ives automaton of General ant, with open-spring chanism, in two movements General turns his head, raises cigarette holder to his lips, ws smoke through his mouth d exhales, slight restoration, erica, c1877, 14in .5cm) high.

,500–9,000 Skinner

ented by Albert H. Dean of dgeport, Connecticut in 1877, s employed a unique piston tem to produce the General's oking action. It is unusual to d a smoking automaton that ually inhales and early vertisements claimed that the omaton was capable of wing perfect smoke rings.

A Leopold Lambert musical automaton of a girl with toys, with a bisque head and forearms, worn, France, c1910, 23in (58.5cm) high.

£1,600–2,000 Bertoia

A Renou musical automaton of a Shrinking Magician, the going-barrel movement playing one air, restored, France, 19thC, 21in (53.5cm) high.

£9,000–11,000 Skinner

This is probably modelled as the Mad Hatter from Alice's Adventures in Wonderland.

A Roullet & Decamps clockwork dancing doll, with a bisque head, France, c1910, 20in (51cm) high.

£2,700–3,000 AutomatomaniA

A Schuco clockwork Charlie Chaplin, Germany, 1920s, 6½in (16.5cm) high, with original box and instructions.

£800–1,000 James D Julia

A painted cast-iron Speaking Dog money bank, stamped 'Shepards Hardware' and 'Oct 20 1885', America, 8in (20.5cm) high.

£1,600–2,000 Northeast Auctions

/ichy automaton of La scotte, with a bisque head d hands, weighted eyes and ng-barrel movement, late thC, 24in (61cm) high.

,800–4,500 Skinner

lassic Vichy automaton, this lady resents a figure from Audran's nic opera, La Mascotte, *which s popular in Paris and London tween 1880 and 1897. The sical movement plays 'La scotte Valse' and one other possibly 'Mme Boniface'.*

A Vichy papier-mâché and wood automaton of a drinking man, France, Paris, c1880, 17in (43cm) high.

£6,800–7,500 AutomatomaniA

A Wolverine clockwork metal Zilotone music box, with six metal discs, America, c1930, 8in (20.5cm) high.

£450–550 Theriault's

ROCKING HORSES

A carved wood rocking horse, on a safety stand, 19thC, 42¼in (107.5cm) long.

£500–600 Cheffins

An F. H. Ayres carved wood rocking horse, retailed by Barkers of Kensington, c safety stand, c1850, 36in (91.5cm) long.

£900–1,000 Sally's

A Victorian rocking horse, with a studded leather saddle and harness, on a safety stand, 59in (150cm) long.

£1,100–1,300 Locke & England

A Victorian wooden rocking horse, on a safety stand, 64in (162.5cm)

£2,800–3,200 John Nicholson

A painted pine rocker, c1880, 41in (104cm) long.

£330–370 Alchemy

A carved wood rocking horse, on a bow rocker, restored, c1890, 54in (137cm) long.

£1,650–1,850 Sally's

A carved wood rocking horse, on a safety stand, pillars replaced, c1900, 48in (122cm) long.

£1,350–1,500 Sally's

A G. & J. Lines carved wood rocking horse, with original thistle badge, on a bow rocker, restored, c1900, 60in (152.5cm) long.

£1,800–2,000 Sally's

TRAINS

American Flyer standard gauge President Special train set, nprising locomotive and three cars, slight damage, America, 1920s.
50–650 James D Julia

An American Flyer standard gauge Pocahontas electric train set, comprising locomotive and three cars, losses, slight damage, America, 1930s.
£1,800–2,200 James D Julia

American Flyer President Special Train set, comprising omotive, club car, Pullman, observation car, diner car, 18 pieces of ck, a transformer and several light bulbs, the four cars with original xes, with American Flyer tape/labels, America, 1940s.
,500–1,800 Skinner

A Bassett-Lowke electric three-rail 4–4–0 locomotive and tender, 'Compound', No. 1082, dated 1955, with original box and bill of sale.
£700–850 Vectis

Bing gauge 1 station and platform, slight damage, Germany, c1902, 'n (33cm) wide, with box, with a Bing clockwork bell.
,400–1,700 Vectis

A Bing clockwork tin train set, comprising a locomotive, tender, passenger car and track, German, c1915, with original box, 12in (30.5cm) wide.
£350–420 Theriault's

. M. Fallow train set, comprising locomotive, tender and two aches, with hand-painted decoration, boiler marked 'Active', aired, America, 1880s, 29in (73.5cm) long overall.
,350–1,600 Bertoia

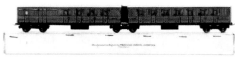

A Hornby Dublo two-coach articulated unit, comprising third class corridor coach and third class corridor brake, slight damage, 1930s, with original box.
£700–850 Wallis & Wallis

Hornby gauge 0 No. 2 Pullman set, comprising 4–4–0 LNER omotive and tender, Pullman coach and dining saloon, with track d track clips, 1930s, with box.
,000–1,200 Vectis

A Hornby gauge 0 electric E320 locomotive, dated 1938, with original box.
£3,000–3,500 Vectis
This is a rare export version of the LMS Royal Scot locomotive.

A Hubley elevated cast-iron clockwork railway set, comprising locomotive, tender and elevated steel track, America, c1895, 30in (76cm) diam.

£5,000–6,000 Bertoia

An Ives standard gauge four-wheel electric locomotive, some losses, America, 193

£1,100–1,300 James D Julia

An Ives standard gauge electric locomotive and observation car, slight damage, America, 1930s.

£250–300 James D Julia

A Lionel standard gauge electric locomotive and four cars, 'Colorado', 'California', 'New York' and 'Illinois', restored, America, 1930s.

£2,300–2,800 James D Julia

A Märklin gauge 0 clockwork steam-type locomotive, tender and two coaches, losses, slight damage, Germany, c1905.

£1,400–1,700 James D Julia

This item was produced for the American market.

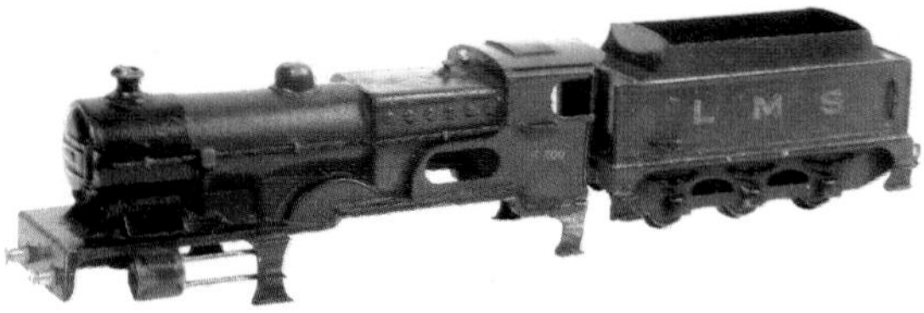

A Märklin 00/H0 gauge 4–4–0 three-rail locomotive and tender, 'Compound', made for the UK market, losses and slight damage, Germany, 1938.

£16,000–20,000 Vectis

A Märklin Paterson train station, Germany, c1910, 16¼in (41.5cm) wide.

£22,000–27,000 James D Julia

This item was produced for the American market.

An Ernest Plank gauge 1 clockwork 2–2–0 locomotive and tender, 'Union', 1930s, with original box.

£1,500–1,800 Vectis

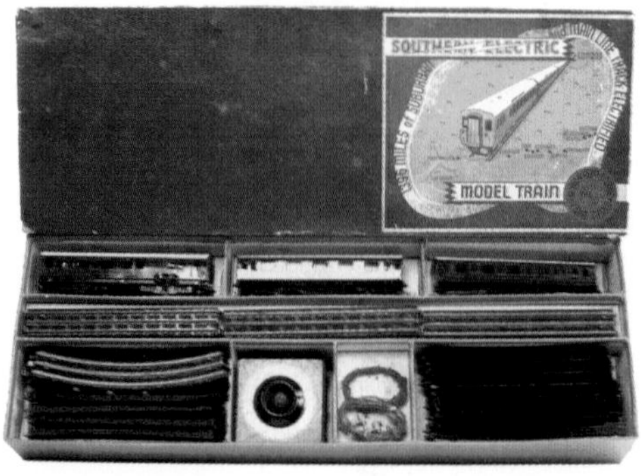

A Trix Twin Southern Electric three-car EMU, comprising a motorcoach, first clas coach, third class brake end coach, Bakelite track and a controller, late 1930s, with bo

£2,300–2,800 Vectis

VEHICLES

An Arcade cast-iron dump trunk, America, early 20thC, 7¼in (18.5cm) long.
£125–150 James D Julia

An Arcade Reo Coupe, with rumble seat, America, c1930, 9in (23cm) long.
£1,700–2,000 James D Julia

An Arcade International dump truck, with tipping bed, iron wheels and rubber tyres, steel spring missing, America, 1930s, 10¼in (26cm) long.
£380–450 James D Julia

A Bing tinplate clockwork double-decker tram, Germany, c1910, 7in (18cm) long.
£700–850 Bertoia

A Bing tinplate car and garage, Germany, c1930, 6½in (16.5cm) long.
£250–275 Roy Laycock

A Carette clockwork Open Roadster, hand-painted, with nickel headlights and rubber tyres, Germany, c1906, 11in (28cm) long.
£5,500–6,500 Bertoia

A tinplate fire wagon, probably by Morton E. Converse & Co, with buckets, ladders and bell, America, c1900, 24in (61cm) long.
£1,000–1,200 James D Julia

A Champion policeman and motorcycle, with rubber tyres, America, early 20thC, 7in (18cm) long.
100–120 Jackson's

An Eichner tinplate clockwork carriage, with glazed panels, Germany, late 19thC, 25in (63.5cm) long, with original shipping box.
£6,000–7,000 James D Julia

A Fischer tinplate wind-up racing motorcycle, Germany, c1905, 7¼in (18.5cm) long, with original box.

£11,000–13,000 James D Julia

A Günthermann lithographed tinplate clockwork Gordon Bennett racing car, drivers replaced, Germany, early 20thC, 12in (30.5cm) long.

£14,000–18,000 James D. Julia

A Hubley cast-iron Packard, with nickel-plated grille and driver, opening doors and hoods, America, 1920s, 11½in (29cm) long.

£6,500–8,000 James D Julia

A Hubley cast-iron Elgin Street Sweeper, rubber tyres replaced, America, 1920s–30s, 9in (23cm) long.

£1,250–1,500 James D Julia

An Ives tinplate clockwork Hook-Behind, the woman with a stamped brass face, the boy with cast-iron legs, repaired, America, 19thC, 17in (43cm) long.

£11,000–13,000 James D Julia

An Ives tinplate Phoenix Fire Pumper, repaired, America, 1890s, 18½in (47cm) long.

£380–450 James D Julia

A tinplate Citroën C6 two-door coupé, steering wheel with Ackermann action, with Michelin rubber tyres, France, late 1920s, 15½in (39.5cm) long.

£400–500 Wallis & Wallis

A tinplate clockwork Citroën C6 four-door saloon, steering wheel with Ackermann action, with Michelin rubber tyres, France, late 1920s, 15½in (39.5cm) long.

£630–750 Wallis & Wallis

A tinplate clockwork Citroën C4 lorry, with drop-down tailgate, steering wheel with Ackermann action, France, c1931, 17in (43cm) long.

£550–650 Wallis & Wallis

A J. R. D. Toys clockwork tinplate Citroën 2CV, c1950, with original box

£250–300 Wallis & Wallis

A Kenton touring car, c1910, America, 9in (23cm) long.
£800–1,000 **James D Julia**

A Kenton Red Devil touring car, passenger later, America, 1910–20, 8¾in (22cm) long.
£300–350 **James D Julia**

A Kenton cast-iron circus wagon, America, early 20thC, 13¾in (35cm) long.
£100–120 **Jackson's**

A Kenton sedan, with cast-iron disc tyres, America, 1920s, 8¼in (21cm) long.
£1,400–1,800 **James D Julia**

A Martin tinplate Train Tortillard, from Les Auto-Transports series, France, 1920s, 25in (63.5cm) long, with box.
£2,000–2,400 **Bertoia**

A Louis Marx tinplate Snoopy Gus wind-up fire truck, America, early 20thC, 8½in (21.5cm) high.
£550–650 **Jackson's**

A Moline Pressed Steel Co Buddy 'L' water tower, working water tank and derrick, water cap missing, America, 1920s, 38½in (98cm) long.
£1,000–1,200 **James D Julia**

A Moline Pressed Steel Co Buddy 'L' Express Line Screen Side van, with disc wheels, America, c1925, 24in (61cm) long.
£1,100–1,300 **Bertoia**

The Moline Pressed Steel Company in East Moline, Illinois began as an automobile parts manufacturer. In 1929 it began to use its pressed steel to manufacture Buddy 'L' toys. These were a great success and the company changed its name to Buddy 'L' Manufacturing Company in 1930.

A Buddy 'L' bus, with aluminium wheels, America, 1930s, 28in (71cm) long.
£5,000–6,000 **James D Julia**

A Schuco tinplate clockwork car and felt monkey, Germany, 1920s, 6½in (16.5cm) long.
£450–550 **Wallis & Wallis**

A Vindex cast-iron John Deere combine, America, c1928, 13½in (34.5cm) long.
£3,500–4,250 **Bertoia**

A Vindex coupé, with rumble seat, America, 1930s, 8in (20.5cm) long.
£800–1,000 **James D Julia**

A Whitanco tinplate clockwork bus, c1915, 14in (35.5cm) long.
£1,000–1,200 **John & Simon Haley**

An A. C. Williams cast-iron Fageol Bus, America, Ohio, c1930, 7¾in (19.5cm) long.
£100–120 **Waddington's**

A Wyandotte pressed-steel sedan and trailer, with a nickel grille, America, late 1930s, 11½in (29cm) long, with box.
£500–600 **Bertoia**

A hand-made wooden horse-drawn wagon, with tin bucket and papier-mâché driver, losses, c1900, 30in (76cm) long.
£1,300–1,600 **James D Julia**

A model of Donald Campbell's *Bluebird* racing car, lithographed signature, 1920s, 16in (40.5cm) long.
£450–550 **James D Julia**

An open touring car, with driver, Germany, 1920s, 10in (25.5cm) long.
£450–550 **James D Julia**

MISCELLANEOUS

A set of W. S. Reed Mother Goose wooden **building blocks,** in a wheeled container lithographed with nursery tales, late 19thC, 18½in (47cm) long.

£430–520 James D Julia

A wooden travelling chess board, late 19thC, 11¾in (30cm) wide.

£160–200 Bloomsbury

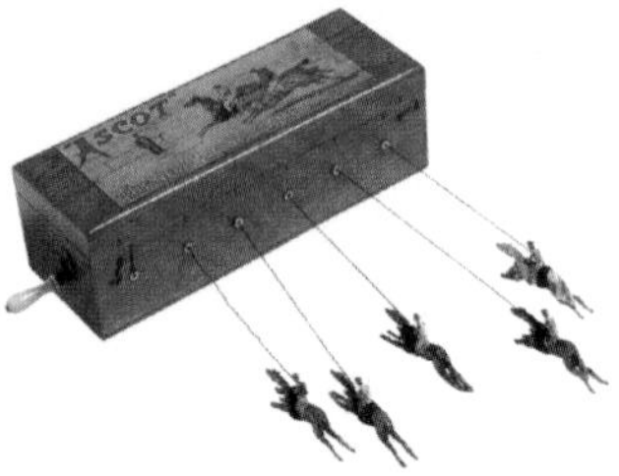

A Jaques Ascot racing game, with lead horses, c1880, in an oak box, 10in (25.5cm) long.

£200–225 Long Street Antiques

A painted Game of the Goose game board, America, early 19thC, 24½ x 25½in (62 x 65cm).

£9,000–11,000 Skinner

The Game of the Goose is a game of disputed origin, but it reached the height of its popularity in the 1700s.

A painted pine Parcheesi game board, America, 19thC, 28¾ x 23¾in (73 x 60.5cm).

£3,200–3,800 Skinner

A marquetry draughts board, the reverse with Parcheesi, Canada, Quebec, c1900, 19 x 32in (48.5 x 81.5cm).

£150–180 Waddington's

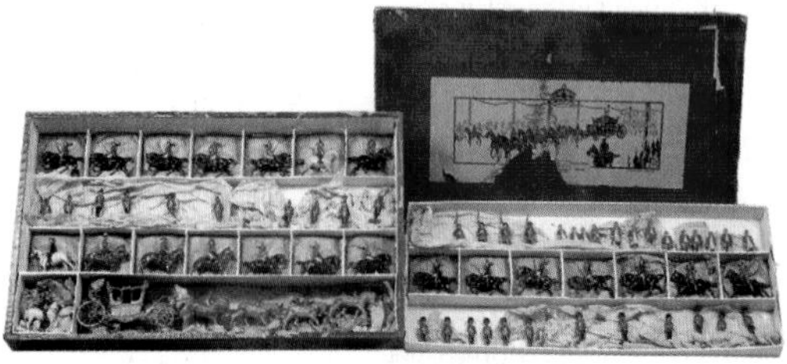

A Britains Coronation presentation set, comprising 71 pieces, No. 1477, slight damage, c1937.

£700–850 Skinner

A set of John Hill & Co Quo Vadis figures, comprising 10 pieces, 1951, in original box.

£400–500 Wallis & Wallis

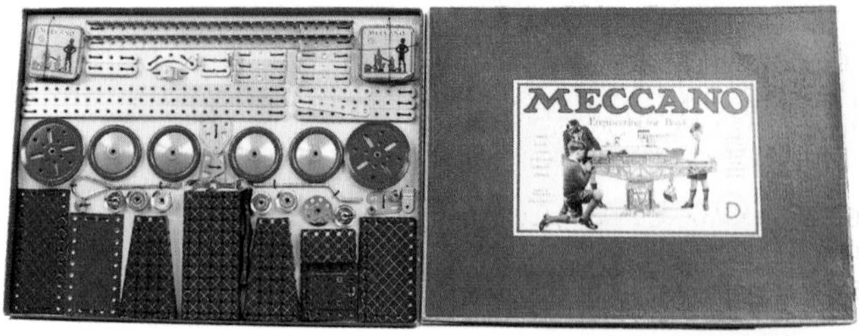

A Meccano set, Set D, with manual, c1935, in original box.

£450–550 Vectis

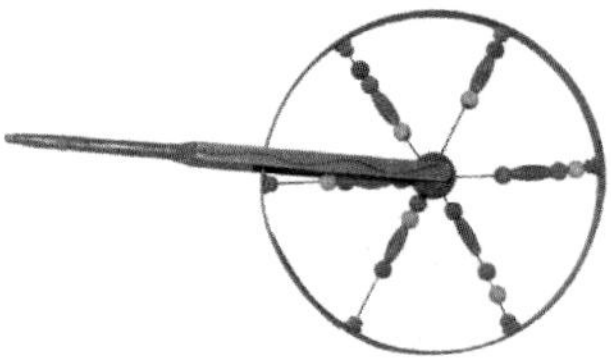

A Victorian painted wood push-along toy, 30in (76cm) long.

£100–120 Humbleyard Fine Art

A painted beech child's rocker, c1900, 27in (68.5cm) wide.

£100–125 Millennia

SPORT

BASEBALL

Hanna Batrite white ash baseball bat, sed and signed by Eddie Matthews, America, 1954, 34in (86.5cm) long.

3,000–3,500 **Mastro Auctions**

Detroit Tigers baseball, signed by 25 embers of the World Championship team cluding Hank Greenberg, Schoolboy Rowe nd Mickey Cochrane, America, 1935.

270–330 Heritage

A Just So tobacco/cigarette card, featuring Jesse Burkett, restored, 1893, 3¾ x 2½in (9.5 x 6.5cm).

£5,500–6,500 Mastro Auctions

A Piedmont cigarette card, featuring Roger Bresnahan, No. T206, America, 1909–11.

£200–240 Heritage

Goudey Gum Co card, featuring Lou Gehrig, No. 92, America, 1933.

500–600 Heritage

A J. & E. Stevens cast-iron Darktown Battery money bank, America, 1880s, 9¾in (25cm) wide.

£3,000–3,600 James D Julia

A cabinet photograph of Mike 'King' Kelly, by G. H. Hastings, America, 1887, 6½ x 4¼in (16.5 x 11cm).

£5,000–6,000
Mastro Auctions

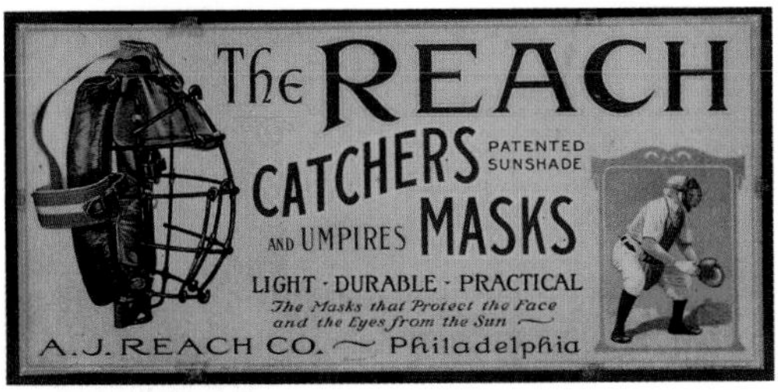

An A. J. Reach Co lithographed tin sign, advertising 'Catchers and Umpires Masks', America, Philadelphia, c1910, 6 x 13in (15 x 33cm).

13,000–16,000 Mastro Auctions

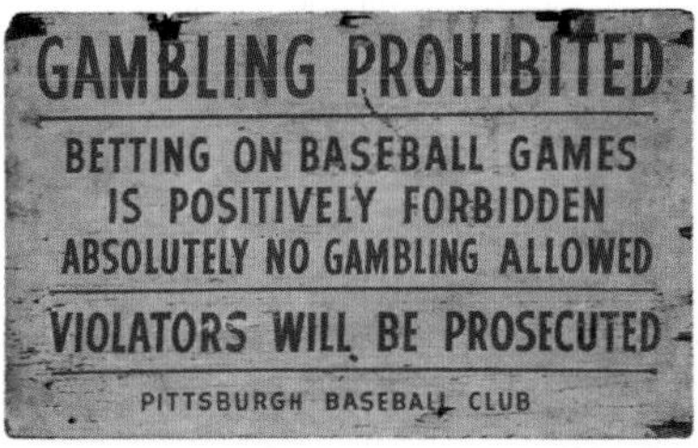

A Pittsburgh Baseball Club painted wood sign, from Forbes Field, inscribed 'Gambling Prohibited', America, 1940s–50s, 18 x 30in (45.5 x 76cm).

£1,500–1,800 Mastro Auctions

BASKETBALL

An Olympic Gold Medal game basketball, signed by the entire US team, America, 1956.

£2,500–3,000 **Heritage**

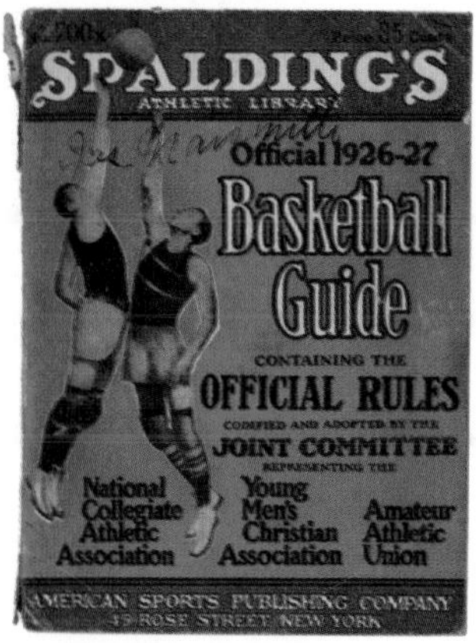

A Spalding's Official Basketball Guide, signed by James Naismith, America, 1926–27, 11¾in (29.5cm) high.

£2,750–3,250 **Heritage**

A San Francisco Warriors je worn by Wilt Chamberlain, America, 1962–63.

£11,000–13,000 **Herita**

BOXING

A Beech-Nut Chewing Tobacco triptych cardboard advertisement, advertising Gene Tunney v Jack Dempsey, America, 1927, 38 x 60in (96.5 x 152.5cm).

£1,000–1,200 **Mastro Auctions**

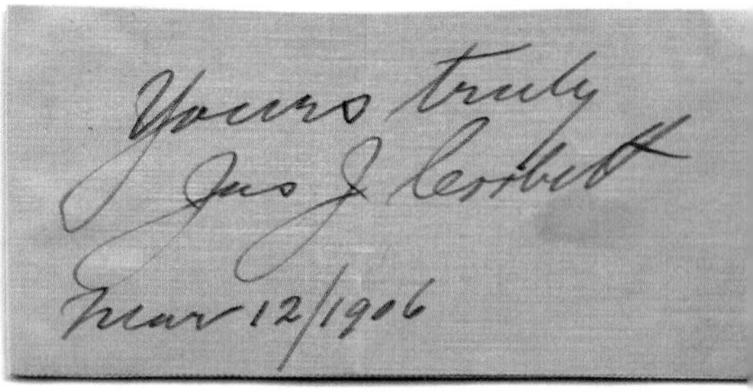

James Corbett, an autograph 'Yours Truly, James J. Corbett, Mar 12/1906', America, 1906, 2½ x 5½in (6.5 x 14cm).

£300–360 **Heritage**

Mecca Cigarettes cards, Champion Prize-Fighters, set of 50, America, 1910.

£6,500–8,000 **Mastro Auctions**

A Topps bubble gum card, Rocky Marciano, No. 32, America, 1951.

£600–700 **Mastro Auctions**

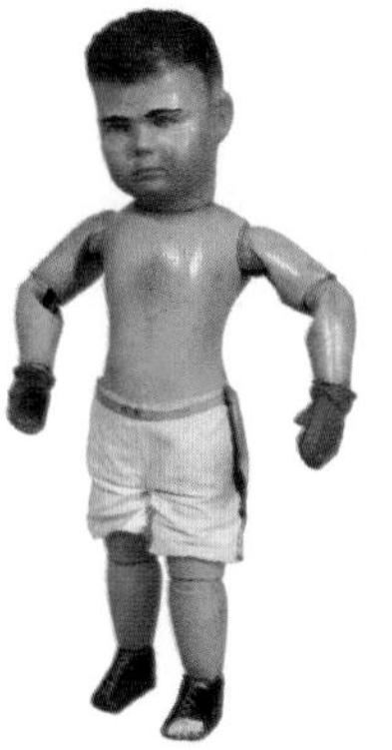

A Schoenhut portrait doll, probably representing Jack Dempsey, with sculpted hair, painted eyes and toddler body, wearing trunks with gold belt and leather boxing gloves, painted boots, one boot damaged, incised Schoenhut marks to back, America, early 20thC, 14in (35.5cm) high.

£6,000–7,000 **Skinner**

This doll was probably a one-off commission. Jack Dempsey won the World Heavyweight boxing title in 1919.

A lustre jug, decorated with named full-le portraits of Tom Molineaux and Tom Cribb the reverse with inscription, restored, early 19thC, 5in (12.5cm) high.

£320–380 **Special Auction Service**

Tom Molineaux was born in 1784, the son a Virginian cotton plantation slave. He was defeated in 1811 by Tom Cribb, who was born in 1781 and was Champion of Engla until 1824. In 1821 Cribb guarded the entrance to Westminster Abbey at the coronation of George IV.

photograph of James Corbett, possibly by seph Hall, America, 1890s, 14 x 11in 5.5 x 28cm).

250–300 Mastro Auctions

A signed photograph of Joe Louis, matted and framed, America, c1940, 8 x 10in (20.5 x 25.5cm).

£170–200 Heritage

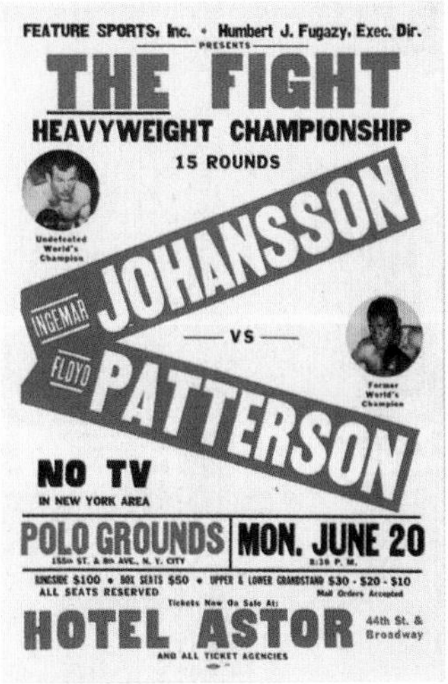

A Heavyweight Championship fight poster, advertising Ingemar Johansson v Floyd Patterson, America, 1960, framed 45 x 31in (114.5 x 78.5cm).

£380–450 Mastro Auctions

Heavyweight Championship programme, r Tommy Burns v Jack Johnson, Australia, ydney, 1908, 8 x 5½in (20.5 x 14cm).

2,000–2,500 Mastro Auctions

A silver pair-cased pocket watch, by William King, the dial later-painted with two boxers, the movement with engraved decoration, 1806.

£330–400 Sworders

CRICKET

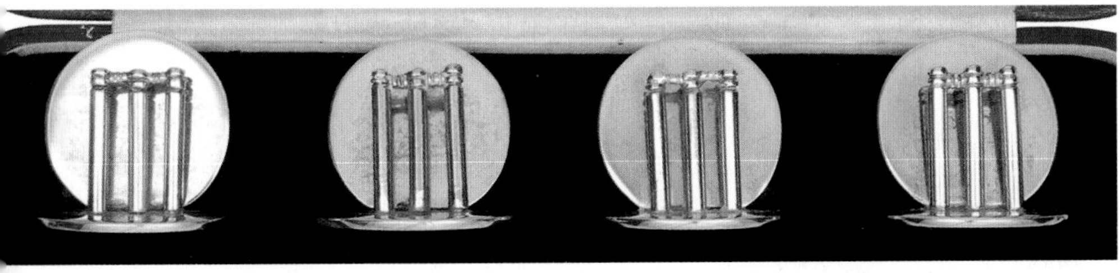

A set of four silver menu holders, in the form of cricket stumps, Chester 1909, in a fitted case, 7½in (19cm) wide.

£1,800–2,000 Nicholas Shaw

promotional poster, 'Cricket on Ice, t Moritz', Switzerland, c1980, 27½ x 19in 70 x 48.5cm).

150–180 Van Sabben

A ceramic tile, probably by Minton, decorated with a cricket scene, c1870, 6in (15cm) square.

£200–220 Manfred Schotten

A silver vesta case, by James Fenton, embossed with a cricket match scene, Birmingham 1906, 1½in (4cm) diam.

£500–600 Gorringes (L)

EQUESTRIAN

A pressed horn box, decorated with a hunting scene, c1820, 3in (7.5cm) diam.

£225–250 Mostly Boxes

A papier-mâché snuff box, decorated with a hunting scene, France, 19thC, 3in (7.5cm) wide.

£110–125 Wooden Bygones

A turned wood container, depicting a view of Derby Da losses, damage, early 19thC 4¾in (12cm) high.

£900–1,100
Canterbury Auctions

A pair of 15ct gold cufflinks, decorated with horseshoes, c1880, ½in (1.5cm) wide.

£180–200 Sylvie Spectrum

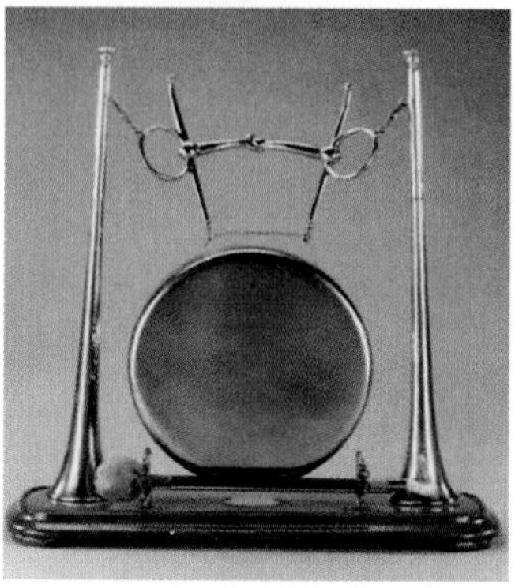

A Victorian metal dinner gong, by Henry Keat & Sons, London, suspended from a horse's bit between two copper hunting horns, on a fitted oak base, the striker a converted bone and cane hunting crop, 23¾in (60.5cm) wide.

£500–600 Graham Budd

A cast-iron jockey hitching stamped 'McKittrick Foundry Union Beach, NJ', America, l 19thC, 46in (117cm) high.

£1,400–1,700
Sotheby's (S)

A horseshoe, worn by Pinza when he won the 1953 Derby, incorporating a silver ashtray, with plaque, on a wooden base.

£2,000–2,500 Graham Budd

A set of jockey scales, by Alexander & Fowler, Liverpool, on a carved oak stool with brass mounts, maker's label, c1905, 28in (71cm) high.

£1,650–1,850 Ronald Chambers

A silver hunting horn, with a ribbed stem, maker's mark for S. Mordan & Co, Chester 1913, 12in (30.5cm) long.

£250–300
Dee, Atkinson & Harrison

A pair of silver-plated and gilt-bronze inkwells, each in the form of a horse's ho c1870, 2in (5cm) high.

£270–300 Walpoles

A Doulton Lambeth jug, commemorating Fred Archer, decorated with a portrait and inscription, the spout in the form of an inverted jockey's cap, the handle moulded with horse tack, c1886, 7in (18cm) high.
£1,000–1,200 Graham Budd

A hand-coloured lithograph, after Henry Alken, depicting a hunting scene, c1822, 22in (56cm) wide.
£110–125 Swan at Tetsworth

A set of three silver napkin rings, by The Goldsmiths & Silversmiths Co, embossed with foxes' heads, London 1937, with original box, 7¾in (19.5cm) wide.
£900–1,000 Nicholas Shaw

A Prattware jug, commemorating Fred Archer, the thumbpiece in the form of a jockey's cap, late 19thC, 7½in (19cm) high.
£1,100–1,300 Graham Budd

An ivory page turner, carved with two horses' heads, c1900, 24in (61cm) long.
£1,000–1,100 Richard Gardner

A photograph of 'Pommern', Triple Crown winner, by Clarence Hailey, signed by the owner Solomon Joel and the jockey Steve Donoghue, dated 1915, 7 x 9in (18 x 23cm).
£140–170 Graham Budd

A glass pin tray, depicting a polo scene, 1920s, 3½in (9cm) wide.
£125–135 Manfred Schotten

A pair of silhouettes, each depicting a racehorse, jockey and trainer, with silver foil highlights, each signed 'Cut by A. W. Pullinger, May 1899', 10¼in (26cm) square.
£230–275 Sworders

A gilt stirrup cup, by C. T. & S., with engine-turned decoration and velvet-lined interior, in a *faux* pocket watch case, 1886, cup 1in (4.5cm) high.
£150–165 Fossack & Furkle

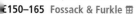

A set of seven Minton, Hollins & Co ceramic tiles, from the Hunting and Racing series, c1880, 6in (15cm) square.
£800–900 Rene Nicholls

A silver-gilt horseracing trophy cup and cover, by Daniel Smith and Robert Sharp, chased with leaves and a frieze of horses and racing scenes, rim inscribed 'Richmond Cup 1780' and 'Earl Fauconberg & Willm. Bethell Esq – Stewards', base inscribed 'Pickett & Rundell Fecit', London 1780, 19in (48cm) high, 113oz.

£32,000–38,000 Woolley & Wallis

A silver-plated horseracing trophy, for the Belmont Stakes, won by 'Sir Barton', 1919, 12¼in (31cm) high.

£9,000–11,000 Mastro Auctions

'Sir Barton' was the first horse to win all three events of the Triple Crown: the Belmont Stakes, the Kentucky Derby and the Preakness.

A silver trainer's trophy, by Boodle & Dunthorpe, for the Centenary Grand Natior in 1937, won by 'Royal Mail', with Pegasus handles and acorn finial, set with medallion Birmingham 1936, 14in (36cm) high, 48oz.

£2,800–3,500 Graham Budd

A silver vesta case, by W. Neale, decorated in relief with racehorses and a grandstand, the reverse monogrammed, Chester 1889, 2in (5cm) wide.

£600–700 Woolley & Wallis

A silver-plated vesta case, in the form of a horseshoe, with wick channel, c1900, 2in (5cm) wide.

£90–100 Swan at Tetsworth

A wooden whip stand, in the form of a horseshoe, carved with two jockeys' heads, c1920, 14in (35.5cm) high.

£750–850 Richard Gardner

FISHING

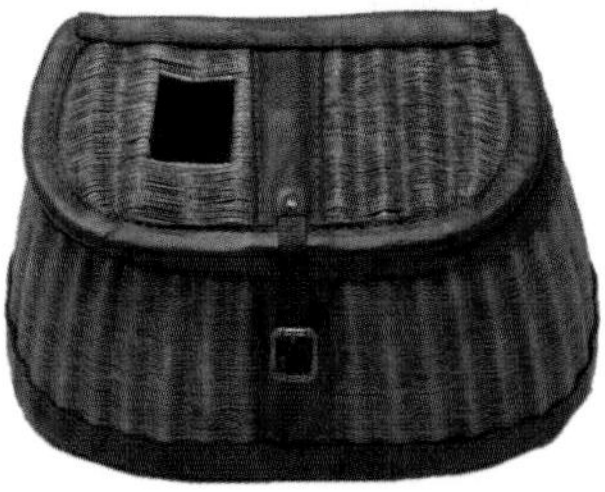

A woven wicker fishing creel, with leather trim, c1900, 14in (35.5cm) wide.

£270–300 Manfred Schotten

A Victorian brass telescopic salmon gaff, 16in (40.5cm) long.

£60–70 Geoffrey Minnis

A telescopic salmon gaff, c1900, 14in (35.5cm) long.

£150–165 Manfred Schotten

A Hardy cast-iron line winder, with brass mechanism, c1897, 10in (25.5cm) diam.

£300–340 Manfred Schotten

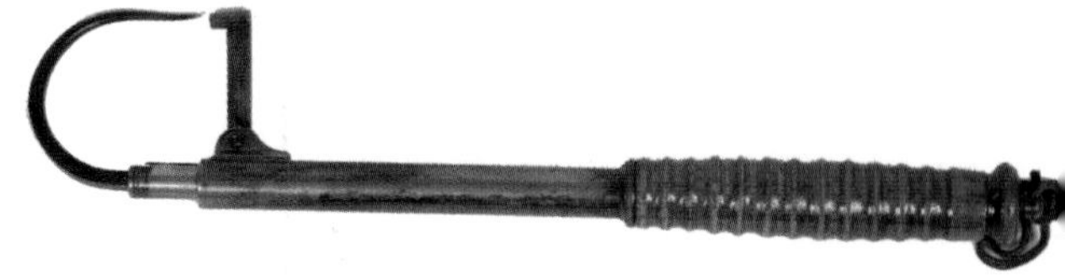

A Gent 185 brass telescopic salmon gaff, with a wooden handle, c1900, 15in (38cm) long.

£100–120 Manfred Schotten

'ictorian brass 4in salmon reel, 'ı folding ivory handle.
80–220 Woolley & Wallis

A walnut starback 6in reel, with perforated brass rear plate and perforated front with ebonized handles, with optional check and centre tensioning screw, c1900.
£200–220 Manfred Schotten

An ebonite or Bakelite 4½in salmon reel, with brass face and nickel rim, c1900.
£160–175 Manfred Schotten

Hardy gunmetal 4½in salmon reel, ıstant check mechanism and horn handle, ımped mark, c1900.
450–500 Manfred Schotten

A Walker Bampton alloy 4in Lennox salmon reel, c1930s.
£110–125 Manfred Schotten

A Hardy Perfect alloy 3¾in salmon fly reel, with double check mechanism, 1958–65.
£200–220 Manfred Schotten

A Hardy split cane Gold Medal salmon fly rod, Palakona No. E114900, c1929, 168in (426.5cm) long.

£270–300 Chiltern Antiques ⊞

A stuffed and mounted trout, by J. Cooper, caught by Austen Mars Waltham Abbey, in a bowfronted glazed case, 1886, 24½in (62cm

£550–650 Woolley & Wallis

A stuffed and mounted roach, by J. Cooper & Sons, caught by E. Cant, River Test, in an ebonized and glazed bowfronted case, 1935, 22in (56cm) wide.

£1,100–1,300 Halls

A Royal Worcester angling trophy, painted with panels of riverside scenes and fishermen within gilt cartouches, signed 'E. Salter', marked, 1899, 8½in (21.5cm) high.

£400–500 Anderson & Garland

A Farlow pigskin cast wallet, c1910, 7in (18cm) wide.

£125–140 Manfred Schotten ⊞

FOOTBALL

A cardboard Coca Cola advertisement, depicting American footballer Red Grange, America, c1947, 15 x 13in (38 x 33cm).

£450–550 Mastro Auctions

A velvet England International cap, worn by Kelly Houlker for Scotland v England, 1902.

£1,200–1,500 Graham Budd

During the Scotland v England match at Ibrox, a section of terracing collapsed. Hundreds of supporters were injured and 26 died.

A Topps bubble gum card, featuring John Unitas, No. 138, America, 1957, 8in (20.5cm) long.

£170–200 Heritage

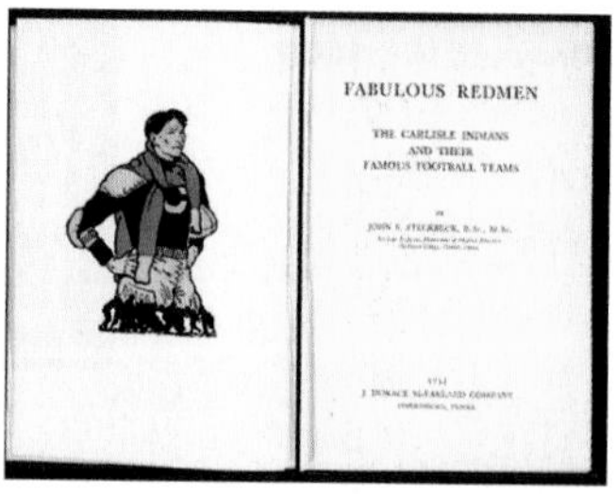

John S. Steckbeck, *Fabulous Redmen, The Carlisle Indians and Their Famous Football Teams*, signed by Jim Thorpe and the author, America, 1951.

£650–800 Mastro Auctions

Jim Thorpe began his athletic career at the Carlisle Indian Industrial School in Pennsylvania, where he led the small school to national fame in football.

A patinated bronze figure of a football player, attributed to Bergman, Austria, c1900, 5in (12.5cm) high.

£500–550 Manfred Schotten ⊞

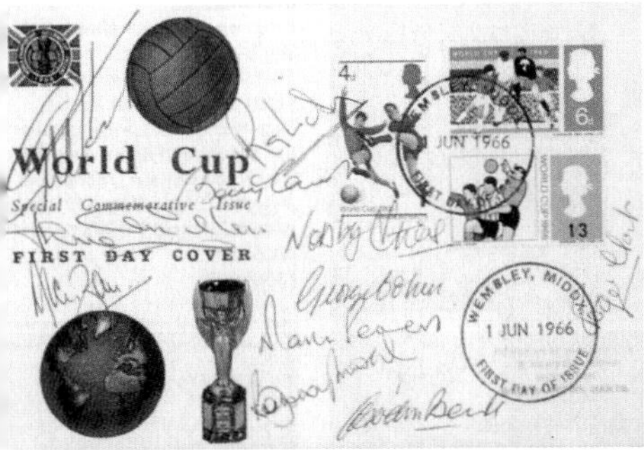

A World Cup first day cover, signed by 11 of the England finalists, postmarked Wembley, 1 June 1966.

£900–1,100 Graham Budd

A England No. 6 international football shirt, as worn by Bobby Moore at the England v West Germany match, 1965.

£4,500–5,500 Graham Budd

A 15ct gold Football League representative medal, awarded to W. Garbutt, the reverse with inscription, 1910.

£500–600 Graham Budd

Garbutt was a Blackburn Rovers player at the time of his selection for the English League v the Scottish League in 1910.

FA Cup Final celebration ıquet menu, for Blackpool v ton Wanderers, signed by Stan ɪrtensen, with dedication, 1953.

.00–240 Graham Budd

ɪnley Mortensen (1921–91) was ɪst famous for his role in the 53 FA Cup Final between ɪckpool and Bolton Wanderers. scored three goals for Blackpool 'ping them to a 4–3 win and :ame the first player to score a t-trick in a final at Wembley.

An Ulster Express railway menu, signed by 11 Manchester United players, dated 1957.

£1,000–1,200 Graham Budd

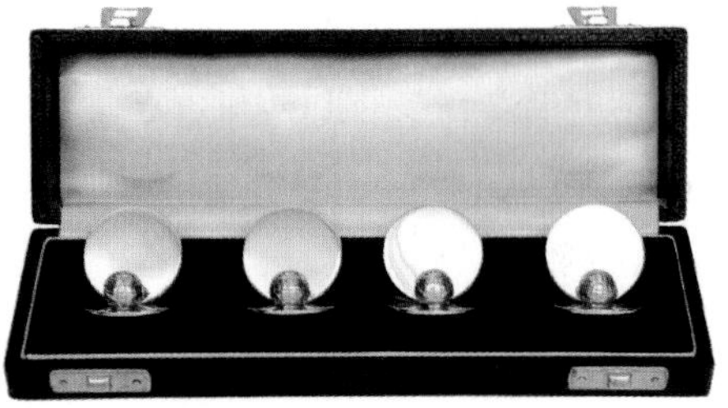

A set of four silver menu holders, in the form of footballs, Scotland, Edinburgh 1935, in a fitted case, 8¼in (21cm) wide.

£1,000–1,100 Nicholas Shaw

photograph of an army American Football game, America, c1900, ımed 23½ x 26in (59.5 x 66cm).

550–800 Mastro Auctions

An FA Cup Final programme, for Barnsley v West Bromwich Albion, restored, 1912.

£8,000–10,000 Graham Budd

ı Air-India poster, 'World Cup 966 London', India, Madras, ɪsigned 1965, 39¼ x 24¾in 9.5 x 63cm).

230–275 Van Sabben

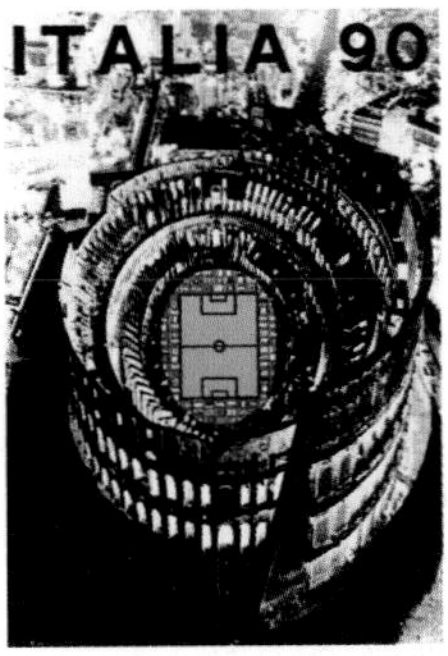

A promotional poster, illustrated by Burri, 'Italia 90', on linen, Italy, 1990, 39¼ x 28in (99.5 x 71cm).

£160–200 Van Sabben

A bound volume of 48 Tottenham Hotspur programmes, cloth covered boards, 1914–15.

£9,000–11,000 Graham Budd

An FA Cup Final programme, for Bolton Wanderers v Manchester City, 1926.

£750–900 Graham Budd

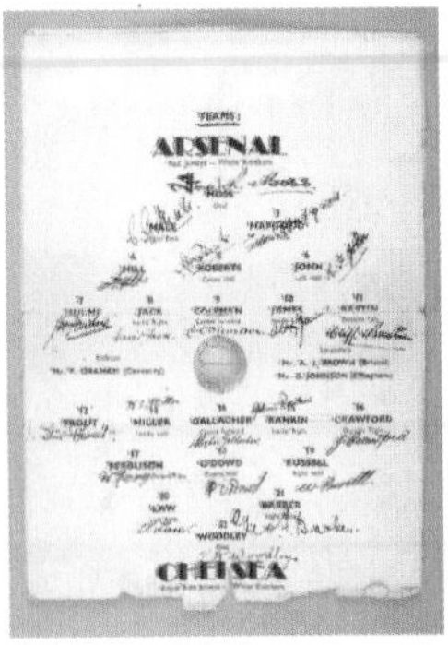

A football programme, for Arsenal v Chelsea, signed by the players, 1932, 9½ x 7in (24 x 18cm).

£160–200 Lawrence Fine Art

A Tourist Information Office programme, for the World Cup, published in German, Italy, 1934.

£900–1,000 Graham Budd

An international football programme, for England v Czechoslovakia, 1937.

£170–220 Graham Budd

An FA Cup Final ticket, for Sheffield United v Tottenham Hotspur, 1901.

£6,000–7,000 Graham Budd

An American Football uniform, worn by a Native American player, the trousers stencilled 'Chief Rain-In-The-Face', America, 1908.

£2,000–2,400 Mastro Auctions

GOLF

A gutta-percha golf ball, c1870, 1½in (4cm) diam.

£55–60 Chiltern Antiques

A Goudy Gum card, featuring Bobby Jones, Sports Kings series, No. 38, America, 1933.

£4,000–5,000 Mastro Auctions

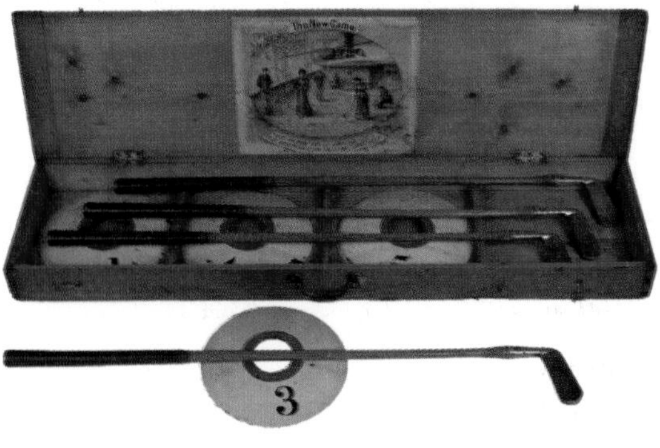

A Marine Golf putting game, with four brass putters and nine discs, 1890s, in original pine box 40in (101.5cm) wide.

£700–800 Manfred Schotten

A Goldscheider figure of a female golfer, Austria, Vienna, 1930s, 10in (25.5cm) high.

£850–950 Andrew Muir

omotional photograph of Bobby Jones, the Warner Brothers Golf series, caption, America, 1930s, 7¾in (21.5 x 19.5cm).
0–600 Mastro Auctions

rles Crombie, *The Rules of Golf*, with 24 trations, cloth bound, c1904.
0–600 Sworder's
se illustrations were used in an advertising paign for Perrier water.

A Royal Doulton plate, by Charles Crombie, decorated with a golfing scene, c1911, 9in (23cm) diam.
£380–430 Manfred Schotten

A silver-plated golf scoring notebook, decorated in relief with a figure of a caddy, with propelling pencil and chain, 1920s, 4in (10cm) high.
£300–350 Manfred Schotten

A Women's National Open Golf Tournament programme, signed by 20 players including Babe Zaharias, Patty Berg, Louise Suggs, Marilynn Smith, Shirley Spork, Marlene Bauer Hagge and Opal Hill, slight damage, America, 1950, 11¾in (29.5cm) high.
£100–120 Heritage
The Ladies' Professional Golf Association was founded in 1950 by a group of 13 female golfers. It is the longest-running women's professional sports organization in America.

A pair of silver salts, in the form of golf balls, London 1894, 1½in (4cm) diam, with case.
£1,650–1,850 Bourbon-Hanby

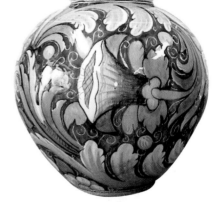

SAILING & ROWING

A silver model of a racing rowing boat, London 1848, 7¼in (18.5cm) long.

£400–500 **Locke & England**

A sterling silver rowing trophy, by Brush & Drummond, the foot engraved 'Victorian Rowing Association', Australia, c1875, 17¼in (44cm) high.

£3,750–4,500 **Leonard Joel**

A sterling silver Cleveland Yacht Club trophy, by Whiting Company, engraved a steam yacht, with inscription, Americ c1896, 11½in (29cm) high.

£2,000–2,500 **James D Julia**

SHOOTING

A Daum glass shooting cup, decorated in enamel with a rooster, thistle and leaves, inscribed 'XIII Concours National et International de Tir, Nancy, 1906', signed, France, c1906, 4½in (11.5cm) high.

£3,000–3,500 **James D Julia**

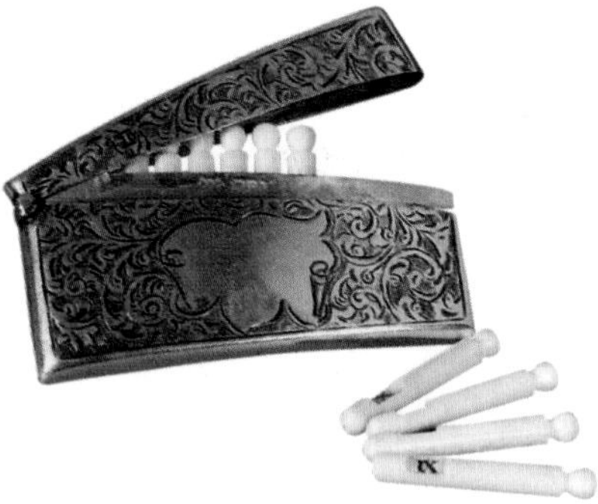

A silver place finder, with hinged cover, enclosing ten sprung ivory pegs, Chester 1905.

£3,000–3,500 **Sotheby's**

A nickel-plated Sykes pow flask, c1860, 9in (23cm) lo

£425–475
Arbour Antiques

A double-barrelled percussion shotgun, by William Rowntree, figured hardwood, cut-down butt, engraved steel trigger-guard, ramrod missing, Birmingham proof marks, signed, 1847–65, barrel 9½in (24cm) long.

£650–800 **Thomas Del Mar**

A double-barrelled sporting gun, by W. Parker, London, inlaid w gold lines and engraved with a flower, pierced platinum plugs, wa half-stock, the trigger-guard decorated with a hound, game and rabbit, signed, c1820, barrel 30¼in (77cm) long.

£850–1,100 **Thomas Del Mar**

A pair of percussion target pistols, by Devisme, Paris, with gold and ebony handles, France, mid 19thC, 15in (38cm) long.

£4,500–5,000 **Arbour Antiques**

A percussion target rifle, with Liège proofs, target sights and dou set trigger, Switzerland, c1870, 52in (132cm) long.

£1,000–1,150 **Michael Long**

ENNIS

ırleigh Ware jug, the handle in the form of a tennis ɣer, 1920–40, 8in (20.5cm) high.

,000–2,200 Gazelles

A wooden miniature tennis racket, 1890s, 12in (30.5cm) long.

£350–400 Manfred Schotten

A tennis racket, 'The Amhurst', c1900, 27in (68.5cm) long.

£250–300 Manfred Schotten

VINTER SPORTS

'arkhurst bubble gum card, ːuring ice hockey player Maurice ːcket' Richard, No. 4, 1951–52.

,750–2,000 ıastro Auctions

A Royal Copenhagen bronze figure of a cross country skier, by S. G. Kelsey, on a marble base with an inscribed brass plaque, No. 256 of 2500, signed, Denmark, dated 1976, 16¼in (41cm) wide.

£230–275 Sworders

A coin-operated Goalee ice hockey game, by Chicago Coin, with chrome goalkeepers, Bakelite handles and lit backglass, America, 1945, 45in (114.5cm) wide.

£900–1,100 Mastro Auctions

promotional poster, by Otto Barth, intersport Im Steir Salzkammergut', on japan, stria, c1915, 39½ x 26in (100.5 x 66cm)

,000–1,200 Van Sabben

A promotional poster, by Abel, 'Beoefent de Skisport in Frankrijk', Holland, 1953, 39¼ x 25¼in (99.5 x 64cm).

£400–500 Van Sabben

A promotional poster, by Roger Excoffon, 'Jeux Olympiques d'Hiver Grenoble', on linen, France, 1968, 20¾ x 12¼in (52.5 x 31cm).

£75–85 Van Sabben

ARMS & ARMOUR

ARMOUR

ESSENTIAL REFERENCE ARMOUR PARTS

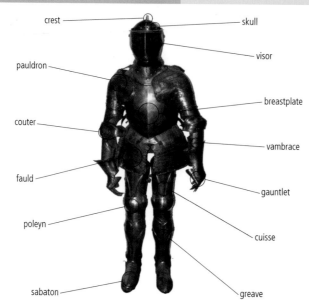

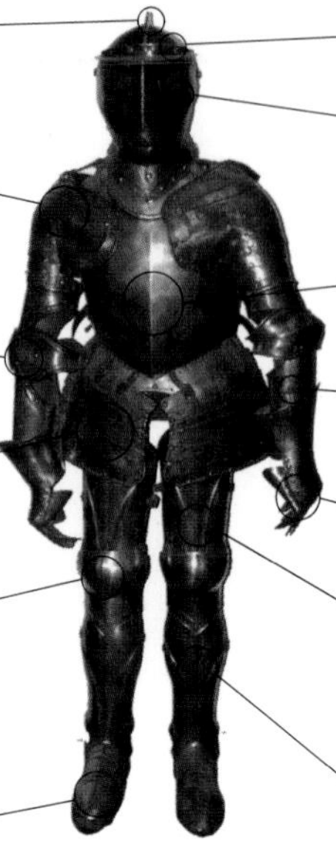

- Armour, in one form or another, has been in use since around 1500 BC and possibly earlier.
- Collecting armour is an expensive hobby. Genuine full suits of armour rarely become available and should be verified by an expert before purchase. They will fetch three- or four-figure sums .
- Armour from the 17th century, particularly the English Civil War, is popular with collectors.
- Reproduction armour is also relatively expensive, with 19th-century German, Spanish and French suits being particularly sought after.

Lanes Armoury

A breastplate, backplate and morion, decorated with etched and gilt foliate pane
Italy, c1580.
£5,000–6,000 **Wallis & Wallis**

A pair of elbow gauntlets, with embossed decoration, c1630.
£2,000–2,300 **Michael German**

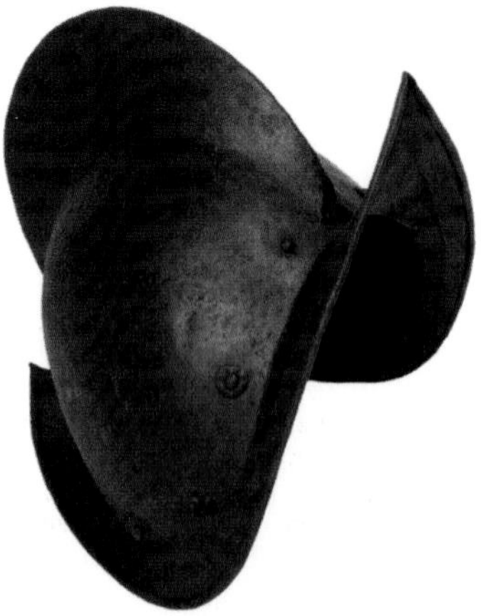

A steel comb morion, Germany, c1580.
£2,000–2,250 **Rod Akeroyd**

A gorget, Germany, 16thC.
£1,600–2,000 **Thomas Del Mar**

A lobster-tail helmet, Germany, mid-17thC
£2,000–2,500 **Thomas Del Mar**

A pair of rowel spurs, with remains of original brass and silver finish, South America, early 19
£400–500 **Thomas Del Mar**

:ANNONS

ronze cannon, relief-decorated with foliage, a wned coat-of-arms, scrollwork cartouches, volutes and le ornament, the top of the chase inscribed 'Taken at tobello NouR 21 1739', the handles formed as a pair narine monsters, on a later wooden carriage, probably ain, c1550, barrel 72in (184cm) long.

4,000–17,000 Thomas Del Mar

erto Bello in Panama was used to export silver for the anish treasure fleets and under Spanish control from the th to the 18th centuries. The Battle of Puerto Bello took ce between the English and Spanish troops on 21 vember 1739 .

A bronze cannon, the barrel with chiselled decoration and inscription 'La Gaiete', cast and chased with a crowned coat-of-arms, on a brass-mounted field carriage, some losses, Flanders, dated 1752, barrel 22½in (57cm) long.

£3,750–4,500 Thomas Del Mar

A pair of brass signal cannon, the cheeks carved with foliage, each with an associated 19thC carriage, one carriage damaged, 18thC, 29¾in (75.5cm) long.

£5,000–6,000 Thomas Del Mar

A cast-iron four-pounder Carronade, cast with a crown over 'B.P.' and impressed 'B.P. & Co 3.2.10', one trunnion impressed 'I' and '4 Pdr', the other trunnion with '1051', on a later wooden carriage, damaged, c1850, 43in (109cm) long.

£1,100–1,300 Wallis & Wallis

:DGED WEAPONS

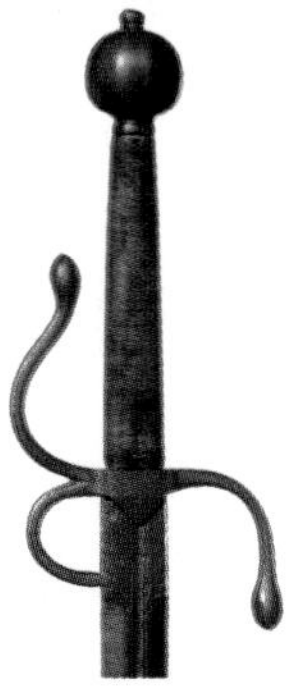

halfsword, the blade fuller nked by a lineal and stippled rder, the ricasso with deep line rders and X control or maker's ark, Italy, early 16thC, 40¾in 03.5cm) long.

2,200–2,500 Faganarms

A steel Bidenhaender sword, the double-edged blade with maker's mark, the wrought and engraved quillons with side rings, with a leather and wood grip, point restored, south Germany, late 16thC, 68½in (174cm) long.

£5,000–6,000 Sotheby's (Am)

dish-hilt rapier, the hilt with scrolling terminals, the later grip bound th plaited wire and 'Turks' heads', the cup-guard formed as an ght-petalled flower, the blade stamped and signed 'Solingen', the ller with pierced decoration, 1630–40, blade 35in (89cm) long.

2,500–3,000 Thomas Del Mar

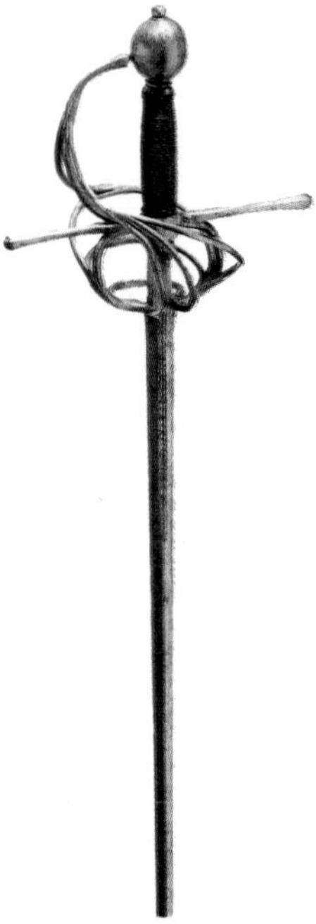

A left-hand rapier, with a bevelled pommel and bevelled iron knucklebow hilt with iron wire wrapping and braided ferrules, the double-edged ridged blade with an inscription, stamped, Germany, c1600, 48½in (123cm) long.

£3,200–3,800 Hermann Historica

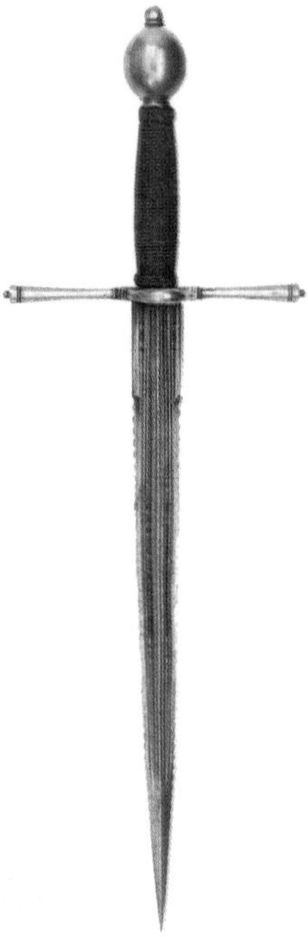

A left-hand dagger, the steel hilt with a wire-bound grip and decorated with 'Turks' heads', the blade with serrated edges, Germany, c1600, 18½in (47cm) long.

£3,250–4,000 Thomas Del Mar

A cavalry sword, the double-edged blade cut with a running wolf to each side, stamped 'Sahagam', bladesmith's mark, Amsterdam Town mark, the scrolling quillon stamped with a clover leaf mark, Holland, c1650, blade 35in (89cm) long.

£1,800–2,200
Thomas Del Mar

A cup-hilt rapier, the cross-guard with baluster terminals, the compressed pommel with baluster button matching the guards, chevron iron wire-wrapped grip with banded iron ferrules, the blade marked 'Iohannes Wvndes/en Solingen', Spain, 1650–70, 34½in (87.5cm) long.

£2,700–3,000 Faganarms

Johannes Wundes is recorded among the swordsmiths of the famed Wundes family. Wundes blades bear a king's head mark but forgeries were widespread.

An officer's sword, the pommel and knucklebow etched with eagles, the forged iron knucklebow hilt with chiselled guard plates, the quillon with dog-head finials, the wooden grip with diamond chequering, the double-edged blade etched with figures, birds and Latin inscriptions, Germany or Holland, c1670, 39½in (100cm) long.

£1,500–1,800
Hermann Historica

A plug bayonet, the swell decorated with a medial hound's-tooth ban flanked by two transverse bands of pellet decoration,the flattened ricasso impressed with two bands of eye-shaped marks, the baluster-form cross-guard with a fluted medial, with a 10½in double-edged blade, northern Europe, 1680–90, 16in (40.5cm) long.

£1,500–1,750 Faganarms

A smallsword, the hilt with chiselled decoration and inlaid with gold leaf, the grip bound with silver and steel wire, with a cruciform blade, c1740, 37¾in (96cm) long.

£1,100–1,250
Michael Long

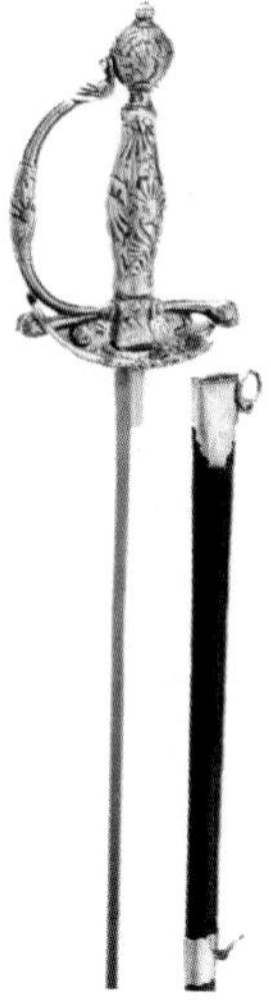

A silver-mounted ceremonial sword, the silver knucklebow decorated with rocaille, the leather scabbard with silver mounts, Germany, c1740, 37½in (95.5cm) long.

£2,750–3,250
Hermann Historica

A boy's sword, with a silver hilt, 18thC, 17½in (44.5cm) long.

£1,600–1,800
Arbour Antiques

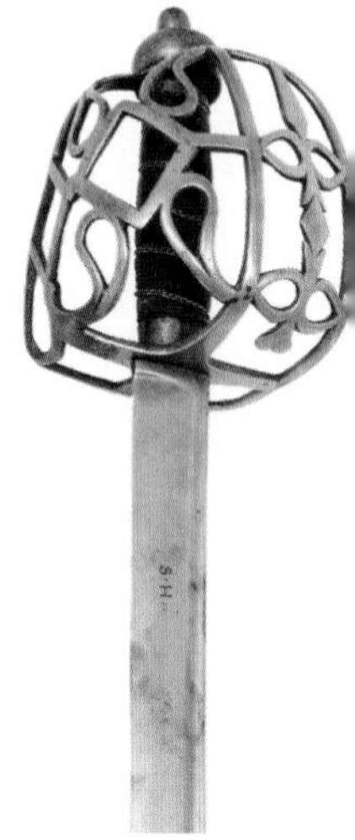

A grenadier's basket-hilt sword, S. Harvey, c1760, 37in (94cm) lo

£1,600–1,850
Rod Akeroyd

A smallsword, the pierced pommel decorated with military trophies and scrolls, the silver hilt hallmarked London 1768, the grip wrapped in twisted wire and ribbon, with a colichemarde-style blade, c1768, 39in (99cm) long.

£1,100–1,250 Michael Long

Colichemarde blades first appeared in 1680 and were popular for the next 40 years in the European royal courts. Considered to be descendants of the rapier, they combined good parrying qualities with good thrusting abilities.

A smallsword, with a silver hilt and colichemarde blade, c1770, 41in (104cm) long.

£2,000–2,400
Michael German

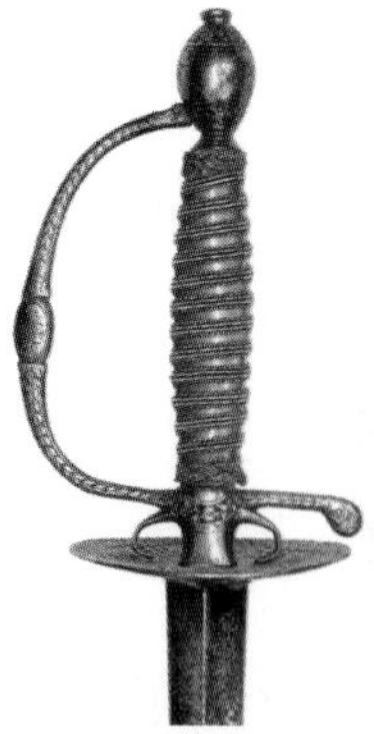

A smallsword, the iron hilt with silver wire and copper-wrapped grip, with a pierced and chisell guard, northern Europe, c1780, blade 30¼in long.

£1,500–1,750 Faganarm

Garth Vincent
Antique Arms, Armour & Medals
LAPADA MEMBER
THE GUN TRADE ASSOCIATION
I have customers worldwide and I am interested in purchasing single items or complete collections, advice freely given
Dealer in antique and reproduction arms and armour for the collector, investor and interior decorator
Commission buying at auction
Access & Visa accepted
Brochure available
The Old Manor House
Allington, Nr Grantham
Lincolnshire NG32 2DH
Telephone: 01400 281358
Fax: 01400 282658
Mobile: 07785 352151
Email: garthvincent@aol.com
Website: http://www.guns.uk.com

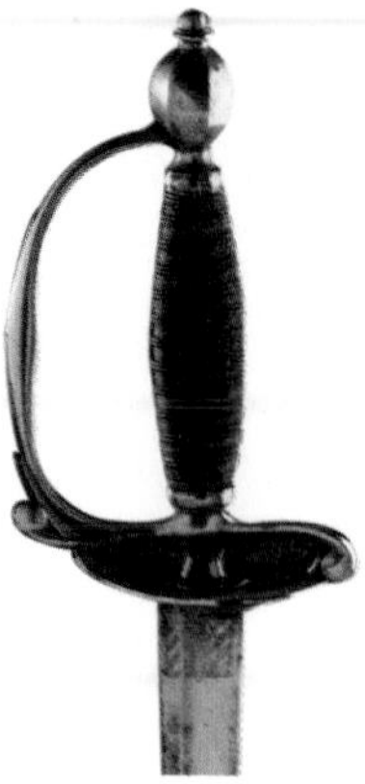

An officer's smallsword, by Bland & Foster, London, the single-edged blade engraved with the crowned Royal arms to either side, slight damage, losses, 1788–91, blade 32½in (82.5cm) long.

£600–700
Thomas Del Mar

John Highmore Bland was Royal sword Cutler and Beltmaker to George III working at 68 St James's Street. He was joined by Robert Foster in 1787.

A court or dress sword, by Edisson & Ravenscroft, London, the ivory grip with a gilded-brass hilt, the guard with a coat-of-arms, c1790, 38in (96.5cm) long.

£270–300
Avrick Antiques

A Light Dragoon officer's sabre, by Gill, the iron beaked pommel inscribed with a crown, the blade signed and etched with a trophy-of-arms, slight damage and losses, late 18thC, blade 33in (84cm) long.

£1,000–1,200
Thomas Del Mar

A Highland officer's broadsword, with a four-flut pommel and a ribbed wooden grip, the steel basket guard wi original cloth and leather liner, with a double-edged blade, l 18thC, blade 32in (81.5cm) l

£1,000–1,200
Wallis & Wallis

A guardsman's sword, with a polished steel hilt and wood grip, the double-edged blade inscribed 'por el rey carlos III' and 'Cavallery A.T. 1771.', Spain, late 18thC, 35¾in (91cm) long.

£650–800 Bearnes

A cutlass, with a brass hilt, leather-covered grip and fulle single-edged blade, English or American, c1812, blade 25¼i (64cm) long.

£475–525 Faganarms

A shortsword, the agate handle with engraved and chased gilt mounts, with hinged quillons, the blade with punched decoration and traces of gilt, in an engraved mounted leather scabbard, France, late 18thC, blade 22¼in (56.5cm) long.

£2,250–2,750
Woolley & Wallis

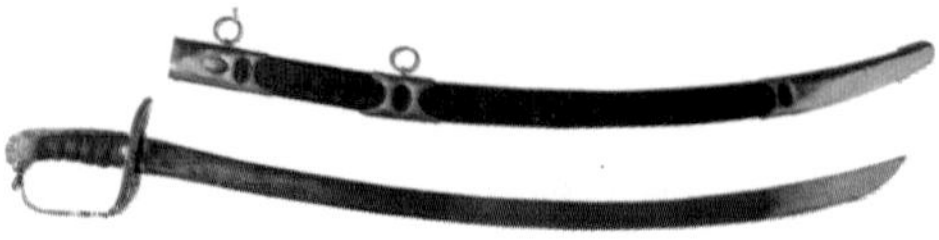

An infantry officer's sword, by Prosser, London, the hilt with lion's-head pommel, the fire-gilt knucklebow with a crowned 'GR' cypher, the fish-skin grip with wire binding, the blade engraved with Georgian coat-of-arms, crowned 'GR' cypher within scrolls and trophies, highlighted in gold, with a gilt-mounted leather scabbard, c1803, 37in (94cm) long.

£1,400–1,600 Michael Long

A 1796 pattern light cavalry trooper's sabre, by Gill, early 19thC, 37in (94cm) long.

£300–350 Avrick Antiques

A boy's military sabre, with original brass scabbard, Continental, c1820, 24in (61cm) long.

£350–400
Michael German

An officer's sword, with French-style brass hilt, the grip bound with twisted gilt wire, the double fullered blade with gilt trophies, the leather scabbard with brass mounts, c1820, 38in (96.5cm) long.

£1,500–1,650 Michael Long

This sword was possibly made for export to America.

A cavalry sword, with a brass handle, France, dated 1825, blade 36in (91.5cm) long.

£200–230
Q & C Militaria

1822 pattern infantry
icer's sword,** with a fish-skin
d wire-bound grip and stepped
mmel, the etched blade with a
yal cipher, signed 'Tatham,
ord cutler to the King,
ndon', with leather and brass-
und scabbard, early 19thC,
¼in (82cm) long.

125–500 Bearnes

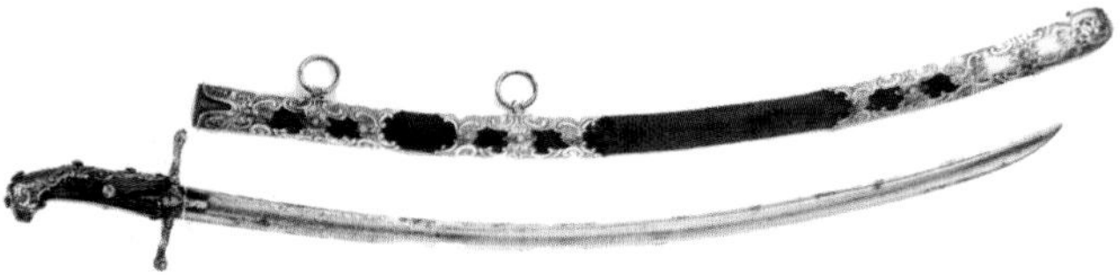

A silver-mounted sabre, the silver hilt cast and chased with scrolls, the quillons with scalloped and bud-shaped terminals, the langets, backstrap, pommel and scabbard set with a turquoise pastes, the pierced back-strap formed as scrolls enclosing scallop shells and flowers, velvet-covered grip, curved double-edged blade with etched decoration and scrollwork wooden grip, with a velvet-covered silver-mounted wooden scabbard, the inner face with traces of gilding, stamped maker's mark 'CW', eastern Europe, early 19thC, blade 28in (71cm) long.

£5,000–6,000 Thomas Del Mar

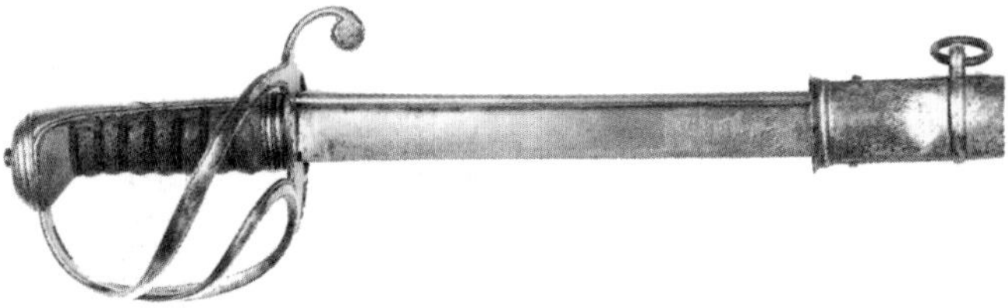

An early Victorian 1821 pattern light cavalry officer's sword, with a triple-bar steel hilt and wirebound fish-skin grip, the blade etched with a crowned VR cypher and wreath within frosted panels, with scabbard, slight damage, blade 35¼in (89.5cm) long.

£180–220 Wallis & Wallis

pioneer sword, with a saw-back blade, c1850, 28in (71cm) long.

340–375 Lanes Armoury

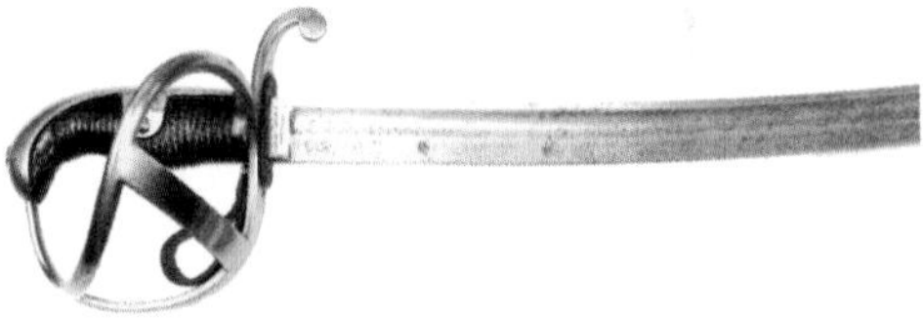

A Royal Engineers driver's sword, by Gebrüder Weyersberg, Solingen, with a steel guard, leather grip and fingerstrap, maker's mark, Prussian and British Liège stamps, Germany, c1850, 34½in (87.5cm) long.

£350–425 Wallis & Wallis

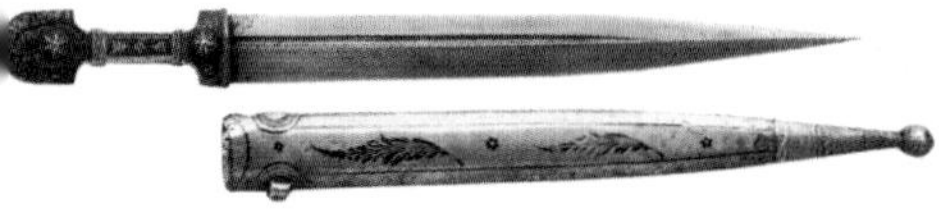

silver-mounted *kindjal*, with a niello silver-decorated wooden hilt, ouble-edged blade and niello silver-covered wooden scabbard, slight amage, Caucasus, 19thC, 17½in (44.5cm) long.

500–600 Thomas Del Mar

A military cadet sword, by Gebruder Weyersberg Solingen, the brass hilt with a reeded grip, the wedge-section blade with a short false edge and blunted tip base, maker's mark, with a brass-mounted leather scabbard, Germany, c1863, blade 16¾in (42.5cm) long.

£250–280 Faganarms

gilt-mounted officer's sabre, Austro/Hungarian, c1900, 6in (91.5cm) long.

525–600 Lanes Armoury

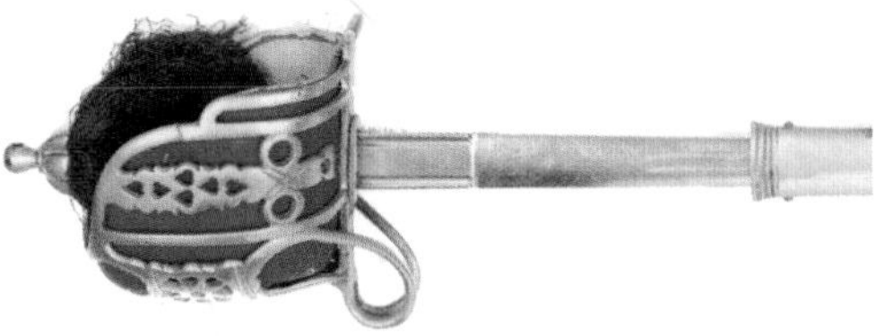

An Edward VII Black Watch Highland officer's broadsword, by W. S. Carver, St James's, the silver-plated basket hilt with a cloth and leather liner, wirebound fish-skin grip, the double-edged claymore blade etched with a Royal cypher, St Andrew and cross, The Black Watch, Royal Highlanders, Sphinx and Egypt within scrolled panels, blade 32½in (82.5cm) long.

£900–1,100 Wallis & Wallis

dagger/knife and fork, by K. Bloner, the stag-horn grip with engraved hite metal fittings, the pommel with three acorn knops, the centre nop pulls out to reveal a two-pronged fork, c1900, 9¾in (25cm) long.

180–200 Michael Long

FIREARMS

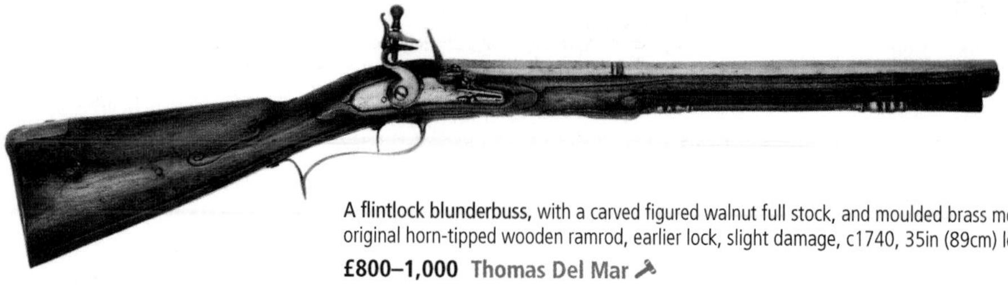

A flintlock blunderbuss, with a carved figured walnut full stock, and moulded brass mounts a original horn-tipped wooden ramrod, earlier lock, slight damage, c1740, 35in (89cm) long.

£800–1,000 Thomas Del Mar

A blunderbuss, the flared steel barrel engraved with a two-tailed naked torso, the walnut full stock with steel mounts, lock and throat pipe associated, signed 'Francesco Gianinno Bargogne in Napoli', repaired, c1750, 35¼in (89.5cm) long.

£600–700 Wallis & Wallis

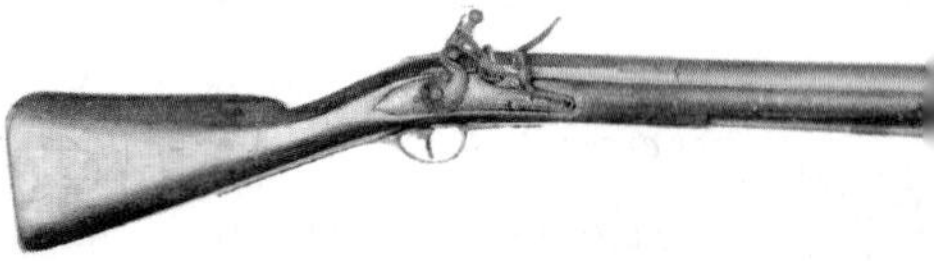

A blunderbuss, the decorated brass barrel engraved 'R. Turner', the full stock with brass furniture, damaged, losses, c1760, barrel c1690, 31in (78.5cm) long.

£1,800–2,200 Wallis & Wallis

A flintlock blunderbuss, the brass barrel inscribed 'Minories-London', proofmarked, the walnut full stock with a brass-mounted wooden ram, the steel action inscribed 'R. Barnett', with brass trigger guard and buttplate, early 19thC, 31in (78.5cm) long.

£1,100–1,300 Andrew Hartley

A model 1865 percussion rifled carbine, the barrel with arsenal mar and dated 1865, the lock with St Etienne Imperial arsenal mark, the stock with traces of arsenal stamps, with steel ramrod, France, barrel 34¼in (87cm) long.

£600–700 Thomas Del Mar

A Brown Bess flintlock musket, by R. Watkin, the butt stock with extra-long butt plate tang, the breech with proof marks and maker's mark, banana lock, acorn finial trigger guard, c1740, 52in (132cm) long.

£2,700–3,000 Michael Long

A Victorian percussion musket, by Parker Field & Sons, with a painte sighted barrel and signed lock, barrel 33½in (85cm) long.

£550–650 Thomas Del Mar

A percussion musket, with Liège proof marks, the back-action lock with a Tula arsenal mark, the full stock with brass mounts, Russia, dated 1861, barrel 37½in (95.5cm) long.

£1,300–1,500 Thomas Del Mar

A brass petronell, c1600, 5in (12.5cm) long.

£270–300 Arbour Antiques

A petronell is a large pistol or carbine that fires a single lead ball. It wa used by the cavalry during the 16th and 17th centuries.

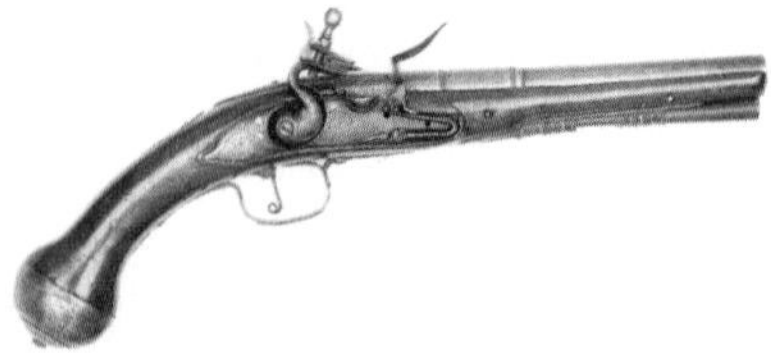

A 28-bore flintlock holster pistol, by C. Warren, the lock engraved with strawberry leaves, the full stock with steel mounts, with London and maker's proof marks, losses, repaired, c1685, 15in (38cm) long.

£850–1,000 Wallis & Wallis

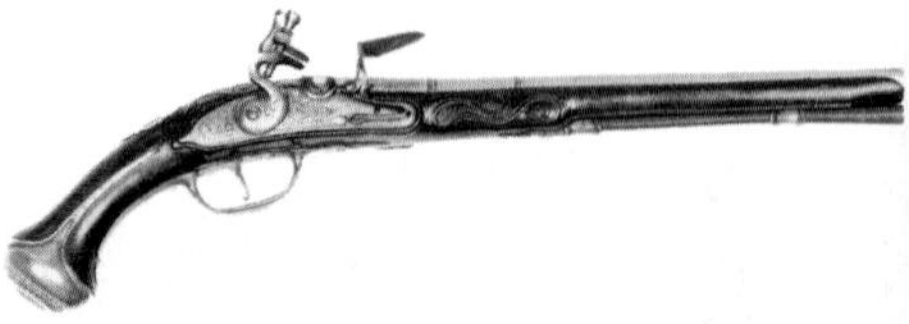

A 20-bore flintlock holster pistol, by Coster, Utrecht, the lock with engraved decoration and maker's name, the scroll-carved walnut full stock with bronze mounts, slight damage, fore-end replaced, Holland, c1685, 20in (51cm) long.

£900–1,100 Wallis & Wallis

An 18-bore flintlock holster pistol, by Nicholson, the plate engraved with a beaded border, winged beast and maker's name, the banded burr-walnut full stock with a scrolled silver sideplate, butt cap replaced, London and maker's proof marks, slight damage, c1700, 20in (51cm) long.

£450–550 Wallis & Wallis

A 50-bore double-barrelled over and under turnover flintlock pistol, the walnut butt and fore-end with steel mounts, cock replaced, c1700, 11in (28cm) long.

£1,600–2,000 Wallis & Wallis

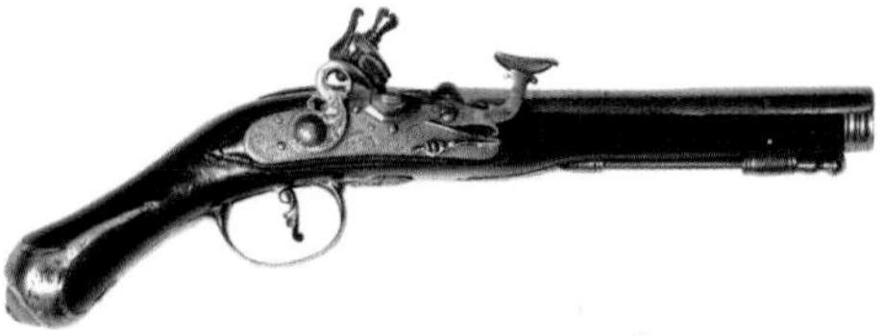

A snaphaunce pistol, with a sliding flash pan and steel mounts, Italy, c1700, 14in (35.5cm) long.

£2,700–3,000 Michael German

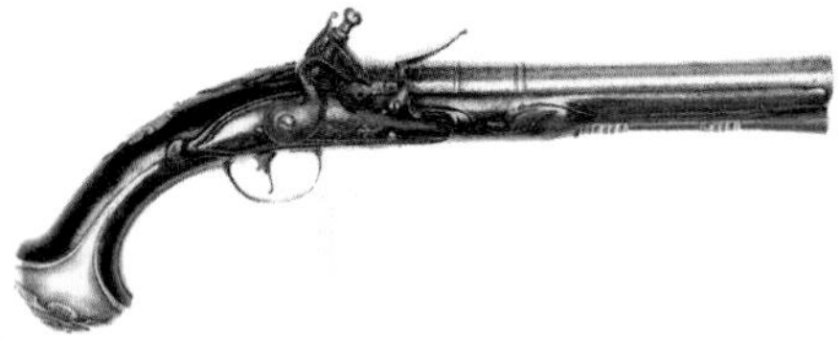

An 18-bore flintlock holster pistol, by Pickfatt, the walnut full stock with silver mounts, slight damage, repair, cock and ramrod replaced, London and maker's proof marks, c1725, 14in (35.5cm) long.

£950–1,150 Wallis & Wallis

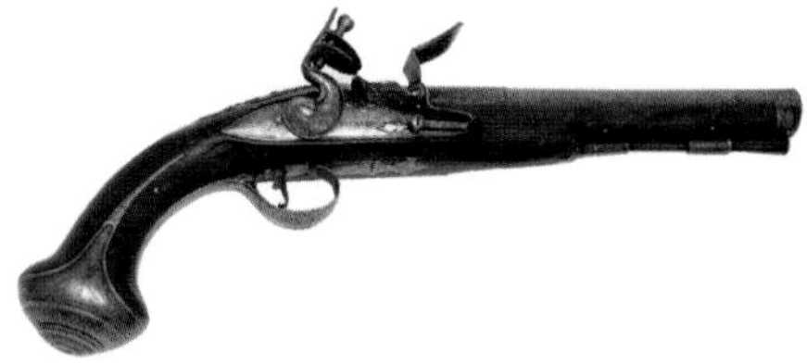

A pair of steel-mounted walnut holster pistols, by T. Richards, with engraved lock plates, c1730, 15½in (39.5cm) long.

£3,400–3,750 Rod Akeroyd

A flintlock service pistol, with a walnut stock, brass pommel and integral ramrod, stamped 'Tower', 18thC, 15½in (39.5cm) long.

£650–800 Bellmans

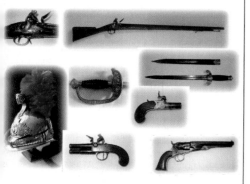

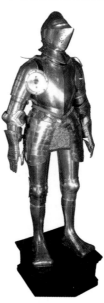

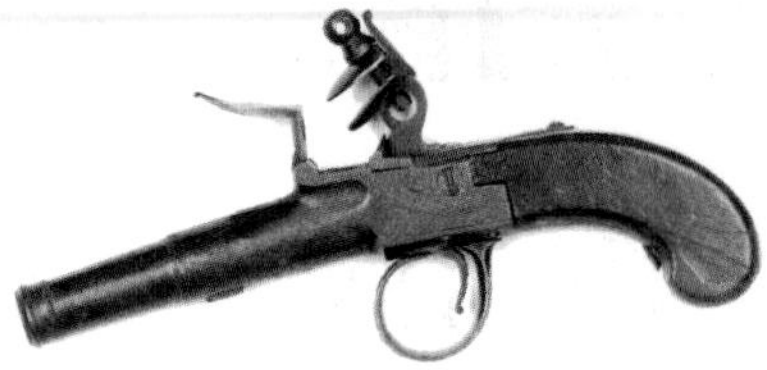

An English-style 80-bore cannon-barrelled flintlock boxlock pocket pistol, engraved 'Josseval a Moudon' within foliate scrolls, with a walnut butt, frissen spring missing, top jaw and screw replaced, France, c1750, 6½in (16.5cm) long.

£130–160 Wallis & Wallis

A double-barrelled Queen Anne pistol, by Stanton, London, with silver mounts, the walnut butt inlaid with silver wire, c1760, 11in (28cm) long.

£2,000–2,250 Rod Akeroyd

A 17-bore flintlock pistol, by I. Barbar, London, c1760, 13¾in (35cm) long.

£600–650 Avrick Antiques

A flintlock duelling pistol, by Jover, London, the carved figured walnut full stock with engraved steel mounts, with signed stepped lock, stamped maker's mark, slight damage, repaired, c1775, 15¼in (38.5cm) long.

£650–800 Thomas Del Mar

A George III pocket percussion pistol, the walnut stock inlaid with white metal, the lock plate engraved 'Joyner London', 7in (17.5cm) long.

£160–200 Penrith Farmers' & Kidd's

A pair of flintlock pistols, with walnut stocks, the lock plate engraved 'Griffin', with turn-off cannon barrels and silver mounts, c1780, 12in (30.5cm) long.

£2,800–3,250 Rod Akeroyd

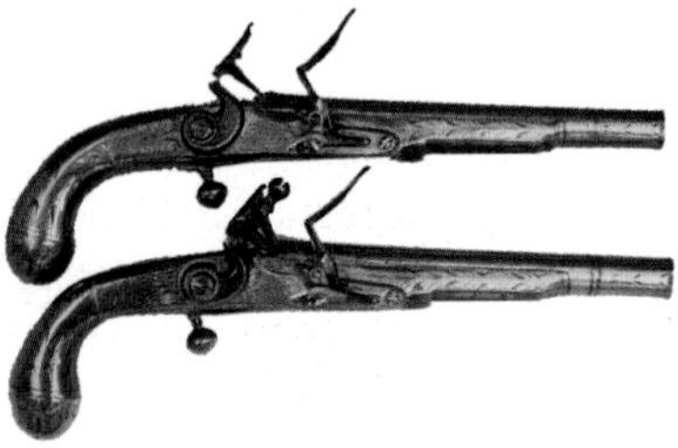

A pair of 26-bore flintlock belt pistols, by T. Murdoch, with engraved barrels, signed, slight damage, top jaw and screw missing from one pistol, ramrods missing, Scotland, c1780, barrel 7¼in (18.5cm) long.

£3,750–4,500 Toovey's

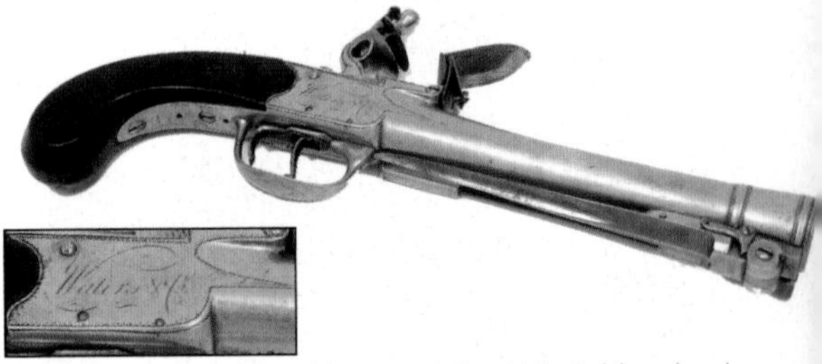

A flintlock blunderbuss pistol, by Waters & Co, with boxlock brass barrel, underflick bayonet and walnut slab-sided butt, c1780, 13in (33cm) long.

£2,800–3,250 Rod Akeroyd

A pair of 24-bore flintlock boxlock pistols, the frames engraved with swags and 'Thomas', with walnut slab butts, with Tower private proof marks, slight damage, c1790, 11½in (29cm) long.

£450–550 Wallis & Wallis

A pair of duelling pistols, by John Manton, London, with walnut stocks, c1790, 15in (38cm) long, with a fitted mahogany case and accessories.

£12,000–14,000 Rod Akeroyd

A 28-bore long sea service flintlock pistol, the lock marked with a crowned 'GR' and 'Tower', the brass butt cap numbered 240 and initialled, early 19thC, 19¼in (49cm) long.

£1,500–1,800 Cheffins

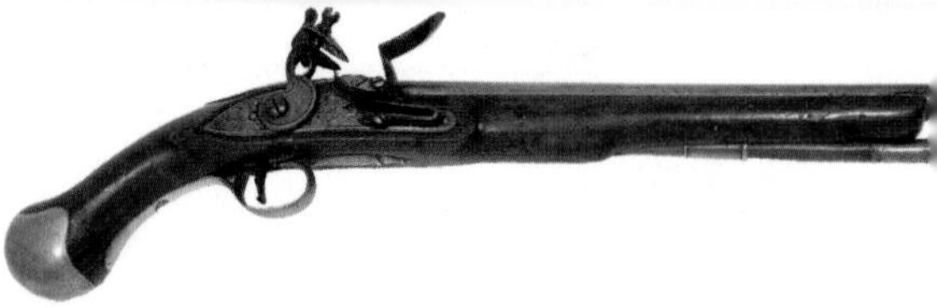

A military long sea service pattern flintlock pistol, with walnut stocks, Tower loc stamped with 'GR' cypher, c1805, 19in (48.5cm) long.

£2,700–3,000 Rod Akeroyd

A pair of flintlock duelling pistols, by Richards, London, with silver mounts, hallmarked 1809, 15in (38cm) long.

£5,000–5,500 Michael German

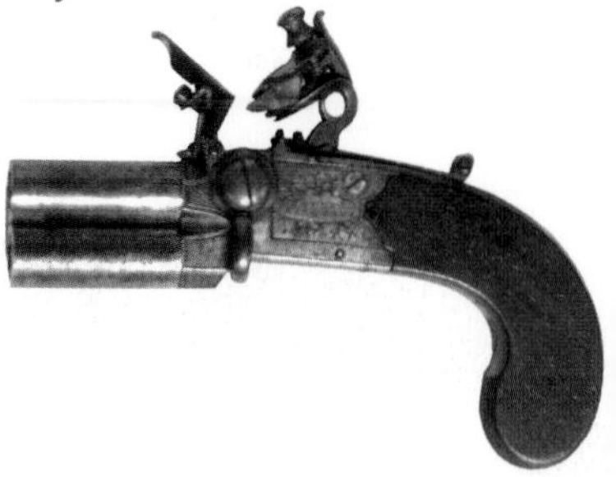

An over-and-under flintlock pocket pistol, by T. Richard London, with a folding trigger and tap action, the walnut grip with a silver escutcheon, c1810, 5in (12.5cm) long.

£1,600–1,800 Arbour Antiques

A pair of flintlock muff pistols, with steel stocks and chequered walnut grips, France, c1810, 5in (12.5cm) long.

£1,600–1,850 Arbour Antiques

A flintlock duelling pistol, by Probin, London, c1810, 15in (38cm) long.

£1,800–2,000 Garth Vincent

A pair of 40-bore flintlock duelling pistols, by Joseph Manton, London, No. 5866, c1813, 15½in (39.5cm) long, in a fitted case.

£20,000–24,000 Waddington's

A pair of flintlock blunderbuss pistols, by Harcourt, Norwich, with brass barrels, boxlock action and walnut butts, Irish registration marks c1815, 7in (18cm) long.

£2,700–3,000 Rod Akeroyd

A naval short sea service flintlock pistol, by Tower Armouries, c1820, 13in (33cm) long.

£550–600 Grimes Militaria

A flintlock rifled travelling pistol, by Alexander Thomson, Edinburgh, the breech inlaid with a platinum line, with a platinum vent, standing back-sight, figured walnut stock and chequered butt, ramrod missing, Scotland, c1820, 12in (30.5cm) long.

£1,200–1500 Thomas Del Mar

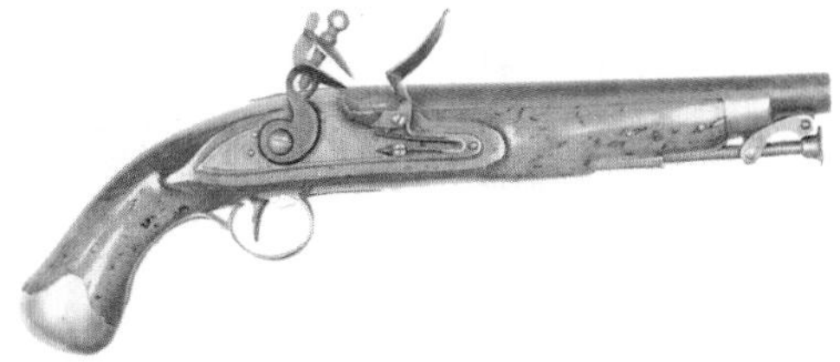

William IV sea service flintlock belt pistol, with brass mounts and Tower proof arks, the walnut full stock with ordnance inspector's marks and stamped with an row and 'BO', the engraved lock stamped 'WR', restored, 15in (38cm) long.

1,300–1,600 Wallis & Wallis

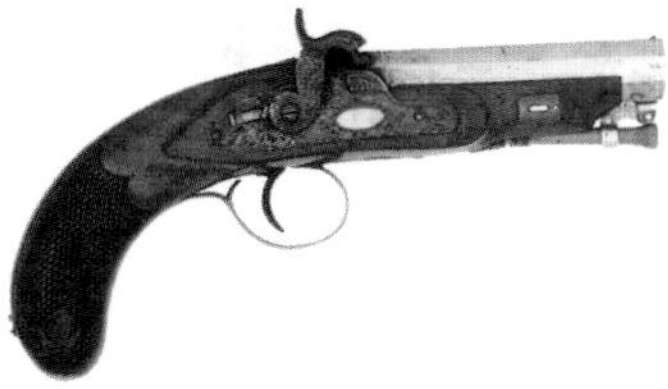

A percussion travelling pistol, the barrel inscribed 'New York', with a silver fore-sight and German silver trigger guard, engraved bolted lock and figured walnut stock, the butt with a chequered panel and hollow for balls, swivel ramrod replaced, possibly America, c1840, 8¼in (21.5cm) long.

£550–650 Thomas Del Mar

pair of flintlock pistols, with steel barrels, the full stocks with hinged ramrod, ass trigger guards and plain grips, lockplates signed 'Richards', 19thC, barrels ¼in (21cm) long.

1,300–1,500 Bearnes

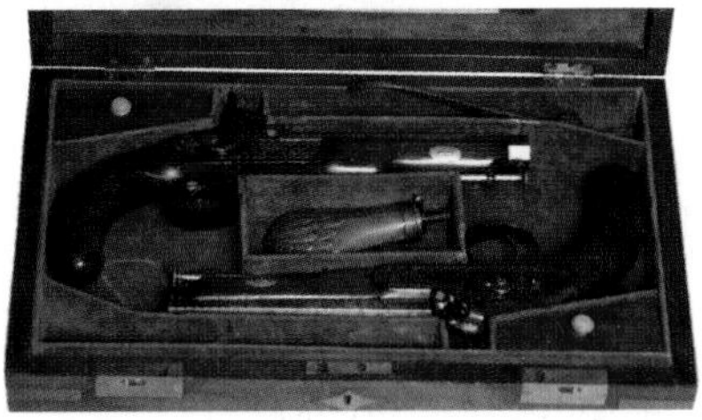

A pair of officer's percussion pistols, by Richards, London, retailed by Mountain & Co, Calcutta, with a belt hook, c1840, in original mahogany case, 17in (43cm) wide.

£3,250–3,750 Arbour Antiques

sea service percussion pistol, by Tower Armouries, 1855, 11in (28cm) long.

270–300 Grimes Militaria

A military officer's over-and-under precision pistol, by Kavanagh, Dublin, with back action locks, captive ramrod and walnut grip, Ireland, c1860, 11in (28cm) long.

£2,800–3,250 Arbour Antiques

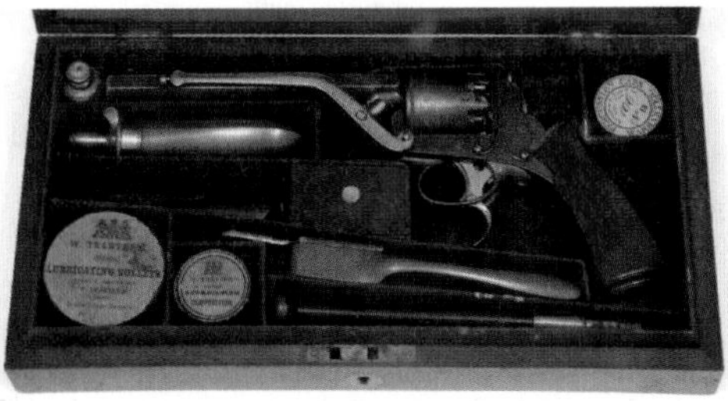

54-bore percussion revolver, by Tranter, with a walnut stock, 1850, 12in (30.5cm) long, in a fitted mahogany case with accessories.

2,500–2,800 Rod Akeroyd

A naval percussion revolver, by Colt, London, 1850, 13in (33cm) long, in a fitted case with original accessories.

£2,600–3,000 Q & C Militaria

five-shot large-bore percussion pepperbox revolver, by Parker, ield & Sons, London, No. 9347, the engraved barrel stamped with roof marks, the scroll-engraved self-cocking German silver action ngraved with maker's details, with figured walnut grips and engraved igger guard, 1845–50, 9½in (24cm) long.

900–1,100 Thomas Del Mar

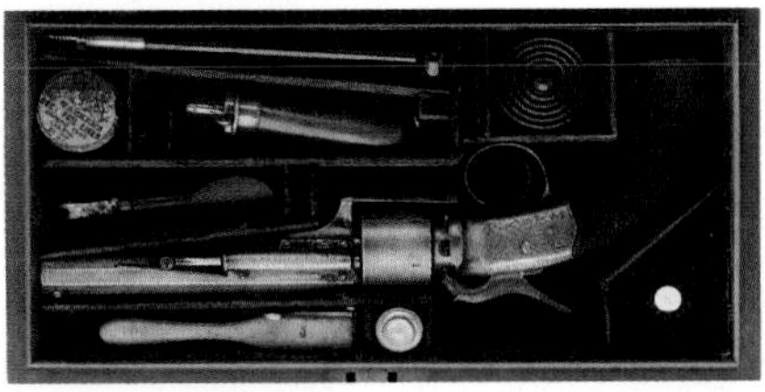

A 54-bore percussion revolver, by Parker, Field & Sons, London, No. 9717, with a signed sighted rifled barrel, the patented rammer signed and engraved 'Regis. June 14th 1852', with a chequered walnut butt, the steel butt cap with engraved decoration, London proof marks, 1852–55, 12½in (32cm) long, in original fitted mahogany velvet-lined case.

£2,500–3,000 Thomas Del Mar

A 10.5 calibre self-cocking transitional revolver, by Hall, with a chequered hardwood grip, 1850s, 12in (30.5cm) long.

£500–550 Avrick Antiques

A .32 revolver, by Tranter, London, retailed by Woodward, London, with gold *koftgari* decoration, c1860, 9in (23cm) long.

£3,000–3,500 Arbour Antiques

To effect koftgari *decoration, the surface of the object is roughened and then the artisan, with a small hammer in one hand and a wire of precious metal (usually gold or silver) in the other, hammers the wire onto the surface while manipulating it to form the design.*

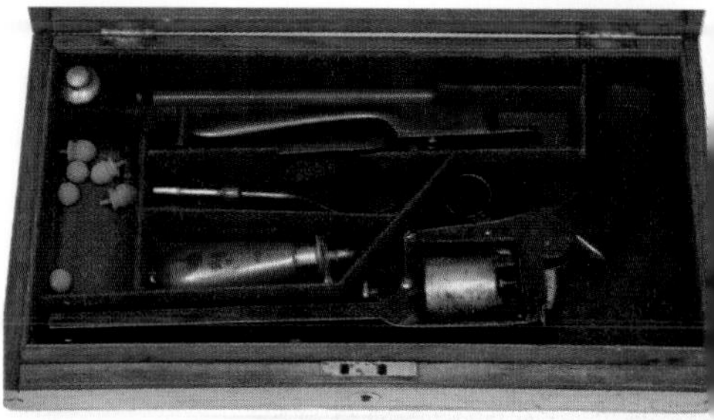

A .38 percussion revolver, by Deane, Adams & Deane, London, with walnut stocks, c1851, 13½in (34.5cm) long, in a fitted oak case with accessories.

£1,700–1,850 Rod Akeroyd

A Schneider-Enfield .577 calibre rifle, with a walnut stock, c1857, barrel 34in (86.5cm) long.

£1,350–1,500 Q & C Militaria

POLEARMS

A ceremonial halberd, fire-etched with foot soldiers, flowers and vines, pole shortened, stamped smith's marks, Germany, c1570, 73½in (186.5cm) long.

£1,600–2,000 Hermann Historica

A forged steel halberd, Italy, c1580, 90in (228.5cm) long.

£900–1,000
Arbour Antiques

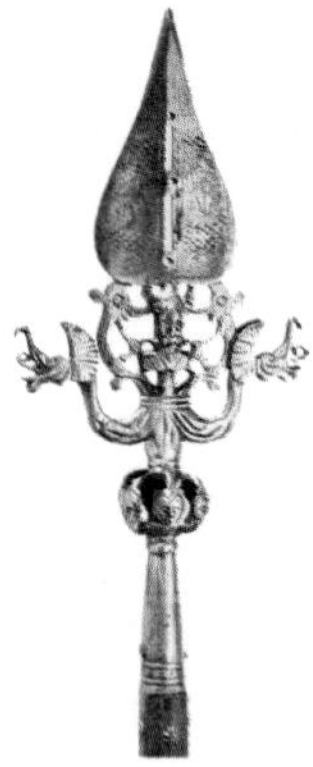

A linstock, the blade with engraved decoration, the root pierced and engraved with Turks' heads, the match holders in the form of elephants' heads, the socket with grotesque masks, the pole with brass rivet heads, Italy, c1600, 83in (211cm) long.

£3,800–4,500
Hermann Historica

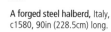

A forged iron mace, the head inlaid with brass dots, the shaft with a replaced leather-covered wooden grip, Poland or Hungary, 17thC, 26in (66cm) long.

£1,800–2,200 Hermann Historica

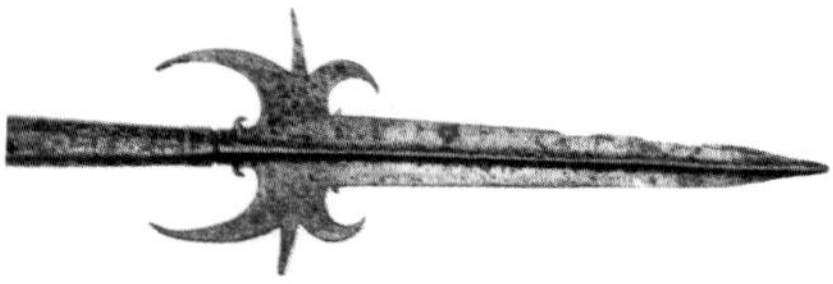

A partizan, slight damage, early 18thC, 15½in (39.5cm) long.

£600–700 Thomas Del Mar

A spontoon, the socket inscribed with an arsenal number, on a later wooden haft adapted for mounting a flag, Germany, possibly Saxony, 1725–50, head 11in (28cm) long.

£500–600 Thomas Del Mar

A spear, the blade engraved with a coat-of-arms and six birds in a shield, the reverse with a bird within a wreath and 'FT', on a fabric-covered wooden haft, slight damage, Italy, 1525–50, head 30in (76cm) long.

£2,250–2,750
Thomas Del Mar

MILITARIA

BADGES

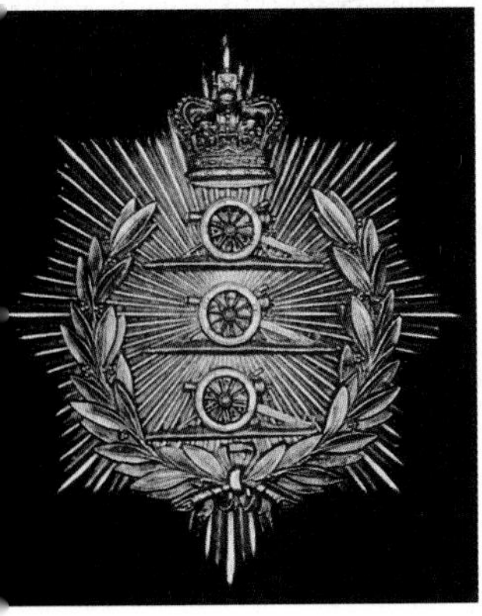

n Artillery Volunteers officer's General attern silver-plated shako plate, c1860.
350–425 Dix Noonan Webb

A Victorian Carnaervonshire Rifle Volunteers white metal Maltese Cross officer's pouch belt badge.
£160–200 Wallis & Wallis

A Forfar & Kincardine Militia Artillery officer's gilt-copper helmet plate, 1889–1900.
£350–425 Dix-Noonan-Webb

COSTUME

n Army miniature brass gorget, c1800, in (15cm) long.
:135–150 Grimes Militaria

his was a remnant of suits of armour and was he last piece of armour worn by the army. It was sed on full dress occasions for decorative and eremonial purposes – it was not substantial nough to be a protective device.

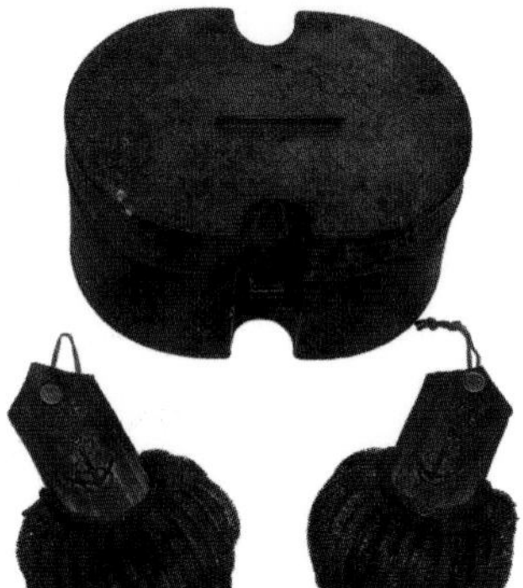

A pair of naval gilt epaulettes, c1800, 6in (15cm) long, in original tin box.
£180–200 Grimes Militaria

A Queen's Own Oxfordshire Hussars officer's full dress cloth and morocco sabretache, with a silver-plated crown and cypher within a silver bullion border, c1850, 13in (33cm) high.
£1,600–2,000 Wallis & Wallis

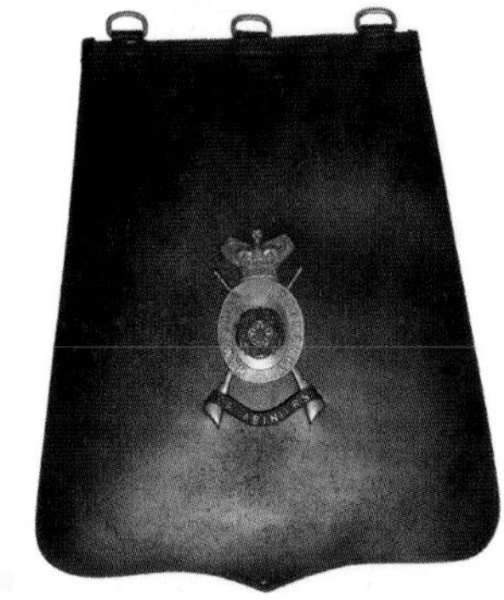

A Yeomanry undress leather sabretache, :1880, 13in (33cm) high.
£180–200 Grimes Militaria

Undress uniform is worn on a daily basis, as opposed to full dress which is worn on special occasions. Sabretaches were worn underneath the sword and were used to carry dispatches.

A Pennsylvania 6th Infantry Civil War jacket and cap, the cap with retailer's label for Wilsons, Philadelphia, America, c1865.
£450–550 Freeman's

An officer's dress uniform, c1876.
£850–950 Paul Cranny

HELMETS & HEADDRESSES

A Montgomeryshire Yeomanry Cavalry japanned tin, silver and gilt helmet and a sabretache, the sabretache with silver bullion work, c1840, sabretache 14in (35.5cm) high.

£6,800–7,500 Rod Akeroyd

A Victorian 7th (The Princess Royal's) Dragoon Guards officer's gilt helmet.

£2,000–2,500 Wallis & Wallis

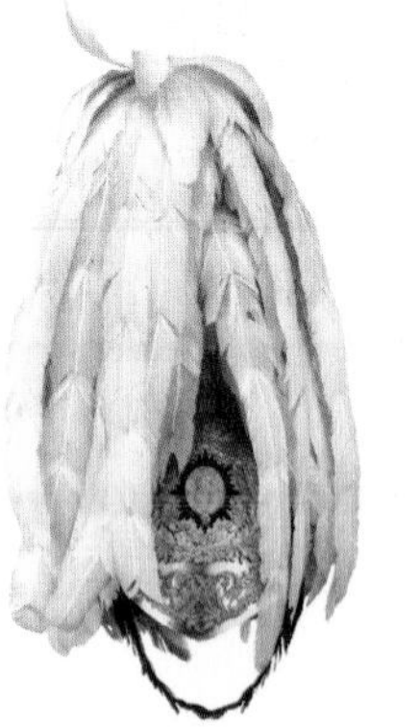

A Victorian Honourable Corps of Gentlemen-at-Arms gilt-metal Albert pattern helmet, with a two-stage swan-feather plume.

£3,000–3,500 Thomas Del Mar

The Honourable Corps of Gentlemen-at-Arm were formed in 1539 as the 'Nearest Guard' to the sovereign.

A 5th Dragoon Guards brass helmet, c1900.

£580–650 Q & C Militaria

A 4th Dragoon Guards helmet, c1900.

£580–650 Q & C Militaria

A Victorian The Princess of Wales's Own Yorkshire Regiment spiked helmet, with a gilt and silver-plated helmet plate.

£550–650 Wallis & Wallis

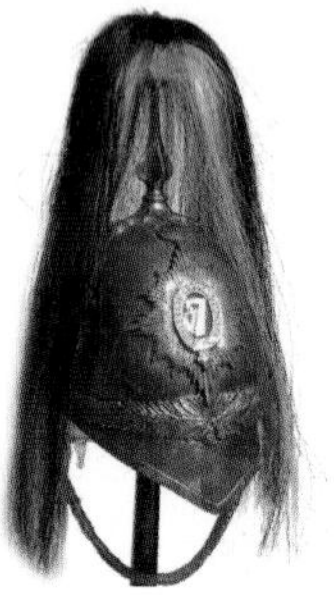

A 7th Dragoon Guards brass helmet, c1900.

£580–650 Q & C Militaria

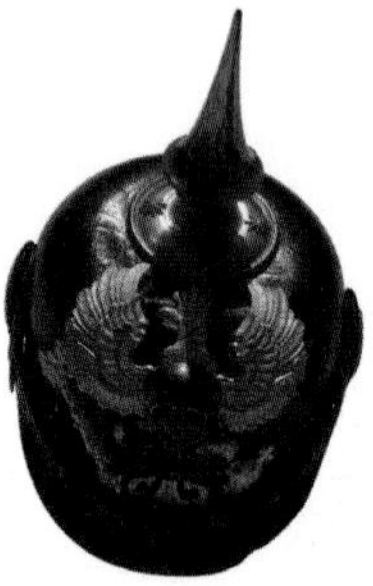

A Brunswick leather and brass *Pickelhaube*, Germany, c1900.

£1,200–1,300 Tussie Mussies

A pith helmet, by Moss Bros & Co, 'The Conforma', with label, c1910, 15in (38cm) wide, with original tin box.

£250–275 Christopher Clarke

An Artillery leather and gilt *Pickelhaube*, cockades and chin scales replaced, Germany, c1915.

£525–585 Michael Long

A French Dragoon Guards brass and white metal helmet, France, c1900.

£675–750 Q & C Militaria

WALLIS & WALLIS EST. 1928

WEST STREET AUCTION GALLERIES, LEWES, SUSSEX, ENGLAND BN7 2NJ
TEL: +44 (0)1273 480208 FAX: +44 (0)1273 476562

Britain's Specialist Auctioneers of Militaria, Arms, Armour & Medals

Distinguished Conduct Medal group of six to Battery Sargeant Major C Gill, Motor Machine Gun Corps, realised £3,400 in a recent auction.

2007 AUCTION DATES

SALE	DAY	LAST ENTRIES
502	July 24th	–
503	September 4th	July 28th
504	October 16th & 17th	September 8th
AUTUMN CONNOISSEUR COLLECTORS' AUCTION	**October 16th & 17th**	**September 8th**
505	November 27th	October 20th

2008 AUCTION DATES AVAILABLE ON REQUEST

Monthly Sale Catalogue £9.50, Europe £10.00, R of W £10.50
Full colour illustrated Connoisseur Sale Catalogue £14.00, Europe £15.00, R of W £15.50 (All prices include postage)

'Get to know the real value of your collection' *– Our last 10 Sale catalogues are available, price £30.00 inc. postage, complete with prices realised*

Entry forms available on request

No charge for payment by credit card

email: auctions@wallisandwallis.co.uk web site: http://www.wallisandwallis.co.uk

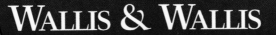

ORDERS & MEDALS

A Military General Service medal, awarded to Sylvester Burke of the 91st Foot Argyle and Sutherland Highlanders, with clasps for Roleia, Vimiera, 21 August 1808.

£1,350–1,500 **Q & C Militaria**

Sylvester Burke was taken by the French and was a prisoner of war for the rest of the campaign.

A Waterloo medal, awarded to George Windus 35th Royal Sussex Regiment.

£1,350–1,500 **Q & C Militaria**

An Army of India medal, awarded to Gunner Patrick Malone, with one clasp Bhurtpoor.

£1,200–1,350 **Q & C Militaria**

A South Africa medal, awarded to Lieutenant and Adjutant Hon R. Monck, 43rd Regiment, 1853.

£1,300–1,500 **Lawrence Fine Art**

A Crimea medal, with one clasp, Sebastopol, awarded to French officer Ctl. Colldt. S. Off. AU9ZE, 1854–56.

£270–300 **Q & C Militaria**

There were a few French recipients of the British Crimea medal.

A Baltic medal, awarded to Lieutenant H. L. T. Inglis, 1854–55.

£1,600–2,000 **Dix Noonan Webb**

This is in mint condition and thus extremely rare.

A Companion of the Order of the Star of India pair, awarded to Surgeon-General J. F. Arthur, Indian Medical Service, Surgeon of the Madras Fusiliers at the Defence of Lucknow: Companion's breast badge, Indian Mutiny 1857–59, two clasps, Defence of Lucknow, Lucknow, naming officially corrected.

£6,000–7,000 **Dix Noonan Webb**

A group of four, awarded to Sailmaker's Mate G. Taylor: Indian General Service medal 1854–95 with one clasp, Burma 1885–87; Egypt medal 1882–89 with one clasp, Suakin 1885; Long Service and Good Conduct medal; Khedive Star; and a Masonic jewel Prince Edward's Lodge No. 25 inscribed 'Bro. George Taylor W. M. 1898–99'.

£1,000–1,200 **Bearnes**

An Ashantee medal, awarded to Capt St A. H. Player, 6th Dragoons, with one clasp, Coomassie 1874–4, with a dress medal.

£1,600–2,000 Bellmans

A Victorian enamel Masonic Order, set with diamonds and emeralds.

£2,000–2,500 Hy Duke

A Kaiser medal and a Franco Prussian medal, the latter with clasps for Weissenburg, Sedan, Würth and Paris, late 19thC.

£130–150 Tussie Mussies

The Kaiser medal was made from melted-down French guns.

A Boxer Rebellion medal, awarded to Lieutenant E. E. Porter, 1900.

£630–700 Q & C Militaria

A gold and enamel Order of St Stanislaus Civil Division, slight damage, Russia, c1870, with sash and box.

£2,500–3,000 Sotheby's (O)

A group of five, awarded to G. Taylor, Royal Horse Guards: Queen's South Africa Medal with three clasps, Cape Colony, Johannesburg, Wittebergen; 1914–15 Star; War and Victory Medals, and Metropolitan Police Coronation Medal 1911, with matching miniatures.

£500–600 **Bearnes**

A pair, awarded to Brigadier-General Monck, CSO, Coldstream Guards: Queen's South Africa medal with three clasps, Belmont, Modder River, Orange Free State, and 1911 Coronation medal, with miniatures.

£1,700–2,000 **Lawrence Fine Art**

A group of four, awarded to Lieut Samuel Foden Moss: Military medal; 1914–15 Star; British War and Victory medals.

£500–600 **Wallis & Wallis**

A group of five, awarded to Edward Holmes, RN: China 1900 medal; 1914–15 Star; British War and Victory medals; Navy Long Service and Good Conduct medal, with a framed HMS *Ajax* certificate dated 17th August 1938.

£350–425 **Bellman's**

A group of five, awarded to Major H. G. Collins: Military Cross; Africa General Service medal, with one clasp, Nyasaland; 1914–15 Star, British War and Victory medals, with five dress miniature medals.

£2,250–2,750 **Toovey's**

A group of seven, awarded to Warrant Officer J. T. Darby, Royal Air Force: Distinguished Flying Cross, GVIR; 1935–45 Star; Air Crew Europe Star; Africa Star; Defence and War medals; Royal Air Force Long Service and Good Conduct medal.

£2,250–2,750 **Dix Noonan Webb**

A group of seven, awarded to Captain Wah Kumje Tang, Burmese Signals, South East Asian Special Operations Force 136: Military Cross; Burma Gallantry; 1939–45 Star; Burma Star; Defence and War medals with MiD oak leaf; USA Bronze Star for Gallantry, 1945.

£7,000–8,000 **Q & C Militaria**

An Order of Burma, awarded to Jadup Sin Wa Naw, 1946.

£2,700–3,000 **Q & C Militaria**

Only three of these medals are known to have been awarded for acts of heroism.

POWDER FLASKS & HORNS

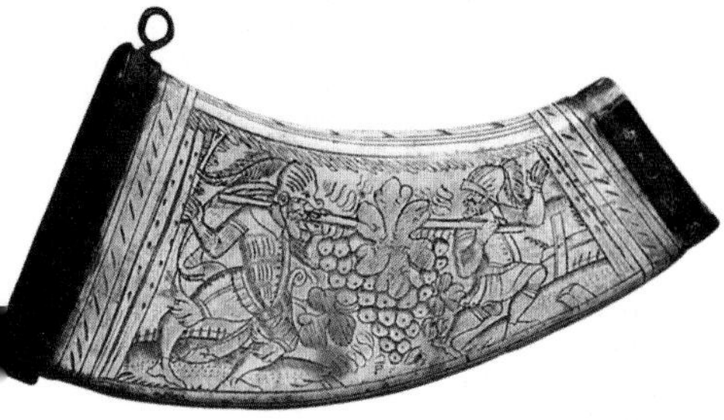

n engraved horn powder flask, iron mounts later, damage and sses, Austria, 16thC, 9¾in (25cm) long.

1,000–1,200 Dorotheum ⊞

An engraved horn powder flask, with steel mounts, losses, Germany, early 17thC, 12¾in (32.5cm) long.

£350–425 Thomas Del Mar ⊞

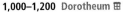

n engraved powder horn, inscribed 'March ye A 1762 Crown Point tephen Dyar', with a carved wood butt plug, slight damage, America, 1762, 11½in (29cm) long.

3,000–3,500 Skinner

ort Crown Point, first constructed by the French c1731, was trategically built halfway between Montreal and Albany at the far outh end of Lake Champlain, to protect the southern reaches of New rance from British colonial expansion. During the French and Indian Var in the 1750s, part of Crown Point and neighbouring installations vere targets of attempts by the British to gain control of Lake Champlain. They did not succeed until it was evacuated by the French nd mostly destroyed by fire in 1759. It was then claimed by the British nd rebuilt in the form of a pentagon. After the conquest of Canada in 760, Crown Point was garrisoned by British troops until 1774, when it vas captured by American revolutionists.

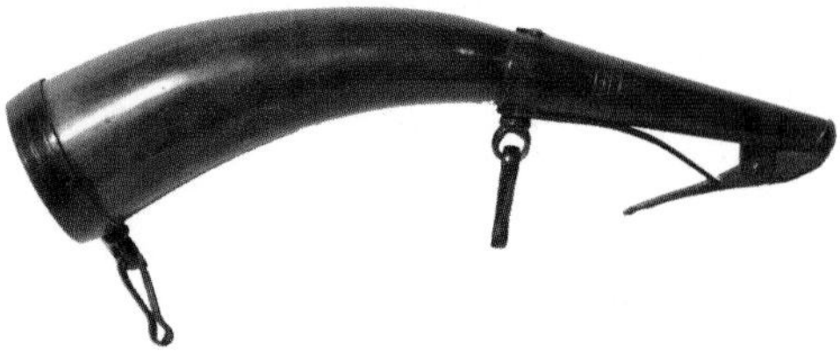

A priming powder horn, with brass mounts, 18thC, 7in (18cm) long.

£280–325 Arbour Antiques ⊞

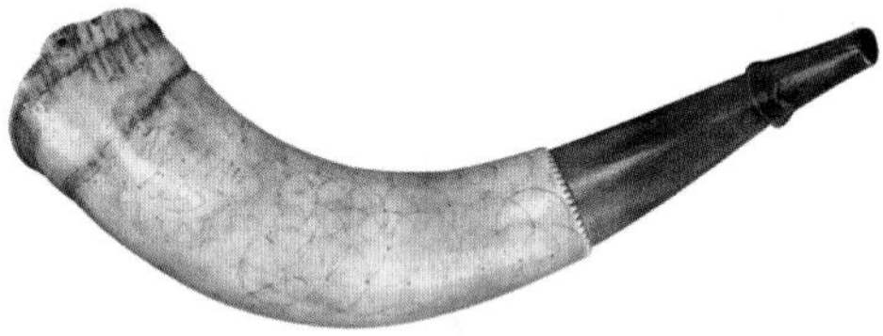

An engraved powder horn, signed 'Wm. M 1799', and 'JM 1814', c1800, 14in (35.5cm) long.

£550–650 James D Julia

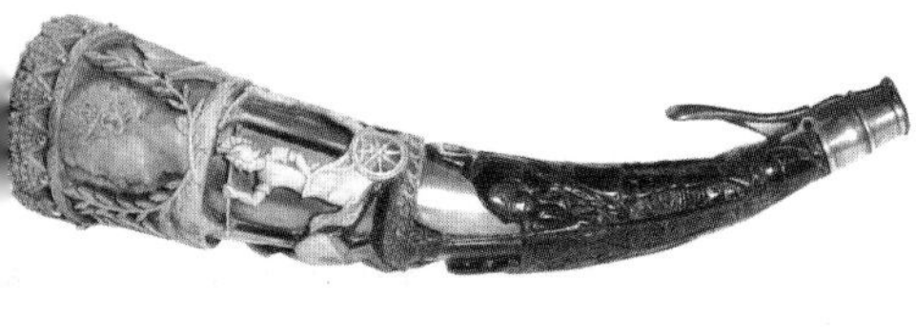

A silver-mounted powder horn, Italy, 19thC, 12in (30.5cm) long.

£1,400–1,600 Arbour Antiques ⊞

A priming powder flask, with steel and brass mounts, Continental, 19thC, 5in (12.5cm) long.

£400–440 Arbour Antiques ⊞

MISCELLANEOUS

A brass-bound mahogany campaign box, with an engraved inscription 'From the Sergeant Major, Staff Sergts & Sergts 1st Batt. Grenadier Gds to Captain the Earl Stanhope. Grenadier Guards. 1908.', 15in (38cm) wide.
£200–225 Christopher Clarke

An officer's mahogany writing desk, the drawer with pair of c1840 double-barrel percussion pistols, c1800, 20in (51cm) wide.
£1,000–1,200 Grimes Militaria

An officer's campaign silver dining compendium, comprising beaker, folding knife, fork and spoon, c1840, 5in (12.5cm) high, in original leather case.
£650–720
Anthony Green Antiques

A Georgian wooden side drum, with painted decoration, losses, 15in (38cm) diam.
£600–700 Wallis & Wallis

A wooden militia drum, with painted decoration, America, Massachusetts, c1860, 17in (43cm) diam.
£2,500–3,000 Northeast Auctions

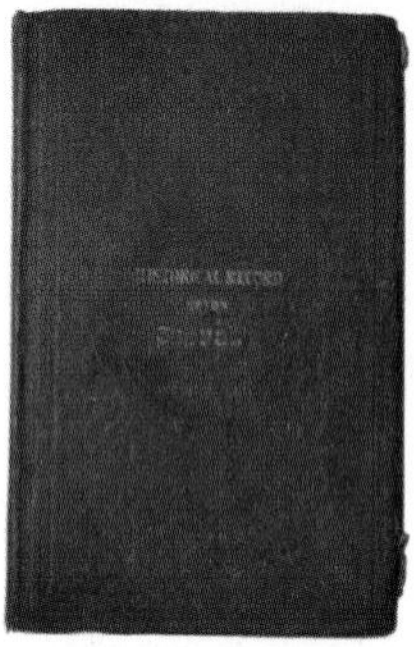

Richard Cannon, *Historical Records of the 36th or the Herefordshire Regiment of Foot*, published by Parker, Furnivall & Parker, London, 1853, 9 x 6in (23 x 15cm).
£150–165 Barter Books

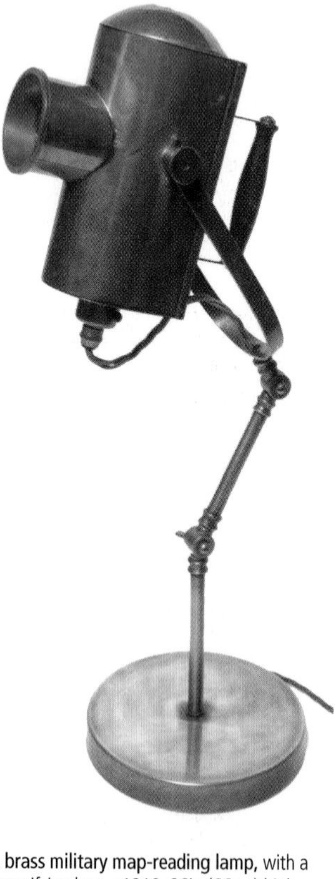

A brass military map-reading lamp, with a magnifying lens, c1910, 26in (66cm) high.
£225–250 Christopher Clarke

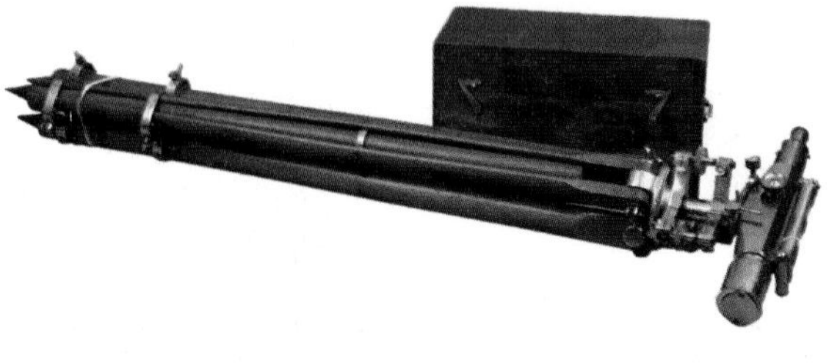

A cast-brass Stanley's Patent Dumpy level, No. 578, dated 1916, in a fitted case, with adjustable folding tripod.
£280–350 Gorringes (L)

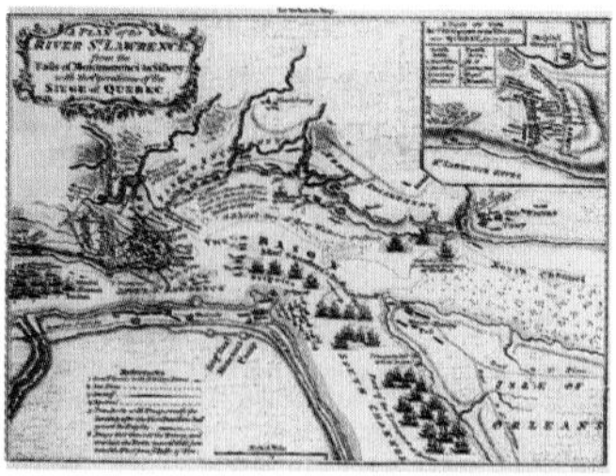

An engraved plan, depicting 'the River St. Lawrence from the falls of Montmorenci to Sillery with the operations of the Siege of Quebec', published by the *London Magazine*, with inset 'Plan of the Action gained by the English near Quebec, Sept. 13, 1759', 1760, 7½ x 9¾in (19 x 25cm).
£375–450 Northeast Auctions

A Boer War steel and horn multi-purpose tool,c1900, 5in (12.5cm) long.
£100–110 Tussie Mussies

SCIENTIFIC INSTRUMENTS

CALCULATING INSTRUMENTS & MACHINES

A mahogany Thatcher's Calculating Instrument, by Keuffel & Esser Co, New York, No. 4012/4142, with outer paper-covered scales on revolving brass rings, and 19in sliding inner cylinder, America, late 19thC, 21½in (54.5cm) wide.

£500–600 Skinner

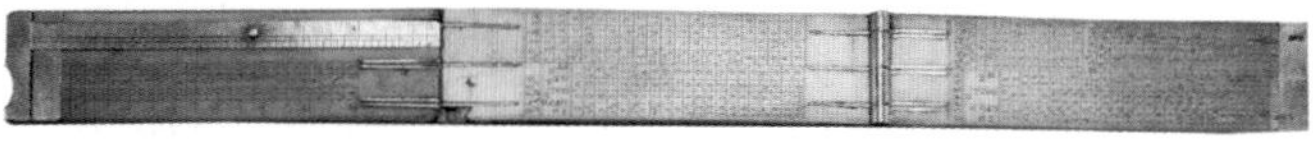

An ivory folding rule, by J. Dobie, Glasgow, with extending calliper and ironmonger's scale, Scotland, 19thC, 15in (38cm) long.

£175–220 Jackson's

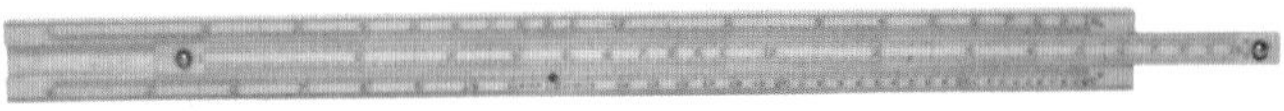

An ivory Soho-type calculating slide rule, by E. Bryan, Manchester, the reverse with Routledge's engineering scales, c1830, 12in (30.5cm) long.

£450–500 Charles Tomlinson

COMPASSES & DIALS

A surveyor's brass compass, by David Rittenhouse, with signed silvered dial, winged brass hub and centre clamp, cast 'tulip' socket, the limb with vial and screw-on sights, America, 18thC, 14½in (37cm) wide.

£11,000–13,000 Skinner

A surveyor's mahogany and brass Vernier compass, by Benjamin Hanks, with engraved paper card, America, late 18thC, 15½in (39.5cm) wide, in a fitted wooden case.

£1,400–1,700 Skinner

A carved ivory pocket compass and thermometer, c1820, 3in (7.5cm) wide, in leather-covered case.

£675–750 Chiltern Antiques

A surveyor's brass compass, by Zehra Peck, needle missing, dial rubbed, one nut replaced, signed, America, 19thC, 13¾in (35cm) wide.

£1,300–1,600 Skinner

A George IV turned ivory sundial, compass and thermometer, by T. Staight, London, with printed card dial, the outer ring with world cities and islands, 4¼in (11cm) diam.

£1,100–1,300 Woolley & Wallis

A brass compass plate, by T. B. Winter, Newcastle-upon-Tyne, each section calibrated in 90°, c1900, 8in (20.5cm) diam.

£100–120 Penrith Farmers' & Kidd's

GLOBES

A terrestrial pocket globe, after Herman Moll, the fish-skin-covered case lined with a celestial map and zodiac calendar, damaged, 18thC, 2¾in (7cm) diam.

£2,000–2,500 **Skinner**

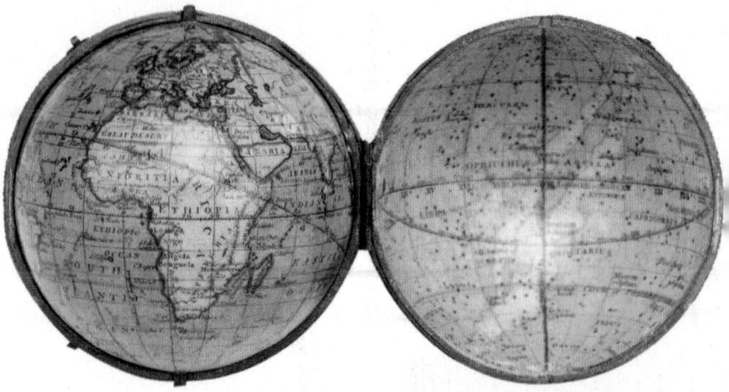

A papier-mâché terrestrial pocket globe, labelled 'Newton's New & Improved Terrestrial Pocket Globe', the fishskin-covered case lined with celestial maps, c1817, 3in (7.5cm) diam.

£5,500–6,500 **Sotheby's**

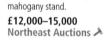

A pair of Wilson's terrestrial and celestial globes, the latter signed by Cyrus Lancaster, America, c1835, 13in (33cm) diam, each on a mahogany stand.

£12,000–15,000
Northeast Auctions

Cyrus Lancaster worked for James Wilson & Sons in Albany, NY. After Wilson's two sons died in 1833, Lancaster continued to produce globes under his own name.

A George III terrestrial pocket globe, by Nathaniel Lane, with inscription, slight damage, 2¾in (7cm) diam.

£900–1,100 **Dreweatt Neate (Ham)**

A celestial globe, by T. Harris & Sons, c1830, 12in (30.5cm) diam.

£10,000–11,000 **Richard Gardner**

A celestial globe, by C. Smith & Son, London, c1860, 19in (48.5cm) diam.

£2,250–2,500 **Mary Cruz Antiques**

A Franklin terrestrial globe, by Nims & Knight, in a calibrated brass horizon ring and paper horizon ring with red-painted rim, divided by the Gregorian and zodiacal calendars, slight damage, America, Troy, NY, 1882–92, 12in (30.5cm) diam, on a mahogany stand.

£3,250–4,000 **Skinner**

A Philip's Merchant Shippers' globe, with lacquered brass meridian and paper-mounted border displaying months of the year and signs of the zodiac, early 20thC, 18in (45.5cm) diam on a mahogany stand set with a compass.

£2,250–2,750 **Gorringes (L)**

MEDICAL, DENTAL & OPTICAL

A George III mahogany apothecary box, by William Stock, London, the hinged cover with a label and enclosing a compartment, the door opening to reveal six bottles and six labelled drawers, on bracket feet, with carrying handles, 13¼in (33.5cm) wide.

£450–550 Sworders

A mahogany apothecary box, with scales, pestle and mortar, c1850, 12½in (32cm) wide.

£900–1,000 Antique Boxes

A Victorian mahogany apothecary box, enclosing glass bottles with paper labels, a mixing bowl, a pair of brass scales and other accessories, inset with an ivory plaque engraved 'Savory & Moore, Chemists to the Queen, London', 10¾in (27cm) wide.

£320–380 Bearnes

A George III glass apothecary jar, with Chester coat-of-arms and inscribed 'Peruv Bark', cover replaced, 24in (61cm) high.

£2,500–2,800 Mary Cruz Antiques

A ruby glass apothecary jar and cover, Germany, c1900, 11½in (29.5cm) high.

£175–200 Sworders

A bleeding bowl, painted with a river scene, China, early 19thC, 10in (25.5cm) wide.

£120–150
Dee, Atkinson & Harrison

A brass bleeding tool, c1810, 2in (5cm) long, in a fitted case.

£750–850 Curious Science

A set of blood letting glasses, c1860, in a fitted box, 13in (33cm) wide.

£300–350 Early Technology

ɔ Victorian mahogany and glass chemist shop signs, n (58.5cm) wide.

25–250 Humbleyard ⊞

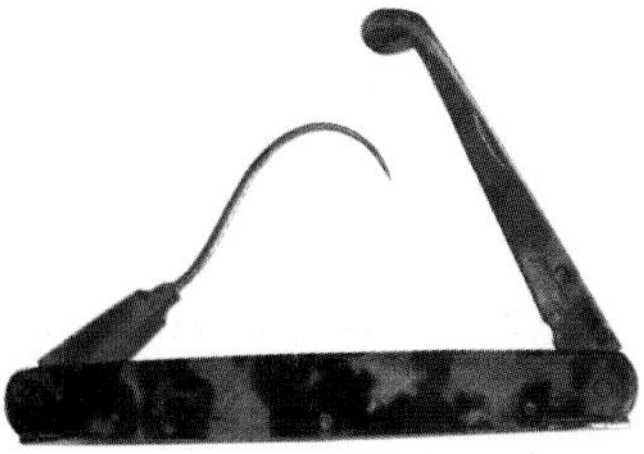

ortoiseshell gum lancet and tenaculum, by Simpson, ɪdon, c1850, 3¾in (9.5cm) long.

30–150 Fossack & Furkle ⊞

ʼum lancet is a spade-shaped blade that could be pushed ɔ an abscess or infected area to drain away the fluid. enaculum is a hook that was used to pull out veins to them off or seal them and so stop the bleeding.

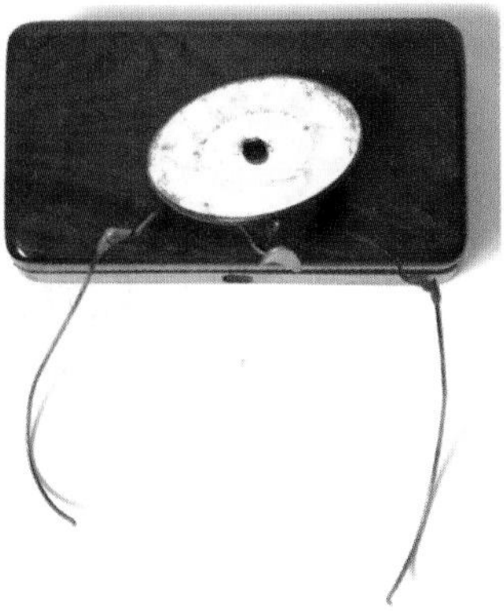

A mahogany head mirror, by Mayer & Meltzer, London, c1890, 7½in (19cm) wide, in a mahogany box.

£100–120 Early Technology ⊞

An optician's metal and brass demonstration eye, c1880, 15in (38cm) high.

£2,000–2,250 Curious Science ⊞

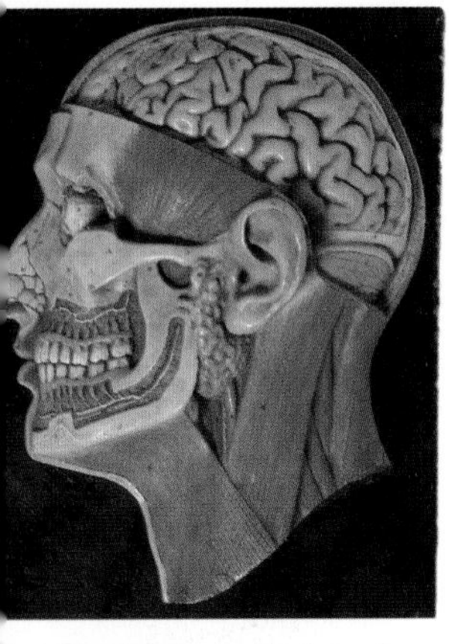

3ock Steger plaster model of a head, ɔwingthe brain and nerves to the teeth, 910, 13in (33cm) high.

ɪ50–950 Curious Science ⊞

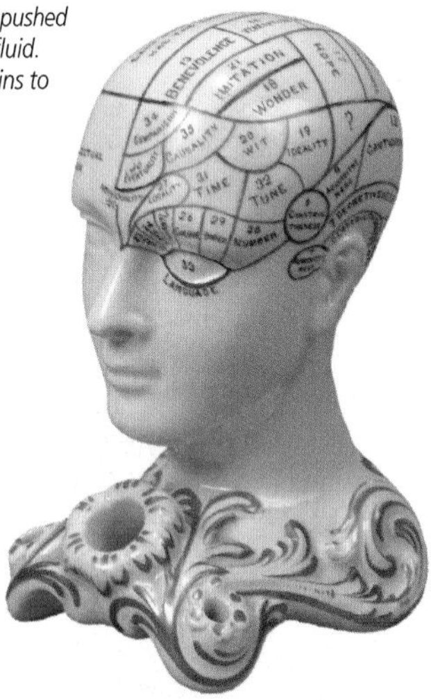

A Staffordshire ceramic phrenology head, 19thC, 5in (12.5cm) high.

£750–850 Walpoles ⊞

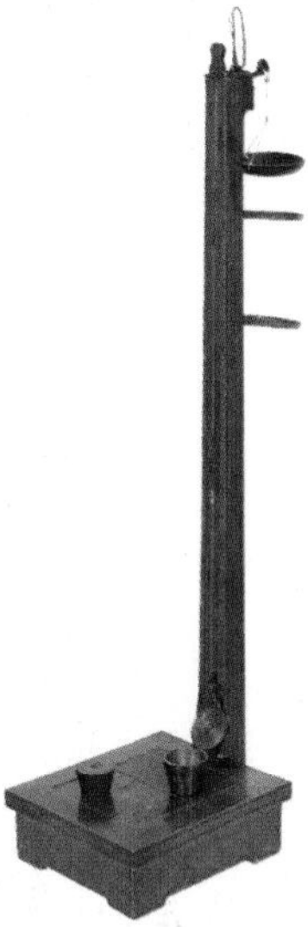

A set of satinwood and tulipwood-banded physician's scales, with sliding height adjustment and recessed folding brass height marker with suspended copper weight bowl, two hinged weight trays and hanging counter-balanced leather-inset standing platform, the column mount inscribed 'Made at Weeks's R'L Museum Tichborne St', c1800, 53¼in (135cm) high, together with a cased set of brass weights.

£2,700–3,300 Bearnes

ɪmahogany postmortem set, by Matcham, London, ɪmprising a capital saw, spine wrench, two Liston knives, iversal handle, six scalpels, two blow pipes, scissors and ːracting hooks, c1840, 9in (23cm) wide.

700–800 Fossack & Furkle ⊞

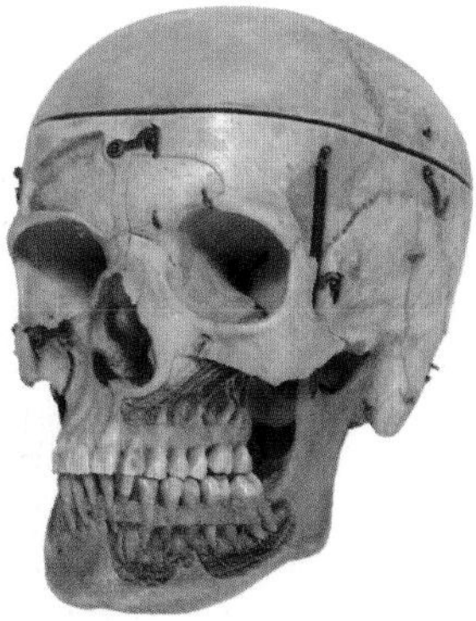

A disarticulated skull, c1890, 6in (15cm) high, with original wooden case.

£1,500–1,650 Curious Science ⊞

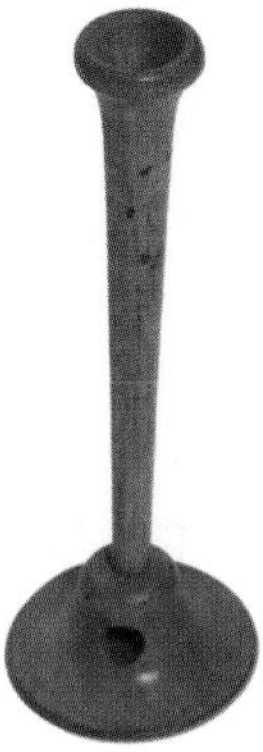

A wooden stethoscope, c1890, 7in (18cm) high.

£135–150 Curious Science ⊞

MICROSCOPES

ESSENTIAL REFERENCE EDMUND CULPEPER c1666–1738

Edmund Culpeper was an important maker of scientific instruments. He trained as an engraver under Walter Hayes and took over Hayes' premises in Moorfields, London before 1700, where he specialized in making mathematical instruments. He diversified into making small simple microscopes from ivory and brass. Although his name is synonymous with the larger tripod microscopes in pyramidal cases, it is widely thought that he did not make these himself, but bought them in from other makers. These tripod microscopes were made by many of the leading makers of the 18th and 19th century, but they are still called Culpeper microscopes to this day. This Culpeper-type microscope from the early 19th century is still in its original shaped box with drawer for accessories.

£1,000–1,200 Charles Tomlinson

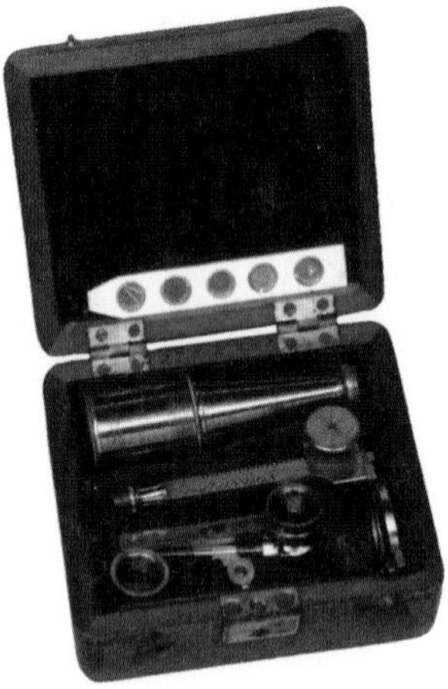

A Regency botanist's brass pocket microscope, by Cary, London, in original fitted mahogany case, 3¾in (9.5cm) wide.

£500–600 Netherhampton

A brass Cuff-type microscope, by W. & S. Jones, London, c1820, 18in (45.5cm) high, in original mahogany case.

£1,800–2,000 Charles Tomlinson

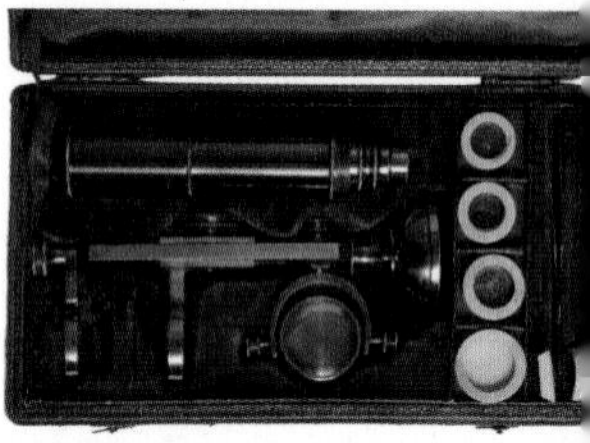

A laquered-brass travelling microscope, Holland, c1810, in original fitted case, 7in (18cm) wide.

£1,100–1,200 Charles Tomlinson

A lacquered-brass travelling microscope, b Dollond, London, 19thC, in fitted mahogany case with accessories including bone slides, 8½in (21.5cm) wide.

£1,000–1,200 Gorringes (L)

A brass microscope, by Baker, London, with accessories, 19thC, 18½in (47cm) high, in a fitted mahogany case.

£700–850 Gardiner Houlgate

A lacquered-brass binocular microscope, by R. & J. Beck, London, with twin pillar stand and tripod base, adjustable stage, with a fitted mahogny case of accessories, mid-19thC, 18in (45.5cm) high, in a fitted mahogany box.

£3,000–3,500 Gorringes (L)

SURVEYING & DRAWING

A low speed anemometer, by Griffin & George, with original instructions, c1940, 4¼in (11cm) wide, in a fitted leather case.

£270–300 Fossack & Furkle

An architect's mahogany travelling box, with brass mounts, fitted with three lift-out trays for watercolour tablets and draughtsmen's instruments, 19thC, 10½in (26.5cm) wide.

£280–320 Dee, Atkinson & Harrison

An architect's/draughtsman's burr-walnut travelling box, by Armstrong, Manchester, with brass mounts, with ivory and nickel instruments, watercolour tablets and set squares, c1890, 14in (35.5cm) wide.

£1,000–1,200 Charles Tomlinson

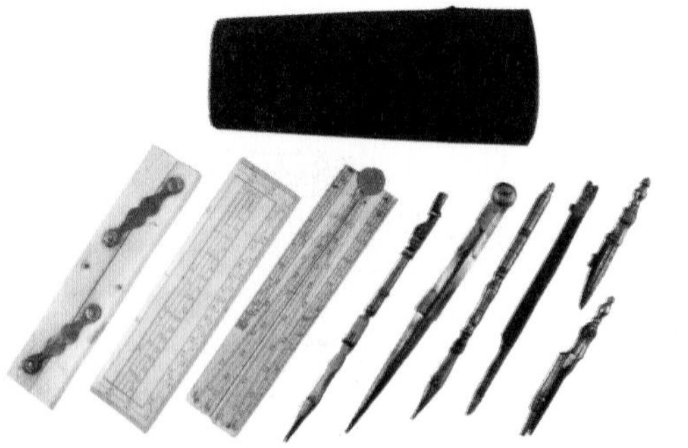

A George II set of drawing instruments, comprising four compasses, a pencil, two ivory rules and a protractor, in a shagreen case.

£370–450 Woolley & Wallis

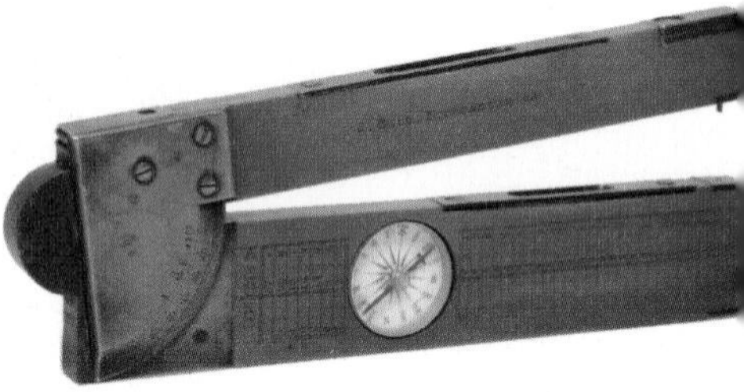

A surveyor's boxwood and brass sighting clinometer, by J. Cale, Newcastle-on-Tyne, c1880, 6in (15cm) long.

£180–200 Charles Tomlinson

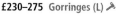

A surveyor's lacquered-brass level, by William & Samuel Jones, London, in original fitted mahogany case, mid-19thC.

£230–275 Gorringes (L)

A bronze surveyor's transit, by W. & L. E. Gurley, New York, with Burt's Patent Solar Attachment and silvered dial, America, 19thC, 16in (40.5cm) high, in a fitted mahogany case.

£4,000–5,000 Skinner

The original version of the solar compass was invented by William Austen Burt in 1835 to solve the problem of aberrations caused by local attractions of the magnetic needle. His invention quickly became a requisite for all U land surveys. Gurley advertised their solar attachment as being 'essentially the solar apparatus of Burt placed upon the cross bar of the ordinary transit'.

A brass level, by Troughton & Simms, London, with a silvered dial, 19thC, 15in (38cm) high.

£250–300 Sworders

A brass 360˚ protractor, by Bithray, London, c1880, 6in (15cm) diam.

£165–185 Chiltern Antiques

'ELESCOPES

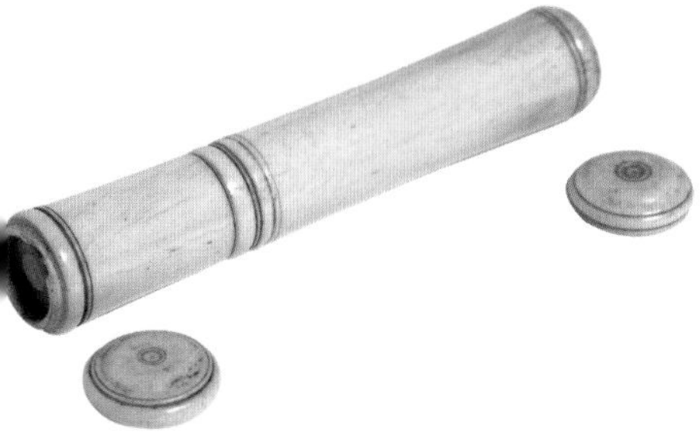

one telescope, with turned end caps, c1700, 5in (12.5cm) long.

.50–500 Charles Tomlinson

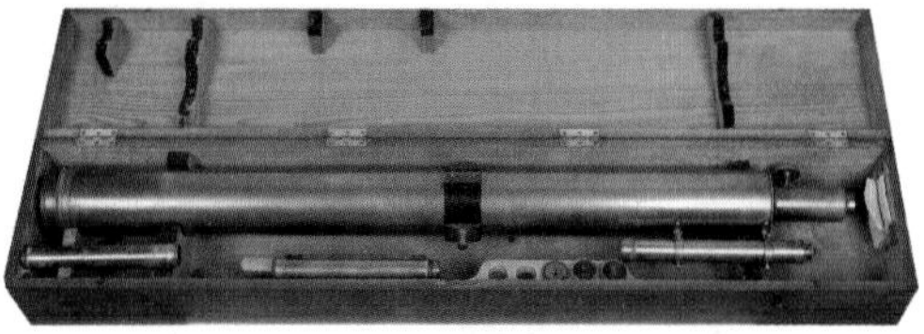

A Victorian 3½in astronomical refracting telescope, the tube with rack-and-pinion focusing, the wooden and brass-mounted tripod with attached label 'Broadhurst Clarkson & Co, 63 Farringdon Road', 51¼in (130cm) extended, in a fitted box with accessories.

£450–550 Bearnes

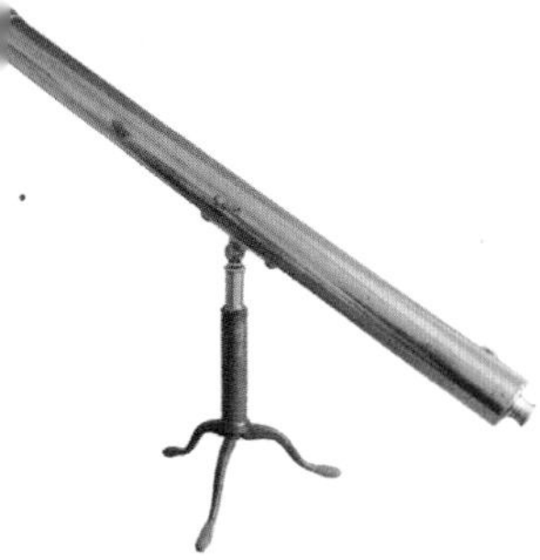

rass astronomical telescope, with tripod nd, late 19thC, 43in (110cm) extended, a fitted pine box with brass accessories.

30–275 Bellmans

A brass telescope, by Broadhurst Clarkson & Co, London, c1900, 39in (99cm) extended, in original case.

£600–675 Grimes Militaria

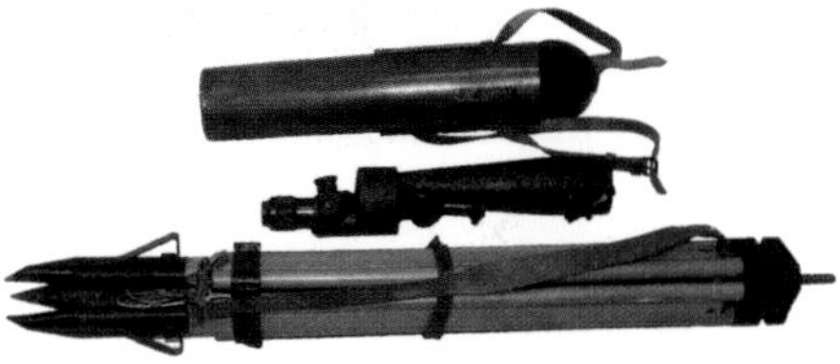

A Carl Zeiss Jena Starmore telescope, with leatherette-covered body and revolving eyepieces, 1930s, 19½in (49.5cm) long, in original fitted leather case with original wooden tripod.

£425–525 Gorringes (L)

VEIGHTS & MEASURES

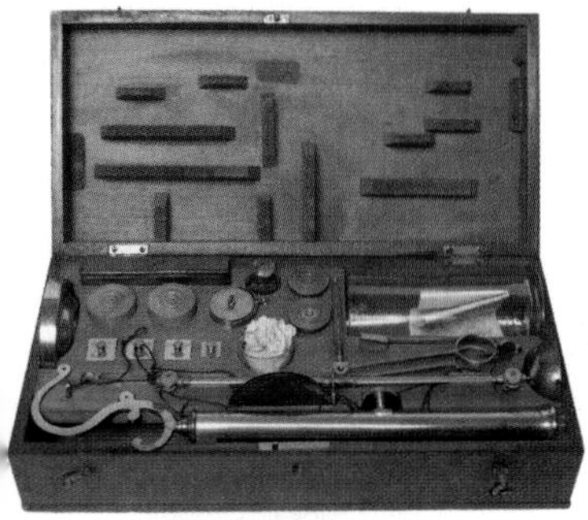

rass Comprehensive Hydrostatic Balance, by W. & S. es, London, c1820, in a fitted mahogany case, in (40.5cm) wide.

,000–3,500 Charles Tomlinson

A set of three bell metal measures, for the Parish of St Catherines, Jamaica, inscribed 'Imperial Half Pint', 'Imperial Gill' and 'Imperial Half Gill', dated 1852.

£600–700 Woolley & Wallis

et of eight imperial measures, for the Borough of Newark, 1 gallon to ¼ gill, 74–90.

,400–1,800 Sworders

A set of eight brass imperial measures, for the County of Norfolk, 1 gallon, ½ gallon, 1 quart, 1 pint, ½ pint, 1 gill and ½ gill, inscribed and dated 1856 and 1877, largest 7½in (19cm) diam.

£4,000–5,000 Dreweatt Neate

MARINE

BAROMETERS

A mahogany marine **sympiesometer,** by Adie & Son, Scotland, Edinburgh, c1820, 10¼in (26cm) high.

£4,500–5,000
D & T Rayment

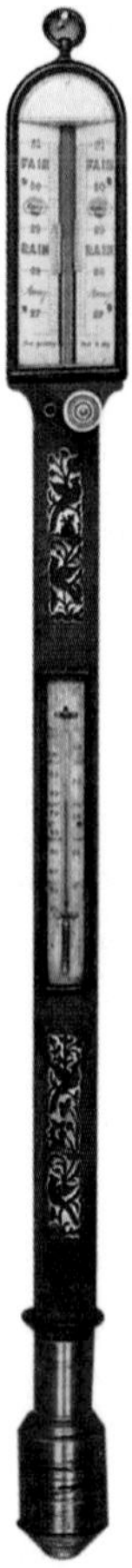

A rosewood marine barometer, with thermometer, ivory twin vernier dial and ivory adjustment knob, the case inlaid with mother-of-pearl, c1850, 35¾in (91cm) high.

£1,200–1,500 Tennants

The prices realized at auction may reflect the fact that some barometers have undergone alterations, or are in unrestored condition.

A mahogany marine barometer, by Robinson, North Shields, with bone scales, c1850, 38in (96.5cm) high.

£3,000–3,500
D & T Rayment

A brass Kew pattern marine **barometer,** by Henry Hughes, London, mounted on gimbals, c1880, 35in (89cm) high.

£1,300–1,500
Alan Walker

CANNONS

A pair of bronze ship's cannons, on hardwood caissons, 1800–25, 52in (132cm) wide.

£22,000–26,000
Northeast Auctions

A brass and oak model of a cannon, 19thC, 5in (12.5cm) long.

£270–300 Arbour Antiques

This model is made from metal taken from the Royal George, *which sank in 1782.*

A brass and boxwood model of a naval cannon, c1860, 6in (15cm) long.

£270–300 Arbour Antiques

HRONOMETERS & TIMEKEEPERS

sewood chronometer, by W. E. Cribb & yneux, London, c1855, 6in (15cm) wide.

000–3,400
: S Pullen

A brass ship's bell clock, by Tiffany & Co, with a silvered dial, the eight-day movement with twin fusee chain, America, 1850–75, 10½in (26.5cm) diam.

£7,000–8,500 Northeast Auctions

A mahogany military deck watch, by Elgin Watch Co, with lever movement, America, c1942, box 5in (13cm) square.

£330–400 Sworders

1ODEL SHIPS

ivory prisoner-of-war model of a ship, the pinned and ıked hull with carved figurehead, three masts with ıding and running rigging, France, early 19thC, ı (38cm) long, in a glazed case.

500–9,000 Heritage

ship can be seen in M's office in the James Bond films Spy Who Loved Me *(1977),* Moonraker *(1979),* opussy *(1983) and* A View to a Kill *(1985). It also eared in the film* The Avengers *(1998).*

A carved and painted wood diorama of the SS *London*, with painted metal sails, c1870, in original glazed teak display case, 38in (96.5cm) wide.

£1,650–1,850 Walpoles

The SS London *was launched from Blackwall in1864. Commanded by Captain Martin, an Australian navigator, she foundered and sank in 1866 in the Bay of Biscay, with the loss of 220 lives.*

ahogany model of a sloop, *Alert*, ı canvas sails, fully rigged, early 20thC, n (178cm) wide.

400–2,800 Freeman's

A sterling silver and parcel-gilt model of a yacht, with three mesh sails, wire rigging and filigree portholes, possibly America, early 20thC, 11½in (29cm) wide.

£700–850 Gorringes (L)

A painted wood model of the *Grand Turk*, America, c1900, 49½in (125.5cm) wide, mounted on a wooden stand.

£1,400–1,700 Skinner

Built in Salem, Massachusetts in 1791, the Grand Turk *was sold to Boston interests and traded to India, China and Russia. In 1797, returning from a long passage from China, she arrived at Portland, Maine in poor condition and two weeks later was ripped from her moorings and wrecked in a gale.*

NAUTICAL HANDICRAFTS

ESSENTIAL REFERENCE BALEEN

Baleen comes from the mouths of the large filter-feeding whales and emerged as a useful by-product of the whaling industry in many cultures and societies. The earliest artefacts were made of baleen produced from Arctic whaling in the 17th century. In the 19th century baleen was an important raw material, comparable to present-day plastics. Its thermoplastic nature and strength meant it could be used to make a wide variety of functional and decorative onjects. Sailors used baleen to make sewing boxes and other small containers and another common use was brush bristles; it was even used as runners on toboggans. Baleen basketry was developed into a craft, with examples of simple baskets to complex woven ones, which could take months to complete. This 19th-century baleen and pine ditty box has a seven-finger point construction and stippled decoration and is 4in (10cm) high.
£375–450 **Northeast Auctions**

A late Victorian shellwork frame, 10in (25.5cm) high.
£270–300 **Walpoles**

A woolwork picture of a frigate and cutter, surmounted by flags and Britannia with the Lion and Unicorn, 1860–70, in original maplewood frame, 28½ x 30½in (72.5 x 77.5cm).
£5,000–5,500 **Walpoles**

A woolwork picture of a Royal Navy battleship, with beadwork gunports, c1890, in original maplewood frame, 30 x 37in (76 x 94cm).
£5,000–5,500 **Walpoles**

A woolwork picture, depicting a man-of-war within a garter and coronet, flanked by the Union flag, French flag and Russian flag and further flags, 19thC, in a maplewood frame, 12¼ x 16½in (31 x 42cm).
£280–330 **Sworders**

ʌILLER'S COMPARES

.) **A Napoleonic prisoner-of-war straw-work picture,** depicting the rison ship *Irresistible*, early 19thC, framed, 9 x 13in (23 x 33cm).
'5,000–5,500 Walpoles

(R) A Napoleonic prisoner-of-war straw-work picture, depicting a harbour, early 19thC, framed, 8 x 10in (20.5 x 25.5cm).
£540–600 Walpoles

.lthough these two Napoleonic prisoner-of-war straw-work pictures are of similar age, size and condition, the ubject matter is the main reason for the large difference in price. The item on the right depicts an unknown French arbour, whereas the picture on the left is of a ship that was initially named HMS *Swiftsure*, built at Deptford, ondon in 1787. She was captured by the French in the Mediterranean on 24 June 1801 and fought on the French ide at the Battle of Trafalgar, where she was recaptured by the British on 21 October 1805. Recommissioned as IMS *Irresistible* she was used as a prison ship until she was scrapped in 1816. This picture is therefore of greater iterest to collectors of naval and Nelson items.

ʌoolwork picture of a three-masted sailing ship, 19thC, x 48in (76 x 122cm).
00–1,100 Sworders

A creamware plate, decorated with a ship in full sail, c1780, 9¾in (25cm) diam.
£200–230 Gillian Shepherd

woolwork picture of HMS *Edgar*, 1908, framed, 20 x 30in (51 x 76cm).
530–700 Piccadilly Antiques

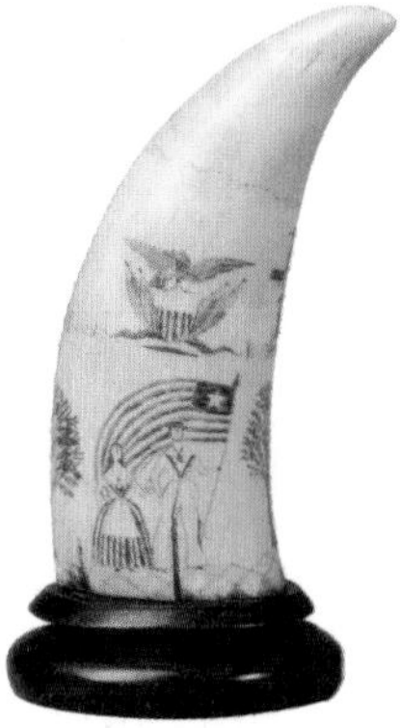

A scrimshaw whale's tooth, carved with various motifs, figures and ships, on a rosewood base, slight damage, America, 1825–50, 7in (18cm) high.
£6,000–7,000 Skinner

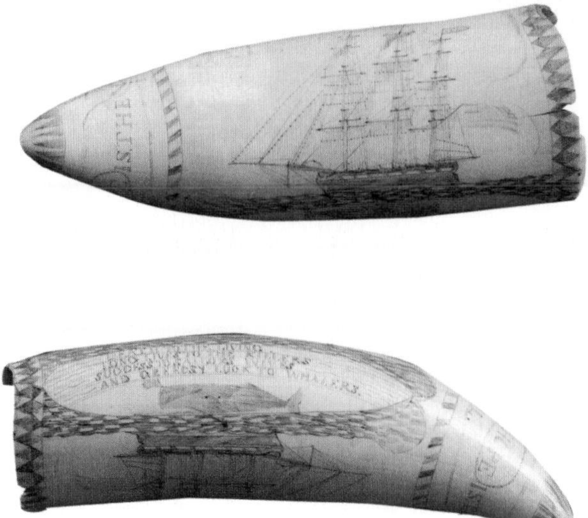

A scrimshaw whale's tooth, carved with an American ship, inscription and a sperm whale, America, 19thC, 6½in (16.5cm) high.

£18,000–22,000 Northeast Auctions

A silver-mounted wooden snuff box, commemorating capture of the *Chesapeake*, engraved with the Broke motto, c1813, 3in (7.5cm) diam.

£3,500–4,250 Sotheby's

The Broke motto, meaning 'We retain the stern trident', and crest were granted to Admiral Sir Philip Bowes Vere Broke, KCB, commander of HMS Shannon, *after his capture in just 15 minutes of the American frigate* Chesapeake *off the Boston shore during the War of 181*

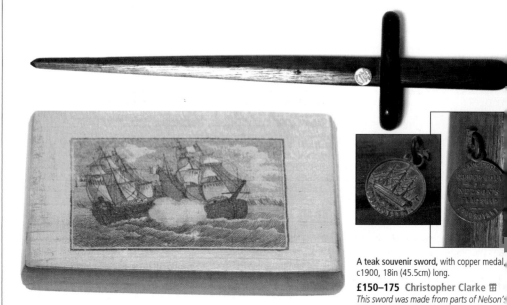

A teak souvenir sword, with copper medal, c1900, 18in (45.5cm) long.

£150–175 Christopher Clarke

This sword was made from parts of Nelson's flagship HMS Foudroyant *at the Battle of th Nile, which was wrecked off Blackpool on Jur 16 1897, 100 years after its launch from Plymouth in 1798.*

A sycamore snuff box, with penwork decoration of two Scottish ships in full sail, Scotland, c1835, 3½in (9cm) wide.

£100–125 Mostly Boxes

A wooden tobacco box, in the form of a boat, c1840, 10in (25.5cm) wide.

£2,000–2,200 Moxhams

A silver-plated Castle Mail Packet Co soup tureen, with engraved crest, 1876–81, 17in (43cm) wide.

£500–550 Castlegate Antiques

The Castle Mail Packet Co shipping line was founded by Donald Currie and so-named because all the ships were named after English castles.

A shellwork valentine, in a glazed mahoga case, 19thC, 10¼in (26cm) wide.

£700–850 Dreweatt Neate (HAM)

AVIGATIONAL INSTRUMENTS

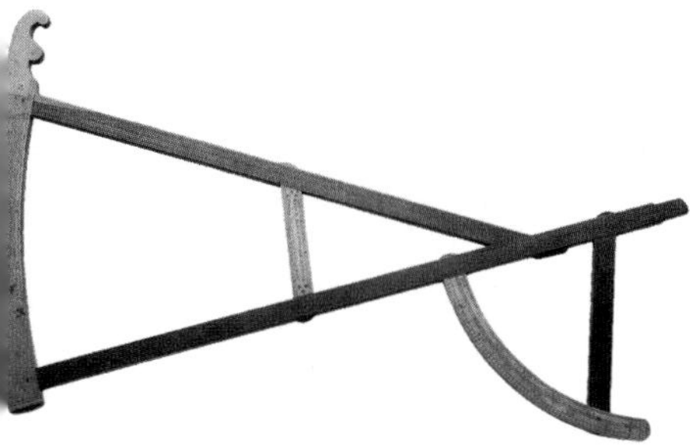

ackstaff, by John Atkinson, London, engraved with fleur-de-lys and or roses, signed and dated 1729, 25in (63.5cm) long.

800–4,500 Northeast Auctions

A brass gunboat binnacle, by Kelvin Bottomley & Baird, pattern No. 185, 1914–18, 18in (45.5cm) high.

£750–900 Anderson & Garland

A brass lifeboat compass, 19thC, 10in (25.5cm) high.

£400–450 Early Technology

early Victorian brass drum/pocket tant, by Cary, London, with silvered e, 3¼in (8.5cm) diam, in a figured nogany box.

50–900 Canterbury Auctions

A Victorian ropework-bound naval telescope, 26½in (67.5cm) long.

£340–380 Walpoles

A brass and mahogany military pattern 155 ship's compass, by E. Dent & Co, London, with viewing window and candle holder, late 19thC, 11¾in (30cm) high.

£3,800–4,500 Sotheby's

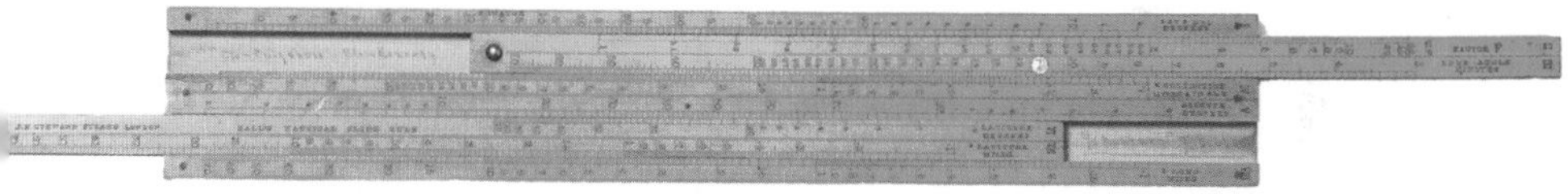

all's boxwood nautical slide rule, late 19thC, 13in (33cm) long.

60–180 Early Technology

HIPS' FITTINGS

rass ship's bell, engraved 'R. A. Emerson 1973', n (25.5cm) high.

25–250
imes Militaria

A carved and painted wood miniature figurehead, from the sloop *Bayadere*, America, 19thC, 13in (33cm) high.

£6,000–7,000 Northeast Auctions

A teak ship's wash unit, with ceramic basin, c1905, 65in (165cm) high.

£900–1,000 LASSCO (bh)

MISCELLANEOUS

A broadsheet, depicting the SS *Great Eastern* printed by T. Goode, c1859, 20 x 30in (51 x 76cm).

£350–425 Netherhampton Salerooms

This ship was nicknamed the 'Leviathan' because of its huge size.

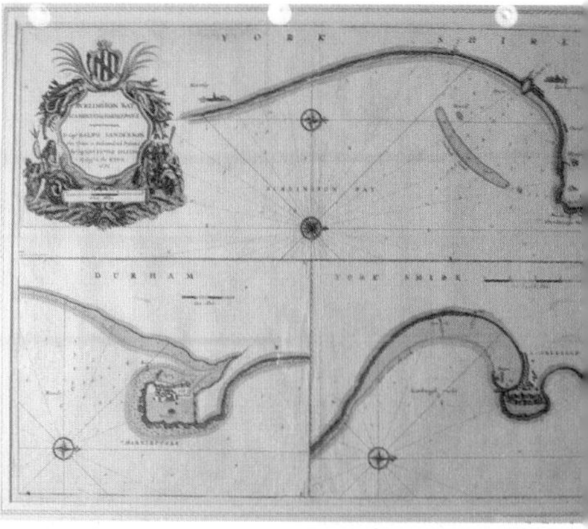

A chart of the approaches to Bridlington, Scarborough and Hartlepool, by Captain Greenville Collins, London, published 1693, 18 x 22in (45.5 x 56cm).

£270–300 Vanbrugh House

A painted pine sea captain's document box, inscribed 'Ship *Omega*', with an iron lock, c1850, 20in (51cm) wide.

£1,000–1,200 Northeast Auctions

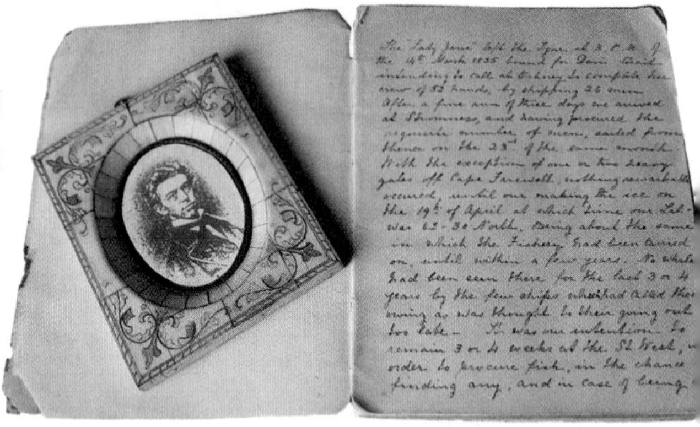

A diary, compiled by Dr James Williamson, surgeon of the whaling ship *Lady Jane*, 1835, 4°, together with a case of six bleeding tools.

£3,000–3,500 Anderson & Garland

The Lady Jane *was the most successful ship in the National Fleet. In this manuscript Williams recounts many of his day-to-day experiences as a surgeon on board ship. He also describes th many horrors the crew endured when the ship was trapped in ice off Greenland in 1835 for year, with 27 crew dying from scurvy.*

A silver table lighter, in the form of a masthead lamp, maker's mark 'D&F', Birmingham 1895, 3¼in (8.5cm) high.

£620–700 Walpoles

A cast-iron umbrella stand, by Jones & Campbell, Stirlingshire, in the form of Admiral Lord Nelson on a plinth supported by two hippocamps, Scotland, c1890, 31in (78.5cm) high.

£1,300–1,500 Christopher Clarke

A silver vinaigrette, by Matthew Linwood, engraved with a portrait of Admiral Lord Nelson, inscribed 'England Expects Every M Will Do His Duty', with gilt interior, the gri pierced with HMS *Victory* and stamped 'Trafalgar October 21', Birmingham 1805, 1¼in (3cm) wide.

£4,500–5,500 Woolley & Wallis

CAMERAS

ɪlair Camera Co Stereo Hawkeye camera, ɪerica, c1905, 6¾in (17cm) wide.

00–350 Antique Photographic

A Dubroni Camera, No. 2, France, Paris, 1860s, 4in (10cm) wide.

£2,700–3,000 Antique Photographic

A J. Lancaster & Sons ¼ plate Stereo Instantograph, 1890s, 7in (18cm) wide.

£450–500 Antique Photographic

Leica III camera, No. 134956 with Leitz Elmar f3.5/5cm lens No. 183678, and a Metraphot ɪeter, c1940.

50–300 Skinner

A Marion & Co mahogany and brass-bound studio camera, with Amey & Barlot Bros lens, together with one wet-plate negative holder complete with a set of reducing masks, and one dry-plate negative holder with double set of reducing masks, on an adjustable tripod base, 1870s, 14in (35.5cm) square.

£850–1,000 Bearnes

Shew & Co ¼ plate Eclipse camera, 1890s, 5½in (14cm) wide.

270–300
ɪtique Photographic

A wet-plate field camera, 1860s, with box 19in (48.5cm) wide.

£550–600 Antique Photographic

OPTICAL INSTRUMENTS

A walnut-veneered parlour graphoscope, by Rowsells, with adjustable support, brass slide, bird's-eye maple interior, c1870, 14in (35.5cm) wide.

£380–425 Chiltern Antiques

An ebonized wood stereo graphoscope, France, 1890s, 13¾in (35cm) wide.

£180–200 Antique Photographic

A wood and paper Zimmerman's Ludoscope, entitled 'A Merry Wheel for Motion Pictures', America, Baltimore, c190 10½in (26.5cm) wide, with six discs.

£650–800 Bertoia

A Magic Lantern, by Gebrüder Bing, Germany, c1910, with box 11in (28cm) wide, with a box of original slides.

£180–220 Theriault's

An achromatic stereoscope, by Smith, Beck & Beck, with box, 1860s, 7½in (19cm) wide.

£540–600 Antique Photographic

A walnut table pedestal stereoscope, with ground-glas screen, double-hinged lid with mirror, internal transport mechanism, ebonized fittings and a pair of rack-and-pinion focusing lenses, 19thC, 17in (43cm) high.

£380–450 Skinner

A mahogany and glass stereoscope, by Jules Richard, 'La Taxiphote', France, c1910, 11in (28cm) wide.

£900–1,100 James D Julia

A Kinora Viewer, by British Kinora Co, 1910, 11¾in (30cm) wide, together with six reels.

£1,600–2,000 Bertoia

A metal Zoetrope, by the London Stereoscopic Co, with original label, on a mahogany wooden pedestal base, together with 20 paper animation strips, c1880, drum 12in (30.5cm) diam.

£650–800 Theriault's

PHOTOGRAPHS

latt D. Babbit, 'Niagara Falls', ambrotype, merica, c1855, 9½ x 7¼in (24 x 18.5cm).

800–1,000 **Jackson's**

Felice Beato, Burmese family in a cart with oxen, c1890, 11½ x 8½in (29 x 21.5cm).

£700–850 **Auction Atrium**

Félix Bonfils, albumen print, numbered 117 in the negative, France, c1870, 9 x 11in (23 x 28cm).

£110–120 **Jubilee Photographica**

ev Borodulin, 'Parade, Moscow', silver print, hotographer's wetstamp, titled and ated, Russia, 1956, printed later, 5¼ x 10in (38.5 x 25.5cm).

3,000–3,600 **Sotheby's**

Margaret Bourke-White, 'Bryantville Auto Service Third Annual Goodyear Dealers Zeppelin Race Winner July – August 1931', signed, slight damage, America, c1931, framed, 20¼ x 26in (51.5 x 66cm).

£1,150–1,400 **Skinner**

This frame is made of Duralumin which was taken from the girder of the US Airship Akron.

amuel Bourne, 'Canal, Kashmir', albumen print from a wet collodion negative, 868, 9½ x 12in (24 x 30.5cm).

1,800–2,000 **Robert Hershkowitz**

Bill Brandt, 'Miner at Evening Meal, Northumberland', silver print, signed, c1937, printed later, 15½ x 12in (39.5 x 30.5in).

£2,800–3,200 **Sotheby's**

Brassaï (Gyula Halász), 'Strongman of the Halles', silver print, titled, 1936, printed later, 11¾ x 9¼in (30 x 23.5cm).

£8,500–10,000 Sotheby's

Julia Margaret Cameron, 'The Dedication (Hatty Campbell)', albumen print from a wet collodion negative, 1868, 9 x 7in (23 x 18cm).

£5,500–6,000 Robert Hershkowitz

André Disderi, *carte de visite*, probably a self portrait, albumen print, c1865, 4 x 2½in (10 x 6.5cm).

£180–200 Jubilee Photographica

John Burke, 'Kandahar', albumen print showing members of the British Expeditionary Force with guns and elephants, 1879, 8 x 11in (20.5 x 28cm).

£180–200 Jubilee Photographica

Les Cleveland, 'Hong Kong Café, Taranaki Street, Wellington', gelatin silver print, title, signed and dated to verso, New Zealand, 1957, 7½ x 5¾in (19.5 x 14.5cm).

£800–950 Webb's

Asahel Curtis, a mountain scene, silver gelatin print, signed and dated, America, 1911, 8 x 10in (20.5 x 25.5cm), framed.

£1,250–1,500 Treadway

Henry Dixon, a sleeping tiger at London Zoo, c1885, 7 x 11in (18 x 28cm).

£450–550 Auction Atrium

Burton Brothers, 'Princess Street, Dunedin', albumen print, New Zealand, c1880, 8 x 11½in (20.5 x 29cm).

£135–150 Jubilee Photographica

Ellis Prentice Cole, 'Utah', sepia gelatin print, titled to verso, America, c1920, 7½ x 9½in (19 x 24cm).

£700–850 Treadway

W. P. Dando, 'Chinchilla', carbon print from a dryplate negative, c1890, 11 x 9in (28 x 23cm).

£450–500 Robert Hershkowitz

Robert Doisneau, 'Le Baiser de l'Hôtel de Ville', silver print, signed, titled and dated 1950, printed later, 11¾ x 15¾in (30 x 40cm).

£12,000–15,000 **Sotheby's**

Peter Henry Emerson, 'Cantley: Wherries waiting for the turn of the tide', platinum print from a dryplate negative, 1886, 7½ x 11in (19 x 28cm).

£4,500–5,000 **Robert Hershkowitz**

Roger Fenton, 'Sedelia, Furness Abbey', albumen print, printed by Francis Frith, 1860s, 8 x 6½in (20.5 x 16.5cm).

£450–500 **Jubilee Photographica**

A. Goddard, 'Doorway, Church, Genoa', salt print from a wet collodion negative, c1855, 10 x 8in (25.5 x 20.5cm).

£3,500–4,000 **Robert Hershkowitz**

Terence Donovan, 'Roland Kirk', silver print, slight damage, c1965, 12 x 10in (30.5 x 25.5cm).

£180–200 **Jubilee Photographica**

Esposito, 'The Spaghetti Factory', albumen print, c1880, 8¼ x 10¼in (21 x 26cm), framed.

£150–180 **Freeman's**

Leon Gerard, 'View in Venice', albumen print from a waxed paper negative, 1858, 10½ x 14in (26.5 x 35.5cm).

£2,700–3,000 **Robert Hershkowitz**

A. C. Gomes, gelatin silver print of a Swahili fiddler or banjo player, Zanzibar, c1900, 5½ x 4in (14 x 10cm).

£90–100 **Jubilee Photographica**

W. & D. Downey, cabinet card, Tsar Alexander II and family, carbon print, c1880, 6½ x 4½in (16.5 x 11.5cm).

£140–160 **Jubilee Photographica**

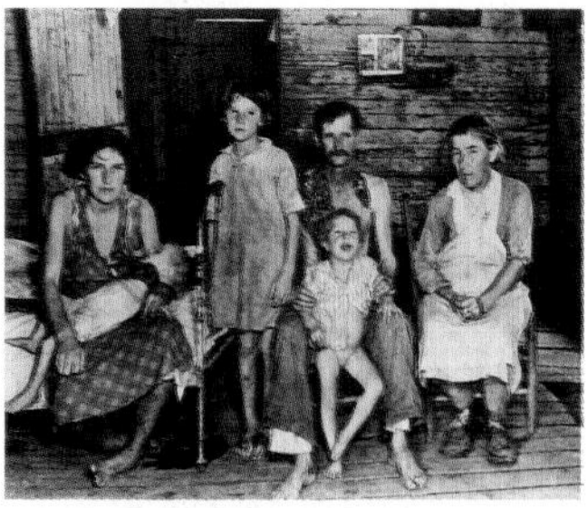

Walker Evans, 'Alabama Cotton Tenant Farmer Family', silver print, annotated 'Bud Fields and his Family – Tenant Sharecroppers, Hale County, Alabama – Summer 1936', America, 1936, printed later, framed and glazed, 7¼ x 9¼in (18.5 x 23.5cm).

£3,500–4,200 **Sotheby's**

F. Jay Haynes, cabinet card, 'Chief White Bull – Shoshone', America, c1883, framed, 6½ x 4¼in (16.5 x 11cm).

£250–300 **Skinner**

Hillers, 'Cheyenne Warrior', matted photograph, America, Oklahoma, c1875, 9 x 7in (23 x 18cm).

£900–1,100 Skinner

Frank Hofmann, untitled study, gelatin silver print, photographer's blind stamp, New Zealand, 15 x 11¾in (38 x 30cm).

£2,000–2,500 Webb's

Horst P. Horst, 'Lisa Fonssagrives, New York', silver print, signed, America, 1951, printed later, 20 x 15¾in (50 x 40cm).

£4,000–5,000 Sotheby's

André Kertész, 'Homing Ship, Central Park, New York', silver print, signed, America, dated 1944, framed and glazed, 9¾ x 7¾in (24.5 x 19.5cm).

£10,000–12,000 Sotheby's

Peter Klier, the Shoay Dagone Pagoda, Rangoon, c1890, 13in x10½in (33 x26.5cm).

£280–350 Auction Atrium

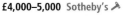

Alberto Korda, 'Che Guevara', silver print, signed, inscribed 'Für Klaus Niermann einen Freund von Kuba', 1960, printed later, 14 x 11in (35.5 x 28cm).

£3,500–4,200 Sotheby's

Atelier Krupp, 'Travelling gin, to lift 30 tons', albumen print from a wet collodion negative, Germany, c1875, 9 x 12in (23 x 30.5cm).

£1,800–2,000 Robert Hershkowitz

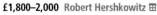

G. R. Lambert & Co, 'Malay Court of Justice' albumen print on an album leaf with a print of the Botanical Gardens on verso, Singapore, c1880, 8 x 11in (20.5 x 28cm).

£180–200 Jubilee Photographica

Annie Leibovitz, 'William Burroughs', silver print from a polaroid negative, 1995, mounted, glazed and framed 23¾ x 25½in (60.5 x 65cm).

£3,000–3,500 Sotheby's

Annie Leibovitz is one of the great contemporary American portraitists. She took this powerful image of Burroughs just two years before his death.

John Dillwyn Llewellyn, 'Kenneth Howard in Brandy Cove', 1854, 7 x 5½in (18 x 14cm).

£300–350 **Jubilee Photographica**

London Stereoscopic Co, stereo card, the American Steam Frigate *Niagara*, albumen prints, c1855, 3½ x 7in (9 x 18cm).

£100–120 **Jubilee Photographica**

Pulman of Auckland, *carte-de-visite* of a Maori, albumen print, New Zealand, c1870, 4 x 2½in (10 x 6.5cm).

£160–180 **Jubilee Photographica**

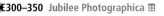

Robert MacPherson, 'Temple of Vesta', coated salt print from a wet collodion negative, c1855, 11 x 16in (28 x 40.5cm).

£2,700–3,000 **Robert Hershkowitz**

Robin Morrison, a portrait of Frank Sargeson, gelatin silver print, New Zealand, dated 1978, 10¼ x 14¾in (26 x 37.5cm).

£900–1,100 **Webb's**

Man Ray, 'Charité Sur Loire', gelatin silver print, signed, America, dated 1933, 6½ x 8¾in (16.5 x 22cm).

£2,000–2,400 **Freeman's**

Marc Riboud, 'Washington', silver print, photographer's wetstamp, signed, titled, France, dated 1967, printed later, 12 x 16in (30.5 x 40.5cm).

£1,200–1,500 **Sotheby's**

James Robertson, 'Olympium, Athens', albumen print from a wet collodion negative, c1853, 13 x 10in (33 x 25.5cm).

£2,700–3,000 **Robert Hershkowitz**

Aleksandr Rodchenko, 'New Buildings on Shabolovka', silver print, photographer's wetstamp, Russia, 1932, 9½ x 11¼in (24 x 28.5cm).

£3,000–3,600 **Sotheby's**

Kurt Schwitters, 'Die Kultpumpe', silver gelatin print, signed, stamped 'Anna Blume', Germany, c1919, 4 x 3in (10 x 7.5cm).

£5,500–6,500 **Freeman's**

Adam Solomon, 'Portrait of Unknown Lady', albumen print from a wet collodion negative, France, c1860, 10in x 7½in (25.5 x 19cm).

£2,700–3,000 **Robert Hershkowitz**

Bert Stern, 'MM Biting the Gem', iris print, numbered 16/36, signed, America, 1962, printed later, 8¼ x 12in (21 x 30.5cm).

£1,250–1,500 **Bukowskis**

Taber, 'California Street from Sansome Street, San Francisco', albumen print, on album leaf, numbered 'B517', America, c1880, 7½ x 9½in (19 x 24cm).

£130–150 **Jubilee Photographica**

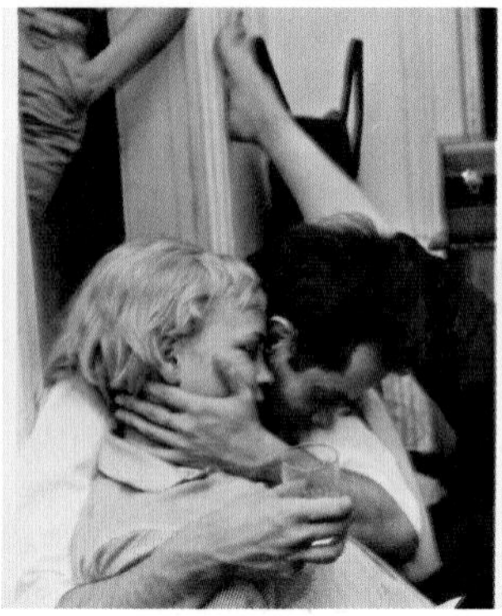

Weegee (Arthur Fellig), 'Rent Party: Have Releases', silver gelatin emulsion print, titled, America, 1956, 9 x 7½in (23 x 19cm).

£1,200–1,500 **Rago Arts**

Linnaeus Tripe, 'HMS *Duke of Wellington* in Keyham Docks', albumen print, titled and signed, dated 1854, 10½ x 13¾in (26.5 x 35cm).

£2,000–2,400 **Sotheby's**

Anon, 'Patio de los Leones, Alhambra', from caolotype negative, slight damage, Europe, 1840s, 5¾ x 8in (14.5 x 20.5cm).

£5,000–6,000 **Sotheby's**

Anon, 'Odalisque', salt print from a wet collodion negative, c1855, 5 x 6in (12.5 x 15cm).

£1,800–2,000 **Robert Hershkowitz**

Anon, 'American Country Life – Summer's Evening', ambrotype, America, c1860, 4 x 6in (10 x 15cm).

£230–275 **Jackson's**

Anon, Golden Gate and Seal Rocks, San Francisco Bay, albumen print, on album leaf, America, c1875, 8 x 9½in (20.5 x 24cm).

£180–200 **Jubilee Photographica**

Anon, delivery carts outside the Mining Exchange Hotel, Cairns, north Queensland, albumen print, Australia, c1880, 7½ x 9½in (19 x 24cm).

£100–120 **Jubilee Photographica**

Anon, Chinese bearers carrying two palanquins, albumen print, c1880, 8 x 10½in (20.5 x 26.5cm).

£100–120 **Jubilee Photographica**

DECORATIVE ARTS

GLASS – DAUM

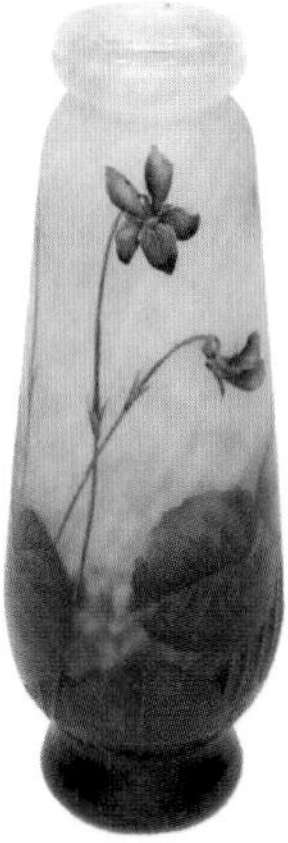

A Daum glass vase, etched and enamelled with violets, France, Nancy, c1895, 8in (20.5cm) high.

£4,500–5,000 Design Gallery

A Daum cameo glass vase, etched and enamelled with mountains and a lake, signed, France, Nancy, c1900, 5in (12.5cm) high.

£2,300–2,600 Ondines

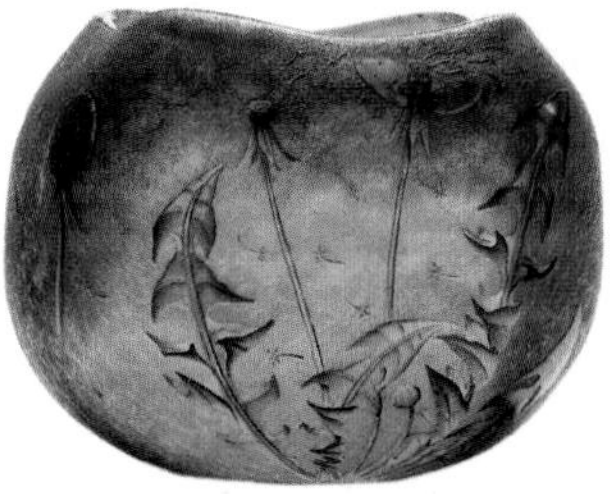

A Daum glass bowl, etched and enamelled with dandelions, signed, France, Nancy, c1900, 4½in (11.5cm) high.

£2,300–2,750 Sotheby's (Am)

A Daum glass vase, etched and enamelled with bleeding hearts, signed, France, Nancy, c1900, 4½in (11.5cm) high.

£1,100–1,300 Rago Arts

A Daum glass vase, etched and enamelled with flowers and leaves, signed, France, Nancy, c1900, 7¼in (18.5cm) high.

£3,000–3,500 Sotheby's (Am)

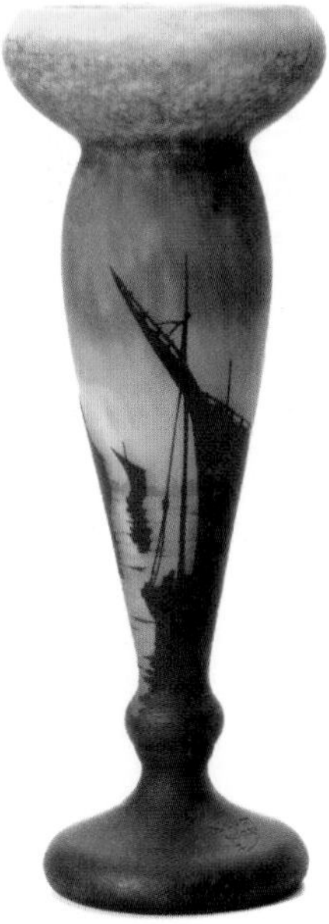

A Daum cameo glass vase, decorated with sailing boats in a harbour, signed, France, Nancy, c1900, 14in (35.5cm) high.

£1,500–1,800 Rago Arts

A Daum cameo glass vase, etched and enamelled with brambles, signed, France, Nancy, c1900, 4¾in (12cm) high.

£1,000–1,200 Jackson's

A Daum glass ewer, etched and enamelled with a Dutch landscape, engraved signature, France, Nancy, c1900, 3½in (9cm) high.

£700–850 Rago Arts

A Daum cameo glass jar and cover, the frosted glass etched and enamelled with flowers, signed, France, Nancy, c1900, 8in (20.5cm) high.

£475–575 Jackson's

A Daum cameo glass vase, decorated with fruiting vine branches, signed, France, Nancy, c1910, 25in (63.5cm) high.

£3,300–4,000
Sotheby's (Am)

A Daum glass vase, etched and enamelled with flowers, signed, painter's monogram, France, Nancy, c1910, 4¾in (12cm) high.

£1,400–1,800
Sotheby's (Am)

A Daum glass vase, etched and enamelled with a winter forest scene, signed, painter's monogram, France, Nancy, c1910, 8in (20.5cm) high.

£1,500–1,800
Sotheby's (Am)

A Daum glass vase, etched and enamelled with geraniums, signed, France, Nancy, c1910, 8in (20.5cm) high.

£3,500–4,200
Sotheby's (Am)

A Daum glass vase, 'Summer', etched and enamelled with woodland and a village, signed, France, Nancy, c1910, 11¼in (28.5cm) high.

£5,000–6,000 **Sotheby's (Am)**

A Daum glass vase, signed, France, Nancy, c1920, 5¼in (13.5cm) high.

£100–120 **Heritage**

A Daum glass vase, with internal decoration and gold inclusions, signed, France, Nancy, c1920, 12in (30.5cm) high.

£1,300–1,500 **Afford Decorative Arts**

A Daum and Louis Majorelle glass vase, with a bronze openwork mount, France, c1930, 11in (28cm) high.

£2,400–2,800 **Ondines**

A Daum glass vase, with gilt foil inclusions, signed, France, Nancy, c1920, 6½in (16.5cm) high.

£500–600 **Bukowskis**

A Daum glass vase, etched with foliage, signed, France, Nancy, c1930, 13in (33cm) high.

£1,200–1,500 **Skinner**

GLASS – GALLE

An Emile Gallé cameo glass vase, decorated with fuchsias, France, Nancy, c1890, 7½in (19cm) high.

£3,300–3,650 **Design Gallery**

An Emile Gallé cameo glass vase, decorated with flowers and foliage, France, Nancy, c1900, 14in (35.5cm) high.

£4,500–5,000 **Mike Weedon**

An Emile Gallé cameo glass vase, decorated with leaves and berries, France, Nancy, c1900, 10in (25.5cm) high.

£1,250–1,400 **Mike Weedon**

An Emile Gallé cameo glass vase, decorated with blossom-laden branches, signed, France, Nancy, c1900, 6½in (16.5cm) high.

£750–900 **Rago Arts**

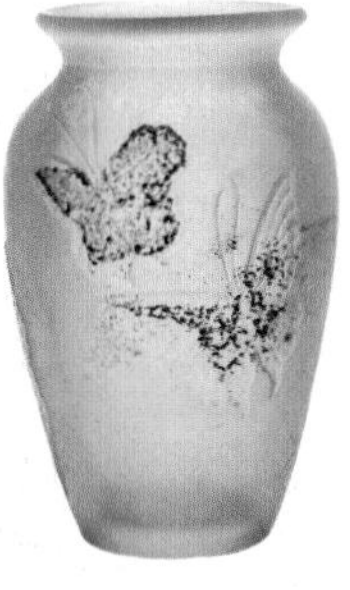

An Emile Gallé glass vase, wheel-carved with three butterflies, engraved mark, France, Nancy, c1900, 5¼in (13.5cm) high.

£5,000–6,000 **Sotheby's (Am)**

An Emile Gallé cameo glass box and cover, decorated with leafy tendrils, signed, France, Nancy, c1900, 5in (13cm) diam.

£700–850 **Waddington's**

ESSENTIAL REFERENCE EMILE GALLE

Emile Gallé was an exceptionally gifted artist/designer who worked for years to understand the necessary skills for the blowing and manipulation of glass. Once Gallé had trained and opened his own glassworks at Nancy in France he rarely made or decorated items of glass himself, but employed skilled craftsmen who worked from his ideas and designs. These stretched the possibilities and potential of glass making with a multi-layered technique known as *pâte-de-verre* (glass paste). Gallé had a broad knowledge of botany and it followed that flowering plants provided a rich source of inspiration for his designs, as did fish, reptiles and insects. *Marqueterie-de-verre* was a highly-skilled technique involving the insertion of hot cut-out panels of vari-coloured glass into the body of the piece while still molten, and then smoothing over and carving decorative motifs to finish. This was a painstaking process which required outstanding technical skill and delicate hand carving to evoke the spirit of nature that Gallé intended. It was hard to achieve and pieces such as this Crocus vase from the beginning of the 20th century are commanding high prices in the current market.

£13,000–16,000 **Freeman's**

An Emile Gallé cameo glass vase, decorated with ferns, signed, France, Nancy, c1900, 10in (25.5cm) high.

£1,100–1,250 Shapiro

An Emile Gallé cameo glass vase, decorated with wisteria, France, Nancy, c1900, 14in (35.5cm) high.

£1,800–2,000 Mike Weedon

An Emile Gallé cameo glass vase, decorated with trees in a mountainous landscape, signed, France, Nancy, c1900, 12½in (32cm) high.

£5,500–6,500 Rago Arts

An Emile Gallé cameo glass vase, overlaid and etched with columbines on an iridescent background, France, Nancy, c1900, 7½in (19cm) high.

£2,500–3,000 Sotheby's (Am)

An Emile Gallé cameo glass vase, decorated with flowers and foliage, signed, France, Nancy, c1900, 5½in (14cm) high.

£800–1,000 Waddington's

An Emile Gallé glass coupe, internally decorated with cameo flowers, signed, France, Nancy, c1900, 5in (12.5cm) high.

£2,000–2,200 Ondines

An Emile Gallé cameo glass vase, with floral decoration, France, Nancy, c1905, 14½in (37cm) high.

£5,500–6,000 Mike Weedon

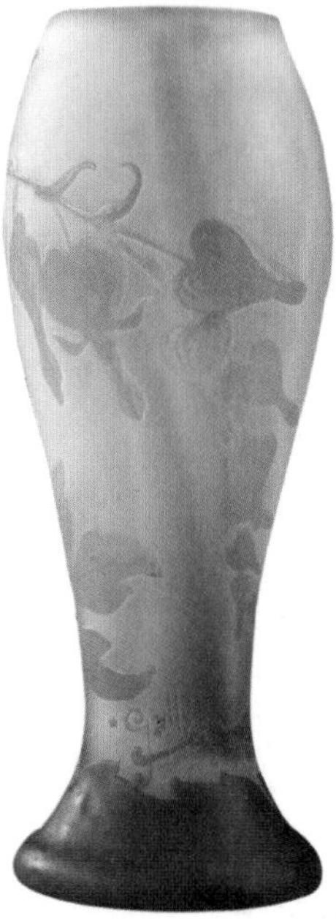

An Emile Gallé cameo glass vase, decorated with bleeding hearts, signed, France, Nancy, c1904, 7½in (19cm) high.

£550–650 Jackson's

An Emile Gallé cameo glass vase, with floral decoration, signed, France, Nancy, c1900, 10in (25.5cm) high.

£5,500–6,500 Galeria Louis C Morton

GLASS – LOETZ

A pair of Loetz iridescent glass candlesticks, with tapering stems, Austria, c1895, 14in (35.5cm) high.

£3,500–4,000 Afford Decorative Arts

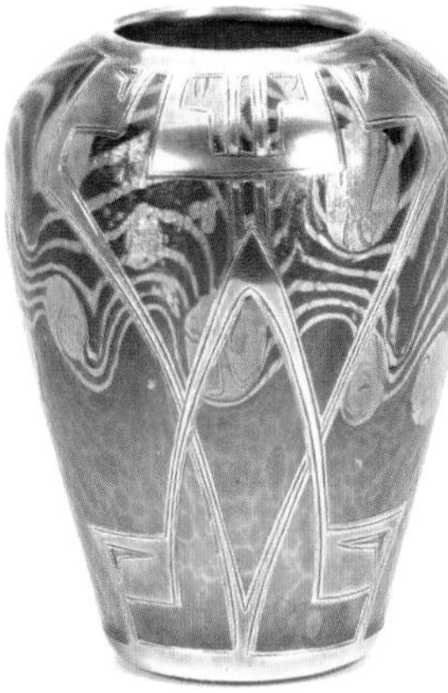

A Loetz iridescent glass vase, decorated with silver overlay, Austria, c1900, 3¾in (9.5cm) high.

£1,800–2,200 Rago Arts

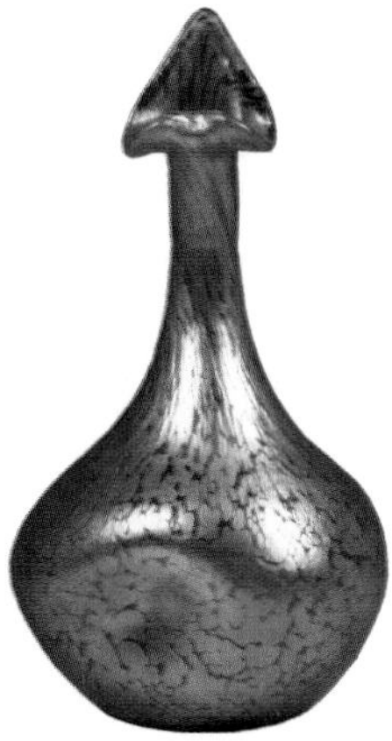

A Loetz Jack-in-the-Pulpit iridescent glass vase, Austria, c1900, 9¾in (25cm) high.

£600–700 Sworders

A Loetz iridescent glass vase, Austria, c1900, 6in (15cm) high.

£135–150 Ruskin Decorative Arts

A Loetz iridescent glass vase, signed, Austria, c1900, 9½in (24cm) high.

£600–700 Heritage

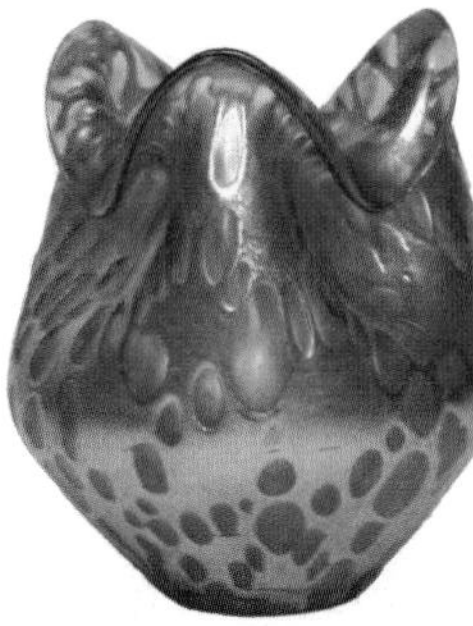

A Loetz iridescent glass Diaspora vase, Austria, c1900, 5½in (14cm) high.

£900–1,000 Afford Decorative Arts

A Loetz iridescent glass Phänomen vase, Austria, c1900, 8½in (21.5cm) high.

£800–1,000 Jackson's

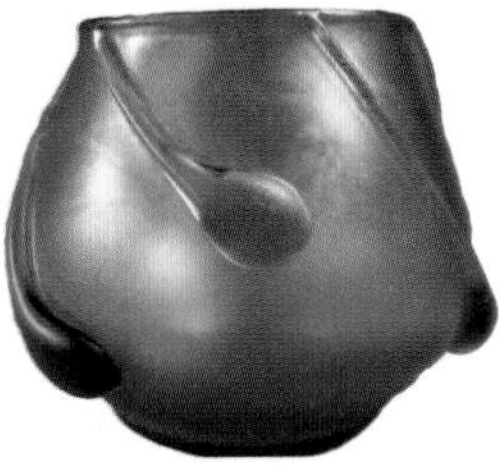

A Loetz iridescent glass vase, applied with teardrop motifs, Austria, c1900, 4¼in (11cm) high.

£200–250 Rosebery's

A pair of Loetz Titania glass vases, Austria, c1906, 8¼in (21cm) high.

£4,250–4,750 Design Gallery

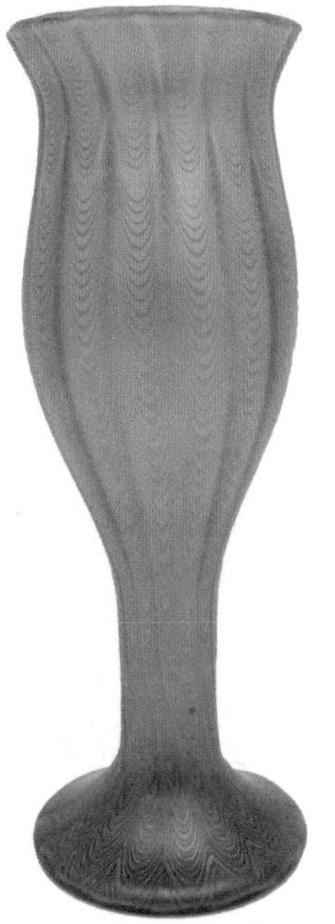

A Loetz iridescent glass vase, decorated with drawn threads, Austria, 1920s, 12½in (32cm) high.

£1,500–1,700 Ondines

GLASS – LALIQUE

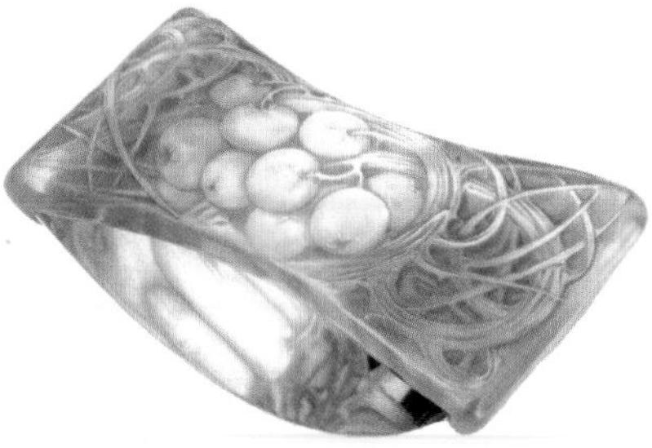

A Lalique glass rocker blotter, 'Cerises', clear and frosted with a sepia patina, on a metal rocker, moulded mark, signed, France, c1920, 6½in (16.5cm) long.

£1,100–1,300 **Rago Arts**

A Lalique glass bowl, 'Vases No. 1', marked, France, c1921, 9¼in (23.5cm) diam.

£180–220 **Heritage**

A Lalique glass bowl, decorated with moulded birds, France, c1935, 9in (23cm) diam.

£500–550 **James Strang**

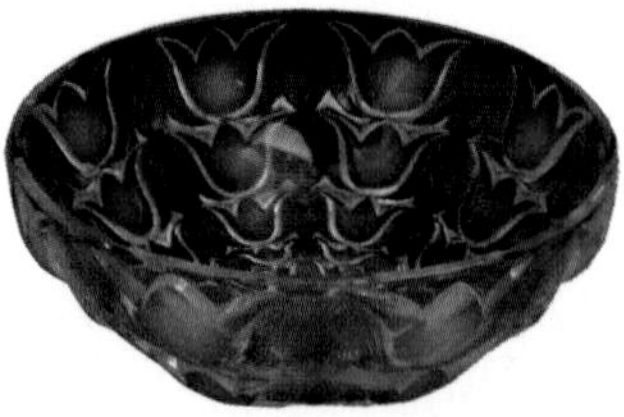

A Lalique opalescent glass bowl, 'Campanules', signed, France, c1930, 9½in (24cm) diam.

£1,100–1,250 **Ondines**

A Lalique glass car mascot, 'Coq Nain', France, c1930, 8in (20.5cm) high.

£1,500–1,650 **Design Gallery**

A Lalique glass dish, 'Martigues', moulded mark, France, c1920, 14in (35.5cm) diam.

£3,500–4,200 **Rago Arts**

A Lalique opalescent glass dish, 'Gazelles', moulded mark, signed, c1925, 11½in (29cm) diam.

£1,100–1,300 **Rago Arts**

A Lalique opalescent glass dish, 'Poissons No. 1', stencilled mark, France, c1930, 11¾in (30cm) diam.

£350–420 **Gorringes (L)**

A Lalique glass dish, 'Fleuron', signed, France, c1930, 10in (25.5cm) diam.

£450–500 **Ondines**

A Lalique opalescent glass plate, 'Bulbes', c1930, 10½in (26.5cm) diam.

£430–480 **Mike Weedon**

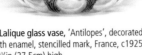

A Lalique glass vase, 'Escargot', moulded mark, France, c1920, 8¼in (21cm) high.
£15,000–18,000 Rago Arts

A Lalique glass vase, 'Antilopes', decorated with enamel, stencilled mark, France, c1925, 10¾in (27.5cm) high.
£18,000–22,000 Rago Arts

A Lalique glass vase, 'Eucalyptus', with moulded decoration, France, c1925, 7in (18cm) high.
£1,300–1,500 Church Hill

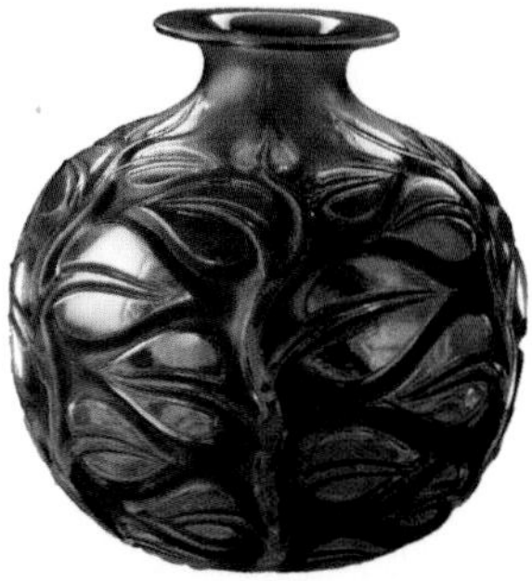

A Lalique glass vase, 'Sophora', marked, France, c1926, 10in (25.5cm) high.
£2,300–2,750 Heritage

A Lalique glass vase, 'Lierre', signed, France, c1927, 7in (18cm) high.
£700–800 Church Hill

A Lalique glass vase, 'Orléans', moulded with flowers, signed, France, c1930, 8in (20.5cm) high.
£2,500–3,000 Sotheby's (P)

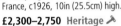

A Lalique glass vase, 'Formose', France, 1930s, 7in (18cm) high.
£1,800–2,000 Ondines

A Lalique glass vase, 'Courlis', stencilled signature, France, c1931, 6½in (16.5cm) high.
£5,000–6,000 Rago Arts

A Lalique glass vase, 'Nefliers', with original staining, raised moulded mark, signed, France, c1930, 5in (12.5cm) high.
£700–800 Afford Decorative Arts

A Lalique opalescent glass vase, 'Saint-Marc', signed, France, c1939, 6¾in (17cm) high.
£1,000–1,200 Rago Arts

GLASS – NAMED MAKERS

A Gabriel Argy-Rousseau *pâte-de-verre* box and cover, decorated with honesty, moulded signature, France, c1920, 3¾in (9.5cm) high.

£2,500–3,000 Rago Arts

A Gabriel Argy-Rousseau *pâte-de-verre* two-handled glass vase, with moulded mark, France, c1930, 3½in (9cm) high.

£5,500–6,200 Ondines

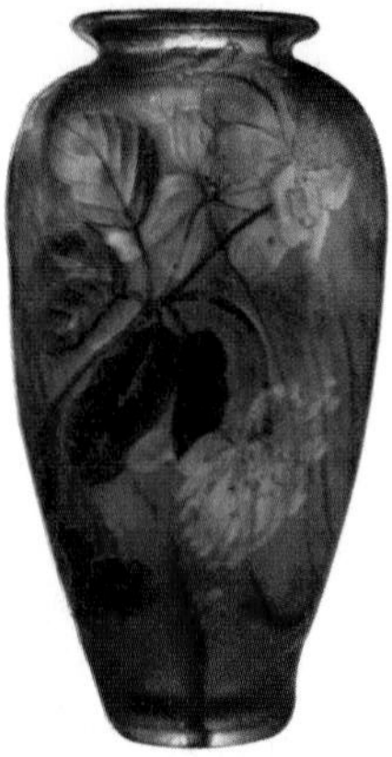

A Burgun & Schverer cameo glass vase, internally decorated with flowers and leafy stems, slight damage, signed, France, c1900, 9½in (24cm) high.

£7,000–8,500 Jackson's

A Georges de Feure cameo glass jar, with a pierced gilt-metal cover and collar, the body decorated with Grecian warriors, signed, France, c1910, 7½in (19cm) high.

£400–500 Jackson's

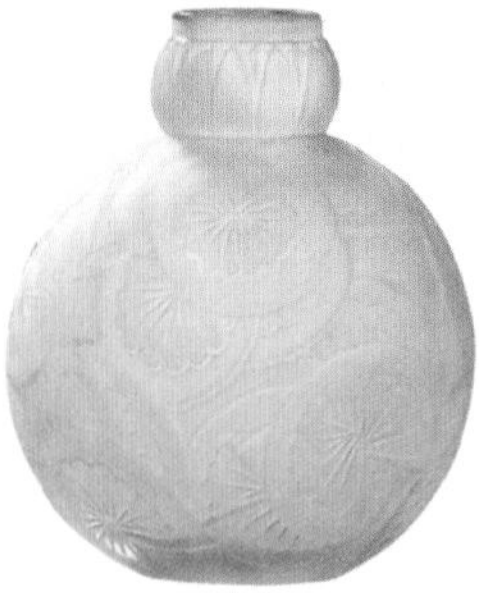

An Etling frosted glass vase, moulded with lily fronds, with traces of blue wash, France, c1930, 10in (25.5cm) high.

£175–200 Skinner

A Francis Jourdain glass aquarium, on a mahogany base, signed, France, 1920, 12½in (32cm) diam.

£4,000–5,000 Sotheby's (P)

An André Hunebelle glass vase, moulded and frosted with three goldfish and wave decoration, France, c1930, 9in (23cm) high.

£350–420 Heritage

A Wilhelm Kralik & Son iridescent glass vase, with four looped handles, Czechoslovakia, c1900, 3½in (9cm) high.

£380–420 Afford Decorative Arts

A Leerdam commemorative glass beaker, designed by Andries D. Copier, etched 'IXe Olympiade Amsterdam Holland 1928', marked, Holland, 6¾in (17cm) high.

£1,400–1,700 Sotheby's (Am)

A Legras & Cie glass vase, with acid-etched, enamel and gilt decoration, marked 'Mont Joye', France, c1900, 4½in (11.5cm) high.

£420–460
Afford Decorative Arts

A Legras & Cie glass vase, with enamel and gilt decoration, marked 'Mont Joye', France, c1900, 10in (25.5cm) high.

£1,000–1,100
Afford Decorative Arts

A Legras & Cie glass vase, with acid-etched, enamel and gilt decoration, signed, France, c1900, 5in (12.5cm) high.

£300–340 Afford Decorative Arts

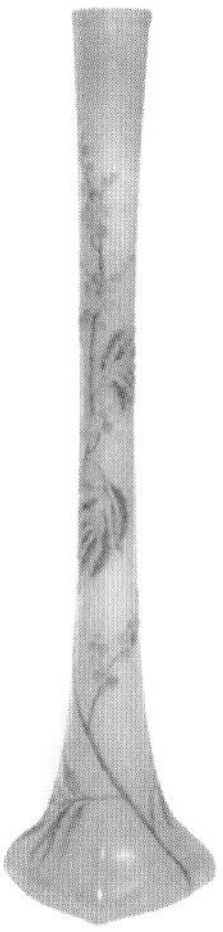

A Legras & Cie glass Solifleur vase, with acid-etched and enamel decoration, France, c1910, 20in (51cm) high.

£1,000–1,200
Afford Decorative Arts

A Koloman Moser glass jug, with a Secessionist brass handle, Austria, c1910, 11½in (29cm) high.

£270–300 James Strang

A Moser Glassworks cameo glass vase, designed by Heinrich Hussman, acid-etched with birds and trees, signed and marked, Bohemia, c1925, 7in (18cm) high.

£900–1,100 Jackson's

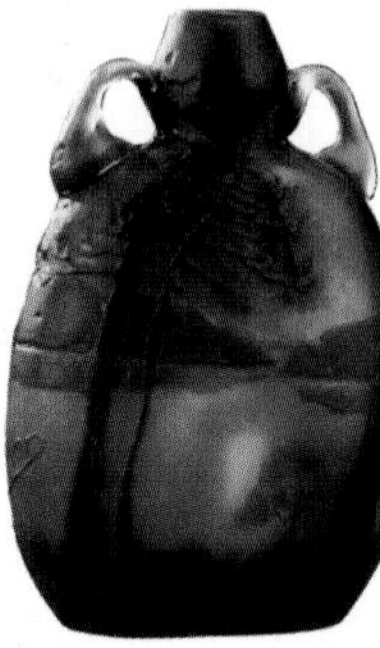

A Muller Frères cameo glass vase, decorated with mountains and a lake, handles repaired, signed, France, c1910, 5¼in (13.5cm) high.

£220–260 Jackson's

A Muller Frères cameo glass vase, decorated with roses, signed, France, c1905, 8½in (21.5cm) high.

£1,300–1,600 Jackson's

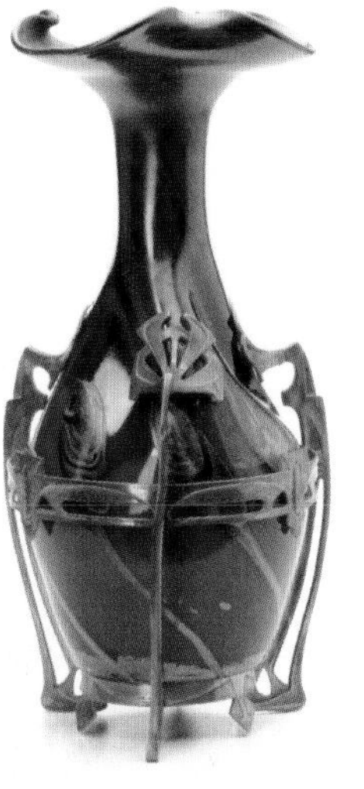

A Rindskopf glass vase, internally decorated with iridescent lappets, with original brass mount, Czechoslovakia, c1905, 14¼in (36cm) high.

£600–700 Rago Arts

A Sabino glass vase, moulded with stylized flowers and geometric forms, France, c1930, 11in (28cm) high.

£425–525 Heritage

A St Louis cameo glass vase, decorated with stylized fronds, signed D'Argenthal, France, c1905, 4½in (11.5cm) high.

£500–600 Rago Arts

A Carlo Scarpa iridescent glass vase, for M. V. M. Cappelin & Co, Italy, c1930, 7in (18cm) high.

£4,000–5,000 Sotheby's

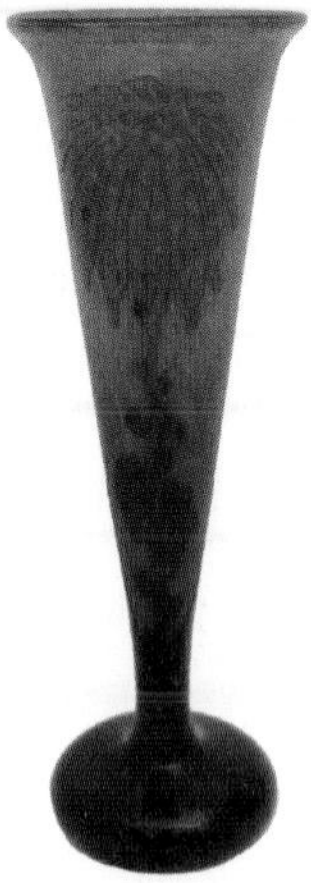

A Schneider glass vase, signed 'Le Verre Français', France, c1930, 12½in (32cm) high.

£1,200–1,300 Ondines

A Schneider glass vase, signed, France, 1925–30, 7½in (19cm) high.

£425–525 Waddington's

This vase is signed 'Schneider', but many pieces from this factory were signed 'Le Verre Français' or 'Charder'.

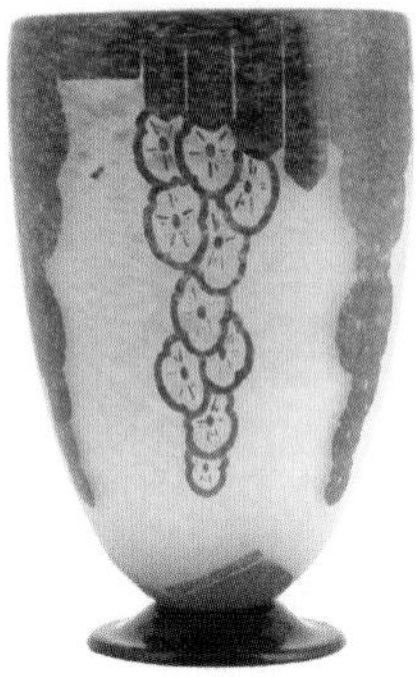

A Schneider cameo glass vase, decorated with stylized wisteria, signed 'Charder' and engraved 'Le Verre Français', stencilled retailer's mark 'Ovington. Est', France, c1930, 12¼in (31cm) high.

£1,200–1,500 Rago Arts

A Steuben Gold Aurene glass comport, with an everted rim, signed, America, c1910, 12in (30.5cm) diam.

£600–700 Jackson's

A Steuben glass vase, retailed by Haviland & Co, America, New York, c1920, 5in (12.5cm) high.

£300–350 Heritage

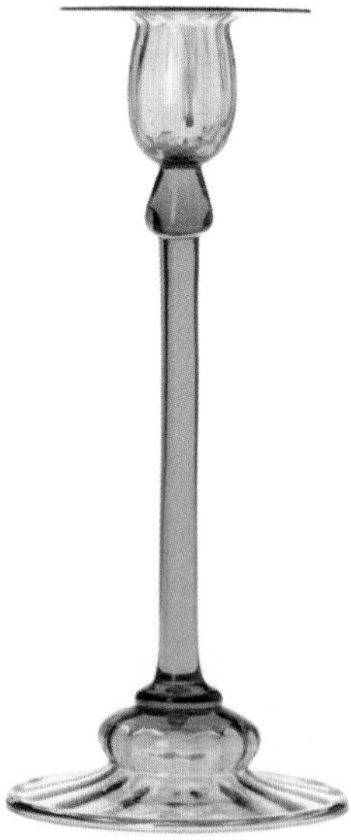

A pair of Steuben glass candlesticks, with waffle mark, America, c1920, 12in (30.5cm) high.

£1,500–1,800 Rago Arts

A group of five glasses, in the manner of Theresienthal, each painted with gilt and enamel stylized flowerheads, painted mark 'WW/D/416', c1900, 9¼in (23.5cm) high.

£2,000–2,400 Lyon & Turnbull

A Tiffany iridescent glass vase, with original paper label, America, c1900, 15in (38cm) high.

£1,800–2,000 Ondines

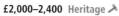

A Tiffany iridescent glass vase, signed 'L.C.T.', America, c1900, 12in (30.5cm) high.
£1,150–1,300 Ondines

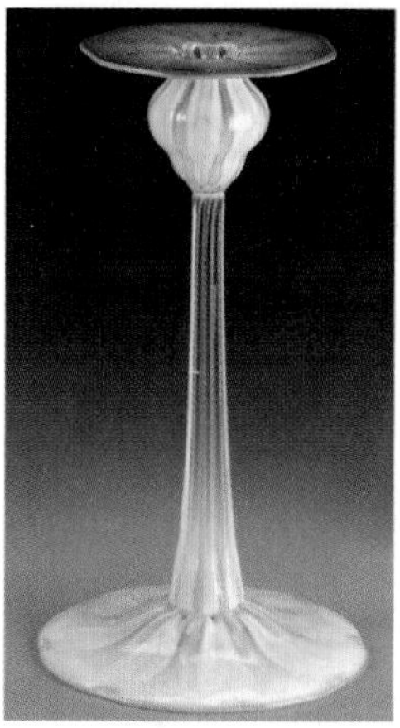

A Tiffany glass candlestick, America, c1900, 10¾in (27.5cm) high.
£2,000–2,400 Heritage

A Tiffany iridescent glass vase, with a floriform bowl, repaired and restored, America, c1912, 17¾in (45cm) high.
£3,500–4,200 Heritage

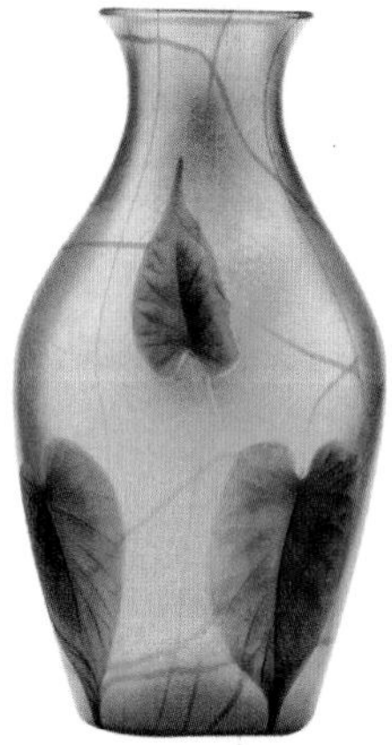

A Tiffany Favrile iridescent glass vase, decorated with intaglio ivy leaves, signed, America, c1915, 9in (23cm) high.
£7,000–8,500 Sotheby's (Am)

A Tiffany Favrile glass vase, signed, America, c1920, 16in (40.5cm) high.
£2,000–2,400 Sotheby's (Am)

A Val St Lambert cut crystal vase, with burgundy overlay, Belgium, c1930, 9in (23cm) high.
£270–300 Art Nouveau Originals

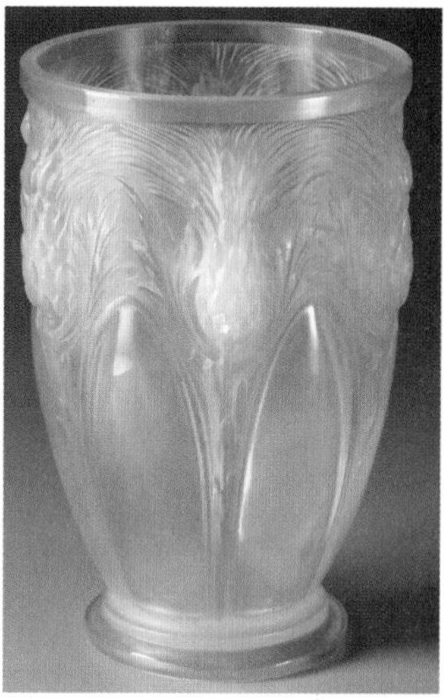

A Verlys opalescent glass vase, moulded with a pattern of thistles, slight damage, France, c1920, 9½in (24cm) high.
£320–380 Heritage

A Thomas Webb & Sons Moorish cameo glass vase, attributed to George Woodall and Gem Cameo, c1890, 10½in (26.5cm) high.
£25,000–30,000 Sotheby's (NY)
This unique vase is listed in the Webb archives as having been sent unfinished to the 1889 Paris Exhibition. It was returned unsold.

A Thomas Webb & Sons Intarsia cameo glass vase, designed by Lionel Pearce, marked, c1900, 7½in (19cm) high.
£5,500–6,500 Sotheby's (NY)

A Thomas Webb & Sons cameo glass scent bottle, with a silver mount and stopper, maker's mark, London 1901, 5in (12.5cm) high.
£1,000–1,200 Sotheby's (NY)

A Thomas Webb & Sons cameo glass vase, decorated with flowerheads and scrolling foliage, signed, c1920, 6in (15cm) high.

£1,100–1,250 Shapiro ⊞

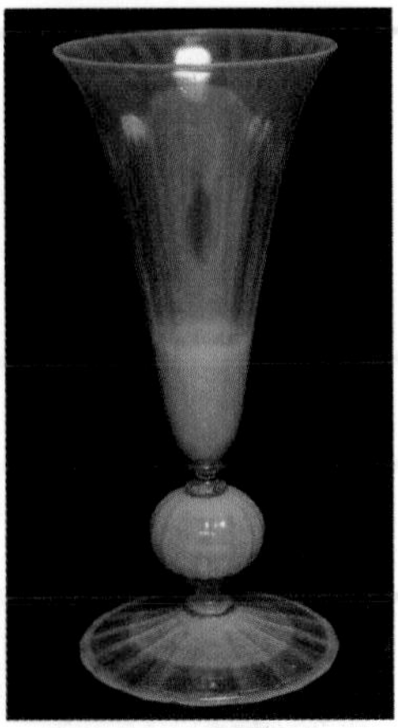

A Whitefriars glass vase, by Harry Powell, c1890, 10in (25.5cm) high.

£2,400–2,700
Country Seat ⊞

A pair of Whitefriars glass vases, by Harry Powell, c1905, 5in (12.5cm) high.

£225–250 Art Nouveau Originals ⊞

GLASS – UNKNOWN MAKERS

An Arts & Crafts glass bowl, c1900, 5in (12.5cm) diam.

£110–125 Shapiro ⊞

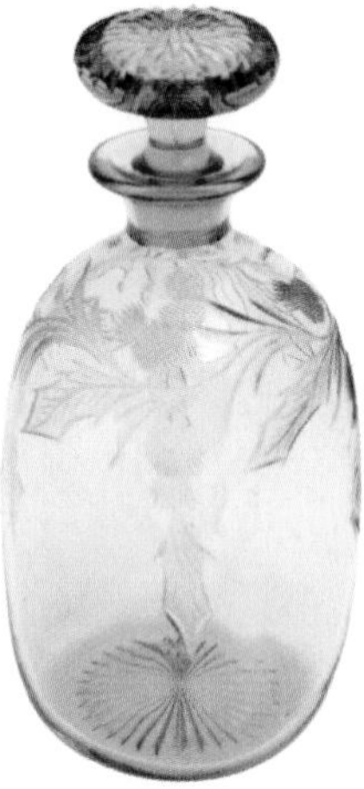

An Arts & Crafts cut-glass decanter, c1900, 9in (23cm) high.

£550–650 Shapiro ⊞

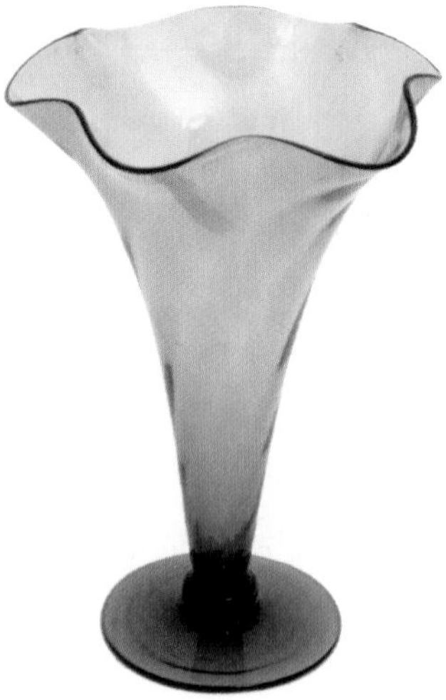

An Arts & Crafts glass vase, c1905, 9in (23cm) high.

£150–175 Shapiro ⊞

A pair of iridescent glass vases, Austria, c1900, 12in (30.5cm) high.

£140–170 Waddington's

A glass scent bottle and stopper, decorated with silver overlay, America, c1900, 4in (10cm) high.

£240–270 Art Nouveau Originals ⊞

GLASS – STAINED GLASS

A pair of Aesthetic Movement stained- and leaded-glass panels, each with a central panel painted with a stork among bullrushes, c1870, each 43¼ x 16¼in (110 x 41.5cm).

£3,000–3,500 Drew Pritchard

A set of stained- and leaded-glass panels, depicting a family in a rural setting, with painted panels and inscriptions, 1870s.

£10,000–11,000 Drew Pritchard

A pair of Ludwig Grandy stained- and leaded-glass panels, painted with flowers and birds, Austria, Vienna, c1890, 41¾ x 17¼in (106 x 44cm).

£320–380 Dorotheum

A stained-glass Hesperiden window, in the manner of Edward Burne-Jones, c1890, 24 x 13¼in (61 x 33.5cm).

£750–900 Jackson's

A stained-glass window, depicting a vase of flowers enclosed by an archway, rosettes and decorative borders, America, 1898, 42½ x 38½in (108 x 98cm).

£9,000–11,000 Freeman's

A pair of stained-glass panels, probably by McCulloch & Co, the design attributed to David Gauld, Scotland, Glasgow, c1900, 16in (40.5cm) high.

£700–800 James Strang

An Art Nouveau leaded-glass window, depicting irises, c1900, 39¼ x 57½in (100x 146cm), with frame.

£2,500–3,000 Sotheby's (Am)

A pair of stained- and leaded-glass windows, attributed to John La Farge, America, c1900, 40¼ x 17¼in (102 x 44cm).

£6,500–8,000 Sotheby's (NY)

CERAMICS – DOULTON

A Royal Doulton chamberstick, by Rosina Brown, decorated with fish amid swirling waves, c1890, 7in (18cm) high.

£580–650 Art Nouveau Originals

A Doulton Lambeth jug, by Hannah Barlow, with sgraffito decoration of a lion and two horses, incised and impressed marks, slight damage, c1870, 9½in (24cm) high.

£650–800 Halls

A Doulton Lambeth salt-glazed stoneware jug, by Arthur Barlow, with incised decoration, c1871, 7½in (19cm) high.

£350–420 Gorringes (L)

A Doulton Lambeth jug, by Hannah Barlow, with sgraffito decoration of a horse, impressed and incised marks, c1885, 10¼in (26cm) high.

£280–320 Tennants

A Royal Doulton oil lamp, by Edith D. Luckton, c1880, 21in (53.5cm) high.

£350–400 Exeter Antique Lighting

A Doulton Slater's Patent tyg, with silver mounts, dated 1899, 6in (15cm) high.

£340–380 Swan at Tetsworth

A Doulton Lambeth stoneware vase, by Emily J. Edwards, incised with flowerheads and foliage, impressed and incised marks, c1876, 15¾in (40cm) high.

£500–600 Toovey's

A pair of Doulton Lambeth stoneware vases, by Hannah Barlow, incised with dogs within cartouches, the ground decorated with birds by Florence Barlow, impressed marks, c1880, 11½in (29cm) high.

£2,000–2,500 Skinner

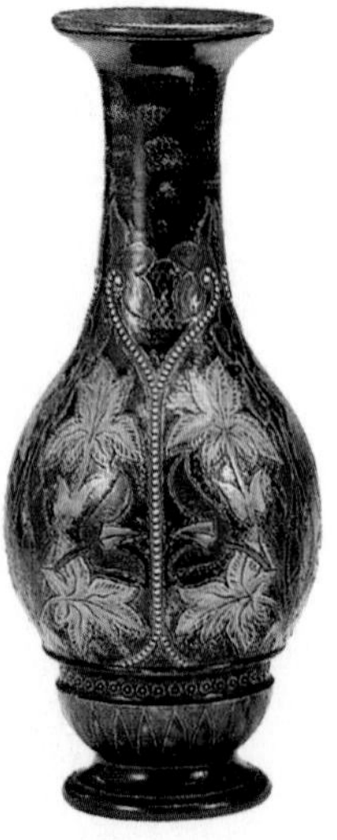

A pair of Doulton Lambeth vases, by George Hugo Tabor, incised with leaves, impressed marks, dated 1880, 17in (43cm) high.

£900–1,100 Freeman's

A Doulton Lambeth stoneware vase, by Eliza Simmance, decorated with lion fish and seaweed, impressed factory mark and inscribed 'Eliza Simmance 466', restored, c1880, 30¾in (78cm) high.

£2,000–2,500 Rosebery's

This vase was probably made as an exhibition piece.

A pair of Doulton Lambeth stoneware vases, by Frank Butler, Elizabeth Adams and Emily London, incised with stylized foliage and embossed with florets, marked, 1882, 9in (23cm) high.

£500–600 Bearnes

A pair of Doulton Lambeth stoneware vases, by Hannah Barlow, incised with cattle, impressed initials, date code for 1883, 10in (25.5cm) high.

£900–1,100 Thomson, Roddick & Medcalf (C)

A pair of Doulton Lambeth stoneware vases, by Mark V. Marshall and Florence Barlow, slip-decorated with birds, fruit and foliage, marked, late 19thC, 17in (43cm) high.

£2,000–2,500 Skinner

A Doulton Lambeth stoneware vase, by Eliza Simmance, impressed and incised marks, 1890s, 11in (28cm) high.

£350–420 Waddington's

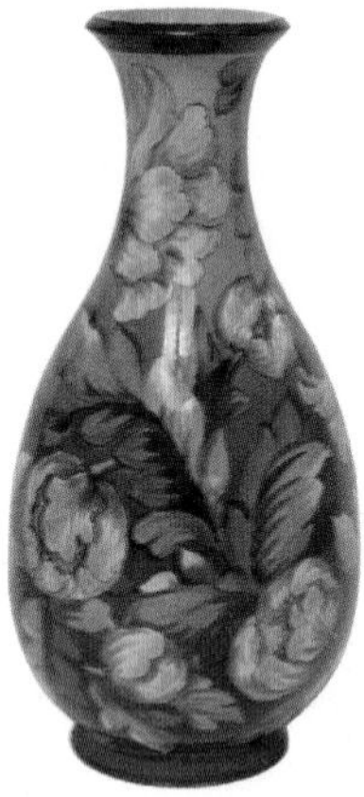

A Doulton faïence vase, decorated with flowers and foliage, c1900, 12in (30.5cm) high.

£300–350 Art Nouveau Originals

A pair of Doulton Lambeth stoneware vases, by Florence Barlow, decorated in *pâte-sur-pâte* with storks and tube-lined with grasses, impressed marks, c1905, 16¼in (41.5cm) high.

£4,250–5,250 Bamfords

A pair of Doulton Lambeth vases, by Mark V. Marshall, decorated with stylized ivy leaves, c1900, 10in (25.5cm) high.

£1,300–1,450 AD Antiques

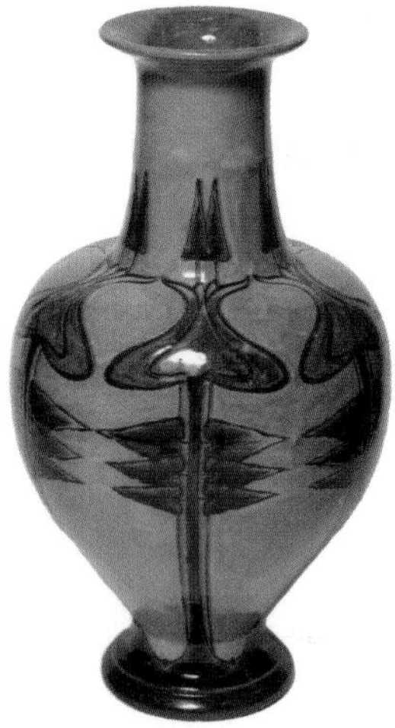

A Doulton Lambeth vase, by Eliza Simmance, decorated with stylized flowers and foliage, 1906, 16in (40.5cm) high.

£1,700–2,000 Brightwells

A pair of Royal Doulton vases, by Eliza Simmance and Bessie Newberry, decorated with flowers and foliage, 1910, 15in (38cm) high.

£2,500–3,000 Brightwells

A Doulton Lambeth vase, by Eliza Simmance and Jane Hurst, c1910, 14in (35.5cm) high.

£1,350–1,500 AD Antiques

CERAMICS – MARTIN BROTHERS

Martin Brothers stoneware tyg, incised with orks, owls and doves, inscribed 'Morning', Joon' and 'Night', incised marks, dated 1875, ⁄in (16cm) high.

1,700–2,000 Lyon & Turnbull

A Martin Brothers stoneware flask, painted with a bearded faun, dated 1894, 8in (20.5cm) high.

£2,700–3,000 Brightwells

A Martin Brothers stoneware jar and cover, in the form of a bird, inscribed signatures, dated 1888, on an ebonized base, 10¼in (26cm) high.

£6,000–7,000 Skinner

Martin Brothers stoneware jar and cover, the form of a bird, incised signature, dated 916, 10¾in (27.5cm) high.

10,000–12,000 Cheffins

A Martin Brothers stoneware jardinière, incised with storks, incised signature, c1892, 9½in (24cm) diam.

£3,000–3,500 Skinner

MARKET INFORMATION DECORATIVE ARTS

- In recent years, exhibitions of Decorative Arts at the Victoria & Albert Museum, London have helped broaden interest and increase awareness.
- As a result of these exhibitions, there has been a revival of interest in 20th-century decorative arts. This remarkable upsurge of interest has meant strong market prices for reconized designers.
- There have been highly successful auctions of the stock of London dealers John Jesse and Gordon Watson, and of Andrew Macintoch Patrick's collection of items by Christopher Dresser.
- The market for Lenci pottery figures and Martin Brothers stoneware birds is particularly buoyant.
- Works by leading designers C. R. Ashbee, the Guild of Handicraft, Omar Ramsden and C. F. A. Voysey have all witnessed a sharp increase in price.
- Furniture by Heal's, Godwin, Shapland & Petter and the Cotswold School is in high demand, as are the finest Art Deco bronze figures by Chiparus and Preiss.
- While heady prices are achieved for the leading names, generic items prove more difficult to sell.
- This trend looks set to continue with collectors eager to upgrade to better and rarer examples and, with limited supply, this can only mean higher prices both at auction and with specialist dealers at the leading fairs.

A Martin Brothers stoneware jug, incised decoration and signature, dated 1876, 5in (13cm) high.
£380–450 Sworders

A Martin Brothers stoneware jug, decorated with fish and seaweed, with inscription, dated 1887, 15¼in (38.5cm) high.
£7,000–8,500 Skinner

A Martin Brothers stoneware face jug, incis signature, dated 1898, 7¾in (19.5cm) high.
£6,000–7,000 Skinner

A Martin Brothers stoneware spoon warmer, restored, dated 1881, 8in (20.5cm) long.
£2,700–3,000 AD Antiques

A Martin Brothers stoneware vase, decorated with fish in a seascape, dated 1887, 7in (18cm) high.
£3,500–4,000 AD Antiques

A Martin Brothers stoneware vase, decorated with monkeys and fruit, dated 1896, 16in (40.5cm) high.
£10,000–12,000 AD Antiques

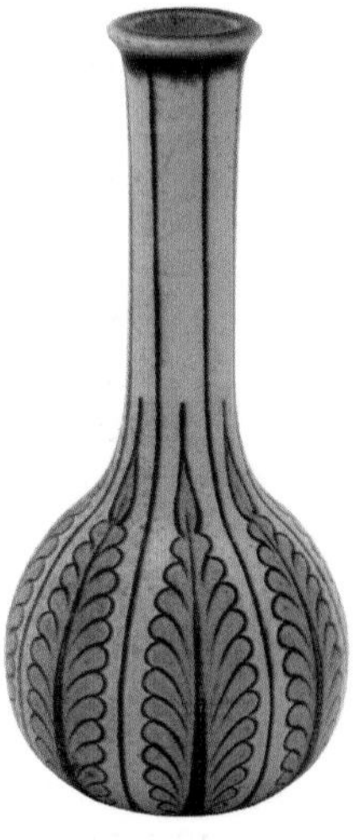

A Martin Brothers stoneware vase, dated 1897, 5in (12.5cm) high.
£550–600 AD Antiques

A Martin Brothers stoneware vase, decorated with a spider crab, marked, dated 1904, 9½in (24cm) high.
£3,000–3,500 Bearnes

CERAMICS – MOORCROFT

A Moorcroft biscuit barrel, decorated with Pomegranate pattern, with silver-plated mounts, c1920, 6in (15cm) high.
£330–400 Greenslade Taylor Hunt

A Moorcroft bowl, decorated with Pomegranate pattern, c1920, 12in (30.5cm) diam.
£1,450–1,600 Time Antiques

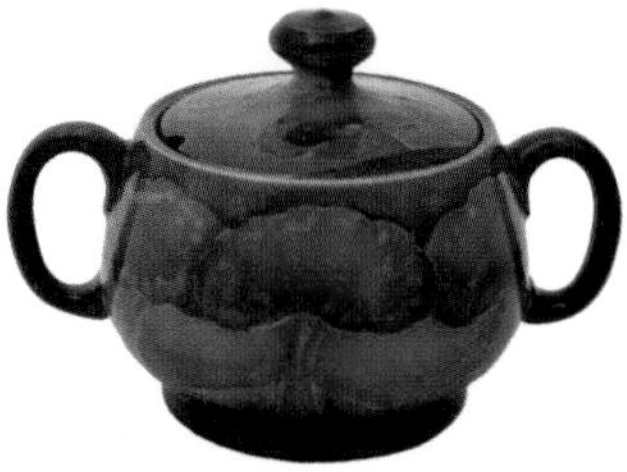

A Moorcroft sugar bowl and cover, decorated with Eventide pattern, c1925, 4in (10cm) diam.
£1,500–1,650 AD Antiques

A Moorcroft bowl, decorated with Moonlit Blue pattern, with a pewter cover, impressed marks, signed, c1925, 6in (15cm) diam.
£1,400–1,700 Paul Beighton

A Moorcroft salt-glazed pottery jug, tube-lined with carp and water lilies, impressed mark and painted signature, c1935, 7in (18cm) high.
£1,100–1,300 Bearnes

A Moorcroft mug, for Liberty & Co, decorated with Pomegranate pattern, painted signature, 1910–12, 4in (10cm) high.
£1,500–1,650 Glazed Over

ESSENTIAL REFERENCE MOORCROFT

William Moorcroft joined James Macintyre's pottery at the very end of the 19th century and introduced Florian ware, which depicted highly organic Art Nouveau motifs in shades of blue. He started the firm of Moorcroft in 1913, just before the outbreak of the WWI. One of the most distinctive features of Moorcroft is the use of tube-lined motifs which give a slightly raised definition to the surface pattern. A wide range of extremely popular floral and fruit patterns were introduced including Wisteria, Clematis, Anemone and Pomegranate among others. Perhaps the most sought after and arguably most artistic patterns were produced during the 1920s when William Moorcroft introduced the celebrated Eventide and Claremont ranges. This bowl is decorated with the Moonlit Blue pattern which was also a popular design, and signed with painted initials. Pieces were retailed through Liberty & Co and rarer examples were mounted with Liberty's Tudric hand-beaten pewter. Items such as these are scarce and command ever increasing prices when they appear on the market.
£1,100–1,200 AD Antiques

A pair of Moorcroft Macintyre vases, decorated in the Imari palette with panels of flowers, printed marks, c1900, 9in (23cm) high.

£300–360 Freeman's

A Moorcroft Macintyre Florian ware vase, printed mark, signed, c1900, 11¾in (30cm) high.

£1,600–2,000 Paul Beighton

A Moorcroft Macintyre Florian ware vase, signed 'W. Moorcroft', 1902–04, 8½in (21.5cm) high.

£2,700–3,000 Glazed Over

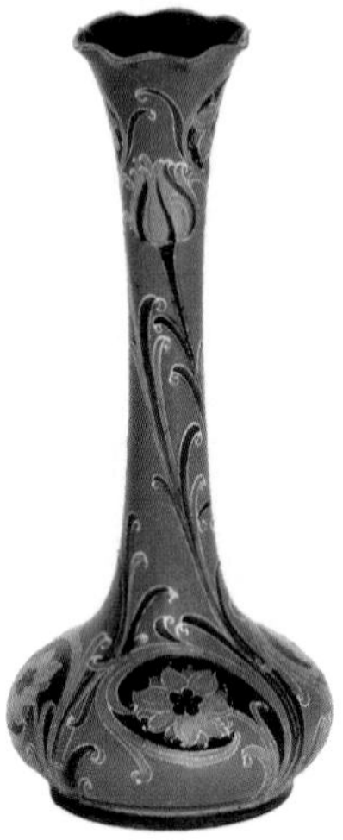

A Moorcroft Macintyre vase, tube-lined with Green and Gold pattern, stamped mark and painted signature, c1903, 9¾in (25cm) high.

£1,000–1,200 Bearnes

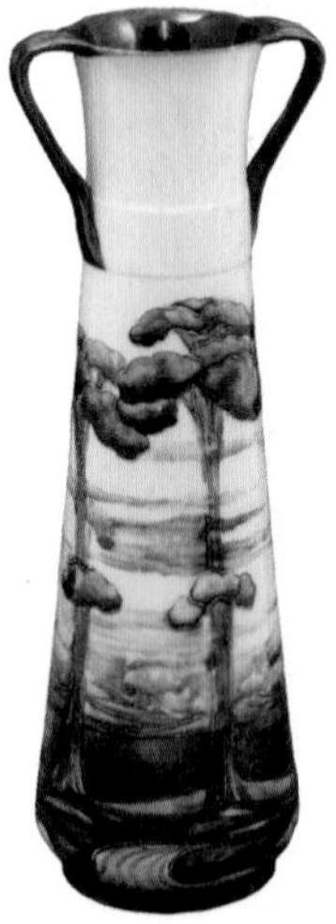

A Moorcroft Macintyre Florian ware vase, decorated with Landscape pattern, printed marks and signature to base, c1903, 11¾in (30cm) high.

£2,800–3,400 Gorringes (L)

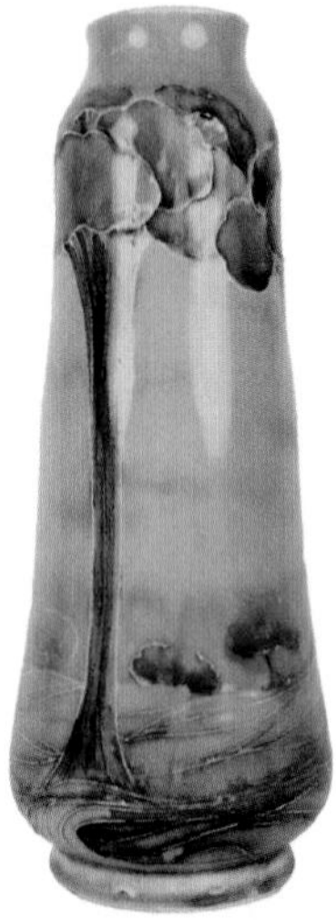

A Moorcroft vase, for Liberty & Co, decorated with Hazeldene pattern, signed 'W Moorcroft', c1905, 7in (18cm) high.

£1,200–1,500 Rosebery's

A Moorcroft Macintyre Florian ware twin-handled vase, painted with Violet pattern, handles repaired, painted signature, c1905, 6in (15.5cm) high.

£380–450 Sworders

A Moorcroft Florian ware vase, decorated with Poppy, Tulip & Forget-me-Not pattern, signed 'W. Moorcroft', 1908–09, 5in (12.5cm) high.

£1,450–1,600 Glazed Over

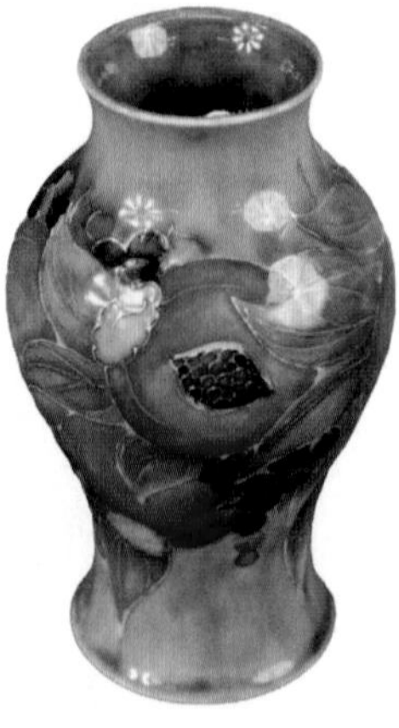

A Moorcroft baluster vase, decorated with Pomegranate pattern, signed, hole drilled in base, dated 1912, 6½in (16.5cm) high.

£700–850 Gorringes (L)

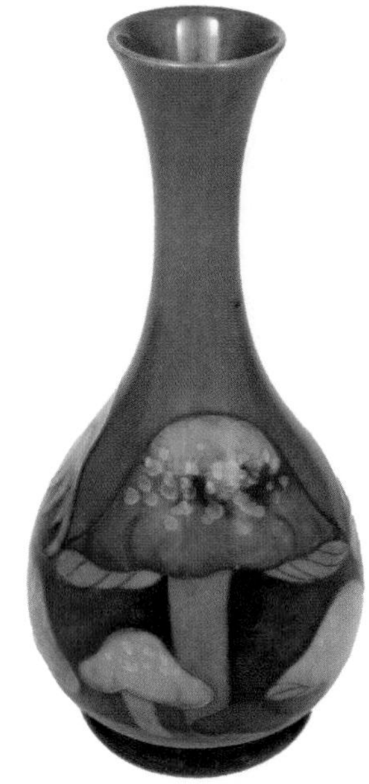

A Moorcroft vase, decorated with Claremont pattern, 1918–25, 8½in (21.5cm) high.
£2,250–2,500 Glazed Over ⊞

A Moorcroft vase, decorated with Large Poppy pattern, c1920, 12in (30.5cm) high.
£3,000–3,300 AD Antiques ⊞

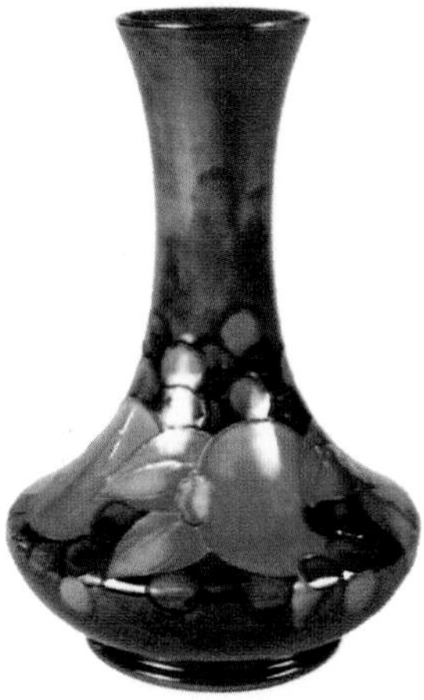

A Moorcroft bottle vase, decorated with Pomegranate pattern, impressed mark, signed, c1920, 8in (20.5cm) high.
£350–420 Paul Beighton ⚒

A Moorcroft vase, decorated with Dawn Landscape pattern, c1924, 6in (15cm) high.
£2,000–2,250 Glazed Over ⊞

A Moorcroft flambé vase, decorated with fish, signed 'W. Moorcroft', 1928–35, 7½in (19cm) high.
£2,700–3,000 Glazed Over ⊞

A Moorcroft salt-glazed vase, decorated with Leaf and Berry pattern in Sunray yellow, 1928–35, 8½in (21.5cm) high.
£750–850 Glazed Over ⊞

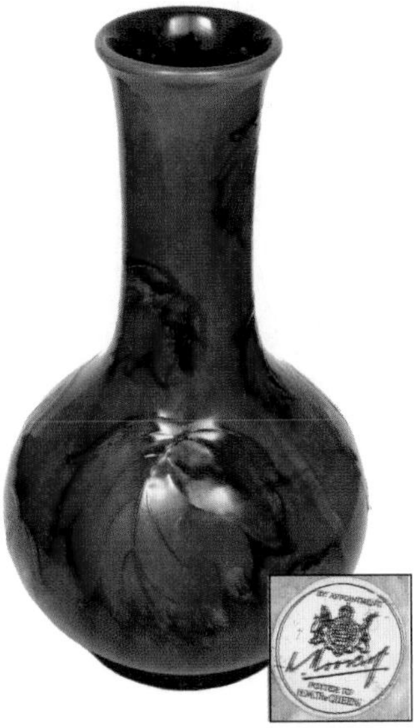

A Moorcroft flambé vase, decorated with Falling Leaves pattern, signed 'W. Moorcroft', with paper label, 1928–35, 9in (23cm) high.
£1,000–1,100 Glazed Over ⊞

A Moorcroft flambé vase, tube-lined with Freesia pattern, impressed mark and painted signature, 1935–40, 12½in (32cm) high.
£750–900 Bearnes ⚒

A Moorcroft vase, decorated with Spring Flowers pattern, c1936, 8in (20.5cm) high.
£380–450
Greenslade Taylor Hunt ⚒

CERAMICS – ROOKWOOD

A Rookwood bowl, No. 956, America, 1908, 5½in (14cm) diam.

£150–180 **Treadway Gallery**

A Rookwood jug, painted by Matthew Daly, America, 1885, 6¼in (16cm) high.

£150–180 **Heritage**

A Rookwood vase, by Albert R. Valentine, decorated with irises, America, dated 1885, 8in (20.5cm) high.

£320–380 **Heritage**

A Rookwood vase, decorated with swallows and trees within gilt bands, impressed mark, America, dated 1892, 21in (53.5cm) high.

£8,500–10,000 **James D Julia**

A Rookwood vase, by Matthew Daly, decorated with Sea Green Glaze and carved with a peacock feather, marked, signed, dated 1900, America, 7in (18cm) high.

£2,200–2,600
Cincinnati Art Galleries

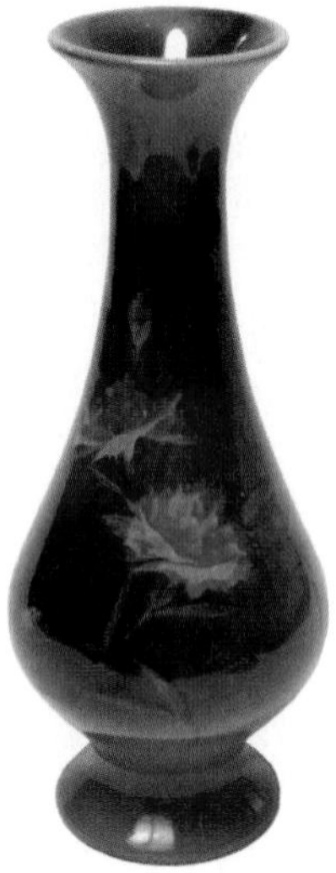

A Rookwood vase, decorated with carnations, America, c1900, 11in (28cm) high.

£580–650 **Art Nouveau Originals**

A Rookwood vase, by Matthew Daly, carved with a peacock feather, marked, America, dated 1900, 14¼in (36cm) high.

£2,700–3,200
Cincinnati Art Galleries

A Rookwood vase, painted by Fred Rothenbusch with a nasturtium, flame mark, America, c1907, 10½in (26.5cm) high.

£700–850 **Rago Arts**

A Rookwood Ombroso vase, by C. S. Todd, decorated with floral rosettes, marked, America, dated 1915, 8¼in (21cm) high.

£1,700–2,000
Cincinnati Art Galleries

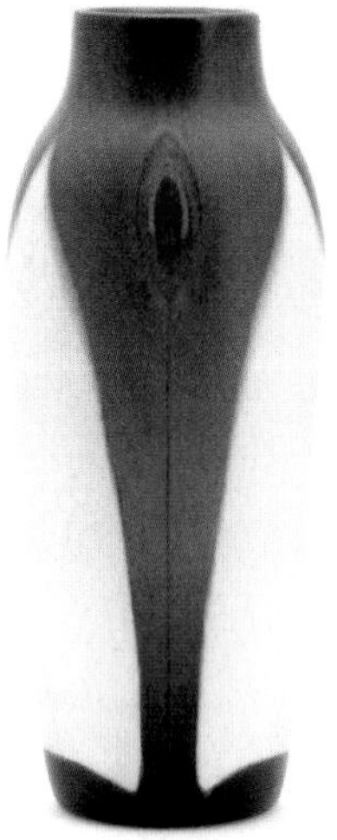

A Rookwood Vellum vase, by Sara Sax, decorated with peacock feathers, slight damage, marked, America, c1915, 8¼in (21cm) high.

£1,000–1,200 Rago Arts

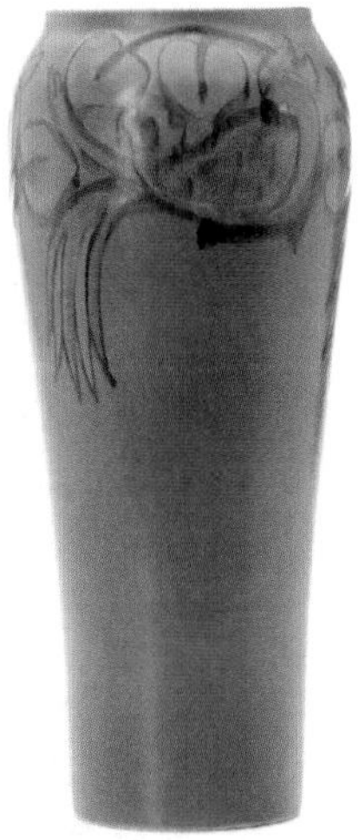

A Rookwood vase, by William Hentschel, decorated with birds of paradise and a matt glaze, rim restored, flame mark, America, 1916, 11¾in (30cm) high.

£700–850 Rago Arts

A Rookwood Vellum vase, by Sallie E. Coyne, painted with pine trees, impressed marks, America, 1916, 6¼in (16cm) high.

£1,400–1,800 Freeman's

A Rookwood Vellum vase, by Kate Curry, slight damage, marked, America, dated 1917, 8in (20.5cm) high.

£800–1,000 Cincinnati Art Galleries

A Rookwood vase, by Carl Schmidt, decorated with trees, marked, America, dated 1919, 13¾in (35cm) high.

£5,000–6,000
Cincinnati Art Galleries

A Rookwood vase, by Sara Sax, marked, America, dated 1925, 14¾in (37.5cm) high.

£1,500–1,800
Cincinnati Art Galleries

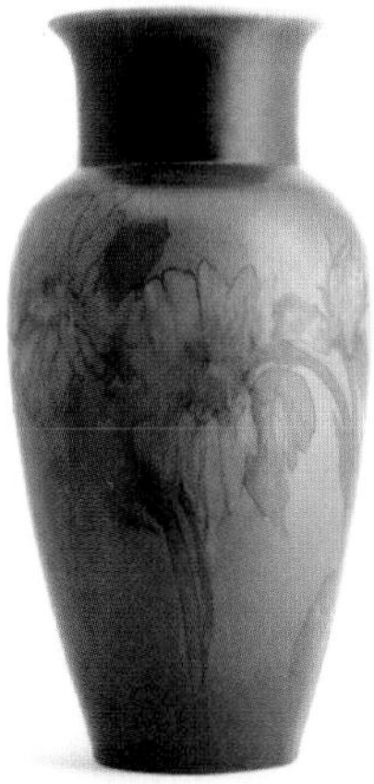

A Rookwood vase, by Elizabeth Lincoln, decorated with birds and sunflowers and a matt glaze, marked, America, 1925, 17¼in (44cm) high.

£3,500–4,200 Rago Arts

A Rookwood vase, by Elizabeth Barrett, with a matt glaze, marked, America, dated 1927, 17¼in (44cm) high.

£1,800–2,200
Cincinnati Art Galleries

A Rookwood vase, by Louise Abel, decorated with a woman swimming with fish, marked, America, dated 1935, 9¼in (23.5cm) high.

£450–550 Cincinnati Art Galleries

CERAMICS – WEDGWOOD

A Wedgwood Fairyland lustre bowl, decorated with Leapfrogging Elves pattern, c1930, 5in (12.5cm) diam.

£1,450–1,600 AD Antiques ⊞

A Wedgwood black basalt model of a tiger and buck, by John Rattenbury Skeaping, 1927, on a wooden base, 12½in (32cm) wide.

£450–550 Dreweatt Neate (N) ⚒

ESSENTIAL REFERENCE WEDGWOOD FAIRYLAND LUSTRE

The Fairyland Lustre range was designed by Daisy Makeig-Jones for Wedgwood in the 1920s. The scenes depicted in elaborate and meticulous patterns on vases, bowls and dishes derived their inspiration from fairy tales. Some of the names were highly evocative such as 'Imps on a Bridge' and 'Flying Humming Birds'. The iridescent effect of the lustre glazes were highlighted with gold borders to increase the dramatic impact. This can be seen in this Fairyland Lustre vase from c1920 which is decorated with the Dragon King pattern. The Fairyland patterns proved to be so popular that other factories started to produce similar ranges, such as those made by Maling, Carlton and Winton. The rarer patterns and shapes continue to achieve very strong prices on the market.

£25,000–30,000 Skinner ⚒

A Wedgwood Fairyland lustre vase and cover, decorated with Jewelled Tree pattern, c1920, 11in (28cm) high.

£4,500–5,000 AD Antiques ⊞

A Wedgwood Fairyland lustre vase, by Daisy Makeig-Jones, decorated with Candlemas pattern, printed mark, c1920, 8¾in (22cm) high.

£5,000–6,000 Freeman's ⚒

A Wedgwood Cane ware vase, by Millicent Taplin, decorated in enamel and copper lustre, impressed mark, c1928, 13¼in (33.5cm) high.

£400–500 Skinner ⚒

A Wedgwood black basalt vase, by Keith Murray, 1932–48, 4in (10cm) high.

£700–800 Gazelles ⊞

CERAMICS – CLARICE CLIFF

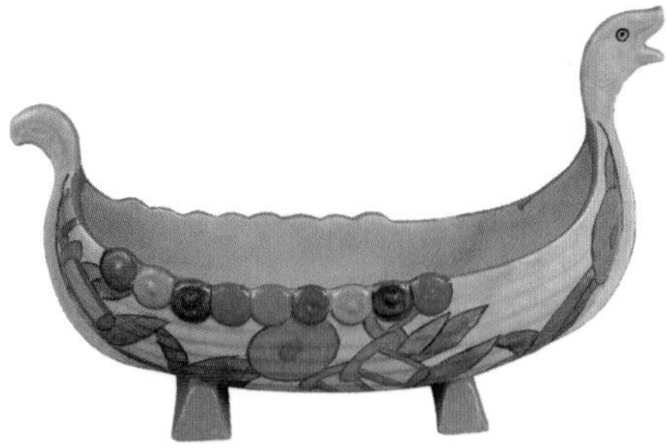

A Clarice Cliff Fantasque Bizarre viking boat, decorated with Bobbins pattern, slight damage, c1930, 16in (40.5cm) long.

£1,700–2,000 Dee, Atkinson & Harrison

A Clarice Cliff Fantasque bowl, decorated in Pebbles pattern, c1929, 7¾in (19.5cm) diam.

£230–275 Greenslade Taylor Hunt

A Clarice Cliff Bizarre bowl, decorated with Patina Coastal pattern, the interior with Delecia ground, marked, c1932, 8¼in (21cm) diam.

£450–550 Bearnes

A Clarice Cliff Bizarre candlestick, printed mark, shape No. 331, c1930, 2in (5cm) high.

£100–120 Halls

A Clarice Cliff Bizarre cigarette box and cover, decorated with Football pattern, c1930, 5½in (14cm) long.

£2,250–2,500 Andrew Muir

A Clarice Cliff Bizarre coffee pot and cover, c1928, 8½in (21.5cm) high.

£600–700 Andrew Muir

A Clarice Cliff Fantasque Bizarre Conical tea service for six, decorated with Crocus pattern, c1931, coffee pot 7in (18cm) high.

£1,600–1,800 Andrew Muir

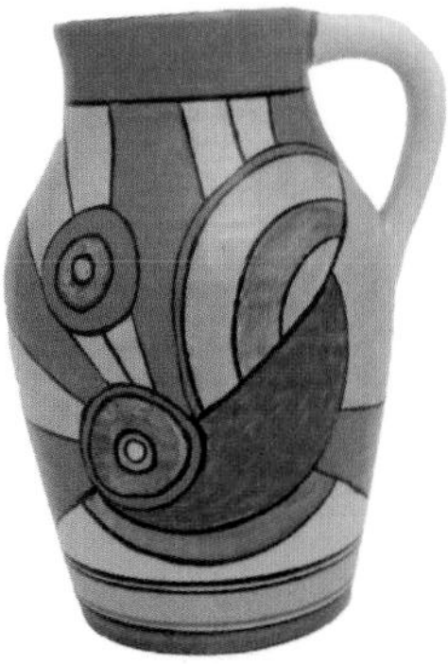

A Clarice Cliff Bizarre Lotus jug, decorated with Sliced Circle pattern, c1929, 12in (30.5cm) high.

£4,000–4,500 Andrew Muir

A Clarice Cliff Bizarre Lotus jug, decorated with Sliced Fruit pattern, marked, c1930, 11¾in (30cm) high.

£1,200–1,500 Leonard Joel

A Clarice Cliff Bizarre Lotus jug, decorated with Autumn pattern, 1930–34, 13in (33cm) high.

£4,000–4,500 Muir Hewitt

A Clarice Cliff Fantasque Bizarre Athens jug, decorated with Honolulu pattern, c1933, 7in (18cm) high.

£800–900 Andrew Muir

A Clarice Cliff Bizarre Lotus jug, decorated with Coral Firs pattern, 1934, 12in (30.5cm) high.

£1,350–1,500 Andrew Muir

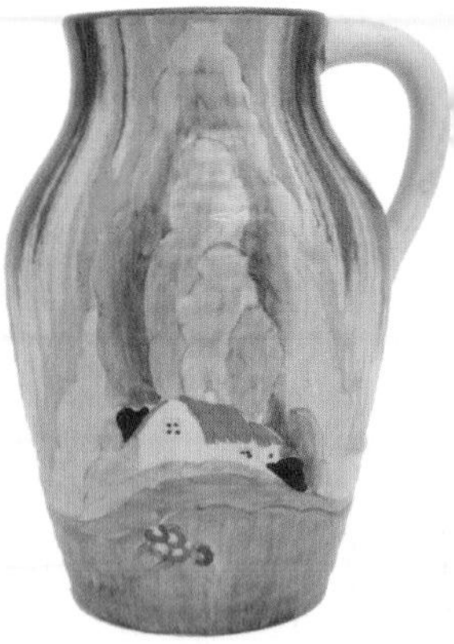

A Clarice Cliff Isis jug, decorated with Forest Glen pattern, c1935, 10in (25.5cm) high.

£1,100–1,250 Andrew Muir

A Clarice Cliff Bizarre Lotus jug, decorated with Sandon pattern, printed mark, c1935, 8in (20.5cm) high.

£250–300 Bearnes

A Clarice Cliff Athens jug, decorated with Forest Glen pattern, c1936, 6in (15cm) high.

£800–900 Muir Hewitt

A Clarice Cliff Lotus jug, decorated with Trees and House pattern, c1930, 11¼in (28.5cm) high.

£1,000–1,200 David Lay

A Clarice Cliff Fantasque Bizarre preserve pot and cover, decorated with House and Bridge pattern, 1930s, 3in (7.5cm) high.

£600–700 Gazelles

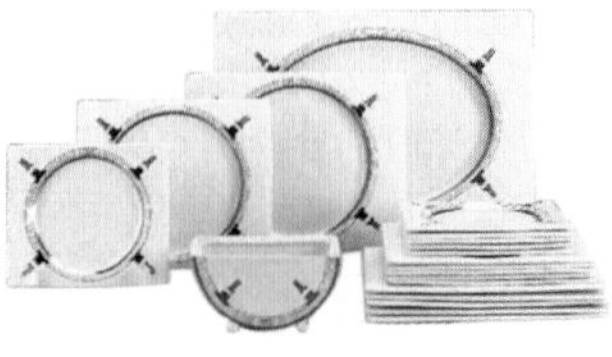

A Clarice Cliff Biarritz dinner service, comprising 20 pieces, printed marks, c1935.

£250–280 Waddington's

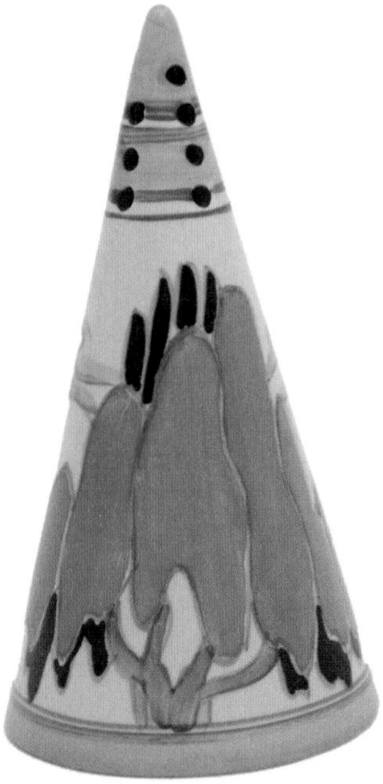

A Clarice Cliff Fantasque Bizarre Conical sugar caster, decorated with Solitude pattern, c1932, 5½in (14cm) high.

£1,600–1,800 Andrew Muir

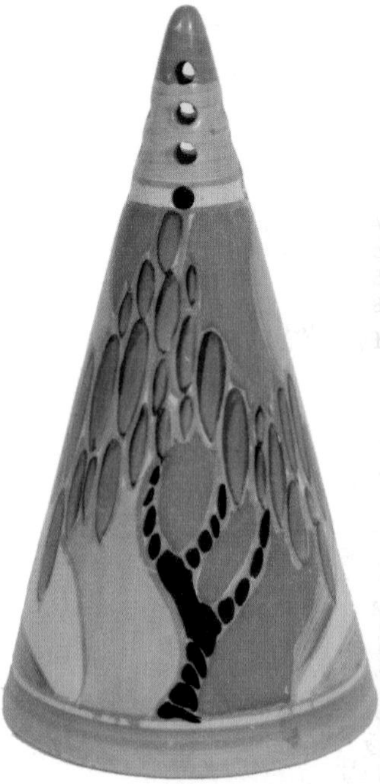

A Clarice Cliff Bizarre Conical sugar caster, decorated with Wind Bells pattern, c1930, 5½in (14cm) high.

£600–700 Charterhouse

A Clarice Cliff Bizarre Athens teapot, decorated with Umbrellas pattern, c1930, 7in (18cm) high.
£175–200 Cheffins

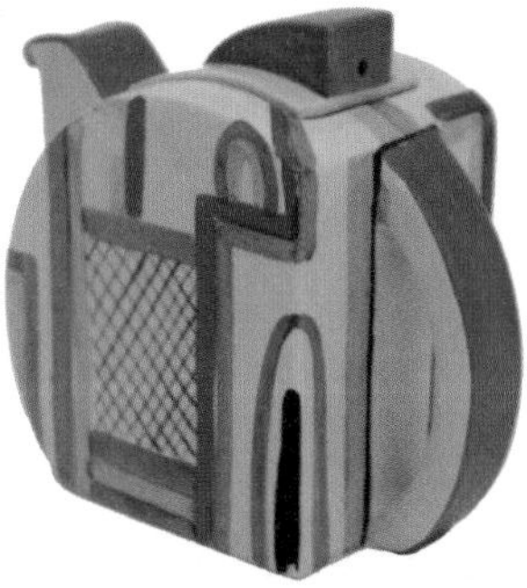

A Clarice Cliff Bizarre Stanford teapot, decorated with Tennis pattern, c1931, 4½in (11.5cm) high.
£2,000–2,200 Andrew Muir

A Wilkinson Clarice Cliff Fantasque vase, decorated with Pebbles pattern, No. 269, c1929, 8in (20.5cm) high.
£700–800 Andrew Muir

A Clarice Cliff Bizarre vase, decorated with Caprice pattern, marked, c1929, 8in (20.5cm) high.
£1,000–1,200 Leonard Joel

A Clarice Cliff Bizarre Applique vase, decorated with Lucerne pattern, c1930, 8in (20.5cm) high.
£7,500–8,500 Andrew Muir

A pair of Clarice Cliff Bizarre Latona vases, decorated with Flowerheads pattern, shape No. 264, painted backstamp, one damaged, c1930, 8in (20.5cm) high.
£600–700 Bearnes

A Clarice Cliff Fantasque Bizarre vase, decorated with Secrets pattern, shape No. 585, printed factory marks, c1930, 8¼in (21cm) wide.
£550–650 Sworder's

A Clarice Cliff Fantasque Bizarre vase, decorated with Red Autumn pattern, shape No. 362, c1931, 8in (20.5cm) high.
£2,700–3,000 Andrew Muir

A Clarice Cliff Isis vase, decorated with Alton pattern, marked, c1934, 9¾in (25cm) high.
£450–550 Rosebery's

A Clarice Cliff Bizarre Latona Yoyo vase, decorated with Red Roses pattern, c1931, 18in (45.5cm) high.
£7,500–8,500 Andrew Muir

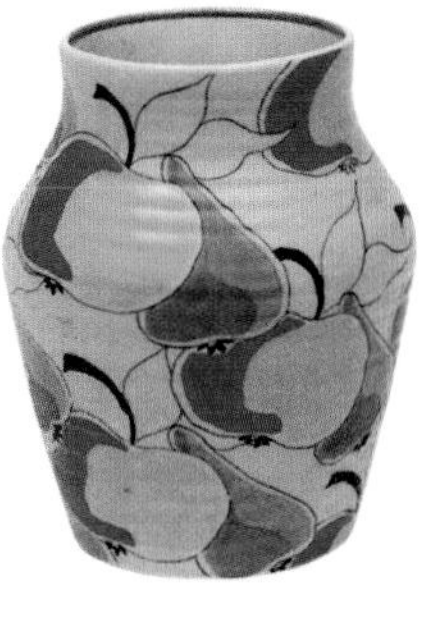

A Clarice Cliff vase, decorated with Eating Apples pattern, marked, c1937, 7in (18cm) high.
£700–850 Leonard Joel

CERAMICS – NAMED MAKERS

An Arequipa pottery bowl, decorated in trail slip with leaves, signed, America, California, dated 1912, 5½in (14cm) wide.
£1,300–1,600 Rago Arts

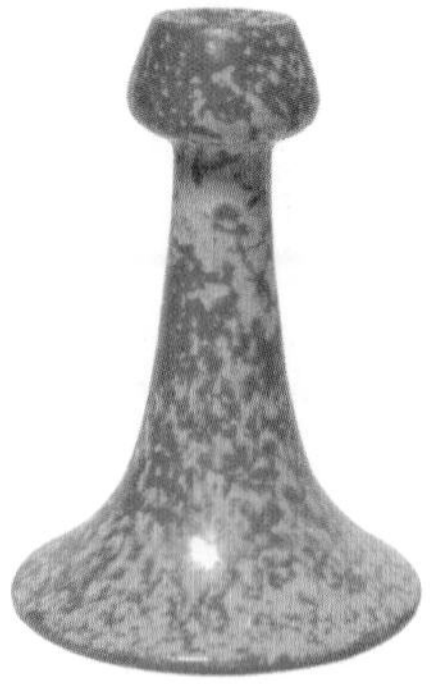

A pair of Ashby Guild candlesticks, c1920, 6in (15cm) high.
£200–225 Art Nouveau Originals

An Ault pottery vase, by Christopher Dresser, decorated with goats' heads, c1890, 11in (28cm) high.
£3,500–4,000 Country Seat

A Brannam Pottery jug, by Thomas Liverton, c1896, 5½in (14cm) high.
£500–600 Country Seat
This jug was made for the Hungarian Millennium Exhibition.

An Eric Bradbury figure of a lady, c1928, 9in (23cm) high.
£250–300 Design Gallery

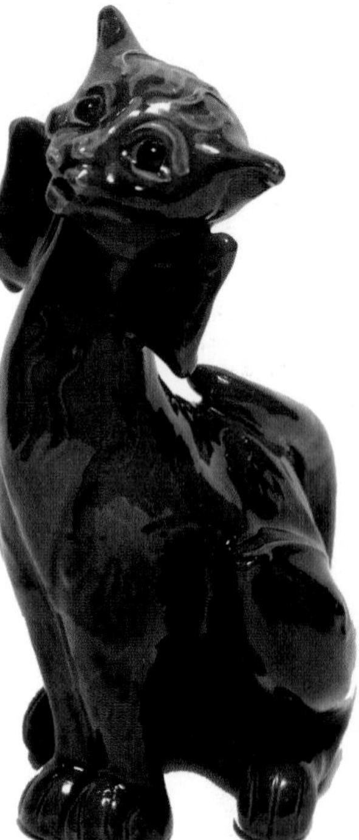

A Brannam Pottery model of a cat, c1895, 10in (25.5cm) high.
£450–500 B Kimber & J Lewis

A Brannam Pottery vase, with three handles, decorated with mythical fishes and foliage, marked, dated 1907, 12in (30.5cm) high.
£475–525 Ruskin Decorative Arts

A Brannam Pottery bowl, decorated with three owls' faces, c1910, 7in (18cm) diam.
£200–230
Ruskin Decorative Arts

A Burmantofts potpourri vase, c1885, 5in (12.5cm) high.
£330–365 Country Seat

A Burmantofts Pottery model of a toad, c1890, 6in (15cm) high.

£320–350
B Kimber & J Lewis ⊞

A Burmantofts Pottery twin-handled vase, c1890, 16in (40.5cm) high.

£600–700 AD Antiques ⊞

A Carlsbad porcelain dinner service, by Carl Knoll, comprising 58 pieces, each painted with tulips, Bohemia, c1900.

£1,800–2,000 Sworders

A Carlton Ware lustre bowl, decorated with Moonlight Cameo pattern, marked, c1925, 11in (28cm) diam.

£250–300 Leonard Joel

A Carlton Ware coffee set, comprising 16 pieces, c1920, coffee pot 8in (20.5cm) high.

£675–750
Hemswell Antique Centres ⊞

A Carlton Ware coffee service, comprising 16 pieces, 1930s.

£230–275 Locke & England

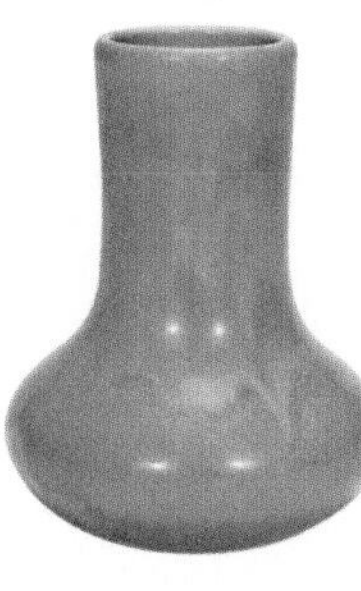

A Clifton Art Pottery Crystal Patina vase, incised maker's mark, shape No. 115, dated 1906, 5¼in (13.5cm) high.

£200–240
Cincinnati Art Galleries

A Castle Hedingham pottery puzzle jug, surmounted by a bird, restored, c1895, 13¾in (35cm) high.

£200–240 Sworders

A Castle Hedingham pottery watch stand, by Edward Bingham, enclosing a four-sided clock, with inscribed banners, the base with figures, one figure missing, incised 'Made at The Royal Essex Art Pottery, No. 108', marked, c1890, 10¼in (26cm) high.

£280–320 Sworders

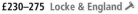

A Susie Cooper pottery model of a fox, c1930, 5in (12.5cm) long.

£1,300–1,500 Gazelles ⊞

A Susie Cooper pottery teapot, hand-painted with Cubist pattern, c1930, 5in (12.5cm) diam.

£700–800 Gazelles

A Susie Cooper pottery jug, hand-painted with Cubist pattern, c1930, 8in (20.5cm) high.

£1,000–1,100 Gazelles

A Susie Cooper pottery beaker, hand-painted with a geometric design and silver lustre, early 1930s, 4in (10cm) high.

£350–400 Gazelles

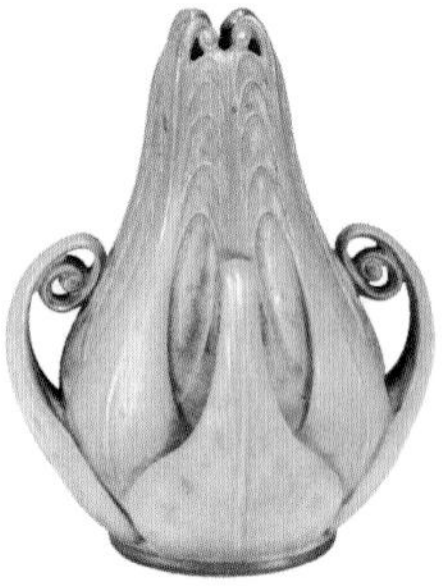

A Paul Dachsel Artichoke vase, with gilt decoration, Bohemia, c1905, 6in (15cm) high.

£1,500–1,800 Freeman's

A Crown Devon vase, decorated with Fairy Castle pattern on a mattajade ground, 1930s, 8in (20.5cm) high.

£850–950 Beverley

A Crown Devon vase, decorated with Fairy Castle pattern on a mattajade ground, 1930s, 8in (20.5cm) high.

£1,000–1,100 Gazelles

A Della Robbia twin-handled vase, by Harry Pearce, c1900, 9½in (24cm) high.

£850–950 AD Antiques

A Della Robbia bowl, signed 'E. L. L. ', c1905, 5in (13cm) diam.

£400–500 AD Antiques

A William de Morgan lustre charger, by Frederick Passenger, decorated with two griffins, marked, c1880, 14½in (37cm) diam.

£1,500–1,800 Sotheby's (O)

A William de Morgan double lustre plaque, decorated with a fish, 1874–75, 9¼in (23.5cm) diam.

£2,700–3,000 AD Antiques

A William de Morgan tile, decorated with Double Rose pattern, 1872–81, 8½in (21.5cm) square.

£1,200–1,400 AD Antiques

A William de Morgan tile, decorated with Berries and Leaves pattern, 1898, 6in (15cm) square.

£380–420 AD Antiques

An Otto Eckmann pottery ewer, with pewter mounts, Germany, c1900, 10in (25.5cm) high.

£300–350 Art Nouveau Originals

A Volkstedt figure, by Karl Ens, entitled 'The Turban Girl', Germany, late 1930s, 7in (18cm) high.

£300–350 Candice Horley

An Essevi figure of a woman on a pedestal, by Sandro Vacchetti, a mouse at the base, Italy, c1935, 16in (40.5cm) high.

£5,500–6,000 Andrew Muir

A Farnham Pottery owl jug, c1905, 12in (30.5cm) high.

£350–400 Ruskin Decorative Arts

A William Fishley Holland slipware bowl, with a resist pattern of leaves, early 20thC, 11in (28cm) diam.

£180–200 Offa's Dyke

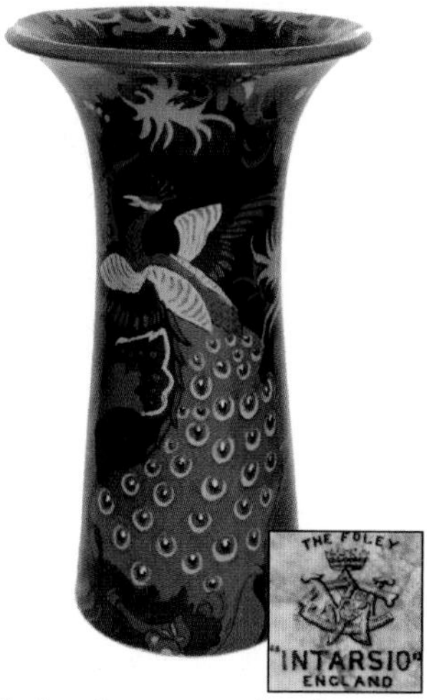

A Foley *intarsio* pottery vase, by Wileman & Co, designed by Frederick Rhead, decorated with Peacock pattern, marked, No. 3047, 1897–1905, 13in (33cm) high.

£1,600–1,800 Gazelles

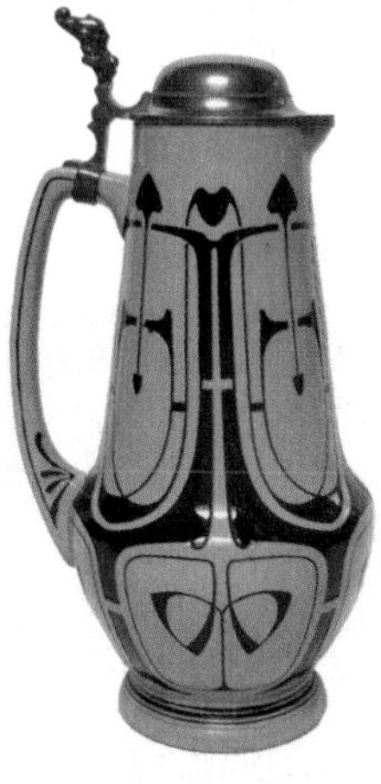

A Simon Gertz pottery jug, by Peter Behrens, with a pewter cover, Germany, c1905, 14in (35.5cm) high.

£340–380 Art Nouveau Originals

A William Goebel pottery wall mask, Austria, 1930s, 7in (18cm) high.

£300–350 Muir Hewitt

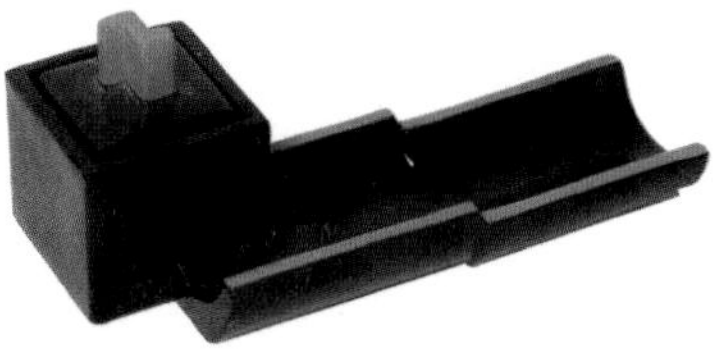

A William Goebel pottery inkwell and pen holder, Austria, c1930, 8in (20.5cm) wide.

£135–150 Muir Hewitt

A Goldscheider terracotta wall mask, Austria, c1890, 15in (38cm) high.

£1,600–1,800
Art Nouveau Originals

A Goldscheider porcelain figure of a woman, Austria, c1930, 13in (33cm) high.

£1,500–1,800
Muir Hewitt

A Goldscheider figure of a dancer, black printed mark, signed 'Lorenzl', Austria, 1930s, 8in (20.5cm) high.

£700–900
Maxwells of Wilmslow

A Goldscheider figure of a woman, Austria, 1930s, 14in (35.5cm) high.

£1,200–1,400 Andrew Muir

A pair of Hancock & Sons Morris ware vases, by George Cartlidge, c1915, 12in (30.5cm) high.

£1,750–2,000
AD Antiques

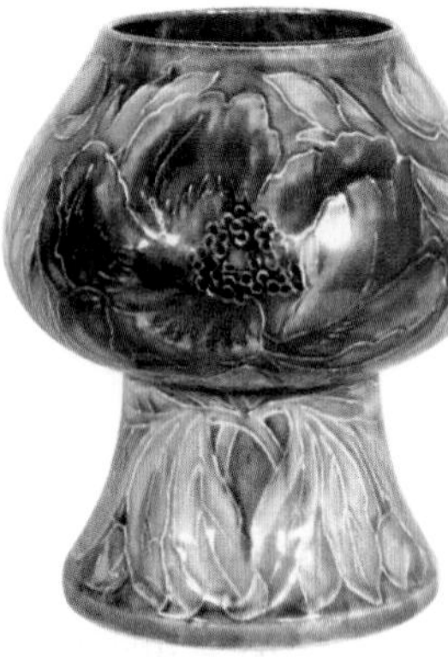

A Hancock & Sons Morris ware vase, by George Cartlidge, signed, early 20thC, 6¾in (17cm) high.

£380–450 Halls

A Heubach figure of a pierrot, Germany, c1940, 4in (10cm) high.

£180–200 Era Antiques

A Hutschenreuther figure, by Karl Tutter, entitled 'Little Red Riding Hood', Germany, c1920, 9in (23cm) high.

£450–500 Candice Horley

A Hutschenreuther figure of a woman, by Karl Tutter, entitled 'The Ball Player', Germany, c1940, 9in (23cm) high.

£300–350 Candice Horley

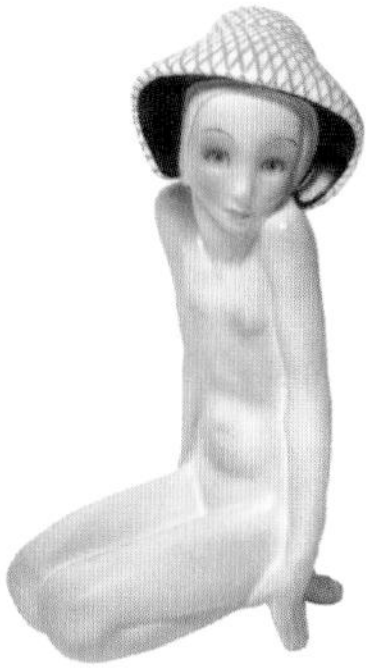

A Lenci porcelain figure of a woman, Italy, c1930, 7in (18cm) high.

£1,500–1,800 Muir Hewitt

A Lenci group, by Abele Jacopi, entitled 'Tritons', Italy, c1935, 22in (56cm) wide.

£4,500–5,000 Andrew Muir

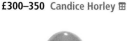

A Leningrad porcelain group of a lady and a gypsy, marked, Russia, dated 1922, 8in (20.5cm) high.

£3,500–4,250 Hy Duke

A Lissitzky plate, Germany, c1920, 7½in (19cm) diam.

£450–500 James Strang

A Lenci figure of a woman, by Elena König Scavini, Italy, dated 1932, 9½in (24cm) high.

£3,750–4,500 Lyon & Turnbull

A Longwy bowl and cover, France, c1930, 5½in (14cm) diam.

£550–600 Design Gallery

A Marguerite Mahood pottery bowl, decorated with a lizard, signed, Australia, c1933, 4¾in (12cm) wide.

£1,800–2,200 Leonard Joel

A Marblehead Pottery vase, possibly by Arthur Baggs and Hanna Tutt, decorated with seven tree trunks, America, dated 1904, 4½in (11.5cm) high.

£2,200–2,600 Skinner

A Marblehead Pottery bowl, decorated with stylized flowers, America, early 20thC, 8½in (21.5cm) diam.

£1,100–1,300 Skinner

A Clément Massier lustre vase, with two handles, the negative space forming a butterfly, painted with butterflies, signed, France, c1900, 11½in (29cm) high.

£2,800–3,200 Rago Arts

A Jérôme Massier fils vase, France, Vallauris, early 20thC, 10in (25.5cm) high.
£200–250 Heritage

A Minton tile inset, printed and painted with flowers, comprising 16 tiles, in a carved mahogany splashback frame, late 19thC, 50¾in (129cm) wide.
£250–300 Halls

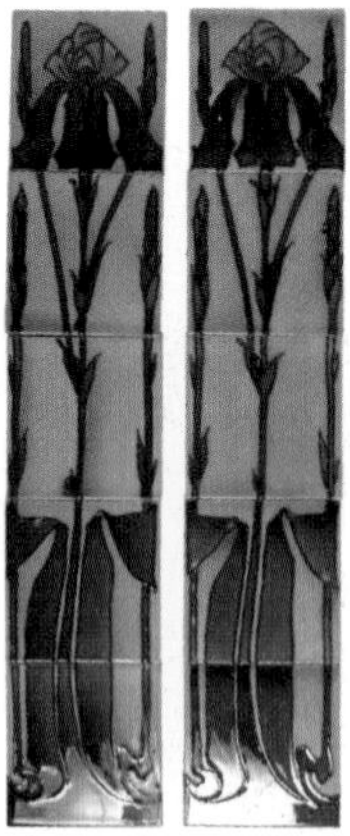

A set of Minton fireplace tiles, tubelined and painted with Secessionist-style irises, c1900, 6in (15cm) high.
£580–650 Time Antiques

A Minton vase, with Secessionist-style decoration, impressed mark, c1900, 16¼in (41.5cm) high.
£230–275 Sworders

A Myott jug, with hand-painted decoration, the handle in the form of a cat, 1930s, 8½in (21.5cm) high.
£1,100–1,300 Gazelles

A Newcomb College desk set, by Roberta Kennon, comprising a quill pot, inkwell with cover and sponge holder, slight damage, stamped mark, America, c1902, quill pot 4¼in (11cm) high.
£5,500–6,500 Rago Arts
This desk set was originally a wedding gift for Beverly Randolph, a decorator for Newcomb from 1895 to 1903.

A Newcomb College candlestick, by Leona Nicholson, decorated with frogs and crescent moons, America, c1902, 11½in (29cm) high.
£11,000–13,000 Rago Arts

A Newcomb College vase, by Mazie Ryan, decorated with wisteria, slight damage, marked, America, 1904, 8½in (21.5cm) high.
£25,000–30,000 Rago Arts

A Newcomb College vase, by Mazie Ryan, slight damage, marked, America, date code for 1905, 7¾in (19.5cm) high.
£2,000–2,500
Cincinnati Art Galleries

A Newcomb College vase, by Sadie Irvine, decorated with grapes and foliage, marked, America, 1917, 7¼in (18.5cm) diam.
£1,500–1,800 Rago Arts

A Newcomb College vase, by Joseph Meyer, decorated with flowers, impressed marks, America, date code for 1918, 5½in (14cm) high.

£2,400–2,800 Freeman's

A Newcomb College vase, by Anna Frances Simpson, decorated with trees, marked, America, date code for 1929, 4¾in (12cm) high.

£1,700–2,000 Cincinnati Art Galleries

A terracotta vase, signed 'A. Otto', the handle in the form of a salamander, Austria, c1890, 12in (30.5cm) high.

£250–280 Art Nouveau Originals

A Eugenio Pattarino wall plaque, depicting the Madonna and Child, No. 168, signed, Italy, c1930, 16¾in (42.5cm) high.

£700–850 Jackson's

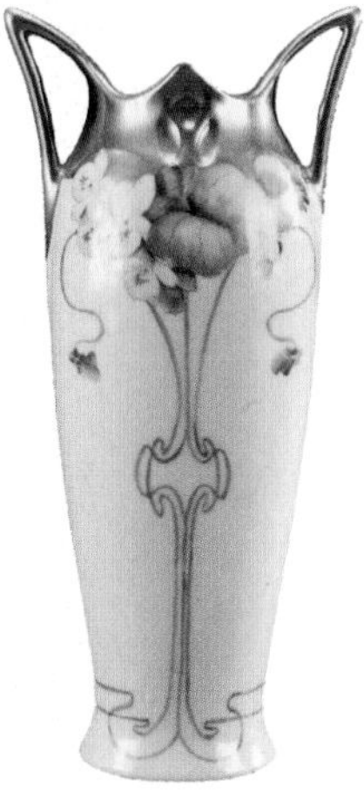

A Pickard porcelain vase, with two handles, decorated with flowers, America, early 20thC, 9in (23cm) high.

£125–150 Jackson's

A Pilkington's Royal Lancastrian vase, by Gladwys Rodgers, painted monogram and impressed marks, c1920, 11in (28cm) high.

£400–450 decorative arts@doune

ESSENTIAL REFERENCE PILKINGTON

Founded in Manchester in the early 1890s, Pilkington was an art pottery whose output tended to be simple in shape with a strong emphasis on ornamentation. Revolutionary and ambitious experiments with technically difficult glazes led to the creation of their spectacular lustre wares. Under the directorship of William and Joseph Burton, decorative artists were encouraged to develop innovative qualities with an emphasis on originality in both colour and form. Some of the most distinguished artists included Walter Crane, Gordon Forsyth, W. S. Mycock, Gladwys Rodgers and Richard Joyce. Joyce's work is notable for a highly individual interpretation of animals and fauna. This vase is from a series designed by Richard Joyce at the beginning of the 20th century and incorporates whimsical vignettes of sub-aquatic life and playful fish on aquamarine and sea blue grounds. Other glaze patterns apart from lustre are Lapis, Sunstone and Eggshell. A variety of marks include painted artists' monograms, an impressed and painted mark depicting bees and the letter 'P'. Pilkington lustre wares in good condition are especially popular and command premium prices.

£650–750 decorative arts @ doune

A Poole Pottery plate, by Olive Bourne and Vera Willis, 1926–27, 11in (28cm) diam.

£2,000–2,200 Gazelles

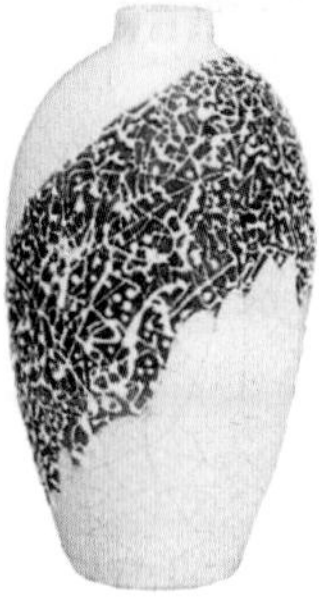

A Primavera vase, with crackle glaze, impressed and incised marks, 1930s, 11¾in (30cm) high.

£300–360 Waddington's

A pair of Rambervillers bookends, by Albert Schneider, in the form of birds, France, c1915, 8in (20.5cm) high.

£135–150 Steven Bishop

A Reissner, Stellmacher & Kessel Amphora vase, impressed and enamelled with a man and a rooster, impressed marks, Austria, early 20thC, 12in (30.5cm) high.

£1,000–1,200 Freeman's

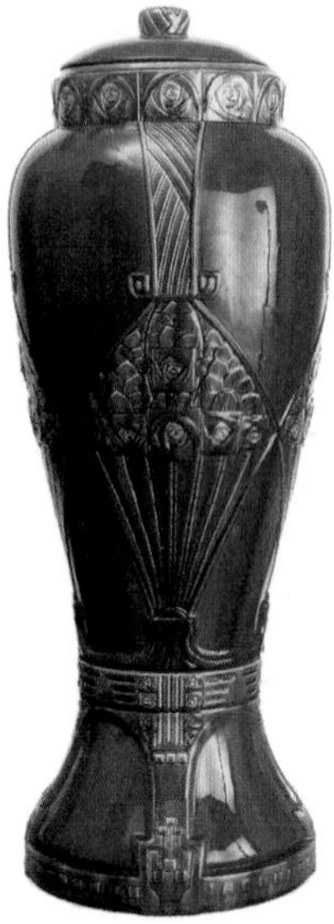

A Rörstrand creamware jar and cover, marked, Sweden, c1909, 52in (132cm) high.

£2,400–2,800 Bukowskis

This jar and cover was exhibited at the Stockholm Exhibition in 1909.

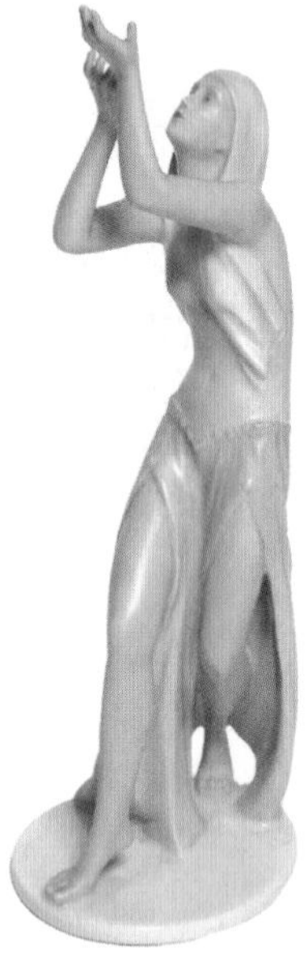

A Rosenthal figure, by Gustav Oppel, entitled 'The Prayer Dancer', Germany, c1936, 8in (20.5cm) high.

£550–600 Candice Horley

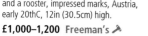

A Roseville Rozane Royal Light vase, by Walter Myers, decorated with an owl, signed, America, c1905, 13½in (34.5cm) high.

£3,000–3,500
Cincinnati Art Galleries

A Royal Dux figure of a woman, entitled 'The Lily Girl', Bohemia, 1930s, 6in (15cm) high.

£380–425 Oakwood Antiques

A Rozenburg vase, decorated with stylized flowers, Holland, 1883–84, 10in (25.5cm) high.

£440–485 Julian's Antiques

This is a very early piece, produced during the first two years of the factory's existence.

A Rozenburg vase, painted with stylized flowers, Holland, c1896, 5in (12.5cm) high.
£350–400 Julian's Antiques

A Ruskin Pottery high-fired vase, impressed mark, dated 1909, 10¾in (27.5cm) high.
£2,000–2,500 Rosebery's

A Ruskin Pottery high-fired stoneware vase, impressed mark, dated 1914, 14½in (37cm) high.
£4,500–5,500 Cincinnati Art Galleries

A Ruskin Pottery high-fired vase, impressed mark, early 20thC, 4¼in (11cm) high.
£380–450 Rosebery's

A Ruskin Pottery high-fired vase, impressed mark, early 20thC, 7in (17.5cm) high.
£900–1,100 Rosebery's

A Ruskin Pottery ginger jar and cover, dated 1917, 5in (12.5cm) diam.
£1,100–1,250 AD Antiques

A Saturday Evening Girls Pottery bowl, decorated with geese, slight damage, signed 'AH/5-14 SEG', America, dated 1914, 11½in (29cm) diam.
£2,500–3,000 Skinner

A Saturday Evening Girls Pottery vase, decorated with a landscape, signed 'SEG/2-17/LS', America, dated 1917, 5¾in (14.5cm) high.
£1,000–1,200 Rago Arts

A Shelley Vogue tea service, decorated with Turkish Blue Blocks pattern, c1930.
£750–900 Charterhouse

A pair of tile panels, by William Butler Simpson & Sons, London, c1880, 27 x 11in (68.5 x 28cm).
£1,600–1,800 Design Gallery

A Van Briggle Pottery jardinière, moulded with stylized morning glories, marked, slight damage, America, dated 1905, 6½in (16.5cm) high.

£750–900 Rago Arts

A Van Briggle Pottery vase, moulded with jonquils, marked, America, dated 1905, 10½in (26.5cm) high.

£1,300–1,600 Rago Arts

An Ernst Wahliss porcelain vase, decorated with stylized flowers and highlighted in gilt, printed mark, Austria, c1900, 16in (40.5cm) high.

£230–275 Rosebery's

A Watcombe Pottery model of a cat, c1900, 9in (23cm) high.

£220–250 B Kimber & J Lewis

A Henry van de Velde stoneware vase, by Reinhold Hanke, impressed monogram, Germany, c1901, 11¾in (30cm) wide.

£13,000–16,000 Sotheby's (NY)

An Elizabeth Mary Watt mug, painted with a band of fruiting branches, inscribed 'Alan Davey Watt', painted inscription to base 'A present from Aunty', early 20thC, 8½in (21.5cm) high.

£400–500 Lyon & Turnbull

A Weller Pottery Greora vase, with four pockets, slight damage, marked, America, 1920s, 8¼in (21cm) high.

£100–120
Cincinnati Art Galleries

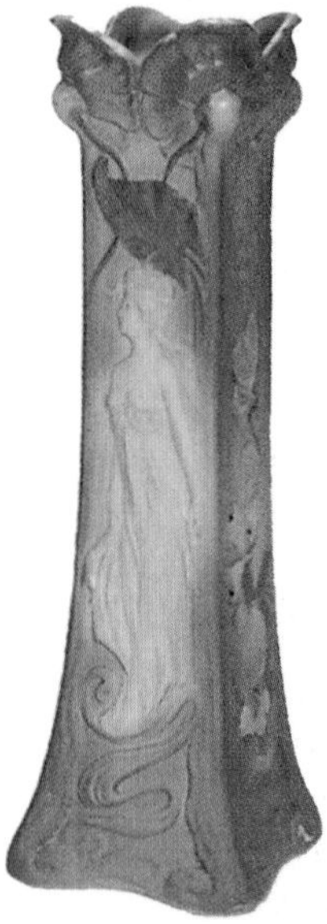

A Weller Pottery vase, decorated with a woman and poppies, America, c1905, 13½in (34.5cm) high.

£400–500
Cincinnati Art Galleries

A Zsolnay Pecs vase, decorated with flowers, stamped and painted marks, Hungary, early 20thC, 5½in (14cm) high.

£2,000–2,500 Sotheby's (O)

SILVER

A silver beaker, engraved with flowers and date, Russia, 1908, 3½in (9cm) high.

£270–300 Art Nouveau Originals

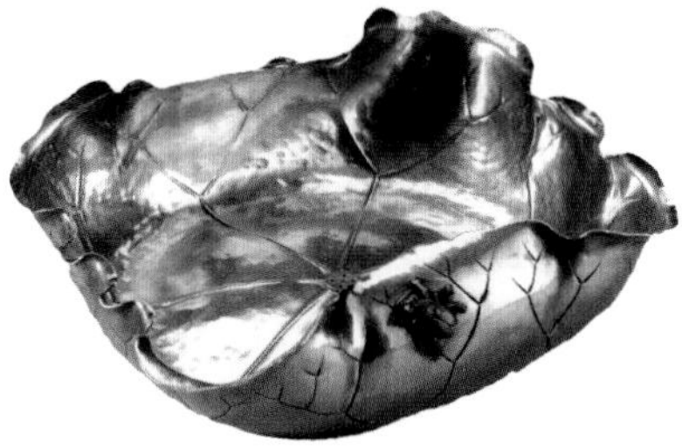

A silver and copper bowl, by George W. Shiebler & Co, America, New York, c1890, 5¾in (14.5cm) wide.

£2,500–3,000 Heritage

An Art Nouveau silver punch bowl, by Reed & Barton, chased and applied with flower heads, embossed with tendrils, stylized plants and scrolling foliage, America, c1900, 20½in (52cm) wide, 123oz.

£6,000–7,000 Freeman's

A silver sugar bowl, by Alexander Ritchie, chased and embossed with Celtic entrelac and zoomorphic birds, maker's mark, Scotland, Glasgow 1936, 3½in (9cm) high.

£1,500–1,750 decorative arts@doune

A Georg Jensen silver bowl, by Arno Malinowski, the stem in the form of a stylized fish, marked, Denmark, 1937, 4½in (11.5cm) high.

£4,000–5,000 Sotheby's

A Boston Society of Arts & Crafts silver box, by Katherine Pratt, decorated with Gothic windows and columns, the cover set with lapis and enamel, impressed marks, America, 1918–27, 6¼in (16cm) diam, 34oz.

£14,000–18,000 Skinner

ESSENTIAL REFERENCE OMAR RAMSDEN

Omar Ramsden was initially in business with Alwyn Carr whom he had met at Sheffield School of Art. Renowned for their highly individual revivalist style, they registered their joint maker's mark in London in 1898. When the partnership was dissolved in 1919 Ramsden set up on his own, running the workshop until his death in 1939. The silver is usually of good heavy gauge and carefully hand-raised with a hammered finish. The designs incorporate repoussé decoration, twisted wirework and are highlighted with coloured enamels or gemstones. Items from this period have Ramsden's distinctive Gothic hallmark and more often than not are inscribed with the Latin inscription 'Omar Ramsden Me Fecit'. Omar Ramsden and Alwyn Carr's work is keenly sought after and prices continue to rise.

This silver and enamel cigarette box has a cast and pierced panel of a man-of-war on an enamelled ground within a rope-twist border. The base has Omar Ramsden's Latin inscription and it is hallmarked London 1925.

£3,500–4,200 Sotheby's (NY)

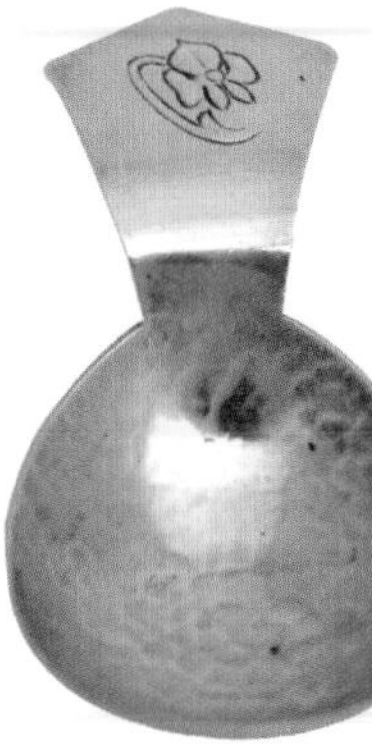

A Keswick School of Industrial Arts silver caddy spoon, with hammered decoration, the stem chased with a flowerhead, maker's mark, Birmingham 1901, 3in (7.5cm) high.

£400–450
decorative arts@doune

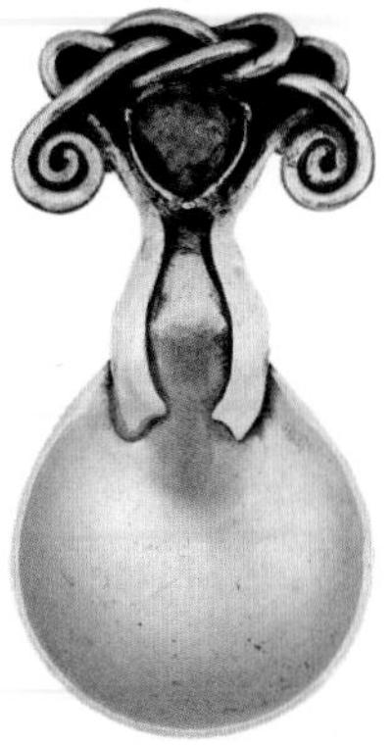

An Arts & Crafts silver caddy spoon, by Ramsden & Carr, with a hammered bowl, the knotted tendril handle set with an enamel boss, London 1906, 3in (7.5cm) long.

£2,300–2,750
Woolley & Wallis

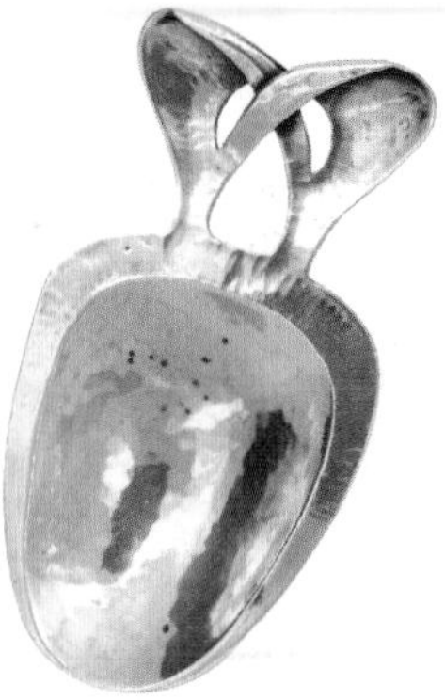

A Liberty Arts & Crafts silver caddy spoon, Birmingham 1907, 3in (7.5cm) long.

£600–700 Nicholas Shaw

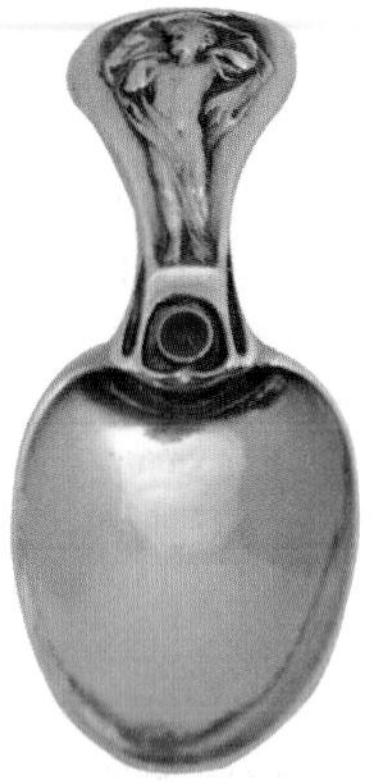

A silver caddy spoon, by John Sidney Reeve for Collis & Co, the stem chased with a classical figure and set with a garnet cabochon, maker's mark, stamped 'Dryad', Birmingham 1911, 4in (10cm) long.

£1,300–1,500
decorative arts@doune

ESSENTIAL REFERENCE CADDY SPOONS

Rituals from the turn of the last century, such as the taking of afternoon tea, have all but disappeared, yet the appeal and pleasure derived from collecting the associated accoutrements still remain. Caddy spoons were produced in all shapes and forms ranging from traditional patterns of the 18th century to striking designs by artist craftsmen. Arts and Crafts caddy spoons in particular show the widest range and diversity of style. At the turn of the 20th century established designers of the day put their own interpretation on traditional forms and caddy spoons were produced in silver, copper, brass and pewter. They are recognized for their simple elegant shapes, hand-hammered finish and are often decorated with enamel or cabochon gemstones. It is a field where collectors can concentrate on specific makers and their individual hallmarks. Enthusiasts are always looking for hitherto unrecorded makers – the more obscure the better. Examples by Omar Ramsden, Alwyn Carr, Edward Spencer and A. E. Jones are scarce and command ever-increasing prices when they appear on the market. This hammered silver caddy spoon by A. E. Jones has a stem with silver wirework and a lapis lazuli finial. It is hallmarked Birmingham 1919.

£580–650 decorative arts@doune

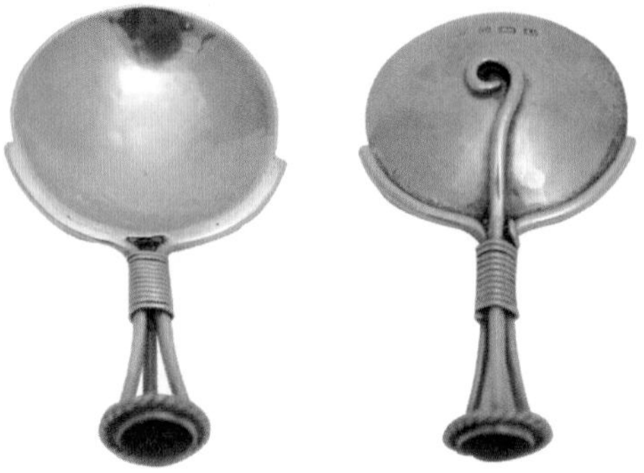

An Arts & Crafts silver and enamel caddy spoon, by Omar Ramsden, 1927, 3¼in (8.5cm) long.

£3,000–3,400
Nicholas Shaw

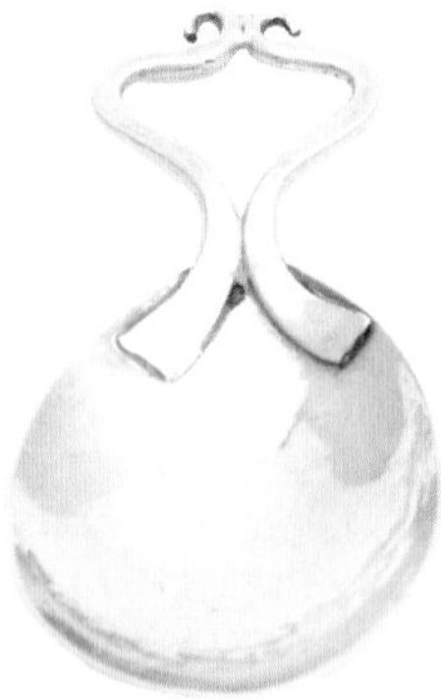

An Arts & Crafts silver caddy spoon, by Greenwood & Watts, London 1929, 3in (7.5cm) long.

£600–650 Shapiro

A silver caddy spoon, by H. G. Murphy, the handle decorated with a Tree of Life, London 1929, 3in (7.5cm) long.

£275–325
Woolley & Wallis

A silver caddy spoon, by Alexander Ritchie, the finial formed as a Celtic knotwork shield above zoomorphic birds' heads, the bowl chased with lotus leaves, stamped maker's mark, Birmingham 1936, 3½in (9cm) high.

£350–400
decorative arts@doune

ESSENTIAL REFERENCE HENRY GEORGE MURPHY

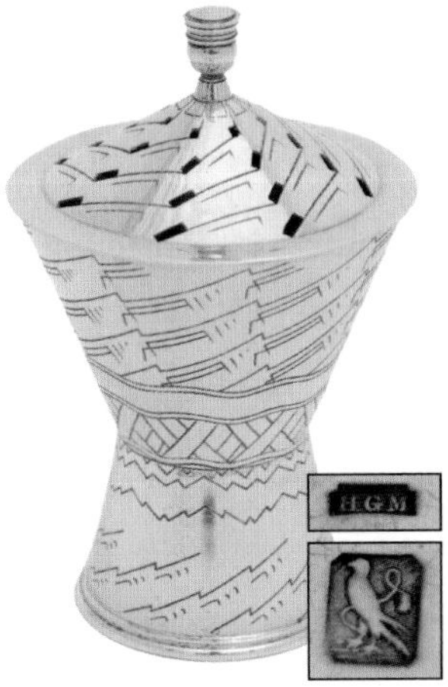

Henry George Murphy (1884–1939) was one of the most influential silversmiths of the Art Deco era. After serving his apprenticeship with Henry Wilson he opened his first workshop in London in 1912. A versatile and innovative designer, he later retailed his silverware through the Falcon Studio in Marylebone. The Falcon Studio motif was registered as part of Murphy's hallmark in 1928 and was reproduced on his designs thereafter. Murphy was also a highly regarded teacher at the Royal College of Art and the Central School of Arts & Crafts, where he later became Principal. Falcon Studio silverware from this period was stylish and strongly Art Deco in shape and was either chased and engraved with bold geometric linear forms or adorned with ivory, enamel or gemset finials. Murphy's work occasionally appears on the market but is attracting a growing number of admirers and collectors following the recent exhibition of his work at the Goldsmith's Hall in London. This sugar caster is hallmarked London 1935 and bears Murphy's mark and marks for the Falcon Studio and the coronation of Edward VIII.

£3,000–3,500 **decorative arts@doune** ⊞

An Art Nouveau silver centrepiece, chased with stylized flowers, the centre bowl above two seated musicians, with silver-plated liners, maker's mark 'AP', Austrian control mark, probably Germany, c1900, 33½in (85cm) wide.

£14,000–17,000 **Sotheby's (NY)**

A silver centrepiece, by C. A. Beumers, mounted with enamels and hardstone, with ivory handles and a gilt-metal liner, marked, Germany, Düsseldorf, c1915, 26¾in (68cm) wide.

£11,000–13,000 **Sotheby's (NY)**

The firm of Conrad Anton Beumers of Düsseldorf was founded in 1858. In the early 20th century they executed modern silver designs by Hugo Leven and Paul Beumers. The workshop closed in 1928.

MILLER'S COMPARES

(L) **An Arts & Crafts hammered silver chamberstick,** by Jacques & Bartholomew, the scrolled handle with a trefoil motif and a detachable sconce, London 1902, 4in (10cm) high.

£1,000–1,100 **decorative arts@doune** ⊞

(R) **An Arts & Crafts brass chamberstick,** the scrolled handle with a trefoil motif and a detachable sconce, c1900, 3½in (9cm) high.

£100–110 **decorative arts@doune** ⊞

These two chambersticks are closely related in design and proportion. While the example on the left is worth more because it is made in silver, the overall quality of the finish is also better. It has a hand-hammered surface with a prouder and more defined wax pan. The example on the right which is made of brass is plainer, of more rudimentary construction and probably produced for the mass market. It is unmarked and therefore unattributed, whereas the chamberstick on the left has the distinctive hallmarks of the silversmiths Jacques & Bartholomew and London hallmarks for 1902. It would have been retailed through more exclusive shops and would therefore command a much higher price than the item on the right.

A silver-mounted glass claret jug, pierced and incised with trailing foliage around a cartouche, possibly America, c1900, 11in (28cm) high.

£450–550 Andrew Hartley

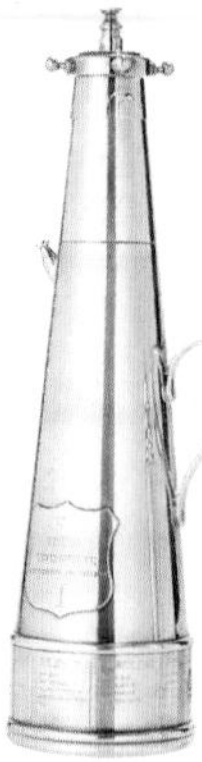

An Asprey & Co silver cocktail shaker, inscribed 'The Thirst Extinguisher' and engraved with recipes for eight cocktails, marked, c1932, 14¾in (37.5cm) high.

£2,500–3,000 Sotheby's (NY)

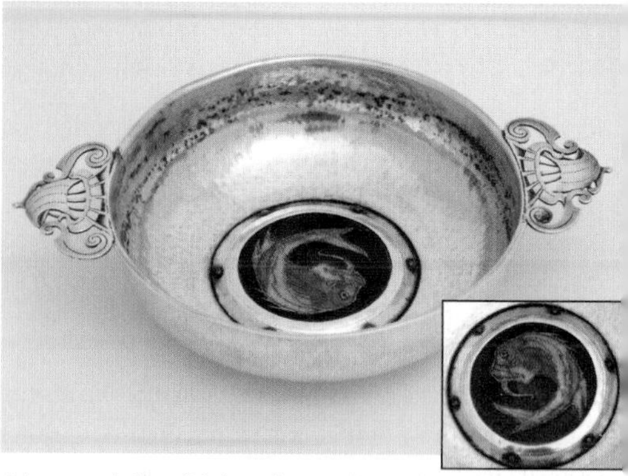

A hammered silver dish, by William Snelling Hadaway, the handles pierced with galleons, the centre set with a polychrome enamelled disc depicting a fish, c1905, 5in (12.5cm) diam.

£1,800–2,000 decorative arts@doune

A Liberty Arts & Crafts silver and gold dish, Birmingham 1918, 5½in (14cm) diam.

£800–900 Daniel Bexfield

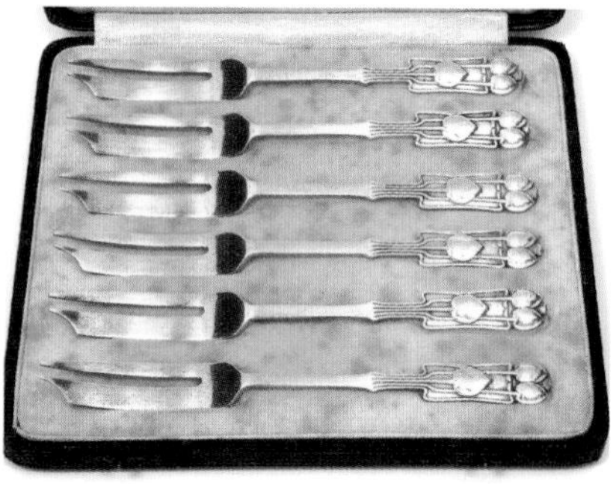

A set of Liberty silver cake forks, by Archibald Knox, the handles with honesty decoration, Birmingham 1913, with original fitted case, 6in (15cm) wide.

£1,000–1,100 Design Gallery

An Art Nouveau silver photograph frame, by Atkin & Ashford, stamped with a geisha girl, easel panel replaced, Birmingham 1905, 9¼in (23.5cm) high.

£350–420 Woolley & Wallis

An Art Nouveau silver photograph frame, decorated with a female head and flowers, Birmingham 1905, 8½in (21.5cm) high.

£500–600 Gorringes (L)

An Art Nouveau silver-mounted glass inkwell, with embossed decoration, America, c1900, 3½in (9cm) high.

£160–200 Heritage

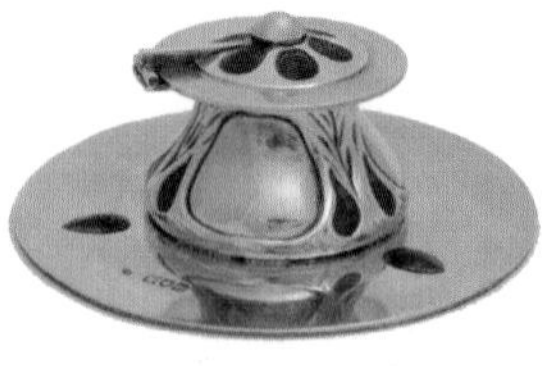

An Art Nouveau silver and enamel inkwell, by Kate Harris for William Hutton & Sons, with embossed, chased and enamel decoration, the hinged cover set with a blister pearl, London 1903, 5½in (14cm) diam.

£5,000–5,500 decorative arts@doune

A silver inkwell, by A. E. Jones, with hammered decoration, Birmingham 1912, 5in (12.5cm) diam.

£1,000–1,200 Shapiro

An Art Deco silver inkwell, by Walker & Hall, Sheffield 1931, 6in (15cm) wide.

£1,100–1,250 Daniel Bexfield

ESSENTIAL REFERENCE ALEXANDER RITCHIE

Alexander Ritchie (1856–1941) established a workshop on the island of Iona at the turn of the 20th century where he produced highly collectable hand-crafted silver. One of several artists involved in the 'Celtic' revival in Scotland, his output ranged from jewellery and silver through to larger items in brass, copper and carved wood. Ritchie drew his inspiration from Celtic mythology and based many of his designs on the Book of Kells or the interlaced scrolls on Pictish standing stones. His pieces were often highlighted with turquoise-blue enamelling to reflect the unusual colour of the sea around the island's white sands and decorated with favourite motifs including galleons, lotus leaves, entrelac and zoomorphic birds. A variety of marks are found on Ritchie's work; earlier and more substantial pieces were inscribed 'AR, Iona' but as output increased wares were sent to the assay offices of Glasgow, Chester and Birmingham to be hallmarked. This silver cream jug is chased and embossed with entwined Celtic foliate motifs and has a zoomorphic bird-head handle. It is stamped with the early mark 'AR, Iona'.

£2,250–2,500 decorative arts@doune

An Art Nouveau silver and silver-gilt loving cup, by Gorham Manufacturing Co, with chased and repoussé panels of daisy stems, the handles with leaf-tip terminals, the base monogrammed 'BAR', marked, America, 1897, 6in (15cm) high, 33oz.

£5,500–6,500 Northeast Auctions

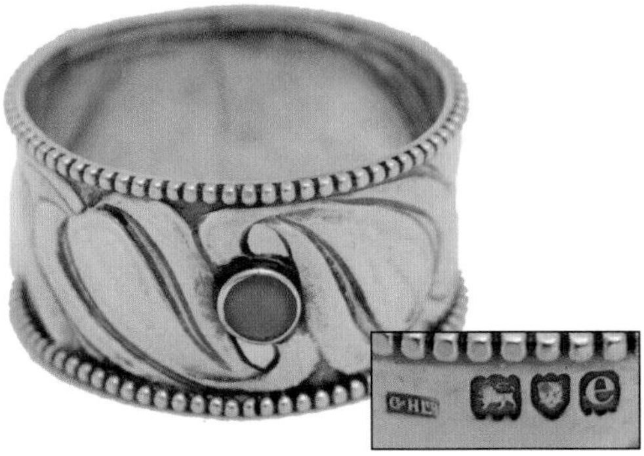

A Guild of Handicrafts silver napkin ring, by C. R. Ashbee, embossed and chased with twin bud motifs, set with a carnelian cabochon, London 1900, 2in (5cm) diam.

£1,000–1,200 decorative arts@doune

A silver quaich, by A. E. Jones, Birmingham 1916, 9½in (24cm) wide.

£1,100–1,250 Shapiro

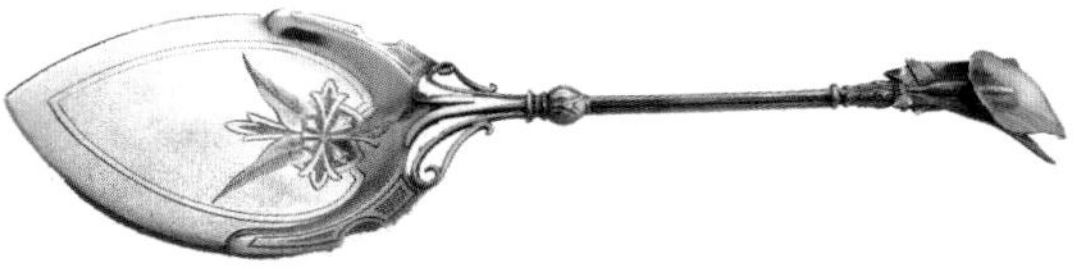

An Aesthetic-style silver serving spoon, engraved and gilt with lily leaves, the handle in the form of a lily, America, late 19thC, 10¾in (27.5cm) long.

£250–300 Heritage

A pair of Tiffany & Co Aesthetic-style silver salts, America, New York, 1870–75, 1½in (4cm) high.

£1,400–1,700 Heritage

A Tiffany & Co Japanese-style five-piece silver and ivory coffee and tea service, maker's marks, America, New York, 1881, coffee pot 8in (20.5cm) high.

£6,500–8,000 Heritage Auctions

A Secessionist four-piece silver tea service, by V. Mayer & Söhne, decorated with stylized ribbons, the teapot with ivory insulators, the cover with a crown finial. Austria, Vienna, 1900–15, 8in (20.5cm) high, with an associated silver-plated tray.

£400–500 Heritage

An Art Deco bachelor's silver four-piece tea and coffee service, by Jean E. Puiforcat, with stylized Louis XIII borders, on stepped bases, France, c1924, teapot 2¾in (7cm) high.

£3,500–4,200 Sotheby's

A silver three-piece coffee service, by Anton Michelsen, with a tray attributed to Kay Fisker, Denmark, 1928 and 1931, coffee pot 4¼in (11cm) high.

£1,500–1,800 Bukowskis

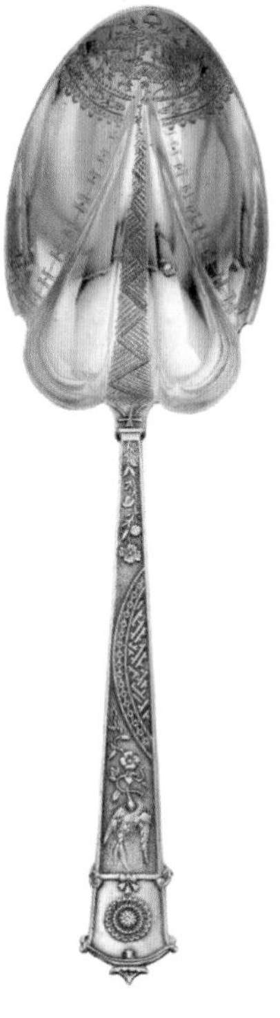

A silver Japanese pattern serving spoon, by Gorham Manufacturing Co, America, Rhode Island, c1880, 9¼in (23.5cm) long.

£500–600 Heritage

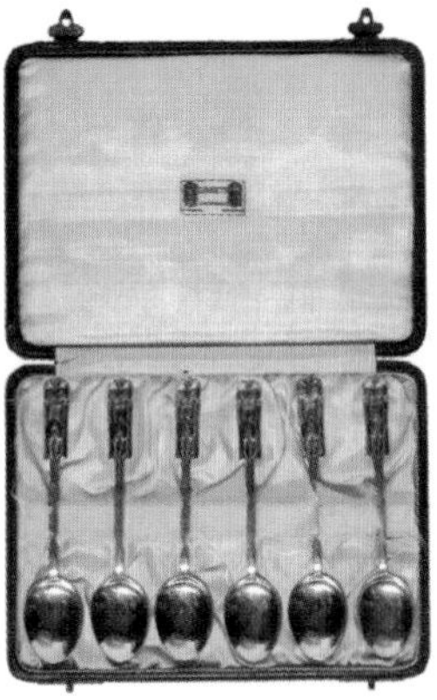

A set of six Liberty silver and enamel teaspoons, by Archibald Knox, 1922, 4in (10cm) long, with original case.

£1,200–1,400 Time Antiques

An Art Nouveau silver Raphael pattern serving fork, marked 'B. Alvin Corporation, Providence, Rhode Island', America, c1902, 7¾in (19.5cm) long.

£350–420 Heritage

An Arts and Crafts silver tazza, with hammered decoration, on three pierced supports, marked 'P. E. & Sons', Scotland, Glasgow 1908, 8in (20.5cm) wide, 20oz.

£350–420 Andrew Hartley

An Art Deco silver and ivory tazza, by Charles Boyton, with a turned ivory stem, marked, facsimile signature, London 1937, 5½in (14cm) diam.

£600–700 Sworders

A Guild of Handicraft silver toast rack, possibly designed by C. R. Ashbee, with repoussé and pierced decoration, set with stone cabochons, London 1907, 4¼in (11cm) high.

£3,300–4,000 Cheffins

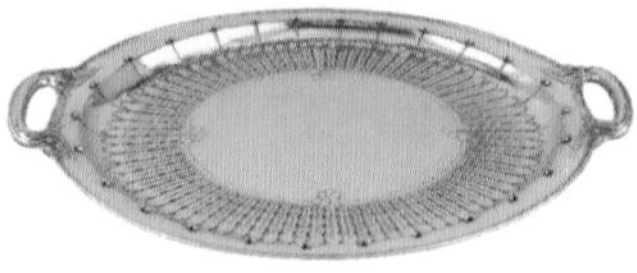

A Tiffany & Co silver presentation tray, with original velvet-lined oak box, America, New York 1903, 30¼in (77cm) wide.

£16,000–20,000 Heritage

SILVER PLATE

A Guild of Handicraft-style silver-plated **biscuit barrel,** embossed with foliate motifs with pierced centres, the cover finial set with a chrysoprase cabochon, with a glass liner, c1905, 6½in (16.5cm) high.

£1,350–1,500
decorative arts@doune

A Duchess of Sutherland's Cripples Guild of Handicrafts **silver-plated bowl,** c1900, 12in (30.5cm) diam.

£580–650 Shapiro

The Duchess of Sutherland's Cripples Guild of Handicrafts was set up to assist crippled children.

A pair of Christofle silver-plated **Flèche candlesticks,** by Gio Ponti, France, Paris, c1928, 8in (20.5cm) high.

£3,250–4,000 Sotheby's (NY)

A pair of **silver-plated sweetmeat dishes,** by Christopher Dresser for Hukin & Heath, c1880, 11in (28cm) wide.

£1,400–1,600 James Strang

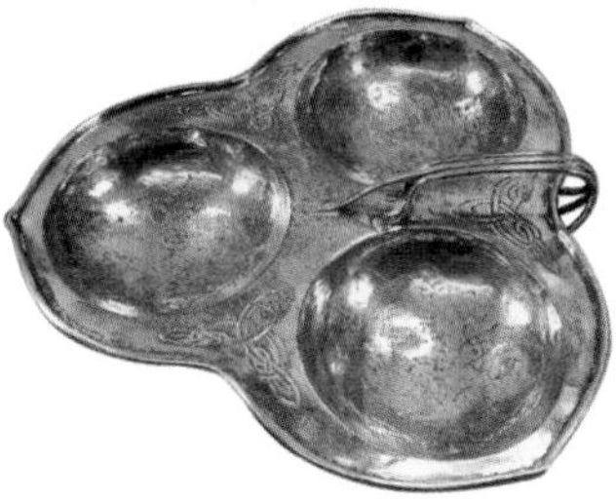

A Keswick School of Industrial Arts **silver-plated hors d'oeuvres dish,** the three divisions decorated with Celtic knotwork designs, the base signed 'J. Richardson, Keswick', c1900, 9½in (24cm) wide.

£180–220 Penrith Farmers' & Kidd's

A Guild of Handicraft **silver-plated muffin dish and cover,** by C. R. Ashbee, with hammered decoration and rope-twist borders, the cover with an enamel finial, with an inscription, c1912, 8¾in (22cm) high.

£600–700 Sworders

A WMF **silver-plated and glass claret jug,** the handle and stopper decorated with berries, the base decorated with the heads of four women emerging from a lily pond, marked, Germany, c1900, 15in (38cm) high.

£1,100–1,300 Canterbury Auctions

An Arts and Crafts **silver-plated inkwell,** set with a Ruskin Pottery ceramic cabochon, Scotland, c1905, 9in (23cm) wide.

£350–400 Durham House Antiques

A **silver-plated claret jug,** by Christopher Dresser for Hukin & Heath, with an ivory handle, dated 1881, 9in (23cm) high.

£750–850
Ruskin Decorative Arts

A **silver-plated Thermos jug,** by W. A. S. Benson, c1890, 10in (25.5cm) high.

£675–750 Shapiro

A **silver-plated jug,** by George Unite, c1900, 9in (23cm) high.

£450–500 Puritan Values

A silver-plated jug, by Sylvia Stave, with a rattan handle, Sweden, Stockholm, 1930s, 7in (18cm) high.

£225–275 Bukowskis

An Art Nouveau silver-plated jam pot and cover, decorated with leaves and flowers, c1910, 4½in (11.5cm) diam.

£110–125 Jeffrey Neal

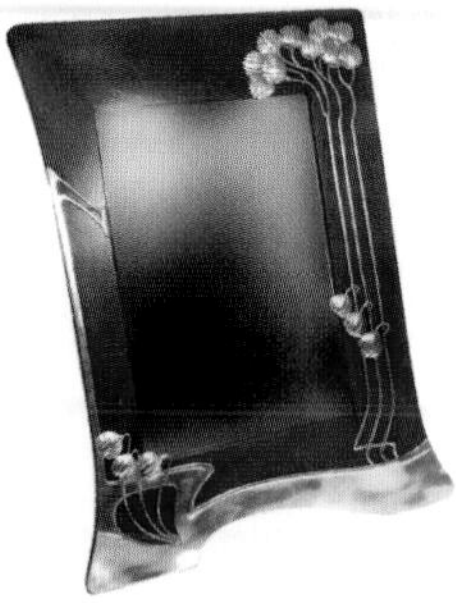

An Art Nouveau silver-plated and stained wood table mirror, c1900, 25in (63.5cm) high.

£3,000–3,500 Esoteric

A silver-plated six-piece tea service, by Richard Hunt, c1860, tray 20in (51cm) diam.

£2,250–2,500
Puritan Values

A silver-plated three-piece tea service, by Christopher Dresser for James Dixon & Son, the teapot with an ebony handle, maker's mark 'JD&S', stamped with facsimile signature, registration mark for 1880, teapot 4½in (11.5cm) high.

£11,000–12,500
decorative arts@doune

A Bauhaus silver-plated tea service for two, the cups with wooden handles, glass liners, covers and spoons, marked, Germany, 1920s, 4¾in (12cm) high.

£500–600 Treadway Gallery

A silver-plated four-piece tea service, by the Wilcox Silver Plate Co, with Bakelite knobs and handles, stamped marks, America, c1928, 3½in (9cm) high.

£3,000–3,600 Sotheby's (NY)

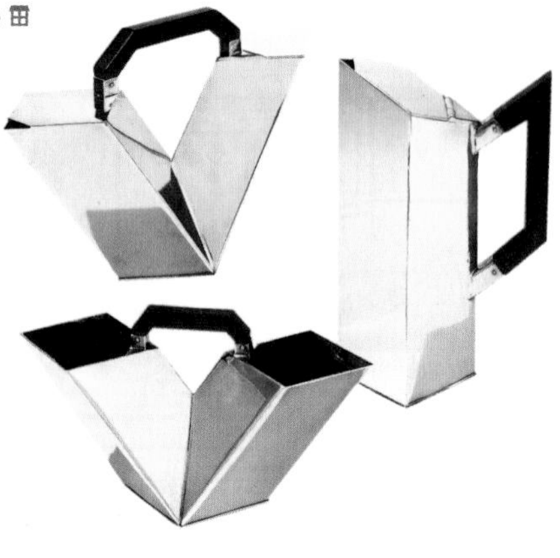

A silver-plated three-piece tea and coffee service, by Joseph Rogers & Sons, with ebonized wood handles, marked, America, c1935, jug 7½in (19cm) high.

£9,500–11,500 Sotheby's (NY)

A WMF Art Nouveau silver-plated vase, with a glass liner, Germany, c1900, 22in (56cm) high.

£2,250–2,500
Worcester Antiques

A Duchess of Sutherland's Cripples Guild of Handicrafts silver-plated vase, marked 'DSCG', c1910, 5in (12.5cm) high.

£100–120 Design Gallery

A pair of Christofle silver-plated Gallia wine coolers, stamped maker's marks, France, c1933, 8in (20.5cm) high.

£2,500–3,000 Sotheby's (O)

PEWTER

A Liberty Tudric pierced pewter bowl, by Archibald Knox, impressed marks, c1903, 10in (25.5cm) wide.

£300–350 Ruskin Decorative Arts

A pair of WMF silverered-pewter candelabra, Germany, c1900, 10¾in (27.5cm) high.

£4,000–4,500 Esoteric

A pair of WMF pewter candlesticks, Germany, c1900, 12in (30.5cm) high.

£1,150–1,300 Ondines

A pair of Liberty Tudric pewter candlesticks, by Archibald Knox, c1905, 12in (30.5cm) high.

£4,000–4,500 Esoteric

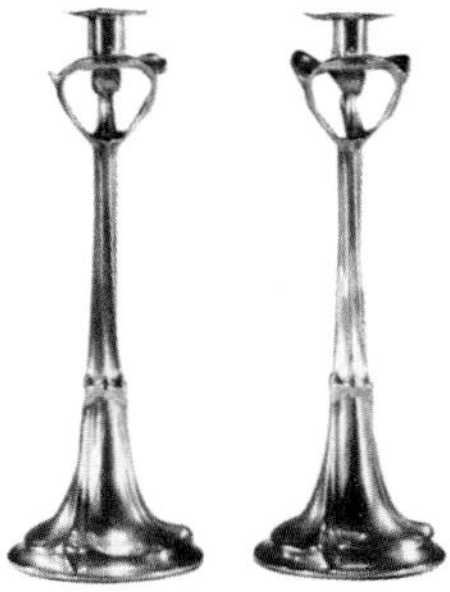

A pair of Kayserzinn pewter candlesticks, by Hugo Leven, with removable sconces, marked, Germany, early 20thC, 16¼in (41.5cm) high.

£1,400–1,650 Sotheby's (O)

A WMF pewter and glass centrepiece, Germany, c1900, 20in (51cm) high.

£600–700 James Strang

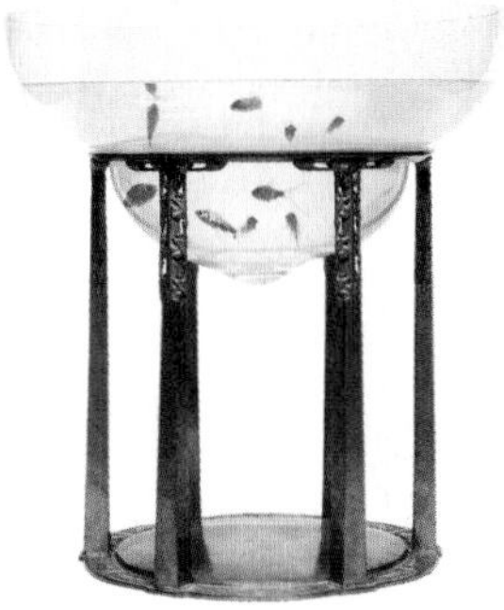

A Liberty pewter and glass centrepiece, cast with 12 panels depicting fish, pierced with leaves and berries, early 20thC, 24½in (62cm) high.

£11,000–13,000 Sotheby's

This piece was probably a special commission produced by Liberty. It is exceptionally rare, not only in its size but also in the skill taken to produce the blown glass liner which is original.

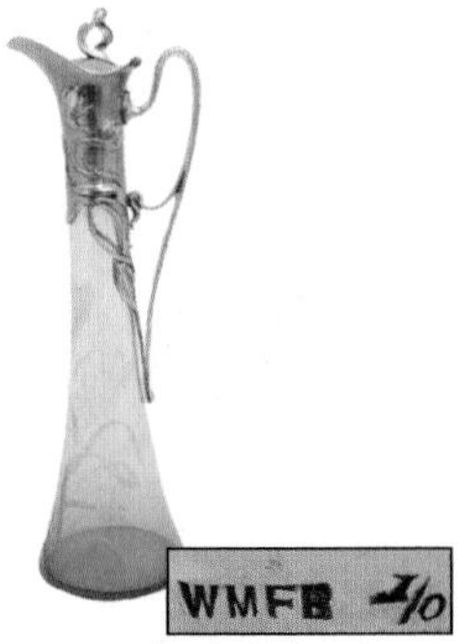

A WMF pewter-mounted etched-glass claret jug, Germany, c1900, 15in (38cm) high.

£1,450–1,600 Ondines

A Liberty pewter coffee pot, with an ebonized handle and finial, c1920, 7in (18cm) high.

£110–125 Ruskin Decorative Arts

A Liberty pewter and glass butter dish, by Archibald Knox, c1905, 3½in (9cm) diam.

£540–600 Design Gallery

A Liberty Tudric pewter jug, in the form of an owl, c1905, 8in (20.5cm) high.

£580–650 Ruskin Decorative Arts

An Argentor silvered-pewter easel mirror, decorated with irises, stamped marks, Austria, c1900, 19¾in (50cm) high.
£800–1,000 Sotheby's (Am)

An Art Nouveau pewter easel mirror, decorated with a maiden, c1900, 24¼in (61.5cm) high.
£1,800–2,200 Sotheby's (O)

A WMF silvered-pewter easel mirror, decorated with a maiden, impressed factory mark, Germany, c1905, 14½in (37cm) high.
£1,500–1,800 Sotheby's (Am)

A Liberty Tudric pewter tankard, c1900, 10in (25.5cm) high.
£600–700 Afford Decorative Arts

An Art Nouveau WMF silvered-pewter tazza, decorated with leaves and berries, stamped mark, Germany, c1900, 10in (25.5cm) high.
£1,000–1,200 Sotheby's (O)

A Liberty Tudric pewter five-piece tea service, by Archibald Knox, stamped marks, c1901, tray 19½in (49.5cm) wide.
£1,100–1,300 Sotheby's (O)

An Art Nouveau pewter tray, decorated with a child and a snail, c1920, 11in (28cm) wide.
£135–150 Ruskin Decorative Arts

A Liberty Tudric pewter vase, by Archibald Knox, c1900, 9¾in (25cm) high.
£600–700 Afford Decorative Arts

A Liberty pewter vase, with three handles and a cabochon mount, c1905, 8in (20.5cm) high.
£350–400 Shapiro

A Liberty Tudric pewter vase, by Archibald Knox, c1910, 9½in (24cm) high.
£700–800 Afford Decorative Arts

COPPER

A copper bowl, by W. A. S. Benson, c1905, 9¾in (25cm) diam.

£135–150 Design Gallery

A copper-covered wooden box, by John Pearson, signed, c1895, 9in (23cm) wide.

£1,100–1,250 Shapiro

A silver and copper box, by A. E. Jones, inset with a ceramic cabochon, with pierced lockplate and riveted corner mounts, on splayed feet, Birmingham 1905, 5½in (14cm) wide.

£900–1,000 Gorringes (L)

EXPERT'S EYE JOHN PAUL COOPER

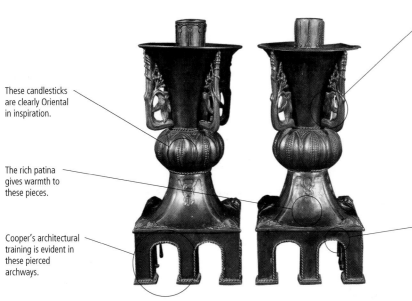

The use of pierced and chased foliage around the upright handles echoes the work of Edward Spencer.
These candlesticks are clearly Oriental in inspiration.
The rich patina gives warmth to these pieces.
Cooper's architectural training is evident in these pierced archways.
In common with his silver mounts on shagreen, Cooper used twisted copper wires applied as decorative borders.

John Paul Cooper (1860–1933) trained as an architect with J. D. Sedding and was appointed Head of Metalwork at Birmingham School of Art in 1902. Cooper's prolific output includes jewellery, silver, gesso and metalwork and he executed over 200 pieces for the Artificers' Guild. He is perhaps best known for his experimental exotic work with shagreen, but he also designed in other materials including tortoiseshell and mother-of-pearl mounted in silver. This pair of patinated-copper candlesticks by John Paul Cooper date from c1909.

£5,500–6,500 Woolley & Wallis

A copper chamberstick, by John Pearson, signed 'J.P.', c1905, 8¼in (21cm) diam.

£250–280 Design Gallery

A Newlyn copper charger, by John Pearson, embossed with a fruit tree, signed, dated 1895, 27½in (70cm) diam.

£1,350–1,600 Diamond Mills

A Newlyn School copper charger, in the manner of John Pearson, set with Ruskin Pottery-style cabochons, decorated with galleons and a bead motif, early 20thC, 21¾in (55.5cm) diam.

£450–550 Gorringes (L)

A Newlyn School Arts & Crafts copper hot water pot, embossed with cormorants and tropical fish on a hammered ground, with bound wicker handle, early 20thC, 8in (20.5cm) high.

£380–450 Gorringes (L)

A Newlyn School copper inkwell, c1900, 7in (18cm) diam.

£500–550 Shapiro

An Arts & Crafts copper inkwell, c1900, 10in (25.5cm) wide.

£110–125 Durham House Antiques

An Arts & Crafts copper jardinière, embossed with heart motifs, c1900, 8in (20.5cm) high.

£400–450 Time Antiques

A copper tray, by Hugh Wallis, c1900, 11in (28cm) diam.

£135–150 Art Nouveau Originals

An Arts & Crafts copper wall box, by John Pearson, with embossed decoration, c1900, 17in (43cm) wide.

£300–350 Worcester Antiques

A WMF copper wall plaque, decorated with crabs and lobsters, Germany, c1900, 15in (38cm) diam.

£280–320 Art Nouveau Originals

A Keswick School of Industrial Arts wall plaque, c1900, 16in (40.5cm) diam.

£850–950 Shapiro

BRASS

EXPERT'S EYE EDWARD SPENCER

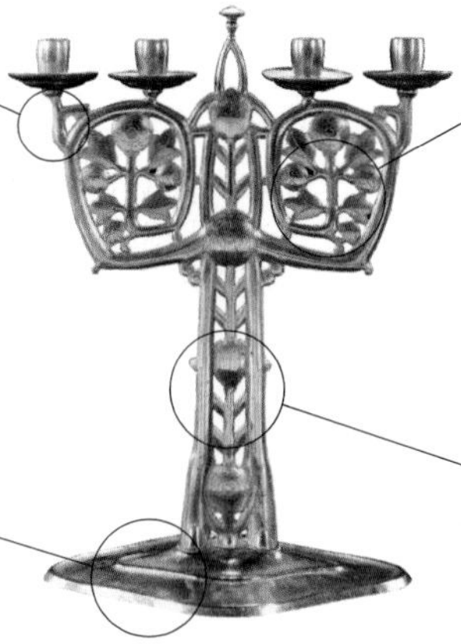

The hand-wrought branches are pierced and engraved with flowering stems supporting the four plain candle sconces.
Spencer's more intricate work had a tendency towards allegorical subjects and he often used a stylized Tree of Life motif.
Spencer's artistry is displayed in this wonderful combination of decorative elegance issuing from a sturdy and solidly rooted base.
This brass candelabrum, probably one of a pair, is formed as an elaborate stylized tree.

The Artificers' Guild was established in 1901 in London by Edward Spencer (1872–1938) and Nelson Dawson (1859–1942), with Spencer becoming chief designer two years later when Montague Fordham took over Dawson's interest in the Guild. The Artificers' Guild produced consistently high-quality jewellery, silver, art metalwork and church furnishings in conjunction with a number of talented designers including Henry Wilson, John Paul Cooper and Phoebe Traquair. Spencer was one of a select group of artist/craftsmen who worked as much for the beauty of their output as they did for commercial gain. This candelabrum by Edward Spencer dates from c1912 and is engraved with roses.

£4,500–5,500 Sotheby's

A Glasgow School brass charger, by Margaret Gilmour, with artist's monogram, c1905, 17in (43cm) diam.

£800–900 James Strang

A pair of Art Nouveau brass fire dogs, c1890, 14in (35.5cm) high.

£180–200 Art Nouveau Originals

An Arts & Crafts brass wall box, with embossed decoration, c1900, 14in (35.5cm) high.

£280–320 Worcester Antiques

ESSENTIAL REFERENCE GLASGOW ROSE

The 'Glasgow rose' became one of the most instantly recognizable features of the Glasgow style. It was used profusely with other trademarks of the Glasgow artists, which include swallows, butterflies and hearts and can be found on metalwork, stained glass, embroidery, jewellery, ceramics, furniture and illustrated works. Charles Rennie Mackintosh used the rose extensively in his furniture and interior design schemes and in particular in The Rose Boudoir installation at the 1902 Turin International Exhibition. The cross-fertilization of ideas across Europe meant that adaptations of the rose motif were used by like-minded artists such as Josef Hoffman and the Vienna Secessionists. This Scottish School brass jardinière dates from c1900 and is embossed with Glasgow roses.

£400–450 Art Nouveau Originals

VARIOUS METALS

A pair of cast-bronze candelabra, attributed to K. M. Seifert & Co for Vereinigte Werkstätten für Kunst im Handwerk, Germany, c1910, 13½in (34.5cm) high.

£2,250–2,750 Bukowskis

A pair of wrought-iron candlesticks, by Goberg, Austria, c1890, 14in (35.5cm) high.

£350–400 Art Nouveau Originals

A Glasgow School polished tin candlestick, by Margaret Gilmour, c1900, 5in (12.5cm) high.

£700–800 James Strang

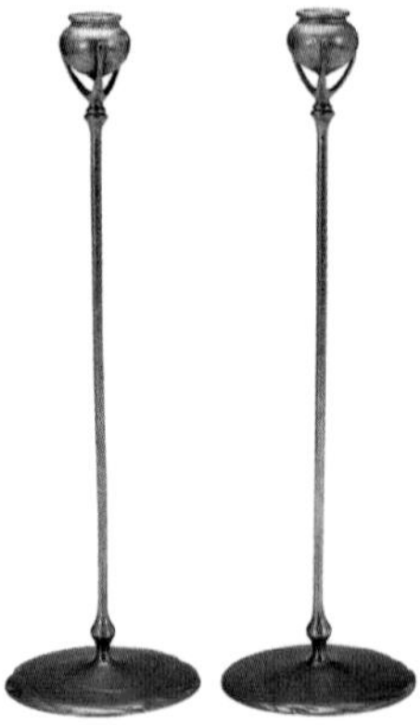

A pair of Tiffany Studios gilt-bronze candlesticks, stamped mark, America, c1910, 18½in (47cm) high.

£1,100–1,300 Freeman's

A pair of bronze candlesticks, by E. T. Hurley, in the form of sea horses, America, dated 1916, 13in (33cm) high.

£2,200–2,600 Rago Arts

A Revere Copper & Brass Co chrome-plated brass Manhattan cocktail set, by Norman Bel Geddes, comprising six goblets, shaker and tray, maker's marks, America, 1937, tray 14½in (37cm) wide.

£6,000–7,000 Sotheby's (NY)

A Tiffany Studios patinated-bronze Scarab inkstand, with glass liner, stamped mark, America, c1910, 4¼in (11cm) high.

£16,000–20,000 Sotheby's (NY)

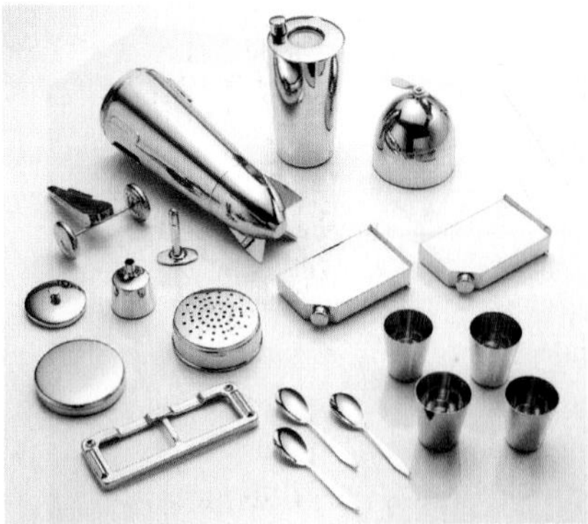

A chrome-plated brass travelling drinks set, by J. A. Henkels Twin Works, in the form an aeroplane, stamped marks, Germany, c1928, 12¾in (32.5cm) long.

£9,500–11,500 Sotheby's (NY)

A bronze vase, with silvered inlay of a dancing woman, and stylized leaves, slight damage, France, c1925, 14in (35.5cm) high.

£450–550 Heritage

ARTS & CRAFTS AND ART NOUVEAU LIGHTING

An Apollo Studios Art Nouveau copper and glass lamp, America, early 20thC, 22in (56cm) high.

£900–1,100 Freeman's

An Arts & Crafts brass and copper oil lamp, by W. A. S. Benson, c1890, 18in (45.5cm) high.

£900–1,000 Puritan Values

A copper lamp, by W. A. S. Benson, c1900, 23in (58.5cm) high.

£2,000–2,200 Country Seat

A bronze and glass table lamp, attributed to Bigelow & Kennard, America, early 20thC, 26½in (67.5cm) high.

£3,500–4,200 Skinner

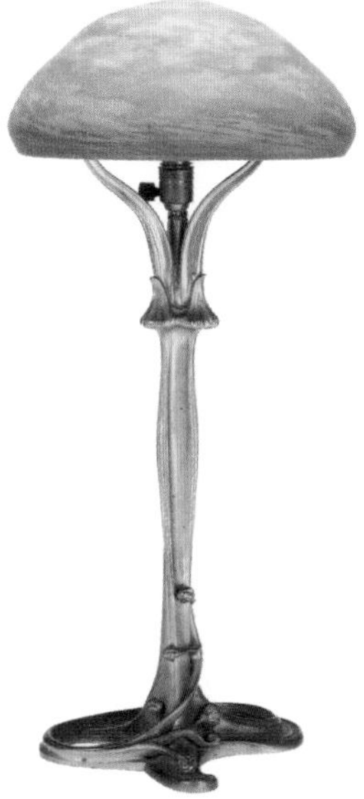

A Daum glass and Louis Majorelle gilt-bronze table lamp, cast with buds, engraved Daum marks, France, early 20thC, 27in (68.5cm) high.

£8,000–10,000 Sotheby's

A Daum glass and metal lamp, the arm with an acanthus leaf, shade with incised mark, France, c1920, 14in (35.5cm) high.

£550–650 Jackson's

A Duffner & Kimberly bronze and leaded-glass hanging lamp, signed, America, early 20thC, 28in (71cm) diam.

£12,000–15,000 Jackson's

A Jefferson glass and gilt-metal table lamp, with reverse-painted decoration, America, early 20thC, 23¼in (59cm) high.

£1,000–1,200 Skinner

A Robert Lorimer wrought iron six-branch light fitting, Scotland, 1927, 23½in (60cm) wide.

£1,350–1,500 Norfolk Decorative

This hand-made light fitting is one of a set of five designed for Glencruitten House, Argyll, Scotland.

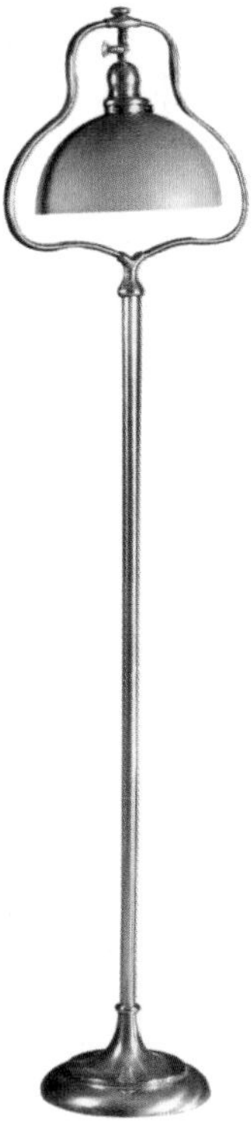

A Handel Mosserine glass and bronze Harp floor lamp, signed, America, early 20thC, 57in (145cm) high.

£650–800 Jackson's

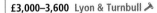

ESSENTIAL REFERENCE MONART GLASS

The name Monart is a combination of the surnames of the company's founders, Isabel Moncrieff and Salvador Ysart. The Ysart family came to Scotland from Barcelona in 1915 and Salvador worked at several glassworks before he was recruited by John Moncrieff Ltd in 1922. Monart's artistic glassware, introduced in 1924, was hand-blown and distinctive in colour, style and decoration. The shapes are based on traditional Chinese porcelain forms and over 300 are recorded in the firm's pattern books. Monart glass was in great demand and quickly became a commercial success. Its popularity grew with a range of vases, bowls and lamps retailed by Liberty & Co in London and Wylie & Lochhead in Glasgow in the 1930s. Today Monart is attracting a growing number of enthusiasts, resulting in a substantial increase in prices. The mushroom lamps, such as this 1930s example, are particularly sought after by collectors.

£3,000–3,600 Lyon & Turnbull

A Muller Frères metal and glass chandelier, with three arms, signed, France, early 20thC, 20in (51cm) high.

£900–1,100 Jackson's

An NW Art Shade Co slag glass and gilt-metal table lamp, decorated with gilt-metal overlays depicting garden-style arbours, impressed marks, America, early 20thC, 32in (81.5cm) high.

£2,000–2,500 Skinner

A Quezal glass and bronze five-branch chandelier, with five arms, modified, signed, America, c1905, 27in (68.5cm) high.

£1,100–1,300 Jackson's

A Pairpoint Manufacturing Co brass and glass Puffy Oxford lamp, America, Massachusetts, c1910, 18½in (47cm) high.

£6,500–8,000 Heritage

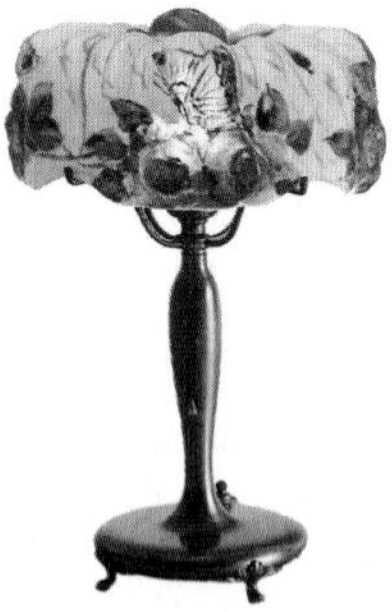

A Pairpoint Manufacturing Co glass and bronze Puffy Oxford lamp, decorated with roses and butterflies, signed, America, c1910, 15in (38cm) high.

£1,000–1,200 Skinner

A Seuss Ornamental Glassworks hanging lamp, decorated with grapes and vines, America, dated 1904, 23½in (59.5cm) diam.

£2,500–3,000 Skinner

A Tiffany Studios glass and bronze table lamp, with oil canister, America, c1895, 20in (51cm) high.

£25,000–30,000 Heritage

A Tiffany Studios Favrile glass and bronze hall lamp, comprising 24 prisms, America, c1900, 14in (35.5cm) high.

£9,000–11,000 Jackson's

A Tiffany Studios Favrile glass and bronze lamp, stamped mark, signed 'L. C. T', America, early 20thC, 10in (25.5cm) high.

£6,500–8,000 Freeman's

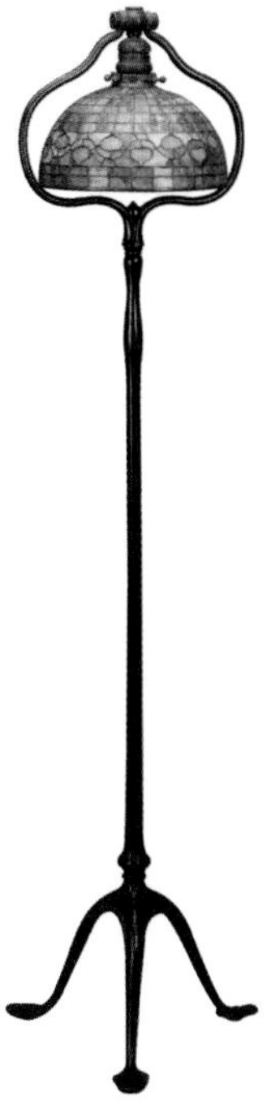

A Tiffany Studios bronze and leaded-glass Acorn floor lamp, stamped marks, America, early 20thC, 54½in (138.5cm) high.

£5,000–6,000 Waddington's

A Tiffany Studios iridescent glass and bronze table lamp, with leaf and wirework decoration, signed, impressed mark, America, early 20thC, 26in (66cm) high.

£14,000–17,000 Skinner

A Maison Vever Art Nouveau patinated-bronze table lamp, decorated with a pine branch and pine cones, the base in the form of an owl, stamped, France, c1900, 17¼in (44cm) high.

£18,000–22,000 Sotheby's

An Arts & Crafts brass hall lantern, with four stained- and leaded-glass panels with Glasgow-style roses, c1900, 12in (30.5cm) high.

£550–600
decorative arts@doune

An Arts & Crafts hammered copper hall lantern, c1910, 12in (30.5cm) high.

£200–220 Exeter Antique Lighting

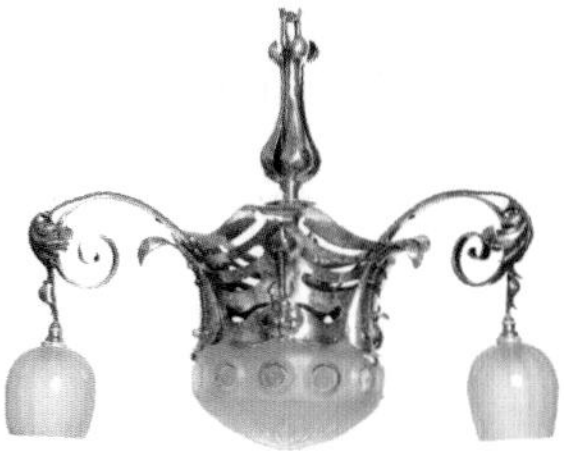

An Art Nouveau silver-plated and glass chandelier, c1900, 27in (68.5cm) wide.

£800–900 Exeter Antique Lighting

A metal and slag glass lampshade, America, early 20thC, 21½in (54.5cm) diam.

£650–800 Skinner

ART DECO LIGHTING

A bronze and ivory lamp, the base in the form of a woman with a hawk, on a marble base, later converted to a lamp, c1920, 15in (38cm) high.

£1,000–1,200 Quay Centre ⊞

A chrome and glass ceiling light, by Ezan, France, c1928, 22in (56cm) diam.

£320–350 Quay Centre ⊞

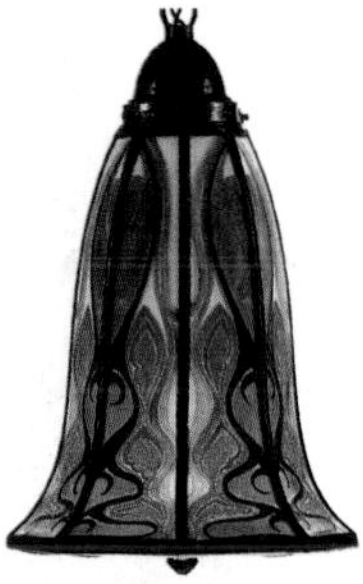

An Amsterdam School stained- and leaded-glass lantern, comprising 16 glass panels, Holland, 1920s, 43¼in (110cm) high.

£3,200–3,800 Sotheby's (Am)

A painted spelter figural table lamp, 1930s, 31in (78.5cm) high.

£425–475 Exeter Antique Lighting ⊞

A pair of nickel-plated and moulded glass wall lights, c1930, 18in (45.5cm) high.

£450–500 Exeter Antique Lighting ⊞

A chromed-metal desk lamp, by Claude Lumière, France, c1930, 17¼in (44cm) high.

£2,800–3,200 Sotheby's (P)

A shagreen and ivory table lamp, attributed to Clément Rousseau, France, c1930, 19¾in (50cm) high.

£3,500–4,200 Sotheby's

A black lacquer and chrome floor-standing uplighter, in the style of Pierre Domanque, France, c1930, 67¾in (172cm) high.

£900–1,000 Robert Mills ⊞

A wrought-iron and porcelain lamp, by Michel Zadounaïsky, enamelled porcelain by François Chanaud, signed, base signed by Zadounaïsky, France, dated 1933, 13¼in (33.5cm) high.

£18,000–22,000 Sotheby's (P)

A gilded spelter and moulded glass figural table lamp, with a man and woman playing musical instruments under a stylized tree, the figures each with Fabrication Française Paris medallions, on a marble base, shade signed 'J. Robert', France, 1930s, 14½in (37cm) high.

£2,700–3,300 Gorringes (L)

A pair of glass floor lamps, France, 1940s, 44½in (113cm) high.

£5,800–6,500 Chameleon ⊞

ART NOUVEAU SCULPTURE

A Franz Bergman gilt-bronze and cold-painted figure of a dancer, the hinged skirt opening to reveal her nudity, impressed mark to reverse, stamped 'Nam Greb', Austria, c1910, 7¾in (19.5cm) high.

£1,000–1,200 Rosebery's

Bergman figures are often stamped 'Nam Greb' – Bergman in reverse.

An Albert Ernst Carrier-Belleuse bronze figure of a nymph, signed, France, 28½in (72.5cm) high.

£3,500–4,200 Freeman's

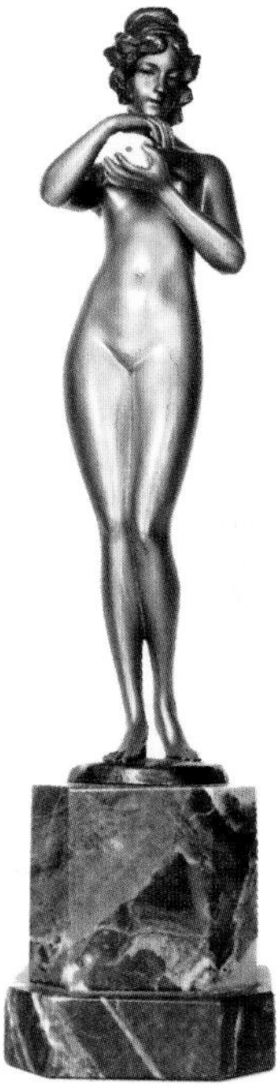

A Hans Keck gilt-bronze and ivory figure of a woman, on a marble plinth, signed, Germany, c1900, 11½in (29cm) high.

£1,300–1,600 Rosebery's

A Mathurin Moreau bronze figure of Summer, c1885, 25in (63.5cm) high.

£6,000–7,000
Garret & Hurst

A Honoré Henri Plé polychromed and patinated bronze bust of a woman, entitled 'Femme de Mequinez', on a socle base, signed and dated, France, 1883, 29½in (75cm) high.

£20,000–24,000
Freeman's

An Emmanuel Villanis bronze bust of La Sybille, signed and numbered, stamped mark, France, c1890, 14¼in (36cm) high.

£3,000–3,300
David Hickmet

Emmanuel Villanis (1858–1914) worked in France and began exhibiting in 1896. Strongly influenced by Art Nouveau, he produced innumerable works, mostly representing feminine figures. The majority were cast in bronze and various tinted metals, often in many dimensions and versions.

An Emmanuel Villanis bronze figure of a girl, entitled 'Prise de Corsaire', with inscription plate, signed, stamped marks, France, c1897, 33½in (85cm) high.

£4,500–5,500 Freeman's

An Ernst Wahliss terracotta figure of a maiden, the base decorated with masks, inscribed with maker's name, marked, Austria, c1900, 26¾in (68cm) high.

£800–1,000 Rosebery's

ART DECO SCULPTURE

A Marcel Bouraine gilt and cold-painted bronze figure of a dancer, entitled 'The Scarf Dancer', on an onyx base, France, c1925, 19½in (49.5cm) wide.

£3,500–4,000 **Clarion Antiques**

A Suzanne Bizzard spelter figure of Diana with a dog and a deer, France, c1925, 16in (40.5cm) high.

£2,500–2,750 **Design Gallery**

A Demêtre Chiparus bronze figure of a young woman, entitled 'Little Sad One', France, on a marble base, signed, c1925, 11¾in (30cm) high.

£2,200–2,500 **David Hickmet**

Romanian-born Demêtre Chiparus (1888–1950) studied in Paris under Mercié and Boucher and exhibited at the Salon des Artistes Français *from 1914 to 1928. Chiparus developed the technique of chryselephantine bronze, pioneered in Belgium at the turn of the century, and gave it its peculiar Art Deco character. He produced numerous figures and small groups of girls, their features carved in ivory set into the bronze, gilded and enamelled.*

A Demêtre Chiparus bronze and ivory figure of a Russian dancer, France, 1920s, 12in (30.5cm) high.

£12,000–14,000 **Mike Weedon**

A Demêtre Chiparus ivory, gilt and cold-painted bronze figural group of a woman and two dogs, entitled 'Friends Forever', on an onyx base, signed, France, 1920s, 11in (28cm) high.

£13,000–16,000 **Freeman's**

A Claire-Jeanne Roberte Colinet painted bronze figure of a woman, on a marble base, signed, c1930, 15in (38cm) high.

£800–1,000 **Rosebery's**

A Hagenauer nickel and brass model of a woman's head, Austria, c1930, 11in (28cm) high.

£1,450–1,600 **James Strang**

A Max Kalish bronze figure of a man, entitled 'Man with a Jackhammer', on a marble base, marked, France, dated 1926, 10¼in (26cm) high.

£5,500–6,500 **Freeman's**

A Georges Lavroff bronze group of a girl with a borzoi, on a marble base, signed, France, c1930, 28½in (72.5cm) wide.

£10,000–12,000 **Sotheby's (Am)**

AUDREY STERNSHINE
tique Galleries
26 Broad St
endleton, Salford
anchester M6 5BY
el: 0161 737 5938
ax: 0161 737 6626
Specialist in Art Nouveau & Art Deco.
www.artnouveau-artdeco.com
Email: as@artnouveau-artdeco.com

A Pierre le Faguays bronze figure of a woman holding two onyx urns, entitled 'Vestal', on an onyx plinth, signed, France, c1925, 20½in (52cm) high.

£9,000–10,000 David Hickmet

Pierre le Faguays (1870–1938), attracted the attention of the public at his first exhibition due to the originality of his dancing subjects. He was a member of the Salon and La Stele *and Evolution groups and was awarded a Medal of Honour in 1927.*

A Pierre le Faguays bronze figure of a dancing woman, with Etling foundry stamp, signed, France, c1930, 22in (56cm) high.

£10,000–11,000 Ondines

A Josef Lorenzl bronze figure of a woman with a flower festoon, on a marble base, Austria, 1920s, 12in (30.5cm) high.

£1,600–1,800 Mike Weedon

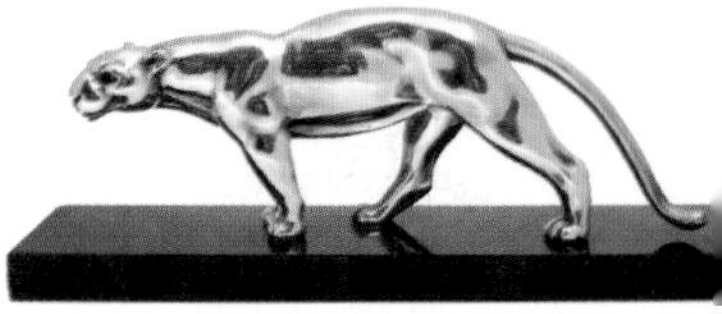

An Ouline silvered-bronze model of panther, on a marble base, France, c1930, 18½in (47cm) wide.

£3,000–3,500 Clarion Antiques

A Fernand Ouillon-Carrère bronze figure of a woman, entitled 'Sword Dance', on an onyx base, France, signed, dated 1919, 14¼in (36cm) high.

£1,300–1,600 Bearnes

A Josef Lorenzl bronze figure of a dancer, on an onyx plinth, signed, Austria, c1930, 11¾in (30cm) high.

£1,300–1,600 Rosebery's

A Fritz Ferdinand Priess bronze and ivory figure of the dancer Ada May, on an onyx plinth, signed, Germany, c1925, 13½in (34cm) high.

£15,000–17,500 David Hickmet

Fritz Ferdinand Priess (1882–1943), was born in Erbach-Odenwald, Germany, studied in Paris and worked with Professor Poertzel in Berlin. Priess' family were renowned ivory carvers and his skill, detailing and modelling in this medium was unsurpassed during the Art Deco era. He combined ivory and bronze with magnificent results – his stunning young ladies captured the energy and seduction of the period and his models of children are exquisite.

A Raphael Charles Peyre gilt-bronze and enamel group of two girls, on a marble base, signed, France, c1930, 14¼in (36cm) wide.

£4,500–5,000 David Hickmet

Raphael Charles Peyre (1872–1949) was born in Paris and studied under Falguière, Mercié and Barrias. He received a Medal of Honour in 1894 from the Salon des Beaux Arts *which was followed by many other awards.*

A C. F. A. Piper bronze figure of a gymnast, signed, stamped marks, 19thC, 15in (38cm) high.

£2,000–2,250 Ronald Chambers

A pair of R. Richard bronze and ivory figures **of child labourers,** on marble plinths, signed, France, c1920, larger 8in (20.5cm) high.
£900–1,100 **Tennants**

A Christa Winsloe-Hatvany bronze model of **a dik-dik,** signed and inscribed, Germany, c1925, 15¼in (38.5cm) high.
£5,200–5,800 **David Hickmet**

A Zabo gilt-bronze and bisque figure of a **clown,** on a marble base, signed, Continental, c1930, 13in (33cm) high.
£900–1,100 **Freeman's**

A Bruno Zach cold-painted bronze figure of **a dancer,** on a marble base, signed and stamped, Austria, c1925, 13in (33cm) high.
£4,000–4,500 **David Hickmet**

Bruno Zach (1891–1935) created tall, athletic, independent women in bronze and ivory. His bronze is occasionally patinated, most often cold-painted and his use of ivory is spare and always well carved. His work was issued by several firms, including S. Altmann & Co and Bergmann.

A Bruno Zach bronze figure of a woman, Austria, c1930, 12in (30.5cm) high.
£9,000–10,000 **Ondines**

A bronze group of a dancing couple, Continental, early 20thC, 14¾in (37.5cm) high.
£850–1,000 **Lyon & Turnbull**

A painted spelter figure of a female **harlequin dancer,** on an onyx base, c1930, 25¾in (65.5cm) high.
£800–1,000 **Andrew Hartley**

A cold-painted spelter figure of a dancer, Austria, c1930, 10in (25.5cm) high.
£700–800 **Muir Hewitt**

A bronze figure of a young girl, on a marble base, indistinct signature to base, probably France, 1930s, 15¾in (40cm) high.
£500–600 **Rosebery's**

ARTS & CRAFTS AND ART NOUVEAU JEWELLERY

A Liberty silver and enamel brooch, by Jessie M. King, c1900, 1in (2.5cm) diam.

£1,100–1,300 James Strang

An Arts & Crafts silver and amethyst brooch, by Theodor Fahrner, retailed by Murrle, Bennett & Co, signed, Germany, c1903, 1¼in (3cm) wide.

£400–500 Skinner

The German company owned by Theodor Fahrner supplied pieces to Murrle, Bennett & Co.

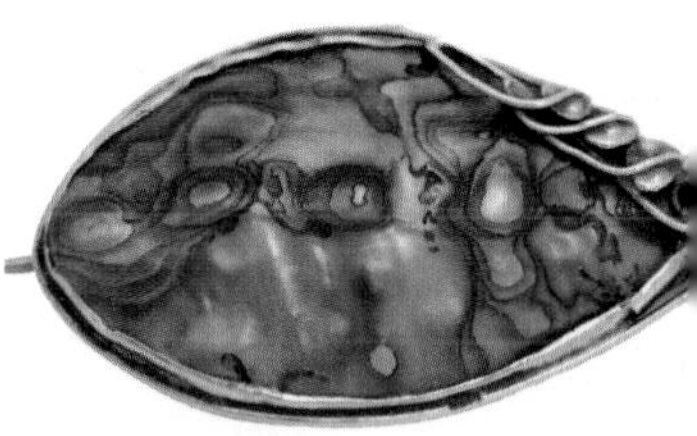

An Arts & Crafts silver and abalone brooch, attributed to Mary Thew, with a silver wirework mount, Scotland, c1905, 2¼in (5.5cm) wide.

£400–450 decorative arts@doune

ESSENTIAL REFERENCE RHODA WAGER

Rhoda Wager (1875–1953) trained at the Glasgow School of Art and received instruction from Bernard Cuzner in Birmingham before moving to Fiji and later Australia where she set up a workshop in 1921. Wager's jewellery is individually hand-wrought in the Arts & Crafts style, and examples from the 1920s usually incorporate Australian motifs such as eucalyptus leaves, nuts and berries, and are set with indigenous gemstones including opals, amethysts, sapphires, pearls and coral. Wager's numerous designs are recorded in her sketchbooks and her jewellery is represented in the collections of the Art Gallery of New South Wales and the Museum of Applied Arts & Sciences, Sydney. Although much jewellery dating from this period is unmarked due to the delicacy and intricacy of design, an artist's signature or monogram such as the Wager mark on the reverse of this brooch is particularly desirable and will ultimately increase value.

This silver wirework brooch was made c1920 and is set with a blister pearl.

£580–650 decorative arts@doune

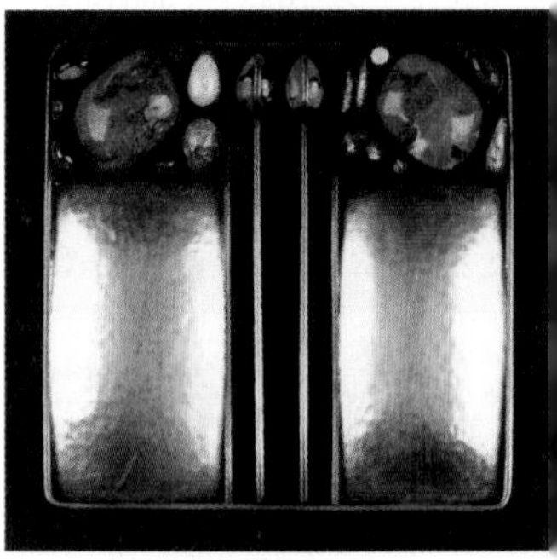

A Wiener Werkstätte silver, gold and opal brooch, by Karl Ponocny, designed by Josef Hoffman for Emilie Flöge, marked, Austria, c1906, with original box.

£140,000–170,000 Waddington's

The Vienna Secession was formed in 1897 with artist and designer Gustav Klimt as President. Its philosophy was to create a mix of art and craft for all people, both rich and poor. Among the original members of this group was the architect Josef Hoffmann who, with Koloman Moser, formed the Wiener Werkstätte or Vienna Workshop in 1903. The Werkstätte's goal was to produce only individual objects of great beauty, with an emphasis on fine craftsmanship, and to move away from the rapidly growing industrialization and mass-production of the era. Their motto was 'better to work ten days at one piece than to manufacture ten pieces in one day.' Emilie Flöge was a wealthy and celebrated Viennese fashion designer and muse of the Werkstätte artists. She and Klimt designed loose-fitting garments, many of which were created from fabrics designed at the Wiener Werkstätte, that freed the wearer from the tight and constricting clothing of the day.

A Wiener Werkstätte silver brooch, by Josef Hoffmann, pierced with two flowers, stamped marks, Austria, early 20thC, 2½in (6.5cm) wide.

£2,500–3,000 Sotheby's

A silver brooch, by Bernard Instone, set with an amber cabochon within a silver wirework mount applied with gold flowerhead clusters, maker's mark, stamped mark, c1925, 1¼in (3cm) wide.

£320–350 decorative arts@doune

A silver brooch, by Alexander Ritchie, decorated with a zoomorphic bird on an enamel ground, marked 'AR', stamped 'ICA, Iona', Birmingham 1937, 2in (5cm) wide.

£270–300 decorative arts@doune

EXPERT'S EYE KATE HARRIS SILVERWARE

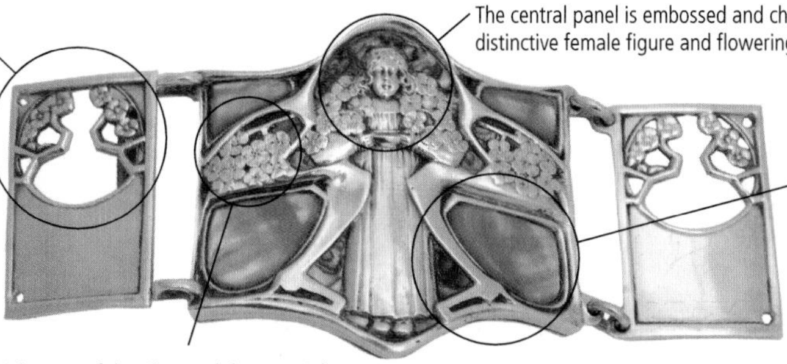

The bold outline of the buckle is softened by plain silver side panels which are chased with Harris's flowering branches against a pierced full moon motif.
The central panel is embossed and chased with Harris's distinctive female figure and flowering shrub motifs.
The combination of abalone shell and mother-of-pearl is typical of the Art Nouveau period.
The designer, the substantial gauge of the silver and the materials used are all factors that add considerably to the value of this piece.

Kate Harris studied sculpture before turning to silverwork in 1898. Her innovative Art Nouveau designs have a strong sculptural quality and often incorporate classical female and stylized tree motifs. She became one of the chief designers for silver manufacturers William Hutton & Sons, who produced her work on a wide variety of objects including centrepieces, caskets, dressing table sets, mirrors and buckles. Her designs were also produced by Connell and the Goldsmiths & Silversmiths Company, among others. This fine example of a silver buckle was designed by Kate Harris and produced by William Hutton & Sons; it is hallmarked London 1901.

£2,250–2,500 **decorative arts@doune** ⊞

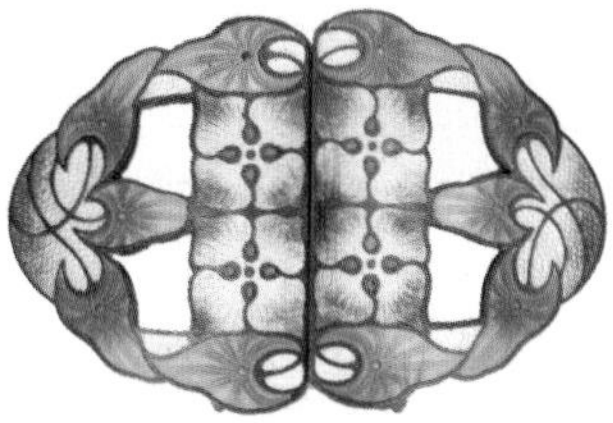

An Art Nouveau enamel buckle, c1900, 3in (7.5cm) wide.

£250–280 **Design Gallery** ⊞

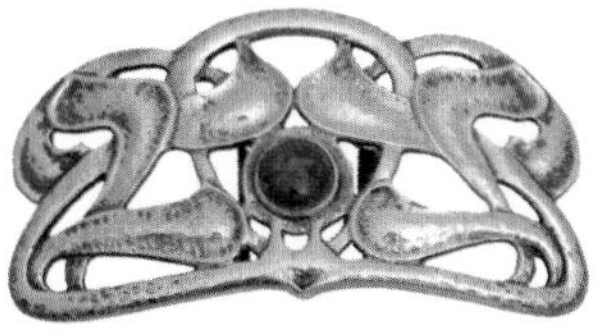

An Arts & Crafts hammered-silver buckle, by A. E. Jones, with entwined stylized foliage and a Ruskin Pottery roundel, maker's mark 'AEJ', Birmingham 1904, 3½in (9cm) wide.

£580–650 **decorative arts@doune** ⊞

A Liberty silver and enamel buckle, Birmingham 1904, 3in (7.5cm) wide.

£550–650 **Lawrence Fine Art** ⚒

A gilt and enamel buckle, c1910, 3in (7.5cm) wide.

£45–50 **Jessie's Button Box** ⊞

An Art Nouveau gold and white-metal necklace, set with ten fire opals and diamonds, c1900.

£4,500–5,000 **Design Gallery** ⊞

An Arts & Crafts, gold, silver, silver-gilt and carved gem necklace, by J. H. Shaw, suspending a rose quartz and tourmaline pendant with a beaded fringe, losses, signed, America, early 20thC, pendant 3½in (9cm) long.

£7,500–9,000 **Skinner** ⚒

A Tiffany gold and emerald necklace, stamped marks, c1915, with a silk satin and velvet case.

£18,000–22,000 **Sotheby's (NY)** ⚒

A 15ct gold and turquoise pendant, by Murrle, Bennett & Co, c1905.

£1,000–1,200
Art Nouveau Originals ⊞

ART DECO JEWELLERY & WATCHES

A **Bakelite bangle,** carved with lip motifs, 1930s, 3in (7.5cm) diam.

£430–480 Design Gallery

A **jadeite, diamond and pearl bracelet,** the jadeite plaques carved with exotic foliage, stamped 'plat 14ct', c1930.

£2,500–3,200 Dreweatt Neate (HAM)

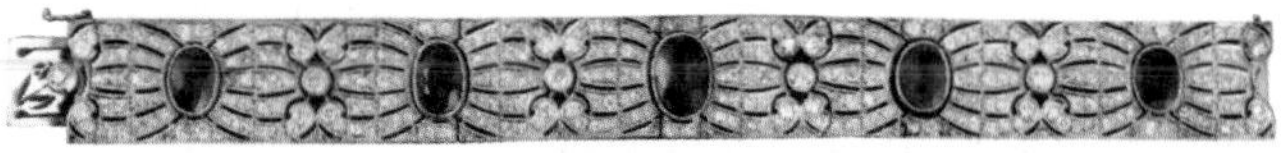

A **sapphire and diamond bracelet,** with pierced and articulated panels, c1930.

£8,000–10,000 Dreweatt Neate (HAM)

An **articulated white-metal, ruby and diamond line bracelet,** c1930.

£6,750–7,500 Grey-Harris

A **platinum and diamond brooch,** with sapphires, rubies, citrines and amethysts set in the form of flowers, c1925.

£2,700–3,250 Sotheby's (NY)

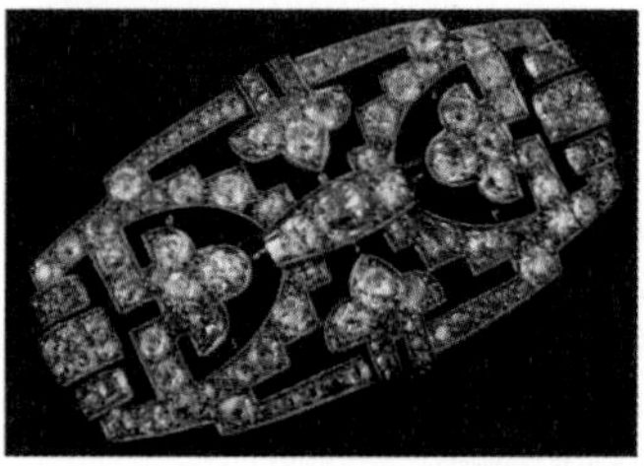

A **diamond brooch,** pierced with geometric scrolls, bands and stylized trefoil motifs, c1925.

£1,750–2,000 Dreweatt Neate (HAM)

A **silver tribal mask brooch,** France, 1924, 2½in (6.5cm) high.

£220–250 James Strang

A **rock crystal and diamond brooch,** marked, France, c1925.

£4,500–5,500 Dreweatt Neate (HAM)

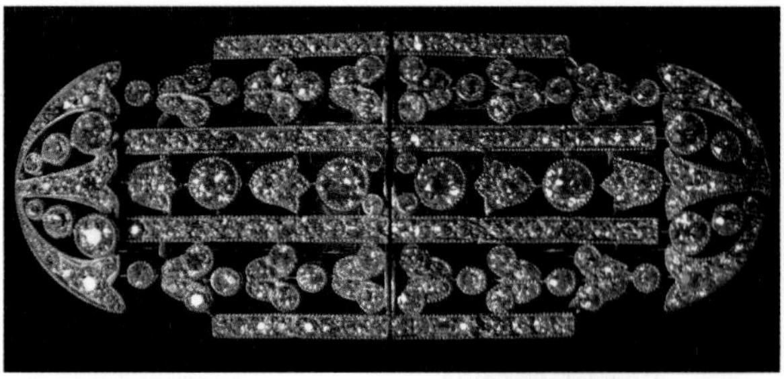

A **platinum and diamond double clip brooch,** c1925, 3in (7.5cm) wide.

£7,500–8,500 Grey-Harris

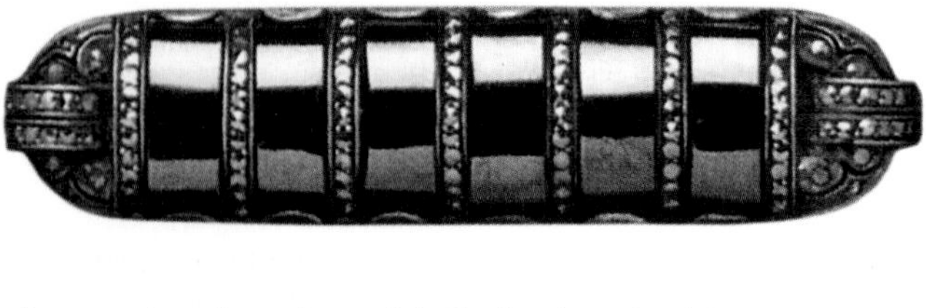

A **silver, marcasite and haematite brooch,** by Theodor Fahrner, signed, Germany, c1926, 5½in (14cm) wide.

£250–300 Skinner

A **platinum and diamond clip brooch,** marked, France, c1930, 1¼in (3cm) high.

£4,750–5,250 Wimpole Antiques

A jade, diamond and silver brooch, c1935, 1½in (4cm) wide.
£1,500–1,750 Swan at Tetsworth

A platinum and diamond brooch, c1930.
£6,500–8,000 Sotheby's (NY)

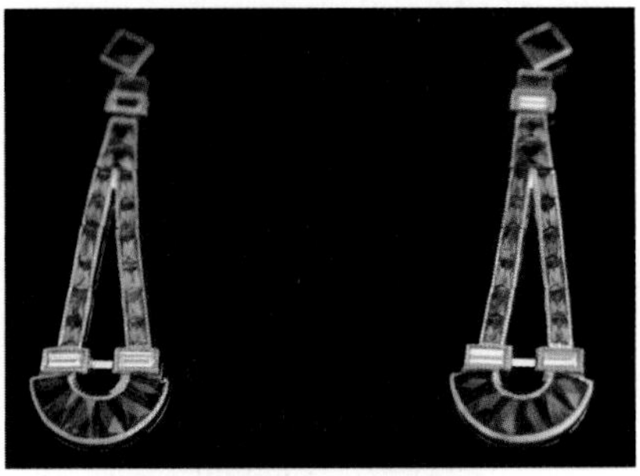

A pair of 18ct white gold, enamel, sapphire and diamond earrings, c1935, 1½in (4cm) long.
£2,000–2,200 Anthony Green Antiques

An enamel, coral and diamond jabot pin, marked, France, 1920s, with a Cartier Paris case.
£2,500–3,000 Sotheby's

An emerald and diamond ring, c1925.
£800–1,000 Dreweatt Neate (HAM)

A Cartier emerald and diamond ring, damaged, signed, c1930.
£2,800–3,400 Dreweatt Neate (HAM)

An 18ct gold, onyx and diamond ring, c1935.
£1,600–1,850 Wimpole Antiques

A platinum, sapphire and diamond ring, c1935.
£1,100–1,250 Wimpole Antiques

An Asprey ebony and ivory watch, the reverse mounted with an ivory panel in the form of a domino, signed, c1920, 2in (5cm) wide.
£1,200–1,500 Sotheby's

A cocktail watch, set with diamonds, with a ribbon strap, mounts stamped '18ct', 1930s.
£850–1,000 Lyon & Turnbull

An emerald and diamond cocktail watch, with a ribbon strap, 1930s.
£1,100–1,300 Lyon & Turnbull

AESTHETIC MOVEMENT FURNITURE

An ebonized cabinet, with three open shelves above shelves, drawers and cupboards, c1880, 68½in (174cm) wide.

£450–550 Penrith Farmers' & Kidd's

A stained-ash open bookcase, c1880, 51¼in (130cm) wide.

£2,500–3,000 Sotheby's (O)

An oak and leather chair, by H. W. Batley for James Shoolbred, c1880, 38¼in (97cm) high.

£750–850 Design Gallery

A pair of ebonized and parcel-gilt shelves, decorated with panels of birds and flowers, c1880, 36¼in (92cm) high.

£900–1,100 Sotheby's (O)

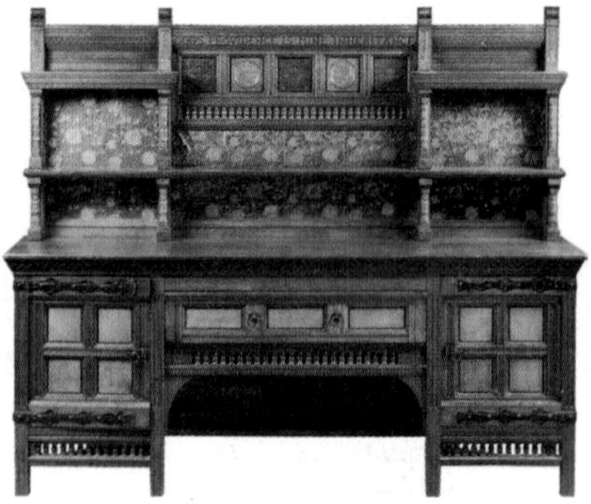

A carved oak sideboard, after Bruce Talbert, the back with carved portrait roundels and embossed leather panels, with inscription, c1885, 81¼in (206.5cm) wide.

£4,500–5,500 Sotheby's (O)

The design of this piece is related to a sideboard designed by Talbert and executed by Gillow & Co for the 1871 International Exhibition in South Kensington. It was bought afterwards by the Victoria & Albert Museum.

A burr-walnut and satinwood sideboard, with mirrored back and painted with vignettes of Venetian scenes, c1885, 92½in (235cm) wide.

£2,800–3,400 Leonard Joel

An Japanese-style mahogany side table, c1870, 27in (68.5cm) high.

£700–800 Design Gallery

An oak-veneered card table, the rotating top opening to reveal a baize cover and compartment, c1890, 34¼in (87cm) wide.

£400–500 Sotheby's (O)

ARTS & CRAFTS FURNITURE

EXPERT'S EYE SHAPLAND & PETTER

This design, typical of the their output, is bold in outline and made from solid oak.

There is pleasing contrast of ornament and simplicity in the applied elongated strapwork hinges, hand-beaten copper lockplate and repoussé copper panel inscribed with a quote from Sir Francis Bacon, 'Reading Maketh A Full Man'.

Clear glass enables easy viewing of the books without detracting attention from the repoussé panel inset into the gallery above.

Renowned for producing a wide range of high quality furniture at their Raleigh Works in Barnstaple, Devon, Shapland & Petter's stock was retailed across Britain. Their Arts & Crafts furniture, characterized by simplicity of line and well-balanced proportions, was predominantly made from oak, mahogany or walnut and often enlivened with various decorative flourishes including long strapwork mounts, pierced heart motifs, inlaid marquetry, embossed panels and mottoes derived from English poets and dramatists. Trademarks to look for are the initials 'S' and 'PB' which can be found on lockplates, and a sequence of numbered design stamps impressed into the furniture.
A recent publication about the firm's Arts & Crafts furniture has raised awareness in the vast range of their products. The Shapland & Petter archive has helped with the attribution of designs and ensured that examples of their solidly-made, well-proportioned furniture are much sought after by collectors today. The oak bookcase illustrated is a perfect example of the type of furniture that established Shapland & Petter as a leading manufacturer of the day.

£1,800–2,000 Puritan Values ⊞

A pair of stained beech library bookcases, by Arthur Simpson, the moulded cornices with Latin inscriptions, each bookcase having three shelves above a cupboard with three panelled sliding doors, on bracket feet, c1900, 53½in (136cm) high.

£5,500–6,500 Charterhouse

An oak bookcase, probably by Shapland & Petter, retailed by Liberty, c1905, 49½in (125.5cm) high.

£1,200–1,300 Design Gallery ⊞

A fruitwood cabinet, by Helen Polénoff, Russia, c1900, 12½in (32cm) high.

£850–950 Design Gallery ⊞

An oak wall cabinet, by Heal's of London, with twin cupboard doors and copper strapwork mounts, stamped mark, c1900, 28in (71cm) high.

£600–650 decorative arts @ doune ⊞

An oak wall cabinet, by Shapland & Petter, the glass door overlaid with a pierced copper panel, stamped mark, c1905, 20in (51cm) high.

£450–500 decorative arts @ doune ⊞

An ebonized reclining armchair, by Philip Webb for Morris & Co, c1866.

£9,000–10,000
Puritan Values ⊞

A set of six Liberty stained beech Windsor armchairs, c1890.

£4,000–4,500
Puritan Values

A pair of oak dining chairs, by George Walton, with rush seats, c1900.

£4,500–5,000
Puritan Values

An oak side chair, by William Birch of High Wycombe, c1900.

£130–160
Thomson, Roddick & Medcalf (C)

A pair of oak chairs, by Robert Lorimer, Scotland, c1900.

£1,100–1,200
James Strang

A stained oak high-back chair, by Charles Rennie Mackintosh, Scotland, c1900.

£20,000–25,000 Sotheby's (NY)
This chair is from the White Dining Room of Miss Cranston's Tea Rooms in Ingram Street, Glasgow.

A mahogany chair, attributed to J. S. Henry, c1905.

£800–900 Strachan Antiques

A pair of inlaid walnut chairs, decorated with Glasgow Rose copper panels, c1905.

£850–1,000 Strachan Antiques

An oak armchair, Glasgow School, fabric designed by Harry Napper, Scotland, c1905.

£600–700 James Strang

A walnut armchair, by E. G. Punnett, c1905.

£2,700–3,000
Puritan Values

An oak chair, by Walter Burley Griffin for Newman College, possibly by James Moore & Sons, Australia, 1916.

£1,500–1,800 Leonard Joel

An oak display cabinet, inlaid with fruitwood floral decoration, the interior lined with velvet, slight damage, c1900, 59¾in (152cm) wide.

£1,300–1,600 Sotheby's (Am)

An oak kneehole desk, by Shapland & Petter, c1900, 48in (122cm) wide.

£1,100–1,250 Strachan Antiques

MITOFSKY
ANTIQUES
ART deco MOdERNISM

A very fine pair of cherrywood *fauteuils*, c1940,
by Jule Leleu (1883–1961), Paris. With original Aubusson
Floral Tapestries and gilt-bronze sabots.
One stamped J. Leleu. 83cm high x 65cm wide x 67cm deep.
Bibliographie: Pierre Kjellberg 'Le Mobilier Duxxe Siécle',
Editions De L'Amateur, Paris 2000,
Modéle Référence Et Reproduit, page 372.

8 Rathfarnham Road, Terenure,
Dublin 6, Ireland

T: +3531 492 0033 F: +353 1 492 0188

M: +353 (0)87 246 1418

W: www.mitofskyantiques.com

E: info@mitofskyantiques.com

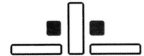

An oak desk, in the manner of C. F. A. Voysey, the fall-front enclosing pigeonholes, c1905, 26½in (67.5cm) wide.

£2,500–3,000 Sotheby's (O)

A mahogany secretaire, the drop-down panelled back enclosing a fitted interior, the sides hung with curtains, c1900, 60in (152.5cm) high.

£300–360 Morphets of Harrogate

A Liberty oak wardrobe, inscribed with motto 'Sleep Doubtless & Secure', c1900, 78½in (199.5cm) high.

£1,600–1,750 Strachan Antiques

A limed oak dining room suite, comprising sideboard, table, one carver and five dining chairs, c1936, 59¾in (152cm) long.

£900–1,100
Special Auction Services

This was designed privately by Mr. E. Davies and was made by J. T. Rogers, Victoria Cabinet Works, Chesterfield, costing £18.2.0 – £845 at today's values.

An oak settle, by Gustav Stickley, the panelled back above a lift-up seat with compartment, signed, America, 1904–12, 47in (119.5cm) wide.

£4,500–5,500 Skinner

An oak sideboard, by John Whittle & Son, the cornice with a tiled panel, signed, c1910, 54in (137cm) wide.

£800–1,000
Penrith Farmers' & Kidd's

A blackwood games table, stamped 'Beard Watson, Sydney', Australia, c1920, 33½in (85cm) diam.

£750–900 Leonard Joel

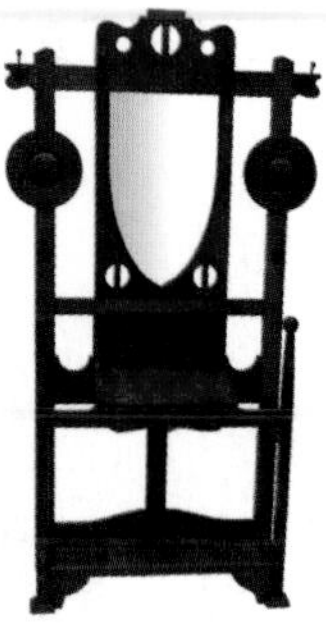

An oak hall stand, by Shapland & Petter, c1900, 80in (203cm) high.

£2,700–3,000
Puritan Values

An oak sideboard, in the style of Baillie-Scott, c1905, 60in (152.5cm) wide.

£3,400–3,800 Design Gallery

An oak trestle table, by Gustav Stickley, slight damage, labelled, America, c1902, 36in (91.5cm) long.

£2,800–3,400 Rago Arts

A mahogany washstand and dressing table, with a tiled back and marble top, the dressing table with swing mirror, drawers and shelves, late 19thC, 45in (114.5cm) wide.

£400–500
Thomson, Roddick & Medcalf (C)

ART NOUVEAU FURNITURE

A mahogany bench, by John Borgensen, France, c1900, 38½in (98cm) wide.

£5,000–6,000 **Sotheby's (P)**

A mahogany display cabinet, inlaid with mother-of-pearl, copper and pewter, inset with silvered embossed copper panels, c1900, 46½in (118cm) wide.

£2,500–3,000 **Sotheby's (O)**

A cabinet, by Carlo Bugatti, with painted decoration by Riccardo Pellegrini, inlaid with pewter, brass, copper and vellum, signed 'Riccardo Pellegrini', Italy, c1900, 33¼in (84.5cm) wide.

£30,000–36,000 **Sotheby's**

A mahogany display cabinet, with a pierced fretwork panel and inlaid decoration, c1905, 53½in (136cm) wide.

£10,000–12,000 **Sotheby's (O)**

This cabinet formerly belonged to George Harrison.

A walnut corner suite, comprising two settees, a desk, a vitrine and a bookshelf, France, Nancy, c1905, 109in (277cm) wide.

£22,000–26,000 **Sotheby's (NY)**

A rosewood armchair, inlaid with a fruitwood and mother-of-pearl panel depicting a maiden, c1900.

£1,350–1,500

decorative arts@doune

EXPERT'S EYE WYLIE & LOCHHEAD

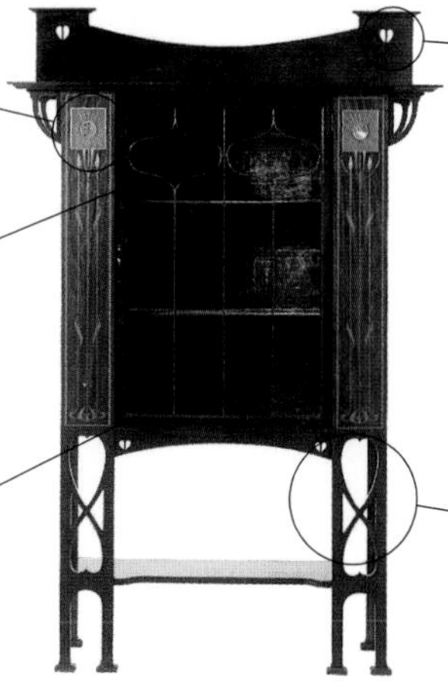

An overall refined elegance is enhanced with rich inlays of holly, sycamore, pewter, abalone and mother-of-pearl.
The clear glass door is punctuated with restrained subtle onion shapes to allow the display shelves to be viewed clearly.
The cabinet retains the original velvet-lined interior.
The shaped surmount is pierced with characteristic split heart motifs. Yin and Yang was another pierced motif much used by Wylie & Lochhead.
Further large heart shapes are repeated on the openwork supports.

Wylie & Lochhead was founded by brothers-in-law Robert Wylie and James Lochhead who established furniture workshops and a showroom in Buchanan Street, Glasgow. By the end of the 19th-century they were producing good quality furniture in the Arts & Crafts style. They exhibited several acclaimed room settings at the Glasgow International Exhibition in 1901 and employed leading designers E. A. Taylor, George Logan and John Ednie, all of whom played a role in the evolution of the Glasgow style at that time. Their designs were stylish and typically of solid construction in heavy gauge oak or mahogany highlighted with pierced motifs, inlays, stained and leaded-glass panels and decorative metal mounts. This mahogany display cabinet was made c1905.

£4,500–5,500 **Sotheby's**

A pair of mahogany chairs, by Louis Majorelle, France, c1900.
£12,000–15,000 **Sotheby's (NY)**

A beechwood chair, by Josef Hoffmann for J. & J. Kohn, entitled 'Sitzmaschine', model No. 670, Austria, c1905.
£10,000–12,000 **Sotheby's (NY)**

A pair of rosewood armchairs, attributed to E. G. Punnett for J. S. Henry, inlaid with boxwood marquetry motifs, c1905.
£4,000–4,500
decorative arts@doune

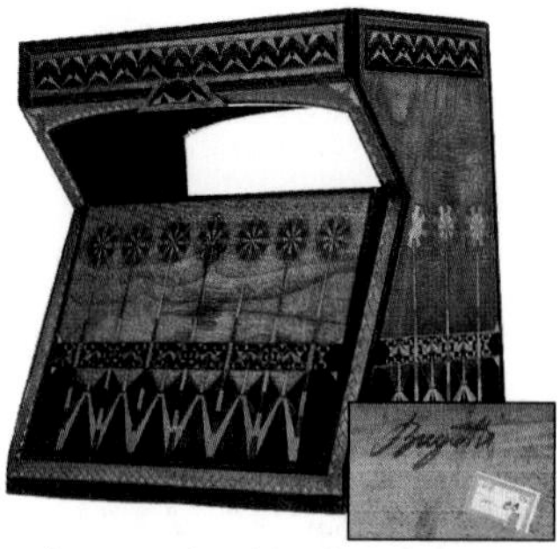

A walnut secretaire cabinet, by Carlo Bugatti, with brass and pewter inlaid decoration, signed, Italy, c1900, 19¾in (50cm) wide.
£13,000–16,000 **Sotheby's (NY)**

An ebonized oak stool, by Adolf Loos for Dr Otto Stoessel, with leather upholstery, Austria, c1901, 24in (61cm) wide.
£5,000–6,000 **Sotheby's (NY)**

A walnut dining room suite, by Henri Rapin, comprising cabinet, six chairs and extending dining table, carved with nasturtiums and thistles, France, branded marks, dated 1909, cabinet 60in (152.5cm) wide.
£23,000–28,000 **Rago Arts**

A walnut dressing table and four chairs, with marble top, France, late 19thC, 52in (132cm) wide.
£750–900 **Jackson's**

An oak centre table, by Henri van de Velde, Belgium, c1900, 36¾in (93.5cm) diam.
£25,000–30,000 **Sotheby's**

A Liberty oak centre table, with pierced stylized floral decoration, early 20thC, 29½in (75cm) diam.
£2,000–2,500 **Sotheby's (O)**

ESSENTIAL REFERENCE LOUIS MAJORELLE FURNITURE

Like Emile Gallé, Louis Majorelle drew his inspiration from natural forms which he translated into free-flowing organic motifs in a highly stylized Art Nouveau manner. It was a modern interpretation of the French rococo tradition. Majorelle was keen for his creations to reach a wide audience and operated a large scale production process through his several workshops. His furniture is noted for its expensive and luxurious appearance suggesting that only the extremely wealthy could afford them. Rich and exotic woods, often with highly elaborate gilt-metal mounts, proved to be a potent combination and his enterprise was a huge commercial success. He was highly acclaimed in Paris and the publicity surrounding his firm's reputation attracted a large audience. This marquetry lamp table from c1900 is inlaid with various woods and depicts a lake scene.
£1,800–2,200 **Jackson's**

ART DECO FURNITURE

A calamander-veneered and ebonized cocktail cabinet, by Paul Boman, the two doors enclosing shelves and a mirrored interior, Finland, 1920s–30s, 59in (150cm) wide.

£8,500–10,000 Bukowskis

A shagreen cocktail cabinet, inlaid with bone, with rising interior, France, 1930s, 17½in (44.5cm) wide.

£13,000–16,000 Sotheby's (P)

A mahogany and gilt-bronze armchair, by Maurice Pré, designed for the First Class Dining Room of the *Normandie*, restored, France, Paris, c1934, 34½in (87.5cm) high.

£3,800–4,500 Heritage

A pair of oak lounge chairs, by René Gabriel, France, c1940.

£3,500–4,200 Sotheby's

A mahogany and painted wood desk, by Joseph Urban, America, c1925, 60in (152.5cm) wide.

£13,000–16,000 Sotheby's (NY)

The set designer Joseph Urban used the money he earned working on films to return to his first love, architecture, and set up his own firm. As always, Urban designed all the interior furnishings and appointments for his New York City office. This desk is an extremely rare surviving work from this commission.

A mahogany writing desk, by Erik Chambert, with a fitted interior, Sweden, 1930s, 34¾in (88.5cm) wide.

£3,500–4,200 Bukowskis

A bird's-eye maple-veneered dressing table, by Jules Leleu, with two covered compartments, France, c1930, 50in (127cm) wide.

£9,000–11,000 Sotheby's

A parchment, sycamore, stamped leather, gilt-bronze and plastic secretaire cabinet, by André Arbus, France, c1937, 27¾in (70.5cm) wide.

£13,000–16,000 Sotheby's (NY)

A walnut sideboard, probably by Epstein, c1930, 66in (167.5cm) wide.
£2,400–2,700 Design Gallery

A Canadian silver birch, glass and brass desk, by T. H. Robsjohn-Gibbings, America, c1938, 52in (132cm) wide.
£5,500–6,500 Sotheby's (NY)

A painted wood stool, by Paul T. Frankl, America, c1925, 23½in (59.5cm) high.
£3,200–3,800 Sotheby's (NY)

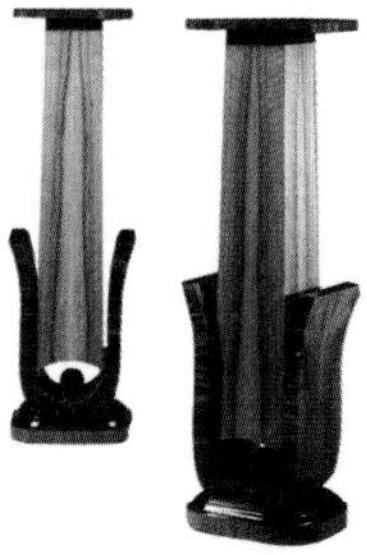

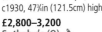

A pair of rosewood-veneered and ebonized stands, c1930, 47¾in (121.5cm) high.
£2,800–3,200 Sotheby's (O)

A chrome-plated steel and leather fire stool, by John Duncan Miller, c1930, 33½in (85cm) wide.
£5,000–6,000 Sotheby's

A walnut and leather stool, by Laszlo Hoenig, signed, c1935, 42½in (108cm) wide.
£7,000–8,500 Sotheby's
The decorator and designer Laszlo Hoenig had a gallery at South Audley Street, London, in the late 1930s.

A mahogany and amboyna-veneered dining suite, comprising a table and eight chairs, c1930, table 90½in (230cm) extended.
£2,300–2,750 Sotheby's (O)

A burr-walnut dining suite, by Epstein, comprising a table, six dining chairs, sideboard and cocktail cabinet, c1938, table 77½in (197cm) wide.
£6,500–8,000 Sotheby's (O)

A lacquered and pewter table, with engraved decoration, slight damage, Sweden, 1920s–30s, 33¾in (85.5cm) diam.
£4,500–5,500 Bukowskis

ESSENTIAL REFERENCE PIERRE CHAREAU

Pierre Chareau (1883–1950) was born in Bordeaux and initially worked in Paris for the famous English firm of Waring & Gillow who specialized in furniture and interior design. In 1919 Chareau set up his own practice as an architect and furniture designer in Paris and opened 'La Boutique' in 1924 specializing in lighting, furniture and interior design. He exhibited at many major exhibitions including the *Salon d'Automne* and the acclaimed *Exposition Internationale des Arts Décoratifs et Industriels Modernes* in 1925. With Jean Puiforcat he joined the *Union des Artistes Modernes* and during this period he formed friendships and artistic links with like-minded designers at the forefront of the avant-garde. Chareau favoured simplicity and functionality and the use of woods such as mahogany, rosewood and walnut. He was acclaimed as an innovator and guiding force behind modernist furniture design and accordingly his works have seen a huge upsurge in interest from collectors. This French walnut table c1924 is an excellent example of his work.

£55,000–65,000 Sotheby's (NY)

A Macassar ebony and brass side table, by Eugène Printz, France, c1928, 70½in (179cm) extended.

£20,000–25,000 Sotheby's (NY)

A maple and sycamore nest of three tables, by Betty Joel for Token Works, 1930s, 24in (61cm) high.

£600–700 Gorringes (L)

A walnut coffee table, c1930, 20in (51cm) high.

£340–380 Design Gallery

A cast-iron and marble centre table, by Edgar Brandt, France, c1930, 32in (81.5cm) wide.

£35,000–42,000 Sotheby's

An oak table, by Emile-Jacques Ruhlmann, entitled 'Bas Ducharne', France, c1930, 38in (96.5cm) diam.

£13,000–16,000 Sotheby's (NY)

A marble and wrought-iron console table, by Raymond Subes, France, c1935, 53¼in (152cm) wide.

£20,000–25,000 Sotheby's (NY)

A chrome and glass centre table, by Marc Lalique, entitled 'Cactus', France, c1949, 61¾in (157cm) diam.

£12,000–15,000 Sotheby's

An Art Deco chrome trolley, c1930, 33in (84cm) high.

£350–400 Design Gallery

WALL MIRRORS

An Arts & Crafts copper mirror, early 20thC, 21in (53.5cm) diam.
£230–260 LASSCO (bh)

An Arts & Crafts Liberty pewter mirror, inlaid with mother-of-pearl, maker's label, c1900, 34¼in (87cm) wide.
£3,200–3,800 Sotheby's (O)

An Arts & Crafts pewter mirror, set with Ruskin Pottery roundels, c1900, 18in (45.5cm) diam.
£400–450 Design Gallery

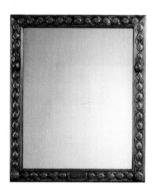

An Arts & Crafts carved oak mirror, entitled '4 Glorious Mysterie', c1900, 45¼ x 37¾in (115 x 96cm).
£1,400–1,800 Sotheby's (O)

An Arts & Crafts brass wall mirror, embossed with Celtic knots and scrolls, c1900, 29½in (75cm) wide.
£1,800–2,200 Sotheby's (O)

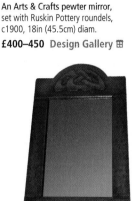

A Liberty patinated copper mirror, by Archibald Knox, c1900, 28in (71cm) high.
£2,700–3,000 James Strang

An oak, ebony, ivory and fruitwood wall mirror, by J. C. Altorf, the top carved with two ducks and four ebony monkeys, Holland, c1905, 30¾in (78cm) wide.
£7,500–9,000 Sotheby's (Am)

An Arts & Crafts copper wall mirror, embossed with stylized foliage, with a ceramic roundel, early 20thC, 30in (76cm) wide.
£1,300–1,600 Sotheby's (O)

An Arts & Crafts brass mirror, in the manner of P. W. Davidson, decorated with swallows and stylized trees, Scotland, dated 1926, 20½in (52cm) square.
£850–1,000 Lyon & Turnbull

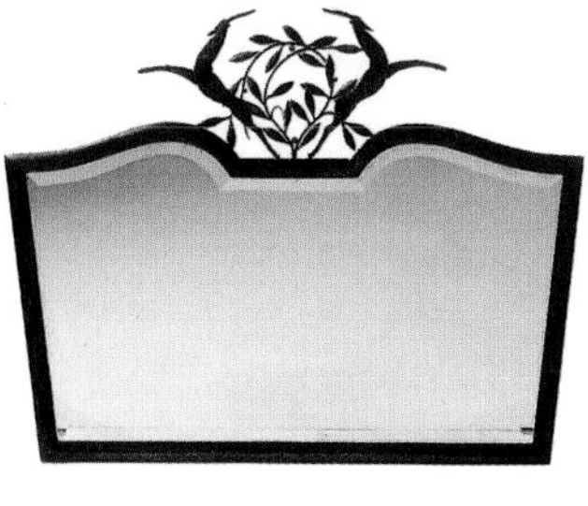

An iron wall mirror, by Edgar Brandt, surmounted with two stylized antelopes and foliage, stamped mark, France, c1930, 42in (106.5cm) wide.
£15,000–18,000 Sotheby's

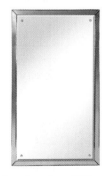

An Art Deco glass mirror, c1930, 38½ x 22½in (98 x 57cm).
£300–330 Design Gallery

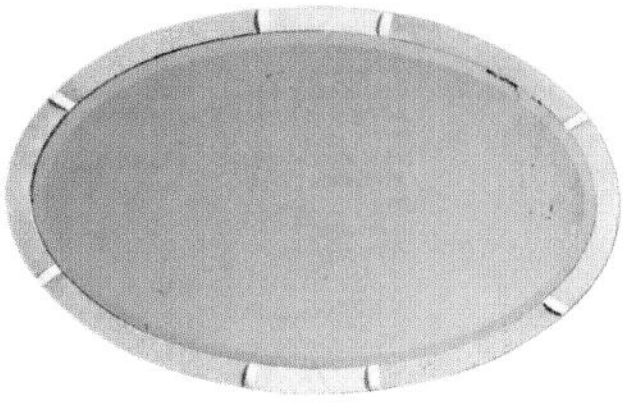

An Art Deco shagreen wall mirror, with ivorine mounts, c1930, 30¾in (78cm) wide.
£2,500–3,000 Sotheby's (O)

DECORATIVE ARTS CLOCKS

An Art Nouveau bronze figural clock, by Sam Grün, the clock with foundry seal for Jollet & Co, on a marble base with gilt-bronze mounts, France, c1890, 16½in (42cm) wide.

£3,200–3,800 Freeman's

A Liberty & Co silver mantel clock, by Archibald Knox, the enamelled dial with a single train movement, the base decorated with a stylized plant motif, Birmingham 1903, 4in (10cm) high.

£4,000–5,000 Lyon & Turnbull

An Art Deco *faux* shagreen, Perspex and tin clock, with an eight-day movement, shagreen restored, slight damage, France, 1930s, 9in (23cm) wide.

£180–200 collectorsworld

ESSENTIAL REFERENCE LIBERTY'S TUDRIC RANGE

Liberty's Tudric pewter range was inspired by early Elizabethan pewter. Eminent designer Archibald Knox produced many designs for the new range which proved to be enormously popular. His individual style was influenced by Celtic and Medieval art and he was employed on many of Liberty's Cymric silver and Tudric pewter wares. Marks included 'English Pewter' and a stamped model number to correspond with those kept in Liberty's pattern books. Some Tudric pewter carries the additional 'Solkets' stamp, which was simply the telegraphic address of Liberty's principal metalware manufacturer W. H. Haseler whose speciality was solitaires and lockets, the name 'Solkets' deriving from a combination of the two words. Liberty metalware has a universal appeal and remains very collectable. This Liberty pewter and enamel clock c1902 was designed by Archibald Knox and is 8in (20.5cm) high.

£5,750–6,500 Esoteric

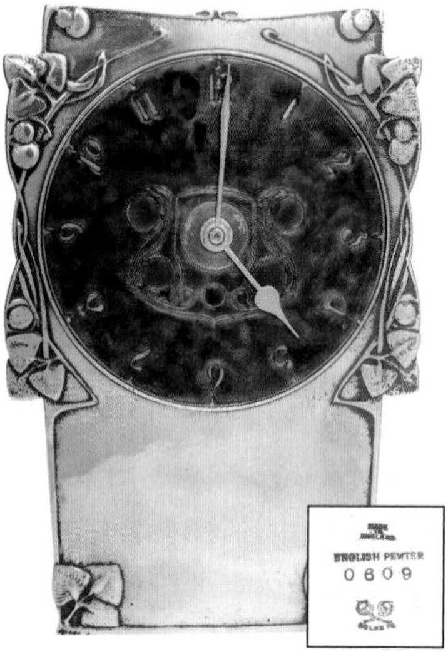

A Tiffany & Co guilloche enamel clock, on an agate scroll-carved base, marked, America, early 20thC, 2½in (6.5cm) high.

£1,400–1,700 Freeman's

A burrwood, metal and glass Telechron clock, by Gilbert Rohde for Herman Miller, with World's Fair label, America, 1934, 13in (33cm) wide.

£2,000–2,400 Sotheby's (NY)

TEXTILES

A Glasgow School silk chairback, worked in wool with Glasgow-style roses and foliage, Scotland, c1905, 25in (63.5cm) wide.

£90–100 decorative arts@doune

An Art Deco crewelwork coverlet, worked in chain lock stitch with a stylized leaf pattern, America, c1925, 69 x 66in (175.5 x 167.5cm).

£270–330 Jackson's

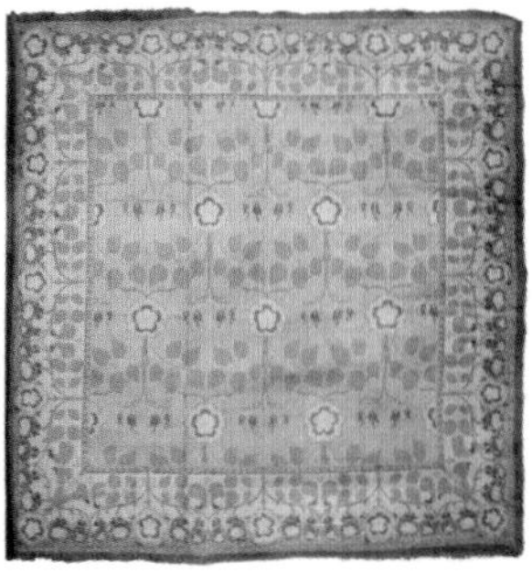

A hand-knotted wool carpet, after a design by C. F. A. Voysey, by Alexander Morton & Co, entitled 'The Rose', slight damage and losses, Ireland, Donegal, c1900, 165 x 161in (419 x 409cm).

£25,000–30,000 Sotheby's

A Celtic Revivalist School hand-knotted wool carpet, Ireland, c1905, 140 x 107in (357 x 272cm).

£11,000–13,000 Sotheby's

A wool carpet, by Ivan da Silva Bruhns, with woven signature, France, c1925, 113 x 92in (287 x 233.5cm).

£25,000–30,000 Sotheby's (NY)

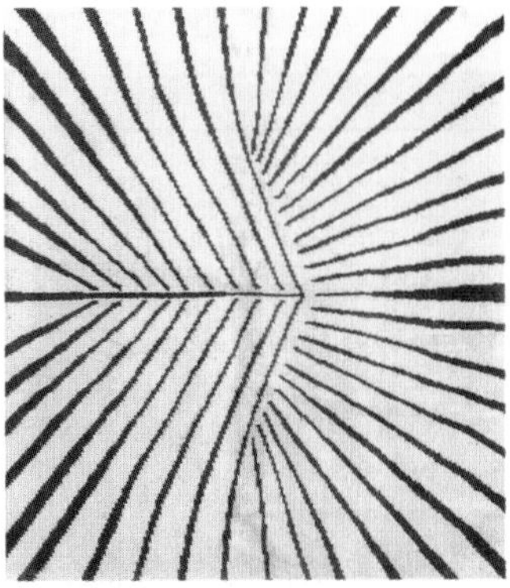

A wool carpet, by Evelyn Wyld, America, c1928, 86 x 82in (218.5 x 208.5cm).

£6,000–7,000 Sotheby's (NY)

An Art Deco wool carpet, decorated with a geometric design, France, 1930s, 80 x 54in (203 x 137cm).

£1,100–1,300 Treadway Gallery

An Art Nouveau glove box, worked in wool with Glasgow-style roses and foliate bands, c1920, 13in (33cm) wide.

£45–50 decorative arts@doune

A Morris & Co wool hanging, by William Morris, decorated with the Tulip and Rose pattern, designed 1875, 82¾ x 32½in (210 x 82.5cm).

£1,200–1,500 Lyon & Turnbull

An embroidered panel, designed by Jessie M. King, worked by Madame Elise Prioleau, c1910, 5in (12.5cm) wide.

£3,400–3,800 James Strang

A Glasgow School fabric panel, worked in wool with Glasgow-style roses and applied beadwork borders, Scotland, c1910, 7in (18cm) wide.

£35–40 decorative arts@doune

BOOK COVERS

William-Cedric Chivers, cover for *The Recuyell of the Historyes of Troye,* published by Kelmscott Press, 1896, large 4°, 2 vols.

£3,000–3,600 Sotheby's

Tom Freud, cover for *David the Dreamer, His Book of Dreams* by Ralph Bergengren, published by Atlantic Monthly Press, Boston, first edition, 1922, oblong 4°, gilt cloth, slight damage.

£200–250 Freeman's

Joseph Conrad and Ford M. Hueffer, cover for *The Inheritors,* first edition, 1901, 8° cloth.

£600–700 Bloomsbury

Jessie Marion King, cover for *The Life of Saint Mary Magdalen,* published by John Lane, 1904, 8in (20.5cm) high.

£230–250 decorative arts@doune

Talwin Morris, cover for *English Literary Criticism,* published by Blackie & Son, 1903, 7½in (19cm) high.

£70–80 decorative arts@doune

Charles Robinson, cover for *A Child's Garden of Verses,* by Robert Louis Stevenson, published by John Lane, The Bodley Head, 1921, 9in (23cm) high.

£115–125 George Bayntun

ESSENTIAL REFERENCE BOOK COVERS

For book collectors there are numerous examples of striking Art Nouveau bindings and the book covers of Talwin Morris and Jessie Marion King are especially popular. Jessie King was a multi-talented artist in a variety of disciplines but is perhaps best known for her finely executed pen and ink drawings. Talwin Morris was art manager for the famous publishing house Blackie & Son of Glasgow from 1893 to 1911. His book covers are both delightful and varied, with strikingly innovative designs and a personal sensitivity to colour. Characteristically they include stylized bud and leaf motifs, a distinctive Glasgow-style sans serif type and architectural framework. Morris's books are collected by enthusiasts throughout the world. Talwin Morris designed this cover for *The Dash for Khartoum* by G. A. Henty, published by Blackie's Colonial Library, c1900, 7½in (19cm) high.

£230–250 decorative arts@doune

ILLUSTRATIONS

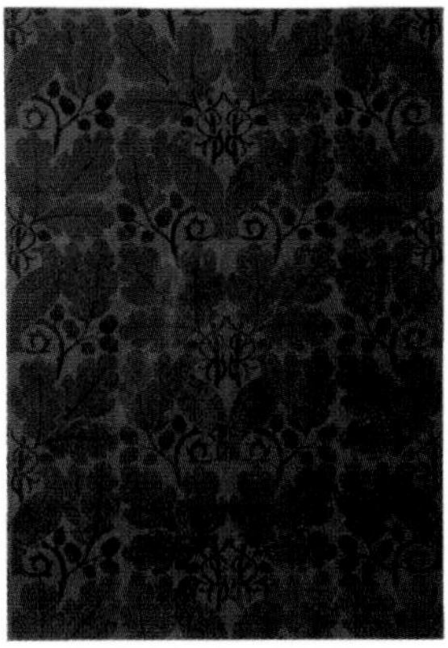

C. F. A. Voysey, a wallpaper/textile proof for Alexander Morton & Co, c1895, 29in (73.5cm) high.

£3,000–3,500 James Strang

Samuel L. Schmucker, 'Autumn', gouache, watercolour and ink on paper, original illustration for the unpublished series 'Woman's Seasons', America, early 20thC, 11 x 7in (28 x 18cm).

£1,400–1,700 Jackson's

A pair of Arts & Crafts Motto prints, 'A Drop of Ink may make a Million Think' and 'There's Naething mair Precious nor Time', by Taber-Prang & Co, in oak frames decorated with copper studs, c1906, 13¾ x 20½in (35 x 52cm).

£160–200 Special Auction Services

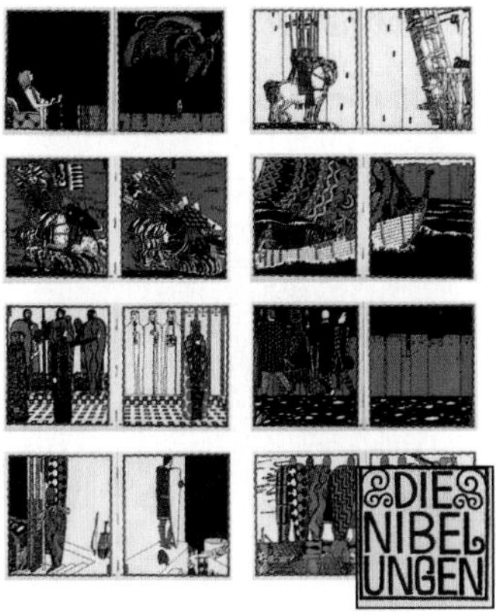

Carl Otto Czeschka, *Die Nibelungen*, with coloured woodblock images and text, each with artist's initials and date, stamped 'Beleg-Exemplar', designed 1908–9, 6 x 5½in (15 x 14cm).

£1,000–1,200 Sotheby's (O)

Leon Bakst, a design for the costumes titled 'Juives', numbered 23, for the ballet *Cleopatra*, hand-written inscription to reverse, France, 1909, 13¼ x 9½in (33.5 x 24cm).

£5,000–6,000 Sotheby's (P)

E. A. Taylor, design on paper for a stained glass window, in a wood frame, Scotland, c1910, 15 x 6in (38 x 15cm).

£3,500–4,000 James Strang

E. A. Taylor was a Glasgow School artist.

Louis Icart, 'Coursing II', a print of a dancing woman with leaping hounds, signed, with 'L. I. Paris' blindstamp and stamped with a windmill motif, No. 415 of edition of 500, France, 1929, 18½ x 28¼in (47 x 72cm).

£2,200–2,700 Sotheby's (O)

Louis Icart, 'Dalila', a colour etching and aquatint, signed and inscribed '159', with 'L.I. Paris' blindstamp, France, 1929, 20¾ x 14in (52.5 x 35.5cm).

£450–550 Freeman's

TWENTIETH-CENTURY DESIGN

GLASS

A Whitefriars moulded glass vase, by William Wilson, 1938, 10in (25.5cm) high.
£100–120 Frank Dux

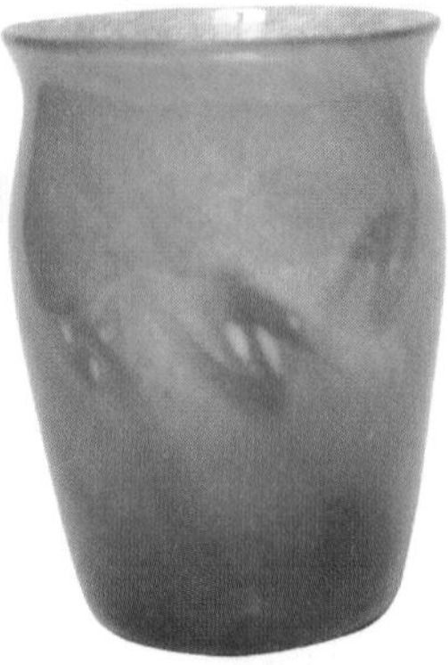

A Nazeing Glassworks glass vase, 1930s, 6½in (16.5cm) high.
£90–100 Ruskin Decorative Arts

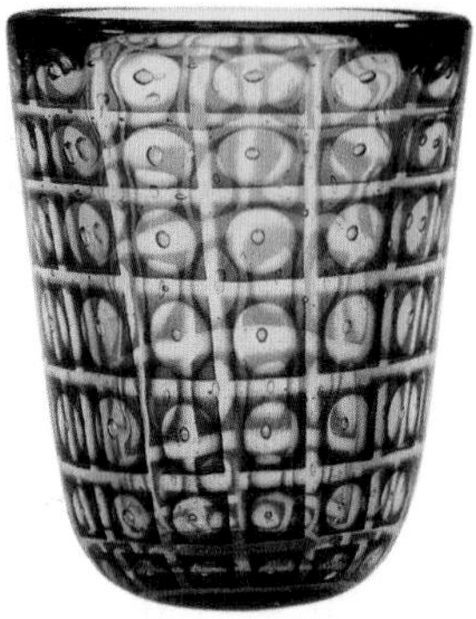

An Orrefors glass Graal vase, by Edward Hald, with presentation inscription, Sweden, 1939, 8¼in (21cm) high.
£2,700–3,300 Bukowskis

A glass bowl, possibly Barovier, with gilt inclusions and bands of bubbles, Italy, c1940, 12in (30.5cm) diam.
£1,200–1,500 Sotheby's (O)

An Orrefors-style glass vase, with red interior, Scandinavia, 1950s–60s, 11in (28cm) diam.
£75–85 Frank Dux

An Orrefors glass vase, by Simon Gate, Sweden, c1940, 12½in (32cm) high.
£450–500 James Strang

An Orrefors glass Edvin vase, by Edvin Öhrström, signed, Sweden, 1945, 6¼in (16cm) high.
£6,500–8,000 Bukowskis

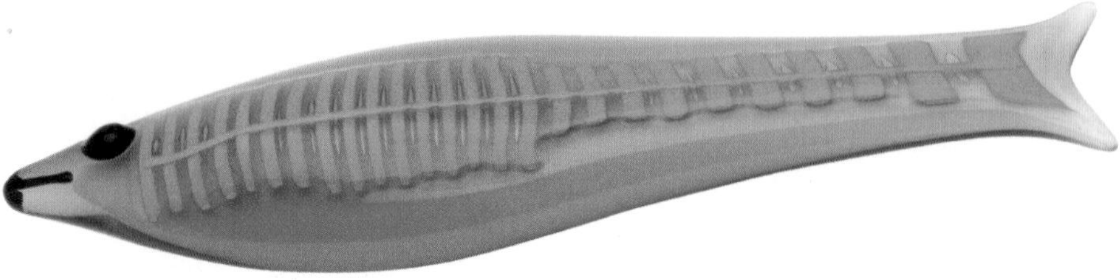

A Venini glass model of a fish, by Kenneth George Scott, Italy, early 1950s, 13½in (34.5cm) long.
£750–900 Rago Arts

A set of 12 Venini drinking glasses, attributed to Gio Ponti, with cane decoration, Italy, Murano, 1950s, largest 4¼in (11cm) high.

£2,200–2,600 **Sotheby's (Am)**

A Venini glass wine jug, Italy, 1950s, 8in (20.5cm) high.

£100–120 **20th Century Marks**

A Venini glass jug, with cane decoration, stamped mark, Italy, mid-1950s, 10in (25.5cm) high.

£550–650 **Rago Arts**

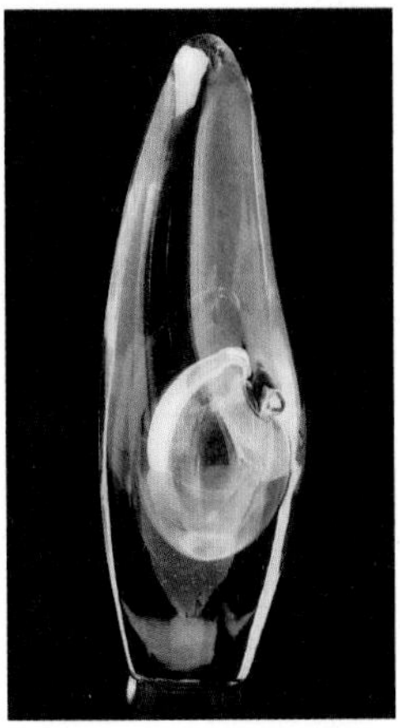

A Iittala glass sculpture, by Timo Sarpaneva, entitled 'Orchid', Finland, 1954, 13in (33cm) high.

£2,000–2,500
Bukowskis (F)

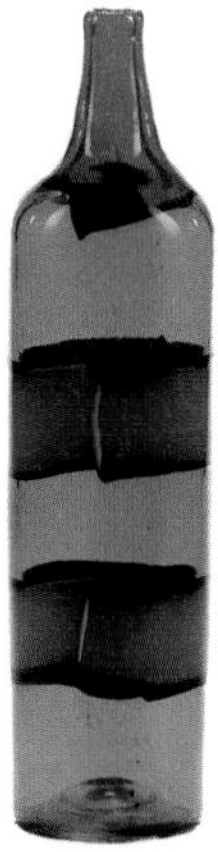

A Venini glass vase, attributed to F. Bianconi, marked, Italy, Murano, 1950s, 14½in (37cm) high.

£1,300–1,600
Sotheby's (Am)

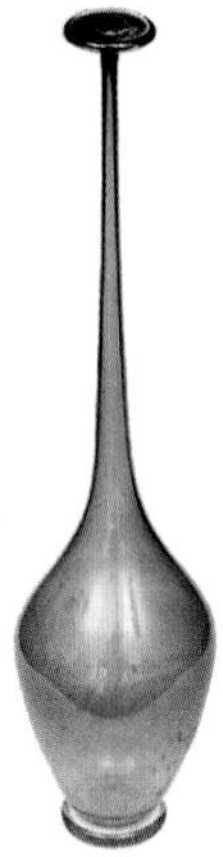

An Orrefors glass Tulip vase, by Nils Landberg, Sweden, c1961, 13¼in (33.5cm) high.

£550–650 **Bamfords**

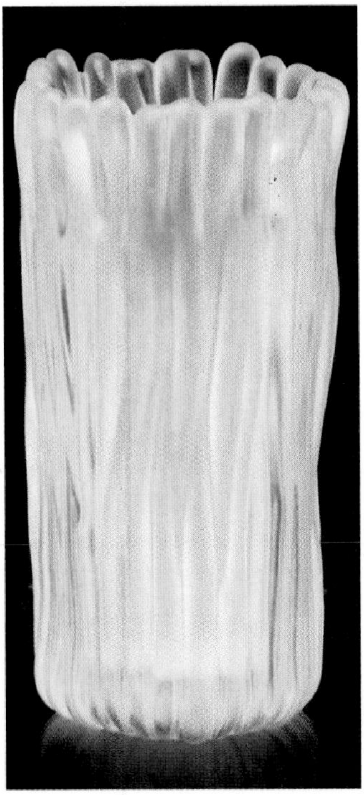

An Iittala glass Jäkälä vase, by Tapio Wirkkala, signed, Finland, 1957, 9in (23cm) high.

£500–600 **Bukowskis (F)**

A Kosta glass vase, by Vicke Lindstrand, engraved with fish, with simulated seaweed, signed with serial number to the base, Sweden, c1959, 9in (23cm) high.

£550–620 **Afford Decorative Arts**

An Orrefors smoked glass vase, Sweden, c1960, 9½in (24cm) high.

£180–200
Ruskin Decorative Arts

A Whitefriars cut-glass vase, by Geoffrey Baxter, c1960, 8in (20.5cm) high.
£180–200 **Ruskin Decorative Arts**

A Whitefriars cased glass vase, by James Powell, 1960s, 12in (30.5cm) high.
£250–280 **Ruskin Decorative Arts**

A Holmegaard cased glass vase, Denmark, c1960, 9in (23cm) high.
£200–225 **Ruskin Decorative Arts**

A Holmegaard-Kastrup cased glass Gul vase, Denmark, 1960s, 17in (43cm) high.
£250–285 **Ruskin Decorative Arts**

An Alsterfors cased glass vase, by Po Ström, Sweden, c1960, 7in (18cm) high.
£120–135 **Ruskin Decorative Arts**

A Whitefriars glass Hoop vase, by Geoffrey Baxter, 1967–73, 11in (28cm) high.
£230–270 **Lawrence Fine Art**

ESSENTIAL REFERENCE VICKE LINDSTRAND

Vicke (Viktor Emanuel) Lindstrand was born in 1904 in Gothenburg, Sweden. In 1928, after studying commercial art for a year, he was hired by glass artist Simon Gate to work at the Orrefors glassworks. Lindstrand added new artistic dimensions to the already famous Orrefors glass with his unique designs and revitalization of classic forms and techniques. During his time at Orrefors he worked on engraved glass and Graal vases and, with sculptor Edvin Öhrström, developed the Ariel technique. Orrefors could not afford to keep Lindstrand during WWII, so between 1943 and 1950 he became creative director at Upsala-Ekeby, working with ceramic. During this period he designed many different stoneware objects ranging from pots to figural sculptures. In 1950 he moved to Kosta, where he once again worked with glass until his retirement in 1973. During that period he developed such forms as 'Trees in the Fog' and 'Autumn'. Vicke Lindstrand died in 1983. This Kosta vase by Vicke Lindstrand is decorated with internal glass canes and bears a date code for 1963. **£700–800** **Afford Decorative Arts**

A Holmegaard glass vase, by Michael Bang, Napoli series, Denmark, 1969–71, 10in (25.5cm) high.
£110–125 Coltman Antiques

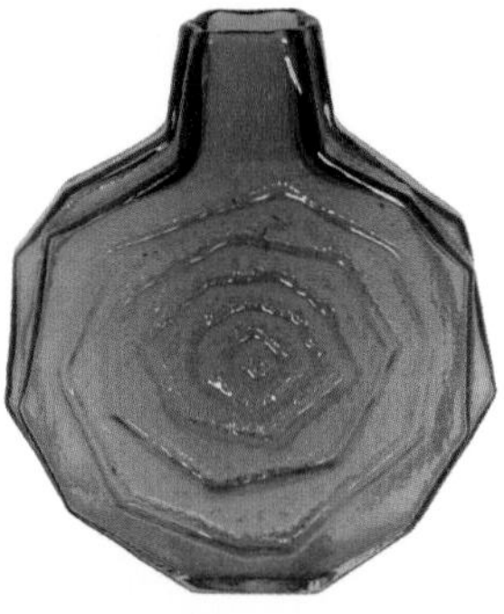

A Whitefriars Banjo glass vase, by Geoffrey Baxter, pattern No. 9681, c1970, 12½in (32cm) high.
£650–800 Bearnes

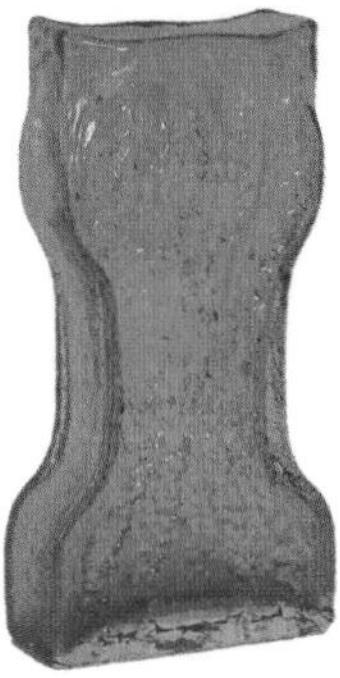

A Whitefriars glass vase, by Geoffrey Baxter, c1970, 12¾in (32.5cm) high.
£650–800 Bearnes

A Sam Herman iridescent glass vase, applied with raised banding and shoulders, engraved mark, America, dated 1971, 9½in (24cm) high.
£500–600 Rosebery's

A Kosta Boda glass bowl, by Kjell Engman, painted with birds, engraved marks, Sweden, c1970, 5¾in (14.5cm) high.
£100–120 Special Auction Services

A Kosta glass bowl, by Paul Hoff, decorated with a fish, Sweden, c1970s, 10in (25.5cm) diam.
£350–400 Coltman Antiques

A glass sculpture, by Tom Patti, signed, America, dated 1978, 2¾in (7cm) high.
£7,000–8,500 Rago Arts

A Holmegaard glass Carnaby vase, by Per Lutken, Denmark, 1970s, 12in (30.5cm) high.
£165–185 Richard Wallis Antiks

A Murano glass decanter with stopper and six tumblers, Italy, 1970s, 16¼in (41.5cm) high.
£100–120 Sotheby's (O)

An Orrefors glass Graal vase, by Eva Englund, signed, Sweden, dated 1979, 15½in (39.5cm) high.
£2,500–3,000 Bukowskis

A glass vase, by Charles Lotton, signed, America, dated 1981, 6in (15cm) high.
£400–500
Cincinnati Art Galleries

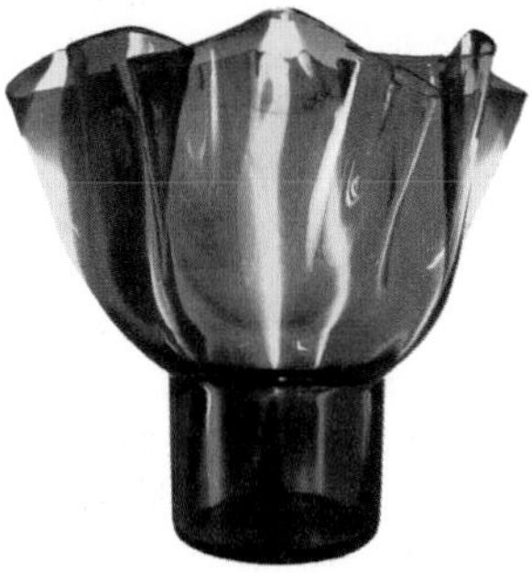

A Venini glass Kukinto handkerchief vase, by Timo Sarpaneva, engraved mark, Italy, Murano, dated 1992, 15¾in (40cm) high.
£750–900 Webb's

CERAMICS

A State Porcelain Manufactory cup and saucer, Imperial cypher for Alexander III, marked, Russia, dated 1922.

£2,500–3,000 Sotheby's (O)

A Sèvres pottery vase, printed mark, France, early 20thC, 11¼in (28cm) high.

£700–850 Sotheby's (O)

An earthenware vase and cover, by Jean Besnard, incised mark, France, 1930s, 9in (23cm) high.

£2,500–3,000 Sotheby's

A Winchcombe Pottery jug, by Michael Cardew, c1930, 5in (12.5cm) high.

£450–500 Offa's Dyke

A Winchcombe Pottery glazed earthenware three-handled vase, by Michael Cardew, with etched decoration, c1940, 7½in (19cm) high.

£450–550 Canterbury Auctions

A Gustavsberg faïence vase, by Stig Lindberg, signed, impressed factory stamp, Sweden, 1940s–50s, 15½in (39.5cm) high.

£500–600 Bukowskis

A Peter Voulkos glazed earthenware vase, incised mark, America, dated 1951, 13¾in (35cm) high.

£15,000–18,000 Sotheby's (NY)

This vase was completed during Voulkos' first year of residence at the Archie Bray Foundation and is typical of the narrow-necked bottle forms with the wax-resistant decoration that dominated his early ceramic output. The Foundation, founded in 1951, is an artistic institution in Helena, Montana, dedicated to developing the skills of ceramic artists since the 1950s.

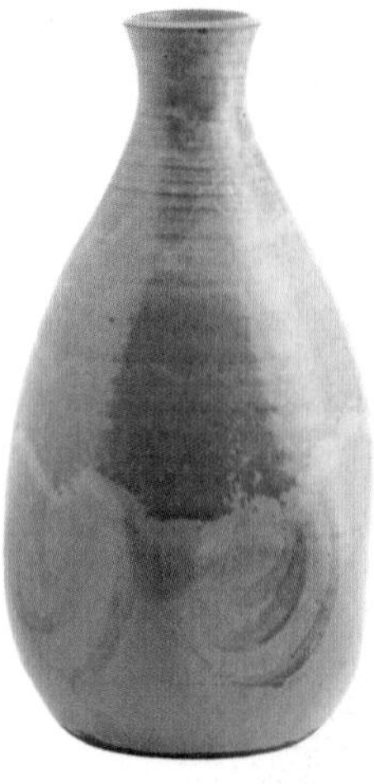

A Peter Voulkos earthenware jug, with celadon glaze, signed, slight damage, America, 1953, 11½in (29cm) high.

£1,400–1,700 Rago Arts

A Wedgwood Persephone tea service, by Eric Ravilious, printed and impressed marks, date code for 1954.

£375–450 Sworders

A Brooklin Pottery vase, by Theo and Susan Harlander, stamped mark, Canada, 1950s, 3in (7.5cm) high.

£180–220 Waddington's

A set of six Piero Fornasetti porcelain cups, Italy, 1950s.
£110–125 20th Century Marks

A ceramic plaque, by Rut Bryk, decorated with butterflies, signed, Finland, 1950s, 10in (25.5cm) wide.
£450–550 Bukowskis (F)

A Tobo stoneware vase, by Erik and Ingrid Triller, signed, Sweden, mid-20thC, 8¼in (21cm) high.
£600–700 Bukowskis
The Tobo stoneware workshop was in production from 1935 to 1973.

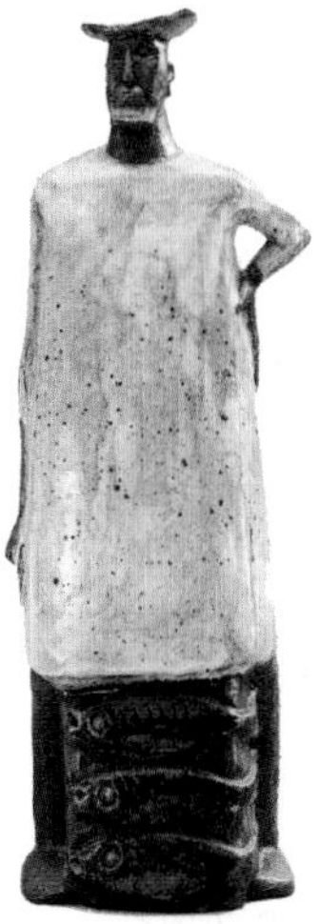

A Höganäs stoneware figure, by Åke Holm, signed, light damage, Sweden, 1950s, 18½in (47cm) high.
£3,000–3,500 Bukowskis

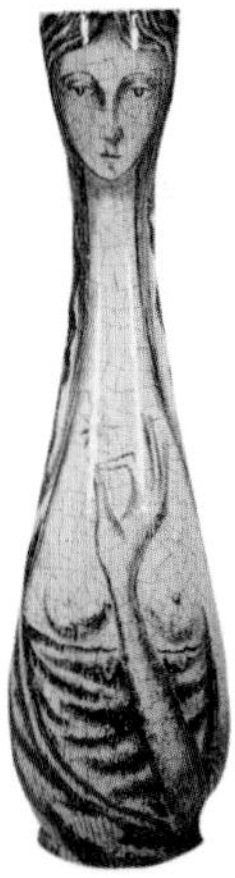

A San Dolo Susanna vase, painted marks, Italy, 1950–75, 40¼in (102cm) high.
£3,800–4,500 Sotheby's (O)

A Gustavsberg Farsta jar, by Wilhelm Kåge, signed, Sweden, 1958, 14¾in (37.5cm) high.
£7,000–8,000 Bukowskis

A Gustavsberg stoneware vase, by Berndt Friberg, signed, Sweden, 1962, 24½in (62cm) high.
£5,750–7,000 Bukowskis

A Gustavsberg stoneware vase, by Stig Lindberg, signed, Sweden, 1962, 16in (40.5cm) high.
£3,200–3,800 Bukowskis

A Troika pottery Urn vase, attributed to Benny Sirota, decorated with Aztec symbols, incised mark, c1963, 10in (25cm) high.
£700–850 Special Auction Services

A pottery vase, by Roy Thomas, 1966, 13in (33cm) high.

£75–85 20th Century Marks

A Troika wheel vase, by Marilyn Pascoe, 1968–74, 7in (18cm) high.

£175–200 Gorringes (L)

A Troika vase, by Marilyn Pascoe, inscribed mark, c1972, 14in (35.5cm) high.

£400–500 Sworders

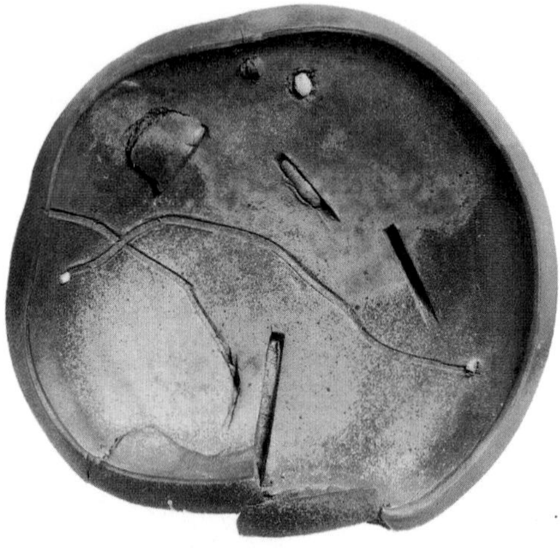

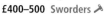

A Peter Voulkos earthenware and porcelain plate, signed, America, dated 1980, 21¾in (55.5cm) diam.

£7,000–8,000 Sotheby's (NY)

A Troika wheel vase, by Colin Carbis, painted mark, 1976–77, 6¾in (17cm) diam.

£180–220 Bearnes

A Harvey Goldman earthenware vessel, marked, America, 1981, 5in (12.5cm) high.

£300–350 Rago Arts

A Robert Turner Ashanti stoneware vessel, incised signature, America, c1982, 13½in (34.5cm) high.

£2,500–3,000 Sotheby's (NY)

PICASSO CERAMICS

YOU TOO COULD OWN a Picasso for £1,000. While auction prices for the artist's major works have started to nudge the £55,000,000 barrier there remains a field of Picasso's oeuvre that continues to perform steadily and reasonably at the heart of the middle market. Picasso's ceramic works were executed during the last few decades of his life, after a period of profound personal and artistic crisis during WWII. Having discovered the Madoura studio at Vallauris in 1946, Picasso demonstrated his remarkable versatility and mastery of colour and expression through this new and unexplored medium. In a wonderfully successful partnership with Suzanne and Georges Ramié between 1947 and 1966 he produced over 600 separate editions that are crucial to understanding his art in the later years of his life. Present across this body of work are all of the hallmarks of his greatest innovative achievements: the faces of his lovers, cubist motifs, the matadors, and his devotion to sensuality all executed in a joyously willful manner.

In 2005, the first of Sotheby's annual auctions of Picasso's work offered examples from the entire series at a variety of estimates from £1,000 to £20,000. The record result for a ceramic work was achieved in 2004 at Sotheby's New York, reaching £120,000 for a unique plate featuring the profile of his young lover Jacqueline. This is perhaps the key to understanding the relative commercial potential of each work; the combination of subject, edition size and sculptural form. Despite being produced in larger editions, colourful faces painted and glazed onto plates tend to achieve the highest prices along with his feminine subjects and naïve animal figures. While the last 18 months have witnessed a strengthening in this market the fact that the works were executed in series ranging between 25 and 500 allows potential bidders to pragmatically put a cap on the level to which they will stay in the game. As a result, while elsewhere at Sotheby's bidders were paying a staggering £48 million for a 1941 portrait of his sometime lover Dora Maar, those present at the Picasso ceramics auction were taking home equally iconic images from the artist's studio for less than £5,000. Demand for Picasso's work will always be strong but in a time where all but the most obscure artists can achieve heady auction results given the right exposure it is refreshing to be able to offer an insight into the work of one of the world's greatest masters at levels that are open to all.

Ralph Taylor

A Pablo Picasso bowl, AR No. 256, edition of 100, stamped mark, France, dated 1955, 7in (18cm) diam.

£1,200–1,500 Leonard Joel

The AR numbers quoted refer to Alain Ramie's *Catalogue de l'Oeuvre Céramique Edité 1947–71*, published by Galerie Madoura in 1988.

A Pablo Picasso earthenware dish, 'Taureau dans l'Arène', AR No. 80, with painted decoration, marked 'Edition Picasso Madoura Plein Feu...Exemplaire Editeur', France, c1948, 15½in (39.5cm) wide.

£13,000–16,000 Sotheby's (O)

An exemplaire éditeur *is effectively a proof for the artist (or Madoura in this case) to keep for their records. They form part of the series but are outside the edition and, in the case of Picasso ceramics, just as valuable. This dish is the artist's proof for an edition of 450.*

A Pablo Picasso earthenware dish, 'Poisson Fond Noir', AR No. 167, edition of 100, with painted decoration, stamped mark, France, 1952, 16½in (42cm) wide.

£3,500–4,200 Sotheby's (O)

A Pablo Picasso earthenware dish, 'Nature Morte à la Cuiller', AR No. 165, edition of 200, with painted decoration, stamped mark, France, 1952, 13in (33cm) square.

£2,000–2,400 Sotheby's (O)

A Pablo Picasso earthenware plate, 'Bouquet à la Pomme', AR No. 307, edition of 400, with painted decoration, stamped mark, France, dated 1956, 10in (25.5cm) diam.

£3,300–4,000 Sotheby's (O)

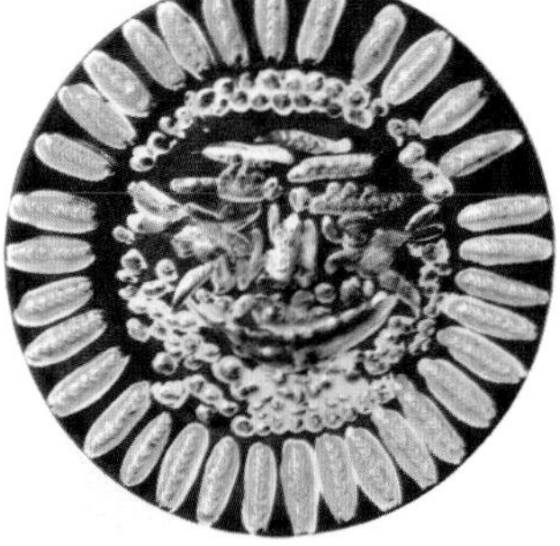

A Pablo Picasso earthenware plate, 'Visage Tourmenté', AR No. 360, edition of 100, with painted decoration, stamped mark, France, 1956, 16½in (42cm) diam.

£4,000–5,000 Sotheby's (O)

A Pablo Picasso earthenware plate, 'Visage aux Feuilles', AR No. 324, proof for edition of 100, with painted decoration, stamped mark, France, 1956, 16½in (42cm) diam.

£4,000–5,000 Sotheby's (O)

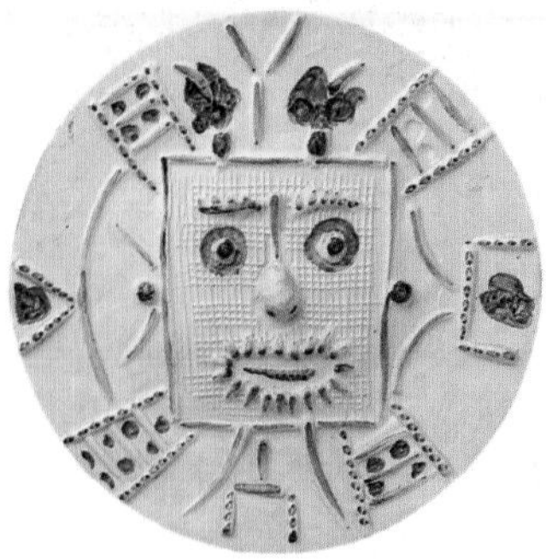

A Pablo Picasso earthenware plate, 'Visage dans un Carré', AR No. 354, edition of 100, with painted decoration, stamped mark, France, 1956, 16½in (42cm) diam.

£14,000–17,000 Sotheby's (O)

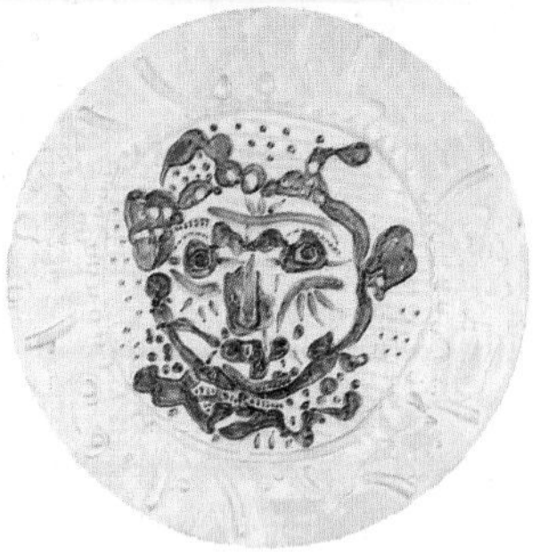

A Pablo Picasso earthenware plate, 'Visage de Faune Tourmenté', AR No. 319, edition of 100, with painted decoration, stamped mark, France, 1956, 16½in (42cm) diam.

£4,000–5,000 Sotheby's (O)

A Pablo Picasso earthenware plate, entitled 'Personnages No. 28', AR No. 463, edition of 150, with painted decoration, marked Exemplaire Editeur, France, 1963, 10in (25.5cm) diam.

£3,800–4,500 Sotheby's (O)

A Pablo Picasso earthenware plate, entitled 'Oiseau No. 83', AR No. 483, edition of 200, with painted decoration, marked Exemplaire Editeur, France, 1963, 10in (25.5cm) diam.

£1,100–1,300 Sotheby's (O)

A Pablo Picasso earthenware jug, entitled 'Pichet Gothique aux Oiseaux', AR No. 187, edition of 100, firing faults, marked, France, 1953, 11½in (29cm) high.

£4,000–5,000 Bukowskis

A Pablo Picasso earthenware jug, 'Visage', AR No. 288, edition of 500, with painted decoration, France, 1955, 12in (30.5cm) high.

£2,000–2,400 Freeman's

A Pablo Picasso earthenware vase, 'Chouetton', AR No. 135, edition of 500, with painted decoration, stamped mark, France, 1952, 10¼in (26cm) high.

£2,500–3,000 Sotheby's (O)

A Pablo Picasso earthenware vase, 'Vase Deux Anses Hautes', AR No. 213, edition of 400, damaged and repaired, stamped mark, France, 1953, 15in (38cm) high.

£3,500–4,200 Freeman's

METALWARE

A chromed-metal tantalus, with a key, c1930, 12in (30.5cm) wide.
£1,400–1,700 Sotheby's (O)

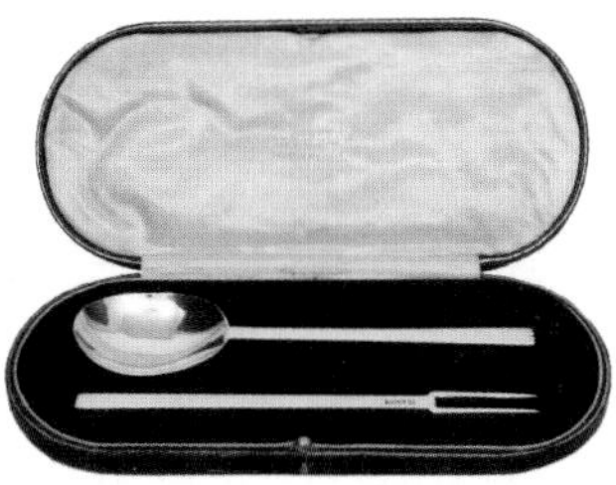

A silver christening set, by Thomas Bradbury & Son, Sheffield 1924, with a fitted case, 8in (20.5cm) long.
£270–300 James Strang

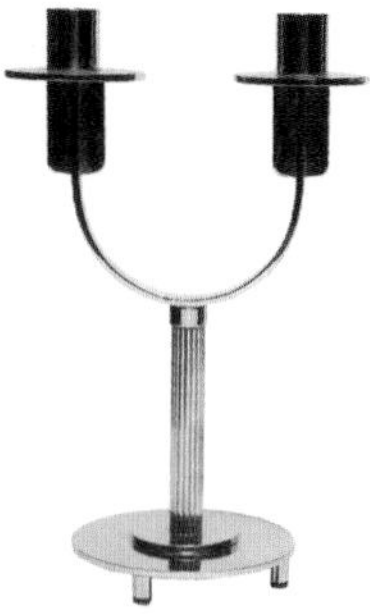

A pair of chrome-plated candlesticks, by Serge Chermayeff, c1936, 13in (33cm) high.
£1,100–1,200 James Strang

A silver powder bowl and cover, by Ian A. R. Davidson, the finial set with moonstones and red cabochons, Scotland, Edinburgh 1952, 6¾in (17cm) high, 11oz.
£1,300–1,600 Lyon & Turnbull

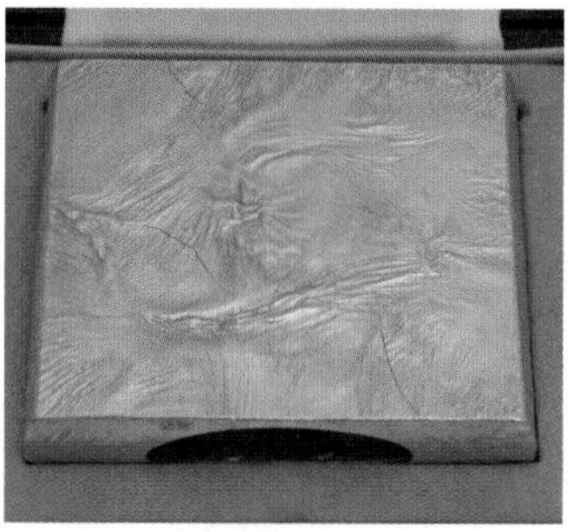

A Cartier 9ct gold cigarette case, 1954, in original case, 3½in (9cm) wide.
£1,600–1,750 Shapiro

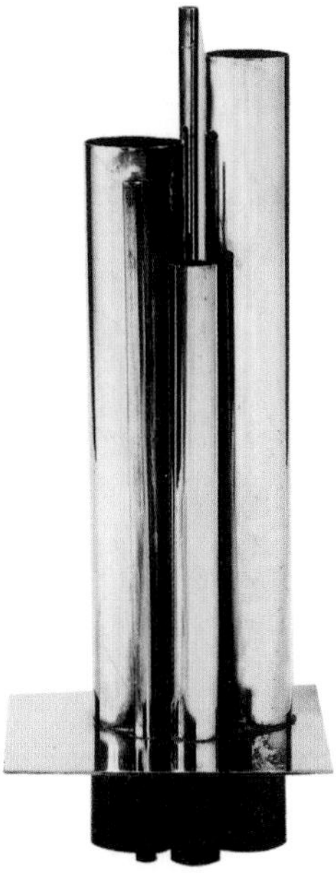

A silver-plated Orgue vase, by Gio Ponti, signed 'Christofle', France, 1956, 13in (33cm) high.
£1,500–1,800 Sotheby's (P)

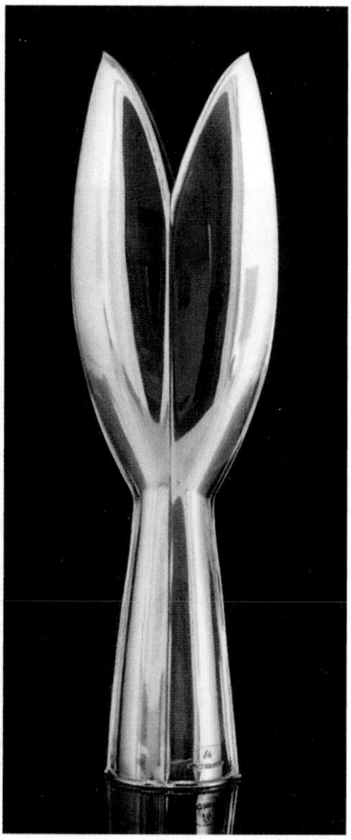

A Kultakeskus silver vase, by Tapio Wirkkala, signed, Finland, 1957, 9¾in (24.5cm) high.
£800–1,000 Bukowskis (F)

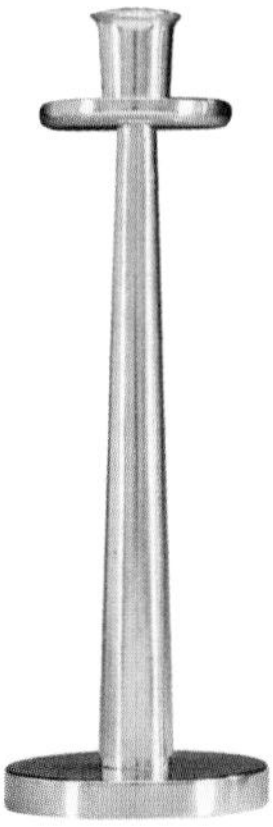

A pair of silver candlesticks, by Åke Strömdahl for Hugo Strömdahl, Sweden, Stockholm 1959, 9in (23cm) high.
£850–1,000 Bukowskis

A silver bowl and cover, by Gerald Benney, London 1964, 8½in (21.5cm) diam, 29oz.
£850–1,000 Lyon & Turnbull

A Dunhill chromed-metal and leatherette cigarette box, in the form of a die, stamped maker's marks, 1960s, 3½in (9cm) wide.
£1,200–1,500 Sotheby's (O)

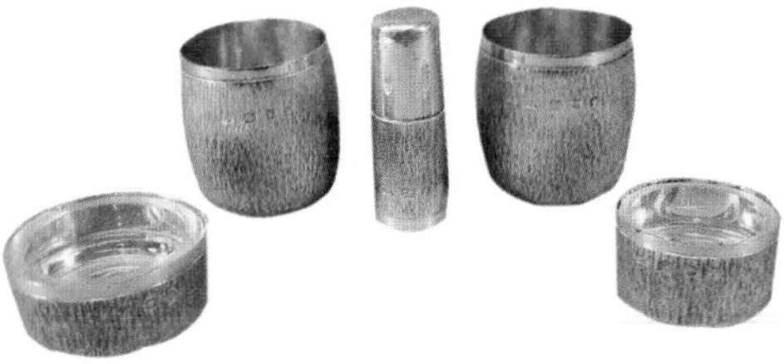

A silver condiment set, by Gerald Benney, comprising five pieces, with gilt lining, London 1972, stirrup cup 4in (10cm) high, 22½oz.

£800–1,000 **Penrith Farmers' & Kidd's**

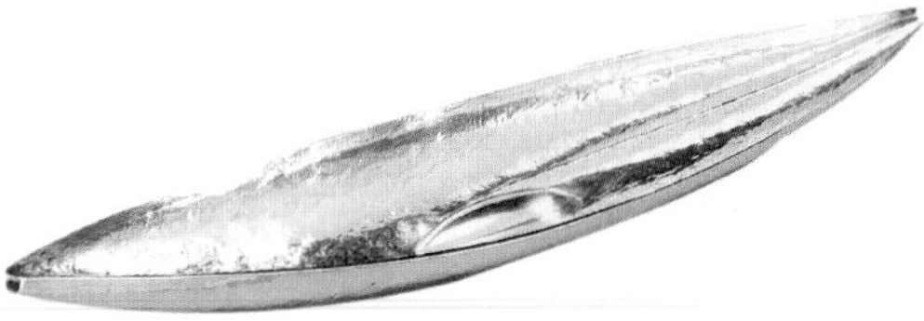

A bowl, by Tapio Wirkkala for Hopeakeskus, in the form of a boat, marked, Swedish import marks, Finland, 1972, designed 1954, 21¼in (54cm) long.

£8,200–9,800 **Bukowskis**

SCULPTURE

A bronze sculpture, by Abbott L. Pattison, on a marble base, signed, America, c1950, 13½in (34.5cm) high.

£800–1,000 **Treadway Gallery**

A bronze sculpture, by Harry Bertoia, entitled 'Panel', America, 1950s, 35¾in (91cm) high.

£6,500–8,000 **Sotheby's (NY)**

An ebony sculpture, by Alexandre Noll, France, 1950s, 10¼in (26cm) high.

£6,500–8,000 **Sotheby's (NY)**

A bronze sculpture, by Lynn Chadwick, entitled 'Maquette for Winged Figure III', edition of four, signed, 1961, 10½in (26.5cm) high.

£20,000–25,000 **Bloomsbury**

Lynn Chadwick (1914–2003) is considered to be one of the foremost British artists of post-WWII. He came to notice at the Venice Biennale *in 1952 and won the International Prize for Sculpture in Venice in 1956. His works are held in many of the great public collections of Europe, North and South America and Japan.*

A copper sculpture, by Satoru Abe, signed, America, dated 1957, 53in (134.5cm) high.

£2,500–3,000 **James D Julia**

A wooden sculpture, by Brian Willsher, signed, c1970, 16in (40.5cm) high.

£450–500 **Retro Centre**

A gilt-bronze sculpture, by Percy Brown, on a stone base, 1970s, 13½in (34.5cm) high.
£250–300 **Rosebery's**

A painted wood sculpture, by Karel Appel, entitled 'Close Together', edition of 65, signed, America, 1977, 30½in (77.5cm) high.
£6,500–8,000 **Freeman's**

A brass sculpture, by Sigurd Persson, on a marble base, signed, Sweden, dated 1979, 11½in (29cm) long.
£1,100–1,300 **Bukowskis**

A granite sculpture, by Laurence Broderick, entitled 'Kneeling Bather', signed, inscribed and dated 1982, 18¼in (46.5cm) long.
£900–1,100 **Lyon & Turnbull**

A bronze sculpture, by Armas Hutri, entitled 'Listening Bear', signed, Finland, 1982, 11in (28cm) high.
£900–1,100 **Bukowskis (F)**

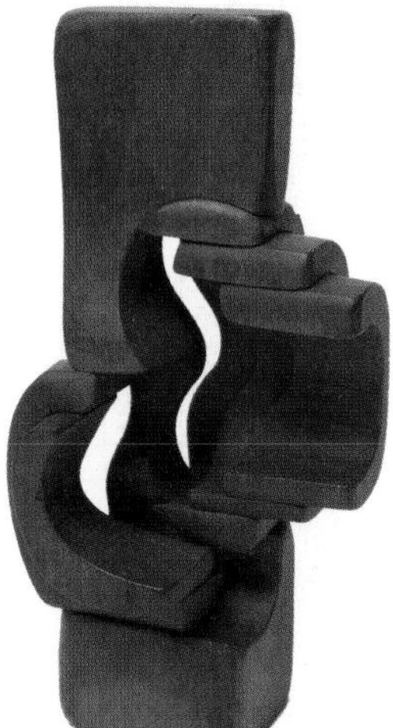

A wooden sculpture, by Brian Willsher, signed dated 1985, 10in (25.5cm) high.
£270–300 **Retro Centre**

A bronze sculpture, by Laila Pullinen, entitled 'Mystical Figure', signed and dated 1989, 13¾in (35cm) high.
£8,500–10,000 **Bukowskis (F)**

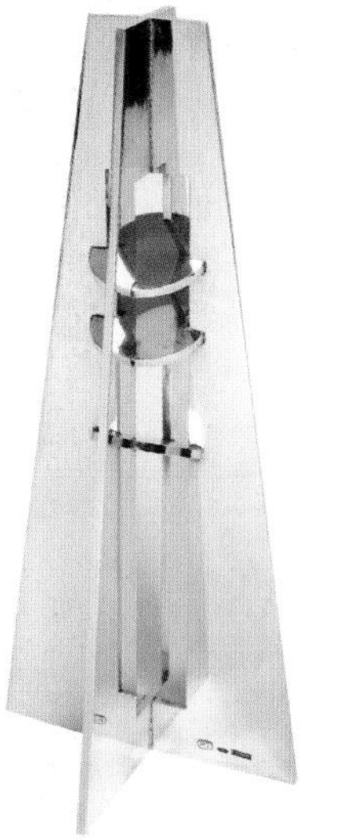

A silver sculpture, by Peter Thrasby, Birmingham, 1991, 10½in (26.5cm) high.
£2,200–2,500 **Daniel Bexfield**

LIGHTING

A nickel-plated copper Giso table lamp, by W. H. Gispen, No. 405, Holland, c1928, 12in (30.5cm) high.

£38,000–45,000 Sotheby's (NY)

A Maison Desny nickeled-bronze and glass lamp, on a mirror base, France, c1930, 4¾in (12cm) high.

£2,300–2,750 Sotheby's (P)

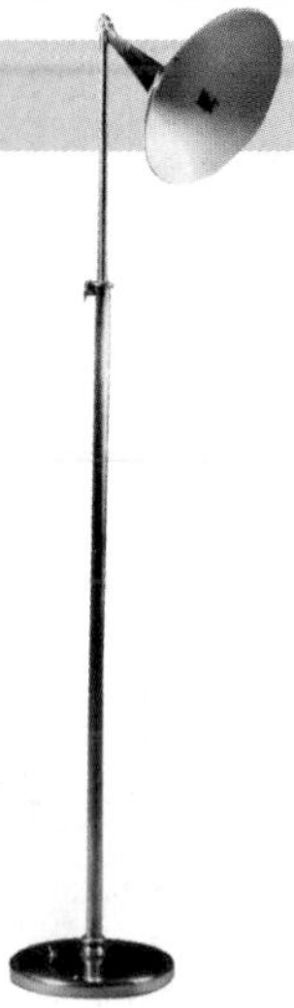

A chromed-brass standard lamp, by Sigfried Giedion for Wohnbedarf AG, Zurich, with an adjustable joint and extendable foot, manufactured by BAG, Turgi, Switzerland, c1932, 72in (183cm) high.

£2,000–2,500 Sotheby's (O)

A pair of brushed-metal table lamps, with articulated shades, stamped 'ESC', 1930s, 7½in (19cm) high.

£550–650 Sotheby's (O)

A pair of brass and glass wall sconces, France, c1940, 13½in (34.5cm) high.

£2,000–2,400 Chameleon

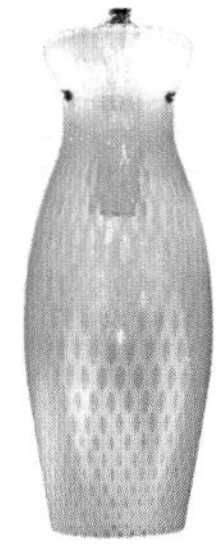

A pair of Murano glass pendant lights, with *latticino* decoration, Italy, c1940, 14½in (37cm) high.

£2,400–2,700 Chameleon

A pair of gilt-bronze three-branch wall lights, by Felix Agostini, Italy, 1940s, 16in (40.5cm) high.

£18,000–22,000 Sotheby's

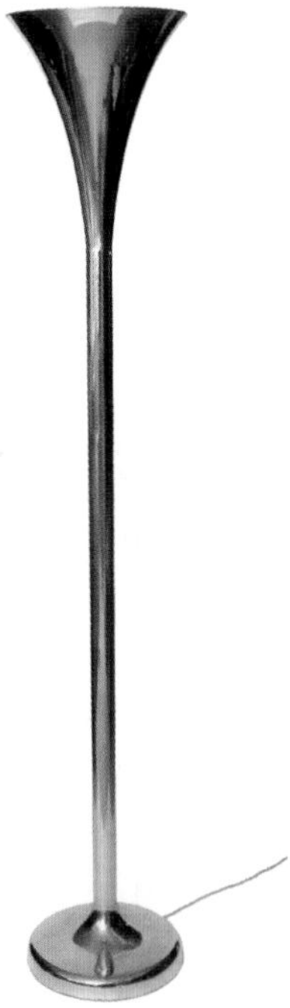

A brass uplighter, 1940s–50s, 71in (180.5cm) high.

£630–700 Design Gallery

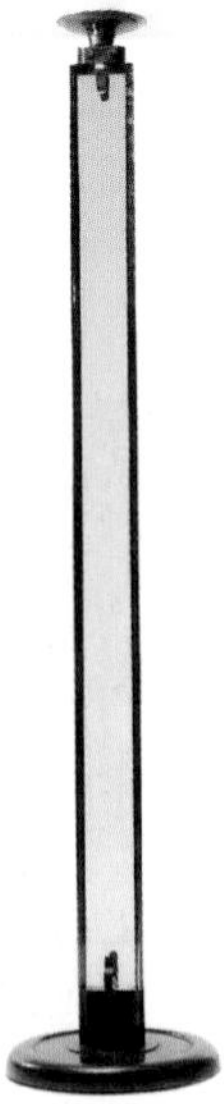

A Fontana Arte glass, metal and brass floor lamp, Italy, 1940s, 74½in (189cm) high.

£9,500–11,500 Sotheby's (NY)

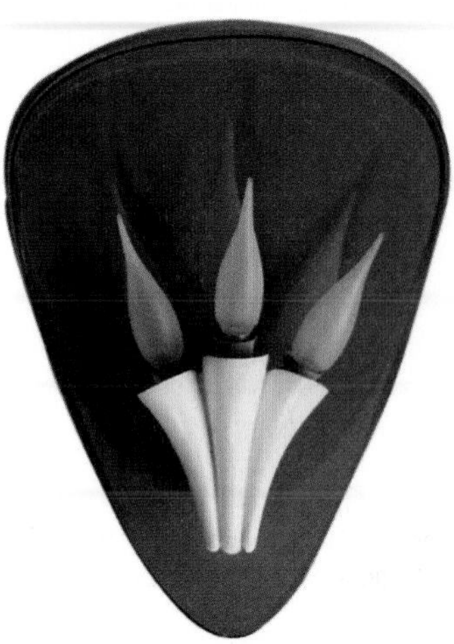

A pair of Fontana Arte glass and painted **metal wall lights,** with later wall attachments, Italy, c1950, 14¼in (36cm) high.

£2,300–2,750 Sotheby's (O)

A pair of glass table lamps, c1950, 7½in (19cm) diam.

£1,100–1,300 Sotheby's (O)

A Heifetz Manufacturing Co enamelled **metal and aluminium table lamp,** by Zahara Schatz, America, c1951, 28¾in (73cm) high.

£3,800–4,500 Sotheby's (NY)

ESSENTIAL REFERENCE PLEXIGLAS

Plexiglas, also known as PMMA (polymethyl-methacrylate), is an amorphous thermoplastic material that is as transparent as glass. It was discovered by accident in the laboratory of Rohm and Haas in Darmstadt, Germany c1930. A research associate was experimenting with an acrylic polymer to see if it would bind two sheets of glass. Instead of acting as an adhesive, however, the polymer dried into a lightweight, clear plastic sheet that was considered to be a promising glass substitute and Plexiglas quickly became an important component of 20th-century design. The artist and designer Zahara Schatz (1916–99) discovered the material and aesthetic possibilities inherent in Plexiglas and developed forms based on wire and metal cut-outs pressed between Plexiglas plates. This American table lamp is made of Plexiglas and brass tubing and dates from c1952.

£850–1,000 Treadway Gallery

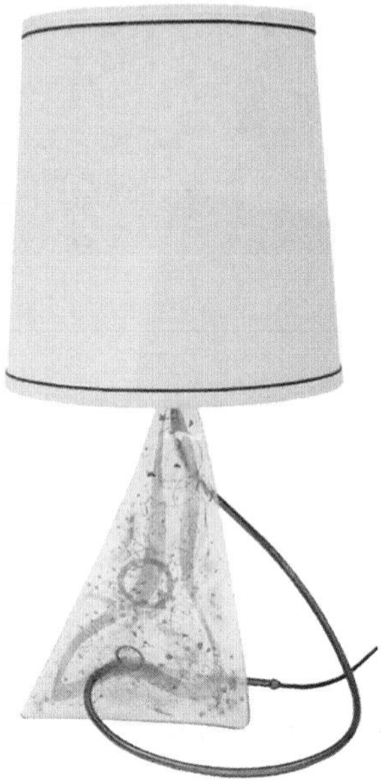

A pair of walnut table lamps, with decorative finials and pleated shades, 1950s, 27in (68.5cm) high.

£160–200 Treadway Gallery

A pair of steel and chrome-plated table **lamps,** by Solé, Paris, with adjustable stems and weighted bases, France, 1950s, 33in (84cm) high.

£230–275 Gorringes (L)

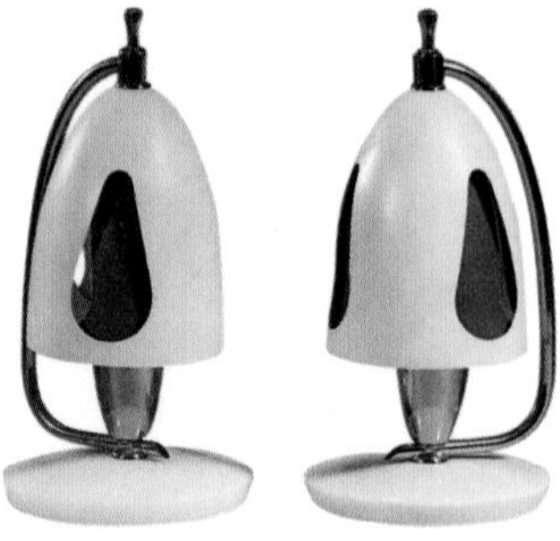

A pair of Arte Luce painted and gilt-metal **table lamps,** with articulated shades, on glass bases, Italy, 1950s, 9in (23cm) high.

£900–1,100 Sotheby's (O)

A Murano glass chandelier, attributed to Gino Vistosi, Italy, 1950s–60s, 43¼in (110cm) high.

£3,200–3,800 Bukowskis

A pair of stainless steel table lamps, Sweden, c1960, 18in (45.5cm) high.

£320–360 Coltman

A pair of Murano glass and silvered-bronze lamps, Italy, c1960, 16in (40.5cm) high.

£2,800–3,250 Chameleon

A pair of Lucite lamps, Italy, c1960, 19in (48.5cm) high.

£3,500–4,000 Chameleon

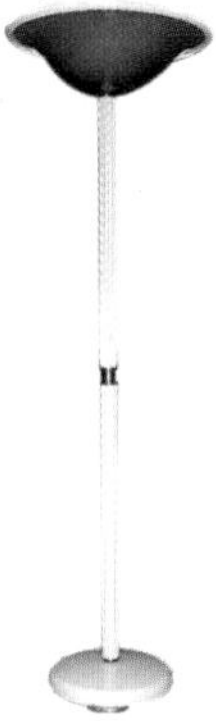

A Murano glass floor lamp, Italy, c1960, 68in (172.5cm) high.

£6,000–6,500 Chameleon

A pair of chrome lamps, Italy, c1960, 12½in (32cm) high.

£2,800–3,200 Chameleon

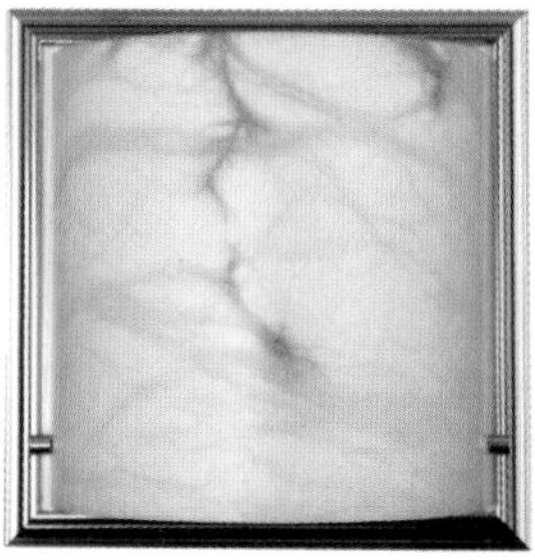

A pair of alabaster and bronze wall sconces, Italy, c1960, 10in (25.5cm) square.

£1,700–2,000 Chameleon

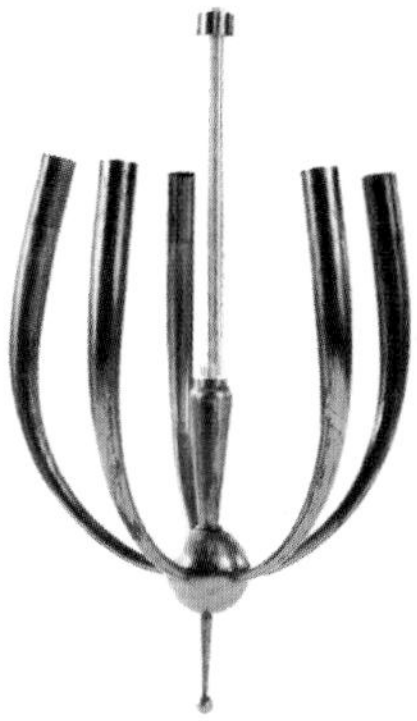

A brass and glass chandelier, by Guglielmo Ulrich, Italy, c1961, 47½in (120.5cm) high.

£2,200–2,700 Sotheby's (NY)

A Lyfa metal and Bakelite wall lamp, by Bent Karlby, Denmark, 1960s, 19¾in (50cm) square.

£500–600 Bukowskis

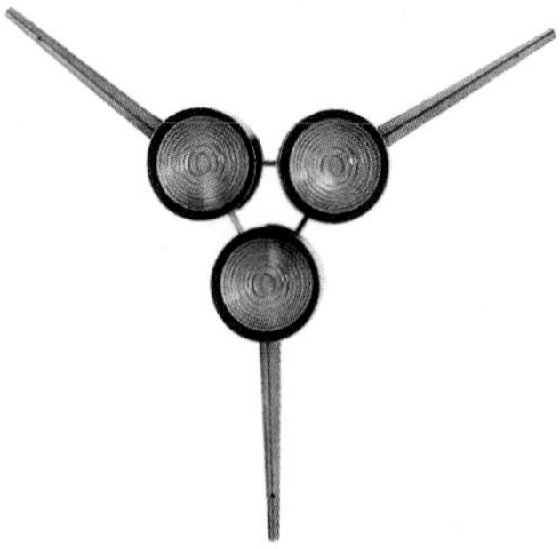

A pair of glass and brass wall lights, by Gio Ponti, Italy, 1960s, 35½in (90cm) wide.

£6,000–7,000 Sotheby's

A pressed-brass table lamp and shade, by Curtis Jere, with stained maple base, labelled, America, c1965.

£270–330 Webb's

A glass table lamp, 1960s, 15in (38cm) high.

£700–850 Sotheby's (O)

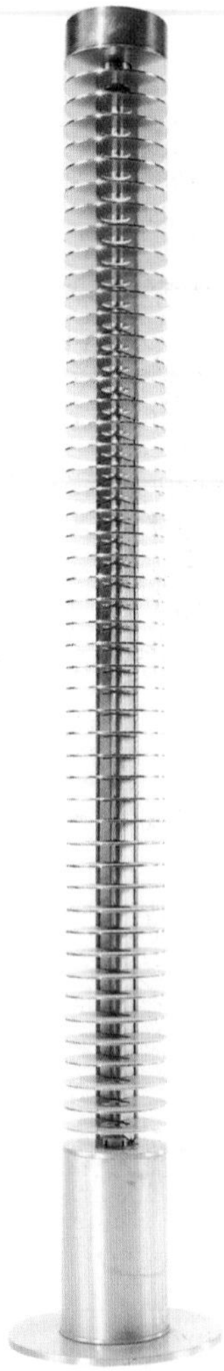

A Bilumen A. Bianchi enamelled aluminium and metal Amalssunta floor lamp, by Vittorio Gregotti, Italy, c1968, 71½in (181.5cm) high.

£7,000–8,500 Sotheby's (NY)

An Martinelli Luce Cobra plastic table lamp, by Elio Martinelli, model 629, with a swivelling shade, marked, Italy, c1969, 16in (40.5cm) diam.

£300–350 Treadway Gallery

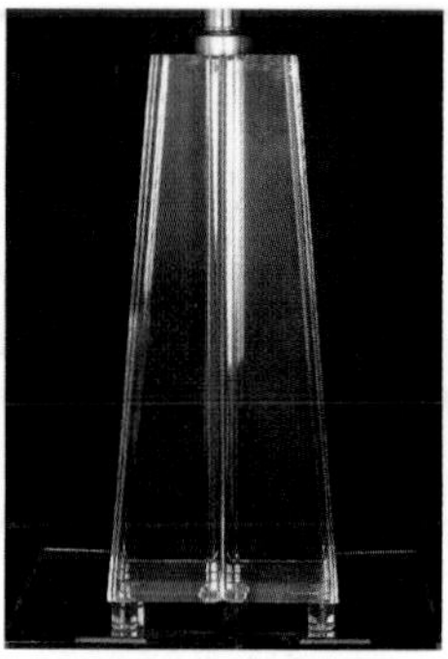

A pair of Lucite lamps, France, c1970, 14¾in (37.5cm) high.

£2,800–3,250 Chameleon

A Perspex and birch candelabra, by Astrid Sjöhede, Sweden, c1972, 58in (147.5cm) high.

£300–350 Coltman Antiques

An aluminium and enamel table lamp, attributed to Mathieu Lustrerie, the swivelling aluminum rings with an enamelled interior, France, 1970s, 21in (53.5cm) high.

£400–500 Treadway Gallery

Mathieu Lustrerie was founded in 1948 by Henri Mathieu and specialized in lighting influenced by kinetic plays of light.

A brushed steel and glass hanging light, 1970s, 43in (109cm) high.

£1,100–1,300 Sotheby's (O)

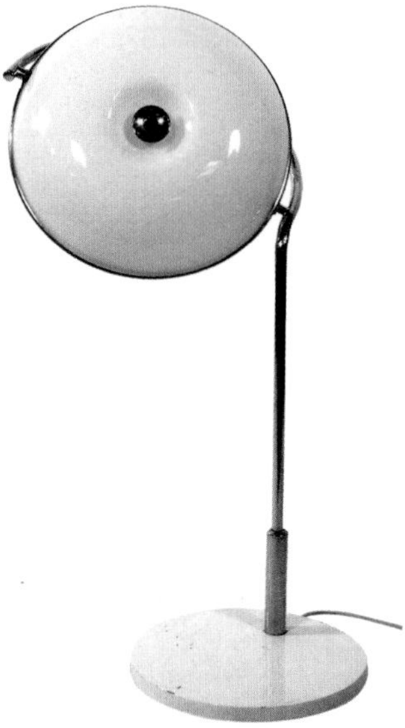

A Reggiani chrome and plastic lamp, marked Italy, 1970s, 31½in (80cm) high.

£140–170 Special Auction Services

A glass standard lamp, by Danny Lane, 1990, 77½in (197cm) high.

£2,300–2,750 Sotheby's

JEWELLERY

A silver monogram brooch, by Wiwen Nilsson, Sweden, Lund 1939, 3¾in (9.5cm) wide.
£440–520 Bukowskis

A Georg Jensen silver bracelet, by Henning Koppel, Denmark, 1970s, 8in (20.5cm) long.
£1,400–1,700 Lyon & Turnbull

An Anton Michelson enamelled brooch, by Eigle Jensen, maker's and designer's marks, Denmark, late 1950s, 2in (7cm) long.
£330–400 Lyon & Turnbull

An 18ct gold, platinum and enamel brooch, by Henryk Kaston, in the form of an eye, set with diamonds and a ruby, after 'The Eye of Time' by Dali, America, 1941, 1½in (4cm) wide.
£3,800–4,500 Skinner

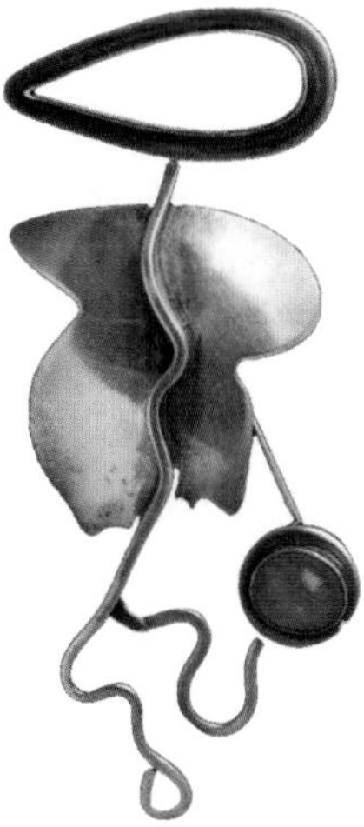

A silver, fire opal and onyx brooch, by Sam Kramer, marked, America, c1950, 4in (10cm) long.
£3,500–4,200 Skinner

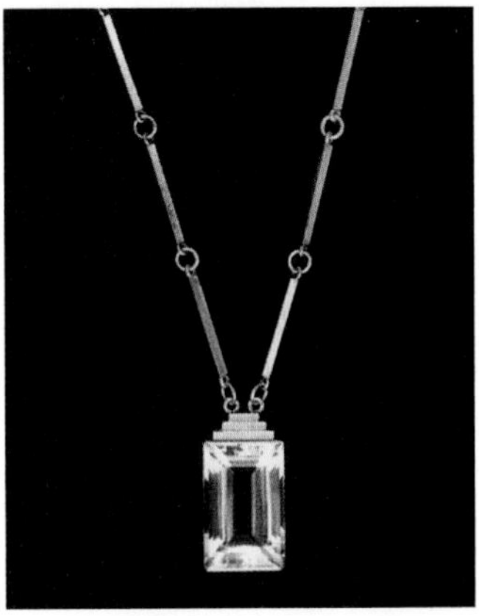

A silver and rock crystal pendant, by Wiwen Nilsson, Sweden, Lund 1944, pendant 1¼in (3cm) long.
£1,000–1,200 Bukowskis

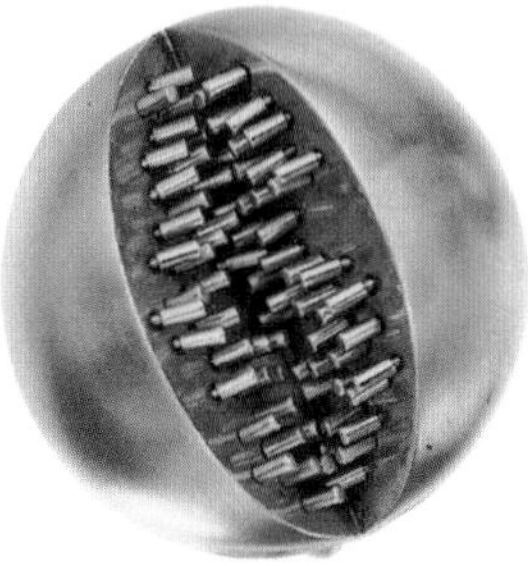

An 18ct gold brooch, by Pol Bury, signed, marked, France, c1950, 1½in (4cm) wide.
£7,000–8,500 Sotheby's (NY)

A silver bracelet, import marks for London 1961, Norway, 8in (20cm) long.
£375–450 Lyon & Turnbull

A Georg Jensen 18ct gold brooch, by Henning Koppel, No. 1327, stamped marks, import marks for London 1962, Denmark, 1950s, 2¼in (5.5cm).
£600–700 Lyon & Turnbull

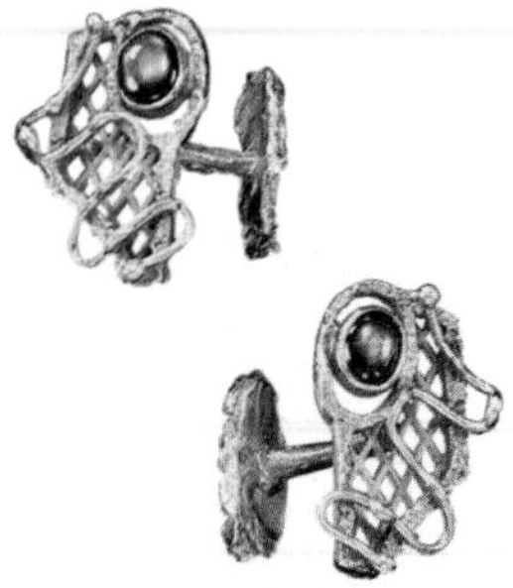

A pair of labradorite cufflinks, 1960s.

£250–300 Sotheby's (O)

An 18ct gold and silver bracelet, by Sven Boltenstern, marked, Austria, c1972, 6¾in (17cm) diam.

£1,700–2,000 Skinner

The son of a Viennese architect, Boltenstern studied sculpture at Salzburg Art Academy and goldsmithing in Vienna and Paris. His work is represented in the Vienna Museum of Applied Art.

A silver corsage bangle, by Soren S. Borup, stamped marks, import marks for London 1972, Denmark, early 1970s, 2¼in (6cm) diam.

£425–525 Lyon & Turnbull

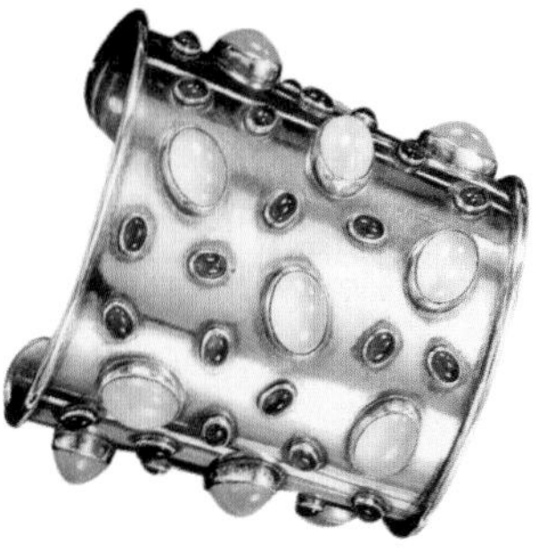

A silver cuff, by Paul Belvoir, set with moonstones and amethysts, marked, London 1990, 7in (18cm) long.

£1,300–1,600 Sotheby's (O)

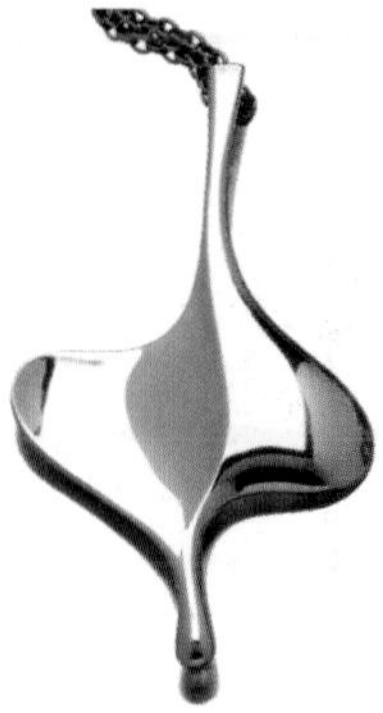

A David-Anderson silver pendant, by Bjørn Sigurd Østern, with maker's marks, Norway, 1960s, on a Georg Jensen belcher link chain with post-WWII maker's marks and later British import marks, Denmark, pendant 4¼in (10.5cm) long.

£500–600 Lyon & Turnbull

Bjørn Sigurd Østern worked at David-Anderson Company in Oslo on a regular basis between 1961 and 1973. He produced vigorous designs, usually in silver, and often set with cabochon cut stones or monochrome enamel.

A rose gold and amethyst crystal ring, 1970s.

£330–400 Lyon & Turnbull

An 18ct gold diamond-set Atlantis bracelet and matching ring, by David Thomas, both signed and numbered '1', with stamped marks, London 1971, bracelet 7in (17.5cm) long.

£4,000–5,000 Lyon & Turnbull

Production of the Atlantis Collection began in 1970 and incorporated approximately 50 different designs. Each piece was signed and numbered and made in strictly limited editions of 150 for rings and earrings and 50 for bracelets. The collection was manufactured to Thomas's patented technique, originally developed by him for his one-off pieces, which involved the lost wax casting method and trapping pre-cut gold wires into his designs.

A Georg Jensen silver pendant and ring, by Astrid Fog, the pendant with import marks for London 1970, the ring with import marks for 1969, Denmark, late 1960s, 2¼in (5.5cm) long.

£650–800 Lyon & Turnbull

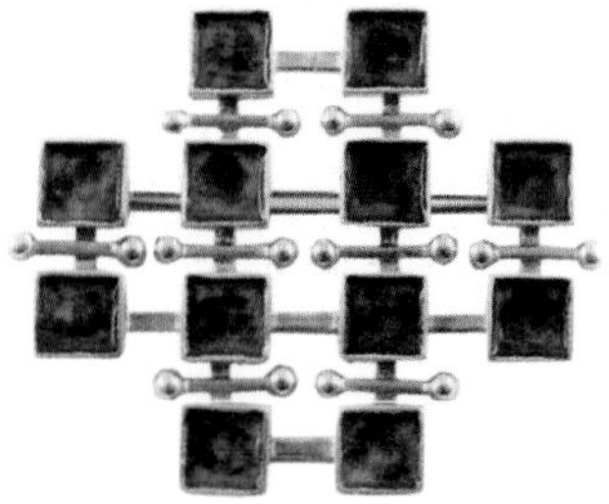

A Uni David-Anderson silver and enamel brooch, marked, English import marks for 1970, Norway, 2in (5cm) wide.

£170–200 Woolley & Wallis

A pair of 18ct gold earrings, by Andrew Grima, set with diamonds, signed, marked, London 1972.

£1,400–1,700 Dreweatt Neate (HAM)

A pair of 22ct gold Noeud hair clips, by Jean Mahie, signed, America, 1993.

£2,300–2,800 Sotheby's (NY)

FURNITURE

A mahogany and upholstered Napoleon armchair, by Edwin Lutyens, c1920.

£12,000–15,000 Sotheby's

It is known that the Napoleon chair was Lutyens' favourite design for an armchair. A person can sit with one leg thrown across the end, and a photograph of Lutyens himself in this pose is recorded. It is believed that this chair belonged to a member of the Lutyens family.

A pair of stained beechwood and plywood chairs, by Josef Hoffmann for Thonet, with pierced backrests, marked Austria, designed 1929.

£2,500–3,000 Sotheby's (Am)

A pair of chrome-plated steel and painted wood bedside cabinets, by Marcel Breuer for Thonet, model No. MM2, with manufacturer's label, Germany, 1930s, 27¼in (69cm) high.

£7,000–8,500 Sotheby's (NY)

An oak table/stool, by Robert 'Mouseman' Thompson, c1930, 24in (61cm) wide.

£580–650 Castlegate Antiques

A walnut wardrobe, by Gordon Russell, design No. 447, the two doors with fielded panels above a single drawer, with maker's label, c1930, 39in (99cm) wide.

£2,000–2,400 Holloway's

A painted wire mesh armchair, some losses, America, 1930–35.

£750–900 Sotheby's (P)

A set of eight steel stacking armchairs, by Robert Mallet-Stevens for Tubor, France, 1930s, 32¾in (83)cm high.

£10,000–12,000 Sotheby's (NY)

MARKET INFORMATION 20TH CENTURY

- Designer goods from the 1970s by such names as Paul Evans, Milo Baughman and Pierre Cardin continue to increase in value.
- Reissued items are becoming more common at auction (Vitra production as opposed to original Herman Miller production, for example) but there is a greater demand for items that have not been reproduced.
- Buyers are focusing more on style and less on scholarship; they are motivated less by pedigree and more by a certain look.
- Auction results for classic 1950s designs are on the rise after having been in the doldrums for several years.
- The current weak US dollar means that more European buyers are spending in the US and fewer Americans are buying in Europe.
- Fewer sales are being made at the large shows and more are being made online and at auction.
- The overall market trend is away from collecting a specific item and more towards achieving a certain style.

ESSENTIAL REFERENCE ISOKON

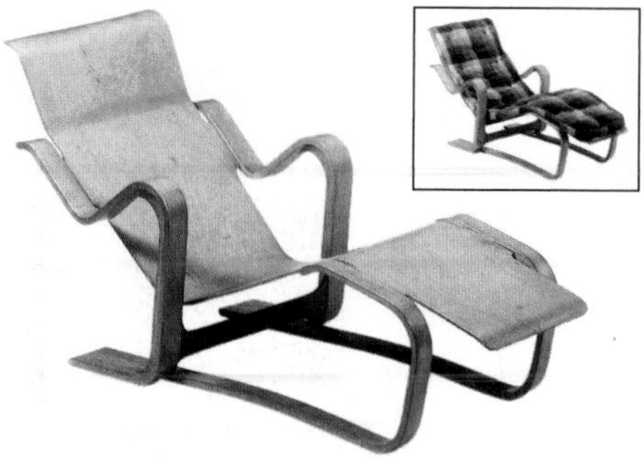

Isokon was founded by Jack Pritchard in late 1935. He wanted to produce pieces which suited the modern home and were aesthetic in their simplicity as well as being comfortable. His primary material of choice was plywood as it was of warmer appearance than tubular steel. Pritchard's first Controller of Design was Walter Gropius, who was replaced by Marcel Breuer after Gropius returned to America. Breuer's first design for Isokon was the plywood Long Chair, which he had previously designed in metal, and production began in December 1935. By 1938 Isokon were only producing between three and six Long Chairs per week as the pre-formed seats were imported from Pritchard's former employers, Venesta, in Estonia. Early versions of the series can also be recognized by by the mortice-and-tenon joints that connect the seat to the frame. This slow production was halted by the outbreak of WWII in 1939, after which the mortice-and-tenon joints were replaced by horizontal members spanning the entire width of the seat, and the bent plywood sections were produced in the UK using a thinner laminate.

The laminated plywood chair shown here was purchased by a student directly from the Isokon stand at the 1936 Ideal Home Exhibition at Olympia, London. Pleading student poverty the Isokon representatives ultimately agreed he could have it for £5 (£235 at today's values) providing he removed it immediately the exhibition ended. Although other pre-war Long Chairs are known, this piece differs in that the veneer on the seat is long grain rather than cross grain, and the squared ends to the feet and arm rest have previously only been known from early photographs and patent documentation held in the Isokon Plus archive. The chair is stamped 'Made in Estonia' and has an upholstered cushion.

£11,000–13,000 Sotheby's

A chromium-plated metal and glass Tugendhat coffee table, by Ludwig Mies van der Rohe probably for Bamberg Metallwerkstätten, No. MR 150, Germany, c1931, 50in (127cm) wide.

£40,000–50,000 Sotheby's (NY)

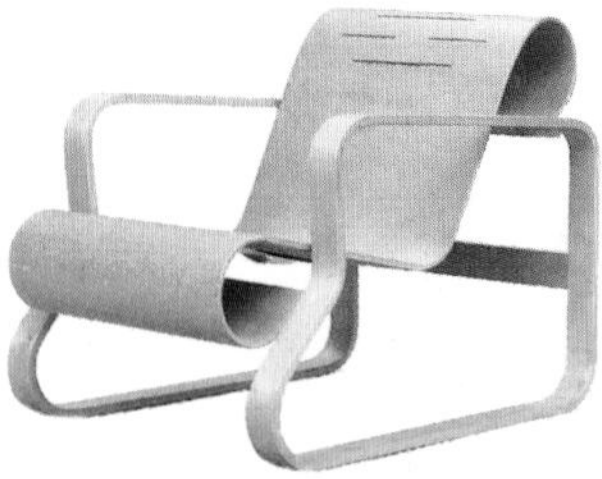

A birchwood Paimio armchair, by Alvar Aalto for Artek, Finland, 1931–32.

£4,500–5,500 Bukowskis

An aluminium and fabric armchair, by Ceateeze Seating, with maker's label, 1930s, 32¼in (82cm) high.

£110–130 Special Auction Services

A tubular steel and leatherette Beta chair, by Nathan George Horwitt for Howell Manufacturing Co, America, Illinois, designed 1930, manufactured 1934, 27¾in (70.5cm) high.

£11,000–13,000 Sotheby's (NY)

A pine Zig-Zag Stoel chair, by Gerrit Rietveld, Holland, 1934–40.

£12,000–14,000 Sotheby's (Am)

A metal cheval mirror, with three plates, possibly France, 1930s, 42in (106.5cm) wide.

£1,400–1,700 Sotheby's (O)

JAMES D. JULIA Inc.
AUCTIONEERS
Antique & Fine Art Division
OOC by Abbott Fuller Graves (20" x 16")
Sold for $201,250!!
Advertising, Toy & Doll Division
Carpenter "Tally Ho" Stewart Collection World Auction Record
Sold for $92,000!!
Rare Firearm & Military Division
Rare & exceptionally fine Colt Walker Percussion Revolver
Sold for $431,250!!
Fine Lamp & Glass Division
Tiffany Studios Fish Lamp
Sold for $161,000!!
One of the nation's leading auctioneers! Our reputation, expertise, marketing plan and international contacts will ensure you strong and, in many cases, record prices for important and rare objects. Call us today for a free, courteous, confidential discussion about what you have to sell.
Consignments Wanted Single items or entire estates
Rembrandt Bugatti Majestic Stag
Sold for $87,400!!
P.O. Box 830 Rte. 201, Skowhegan Rd., Fairfield, ME 04937, USA Tel: 1 (207) 453-7125 Fax: 1 (207) 453-2502
Website: www.juliaauctions.com James D. Julia Auctioneer License: ME: AR83 NH: 2511 MA: 1406

Clarion Antiques Ltd.
Art Deco and Art Nouveau
Statuary, Sculptures
and Fine Art,
Ceramics, Glass, Lighting
Antique Search Service
Valuations
Antique Style
for your
Special Home
Contact us on 01253 721903
Mobile:07985 191623
e-mail:
clarion2000@btinternet.com
website:clarionantiquesltd.co.uk

W.M.F. Loetz Tiffany & Co. Orrefors Liberty
Moorcroft Doulton Clarice Cliff Studio Pottery Troika Poole Susie Cooper
Eames G-Plan Ercol Gordon Russell Liberty Herman Miller France & Sons
SPECIAL AUCTION SERVICES
ESTABLISHED 1991
Decorative Arts & Modern Design
We hold regular specialist auctions of late 19th and 20th Century Ceramics and Porcelain, Glass, Furniture, Works of Art, Lighting and Fabrics
For a FREE valuation call or email Thomas Plant
(as seen on BBC's Flog It! & Bargain Hunt)
Tel: 0118 971 2949
Email: thomas@specialauctionservices.com
Visit: www.specialauctionservices.com
Whitefriars Murano Holmegaard Kosta Boda

ESSENTIAL REFERENCE ALVAR AALTO

Alvar Aalto (1898–1976) developed numerous designs for moulded plywood during the 1930s, including a revolutionary L-shaped leg that was used in much of his furniture. The success of these designs enabled him and his wife to found the manufacturing company Artek in Helsinki in 1935. Aalto's work, which was well received in Britain and America during the 1930s and '40s, was produced by Finmar, a British subsidiary, and later by Artek-Pascoe in New York. Artek also began production in Sweden when exports from Finland to America were prohibited during WWII. This birch occasional table with bentwood legs is a simple piece of Artek furniture, manufactured in Sweden c1940.

£250–300 Treadway Gallery

An oak Funkis sideboard, by Axel Einar Hjort for Nordiska Kompaniet, with a leather writing surface, Sweden, Stockholm, 1930s, 43in (109cm) wide.

£5,000–6,000 Bukowskis

A lacquered steel, wood and upholstery Flavigny bed, by Jean Prouvé, France, c1940, 74½in (189.5cm) long.

£3,200–3,800 Sotheby's (NY)

A burr-maidou and mahogany Formal Dining Group table, by Herman Miller for Gilbert Rohde, with a chequerboard veneered top, on two curved plinth supports, one leaf replaced, America, c1940, 72in (183cm) wide.

£1,400–1,700 Treadway Gallery

A jacaranda and walnut-veneered cabinet, by Erik Matsson for Mjölby Intarsia, signed and dated 1940, Sweden, 38½in (98cm) wide.

£2,200–2,600 Bukowskis

A mahogany Flora cabinet, by Josef Frank for Svenskt Tenn, papered with illustrations of flora by Palmstruchs, the two doors enclosing shelves, Sweden, c1940, 47in (119.5cm) wide.

£8,000–10,000 Bukowskis

A birch cabinet, by Alvar Aalto for Artek, the two doors enclosing five drawers and one adjustable shelf, stamped 'Aalto Design Artek Made in Sweden', c1940, 47¼in (120cm) wide.

£1,500–1,800 Treadway Gallery

A set of eight oak dining chairs, by Robert 'Mouseman' Thompson, comprising six dining chairs and two carvers with lattice backs, c1940.

£4,300–4,800 Fair Finds

A calico ash and plywood DCW chair, by Charles and Ray Eames for Evans Products, the spine and legs with a rubber shock mount assembly, with Evans product label to base, America, 1946–58.

£500–600 Rosebery's

A walnut chest of drawers, the six drawers with Bakelite handles, 1940s, 33in (84cm) wide.

£500–550 Burford Antiques

A teak and leather Chieftain armchair, by Finn Juhl for Niels Vodder, stamped marks, Denmark, Copenhagen, c1949.
£14,000–17,000 Sotheby's (NY)

A fibreglass, wood and steel La Chaise chaise longue, by Charles and Ray Eames for Vitra Basle, with paper label, Switzerland, designed 1948, manufactured 1990s, 34in (86.5cm) high.
£3,200–3,800 Sotheby's (Am)

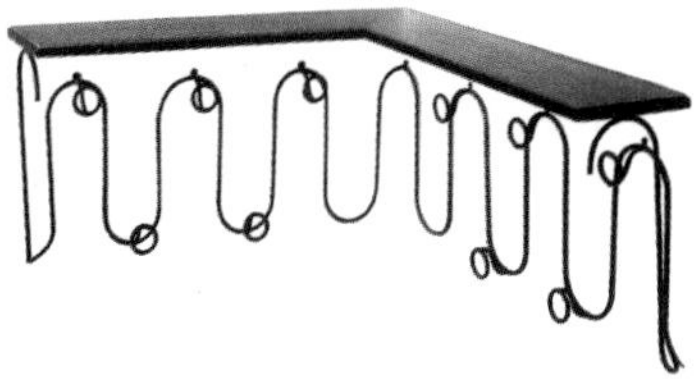

An enamelled steel and oak corner coat rack, by Jean Royère, France, c1950, 21in (53.5cm) high.
£6,000–7,000 Sotheby's (NY)

A painted metal and Formica Compass desk, by Jean Prouvé, France, c1950, 47¼in (120cm) wide.
£3,800–4,500 Sotheby's (O)

A lacquered steel, aluminium and wood Compass desk, by Jean Prouvé, France, 1950s, 76¾in (195cm) wide.
£10,000–12,000 Sotheby's (NY)

A teak and oak desk, by Hans J. Wegner for Andreas Tuck, branded mark, Denmark, 1950s, 53½in (136cm) wide.
£1,200–1,400 Bukowskis

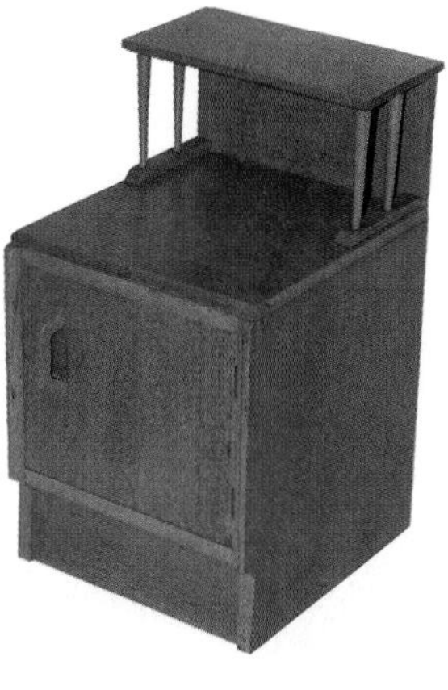

An oak bedside cabinet, by E. Gomme for G-Plan, 1950s, 24in (61cm) high.
£90–100 North Wilts Exporters

A Waring & Gillow-style satinwood dressing table and two bedside tables, each with a plate glass top, the dressing table with a drawer flanked by hinged swing-out drawers, c1950.
£650–800 Anderson & Garland

ESSENTIAL REFERENCE HEYWOOD-WAKEFIELD

Formed in 1897 by the merger of two companies, Heywood-Wakefield was based in Gardner, Massachusetts. The company initially produced wicker and rattan furniture, but from the 1930s to the 1960s it was famous for its sleek, streamlined furniture made from solid birch. Much of the timber was from Heywood-Wakefield's own mill in Connifer, New York. The logs were separated at the mill, the outer lighter portion being used for their Modern line and the darker inner section used for the Old Colony line. At the factory the timber was air- and kiln-dried and then 'equalized' to prevent warping, shrinking and swelling. It was cut into boards that were matched according to colour and grain and glued together for use as table tops, chair backs, etc. Smaller parts such as handles and legs were machined. This birch kneehole desk and side chair was made c1950; the desk is 50in (127cm) wide.
£180–220 Jackson's

An oak and iron Portemanteau, by Le Corbusier, with four hooks and two shelves, France, c1950, 34½in (87.5cm) wide.

£15,000–18,000 Sotheby's (NY)

A set of six teak and fabric Egyptian dining chairs, by Finn Juhl for Neils Vodder, branded mark, Denmark, 1950s.

£5,000–6,000 Bukowskis

A birch and fabric armchair, by Alvar Aalto, Finland, c1950.

£1,350–1,600 Skinner

A dyed birch plywood DCW chair, by Charles and Ray Eames for Herman Miller, slight damage, America, 1950s.

£350–420 Treadway Gallery

A pair of walnut and beech Shell chairs, by Hans Wegner for Fritz Hansen, branded mark, Denmark, Copenhagen, 1950s.

£3,500–4,200 Sotheby's (NY)

A teak and oak Valet chair, by Hans Wegner for Johannes Hansen, branded mark, Denmark, Copenhagen, 1950s.

£3,000–3,500 Sotheby's (NY)

A painted plywood and oak cabinet, by Le Corbusier, France, c1952, 61in (155cm) wide.

£5,000–6,000 Sotheby's (NY)

A wood and goatskin cocktail cabinet, by Aldo Tura, with a mirrored interior and yellow metal mounts, Italy, 1950s, 31¾in (80.5cm) wide.

£11,000–13,000 Bukowskis

A brushed-chrome and upholstery Florence sofa, by Knoll Associates, with maker's labels, America, c1954, 73in (185.5cm) wide.

£475–575 Treadway Gallery

A chromium-plated steel, teak and leather swivel chair, by Hans Wegner for Johannes Hansen, with manufacturer's metal tag, Denmark, Copenhagen, c1955.

£20,000–25,000 Sotheby's (NY)

A pair of rosewood and leather Contour side chairs, by Vladimir Kagan for Kagan-Dreyfuss, America, New York, 1950s.

£7,000–8,500 Sotheby's (NY)

A rosewood, Venetian glass and brass coffee table, by Vladimir Kagan for Kagan-Dreyfuss, America, New York, 1950s, 46in (117cm) diam.

£20,000–24,000 **Sotheby's (NY)**

A walnut and glass two-tiered side table, by Vladimir Kagan for Kagan Dreyfuss, branded mark, America, New York, 1950s, 32in (81.5cm) wide.

£2,800–3,300 **Sotheby's (NY)**

A nest of three walnut and glass occasional tables, Italy, c1950, largest 24½in (62cm) wide.

£1,800–2,200 **Sotheby's (O)**

An oak and ceramic sofa table, ceramic by Stig Lindberg at Gustavsburg, frame designed by David Rosén, for Nordiska Kompaniet, marked, Sweden, Stockholm, 1950s, 48¾in (124cm) wide.

£370–450 **Bukowskis**

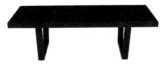

An ebonized wood Slat bench, by George Nelson for Herman Miller, America, 1950s, 48in (122cm) wide.

£380–450 **Treadway Gallery**

A painted metal trolley, by Mathieu Matégot, France, 1950s, 27½in (70cm) wide.

£2,500–3,000 **Sotheby's (NY)**

An ebonized plywood CTW table, by Charles and Ray Eames for Herman Miller, America, 1950s, 34in (86.5cm) diam.

£600–700 **Treadway Gallery**

A lacquer and brass shelving unit, by Dunbar, with five adjustable shelves, lighting and cross-bracing, America, c1956, 48in (122cm) wide.

£4,500–5,500 **Rago Arts**

A walnut storage and display unit, by Terence Conran for Conran Furniture, the cupboard with two glazed doors enclosing three drawers, above a two-tier open shelf on metal legs, 1950s, 60in (152.5cm) wide.

£450–550 **Morphets**

A teak chest of drawers, by Schulim Krimper, with three short and four long drawers, on stylized supports, signed, Australia, c1956, 33in (84cm) wide.

£2,000–2,500 **Leonard Joel**

A walnut chest of drawers, by George Nakashima, with dovetailed joints, America, c1955, 36in (91.5cm) wide.

£6,500–8,000 Rago Arts

A birch credenza, by Heywood-Wakefield, No. 593, c1955, 54in (137cm) wide.

£180–220 Jackson's

A teak side table, by Schulim Krimper, with a shaped rail above a frieze drawer, on stylized supports, Australia, c1955, 24in (61cm) wide.

£900–1,100 Leonard Joel

A rosewood, enamelled-aluminium and leather Lounge Chair and Ottoman, by Charles and Ray Eames for Herman Miller, c1956, marked, ottoman 26in (66cm) wide.

£1,600–2,000 Treadway Gallery

A walnut, mahogany, oak and brass cabinet, by Josef Frank for Svenskt Tenn, Sweden, c1957, 35½in (90cm) wide.

£23,000–28,000 Sotheby's (NY)

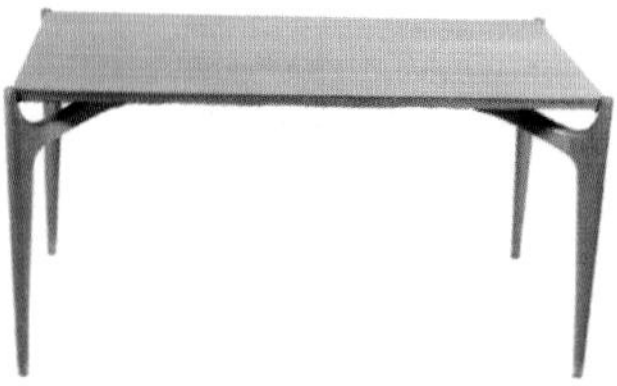

A satin-birch and veneer coffee table, Continental, c1958, 45in (114.5cm) wide.

£180–220 Special Auction Services

A teak sofa table, by Johannes Andersen for CFC Silkeborg, Denmark, 1950s–60s, 20½in (52cm) wide.

£700–850 Bukowskis

A brass and silvered glass mirror, by Ettore Sottsass for Poltronova, with paper label, Italy, c1959, 17½in (44.5cm) wide.

£4,000–5,000 Sotheby's (NY)

MARKET INFORMATION TIPS FOR BUYERS

- Be discriminating – provenance of an item is not always as important as condition and authenticity.
- Be careful – there is a great deal of creative license in the marketplace regarding the attribution of items to certain designers/manufacturers, both online and in auction catalogues.
- Be cautious – an attribution means just that. It is not a factual statement.
- Be inquisitive – when buying at auction it is the buyer's responsibility to be aware of the condition of an item.
- Be instinctive – buying on speculation may be a good strategy for dealers; collectors should buy items that they intend to keep and enjoy.

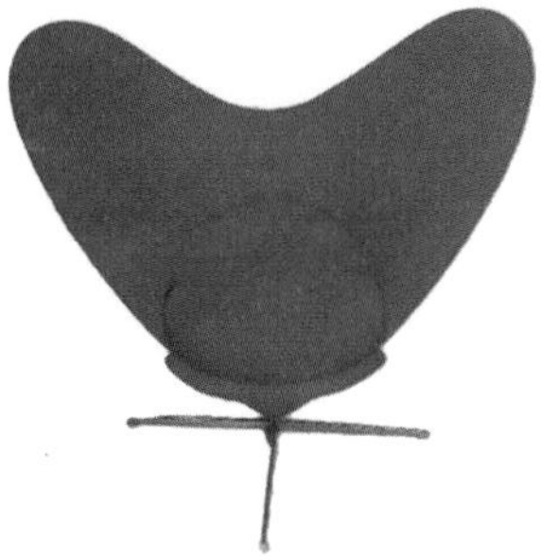

A metal and fabric Heart Cone chair, by Verner Panton, designed 1959, manufactured by Vitra, Germany, c2000.
£600–700 Waddington's

A plywood Wilhelmiina stacking chair, by Ilmari Tapiovaara for W. Schauman, with an ebonized seat and backrest, marked, Finland, 1959.
£800–1,000 Sotheby's (Am)

A mirror, by Jacques Adnet, with leather-covered frame, with strap and brass buckles, slight damage, France, 1950s, 12in (30.5cm) diam.
£550–650 Treadway Gallery

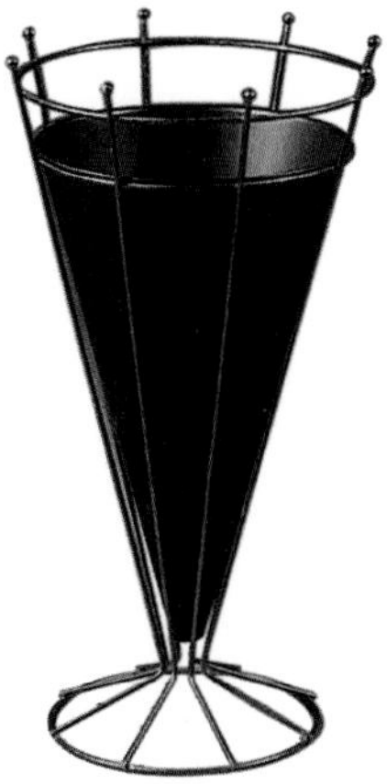

A brass umbrella stand, with metal inset, 1950s, 21¾in (55.5cm) high.
£600–700 Sotheby's (O)

An Italian School painted and gilt birch wardrobe, the doors decorated with scenes from a ball and a theatre, enclosing a glass shelf above five carved coat hooks, marked, Italy, Milan, 1950s, 67in (170cm) wide.
£11,000–13,000 Sotheby's

A teak and oak desk and teak and leather armchair, by Arne Vodder for Bovirke, branded marks, Denmark, Copenhagen, 1950s–60s, desk 61in (155cm) wide.
£1,000–1,200 Bukowskis

A leather two-seater sofa, Italy, c1960, 87in (221cm) wide.
£680–750 Burford Antiques

A travertine and steel coffee table, Italy, c1960, 16¼in (41cm) wide.
£350–420 Sotheby's (O)

A rosewood and ebonized fold-over table, Sweden, c1960, 40in (101.5cm) wide.
£600–700 Pure Imagination

A pair of walnut and upholstery armchairs, by Eero Saarinen, America, c1960.
£1,000–1,200 Webb's

A leather Ox chair, by Hans Wegner, Denmark, c1960.
£2,800–3,250 20th Century Marks

A pair of rosewood and leather armchairs, Denmark, c1960.

£700–800 **Pure Imagination**

A teak and upholstery armchair and footstool, by Povl Dinesen, marked, Denmark, c1960.

£1,200–1,400 **Skinner**

A nickel-plated metal and wool upholstered armchair, by Hans Wegner for AP Stolen, Denmark, 1960s.

£11,000–13,000
Sotheby's (NY)

This armchair, an extremely limited production by AP Stolen in the 1960s, was never made available in a large-scale edition.

A steel and leather Tulip armchair, by Preben Fabricius and Jørgen Kastholm for Alfred Kill International, Denmark, 1960s.

£1,800–2,200 **Bukowskis**

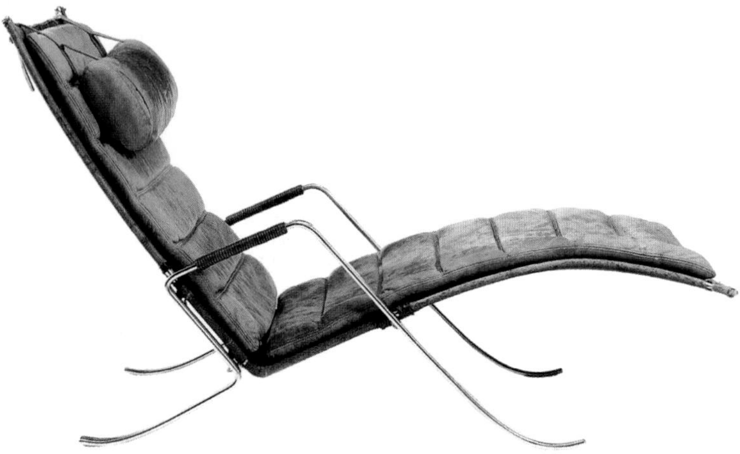

A chromium-plated steel, canvas and leather Grasshopper chaise longue, by Preben Fabricius and Jørgen Kastholm for Alfred Kill International, Denmark, 1960s, 59in (150cm) long.

£4,000–5,000 **Sotheby's (Am)**

ESSENTIAL REFERENCE POUL KJAERHOLM

Born in 1929 in Denmark, Poul Kjaerholm began his career as a cabinet-maker's apprentice. An extensive range of his furniture was produced from the 1950s by his friend Ejvind Kold Christensen, who gave him tremendous artistic freedom. Although formally trained as a cabinet-maker, Kjaerholm was a strong proponent of industrial production, and his work stands out among that of his Danish contemporaries because of his extensive use of steel frames rather than the more traditional wood. During his career Kjaerholm received several awards for his work, including two Grand Prix awards at the Milan Triennale in 1957 and 1960. Since 1982, a wide selection of Kjaerholm's furniture that was originally produced by his friend E. Kold Christensen in Hellerup, has been reissued by the Danish manufacturing firm of Fritz Hansen. This leather and steel armchair was made by E. Kold Christensen c1960.

£1,300–1,600 **Bukowskis**

An oak and upholstery sofa, by Hans J. Wegner for Johannes Hansen, marked, Denmark, early 1960s, 57in (145cm) wide.

£1,000–1,200 Bukowskis

A brushed-steel and leather PK33 stool, by Poul Kjaerholm for E Kold Christensen, marked, Denmark, early 1960s, 21¾in (55.5cm) diam.

£3,500–4,200 Bukowskis

A walnut and ash stool, by Wharton Esherick, with carved inscription 'W.E. 1962', America, 14½in (37cm) wide.

£2,800–3,200 Treadway Gallery

A walnut dining/conference table, signed 'D. Johnson', stamped 'August 30, 1962', restored, America, 95in (241.5cm) long.

£550–650 Treadway Gallery

A fibreglass reinforced polyester Globe chair, by Eero Aarnio, Finland, designed 1963, reissued by Adelta, Germany, c2000.

£750–900 Waddington's

A set of four teak and beech Grand Prix chairs, by Arne Jacobsen for Fritz Hansen, labelled Denmark, 1964–65.

£1,300–1,600 Bukowskis

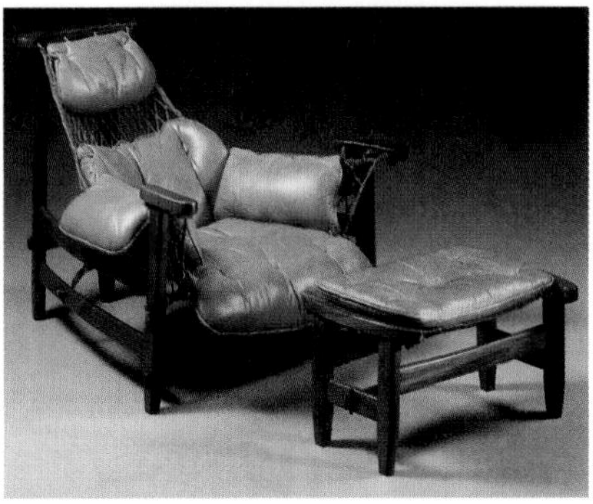

A rosewood and leather armchair and footstool, by Jean Gillon for Italima Wood Art, Brazil, with paper label, c1965.

£2,500–3,000 Sotheby's (O)

A rosewood desk, Sweden, 1960s, 54in (137cm) wide.

£1,350–1,500 Pure Imagination

A teak and glass coffee table, by G-Plan, 1960s.

£90–100 North Wilts Exporters

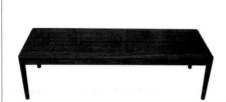

A jacaranda coffee table, Jørgen Hoj, Denmark, c1965, 59in (150cm) long.
£800–900 Boom Interiors

A black-painted occasional table, with a tiled top depicting three dancers, signed 'Kumar', 1960s, 30¼in (77cm) wide.
£45–55 Special Auction Services

A carved and laminated cherry table, by Wendell Castle, incised 'W.C.65', America, 1965, 32¾in (83cm) high.
£12,000–14,000 Sotheby's (NY)

A bronze, copper, wood and pewter double-sided cabinet, by Paul Evans for the Paul Evans Studio, America, 1965, 30½in (77.5cm) wide.
£6,000–7,000 Sotheby's (NY)

A lacquered vellum-covered dining suite, by Aldo Tura, comprising a table, four chairs and a sideboard, sideboard with paper label, Italy, Milan, 1960s, table 74¾in (190cm) wide.
£7,500–9,000 Sotheby's (O)

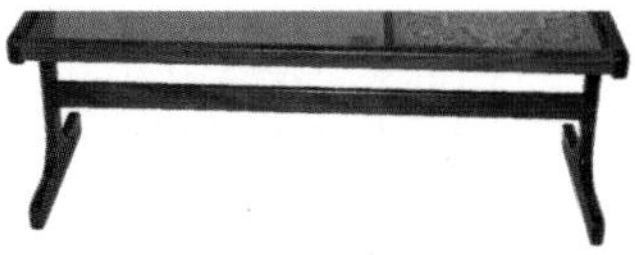

A teak coffee table, by G-Plan, with a tiled and glass top, 1960s, 48in (122cm) wide.
£90–100 North Wilts Exporters

A part-painted steel and slate sideboard, by Paul Evans for the Directional Furniture Company, from the Sculptured Steel series, with a welded signature, America, 1960s, 72½in (184cm) wide.
£20,000–25,000 Sotheby's (NY)

A jacaranda double pedestal desk, by Arne Vodder, with six drawers and open shelving to reverse, Denmark, c1967, 55in (140cm) wide.
£1,400–1,600 Boom Interiors

A rosewood veneer cabinet, the eight drawers with moulded plastic three-dimensional plates with *faux* marble finish, 1960s, 79in (200.5cm) wide.
£600–700 Treadway Galleries

A mahogany and lacquered-metal jardinière, by Josef Frank for Svenskt Tenn, with later paint and lamp fitting, Sweden, 1960s, 27¼in (69cm) wide.
£750–900 Bukowskis

A glass and metal mirror, Italy, 1960s, 23½in (59.5cm) wide.
£600–700 Sotheby's (O)

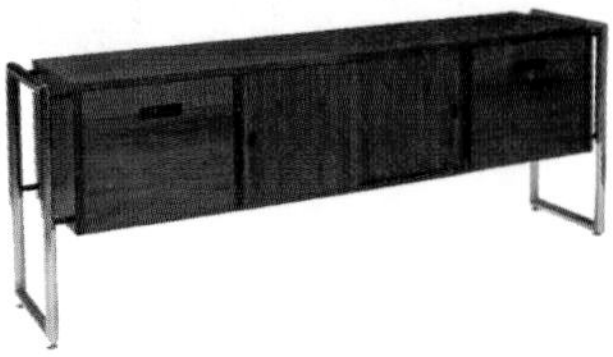

A rosewood cabinet, with two sliding doors, two shallow drawers and two file drawers, on chromed-steel end supports, 1960s, 68in (172.5cm) wide.
£1,300–1,600 Treadway Galleries

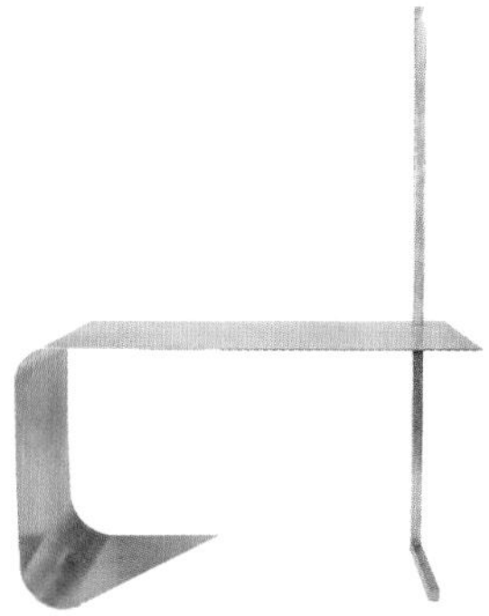

A stainless steel student's desk, by Maria Pergay, France, c1968, 62½in (157.5cm) wide.
£16,000–20,000 Sotheby's (NY)

An elm sideboard, by Priory, with two shelves above three drawers, over three doors, 1960s, 48in (122cm) wide.
£180–200 North Wilts Exporters

A rosewood and smoked glass coffee table, Denmark, c1960s, 58in (147.5cm) long.
£330–370 Coltman Antiques

A walnut End table, by George Nakashima, America, 1969, 26½in (67.5cm) wide, with a copy of the original bill of sale.
£8,500–10,000 Freeman's
Nakashima is regarded as one of the most original voices in American design, a visionary craftsman with the ability to reveal in his work the soul of a tree. Born to Japanese immigrants in the Pacific Northwest, Nakashima's early career was spent as an architect, working for the firm of Antonin Raymond and completing projects in the United States, Japan and India. His internment along with his wife in a Japanese-American internment camp brought a halt to his architectural career, but in the Washington camp he began to develop his skills as a furniture maker under the guidance of a Japanese master carpenter. After his former employer Raymond sponsored the family's release, Nakashima opened his first furniture studio in New Hope, Pennsylvania.

A wooden bench, by José Zanine Caldas, branded signature, Brazil, 1970s, 67in (170cm) wide.
£13,000–16,000 Sotheby's (NY)

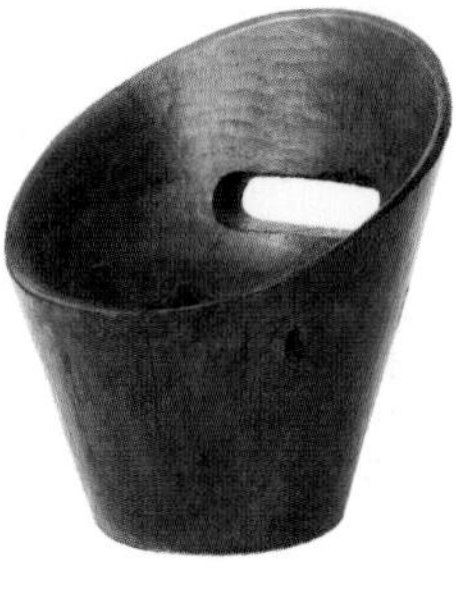

A pair of pequi wood chairs, by José Zanine Caldas, each with a branded signature, Brazil, c1970, 31¾in (80.5cm) high.
£18,000–22,000 Sotheby's (NY)

A fibreglass, aluminium and upholstery swivel chair, by Lurashell, with label to underside, c1970.
£110–130 Special Auction Services

A chrome and metal chair, the tubular chrome frame supporting a series of springs for the seat and backrest, with painted bentwood arms, 1970s.
£120–150 Special Auction Services

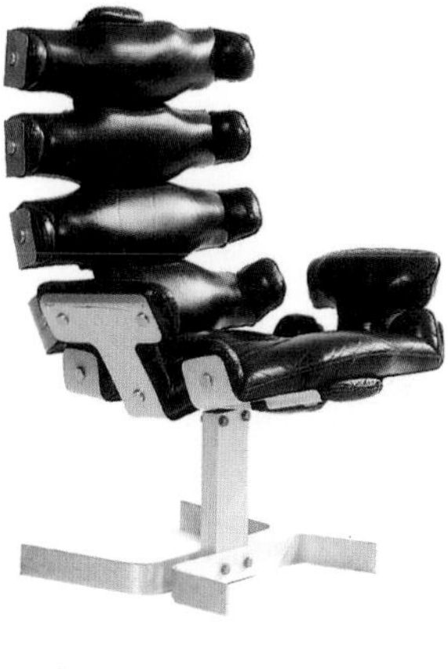

A pair of steel and leather Rib chairs, by Pierre Vandel, France, 1970s.
£6,500–8,000 Sotheby's (NY)

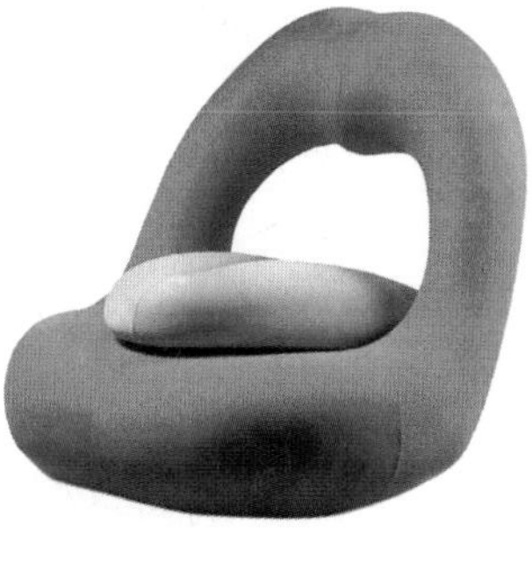

A fabric Mouth chair, with a sliding tongue seat, Italy, 1970s.
£1,000–1,200 Sotheby's (O)

A glass and chrome dining suite, by Richard Young for Merrow Associates, comprising a table and four chairs, c1970.
£500–600 Special Auction Services

A rosewood dining suite, by Hove Møbler, after a design by Hans Brattrud, comprising a quarter-veneered table with a rotating melamine centre and chrome legs, a sideboard with an ebonized top over two cupboards and two drawers and a set of six chairs with lath seats and backs and chrome bases, Norway, 1970s.

£3,000–3,500 Maxwells of Wilmslow

A rosewood-veneered and chrome-plated extending dining table, by Dyrlund, the top with four folding draw leaves, on six curved legs, with paper label, Denmark, c1970, 59in (150cm) diam, extended.

£900–1,100 Penrith Farmers' & Kidd's

A chrome and glass coffee table, on a tubular chrome base, 1970s, 31½in (80cm) diam.

£130–160 Special Auction Services

A teak sideboard, with three graduated drawers and three cupboards, one with a fall-front, c1971, 78in (198cm) wide.

£600–700 Webb's

A maple and leather PK27 chair, by Poul Kjaerholm, Denmark, c1972.

£2,700–3,000 20th-Century Marks

A walnut Conoid coffee table, by George Nakashima, inscribed to the underside 'to the Donches George Nakashima May 1972', America, 37in (94cm) wide, with a copy of the original invoice dated 1972.

£11,000–13,000 Freeman's

A pine Effe table, by Enzo Mari for Simon International, from the Metamobile series, Italy, c1974, 78¾in (200cm) wide.

£7,500–9,000 Sotheby's (NY)

ESSENTIAL REFERENCE PAUL EVANS

Paul Evans (1931–87) studied sculpture, metalwork and silver- and goldsmithing at the Cranbrook Academy of Art, Michigan. He began making metal furniture and exhibited in a group show in 1957 at the Museum of Contemporary Crafts in New York. In 1964 Evans was appointed designer for furniture manufacturer Directional, where he introduced his very collectable editions such as the Argente, Sculpted Bronze and Cityscape. Paul Evans signed and dated most of his pieces and his furniture has been bringing record-breaking prices at antiques shows and auctions across America and Europe. This sculpted-bronze bar cabinet has two half-round doors enclosing a cabinet, a drawer and two shelves, signed 'PE73', America, 1973, 72in (183cm) diam.

£13,000–16,000 Treadway Gallery

A walnut Conoid chair, by George Nakashima, America, Pennsylvania, 1976, with a copy of the original invoice.

£6,000–7,000 Skinner

A woven grass and wood stool, by George Nakashima, America, 1976, 17½in (44.5cm) wide, with a copy of the original invoice.

£1,600–2,000 Freeman's

A chrome and glass shelving unit, the three smoked glass shelves supported by a pair of chrome cylindrical stems on circular bases, 1970s, 59in (150cm) wide.

£230–280 Special Auction Services

A moulded plastic storage unit, slight damage, Italy, 1970s, 49½in (125.5cm) wide.

£650–800 Treadway Gallery

A moulded plastic Plana coat rack and Pluvium umbrella stand, by Giancarlo Piretti for Castelli, the coat rack with drop-down arms above an umbrella holder, the umbrella stand with swivelling disks, each with marked weighted bases, Italy, 1970s, coat rack 65in (165cm) high .

£250–300 Treadway Gallery

A rosewood, amboyna-veneered and ebony-inlaid Africa dining suite, by Tobia and Afra Scarpa for Maxalto, comprising a table and six chairs, each stamped with manufacturer's mark, Italy, designed 1975, table 74¾in (190cm) diam.

£6,000–7,000 Sotheby's (O)

Tobia Scarpa (b1935) was the son of architect Carlo Scarpa and he and his wife Afra Bianchin designed furniture for Gavina from 1960. Soon afterwards they opened their own office and designed pieces for firms such as B&B Italia, Knoll, Maxalto and Benetton.

A rosewood, chromed steel and corduroy dining suite, by Claude Megson, comprising a table and eight chairs, New Zealand, 1970s.

£2,250–2,750 Webb's

A bentwood, cane and leather Rio chaise longue, by Oscar Niemeyer, Brazil, c1978, 31¼in (79.5cm) high.

£10,000–12,000 Sotheby's (NY)

A rosewood coffee table, the top with ceramic insert and two slides, Denmark, 1980s, 63in (160cm) wide.

£300–350 Coltman Antiques

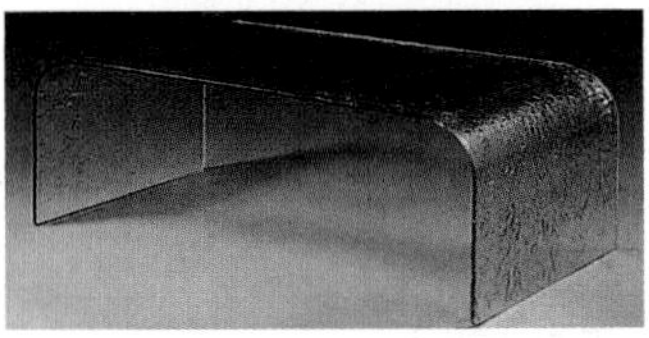

A textured glass coffee table, Italy, c1980, 41in (104cm) wide.

£450–550 Sotheby's (O)

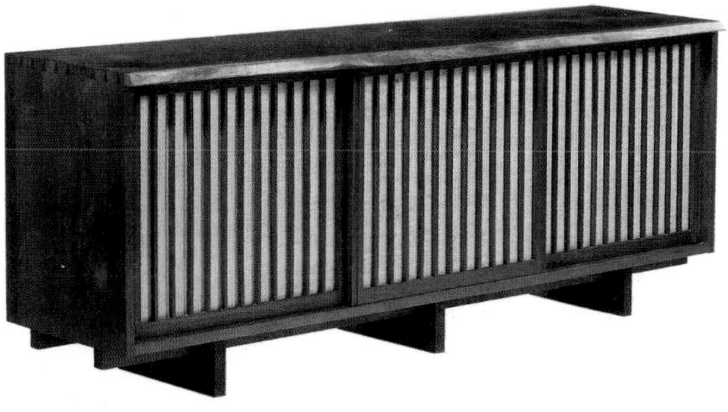

A walnut credenza, by George Nakashima, the three sliding grilled doors backed with pandanus cloth, enclosing four drawers and four adjustable shelves, signed and dated 1980, America, 84in (213.5cm) wide, with a copy of the original invoice.

£25,000–30,000 Freeman's

A walnut Conoid dining table, by George Nakashima, signed and dated 1980, America, 60in (152.5cm) wide, with original invoice.

£17,000–20,000 Freeman's

A set of eight steel and leather Brno chairs, by Ludwig Mies van der Rohe for Knoll, some signed with Knoll International labels, America, dated 1982.

£2,500–3,000 Treadway Gallery

A walnut Mira high stool, by George Nakashima, America, Pennsylvania, c1984, 35in (89cm) high, with a copy of the original invoice

£900–1,100 Skinner

A bentwood beech and upholstery Duet chair, designed by Rud Thygesen and Johnny Sorensen, Denmark, c1986.

£130–150 Special Auction Services

A fiddleback maple and ebony rocking chair, by Sam Maloof, inscribed 'No. 1986/Sam Maloof F.A.C.C.', America.

£20,000–25,000 Sotheby's (NY)

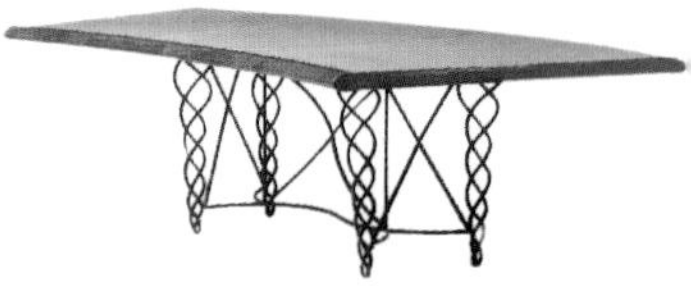

A wrought-iron and leather table, by Bill Amberg and André Dubreuil, c1987, 108¾in (276cm) wide.

£9,000–11,000 Sotheby's (O)

This unique piece was produced in a rare partnership between Bill Amberg and André Dubreuil when designing the interior of a west London house.

An aluminium, beech and woven birch bark armchair, by Mats Theselius for Källemo, marked and numbered, Sweden, c1990.

£4,500–5,500 Bukowskis

Two hundred of these chairs were made, of which 50 had woven birch bark seats and back rests, and those of the remaining 150 were of woven leather.

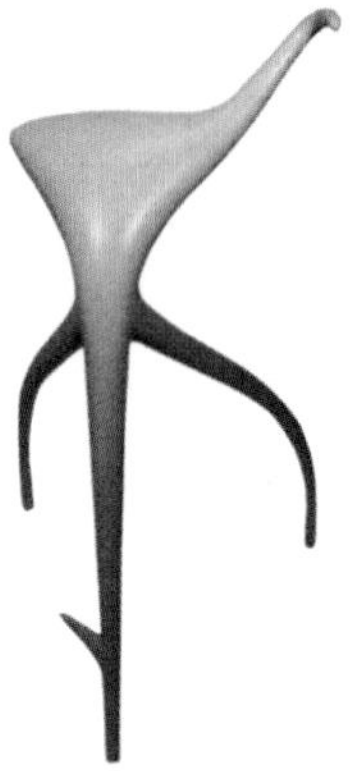

A burnished aluminium WW stool, by Philippe Starck for Vitra, signed, Germany, 1990s.

£750–900 Waddington's

A laminate four-fold screen, by Piero Fornasetti, decorated with books and accessories and *faux* wood panelling with hung *objets d'art* to the reverse, Italy, Milan, late 20thC, 55½in (141cm) wide.

£5,000–6,000 Skinner

In Piero Fornasetti's atelier each piece is executed by hand. As a designer and visionary he was interested in the transition of one medium to another, such as newspaper print used to decorate plates. His work appears to be bits of history, memories and new ideas all used to decorate a variety of media. This characterized his design style and makes his work easy to identify. Fornasetti's decorative arts were offered through fine department stores and shops thoughout the world.

A metal umbrella stand, by Piero Fornasetti, decorated with a screened design, with paper label, Italy, Milan, signed & dated 1996, 29½in (75cm) high.

£250–300 Treadway Gallery

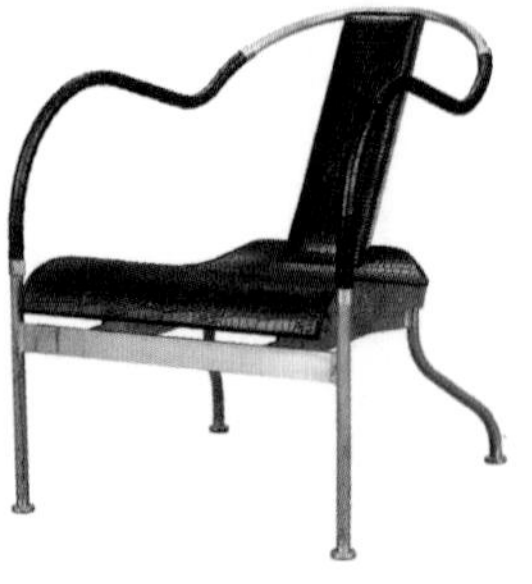

A brass and embossed leather El Rey armchair, by Mats Theselius for Källemo, signed and numbered, Sweden, 1999.

£3,500–4,200 Bukowskis

CLOCKS

A chrome clock, by K. E. M. Weber for Lawson Time Inc, America, c1930, 8in (20.5cm) wide.
£1,100–1,200
James Strang

A glass and chrome-plated mantel clock, with a partly-mirrored dial, fitted for electricity, 1930s, 9in (23cm) diam.
£1,300–1,600
Sotheby's (Am)

A mahogany and inlaid marquetry longcase clock, Sweden, 1940s, 66in (167.5cm) high.
£1,600–1,800
Pure Imagination

A wood, metal and brass clock, by Henning Koppel, Denmark, c1960, 11½in (29cm) diam.
£1,200–1,500
Sotheby's (NY)

A plastic table clock, by Angelo Mangiarotti for Secticon, with a gilt dial, signed, Switzerland, 1960s, 9½in (24cm) high.
£125–150
Treadway Gallery

TEXTILES

A rug, signed 'S.W.T.', slight damage and losses, Sweden, c1950, 102¾ x 69¾in (261 x 177cm).
£7,000–8,500 **Bukowskis**

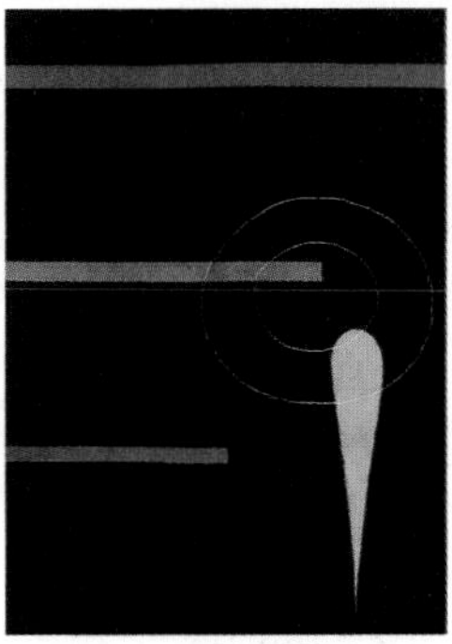

A rug, machine-woven with geometrical motifs, 1950s, 154¼ x 114½in (392 x 291cm).
£1,250–1,500
Sotheby's (Am)

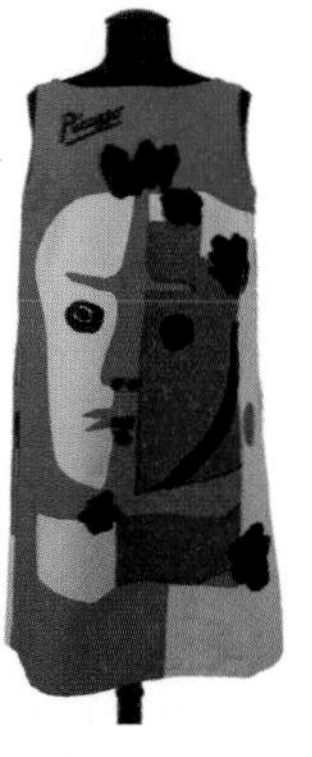

A cotton Clown print dress, by Picasso for dead-stock, decorated with 'Suite de 180' print, 1963.
£1,500–1,800 **Whitaker**

An Op Art gown, by Marco Correa, with label, c1970.
£500–600 **Kerry Taylor**

POSTERS

An advertising poster, by Aubrey Beardsley, 'The Yellow Book, Vol III', 1894, 20¼ x 12¾in (51.5 x 32.5cm).

£550–650 **Freeman's**

A lithograph poster, by Edward Penfield, 'Harpers Christmas', signed, America, 1894, 22¼ x 16⅓in (56.5 x 41.5cm).

£400–500 **Freeman's**

An advertising poster, by Florence Lundborg, 'The Lark', America, 1895, 20¾ x 14⅓in (52 x 37.5cm).

£400–500 **Freeman's**

A poster, by Edward Penfield, 'Western Lawn Tennis Tournament', on linen, America, 1896, 28 x 19¼in (71 x 49cm).

£5,500–6,500 **Freeman's**

A lithograph advertising poster, by Akseli Gallen-Kallela, 'Bil-Bol Cars', signed, Finland, 1907, 32½ x 42½in (81.5 x 108cm).

£35,000–42,000 **Bukowskis (F)**

A General Bus Co poster, by Grainger Johnson, 'Godstone by Motorbus', 1922 , 39¼ x 24½in (100 x 62cm).

£1,650–1,850 **P & K Rennie**

A poster, by Sep. E. Scott, 'Eat More Fruit and be more Beautiful', c1925, 30 x 20in (76 x 51cm).

£320–380 **Onslow's**

A poster, by André Daude, 'Pianos Daude', on linen, France, c1925, 61¾ x 46in (157 x 117cm).

£1,000–1,200 **Freeman's**

An LNER poster, by Tom Purvis, 'Northumberland, It's Quicker By Rail', on linen, c1930, 40¼ x 50in (102 x 127cm).

£2,250–2,750 Onslow's

An LNER poster, by Frank Brangwyn, 'The Forth-Bridge, East Coast Route', on linen, c1930, 39¼ x 50½in (100 x 128cm).

£3,000–3,500 Onslow's

A poster, by Prieto, 'San Sebastian', on japan paper, c1930, 39½ x 27¼in (100.5 x 69cm).

£400–500 Van Sabben

A film poster, 'King Kong', on linen, America, 1933, reprinted 1956, 41 x 27in (104 x 68.5cm).

£700–850 Ritchies Inc

A travel poster, by Julien Lacaze, 'Côte d'Azur', France, 1935, 39½ x 24½in (100.5 x 62cm).

£300–350 Van Sabben

A London Underground poster, by Maurice A. Miles, 'For the Zoo', slight damage, c1933, 40 x 24¾in (101.5 x 63cm).

£1,800–2,200 Onslow's

Maurice Miles exhibited at the Royal Academy in 1931. He designed two posters for the Underground in the Cubist style, the other being for Kew Gardens, and one other featuring Polperro for Shell in 1933.

A British Communist Party poster, 'Hendon War Display, Only Mass Action Of Workers Can Stop War', 1930s, 30 x 20in (76 x 51cm).

£900–1,100 Onslow's

A lithograph poster, by Alexei Evgenievich Zelensky, 'The Circus', signed, edition of 500, Russia, 1936, 35 x 49in (88.5 x 124cm).

£2,800–3,300 Sotheby's (O)

A London Underground poster, by Barnett Freedman, 'Circus', on japan paper, 1936, 24¾ x 40in (63 x 101.5cm).

£650–800 Onslow's

A London Transport poster, by Paul Nash, 'Come Out To Live, Buy A Season Ticket', 1936, 39¼ x 24½in (100 x 62cm).

£680–750 P & K Rennie

A propaganda poster, by Philip Zec, 'Women of Britain. Come into the Factories', c1940, 28 x 19in (71 x 48.5cm), framed and glazed.

£150–180 Dominic Winter

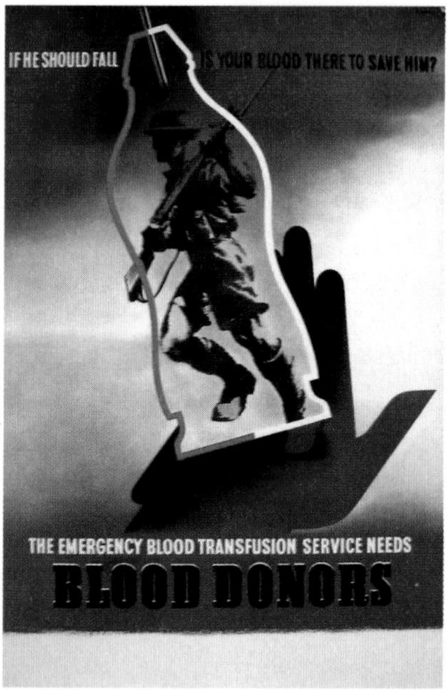

A Blood Transfusion Service poster, by Abram Games, 'If he should fall is your blood there to save him?', 1940s, 25½ x 19¼in (65 x 49cm).

£140–170 Onslow's

A Fox film poster, *The Day The Earth Stood Still*, on linen, America, 1951, 27 x 41in (68.5 x 104cm).

£4,000–5,000 Ritchies

An RKO film poster, *Pluto's Party*, America, 1952, 41 x 27in (104 x 68.5cm).

£450–550 Ritchies

A film poster, *Devil Girl from Mars*, America, 1954, 41 x 27in (104 x 68.5cm).

£650–750 Ritchies

A British Railways poster, by Kenneth Steel, 'Selby Abbey', 1950s, 39¼ x 24½in (100 x 62cm).

£450–500 P & K Rennie

A British Railways poster, by Frederick D. Blake, 'London', c1955, 40 x 25in (101.5 x 63.5cm).

£160–200 Van Sabben

A Universal film poster, *Tarantula*, on linen, America, 1955, 41 x 27in (104 x 68.5cm).

£750–900 Ritchies

An American International film poster, *Invasion of the Saucer-Men*, America, 1957, 41 x 27in (104 x 68.5cm).

£3,200–3,800 Ritchies

A Beijing People's Republic Art Publishing House poster, 'Young People Are Like The Rising Sun For Our Country, All Our Hopes Are Placed On Them', damaged, China, 1958, 21 x 30in (53.5 x 76cm).

£350–420 Bloomsbury

A Shanghai People's Art Publishing House poster, 'Working People Must Be The Masters of Culture', China, 1958, 30 x 19¾in (76 x 50cm).

£230–280 Bloomsbury

A Shan Xi People's Publishing House sposter, 'Long Live the Great Marxism, Leninism and Mao Tse-Tung's Thoughts', China, 1971, 30¼ x 42¼in (77 x 107.5cm).

£700–850 Bloomsbury

PRINTS

OVER THE PAST four years the market for modern prints has almost quadrupled, particularly Modern British and Contemporary American examples. This increase rides on the back of the ever strengthening art market as a whole. As ownership of original paintings by the likes of Damien Hirst, Bridget Riley, Richard Hamilton, Andy Warhol and Roy Lichtenstein becomes available only to those with a very large disposable income, original prints by these artists are increasingly being seen as the only affordable way of owning a work of art by a so called 'blue chip' artist. While a Bridget Riley painting from the 1960s recently sold for over £1,000,000, her prints sell for between £1,000 and £15,000, and as her popularity soars so do her prices. Warhol is another good example – images from his Mick Jagger series of prints could be bought for around £3,000 at auction in the mid- to late 1990s. These days if you want to own one expect to pay in the region of £15,000. In terms of where the market is going, my prediction is ever upwards. For UK collectors of modern British art, the big name artists will continue to increase in popularity, particularly those artists whose main output was primarily in other media, such as sculpture – for example Reg Butler, Geoffrey Clarke and Lynn Chadwick. I would also look at important painters who produced relatively few prints, such as William Scott, Keith Vaughan and Christopher Richard Wynne Nevinson.

For any collector thinking about buying prints the most important factor to consider after confirmation of the authenticity of the work, is condition. Prints are multiples and it is therefore vital that the impression bought is in the best possible state; tears, creases, staining and other visible damage to the sheet of paper dramatically affect its value, in severe cases making the work almost valueless. Any good dealer or auctioneer will disclose the condition of the work to you, and if it is not clear ask. I would also always recommend inspecting prints at first hand before buying. At any print auction you will see dealers asking to view prints out of their frames, carefully handling the works to closely inspect the condition. This is expected, particularly by auctioneers, so do not be afraid to ask to do this. If you cannot attend an auction, ask for a condition report, which will give you some protection if the work you have bought is very different to its catalogue description. **Alexander Hayter**

Karel Appel
Dutch (1921–2006)
Face, 1977
Signed, lithograph, numbered
12 x 16in (30.5 x 40.5cm)
£750–900 Auction Atrium

Romare Bearden
American (1912–88)
Jamming at the Savoy, 1981–82
Signed, etching and aquatint, edition of 180
16½ x 23½in (42 x 59.5cm)
£2,750–3,250 Freeman's

Sir Peter Blake
British (b1932)
The Tattooed Lady, c1982
Silk screen on Somerset satin paper,
16 colourways, 5 prints in each colourway,
6 versions
40 x 30in (101.5 x 76cm)
£2,700–3,000 CCA Galleries

Sandra Blow, RA
British (1925–2006)
Untitled 1968
Edition of 50
18½ x 23½in (47 x 60cm)
£1,100–1,250 CCA Galleries

Lynn Chadwick
British (1914–2003)
Reclining Figure on Green Wave, 1971
Signed and dated, lithograph, artist's proof
for edition of 90
19¾ x 30in (50 x 76cm)
£400–500 Bloomsbury

Marc Chagall
Russian/French (1887–1985)
Ruse de Dorcon, 1961
Signed, colour lithograph on Arches paper, edition of 60
16¾ x 12½in (42.5 x 32cm)
£8,500–10,000 **Freeman's**

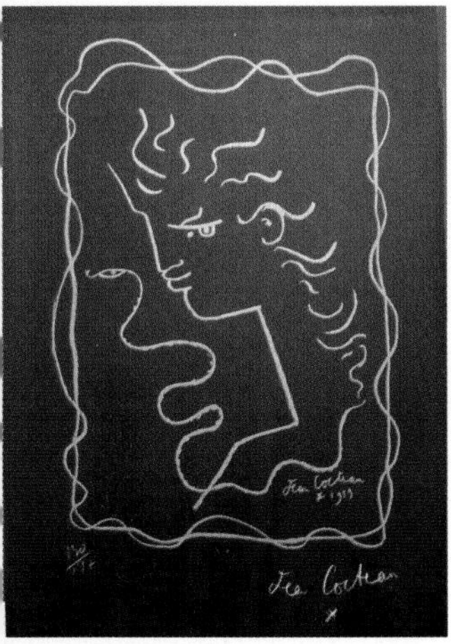

Jean Cocteau
French (1889–1963)
Visage 2, 1959
Signed, lithograph on wove paper
24x 18in (61 x 45.5cm)
£500–600 **Auction Atrium**

Tracey Emin
British (b1963)
Sixty a Day Woman, 1986
Signed, lithograph printed in colours, edition of 18
21¾ x 29¾in (55.5 x 75.5cm)
£850–1,000 **Rosebery's**
This rare and early work by Tracey Emin displays her early interest in German Expressionist art. Many subjects such as love, war and hate are bound up in her mature works.

Mikhail Mikhailovich Chemiakin
Russian (b1943)
Untitled
A pair, signed, one dated 1976
25¼ x 18¼in (64 x 46.5cm)
£1,200–1,500 **Sotheby's (O)**

Beryl Cook
British (b1926)
Russian Tea Room, 2002
Edition of 300
26¾ x 31¼in (68 x 79.5cm)
£2,000–2,400 **CCA Galleries**

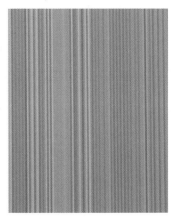

Johnny Friedlaender
German (1912–92)
Composition, 1978
Signed and inscribed, etching
29½ x 22in (75 x 56cm)
£220–260 **Skinner**

Prunella Clough
British (1919–99)
Cranes, c1952
Signed, lithograph on wove paper
17 x 14½in (43 x 37cm)
£4,000–5,000 **Bloomsbury**
Lithographs by Prunella Clough from this period are rare. They were printed in very small editions, in some cases fewer than 10.

Ronald Davis
American (b1937)
Vertical Stripes, 1972
Signed and dated, Serigraph on paper, edition of 150
35 x 24¼in (89 x 61.5cm)
£250–300 **Skinner**

Dame Elizabeth Frink, CH, RA
British (1930–93)
Man, 1985
Signed, etching and aquatint, one of ten artist's proofs for edition of 30
8¼ x 8in (21 x 20.5cm)
£1,000–1,100 **Caroline Wiseman**

MILLER'S COMPARES

(L) William Scott
(1913–89)
Untitled, 1973
Signed and dated, lithograph on wove paper, edition of 75
18½ x 20½in (47 x 52cm)
£3,000–3,600 Bloomsbury

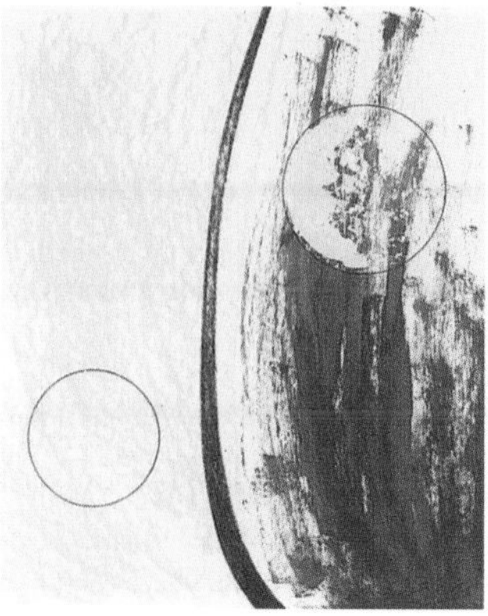

(R) Barbara Hepworth, DBE
British (1903–75)
Orchid, 1970
Colour lithograph on wove paper, edition of 60
16¼ x 17¾in (41 x 45cm)
£400–500 Bloomsbury

Both William Scott and Dame Barbara Hepworth are of the Cornish School and leading figures in modern British art. However, these lithographs dating from the early 1970s recently achieved vastly different prices at auction. One key reason is that the item on the left is signed. A signature is vital – it is this act of artist authentication that enables a work to sell for £4,000 rather than £400 and the difference can really be that wide. The item on the left, if unsigned, would sell for around £500; the item on the right, if signed, would fetch closer to £1,500. Another area of note is that, stylistically, the Scott is immediately recognizable – the use of broad areas of colour and the abstracted still life image are what define this artist's output. By contrast Hepworth is known primarily as a sculptor and so her works on paper lack the three-dimensionality that, for many, defines her art. However, perhaps it is this slightly under appreciated aspect of Hepworth's output that keen collectors should look out for over the coming years.

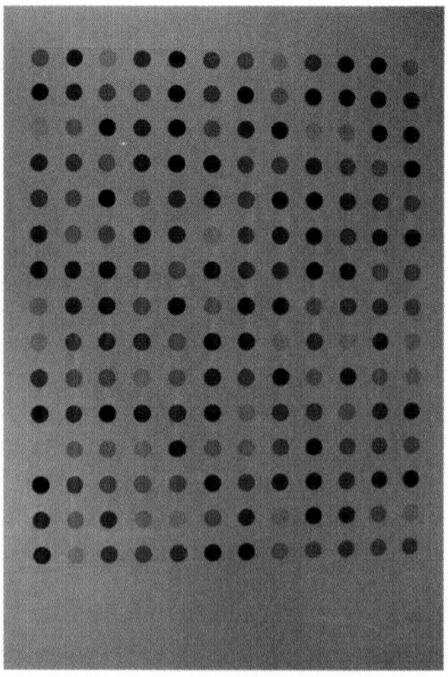

Damien Hirst
British (b1966)
Ethidium Bromide Aqueous Solution 2005
Signed, etching on Hahnemuehle paper
118½ x 99½in (301 x 252.5cm)
£10,000–11,000 Caroline Wiseman

David Hockney
British (b1937)
Cleanliness is next to Godliness, 1964
Signed and dated, silkscreen printed in colours, edition of 40
33 x 21¾in (84 x 55.5cm)
£3,300–4,000 Bloomsbury

Sir Terry Frost, RA
British (1915–2003)
Tolcarne Moon Blue, Newlyn, 1997
Edition of 150
25½ x 25in (65 x 63.5cm)
£1,100–1,250 CCA Galleries

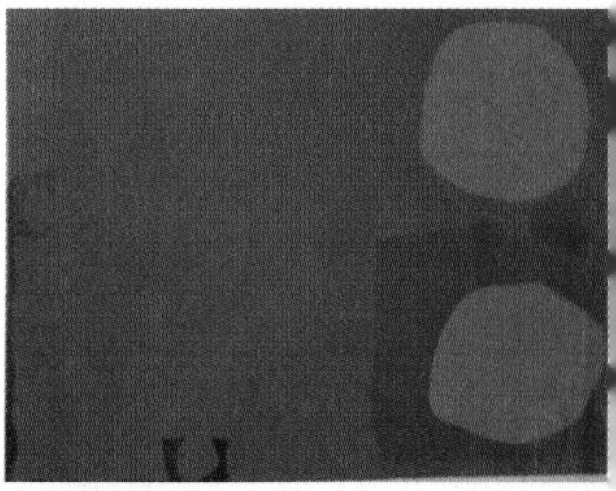

Patrick Heron
British (1920–99)
Red and Pink, 1970
Signed and dated, silkscreen, edition of 100
23½ x 31in (59.5 x 79cm)
£4,500–5,000 Caroline Wiseman

Howard Hodgkin
British (b1932)
Still Life, 1980
Initialled, screen print, edition of 100
31½ x 29in (80 x 73.5cm)
£2,000–2,400 David Lay

Patrick Hughes
British (b1939)
Splash of Colours, 1982
Edition of 20
30¾ x 42¼in (78 x 107cm)
£700–770 CCA Galleries

Rockwell Kent
American (1882–1971)
Resting, 1929
Signed, lithograph, edition of 100
9½ x 5¾in (24 x 14.5cm)
£500–600 **Freeman's**

Laura Knight, DBE
British (1877–1972)
Some Clowns, 1930
Signed, drypoint on laid paper, edition of 50
13¾ x 9¾in (35 x 25cm)
£700–850 **Bloomsbury**

Willem De Kooning
Dutch (1904–1997)
Untitled, 1986
Signed, lithograph printed in colours, edition of 100, from Quatre Lithographies
28¼ x 24¾in (72 x 63cm)
£4,000–5,000 **Bloomsbury**

Roy Lichtenstein
American (1923–97)
Crak!, 1963–64
Signed, offset lithograph printed in colours
18¾ x 27in (47.5 x 68.5cm)
£9,500–11,500 **Bloomsbury**

Louis Lozowick
Russian/American (1892–1973)
Oil Country, 1936
Lithograph, edition of 200
12½ x 7½in (29 x 19cm)
£280–330 **Freeman's**

John Minton
British (1917–57)
Apple Orchard, Kent, 1951
Lithograph, 19¼ x 28¾in (49 x 73cm)
£650–750 **P & K Rennie**
This is one of a series of three lithographs commissioned by J. Lyons & Co between 1947 and 1955 to display in their teashops.

Joan Miró
Spanish (1893–1983)
Fusees, 1959
Signed, colour etching and aquatint
5 x 7in (12.5 x 18cm)
£2,000–2,400 **Freeman's**

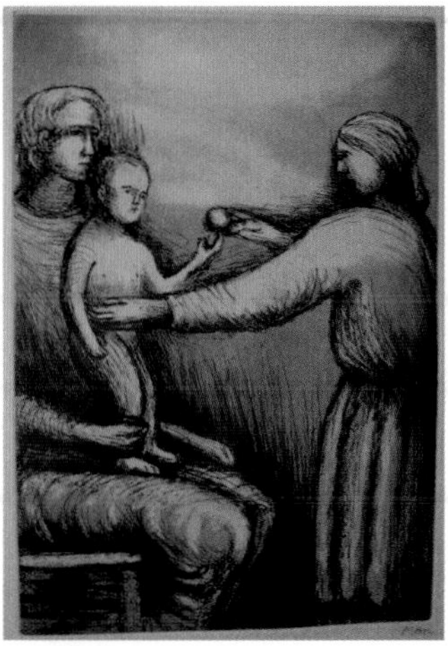

Henry Moore, OM, CH, FBA
British (1898–1986)
Mother and Child XXI, 1983
Etching, aquatint and roulette, edition of 65
24½ x 20½in (62 x 52cm)
£3,000–3,500 **Caroline Wiseman**

Christopher Richard Wynne Nevinson, ARA
British (1889–1946)
The Temples of New York, 1921
Signed, drypoint, edition of 50
7¾ x 5¾in (19.5 x 14.5cm)
£3,500–4,200 **Freeman's**

Eduardo Paolozzi, CBE, FRA
Scottish (1924–2005)
Bash, 1971
Signed and dated, silkscreen printed in colours, printer's proof
29¼ x 19½in (74.5 x 49.5cm)
£380–450 **Bloomsbury**

Pablo Picasso
Spanish (1881–1973)
Exposition 1958 Vallauris
Signed, colour lino cut, edition of 300
25¼ x 20¾in (64 x 52.5cm)
£2,500–3,000 **Freeman's**

John Piper
British (1903–92)
Llyn Teifi 1987
Etching on Velin Arches paper, edition of 70,
15½ x 22¾in (39.5 x 58cm)
£1,400–1,600 **Caroline Wiseman**

Barbara Rae, RA, RSA
Scottish (b1943)
Spanish Farm – Puerto Romano, 1992
Signed, dated and titled, monoprint in colours
11 x 11½in (28 x 29cm)
£550–650 **Rosebery's**

Man Ray
American (1890–1986)
Electro Magie, Electro Image, 1969
Signed, etching in colours on BFK Rives paper, edition of 25
11¼ x 8¾in (28.5 x 22.5cm)
£750–900 **Auction Atrium**

Bridget Riley
British (b1931)
Elapse, 1982
Signed, silkscreen printed in colours, edition of 260
45¾ x 30in (116 x 76cm)
£3,800–4,500 **Bloomsbury**

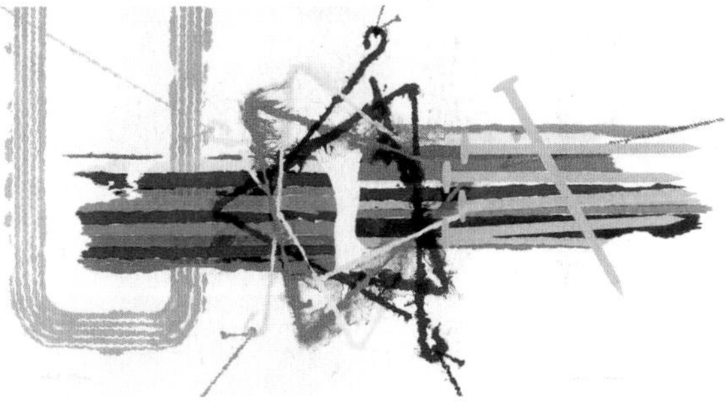

James Rosenquist
American (b1933)
Violent Turn, 1977
Signed, colour lithograph on Arches paper, edition of 100
36½ x 70in (92.5 x 178cm)
£3,000–3,500 Freeman's

Michael Rothenstein
British (1908–93)
Birds and Branches, 1995
Edition of 100
17¼ x 21¼in (44 x 54cm)
£680–750 CCA Galleries

Georges Rouault
French (1871–1958)
In These Dark Times of Vainglory and Unbelief, Our Lady of Land's End Keeps Vigil, 1924
Signed and dated, etching and aquatint
25¾ x 20in (65.5 x 51cm)
£1,350–1,500 Caroline Wiseman

Aldo Salvadori
Italian (1905–2002)
Woman in Studio, 1995
Edition of 200
32 x 19in (81 x 48.5cm)
£680–750 CCA Galleries

Rufino Tamayo
Mexican (1899–1991)
Hombre, Luna y Estrellas, 1950
Signed, colour lithograph, edition of 200
19¾ x 13½in (50 x 34.5cm)
£750–900 Freeman's

Gordon Walters
New Zealander (1919–95)
Karaka, 1979
Signed and dated, screenprint, artist's proof
22 x 17¼in (56 x 44cm)
£3,200–3,800 Webb's

Andy Warhol
American (1928–87)
Flowers, 1964
Signed and dated, offset lithograph, edition of c300, slight damage
23in (58.5cm) square
£6,500–8,000 Bloomsbury

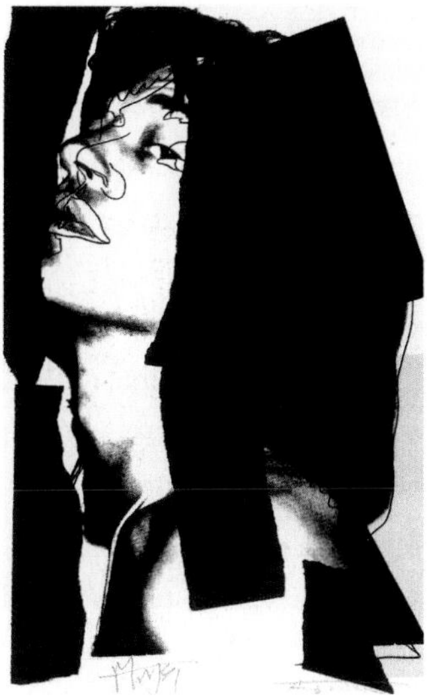

Andy Warhol
American (1928–87)
Mick Jagger, 1975
Signed, screenprint on Arches paper,edition of 50, signed by Jagger
43¼ x 28½in (110 x 72.5cm)
£13,000–16,000 Freeman's

GLOSSARY

abrash: Slight shift in colour tone in a rug or carpet, due to a new batch of yarn being used – each batch of a natural dye will differ slightly from the others.

***albarello*:** Drug jar, usually of waisted cylindrical form, used in most major European countries from the 15thC.

ambrotype: Early type of glass negative that could be made to appear as a positive by backing it with black varnish or paper.

anchor escapement: Said to have been invented c1670 by Robert Hooke or William Clement. A type of escape mechanism shaped like an anchor, which engages at precise intervals with the toothed escape wheel. The anchor permits the use of a pendulum (either long or short), and gives greater accuracy than was possible with the verge escapement.

***anhua*:** Hidden decoration on Chinese porcelain.

argyle: Silver gravy-warmer shaped like a coffee pot with a central well for the gravy and an outer casing for hot water, said to have been invented by one of the Dukes of Argyll.

askos: Small ancient Greek vessel to contain liquids, in the form of a closed pot with a spout and handle.

associated: Term used in antiques, in which one part of an item is of the same design but not originally made for it. See *marriage* and *made up*.

automaton: Any moving toy or decorative object, usually powered by a clockwork mechanism.

aventurine: Brown or blue quartz with gold inclusions, hence anything that resembles the mineral, such as aventurine glass, that is flecked with gold-coloured mica or other metals, or lacquer work of gold strands on a red or black background.

barbotine: Painting on pottery using coloured kaolin pastes, invented in 1865 by Ernest Chaplet.

bat printing: Type of transfer printing used to produce fine detail on porcelain and bone china by English factories in the early 19thC.

bezel: Ring, usually brass, surrounding the dial of a clock, and securing the glass dial cover.

***bianco-sopra-bianco*:** Literally white-on-white. Used in ceramics to describe an opaque white pattern painted on an off-white background.

Biedermeier: Style of furniture made principally in the 1820s and '30s in Austria, Germany and parts of Scandinavia and characterized by simple, heavy Classical forms. It is named after a fictional character who symbolized the German bourgeoisie of the early 19thC.

biggin: Form of coffee percolator invented c1799 by George Biggin.

***bijin*:** Japanese term for a beautiful woman.

bisque: French term for biscuit ware, or unglazed porcelain.

***blanc-de-Chine*:** Translucent white Chinese porcelain, unpainted and with a thick glaze, made in kilns in Dehua in the Fujian province from the Song Dynasty and copied in Europe.

***bleu de Nevers*:** A brilliant blue glaze first found on pottery from Nevers in France from the 17th or early 18thC.

Bodhisattva: Attendant of Buddha.

***bombé*:** Bulbous, curving form, a feature often seen on wares produced during the rococo period.

***bonbonnière*:** Sweet jar or box.

***bordalou*:** Lady's portable commode.

***boteh*:** Stylized design of a floral bush found on rugs, similar to a Paisley design.

Britannia standard: Higher standard of silver required between 1697 and 1720. Denoted by Britannia and a lion's head in profile on the hallmark.

***bureau de dame*:** Writing desk of delicate appearance and designed for use by ladies. Usually raised above slender cabriole legs and with one or two external drawers.

***bureau plat*:** French writing table with a flat top and drawers in the frieze.

cabaret set: Tea set on a tray for three or more people.

calamander: Hardwood, imported from Sri Lanka (of the same family as ebony), used in the Regency period for making small articles of furniture, as a veneer and for crossbanding.

cameo glass: Two or more layers of coloured glass in which the top layers are then cut or etched away to create a multi-coloured design in relief. An ancient technique popular with Art Nouveau glassmakers in the early 20thC.

cannetille: Extremely thin gold wirework decoration.

cartouche: Ornate tablet or shield surrounded by scrollwork and foliage, often bearing an inscription, monogram or coat-of-arms.

cash motif: Chinese ceramic pattern based on the design of Chinese coins with a square central hole.

catlinite: Red stone composed of compressed clay, often used by Native Americans to make pipes.

celadon: Chinese stoneware with an opaque grey-green glaze, first made in the Song Dynasty and still made today, principally in Korea.

cellaret: Lidded container on legs designed to hold wine. The interior is often divided into sections for individual bottles.

***champlevé*:** Enamelling on copper or bronze, similar to cloisonné, in which a glass paste is applied to the hollowed-out design, fired and ground smooth.

character doll: One with a naturalistic face, especially laughing, crying, pouting, etc.

***chilong*:** Small lizard, often portrayed on Chinese ceramics.

Chinese Imari: Chinese imitations of Japanese blue, red and gold painted Imari wares, made from the early 18thC.

chinoiserie: The fashion, prevailing in the late 18thC, for Chinese-style ornamentation on porcelain, wallpapers, fabrics, furniture and garden architecture.

chryselephantine: Combination of ivory and a metal, usually bronze; used for Art Deco figures.

chrysoprase: opaque green glass.

***chuval*:** Turkic word meaning bag.

cistern tube: Mercury tube fitted into stick barometers, the lower end of which is sealed into a boxwood cistern.

Cizhou: Chinese porcelain wares characterized by bold shapes and decoration on a slip-covered body. They were named after the most important centre of production, Cixian (Cizhou), but were also produced in many different places in northern China.

clock garniture: Matching group of clock and vases or candelabra made for the mantel shelf. Often highly ornate.

cloisonné: Enamelling on metal with divisions in the design separated by lines of fine metal wire. A speciality of the Limoges region of France in the Middle Ages, and of Chinese craftsmen to the present day.

close-concentric paperweight: One which consists of concentric circles of canes arranged tightly together so that the clear glass cannot be seen between the rings of canes.

close-pack paperweight: One which is characterized by canes closely packed together without a pattern.

***coiffeuse*:** French dressing table.

coin silver: Silver of the standard used for coinage, ie .925 or sterling.

colza lamp: Lamp that burned a thick heavy oil made from rapeseed that was stored to one side in a reservoir shaped like a classical urn.

coromandel: Imported wood from the Coromandel coast of India, of similar blackish appearance to calamander and used from c1780 for banding, and for small pieces of furniture.

countwheel: Wheel with segments cut out of the edge or with pins fitted to one face, which controls the striking of a clock. Also known as a locking plate.

***crespina*:** Shallow Italian dish with a fluted border.

***cuerda seca*:** Technique of tile-making, developed in Iran in the 15thC, whereby the colours of the design were separated by an oily substance which leaves a brownish outline.

***cwpwrdd deuddarn*:** Welsh variety of the press cupboard with two tiers.

cyma: Double-carved moulding. Cyma recta is concave above and convex below; cyma reversa the other way round. Also known as ogee and reverse ogee moulding. Popular with 18thC cabinet makers.

Cymric: Trade-name used by Liberty & Co for a mass-produced range of silverware inspired by Celtic art, introduced in 1899 and often incorporating enamelled pictorial plaques.

deadbeat escapement: Type of anchor escapement, possibly invented by George Graham and used in precision pendulum clocks.
Dehua: Town in southern China where much *blanc-de-Chine* was produced.
Delft: Dutch tin-glazed earthenwares named after the town of Delft, the principal production centre, from the 16thC onwards. Similar pottery made in England from the late 16thC is also termed 'delft' or 'delftware'.
dentils: Small rectangular blocks applied at regular intervals as a decorative feature.
déposé: Term indictating a registered patent. Used on French and German bisque dolls and often appearing as an incised mark on the head.
***deutsche Blumen*:** Naturalistically painted flowers, either single or tied into bunches, used as a popular decorative motif on 18thC pottery and porcelain.
***dhurrie*:** Cotton flatweave rug or carpet from India.
diaper: Surface decoration composed of repeated diamonds or squares, often carved in low relief.
ding: Chinese three-legged vessel.
dog of *Fo*: Buddhist guardian lion.
***doucai*:** Decoration on Chinese porcelain using five colours.
***duchesse brisée*:** Type of chaise longue of French origin, consisting of one or two tub-shaped chairs and a stool to extend the length. Popular in Britain during the late 18thC.
Durham quilt: A type of quilt with fancy stitching on a plain background, made in the northeast of England.
***encre-de-Chine*:** Indian ink.
***en grisaille*:** Painted decoration using a mainly black and grey palette and resembling a print.
***ensi*:** Rug used as a tent door by Turkoman tribes.
escapement: Means or device which regulates the release of the power of a timepiece to its pendulum or balance.
***façon de Venise*:** Literally 'in the Venetian style', used to describe high quality, Venetian-influenced glassware made in Europe during the 16th to 17thC.
***fahua*:** Type of sancai (Chinese three-coloured ware). Usually has a turquoise or purple-blue ground and dates from the late 15th/early 16thC.
faïence: Tin-glazed earthenware named after the town of Faenza in Italy, but actually used to describe products made anywhere but Italy, where they are called maiolica.
***famille jaune/noire/rose/verte*:** Chinese porcelain in which yellow, black, pink or green respectively are the predominant ground colours.
***fauteuil*:** French open-armed drawing room chair.
fielded panel: Panel with bevelled or chamfered edges.
Fitzhugh pattern: Design in Chinese ceramics characterized by a border of four split pomegrantes and butterflies. Made for the American market and named after the person who first ordered it.
flambé: Glaze made from copper, usually deep crimson, flecked with blue or purple, and often faintly crackled.
flatware (1): Collective name for flat pottery and porcelain, such as plates, dishes and saucers.
flatware (2): Cutlery.
flatweave: Term sometimes used to describe kilims and *soumakhs.*
flow blue: Process used principally after 1840 in which powder is added to the dye used in blue and white transfer-printed ceramics so that the blue flows beyond the edges of the transfer, making the pattern less sharply defined. Items using this process were made primarily for the American market.
fluted: Border that resembles a scalloped edge, used as a decoration on furniture, glass, silver and porcelain items.
***fuku*:** Chinese term for happiness.
***fu shou*:** Chinese decorative motif meaning happiness and longevity.
fusee: 18thC clockwork invention; a cone-shaped drum, linked to the spring barrel by a length of gut or chain. The shape compensates for the declining strength of the mainspring thus ensuring constant timekeeping.
gadroon: Border or ornament comprising radiating lobes of either curbed or straight form. Used from the late Elizabethan period.
garrya: Catkin-bearing evergreen shrub used as carved or inlaid decoration, usually on furniture in the styles of Hepplewhite or Adam.
girandole: Carved and gilt candle sconce incorporating a mirror.
Gnathian ware: A unique style of ancient Greek pottery from the town of Gnathia, characterized by painted decoration on a black gloss body.
Guanyin: Buddhist Bodhisattva of Compassion.
***guéridon*:** Small circular table designed to carry some form of lighting.
guglet: Type of water bottle, often accompanied by a small basin and used for minor ablutions.
***guilloche*:** Decorative motif of interlacing circles forming a continuous figure-of-eight pattern.
***gül*:** From the Persian word for flower – usually used to describe a geometric flowerhead on a rug.
***guttus*:** Ancient Greek closed vessel with a spout and handle for pouring oil into lamps.
halberd: Spear fitted with a double axe.
hard paste: True porcelain made of china stone (petuntse) and kaolin; the formula was long known to, and kept secret by, Chinese potters but only discovered in the 1720s at Meissen, Germany, from where it spread to the rest of Europe and the Americas. Recognized by its hard, glossy feel.
***hatchli*:** Rug used as a door by Turkomans on their tents.
***hiramakie*:** Japanese term for sponged gold applied level with the surface.
***hongmu*:** Type of wood used in the manufacture of Chinese furniture.
***ho-o*:** Mythical Chinese bird, similar to a phoenix, symbolizing wisdom and energy.
Hotei: Japanese Shinto god of Luck, Happiness, Laughter and Wisdom of Contentment.
***hu*:** Bronze Chinese ritual vessel.
***huanghuali*:** Type of Oriental wood, much admired for its colour.
Imari: Export Japanese porcelain of predominantly red, blue and gold decoration which, although made in Arita, is called Imari after the port from which it was shipped.
impasto: Technique of applying paint thickly to ceramics so that the brush or palette knife marks are visible.
***indianische Blumen*:** German for 'indian flowers'; painting on porcelain in the Oriental style, especially on mid-18thC Meissen.
***inro*:** Japanese multi-compartmental medicine or seal container, carried suspended from the sash of a kimono.
***intarsio*:** Dramatic form of underglaze decoration featured on wares designed and decorated by Frederick Rhead.
ironstone: Stoneware, patented 1813 by Charles James Mason, containing ground glassy slag, a by-product of iron smelting, for extra strength.
***kachina*:** Native American supernatural ancestor figure.
Kakiemon: Family of 17thC Japanese porcelain decorators who produced wares decorated with flowers and figures on a white ground in distinctive colours: azure, yellow, turquoise and soft red. Widely imitated in Europe.
***kasa*:** Scandinavian drinking vessel.
***katana*:** Long Japanese sword.
***kelleh*:** Long narrow carpets which are wider than runners.
***kendi*:** Chinese or Japanese globular drinking vessel which is filled through the neck, the liquid being drunk through the spout.
***khula khud*:** Indo-Persian term for helmet.
kiku: Japanese term for a chrysanthemum.
kilim: Flat woven rug without a pile.
***klapmuts*:** Chinese dish with rounded wall and flattened rim, said to resemble a type of woollen hat of this name worn by the Dutch in the 16th and 17thC.
knop: Knob, protuberance or swelling in the stem of a wine glass, of various forms which can be used as an aid to dating and provenance.
***Komai*:** Style of Japanese lacquerwork made famous by the Komai family.
***koro*:** Japanese incense burner.
***kotile*:** Ancient Greek vessel in the form of a bowl.
***kovsh*:** Russian vessel used for measuring drink, often highly decorated for ornamental purposes.
***kozuka*:** Small Japanese utility knife.
kraak porselein: Dutch term for porcelain raided from Portuguese ships, used to describe the earliest Chinese export porcelain.
krater: Ancient Greek vessel for mixing water and wine in which the mouth is always the widest part.
***kris*:** Indonesian or Malaysian dagger with a scalloped edge.
***kylin*:** Chinese mythical beast.
lambrequin: Ornamental hanging covering the edge of a shelf or the upper part of a window or door.

laque burgauté: Asian lacquer wares, inlaid with mother-of-pearl, gold or precious stones.

latticinio: Fine threads of white or clear glass forming a filigree mesh effect enclosed in clear glass.

lattimo: from the Italian *latte* meaning milk; an opaque white glass made by adding bone ash or tin oxide to the glass batch.

lekythos: Ancient Greek flask used for oil or perfume.

lingzhi: Type of fungus or mushroom, used as a motif on Chinese works of art.

loaded: Term used for a silver candlestick with a hollow stem filled with pitch or sand for weight and stability.

Longquan: Chinese ceramics with a pale grey body covered by a thick, opaque, bluish-green, slightly bubbly glaze.

Lucite: Type of solid, transparent plastic, often used instead of glass.

Luohan: Saintly person in Buddhist religion.

made up: Piece of furniture that has been put together from parts of other pieces of furniture. See *associated* and *marriage*.

maiolica: Tin-glazed earthenware produced in Italy from the 15thC to the present day.

majolica: Heavily-potted, moulded ware covered in transparent glazes in distinctive, often sombre colours, developed by the Minton factory in the mid-19thC.

Mandarin palette: design that portrays the day-to-day life of the Mandarin class in China. A very popular subject matter in the West and therefore common on Chinese export wares.

marriage: Joining together of two unrelated parts to form one piece of furniture. See *associated* and *made up*.

martelé: Term for silverware with a fine, hammered surface, first produced in France and later revived by the American silversmiths Gorham Manufacturing Co during the Art Nouveau period.

matched pair: Two items that are very similar in appearance and give the appearance of being a pair.

meiping: Chinese for cherry blossom, used to describe a tall vase with high shoulders, small neck and narrow mouth, used to display flowering branches.

meiren: Chinese term for a beautiful, elegant lady.

merese: Flat disc of glass which links the bowl and stem, and sometimes the stem and foot, of a drinking glass.

mihrab: Prayer niche with a pointed arch; the motif which distinguishes a prayer rug from other types.

milk glass: (*milchglass*) Term for glass made with tin oxide, which turns it an opaque white. Developed in Venice in the late 15thC.

millefiori: Italian term meaning 'thousand flowers'. A glassmaking technique whereby canes of coloured glass are arranged in bundles so that the cross-section creates a pattern. Commonly used in paperweights.

minogame: Mythical Japanese character, half turtle, half beast.

mon: Japanese crest or coat-of-arms.

monteith: Large bowl with detachable collar and scalloped rim from which wine glasses were suspended to cool over iced water.

nashiji: Multitude of gold flakes in Japanese lacquer.

near pair: Two items that are very similar in appearance and give the appearance of being a pair. Also known as a matched pair.

netsuke: Japanese carved toggles made to secure *sagemono* (hanging things) to the *obi* (waist belt) from a cord; usually of ivory, lacquer, silver or wood, from the 16thC.

nonome: Japanese term for false damascening or inlay.

niello: Black metal alloy or enamel used for filling in engraved designs on silverware.

nulling (knulling): Decorative carving in the form of irregular fluting, usually found on early oak furniture.

ogee: Double curve of slender S shape.

oinochoe: Ancient Greek small jug with handles.

ojime: Japanese word meaning bead.

okimono: Small, finely carved Japanese ornament.

olla: Ancient earthenware pot for cooking or carrying water.

olpe: Type of ancient Greek jug with a round lip.

oni: Chinese devil.

opaline: Semi-translucent glass.

ormolu: Strictly, gilded bronze but used loosely for any yellow metal. Originally used for furniture handles and mounts but, from the 18thC, for inkstands, candlesticks etc.

overlay: In cased glass, the top layer, usually engraved to reveal a different coloured layer beneath.

paktong: Alloy of copper, zinc and nickel resembling silver. Made in China in the 18thC for export to Europe and used especially for candlesticks, fireside furniture and ornaments.

palmette: Stylized palm-leaf motif.

pardah: A rug which is suspended in a tent doorway.

pâte-de-cristal: Glass that is crushed into fine crystals and then bound together so that it can be moulded rather than having to be worked in its molten state.

***pâte-de-verre* (glass paste) :** Translucent glass created by melting and applying powdered glass in layers or by casting it in a mould.

pâte-sur-pâte: 19thC Sèvres porcelain technique, much copied, of applying coloured clay decoration to the body before firing.

pavé: Setting that has been paved with snugly fitting gemstones, so that little or no metal shows through.

penwork: Type of decoration applied to japanned furniture, principally in England in the late 18th/early 19thC. Patterns in white japan were applied to a piece which had already been japanned black, and then the details and shading were added using black Indian ink with a fine quill pen.

pier glass: Mirror designed to be fixed to the pier, or wall, between two tall window openings, often partnered by a matching pier table. Made from the mid-17thC.

pietra dura: Italian term for hardstone, applied to a mosaic pattern of semi-precious stones and marble.

piqué: Technique in which a material such as tortoiseshell is inlaid with metal decoration.

plique-à-jour: Enamelling technique in which a structure of metal strips is laid on a metal background to form enclosed areas which are then filled with transparent enamels. When the backing is removed, a transparent 'stained glass' effect is achieved.

plum pudding: Type of figuring in some veneers, produced by dark oval spots in the wood. Found particularly in mahogany.

point-de-France: Type of needlelace developed in the late 17thC.

point-de-gaze: Type of lace developed in Belgium in the latter half of the 19thC, so-called because of its light, gauzy appearance.

pole screen: Small adjustable screen mounted on a pole and designed to stand in front of an open fire to shield a lady's face from the heat.

powder flask: Device for measuring out a precise quantity of priming powder, suspended from a musketeer's belt or bandolier and often ornately decorated. Sporting flasks are often made of antler and carved with hunting scenes.

powder horn: Cow horn hollowed out, blocked at the wide end with a wooden plug and fitted with a measuring device at the narrow end, used by musketeers for dispensing a precise quantity of priming powder.

prie-dieu: Chair with a low seat and a tall back designed for prayer. Usually dating from the 19thC.

printie/printy: Circular or oval hollow cut into glass for decorative effect, sometimes called a lens.

prochous: Ancient Greek pitcher.

proto-porcelain: Early high-fired stoneware that preceded true porcelain, developed in China as kilns became more efficient and capable of reaching higher temperatures.

prunt: Blob of glass applied to the stem of a drinking vessel both as decoration and to stop the glass from slipping in the hand. Sometimes impressed with a decorative stamp to form a 'raspberry'.

punchong: Style of 15thC Korean ceramics.

***Qianjian* palette:** Range of light brown colours used in the decoration of Chinese ceramics.

qilin: Chinese mythical beast. Also spelt *kilin*.

Qingbai: White ware produced by potters in the Jingdezhen area of China throughout the Song Dynasty.

quarter-veneered: Four consecutively cut, and therefore identical, pieces of veneer laid at opposite ends to each other to give a mirrored effect.

religieuse: Early clocks of the Louis XIV period in France, influenced by the sober Protestantism of the Dutch taste.

repoussé: Relief decoration on metal made by hammering on the reverse so that the decoration projects.

register plate: Scale of a barometer against which the mercury level is read.

regulator: Clock of great accuracy, thus sometimes used for controlling or checking other timepieces.

rocaille: Shell and rock motifs found in rococo work.

***rouge de fer*:** Iron-red colour produced with iron oxide, used on Chinese ceramics.
rouleau vase: Type of Chinese vase of cylindrical shape with a rolled over rim.
rummer: 19thC English low drinking goblet.
***ruyi*:** Chinese presentation sceptre.
***ruyi* clouds:** Cloud-like decorative feature often used as a design in Chinese art.
***sancai*:** Three-colour decoration on Chinese porcelain.
S. F. B. J.: *Société de Fabrication de Bébés et Jouets*; association of doll makers founded 1899 by the merger of Jumeau, Bru and others.
***sang-de-boeuf*:** Bright red glaze used extensively on Chinese ceramics during the Qing Dynasty.
***Sennin*:** Japanese immortal.
Sgraffito: Form of ceramic decoration incised through a coloured slip, revealing the ground beneath.
***shamshir*:** Indian sword.
***shakudo*:** Japanese term for an alloy of copper and gold.
***Shibayama*:** Japanese term for lacquer applied with semi-precious stones and ivory.
***Shibuichi*:** Japanese term for an alloy of copper and silver.
***shishi*:** Japanese mythical beast, a lion-dog.
***shou* symbol:** Chinese decorative motif, symbolizing longevity.
***Shoulao*:** Chinese Star God of Longevity – one of the three most senior Chinese gods.
shoulder-head: Term for a doll's head and shoulders.
shoulderplate: Area of a doll's shoulder-head below the neck.
silver resist: Decorative technique normally found on pearlware ceramics c1800–20, whereby a design is painted in wax onto an object and then silver lustre is applied to the surface. When the wax is burnt off in the kiln, the painted design appears on a silver lustre ground.
siphon tube: U-shaped tube fitted into wheel barometers where the level of mercury in the short arm is used to record air pressure.
soft paste: Artificial porcelain made with the addition of ground glass, bone-ash or soap-stone. Used by most European porcelain manufacturers during the 18thC. Recognized by its soft, soapy feel.
spadroon: Cut-and-thrust sword.
spandrel: Element of design, closing off a corner.
spelter: Zinc treated to look like bronze and much used as an inexpensive substitute in Art Nouveau appliqué ornament and Art Deco figures.
strapwork: Repeated carved decoration suggesting plaited straps.
strip quilt ('strippy'): Quilt composed of alternating strips of different fabrics, either solid colours or prints. Very often used as the back of a patchwork or floral quilt.
stuff-over: Descriptive of upholstered furniture where the covering extends over the frame of the seat.
stumpwork: Embroidery which incorporates distinctive areas of raised decoration, formed by padding certain areas of the design.
***sugán*:** Twisted lengths of straw: referring to a type of Irish country chair that has a seat of this type.
***susani*:** Central Asian hand-embroidered bridal bed-cover.
***table ambulante*:** French term for a small, portable occasional table.
***takamakie*:** Technique used in Japanese lacquerware in which the design is built up and modelled in a mixture of lacquer and charcoal or clay dust, and then often gilded.
***takazogan*:** Japanese high relief inlay.
***taotie*:** Chinese mythical animal that devours wrong-doers.
tazza: Wide but shallow bowl on a stem with a foot; ceramic and metal tazzas were made in antiquity and the form was revived by Venetian glassmakers in the 15thC. Also made in silver from the 16thC.
teapoy: Piece of furniture in the form of a tea caddy on legs, with a hinged lid opening to reveal caddies, mixing bowl and other tea drinking accessories.
tear: Tear-drop-shaped air bubble in the stem of an early 18thC wine glass, from which the air-twist evolved.
tête-à-tête: Tea set for two people.
thuyawood: Reddish-brown wood with distinctive small 'bird's-eye' markings, imported from Africa and used as a veneer.
***tiki*:** Symbol of the procreative power of the Maori god Tane.
timepiece: Clock that does not strike or chime.
tin glaze: Glassy opaque white glaze of tin oxide; re-introduced to Europe in the 14thC by Moorish potters; the characteristic glaze of delftware, faïence and maiolica.
***togidashi*:** Japanese lacquer technique in which further layers of lacquer are added to *hiramake* (qv) then polished flush with the original surface.
***tôle-peinte*:** Polychrome painted metal.
toleware: Items made from tinplated sheet iron which is varnished and then decorated with brightly coloured paints.
tombak: Alloy of copper and zinc.
***Tosei Gusoku*:** Japanese term meaning 'modern equipment', used to describe a new style of armour introduced in the late 16thC.
Trafalgar chair: Type of dining chair with sabre legs and a ropetwist bar, made during the Regency period to commemorate the Battle of Trafalgar.
Trafalgar seat: Seat that is held in position by a small peg in the top centre of the front rail of the chair, which fits into a corresponding hole in the underside of the front seat frame.
***trembleuse*:** French term for a cup and saucer with a raised rim that holds the cup steady to avoid spillages.
trumeau: Section of wall between two openings; a pier mirror.
***tsuba*:** Guard of a Japanese sword, usually consisting of an ornamented plate.
Tudric: Range of Celtic-inspired Art Nouveau pewter of high quality, designed for mass-production by Archibald Knox and others, and retailed through Liberty & Co.
tyg: Three-handled mug.
***ushabti*:** Literally 'answerer'. Ancient Egyptian ceramic figure placed in a tomb to work in the afterworld in the place of the dead person it represented.
wan: Chinese character meaning 'myriad' or 'ten thousand', often used as a decorative ground in cloisonné to indicate 'may this vessel last for ten thousand years'.
***vargueño*:** Spanish cabinet with a fall-front enclosing drawers.
vaseline glass: Type of opalescent glass developed in Britain in the late 1870s and designed to resemble 15th- and 16thC Venetian glass.
***vase parlant*:** Glass vase of Art Nouveau design engraved or decorated in cameo with verses from French poetry.
verge escapement: Oldest form of escapement, found on clocks as early as 1300 and still in use in 1900. Consisting of a bar (the verge) with two flag-shaped pallets that rock in and out of the teeth of the crown or escape wheel to regulate the movement.
vernier scale: Short scale added to the traditional 3in (7.5cm) scale on stick barometers to give more precise readings than had previously been possible.
***vernis Martin*:** Type of japanning or imitation lacquerwork invented by the Martin family in Paris in the 18thC.
***verre églomisé*:** Painting on glass. Often the reverse side of the glass is covered in gold or silver leaf through which a pattern is engraved and then painted black.
vesta case: Ornate flat case of silver or other metal for carrying vestas, an early form of match. Used from the mid-19thC.
vitrine: French display cabinet which is often of *bombé* or serpentine outline and ornately decorated with marquetry and ormolu.
***wakizashi*:** Short Japanese sword.
Warwick cruet: Cruet of open design usually containing three silver casters and two silver-mounted glass bottles, named after an example made by Anthony Nelme in 1715 for William Greville, Earl of Warwick.
WMF: Short for Württembergische Metallwarenfabrik, a German foundry that was one of the principal producers of Art Nouveau metalware.
***wucai*:** Type of five-colour Chinese porcelain decoration, executed in vigorous style.
***wufu*:** Chinese term meaning 'the five happinesses' (long life, riches, tranquility, love of virtue and a good end to one's life).
***yaki*:** Japanese term for ware.
***yen yen*:** Chinese term for a long-necked vase with a trumpet mouth.
Yingqing: Type of porcelain from Jingdezhen in China, first produced during the Song dynasty. Also known as Qingbai.
Zitan: Type of dense wood used for making chinese furniture.

DIRECTORY OF SPECIALISTS

If you wish to be included in next year's directory, or if you have a change of address or telephone number, please contact Miller's Advertising Department on +44 (0) 1580 766411 by March 2008. We advise readers to make contact by telephone before visiting a dealer, therefore avoiding a wasted journey.

CANADA

Can/Am Antiques, 760 Golf Club Road, Fredericton, New Brunswick, E3B 7S6 Tel: 506 455 2005 jon@theoldriverlodge.net www.rubylane.com/shops/cantiquesnb
Antiques, furniture, ceramics, clocks, fine art and collectibles.

JEWELLERY

Fiona Kenny Antiques Tel: 905 682 0090 merday@cogeco.ca www.tocadero.com/merday fionakennyantiques.com
18th–20thC jewellery and antiques, sterling and silver plate, china and pottery, 20thC modern, collectibles and advertising.

LIGHTING

Andrew W Zegers Antiques, 25 Rodman Street, St Catherines, Ontario, L2R 5C9 Tel: 905 685 4643
Also art and accessories, antique formal upholstered & country furniture.

U.S.A.

AMERICANA

American West Indies Trading Co. Antiques & Art Tel: 305 872 3948 awindies@att.net www.goantiques.com/members/awindiestrading
Ethnographic, Folk, Tribal, Spanish Colonial, Santos & Retablos, American Indian, Indonesian Keris, southeast Asian antiquities, orientalia, Art Deco, Floridiana.

Allan Katz Americana, 25 Old Still Road, Woodbridge, Connecticut 06525 Tel: 203 393 9356
Folk Art, trade signs and weather vanes.

Antiquities

Hurst Gallery, 53 Mt. Auburn Street, Cambridge, MA 02138 Tel: 617 491 6888 manager@hurstgallery.com www.hurstgallery.com
Art of the Pacific, Africa, Asia, The Americas and the ancient world.

Appraiser

Anne Weston & Associates, LLC, 43 Pray Street, Portsmouth, New Hampshire 03801 Tel: 603 431 0385 Cell: 603 521 4001 anne-weston@comcast.net www.anne-weston.com

ARMS & MILITARIA

Faganarms, Box 425, Fraser, MI48026 Tel: 586 465 4637 info@faganarms.com www.faganarms.com

BAROMETERS

Barometer Fair, P.O. Box 25502, Sarasota, FL 34277 Tel: 941 400 7044 john@barometerfair.com www.barometerfair.com
Buys, sells and restores antique barometers.

BOOKS

Bauman Rare Books, 1608 Walnut Street, 19th Floor, Philadelphia, PA 19104 Tel: 215 546 6466 brb@baumanrarebooks.com www.baumanrarebooks.com

CLOCKS

R. O. Schmitt Fine Art, P.O. Box 162, Windham, NH 03087 Tel: 603 432 2237 www.antiqueclockauction.com
Specialist antique clock auctions.

DECORATIVE ARTS

Anne Weston & Associates, LLC, 43 Pray Street, Portsmouth, New Hampshire 03801 Tel: 603 431 0385 Cell 603 521 4001 anne-weston@comcast.net www.anne-weston.com

DOLLS

Sara Bernstein Antique Dolls & Bears, Englishtown, New Jersey 07726 Tel: 732 536 4101 santiqbebe@aol.com www.sarabernsteindolls.com
Dolls and Teddy bears.

Theriault's, P.O. Box 151, Annapolis, MD 21404 Tel: 410 224 3655 info@theriaults.com www.theriaults.com
Doll auctions.

FURNITURE

American Art Display, 514 14th West Palm Beach, Florida 33401 Tel: 561 379 9367 americanartdisplay@msn.com
Display stands.

Antique Associates at West Townsend, P.O. Box 129W, 473 Main Street, West Townsend, MA 01474 Tel: 978 597 8084 drh@aaawt.com

Antiquebug, Frank & Cathy Sykes, 85 Center Street, Wolfeboro, New Hampshire 03894 Tel: 603 569 0000 dragonfly@antiquebug.com www.antiquebug.com
Also Folk Art, mahogany speed boat models, maps and antiquarian books.

Axe Antiques, 275 Alt, A1A (SR811) Jupiter, Florida 33477, Palm Beach County Tel: 561 743 7888/877 689 1730 www.axeantiques.com
Also stocks fine art, vintage pillows, seals, militaria and architectural elements.

Douglas Hamel Antiques, 56 Staniels Road, Chichester, New Hampshire 03234 Tel: 603 798 5912 doughamel@shakerantiques.com www.shakerantiques.com
We buy, sell and locate Shaker antiques.

Warehouse Provence, 1120 Massachusetts Ave, (Rte.111) Boxborough, Maine, MA 01719 Tel: 978 266 0200 warehouseprovence@aics.net www.warehouseprovence.com

LIGHTING

Chameleon Fine Lighting, 223 East 59th Street, New York 10022 Tel: 212 355 6300 mail@chameleon59.com www.chameleon59.com

MARKETS & CENTRES

Chesapeake Antique Center, Inc,Route 301, P.O. Box 280, Queenstown, MD 21658 Tel: 410 827 6640 admin@chesapeakeantiques.com www.chesapeakantiques.com

Santa Monica Antique Market, 1607 Lincoln Boulevard, Santa Monica, California 90404 Tel: 310 673 7048

ORIENTAL

Mimi's Antiques, Peter Stiltz Tel: 443 250 0930 mimisantiques@comcast.net www.mimisantiques.com www.trocadero.com/mimisantiques
18th and 19th century Chinese export porcelain, American and English furniture, continental porcelain, paintings, Sterling, oriental rugs.

PAPERWEIGHTS

The Dunlop Collection, P.O. Box 6269, Statesville, NC 28687 Tel: 704 871 2626 or Toll Free Telephone (800) 227 1996

PUBLICATIONS
Antique Collectors Club Ltd, Market Street Industrial Park, Wappinger Falls, New York 12590
Tel: 914 297 0003

SILVER
Alter Silver Gallery Corp, Gallery 49A & 50, 1050 Second Avenue, New York 10022
Tel: 212 750 1928/ 917 848 1713
altersilvergallery@mac.com

Antique Elegance, Tel: 617 484 7556
Also jewelry, pottery, porcelain, orientalia, cut glass, paintings, rugs and furniture.

Argentum, The Leopard's Head, 472 Jackson Street, San Francisco, CA 94111
Tel: 415 296 7757
info@argentumtheleopard.com
www.argentumtheleopard.com

Imperial Half Bushel, 831 North Howard Street, Baltimore, Maryland 21201
Tel: 410 462 1192
www.imperialhalfbushel.com

TEXTILES
Antique European Linens, Pandora de Balthazar, Timeles Down and Textiles, 106 N. Washington St., Rond Top, TX 78954
Tel: 979 249 2070
roundtop@antiqueeuropeanlinens.com
www.pandoradebalthazar.com

Antique European Linens, Pandora de Balthazar, Timeles Down and Textiles, 9 S. 9th Avenue, Pensacola, FL 32502
Tel: 859 432 4777
sales@antiqueeuropeanlinens.com
www.pandoradebalthazar.com
Hungarian goose down pillows & european duvets.

TRIBAL ART
Hurst Gallery, 53 Mt. Auburn Street, Cambridge, MA 02138
Tel: 617 491 6888
manager@hurstgallery.com
www.hurstgallery.com
Art of the Pacific, Africa, Asia, the Americas and the ancient world.

UK & IRELAND

20TH DESIGN
Berkshire
Special Auction Services, Kennetholme, Midgham, Reading, RG7 5UX
Tel: 0118 971 2949
www.specialauctionservices.com
Specialist auctions of 20th century designer furniture.

ANTIQUITIES
Dorset
Ancient & Gothic, P O Box 5390, Bournemouth, BH7 6XR
Tel: 01202 431721
Bi-monthly sales of Greek, Roman, Anglo-Saxon and Medieval antiquities.

ARCHITECTURAL
Somerset
Robert Mills Ltd, Narroways Road, Eastville, Bristol, BS2 9XB
Tel: 0117 955 6542
info@rmills.co.uk
www.rmills.co.uk

ARMS & MILITARIA
Gloucestershire
Q & C Militaria, 22 Suffolk Road, Cheltenham, GL50 2AQ
Tel: 01242 519815 or 07778 613977
qcmilitaria@btconnect.com
www.qcmilitaria.com

Kent
Dennis Exall,
Tel: 07810 118338
Edged weapons, world medals, general militaria, postcards and badges.

Lancashire
Rod Akeroyd & Son, 20 Ribblesdale Place, Preston, PR1 3NA
Tel: 01772 203845
info@firearmscollector.com
www.firearmscollector.com

Lincolnshire
Garth Vincent, The Old Manor House, Allington, Nr Grantham, NG32 2DH
Tel: 01400 281358 or 07785 352151
garthvincent@aol.com
www.guns.uk.com

Oxfordshire
Avrick Antiques
Tel: 01295 738 318 or 07762 272846
avrick_antiques@tiscali.co.uk
www.avrick-antiques.co.uk
Antique firearms and edged weapons.

Surrey
West Street Antiques, 63 West Street, Dorking, RH4 1BS Tel: 01306 883487
weststant@aol.com
www.antiquearmsandarmour.com

East Sussex
Wallis & Wallis, West Street Auction Galleries, Lewes, BN7 2NJ Tel: 01273 480208
auctions@wallisandwallis.co.uk
www.wallisandwallis.co.uk
Auctioneers of militaria, arms and armour and medals.

BAROGRAPHS
Somerset
Richard Twort,
Tel: 01934 612439 or 07711 939789
walls@mirage-interiors.com

BAROMETERS
Berkshire
Alan Walker, Halfway Manor, Halfway, Newbury, RG20 8NR
Tel: 01488 657670 or 07770 728397
enquiries@alanwalker-barometers.com
www.alanwalker-barometers.com

Cheshire
Derek & Tina Rayment Antiques, Orchard House, Barton Road, Barton, Nr Farndon, SY14 7HT
Tel: 01829 270429 07860 666629 and 07702 922410
raymentantiques@aol.com
www.antique-barometers.com
Also repair & restoration

Wiltshire
P A Oxley Antique Clocks & Barometers, The Old Rectory, Cherhill, Calne, SN11 8UX
Tel: 01249 816227
info@paoxley.com
www.britishantiqueclocks.com

BOOKS
Gloucestershire
Dominic Winter Book Auctions, Mallard House, Broadway Lane, South Cerney, GL7 5UQ
Tel: 01285 860006
info@dominicwinter.co.uk
www.dominicwinter.co.uk
Specialist book and works on paper auctions.

Northumberland
Barter Books, Alnwick Station, Alnwick, NE66 2NP
Tel: 01665 604888
www.barterbooks.co.uk

Somerset
George Bayntun, Manvers Street, Bath, BA1 1JW
Tel: 01225 466000

Surrey
David Aldous-Cook, P.O. Box 413, Sutton, SM3 8SZ Tel: 020 8642 4842
office@davidaldouscook.co.uk
www.davidaldouscook.co.uk
Reference books on antiques and collectables.

BOXES & TREEN
Berkshire
Mostly Boxes, 93 High Street, Eton, Windsor, SL4 6AF
Tel: 01753 858470

CERAMICS
Oxfordshire
Julian Eade
Tel: 01865 300349 or 07973 542971
Doulton Lambeth stoneware and Burslem wares. Royal Worcester, Minton and Derby.

CLOCKS
Cheshire
Coppelia Antiques, Holford Lodge, Plumley Moor Road, Nr Knutsford, Plumley, WA16 9RS
Tel: 01565 722197
www.coppeliaantiques.co.uk

Gloucestershire
The Grandfather Clock Shop, Styles of Stow, The Little House, Sheep Street, Stow-on-the-Wold, GL54 1JS
Tel: 01451 830455
info@stylesofstow.co.uk
www.stylesofstow.co.uk

Jillings Antique Clocks, Croft House, 17 Church Street, Newent, GL18 1PU
Tel: 01531 822100
www.jillings.com

Woodward Antique Clocks, 21 Suffolk Parade, Cheltenham, GL50 2AE
Tel: 01242 245667
enquiries@woodwardclocks.co.uk
www.woodwardclocks.co.uk

Greater Manchester
Northern Clocks, Boothsbank Farm Worsley, Manchester, M28 1LL
Tel: 0161 790 8414
info@northernclocks.co.uk
www.northernclocks.co.uk

Hampshire
The Clock-Work-Shop (Winchester), 6A Parchment Street, Winchester,

SO23 8AT Tel: 01962 842331
www.clock-work-shop.co.uk

Kent
The Old Clock Shop, 63 High Street, West Malling, ME19 6NA
Tel: 01732 843246
www.theoldclockshop.co.uk

Derek Roberts Antiques, 25 Shipbourne Road, Tonbridge, TN10 3DN
Tel: 01732 358986
drclocks@clara.net
www.qualityantiqueclocks.com

London
The Clock Clinic Ltd, 85 Lower Richmond Road, Putney, SW15 1EU
Tel: 020 8788 1407
clockclinic@btconnect.com
www.clockclinic.co.uk

Roderick Antique Clocks, 23 Vicarage Gate, W8 4AA
Tel: 020 7937 8517
rick@roderickantiqueclocks.com
www.roderickantiqueclocks.com

Somerset
The Clock Shop, The Pitching, Market Place, Castle Cary, BA7 7AL Tel: 01963 359100
www.castlecaryclockshop.co.uk

Kembery Antique Clocks Ltd, George Street Antique Centre, 8 Edgar Buildings, George Street, Bath, BA1 2EH Tel: 0117 956 5281
kembery@kdclocks.co.uk
www.kdclocks.co.uk

Staffordshire
The Essence of Time Antique Clocks, Unit 2, Curborough Antiques & Craft Centre, Curborough Hall Farm, Watery Lane, off Eastern Avenue By-Pass, Lichfield, WS13 8ES
Tel: 01543 418239

Surrey
The Clock House, 75 Pound Street, Carshalton, SM5 3PG
Tel: 020 8773 4844 or 07850 363317
markcocklin@theclockhouse.co.uk
www.theclockhouse.co.uk

Wiltshire
P A Oxley Antique Clocks & Barometers, The Old Rectory, Cherhill, Calne, SN11 8UX Tel: 01249 816227
info@paoxley.com
www.britishantiqueclocks.com

Allan Smith Clocks, Amity Cottage, 162 Beechcroft Road, Upper Stratton, Swindon, SN2 7QE
Tel: 01793 822977
allansmithclocks@ntlworld.com
www.allansmithantiqueclocks.co.uk

North Yorkshire
Brian Loomes, Calf Haugh Farm, Pateley Bridge, HG3 5HW
Tel: 01423 711163
clocks@brianloomes.com
www.brianloomes.com

COMICS
East Sussex
phil-comics auctions, P.O. Box 3433, Brighton, BN50 9JA
Tel: 01273 673462 or 07739 844703
phil@phil-comics.com
www.phil-comics.com
A collector and trader/auctioneer with 15 years experience specialising in Beano and Dandy children's annuals and comics. phil-comics auctions will sell your single items to entire collections through live online auctions. We seek all types of children's books, annuals and comics, including: Beano, Beezer, Black Bob, Broons, Dandy, Giles, Hotspur, Knockout, Lion, Marvelman, Mickey Mouse, Oor Wullie, Superman, Rupert Bear, Radio Fun, Rover, Topper, Victor, Wizard and many, many more! Please quote single items to entire collections from 1900 to 1980. Books, annuals, comics, summer specials, free gifts, flyers, original artwork, ephemera, etc. Please see www.phil-comics.com for full details and write, telephone or email with any queries. We look forward to hearing from you and will provide a fast courteous response.

DECORATIVE ARTS
Greater Manchester
A. S. Antique Galleries, 26 Broad Street, Pendleton, Salford, M6 5BY
Tel: 0161 737 5938
as@artnouveau-artdeco.com
www.artnouveauartdeco.com

Kent
The Design Gallery 1850–1950, 5 The Green, Westerham, TN16 1AS
Tel: 01959 561234
sales@designgallery.co.uk
www.designgallery.co.uk

Lancashire
Clarion Antiques and Fine Art, Ground Floor, 2 St Georges Square, Lytham St Anns, FY8 2NY
Tel: 01253 721903 or 07985 191623
clarion2000@btinternet.com
www.clarionantiquesltd.co.uk

London
Crafts Nouveau, 112 Alexandra Park Road, Muswell Hill, N10 2AE
Tel: 0208 444 3300
www.craftsnouveau.co.uk

Republic of Ireland
Mitofsky Antiques, 8 Rathfarnham Road, Terenure, Dublin 6
Tel: 492 0033
info@mitofskyantiques.com
www.mitofskyantiques.com

EXHIBITION & FAIR ORGANISERS
Nottinghamshire
DMG Fairs, P.O. Box 100, Newark, NG24 1DJ
Tel: 01636 702326
www.dmgantiquefairs.com

West Midlands
Clarion Events Ltd, Antiques For Everyone, The NEC, Birmingham
Tel: 0870 736 6060 or 0121 67 2947
www.antiquesforeveryone.co.uk

EXPORTERS
East Sussex
International Furniture Exporters Ltd, Old Cement Works, South Heighton, Newhaven, BN9 0HS
Tel: 01273 611251
ife555@aol.com
www.int-furniture-exporters.co.uk

Wiltshire
North Wilts. Exporters, Farm Hill House, Brinkworth, SN15 5AJ Tel: 01666 510876 or 07836 260730
mike@northwilts.demon.co.uk
www.northwiltsantiqueexporters.com

FISHING
Kent
The Old Tackle Box, P.O. Box 55, High Street, Cranbrook, TN17 3ZU
Tel: 01580 713979 or 07729 278 293
tackle.box@virgin.net

London
Angling Auctions, P. O. Box 2095, W12 8RU
Tel: 020 8749 4175 or 07785 281349
neil@anglingauctions.demon.co.uk

FURNITURE
Herefordshire
Pugh's Antiques, Portley House, Old Ludlow Road, Leominster, H36 0AA
Tel: 01568 616546
sales@pughsantiques.com
www.pughsantiques.com

Northamptonshire
Lorraine Spooner Antiques, 211 Watling Street West, Towcester, NN12 6BX
Tel: 01327 358777
lorraine@lsantiques.com
www.lsantiques.com
Period furniture, clocks, silver, porcelain, glass, paintings & prints, linens, books.

Scotland
Destiny Antiques, Art & Design, Nugent Drive, Perth Airport, Scone, Perthshire, PH2 6PL
Tel: 01738 553273

Jeremy Gow Antique Restoration, Pitscandly Farm, Forfar, Angus, DD8 3NZ
Tel: 01307 465342
jeremy@knowyourantiques.com
www.knowyourantiques.com
17th & 18thc marquetry English & continental furniture and restoration. BAFRA member.

West Sussex
British Antique Replicas, 45 School Close, Queen Elizabeth Avenue, Burgess Hill, RH15 9RX
Tel: 01444 245577
www.1760.com
Replica antique furniture.

Wiltshire
Cross Hayes Antiques, Unit 21, White Walls, Easton Grey, Malmesbury, SN16 0RD Tel: 01666 822877
david@crosshayes.co.uk
www.crosshayes.co.uk
Shipping furniture.

Worcestershire
S.W. Antiques, Abbey Showrooms, Newlands (road), Pershore, WR10 1BP
Tel: 01386 555580
sales@sw-antiques.co.uk
www.sw-antiques.co.uk

GLASS
Gloucestershire
Grimes House Antiques, High Street, Moreton-in-Marsh, GL56 0AT
Tel: 01608 651029
grimes_house@cix.co.uk
www.grimeshouse.co.uk
www.cranberryglass.co.uk

JEWELLERY
London
Shapiro & Co, Stand 380, Gray's Antique Market, 58 Davies Street, W1Y 5LP
Tel: 020 7491 2710 or 07768 840930
Faberge.

Norfolk
T. Robert, P.O. Box 9, Cromer, NR27 0HE
Tel: 01263 511865
enquiries@t-robert.com
www.t-robert.com

MARKETS & CENTRES
Lincolnshire
Hemswell Antique Centres, Caenby Corner Estate, Hemswell Cliff, Gainsborough, DN21 5TJ
Tel: 01427 668389
enquiries@hemswell-antiques.com
www.hemswell-antiques.com

London
Bourbon-Hanby Arcade Antiques & Interiors, 151 Sydney Street, Chelsea, SW3 6NT
Tel: 0870 1423403
www.bourbonhanby.co.uk
www.antiqueschelsea.co.uk

Alfie's Antique Market, 13-25 Church Street, London, NW8 8DT
Tel: 020 7723 6066
www.alfiesantiques.com

Grays Antique Markets, South Molton Lane, W1K 5AB Tel: 020 7629 7034
www.graysantiques.com

East Sussex
Church Hill Antiques Centre, 6 Station Street, Lewes, BN7 2DA Tel: 01273 474 842
churchhilllewes@aol.com

MUSICAL
Kent
Stephen T. P. Kember LTD, Pamela Goodwin, 11 The Pantiles, Royal Tunbridge Wells, TN2 5TD Tel: 01959 574067 or 07850 358067
steve.kember@btinternet.com
www.antique-musicboxes.co.uk
Antique cylinder & disc musical boxes.

Nottinghamshire
Turner Violins, 1-5 Lily Grove, Beeston, NG9 1QL
Tel: 0115 943 0333
info@turnerviolins.co.uk

OAK & COUNTRY FURNITURE
Northamptonshire
Paul Hopwell Antiques, 30 High Street, West Haddon, NN6 7AP Tel: 01788 510636
paulhopwell@antiqueoak.co.uk
www.antiqueoak.co.uk

PAPERWEIGHTS
Cheshire
Sweetbriar Gallery Ltd., 29 Beechview Road, Kingsley, WA6 8DF
Tel: 01928 788225
sales@sweetbriar.co.uk
www.sweetbriar.co.uk

PINE
Wiltshire
North Wilts. Exporters, Farm Hill House, Brinkworth, SN15 5AJ Tel: 01666 510876 or 07836 260730
mike@northwilts.demon.co.uk
www.northwiltsantiqueexporters.com

PORCELAIN
Essex
Barling Porcelain
Tel: 01621 890058
www.barling.uk.com

East Sussex
Tony Horsley, P.O. Box 3127, Brighton, BN1 5SS Tel: 01273 550770
Candle extinguishers, Royal Worcester and other fine porcelain.

POTTERY
Berkshire
Special Auction Services, Kennetholme, Midgham, Reading, RG7 5UX
Tel: 0118 971 2949
www.specialauctionservices.com
www.antiquestradegazette.com/sas
Specialist auctions of commemoratives, pot lids & Prattware, Fairings, Goss & Crested, Baxter & Le Blond prints.

Buckinghamshire
Gillian Neale Antiques, P.O. Box 247, Aylesbury, HP20 1JZ Tel: 01296 423754 or 07860 638700
gillianneale@aol.com
www.gilliannealeantiques.co.uk
Blue & white transfer printed pottery 1780—1860.

Dorset
Greystoke Antiques, 4 Swan Yard, Sherborne, DT9 3AX
Tel: 01935 812833
English blue transfer printed pottery.

Gloucestershire
Styles of Stow, The Little House, Sheep Street, Stow-on-the-Wold, GL54 1JS
Tel: 01451 830455
www.stylesofstow.co.uk
Staffordshire figures.

Oxfordshire
Winson Antiques, Unit 11, Langston Priory Workshops, Kingham, OX7 6UP Tel: 01608 658856 or 07764 476776
clive.payne@virgin.net
www.clivepayne.co.uk
Mason's Ironstone china and period furniture.

Surrey
Judi Bland Antiques
Tel: 01276 857576 or 01536 724145
18th & 19th century English Toby jugs.

PUBLICATIONS
London
Antiques Trade Gazette, 115 Shaftesbury Avenue, WC2H 8AD
Tel: 0207 420 6646
www.antiquestradegazette.com

West Midlands
Antiques Magazine, H.P. Publishing, 2 Hampton Court Road, Harborne, Birmingham, B17 9AE
Tel: 0121 681 8003
subscriptions@antiquesmagazine.com
www.hp-publishing.co.uk

Art Loss Review, H.P. Publishing, 2 Hampton Court Road, Harborne, Birmingham, B17 9AE
Tel: 0121 681 8003
subscriptions@artlossreview.com
www.hp-publishing.co.uk

SCIENTIFIC INSTRUMENTS
Cheshire
Charles Tomlinson, Chester Tel: 01244 318395
charlestomlinson@tiscali.co.uk

Scotland
Early Technology, Monkton House, Old Craighall, Musselburgh, Midlothian, EH21 8SF
Tel: 0131 665 5753
michael.bennettlevy@virgin.net
www.earlytech.com
www.rare78s.com
www.tvhistory.tv

SCULPTURE
West Sussex
Garret & Hurst Sculpture, P.O. Box 658, East Grinstead, RH19 3GH
Tel: 01342 311729 or 07976 247942
garhurst@btinternet.com
www.garretandhurst.co.uk

SILVER
London
Daniel Bexfield Antiques, 26 Burlington Arcade, W1J 0PU
Tel: 020 7491 1720
antiques@bexfield.co.uk
www.bexfield.co.uk
Specialising in fine quality silver, jewellery and objects of vertu dating from the 17th to the 20thC.

TEDDY BEARS
Oxfordshire
Teddy Bears of Witney, 99 High Street, Witney, OX28 6HY Tel: 01993 702616 or 706616
alfonzo@witneybears.co.uk
www.teddybears.co.uk

TEXTILES
London
Erna Hiscock & John Shepherd, Chelsea Galleries, 69 Portobello Road, W11
Tel: 01233 661407
erna@ernahiscockantiques.com
www.ernahiscockantiques.com
Antique samplers.

TOYS
Berkshire
Special Auction Services, Kennetholme, Midgham, Reading, RG7 5UX
Tel: 0118 971 2949
www.specialauctionservices.com
Specialist auctions of toys for the collector including Dinky, Corgi, Matchbox, lead soldiers and figures, tinplate and model railways, etc.

East Sussex
Wallis & Wallis, West Street Auction Galleries, Lewes, BN7 2NJ
Tel: 01273 480208
grb@wallisandwallis.co.uk
www.wallisandwallis.co.uk
Auctioneers of diecast toys, model railways, tin plate toys and models.

DIRECTORY OF AUCTIONEERS

Auctioneers who hold frequent sales should contact the advertising department on +44 (0) 1580 766411 by March 2008 for inclusion in the next edition.

U.S.A.

Alderfer Auction Company,
501 Fairgrounds Road,
Hatfield, PA 19440
Tel: 215 393 3037
www.alderferauction.com

Bertoia Auctions, 2141 DeMarco Drive,
Vineland, New Jersey 08360
Tel: 856 692 1881
toys@bertoiaauctions.com
www.bertoiaauctions.com

Bloomington Auction Gallery,
300 East Grove St, Bloomington,
Illinois 61701 Tel: 309 828 5533
joyluke@verizon.net
www.joyluke.com

Frank H Boos Gallery,
420 Enterprise Court,
Bloomfield Hills, Michigan 48302
Tel: 248 332 1500
artandauction@boosgallery.com
www.boosgallery.com

Braswell Galleries,
125 West Ave, Norwalk, CT 06854
Tel: 203 899 7420

William Bunch Auctions,
1 Hillman Drive, Chadds Ford,
Philadelphia 19317
Tel: 610 558 1800
info@williambunchauctions.com
www.williambunchauctions.com

Concept Art Gallery, 1031 South
Braddock Avenue, Pittsburgh, PA
15218 Tel: 412 242 9200
info@conceptgallery.com
www.conceptgallery.com

The Chicago Wine Company,
5663 West Howard Street,
Niles, Illinois 60714
Tel: 847 647 8789
info@tcwc.com
www.tcwc.com

Cincinnati Art Galleries, LLC,
225 East 6th Street, Cincinnati,
Ohio 45202 Tel: 513 381 2128
www.cincinnatiartgalleries.com

The Cobbs Auctioneers LLC,
Noone Falls Mill, 50 Jaffrey Rd,
Peterborough, NH 03458
Tel: 603 924 6361
info@thecobbs.com
www.thecobbs.com

Copake Auction, Inc., 266 RT. 7A,
Copake, NY 12516
Tel: 518 329 1142
info@copakeauction.com
www.copakeauction.com

Craftsman Auctions, Rago Arts &
Auction Center, 333 North Main Street,
Lambertville, New Jersey 08530
Tel: 609 397 9374 info@ragoarts.com
www.ragoarts.com

Doyle New York, 175 East 87th Street,
New York 10128 Tel: 212 427 2730
info@doylenewyork.com
www.doylenewyork.com

Du Mouchelles, 409 East Jefferson,
Detroit, Michigan 48226
Tel: 313 963 6255
info@dumouchelles.com

Eldred's, Robert C Eldred Co Inc.,
1475 Route 6A, East Dennis,
Massachusetts 0796
Tel: 508 385 3116 www.eldreds.com

Freeman's Fine Art Of Philadelphia Inc.,
Samuel T. Freeman & Co.,
1808 Chestnut Street,
Philadelphia 19103 Tel: 215 563 9275
www.freemansauctions.com

The Great Atlantic Auction Company,
2 Harris & Main Street, Putnam,
CT 06260 Tel: 860 963 2234
www.thegreatatlanticauction.com

Green Valley Auctions, Inc.,
2259 Green Valley Lane, Mt. Crawford,
VA 22841 Tel: 540 434 4260
gvai@shentel.net
www.greenvalleyauctions.com

Gene Harris Antique Auction Center,
203 S. 18th Avenue, P.O. Box 476,
Marshalltown, Iowa 50158
Tel: 641 752 0600
geneharris@geneharrisauctions.com
geneharrisauctions.com

Heritage Auction Galleries,
3500 Maple Avenue,
17th Floor, Dallas, Texas 75219-3941
Tel: 214 528 3500/800 872 6467
bid@HeritageAuctions.com
www.HeritageAuctions.com

Leslie Hindman, Inc.,
122 North Aberdeen Street, Chicago,
Illinois 60607 Tel: 312 280 1212
www.lesliehindman.com

Hunt Auctions, Inc., 75 E. Uwchlan
Avenue, Suite 130, Exton,
Pennsylvania 19341
Tel: 610 524 0822
info@huntauctions.com
www.huntauctions.com

Randy Inman Auctions Inc.,
P.O. Box 726, Waterville,
Maine 04903-0726
Tel: 207 872 6900
inman@inmanauctions.com
www.inmanauctions.com

Jackson's International, Auctioneers &
Appraisers of Fine Art & Antiques,
2229 Lincoln Street, Cedar Falls,
IA 50613 Tel: 319 277 2256
www.jacksonsauction.com

Arthur James Galleries,
615 East Atlantic Ave.,
Delray Beach, FL 33483
Tel: 561 278 2373
www.arthurjames.com

James D Julia, Inc., P. O. Box 830,
Rte.201 Skowhegan Road,
Fairfield, ME 04937
Tel: 207 453 7125
jjulia@juliaauctions.com
www.juliaauctions.com

Mastro Auctions, 7900 South Madison
Street, Burr Ridge, Illinois 60527
Tel: 630 472 1200
www.mastroauctions.com

Paul McInnis Inc. Auction Gallery,
21, Rockrimmon Road,
Northampton, New Hampshire
Tel: 603 964 1301
www.paulmcinnis.com

New Orleans Auction Galleries, Inc.,
801 Magazine Street, AT 510 Julia,
New Orleans, Louisiana 70130
Tel: 504 566 1849
info@neworleansauction.com

Northeast Auctions, 93 Pleasant St,
Portsmouth, NH 03801-4504
Tel: 603 433 8400
www.northeastauctions.com

Pook & Pook Inc. Auctioneers and
Appraisers, 463 East Lancaster Ave.,
Downington, PA 19335
Tel: 610 269 4040
info@pookandpook.com
www.pookandpook.com

Rago Arts & Auction Center,
333 North Main Street,
Lambertville, New Jersey 08530
Tel: 609 397 9374
info@ragoarts.com
www.ragoarts.com

R. O. Schmitt Fine Art,
P.O. Box 162, Windham,
NH 03087 Tel: 603 432 2237
www.antiqueclockauction.com

Skinner Inc., 357 Main Street,
Bolton, MA 01740
Tel: 978 779 6241
www.skinnerinc.com

Skinner Inc.,
The Heritage On The Garden,
63 Park Plaza, Boston,
MA 02116
Tel: 617 350 5400

Sloan's & Kenyon,
4605 Bradley Boulevard,
Bethesda, Maryland 20815
Tel: 301 634 2330
info@sloansandkenyon.com
www.sloansandkenyon.com

Sotheby's, 1334 York Avenue at 72nd
St, New York 10021
Tel: 212 606 7000
www.sothebys.com

Sotheby's, 215 West Ohio Street,
Chicago, Illinois 60610
Tel: 312 670 0010

Sotheby's, 9665 Wilshire Boulevard,
Beverly Hills, California 90212
Tel: 310 274 0340

Sprague Auctions, Inc., Route 5,
Dummerston, VT 05301
Tel: 802 254 8969
www.spragueauctions.com

Stair Galleries, P O Box 418,
33 Maple Avenue,
Claverack, NY 12513
Tel: 212 860 5446/518 851 2544
www.stairgalleries.com

Strawser Auctions, Michael G.
Strawser, 200 North Main Street,
Wolcottville, Indiana 46795
Tel: 260 854 2859
info@strawserauctions.com
www.strawserauctions.com
www.majolicaauctions.com

Swann Galeries, 104 East 25th Street,
New York 10010 Tel: 212 254 4710
swann@swanngalleries.com

Theriault's, P.O. Box 151, Annapolis,
MD 21404 Tel: 410 224 3655
info@theriaults.com
www.theriaults.com

Time & Again Auction Gallery,
1080 Edward Street, Linden, NJ 07036
Tel: 800 290 5401 or 908 862 0200
tandagain@aol.com
www.timeandagainantiques.com

John Toomey Gallery,
818 North Boulevard, Oak Park,
IL 60301 Tel: 708 383 5234
info@johntoomeygallery.com
www.johntoomeygallery.com

Treadway Gallery, Inc.,
2029 Madison Road, Cincinnati,
Ohio 45208 Tel: 513 321 6742
info@treadwaygallery.com
www.treadwaygallery.com

TreasureQuest Auction Galleries, Inc.,
TreasureQuest Appraisal Group, Inc.,
8447 S.E. Retreat Dr., Hobe Sound,
Florida 33455 Tel: 772 781 8600
www.TQAG.com

Weschler's Auctioneers & Appraisers,
909 E Street, NW,
Washington, DC2004
Tel: 202 628 1281/800 331 1430
info@weschlers.com
www.weschlers.com

Charles A. Whitaker Auction Company,
1002 West Cliveden St, Philadelphia,
PA 19119 Tel: 215 817 4600
caw@whitakerauction.com
www.whitakerauction.com

Wolf's Auction Gallery,
1239 W 6th Street, Cleveland,
OH 44113 Tel: 216 575 9653

AUSTRALIA

Shapiro Auctioneers, 162 Queen Street,
Woollahra, Sydney, NSW 2025
Tel: 612 9326 1588
info@shapiroauctioneers.com.au
www.shapiroauctioneers.com.au

Vickers & Hoad Antique & Fine Art
Auctioneers, Sydney
Tel: 612 9693 5199
info@vickhoad.com
www.vickersandhoad.com

AUSTRIA

Dorotheum, Palais Dorotheum,
A-1010 Wien, Dorotheergasse 17,
1010 Vienna Tel: 515 60 229
client.services@dorotheum.at

BELGIUM

Amberes Auctioneers,
Terninckstraat 6-8-10,
2000 Antwerp
Tel: 32 3 226 99 69
www.amberes.be

Galerie Moderne, 3 rue du Parnasse,
1050 Brussels Tel: 32 2 511 54 15
info@galeriemoderne.be
www.galeriemoderne.be

Horta, Hôtel de Ventes - Auctioneers,
70/74 av. de Roodebeek,
1030 Brussels Tel: 32 27416060
info@horta.be
www.horta.be

The Romantic Agony Auctions,
Devroe & Stubbe,
Aquaductstraat 38-40, B-1060,
Brussels Tel: 32 2 544 10 55
auction@romanticagony.com
www.romanticagony.com

CANADA

Bailey's Auctioneers & Appraisers
Tel: 519 823 1107
www.BaileyAuctions.com

Deveau Galleries,
Robert Fine Art Auctioneers,
297-299 Queen Street, Toronto,
Ontario M5A 1S7
Tel: 416 364 6271

Heffel Fine Art Auction House,
Toronto, Ontario
Tel: 416 961 6505
mail@heffel.com
www.heffel.com

Heffel Fine Art Auction House,
Vancouver, BC Tel: 604 732 6505

Ritchies Inc., Auctioneers & Appraisers
of Antiques & Fine Art,
380 King Street East, Toronto,
Ontario, M5A 1K4
Tel: (416) 364 1864
auction@ritchies.com
www.ritchies.com

Sotheby's, 9 Hazelton Avenue,
Toronto, Ontario, M5R 2EI
Tel: (416) 926 1774
www.sothebys.com

A Touch of Class Auction & Appraisal
Service Tel: 705 726 2120
info@atouchofclassauctions.com
www.atouchofclassauctions.com

Waddington's Auctions,
111 Bathurst Street, Toronto,
M5V 2R1 Tel: 416 504 9100
info@waddingtons.ca
www.waddingtons.ca

When the Hammer Goes Down,
440 Douglas Avenue, Toronto,
Ontario, M5M 1H4 Tel: 416 787 1700
TOLL FREE 1 (866) BIDCALR (243 2257)
BIDCALR@rogers.com
www.bidcalr.com

CHINA

Sotheby's, Suites 3101-3106,
One Pacific Place,
88 Queensway, Hong Kong
Tel: (852) 2524 8121
www.sothebys.com

FINLAND

Bukowskis, Horhammer,
Iso Roobertink, 12 Stora Robertsg,
00120 Helsinki Helsingfors
Tel: 358 9 668 9110
www.bukowskis.fi

FRANCE

Artcurial, Paris
Tel: 33 1 42 99 20 13
www.artcurial.com

Sotheby's France SA,
76 rue du Faubourg,
Saint Honore, Paris 75008
Tel: 33 1 53 05 53 05
www.sothebys.com

GERMANY

Hampel Fine Art Auctions,
Schellingstrasse 44, 80799 Munich
Tel: 49 89 28 80 4 0
office@hampel-auctions.com
www.hampel-auctions.com

Hermann Historica OHG,
Postfach 201009, 80010 Munchen
Tel: 49 89 5237296
www.hermann-historica.com

Nagel Auktionen GMBH & Co. KG,
Neckarstrasse 189-191,
70190 Stuttgart
Tel: 49 711 649 690
contact@auction.de
www.auction.de

Sotheby's Berlin, Palais
anmFestungsgraben, Unter den Linden,
Neue Wache D-10117
Tel: 49 (30) 201 0521
www.sothebys.com

Sotheby's Munich, Odeonsplatz 16,
D-80539 Munchen
Tel: 49 (89) 291 31 51

Venator & Hanstein Book & Print
Auctions, Cacilienstrasse 48,
50667 Cologne
Tel: 49 221 257 54 19
www.venator-hanstein.de

ISRAEL

Sotheby's Israel,
46 Rothschild Boulevard,
Tel Aviv 66883
Tel: 972 3 560 1666
www.sothebys.com

ITALY

Bloomsbury Auctions, Palazzo Colonna,
Via della Pilotta 18, 00187,
Roma Tel: 39 06 679 1107
info@bloomsburyauctions.com
www.bloomsburyauctions.com

Della Rocca, Via Della Rocca 33,
Turin Tel: 39 01 188 8226
info@dellarocca.net
www.dellarocca.net

Il Ponte, Palazzo Crivelli,
Via Pontaccio 12, 20122 Milano
Tel: 39 02 86 31 41
info@ponteonline.com
www.ponteonline.com

San Marco
Tel: 39 041 2777981
info@sanmarcoaste.com
www.sanmarcoaste.com

Sotheby's, Palazzo Broggi,
Via Broggi, 19, Milan 20129
Tel: 39 02 295 001
www.sothebys.com

Sotheby's Rome,
Piazza d'Espana 90,
Rome 00186
Tel: 39(6) 69941791/6781798

JAPAN

Est-Ouest Auctions Co Ltd,
2-5-15 Higashigotanda,
Shinagawa-ku, Tokyo 141-0022
Tel: 81 3 5791 3131
info@est-ouest.co.jp
www.est-ouest.co.jp

MEXICO

Galeria Louis C. Morton,
GLC A7073L IYS,
Monte Athos 179, Col. Lomas de
Chapultepec CP11000
Tel: 52 5520 5005
www.lmorton.com

MONACO

Sotheby's Monaco, B.P.
45 Le Sporting d'Hiver,
Place du Casino, Monte Carlo,
Cedex MC 98001
Tel: 377 93 30 88 80
www.sothebys.com

NETHERLANDS

Sotheby's Amsterdam,
De Boelelaan 30, Amsterdam 1083 HJ
Tel: 31 20 550 2200
www.sothebys.com

Van Sabben Poster Auctions,
Appelsteeg 1-B,
NL-1621 BD, Hoorn
Tel: 31 (0)229 268203
uboersma@vansabbenauctions.nl
www.vansabbenauctions.nl

NEW ZEALAND

Webb's,
18 Manukau Rd,
Newmarket, P.O. Box 99251,
Auckland Tel: 09 524 6804
auctions@webbs.co.nz
www.webbs.co.nz

SINGAPORE

Sotheby's (Singapore) Pte Ltd,
1 Cuscaden Road,
01-01 The Regent, 249715
Tel: 65 6732 8239
www.sothebys.com

SWEDEN

Bukowskis, Arsenalsgatan 4,
Stockholm Tel: 46 (8) 614 08 00
info@bukowskis.se
www.bukowskis.se

SWITZERLAND

Galerie Koller AG, Hardturmstrasse
102, CH-8031 Zürich
Tel: 41 44 445 63 63
office@galeriekoller.ch
www.galeriekoller.ch

Sotheby's, 13 Quai du Mont Blanc,
Geneva CH-1201
Tel: 41 22 908 4800
www.sothebys.com

Sotheby's Zurich, Gessneralee 1,
CH-8021 Zurich

TAIWAN R.O.C.

Sotheby's Taipei, 1st Floor,
No 79 Secl, An Ho Road, Taipei
Tel: 886 2 755 2906

UK & IRELAND

Bedfordshire

Piano Auctions Ltd,
Maltings Farm House,
Cardington, Bedford,
MK44 3SU Tel: 01234 831742
www.pianoauctions.co.uk

Sheffield Railwayana Auctions,
4 The Glebe, Clapham, Bedford,
MK41 6GA Tel: 01234 325341
www.sheffieldrailwayana.co.uk

W&H Peacock,
26 Newnham Street,
Bedford, MK40 3JR
Tel: 01234 266366
www.peacockauction.co.uk

Berkshire

Cameo Auctions,
Kennet Holme Farm, Bath Road,
Midgham, Reading,
RG7 5UX Tel: 01189 713772
office@cameo-auctioneers.co.uk
www.cameo-auctioneers.co.uk

Dreweatt Neate, Donnington Priory,
Donnington, Newbury, RG14 2JE
Tel: 01635 553553
donnington@dnfa.com
www.dnfa.com/donnington

Special Auction Services,
Kennetholme, Midgham, Reading,
RG7 5UX Tel: 0118 971 2949
www.specialauctionservices.com

Buckinghamshire

Amersham Auction Rooms,
Station Road, Amersham, HP7 0AH
Tel: 01494 729292
info@amershamauctionrooms.co.uk
www.amershamauctionrooms.co.uk

Bourne End Auction Rooms,
Station Approach, Bourne End,
SL8 5QH Tel: 01628 531500
be.auctions@virgin.net
www.bourneendauctionrooms.com

Dickins Auctioneers Ltd,
The Claydon Saleroom, Calvert Road,
Middle Claydon, MK18 2EZ
Tel: 01296 714434
info@dickinsauctioneers.com
www.dickinsauctioneers.com

Cambridgeshire
Cheffins, Clifton House,
1 & 2 Clifton Road, Cambridge,
CB1 7EA Tel: 01223 213343
www.cheffins.co.uk

Willingham Auctions,
25 High Street, Willingham,
CB4 5ES Tel: 01954 261252
info@willinghamauctions.com
www.willinghamauctions.com

Cheshire
Halls Fine Art Auctions,
Booth Mansion,
30 Watergate Street,
Chester, CH1 2LA
Tel: 01244 312300/312112

Maxwells of Wilmslow inc Dockree's,
133A Woodford Road, Woodford,
SK7 1QD
Tel: 0161 439 5182
info@maxwells-auctioneers.co.uk
www.maxwells-auctioneers.co.uk

Wright Manley, Beeston Castle
Salerooms, Tarporley, CW6 9NZ
Tel: 01829 262150
www.wrightmanley.co.uk

Cleveland
Vectis Auctions Ltd,
Fleck Way, Thornaby,
Stockton-on-Tees,
TS17 9JZ Tel: 01642 750616
admin@vectis.co.uk
www.vectis.co.uk

Cornwall
W H Lane & Son, Jubilee House,
Queen Street, Penzance, TR18 2DF
Tel: 01736 361447
www.invaluable.com/whlane

David Lay ASVA, Auction House,
Alverton, Penzance, TR18 4RE
Tel: 01736 361414

Cumbria
Mitchells Auction Company,
The Furniture Hall,
47 Station Road, Cockermouth,
CA13 9PZ Tel: 01900 827800
info@mitchellsfineart.com
www.mitchellsauction.co.uk

Penrith Farmers' & Kidd's plc,
Skirsgill Salerooms, Penrith,
CA11 0DN Tel: 01768 890781
info@pfkauctions.co.uk
www.pfkauctions.co.uk

Thomson, Roddick & Medcalf Ltd,
Coleridge House, Shaddongate,
Carlisle, CA2 5TU
Tel: 01228 528939
www.thomsonroddick.com

Derbyshire
Bamfords Ltd,
The Derby Auction House,
Chequers Road,
off Pentagon Island, Derby,
DE21 6EN Tel: 01332 210000
bamfords-auctions@tiscali.co.uk
www.bamfords-auctions.co.uk

Bamfords Ltd,
The Matlock Auction Gallery,
The Old Picture Palace,
133 Dale Road, Matlock, DE4 3LU
Tel: 01629 57460
bamfords-matlock@tiscali.co.uk
www.bamfords-auctions.co.uk

Devon
Bearnes,
St Edmund's Court,
Okehampton Street, Exeter,
EX4 1DU Tel: 01392 207000
enquiries@bearnes.co.uk
www.bearnes.co.uk

Michael J Bowman,
6 Haccombe House, Nr Netherton,
Newton Abbott, TQ12 4SJ
Tel: 01626 872890
www.invaluable.com/bowman

Dreweatt Neate,
205 High Street, Honiton,
EX14 1LQ Tel: 01404 42404
honiton@dnfa.com
www.dnfa.com/honiton

Rendells, Stonepark,
Ashburton, TQ13 7RH
Tel: 01364 653017
stonepark@rendells.co.uk
www.rendells.co.uk

S.J. Hales Auctioneers,
Tracey House Salerooms,
Newton Road, Bovey Tracey,
Newton Abbot, TQ13 9AZ
Tel: 01626 836684
info@sjhales.com
www.sjhales.com
www.the-saleroom.com/sjhales

Dorset
Chapman, Moore & Mugford,
9 High Street,
Shaftesbury, SP7 8JB
Tel: 01747 822244

Charterhouse,
The Long Street Salerooms,
Sherborne, DT9 3BS
Tel: 01935 812277
enquiry@charterhouse-auctions.co.uk
www.charterhouse-auctions.co.uk

Cottees of Wareham,
The Market, East Street, Wareham,
BH20 4NR Tel: 01929 552826
www.auctionsatcottees.co.uk

Duke's, The Dorchester Fine Art
Salerooms, Weymouth Avenue,
Dorchester, DT1 1QS
Tel: 01305 265080
enquiries@dukes-auctions.com
www.dukes-auctions.com

Onslow's Auctions Ltd,
The Coach House, Manor Road,
Stourpaine, Blandford Forum,
DT8 8TQ Tel: 01258 488838
onslowauctions@btinternet.com
www.onslows.co.uk

Riddetts of Bournemouth,
1 Wellington Road,
Bournemouth, BH8 8JQ
Tel: 01202 555686
auctions@riddetts.co.uk
www.riddetts.co.uk

Essex
Ambrose, Ambrose House,
Old Station Road, Loughton, IG10 4PE
Tel: 020 8502 3951
www.ambroseauction.co.uk

Brentwood Antique Auctions,
45 North Road,
Brentwood, CM14 4UZ
Tel: 01277 224599
www.brentwoodantiqueauction.co.uk

Cooper Hirst Auctions,
The Granary Saleroom,
Victoria Road, Chelmsford, CM2 6LH
Tel: 01245 260535

Mullucks Wells Inc.,
The Old Town Hall, Great Dunmow,
CM6 1AU Tel: 01371 873014
saleroom@mullucks.co.uk
www.mullucks.co.uk

Sworders,
14 Cambridge Road,
Stansted Mountfitchet, CM24 8BZ
Tel: 01279 817778
auctions@sworder.co.uk
www.sworder.co.uk

Gloucestershire
Clevedon Salerooms,
The Auction Centre, Kenn Road,
Kenn, Clevedon,
Bristol, BS21 6TT
Tel: 01934 830111
clevedon.salerooms@blueyonder.co.uk
www.clevedon-salerooms.com

The Cotswold Auction Company Ltd,
incorporating Short Graham & Co and
Hobbs and Chambers Fine Arts,
4–6 Clarence Street,
Gloucester, GL1 1DX
Tel: 01452 521177
info@cotswoldauction.co.uk
www.cotswoldauction.co.uk

The Cotswold Auction Company Ltd,
incorporating Short Graham & Co and
Hobbs and Chambers Fine Arts,
Chapel Walk Saleroom,
Cheltenham, GL50 3DS
Tel: 01242 256363

The Cotswold Auction Company Ltd, incorporating Short Graham & Co and Hobbs and Chambers Fine Arts, The Coach House, Swan Yard, 9-13 West Market Place, Cirencester, GL7 2NH
Tel: 01285 642420

Dreweatt Neate, St John's Place, Apsley Road, Clifton, Bristol, BS8 2ST
Tel: 0117 973 7201
bristol@dnfa.com
www.dnfa.com/bristol

Moore, Allen & Innocent, The Salerooms, Norcote, Cirencester, GL7 5RH
Tel: 01285 646050
fineart@mooreallen.co.uk
www.mooreallen.co.uk

Smiths, Newent Auction Rooms, 16 Broad Street, Newent, GL18 1AJ
Tel: 01531 820767
enquiries@smithsnewentauctions.co.uk
www.auctionbox.com
www.invaluable.com/smiths newentauctions

Specialised Postcard Auctions, 25 Gloucester Street, Cirencester, GL7 2DJ
Tel: 01285 659057

Tayler & Fletcher, London House, High Street, Bourton-on-the-Water, Cheltenham, GL54 2AP
Tel: 01451 821666
bourton@taylerfletcher.com
www.taylerfletcher.com

Dominic Winter Book Auctions, Mallard House, Broadway Lane, South Cerney, GL7 5UQ
Tel: 01285 860006
info@dominicwinter.co.uk
www.dominicwinter.co.uk

Wotton Auction Rooms, Tabernacle Road, Wotton-under-Edge, GL12 7EB
Tel: 01453 844733
info@wottonauctionrooms.co.uk
www.wottonauctionrooms.co.uk

Greater Manchester

Capes Dunn & Co, The Auction Galleries, 38 Charles Street, Off Princess Street, M1 7DB
Tel: 0161 273 6060/1911
capesdunn@yahoo.co.uk
www.ukauctioneers.com

Hampshire

Jacobs & Hunt, 26 Lavant Street, Petersfield, GU32 3EF
Tel: 01730 233933
www.jacobsandhunt.co.uk

George Kidner Auctioneers and Valuers, The Lymington Saleroom, Emsworth Road, Lymington, SO41 9BL
Tel: 01590 670070
info@georgekidner.co.uk
www.georgekidner.co.uk

May & Son Auctioneers & Valuers, Delta Works, Salisbury Road, Shipton Bellinger, SP9 7UN
Tel: 01980 846000
enquiries@mayandson.com
www.mayandson.com

D M Nesbit & Co, Fine Art and Auction Department, Southsea Salerooms, 7 Clarendon Road, Southsea, PO5 2ED
Tel: 02392295568
auctions@nesbits.co.uk
www.nesbits.co.uk

Odiham Auction Sales/May & Sons, Unit 4, Priors Farm, West Green Road, Mattingley, RG27 8JU
Tel: 01189 326824
auction@dircon.co.uk

Herefordshire

Brightwells Fine Art, The Fine Art Saleroom, Easters Court, Leominster, HR6 0DE Tel: 01568 611122
fineart@brightwells.com
www.brightwells.com

Morris Bricknell, Stroud House, 30 Gloucester Road, Ross-on-Wye, HR9 5LE
Tel: 01989 768320
morrisbricknell@lineone.net
www.morrisbricknell.com

Williams & Watkins, Ross Auction Rooms, Ross-on-Wye, HR9 7QF
Tel: 01989 762225
info@williamsandwatkins.co.uk
www.williamsandwatkins.co.uk

Nigel Ward & Co, The Border Property Centre, Pontrilas, HR2 0EH
Tel: 01981 240140
office@nigel-ward.co.uk
www.nigel-ward.co.uk

Hertfordshire

Sworders, The Hertford Saleroom, 42 St Andrew Street, Hertford, SG14 1JA Tel: 01992 583508
auctions@sworder.co.uk
www.sworder.co.uk

Tring Market Auctions, The Market Premises, Brook Street, Tring, HP23 5EF Tel: 01442 826446
sales@tringmarketauctions.co.uk
www.tringmarketauctions.co.uk

Kent

Bentley's Fine Art Auctioneers, The Old Granary, Waterloo Road, Cranbrook, TN17 3JQ Tel: 01580 715857
BentleysKent@aol.com
www.bentleysfineartauctioneers.co.uk

Calcutt Maclean Standen Fine Art Ltd, The Estate Office, Stone Street, Cranbrook, TN17 3HD
Tel: 01580 713828
auctions@cmsfineart.co.uk
www.calcuttmacleanstanden.co.uk

The Canterbury Auction Galleries, 40 Station Road West, Canterbury, CT2 8AN
Tel: 01227 763337
www.thecanterburyauctiongalleries.com

Dreweatt Neate, The Auction Hall, The Pantiles, Tunbridge Wells, TN2 5QL
Tel: 01892 544500
tunbridgewells@dnfa.com
www.dnfa.com/tunbridgewells

Gorringes, 15 The Pantiles, Tunbridge Wells, TN2 5TD
Tel: 01892 619670
www.gorringes.co.uk

Hobbs Parker Auctioneers LLP, Romney House, Monument Way, Orbital Park, Ashford, TN24 0HB
Tel: 01233 502222
antiques@hobbsparker.co.uk
www.hobbsparker.co.uk

Ibbett Mosely, 125 High Street, Sevenoaks, TN13 1UT
Tel: 01732 456731
auctions@ibbettmosely.co.uk
www.ibbettmosely.co.uk

Lambert & Foster, 102 High Street, Tenterden, TN30 6HT
Tel: 01580 762083
saleroom@lambertandfoster.co.uk
www.lambertandfoster.co.uk

Lambert & Foster, 77 Commercial Road, Paddock Wood, TN12 6DR
Tel: 01892 832325

South Eastern Auctions Ltd, The Auction Rooms, 104 Branbridges Road, East Peckham, TN12 5HH
Tel: 01622 878344
seauctionrooms@btconnect.com
www.southeasternauctions.co.uk

Lancashire

Smythes Fine Art, Chattel & Property Auctioneers & Valuers, 174 Victoria Road West, Cleveleys, FY5 3NE
Tel: 01253 852184
smythes@btinternet.com
www.smythes.net

Leicestershire

Gilding's Auctioneers and Valuers, 64 Roman Way, Market Harborough, LE16 7PQ
Tel: 01858 410414
sales@gildings.co.uk
www.gildings.co.uk

Lincolnshire
Golding Young,
Old Wharf Road, Grantham,
NG31 7AA Tel: 01476 565118
enquiries@goldingyoung.com
www goldingyoung.com

Thomas Mawer & Son,
Dunston House, Portland Street,
Lincoln, LN5 7NN
Tel: 01522 524984
mawer.thos@lineone.net

Marilyn Swain Auctions,
The Old Barracks, Sandon Road,
Grantham, NG31 9AS
Tel: 01476 568861
marilynswain@btconnect.com
www.marilynswainauctions.co.uk

London
Angling Auctions,
P. O. Box 2095, W12 8RU
Tel: 020 8749 4175 or
07785 281349
neil@anglingauctions.demon.co.uk

Auction Atrium,
58-60 Kensington Church Street,
W8 4DB Tel: 020 7937 3259
info@auctionatrium.com
www.auctionatrium.com

Baldwins,
11 Adelphi Terrace, WC2N 6BJ
Tel: 020 7930 9808
auctions@baldwin.sh
www.baldwin.sh

Bloomsbury Auctions,
Bloomsbury House,
24 Maddox Street, W1S 1PP
Tel: 020 7495 9494
info@bloomsburyauctions.com
www.bloomsburyauctions.com

Graham Budd Auctions Ltd.
Auctioneers & Valuers
Tel: 020 8366 2525
gb@grahambuddauctions.co.uk
www.grahambuddauctions.co.uk

Comic Book Postal Auctions Ltd,
40-42 Osnaburgh Street,
NW1 3ND Tel: 020 7424 0007
comicbook@compalcomics.com
www.compalcomics.com

Criterion Auctioneers,
53 Essex Road,
Islington, N1 2BN
Tel: 020 7359 5707
info@criterion-auctioneers.co.uk
www.criterionauctions.co.uk

Dix-Noonan-Webb,
16 Bolton Street, W1J 8BQ
Tel: 020 7016 1700
coins@dnw.co.uk
medals@dnw.co.uk
www.dnw.co.uk

Lots Road Auctions, 71 Lots Road,
Chelsea, SW10 0RN
Tel: 020 7376 6800
info@lotsroad.com www.lotsroad.com

MacDougall Arts Ltd.,
33 St James's Square, SW1Y 4JS
Tel: 0207661 9325
info@macdougallauction.com
www.macdougallauction.com

Morton & Eden Ltd,
45 Maddox Street, W1S 2PE
Tel: 020 7493 5344
info@mortonandeden.com
www.mortonandeden.com

Rosebery's Auctioneers & Valuers,
74/76 Knights Hill, SE27 0JD
Tel: 020 8761 2522
info@roseberys.co.uk
www.roseberys.co.uk

Sotheby's, 34-35 New Bond Street,
W1A 2AA Tel: 020 7293 5000
www.sothebys.com

Sotheby's Olympia,
Hammersmith Road, W14 8UX
Tel: 020 7293 5555

Spink & Son Ltd,
69 Southampton Road,
Bloomsbury, WC1B 4ET
Tel: 020 7563 4000
info@spink.com www.spink.com

Kerry Taylor Auctions in Association
with Sotheby's, St George Street
Gallery, Sotheby's New Bond Street,
W1A 2AA Tel: 07785 734337
fashion.textiles@sothebys.com

Vault Auctions Ltd, P.O. Box 257,
South Norwood, SE25 6JN
Tel: 01342 300 900
contact@vaultauctions.com
www.vaultauctions.com

Merseyside
Cato Crane & Company,
Antiques & Fine Art Auctioneers,
6 Stanhope Street, Liverpool,
L8 5RF Tel: 0151 709 5559
johncrane@cato-crane.co.uk
www.cato-crane.co.uk

Norfolk
Garry M. Emms & Co. Ltd.,
Auctioneers, Valuers & Agents,
Great Yarmouth Salerooms,
Beevor Road (off South Beach Parade),
Great Yarmouth, NR30 3PS
Tel: 01493 332668
garry@greatyarmouthauctions.com
www.greatyarmouthauctions.com

Thomas Wm Gaze & Son,
Diss Auction Rooms,
Roydon Road, Diss, IP22 4LN
Tel: 01379 650306
sales@dissauctionrooms.co.uk
www.twgaze.com

Holt's Auctioneers,
Church Farm Barns,
Wolferton, E31 6HA
Tel: 01485 542822
enquiries@holtandcompany.co.uk
www.holtandcompany.co.uk

Keys, Off Palmers Lane,
Aylsham, NR11 6JA
Tel: 01263 733195
mail@aylshamsalerooms.co.uk
www.aylshamsalerooms.co.uk

Nottinghamshire
Dreweatt Neate, Neales,
192 Mansfield Road,
Nottingham, NG1 3HU
Tel: 0115 962 4141 fineart@neales-auctions.com
www.dnfa.com/nottingham

Arthur Johnson & Sons Ltd,
The Nottingham Auction Centre,
Meadow Lane, Nottingham,
NG2 3GY Tel: 0115 986 9128
antiques@arthurjohnson.co.uk

T Vennett-Smith,
11 Nottingham Road,
Gotham, NG11 0HE
Tel: 0115 983 0541
info@vennett-smith.com
www.vennett-smith.com

Oxfordshire
Holloway's,
49 Parsons Street, Banbury,
OX16 5NB Tel: 01295 817777
enquiries@hollowaysauctioneers.co.uk
www.hollowaysauctioneers.co.uk

Jones & Jacob, Watcomb Manor
Saleroom, Ingham Lane, Watlington,
OX49 5EJ Tel: 01491 612810
saleroom@jonesandjacob.com
www.jonesandjacob.com
www.simmonsandsons.com

Mallams, Bocardo House,
24a St Michaels Street,
Oxford, OX1 2EB
Tel: 01865 241358
oxford@mallams.co.uk
www.mallams.co.uk
www.the-saleroom.com/mallamsoxford

Republic of Ireland
James Adam & Sons,
26 St Stephen's Green,
Dublin 2 Tel: 1 676 0261
www.jamesadam.ie/

Hamilton Osborne King,
4 Main Street, Blackrock,
Co. Dublin Tel: 1 288 5011
blackrock@hok.ie www.hok.ie

Mealy's, Chatsworth Street,
Castle Comer, Co Kilkenny
Tel: 564 441 229
info@mealys.com www.mealys.com

Whyte's Auctioneers,
38 Molesworth Street, Dublin 2
Tel: 1 676 2888 info@whytes.ie
www.whytes.ie

Scotland
Lyon & Turnbull, 33 Broughton Place,
Edinburgh, EH1 3RR
Tel: 0131 557 8844
info@lyonandturnbull.com
www.lyonandturnbull.com

Sotheby's, 112 George Street, Edinburgh, EH2 4LH Tel: 0131 226 7201 www.sothebys.com

Thomson, Roddick & Medcalf Ltd, 43/44 Hardengreen Business Park, Eskbank, Edinburgh, EH22 3NX Tel: 0131 454 9090 www.thomsonroddick.com

Thomson, Roddick & Medcalf Ltd, 60 Whitesands, Dumfries, DG1 2RS Tel: 01387 279879 trmdumfries@btconnect.com www.thomsonroddick.com

Shropshire

Brettells Antiques & Fine Art, 58 High Street, Newport Tel: 01952 815925 auction@brettells.com www.brettells.com

Halls Fine Art Auctions, Welsh Bridge, Shrewsbury, SY3 8LA Tel: 01743 231212 www.hallsestateagents.co.uk

Mullock & Madeley, The Old Shippon, Wall-under-Heywood, Nr Church Stretton, SY6 7DS Tel: 01694 771771 auctions@mullockmadeley.co.uk www.mullockmadeley.co.uk

Walker, Barnett & Hill, Cosford Auction Rooms, Long Lane, Cosford, TF11 8PJ Tel: 01902 375555 wbhauctions@lineone.net www.walker-barnett-hill.co.uk

Somerset

Greenslade Taylor Hunt Fine Art, Magdelene House, Church Square, Taunton, TA1 1SB Tel: 01823 332525 www.gth.net

Lawrence Fine Art Auctioneers, South Street, Crewkerne, TA18 8AB Tel: 01460 73041 www.lawrences.co.uk

Gardiner Houlgate, The Bath Auction Rooms, 9 Leafield Way, Corsham, Nr Bath, SN13 9SW Tel: 01225 812912 www.invaluable.com/gardiner-houlgate

Staffordshire

Louis Taylor Auctioneers & Valuers, Britannia House, 10 Town Road, Hanley, Stoke on Trent, ST1 2QG Tel: 01782 214111 louis.taylor@ukonline.co.uk www.louistaylorfineart.co.uk

Potteries Specialist Auctions, 271 Waterloo Road, Cobridge, Stoke on Trent, ST6 3HR Tel: 01782 286622 www.potteriesauctions.com

Wintertons Ltd, Lichfield Auction Centre, Fradley Park, Lichfield, WS13 8NF Tel: 01543 263256 enquiries@wintertons.co.uk www.wintertons.co.uk

Suffolk

Dyson & Son, The Auction Room, Church Street, Clare, CO10 8PD Tel: 01787 277993 info@dyson-auctioneers.co.uk www.dyson-auctioneers.co.uk

Sworders incorporating Olivers, The Saleroom, Burkitts Lane, Sudbury, CO10 1HB Tel: 01787 880305 olivers@sworder.co.uk www.sworder.co.uk www.invaluable.com

Vost's, Newmarket, CB8 9AU Tel: 01638 561313

Surrey

Clarke Gammon Wellers, The Sussex Barn, Loseley Park, Guildford, GU3 1HS Tel: 01483207570 fine.art@clarkegammon.co.uk www.invaluable.com/clarke gammonwellers

Cooper Owen, 74 Station Road, Egham, TW20 9LF Tel: 01784 434 900 customerservice@cooperowen.com www.cooperowen.com

Crow's Auction Gallery, The Car Park, r/o Dorking Halls, Reigate Road, Dorking, RH4 1SG Tel: 01306 740382 enquiries@crowsauctions.co.uk www.crowsauctions.co.uk

Dreweatt Neate, Baverstock House, 93 High Street, Godalming, GU7 1AL Tel: 01483 423567 godalming@dnfa.com www.dnfa.com/godalming

Ewbank Auctioneers, Burnt Common Auction Rooms, London Road, Send, Woking, GU23 7LN Tel: 01483 223101 antiques@ewbankauctions.co.uk www.ewbankauctions.co.uk

Lawrences Auctioneers Limited, Norfolk House, 80 High Street, Bletchingley, RH1 4PA Tel: 01883 743323 www.lawrencesbletchingley.co.uk

John Nicholson, The Auction Rooms, Longfield, Midhurst Road, Fernhurst, GU27 3HA Tel: 01428 653727 sales@johnnicholsons.com www.johnnicholsons.com

P F Windibank, The Dorking Halls, Reigate Road, Dorking, RH4 1SG Tel: 01306 884556/876280 sjw@windibank.co.uk www.windibank.co.uk

Richmond & Surrey Auctions Ltd, Richmond Station, Kew Road, Old Railway Parcels Depot, Richmond, TW9 2NA Tel: 020 8948 6677 rsatrading.richmond@virgin.net

East Sussex

Burstow & Hewett, Abbey Auction Galleries, Lower Lake, Battle, TN33 0AT Tel: 01424 772374 auctions@burstowandhewett.co.uk www.burstowandhewett.co.uk

Dreweatt Neate, 46-50 South Street, Eastbourne, BN21 4XB Tel: 01323 410419 eastbourne@dnfa.com www.dnfa.com/eastbourne

Eastbourne Auction Rooms, Auction House, Finmere Road, Eastbourne, BN22 8QL Tel: 01323 431444 sales@eastbourneauction.com www.eastbourneauction.com

Gorringes, Terminus Road, Bexhill-on-Sea, TN39 3LR Tel: 01424 212994 bexhill@gorringes.co.uk www.gorringes.co.uk

Gorringes, 15 North Street, Lewes, BN7 2PD Tel: 01273 472503 clientservices@gorringes.co.uk www.gorringes.co.uk

Raymond P Inman, 98a Coleridge Street, Hove, BN3 5AA Tel: 01273 774777 r.p.inman@talk21.com www.invaluable.com/raymondinman

Rye Auction Galleries, Rock Channel, Rye, TN31 7HL Tel: 01797 222124 sales@ryeauctiongalleries.co.uk www.ryeauctiongalleries.co.uk

Wallis & Wallis, West Street Auction Galleries, Lewes, BN7 2NJ Tel: 01273 480208 auctions@wallisandwallis.co.uk www.wallisandwallis.co.uk

West Sussex

Henry Adams Fine Art, Baffins Hall, Baffins Lane, Chichester, PO19 1UA Tel: 01243 532223 enquiries@henryadamsfineart.co.uk www.henryadamsfineart.co.uk

Bellmans Auctioneers & Valuers, New Pound, Wisborough Green, Billingshurst, RH14 0AZ Tel: 01403 700858 enquiries@bellmans.co.uk www.bellmans.co.uk

Denham's, The Auction Galleries, Warnham, Nr Horsham, RH12 3RZ Tel: 01403 255699 or 253837 enquiries@denhams.com www.denhams.com

Sotheby's Sussex, Summers Place, Billingshurst, RH14 9AD Tel: 01403 833500 www.sothebys.com

Stride & Son Auctions,
Southdown House,
St John's Street, Chichester,
PO19 1XQ Tel: 01243 780207
enquiries@stridesauctions.co.uk
www.stridesauctions.co.uk

Toovey's Antiques & Fine Art
Auctioneers & Valuers,
Spring Gardens, Washington,
RH20 3BS Tel: 01903 891955
auctions@tooveys.com
www.tooveys.com

Worthing Auction Galleries Ltd,
Fleet House, Teville Gate,
Worthing, BN11 1UA
Tel: 01903 205565
info@worthing-auctions.co.uk
www.worthing-auctions.co.uk

Tyne & Wear

Anderson & Garland (Auctioneers),
Marlborough House,
Marlborough Crescent,
Newcastle-upon-Tyne, NE1 4EE
Tel: 0191 430 3000
www.andersonandgarland.com

Boldon Auction Galleries,
Front Street, East Boldon,
NE36 0SJ Tel: 0191 537 2630
boldon@btconnect.com
www.boldonauctions.co.uk
www.the-saleroom.com/boldon

Wales

Anthemion Auctions,
15 Norwich Road, Cardiff,
CF23 9AB Tel: 029 2047 2444
auction@anthemionauctions.com
www.anthemionauctions.com

Peter Francis,
Curiosity Sale Room,
19 King Street, Carmarthen,
SA31 1BH Tel: 01267 233456
nigel@peterfrancis.co.uk
www.peterfrancis.co.uk

Morgan Evans, 30 Church Street,
Llangefni, Anglesey, LL77 7DU
Tel: 01248 723303/421582
auctions@morganevans.com
www.morganevans.com

Rogers Jones & Co,
The Saleroom, 33 Abergele Road,
Colwyn Bay, LL29 7RU
Tel: 01492 532176
www.rogersjones.co.uk

Wingetts Auction Gallery,
29 Holt Street, Wrexham,
Clwyd, LL13 8DH
Tel: 01978 353553
auctions@wingetts.co.uk
www.wingetts.co.uk

Warwickshire

Locke & England,
18 Guy Street, Leamington Spa,
CV32 4RT Tel: 01926 889100
info@leauction.co.uk
www.auctions-online.com/locke

West Midlands

Biddle and Webb Ltd,
Ladywood, Middleway,
Birmingham, B16 0PP
Tel: 0121 455 8042
antiques@biddleandwebb.freeserve.co.uk
www.biddleandwebb.co.uk

Black Country Auctions Ltd,
Baylies' Hall, Tower Street,
Dudley, DY1 1NB
Tel: 01384 250220
info@blackcountryauctions.co.uk
www.blackcountryauctions.co.uk

Fellows & Sons,
Augusta House, 19 Augusta Street,
Hockley, Birmingham, B18 6JA
Tel: 0121 212 2131
info@fellows.co.uk
www.fellows.co.uk

Wiltshire

Henry Aldridge & Son Auctions,
Unit 1, Bath Road Business Centre,
Devizes, SN10 1XA
Tel: 01380 729199
www.henry-aldridge.co.uk

Dreweatt Neate,
Hilliers Yard, High Street,
Marlborough, SN8 1AA
Tel: 01672 515161
marlborough@dnfa.com
www.dnfa.com/marlborough

Netherhampton Salerooms,
Salisbury Auction Centre,
Netherhampton, Salisbury,
SP2 8RH Tel: 01722 340041
www.salisburyauctioncentre.co.uk
www.the-saleroom.com/netherhampton
www.invaluable.com

Woolley & Wallis,
Salisbury Salerooms,
51-61 Castle Street,
Salisbury, SP1 3SU
Tel: 01722 424500/411854
enquiries@woolleyandwallis.co.uk
www.woolleyandwallis.co.uk

Worcestershire

Philip Laney,
The Malvern Auction Centre,
Portland Road, off Victoria Road,
Malvern, WR14 2TA
Tel: 01684 893933
philiplaney@aol.com
www.invaluable.com/philiplaney

Philip Serrell,
The Malvern Saleroom,
Barnards Green Road, Malvern,
WR14 3LW Tel: 01684 892314
serrell.auctions@virgin.net
www.serrell.com

Yorkshire

BBR,
Elsecar Heritage Centre,
Elsecar, Nr Barnsley, S74 8HJ
Tel: 01226 745156
sales@onlinebbr.com
www.onlinebbr.com

Paul Beighton,
Woodhouse Green, Thurcroft,
Rotherham, S66 9AQ
Tel: 01709 700005
www.paulbeightonauctioneers.co.uk

Boulton & Cooper,
St Michael's House,
Market Place, Malton, YO17 7LR
Tel: 01653 696151
antiques@boultoncooper.co.uk
www.boultoncooper.co.uk

H C Chapman & Son,
The Auction Mart, North Street,
Scarborough, YO11 1DL
Tel: 01723 372424

Cundalls,
15 Market Place, Malton, YO17 7LP
Tel: 01653 697820
www.cundalls.co.uk

David Duggleby,
The Vine St Salerooms,
Scarborough, YO11 1XN
Tel: 01723 507111
auctions@davidduggleby.com
www.davidduggleby.com

Hartleys,
Victoria Hall Salerooms,
Little Lane, Ilkley, LS29 8EA
Tel: 01943 816363
info@hartleysauctions.co.uk
www.hartleysauctions.co.uk

Lithgow Sons & Partners,
The Auction Houses,
Station Road, Stokesley,
Middlesbrough, TS9 7AB
Tel: 01642 710158
info@lithgowsauctions.com
www.lithgowsauctions.com

Malcolm's No1 Auctions
Tel : 01977 684971 or 07774 130784
info@malcolmsno1auctions.co.uk
www.malcolmsno1auctions.co.uk

Christopher Matthews,
23 Mount Street,
Harrogate, HG2 8DQ
Tel: 01423 871756

Morphets of Harrogate,
6 Albert Street,
Harrogate, HG1 1JL
Tel: 01423 530030
www.morphets.co.uk

Tennants,
34 Montpellier Parade, Harrogate, HG1
2TG Tel: 01423 531661
enquiry@tennants-ltd.co.uk
www.tennants.co.uk

Tennants, The Auction Centre,
Harmby Road, Leyburn, DL8 5SG
Tel: 01969 623780

Wilkinson's Auctioneers Ltd,
The Old Salerooms, 28 Netherhall
Road, Doncaster, DN1 2PW
Tel: 01302 814884
www.wilkinsons-auctioneers.co.uk

NORTHEAST AUCTIONS
BY RONALD BOURGEAULT, LLC
NORTHEASTAUCTIONS.COM

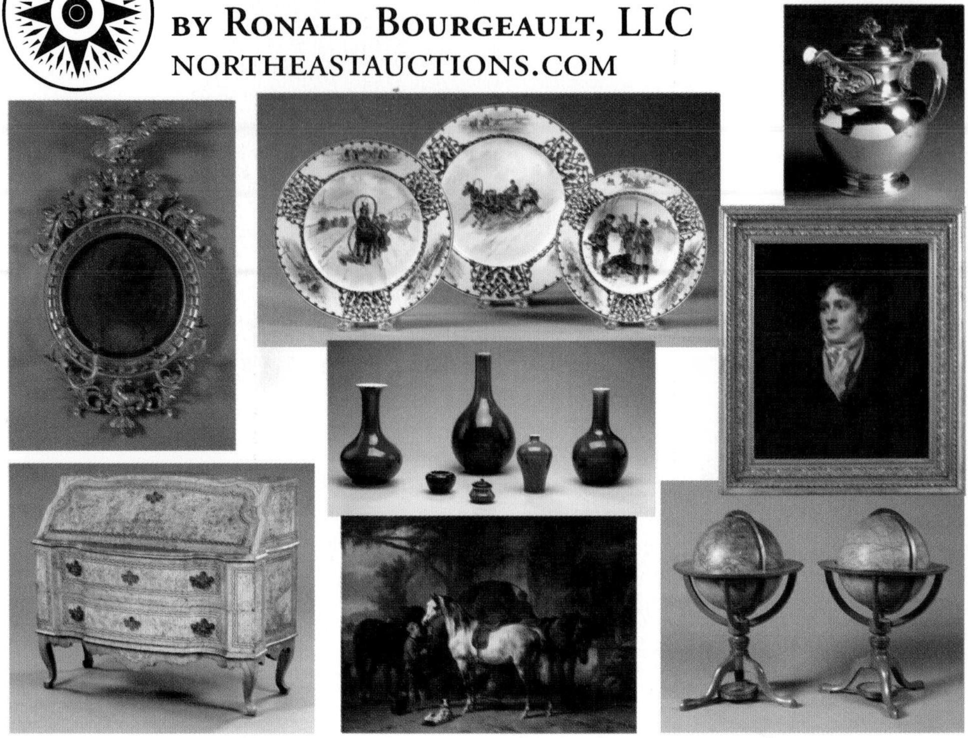

93 PLEASANT STREET PORTSMOUTH, NH 03801 USA
TEL. +1 603.433.8400

International Client Services
Anne Weston
email: aweston@northeastauctions.com

R. O. Schmitt Fine Art

SPECIALISTS IN
ANTIQUE CLOCKS

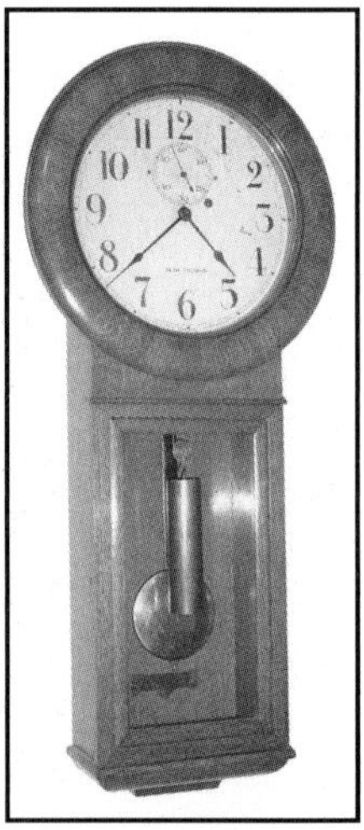

Estate valuation and liquidation is our specialty. We have thirty years of experience and a clientele of several thousand collectors worldwide. We also provide a venue for cylinder and disc music boxes, and clocks with these same attachments.

R. O. SCHMITT
P. O. BOX 162
WINDHAM, NH 03087, USA
603-432-2237
www.antiqueclockauction.com

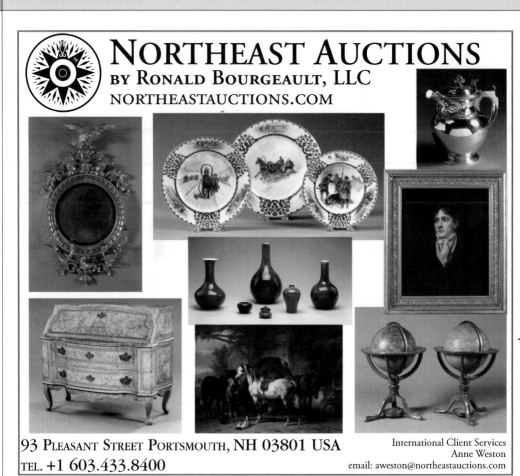

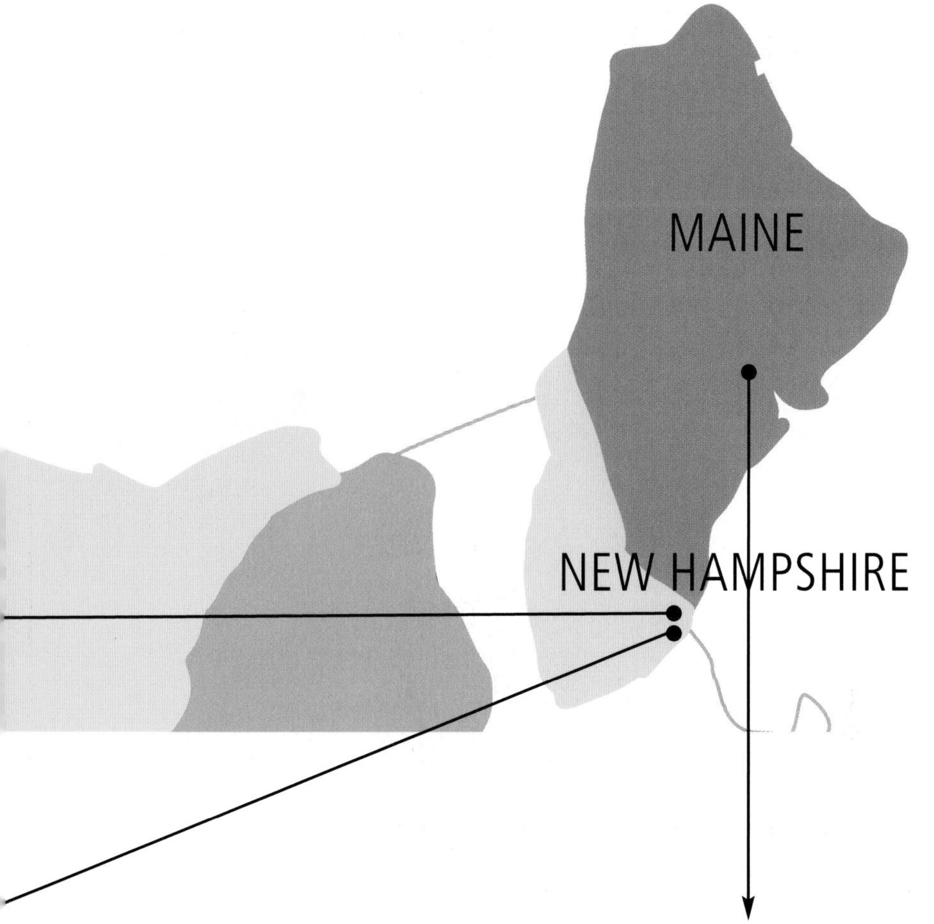
MAINE
NEW HAMPSHIRE

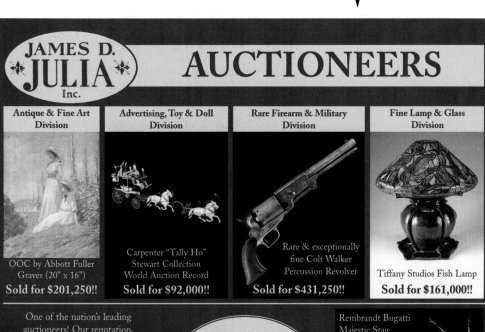

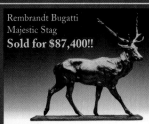

Waddington's
Canada's Auction House Since 1850
Waddington's has been serving the Canadian and International markets for over 150 years. We feature a wide variety of both antique and modern silver in our Decorative Arts auctions.
111 Bathurst Street
Toronto Ontario Canada M5V 2R1
Tel: 416.504.9100 Toll Free: 1.877.504.5700
Fax: 416.504.0033 Email: info@waddingtons.ca
www.waddingtons.ca
George III
Silver Tray
by Paul Storr, 1812
engraved with
the arms of
Sir Robert Peel
SOLD: $9600
Georg Jensen bowl
by Henning Koppel
c. 1950
SOLD: $23,000
Rare Guildford
Silver Kettle
c.1730-40
maker: Richard Croker
SOLD: $15,000

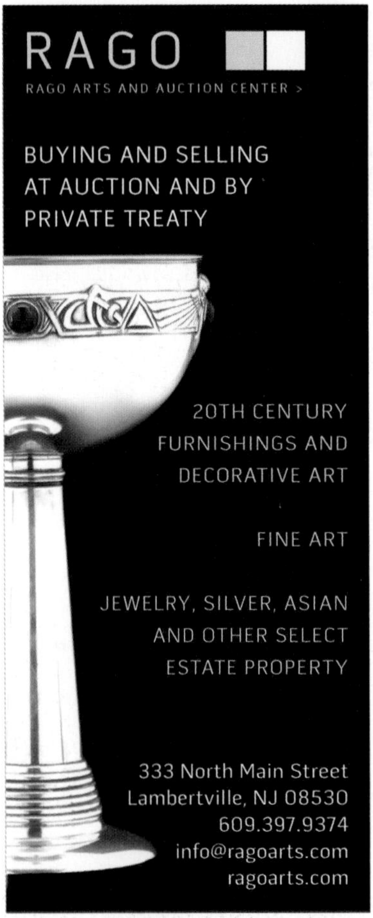
RAGO
RAGO ARTS AND AUCTION CENTER >
BUYING AND SELLING
AT AUCTION AND BY
PRIVATE TREATY
20TH CENTURY
FURNISHINGS AND
DECORATIVE ART
FINE ART
JEWELRY, SILVER, ASIAN
AND OTHER SELECT
ESTATE PROPERTY
333 North Main Street
Lambertville, NJ 08530
609.397.9374
info@ragoarts.com
ragoarts.com

Bertoia auctions
Over 45 million dollars experience in antique toy auctions and collectibles. The world over.
For confidential consignment inquiries, please contact:
Bertoia Auctions
2141 DeMarco Drive
Vineland, NJ 08360
Phone 856-692-1881
Fax 856-692-8697
Email toys@bertoiaauctions.com
Website www.bertoiaauctions.com

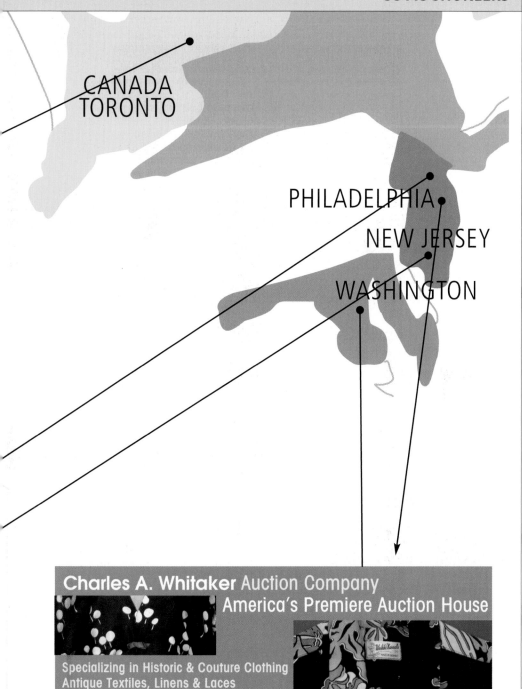

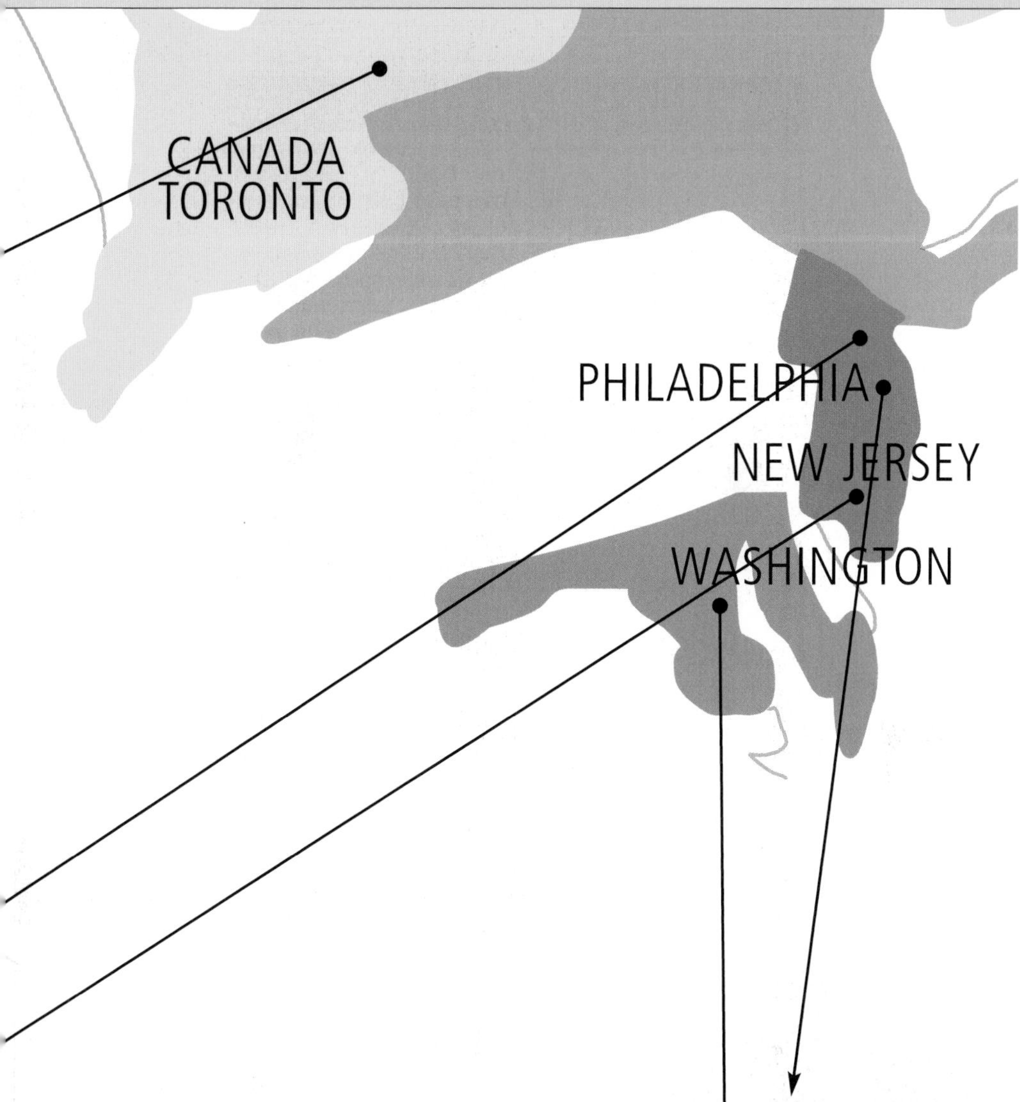
CANADA
TORONTO
PHILADELPHIA
NEW JERSEY
WASHINGTON

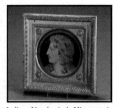

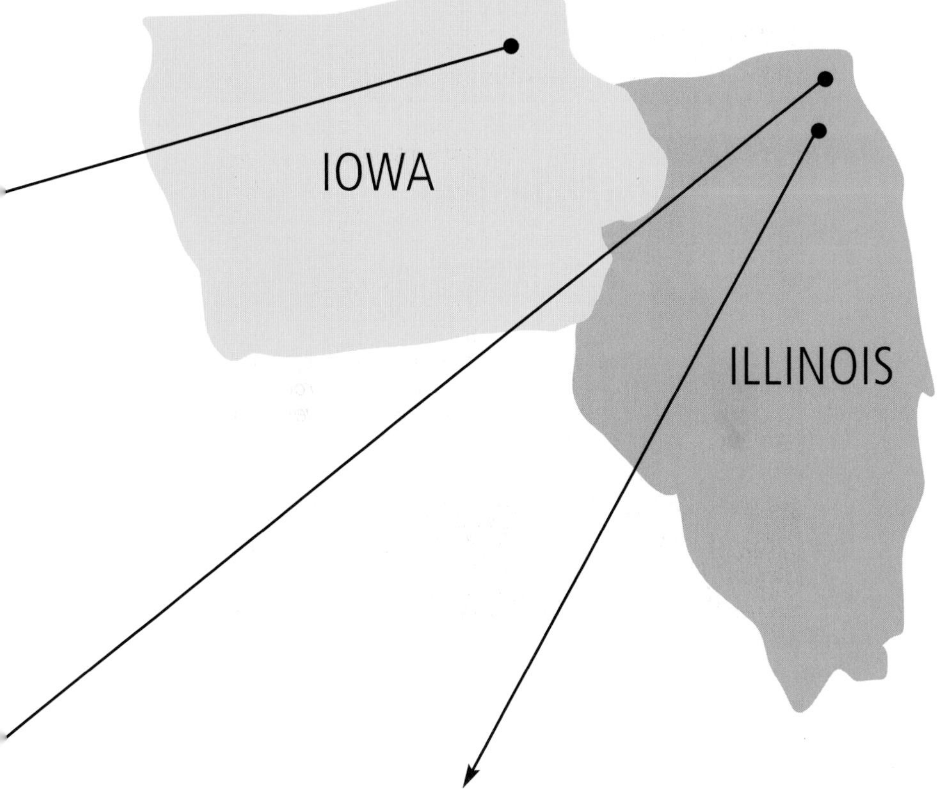

Bloomington Auction Gallery

Auctioneers & Appraisers

300 East Grove St., Bloomington, IL 61701
Phone (309) 828-5533 • Fax (309) 829-2266
joyluke@verizon.net©

Specializing in Fine Estates

Selling the Best in the Mid-West

Under the personal supervision of Robert & Joy Luke since 1977

Visit our website for illustrated catalogues at www.joyluke.com

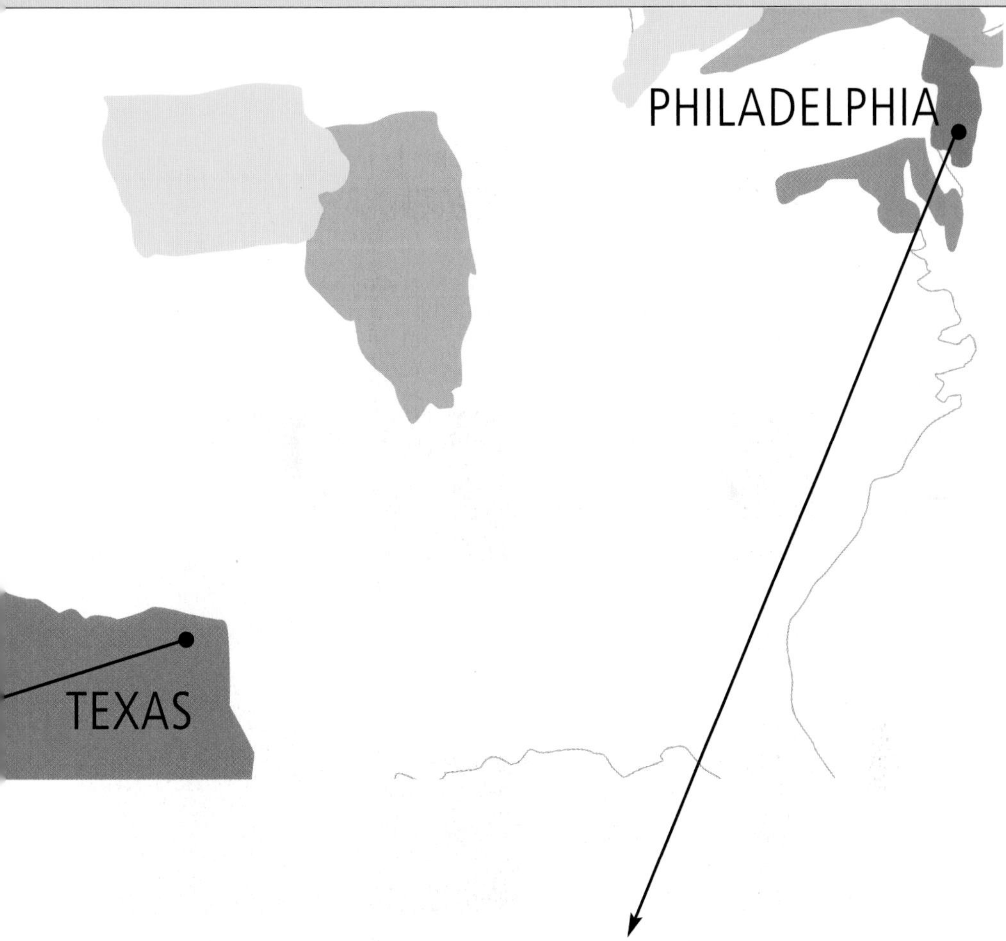
PHILADELPHIA
TEXAS

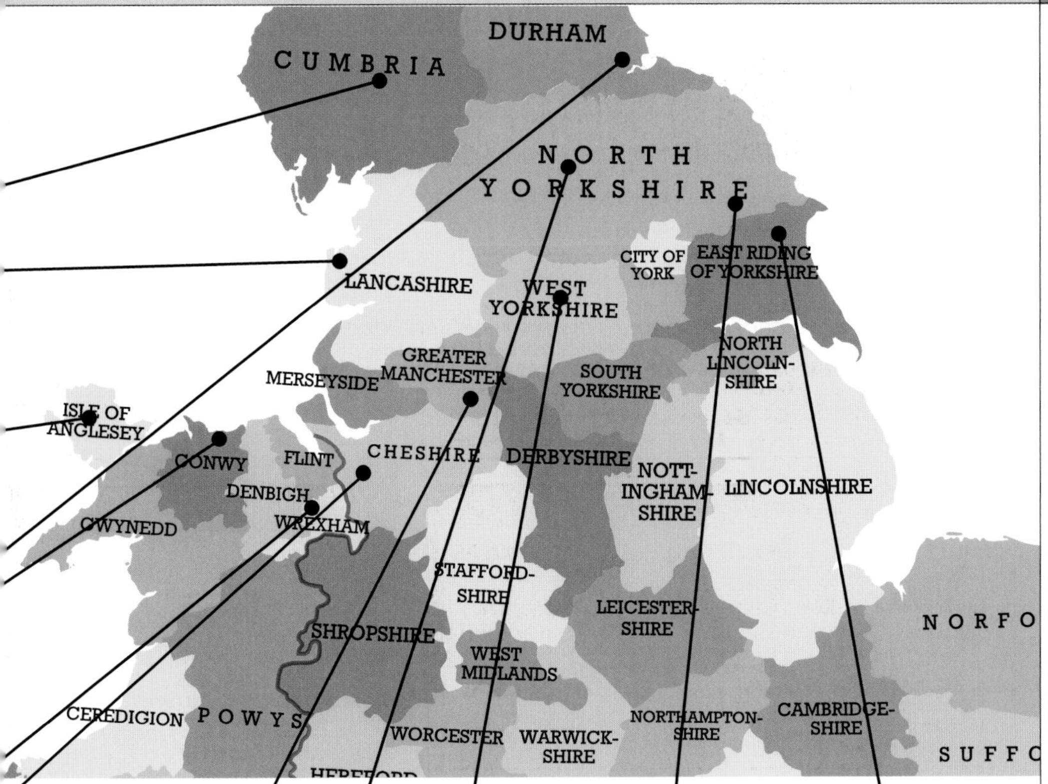

Tennants

AUCTIONEERS

Over 45,000 Lots Sold Annually
Weekly 800–1000 Lot Sales
Our Valuation & House Clearance Service Operates Throughout the UK
Important International Catalogue Sales
Specialist Collectors Sales & Country House Sales

Head Office: The Auction Centre, Leyburn
North Yorkshire DL8 5SG. Tel: 01969 623780
www.tennants.co.uk Email: enquiry@tennants-ltd.co.uk

Also at: 34 Montpelier Parade, Harrogate, North Yorkshire
Tel: 01423 531661
Mill House, South Street, Oakham, Rutland
Tel: 01572 724666

Chartered Surveyors • Estate Agents • Property & Planning Consultants • Valuers & Auctioneers • Fine Arts Saleroom

Dee Atkinson & Harrison

www.dahauctions.com

Regular Catalogued Fine Art Sales

Fortnightly Sales of Victorian and General Furniture and Effects

Biannual Sales of Collectors', Toys, Sporting & Other Nostalgia

Valuations for Probate & Insurance
Free Verbal Valuations

Valuation Days Held Throughout The Region

House Clearance

THE EXCHANGE SALEROOM, DRIFFIELD, EAST YORKSHIRE
TEL: 01377 253151 FAX: 01377 241041
EMAIL: info@dahauctions.com

HARTLEYS

AUCTIONEERS AND VALUERS

Victoria Hall Salerooms
Little Lane, Ilkley, West Yorkshire LS29 8EA
Tel: 01943 816363 Fax: 01943 817610
E-Mail: info@hartleysauctions.co.uk
www.hartleysauctions.co.uk

Independent
Furniture and Fine Arts Auctioneers for four generations. Now fully extended and computerised premises with two salerooms and carefully graded general and specialist sales every week.

Cundalls

ANTIQUE AND FINE ART SALES AT THE MILTON ROOMS, MALTON

Regular Sales of Railwayana and Collectors Items
Valuations for Insurance, Probate and all other purposes

15 Market Place, Malton, North Yorkshire YO17 7LP
Tel: 01653 697820 Fax: 01653 698305
www.cundalls.co.uk

Brightwells
FINE ART
Established 1846

The Fine Art Saleroom
Easters Court, Leominster,
Herefordshire HR6 0DE

FINE NEW SALEROOMS - with on site parking & café
Monthly catalogue sales of ANTIQUES

Regular Specialist Sales of:

- PICTURES
- SILVER & JEWELLERY
- SPORTING ITEMS
- PORCELAIN, POTTERY & GLASS
- CLASSIC & VINTAGE CARS & AUTOMOBILIA
- TOYS & TEXTILES
- ROCK, POP & 20TH CENTURY DESIGN
- BOOKS & STAMPS

Sales fixtures list on request

VALUATIONS for ALL PURPOSES
Tel: 01568 611122 Fax: 01568 610519
E-mail: fineart@brightwells.com Website: www.brightwells.com

PHILIP SERRELL
auctioneers & valuers

REGULAR SALES OF ANTIQUES & FINE ART

TWO SALES EACH MONTH OF VICTORIAN, EDWARDIAN, CONTEMPORARY FURNITURE & EFFECTS

FREE SALES ESTIMATES FOR A SINGLE ITEM OR COMPLETE HOUSE CONTENTS

VALUATIONS FOR INHERITANCE TAX & INSURANCE PURPOSES

SPECIALISTS IN THE SALE OF WORCESTER PORCELAIN

SALEROOM
The Malvern Saleroom
Barnards Green Road, Malvern WR14 3LW
Tel: 01684 892314 Fax: 01684 569832
www.serrell.com

Nigel Ward & Co.
CHARTERED SURVEYOR,
LAND & ESTATE AGENT, AUCTIONEER & VALUER

Regular Saturday Auctions of Antique and Country Furniture, Porcelain, Objets D'art & Collectables at our New Salesrooms in Pontrilas

Complete House Clearances &
On the Premises sales arranged.

Free advice without obligation for
Sale purposes. Distance no object.
Valuations for Probate, Insurance, etc.

The Border Property Centre,
Pontrilas, Hereford, HR2 0EH
Tel: 01981 240140
See us on: **www.nigel-ward.co.uk**

NIGEL L. WARD, A.R.I.C.S., A.S.V.A., F.A.A.V., M.R.A.C.

Wotton Auction Rooms Ltd

Two day monthly auctions – the largest on the Cotswolds always exceeding 1500 lots, all categories, all prices.

Valuations for all purposes.

Call for a calendar of sales.

Tabernacle Road,
Wotton-under-Edge,
Gloucestershire GL12 7EB
Tel: 01453 844733
info@wottonauctionrooms.co.uk
www.wottonauctionrooms.co.uk

MOORE ALLEN
& INNOCENT

Regular General and Antique Sale to include Antique and Later Furniture, Porcelain, Glass, Clocks, Metalware, Silver, Plate, Jewellery, Collectables, Pictures, Textiles, Books, etc.

- Also Specialist Pictures Sales held twice yearly
- Specialist Sporting Sales held twice yearly
- Selected Antique Sale held quarterly

General Sales Commence 9.30am.
All Other Sales Commence 10.00am

- Free Pre-Sale Valuations

Catalogue available on our website week of sale at
www.mooreallen.co.uk

Valuations also conducted for Probate, Insurance, Private Treaty and Family Division
Telephone: 01285 646050 Fax: 01285 652862
email: fineart@mooreallen.co.uk

www.mooreallen.co.uk

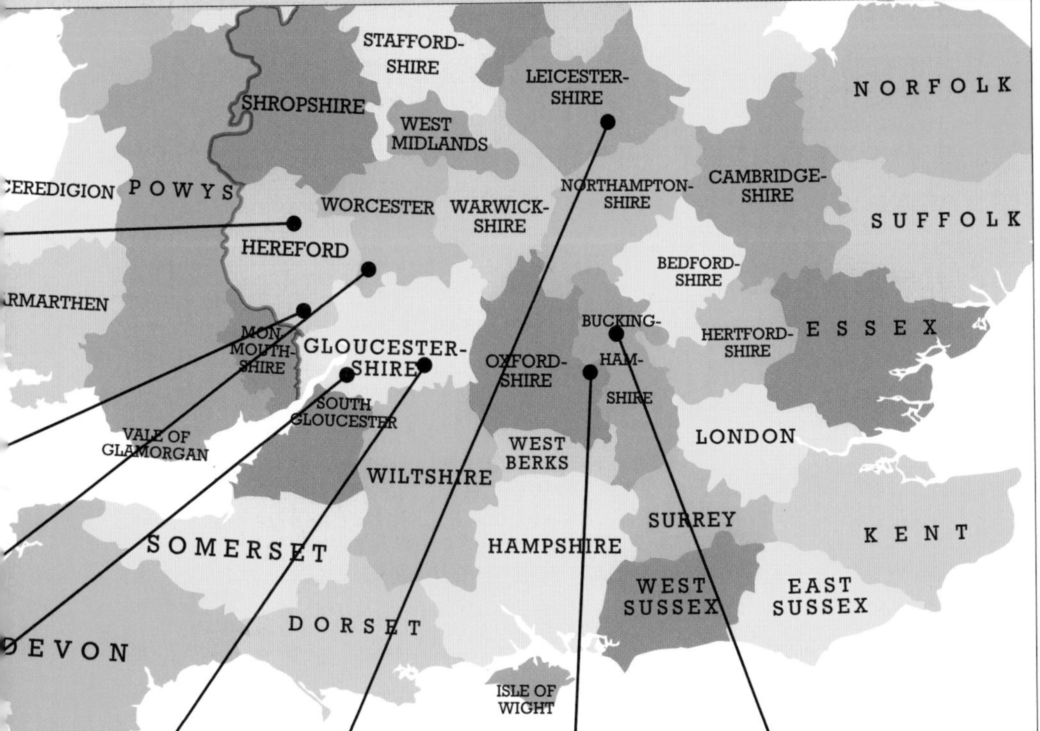
STAFFORD-
SHIRE
LEICESTER-
SHIRE
NORFOLK
SHROPSHIRE
WEST
MIDLANDS
CEREDIGION
POWYS
WORCESTER
WARWICK-
SHIRE
NORTHAMPTON-
SHIRE
CAMBRIDGE-
SHIRE
SUFFOLK
HEREFORD
BEDFORD-
SHIRE
RMARTHEN
BUCKING-
HAM-
SHIRE
HERTFORD-
SHIRE
ESSEX
MON
MOUTH-
SHIRE
GLOUCESTER-
SHIRE
OXFORD-
SHIRE
SOUTH
GLOUCESTER
VALE OF
GLAMORGAN
LONDON
WEST
BERKS
WILTSHIRE
SURREY
SOMERSET
HAMPSHIRE
KENT
WEST
SUSSEX
EAST
SUSSEX
DORSET
DEVON
ISLE OF
WIGHT

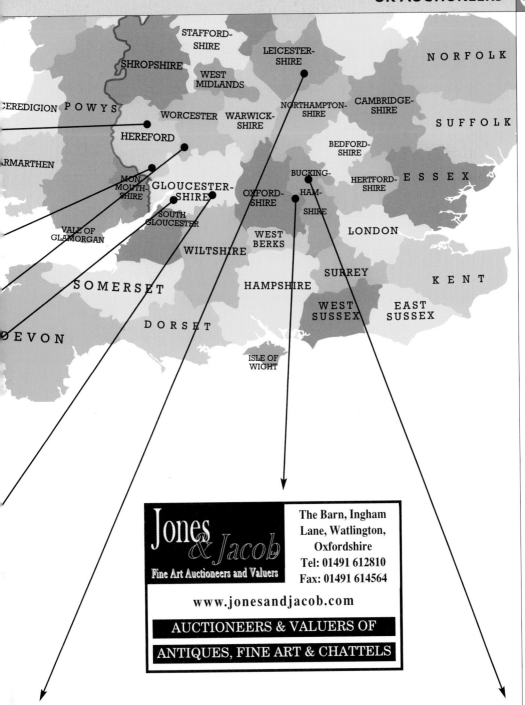

WILLIAMS & WATKINS
AUCTIONEERS

ROSS AUCTION ROOMS
Ross Auction Rooms, Ross-on-Wye,
Herefordshire HR9 7QF

REGULAR MONTHLY SALES OF
ANTIQUE FURNISHINGS & EFFECTS

Transport Arranged, Free Pre-Sale Storage,
Insurance and Valuations

Open 5 days a Week, Excellent Purpose-Built
Premises with Easy Access and Parking

info@williamsandwatkins.co.uk
www.williamsandwatkins.co.uk

TEL: 01989 762225

PHILIP LANEY
Chartered Surveyor
THE MALVERN AUCTION CENTRE

REGULAR SALES OF ANTIQUES,
WORCESTER AND OTHER PORCELAIN
AND COLLECTABLES

Portland Road, off Victoria Road, Malvern
Worcestershire WR14 2TA. Tel: 01684 893933

HOLLOWAY'S
Auctioneers and Valuers of Fine Art and Furniture

Fine Art sales every two months
General sales every fortnight
Illustrated catalogues on our website
Valuations for all purposes

SOFAA

49 Parsons Street, Banbury, Oxfordshire OX16 5NB
Tel: 01295 817777 Fax: 01295 817701
E-mail: enquiries@hollowaysauctioneers.co.uk
Website: www.hollowaysauctioneers.co.uk

Henry Aldridge & Son Auctions

DEVIZES AUCTION ROOMS
Unit 1, Bath Road Business Centre, Devizes,
Wiltshire SN10 1XA Tel: 01380 729199
Website: www.henry-aldridge.co.uk

Auctioneers of Antique & General Furniture,
Specialist Sales, Collectors Items

***Titanic*, White Star & Maritime Specialists**

BOURNE END AUCTION ROOMS

Est. 1992

Antiques and Collectors sales
held on a monthly basis
General household furniture and
effects on a weekly basis

Auctions every Wednesday
at 10.30am
Viewing Tuesdays
9.30am – 7pm

Probate, Insurance and Pre-Sale Valuations

For further information please contact:
Bourne End Auction Rooms, Station Approach,
Bourne End SL8 5QH
Telephone: 01628 531500 Fax: 01628 522158

Email: be.auctions@virgin.net
www.bourneendauctionrooms.com

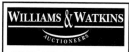

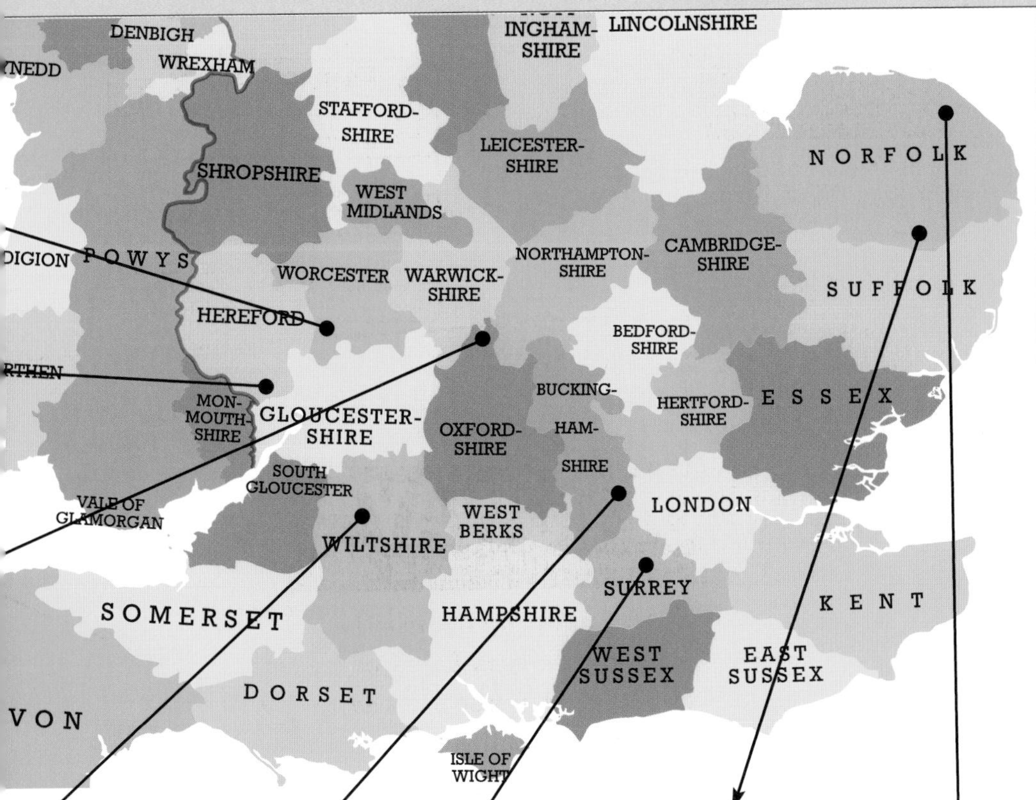
DENBIGH
WREXHAM
NEDD
STAFFORD-SHIRE
INGHAM-SHIRE
LINCOLNSHIRE
LEICESTER-SHIRE
NORFOLK
SHROPSHIRE
WEST MIDLANDS
DIGION
POWYS
NORTHAMPTON-SHIRE
CAMBRIDGE-SHIRE
WORCESTER
WARWICK-SHIRE
SUFFOLK
HEREFORD
BEDFORD-SHIRE
RTHEN
BUCKING-HAM-SHIRE
MON-MOUTH-SHIRE
GLOUCESTER-SHIRE
OXFORD-SHIRE
HERTFORD-SHIRE
ESSEX
SOUTH GLOUCESTER
VALE OF GLAMORGAN
WEST BERKS
LONDON
WILTSHIRE
SURREY
SOMERSET
HAMPSHIRE
KENT
WEST SUSSEX
EAST SUSSEX
DORSET
VON
ISLE OF WIGHT

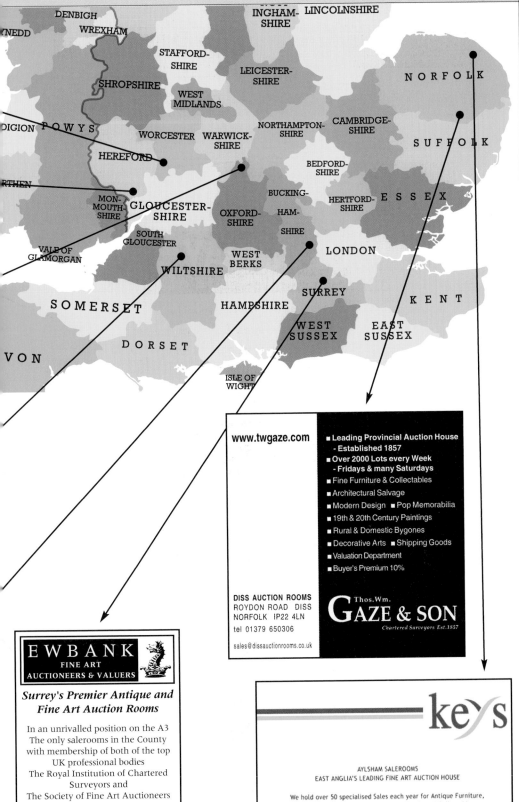

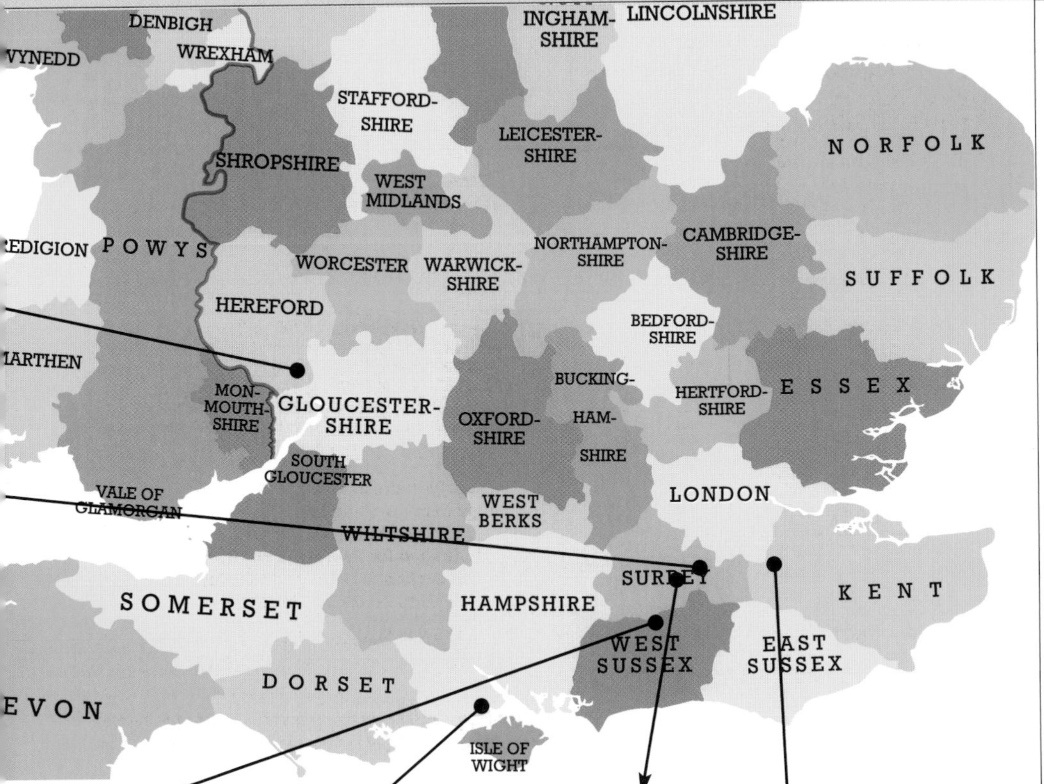
DENBIGH
WREXHAM
STAFFORD-SHIRE
INGHAM-SHIRE
LINCOLNSHIRE
LEICESTER-SHIRE
NORFOLK
SHROPSHIRE
WEST MIDLANDS
POWYS
WORCESTER
WARWICK-SHIRE
NORTHAMPTON-SHIRE
CAMBRIDGE-SHIRE
SUFFOLK
HEREFORD
BEDFORD-SHIRE
BUCKING-HAM-SHIRE
HERTFORD-SHIRE
ESSEX
MON-MOUTH-SHIRE
GLOUCESTER-SHIRE
OXFORD-SHIRE
SOUTH GLOUCESTER
LONDON
VALE OF GLAMORGAN
WEST BERKS
WILTSHIRE
SURREY
KENT
SOMERSET
HAMPSHIRE
WEST SUSSEX
EAST SUSSEX
DORSET
EVON
ISLE OF WIGHT

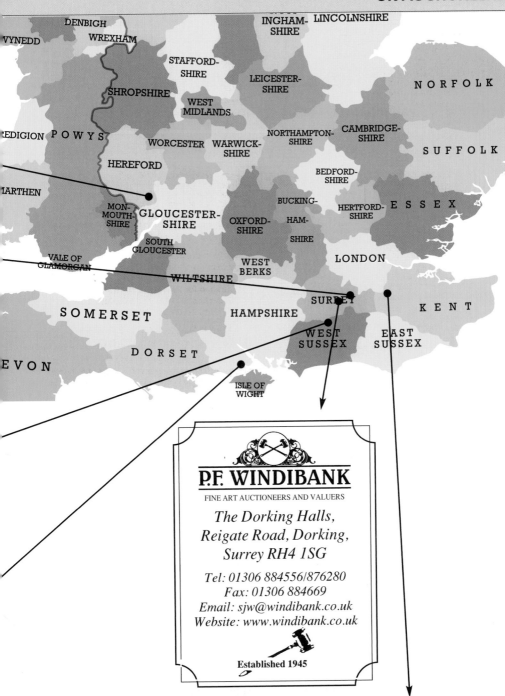

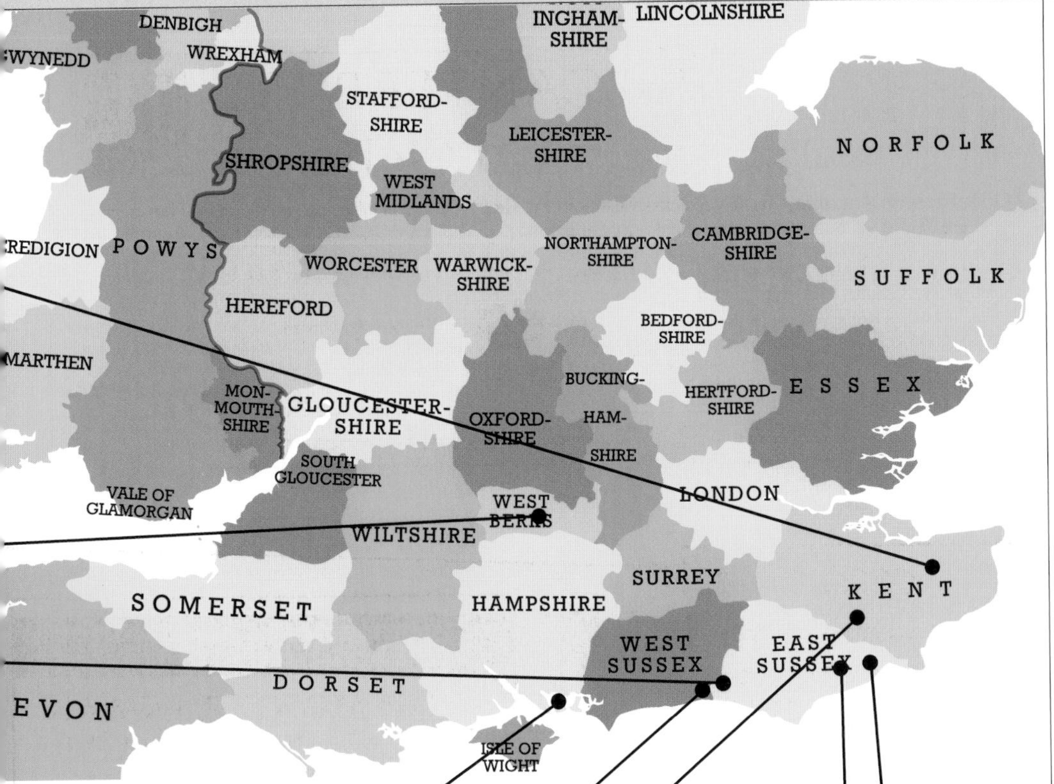
DENBIGH
WYNEDD
WREXHAM
INGHAM-SHIRE
LINCOLNSHIRE
STAFFORD-SHIRE
LEICESTER-SHIRE
NORFOLK
SHROPSHIRE
WEST MIDLANDS
REDIGION
POWYS
WORCESTER
WARWICK-SHIRE
NORTHAMPTON-SHIRE
CAMBRIDGE-SHIRE
SUFFOLK
HEREFORD
BEDFORD-SHIRE
MARTHEN
BUCKING-HAM-SHIRE
HERTFORD-SHIRE
ESSEX
MON-MOUTH-SHIRE
GLOUCESTER-SHIRE
OXFORD-SHIRE
SOUTH GLOUCESTER
VALE OF GLAMORGAN
WEST BERKS
LONDON
WILTSHIRE
SURREY
KENT
SOMERSET
HAMPSHIRE
WEST SUSSEX
EAST SUSSEX
DORSET
EVON
ISLE OF WIGHT

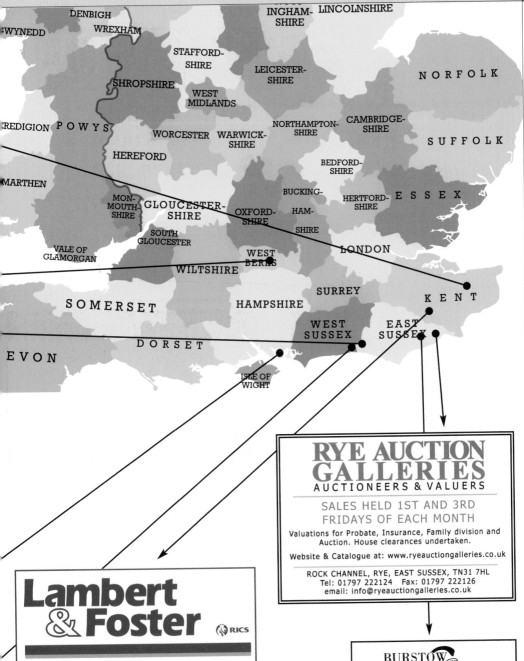

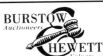

KEY TO ILLUSTRATIONS

Each illustration and descriptive caption is accompanied by a letter code. By referring to the following list of auctioneers (denoted by ⚒) and dealers (⊞) the source of any item may be immediately determined. Inclusion in this edition in no way constitutes or implies a contract or binding offer on the part of any of our contributors to supply or sell the goods illustrated, or similar articles, at the prices stated. Advertisers in this year's directory are denoted by †.

If you require a valuation for an item, it is advisable to check whether the dealer or specialist will carry out this service and if there is a charge. Please mention Miller's when making an enquiry. Having found a specialist who will carry out your valuation it is best to send a photograph and description of the item to the specialist together with a stamped addressed envelope for the reply. A valuation by telephone is not possible.

Most dealers are only too happy to help you with your enquiry; however, they are very busy people and consideration of the above points would be welcomed.

20th Century Marks
⊞ 20th Century Marks, 'The Office', Whitegates, Rectory Road, Little Burstead, Essex, CM12 9TR Tel: 01268 411 000 or 07831 778992 info@20thcenturymarks.co.uk www.20thcenturymarks.co.uk

AD Antiques
⊞ AD Antiques, P.O. Box 2407, Stone, Staffordshire, ST15 9WY Tel: 07811 783518 alison@adantiques.com www.adantiques.com

Addyman Books
⊞ Addyman Books, 39 Lion Street, Hay-on-Wye, Herefordshire, HR3 5AD Tel: 01497 821136

Adrian Harrington
⊞ Adrian Harrington, 64a Kensington Church Street, London, W8 4DB Tel: 020 7937 1465 rare@harringtonbooks.co.uk www.harringtonbooks.co.uk

Afford Decorative
⊞ Afford Decorative Arts By appointment Tel: 01827 330042 or 07831 114909 afforddecarts@fsmail.net www.afforddecarts.com

Alan Walker
⊞† Alan Walker, Halfway Manor, Halfway, Newbury, Berkshire, RG20 8NR Tel: 01488 657670 or 07770 728397 enquiries@alanwalker-barometers.com www.alanwalker-barometers.com

Alchemy
⊞ Alchemy Antiques, The Old Chapel, Long Street, Tetbury, Gloucestershire, GL8 8AA Tel: 01666 505281

Alter Silver Gallery
⊞ Alter Silver Gallery Corp., Gallery 49A & 50, 1050 Second Avenue, New York 10022, U.S.A. Tel: 212 750 1928 or 917 848 1713 altersilvergallery@mac.com

Amelia Dolls
⊞ Amelia Dolls, Pantiles Spa Antiques, The Pantiles, Tunbridge Wells, Kent, TN4 8HE Tel: 01892 541377 or 01342 713223 amedoll@tiscali.co.uk http://myweb.tiscali.co.uk/amedoll

Amelie Caswell
⊞ Amelie Caswell Tel: 0117 9077960

Ancient & Gothic
⊞ Ancient & Gothic, P. O. Box 5390, Bournemouth, Dorset, BH7 6XR Tel: 01202 431721

Anderson & Garland
⚒ Anderson & Garland (Auctioneers), Marlborough House, Marlborough Crescent, Newcastle-upon-Tyne, Tyne & Wear, NE1 4EE Tel: 0191 430 3000

Andrew Campbell
⊞ Andrew Campbell, 83 Fern Avenue, Jesmond, Newcastle-upon-Tyne, Tyne & Wear, NE2 2RA Tel: 0191 281 5065 or 07836 286218 enquiries@acsilver.co.uk www.acsilver.biz

Andrew Hartley
⚒† Hartleys, Victoria Hall Salerooms, Little Lane, Ilkley, Yorkshire, LS29 8EA Tel: 01943 816363 info@hartleysauctions.co.uk www.hartleysauctions.co.uk

Andrew Muir
⊞ Andrew Muir Tel: 07976 956208 andrewmuir@blueyonder.co.uk www.andrew-muir.com

Andy Gibbs
⊞ Andy Gibbs, 29 Brookend Street, Ross-on-Wye, Herefordshire, HR9 7EE Tel: 01989 566833 or 07850 354480 andy.gibbs@clara.co.uk www.andygibbs-antiques.co.uk

Anthony Green Antiques
⊞ Anthony Green Antiques, Vault 54, The London Silver Vaults, Chancery Lane, London, WC2A 1QS Tel: 020 7430 0038 vintagewatches@hotmail.com www.anthonygreen.com

Antiquated
⊞ Antiquated, 10 New Street, Petworth, West Sussex, GU28 0AS Tel: 01798 344011

Antique Boxes
⊞ Antique Boxes Tel: 01694 722735 or 07759 803016 bevstella@whistons.freeserve.co.uk

Antique Garden
⊞ The Antique Garden, Grosvenor Garden Centre, Wrexham Road, Belgrave, Chester, CH4 9EB Tel: 01244 629191 or 07976 539 990 antigard@btopenworld.com www.antique-garden.co.uk

Antique Photographic
⊞ Antique Photographic Company Ltd Tel: 01949 842192 alpaco47@aol.com www.rubylane.com/shops/woodstoneantiques

Antique Print Shop
⊞ The Antique Print Shop, 11 Middle Row, East Grinstead, West Sussex, RH19 3AX Tel: 01342 410501 printsandmaps@theantiqueprintshop.com www.theantiqueprintshop.com

Antiquesales.com
⊞ Antiquesales.com.au, By appointment, 24 Albert Road, South Melbourne, Victoria 3205, Australia Tel: 61 03 9317 3500 or 0412 55 66 76 info@antiquesales.com.au

Arbour Antiques
⊞ Arbour Antiques, Poet's Arbour, Sheep Street, Stratford-on-Avon, Warwickshire, CV37 6EF Tel: 01789 293453 info@arbourantiques.co.uk www.arbourantiques.co.uk

Arcadia Antiques
⊞ Arcadia Antiques, 30 Long Street, Tetbury, Gloucestershire, GL8 8AQ Tel: 01666 500236 or 07768 666833 jackharness1@aol.com www.arcadiaantiques.co.uk

Art Nouveau Originals
⊞ Art Nouveau Originals, The Bindery Gallery, 69 High Street, Broadway, Worcestershire, WR12 7DP Tel: 01386 854645 or 07774 718 096 cathy@artnouveauoriginals.com www.artnouveauoriginals.com

Auction Atrium
⚒ Auction Atrium, 58-60 Kensington Church Street, London, W8 4DB Tel: 020 7937 3259 info@auctionatrium.com www.auctionatrium.com

Augustus Brandt
⊞ Augustus Brandt Antiques, Media House, Pound Street, Petworth, West Sussex, GU28 0DX Tel: 01798 344722 or 0794 7732729 brandt@easynet.co.uk www.augustus-brandt-antiques.co.uk

Aurum
⊞ Aurum, 310/311 Grays Antique Market, 58 Davies Street, London, W1K 5LP Tel: 020 7409 0215 aurum@tinyworld.co.uk www.graysantiques.com

AutomatomaniA
⊞ AutomatomaniA, Logie Steading, Forres, Morayshire, IV36 2QN, Scotland Tel: 01309 694828 or 07790 719097 magic@automatomania.com www.automatomania.com

Avon Antiques
⊞ Avon Antiques, 25-26-27 Market Street, Bradford on Avon, Wiltshire, BA15 1LL Tel: 01225 862052 avonantiques@aol.com www.avon-antiques.co.uk

Avrick Antiques
⊞† Avrick Antiques Tel: 01295 738 318 or 07762 272846 avrick_antiques@tiscali.co.uk www.avrick-antiques.co.uk

B Kimber & J Lewis
⊞ Brenda Kimber & John Lewis, The Victoria Centre, 3-4 Victoria Road, Saltaire, Shipley, West Yorkshire Tel: 01274 611478 or 01482 442265

Bac to Basic
⊞ Bac to Basic Antiques Tel: 07787 105609 bcarruthers@waitrose.com

Bamfords
Bamfords Ltd, The Matlock Auction Gallery, The Old Picture Palace, 133 Dale Road, Matlock, Derbyshire, DE4 3LU Tel: 01629 57460 bamfords-matlock@tiscali.co.uk www.bamfords-auctions.co.uk

Bamfords
Bamfords Ltd, The Derby Auction House, Chequers Road, off Pentagon Island, Derby, DE21 6EN Tel: 01332 210000 bamfords-auctions@tiscali.co.uk www.bamfords-auctions.co.uk

Barbara Ann Newman
⊞ Barbara Ann Newman Tel: 07850 016729

Barter Books
⊞ Barter Books, Alnwick Station, Alnwick, Northumberland, NE66 2NP Tel: 01665 604888 www.barterbooks.co.uk

Bauman Rare Books
⊞ Bauman Rare Books, 1608 Walnut Street, 19th Floor, Philadelphia, PA 19104, U.S.A. Tel: 215 546 6466 brb@baumanrarebooks.com www.baumanrarebooks.com

BBR
BBR, Elsecar Heritage Centre, Elsecar, Nr Barnsley, South Yorkshire, S74 8HJ Tel: 01226 745156 sales@onlinebbr.com www.onlinebbr.com

Bearnes
† Bearnes, St Edmund's Court, Okehampton Street, Exeter, Devon, EX4 1DU Tel: 01392 207000 enquiries@bearnes.co.uk www.bearnes.co.uk

Bellmans
Bellmans Auctioneers & Valuers, New Pound, Wisborough Green, Billingshurst, West Sussex, RH14 0AZ Tel: 01403 700858 enquiries@bellmans.co.uk www.bellmans.co.uk

Berry Bros & Rudd
⊞ Berry Bros & Rudd, Hamilton Close, Houndmills, Basingstoke, Hampshire, RG21 6YB Tel: 0870 900 4300 www.bbr.com

Berry Bros & Rudd
⊞ Berry Bros & Rudd, 3 St. James's Street, London, SW1A 1EG Tel: 020 7396 9600 www.bbr.com

Bertoia
† Bertoia Auctions, 2141 DeMarco Drive Vineland, New Jersey 08360, U.S.A. Tel: 856 692 1881 toys@bertoiaauctions.com www.bertoiaauctions.com

Beverley
⊞ Beverley, 30 Church Street, Marylebone, London, NW8 8EP Tel: 020 7262 1576 or 07776136003

Beverley R
⊞ Beverley R Ltd, Gray's Antiques, Stand 342-344, 58 Davies Street, London, W1 Tel: 020 7408 1129 or 07836 205761 BeverleyRltd@aol.com

Daniel Bexfield
⊞† Daniel Bexfield Antiques, 26 Burlington Arcade, London, W1J 0PU Tel: 020 7491 1720 antiques@bexfield.co.uk www.bexfield.co.uk

Biblion
⊞ Biblion, Grays Antique Market, 1-7 Davies Mews, London, W1K 5AB Tel: 020 7629 1374 info@biblion.com www.biblion.com www.biblionmayfair.com

Steven Bishop
⊞ Steven Bishop Antiques & Decorative Arts Tel: 07761563095 meridian34all@btinternet.com www.meridiangallery.co.uk

Bloomsbury
Bloomsbury Auctions, Bloomsbury House, 24 Maddox Street, London, W1S 1PP Tel: 020 7495 9494 info@bloomsburyauctions.com www.bloomsburyauctions.com

Boom Interiors
⊞ Boom Interiors, 115-117 Regents Park Road, Primrose Hill, London, NW1 8UR Tel: 020 7722 6622 or 07973 114 396 info@boominteriors.com www.boominteriors.com

Bourbon-Hanby
⊞ Bourbon-Hanby Arcade Antiques & Interiors, 151 Sydney Street, Chelsea, London, SW3 6NT Tel: 0870 1423403 www.bourbonhanby.co.uk www.antiqueschelsea.co.uk

Bourton Bears
⊞ Bourton Bears Tel: 01993 824756 help@bourtonbears.co.uk www.bourtonbears.com

Bradley Gent
⊞ Bradley Gent Tel: 07711 158005 www.antiques-shop.co.uk

Brandt
See Augustus Brandt

Brian Watson
⊞ Brian Watson Antique Glass By appointment only, Foxwarren Cottage, High Street, Marsham, Norwich NR10 5QA Tel: 01263 732519 brian.h.watson@talk21.com

Brightwells
⊞ Brightwells Decorative Arts Tel: 01744 24899 or 07802 561951 stanmoore@brightwells.demon.co.uk

Britannia
⊞ Britannia, Grays Antique Market, Stand 101, 58 Davies Street, London, W1Y 1AR Tel: 020 7629 6772 britannia@grays.clara.net

Bukowskis
Bukowskis, Arsenalsgatan 4, Stockholm, Sweden Tel: 46 (8) 614 08 00 info@bukowskis.se www.bukowskis.se

Bukowskis (F)
Bukowskis, Horhammer, Iso Roobertink, 12 Stora Robertsg, 00120 Helsinki Helsingfors, Finland Tel: 358 9 668 9110 www.bukowskis.fi

Burford Antiques
⊞ Burford Antiques Centre, at the Roundabout, Cheltenham Road, Burford, Oxfordshire, OX8 4JA Tel: 01993 823227 www.burfordantiquecentre.co.uk

Candice Horley
⊞ Candice Horley Antiques Tel: 01883 716056 or 0705 0044855 cjhorleyantiques@aol.com

Canterbury Auctions
† The Canterbury Auction Galleries, 40 Station Road West, Canterbury, Kent, CT2 8AN Tel: 01227 763337 www.thecanterburyauctiongalleries.com

Caroline Wiseman
⊞ Caroline Wiseman Tel: 020 7622 2500 caroline@carolinewiseman.com www.carolinewiseman.com

Castlegate Antiques
⊞ Castlegate Antiques Centre, 55 Castlegate, Newark, Nottinghamshire, NG24 1BE Tel: 01636 700076 or 07860 843739

Catchpole & Rye
⊞ Catchpole & Rye, Saracens Dairy, Jobbs Lane, Pluckley, Ashford, Kent, TN27 0SA Tel: 01233 840840 info@crye.co.uk www.crye.co.uk

CCA Galleries
⊞ CCA Galleries Ltd, The Studio, Greenhills Estate, Tilford Road, Tilford, Surrey, GU10 2DY Tel: 01252 797 201 gillian.duke@ccagalleries.com www.ccagalleries.com

Chair Set
⊞ The Chair Set, 18 Market Place, Woodstock, Oxfordshire, OX20 1TA Tel: 01428 707301 or 07711 625 477 allanjames@thechairset.com www.thechairset.com

Chameleon
⊞ Chameleon Fine Lighting, 223 East 59th Street, New York 10022, U.S.A. Tel: 212 355 6300 mail@chameleon59.com www.chameleon59.com

Charles Tomlinson
† Charles Tomlinson, Chester Tel: 01244 318395
charlestomlinson@tiscali.co.uk

Charterhouse
Charterhouse, The Long Street Salerooms, Sherborne, Dorset, DT9 3BS Tel: 01935 812277 enquiry@charterhouse-auctions.co.uk www.charterhouse-auctions.co.uk

Cheffins
Cheffins, Clifton House, 1 & 2 Clifton Road, Cambridge, CB1 7EA Tel: 01223 213343
www.cheffins.co.uk

Chicago Wine Co
The Chicago Wine Company, 5663 West Howard Street, Niles, Illinois 60714, U.S.A. Tel: 847 647 8789 info@tcwc.com
www.tcwc.com

Chiltern Antiques
Chiltern Antiques, P. O. BOX 4694, Henley on Thames, Oxfordshire, RG9 5WY Tel: 0118 924 2582
frednickson@chilternantiques.com

Chislehurst
Chislehurst Antiques, 7 Royal Parade, Chislehurst, Kent, BR7 6NR Tel: 020 8467 1530

Christopher Clarke
Christopher Clarke (Antiques) Ltd, The Fosseway, Stow-on-the-Wold, Gloucestershire, GL54 1JS Tel: 01451 830476
cclarkeantiques@aol.com www.campaignfurniture.com

Church Hill Antiques
† Church Hill Antiques Centre, 6 Station Street, Lewes, East Sussex, BN7 2DA Tel: 01273 474 842
churchhilllewes@aol.com

Cincinnati Art Galleries
Cincinnati Art Galleries, LLC, 225 East 6th Street, Cincinnati, Ohio 45202, U.S.A. Tel: 513 381 2128
www.cincinnatiartgalleries.com

Clarenbridge Antiques
Clarenbridge Antiques, Limerick Road, Clarenbridge, Co Galway, Republic of Ireland Tel: 091 796522
clarenbridgeantiques@tinet.ie

Clarion Antiques
Clarion Antiques Ltd
Tel: 01253 721903 or 07985 191623
clarion2000@btinternet.com
www.clarionantiquesltd.co.uk

Clive & Lynne Jackson
Clive & Lynne Jackson Tel: 01242 254375

Clock-Work-Shop
† The Clock-Work-Shop (Winchester), 6A Parchment Street, Winchester, Hampshire, SO23 8AT Tel: 01962 842331 or 07885 954302 www.clock-work-shop.co.uk

Cohen & Cohen
Cohen & Cohen, 101b Kensington Church Street, London, W8 7LN Tel: 020 7727 7677 info@cohenandcohen.co.uk
www.cohenandcohen.co.uk

collectorsworld
www.collectorsworld.net, P.O. Box 4922, Bournemouth, Dorset, BH1 3JA Tel: 01202 555223 info@collectorsworld.biz
www.collectorsworld.net www.collectorsworld.biz

Coltman Antiques
Coltman Antiques, 18 Blandford Square, Newcastle on Tyne, Tyne & Wear, NE1 4HZ Tel: 0191 233 1430
www.coltmanantiques.com

Corney & Barrow
Corney & Barrow Ltd, No 1 Thomas More Street, London, EW1 1YZ Tel: 020 7265 2400 www.corneyandbarrow.com

Country Seat
The Country Seat, Huntercombe Manor Barn, Henley-on-Thames, Oxfordshire, RG9 5RY Tel: 01491 641349
ferry&clegg@thecountryseat.com www.thecountryseat.com

C S Moreton Antiques
C. S. Moreton Antiques, Inchmartine House, Inchture, Perth, PH14 9QQ, Scotland Tel: 01828 686412
moreton@inchmartine.freeserve.co.uk

Curious Science
Curious Science, 307 Lillie Road, Fulham, London, SW6 7LL Tel: 020 7610 1175 or 07956 834094 props@curiousscience.com
www.curiousscience.com

D & A North
Desmond & Amanda North, The Orchard, 186 Hale Street, East Peckham, Kent, TN12 5JB Tel: 01622 871353

D & S Pullen
David & Sarah Pullen, P.O. Box 24, Bexhill on Sea, East Sussex, TN39 4ZN Tel: 01424 848035

D & T Rayment
Derek & Tina Rayment Antiques, Orchard House, Barton Road, Barton, Nr Farndon, Cheshire, SY14 7HT Tel: 01829 270429 or 07860 666629 and 07702 922410 raymentantiques@aol.com
www.antique-barometers.com

Daniels Antiques
Daniels Antiques, 431 East Hyman Ave., Aspen, Co 81611, U.S.A. Tel: 970 544 9282 danielsantiques@comcast.net

David Bowden
David Bowden, 304/306 Grays Antique Market, 58 Davies Street, London, W1K 5LP Tel: 020 7495 1773

David Brower
David Brower, 113 Kensington Church Street, London, W8 7LN Tel: 0207 221 4155 David@davidbrower-antiques.com
www.davidbrower-antiques.com

David Hickmet
David Hickmet, 75 Portobello Road, London, W11 2QB Tel: 07971850405 david@hickmet.com www.hickmet.com

David Lay
David Lay, ASVA, Auction House, Alverton, Penzance, Cornwall, TR18 4RE Tel: 01736 361414

David March
David & Sally March By appointment only
Tel: 01275 372422
david.march@lineone.net www.antiquesweb.co.uk

Debden Antiques
Debden Antiques, Elder Street, Debden, Saffron Walden, Essex, CB11 3JY Tel: 01799 543007
info@debden-antiques.co.uk debden-antiques.co.uk

decorative arts@doune
decorative arts@doune, Scottish Antique & Arts Centre, By Doune, Stirling, FK16 6HD, Scotland Tel: 01786 834401 or 07778 475974 decorativearts.doune@btinternet.com
www.decorativearts-doune.com

Dee, Atkinson & Harrison
†Dee, Atkinson & Harrison, The Exchange Saleroom, Driffield, East Yorkshire, YO25 6LD Tel: 01377 253151 info@dahauctions.com
www.dahauctions.com

Design Gallery
† The Design Gallery 1850–1950, 5 The Green, Westerham, Kent, TN16 1AS Tel: 01959 561234 or 07974 322858
sales@designgallery.co.uk www.designgallery.co.uk

Diamond Mills
Diamond Mills & Co, 117 Hamilton Road, Felixstowe, Suffolk, IP11 7BL Tel: 01394 282281

Dix Noonan Webb
Dix Noonan Webb, 16 Bolton Street, London, W1J 8BQ
Tel: 020 7016 1700
coins@dnw.co.uk medals@dnw.co.uk www.dnw.co.uk

Doll Antiques
Doll Antiques Tel: 0121 449 0637

Dollectable
Dollectable, 53 Lower Bridge Street, Chester, CH1 1RS
Tel: 01244 344888/679195

Dolls and Lace
Dolls and Lace, P.O. Box 743, Lehi, Utah 84043, U.S.A.
Tel: 801 836 8769 susan@dollsandlace.com
www.dollsandlace.com

Dominic Winter
†Dominic Winter Book Auctions, Mallard House, Broadway Lane, South Cerney, Gloucestershire, GL7 5UQ Tel: 01285 860006
info@dominicwinter.co.uk www.dominicwinter.co.uk

Dorotheum
Dorotheum, Palais Dorotheum, A-1010 Wien, Dorotheergasse 17, 1010 Vienna, Austria Tel: 515 60 229 client.services@dorotheum.at

Dreweatt Neate
†Dreweatt Neate, Donnington Priory, Donnington, Newbury, Berkshire, RG14 2JE Tel: 01635 553553 donnington@dnfa.com www.dnfa.com/donnington

Dreweatt Neate (Bri)
†Dreweatt Neate, St John's Place, Apsley Road, Clifton, Bristol, Gloucestershire, BS8 2ST Tel: 0117 973 7201 bristol@dnfa.com www.dnfa.com/bristol

Dreweatt Neate (HAM)
†Dreweatt Neate, Baverstock House, 93 High Street, Godalming, Surrey, GU7 1AL Tel: 01483 423567 godalming@dnfa.com www.dnfa.com/godalming

Dreweatt Neate (N)
†Dreweatt Neate, 192 Mansfield Road, Nottingham, NG1 3HU Tel: 0115 962 4141 fineart@neales-auctions.com www.dnfa.com/nottingham

Dunlop Collection
† The Dunlop Collection, P.O. Box 6269, Statesville, NC 28687, U.S.A. Tel: 704 871 2626 or Toll Free Telephone (800) 227 1996

Durham House Antiques
Durham House Antiques, Sheep Street, Stow-on-the-Wold, Gloucestershire, GL54 1AA Tel: 01451 870404 DurhamHouseGB@aol.com www.DurhamHouseGB.com

Dwyer Antiques
T. L. Dwyer Antiques, 121 Old Company Road, Barto, PA 19504, U.S.A. Tel: 215 679 5036 tleed@enter.net

Early Technology
† Early Technology, Monkton House, Old Craighall, Musselburgh, Midlothian, EH21 8SF, Scotland Tel: 0131 665 5753 michael.bennett-levy@virgin.net www.earlytech.com www.rare78s.com www.tvhistory.tv

Elizabeth Gibbons
Elizabeth Gibbons Antique Textiles By appointment only London & Herefordshire Tel: 020 7352 1615, 01989 750243 or 07754 189842 elizabeth@egantiquetextiles.co.uk

Ellison Fine Art
Claudia Hill at Ellison Fine Art By appointment only Tel: 01494 678880 or 077203 17899 www.ellisonfineart.com

Era Antiques
Era Antiques ikar66@aol.com

Erna Hiscock
† Erna Hiscock & John Shepherd, Chelsea Galleries, 69 Portobello Road, London, W11 Tel: 01233 661407 erna@ernahiscockantiques.com www.ernahiscockantiques.com

Esoteric
Esoteric Tel: 0780 151 4528 rscobie@ic24.net www.esoteric20th.co.uk

Eureka Antiques
Eureka Antiques, Saturdays: 105 Portobello Road, London, W11 2QB Tel: 020 7229 5577 or 07798 573332

Ewbank Auctioneers
†Ewbank Auctioneers, Burnt Common Auction Rooms, London Road, Send, Woking, Surrey, GU23 7LN Tel: 01483 223101 antiques@ewbankauctions.co.uk www.ewbankauctions.co.uk

Exeter Antique Lighting
The Exeter Antique Lighting Co., Cellar 15, The Quay, Exeter, Devon, EX2 4AP Tel: 01392 490848 or 07702 969438 www.antiquelightingcompany.com

Faganarms
Faganarms, Box 425, Fraser, MI48026, U.S.A. Tel: 586 465 4637 info@faganarms.com www.faganarms.com

Fair Finds
Fair Finds Antiques, Rait Village Antiques Centre, Rait, Perthshire, PH2 7RT, Scotland Tel: 01821 670379

Farr Vintners
Farr Vintners Tel: 020 7821 2000 enquiries@farrvintners.com www.farrvintners.com

Fenwick & Fenwick
Fenwick & Fenwick, 88-90 High Street, Broadway, Worcestershire, WR12 7AJ Tel: 01386 853227/841724

Fine & Rare Wines
Fine & Rare Wines Ltd. London Tel: 020 8960 1995

Fossack & Furkle
Fossack & Furkle, P.O. Box 733, Abington, Cambridgeshire, CB1 6BF Tel: 01223 894296 or 07939078719 fossack@btopenworld.com www.fossackandfurkle.freeservers.com

Frank Dux
Frank Dux Antiques, 33 Belvedere, Bath, Somerset, BA1 5HR Tel: 01225 312367 m.hopkins@antique-glass.co.uk www.antique-glass.co.uk

Freeman's
†Freeman's Fine Art Of Philadelphia Inc., Samuel T. Freeman & Co., 1808 Chestnut Street, Philadelphia, PA 19103, U.S.A. Tel: 215 563 9275 www.freemansauctions.com
Photographer Elizabeth Field

Galeria Louis C Morton
Galeria Louis C. Morton, GLC A7073L IYS, Monte Athos 179, Col. Lomas de Chapultepec CP11000, Mexico Tel: 52 5520 5005 glmorton@prodigy.net.mx www.lmorton.com

Gardiner Houlgate
Gardiner Houlgate, The Bath Auction Rooms, 9 Leafield Way, Corsham, Nr Bath, Somerset, SN13 9SW Tel: 01225 812912 www.invaluable.com/gardiner-houlgate

Garret & Hurst
† Garret & Hurst Sculpture, P.O. Box 658, East Grinstead, West Sussex, RH19 3GH Tel: 01342 311729 or 07976 247942 garhurst@btinternet.com www.garretandhurst.co.uk

Garth Vincent
† Garth Vincent, The Old Manor House, Allington, Nr Grantham, Lincolnshire, NG32 2DH Tel: 01400 281358 or 07785 352151 garthvincent@aol.com www.guns.uk.com

Gazelles
Gazelles Ltd Tel: 023 8081 1610 or 07778 020 104 allan@gazelles.co.uk www.gazelles.co.uk

G D Blay
G D Blay Antiques, 56 West Street, Dorking, Surrey, RH4 1BS Tel: 07785 767718 gdblay@hotmail.com www.gdblayantiques.com

Geoffrey Breeze
Geoffrey Breeze Antiques Tel: 077 404 35844 www.antiquecanes.co.uk

Geoffrey Minnis
Geoffrey T. Minnis, Hastings Antique Centre, 59–61 Norman Road, St Leonards-on-Sea, East Sussex, TN38 0EG Tel: 01424 428561

George Bayntun
George Bayntun, Manvers Street, Bath, Somerset, BA1 1JW Tel: 01225 466000 ebc@georgebayntun.com

Georgian Antiques
Georgian Antiques, 10 Pattinson Street, Leith Links, Edinburgh, EH6 7HF, Scotland Tel: 0131 553 7286 info@georgianantiques.net JDixon7098@aol.com www.georgianantiques.net

Gilbert & Dale
Gilbert & Dale Antiques, The Old Chapel, Church Street, Ilchester, Nr Yeovil, Somerset, BA22 8ZA Tel: 01935 840464

Gilding's
†Gilding's Auctioneers and Valuers, 64 Roman Way, Market Harborough, Leicestershire, LE16 7PQ Tel: 01858 410414 sales@gildings.co.uk www.gildings.co.uk

Gillian Neale
† Gillian Neale Antiques, P.O. Box 247, Aylesbury, Buckinghamshire, HP20 1JZ Tel: 01296 423754 or 07860 638700 gillianneale@aol.com www.gillianneaIeantiques.co.uk

Gillian Shepherd
Gillian Shepherd, Old Corner House Antiques, 6 Poplar Road, Wittersham, Kent, TN30 7PG Tel: 01797 270236

Glade Antiques
Glade Antiques, P.O. Box 873, High Wycombe, Buckinghamshire, HP14 3ZQ Tel: 01494 882818 or 07771 552 328 sonia@gladeantiques.com www.gladeantiques.com

Glass etc
Glass etc, 18–22 Rope Walk, Rye, East Sussex, TN31 7NA Tel: 01797 226600 decanterman@freezone.co.uk www.decanterman.com

Glazed Over
Glazed Over Tel: 0773 2789114

Gordon Reece Gallery
Gordon Reece Galleries, Finkle Street, Knaresborough, Yorkshire, HG5 8AA Tel: 01423 866219 www.gordonreecegalleries.com

Gorringes
† Gorringes, 15 North Street, Lewes, East Sussex, BN7 2PD Tel: 01273 472503 clientservices@gorringes.co.uk www.gorringes.co.uk

Graham Budd
Graham Budd Auctions Ltd, Auctioneers & Valuers gb@grahambuddauctions.co.uk

Graham Smith Antiques
Graham Smith Antiques, 83 Fern Avenue, Jesmond, Newcastle upon Tyne, Tyne & Wear, NE2 2RA Tel: 0191 281 5065 or 07836 251873 gsmithantiques@aol.com

Greenslade Taylor Hunt
Greenslade Taylor Hunt Fine Art, Magdelene House, Church Square, Taunton, Somerset, TA1 1SB Tel: 01823 332525

Grey-Harris
Grey-Harris & Co, 12 Princess Victoria Street, Clifton, Bristol, Somerset, BS8 4BP Tel: 0117 973 7365

Greystoke Antiques
† Greystoke Antiques of Sherborne, 4 Swan Yard, Sherborne, Dorset, DT9 3AX Tel: 01935 812833

Griffin
Griffin Fine Art Tel: 01488 684667 or 0780 8741823 johnriordan@griffinfineart.co.uk www.bronzegriffin.com

Grimes Militaria
Grimes Militaria, 13 Lower Park Row, Bristol, Somerset, BS1 5BN Tel: 0117 929 8205

Guest & Gray
Guest & Gray, 1-7 Davies Mews, London, W1K 5AB Tel: 020 7408 1252 info@chinese-porcelain-art.com www.chinese-porcelain-art.com

Hallidays
Hallidays, The Old College, Dorchester- on-Thames, Oxfordshire, OX10 7HL Tel: 01865 340028/68 or 07860 625917 antiques@hallidays.com www.hallidays.com

Halls
Halls Fine Art Auctions, Welsh Bridge, Shrewsbury, Shropshire, SY3 8LA Tel: 01743 231212

Harlequin Antiques
Harlequin Antiques, 79-81 Mansfield Road, Daybrook, Nottingham, NG5 6BH Tel: 0115 967 4590 sales@antiquepine.net www.antiquepine.net

Helen Girton
Helen Girton Antiques, P.O. Box 2022, Buckingham, MK18 4ZH Tel: 01280 815012 www.helengirtonantiques.co.uk

Helios Gallery
Helios Gallery, 292 Westbourne Grove, London, W11 2PS Tel: 077 11 955 997 info@heliosgallery.com www.heliosgallery.com

Hemswell Antique Centres
† Hemswell Antique Centres, Caenby Corner Estate, Hemswell Cliff, Gainsborough, Lincolnshire, DN21 5TJ Tel: 01427 668389 enquiries@hemswell-antiques.com www.hemswell-antiques.com

Henry Baines
Henry Baines Tel: 07973 214406 henrybaines@onetel.com

Heritage
† Heritage Auction Galleries, 3500 Maple Avenue, 17th Floor, Dallas, Texas 75219-3941, U.S.A. Tel: 214 528 3500/800 872 6467 bid@HeritageAuctions.com www.HeritageAuctions.com

Hermann Historica
Hermann Historica OHG, Postfach 201009, 80010 Munchen, Germany Tel: 00 49 89 5237296

Hillhaven
Hillhaven Antique Linen & Lace Tel: 0121 358 4320

Hiscock & Shepherd
See Erna Hiscock

Holloway's
† Holloway's, 49 Parsons Street, Banbury, Oxfordshire, OX16 5NB Tel: 01295 817777 enquiries@hollowaysauctioneers.co.uk www.hollowaysauctioneers.co.uk

Hugh Mote
Hugh C. Mote By appointment only Tel: 01737 842254 Hugh.C.Mote@btinternet.com

Humbleyard Fine Art
Humbleyard Fine Art, Unit 32 Admiral Vernon Arcade, Portobello Road, London, W11 2DY Tel: 01362 637793 or 07836 349416

Hurst Gallery
Hurst Gallery, 53 Mt. Auburn Street, Cambridge, MA 02138, U.S.A. Tel: 617 491 6888 manager@hurstgallery.com www.hurstgallery.com

Hy Duke
Hy Duke & Son, The Dorchester Fine Art Salerooms, Weymouth Avenue, Dorchester, Dorset, DT1 1QS Tel: 01305 265080 enquiries@dukes-auctions.com www.dukes-auctions.com

Islwyn Watkins
Islwyn Watkins, Offa's Dyke Antique Centre, 4 High Street, Knighton, Powys, LD7 1AT, Wales Tel: 01547 520145

Jackson's
† Jackson's International, Auctioneers & Appraisers of Fine Art & Antiques, 2229 Lincoln Street, Cedar Falls, IA 50613, U.S.A. Tel: 319 277 2256 sandim@jacksonsauctions.com www.jacksonsauction.com

James Adam
James Adam & Sons, 26 St Stephen's Green, Dublin 2, Republic of Ireland Tel: 676 0261 www.jamesadam.ie/

James D Julia
† James D Julia, Inc., P. O. Box 830, Rte.201 Skowhegan Road, Fairfield, ME 04937, U.S.A. Tel: 207 453 7125 jjulia@juliaauctions.com www.juliaauctions.com

James Strang
James Strang Tel: 01334 472 566 or 07950 490088 james@mod-i.com www.mod-i.com

J Collins
J Collins & Son, P.O. Box No 119, Bideford, Devon, EX39 1WX Tel: 01237 473103 biggs@collinsantiques.co.uk www.collinsantiques.co.uk

Jeanette Hayhurst
Jeanette Hayhurst Fine Glass, 32a Kensington Church Street, London, W8 4HA Tel: 020 7938 1539 www.antiqueglass-london.com

Jeffrey Neal
Jeffrey Neal, Vault 27, The London Silver Vaults, Chancery Lane, London, WC2A 1QS Tel: 020 8421 8848 or 07768 533055 jeffrey@bloomvault.com www.bloomvault.com

Jennifer Lloyd
Jennifer Lloyd, Chelsea Galleries, 69 Portobello Road, London, W11 2QB Tel: 07768 071400 lloydantiques@hotmail.com

Jeremy Knowles
Jeremy Knowles, 6 Georgian House, 10 Bury Street, St James's, London, SW1Y 6AA Tel: 020 7930 4929 or 07973 618602 jeremy@jeremyknowles.com www.jeremyknowles.com

Jessie's Button Box
Jessie's Button Box, Bartlett Street Antique Centre, Bath, Somerset, BA1 2QZ Tel: 0117 929 9065

Joanna Proops
Joanna Proops Antique Textiles & Lighting, 34 Belvedere, Lansdown Hill, Bath, Somerset, BA1 5HR Tel: 01225 310795 antiquetextiles@aol.co.uk www.antiquetextiles.co.uk

John Howard
John Howard at Heritage, 6 Market Place, Woodstock, Oxfordshire, OX20 1TA Tel: 0870 4440678 or 07831 850544 john@johnhoward.co.uk www.antiquepottery.co.uk

John Newton
John Newton Antiques By appointment Tel: 01482 445785 or 07749 872918 jnantiques@g127.karoo.co.uk www.johnnewtonantiques.com

John Nicholson
John Nicholson, The Auction Rooms, Longfield, Midhurst Road, Fernhurst, Surrey, GU27 3HA Tel: 01428 653727 sales@johnnicholsons.com

John Rogers
John Rogers Tel: 01643 863170 or 07710 266136 johnrogers024@btinternet.com

John Travers
John Travers Antique Prints & Maps, Talbot Court Galleries, 7 Talbot Court, Stow-on-the-Wold, Gloucestershire, GL54 1BQ Tel: 01451 832169 www.talbotcourtgalleries.co.uk

Jonathan Potter
Jonathan Potter Ltd Antique Maps, 125 New Bond Street, London, W1S 1DY Tel: 020 7491 3520 jpmaps@attglobal.net www.jpmaps.co.uk

Jubilee Photographica
Jubilee Photographica, 10 Pierrepoint Row, Camden Passage, London, N1 8EE Tel: 07860 793707 meara@btconnect.com

Judi Bland
† Judi Bland Antiques Tel: 01276 857576 or 01536 724145

Judy & Brian Harden
Judy & Brian Harden, P.O. Box 14, Bourton on the Water, Cheltenham, Gloucestershire, GL54 2YR Tel: 01451 810684 or 07831 692252 harden@portraitminiatures.co.uk www.portraitminiatures.co.uk

Julian's Antiques
Julian's Antiques By appointment only Tel: 01904 796248 or 07798 840994

Junktion
Junktion, The Old Railway Station, New Bolingbroke, Boston, Lincolnshire, PE22 7LB Tel: 01205 480068 or 07836 345491 junktionantiques@hotmail.com

Just Glass
Just Glass, Cross House, Market Place, Alston, Cumbria, CA9 3HS Tel: 01434 381263 or 0783 3994948

Justerini & Brooks
Justerini & Brooks, 61 St James's Street, London, SW1A 1LZ Tel: 020 7484 6400 www.justerinis.com

J W Weldon
J. W. Weldon, 55 Clarendon Street, Dublin 2, Republic of Ireland Tel: 1 677 1638

K & M Antiques
K & M Antiques, 369-370 Grays Antique Market, 58 Davies Street, London, W1K 5LP Tel: 020 7491 4310 or 07787 565 505 Kandmantiques@aol.com

Karel Weijand
Karel Weijand, Lion & Lamb Courtyard, Farnham, Surrey, GU9 7LL Tel: 01252 726215 carpets@karelweijand.com www.karelweijand.com

Kembery Clocks
† Kembery Antique Clocks Ltd, George Street Antique Centre, 8 Edgar Buildings, George Street, Bath, Somerset, BA1 2EH Tel: 0117 956 5281 kembery@kdclocks.co.uk www.kdclocks.co.uk

Kerry Taylor
Kerry Taylor Auctions, in Association with Sotheby's, St George Street Gallery, Sotheby's New Bond Street, London, W1A 2AA Tel: 07785 734337 fashion.textiles@sothebys.com

Key Antiques
Key Antiques of Chipping Norton, 11 Horsefair, Chipping Norton, Oxfordshire, OX7 5AL Tel: 01608 644992 or 643777 info@keyantiques.com www.keyantiques.com

Knights Antiques
Knights Antiques, 5 Friday Street, Henley-on-Thames, Oxfordshire, RG9 1AN Tel: 01491 414124 or 07774 644478 simon@knightsantiques.co.uk www.knightsantiques.co.uk

Koh I Noor Antiques
Koh I Noor Antiques Tel: 020 8950 7755 or 07802 196089 casalizard@yahoo.co.uk

Lanes Armoury
The Lanes Armoury, 26 Meeting House Lane, The Lanes, Brighton, East Sussex, BN1 1HB Tel: 01273 321357 enquiries@thelanesarmoury.co.uk www.thelanesarmoury.co.uk

Langton Green Antiques
Langton Green Antiques, Langton Road, Langton Green, Tunbridge Wells, Kent, TN3 0HP Tel: 01892 862004 antiques@langtongreen.fsbusiness.co.uk www.langtongreenantiques.co.uk

LASSCO (bh)
LASSCO, Brunswick House, 30 Wandsworth Road, Vauxhall, London, SW8 2LG Tel: 0207394 2100 brunswick@lassco.co.uk www.lassco.co.uk

LASSCO (sm)
LASSCO, St Michael's, Mark Street, London, EC2A 4ER Tel: 020 7749 9949 st.michaels@lassco.co.uk

Laura Bordignon
Laura Bordignon Antiques, P.O. Box 6247, Finchingfield, Essex, CM7 4ER Tel: 01371 811 791 or 07778 787929 laurabordignon@hotmail.com

Lawrence Fine Art
Lawrence Fine Art Auctioneers, South Street, Crewkerne, Somerset, TA18 8AB Tel: 01460 73041 www.lawrences.co.uk

Le Boudoir
Le Boudoir Collectables, The Basement, George Street Antique Centre, 8 Edgar Buildings, Bath, Somerset, BA1 2EE Tel: 01225 311061 or 07974 918630 www.le-boudoir-online.com

Leonard Joel
Leonard Joel Auctioneers, 333 Malvern Road, South Yarra, Victoria 3141, Australia Tel: 03 9826 4333 decarts@ljoel.com.au jewellery@ljoel.com.au www.ljoel.com.au

Lewis & Lewis Deco
Lewis & Lewis Deco Tel: 07739 904681 lewis_robin@hotmail.com

Locke & England
Locke & England, 18 Guy Street, Leamington Spa, Warwickshire, CV32 4RT Tel: 01926 889100 info@leauction.co.uk www.auctions-online.com/locke

Long Street Antiques
Long Street Antiques, Stamford House, 14 Long Street, Tetbury, Gloucestershire, GL8 8AQ Tel: 01666 500850 longstantiques@aol.com www.longstreetantiques.co.uk

Lorfords
Lorfords, 57 Long Street, Tetbury, Gloucestershire, GL8 8AA Tel: 01666 505111 or 07815 802862 toby@lorfordsantiques.co.uk www.lorfordsantiques.co.uk

Louisa Francis & Walker
Louisa Francis & Walker Fine Antiques, High Street, Brasted, Nr Westerham, Kent, TN16 1JA Tel: 01959 565623 or 07879 626721 sharon10.t21@btinternet.com

Lucy Harris
Lucy Harris Antiques By appointment Tel: 0207 405 0505 or 07957 144492 lucy@vault39.com

Lynda Brine
Lynda Brine By Appointment only lyndabrine@yahoo.co.uk www.scentbottlesandsmalls.co.uk

Lyon & Turnbull
Lyon & Turnbull, 33 Broughton Place, Edinburgh, EH1 3RR, Scotland Tel: 0131 557 8844 or 07714699802 info@lyonandturnbull.com

M&N Oriental
M&N Oriental Rugs, P.O. Box 55, Greater Manchester, M23 9RU Tel: 0161 905 3112 or 07710 570610 mnorientalrugs@aol.com www.mnorientalrugs.com

Manfred Schotten
Manfred Schotten, 109 High Street, Burford, Oxfordshire, OX18 4RG Tel: 01993 822302 sport@schotten.com www.schotten.com

Manor House Antiques
Manor House Antiques Tel: 01691 682558 hughbach@aol.com

Mario's Antiques
Mario's Antiques, 75 Portobello Road, London, W11 2QB Tel: 020 8902 1600 or 07919 254000 marwan@barazi.screaming.net www.marios_antiques.com

Marion Langham
Marion Langham Limited marion@ladymarion.co.uk www.ladymarion.co.uk

Mark Seabrook
⊞ Mark Seabrook Antiques, P.O. Box 396, Huntingdon, Cambridgeshire, PE28 0ZA Tel: 01480 861935 or 07770 721931 enquiries@markseabrook.com www.markseabrook.com

Marsh-McNamara
⊞ Marsh-McNamara Tel: 07790 759162

Martin Taylor
⊞ Martin Taylor Antiques, 323 Tettenhall Road, Wolverhampton, West Midlands, WV6 0JZ Tel: 01902 751166 or 07836 636524 enquiries@mtaylor-antiques.co.uk www.mtaylor-antiques.co.uk

Mary Cruz Antiques
⊞ Mary Cruz Antiques, 5 Broad Street, Bath, Somerset, BA1 5LJ Tel: 01225 334174

Mastro Auctions
⚒ Mastro Auctions, 7900 South Madison Street, Burr Ridge, Illinois 60527, U.S.A. Tel: 630 472 1200 jmarren@mastroauctions.com www.mastroauctions.com

Maxwells of Wilmslow
⚒† Maxwells of Wilmslow inc Dockree's, 133A Woodford Road, Woodford, Cheshire, SK7 1QD Tel: 0161 439 5182 info@maxwells-auctioneers.co.uk www.maxwells-auctioneers.co.uk

McBains
⊞ McBains of Exeter, Exeter Airport, Clyst, Honiton, Exeter, Devon, EX5 2BA Tel: 01392 366261 mcbains@netcom.co.uk

Mealy's
⚒ Mealy's, Chatsworth Street, Castle Comer, Co Kilkenny, Republic of Ireland Tel: 564 441 229 info@mealys.com www.mealys.com

Mere Antiques
⊞ Mere Antiques, 13 Fore Street, Topsham, Exeter, Devon, EX3 0HF Tel: 01392 874224 info@mereantiques.com www.mereantiques.com

Michael German
⊞ Michael German Antiques Ltd, 38B Kensington Church Street, London, W8 4BX Tel: 020 7937 2771 or 020 7937 1776 info@antiquecanes.com info@antiqueweapons.com www.antiquecanes.com

Michael Long
⊞ Michael D Long Ltd, 96-98 Derby Road, Nottingham, NG1 5FB Tel: 0115 941 3307 sales@michaeldlong.com www.michaeldlong.com

Mike Weedon
⊞ Mike Weedon, 7 Camden Passage, Islington, London, N1 8EA Tel: 020 7226 5319 (Wed/Sat) or 020 7609 6826 info@mikeweedonantiques.com www.mikeweedonantiques.com

Millennia
⊞ Millennia Antiquities Tel: 01204 690175 or 07930 273998 millenniaant@aol.com www.AncientAntiquities.co.uk

Millers
⊞ Millers Antiques Ltd, Netherbrook House, 86 Christchurch Road, Ringwood, Hampshire, BH24 1DR Tel: 01425 472062 mail@millers-antiques.co.uk www.millers-antiques.co.uk

Millroyale Antiques
⊞ Millroyale Antiques Tel: 01902 375006 www.whiteladiesantiques.com

Morphets
⚒ Morphets of Harrogate, 6 Albert Street, Harrogate, Yorkshire, HG1 1JL Tel: 01423 530030

Mostly Boxes
⊞ Mostly Boxes, 93 High Street, Eton, Windsor, Berkshire, SL4 6AF Tel: 01753 858470

Moxhams
⊞ Moxhams Antiques, 17, 23 & 24 Silver Street, Bradford on Avon, Wiltshire, BA15 1JZ Tel: 01225 862789 info@moxhams-antiques.demon.co.uk www.moxhams-antiques.co.uk

Muir Hewitt
⊞ Muir Hewitt Art Deco Originals, Halifax Antiques Centre, Queens Road Mills, Queens Road/Gibbet Street, Halifax, Yorkshire, HX1 4LR Tel: 01422 347377 muir.hewitt@virgin.net muir.hewitt@btconnect.com www.muirhewitt.com

M V S Antiques
⊞ M.V.S. Tel: 01564 742950 or 07970 629848 max@mvsantiques.fsnet.co.uk

Neptune Gallery
⊞ Neptune Gallery Tel: 086 8064542 or 01 2353920 www.Neptuneonline.ie

Netherhampton Salerooms
⚒ Netherhampton Salerooms, Salisbury Auction Centre, Netherhampton, Salisbury, Wiltshire, SP2 8RH Tel: 01722 340 041

Newel Art Galleries
⊞ Newel Art Galleries, Inc., 425 East 53rd Street, New York 10022, U.S.A. Tel: 212 758 1970 info@newel.com www.Newel.com

Nicholas Shaw
⊞ Nicholas Shaw Antiques, Virginia Cottage, Lombard Street, Petworth, West Sussex, GU28 0AG Tel: 01798 345146/01798 345147 or 07885 643000 silver@nicholas-shaw.com www.nicholas-shaw.com

Norfolk Decorative
⊞ Norfolk Decorative Antiques, Antique Lighting Sales & Restoration, Fakenham Industrial Estate, Fakenham, Norfolk, NR21 8NW Tel: 01328 856333 enquiries@norfolkdecorativeantiques.co.uk www.norfolkdecorativeantiques.co.uk

North Wilts Exporters
⊞† North Wilts. Exporters, Farm Hill House, Brinkworth, Wiltshire, SN15 5AJ Tel: 01666 510876 or 07836 260730 mike@northwilts.demon.co.uk www.northwiltsantiqueexporters.com

Northeast Auctions
⚒† Northeast Auctions, 93 Pleasant St. Portsmouth, NH 03801-4504, U.S.A. Tel: 603 433 8400 rbourgeault@northeastauctions.com www.northeastauctions.com

Oak & Country
⊞ The Oak & Country Furniture Partnership, Antiques of Woodstock, 18/20 Market Place, Woodstock, Oxfordshire, OX20 1TA Tel: 07703 532980 www.antiqueoakfurniture.co.uk

Oakwood Antiques
⊞ Oakwood Antiques Tel: 01204 304309 or 07813 386415

Offa's Dyke
⊞ Offa's Dyke Antique Centre, 4 High Street, Knighton, Powys, Wales, LD7 1AT Tel: 01547 528635/520145

Old Cinema
⊞ The Old Cinema, 160 Chiswick High Road, London, W4 1PR Tel: 020 8995 4166 theoldcinema@antiques-uk.co.uk www.theoldcinema.co.uk

Old Corner House
See Gillian Shepherd

Old Malthouse
⊞ The Old Malthouse, 15 Bridge Street, Hungerford, Berkshire, RG17 0EG Tel: 01488 682209 hunwick@oldmalthouse30.freeserve.co.uk

Olivers
⚒ Sworders incorporating Olivers, The Saleroom, Burkitts Lane, Sudbury, Suffolk, CO10 1HB Tel: 01787 880305 olivers@sworder.co.uk www.sworder.co.uk www.invaluable.com

Olliff's Architectural
⊞ Olliff's Architectural Antiques Tel: 07850 235793 marcus@olliffs.com www.olliffs.com

Ondines
⊞ Ondines Tel: 01865 882465

Onslow's
⚒ Onslow's Auctions Ltd, The Coach House, Manor Road, Stourpaine, Blandford Forum, Dorset, DT8 8TQ Tel: 01258 488838 onslowauctions@btinternet.com

P & K Rennie
⊞ Paul & Karen Rennie, Rennies Seaside Modern, 47 The Old High Street, Folkestone, Kent, CT20 1RN Tel: 01303 242427 info@rennart.co.uk www.rennart.co.uk

Pantiles Spa Antiques
⊞ Pantiles Spa Antiques, 4, 5, 6 Union House, The Pantiles, Tunbridge Wells, Kent, TN4 8HE Tel: 01892 541377 or 07711 283655 psa.wells@btinternet.com www.antiques-tun-wells-kent.co.uk

Pastimes
⊞ Pastimes (OMRS), 22 Lower Park Row, Bristol, Gloucestershire, BS1 5BN Tel: 0117 929 9330

Paul Beighton
⚒ Paul Beighton, Woodhouse Green, Thurcroft, Rotherham, Yorkshire, S66 9AQ Tel: 01709 700005 www.paulbeightonauctioneers.co.uk

Paul Cranny
⊞ Paul Cranny Antiques, Bank Square Gallery, 63 Maghera Street, Kilrea, Co. Derry, Northern Ireland, BT51 5QL Tel: 028 2954 0279 or 07802708656 paulcrannyantiques@yahoo.co.uk

Paul Weatherell
⊞ Paul Weatherell Antiques, 30–31 Montpellier Parade, Harrogate, Yorkshire, HG1 2TG Tel: 01423 507810 paul@weatherells.com www.weatherells.com

Pennard House
⊞ Pennard House Antiques, Pennard House, East Pennard, Shepton Mallet, Somerset, BA4 6TP Tel: 01749 860731 www.pennardantiques.com

Penrith Farmers' & Kidd's
† Penrith Farmers' & Kidd's plc, Skirsgill Salerooms, Penrith, Cumbria, CA11 0DN Tel: 01768 890781 info@pfkauctions.co.uk www.pfkauctions.co.uk

Percy's
⊞ Percy's, Vault 16, The London Silver Vaults, Chancery Lane, London, WC2A 1QS Tel: 020 7242 3618 sales@percys-silver.com www.claretjugs.co.uk www.percys-silver.com

Period Furniture
⊞ Period Furniture Showrooms, 49 London End, Beaconsfield, Buckinghamshire, HP9 2HW Tel: 01494 674112 sales@periodfurniture.net www.periodfurniture.net www.englishoak.com

Period Oak
⊞ Period Oak of Petworth, Marston House, Lombard Street, Petworth, West Sussex, GU28 0AG Tel: 01798 344111 or 07917 571350 sales@periodoakantiques.co.uk www.periodoakantiques.com

Peter Francis
Peter Francis, Curiosity Sale Room, 19 King Street, Carmarthen, Wales, SA31 1BH Tel: 01267 233456 nigel@peterfrancis.co.uk www.peterfrancis.co.uk

Peter Harrington
⊞ Peter Harrington, 100 Fulham Road, London, SW3 6HS Tel: 020 7591 0220/0330 www.peter-harrington-books.com

Peter Norden Antiques
⊞ Peter Norden Antiques, 61 Long Street, Tetbury, Gloucestershire, GL8 8AA Tel: 01666 503 854 peternorden_antiques@lineone.net www.peter-norden-antiques.co.uk

Peter Scott
⊞ Peter Scott Tel: 0117 986 8468 or 07850 639770

Peter Wain
⊞ Peter Wain, Mor Awel, Marine Terrace, Camaes Bay, Anglesey, LL67 0ND Tel: 1407 710077 or 07860 302945 peterwain@supanet.com

Piccadilly Antiques
⊞ Piccadilly Antiques, 280 High Street, Batheaston, Bath, Somerset, BA1 7RA Tel: 01225 851494 or 07785 966132 piccadillyantiques@ukonline.co.uk

Pieces of Time
⊞† Pieces of Time, 1-7 Davies Mews, London, W1K 5AB Tel: 020 7629 2422 info@antique-watch.com www.antique-watch.com www.cufflinksworld.com

Pollyanna
⊞ Pollyanna, 34 High Street, Arundel, West Sussex, BN18 9AB Tel: 01903 885198 or 07949903457

Pure Imagination
⊞ Pure Imagination, P.O. Box 140, South Shields, Tyne & Wear, NE33 3WU Tel: 0191 4169090 or 0771 5054919 www.pureimaginations.co.uk

Puritan Values
⊞ Puritan Values at the Dome, St Edmunds Business Park, St Edmunds Road, Southwold, Suffolk, IP18 6BZ Tel: 01502 722211 or 07966 371676 sales@puritanvalues.com www.puritanvalues.com

Q & C Militaria
⊞† Q & C Militaria, 22 Suffolk Road, Cheltenham, Gloucestershire, GL50 2AQ Tel: 01242 519815 or 07778 613977 qcmilitaria@btconnect.com www.qcmilitaria.com

Quay Centre
⊞ Quay Centre, Topsham, Nr Exeter, Devon, EX3 0JA Tel: 01392 874006 office@quayantiques.com www.quayantiques.com

Quayside Antiques
⊞ Quayside Antiques, 9 Frankwell, Shrewsbury, Shropshire, SY3 8JY Tel: 01743 360490 or 07715 748223 www.quaysideantiques.co.uk www.quaysideantiquesshrewsbury.co.uk

R & G McPherson
⊞ R & G McPherson Antiques, 40 Kensington Church Street, London, W8 4BX Tel: 020 7937 0812 or 07768 432 630 rmcpherson@orientalceramics.com www.orientalceramics.com

Raccoon Creek
⊞ Raccoon Creek Antiques, U.S.A. Tel: 610 689 2200 raccooncreek@msn.com www.raccooncreekantiques.com

Rago Arts
† Rago Arts & Auction Center, 333 North Main Street, Lambertville, New Jersey 08530, U.S.A. Tel: 609 397 9374 info@ragoarts.com www.ragoarts.com

Rapparee
⊞ Rapparee Antiques at Louisa Francis & Walker, High Street, Brasted, Westerham, Kent, TN16 1JA Tel: 01959 565623

Red Lion Antiques
⊞ Red Lion Antiques, New Street, Petworth,West Sussex, GU28 0AS Tel: 01798 344485 www.redlion-antiques.com

Rene Nicholls
⊞ Rene Nicholls, 56 High Street, Malmesbury, Wiltshire, SN16 9AT Tel: 01666 823089

Retro Centre
⊞ Retro Centre Tel: 0118 950 7224 al@retro-centre.co.uk www.retro-centre.co.uk

Riccardo Sansoni
⊞ Riccardo Sansoni

Richard Gardner
⊞ Richard Gardner Antiques, Swanhouse, Market Square, Petworth, West Sussex, GU28 0AN Tel: 01798 343411 rg@richardgardnerantiques.co.uk www.richardgardnerantiques.co.uk

Richard Wallis Antiks
⊞ Richard Wallis Antiks Tel: 020 8529 1749 www.richardwallisantiks.com

Ritchies
Ritchies Inc., Auctioneers & Appraisers of Antiques & Fine Art, 380 King Street East, Toronto, Ontario, M5A 1K4, Canada Tel: (416) 364 1864 auction@ritchies.com www.ritchies.com

Robert Hershkowitz
⊞ Robert Hershkowitz Limited, Cockhaise, Monteswood Lane, Lindfield, Sussex, RH16 2QP Tel: 01444 482240 prhfoto@hotmail.com

Robert Mills
⊞† Robert Mills Ltd, Narroways Road, Eastville, Bristol, Somerset, BS2 9XB Tel: 0117 955 6542 info@rmills.co.uk www.rmills.co.uk

Robert Young Antiques
⊞ Robert Young Antiques, 68 Battersea Bridge Road, London, SW11 3AG Tel: 020 7228 7847 office@robertyoungantiques.com www.robertyoungantiques.com

Rocky Mountain
⊞ Rocky Mountain Quilts, 130 York Street York Villiage, Maine 03909, U.S.A. Tel: 207 363 6800 rmqoffice@rockymountainquilts.com www.rockymountainquilts.com

Rod Akeroyd & Son
⊞ Rod Akeroyd & Son, 20 Ribblesdale Place, Preston, Lancashire, PR1 3NA Tel: 01772 203845 info@firearmscollector.com www.firearmscollector.com

Roger Bradbury
⊞ Roger Bradbury Antiques, Church Street, Coltishall, Norfolk, NR12 7DJ Tel: 01603 737444

Roger de Ville
⊞ Roger de Ville Antiques, Bakewell Antiques Centre, King Street, Bakewell, Derbyshire, DE45 1DZ Tel: 01629 812496 or 07798 793857 contact@rogerdeville.co.uk www.rogerdeville.co.uk

Rogers de Rin
⊞ Rogers de Rin, 76 Royal Hospital Road, London, SW3 4HN Tel: 020 7352 9007 rogersderin@rogersderin.co.uk www.rogersderin.co.uk

Ronald Chambers
Ronald G.Chambers Fine Antiques, Market Square, Petworth, West Sussex, GU28 0AH Tel: 01798 342305 jackie@ronaldchambers.com www.ronaldchambers.com

Rosebery's
Rosebery's Auctioneers & Valuers, 74/76 Knights Hill, London, SE27 0JD Tel: 020 8761 2522 info@roseberys.co.uk www.roseberys.co.uk

Roy Laycock
Roy Laycock Tel: 01430 860313

Ruskin Decorative Arts
Ruskin Decorative Arts, 5 Talbot Court, Stow-on-the-Wold, Gloucestershire, GL54 1DP Tel: 01451 832254 william.anne@ruskindecarts.co.uk

S & P Rumble
Simon & Penny Rumble, Causeway End Farm House, Chittering, Cambridgeshire, CB5 9PW Tel: 01223 861831 rumbleantiques@btinternet.com www.rumbleantiques.com

Sally's
Sally's Rocking Horses, Unit 1 The Fox Building, Severn Road, Welshpool, Powys, SY21 7AZ, Wales Tel: 01938 558075 sally@sallysrockinghorses.com

Samarkand Rugs
Samarkand Rugs, 7 & 8 Brewery Yard, Sheep Street, Stow-on-the-Wold, Gloucestershire, GL54 1AA Tel: 01451 832322 samarkandrugs@tiscali.co.uk

Schredds
Schredds of Portobello, P.O. Box 227, London, N6 4EW Tel: 020 8348 3314 or 07831 155376 silver@schredds.demon.co.uk www.schredds.com

Scottish Antique and Arts
Scottish Antique and Arts Centre, Carse of Cambus, Doune, Perthshire, FK16 6HG, Scotland Tel: 01786 841203 sales@scottish-antiques.com www.scottish-antiques.com

Scottow Antiques
Scottow Antiques, Green Street Green, Orpington, Kent Tel: 07860 795909

Serendipity
Serendipity, 125 High Street, Deal, Kent, CT14 6BB Tel: 01304 369165 or 01304 366536 dipityantiques@aol.com

Serendipity
Serendipity, The Tythings, Preston Court, Nr Ledbury, Herefordshire, HR8 2LL Tel: 01531 660245 or 07711 245004 www.serendipity-antiques.co.uk

Shapiro
† Shapiro & Co, Stand 380, Gray's Antique Market, 58 Davies Street, London, W1Y 5LP Tel: 020 7491 2710 or 07768 840930

Silver Shop
The Silver Shop, Powerscourt Townhouse Centre, St Williams Street, Dublin 2, Republic of Ireland Tel: 01 679 4147 ianhaslam@eircom.net

Simply Antiques
Simply Antiques, Windsor House, High Street, Moreton-in-Marsh, Gloucestershire, GL56 0AD Tel: 07710 470877 info@callingcardcases.com www.callingcardcases.com

Skinner
Skinner Inc., 357 Main Street, Bolton, MA 01740, U.S.A. Tel: 978 779 6241 pamv@skinnerinc.com/creidel@skinnerinc.com www.skinnerinc.com

Skip & Janie Smithson
Skip & Janie Smithson Antiques Tel: 01754 810265 or 07831 399180 smithsonantiques@hotmail.com

Sotheby's
Sotheby's, 34-35 New Bond Street, London, W1A 2AA Tel: 020 7293 5000 www.sothebys.com

Sotheby's (Am)
Sotheby's Amsterdam, De Boelelaan 30, Amsterdam 1083 HJ, Netherlands Tel: 31 20 550 2200

Sotheby's (G)
Sotheby's, 13 Quai du Mont Blanc, Geneva, CH-1201, Switzerland Tel: 41 22 908 4800

Sotheby's (HK)
Sotheby's, Suites 3101-3106, One Pacific Place, 88 Queensway, Hong Kong, China Tel: (852) 2524 8121

Sotheby's (NY)
Sotheby's, 1334 York Avenue at 72nd St, New York 10021, U.S.A. Tel: 212 606 7000

Sotheby's (O)
Sotheby's Olympia, Hammersmith Road, London, W14 8UX Tel: 020 7293 5555

Sotheby's (P)
Sotheby's France SA, 76 rue du Faubourg, Saint Honore, Paris 75008, France Tel: 33 1 53 05 53 05 www.sothebys.com

Sotheby's (S)
Sotheby's Sussex, Summers Place, Billingshurst, West Sussex, RH14 9AD Tel: 01403 833500

Special Auction Services
†Special Auction Services, Kennetholme, Midgham, Reading, Berkshire, RG7 5UX Tel: 0118 971 2949 www.specialauctionservices.com

Spurrier-Smith
Spurrier-Smith Antiques, 39 Church Street, Ashbourne, Derbyshire, DE6 1AJ Tel: 01335 342198/343669 or 07970 720130 ivan@spurrier-smith.fsnet.co.uk

Stockspring Antiques
Stockspring Antiques, 114 Kensington Church Street, London, W8 4BH Tel: 020 7727 7995 stockspring@antique-porcelain.co.uk www.antique-porcelain.co.uk

Sue Killinger
Sue Killinger Antiques Tel: 01494 862975 or 07836684815

Styles of Stow
† Styles of Stow, The Little House, Sheep Street, Stow-on-the-Wold, Gloucestershire, GL54 1JS Tel: 01451 830455 www.stylesofstow.co.uk

S W Antiques
† S W Antiques, Abbey Showrooms, Newlands (road), Pershore, Worcestershire, WR10 1BP Tel: 01386 555580 sales@sw-antiques.co.uk www.sw-antiques.co.uk

Swan at Tetsworth
The Swan at Tetsworth, High Street, Tetsworth, Nr Thame, Oxfordshire, OX9 7AB Tel: 01844 281777 antiques@theswan.co.uk www.theswan.co.uk

Swan Gallery
Swan Gallery, High Street, Burford, Oxfordshire, OX18 4RE Tel: 01993 822244

Sweetbriar Gallery
† Sweetbriar Gallery Ltd., 29 Beechview Road, Kingsley, Cheshire, WA6 8DF Tel: 01928 788225 sales@sweetbriar.co.uk www.sweetbriar.co.uk www.sweetbriarartglass.co.uk

Sworders
Sworders, The Hertford Saleroom, 42 St Andrew Street, Hertford, SG14 1JA Tel: 01992 583508 auctions@sworder.co.uk www.sworder.co.uk

Sylvie Spectrum
Sylvie Spectrum, Stand 372, Grays Market, 58 Davies Street, London, W1K 5LB Tel: 020 7629 3501

Teddy Bears of Witney
† Teddy Bears of Witney, 99 High Street, Witney, Oxfordshire, OX28 6HY Tel: 01993 702616 or 706616 alfonzo@witneybears.co.uk www.teddybears.co.uk

Tempus
Tempus Tel: 01344 874007 www.tempus-watches.co.uk

Tennants
†Tennants, The Auction Centre, Harmby Road, Leyburn, Yorkshire, DL8 5SG Tel: 01969 623780 enquiry@tennants-ltd.co.uk www.tennants.co.uk

Theriault's
Theriault's, P.O. Box 151, Annapolis, MD 21404, U.S.A. Tel: 410 224 3655 info@theriaults.com www.theriaults.com

Thomas Del Mar
Thomas Del Mar Ltd, c/o Sotheby's Olympia, Hammersmith Road, London, W14 8UX Tel: 020 7602 4805 enquiries@thomasdelmar.com www.thomasdelmar.com www.antiquestradegazette.com/thomasdelmar

Thomson, Roddick & Medcalf (C)
Thomson, Roddick & Medcalf Ltd, Coleridge House, Shaddongate, Carlisle, Cumbria, CA2 5TU Tel: 01228 528939 www.thomsonroddick.com

Thomson, Roddick & Medcalf (D)
Thomson, Roddick & Medcalf Ltd, 60 Whitesands, Dumfries, DG1 2RS, Scotland Tel: 01387 279879 trmdumfries@btconnect.com

Thomson, Roddick & Medcalf (E)
Thomson, Roddick & Medcalf Ltd, 43/44 Hardengreen Business Park, Eskbank, Edinburgh, EH22 3NX, Scotland Tel: 0131 454 9090

Time Antiques
Time Antiques, The Antique Centre, 2nd floor, 142 Northumberland Street, Newcastle-upon-Tyne, Tyne & Wear, NE1 7DQ Tel: 0191 232 9832 timeantiques@talktalk.net

Tony Horsley
† Tony Horsley, P.O. Box 3127, Brighton, East Sussex, BN1 5SS Tel: 01273 550770

Toovey's
† Toovey's Antiques & Fine Art Auctioneers & Valuers, Spring Gardens, Washington, West Sussex, RH20 3BS Tel: 01903 891955 auctions@tooveys.com www.tooveys.com

Top Banana
The Top Banana Antiques Mall, 1 New Church Street, Tetbury, Gloucestershire, GL8 8DS Tel: 0871 288 1102 info@topbananaantiques.com www.topbananaantiques.com

Top Banana
The Top Banana Antiques Mall, 32 Long Street, Tetbury, Gloucestershire, GL8 8AQ Tel: 0871 288 1110

Top Banana
The Top Banana Antiques Mall, 48 Long Street, Tetbury, Gloucestershire, GL8 8AQ Tel: 0871 288 3058

Top Banana
The Top Banana Antiques Mall, 46 Long Street, Tetbury, Gloucestershire, GL8 8AQ Tel: 0871 288 3058

Treadway Gallery
† Treadway Gallery, Inc., 2029 Madison Road, Cincinnati, Ohio 45208, U.S.A. Tel: 513 321 6742 davew@treadwaygallery.com www.treadwaygallery.com

Tredantiques
Tredantiques, The Antiques Complex, Exeter Airport Industrial Complex, Exeter, Devon, EX5 2BA Tel: 01392 447082 or 07967 447082 j.tredant@btinternet.com www.tredantiques.com

Tribal Gathering
Tribal Gathering, No 1 Westbourne Grove Mews, Notting Hill, London, W11 2RU Tel: 020 7221 6650 or 07720 642539 bryan@tribalgathering.com www.tribalgatheringlondon.com

Tussie Mussies
† Tussie Mussies, The Old Stables, 2b East Cross, Tenterden, Kent, TN30 6AD Tel: 01580 766244 tussiemussies@btinternet.com www.tussiemussies.co.uk

Typically English
Typically English Antiques Tel: 01249 721721 or 07818 000704 typicallyeng@ukonline.co.uk

Van Sabben
Van Sabben Poster Auctions, Appelsteeg 1-B, NL-1621 BD, Hoorn, Netherlands Tel: 31 (0)229 268203 uboersma@vansabbenauctions.nl www.vansabbenauctions.nl

Vanbrugh House
Vanbrugh House Antiques, Park Street, Stow-on-the-Wold, Gloucestershire, GL54 1AQ Tel: 01451 830797 johnsands@vanbrughhouse.co.uk www.vanbrughhouse.co.uk

Vanessa Parker
Vanessa Parker Rare Books, The Old Rectory, Polranny, Achill Sound, Co Mayo, Republic of Ireland Tel: (098) 20984 or (087) 2339221

Vectis
Vectis Auctions Ltd, Fleck Way, Thornaby, Stockton-on-Tees, Cleveland, TS17 9JZ Tel: 01642 750616 admin@vectis.co.uk www.vectis.co.uk

Vetta Decorative Arts
Vetta Decorative Arts, P.O. Box 247, Oxford, OX1 5XH Tel: 0780 905 4969 vettaatam@aol.com

Vivienne King
Vivienne King of Panache Tel: 01934 814759 or 07974 798871 Kingpanache@aol.com

Waddington's
† Waddington's Auctions, 111 Bathurst Street, Toronto, M5V 2R1, Canada Tel: 416 504 9100 info@waddingtons.ca www.waddingtons.ca

Wadsworth's
Wadsworth's, 2 St Nicholas, Houghton, Arundel, West Sussex, BN18 9LW Tel: 01798 839017 or 07770 942489 info@wadsworthsrugs.com www.wadsworthsrugs.com

Walcot Reclamations
Walcot Reclamations, 108 Walcot Street, Bath, Somerset, BA1 5BG Tel: 01225 444404 rick@walcot.com www.walcot.com

Wallis & Wallis
† Wallis & Wallis, West Street Auction Galleries, Lewes, East Sussex, BN7 2NJ Tel: 01273 480208 auctions@wallisandwallis.co.uk grb@wallisandwallis.co.uk www.wallisandwallis.co.uk

Walpoles
Walpoles Antiques, 18 Nelson Road, Greenwich, London, SE10 9JB Tel: 07831 561042 info@walpoleantiques.com www.walpoleantiques.com

Wartski
Wartski Ltd, 14 Grafton Street, London, W1S 4DE Tel: 020 7493 1141 wartski@wartski.com www.wartski.com

Webb's
Webb's, 18 Manukau Rd, Newmarket, P.O. Box 99251, Auckland, New Zealand Tel: 09 524 6804 auctions@webbs.co.nz www.webbs.co.nz

Weschler's
† Weschler's Auctioneers & Appraisers, 909 E Street, NW Washington DC2004, U.S.A. Tel: 202 628 1281 or 800 331 1430 karen@weschlers.com www.weschlers.com

Westville House Antiques
Westville House Antiques, Westville House, Littleton, Nr Somerton, Somerset, TA11 6NP Tel: 01458 273376 or 07799 533990 info@westville.co.uk www.westville.co.uk

Whitaker
† Courtesy of Whitakerauction.com, Charles A. Whitaker Auction Company, 1002 West Cliveden St, Philadelphia, PA 19119, U.S.A. Tel: 215 817 4600 caw@whitakerauction.com www.whitakerauction.com

William Cook
William Cook, High Trees House, Savernake Forest, Marlborough, Wiltshire, SN8 4NE Tel: 01672 512561 info@williamcookantiques.com www.williamcookantiques.com

Wimpole Antiques
Wimpole Antiques, Stand 349, Grays Antique Market, 58 Davies Street, London, W1K 5LP Tel: 020 7499 2889 lynn@wimpoleantiques.plus.com

Winson Antiques
† Winson Antiques, Unit 11, Langston Priory Workshops, Kingham, Oxfordshire, OX7 6UP Tel: 01608 658856 or 07764 476776 clive.payne@virgin.net www.clivepayne.co.uk

Woburn Abbey Antiques
Woburn Abbey Antiques Centre, Woburn, Bedfordshire, MK17 9WA Tel: 01525 290666 antiques@woburnabbey.co.uk www.discoverwoburn.co.uk

Wooden Bygones
Wooden Bygones Tel: 01442 842992

Woolley & Wallis
Woolley & Wallis, Salisbury Salerooms, 51-61 Castle Street, Salisbury, Wiltshire, SP1 3SU Tel: 01722 424500 or 411854 enquiries@woolleyandwallis.co.uk www.woolleyandwallis.co.uk

Worcester Antiques
Worcester Antiques Centre, Reindeer Court, Mealcheapen Street, Worcester, WR1 4DF Tel: 01905 610680 info@worcesterantiquecentre.com www.worcesterantiquecentre.com

Yoxall Antiques
Yoxall Antiques, 68 Yoxall Road, Solihull, West Midlands, B90 3RP Tel: 0121 744 1744 or 07860 168078 sales@yoxallantiques.co.uk www.yoxall-antiques.co.uk

INDEX TO ADVERTISERS

INDEX

Bold page numbers refer to information and pointer boxes

D

G

H